THE AUTOBIOGRAPHY OF
GEORGE MÜLLER

A NARRATIVE OF SOME OF THE LORD'S DEALINGS WITH GEORGE MÜLLER

WRITTEN BY HIMSELF

PARTS I -- IV

1805-1856

© 2008 Benediction Classics, Oxford. .

Contents

FIRST PART 1
SECOND PART 143
THIRD PART 277
FOURTH PART 443

FIRST PART

Prefaces

PREFACE

TO THE

FIRST EDITION OF THE FIRST PART.

It was only after the consideration of many months, and after much self-examination as to my motives, and after much earnest prayer, that I came to the conclusion to write this little work. I have not taken one single step in the Lord's service, concerning which I have prayed so much. My great dislike to increasing the number of religious books would, in itself, have been sufficient to have kept me for ever from it, had I not cherished the hope of being instrumental in this way to lead some of my brethren to value the Holy Scriptures more, and to judge by the standard of the word of God the principles on which they act. But that which weighed more with me than any thing was, that I have reason to believe from what I have seen among the children of God, that many of their trials arise, either from want of confidence in the Lord as it regards temporal things, or from carrying on their business in an unscriptural way. On account, therefore, of the remarkable way in which the Lord has dealt with me in temporal things, within the last ten years, I feel that I am a debtor to the Church of Christ, and that I ought, for the benefit of my poorer brethren especially, to make known, as much as I can, the way in which I have been led. In addition to this, I know it to be a fact, that to many souls the Lord has blessed what I have told them about the way in which He has led me, and therefore it seemed to me a duty to use such means, whereby others also, with whom I could not possibly converse, might be benefited. That which at last, on May 6, 1836, induced me finally to determine to write this Narrative was, that, if the Lord should permit the book to sell, I might, by the profits arising from the sale, be enabled in a greater degree to help the poor brethren and sisters among whom I labour, a matter which just at that time weighed much on my mind. I therefore at last began to write. But after three days I was obliged to lay the work again aside, on account of my other pressing engagements. On May 15th I was laid aside on account of an abscess and now being unable, for many weeks, to walk about as usual, though able to work at home, I had time for writing. When the manuscript was nearly completed, I gave it to a brother to look it over, that I might have his judgment; and the Lord so refreshed his spirit through it, that he offered to advance the means for having it printed, with the understanding that if the book should not sell, he would never consider me his debtor. By this offer not a small obstacle was removed, as I have no means of my own to defray the expense of printing. These two last circumstances, connected with many other points, confirmed me that I had not been mistaken, when I came to the conclusion that it was the will of God, that I should serve His church in this way.

The fact of my being a foreigner, and therefore but very imperfectly acquainted with the English language, I judged to be no sufficient reason for keeping me from writing. The Christian reader being acquainted with this fact, will candidly excuse any inaccuracy of expression.

For the poor among the brethren this Narrative is especially intended, and to their prayers I commend it in particular.

GEORGE MÜLLER.

Bristol, July 5, 1837.

EXTRACT FROM THE PREFACE TO THE SECOND EDITION OF THE FIRST PART

As to this second edition I would mention, that, while in substance it is the same as the first, yet, on account of my increased acquaintance with the English language, many verbal alterations have been made; also several alterations have been made on account of the increased light which the Lord has been pleased to grant me since July, 1937; a few paragraphs have been entirely left out, and a few new paragraphs have been added.

GEORGE MÜLLER.

Bristol, October 28, 1840.

EXTRACT FROM THE PREFACE TO THE THIRD EDITION OF THE FIRST PART

As the second edition of four thousand copies is exhausted, and as the Lord condescends to bless this Narrative more and more, both to believers and unbeliev-

FIRST PART

ers, it has appeared to me a debt which I owe to the church of God to publish this third edition. Several new paragraphs of considerable length have been introduced.

GEORGE MÜLLER.

Bristol, June 17, 1845.

PREFACE TO THE EIGHTH EDITION OF THE FIRST PART

The Seventh edition of eight thousand copies is also exhausted, and the Lord condescends to bless yet more and more this Narrative, both to the the conversion of unbelievers, and to the edification of His own children. On this account I feel it my duty, as well as my privilege, to send forth this new edition, in which scarcely any alterations have been made.

GEORGE MÜLLER.

Bristol, December, 1881.

PREFACE TO THE NINTH EDITION

The reason which led me to the publication of the Eighth edition of this Narrative, has influenced me also to publish this Ninth edition.

GEORGE MÜLLER.

Bristol, March, 1895.

A NARRATIVE OF SOME OF THE LORD'S DEALINGS WITH GEORGE MÜLLER
FIRST PART

I was born at Kroppenstaedt, near Halberstadt, in the kingdom of Prussia, on September 27th, 1805. In January 1810 my parents removed to Heimersleben, about four miles from Kroppenstaedt, where my father was appointed collector in the excise. As a warning to parents I mention, that my father preferred me to my brother, which was very injurious to both of us. To me, as tending to produce in my mind a feeling of self-elevation; and to my brother, by creating in him a dislike both towards my father and me.

My father, who educated his children on worldly principles, gave us much money, considering our age; not in order that we might spend it, but, as he said, to accustom us to possess money without spending it. The result was, that it led me and my brother into many sins. For I repeatedly spent a part of the money in a childish way, and afterwards, when my father looked over my little treasure, I sought to deceive him in making up the accounts, either by not putting down all the money which he had given me, or by professing to have more money in hand than was the case, and counting it out accordingly before him. Now, though this deceit was found out at last, and I was punished, yet I remained the same. For before I was ten years old I repeatedly took of the government money which was intrusted to my father, and which he had to make up; till one day, as he had repeatedly missed money, he detected my theft, by depositing a counted sum in the room where I was, and leaving me to myself for a while. Being thus left alone, I took some of the money, and hid it under my foot in my shoe. When my father, after his return, had counted and missed the money, I was searched and my theft detected.

Though I was punished on this and other occasions, yet I do not remember that at any time, when my sins were found out, it made any other impression upon me than to make me think how I might do the thing the next time more cleverly, so as not to be detected. Hence it came, that this was not the last time that I was guilty of stealing.

THE LORD'S DEALINGS WITH GEORGE MÜLLER

When I was between ten and eleven years of age, I was sent to Halberstadt, to the cathedral classical school, there to be prepared for the university; for my father's desire was, that I should become a clergyman: not, indeed, that thus I might serve God, but that I might have a comfortable living. My time was now spent in studying, reading novels, and indulging, though so young, in sinful practices. Thus it continued till I was fourteen years old, when my mother was suddenly removed. The night she was dying, I, not knowing of her illness, was playing at cards till two in the morning, and on the next day, being the Lord's day, I went with some of my companions in sin to a tavern, and then we went about the streets, half intoxicated.

The following day I attended, for the first time, the religious instruction, which I was to receive previous to my confirmation. This likewise was attended to in a careless manner; and when I returned to my lodgings, my father had arrived to fetch my brother and me home to our mother's funeral. This bereavement made no lasting impression on my mind. I grew worse and worse. Three or four days before I was confirmed, (and thus admitted to partake of the Lord's supper,) I was guilty of gross immorality; and the very day before my confirmation, when I was in the vestry with the clergyman to confess my sins, (according to the usual practice,) after a formal manner, I defrauded him; for I handed over to him only the twelfth part of the fee which my father had given me for him.

In this state of heart, without prayer, without true repentance, without faith, without knowledge of the plan of salvation, I was confirmed, and took the Lord's supper, on the Sunday after Easter 1820. Yet I was not without some feeling about the solemnity of the thing, and I stayed at home in the afternoon and evening, whilst the other boys and girls, who had been confirmed with me, walked about in the fields I also made resolutions to turn from those vices in which I was living, and to study more. But as I had no regard to God, and attempted the thing in my own strength, all soon came to nothing, and I still grew worse.

Six weeks after my confirmation I went for a fortnight to Brunswick, to a sister of my father, where I became attached to a young female, who was a Roman catholic. My time till Midsummer 1821 was spent partly in study, but in a great degree in playing the piano-forte and guitar, reading novels, frequenting taverns, forming resolutions to become different, yet breaking them almost as fast as they were made. My money was often spent on my sinful pleasures, through which I was now and then brought into trouble, so that once, to satisfy my hunger, I stole a piece of coarse bread, the allowance of a soldier who was quartered in the house where I lodged. What a bitter, bitter thing is the service of Satan, even in this world!!

At Midsummer 1821 my father obtained an appointment at Schoenebeck, near Magdeburg, and I embraced the opportunity of entreating him to remove me to the cathedral classical school of Magdeburg; for I thought, that, if I could but leave my companions in sin, and get out, of certain snares, and be placed under other tutors, I should then live a different life. But as my dependence in this matter also was not upon God, I fell into a still worse state. My father consented, and I was allowed to

FIRST PART

leave Halberstadt, and to stay at Heimersleben till Michaelmas. During that time I superintended, according to my father's wish, certain alterations, which were to be made in his house there, for the sake of letting it profitably. Being thus quite my own master, I grew still more idle, and lived as much as before in all sorts of sin.

When Michaelmas came, I persuaded my father to leave me at Heimersleben till Easter, and to let me read the classics with a clergyman living in the same place. As Dr. Nagel was a very learned man, and also in the habit of having pupils under his care, and a friend of my father, my request was granted. I was now living on the premises belonging to my father, under little real control, and intrusted with a considerable sum of money, which I had to collect for my father, from persons who owed it to him. My habits soon led me to spend a considerable part of this money, giving receipts for different sums, yet leaving my father to suppose I had not received them.

In November I went on a pleasure excursion to Magdeburg, where I spent six days in much sin; and though my absence from home had been found out by my father, before I returned from thence; yet I took all the money I could obtain, and went to Brunswick, after I had, through a number of lies, obtained permission from my tutor. The reason of my going to Brunswick was, the attachment I had formed eighteen months previously to the young female residing there. I spent a week at Brunswick, in an expensive hotel. At the end of the week my money was expended. This, as well as the want of a passport, prevented my staying any longer in the hotel; but as I still wished to remain at Brunswick, I went to my uncle, the husband of my father's sister, and made some excuse for not having gone to him in the first instance. My uncle, seeing I suppose my unsteady life, intimated after a week, that he did not wish me to remain with him any longer.

I then went, without money, to another hotel, in a village near Brunswick, where I spent another week in an expensive way of living. At last, the owner of the hotel suspecting that I had no money, asked for payment, and I was obliged to leave my best clothes as a security, and could scarcely thus escape from being arrested. I then walked about six miles, to Wolfenbuttel, went to an inn, and began again to live as if I had plenty of money. Here I stayed two days, looking out for an opportunity to run away; for I had now nothing remaining to leave as a pledge. But the window of my room was too high to allow of my escaping, by getting down at night. On the second or third morning I went quietly out of the yard, and then ran off; but being suspected and observed, and therefore seen to go off, I was immediately called after, and so had to return.

I now confessed my case, but found no mercy. I was arrested, and taken between two soldiers to a police officer. Being suspected by him to be a vagabond or thief, I was examined for about three hours, and then sent to gaol. I now found myself at the age of sixteen, an inmate of the same dwelling with thieves and murderers, and treated accordingly. My superior manners profited nothing. For though, as a particular favour, I received the first evening some meat with my bread, I had the next day the common allowance of the prisoners,--very coarse bread and water, and for dinner vegetables, but no meat. My situation was most wretched. I was locked up in this place day and night, without permission to leave my cell. The dinner was such that on the first day I completely loathed it; and left it untouched. The second day I took a little, the third day all, and the fourth and following days I would fain have had more. On the second day I asked the keeper for a Bible, not to consider its blessed contents, but to pass away the time. However, I received none. Here then I was; no creature with me; no book, no work in my hands, and large iron rails before my narrow window.

During the second night I was awakened out of my sleep by the rattling of the bolts and keys. Three men came into my room. When I asked them in my fright what it meant, they laughed at me, continuing quietly to try the iron rails, to see whether I could escape.--After a few days I found out, that a thief was imprisoned next to me, and, as far as a thick wooden partition would allow of it, I conversed with him; and shortly after the governor of the prison allowed him, as a favour to me, to share my cell. We now passed away our time in relating our adventures, and I was by this time so wicked, that I was not satisfied with relating things of which I had been really guilty, but I even invented stories, to show him what a famous fellow I was.

I waited in vain day after day to be liberated.--After about ten or twelve days my fellow prisoner and I disagreed, and thus we two wretched beings, to increase our wretchedness, spent day after day without conversing together.--I was in prison from December 18th, 1821, till January 12th, 1822, when the keeper came and told me to go with him to the police office. Here I found, that the Commissioner, before whom I had been tried, had first written to my uncle at Brunswick, and when he had written in reply, that it was better to acquaint my father with my conduct, the Commissioner had done so; and thus I was kept in prison till my father sent the money which was needed for my traveling expenses, to pay my debt in the inn, and for my maintenance in the prison. So ungrateful was I now, for certain little kindnesses shown to me by my fellow-prisoner, that, although I had promised to call on his sister, to deliver a message from him, I omitted to do so; and so little had I been benefited by this my chastisement, that, though I was going home to meet an angry father, only two hours after I had left the town where I had been imprisoned, I chose an avowedly wicked person as my traveling companion for a great part of my journey.

My father, who arrived two days after I had reached Heimersleben, after having severely beaten me, took me home to Schoenebeck, intending to keep me there till Easter, and then to send me to a classical school at Halle, that I might be under strict discipline and the continual inspection of a tutor. In the meantime I took pupils, whom I instructed in Latin, French, arithmetic, and German Grammar. I now endeavoured, by diligence in study, to regain the favour of my father. My habits were, as to outward appearance, exemplary. I made progress in my own studies, benefited my pupils, and was soon liked by every body around me, and in a short time my father had forgotten all. But all this time I was in heart as bad as ever; for I was still in secret habitually guilty of great sins.

FIRST PART

Easter came, and on account of my good behaviour, my diligence in study, and also because I was no expense to my father, but earned much more than I cost him, I easily persuaded him to let me stay at home till Michaelmas. But after that period he would not consent to my remaining any longer with him, and therefore I left home, pretending to go to Halle to be examined. But having a hearty dislike to the strict discipline of which I had heard, and knowing also that I should meet there young men attending the university with whom I was acquainted, enjoying all the liberty of German students, whilst I myself was still at school: for these and other reasons I went to Nordhausen, and had myself examined by the director of the gymnasium, to be received into that school. I then went home, but never told my father a word of all this deception, till the day before my departure, which obliged me to invent a whole chain of lies. He was then very angry; but at last, through my entreaties and persuasion, he gave way and allowed me to go. This was in the beginning of October, 1822.

I continued at Nordhausen two years and six months, till Easter, 1825. During this time I studied with considerable diligence the Latin classics, French, history, my own language, &c.; but did little in Hebrew, Greek, and the Mathematics. I lived in the house of the director, and got, through my conduct, highly into his favour, so much so, that I was held up by him in the first class as an example to the rest, and he used to take me regularly with him in his walks, to converse with me in Latin. I used now to rise regularly at four, winter and summer, and generally studied all the day, with little exception, till ten at night.

But whilst I was thus outwardly gaining the esteem of my fellow-creatures, I did not care in the least about God, but lived secretly in much sin, in consequence of which I was taken ill, and for thirteen weeks confined to my room. During my illness I had no real sorrow of heart, yet being under certain natural impressions of religion, I read through Klopstock's works without weariness. I cared nothing about the word of God. I had about three hundred books of my own, but no Bible. I practically set a far higher value upon the writings of Horace and Cicero, Voltaire and Moliere, than upon the volume of inspiration. Now and then I felt that I ought to become a different person, and I tried to amend my conduct, particularly when I went to the Lord's supper, as I used to do twice every year, with the other young men. The day previous to attending that ordinance, I used to refrain from certain things; and on the day itself I was serious, and also swore once or twice to God, with the emblem of the broken body in my mouth, to become better, thinking that for the oath's sake I should be induced to reform. But after one or two days were over, all was forgotten, and I was as bad as before.

I had now grown so wicked, that I could habitually tell lies without blushing. And further, to show how fearfully wicked I was, I will mention, out of many others, only one great sin, of which I was guilty, before I left this place. Through my dissipated life I had contracted debts, which I had no means of discharging; for my father could allow me only about as much as I needed for my regular maintenance. One day, after having received a sum of money from him, and having purposely shown it to some of my companions, I afterwards feigned that it was stolen, having myself by force injured the lock of my trunk, and having also designedly forced open my guitar case. I also feigned myself greatly frightened at what had happened, ran into the director's room with my coat off, and told him that my money was stolen. I was greatly pitied. Some friends also gave me now as much money as I pretended to have lost, and the circumstance afforded me a ground upon which to ask my creditors to wait longer. But this matter turned out bitterly; for the director, having ground to suspect me, though he could not prove anything, never fully restored me to his confidence.

As it regards my own feeling, though I was very wicked, yet this desperate act of depravity was too much, even for my hardened conscience; for it never afterwards allowed me to feel easy in the presence of the director's wife, who, like a kind mother, had waited on me in my illness, and on whom I had now so willfully brought trouble. How long-suffering was God at this time, not to destroy me at once! And how merciful that he did not suffer me to be tried before the police, who easily would have detected that the whole was a fabrication! I was heartily glad for many reasons, but particularly on account of this latter circumstance, to be able soon after to exchange the school for the university.

I had now obtained what I had fondly looked forward to. I became a member of the university, and that with very honourable testimonials. I had thus obtained permission to preach in the Lutheran Establishment, but I was as truly unhappy, and as far from God as ever. I had made strong resolutions, now at last, to change my course of life, for two reasons: first, because, without it, I thought no parish would choose me as their pastor; and secondly, that without a considerable knowledge of divinity I should never get a good living, as the obtaining of a valuable cure, in Prussia, generally depends upon the degree which the candidates of the ministry obtain in passing the examination. But the moment I entered Halle, the university town, all my resolutions came to nothing.--Being now more than ever my own master, and without any control as long as I did not fight a duel, molest the people in the streets, &c., I renewed my profligate life afresh, though now a student of divinity. When my money was spent, I pawned my watch and a part of my linen and clothes, or borrowed in other ways. Yet in the midst of it all I had a desire to renounce this wretched life, for I had no enjoyment in it, and had sense enough left to see, that the end one day or other would be miserable; for I should never get a living. But I had no sorrow of heart on account of offending God.

One day when I was in a tavern with some of my wild fellow-students, I saw among them one of my former school-fellows, named Beta, whom I had known four years before at Halberstadt, but whom at that time had despised, because he was so quiet and serious. It now appeared well to me to choose him as my friend, thinking that if I could but have better companions, I should by that means improve my own conduct. I entered into familiar discourse with him, and we were soon much knit to one another. "Cursed be the man that trusteth in man, and maketh flesh his arm." Jeremiah xvii. 5.

FIRST PART

This Beta was a backslider. When formerly he was so quiet at school, I have reason to believe it was because the Spirit of God was working on his heart; but now, having departed from the Lord, he tried to put off the ways of God more and more, and to enjoy the world of which he had known but little before. I sought his friendship because I thought it would lead me to a steady life; and he gladly formed an acquaintance with me, as he told me afterwards, because he thought it would bring him into gay society. Thus my poor foolish heart was again deceived. And yet, God, in His abundant mercy, made him, after all, in a way which was never thought of by me, the instrument of doing me good, not merely for time, but for eternity.

About this period, June 1825, I was again taken ill in consequence of my profligate and vicious life. My state of health would therefore no longer allow me to go on in the same course, but my desires were still unchanged. About the end of July I recovered. After this, my conduct was outwardly rather better; but this arose only from want of money. At the commencement of August, Beta and I with two other students, drove about the country, for four days. All the money for this expensive pleasure had been obtained by pledging some of our remaining articles. When we returned, instead of being truly sorry on account of this sin, we thought of fresh pleasures, and, as my love for traveling was stronger than ever, through what I had seen on this last journey, I proposed to my friends to set off for Switzerland. The obstacles in the way, the want of money, and the want of the passports, were removed by me. For, through forged letters from our parents, we procured passports; and through pledging all we could, particularly our books, we obtained as much money as we thought would be enough. Beta was one of the party.

On August 18th we left Halle. It will be enough to say that we went as far as Mount Rigi in Switzerland, by the way of Erfurt, Frankfort, Heidelberg, Stuttgart, Zurich, and returned by the way of Constance, Ulm, and Nuremberg. Forty-three days we were, day after day, traveling, almost always on foot. I had now obtained the desire of my heart. I had seen Switzerland. But still I was far from being happy. The Lord most graciously preserved us from many calamitous circumstances, which, but for His gracious providence, might have overtaken us. But I did not see His hand at that time, as I have seen it since. Sickness of one or more of us, or separation from one another, which might have so easily befallen us, would have brought us, being so far from home, and having but just as much money as was absolutely needed, into a most miserable condition. I was on this journey like Judas; for, having the common purse, I was a thief. I managed so, that the journey cost me but two-thirds of what it cost my friends. Oh! how wicked was I now. At last all of us became tired of seeing even the most beautiful views; and whilst at first, after having seen certain scenes, I had been saying with Horace, at the end of the day, in my pagan heart, "Vixi," (I have lived), I was now glad to get home again.

September 29th we reached Halle, from whence each of us, for the remainder of the vacation, went to his father's house. I had now, by many lies, to satisfy my father concerning the traveling expenses, and succeeded in deceiving him. During the three weeks I stayed at home I determined to live differently for the future. Once more the Lord showed me what resolutions come to, when made in man's strength. I was different for a few days; but when the vacation was over, and fresh students came, and, with them, fresh money, all was soon forgotten.

At that time Halle was frequented by 1260 students, about 900 of whom studied divinity, all of which 900 were allowed to preach, although, I have reason to believe, not nine of them feared the Lord.

The time was now come when God would have mercy upon me. His love had been set upon such a wretch as I was before the world was made. His love had sent His Son to bear the punishment due to me on account of my sins, and to fulfill the law which I had broken times without number. And now at a time when I was as careless about Him as ever, He sent His Spirit into my heart. I had no Bible, and had not read in it for years. I went to church but seldom; but, from custom, I took the Lord's supper twice a year. I had never heard the gospel preached, up to the beginning of November 1825. I had never met with a person who told me that he meant, by the help of God, to live according to the Holy Scriptures. In short, I had not the least idea, that there were any persons really different from myself, except in degree.

One Saturday afternoon, about the middle of November 1825, I had taken a walk with my friend Beta. On our return he said to me, that he was in the habit of going on Saturday evenings to the house of a Christian, where there was a meeting. On further enquiry he told me that they read the Bible, sang, prayed, and read a printed sermon. No sooner had I heard this, than it was to me as if I had found something after which I had been seeking all my life long. I immediately wished to go with my friend, who was not at once willing to take me; for knowing me as a gay young man, he thought I should not like this meeting. At last, however, he said he would call for me.--I would here mention, that Beta seems to have had conviction of sin, and probably also a degree of acquaintance with the Lord, when about fifteen years old. Afterwards, being in a cold and worldly state, he joined me in this sinful Journey to Switzerland. On his return, however, being extremely miserable, and convinced of his guilt, he made a full confession of his sin to his father; and whilst with him, sought the acquaintance of a Christian brother, named Richter. This Dr. Richter, who himself had studied a few years before at Halle, gave him, on his return to the university, a letter of introduction to a believing tradesman, of the name of Wagner. It was this brother, concerning whom Beta spoke to me, and in whose house the meeting was held.

We went together in the evening. As I did not know the manners of believers, and the joy they have in seeing poor sinners, even in any measure caring about the things of God, I made an apology for coming. The kind answer of this dear brother I shall never forget. He said: "Come as often as you please; house and heart are open to you." We sat down and sang a hymn. Then brother Kayser, now a missionary in Africa, in connection with the London Missionary Society, who was then living at Halle, fell on his knees, and asked a blessing on our meeting. This kneeling down

FIRST PART

made a deep impression upon me; for I had never either seen any one on his knees, nor had I ever myself prayed on my knees. He then read a chapter and a printed sermon; for no regular meetings for expounding the Scriptures were allowed in Prussia, except an ordained clergyman was present. At the close we sang another hymn, and then the master of the house prayed. Whilst he prayed, my feeling was something like this: "I could not pray as well, though I am much more learned than this illiterate man." The whole made a deep impression on me. I was happy; though, if I had been asked, why I was happy, I could not have clearly explained it.

When we walked home, I said to Beta, "All we have seen on our journey to Switzerland, and all our former pleasures, are as nothing in comparison with this evening." Whether I fell on my knees when I returned home, I do not remember; but this I know, that I lay peaceful and happy in my bed. This shows that the Lord may begin His work in different ways. For I have not the least doubt, that on that evening, He began a work of grace in me, though I obtained joy without any deep sorrow of heart, and with scarcely any knowledge. That evening was the turning point in my life.--The next day, and Monday, and once or twice besides, I went again to the house of this brother, where I read the Scriptures with him and another brother; for it was too long for me to wait till Saturday came again.

Now my life became very different, though not so, that all sins were given up at once. My wicked companions were given up; the going to taverns was entirely discontinued; the habitual practice of telling falsehoods was no longer indulged in, but still a few times after this I spoke an untruth.--At the time when this change took place, I was engaged in translating a novel out of French into German, for the press, in order to obtain the means of gratifying my desire to see Paris, &c. This plan about the journey was now given up, though I had not light enough to give up the work in which I was engaged, but finished it. The Lord, however, most remarkably put various obstacles in the way and did not allow me to sell the manuscript. At last, seeing that the whole was wrong, I determined never to sell it, and was enabled to abide by this determination. The manuscript was burnt.

I now no longer lived habitually in sin, though I was still often overcome, and sometimes even by open sins, though far less frequently than before, and not without sorrow of heart. I read the Scriptures, prayed often, loved the brethren, went to church from right motives, and stood on the side of Christ; though laughed at by my fellow-students.

It had pleased God to teach me something of the meaning of that precious truth: "God so loved the world, that He gave His only begotten Son, that whosoever believeth in Him should not perish, but have everlasting life." I understood something of the reason why the Lord Jesus died on the cross, and suffered such agonies in the Garden of Gethsemane: even that thus, bearing the punishment due to us, we might not have to bear it ourselves. And, therefore, apprehending in some measure the love of Jesus for my soul, I was constrained to love Him in return. What all the exhortations and precepts of my father and others could not effect; what all my own resolutions could not bring about, even to renounce a life of sin and profligacy: I was enabled to do, constrained by the love of Jesus. The individual who desires to have his sins forgiven, must seek for it through the blood of Jesus. The individual who desires to get power over sin, must likewise seek it through the blood of Jesus.

In January 1826, I began to read missionary papers, and was greatly stirred up to become a missionary myself. I prayed frequently concerning this matter, and thus made more decided progress for a few weeks. But soon, alas! I was drawn aside. I used frequently to meet a young female, who also came to the meetings on Saturday evenings; and being the only pious female of my own age, whom I knew, I soon felt myself greatly attached to her. This led away my heart from missionary work, for I had reason to believe that her parents would not allow her to go with me. My prayers now became cold and formal, and at length were almost entirely given up. My joy in the Lord left me. In this state I continued for about six weeks. At the end of that time, about Easter 1826, I saw a devoted young brother, named Hermann Ball, a learned man, and of wealthy parents, who, constrained by the love of Christ, preferred labouring in Poland among the Jews as a missionary, to having a comfortable living near his relations. His example made a deep impression on me. I was led to apply his case to my own, and to compare myself with him; for I had given up the work of the Lord, and, I may say, the Lord Himself, for the sake of a girl. The result of this comparison was, that I was enabled to give up this connexion, which I had entered into without prayer, and which thus had led me away from the Lord. When I was enabled to be decided, the Lord smiled on me, and I was, for the first time in my life, able fully and unreservedly to give up myself to Him.

It was at this time that I began truly to enjoy the peace of God, which passeth all understanding. In this my joy I wrote to my father and brother, entreating them to seek the Lord, and telling them how happy I was; thinking, that if the way to happiness were but set before them, they would gladly embrace it. To my great surprise an angry answer was returned.--About this period the Lord sent a believer, Dr. Tholuck, as professor of divinity to Halle, in consequence of which a few believing students came from other universities. Thus also, through becoming acquainted with other brethren, the Lord led me on.

With the revival of the work of grace in my heart, after the snare above referred to had been broken, my former desire, to give myself to missionary service, returned, and I went at last to my father to obtain his permission, without which I could not be received into any of the German missionary institutions. My father was greatly displeased, and particularly reproached me, saying that he had expended so much money on my education, in hope that he might comfortably spend his last days with me in a parsonage, and that he now saw all these prospects come to nothing. He was angry, and told me he would no longer consider me as his son. But the Lord gave me grace to remain steadfast. He then entreated me, and wept before me; yet even this by far harder trial the Lord enabled me to bear. Before I went away I took an opportunity of reminding my brother of my former wicked life, and told him that now, having been thus blessed by God, I could not but live for Him. After I had left my father, though I wanted more money than at any previous period of my life, as I had to remain two years longer in the university, I determined, never to take any more from him; for it seemed to me wrong, so far as I remember, to suffer myself to be supported by him, when he had no prospect that I should become, what he would wish me to be, namely, a clergyman with a good living. This resolution I was enabled to keep.

By the way I would here observe, that the Lord afterwards, in a most remarkable way, supplied my temporal wants. For shortly after this had occurred, several American gentlemen, three of whom were professors in American colleges, came to Halle for literary purposes; and as they did not understand German, I was recommended by Dr. Tholuck to teach them. These gentlemen, some of whom were believers, paid so handsomely for the instruction which I gave them, and for the lectures of certain professors which I wrote out for them, that I had enough and to spare. Thus did the Lord richly make up to me the little which I had relinquished for His sake. "0 fear the Lord, ye His saints; for there is no want to them that fear Him." Psalm xxxiv. 9.

On my return from my father to Halle, I found that the more experienced brethren thought that I ought for the present to take no further steps respecting my desire to go out as a missionary. But still it was more or less in my mind.-- Whitsuntide and the two days following I spent in the house of a pious clergyman in the country: for all the ministers at Halle, a town of more than 30,000 inhabitants, were unenlightened men, God greatly refreshed me through this visit. Dear Beta was with me. On our return we related to two of our former friends, whose society we had not quite given up, though we did not any longer live with them in sin, how happy we had been on our visit. I then told them how I wished they were as happy as ourselves. They answered, we do not feel that we are sinners. After this I fell on my knees, and asked God to show them that they were sinners. Having done so, I left them, and went into my bed-room, where I continued to pray for them. After a little while I returned to my sitting-room, and found them both in tears, and both told me that they now felt themselves to be sinners. From that time a work of grace commenced in their hearts.

Shortly after this, being still greatly exercised about going out as a missionary, and wishing much (according to my natural mind, as I now see,) to have the matter settled, in one way or the other, without being willing quietly, patiently, and prayerfully to wait on the Lord, I came to the conclusion to ascertain the Lord's mind by the lot. To this end I not merely drew a lot in private, but I bought a ticket in the royal lottery; and I left it thus with the Lord, that if I gained any thing, I should take it to be His will that I should become a missionary, if not, that I should remain at home. My ticket came out with a small sum, on account of which it appeared to me that I should be a missionary. I therefore applied to the Berlin Missionary Society, but was not accepted, because my father had not given his consent.

THE LORD'S DEALINGS WITH GEORGE MÜLLER

Very soon afterwards I was led to see in some degree, and since then much more fully, the error into which I had fallen respecting the lot. In the first place it was altogether wrong, that I, a child of God, should have any thing to do with so worldly a system as that of the lottery. But it was also unscriptural to go to the lot at all for the sake of ascertaining the Lord's mind, and this I ground on the following reasons. We have neither a commandment of God for it, nor the example of our Lord, nor that of the apostles, after the Holy Spirit had been given on the day of Pentecost. 1. We have many exhortations in the word of God to seek to know His mind by prayer and searching the Holy Scriptures, but no passage which exhorts us to use the lot. 2. The example of the apostles (Acts i.) in using the lot, in the choice of an apostle, in the room of Judas Iscariot, is the only passage, which can be brought in favour of the lot, from the New Testament, (and to the Old we have not to go under this dispensation, for the sake of ascertaining how we ought to live as disciples of Christ). Now concerning this circumstance we have to remember, that the Spirit was not yet given (John vii. 39; ch. xiv. 16, 17; ch. xvi. 7, 13), by whose teaching especially it is that we may know the mind of the Lord; and hence we find, that, after the day of Pentecost, the lot was no more used, but the apostles gave themselves to prayer and fasting to ascertain how they ought to act.

In addition to this I would give my own experience concerning the lot, but only by way of illustrating the view just given; for the word of God is quite sufficient on the subject. And first as it regards my using the lot in the above case. How did it turn out? I had repeatedly asked the Lord to show me His mind, whether He would have me to be a missionary or not. But not coming to a satisfactory assurance, and being very anxious to have the matter settled, I found out in my own judgment a much shorter way, namely, the lot. I ought to have said to myself, how can an individual, so ignorant as you are, think about being a teacher to others? For though I was truly begotten again, and rested upon Christ alone for salvation, still I should not have been able to give a clear explanation of even the most elementary truths of the Gospel. How then could I be fit to teach others? The first thing therefore I ought to have done, was, to seek through much prayer, and searching the Scriptures, and a holy life, to obtain more knowledge of divine things. Further, as to my impatience in wishing the matter settled, how could I have been fit to endure in that state the hardships and trials of a missionary life, in which my patience, no doubt, would have been much more severely tried? I therefore ought to have said to myself, if I cannot wait quietly, though it be many months longer, before the Lord shows me clearly His will concerning the matter, how then can I be fit for missionary work? Instead of thus comparing my state of heart and knowledge, with what is required in the Scriptures from him who is to be a teacher, I ran hastily to the lot, and thought I had done it prayerfully. And how did it end? According to my prayers the lot decided I should be a missionary among the heathen (and my mind, at that time, especially inclined to the East Indies). But the way in which the Lord has led me since has been very different. And it ought not to be said in defense of the practice of deciding by lot-- Perhaps the Lord meant you to be a missionary among the heathen, but you did not give yourself to the work? for I actually offered myself to a society, but was not accepted. Moreover, since 1826 I have repeatedly offered myself most solemnly to the

FIRST PART

Lord for this work, and am as sure that it is not His will that I should go out a missionary for the present, as I am sure of any thing. Nor could it be said, that perhaps the Lord yet may call me for this work. For if He should be pleased to do so tomorrow, yet that would prove nothing concerning the above point. For I did not use the lot to ascertain whether at any period of my life I should be engaged in missionary work, but whether I should then set about it. And to put such an explanation on the matter, would be acting as false prophets, who, when their prophecies fail, try to find out some way or other, whereby they may show that their prophecies were true.

About two years after I used the lot in another instance. I went one day to a village about fifteen miles from Halle, to see the few believers there. When I was about three miles from the place, it began to get dark; and finding myself in a spot where the road divided, and not knowing which way I should choose, I was greatly perplexed. I stood a moment, and then prayed to God to show me by the lot, which was the right way. Now, truly one may say, if the use of the lot in our day is according to the will of God, this was particularly a case for the Lord to direct me through this means. For here was one of His children in need, looking up to his Father to help him, through the lot, out of his difficulty, and this His child also on a journey in His service. I drew the lot and went the way to the left. After some time I found I was on the wrong road. Now, at last, as I did not know how to get into the right one, I did what I ought to have done before, and what I believe to be a scriptural way of acting; I prayed that the Lord graciously would send some one to put me into the right way; and almost immediately a carriage came up, and I was directed on my journey.

In one other instance I used the lot some years after. It concerned a most important matter, important for my whole life. I had then a degree of conviction, that I ought prayerfully and patiently to wait for the Lord's decision. But my natural mind would have the decision at once, and thus after prayer I drew the lot, to have the matter in one way or other settled. But facts turned out completely different from what the lot decided.

To ascertain the Lord's will we ought to use scriptural means. Prayer, the word of God, and His Spirit should be united together. We should go to the Lord repeatedly in prayer, and ask Him to teach us by His Spirit through His word. I say, by His Spirit through His word. For if we should think that His Spirit led us to do so and so, because certain facts are so and so, and yet His word is opposed to the step which we are going to take, we should be deceiving ourselves.

For instance: A brother in business thinks he ought to leave the house in which he lives, because it is not in a good situation. He wishes to know the Lord's mind, as he says, and prays about the matter. After a few days, unexpectedly, a house is offered to him without seeking after it, in a much better situation. The house is very suitable, as he thinks; the rent very moderate; and moreover the person who offers him the house tells him, that, because he is a believer he will let him have it at this cheap rent. There is, however, this scriptural objection in the way. If he goes into this house, he must carry on so large a business, to cover his expenses, that his time will be so occupied as to encroach upon those hours, which ought to be devoted to his spiritual interests. Now the scriptural way of deciding would be this: No situation, no business will be given to me by God, in which I have not time enough to care about my soul (Matthew vi. 33). Therefore, however outward circumstances may appear, it can only be considered as permitted of God, to prove the genuineness of my love, faith, and obedience, but by no means as the leading of His providence to induce me to act contrary to His revealed will.

In connexion with this I would mention, that the Lord very graciously gave me, from the very commencement of my divine life, a measure of simplicity and of childlike disposition in spiritual things, so that whilst I was exceedingly ignorant of the Scriptures, and was still from time to time overcome even by outward sins, yet I was enabled to carry most minute matters to the Lord in prayer. And I have found "godliness profitable unto all things, having promise of the life that now is, and of that which is to come." Though very weak and ignorant, yet I had now, by the grace of God, some desire to benefit others, and he who so faithfully had once served Satan, sought now to win souls for Christ.

I may mention a few instances. I circulated every month, in different parts of the country, about 300 missionary papers. I also sold and distributed a considerable number of tracts, and often took my pockets full in my walks, and distributed them, and spoke to poor people whom I met. I also wrote letters to some of my former companions in sin. I visited for thirteen weeks a sick man, who, when I first began to speak to him about the things of God, was completely ignorant of his state as a sinner, trusting for salvation in his upright and moral life. After some weeks, however, the Lord allowed me to see a decided change in him, and he afterwards repeatedly expressed his gratitude, that I had been sent to him by God, to be the means of opening his blind eyes. May this encourage the believing reader to sow the seed, though he does not see it spring up at once.

Thus the Lord condescended to begin to use me soon after my conversion, though but little; for I could bear but very little, as I did not see at that time, as I do now, that God alone can give spiritual life at the first, and keep it up in the soul afterwards. How imperfectly, however, on account of my ignorance, some of these things were done, I will show by the following instance. Once I met a beggar in the fields, and spoke to him about his soul. But when I perceived it made no impression upon him, I spoke more loudly; and when he still remained unmoved, I quite bawled in talking to him; till at last I went away, seeing it was of no use. Though none had sought the Lord less than myself, when He was pleased to begin His work in me; yet so ignorant was I of the work of the Spirit, that I thought my speaking very loudly would force him into repentance towards God, and faith in the Lord Jesus.

Having heard that there was a schoolmaster living in a village, about six miles from Halls, who was in the habit of holding a prayer meeting at four o'clock every morning, with the miners, before they went into the pit, giving them also an address, I thought he was a believer; and as I knew so very few brethren, I went to see him, in

FIRST PART

order, if it might be, to strengthen his hands. About two years afterwards he told me, that when I came to him first, he knew not the Lord, but that he had held these prayer-meetings merely out of kindness to a relative, whose office it was, but who bad gone on a journey; and that those addresses which lie had read were not his own, but copied out of a book. He also told me, that he was much impressed with my kindness, and, what he considered condescension on my part in coming to see him, and this, together with my conversation, had been instrumental in leading him to care about the things of God; and I knew him ever afterwards as a true believer.

This schoolmaster asked me, whether I would not preach in his parish, as the aged and infirm clergyman would be very glad of my assistance. Up to this time I had never preached, though for fifteen months past I might have done so as a student of divinity; for before Christmas 1825 I had been mercifully kept from attempting to preach, (though I wrote to my father about July that I had preached, because I knew it would please him), and after Christmas, when I knew the Lord, I refrained from doing so, because I felt that I was yet too little instructed in the things of God. The same reason ought to have still kept me from preaching; yet I thought, that, by taking a sermon, or the greater part of one, written by a spiritual man, and committing it to memory, I might benefit the people. Had I reasoned scripturally, I should have said, surely it cannot be the will of God, that I should preach in this way, if I have not enough knowledge of the Scriptures to write a sermon. Moreover, I had not enough light nor tenderness of conscience to see, that I was a deceiver in the pulpit; for every body supposes, that the sermon a man preaches is, if not entirely, at least as to the most part, his own composition.

I now set about putting a printed sermon into a suitable form, and committing it to memory. It was hard work. There is no joy in man's own doings and choosings. It took me nearly a whole week to commit to memory such a sermon as would take up nearly an hour in repeating. I got through it, but had no enjoyment in the work. It was on August 27, 1826, at eight in the morning, in a chapel of ease, in connexion with which my friend was schoolmaster.5 At eleven I repeated the same sermon verbatim in the parish church. There was one service more, in the afternoon, at which I needed not to have done any thing; for the schoolmaster might have read a printed sermon, as he used to do. But having a desire to serve the Lord, though I often knew not how to do it scripturally; and knowing that this aged and unenlightened clergyman had had this living for forty-eight years, and having therefore reason to believe, that the gospel scarcely ever had been preached in that place; I had it in my heart to preach again in the afternoon. But I had no second sermon committed to memory. It came, however, to my mind to read the 5th chapter of Matthew, and to make such remarks as I was able. I did so. Immediately upon beginning to expound "Blessed are the poor in spirit, &c." I felt myself greatly assisted; and whereas in the morning my sermon had not been simple enough for the people to understand it, I now was listened to with the greatest attention, and I think was also understood. My own peace and joy were great. I felt this a blessed work. After the service I left the aged clergyman as soon as possible, lest I should lose my enjoyment.

On my way to Halle I thought, this is the way I should like always to preach. But then it came immediately to my mind, that such sort of preaching might do for illiterate country people, but that it never would do before a well educated assembly in town. I thought, the truth ought to be preached at all hazards, but it ought to be given in a different form, suited to the hearers. Thus I remained unsettled in my mind as it regards the mode of preaching; and it is not surprising that I did not then see the truth concerning this matter, for I did not understand the work of the Spirit, and therefore saw not the powerlessness of human eloquence. Further, I did not keep in mind, that if the most illiterate persons in the congregation can comprehend the discourse, the most educated will understand it too; but that the reverse does not hold true.

It was not till three years afterwards that I was led, through grace, to see what I now consider the right mode of preparation for the public preaching of the Word. But about this, if God permit, I will say more when I come to that period of my life.

I now preached frequently, both in the churches of villages and towns, but never had any enjoyment in doing so, except when speaking in a simple way; though the repetition of sermons, which had been committed to memory, brought more praise from my fellow-creatures. But from neither way of preaching did I see any fruit. It may be, that the last day may show the benefit even of these feeble endeavours. One reason why the Lord did not permit me to see fruit, seems to me, that I should have been most probably lifted up by success. It may be also, because I prayed exceedingly little respecting the ministry of the Word, and because I walked so little with God, and was so rarely a vessel unto honour, sanctified, and meet for the Master's use.

About the time that I first began to preach I lived for about two months in free lodgings, provided for poor students of divinity in the Orphan-House, built in dependence upon God, by that devoted and eminent servant of Christ, A. H. Franke, Professor of Divinity at Halle, who died 1727. I mention this, as some years afterwards I was benefited myself through the faith of this dear man of God.--About that time I was still so weak that I fell repeatedly into open sins, yet could not continue in them, nay, not even for a few days, without sorrow of heart, confession before God, and fleeing to the blood of the Lamb. And so ignorant was I still, that I bought a crucifix in a frame, and hung it up in my room, hoping that being thus frequently reminded of the sufferings of my Saviour, I should not fall so frequently into sin. But in a few days the looking to the crucifix was as nothing, and I fell about that very time more than once deeply.

About this time I formed an intimate acquaintance with a brother, who was also a divinity student: and as we loved one another so much, and were so happy in one another's society, we thought that it would greatly add to our joy, and to one another's benefit, to live together, and that thus we might mutually help one another. Accordingly in September 1826, I left the free lodgings in the Orphan-House, and lived with him. But alas! we were not aware, that because God is greatly glorified by

FIRST PART

the love and union of His people, for this very reason Satan particularly hates it, and will, therefore, in every possible way, seek to divide them. We ought to have especially prayed, and that frequently, that the Lord would keep us together in love; instead of which, I do not think that we at all feared disunion, as we loved one another so much. For this reason our great adversary soon got an advantage by our neglecting prayer concerning this point, and we were disunited, and love and union were not fully restored between us till after we had been for some time separated.

Having heard that a very rich lady of title, residing at Frankfort-on-the-Maine, about two hundred miles from Halle, was a very pious person, and, in visiting a charitable institution at Dusselthal, had given very liberally; and wishing much about the commencement of the year 1827 to help a poor relative with a small sum of money, and also to pay the remainder of the debt which I had contracted for my traveling expenses to Switzerland: I wrote to this lady, asking her to lend me a small sum of money, in actual amount only little above £5., but, as money in the North of Germany has much more value than in England, it was as much as £ 12. or £ 15. in this country. Whilst I was writing, however, the thought occurred to me, Suppose this lady should not be a believer? I, therefore, pointed out to her the way of salvation, and related to her how I had been brought to the knowledge of the truth. But I received no answer by the time I might have had one.--I would just notice, that since 1829 my practice, on account of what I found in the Scriptures, Rom. xiii. 8, as it regards borrowing money, has been different. And, moreover, I have considered that there is no ground to go away from the door of the Lord to that of a believer, so long as He is so willing to supply our need.

About January 20th I was one day very wretched. Satan obtained an advantage over me through over-much work; for I was in the habit of writing about fourteen hours a day. One morning I was in so wretched a state, that I said in my heart, what have I now gained by becoming a Christian? Afterwards I walked about in the streets in this wretched state of heart, and at last I went into a confectioner's shop, where wine and ardent spirits were sold, to eat and to drink. But as soon as I had taken a piece of cake I left the shop, having no rest, as I felt that it was unbecoming a believer, either to go to such places, or to spend his money in such a way. In the afternoon of the very day on which, in the ingratitude of my heart, I had had such unkind thoughts about the Lord, (who was at that very time in so remarkable a manner supplying my temporal wants, by my being employed in writing for an AMERICAN Professor), He graciously showed me my sin, not by a severe chastisement, as I most righteously deserved, but by adding another mercy to the many He had already shown me. Oh! how long-suffering is our Lord. How does He bear with us! May I at least now seek, for the few days whilst I may stay in this world, to be more grateful for all His mercies!

At two o'clock I received a parcel from Frankfort, containing the exact sum of money of which I had requested the loan. There was no letter to be found. I was overwhelmed with the Lord's mercy, but very much regretted that there was no letter.

At last, on carefully examining the paper in which the silver had been packed, I found one, which I have kept, and which I translate from the German.

"A peculiar providence has brought me acquainted with the letter which you have written to Lady B. But you are under a mistake concerning her, both as it regards her character, and her stay at D., where she never was. She has been taken for another individual. But that I may lessen in some measure the difficulties in which you seem to be, I send you the enclosed small sum, for which you may thank, not the unknown giver, but the Lord, who turneth the hearts like rivers of water. Hold fast the faith which God has given you by His Holy Spirit; it is the most precious treasure in this life, and it contains in itself true happiness. Only seek by watching and prayer more and more to be delivered from all vanity and self-complacency, by which even the true believer may be ensnared when he least expects it. Let it be your chief aim to be more and more humble, faithful, and quiet. May we not belong to those who say and write continually,' Lord,' 'Lord,' but who have Him not deeply in their hearts. Christianity consists not in words, but in power. There must be life in us. For, therefore, God loved us first that we might love Him in return; and that loving we might receive power, to be faithful to Him, and to conquer ourselves, the world, distress, and death. May His Spirit strengthen you for this, that you may be an able messenger of His Gospel! Amen.

"AN ADORING WORSHIPPER OF THE

SAVIOUR, JESUS CHRIST."

Frankfort-on-the-Maine, January 14th, 1827.

I saw, in some measure, at the time when I received t letter, how much I needed such a faithful, and, at the same time, loving word of admonition; but I have seen it more fully since. Self-complacency, and a want of quietness and saying and writing more frequently "Lord," "Lord," than acknowledging Him by my life as such; these were the evils against which at that time I particularly needed to be cautioned; and up to this day I am still much, very much, lacking in these points: though the Lord, to His praise I would say it, has done much for me in these particulars since that time.

After having read this letter, my heart was full of joy, shame and gratitude. Truly it was the goodness of God which brought my heart into this state, and not the money for that was gone in a few hours after for the two purposes above referred to. With my heart full of peculiar feelings, and ashamed of my conduct in the morning, I left the town towards the evening, to walk alone in a solitary place. And now, being particularly conscious of my ingratitude to the Lord for all His mercies, and of my want of steadfastness in His ways, I could not forbear falling down on my knees behind a hedge, though the snow was a foot deep, anew to surrender myself wholly to Him, and to pray for strength that I might for the future live more to His glory, and

FIRST PART

also to thank Him for His late mercy. It was a blessed time, I continued about half an hour in prayer.

After such an experience, it may be difficult for one, who does not know the plague of his own heart, to think that I was at that time a true believer, when I tell hint that so base was I, so altogether like a beast before my God, and unmindful of His mercies to me in Christ, that only a few weeks after I fell into a wretched backsliding state, in which I continued for many days, during which time prayer was almost entirely given up. It was on one of these days that I rang my bell, and ordered the servant to fetch me wine. And now I began to drink. But how good was the Lord! Though I desired to drink, that I might be able more easily to go on in sin, yet He would not allow me to give up myself to the wickedness of my heart. For whilst in my ungodly days I had drunk once about five quarts of strong beer in one afternoon, in the way of bravado, and once also much wine at one time, without remorse of conscience, I could now take only two or three glasses before the wickedness of my conduct was brought before me; and my conscience told me that I drank merely for the sake of drinking, and thus I gave it up.

It was about this time that I formed the plan of exchanging the University of Halle for that of Berlin, on account of there being a greater number of believing professors and students in the latter place. But the whole plan was formed without prayer, or at least without earnest prayer. When, however, the morning came on which I had to take decided steps concerning it, and to apply for the university-testimonials, the Lord graciously stirred me up, prayerfully to consider the matter; and finding that I bad no sufficient reason for leaving Halle, I gave up the plan, and have never had reason to regret having done so.

In the vacations, Michaelmas, 1826, and Easter, 1827, and at other times, I visited a Moravian settlement, called Gnadau, which was only about three miles distant from the place where my father then resided. Through the instrumentality of the brethren, whom I met there, my spirit was often refreshed.

The public means of grace by which I could be benefited were very few. Though I went regularly to church when I did not preach myself, yet I scarcely ever heard the truth; for there was no enlightened clergyman in the town. And when it so happened that I could bear Dr. Tholuck, or any other godly minister, the prospect of it beforehand, and the looking back upon it afterwards, served to fill me with joy. Now and then I walked ten or fifteen miles to enjoy this privilege. May those who enjoy the faithful ministry of the Word feel exceedingly thankful for it. There are few blessings on earth greater for a believer; and yet the Lord is frequently obliged to teach us the value of this blessing by depriving us of it for a season.

Another means of grace which I attended, besides the Saturday evening meetings in brother Wagner's house, was a meeting every Lord's day evening with the believing students, which consisted of six or more in number, and increased, before I left Halle, to about 20; and which, after the Easter vacation of 1827, was held in my room till I left Halle. In these meetings one, or two, or more of the brethren prayed, and we read the Scriptures, sang hymns, and sometimes also one or another of the brethren spoke a little in the way of exhortation, and we read also such writings of godly men as were calculated for edification. I was often greatly stirred up and refreshed in these meetings; and twice, being in a backsliding state, and therefore cold and miserable, I opened my heart to the brethren, and was brought out of that state through the means of their exhortations and prayers. "Forsake not the assembling of yourselves together," is a most important exhortation. Even if we should not derive any especial benefit, at the time, so far as we are conscious, yet we may be kept from much harm. And very frequently the beginning of coldness of heart is nourished by keeping away from the meetings of the saints. I know, when I was cold, and had no real desire to be brought out of that state, I went a few times into the villages, where I was sure not to meet with brethren, that I might not be spoken to about the things of God. Yet so gracious was the Lord, that my very wretchedness brought me back after a few hours. The Lord had begun a good work in me; and being faithful, though I was faithless, He would not give me up, but carried on His gracious work in me; though it would have progressed much more rapidly, had not my rebellious heart resisted. As to the other means of grace I would say: I fell into the snare, into which so many young believers fall, the reading of religious books in preference to the Scriptures. I could no longer read French and German novels, as I had formerly done, to feed my carnal mind; but still I did not put into the room of those books the best of all books. I read tracts, missionary papers, sermons, and biographies of godly persons. The last kind of books I found more profitable than others, and had they been well selected, or had I not read too much of such writings, or had any of them tended particularly to endear the Scriptures to me, they might have done me much good.--I never had been at any time in my life in the habit of reading the Holy Scriptures. When under fifteen years of age, I occasionally read a little of them at school; afterwards God's precious book was entirely laid aside, so that I never read one single chapter of it, as far as I remember, till it pleased God to begin a work of grace in my heart. Now the scriptural way of reasoning would have been: God Himself has condescended to become an author, and I am ignorant about that precious book, which His Holy Spirit has caused to be written through the instrumentality of His servants, and it contains that which I ought to know, and the knowledge of which will lead me to true happiness; therefore I ought to read again and again this most precious book, this book of books, most earnestly, most prayerfully, and with much meditation; and in this practice I ought to continue all the days of my life. For I was aware, though I read it but little, that I knew scarcely anything of it. But instead of acting thus, and being led by my ignorance of the word of God to study it more, my difficulty in understanding it, and the little enjoyment I had in it, made me careless of reading it (for much prayerful reading of the Word, gives not merely more knowledge, but increases the delight we have in reading it); and thus, like many believers, I practically preferred, for the first four years of my divine life, the works of uninspired men to the oracles of the living God. The consequence was, that I remained a babe, both in knowledge and grace. In knowledge I say; for all true knowledge must be derived, by the Spirit, from the Word. And as I neglected the Word, I was for nearly four years so ignorant, that I did not clearly know even the fundamental points

FIRST PART

of our holy faith. And this lack of knowledge most sadly kept me back from walking steadily in the ways of God. For it is the truth that makes us free, (John viii. 31, 32,) by delivering us from the slavery of the lusts of the flesh, the lusts of the eyes, and the pride of life. The Word proves it. The experience of the saints proves it; and also my own experience most decidedly proves it. For when it pleased the Lord in Aug. 1829, to bring me really to the Scriptures, my life and walk became very different. And though even since that I have very much fallen short of what I might and ought to be, yet, by the grace of God, I have been enabled to live much nearer to Him than before.

If any believers read this, who practically prefer other books to the Holy Scriptures, and who enjoy the writings of men much more than the word of God, may they be warned by my loss. I shall consider this book to have been the means of doing much good, should it please the Lord, through its instrumentality, to lead some of His people no longer to neglect the Holy Scriptures, but to give them that preference, which they have hitherto bestowed on the writings of men. My dislike to increase the number of books would have been sufficient to deter me from writing these pages, had I not been convinced, that this is the only way in which the brethren at large may be benefited through my mistakes and errors, and been influenced by the hope, that in answer to my prayers, the reading of my experience may be the means of leading them to value the Scriptures more highly, and to make them the rule of all their actions.

Before I leave this subject I would only add: If the reader understands very little of the word of God, he ought to read it very much; for the Spirit explains the Word by the Word. And if he enjoys the reading of the Word little, that is just the reason why he should read it much; for the frequent reading of the Scriptures creates a delight in them, so that the more we read them, the more we desire to do so. And if the reader should be an unbeliever, I would likewise entreat him to read the Scriptures earnestly, but to ask God previously to give him a blessing. For in doing so, God may make him wise unto salvation, 2 Tim. iii. 16.

If any one should ask me, how he may read the Scriptures most profitably, I would advise him, that

I. Above all he should seek to have it settled in his own mind, that God alone, by His Spirit, can teach him, and that therefore, as God will be inquired of for blessings, it becomes him to seek God's blessing previous to reading, and also whilst reading.

II. He should have it, moreover, settled in his mind, that although the Holy Spirit is the best and sufficient teacher, yet that this teacher does not always teach immediately when we desire it, and that, therefore, we may have to entreat Him again and again for the explanation of certain passages; but that He will surely teach us at last, if indeed we are seeking for light prayerfully, patiently, and with a view to the glory of God.

III. It is of immense importance for the understanding of the word of God, to read it in course, so that we may read every day a portion of the Old and a portion of the New Testament, going on where we previously left off. This is important--1, because it throws light upon the connexion, and a different course, according to which one habitually selects particular chapters, will make it utterly impossible ever to understand much of the Scriptures. 2, Whilst we are in the body, we need a change even in spiritual things, and this change the Lord has graciously provided in the great variety which is to be found in His word. 3, It tends to the glory of God; for the leaving out some chapters here and there, is practically saying, that certain portions are better than others; or, that there are certain parts of revealed truth unprofitable or unnecessary. 4, It may keep us, by the blessing of God, from erroneous views, as in reading thus regularly through the Scriptures, we are led to see the meaning of the whole, and also kept from laying too much stress upon certain favourite views. 5, The Scriptures contain the whole revealed will of God, and therefore we ought to seek to read from time to time through the whole of that revealed will. There are many believers, I fear, in our day, who have not read even once through the whole of the Scriptures; and yet in a few months, by reading only a few chapters every day, they might accomplish it.

IV. It is also of the greatest importance to meditate on what we read, so that perhaps a small portion of that which we have read, or, if we have time, the whole may be meditated upon in the course of the day. Or a small portion of a book, or an epistle, or a gospel, through which we go regularly for meditation, may be considered every day, without, however, suffering oneself to be brought into bondage by this plan.

Learned commentaries I have found to store the head with many notions, and often also with the truth of God; but when the Spirit teaches, through the instrumentality of prayer and meditation, the heart is affected. The former kind of knowledge generally puffs up, and is often renounced, when another commentary gives a different opinion, and often also is found good for nothing, when it is to be carried out into practice. The latter kind of knowledge generally humbles, gives joy, leads us nearer to God, and is not easily reasoned away; and having been obtained from God, and thus having entered into the heart, and become our own, is also generally carried out. If the inquirer after truth does not understand the Hebrew and Greek languages, so as to be able to compare the common translation with the original, he may, concerning several passages, get light by an improved rendering, provided he can be sure that the translator was a truly spiritual person.

The last and most important means of, grace, namely, prayer, was comparatively but little improved by me. I prayed, and I prayed often. I also prayed, in general, by the grace of God, with sincerity; but had I been more earnestly praying, or even only as much, as I have prayed of late years, I should have made much more rapid progress.

FIRST PART

In August, 1827, I heard that the Continental Society in England intended to send a minister to Bucharest, the residence of many nominal German Christians, to help an aged brother in the work of the Lord; the two other German Protestant ministers in that place being, the one a Socinian, and the other an unenlightened orthodox preacher. After consideration and prayer I offered myself for this work to professor Tholuck, who was requested to look out for a suitable individual; for with all my weakness I had a great desire to live wholly for God. Most unexpectedly my father gave his consent, though Bucharest was above a thousand miles from my home, and as completely a missionary station as any other. I considered this a remarkable providence; though I see now, that a servant of Christ has to act for his Master, whether it be according to the will of his earthly father or not. I then went home to, spend a short time with my father. In the town where he lived, containing about 3000 inhabitants, I could not hear of a single believer, though I made many inquiries. The time I stayed with my father was more profitably spent than it had formerly been. I was enabled more than ever before to realize my high calling. I had by the grace of God power over sin; at least much more than at any former period of my life.

I returned to Halle, and now prepared with earnestness for the work of the Lord. I set before me the sufferings which might await me. I counted the cost. And he, who once so fully-served Satan, was now willing, constrained by the love of Christ, rather to suffer affliction for the sake of Jesus, than to enjoy the pleasures of sin for a season. I also prayed with, a degree of earnestness concerning my future work.

One day, at the end of October, the above-mentioned brother, Hermann Ball, missionary to the Jews, attended the Lord's day evening meeting in my room, on his way through Halle, and stated that he feared, on account of his health, his should be obliged to give up labouring among the Jews. When I heard this, I felt a peculiar desire to fill up his place. About this very time also I became exceedingly fond of the Hebrew language, which I had cared about very little up to that time, and which I had merely studied now and then, from a sense of duty. But now I studied it, for many weeks, with the greatest eagerness and delight. Whilst I thus from time to time felt a desire to fill up Brother Ball's place as a missionary to the Jews, (about which, however, I did not seriously think, because Dr. Tholuck daily expected a letter from London, finally to settle the particulars respecting my going to Bucharest); and whilst I thus greatly delighted in the study of Hebrew: I called in the evening of Nov. 17th on Dr. Tholuck. In the course of conversation he asked me, whether I had ever had a desire to be a missionary to the Jews, as I might be connected with the London Missionary Society, for promoting Christianity among them, for which he was an agent. I was struck with the question, and told him what had passed in my mind, but added that it was not proper to think anything about that, as I was going to Bucharest: to which he agreed.

When I came home, however, these few words were like fire within me. The next morning I felt all desire for going to Bucharest gone, which appeared to me very wrong and fleshly, and I therefore entreated the Lord, to restore to me the former desire for labouring on that missionary station. He graciously did so almost immediately. My earnestness in studying Hebrew, and my peculiar love for it, however, continued. About this time I had an offer of becoming tutor to the sons of a pious Gentleman of title, which I did not accept on account of my purpose of going to Bucharest, and if that should come to nothing, on account of my desire of being a missionary to the Jews.

About ten days after, Dr. Tholuck received a letter from the Continental Society, stating, that, on account of the war between the Turks and Russians, it appeared well to the committee, for the time being to give up the thought of sending a minister to Bucharest, as it was the seat of war between the two armies. Dr. Tholuck then asked me again, what I now thought about being a missionary to the Jews. My reply was, that I could not then give an answer, but that I would let him know, after I had prayerfully considered the matter. After prayer and consideration, and consulting with experienced brethren, in order that they might probe my heart as to my motives, I came to this conclusion, that, though I could not say with certainty it was the will of God that I should be a missionary to the Jews, yet, that I ought to offer myself to the committee, leaving it with the Lord to do with me afterwards, as it might seem good in His sight. Accordingly Dr. Tholuck wrote, about the beginning of December, 1827, to the committee in London.

At Christmas I spent a few days at Belleben, a village about fifteen miles from Halle, where I had been once or twice before, both for the sake of refreshing the few brethren living there, and also of having my own spirit refreshed by their love. One evening, when I was expounding the Scriptures to them, an unconverted young man happened to be present, and it pleased the Lord to touch his heart, so that he was brought to the knowledge of the truth.

In the beginning of the year 1828 there was a new workhouse established at Halle, into which persons of bad character were put for a time, and made to work. Being disposed to benefit unbelievers, I heartily desired to have permission statedly to preach the word of truth to them while I stayed at Halle, particularly as I understood that one of the lecturers of divinity in the university, who was a Socinian, had applied for this living. I wrote to the magistrates of the city, and offered to preach to those criminals gratuitously, hoping that in this way there would be less objection to my doing so. The reply was, that Dr.--had applied for this living, and that it had been laid before the provincial government for consideration, but that they would be glad if I would preach in the workhouse till the matter was decided. The decision did not come for some time, and I had thus an opportunity of preaching twice every Lord's day, and once or twice on the week evenings; and besides this I took the criminals one by one into a room, to converse with them about their souls. Thus the Lord condescended to give to one so unworthy, so ignorant, so weak in grace, and so young in the faith and in years, a most important field of labour. However, it was well, that even under these circumstances I should have laboured there; for humanly speaking, had I not been there, they would have had either no instruction at all, or a Socinian, or an unenlightened preacher would have preached to them. And besides this, I had at least some qualification for ministering there; for I knew the state of those poor sinners, having been myself formerly, in all probability, a great deal worse than most of them, and my simplicity and plainness of speech they would not have found in every minister. After some months the matter was decided, the Socinian lecturer of divinity, Dr. --, was appointed to the living, and I had to discontinue my labours.

It was not before March 1828, that Professor Tholuck received an answer from London respecting me, in which the committee put a number of questions to me, on the satisfactory answers to which my being received by them would depend. After replying to this first communication, I waited daily for an answer, and was so much the more desirous of having it, as my course in the university was completed. But no answer came. Had my desire, to serve the Lord among the Jews, been of the flesh, it would in all likelihood not have continued; but I still thought about it, and continued to make it a subject of prayer. At last, on June 13th, I received a letter from London, stating that the committee had determined, to take me as a missionary student for six months on probation, provided that I would come to London.

I had now had the matter before me about seven months, having supposed, not only that it would have been settled in a few weeks, but also, that, if I were accepted, I should be sent out immediately, as I had passed the university. Instead of this, not only seven months passed over before the decision came, but I was also expected to come to London, and not only so, but, though I had from my infancy been more or less studying, and now at last wished actively to be engaged, it was required that I should again become a student. For a few moments, therefore, I was greatly disappointed and tried. But, on calmly considering the matter, it appeared to me but right that the committee should know me personally, and that it was also well for me to know them more intimately than merely by correspondence, as this afterwards would make our connexion much more comfortable. I determined therefore, after I had seen my father, and found no difficulty on his part, to go to London.

There was, however, an obstacle in the way of my leaving the country. Every Prussian male subject is under the necessity of being for three years a soldier, provided his state of body allows it; but those who have had a classical education up to a certain degree, and especially those who have passed the university, need to be only one year in the army, but have to equip and maintain themselves during that year. Now, as I had been considered fit for service, when I was examined in my twentieth year, and had only been put back, at my own request, till my twenty-third year, and as I was now nearly twenty-three, I could not obtain a passport out of the country, till I had either served, my time, or had been exempted by the King himself. The latter I hoped would be the case; for it was a well known fact that those who had given themselves to missionary service, had been always exempted. Certain brethren of influence, living in the capital, to whom I wrote on the subject, advised me, however, to write first to the president of the government of the province to which I belonged. This was done, but I was not exempted. Then those brethren wrote to the King himself; but he replied, that the matter must be referred to the ministry and to the law, and no exception was made in my favour.

I now knew not what to do. In the meantime, at the beginning of August, I was taken ill. It was a common cold at first, but I could not get rid of it, as formerly. At last a skillful physician was consulted, and powerful means were used. After some time, he prescribed tonics and wine. For a day or two I seemed to get better, but after that it appeared, by the return of giddiness in my head, that the tonics had been too soon resorted to. At last, having used still other means, I seemed in a fit state for tonics, and began again to take them. At the same time one of my friends, an American Professor, took me as a companion with him to Berlin and other places, so that we rode about the country for about ten days together. As long as I was day after day in the open air, going from place to place, drinking wine and taking tonics, I felt well; but as soon as I returned to Hale, the old symptoms returned. A second time the tonics were given up, and the former means used.

About ten weeks had by this time passed away, since I was first taken ill. This illness, in which a particular care for the body seemed to be so right, and in which therefore frequent walks were taken, and in which I thought myself justified in laying aside the study of Hebrew, &c., had not at all a beneficial effect on my soul. In connexion with this one of my chief companions at this time, the last-mentioned American Professor, was a backslider. If the believing reader does not know much of his own heart and of man's weakness, he will scarcely think it possible that, after I had been borne with by the Lord so long, and had received so many mercies at His hands, and had been so fully and freely pardoned through the blood of Jesus, which I both knew from His word, and had also enjoyed; and after that I had been in such various ways engaged in the work of the Lord; I should have been once more guilty of great backsliding, and that at the very time when the hand of God was lying heavily upon me. Oh! how desperately wicked is the human heart.

It was in this cold state of heart, that I rode with my friend to Leipsic, at the time of the famous Michaelmas fair. He wished me to go with him to the Opera. I went, but had not the least enjoyment. After the first act I took a glass of ice for refreshment. After the second act I was taken faint in consequence of this, my stomach being in a very weak state; but I was well enough; after a while, to go to the hotel, where I passed a tolerable night. On the next morning my friend ordered the carriage for our return to Halle. This circumstance the Lord graciously used as a means of arousing me; and on our way home, I freely opened my mind to my friend about the way in which we had been going on; and he then told me that he was in a different state of heart, when he left America. He also told me, when I was taken faint, that he thought it was an awful place to die in. This was the second and last time, since I have believed in the Lord Jesus, that I was in a theatre; and but once, in the year 1827, I went to a concert, when I likewise felt, that it was unbecoming for me, as a child of God, to be in such a place. On my return to Halle I broke a blood-vessel in my stomach, in consequence of the glass of ice. I was now exceedingly weak, in which state I continued far several weeks, and then went for change of air into the country, to the house of a beloved brother in the Lord, who, up to this day, has continued a kind and faithful friend to me. My heart was now again in a better state than

FIRST PART

it had been before the rupture of the blood-vessel, Thus the Lord, in the faithful love of His heart, seeing that I was in a backsliding state, chastised me for my profit; and the chastisement yielded, in a measure at least, the peaceable fruit of righteousness. Heb. xii. 10, 11.

Whilst I was staying in the country, I received a letter from the American Professor, who had in the meantime changed Halle for Berlin, and who wished me to come to Berlin, where, being near the Court, I should be more likely to obtain an exemption from my military duty; and he mentioned, at the same time, that all the expenses, connected with my staying in Berlin, would be fully covered by the remuneration I should receive for teaching German to himself and two of his friends, for a few hours every week. As I had no more connexion with the university at Halle, my course having been finished for more than six months past, and as I had the prospect of being spiritually benefited through my stay in Berlin, and there was no probability, if I remained at Halle, of obtaining the above-mentioned exemption, I came to the conclusion to go to Berlin.

Two ladies of title traveled with me to Berlin in a hired carriage. As I knew that we should be for two days together, I thought, in my fleshly wisdom, that though I ought to speak to them about the things of God, I should first show them kindness and attention, and that, after having thus opened a way to their hearts, I might fully set before them their state by nature, and point them to the Lamb of God. We went on together most amicably, I making only a few general remarks about divine things. On the second evening, however, when we were near the end of our journey, I felt that it was high time to speak. And no sooner had I begun plainly to do so, than one of them replied, "Oh! Sir, I wish you had spoken sooner about these things, for we have, for a long time, wished to have some one to whom we might open our hearts; but seeing that the ministers whom we know do not live consistently, we have been kept from speaking to them." I now found that they had been under conviction of sin for some time, but did not know the way to obtain peace, even by faith in the Lord Jesus. After this I spoke freely to them during the hour that yet remained. They parted from me under feelings of gratitude and regret that they could hear no more, for they only passed through Berlin. I felt myself greatly reproved, and all I could do was, by a long letter, to seek to make up for my deficiency in ministering to them on the journey. May this circumstance never be forgotten by me, and may it prove a blessing to the believing reader.

My chief concern now was how I might obtain a passport for England, through exemption from military duty. But the more certain brethren tried, though they knew how to set about the matter, and were also persons of rank, the greater difficulty there appeared to be in obtaining my object; so that in the middle of January 1829 it seemed as if I must immediately become a soldier. There was now but one more way untried, and it was at last resorted to. A believing major, who was on good terms with one of the chief generals, proposed that I should actually offer myself for entering the army, and that then I should be examined as to my bodily qualifications, in the hope, that, as I was still in a very weak state of body, I should be found unfit for military service. In that case it would belong to the chief general finally to settle the matter; who, being a godly man himself, on the major's recommendation would, no doubt, hasten the decision, on account of my desire to be a missionary to the Jews. At the same time it stood so, that, if I should be found fit for service, I should have to enter the army immediately.

Thus far the Lord had allowed things to go, to show me, it appears, that all my friends could not procure me a passport till His time was come. But now it was come. The King of kings had intended that I should go to England, because He would bless me there, and make me a blessing, though I was at that time, and am still most unworthy of it; and, therefore, though the King of Prussia had not been pleased to make an exemption in my favour, yet now all was made plain, and that at a time when hope had almost been given up, and when the last means had been resorted to. I was examined, and was declared to be unfit for military service. With a medical certificate to this effect, and a letter of recommendation from the major I went to this chief general, who received me very kindly and who himself wrote instantaneously to a second military physician, likewise to examine me at once. This was done, and it was by him confirmed that I was unfit. Now the chief general himself, as his adjutants happened to be absent, in order to hasten the matter, wrote with his own hands the papers which were needed, and I got a complete dismissal, and that for life, from all military engagements. This was much more than I could have expected. This military gentleman spoke to me in a very kind way, and pointed out certain parts of the Scriptures, which he in particular advised me to bring before the Jews, especially Romans xi.

On considering why the Lord delayed my obtaining this permission, I find that one of the reasons may have been, that I might both be profited myself by my stay in Berlin, and that I also might be instrumental in benefiting others. As to the first, I would mention, that I learned a lesson in Berlin which I did not know before. Whilst I was at Halle, I thought I should much enjoy being among so many christians as there are in Berlin. But when I was there I found, that enjoyment in the Lord does not depend upon the multitude of believers, by whom we are surrounded. As to the second point, perhaps the last day may show, that the Lord had some work for me in Berlin: for, from the time of my coming until I left, I preached three, four, or five times every week in the wards of a poorhouse, which was inhabited by about three hundred aged and infirm people. I also preached once in a church, and likewise visited one of the prisons several times on Lord's days to converse with the prisoners about their souls, where I was locked in by the keeper with the criminals in their cells.

On the whole my time in Berlin was not lost; and I was in a better state of heart than I had been for any length of time before, I was not once overcome by my former outward besetting sins, though I have nothing to boast of even as it regards that period; and were only the sins of those days brought against me, had I not the blood of Jesus to plead, I should be most miserable. But I think it right to mention, for the glory of God, as I have so freely spoken about my falls, that whilst I was more than ever unobserved by others; and whilst I was living in the midst of more gaiety and temptations than ever; and had far more money than at any previous time of my life; I was kept from things of which I had been habitually guilty in my unconverted days!--My health was in a very weak state, almost the whole time whilst I was staying in Berlin, and was in no degree better, till, on the advice of, a believing medical professor, I gave up all medicine.

Having now without any further difficulty obtained my passport, I left Berlin on February 3rd, 1829, for London. The Lord gave me more grace on my way from Berlin than on my way to it; for my mouth was almost immediately opened to my fellow-travelers, and the message of the Gospel seemed to be listened to with interest, particularly by one. On February 5th I arrived at my father's house; it was the place where I had lived as a boy, and the scene of many of my sins, my father having now returned to it after his retirement from office. I came to it with peculiar feelings. These feelings were not excited merely by the fact of my having been seven years absent from it, but arose from the spiritual change I had undergone since I last saw the place; for I had never been at Heimersleben since my father fetched me from thence, which was a few days after my imprisonment at Wolfenbüttel had come to an end. There were but three persons in the whole town with whom my soul had any fellowship. One of them had spent all his money in coal mines, and was then earning his daily bread by thrashing corn. As a boy I had in my heart laughed at him, for he seemed so different from all other people. Now I sought him out, having previously been informed that he was a believer, to acknowledge him as such, by having fellowship with him, and attending, a meeting in his house on the Lord's day evening. My soul was refreshed, and his also. Such a spiritual feast, as meeting with a brother, was a rare thing to him. May we believers who live in Great Britain, and especially those of us who are surrounded by many children of God, seek for grace, more highly to prize the blessings which, we enjoy through fellowship with brethren! This dear brother, who had then been a believer for more than twenty years, had only a few times heard the gospel preached during all that period. What a wonderful thing that I, one of the vilest of those brought up in that small town, should have been so abundantly favoured, as to have been brought to the knowledge of the truth, whilst none of all my relations, and scarcely one of those who grew up with me, so far as it has come to my knowledge, know the Lord!

I left my father's house on February 10th, with the prospect of seeing him again in about a twelvemonth, as a missionary among the Jews. But how has the Lord graciously altered matters!--I was kindly lodged for a night at Halberstadt by an aged brother, and then proceeded towards Rotterdam, by the way of Munster. At Munster I rested a few days, and was very kindly received by several brethren. They were officers in the army, and two of them had been, but a little while before this, Roman Catholics. I lodged in the house of a beloved brother, a tailor, who likewise had been a Roman Catholic.

About February 22nd I arrived at Rotterdam. I took lodgings in the house of a believer, where two German brethren lodged, whom I had known at Halle, and who intended to go out as missionaries in connexion with the Dutch Missionary Society. It was a peculiar feeling to me, for the first time in my life to find myself among Christians of another nation, to attend their family prayer, hear them sing, &c. In spirit I had fellowship with them, though our communication was but broken, as I understood but little of the Dutch language. Here also I heard for the first time the preaching of the Gospel in English, of which I knew enough to understand a part of what was said.--My going to England by the way of Rotterdam was not the usual way; but consulting with a brother in Berlin, who had been twice in England, I was told that this was the cheapest route. My asking this brother, to be profited by his experience, would have been quite right, had I, besides this, like Ezra, sought of the Lord the right way. Ezra viii. 21. But I sought unto men only, and not at all unto the Lord, in this matter. When I came to Rotterdam, I found that no vessels went at that time from that port to London, on account of the ice having just broken up in the river, and that it would be several weeks before the steamers would again begin to ply. Thus I had to wait nearly a month at Rotterdam, and, therefore, not only needed much more time than I should have required to go by way of Hamburgh, but also much more money.

On March 19th, 1829, I landed in London. I now found myself, in a great measure, as it regards liberty, brought back to the years when I was at school; yea, almost all the time I had been at school, and certainly for the last four years, previous to my coming to England, I was not so much bound to time and order as I was in this seminary; and had not there been a degree of grace in me, yea, so much as not to regard the liberty of the flesh, I should now probably have given up all idea of being a missionary to the Jews. But as I did not see that anything was expected from me which I could not conscientiously accede to, I thought it right to submit myself, for the Lord's sake, to all the regulations of the institution.

My brethren in the seminary, most of them Germans, had instruction in Hebrew, Latin, Greek, French, German, &c., scarcely any of them having had a classical education; I read only Hebrew, and was exempted from all the rest. I remember how I longed to be able to expound the Scriptures in English, when I heard a German brother do so, a few days after my arrival. And I also remember what joy it gave me, when a few weeks after, for the first time, I spoke in English to a little boy, whom I met alone in the fields, about his soul, thinking that he would bear with my broken English.--I now studied much, about twelve hours a day, chiefly Hebrew; commenced Chaldee; perfected myself in reading the German-Jewish in Rabbinic characters, committed portions of the Hebrew Old Testament to memory, &c.; and this I did with prayer, often falling on my knees, leaving my books for a little, that I might seek the Lord's blessing, and also, that I might be kept from that spiritual deadness, which is so frequently the result of much study. I looked up to the Lord even whilst turning over the leaves of my Hebrew dictionary, asking His help, that I might quickly find the words. I made comparatively little progress in English; for living with some of my countrymen, I was continually led to converse in German.

FIRST PART

My experience in this particular leads me to remark, that, should this fall into the hands of any who are desirous to labour as missionaries among a people whose language is not their own, they should seek not merely to live among them, for the sake of soon learning their language, but also, as much as possible, to be separated from those who speak their own language; for, when, some months after, I was in Devonshire, completely separated from those who spoke German, I daily made much progress, whilst I made comparatively little in London.

Soon after my arrival in England, I heard one of the brethren in the seminary speak about a Mr. Groves, a dentist in Exeter, who, for the Lord's sake, had given up his profession, which brought him in about fifteen hundred pounds a year, and who intended to go as a missionary to Persia, with his wife and children, simply trusting in the Lord for temporal supplies. This made such an impression on me, and delighted me so, that I not only marked it down in my journal, but also wrote about it to my German friends.

I came to England weak in body, and in consequence of much study, as I suppose, I was taken ill on May 15, and was soon, at least in my own estimation, apparently, beyond recovery. The weaker I became in body, the happier I was in spirit. Never in my whole life had I seen myself so vile, so guilty, so altogether what I ought not to have been, as at this time. It was as if every sin, of which I had been guilty, was brought to my remembrance; but, at the same time, I could realize that all my sins were completely forgiven that I was washed and made clean, completely clean, in the blood of Jesus. The result of this was, great peace. I longed exceedingly to depart and to be with Christ. When my medical attendant came to see me, my prayer was something like this: "Lord, Thou knowest that he does not know what is for my real welfare, therefore do Thou direct him." When I took my medicine, my hearty prayer each time was something like this: "Lord, Thou knowest that this medicine is in itself nothing, no more than as if I were to take a little water. Now please, 0 Lord, to let it produce the effect which is for my real welfare, and for Thy glory. Let me either be taken soon to Thyself or let me be soon restored; let me be ill for a longer time, and then taken to Thyself, or let me be ill for a longer time, and then restored. 0 Lord, do with me as seemeth Thee best!" One sin in particular was brought to my mind, which I never had seen before, viz., that whilst all my life, even in former sicknesses, I had been blessed with uninterrupted refreshing sleep, which now, for some nights, had almost entirely fled from my eyes, I had never heartily thanked God for it.

After I had been ill about a fortnight, my medical attendant unexpectedly pronounced me better. This, instead of giving me joy, bowed me down, so great was my desire to be with the Lord; though almost immediately afterwards grace was given me to submit myself to the will of God. After some days I was able to leave my room. Whilst recovering I still continued in a spiritual state of heart, desiring to depart and to be with Christ. As I recovered but slowly, my friends entreated me to go into the country for change of air; but my heart was in such a happy and spiritual frame, that I did not like the thought of traveling and seeing places. So far was I changed, who once had been so passionately fond of traveling. But as my friends continued to advise me to go into the country, I thought at last that it might be the will of God that I should do so, and I prayed therefore thus to the Lord: "Lord, I will gladly submit myself to Thy will, and go if Thou wilt have me to go. And now let me know Thy will by the answer of my medical attendant. If, in reply to my question, he says it would be very good for me, I will go; but if he says it is of no great importance, then I will stay." When I asked him, he said that it was the best thing I could do. I was then enabled willingly to submit, and accordingly went to Teignmouth. It was there that I became acquainted with my beloved brother, friend, and fellow-labourer, Henry Craik.

A few days after my arrival at Teignmouth, the chapel, called Ebenezer, was reopened, and I attended the opening. I was much impressed by one of those who preached on the occasion. For though I did not like all he said, yet I saw a gravity and solemnity in him different from the rest. After he had preached, I had a great desire to know more of him; and being invited by two brethren of Exmouth, in whose house he was staying, to spend some time with them, I had an opportunity of living ten days with him under the same roof. Through the instrumentality of this brother the Lord bestowed a great blessing upon me, for which I shall have cause to thank Him throughout eternity.

I will mention some points which God then began to show me.

1. That the word of God alone is our standard of judgment in spiritual things; that it can be explained only by the Holy Spirit; and that in our day, as well as in former times, He is the teacher of His people. The office of the Holy Spirit I had not experimentally understood before that time. Indeed, of the office of each of the blessed persons, in what is commonly called the Trinity, I had no experimental apprehension. I had not before seen from the Scriptures that the Father chose us before the foundation of the world; that in Him that wonderful plan of our redemption originated, and that He also appointed all the means by which it was to be brought about. Further, that the Son, to save us, had fulfilled the law, to satisfy its demands, and with it also the holiness of God; that He had borne the punishment due to our sins, and had thus satisfied the justice of God. And further, that the Holy Spirit alone can teach us about our state by nature, show us the need of a Saviour, enable us to believe in Christ, explain to us the Scriptures, help us in preaching, &c. It was my beginning to understand this latter point in particular, which had a great effect on me; for the Lord enabled me to put it to the test of experience, by laying aside commentaries, and almost every other book, and simply reading the word of God and studying it. The result of this was, that the first evening that I shut myself into my room, to give myself to prayer and meditation over the Scriptures, I learned more in a few hours than I had done during a period of several months previously. But the particular difference was, that I received real strength for my soul in doing so. I now began to try by the test of the Scriptures the things which I had learned and seen, and found that only those principles, which stood the test, were really of value.

FIRST PART

2. Before this period I had been much opposed to the doctrines of election, particular redemption, and final persevering grace; so much so that, a few days after my arrival at Teignmouth, I called election a devilish doctrine. I did not believe that I had brought myself to the Lord, for that was too manifestly false; but yet I held, that I might have resisted finally. And further, I knew nothing about the choice of God's people, and did not believe that the child of God, when once made so, was safe for ever. In my fleshly mind I had repeatedly said, If once I could prove that I am a child of God for ever, I might go back into the world for a year or two, and then return to the Lord, and at last be saved. But now I was brought to examine these precious truths by the word of God. Being made willing to have no glory of my own in the conversion of sinners, but to consider myself merely as an instrument; and being made willing to receive what the Scriptures said; I went to the Word, reading the New Testament from the beginning, with a particular reference to these truths. To my great astonishment I found that the passages which speak decidedly for election and persevering grace, were about four times as many as those which speak apparently against these truths; and even those few, shortly after, when I had examined and understood them, served to confirm me in the above doctrines. As to the effect which my belief in these doctrines had on me, I am constrained to state, for God's glory, that though I am still exceedingly weak, and by no means so dead to the lusts of the flesh, and the lust of the eyes, and the pride of life, as I might and as I ought to be, yet, by the grace of God, I have walked more closely with Him since that period. My life has not been so variable, and I may say that I have lived much more for God than before. And for this have I been strengthened by the Lord, in a great measure, through the instrumentality of these truths. For in the time of temptation, I have been repeatedly led to say: Should I thus sin? I should only bring misery into my soul for a time, and dishonour God; for, being a son of God for ever, I should have to be brought back again, though it might be in the way of severe chastisement. Thus, I say, the electing love of God in Christ (when I have been able to realize it) has often been the means of producing holiness, instead of leading me into sin. It is only the notional apprehension of such truths, the want of having them in the heart, whilst they are in the head, which is dangerous.

3. Another truth, into which, in a measure, I was led during my stay in Devonshire, respected the Lord's coming. My views concerning this point, up to that time, had been completely vague and unscriptural. I had believed what others told me, without trying it by the Word. I thought that things were getting better and better, and that soon the whole world would be converted. But now I found in the Word, that we have not the least Scriptural warrant to look for the conversion of the world before the return of our Lord. I found in the Scriptures, that that which will usher in the glory of the church, and uninterrupted joy to the saints, is the return of the Lord Jesus, and that, till then, things will be more or less in confusion. I found in the Word, that the return of Jesus, and not death, was the hope of the apostolic Christians; and that it became me, therefore, to look for His appearing. And this truth entered so into my heart, that, though I went into Devonshire exceedingly weak, scarcely expecting that I should return again to London, yet I was immediately, on seeing the truth, brought off from looking for death, and was made to look for the

return of the Lord. Having seen this truth, the Lord also graciously enabled me to apply it, in some measure at least, to my own heart, and to put the solemn question to myself--What may I do for the Lord, before He returns, as He may soon come?

4. In addition to these truths, it pleased the Lord to lead me to see a higher standard of devotedness than I had seen before. He led me, in a measure, to see what is my true glory in this world, even to be despised, and to be poor and mean with Christ. I saw then, in a measure, though I have seen it more fully since, that it ill becomes the servant to seek to be rich, and great, and honoured in that world, where his Lord was poor, and mean, and despised.

I do not mean to say that all that which I believe at present concerning these truths, and those which, in connexion with them, the Lord has shown me since August 1829, were apprehended all at once; and much less did I see them all at once with the same clearness, as, by the grace of God, I do now; yet my stay in Devonshire was a most profitable time to my soul. My prayer had been, before I left London, that the Lord would be pleased to bless my journey to the benefit of my body and soul. This prayer was answered in both respects; for in the beginning of September I returned to London much better in body; and, as to my soul, the change was so great, that it was like a second conversion.

After my return to London, I sought to benefit my brethren in the seminary, and the means which I used were these. I proposed to them to meet together every morning from six to eight for prayer and reading the Scriptures, and that then each of us should give out what he might consider the Lord had shown him to be the meaning of the portion read. One brother in particular was brought into the same state as myself; and others, I trust, were more or less benefited. Several times, when I went to my room after family prayer in the evening, I found communion with God so sweet, that I continued in prayer till after twelve, and then, being full of joy, went into the room of the brother just referred to; and, finding him also in a similar frame of heart, we continued praying until one or two and even then I was a few times so full, of joy, that I could scarcely sleep, and at six in the morning again called the brethren together for prayer.

All this moreover did not leave me idle, as it regards actual engagements in the Lord's work, as I will now show. After I had been for about ten days in London, and had been confined to the house on account of my studies, my health began again to decline; and I saw that it would not be well, my poor body being only like a wreck or brand brought out of the devil's service, to spend my little remaining strength in study, but that I now ought to set about actual engagements in the Lord's work, particularly as He had now given me more light about His truth, and also a heart to serve Him. I consequently wrote to the committee of the Society, requesting them to send me out at once, as they had now had an opportunity of knowing me; and, that they might do so with more confidence, to send me as a fellow-labourer to an experienced brother. However I received no answer.

FIRST PART

After having waited about five or six weeks, in the meantime seeking in one way or other to labour for the Lord, it struck me that I was wrong and acting unscripturally, in waiting for the appointment to missionary work from my fellow-men; but that, considering myself called by the Lord to preach the gospel, I ought to begin at once to labour among the Jews in London, whether I had the title of missionary or not. In consequence of this I distributed tracts among the Jews, with my name and residence written on them, thus inviting them to conversation about the things of God; preached to them in those places where they most numerously collect together; read the Scriptures regularly with about fifty Jewish boys; and became a teacher in a Sunday school. In this work I had much enjoyment and the honour of being reproached and ill-treated for the name of Jesus. But the Lord gave me grace, never to be kept from the work by any danger, or the prospect of any suffering.

My light increased more and more during the months of September, October, and November. At the end of November it became a point of solemn consideration with me, whether I could remain connected with the Society in the usual way. My chief objections were these: 1. If I were sent out by the Society, it was more than probable, yea, almost needful, if I were to leave England, that I should labour on the Continent, as I was unfit to be sent to eastern countries on account of my health, which would probably have suffered, both on account of the climate, and of my having to learn other languages. Now, if I did go to the Continent, it was evident, that without ordination I could not have any extensive field of usefulness, as unordained ministers are generally prevented from labouring freely there; but I could not conscientiously submit to be ordained by unconverted men, professing to have power to set me apart for the ministry, or to communicate something to me for this work which they do not possess themselves. Besides this, I had other objections to being connected with any state church or national religious establishment, which arose from the increased light which I had obtained through the reception of this truth, that the word of God is our only standard, and the Holy Spirit our only teacher. For as I now began to compare what I knew of the establishment in England and those on the Continent, with this only true standard, the word of God, I found that all establishments, even because they are establishments, i.e. the world and the church mixed up together, not only contain in them the principles which necessarily must lead to departure from the word of God; but also, as long as they remain establishments, entirely preclude the acting throughout according to the Holy Scriptures.--Then again, if I were to stay in England, the Society would not allow me to preach in any place indiscriminately, where the Lord might open a door for me; and to the ordination of English bishops I had still greater objections, than to the ordination of a Prussian Consistory. 2. I further had a conscientious objection against being led and directed by men in my missionary labours. As a servant of Christ it appeared to me, I ought to be guided by the Spirit, and not by men, as to time and place; and this I would say, with all deference to others, who may be much more taught and much more spiritually minded than myself. A servant of Christ has but one Master. 3. I had love for the Jews, and I had been enabled to give proofs of it; yet I could not conscientiously say, as the committee would expect from me, that I would spend the greater part of my time only among them. For the scriptural plan seemed to me, that, in coming to a place, I should seek out the Jews, and commence my labour particularly among them; but that, if they rejected the gospel, I should go to the nominal Christians--The more I weighed these points, the more it appeared to me that I should be acting hypocritically, were I to suffer them to remain in my mind, without making them known to the committee.

The question that next occurred to me was, how I ought to act if not sent out by the Society. With my views I could not return to Prussia; for I must either refrain from preaching, or imprisonment would be the result. The only plan that presented itself to me was, that I should go from place to place throughout England, as the Lord might direct me, and give me opportunity, preaching wherever I went, both among Jews and nominal Christians. To this mode of service I was especially stirred up through the recently received truth of the Lord's second coming, having it impressed upon my heart to seek to warn sinners, and to stir up the saints; as He might soon come. At the same time it appeared to me well, that I should do this in connexion with the Society for promoting Christianity among the Jews, serving them without any salary, provided they would accept me on these conditions. An objection which came to my mind against taking any step which might lead to the dissolution of my connexion with the Society, namely, that I had been some expense to it, and that thus I should appear ungrateful, and the money would seem to have been thrown away, was easily removed in this way:

1. When I engaged with the Society, I did it according to the light I then had. 2. I have but one Master; His is the money, and to Him I have to give an account. 3. Though I have nothing to boast of, but much reason to be ashamed before God on account of my lack of service; yet, speaking after the manner of men, in some measure I did work, not only in the Lord's service, but even in that particular line for which the money had been put into the hands of the committee.

There remained now only one point more to be settled:

How I should do for the future as it regarded the supply of my temporal wants, which naturally would have been a great obstacle, especially as I was not merely a foreigner, but spoke so little English, that whilst I was greatly assisted in expounding the Scriptures, it was with difficulty I could converse about common things. On this point, however, I had no anxiety; for I considered that, as long as I really sought to serve the Lord, that is, as long as I sought the kingdom of God and His righteousness, these my temporal supplies would be added to me. The Lord most mercifully enabled me to take the promises of His word, and rest upon them, and such as Matthew vii. 7, 8, John xiv. 13, 14, Matthew vi. 25-34, were the stay of my soul concerning this point. In addition to this, the example of brother Groves, the dentist before alluded to, who gave up his profession, and went out as a missionary, was a great encouragement to me. For the news, which by this time had arrived, of how the Lord had aided him on his way to Petersburg, and at Petersburg, strengthened my faith.

FIRST PART

At last, on December 12, 1829, I came to the conclusion to dissolve my connexion with the Society, if they would not accept my services under the above conditions, and to go throughout the country preaching, (being particularly constrained to do so from a desire to serve the Lord as much as in me lay, BEFORE HIS RETURN), and to trust in Him for the supply of my temporal wants. Yet at the same time it appeared well to me to wait a month longer, and to consider the matter still further, before I wrote to the committee, that I might be sure I had weighed it fully.

On December 24th I went to the Church Missionary Institution at Islington, in the hope of benefiting the students there, if it were the Lord's will. I returned very happy, as I almost invariably was at that time, and went to bed full of joy. Next morning, (being that of Christmas day), I awoke in a very different state of heart from what I had experienced for many weeks past. I had no enjoyment, and felt cold and lifeless in prayer. At our usual morning meeting, however, one of the brethren exhorted me to continue to pray, saying that the Lord surely would again smile on me, though now for a season, for wise purposes, He seemed to have withdrawn Himself. I did so. At the Lord's table, in the morning, a measure of enjoyment returned. Afterwards I dined in a family, in company with the brother just referred to. My former enjoyment gradually returned. Towards evening the Lord gave me an opportunity of speaking about His return, and I had great enjoyment in doing so. At eight o'clock I was asked to expound at family prayer, and was much assisted by the Lord. About half an hour after the exposition was over, I was requested to come out of the room to see one of the servants, and the mother of another of the servants, who had been present at family prayer. I found them in tears, and both deeply impressed and under concern about their souls. I then went home, at least as happy as on the previous evening. I have related this circumstance, because I am aware that it is a common temptation of Satan to make us give up the reading of the Word and prayer when our enjoyment is gone; as if it were of no use to read the Scriptures when we do not enjoy them, and as if it were of no use to pray when we have no spirit of prayer; whilst the truth is, in order to enjoy the Word, we ought to continue to read it, and the way to obtain a spirit of prayer, is, to continue praying; for the less we read the word of God, the less we desire to read it, and the less we pray, the less we desire to pray.

About the beginning of the next year my fellow students had a fortnight's vacation, and as with them I had conformed myself to the order of the Institution, I felt that I might also partake of their privileges; not indeed to please the flesh, but to serve the Lord. On December 30th, I therefore left London for Exmouth, where I intended to spend my vacation in the house of my Christian friends, who had kindly lodged me the summer before, that I might preach there during this fortnight, and still more fully weigh the matter respecting my proposal to time Society. I arrived at Exmouth on December 31st, at six in the evening, an hour before the commencement of a prayer-meeting at Ebenezer Chapel. My heart was burning with a desire to tell of the Lord's goodness to my soul, and to speak forth what I considered might not be known to most with whom I met. Being, however, not called on, either to speak or pray, I was silent. The next morning I spoke on the difference between being a Christian and a happy Christian, and showed, whence it generally comes, that we rejoice so little in the Lord. This my first testimony was blessed to many believers, that God, as it appears, might show me that He was with me. Among others it proved a blessing to a Christian female, who had been for ten years in bondage, and who, in the providence of God, had been brought from Exeter to be present that morning. This she told me many months after, when I met her on a journey.

At the request of several believers I spoke again in the afternoon, and also proposed a meeting in the chapel every morning at ten, to expound the epistle to the Romans. I had also most days a meeting in a room with several ladies, for reading the Scriptures with them. This I did that I might make the best of my fortnight. The second day after my arrival, a brother said to me: "I have been praying for this month past that the Lord would do something for Lympstone, a large parish where there is little spiritual light. There is a Wesleyan chapel, and I doubt not you would be allowed to preach there." Being ready to speak of Jesus wherever the Lord might open a door, yet so, that I could be faithful to the truths which he had been pleased to teach me, I went, and easily obtained liberty to preach twice on the next day, being the Lord's day. Besides this I preached in another village near Exmouth; so that I spoke once, twice, or three times in public or private meetings every day for the first ten or twelve days, and that with great enjoyment to my own soul.

During the first days of January, 1830, whilst at Exmouth, it became more and more clear to me, that I could not be connected with the Society under the usual conditions; and as I had an abundance of work where I was, and little money to spend in traveling (for all I possessed was about five pounds), it appeared best to me to write at once to the committee, that, whilst they were coming to a decision respecting me, I might continue to preach. I therefore wrote to them, stating what had been my views before I became acquainted with them, and what they were now. I also stated my difficulty in remaining, connected with them on the usual terms, as stated in substance above; and then concluded, that as, however, I owed them much, as having been instrumental in bringing me to England, where the Lord had blessed me so abundantly: and as I, also, should like to obtain from them the Hebrew Scriptures and tracts for the Jews: I would gladly serve them without any salary, if they would allow me to labour in regard to time and place as the Lord might direct me. Some time after I received a very kind private letter from one of the secretaries, who always had been very kind to me, together with the following official communication from the committee.

"London Society for promoting Christianity amongst the Jews."

At a Meeting of the Missionary Sub-Committee, held January 27, 1830, Society House, 10, Wardrobe Place, Doctors' Commons, a Letter was read from Mr. G. F. Müller.

"Resolved, That Mr. Müller be informed, that while the committee cordially rejoice in any real progress in knowledge and grace which he may have made under the teaching of the Holy Spirit, they, nevertheless, consider it inexpedient for any society to employ those who are unwilling to submit themselves to their guidance with respect to missionary operations; and that while, therefore, Mr. Müller holds his present opinions on that point, the committee cannot consider him as a missionary student; but should more mature reflection cause him to alter that opinion, they will readily enter into further communication with him."

Thus my connexion with the Society was entirely dissolved. Fifty-two years have passed away since, and I never have, even for one single moment, regretted the step I took, but have to be sorry that I have been so little grateful for the Lord's goodness to me in that matter. The following part of the Narrative also will prove to the enlightened reader, how God blessed my acting out the light He had been pleased to give me. But I cannot leave this subject, without adding, that it is far from my intention to throw any blame upon the Society. I have no wish to do so: nay, I confess, were the last-mentioned circumstances not so intimately connected with my being in England, I would rather have left out the matter altogether. But being under the necessity of saying something about my connexion with it, it appeared best to me to relate the circumstances just as they were. Yet I do testify that I have not done it in the least for the sake of injuring the Society; for I have received much kindness from some of those connected with it, particularly from two worthy men, then taking a prominent part in managing its affairs. If I be judged differently, I can only say, "Judge nothing before the time, until the Lord come."

After I had preached about three weeks at Exmouth and its neighbourhood, I went to Teignmouth, with the intention of staying there ten days, to preach the Word among the brethren with whom I had become acquainted during the previous summer, and thus to tell them of the Lord's goodness to me. One of the brethren said almost immediately on my arrival at Teignmouth, I wish you would become our minister, as the present one is going to leave us. My answer was, I do not intend to be stationary in any place, but to go through the country, preaching the Word as the Lord may direct me. In the evening, Monday, I preached for brother Craik, at Shaldon, in the presence of three ministers, none of whom liked the sermon; yet it pleased God, through it, to bring to the knowledge of His dear Son, a young woman who had been servant to one of these ministers, and who had heard her master preach many times. How differently does the Lord judge from man! Here was a particular opportunity for the Lord to get glory to Himself. A foreigner was the preacher, with great natural obstacles in the way, for he was not able to speak English with fluency; but he had a desire to serve God, and was by this time also brought into such a state of heart as to desire that God alone should have the glory, if any good were done through his instrumentality. How often has it struck me, both at that time and since, that His strength was made perfect in my weakness.

On Tuesday evening I preached at Ebenezer Chapel, Teignmouth, the same chapel at the opening of which I became acquainted with the brother, whom the Lord had afterwards used as an instrument of benefiting me so much. My preaching was also disliked there by many of the hearers; but the Lord opened the hearts of a few to receive the truth, and another young woman was brought to the Lord through the instrumentality of the word then preached. On Wednesday I preached again in the same chapel, and the word was disliked still, perhaps more, though the few, who received the truth in the love of it, increased in number. On Thursday I preached again at Shaldon, and on Friday at Teignmouth. The effect was the same; dislike on the one side, and joy and delight in the truth on the other. By this time I began to reflect about the cause of this opposition; for the same brethren who had treated me with much kindness the summer previous, when I was less spiritually minded, and understood much less of the truth, now seemed to oppose me, and I could not explain it in any other way than this, that the Lord intended to work through my instrumentality at Teignmouth, and that therefore Satan, fearing this, sought to raise opposition against me.

On the Lord's day I dined with a brother, whose heart the Lord had opened to receive me as a servant of Christ. After dinner I talked to a young woman, his servant, at the request of her sister, who on the Tuesday previous had been convinced of sin, and on the Friday brought to enjoy peace in the Lord. This young woman also was, through the instrumentality of this conversation, brought to see her sinful state, though she could not rejoice in the Lord until about seven months after. How differently the Lord dealt with her sister, and yet the work of grace was as real in the one as in the other, as I had full opportunity of seeing afterwards! On this same Lord's day I preached twice at Teignmouth, and once at Shaldon; for so precious did every opportunity seem to me, and so powerfully did I feel the importance of those precious truths, which I had so recently been led to see, that I longed to be instrumental in communicating them to others.

By this time the request, that I might stay at Teignmouth, and be the minister of the above chapel, had been repeatedly expressed by an increasing number of the brethren; but others were decidedly against my remaining there. This opposition was instrumental in settling it in my mind that I should stay for awhile, at least until I was formally rejected. In consequence of this conclusion I took the following step, which, it may be, I should not repeat under similar circumstances, but which was certainly taken in love to those who were concerned in the matter, and for the glory of God, as far as I then had light.

On the Tuesday following, after preaching, I told the brethren how, in the providence of God, I had been brought to them without the least intention of staying among them, but that, on finding them without a minister, I had been led to see it to be the will of God to remain with them. I also told them, as far as I remember, that I was aware of the opposition of some, but that I nevertheless intended to preach to them till they rejected me; and if they should say, I might preach, but they would give me no salary, that would make no difference on my part, as I did not preach for the sake of money; but I told them, at the same time, that it was an honour, to be allowed to supply the temporal wants of any of the servants of Christ. The latter point I added, as it seemed right to me, to give out the whole counsel of God, as far as I

FIRST PART

knew it. On the next day, Wednesday, I left, and having preached in two or three places near Exmouth, and taken leave of my friends there, I returned to Teignmouth.

Here I preached again three times on the Lord's day, none saying we wish you not to preach, though many of the hearers did not hear with enjoyment. Some of them left, and never returned; some left, but returned after awhile. Others came to the chapel, who had not been in the habit of attending there previous to my coming. There was sufficient proof that the work of God was going on, for there were those who were glad to hear what I preached, overlooking the infirmities of the foreigner, delighting in the food for their souls, without caring much about the form in which the truth was set before them; and these were not less spiritual than the rest: and there were those who objected decidedly; some, however, manifesting merely the weakness of brethren, and others the bitterness of the opposers of the cross. There was, in addition to this, a great stir, a spirit of inquiry, and a searching of the Scriptures, whether these things were so. And what is more than all, God set His seal upon the work, in converting sinners. Twelve weeks I stood in this same position, whilst the Lord graciously supplied my temporal wants, through two brethren, unasked for. After this time, the whole little church, eighteen in number, unanimously gave me an invitation to become their pastor. My answer to them was, that their invitation did not show me more than I had seen before, that it was the will of God that I should remain with them, yet that for their sakes I could not but rejoice in this invitation, as it was a proof to me that God had blessed them through my instrumentality, in making them thus of one mind. I also expressly stated to the brethren, that I should only stay so long with them, as I saw it clearly to be the will of the Lord; for I had not given up my intention of going from place to place, if the Lord would allow me to do so. The brethren, at the same time, now offered to supply my temporal wants, by giving me £55. a year, which sum was afterwards somewhat increased, on account of the increase of the church.

I now had Teignmouth for my residence, but I did not confine my labours to this place; for I preached regularly once a week in Exeter, once a fortnight at Topsham, sometimes at Shaldon, often at Exmouth, sometimes in the above-mentioned villages near Exmouth, regularly once a week at Bishopsteignton, where a part of the church lived, and afterwards repeatedly at Chudleigh, Collumpton, Newton Bushel, and elsewhere.

That which I now considered the best mode of preparation for the public ministry of the Word, no longer adopted from necessity, on account of want of time, but from deep conviction, and from the experience of God's blessing upon it, both as it regards my own enjoyment, the benefit of the saints, and the conversion of sinners, is as follows:--1. I do not presume to know myself what is best for the hearers, and I therefore ask the Lord in the first place, that He would graciously be pleased to teach me on what subject I shall speak, or what portion of His word I shall expound. Now sometimes it happens, that previous to my asking Him, a subject or passage has been in my mind, on which it has appeared well for me to speak. In that case I ask the Lord, whether I should speak on this subject or passage. If, after prayer, I feel persuaded that I should I fix upon it, yet so, that I would desire to leave myself open to the Lord to change it, if He please. Frequently, however, it occurs, that I have no text or subject in my mind, before I give myself to prayer for the sake of ascertaining the Lord's will concerning it. In this case I wait some time on my knees for an answer, trying to listen to the voice of the Spirit to direct me. If then a passage or subject, whilst I am on my knees, or after I have finished praying for a text, is brought to my mind, I again ask the Lord, and that sometimes repeatedly, especially if, humanly speaking, the subject or text should be a peculiar one, whether it be His will that I should speak on such a subject or passage. If after prayer my mind is peaceful about it, I take this to be the text, but still desire to leave myself open to the Lord for direction, should He please to alter it, or should I have been mistaken. Frequently also, in the third place, it happens, that I not only have no text nor subject on my mind previous to my praying for guidance in this matter, but also I do not obtain one after once, or twice, or more times praying about it. I used formerly at times to be much perplexed, when this was the case, but for more than forty-five years it has pleased the Lord, in general at least, to keep me in peace about it. What I do is, to go on with my regular reading of the Scriptures, where I left off the last time, praying (whilst I read) for a text, now and then also laying aside my bible for prayer, till I get one. Thus it has happened, that I have had to read five, ten; yea twenty chapters, before it has pleased the Lord to give me a text: yea, many times I have even had to go to the place of meeting without one, and obtained it perhaps only a few minutes before I was going to speak; but I have never lacked the Lord's assistance at the time of preaching, provided I had earnestly sought it in private. The preacher cannot know the particular state of the various individuals who compose the congregation, nor what they require, but the Lord knows it; and if the preacher renounces his own wisdom, he will be assisted by the Lord; but if he will choose in his own wisdom, then let him not be surprised if he should see little benefit result from his labours.

Before I leave this part of the subject, I would just observe one temptation concerning the choice of a text. We may see a subject to be so very full, that it may strike us it would do for some other occasion. For instance, sometimes a text, brought to one's mind for a week-evening meeting, may appear more suitable for the Lord's day, because then there would be a greater number of hearers present. Now, in the first place, we do not know whether the Lord ever will allow us to preach on another Lord's day; and, in the second place, we know not whether that very subject may not be especially suitable for some or many individuals present just that week-evening. Thus I was once tempted, after I had been a short time at Teignmouth, to reserve a subject, which had been just opened to me, for the next Lord's day. But being able, by the grace of God, to overcome the temptation by the above reasons, and preaching about it at once, it pleased the Lord to bless it to the conversion of a sinner, and that too an individual who meant to come but that once more to the chapel, and to whose case the subject was most remarkably suited.

2. Now when the text has been obtained in the above way, whether it be one or two or more verses, or a whole chapter or more, I ask the Lord that He would graciously be pleased to teach me by His Holy Spirit, whilst meditating over it. Within

FIRST PART

the last fifty years, I have found it the most profitable plan to meditate with my pen in my hand, writing down the outlines, as the Word is opened to me. This I do, not for the sake of committing them to memory, nor as if I meant to say nothing else, but for the sake of clearness, as being a help to see how far I understand the passage. I also find it useful afterwards to refer to what I have thus written. I very seldom use any other help besides the little I understand of the original of the Scriptures, and some good translations in other languages. My chief help is prayer. I have NEVER in my life begun to study one single part of divine truth, without gaining some light about it, when I have been able really to give myself to prayer and meditation over it. But that I have often found a difficult matter, partly on account of the weakness of the flesh, and partly also on account of bodily infirmities and multiplicity of engagements. This I most firmly believe, that no one ought to expect to see much good resulting from his labours in word and doctrine, if he is not much given to prayer and meditation.

3. Having prayed and meditated on the subject or text, I desire to leave myself entirely in the hands of the Lord. I ask Him to bring to my mind what I have seen in my room, concerning the subject I am going to speak on, which He generally most kindly does, and often teaches me much additionally, whilst I am preaching.

In connection with the above, I must, however, state, that it appears to me there is a preparation for the public ministry of the Word, which is even more excellent than the one spoken of. It is this: to live in such constant and real communion with the Lord, and to be so habitually and frequently in meditation over the truth, that without the above effort, so to speak, we have obtained food for others, and know the mind of the Lord as to the subject or the portion of the Word on which we should speak. But this I have only in a small measure experienced, though I desire to be brought into such a state, that habitually "out of my belly may flow rivers of living water."

That which I have found most beneficial in my experience for the last fifty-one years in the public ministry of the Word, is, expounding the Scriptures, and especially the going now and then through a whole gospel or epistle. This may be done in a two-fold way, either by entering minutely into the bearing of every point occurring in the portion, or by giving the general outlines, and thus leading the hearers to see the meaning and connexion of the whole. The benefits which I have seen resulting from expounding the Scriptures are these: 1. The hearers are thus, with God's blessing, led to the Scriptures. They find, as it were, a practical use of them in the public meetings. This induces them to bring their bibles, and I have observed that those who at first did not bring them, have afterwards been induced to do so: so that in a short time few, of the believers at least, were in the habit of coming without them. This is no small matter; for every thing, which in our day will lead believers to value the Scriptures, is of importance. 2. The expounding of the Scriptures is in general more beneficial to the hearers than if, on a single verse, or half a verse, or two or three words of a verse some remarks are made, so that the portion of Scripture is scarcely anything but a motto for the subject; for few have grace to meditate much over the Word, and thus exposition may not merely be the means of opening up to them the Scriptures, but may also create in them a desire to meditate for themselves. 3. The expounding of the Scriptures leaves to the hearers a connecting link, so that the reading over again the portion of the Word, which has been expounded, brings to their remembrance what has been said; and thus, with God's blessing, leaves a more lasting impression on their minds. This is particularly of importance as it regards the illiterate, who sometimes have neither much strength of memory nor capacity of comprehension. 4. The expounding of large portions of the Word, as the whole of a gospel or an epistle, besides leading the hearer to see the connexion of the whole, has also this particular benefit for the teacher, that it leads him, with God's blessing, to the consideration of portions of the Word, which otherwise he might not have considered, and keeps him from speaking too much on favourite subjects, and leaning too much to particular parts of truth, which tendency must surely sooner or later injure both himself and his hearers.--Expounding the word of God brings little honour to the preacher from the unenlightened or careless hearer, but it tends much to the benefit of the hearers in general.

Simplicity in expression, whilst the truth is set forth, is, in connexion with what has been said, of the utmost importance. It should be the aim of the teacher to speak so, that children, servants, and people who cannot read, may be able to understand him, so far as the natural mind can comprehend the things of God. It ought also to be remembered, that there is, perhaps, not a single congregation in which there are not persons of the above classes present, and that if they can understand, the well-educated or literary persons will understand likewise; but the reverse does not hold good. It ought further to be remembered that the expounder of the truth of God speaks for God, for eternity, and that it is not in the least likely that he will benefit the hearers, except he uses plainness of speech, which nevertheless needs not to be vulgar or rude. It should also be considered, that if the preacher strive to speak according to the rules of this world, he may please many, Particularly those who have a literary taste; but, in the same proportion, he is less likely to become an instrument in the hands of God for the conversion of sinners, or for the building up of the saints. For neither eloquence nor depth of thought make the truly great preacher, but such a life of prayer and meditation and spirituality, as may render him a vessel meet for the Master's use, and fit to be employed both in the conversion of sinners and in the edification of the saints.

About the beginning of April I went to preach at Sidmouth. While I was staying there, three sisters in the Lord had, in my presence, a conversation about baptism, one of whom had been baptized after she had believed. When they had conversed a little on the subject, I was asked to give my opinion concerning it. My reply was, "I do not think, that I need to be baptized again." I was then asked by the sister who bad been baptized, "But have you been baptized?" I answered, "Yes, when I was a child." She then replied, "Have you ever read the Scriptures, and prayed with reference to this subject?" I answered, "No." "Then," she said, "I entreat you, never to speak any more about it till you have done so." It pleased the Lord to show me the importance of this remark; for whilst at that very time I was exhorting every one to receive noth-

FIRST PART

ing which could not be proved by the word of God, I had repeatedly spoken against believers' baptism, without having ever earnestly examined the Scriptures, or prayed concerning it; and now I determined, if God would help me, to examine that subject also, and if infant baptism were found to be scriptural, I would earnestly defend it; and if believers' baptism were right, I would as strenuously defend that, and be baptized.

As soon as I had time, I set about examining the subject. The mode I adopted was as follows: I repeatedly asked God to teach me concerning it, and I read the New Testament from the beginning, with a particular reference to this point. But now, when I earnestly set about the matter, a number of objections presented themselves to my mind.

1. Since many holy and enlightened men have been divided in opinion concerning this point, does this not prove, that it is not to be expected we should come to a satisfactory conclusion about this question in the present imperfect state of the church?--This question was thus removed: If this ordinance is revealed in the Bible, why may I not know it, as the Holy Spirit is the teacher in the church of Christ now as well as formerly? 2. There have been but few of my friends baptized, and the greater part of them are opposed to believers' baptism, and they will turn their backs on me. Answer: Though all men should forsake me, if the Lord Jesus takes me up, I shall be happy. 3. You will be sure to lose one half of your income if you are baptized. Answer: As long as I desire to be faithful to the Lord, He will not suffer me to want. 4. People will call you a baptist, and you will be reckoned among that body, and you cannot approve of all that is going on among them. Answer: It does not follow that I must in all points go along with all those who hold believers' baptism, although I should be baptized. 5. You have been preaching for some years, and you will have thus publicly to confess, that you have been in an error, should you be led to see that believers' baptism is right. Answer: It is much better to confess that I have been in error concerning that point than to continue in it. 6. Even if believers' baptism should be right, yet it is now too late to attend to it, as you ought to have been baptized immediately on believing. Answer: It is better to fulfill a commandment of the Lord Jesus ever so late, than to continue in the neglect of it.

It had pleased God, in his abundant mercy, to bring my mind into such a state, that I was willing to carry out into my life whatever I should find in the Scriptures concerning this ordinance, either the one way or the other. I could say, "I will do His will," and it was on that account, I believe, that I soon saw which "doctrine is of God," whether infant baptism or believers' baptism. And I would observe here, by the way, that the passage to which I have just now alluded, John vii. 17, has been a most remarkable comment to me on many doctrines and precepts of our most holy faith. For instance: "Resist not evil: but whosoever shall smite thee on thy right cheek, turn to him the other also. And if any man will sue thee at the law, and take away thy coat, let him have thy cloak also. And whosoever shall compel thee to go a mile, go with him twain. Give to him that asketh thee, and from him that would borrow of thee turn not thou away. Love your enemies, bless them that curse you, do good to them that hate you, and pray for them which despitefully use you, and persecute you." Matthew v. 39-44. "Sell that ye have, and give alms." Luke xii. 33. "Owe no man any thing, but to love one another." Rom. xiii. 8. It may be said, surely these passages cannot be taken literally, for how then would the people of God be able to pass through the world. The state of mind enjoined in John vii. 17, will cause such objections to vanish. Whosoever is WILLING To ACT OUT these commandments of the Lord LITERALLY, will, I believe, be led with me to see that, to take them LITERALLY, is the will of God.--Those who do so take them will doubtless often be brought into difficulties, hard to the flesh to bear, but these will have a tendency to make them constantly feel that they are strangers and pilgrims here, that this world is not their home, and thus to throw them more upon God, who will assuredly help us through any difficulty into which we may be brought by seeking to act in obedience to His word.

As soon as I was brought into this state of heart, I saw from the Scriptures that believers ONLY are the proper subjects for baptism, and that immersion is the only true Scriptural mode, in which it ought to be attended to. The passage which particularly convinced me of the former, is Acts viii. 36-38, and of the latter, Rom. vi. 3-5. Some time after, I was baptized. I had much peace in doing so, and never have I for one single moment regretted it.--Before I leave this point, I would just say a few words concerning the result of this matter, so far as it regards some of the objections which occurred to my mind when I was about to examine the Scriptures concerning baptism.

1. Concerning the first objection, my conviction now is, that of all revealed truths not on is more clearly revealed in the Scriptures, not even the doctrine of justification by faith, and that the subject has only become obscured by men not having been willing to take the Scriptures alone to decide the point.

2. Not one of my true friends in the Lord has turned his back on me, as I supposed, and almost all of them have been themselves baptized since.

3. Though in one way I lost money in consequence of being baptized, yet the Lord did not suffer me to be really a loser, even as it regards temporal things; for He made up the loss most bountifully. In conclusion, my example has been the means of leading many to examine the question of baptism, and to submit, from conviction, to this ordinance and seeing this truth I have been led to speak on it as well as on other truths; and during the forty-five years that I have now resided in Bristol, more than three thousand believers have been baptized among us.

In June of this year (1830) I went to preach at the opening of a chapel in a village near Barnstaple, built by that blessed man of God, Thomas Pugsley, now with the Lord. It pleased God to bring two souls to Himself through this my visit, and one more was converted on another visit. So graciously did the Lord condescend to use me, that almost everywhere He blessed the Word which I preached, thereby testifying that He had sent me, and thereby also getting glory to Himself in using such an

FIRST PART

instrument. It was so usual for me to preach with particular assistance, especially during the first months of this year, that once, when it was otherwise, it was much noticed by myself and others. The circumstance was this. One day, before preaching at Teignmouth, I had more time than usual, and therefore prayed and meditated about six hours, in preparation for the evening meeting, and I thought I saw many precious truths in the passage on which I had meditated. It was the first part of the first chapter of the epistle to the Ephesians. After I had spoken a little time, I felt that I spoke in my own strength, and I, being a foreigner, felt particularly the want of words, which had not been the case before. I told the brethren, that I felt I was left to myself, and asked their prayers. But after having continued a little longer, and feeling the same as before, I closed, and proposed that we should have a meeting for prayer, that the Lord still might be pleased to help me. We did so, and I was particularly assisted the next time.

During this summer also it appeared to me scriptural, according to the example of the Apostles, Acts xx. 7, to break bread every Lord's day, though there is no commandment given to do so, either by the Lord, or by the Holy Ghost through the Apostles. And at the same time it appeared to me scriptural, according to Eph. iv., Rom. xii., &c., that there should be given room for the Holy Ghost to work through any of the brethren whom He pleased to use; that thus one member might benefit the other with the gift which the Lord has bestowed upon him. Accordingly at certain meetings any of the brethren had an opportunity to exhort or teach the rest, if they considered that they had any thing to say which might be beneficial to the hearers.--I observe here, that, as the Lord gave me grace to endeavour at once to carry out the light which He had been pleased to give me on this point, and as the truth was but in part apprehended, there was much infirmity mixed with the manner of carrying it out. Nor was it until several years after that the Lord was pleased to teach me about this point more perfectly. That the disciples of Jesus should meet together, on the first day of the week, for the breaking of bread, and that that should be their principal meeting, and that those, whether one or several, who are truly gifted by the Holy Spirit for service, be it for exhortation, or teaching, or rule, &c., are responsible to the Lord for the exercise of their gifts: these are to me no matters of uncertainty, but points on which my soul, by grace, is established, through the revealed will of God.

On October 7th, 1830, I was united by marriage to Miss Mary Groves, sister of the brother whose name has already been mentioned. This step was taken after prayer and deliberation, from a full conviction that it was better for me to be married: and I have never regretted since, either the step itself or the choice, but desire to be truly grateful to God for having given me such a wife.

About this time I began to have conscientious objections against any longer receiving a stated salary. My reasons against it were these:--

1. The salary was made up by pew-rents; but pew-rents are, according to James ii. 1-6, against the mind of the Lord, as, in general, the poor brother cannot have so good a seat as the rich. (All pew-rents were therefore given up, and all the

seats made free, which was stated at the entrance of the chapel). 2. A brother may gladly do something towards my support if left to his own time; but when the quarter is up, he has perhaps other expenses, and I do not know, whether he pays his money grudgingly, and of necessity, or cheerfully; but God loveth a cheerful giver. Nay, I knew it to be a fact, that sometimes it had not been convenient to individuals to pay the money, when it had been asked for by the brethren who collected it. 3. Though the Lord had been pleased to give me grace to be faithful, so that I had been enabled not to keep back the truth, when He had shown it to me; still I felt that the pew-rents were a snare to the servant of Christ. It was a temptation to me, at least for a few minutes, at the time when the Lord had stirred me up to pray and search the Word respecting the ordinance of baptism, because £30. of my salary was at stake, if I should be baptized.

For these reasons I stated to the brethren, at the end of October, 1830, that I should for the future give up having any regular salary. After I had given my reasons for doing so, I read Philippians iv., and told the saints, that if they still had a desire to do something towards my support, by voluntary gifts, I had no objection to receive them, though ever so small, either in money or provisions. A few days after it appeared to me, that there was a better way still; for if I received personally every single gift, offered in money, both my own time and that of the donors would be much taken up; and in this way also the poor might, through temptation, be kept from offering their pence, a privilege of which they ought not to be deprived; and some also might in this way give more than if it were not known who was the giver; so that it would still be doubtful whether the gifts were given grudgingly or cheerfully. For these reasons especially, there was a box put up in the chapel, over which was written, that whoever had a desire to do something towards my support, might put his offering into the box.

At the same time it appeared to me right, that henceforth I should ask no man, not even my beloved brethren and sisters, to help me, as I had done a few times according to their own request, as my expenses, on account of traveling much in the Lord's service, were too great to be met by my usual income. For unconsciously I had thus again been led, in some measure, to trust in an arm of flesh; going to man, instead of going to the Lord at once. To come to this conclusion before God, required more grace than to give up my salary.

About the same time also my wife and I had grace given to us to take the Lord's commandment, "Sell that ye have, and give alms," Luke xii. 33, literally, and to carry it out. Our staff and support in this matter were Matthew vi. 19-34, John xiv. 13, 14. We leaned on the arm of the Lord Jesus. It is now fifty-one years, since we set out in this way, and we do not in the least regret the step we then took. Our God also has, in His tender mercy, given us grace to abide in the same mind concerning the above points, both as it regards principle and practice; and this has been the means of letting us see the tender love and care of our God over His children, even in the most minute things, in a way in which we never experimentally knew them before; and it has, in particular, made the Lord known to us more fully than we knew

FIRST PART

Him before, as a prayer hearing God. As I have written down how the Lord has been pleased to deal with us since, I shall be able to relate some facts concerning this matter, as far as they may tend to edification.

Extracts from my Journal.

Nov. 18th, 1830.--Our money was reduced to about eight shillings. When I was praying with my wife in the morning, the Lord brought to my mind the state of our purse, and I was led to ask Him for some money. About four hours after, we were with a sister at Bishopsteignton, and she said to me, "Do you want any money?" "I told the brethren," said I, "dear sister, when I gave up my salary, that I would for the future tell the Lord only about my wants." She replied, "But He has told me to give you some money. About a fortnight ago I asked Him, what I should do for Him, and He told me to give you some money; and last Saturday it came again powerfully to my mind, and has not left me since, and I felt it so forcibly last night, that I could not help speaking of it to Brother P." My heart rejoiced, seeing the Lord's faithfulness, but I thought it better not to tell her about our circumstances, lest she should be influenced to give accordingly; and I also was assured, that, if it were of the Lord, she could not but give. I therefore turned the conversation to other subjects, but when I left she gave me two guineas. We were full of joy on account of the goodness of the Lord.--I would call upon the reader to admire the gentleness of the Lord, that He did not try our faith much at the commencement, but gave us first encouragement, and allowed us to see His willingness to help us, before He was pleased to try it more fully.

The next Wednesday I went to Exmouth, our money having then again been reduced to about nine shillings. I asked the Lord on Thursday, when at Exmouth, to be pleased to give me some money. On Friday morning, about eight o'clock, whilst in prayer, I was particularly led to ask again for money; and before I rose from my knees I had the fullest assurance, that we should have the answer that very day. About nine o'clock I left the brother with whom I was staying, and he gave me half a sovereign, saying, "Take this for the expenses connected with your coming to us." I did not expect to have my expenses paid, but I saw the Lord's fatherly hand in sending me this money within one hour after my asking Him for some. But even then I was so fully assured that the Lord would send more that very day, or had done so already, that, when I came home about twelve o'clock, I asked my wife whether she had received any letters. She told me she had received one the day before from a brother in Exeter, with three sovereigns. Thus even my prayer on the preceding day had been answered. The next day one of the brethren came and brought me £4., which was due to me of my former salary, but which I could never have expected, as I did not even know that this sum was due to me. Thus I received, within thirty hours, in answer to prayer, £7. 10s.

In the commencement of December I went to Collumpton, where I preached several times, and likewise in a neighbouring village. In driving home from the village late at night, our driver lost his way. As soon as we found out our mistake, being then near a house, it struck me that the hand of God was in this matter; and having awakened the people of the house, I offered a man something if he would be kind enough to bring us into the right road. I now walked with the man before the gig, and conversed with him about the things of God, and soon found out that he was an awful backslider. May God, in mercy, bless the word spoken to him, and may we learn from this circumstance, that we have to ask on such occasions, why the Lord has allowed such and such things to happen to us.--Since the publication of the first edition, one day, about eight years after this circumstance had happened, the individual who drove me that night introduced himself to me as a believer, and told me that on that evening he received his first impressions under the preaching of the Word. The missing of the right road may have been connected with his state of mind. May I and my fellow-labourers in the Gospel be encouraged by this, patiently to continue to sow the seed, though only after eight years or more we should see the fruit of it. I only add, that up to that time, the individual had been a very dissipated young man, who caused his believing parents very much grief. Their love led them to convey me and my wife to this village and back again, and truly the Lord gave them a reward in doing so.

Between Christmas and the new year, when our money was reduced to a few shillings, I asked the Lord for more; when a few hours after there was given to us a sovereign by a brother from Axminster. This brother had heard much against me, and was at last determined to hear for himself, and thus came to Teignmouth, a distance of forty miles; and having heard about our manner of living, gave us this money.

With this closes the year 1830. Throughout it the Lord richly supplied all my temporal wants, though at the commencement of it I had no certain human prospect for one single shilling; so that, even as it regards temporal things, I had not been in the smallest degree a loser in acting according to the dictates of my conscience; and, as it regards spiritual things, the Lord had indeed dealt bountifully with me, and led me on in many respects, and, moreover, had condescended to use me as an instrument in doing His work.

On January 6th, 7th, and 8th, 1831, I had repeatedly asked the Lord for money, but received none. On the evening of January 8th I left my room for a few minutes, and was then tempted to distrust the Lord, though He had been so gracious to us, in that He not only up to that day had supplied all our wants, but had given us also those answers of prayer, which have been in part just mentioned. I was so sinful, for about five minutes, as to think it would be of no use to trust in the Lord in this way. I also began to say to myself, that I had perhaps gone too far in living in this way. But, thanks to the Lord! this trial lasted but a few minutes. He enabled me again to trust in Him, and Satan was immediately confounded; for when I returned to my room (out of which I had not been absent ten minutes), the Lord had sent deliverance. A sister in the Lord, who resided at Exeter, had come to Teignmouth, and brought us £2. 4s.; so the Lord triumphed, and our faith was strengthened.

FIRST PART

Jan. 10. Today, when we had again but a few shillings, £5. was given to us, which had been taken out of the box. I had, once for all, told the brethren, who had the care of these temporal things, to have the kindness to let me have the money every week; but as these beloved brethren either forgot to take it out weekly, or were ashamed to bring it in such small sums, it was generally taken out every three, four, or five weeks. As I had stated to them, however, from the commencement, that I desired to look neither to man nor the box, but to the living God, I thought it not right on my part, to remind them of my request to have the money weekly, lest it should hinder the testimony which I wished to give, of trusting in the living God alone. It was on this account that on January 28th, when we had again but little money, though I had seen the brethren on January the 24th open the box and take out the money, I would not ask the brother, in whose hands it was, to let me have it; but, standing in need of it, as our coals were almost gone, I asked the Lord to incline his heart to bring it, and but a little time afterwards it was given to us, even £1. 8s. 6d.

I would here mention, that since the time I began living in this way, I have been kept from speaking, either directly or indirectly, about my wants, at the time I was in need. But whilst I have refrained, and do still habitually refrain, from speaking to my fellow creatures about my wants at the time, I desire to speak well of the Lord's goodness, after He has delivered me; not only in order that He thus may get glory, but also that the children of God may be encouraged to trust in Him.

On February 14th we had again very little money, and, whilst praying, I was led to ask the Lord, graciously to supply our wants; and the instant that I rose from my knees, a brother gave me £1., which had been taken out of the box.

On March 7th I was again tempted to disbelieve the faithfulness of the Lord, and though I was not miserable, still I was not so fully resting upon the Lord, that I could triumph with joy. It was but one hour after, when the Lord gave me another proof of His faithful love. A Christian lady at Teignmouth had been from home for some time, and on her return she brought from the sisters in the Lord, with whom she had been staying, five sovereigns for us, with these words written in the paper;--"I was an hungered, and ye gave me meat; I was thirsty, and ye gave me drink. Lord, when saw we Thee an hungered, and fed Thee? or thirsty, and gave Thee drink? The King shall answer and say unto them, "Verily, verily, I say unto you, inasmuch as ye have done it unto one of the least of these my brethren, ye have done it unto me."

On March 16th I went to Axminster, and preached in several places in that neighbourhood, besides holding a meeting at Axminster. Whilst staying there I was requested to preach at Chard; but as I had never been away from Teignmouth on the Lord's day, I had to pray much, before I came to the conclusion to comply with the request. At last I had the fullest assurance that I ought to preach at Chard. I have since heard that the Lord used me in edifying the brethren, and through a general exhortation to all, to read the Scriptures with earnestness, a woman was stirred up to do so, and this was the means of her conversion. As to myself, I had a most refreshing season. I mention this circumstance to show how important it is to ascertain the will of God, before we undertake any thing, because we are then not only blessed in our own souls, but also the work of our hands will prosper.--One of the brethren at Chard forced a sovereign upon me, against the acceptance of which I strove much, lest it should appear as if I had preached for money. Another would give me a paper with money. I refused it for the same reason. At last he put it by force into my pocket, and ran away. The paper contained 11s. 6d.

April 16th. This morning I found that our money was reduced to 3s., and I said to myself, I must now go and ask the Lord earnestly for fresh supplies. But before I had prayed, there was sent from Exeter £2, as a proof that the Lord hears before we call.

I would observe here, by the way, that if any of the children of God should think that such a mode of living leads away from the Lord, and from caring about spiritual things, and has the effect of causing the mind to be taken up with the question, What shall I eat? What shall I drink?--and Wherewithal shall I be clothed? and that on that account it would be much better to have a stated salary, particularly for one who labours in the word and doctrine, in order that he may be above these cares; I say, should any believer think so, I would request him, prayerfully to consider the following remarks:--1. I have had experience of both ways, and know that my present mode of living, as to temporal things, is connected with less care. 2. Confidence in the Lord, to whom alone I look for the supply of my temporal wants, keeps me, at least whilst faith is in exercise, when a case of distress comes before me, or when the Lord's work calls for my pecuniary aid, from anxious reckoning like this: Will my salary last out? Shall I have enough myself the next month? &c. In this my freedom, I am, by the grace of God, generally at least, able to say to myself something like this:--My Lord is not limited; He can again supply; He knows that this present case has been sent to me; and thus, this way of living, so far from leading to anxiety, as it regards possible future want, is rather the means of keeping from it. And truly it was once said to me by an individual,--You can do such and such things, and need not to lay by, for the church in the whole of Devonshire cares about your wants. My reply was: The Lord can use not merely any of the saints throughout Devonshire, but those throughout the world, as instruments to supply my temporal wants. 3. This way of living has often been the means of reviving the work of grace in my heart, when I have been getting cold; and it also has been the means of bringing me back again to the Lord, after I have been backsliding. For it will not do,--it is not possible, to live in sin, and, at the same time, by communion with God, to draw down from heaven every thing one needs for the life that now is. 4. Frequently, too, a fresh answer to prayer, obtained in this way, has been the means of quickening my soul, and filling me with much joy.

About April 20th I went to Chumleigh. Here and in the neighbourhood I preached repeatedly, and from thence I went to Barnstaple. Whilst we were at Barnstaple, there was found in my wife's bag a sovereign, put there anonymously. A sister also gave us £2. On our return to Teignmouth, May 2, when we emptied our travelling bag, there fell out a paper with money. It contained two sovereigns and threepence, the latter put in, no doubt, to make a noise in emptying the bag. May the Lord bless and reward the giver! In a similar way we found 4s. put anonymously into one of our drawers, a few days after.

June 6. Having prayed much on the previous days, that, when we wanted money, the Lord would be pleased to send some, today, after I had again asked for it, a poor sister brought half a sovereign, 5s. from herself, and 5s. from another very poor sister. This is not only a fresh proof that the Lord hears prayer, but also that He sends by whom He will. Our money had been reduced to 8s.

June 12. Lord's day. On Thursday last I went with brother Craik to Torquay, to preach there. I had only about 3s. with me and left my wife with about 6s. at home. The Lord provided beds for us through the hospitality of a brother. I asked the Lord repeatedly for money; but when I came home my wife had only about 3s. left, having received nothing. We waited still upon the Lord. Yesterday passed away, and no money came. We had 9d. left. This morning we were still waiting upon the Lord, and looking for deliverance. We had only a little butter left for breakfast, sufficient for brother E. and a relative living with us, to whom we did not mention our circumstances, that they might not be made uncomfortable. After the morning meeting, brother Y. most unexpectedly opened the box, and, in giving me quite as unexpectedly the money at such a time, he told me that he and his wife could not sleep last night on account of thinking that we might want money. The most striking point is, that, after I had repeatedly asked the Lord, but received nothing, I then prayed yesterday, that the Lord would be pleased to impress it on brother Y. that we wanted money, so that he might open the box. There was in it £1. 8s. 10 1/2d. Our joy on account of this fresh deliverance was great, and we praised the Lord heartily.

June 18. Brother Craik called on us today, and he then had only 1 1/2d. left. A few minutes after, he received: a sum of money, and in returning to us on his way home, he gave us 10s., when we had but 3s. left.

July 20. A shoulder of mutton and a loaf were sent to us anonymously.--I understood some time afterwards, that Satan had raised the false report that we were starving, in consequence of which a believer sent these provisions. I would mention by the way, that various reports have been circulated, on account of this our way of living. Sometimes it has been said that we had not enough to eat, and that surely such and such an infirmity of body we had brought on us, because we had not the necessaries of life. Now, the truth is, that, whilst we have been often brought low; yea, so low, that we have not had even as much as one single penny left; or so as to have the last bread on the table, and not as much money as was needed to buy another loaf;-- yet never have we had to sit down to a meal, without our good Lord having provided nourishing food for us. I am bound to state this, and I do it with pleasure. My Master has been a kind Master to me, and if I had to choose this day again, as to the way of living, the Lord giving me grace, I would not choose differently. But even these very reports, false as they were, I doubt not the Lord has sometimes used as a means, to put it into the hearts of His children, to remember our temporal necessities.

THE LORD'S DEALINGS WITH GEORGE MÜLLER

About July 25th I preached several times at Collumpton, and in a neighbouring village, in the open air. My experience as it regards preaching in the open air has been very different from what I might have expected. I have often preached out of doors, and but once has it been blessed, as far as I know, and that was in the case of an officer in the army, who came to make sport of it; whilst almost in every place, if not in every place, where I have preached in rooms or chapels, the Lord has given testimony to the Word. Perhaps the Lord has not been pleased to let me see fruit from this part of my work, though I have been many times engaged in it; or it may be, that, because I did not pray so earnestly respecting my out-door preaching as respecting my in-door preaching, the former has not been so much blessed as the latter. But this testimony I cannot but bear, that, though I do not consider it at present my work, on account of want of bodily strength, yet it is a most important work, and I should delight in being so honoured now, as to be allowed to be engaged in it.

August 9. After extreme suffering, which lasted about seventeen hours, my wife was this day delivered of a still-born child.--Who of my readers would suppose, that whilst I was so abundantly blessed by God, and that in so many respects, my heart should have been again many times during several months previous to this day, cold, wretched, carnal? How long-suffering is the Lord! Repeatedly, during this time, I could let hours run on, after I had risen in the morning, before I prayed; at least, before I retired for prayer. And at that time when I appeared most zealous for God, perhaps more so than at any time before or since, I was often far from being in a spiritual state. I was not now, indeed, indulging in gross outward sins, which could be noticed by my brethren; but often--very often, the eye of my kind loving Father must have looked on me with much grief. On this account, I have no doubt, the Lord now, in great compassion, sent this heavy blow. I had not seriously thought of the great danger connected with childbearing, and therefore had never earnestly prayed about it. Now came this solemn time. The life of my dear wife was hanging, as it were, on a thread, and, in the midst of it, my conscience told me, that my state of heart made such a chastisement needful. Yet, at the same time, I was much supported.--When the child was still-born, I saw almost immediately afterwards, that this could not have been expected otherwise, for I had not looked on the prospect of having a child as on a blessing, which I was about to receive from God, but rather considered it as a burden and a hindrance in the Lord's work; for I did not know then, that, whilst a wife and children may be in certain respects, on the one hand, a hindrance to the servant of Christ, they also may fit him, on the other hand, for certain parts of his work, in teaching him things which are important to be known, especially for the pastoral work. The Lord now brought, in addition to this, very great sufferings upon my beloved wife, which lasted for six weeks, combined with a partial lameness of the left side.--Immediately after the eventful time of August 8th and 9th, the Lord brought me, in His tender mercy, again into a spiritual state of heart, so that I was enabled to look on this chastisement as a great blessing. May this my experience be a warning to believing readers, that the Lord may not need to chastise them, on account of their state of heart! May it also be a fresh proof to them, that the Lord,

FIRST PART

in His very love and faithfulness, will not, and cannot let us go on in backsliding, but that He will visit us with stripes, to bring us back to Himself!

There was one point, however, in which, by grace, I had continued to be faithful to God, i.e. in my mode of living, and, therefore, in as far as I had been faithfully sowing, I now reaped abundantly; for the Lord most graciously supplied, in rich abundance, all our temporal wants, though they were many. Another reason for this may have been, that the Lord never lays more on us, in the way of chastisement, than our state of heart makes needful; so that whilst He smites with the one hand, He supports with the other.--We saw it to be against the Lord's mind to put by any money for my wife's confinement, though we might have, humanly speaking, very easily saved £20. or £30. during the six months previous to August 7th. I say, humanly speaking, and judging from what we had received during all these months, we might have laid by as much as the above sums; but I have every reason to believe, that, had I begun to lay up, the Lord would have stopped the supplies, and thus, the ability of doing so was only apparent. Let no one profess to trust in God, and yet lay up for future wants, otherwise the Lord will first send him to the hoard he has amassed, before He can answer the prayer for more. We were persuaded, that, if we laid out our money in the Lord's service, He would send more when we needed it; and this our faith, His own gift, He graciously honoured, inasmuch as He not merely gave us what we needed, but much more.

On August 6th, just before this time of need, the Lord sent us £5. from a distance of about forty miles, and that from a sister, whom, up to this day, neither of us know personally. On August 7th I received £1. 0s. 9 1/2d. out of the box. August 15th, from a distance of twenty-five miles was sent £5., and from a distance of about seventy miles £1. August 18th, whilst preaching at Chudleigh, £1. was sent to me, and a brother sent from Exeter £2. August 21st was again sent from a distance of seventy miles £5., and August 23rd another £5. from the same place. Also, August 22nd, 16s. 9d. was given out of the box. August 24th, a brother, who is a day labourer, gave me 2s. 6d. August 31st, 5s. was given to me. September 3rd, whilst preaching at Chudleigh, £3. 10s. was given to me by a brother and three sisters. September 4th, a sister gave me a guinea, and also out of the box was given 9s. 8d. September 10th, £6. was given to me. Thus, within about one month, the Lord not only sent us nearly £40., but likewise all sorts of suitable provisions and refreshments, needful at such a time; and, in addition to this, the two medical gentlemen who attended my wife would not take any remuneration for their unwearied attention and kindness, during the space of six weeks. Thus the Lord gave us even more than we could have saved, if we had endeavoured to do so.

November 16th. This morning I proposed united prayer respecting our temporal wants. Just as we were about to pray, a parcel came from Exmouth. In prayer we asked the Lord for meat for dinner, having no money to buy any. After prayer, on opening the parcel, we found, among other things, a ham, sent by a brother at Exmouth, which served us for dinner. Thus not only our own family was provided for, but also a sister in the Lord then staying with us.

November 17th. Today we had not a single penny left. We had asked the Lord yesterday and today. We desired only enough money to be able to buy bread. We were reduced more than ever we had been before. But our gracious and faithful Lord, who never lays more upon His children than He enables them to bear, delivered us again this time, by sending us £1. 10s. 6d., about an hour before we wanted money to buy bread.

November 19th. We had not enough to pay our weekly rent; but the Lord graciously sent us again today 14s. 6d. I would just observe, that we never contract debts, which we believe to be unscriptural (according to Romans xiii. 8;) and therefore we have no bills with our tailor, shoemaker, grocer, butcher, baker, &c.; but all we buy we pay for in ready money. The Lord helping us, we would rather suffer privation, than contract debts. Thus we always know how much we have, and how much we have a right to give away. May I entreat the believing reader, prayerfully to consider this matter; for I am well aware that many trials come upon the children of God, on account of not acting according to Rom. xiii. 8.

November 27th, Lord's day. Our money had been reduced to 2 1/2d.; our bread was hardly enough for this day. I had several times brought our need before the Lord. After dinner, when I returned thanks, I asked Him to give us our daily bread, meaning literally that He would send us bread for the evening. Whilst I was praying, there was a knock at the door of the room. After I had concluded, a poor sister came in, and brought us some of her dinner, and from another poor sister, 5s. In the afternoon she also brought us a large loaf. Thus the Lord not only literally gave us bread, but also money.

In reading about all these answers to prayer, the believing reader may be led to think that I am spiritually minded above most of the children of God, and that, therefore, the Lord favours us thus. The true reason is this. Just in as many points as we are acting according to the mind of God, in so many are we blessed and made a blessing. Our manner of living is according to the mind of the Lord, for He delights in seeing His children thus come to Him (Matt. vi.); and therefore, though I am weak and erring in many points, yet He blesses me in this particular, and, I doubt not, will bless me, as long as He shall enable me to act according to His will in this matter.

After we had, on December 31st, 1831, looked over the Lord's gracious dealings with us during the past year, in providing for all our temporal wants, we had about 10s. left. A little while after, the providence of God called for that, so that not a single farthing remained. Thus we closed the old year, in which the Lord had been so gracious in giving to us, without our asking any one:--

1. Through the instrumentality of the box, £31. 14s.--

2. From brethren of the Church at Teignmouth, in presents of money, £6. 18s. 6d.

FIRST PART

3. From brethren living at Teignmouth and elsewhere, not connected with the Church at Teignmouth, £93. 6s. 2d. Altogether, £131. 18s. 8d.

There had been likewise many articles of provision and some articles of clothing given to us, worth at least £20. I am so particular in mentioning these things, to show that we are never losers by acting according to the mind of the Lord. For had I had my regular salary, humanly speaking, I should not have had nearly as much; but whether this would have been the case or not, this is plain, that I have not served a hard Master, and that is what I delight to show. For, to speak well of His name, that thus my beloved fellow-pilgrims, who may read this, may be encouraged to trust in Him, is the chief purpose of my writing.

We had now in the new year to look up to our kind Father for new mercies, and during the year 1832 also we found Him as faithful and compassionate as before, not laying more on us than He enabled us to bear, though space will only permit me to mention a few particulars.

January 7, 1832. We had been again repeatedly asking the Lord today and yesterday to supply our temporal wants, having no means to pay our weekly rent; and this evening, as late as eleven o'clock, a brother gave us 19s. 6d., a proof that the Lord is not limited to time.

January 13. The Lord has again graciously fed us today. We have 5d. left, some bread, rice, meat, potatoes, and other good things, and, above all, the Lord Jesus. He who has provided will provide.

January 14. This morning we had nothing but dry bread with our tea; only the second time since we have been living by simple faith upon Jesus for temporal supplies. We have more than £40. of ready money in the house for two bills,[2] which will not be payable for several weeks; but we do not consider this money to be our own, and would rather suffer great privation, God helping us, than take of it. I thank the Lord, who gives me grace to be more faithful in these matters than I used to be formerly, when I would have taken of it, and said, that by the time the money was actually due, I should be able to replace it. We were looking to our Father, and He has not suffered us to be disappointed. For when now we had but 3d. left, and only a small piece of bread, we received 2s. and 5s., the particulars concerning which would take up too much space.

February 18. This afternoon I broke a blood vessel in my stomach, and lost a considerable quantity of blood. I was very happy immediately afterwards. February 19. This morning, Lord's day, two brethren called on me, to ask me what arrangement there should be made today, as it regarded the four villages, where some of the brethren were in the habit of preaching, as, on account of my not being able to preach, one of the brethren would need to stay at home to take my place. I asked them, kindly to come again in about an hour, when I would give them an answer.

After they were gone, the Lord gave me faith to rise. I dressed myself, and determined to go to the chapel. I was enabled to do so, though so weak when I went, that walking the short distance to the chapel was an exertion to me. I was enabled to preach this morning with as loud and strong a voice as usual, and for the usual length of time. After the morning meeting, a medical friend called on me, and entreated me not to preach again in the afternoon, as it might greatly injure me. I told him, that I should indeed consider it great presumption to do so, had the Lord not given me faith. I preached again in the afternoon, and this medical friend called again, and said the same concerning the evening meeting. Nevertheless, having faith, I preached again in the evening. After each meeting I became stronger, which was a plain proof that the hand of God was in the matter. After the third meeting I went immediately to bed, considering that it would be presumption to try my strength needlessly.

February 20. The Lord enabled me to rise early in the morning, and to go to our usual prayer-meeting, where I read, spoke, and prayed. Afterwards I wrote four letters, expounded the scriptures at home, and attended the meeting again in the evening. February 21. I attended the two meetings as usual, preached in the evening, and did my other work besides. February 22. Today I attended the meeting in the morning, walked afterwards six miles with two brethren to Newton Bushel, and rode from thence to Plymouth: February 23. I am now as well as I was before I broke the blood vessel.--In relating the particulars of this circumstance I would earnestly warn every one who may read this, not to imitate me in such a thing if he has no faith; but if he has, it will, as good coin, most assuredly be honoured by God. I could not say, that, if such a thing should happen again, I would act in the same way; for when I have been not nearly so weak as when I had broken the blood-vessel, having no faith, I did not preach; yet if it were to please the Lord to give me faith, I might be able to do the same, though even still weaker than at the time just spoken of.

About this time I repeatedly prayed with sick believers till they were restored. Unconditionally I asked the Lord for the blessing of bodily health, (a thing which I could not do now), and almost always had the petition granted. In some instances, however, the prayer was not answered. In the same way, whilst in London, Nov. 1829, in answer to my prayers, I was immediately restored from a bodily infirmity under which I had been labouring for a long time, and which has never returned since. The way in which I now account for these facts is as follows. It pleased the Lord, I think, to give me in such cases something like the gift (not grace) of faith, so that unconditionally I could ask and look for an answer. The difference between the gift and the grace of faith seems to me this. According to the gift of faith I am able to do a thing, or believe that a thing will come to pass, the not doing of which, or the not believing of which would not be sin; according to the grace of faith I am able to do a thing, or believe that a thing will come to pass, respecting which I have the word of God as the ground to rest upon, and, therefore, the not doing it, or the not believing it would be sin. For instance, the gift of faith would be needed, to believe that a sick person should be restored again though there is no human probability: for there is no promise to that effect; the grace of faith is needed to believe that the Lord will give me the necessaries of life, if I first seek the kingdom of God and His righteousness: for there is a promise to that effect." Matt. vi.

March 18. These two days we have not been able to purchase meat. The sister in whose house we lodge gave us today part of her dinner. We are still looking to Jesus for deliverance. We want money to pay the weekly rent and to buy provisions. March 19. Our landlady sent again of her meat for our dinner. We have but a half-penny left. I feel myself very cold in asking for money: still I hope for deliverance, though I do not see whence money is to come. We were not able to buy bread today as usual. March 20. This has been again a day of very great mercies. In the morning we met round our breakfast which the Lord had provided for us, though we had not a single penny left. The last half-penny was spent for milk. We were then still looking to Jesus for fresh supplies. We both had no doubt that the Lord would interfere. I felt it a trial that I had but little earnestness in asking the Lord, and had this not been the case, perhaps we might have had our wants sooner supplied. We have about £7. in the house; but considering it no longer our own, the Lord kept us from taking of it, with the view of replacing what we had taken, as formerly I might have done. The meat which was sent yesterday for our dinner, was enough also for today. Thus the Lord had provided another meal. Two sisters called upon us about noon, who gave us two pounds of sugar, one pound of coffee, and two cakes of chocolate. Whilst they were with us, a poor sister came and brought 1s. from herself, and 2s. 6d. from another poor sister. Our landlady also sent us again of her dinner, and also a loaf. Our bread would scarcely have been enough for tea, had the Lord not thus graciously provided. In the afternoon the same sister who brought the money, brought us also from another sister, one pound of butter and 2s., and from another sister 5s. Thus the Lord graciously has again answered our feeble and cold breathings. Lord, strengthen our faith.

March 29. I went to Shaldon this morning. Brother Craik has left for Bristol for four weeks. I think he will only return to take leave, and that the Lord will give him work there. [What a remarkable presentiment, which came to pass, concerning my beloved brother and fellow-labourer!]

April 4. Besides our own family, there are now four visitors staying with us, and we have but 2s. April 5. Four pounds of cheese, and one pound of butter were sent to us. April 7. Anonymously was sent to us, from Plymouth, a large ham, with two sovereigns tied in the corner of the cloth in which the ham was wrapped up. Thus the Lord, once more, in this our time of need, when our expenses are double, has graciously appeared for us.

April 8. I have again felt much this day that Teignmouth is no longer my place, and that I shall leave it.

I would observe that in August of the preceding year (1831), I began greatly to feel as if my work at Teignmouth were done, and that I should go somewhere else. On writing about this to a friend, I was led, from the answer I received, to consider the matter more maturely, and at last had it settled in this way, that it was not likely to be of God, because, for certain reasons, I should naturally have liked to leave Teignmouth. Afterwards I felt quite comfortable in remaining there. In the commencement of the year 1832 I began again much to doubt whether Teignmouth was my place, or whether my gift was not much more that of going about from place to place, seeking to bring believers back to the Scriptures, than to stay in one place and to labour as a pastor. I thought so particularly whilst at Plymouth, in February. On my return, however, I resolved to try whether it were not the will of God that I should still give myself to pastoral work among the brethren at Teignmouth; and, with more earnestness and faithfulness than ever, I was enabled to attend to this work, and was certainly much refreshed and blessed in it; and I saw immediately blessings result from it. This my experience seemed more than ever to settle me at Teignmouth. But notwithstanding this, the impression that my work was done there, came back after some time, as the remark in my journal of April 8th shows, and it became stronger and stronger. There was one point remarkable in connexion with this. Wherever I went, I preached with much more enjoyment and power than at Teignmouth, the very reverse of which had been the case on my first going there. Moreover, almost every where I had many more hearers than at Teignmouth, and found the people hungering after food, which, generally speaking, was no longer the case at Teignmouth.

April 10. I asked the Lord for a text, but obtained none. At last; after having again much felt that Teignmouth is not my place, I was directed to Isaiah li. 9-11. April 11. Felt again much that Teignmouth will not much longer be my residence. April 12. Still feel the impression that Teignmouth is no longer my place. April 13. Found a letter from Brother Craik, from Bristol, on my return from Torquay, where I had been to preach. He invites me to come and help him. It appears to me from what he writes, that such places as Bristol more suit my gifts. O Lord, teach me! I have felt this day more than ever, that I shall soon leave Teignmouth. I fear, however, there is much connected with it which savours of the flesh, and that makes me fearful. It seems to me as if I should shortly go to Bristol, if the Lord permit. April 14. Wrote a letter to Brother Craik, in which I said I should come, if I clearly saw it to be the Lord's will. Have felt again very much today, yea, far more than ever, that I shall soon leave Teignmouth. At last I was pressed in spirit to determine that tomorrow I would tell the brethren so, in order that by the result of this I might see more of the Lord's mind; and that, at all events, I might have their prayers, to be directed in this matter by the Lord.

April 15. Lord's day. This evening I preached again once more, as fully as time would permit, on the Lord's second coming. After having done so, I told the brethren what effect this doctrine had had upon me, on first receiving it, even to determine me to leave London, and to preach throughout the kingdom; but that the Lord had kept me chiefly at Teignmouth for these two years and three months, and that it seemed to me now that the time was near when I should leave them. I reminded them of what I told them when they requested me to take the oversight of them, that I could make no certain engagement, but stay only so long with them as I

FIRST PART

should see it to be the Lord's will to do so. There was much weeping afterwards. But I am now again in peace. [This would not have been the case, had the matter not been of God. I knew of no place to go to. My mind was much directed to Torquay, to preach there for a month or so, and then to go further. For though I had written that I would come to Bristol, I meant only to stay there for a few days, and to preach a few times.]

April 16. This morning I am still in peace. I am glad I have spoken to the brethren, that they may be prepared, in case the Lord should take me away.--Having again little money, and being about to leave Teignmouth for several days, I asked the Lord for a fresh supply, and within about four hours afterwards he sent me, from six different quarters, £3. 7s. 6d. I left today for Dartmouth, where I preached in the evening.--There was much weeping today among the saints at Teignmouth. This is already a trial to me, and it will be still more so should I actually leave.--It is a most important work to go about and stir up the churches; but it requires much grace, much self-denial, much saying over the same things, and the greatest watchfulness and faithfulness, in making use of one's time for prayer, meditation, and reading the Scriptures.--I had five answers to prayer today. 1. I awoke at five, for which I had asked the Lord last evening. 2. The Lord removed from my dear wife an indisposition, under which she had been suffering. It would have been trying to me to have had to leave her in that state. 3. The Lord sent us money. 4. There was a place vacant on the Dartmouth coach, which only passes through Teignmouth. 5. This evening I was assisted in preaching, and my own soul refreshed.

April 17. I preached again at Dartmouth. April 18. I am still at Dartmouth. I wrote to Brother Craik, that, the Lord willing, I should be with him at Bristol on the 21st. I preached again this evening, with especial assistance, before a large congregation. April 19. I awoke early, and had a good while to myself for prayer and reading the Word, and left happy in spirit for Torquay, where I preached in the evening with much help. The brethren are sorry, that, on account of my going to Bristol, my regular weekly preaching will be given up there for a while. I walked home after preaching, and arrived at Teignmouth at twelve o'clock.

April 20. I left this morning for Bristol. I preached with little power (as to my own feeling) in Exeter, from three till half-past four. At five I left for Taleford, where I preached in the evening, likewise with little power. I was very tired in body, and had had therefore little prayer. But still, in both places, the believers seemed refreshed. I went to bed at eleven, very, very tired.

April 21. This morning I rose a little before five, and attended a prayer meeting from a quarter past five, to a quarter past six. I spoke for some time at the meeting. Afterwards I prayed and read again with some believers, and likewise expounded the Scriptures. The Bristol coach took me up about ten. I was very faithless on the journey.

I did not speak a single word for Christ, and was therefore wretched in my soul. This has shown me again my weakness. Though the Lord had been so gracious to me yesterday, in this particular, both on my way from Teignmouth to Exeter, and from Exeter to Taleford, and had given me much encouragement, in that He made my fellow-travellers either thankfully to receive the word, or constrained them quietly to listen to the testimony; yet I did not confess Him today. Nor did I give away a single tract, though I had my pockets full on purpose. O wretched man that I am!

I would offer here a word of warning to my fellow-believers. Often the work of the Lord itself may be a temptation to keep us from that communion with Him which is so essential to the benefit of our own souls.--On the 19th I had left Dartmouth, conversed a good deal that day, preached in the evening, walked afterwards eight miles, had only about five hours sleep, traveled again the next day twenty-five miles, preached twice, and conversed very much besides, went to bed at eleven, and rose before five. All this shows that my body and spirit required rest, and, therefore, however careless about the Lord's work I might have appeared to my brethren, I ought to have had a great deal of quiet time for prayer and reading the Word, especially as I had a long journey before me that day, and as I was going to Bristol, which in itself required much prayer. Instead of this, I hurried to the prayer meeting after a few minutes' private prayer. But let none think that public prayer will make up for closet communion. Then again, afterwards, when I ought to have withdrawn myself, as it were, by force, from the company of beloved brethren and sisters, and given my testimony for the Lord (and, indeed, it would have been the best testimony I could have given them), by telling them that I needed secret communion with the Lord: I did not do so, but spent the time, till the coach came, in conversation with them. Now, however profitable in some respects it may have been to those with whom I was on that morning, yet my own soul needed food; and not having had it, I was lean, and felt the effects of it the whole day, and hence I believe it came that I was dumb on the coach.

April 22. This morning I preached at Gideon Chapel, Bristol. [Though this sermon gave rise to false reports, yet the Lord was pleased to bless it to several; and the false reports were likewise instrumental in bringing many individuals under the sound of the Word.] In the afternoon I preached at the Pithay Chapel. [This sermon was a blessing to many, many souls; and many were brought through it, to come afterwards to hear Brother Craik and me. Among others it was the means of converting a young man who was a notorious drunkard, and who was just again on his way to a public house, when an acquaintance of his met him, and asked him to go with him to hear a foreigner preach. He did so; and from that moment he was so completely altered, that he never again went to a public house, and was so happy in the Lord afterwards that he often neglected his supper, from eagerness to read the Scriptures, as his wife told me. He died about five months afterwards.] This evening I was much instructed in hearing Brother Craik preach. I am now fully persuaded that Bristol is the place where the Lord will have me to labour.

FIRST PART

April 23. This evening I preached again with much assistance at Gideon. I was very happy. [The Lord made this testimony a blessing to several.] I feel that Bristol is my place for a while. The Lord mercifully teach me!

April 27. It seems to Brother Craik and myself the Lord's will that we should go home next week, in order that in quietness, without being influenced by what we see here, we may more inquire into the Lord's will concerning us. It especially appears to us much more likely that we should come to a right conclusion among the brethren and sisters in Devonshire, whose tears we shall have to witness, and whose entreaties to stay with them we shall have to hear, than here in Bristol, where we see only those who wish us to stay. Some asked me to stay with them while Brother Craik goes home. But it seems better that we should both go. [I observe here, it was evident that many preferred my beloved brother's gifts to my own; yet, as he would not come, except I came with him: and as I knew that I also had been called by the Lord for the ministry of the Word, I knew that I also should find my work in Bristol, and that though it might be a different one, yet I should fill up in some measure his lack, whilst he supplied my deficiencies; and that thus we might both be a benefit to the church and to the world in Bristol. The result has evidently confirmed this. I am, moreover, by the grace of God, strengthened to rejoice in my fellow-labourer's honour, instead of envying him; having, in some measure, been enabled to enter into the meaning of that word: "A man can receive nothing, except it be given him from above."]

April 28. It still seems to us the Lord's will that we should both leave soon, to have quiet time for prayer concerning Bristol. This afternoon I felt the want of retirement, finding afresh, that the society of brethren cannot make up for communion with the Lord. I spent about three hours over the Word and in prayer, this evening, which has been a great refreshment to my inner man.

April 29. I preached this morning with much outward power, but with little inward enjoyment, on Rev. iii. 14-22. [As it afterwards appeared, that testimony was blessed to many, though I lacked enjoyment in my own soul. May this be an encouragement to those who labour in word and doctrine!] This afternoon Brother Craik preached in a vessel called the Clifton Ark, fitted up for a chapel. In the evening I preached in the same vessel. [These testimonies also God greatly honoured, and made them the means of afterwards bringing several, who then heard us, to our meeting places. How did God bless us in everything we took into our hands! How was He with us, and how did He help us, thereby evidently showing that He Himself had sent us to this city!] Brother Craik preached this evening at Gideon for the last time previous to our going. The aisles, the pulpit stairs, and the vestry were filled, and multitudes went away on account of the want of room.

April 30. It was most affecting to take leave of the dear children of God, dozens pressing us to return soon, many with tears in their eyes. The blessing which the Lord has given to our ministry, seems to be very great.

We both see it fully the Lord's will to come here, though we do not see under what circumstances. A brother has promised to take Bethesda Chapel for us, and to be answerable for the payment of the rent: so that thus we should have two large chapels.-I saw, again, two instances today, in which my preaching has been blessed.

May 1. Brother Craik and I left this morning for Devonshire. May 2. I preached this evening at Bishopsteignton, and told the brethren, that, the Lord willing, I should soon leave them. May 3. I saw several of the brethren today, and felt so fully assured that it is the Lord's will that I should go to Bristol, that I told them so. This evening I had a meeting with the three deacons, when I told them plainly about it; asking them, if they see any thing wrong in me concerning this matter, to tell me of it. They had nothing to say against it; yea, though much wishing me to stay, they were convinced themselves that my going is of God.

May 4. I saw again several brethren today, and told them about my intention to go to Bristol. There is much sorrowing and sighing, but it does not move me in the least, though I desire to sympathize with them. I am still fully persuaded that the Lord will have us go to Bristol. May 5. One other striking proof to my mind, that my leaving Teignmouth is of God, is, that some truly spiritual believers, though they much wish me to stay, themselves see that I ought to go to Bristol.

May 7. Having received a letter from Bristol on May 5th, it was answered today in such a way that the Lord may have another opportunity, to prevent our going thither, if it be not of Him. Especially we will not move a single stone out of the way in our own strength, and much less still be guilty of a want of openness and plainness, nor would we wish by such means to obtain Bethesda chapel.

May 11. The Lord seems to try us about Bristol. There was reason to expect a letter the day before yesterday, but none came; also today there is no letter. Even this is very good for us. Yea, I do wish most heartily that we may not have Bethesda chapel, if it be not good for us.

May 15. Just when I was in prayer concerning Bristol, I was sent for to come to Brother Craik. Two letters had arrived from Bristol. The brethren assembling at Gideon accept our offer to come under the conditions we have made, i.e., for the present to consider us only as ministering among them, but not in any fixed pastoral relationship, so that we may preach as we consider it to be according to the mind of God, without reference to any rules among them; that the pew-rents should be done away with and that we should go on, respecting the supply of our temporal wants, as in Devonshire. We intend, the Lord willing, to leave in about a week, though there is nothing settled respecting Bethesda chapel.

May 16. I preached for the last time at Bishopsteignton, and took leave of the brethren. May 17. I went to Exmouth, and, after preaching, took leave of the brethren. May 21. I began today to take leave of the brethren at Teignmouth, calling on each of them. In the evening I went over to Shaldon to take leave of the brethren, of whom brother Craik has had the oversight. It has been a trying day. Much weeping on the part of the saints. Were I not so fully persuaded that it is the will of God we should go to Bristol, I should have been hardly able to bear it.

May 22. The brethren at Shaldon and Teignmouth say, that they expect us soon back again. As far as I understand the way in which God deals with his children, this seems very unlikely. In every respect we have seen the Lord's goodness, and all proves that it is His will that we should go to Bristol. This full persuasion has helped me to withstand all the tears of the saints. Towards the evening the Lord, after repeated prayer, gave me Col. i. 21-23, as a text, for the last word of exhortation. It seemed to me best to speak as little as possible about myself, and as much as possible about Christ. I scarcely alluded to our separation, and only commended myself and the brethren, in the concluding prayer, to the Lord. The parting scenes are very trying, but my full persuasion is, that the separation is of the Lord.

May 23. My beloved wife, Mr. Groves, my father-in-law, and I left this morning for Exeter. Dear brother Craik intends to follow us tomorrow.

Review of the time since I left London, up to my removal from Teignmouth.

I. All this time the Lord never allowed me to regret the step I had taken, in separating from the Society.

II. The results have most abundantly shown, that it was of God; for, by His help, 1, I have not lost in truth or grace since. 2, I have been in peace concerning the matter. 3, the Lord made it a blessing to many souls.

III. During this period it pleased the Lord, to convert, through my instrumentality, many souls at Teignmouth, Exmouth, Bishopsteignton, Exeter, Chudleigh, in the neighbourhood of Barnstaple, at Chard, and elsewhere. The church at Teignmouth increased from eighteen to fifty-one.

IV. The Lord most graciously supplied all my temporal wants during this period, so that I lacked no good thing.

V. We had unexpectedly received, just before we left Teignmouth, about £15., else we should not have been able to defray all the expenses connected with leaving, traveling, &c. By this also the Lord showed His mind concerning our going to Bristol.

VI. During these two years and five months, since I left London, I have sinned in many respects, though walking, it may be, in the eyes of the brethren, very near to God. Indeed, my confession concerning this time also is, that I have been an unprofitable servant.

THE LORD'S DEALINGS WITH GEORGE MÜLLER

The following record will now show to the believing reader how far, what I have said concerning my persuasion, that it was the will of God that we should go to Bristol, has been proved by facts.

May 25th, 1832. This evening we arrived in Bristol. May 27. This morning we received a sovereign, sent to us by a sister residing in Devonshire, which we take as an earnest that the Lord will provide for us here also. May 28. When we were going to speak to the brethren, who manage the temporal affairs of Gideon chapel, about giving up the pew-rents, having all the seats free, and receiving the free-will offerings through a box, a matter which was not quite settled on their part, as brother Craik and I had thought; we found that the Lord had so graciously ordered this matter for us, that there was not the least objection on the part of these brethren.

June 4. For several days we have been looking about for lodgings, but finding none plain and cheap enough, we were led to make this also a subject of earnest prayer; and now, immediately afterwards, the Lord has given us such as are suitable. They are the plainest and cheapest we can find, but still too good for servants of Jesus, as our Master had not where to lay His head. We pay only 18s. a week for two sitting-rooms and three bedrooms, coals and attendance. It was particularly difficult to find cheap furnished lodgings, having five rooms in the same house, which we need, as brother Craik and we live together. How good is the Lord to have thus appeared for us, in answer to prayer, and what an encouragement to commit every thing to Him in prayer!

June 5. Today we had already a testimony of a sinner having been converted by brother Craik's instrumentality, on the first Lord's day in April, simply through hearing the text read. [This aged sister lived eleven years afterwards, during which time her walk was according to the profession she made. She fell asleep in 1843.] June 7. We have daily fresh encouragements, and fresh proofs that our being here is of God. June 16. We saw another instance of conversion through brother Craik's instrumentality.

June 25. Today it was finally settled to take Bethesda chapel for a twelvemonth, on condition that a brother at once paid the rent, with the understanding, that, if the Lord shall bless our labours in that place, so that believers are gathered together in fellowship, he expects them to help him; but, if not, that he will pay all. This was the only way in which we could take the chapel; for we could not think it to be of God to have had this chapel, though there should have been every prospect of usefulness, if it had made us in any way debtors. We had tried to obtain a cheaper meeting-place, but could find none large enough to accommodate the hearers.

July 6. Today we commenced preaching at Bethesda Chapel. It was a good day. July 13. Today we heard of the first cases of cholera in Bristol. July 16. This evening, from six to nine o'clock, we had appointed for conversing at the vestry, one by one, with individuals, who wished to speak to us about their souls. There were so many, that we were engaged from six till twenty minutes past ten.

FIRST PART

These meetings we have continued ever since twice a week, or once a week, or once a fortnight, or once a month, as our strength and time allowed it, or as they seemed needed. We have found them beneficial in the following respects:

1. Many persons, on account of timidity, would prefer coming at an appointed time to the vestry to converse with us, to calling on us in our own house. 2. The very fact of appointing a time for seeing people, to converse with them in private concerning the things of eternity, has brought some, who, humanly speaking, never would have called on us under other circumstances; yea, it has brought even those who, though they thought they were concerned about the things of God, yet were completely ignorant; and thus we have had an opportunity of speaking to them. 3. These meetings have also been a great encouragement to ourselves in the work, for often, when we thought that such and such expositions of the Word had done no good at all, it was, through these meetings, found to be the reverse; and likewise, when our hands were hanging down, we have been afresh encouraged to go forward in the work of the Lord, and to continue sowing the seed in hope, by seeing at these meetings fresh cases, in which the Lord had condescended to use us as instruments, particularly as in this way instances have sometimes occurred in which individuals have spoken to us about the benefit which they derived from our ministry, not only a few months before, but even as long as two, three, and four years before.

For the above reasons I would particularly recommend to other servants of Christ, especially to those who live in large towns, if they have not already introduced a similar plan, to consider whether it may not be well for them also to set apart such times for seeing inquirers. Those meetings, however, require much prayer, to be enabled to speak aright, to all those who come, according to their different need; and one is led continually to feel that one is not sufficient of one's self for these things, but that our sufficiency can be alone of God. These meetings also have been by far the most wearing out part of all our work, though at the same time the most refreshing.

July 18. Today I spent the whole morning in the vestry, to procure a quiet season. This has now for some time been the only way, on account of the multiplicity of engagements, to make sure of time for prayer, reading the Word and meditation. July 19. I spent from half-past nine till one in the vestry, and had real communion with the Lord. The Lord be praised, who has put it into my mind to use the vestry for a place of retirement!

August 5. When all our money was gone today, the Lord again graciously supplied our wants. August 6. This afternoon, from two till after six, brother Craik and I spent in the vestry, to see the inquirers. We have had again, in seeing several instances of blessing upon our labours, abundant reason brought before us to praise the Lord for having sent us to Bristol.

August 13, 1832. This evening one brother and four sisters united with brother Craik and me in church fellowship at Bethesda, without any rules, desiring only to act as the Lord shall be pleased to give us light through His word.

August 14. This day we set apart for prayer concerning the cholera, and had three meetings.

August 17. This morning, from six to eight, we had a prayer meeting at Gideon, on account of the cholera. Between two and three hundred people were present. [We continued these meetings every morning, as long as the cholera raged in Bristol, and afterwards changed them into prayer meetings for the church at large, so that we had them for about four months.]

August 24. This morning a sister in the Lord, within fifty yards of our lodging, was taken ill in the cholera, and died this afternoon. Her husband, also a believer, has been attacked, and may be near death. The ravages of this disease are becoming daily more and more fearful. We have reason to believe that great numbers die daily in this city. Who may be the next, God alone knows. I have never realised so much the nearness of death. Except the Lord keep us this night, we shall be no more in the land of the living tomorrow. Just now, ten in the evening, the funeral bell is ringing, and has been ringing the greater part of this evening. It rings almost all the day. Into Thine hands, O Lord, I commend myself! Here is Thy poor worthless child! If this night I should be taken in the cholera, my only hope and trust is in the blood of Jesus Christ, shed for the remission of all my many sins. I have been thoroughly washed in it, and the righteousness of God covers me.--As yet there have not been any of the saints, among whom brother Craik and I labour, taken in the cholera. [Only one of them fell asleep afterwards in consequence of this disease. I would observe, that though brother Craik and I visited many cholera cases, by day and by night, yet the Lord most graciously preserved us and our families from it.]

September 17. This morning the Lord, in addition to all His other mercies, has given us a little girl, who, with her mother, are doing well.

September 21. On account of the birth of our little one, and brother Craik's intended marriage, it is needful that we change our lodgings, as they will now be too small for us, because we shall want one room more. Just when we were thinking about this, the house belonging to Gideon chapel, which had been let for three years, was unexpectedly given up by the tenant, and it was now offered to us by the church. We said we could not think of going into it, as we had no furniture, and no money to buy any. The brother who proposed our going into that house, however, replied that the brethren would gladly furnish it for us, to which we objected, fearing it would burthen them. When, however, the matter was repeatedly mentioned, and when it was particularly expressed that it would be a pleasure to the brethren to furnish the house, we began to consider the subject in prayer, and we saw no scriptural objection to accept this kindness, provided the furniture was very plain. This was promised.

FIRST PART

The house was furnished, yet the love of the brethren had done it more expensively than we wished it.

September 23. Today an individual desired publicly to return thanks to the Lord, for having been supported under the loss of a child, mother, brother, and wife, in the cholera, within one month.

September 25. Last night brother Craik and I were called out of bed to a poor woman ill in the cholera. She was suffering intensely. We never saw a case so distressing. We could hardly say any thing to her on account of her loud cries. I felt as if the cholera was coming upon me. We commended ourselves into the hands of the Lord when we came home, and He mercifully preserved us. The poor woman died today.

Oct. 1. A meeting for inquirers this afternoon from two to five. Many more are convinced of sin through brother Craik's preaching than my own. This circumstance led me to inquire into the reasons, which are probably these:--1. That brother Craik is more spiritually minded than I am. 2. That he prays more earnestly for the conversion of sinners than I do. 3. That he more frequently addresses sinners, as such, in his public ministrations, than I do.--This led me to more frequent and earnest prayer for the conversion of sinners, and to address them more frequently as such. The latter had never been intentionally left undone, but it had not been so frequently brought to my mind as to that of brother Craik. Since then, the cases in which it has pleased the Lord to use me as an instrument of conversion have been quite as many as those in which brother Craik has been used. May the Lord be pleased to use this as a means to lead any of His servants, who may not have acted according to these two last points, to seek to do so, and may He graciously enable me to do so more abundantly!

October 3. This day we set apart as a day of thanksgiving, the cholera having decreased. Oct. 5. Prayer meeting this morning as usual. The cholera is very much decreasing, and the number at our morning prayer meetings likewise.--Hundreds of people were stirred up at that time, but many of them, when the judgment of God had passed away, cared no longer about their souls. Yet a goodly number, who were first led through the instrumentality of the cholera to seek the Lord, are now breaking bread with us, and are walking in the fear of the Lord. How merciful in its results has this heavy judgment been to many!

January 4, 1833. This morning we received letters from Bagdad. The missionary brethren there invite brother Craik and me to come and join them in their labours. The invitation was accompanied by drafts to the amount of £200., for our traveling expenses. What wilt Thou have me to do, gracious Lord? I do not know what may be the Lord's mind. There are points which ought to be much considered and prayed over: There are German villages not very far from Bagdad, where I might labour; upon our going, that of certain other individuals may depend; the brethren at Bagdad are of one mind respecting our going out; good may be done on the way; the going out without any visible support from a society, simply trusting in the Lord for the supply of our temporal wants, would be a testimony for Him; I have had for years a feeling as if one day I should go out as a missionary to the heathen or Mahomedans; and lastly, the hands of the brethren at Bagdad may be strengthened; these are the points, which must appear of no sufficient weight in comparison with the importance of our work here, before I can determine not to go.

January 5. I considered with brother Craik about going to Bagdad. We see nothing clearly. If the Lord will have me to go, here I am. January 7. I spent again some time in prayer, respecting our going to Bagdad, and examined more fully into it. January 8. I had from half-past five till eight this morning to myself in prayer and reading the Word. I prayed then, and repeatedly besides this day, respecting our going to Bagdad. I wrote also a letter to some believers at and near Barnstaple, to ask their prayers concerning this matter. I do not see more clearly than I did before. January 9. I again asked the Lord concerning Bagdad, but see nothing clearly respecting it. I told the Lord I should stay at my post, unless He Himself should most evidently take me away, and I did not feel afterwards my remaining here to be against His will. January 14. I feel more and more satisfied that it is not of the Lord that I should go to Bagdad. January 19. For some days past I have been reading brother Groves' journal of his residence at Bagdad, both for the sake of information respecting his position there, and also, if it please the Lord, that He may use this as a means to show me clearly wether I should go or stay. Blessed be His name that I have no desire of my own in this matter! [Forty-seven years have since passed away, and I think I may say this day still, according to the best of my knowledge, I had no desire of my own in this matter; but I never saw it to be the Lord's will to leave the work which He Himself had so evidently given me.]

February 9. I read a part of Franke's life. The Lord graciously help me to follow him, as far as he followed Christ. The greater part of the Lord's people whom we know in Bristol are poor, and if the Lord were to give us grace to live more as this dear man of God did, we might draw much more than we have as yet done out of our Heavenly Father's bank, for our poor brethren and sisters.

May 27. Today the two churches, assembling at Gideon and Bethesda, met together at tea.--These meetings we have often repeated, and found them profitable on several accounts. 1. They give a testimony to the world of the love of the brethren, by rich and poor meeting thus together to partake of a meal. 2. Such meetings may be instrumental in uniting the saints more and more together. 3. They give us a sweet foretaste of our meeting together at the marriage supper of the Lamb.--At these meetings we pray and sing together, and any brother has an opportunity to speak what may tend to the edification of the rest.

May 28. This morning, whilst sitting in my room, the distress of several brethren and sisters was brought to my mind, and I said to myself, "Oh that it might please the Lord to give me means to help them!" About an hour afterwards I received £60. from a brother, whom up to this day I never saw, and who then lived, as he does still,

FIRST PART

at a distance of several thousand miles. This shows how the Lord can provide in any way for His people, and that He is not confined to places. Oh that my heart might overflow with gratitude to the Lord! [Since the first edition was printed, I have become personally acquainted with the donor.]

May 29. Review of the last twelve months, since we have been in Bristol, as it regards the fruits of our labours. 1. It has pleased the Lord to gather a church, through our instrumentality, at Bethesda, which is increased to 60 in number, and there have been added to Gideon church 49; therefore the total number of those added to us within the year, has been 109. 2. There have been converted through our instrumentality, so far as we have heard and can judge respecting the individuals, 65. 3. Many backsliders have been reclaimed, and many of the children of God have been encouraged and strengthened in the way of truth. What clear proofs that we were not suffered to be mistaken, as it regards our coming to Bristol.

June 12. I felt, this morning, that we might do something for the souls of those poor boys and girls, and grown-up or aged people, to whom we have daily given bread for some time past, in establishing a school for them, reading the Scriptures to them, and speaking to them about the Lord. As far as I see at present, it appears well to me to take a place in the midst of those poor streets near us, to collect the children in the morning about eight, giving them each a piece of bread for breakfast, and then to teach them to read, or to read the Scriptures to them, for about an hour and a half. Afterwards the aged, or grown-up people, may have their appointed time, when bread may be given to them, and the Scriptures read and expounded to them, for, perhaps, half an hour. About similar things I have now and then thought these two years.--There was bread given to about 30 or 40 persons today; and though the number should increase, in the above way, to 200 or more, surely our gracious and rich Lord can give us bread for them also. No sooner had these thoughts arisen, and I communicated them to my dear brother Craik, than I was also directed to a place where the people may be assembled, holding comfortably 150 children. We went about it, and may have it at the rent of 10l., yearly. The Lord directed us, also, to an aged brother as a teacher, and he gladly accepted of our offer. Surely, this matter seems to be of God. Moreover, as I have just now a good deal of money left of the 60l., we have wherewith to begin; and if it be the Lord's will, and if He will accept it, I am willing to lay out at once 20l. of it in this way, yea, all that is left, if He will but speak; and, by the time that this is gone, He can send more. O Lord, if this matter be of Thee, then prosper it! [This desire was not carried out. As far as I remember, the chief obstacle in the way was a pressure of work coming upon brother Craik and me just about that time. Shortly after, the number of the poor who came for bread increased to between 60 and 80 a day, whereby our neighbours were molested, as the beggars were lying about in troops in the streets, on account of which we were obliged to tell them no longer to come for bread. But though, at this time, this matter was not carried out, the thought was, from time to time, revived and strengthened in my mind, and it ultimately issued in the formation of the Scriptural Knowledge Institution, and in the establishment of the Orphan-Houses.]

THE LORD'S DEALINGS WITH GEORGE MÜLLER

June 22. A brother sent a hat to brother Craik, and one to me, as a token of his love and gratitude, like a thank-offering, as he says. This is now the fourth hat which the Lord has kindly sent me successively, whenever, or even before, I needed one. Between August 19th and 27th was sent to us, by several individuals, a considerable quantity of fruit. How very kind of the Lord, not merely to send us the necessaries of life, but even such things as, on account of the weakness of our bodies, or the want of appetite, we might have desired! Thus the Lord has sent wine or porter when we required it; or, when there was want of appetite, and, on account of the poverty of our brethren, we should not have considered it right to spend money upon such things, He has kindly sent fowls, game, &c., to suit our appetite. We have, indeed, not served a hard Master. I am quite ashamed when I still, sometimes, find my heart dissatisfied, or, at least, not grateful as it ought to be.

December 17. This evening brother Craik and I took tea with a family, of whom five have been brought to the knowledge of the Lord through our instrumentality. [When we took tea with them again, about a twelvemonth afterwards, the number had increased to seven.] As an encouragement to brethren who may desire to preach the Gospel in a language not their own, I would mention, that the first member of this family who was converted, came merely out of curiosity to hear my foreign accent, some words having been mentioned to her which I did not pronounce properly. Scarcely had she entered the chapel, when she was led to see herself a sinner. Her intention had been, to stay only a few minutes. But she felt herself as if bound to the seat whilst I was speaking, and remained to the close of the meeting. She then went hastily home, instead of pursuing her pleasures, washed the paint off her face, stayed at home that Lord's day, till the meeting began again, and from that day was truly converted. Having found the Lord, she entreated her brothers and sisters to go and hear the Gospel preached, who, in doing so, were likewise converted. May my dear missionary brethren always be mindful that the Lord can bless a few broken sentences, however badly the words are pronounced, as a means in the conversion of sinners!

December 31, 1833. In looking over my journal, I find:--I. That at least 260 persons (according to the number of names we have marked down, but there have been many more,) have come to converse with us about the concerns of their souls. Out of these, 153 have been added to us in fellowship these last eighteen months, 60 of whom have been brought to the knowledge of the Lord through our instrumentality. Besides these 60, five have fallen asleep before they were received into communion. In addition to these, there are many among the inquirers and candidates for fellowship, whom we have reason to believe God has given to us as seals to our ministry in this city. Some also were converted through our instrumentality who are in fellowship with other churches in this city.

II. In looking over the Lord's dealings with me as to temporal things, I find that He has sent me, during the past year,--

1. In freewill offerings through the boxes, as my part £152 14s. 5 1/4d.

FIRST PART

2. Presents in money given to me £25 1s. 3d.

3. Presents in clothes and provisions worth at least £20 0s. 0d.

Altogether from the brethren in Bristol £197 15s. 8 1/4d.

4. A brother sent me, from a distance of several thousand miles £60 0s. 0d.

5. We live free of rent, which is worth for our part £10 0s. 0d.

Totaling £267 15s 8 1/4d.

It is just now four years since I first began to trust in the Lord alone for the supply of my temporal wants. My little all I then had, at most worth 100l. a year, I gave up to the Lord, having then nothing left but about 5l. The Lord greatly honoured this little sacrifice, and He gave me, in return, not only as much as I had given up, but considerably more. For during the first year, He sent me already, in one way or other, (including what came to me through family connexion) about 130l. During the second year, 151l. 18s. 8d. During the third year, 195l. 3s. During this year, 267l. 15s. 8 1/4d. The following points require particular notice:--1. During the last three years and three months I never have asked any one for any thing; but, by the help of the Lord, I have been enabled at all times to bring my wants to Him, and He graciously has supplied them all. And thus, the Lord helping me, I hope to be enabled to go on to the last moment of my life. 2. At the close of each of these four years, though my income has been comparatively great, I have had only a few shillings, or nothing at all left; and thus it is also today, by the help of God. 3. During the last year a considerable part of my income has come from a distance of several thousand miles, from a brother whom I never saw. 4. Since we have been obliged to discontinue the giving away bread to about 50 poor people every day, on account of our neighbours, our income has not been, during the second part of this year, nearly so great, scarcely one-half as much, as during the first part of it; as if the Lord would thereby show us that when the calls upon us are many, He is able to send in accordingly. Observe this!

January 1, 1834. It seemed well to brother Craik and me, to have an especial public meeting for thanksgiving to the Lord, for His many mercies towards us since we have been in Bristol, and for the great success which it has pleased Him to grant to our labours; and also for confession of our sinfulness and unworthiness, and to entreat Him to continue His goodness towards us. Accordingly we met last evening, and continued together from seven o'clock till half-past twelve. About four hundred individuals, or more, met with us on the occasion.

January 3. This evening, from six to a quarter past ten, we conversed with inquirers. After we had seen twelve, we had to send away six. There were several fresh cases of conversion among them. The work of the Lord is still going on among us.

One of the individuals, who has lately been brought to the knowledge of the truth, used to say in his unconverted state, when he was tempted not to go to the chapel,--"I will go; the Lord may bless me one day, and soften my hard heart."--His expectation has not come to nothing.

January 9. Brother Craik and I have preached during these eighteen months, once a month, at Brislington, a village near Bristol, but have not seen any fruit of our labours there. This led me, today, very earnestly to pray to the Lord for the conversion of sinners in that place. I was also, in the chapel, especially led to pray again about this, and asked the Lord in particular that He would be pleased to convert, at least, one soul this evening, that we might have a little encouragement. I preached with much help, and I hope there has been good done this evening. [The Lord did according to my request. There was, that evening, a young man brought to the knowledge of the truth.]

January 13. The Lord verified in our experience the truths which I had preached last evening in speaking on "Hast thou not made an hedge about him, and about his house, and about all that he hath, on every side?" Job i. 10. Thieves attempted to break into Gideon Chapel. They had broken it open, but were either smitten with blindness, so as not to see a certain door which had been left unlocked, or were disturbed before accomplishing their design; for there was nothing missing.

January 14. I was greatly tried by the difficulty of fixing upon a text, from which to preach, on the morning of October 20, and at last preached without enjoyment. Today I heard of a NINTH instance in which this very sermon has been blessed. May my brethren in the ministry of the Word be encouraged by this to go quietly, yet prayerfully, forward in the work of the Lord!

January 31. This evening a Dorcas Society was formed among the sisters in communion with us, but not according to the manner in which we found one when we came to Bristol; for as we have dismissed all teachers from the Sunday School who were not believers, so now believing females only will meet together to make clothes for the poor. The being mixed up with unbelievers had not only proved a barrier to spiritual conversation among the sisters, but must have been also injurious to both parties in several respects. One sister, now united to us in fellowship, acknowledged that the being connected with the Dorcas Society, previous to her conversion, had been, in a measure, the means of keeping her in security; as she thought, that, by helping on such like things, she might gain heaven at last. Oh that the saints in faithful love, according to the word of God, (2 Cor. vi. 14-18) might be more separated, in all spiritual matters, from unbelievers, and not be unequally yoked together with them!

February 12. I prayed little, read little of the Word, and laboured little to day. On the whole an unprofitable day. May the Lord in mercy give me fervency of spirit!

FIRST PART

February 19. Brother Craik preached this evening on Mark iv. 30-41, and was enabled to give out precious truths. Oh that I did feed more upon them! For several weeks I have had very little real communion with the Lord. I long for it. I am cold. I have little love to the Lord. But I am not, yea, I cannot be satisfied with such a state of heart. Oh that once more I might be brought to fervency of spirit, and that thus it might continue with me forever! I long to go home that I maybe with the Lord, and that I may love Him with all my heart. I fear that the Lord will chastise me at the time of my dear wife's confinement. Lord Jesus, take Thy miserable sinful servant soon to Thyself, that I may serve Thee better! Within the last week I have repeatedly set out, as it were, afresh; but soon, very soon, all has come again to nothing. The Lord alone can help me. Oh that it might please Him to bring me into a more spiritual state!

February 20. By the mercy of God I was today melted into tears on account of my state of heart. Oh that it might please the Lord to bring me into a more spiritual state! February 21. Through the help of the Lord I am rather in a better state of heart than for some time past.--I was led this morning to form a plan for establishing, upon scriptural principles, an Institution for the spread of the Gospel at home and abroad. I trust this matter is of God.--This evening we had again, from six to half-past ten, a meeting with inquirers. The work of the Lord is going on among us as much as ever. Oh that our hearts might overflow with gratitude! Even after we were worn out to the utmost, we could not see all, but had to send away several individuals.

February 25. The inquiries were so many yesterday, that though we conversed more than four hours with them, we had to appoint another meeting for today, and saw again several from two till five. I was led again this day to pray about the forming of a new Missionary Institution, and felt still more confirmed that we should do so.

[Some readers may ask why we formed a new Institution for the spread of the Gospel, and why we did not unite with some of the religious societies, already in existence, seeing that there are several Missionary-, Bible-, Tract-, and School Societies. I give, therefore, our reasons, in order to show, that nothing but the desire to maintain a good conscience led us to act as we did. For as, by the grace of God, we acknowledged the word of God as the only rule of action for the disciples of the Lord Jesus, we found, in comparing the then existing religious Societies with the word of God, that they departed so far from it, that we could not be united with them, and yet maintain a good conscience. I only mention here the following points.

1. The end which these religious societies propose to themselves, and which is constantly put before their members, is, that the world will gradually become better and better, and that at last the whole world will be converted. To this end there is constantly reference made to the passage in Habakkuk ii. 14. "For the earth shall be filled with the knowledge of the glory of the Lord, as the waters cover the sea," or the one in Isaiah xi. 9, "For the earth shall be full of the knowledge of the Lord, as the waters cover the sea." But that these passages can have no reference to the pre-

sent dispensation, but to the one which will commence with the return of the Lord, that in the present dispensation things will not become spiritually better, but rather worse, and that in the present dispensation it is not the whole world that will be converted, but only a people gathered out from among the Gentiles for the Lord, is clear from many passages of the divine testimony, of which I only refer to the following: Matt. xiii. 24-30, and verse 36-43, 2 Tim. iii. 1-13, Acts. xv. 14.

A hearty desire for the conversion of sinners, and earnest prayer for it to the Lord, is quite scriptural; but it is unscriptural to expect the conversion of the whole world. Such an end we could not propose to ourselves in the service of the Lord.

2. But that which is worse, is the connexion of those religious societies with the world, which is completely contrary to the word of God (2 Cor. vi. 14-18). In temporal things the children of God need, whilst they remain here on earth, to make use of the world; but when the work to be done requires, that those who attend to it should be possessed of spiritual life (of which unbelievers are utterly destitute), the children of God are bound, by their loyalty to their Lord, entirely to refrain from association with the unregenerate. But alas! The connexion with the world is but too marked in these religious societies; for every one who pays a guinea, or, in some societies, half-a-guinea, is considered as a member. Although such an individual may live in sin; although he may manifest to every one that he does not know the Lord Jesus; if only the guinea or the half-guinea be paid, he is considered a member, and has a right as such to vote. Moreover, whoever pays a larger sum, for instance, £10. or £20. can be, in many societies, a member for life, however openly sinful his life should be for the time, or should became afterwards. Surely, such things aught not to be!

3. The means which are made use of in these religious societies, to obtain money for the work of the Lord, are also, in other respects, unscriptural; for it is a most common case to ask the unconverted for money, which even Abraham would not have done (Genesis xiv. 21-24): and how much less should we do it, who are not only forbidden to have fellowship with unbelievers in all such matters (2 Cor. vi. 14-18), but who are also in fellowship with the Father and the Son, and can therefore obtain everything from the Lord which we possibly can need in His service, without being obliged to go to the unconverted world! How altogether differently the first disciples acted in this respect, we learn from 3 John 7.

4. Not merely, however, in these particulars is there a connexion with the world in these religious societies; but it is not a rare thing for even Committee Members (the individuals who manage the affairs of the societies) to be manifestly unconverted persons, if not open enemies to the truth; and this is suffered because they are rich, or of influence, as it is called.

5. It is a most common thing to endeavour to obtain for patrons and presidents of these societies, and for chairmen at the public meetings, persons of rank or wealth to attract the public. Never once have I known a case of a POOR, but very devoted,

wise, and experienced servant of Christ being invited to fill the chair at such public meetings. Surely, the Galilean fishermen, who were apostles, or our Lord Himself, who was called the carpenter, would not have been called to this office, according to these principles. These things ought not so to be among the disciples of the Lord Jesus, who should not judge with reference to a person's fitness for service in the Church of Christ by the position he fills in the world, or by the wealth he possesses!

6. Almost all these societies contract debts, so that it is a comparatively rare case to read a Report of any of them, without finding that they have expended more than they have received, which, however, is contrary both to the spirit and to the letter of the New Testament. (Rom. xiii. 8).

Now, although brother Craik and I were ready, by the grace of God, heartily to acknowledge that there are not only many true children of God connected with these religious societies, but that the Lord has also blessed their efforts in many respects, notwithstanding the existence of these and other principles and practices which we judged to be unscriptural, yet it appeared to us to be His will, that we should be entirely separate from these societies, (though we should be considered as singular persons, or though it should even appear that we despised other persons, or would elevate ourselves above them), in order that, by the blessing of God, we might direct the attention of the children of God in these societies to their unscriptural practices; and we would rather be entirely unconnected with these societies than act contrary to the Holy Scriptures. We therefore separated entirely from them, although we remained united in brotherly love with individual believers belonging to them; and would by no means judge them for remaining in connexion with them, if they do not see that such things are contrary to Scripture. But seeing them to be so ourselves, we could not with a clear conscience remain. After we had thus gone on for some time, we considered that it would have an injurious tendency upon the brethren among whom we laboured, and also be at variance with the spirit of the Gospel of Christ, if we did nothing at all for Missionary objects, the circulation of the Holy Scriptures, Tracts, etc.; and we were therefore led for these and other reasons to do something for the spread of the Gospel at home and abroad, however small the beginning might be. This was the origin of the Institution, of which the following part of my Narrative speaks.]

March 5. This evening, at a public meeting, brother Craik and I stated the principles on which we intend to carry on the institution which we propose to establish for the spread of the Gospel at home and abroad. There was nothing outwardly influential, either in the number of people present, or in our speeches. May the Lord graciously be pleased to grant His blessing upon the institution, which will be called "The Scriptural Knowledge Institutions for Home and Abroad."

I. THE PRINCIPLES OF THE INSTITUTION.

1. We consider every believer bound, in one way or other, to help the cause of Christ, and we have Scriptural warrant for expecting the Lord's blessing upon our

work of faith and labour of love: and although, according to Matt. xiii. 24-43, 2 Tim. iii. 1-13, and many other passages, the world will not be converted before the coming of our Lord Jesus, still, while He tarries; all Scriptural means ought to be employed for the ingathering of the elect of God.

2. The Lord helping us, we do not mean to seek the patronage of the world; i.e., we never intend to ask unconverted persons of rank or wealth to countenance this Institution, because this, we consider, would be dishonourable to the Lord. In the name of our God we set up our banners, Ps. xx. 5; He alone shall be our Patron, and if He helps us we shall prosper, and if He is not on our side, we shall not succeed.

3. We do not mean, to ask unbelievers for money (2 Cor. vi. 14-18); though we do not feel ourselves warranted to refuse their contributions, if they, of their own accord should offer them. Acts xxviii. 2-10.

4. We reject altogether the help of unbelievers in managing or carrying on the affairs of the Institution. 2 Cor, vi. 14-18.

5. We intend never to enlarge the field of labour by contracting debts (Rom. xiii. 8), and afterwards appealing to the Church of Christ for help, because this we consider to be opposed both to the letter and the spirit of the New Testament; but in secret prayer, God helping us, we shall carry the wants of the Institution to the Lord, and act according to the means that God shall give.

6. We do not mean to reckon the success of the Institution by the amount of money given, or the number of Bibles distributed, &c, but by the Lord's blessing upon the work (Zech. iv. 6); and we expect this, in the proportion in which He shall help us to wait upon Him in prayer.

7. While we would avoid aiming after needless singularity, we desire to go on simply according to Scripture, without compromising the truth; at the same time thankfully receiving any instruction which experienced Believers, after prayer, upon Scriptural ground, may have to give us concerning the Institution.

II. THE OBJECTS OF THE INSTITUTION ARE:

1. To assist Day-Schools, Sunday-Schools, and Adult-Schools, in which instruction is given upon Scriptural principles, and, as far as the Lord may give the means, and supply us with suitable teachers, and in other respects make our path plain, to establish Schools of this kind.

a. By Day-Schools upon Scriptural principles, we understand Day Schools in which the teachers are godly persons,--in which the way of salvation is scripturally pointed out,--and in which no instruction is given opposed to the principles of the gospel.

FIRST PART

b. Sunday-Schools, in which all the teachers are believers, and in which the Holy Scriptures alone are the foundation of instruction,--are such only as the Institution assists with the supply of Bibles, Testaments, &c.; for we consider it unscriptural, that any persons, who do not profess to know the Lord themselves, should be allowed to give religious instruction.

c. The Institution does not assist any Adult-Schools with the supply of Bibles, Testaments, Spelling Books, &c., except the teachers are believers.

2. To circulate the Holy Scriptures.

We sell Bibles and Testaments to poor persons at a reduced price. But while we, in general, think it better that the Scriptures should be sold, and not given altogether gratis, still, in cases of extreme poverty, we think it right to give, without payment, a cheap edition.

3. The third object of this Institution is, to aid Missionary efforts.

We desire to assist those Missionaries whose proceedings appear to be most according to the Scriptures. It is proposed to give such a portion of the amount of the donations to each of the fore-mentioned objects, as the Lord may direct; but if none of the objects should claim a more particular assistance, to lay out an equal portion upon each; yet so, that if any donor desires to give for one of the objects exclusively, the money shall be appropriated accordingly.

March 7. Today we have only one shilling left. Many times also in Bristol our purse has been either empty or nearly so, though we have not been brought quite so low as it regards provisions, as was sometimes the case at Teignmouth. This evening, when we came home from our work, we found a brother, our tailor, waiting for us, who brought a new suit of clothes both for brother Craik and me, which a brother, whose name was not to be mentioned, had ordered for us. March 8. Our brother brought us this evening also, from the same friend, a new hat for each of us.

March 10. Some time since, a brother who had been brought to the knowledge of the Lord through our instrumentality, having been previously guilty of habitual drunkenness and other open sins, requested with tears our prayers on behalf of his wife, who, like himself formerly, was still given to drinking, and who grew worse and worse. About ten days, after he had spoken to us, it pleased God to begin a work of grace in her heart, in answer to the many prayers of her husband, and this evening she was added to us in fellowship. There have come many instances before us, since we have been in Bristol, in which unbelieving partners have been given to believing ones, in answer to their prayers; yea, even such as had threatened to murder their wives, or leave them, they would still continue to go to our chapels.

March 19. This afternoon at five, my wife was in much pain, which she shortly afterwards considered as the token of her hour being near. I therefore set off to call in a sister, and then I went for the nurse, and my wife's sister, and our servant, who were at Clifton. The Lord having graciously speeded all this, I went to Bethesda Chapel, where I had to preach shortly after. I thought it better to spend the few minutes, which I had before preaching, in prayer for my wife, than to return home again, as I should have had to set off directly afterwards, believing that my mind would be thus more quiet and calm, and that I also might thus help my dearest wife much more effectually. The Lord most graciously kept me from excitement and anxiety, so that I went in peace, preached in peace, and walked home in peace, looking up to Jesus to prepare me for all that might await me, as I remembered but too well the two former times of my wife's confinement. I might have asked brother Craik to preach, and have gone home; but I thought it more honouring the Lord to do His work. In walking home, the following words were a particular refreshment to me:--

Make you His service your delight,

Your wants shall be His care.

When I came home, I heard the joyful news, that all was over, and that my dear Mary had been delivered at twenty minutes past eight of a little boy. Observe! 1. The Lord graciously sent the medical attendant and the nurse (the latter nearly three miles off), in the right time. 2. The Lord put it into my heart to honour Him, by preferring the care of His house to that of my own, and thus He lovingly spared me three painful hours. May He be pleased to give me grace more than ever to love and serve Him!

March 31. Today the brethren and sisters in communion at Bethesda dined together, having been invited by a sister; and in the evening the churches of Gideon and Bethesda took tea together. Both times were refreshing seasons. At dinner we were together from one till half past three, at tea from five to nine. Both times we prayed repeatedly, sang hymns, read a little of the Word, and several brethren spoke of the Lord's dealings with them.

April 3. Today I have had again much reason to see how weak I am, and how prone to give way to every sin if I am not kept by God. May He have mercy upon me, and keep me from bringing an open disgrace upon His holy name! O wretched man that I am!!

April 14. Brother and sister Craik and ourselves have been living together hitherto; but now, as the Lord has given to them one child, and to us two, and there are but six rooms in our house, so that of late dear brother Craik and I have had repeatedly to go to another house to be uninterrupted: we came at last to the conclusion, that it would be better for our souls and the Lord's work that we should separate. April 15. Today I received from several sisters 25l. towards furnishing a house.

FIRST PART

April 23. Yesterday and today I had asked the Lord to send us 20l., that we might be able to procure a larger stock of Bibles and Testaments than our small funds of the Scriptural Knowledge Institution would allow us to purchase; and this evening a sister, unasked, promised to give us that sum, adding that she felt a particular pleasure in circulating the Holy Scriptures, as the simple reading of them had been the means of bringing her to the knowledge of the Lord.

April 26. We have repeatedly conversed about the name which we should give to our babe; but, being unsettled about it, and considering that in all our ways we ought to acknowledge the Lord, I gave myself today to prayer concerning this matter, and the name Elijah, about which I never had thought, was particularly, whilst praying, impressed on my mind, and therefore we intend to name the child Elijah, i. e., my God is Jah, Jehovah. May the Lord in mercy grant Elijah's spirit and Elijah's blessing to our little one!

May 4. Today 15l. more was given to me towards furnishing a house. Thus the Lord has now graciously supplied our need in this particular also. May 13. Today 2l. more was given to us towards furnishing the house, and also some carpet. May 15. Today we moved into our house, having lived nearly two years with brother and sister Craik.

June 4. Today a sister called on me, and I felt irritated at her staying, after having given her to understand that I had but a few minutes time. I sinned thus against the Lord. Help Thou me, blessed Jesus, in future!

June 8. Lord's day. I obtained no text yesterday, notwithstanding repeated prayer and reading of the Word. This morning I awoke with these words:--"My grace is sufficient for thee." As soon as I had dressed myself, I turned to 2 Cor. xii. to consider this passage; but in doing so, after prayer, I was led to think that I had not been directed to this portion for the sake of speaking on it as I at first thought, and I therefore followed my usual practice in such cases, i. e., to read on in the Scriptures where I left off last evening. In doing so, when I came to Heb. xi. 13-16, I felt that this was the text. Having prayed, I was confirmed in it, and in a few minutes the Lord was pleased to open this passage to me. I preached on it with great enjoyment, both at Gideon and at Bethesda, particularly in the evening at Bethesda. This help was evidently from God. May He fill my heart with gratitude, and encourage me by this, to trust in Him for the future! I now understand why those words, "My grace is sufficient for thee," were brought to my mind when I awoke this morning.--[It pleased God, as I have heard since, greatly to bless what I said on that passage, and at least one soul was brought through it to the Lord.]

June 25. These last three days I have had very little real communion with God, and have therefore been very weak spiritually, and have several times felt irritability of temper. May God in mercy help me to have more secret prayer!--Let none expect to have the mastery over his inward corruption in any degree, without going in his weakness again and again to the Lord for strength. Nor will prayer with others, or conversing with the brethren, make up for secret prayer; for I had been engaged in both repeatedly, during the three previous days, as my journal shows.

June 26. I was enabled, by the grace of God, to rise early, and I had nearly two hours in prayer before breakfast. I feel now this morning more comfortable. May God in mercy help me to walk before Him this day, and to do His work; and may He keep me from all evil!

July 5. The Lord very mercifully kept us today from a great calamity, the apron of our Christian servant having caught fire; but the fire was extinguished, and she was kept from being burned!

July 11. I have prayed much about a master for a boys' school, to be established in connexion with our little Institution. Eight have applied for the situation, but none seemed to be suitable. Now at last the Lord has given us a brother, who will commence the work. The Lord allowed us to call upon Him many times before He answered, but at last He granted our request.

July 13. Today we finished reading through the Scriptures, at family prayer, the second time since we came to Bristol, which is little more than two years. I mention this circumstance to show how often we may read through the whole of the Scriptures, though we should read but little every day, if we go regularly onward.

August 18. Today brother Craik and I engaged a sister to be governess of another girls' school, which we intend to establish, in dependence upon the Lord for supplies. August 27. I had prayed repeatedly, and had read ten chapters of the Word to get a text, but obtained none, and had to go this evening to the chapel without knowing on what portion of His Holy Word the Lord would have me to speak. At the commencement of the meeting I was directed to Lament. iii. 22-26, on which I spoke with much assistance and enjoyment.

September 18. A brother, a tailor, was sent to measure me for new clothes. My clothes are again getting old, and it is therefore very kind of the Lord to provide thus. September 25. A brother sent me a new hat today.

October 9. Our little institution, established in dependence upon the Lord, and supplied by Him with means, has now been seven months in operation, and through it have been benefited with instruction,--1. In the Sunday-School, about 120 children. 2. In the Adult-School, about 40 Adults. 3. In the two Day-Schools for boys and, the two Day-Schools for girls, 209 children, of whom 54 have been entirely free; the others pay about one-third of the expense. There have been also circulated 482 Bibles, and 520 New Testaments. Lastly, 57l. has been spent to aid missionary exertions. The means which the Lord has sent us, as the fruit of many prayers, during these seven months, amount to 167l. 10s. 0 1/2d.

FIRST PART

October 28. This afternoon brother Craik and I took tea with seven brethren and sisters, whom the Lord has brought to a knowledge of Himself through our instrumentality, within the last two years; all but one belonging to the same family. We heard there a most affecting account of a poor little orphan boy, who for some time attended one of our schools, and who seems there, as far as we can judge, to have been brought to a real concern about his soul, through what I said concerning the torments of hell, and who some time ago was taken to the poor-house some miles out of Bristol. He has expressed great sorrow that he can no longer attend our school and ministry. May this, if it be the Lord's will, lead me to do something also for the supply of the temporal wants of poor children, the pressure of which has occasioned this poor boy to be taken away from our school!

November 1. Today, our means being completely gone, we had them supplied in the following manner:--some time since some silver spoons were given to us, which we never used, from the consideration, that for servants of Christ it was better, for the sake of example, to use cheaper ones, and for that reason we had sold our plate at Teignmouth. Yet up to this day those spoons remained unsold. But now, as we wanted money, we disposed of them, considering that the kind giver would not be displeased at our doing so to supply our need.

November 4. I spent the greater part of the morning in reading the Word and in prayer, and asked also for our daily bread, for we have scarcely any money left.--We obtained today two large school-rooms, which we much needed. Thus the Lord graciously helps us concerning the Institution, and gives us faith to go forward in the work, enlarging the field more and more (though we have but little money), yet so that we do not contract debts.

November 5. I spent almost the whole of the day in prayer and reading the Word. I prayed also again for the supply of our own temporal wants, but the Lord has not as yet appeared. Still my eyes are up to Him. November 8. Saturday. The Lord has graciously again supplied our temporal wants during this week, though at the commencement of it we had but little left. I have prayed much this week for money, more than any other week, as far as I remember, since we have been in Bristol. The Lord has not answered our prayers by causing means to be sent in the way of a gift, but has supplied us through our selling what we did not need, or by our being paid what was awed to us.

December 10. Today we found that a departed brother had left both to brother Craik and me 12l. December 31, 1834.--I. Since brother Craik and I have been labouring in Bristol, 227 brethren and sisters have been added to us in fellowship. We found 68 believers in the church at Gideon, so that now the whole number would be 295, had there been no changes, but it is only 257; for twelve have fallen asleep; six have left Bristol; twelve have left the churches during the two years and six months, but are still in Bristol; eight are under church discipline, respecting some of whom, however, we hope that they maybe soon restored to communion. Of those 257, there belong 125 to Bethesda church, and 132 to Gideon church. Out of the 227 who have been added to us, 103 have been converted through our instrumentality, and many have been brought into the liberty of the Gospel, or reclaimed from backsliding. Forty-seven young converts are at Gideon, and fifty-six at Bethesda. Considering that some have fallen asleep who never were in communion with us, and yet converted through our instrumentality; and that some are united to other churches in and out of Bristol; and that many are now standing as candidates for fellowship, of those who have been given to us in this city, as seals to our ministry; the number added may be only one-half, or two-thirds of the real number. May the Lord fill our hearts with gratitude, for having thus condescended to use us! II. The income which the Lord has given me during this year is:--

1. My part of the freewill offerings through the boxes £135 13s. 2 1/4d.

2. Money given to me by saints in and out of Bristol £92 7s. 6d.

Altogether... £228 0s. 8 1/4d.

3. Besides this, many articles in provisions, clothing, and furniture, worth to us about £60 0s. 0d.

January 1, 1835. We had last evening an especial prayer-meeting of the two churches, and any other persons hat chose to attend, for the sake of praising the Lord for all His many mercies which we have received during the past year, and to ask Him to continue to us His favour during this year also. It was open to any of the brethren to pray, as they felt disposed, and eighteen did so, as I afterwards reckoned. We continued in prayer and praise, mixed with singing, reading the Word, and exhortation, from seven in the evening till one in the morning. January 13. From ten till one in the first part of the day, and from six to half-past eight this evening, I visited, from house to house, the people living in Orange Street, and saw in this way the families living in nine houses, to ascertain whether any individuals wanted Bibles, whether they could read, whether they wished their children to be put to our Day-Schools or Sunday-School, with the view of helping them accordingly. This afforded opportunities to converse with them about their souls. In this way I sold eight Bibles and two Testaments at reduced prices, and gave away one Testament; engaged one woman as an adult scholar, one boy as a day scholar; and spoke besides this to about thirty people about their souls.--January 15. This morning, from ten till one, I went again from house to house in Orange Street. I visited nine houses, sold a Bible and Testament at reduced prices, and engaged, a few children for the schools, and conversed with fifteen persons about their souls. I should greatly delight in being frequently engaged in such work, for it is a most important one; but our hands are so full with other work, that we can do but little in this way.--January 17. Today brother Groves arrived from the East Indies. One reason of his coming to England is, to go to Germany to obtain missionary brethren for the East Indies, having reason to believe that he will find them there; and he asked me, on account of my acquaintance with the language, to accompany him, that thus, through me, he may be enabled to judge about the state of the brethren, and to communicate to them what he thinks needful

FIRST PART

for them to know. This is a most important work. May the Lord direct me in this matter, and make me to act according to His will!--I received again today, after prayer respecting the funds, 10l. for the Scriptural Knowledge Institution.--January 21. Received, in answer to prayer, from an unexpected quarter, 5l. for the Scriptural Knowledge Institution. The Lord pours in, whilst we seek to pour out. For during the past week, merely among the poor, in going from house to house, fifty-eight copies of the Scriptures were sold at reduced prices, the going on with which is most important, but it will require much means.

January 28. I have, for these several days, again prayed much to ascertain whether the Lord will have me to go as a missionary to the East Indies, and I am most willing to go, if He will condescend to use me in this way. January 29. I have been greatly stirred up to pray about going to Calcutta as a missionary. May the Lord guide me in this matter! [After all my repeated and earnest prayer in the commencement of 1835, and willingness on my part to go, if it were the Lord's will, still He did not send me.]

February 4. I have been praying repeatedly and earnestly of late respecting my journey to the Continent. I desire to go, or not to go, just as the Lord will have it to be. May He graciously direct me! I feel the same about going to India. As a means to ascertain the Lord's will, I have been reading about the Hindoos, that I may know more clearly the state in which they are. May the Lord in mercy stir me up to care more about their state, whether it be His will that I should labour personally among them, or not!

February 16. I mentioned this evening, before the church at Bethesda, as also on the 13th before the church at Gideon, that I see it the Lord's will to go to the Continent, for the sake of assisting brother Groves by my knowledge of the German language, in conferring with those who may desire to go out as missionaries. There is not one believer amongst us who sees any objection to it, and several have expressed that it seems to be of the Lord, and that thus we could help, as churches, in the going forth of missionaries. This is very comforting to me, as the Lord confirms me still more, through this unanimity, in its being His will that I should go.

February 25. In the name of the Lord, and in dependence upon Him alone for support, we have established a fifth Day-School for poor children, which today has been opened. We have now two boys' schools, and three girls' schools. February 26. This afternoon I left Bristol for the Continent.

February 27. London. This morning I went to the Alien Office for my passport. On entering the office I saw a printed paper, in which it is stated that every alien neglecting to renew, every six months, his certificate of residence which he receives on depositing his passport, subjects himself to a penalty of £50, or imprisonment. This law I have ignorantly broken ever since I left London in 1829. It appeared to me much better to confess at once that I had ignorantly done so, than now willfully break it; trusting in the Lord as it regarded the consequences of the step. I did so, and the Lord inclined the heart of the officer with whom I had to do, to pass over my noncompliance with the law, on account of my having broken it ignorantly. Having obtained my passport, I found an unexpected difficulty in the Prussian ambassador refusing to sign it, as it did not contain a description of my person, and therefore I needed to prove that I was the individual spoken of in the passport. This difficulty was not removed for three days, when, after earnest prayer, through a paper signed by same citizens of London, to whom I am known, the ambassador was satisfied. This very difficulty, when once the Lord had removed it, afforded me cause for thanksgiving; for I now obtained a new passport, worded in such a way, that, should I ever need it again, will prevent similar difficulties.

March 3. This evening I preached comfortably in Johnstreet Chapel, for Brother Evans. I never preached in any place where I so much felt that he who statedly ministers was more worthy than myself. This feeling led me to earnest prayer, and the Lord heard and assisted me.

March 7. Dover. Last evening I left London, and arrived here this morning. The Lord enabled me to confess Him before my fellow-passengers. I have had a good deal of prayer and reading the Word in quietness, though staying in an hotel.-- March 8. I preached this morning and evening comfortably in one of the chapels at Dover. March 9. All this day too we have been obliged to remain at Dover, the sea being so rough that no packet sails. I spent the day in writing letters, in reading the Word, and in prayer. We depend entirely upon the Lord as it regards our movements. This evening we asked the Lord twice, unitedly, that He would be pleased to calm the wind and the waves, and I now feel quite comfortable in leaving the matter with Him!

March 10. The Lord heard our prayer. We awake early in the morning, and found the wind comparatively calm. We left the hotel before break of day, to go to the packet. All being in great hurry, on our way towards the sea, I was separated from brothers G. and Y. I now lifted up my heart to the Lord, as He generally helps me to do on such occasions, to direct my steps towards the boat which went out to meet the packet, and I found it almost immediately. We had, in answer to prayer, a good passage. At Calais we obtained our passports, luggage out of the custom house, and places in the diligence without difficulty, and left a little after ten in the morning for Paris. What a blessed thing it is, in all such matters, to have a Father to go to for help! What a different thing, also, to travel in the service of the Lord Jesus, from what it is to travel in the service of the flesh!

March 11. Paris. We arrived here about ten this evening. March 12. Today we went about our passports, and I saw thus a good deal of the best part of Paris. Blessed be God, my heart is above these things! If ten years ago, when my poor foolish heart was full of Paris, I had come here, how should I have been taken up with these palaces, &c.; but now I look at these things, and my heart does not care about them, What a difference grace makes! There were few people, perhaps, more passionately fond of traveling, and seeing fresh places, and new scenes, than myself; but

FIRST PART

now, since, by the grace of God, I have seen beauty in the Lord Jesus, I have lost my taste for these things.

March 13. We again found difficulty in obtaining our passports, arising, probably, from a mistake of the police officers. May the Lord order this matter so, that it shall be for our real welfare!--March 14. By the help of the Lord we obtained our passports, and brother Groves and I took our places in the Malle Poste for Strasburg, to leave tomorrow evening. Brother Y. intends to remain here a few days, on account of his health.

March 15. This morning I preached in a little chapel in Palais Royal. We left Paris this evening at six.--March 17. From six o'clock in the evening of the 15th, till this afternoon at half-past one, when we arrived at Strasburg, We were continually shut up in the Malle Poste, with the exception of yesterday morning about seven, and last night about eleven, when we were allowed half an hour for our meals. I had refreshing communion with my beloved brother. This quickest of all conveyances in France carries only two passengers, and we were thus able freely to converse and to pray together, which was refreshing indeed. Though we had traveled forty-four hours, yet as we had soon finished our business at Strasburg, we left this evening for Basle, trusting in the Lord for strength for the third night's traveling. A little after we had started, we stuck fast in a new road. I lifted up my heart to the Lord, and we were soon delivered, otherwise the circumstance, in a cold night, and during a fall of snow, would have been trying, as we had to get out of the mail. I now found myself again, after six years, amidst fellow-passengers who spoke my native language; but alas! they spoke not for Christ.

March 18. This afternoon we arrived at Basle, where we were very kindly received by the brethren.--March 23. Basle. These six days we have received great kindness from the brethren. The Lord has given me an opportunity of bringing before several who are already engaged in the ministry of the Word, and before many who intend to give themselves to this work, many important truths, so that in these opportunities I have been richly repaid for the journey. This morning I conversed also with three brethren, journeymen, who have a desire to give themselves to missionary work; but nothing could be decided now. I awake very faint, but have been mercifully helped through the work. Brother Groves intends to go to Geneva, and I to Tubingen, in order to become acquainted with a brother, a student, who is likely to go out with Brother Groves as a tutor to his sons, and to combine with this, missionary service.

During my stay at Basle I attended one day a meeting at which a venerable pious clergyman expounded the Greek New Testament to several brethren, who purposed to give themselves to missionary service. The passage to which this dear aged brother had then come, in the original of the New Testament, was 1 Peter iii. 1, 2, which, in our English translation, reads thus: "Likewise, ye wives, be in subjection to your own husbands; that, if any obey not the word, they also may without the word be won by the conversation of the wives; while they behold your chaste conversation coupled with fear." After this aged brother had expounded the passage, he related a circumstance which had occurred in his own days, and under his own eyes, at Basle, which has appeared to me so encouraging for those children of God who have unbelieving relatives, and especially for sisters in the Lord who have unbelieving husbands; and which, at the same time, is such a beautiful illustration of 1 Peter iii, 1.; that I judge it desirable to insert the narrative of this fact here. I will do so as exactly as I remember it. There lived at Basle an opulent citizen, whose wife was a believer, but he himself feared not the Lord. His practice was, to spend his evenings in a wine-house, where he would often tarry till eleven, twelve, or even one o'clock. On such occasions his wife always used to send her servants to bed, and sat up herself; to await the return of her husband. When at last he came, she used to receive him most kindly, never reproach him in the least, either at the time or afterwards, nor complain at all on account of his late hours, by which she was kept from seasonable rest. Moreover, if it should be needful to assist him in undressing himself, when he had drunk to excess, she would do this also in a very kind and meek way. Thus it went on for a long time. One evening, this gentleman was again, as usual, in a wine-house, and having tarried there with his merry companions till midnight, he said to them: "I bet, that if we go to my house, we shall find my wife sitting up and waiting for me, and she herself will come to the door and receive us very kindly; and if I ask her to prepare us a supper, she will do it at once without the least murmur, or unkind expression, or look." His companions in sin did not believe his statement. At last, however, after some more conversation about this strange statement, (as it appeared to them,) it was agreed that they would all go, to see this kind wife. Accordingly they went, and, after they had knocked, found the door immediately opened by the lady herself, and they were all courteously and kindly received by her. The party having entered, the master of the house asked his wife to prepare supper for them, which she, in the meekest way, at once agreed to do; and, after awhile, supper was served by herself; without the least sign of dissatisfaction, or murmur, or complaint. Having now prepared all for the company, she retired from the party to her room. When she had left the party, one of the gentlemen said: "What a wicked and cruel man you are, thus to torment so kind a wife." He then took his hat and stick, and, without touching a morsel of the supper, went away. Another made a similar remark, and left, without touching the supper. Thus one after another left, till they were all gone, without tasting the supper. The master of the house was now left alone, and the Spirit of God brought before him all his dreadful wickedness, and especially his great sins towards his wife; and the party had not left the house half an hour, before he went to his wife's room, requesting her to pray for him, told her that he felt himself a great sinner, and asked her forgiveness for all his behaviour towards her. From that time he became a disciple of the Lord Jesus.

Observe here, dear reader, the following points in particular, which I affectionately commend to your consideration: 1, The wife acted in accordance with 1 Peter iii. 1. She kept her place as being in subjection, and the Lord owned it. 2, She reproached not her husband, but meekly and kindly served him when he used to come home. 3, She did not allow the servants to sit up for their master, but sat up herself; thus honouring him as her head and superior, and concealed also, as far as she was able, her husband's shame from the servants. 4, In all probability a part of those hours, during which she had to sit up, was spent in prayer for her husband, or in reading the word of God, to gather fresh strength for all the trials connected with her position. But whether this was the case or not, it is certain that thus, under similar circumstances, the time might be spent, and it would then indeed be spent profitably. 5, Be not discouraged if you have to suffer from unconverted relatives. Perhaps very shortly the Lord may give you the desire of your heart, and answer your prayer for them; but in the meantime seek to commend the truth, not by reproaching them on account of their behaviour towards you, but by manifesting towards them the meekness, gentleness, and kindness of the Lord Jesus Christ.

March 25. Tubingen in Wirtemberg. The day before yesterday I left Basle in the afternoon. The Lord enabled me to confess Him before a young man and his wife, who were going to Vienna to increase their riches. What a mercy that grace has made me to differ, and that I travel the service of another master! They listened very attentively, and were not at all opposed. They also esteem the people of God, and have been in the habit of meeting with them. Our parting was very affectionate and solemn, after I had charged them to care earnestly about the one thing needful.

I arrived, yesterday morning at six, at Schaffhausen. I found a brother waiting for me at the post office, a gentleman of title, who, having been informed by brethren at Basle of my arrival, kindly took me to his house for the two hours I had to stay in that town, to refresh my body with breakfast, and my soul with communion with the brethren whom he had invited to meet me. I was in this town about ten years ago. I was now again within a short distance of the fall of the Rhine, which was then most attractive to me. Now I considered that my time could be spent much more profitably than by going there. The little time that I was at Schaffhausen, I received much information concerning the state of the church in many parts of the Continent, from a believing physician and a clergyman; and I also communicated things which, with God's blessing, may be profitable. After this I continued my journey to Tubingen. It was with peculiar feelings; for all this way I had traversed nearly ten years ago, to gratify my natural desire for travelling, and now I went over the same ground in the service of the Lord Jesus.

I arrived here this morning at nine, having been strengthened to travel two nights and a day and a half, though I left Basle very weak. This morning I saw brother Gundert, the student of divinity, on whose account I am here, and spent about three hours in conversation with him. Afterwards I called on a Christian professor in the university, who received me kindly. This evening I had a meeting with the believing students, for whom the Lord gave me a word.

March 26. This morning I drove with brother Gundert to Stuttgart, both for the sake of seeing more of him, and also that we might unitedly talk over the matter with his father, who lives there. I am now staying at the house of brother Gundert senior, where I am kindly lodged. I think brother Gundert junior, will go to the East Indies. His father is not only willing to give him up for the Lord's sake, but seems to consider it an honour to have a son to give to the Lord in this way. This evening I again met several brethren, to whom I spoke about the things of God.

March 30. Halle. From the evening of the 27th till this afternoon, when I arrived here, I have traveled day and night, and have been strengthened by the Lord for it. The whole of this way, several hundred miles, I had gone step by step before. My thoughts were peculiarly affecting, as I retraced the mercies which I had experienced at the hands of God.--The Lord enabled me repeatedly to confess His name before my changing fellow-travelers. A student spoke to me about the peculiarly good and cheap wine of Weinheim, near Heidelberg. I told him that when, years ago, as a student like himself, I came through that place, I cared about such things, but that now I knew what was much better than wine.--Yesterday a Frenchman, having heard my testimony for Jesus once or twice, when the last merry companion had left the coach, quitted my society, it being too dull for him, and joined himself to an officer in the army, sitting in the forepart of the coach. (The coach was divided into the forepart and inside.) This gave me a blessed and most refreshing opportunity to pray for about an hour aloud in the coach, which strengthened and refreshed my soul. It was particularly kind of the Lord to give me an opportunity of praying aloud, as, on account of having then already traveled forty-eight hours uninterruptedly, my body was too tired to allow me to continue for any length of time in mental prayer.--Yesterday afternoon, at Eisenach (situated just under the hill on which stands the decayed castle called the Wartburg, where Luther translated the Holy Scriptures), I saw fearful scenes of profanity. How has the candlestick been removed!--This afternoon I reached Halle, where it pleased the Lord to bring me to the knowledge of Himself, having been graciously preserved hitherto, though a spring was found broken when I got out of the mail. I greatly needed rest, but my heart was too full. I could not sleep. I went first to the house of the brother, where I was first impressed, and afterwards I called on my esteemed tutor, professor Dr. Tholuck, counsellor of the Consistory, who received me, after seven years' separation, with his former kindness and brotherly love. (He made me lodge with him, and gave thereby a testimony that differences of views, concerning certain parts of God's truth, ought not to separate the children of God; for I had written to him my mind from Bristol two years before.)

March 31. Today I rode with Dr. Tholuck and two young brethren to a believing clergyman, living in the neighbourhood of Halle, where we spent the day. Dr. Tholuck told me many encouraging things, particularly this, that several of my former fellow-students, who, at the time when I was at Halle, knew not the Lord, had been brought to know Him since, and are now labouring in His vineyard. And further, that certain brethren, formerly very weak in the faith, had been established, and are now going on well. May this encourage the heart of the believing reader still to pray for his unconverted friends, and may it strengthen him to hope for better days concerning those of his brethren in the Lord who are now weak in the faith!

April 1. Today I saw a clergyman, in whom I recognized an individual who studied at Halle, whilst I was there, living then in open sin, and who is now, by divine mercy, pointing sinners to the Lamb of God. In the evening I went to the large

FIRST PART

Orphan-house, built, in dependence on the Lord, by A. H. Franke, to see one of the classical teachers, who is the son of my father's neighbour, and whom I had not seen for about fifteen years. I found him, to the joy of my heart, to be a brother in the Lord. This evening I spent in the same room where it pleased the Lord to begin a work of grace in my heart, with several of the same brethren and sisters with whom I used to meet seven years ago, and told them of the Lord's faithfulness, gentleness, kindness, and forbearance towards me, since I had seen them last. Truly how good has the Lord been to me since!

April 2. This morning I again spent in calling on the brethren and sisters, being enabled, every where, before learned and unlearned, to testify about the blessedness of adhering to the Scriptures as our only guide in spiritual things. I left Halle this afternoon, having received much love from the brethren, and drove fifteen miles further, to a beloved brother and old friend, brother Stahlschmidt at Sandersleben, who has shown me much kindness even since I have been in England. I was received with much love by this brother and his dear wife, and his man servant, also a beloved brother. [This brother (the man servant) I met fifty-four years ago at Gnadau, a Moravian settlement, where I several times spent a few days for the refreshment of my soul, to which place he also came, a distance of about forty-five miles, for the same purpose. He was then living with a farmer, ploughing his fields, &c. At that time our hearts were knit together; for I wish it to be understood by any unconverted reader, that, whilst I should at one time have looked with scorn upon such a person, if he had attempted to be familiar with me, now the love of Jesus, in whom we were one, filled my heart with love to him, and these outward distinctions were broken down. In consequence of this acquaintance, he wrote me several letters to Halle, and I wrote to him. Those letters were particularly refreshing and spiritual, and therefore I read them to other brethren, and also to brother Stahlschmidt, a wine merchant. On account of this, he had a great desire to have brother Kroll living in his house. The Lord, after a time, brought it about, and this brother lived with him above forty years, and was a friend, a brother, and a most faithful servant to this merchant, so that his considerable business was in a great measure intrusted to him; and yet he treated his master with all due respect, and kept his place as a servant. This latter point is very important, and brings glory to God. For whilst a believing master should treat a believing servant with all kindness and brotherly love; yet the believing servant should with all obedience, with all faithfulness, and particularly with due respect, treat his believing master or mistress.]

April 3. Sandersleben. Today I saw several brethren and sisters, and among others a brother, who is in about the same state in which he was eight years ago. He has very little enjoyment, and makes no progress in the things of God. The reason is, that, against his conscience, he remains in a calling, which is opposed to the profession of a believer. We are exhorted in Scripture to abide in our calling; but only if we can abide in it "with God." 1 Cor. vii. 24.--This evening a believing clergyman, and the brethren and sisters of this small town and some neighbouring villages, were collected together in brother Stahlschmidt's house, and I spoke to them for two hours about the things of God, particularly about the way in which God has led me, since I saw them, and sought to strengthen their hands in God, and exhorted them to give themselves fully to the Lord. It was a time of refreshing. Indeed, the Lord has greatly refreshed my own soul, at Basle, Tubingen, Stuttgart, Halle, and elsewhere, whenever I have spoken well of His name. The child of God should make it his particular business to encourage sinners to seek after the Lord, and to increase the faith and love of the brethren, through speaking well of the name of the Lord.

April 4. I left Sandersleben this morning. My brother and host acted according to 3 John, 5 and 6; for he sent me on ten miles in his carriage.

When I arrived at Aschersleben, to which place brother Stahlschmidt had conveyed me, I had but one station more to my father's house. On the way I asked the driver about a certain individual, with whom I studied at Halle, once a companion with me in open sin. I found that he is still in the same state. What a difference has grace made between him and me! Nothing, nothing but grace has made this difference! I, guilty sinner, might now be still on the same road, and he, in my room, might have been plucked as a brand out of the fire. But it is not so. May the Lord help me to love him much, very much, for His distinguishing grace!--Such feelings I had in particular this afternoon, when I saw the town before me in which my father lives, as there are but two in the whole place, as far as I can find out, who love the Lord. How different is everything with me now from what it was when, as a wicked youth, I used to go to this town, at the time of my vacation. How truly happy am I now! How is my heart now raised above all those things in which I sought, and also fancied I found happiness! Truly all these things are like bubbles to me now! My heart is not here; yea, my heart is not even in England. My heart is, at least in a measure, in heaven, though I am still nothing but a poor weak worm. I felt the solemnity and importance of having once more the privilege of seeing my aged father. I also felt the importance of being at the place, where I had spent much of my time in my youth, and where I had been known as living in sin. My desire was, that I might be enabled to walk, the three days I intended to stay there, as it becomes a servant of Christ. For this I had been led to prayer before I left Bristol, and since I have been on the Continent. At last I arrived at my father's house. How affecting to meet him once more!

April 5. Heimersleben. This afternoon a friend of my father called-one who knows not the Lord. After a few minutes the Lord gave me an opportunity of setting before him the fundamental truths of the Gospel, and the joy and comfort they afford, and have afforded to me. Thus a way was opened to me of stating the truth more fully than ever I had been able to do before, by word of mouth, in the presence of my father and brother, without saying to them, "Thou art the man." I was assisted by the Lord. May He water the seed sown! This evening I went to the only two brethren in this little town, thus to own them as such. It has appeared well to me to call on none whom I know, else I should be expected to call on all; and as I see it right to spend but three days here, I consider that that little time should be wholly given to my father, as it may be the last time that I shall see him; yet, at the same

FIRST PART

time, I judged that it was well pleasing in the sight of the Lord, that I should call on these brethren to strengthen their hands.

When I saw these brethren last, in February, 1829, two or three more used to meet with them; but since then the reproach of the cross has driven the others back into the world. From that time, these brethren have scarcely seen a believer, and never hear the Gospel preached; it was therefore a great joy to them to see me. They told me that the Lord had blessed my last visit to them; and having been informed of my coming, they were prepared to ask me many questions. One of them, Knabe, about thirty years ago being possessed of property, was persuaded to lay it out in coal mines. He joined with two men who spent his property, and after some time they became bankrupts, so that there was not money enough to pay the workmen and some other creditors, even after all their goods had been sold. This evening brother Knabe asked me what he ought to do about the money which had been left unpaid three and twenty years; whether he was still under an obligation to pay it, if he could. My answer was at once that he was, being in the sight of the Lord still a debtor, though cleared by the laws of men. He then told me, that some years since some property was left to him, and that he also, in the years 1816, 1817, and 1818, when the corn prices were very high, had laid by some money, and that therefore he was fully able to pay the debt. He saw immediately that this was the right way, and said that he would act accordingly. He added that now he saw why he had made so little progress in divine things. I have learned that this brother has lately taken two destitute orphans into his house, whom he entirely supports by the labour of his hands (he earns his bread by thrashing corn), and that the people, though they consider him, on account of his love for the Lord, a weak and foolish person, yet look upon him with respect.

April 6. I spent this morning in answering questions which my father put to me about secular things in England. This I did for the following reasons:--1. I had scarcely ever spoken about these things in my letters, indeed so little, that my father told me, he had often intended to ask me whether it was forbidden in England to send letters abroad about such matters, as I never wrote about them. I had refrained from doing so, partly, on account of want of time; and, partly, because I had better things to write about, wishing to direct his mind to the things of God. 2. Now, however, I spoke on these subjects, because I particularly desired to be as kind, affectionate, and obliging as I conscientiously could, considering that this was the testimony I was especially called on to give. Formerly I had much pressed the things of God on him, and not with sufficient tenderness, knowing not then experimentally the helplessness of the creature. After it had pleased the Lord to show me the truth more clearly, in the summer of 1829, I wrote in a different way; but in the commencement of the year 1833 I felt pressed in spirit once more, most fully, not so much as a son, but as a servant of Christ, to write, and to point out to him minutely his state, showing him the danger of his soul, the grounds of which I fully laid before him. When this, as formerly, greatly displeased him, I ceased to speak any more in this way, and from that time I aimed and still aim more and more to show him love in action, as it becomes a believing son, telling him only how happy I am--how I am supported under such and such trials--how I am not caring about certain things as formerly I did--in what an awful state I was once living, and how God brought me out of it; and how any sinner, by forsaking his evil ways, and believing on the Lord Jesus, may be brought to the same joy and happiness, and what a delight it would be to me to meet my father at last in heaven, &c. Since I have corresponded with him in this way, things have been very comfortable, though I have brought as much truth before him as formerly, and though I have never sent a letter without speaking, comparatively, much about these things. On the same ground I have not on this visit spoken directly to my father about the state of his soul, though he has more than ever heard the truth from my lips. God has indeed been with me, and I believe that I have been led by Him to pursue this course. Different, however, has been the way in which I have dealt with my unconverted brother; for the relationship in which I stand to him is a different one. For this afternoon, I not only pointed out to him his danger, but spoke also respecting his sins, and have done so in my letters, and intend to do so still, if the Lord permit.

This afternoon brother Knabe called on me. He told me that he had already experienced a trial on account of his intention to pay the money, as his wife tried to keep him from it, by endeavouring to persuade him that God does not require him to do such a thing, as he has taken two orphan children into his house. He nevertheless is determined to do it. He saw, however, another difficulty, which was, that, when he looked over the papers containing the names of his creditors, it was found that all but three, out of about thirty, were dead, and he did not know what to do concerning them. I told him to go to those places where his creditors used to live, and he might find, perhaps, some needy widows and fatherless children, whom they had left behind; and, if not, he should inquire after the lawful heirs, and pay the money to them. He saw with me, and declared his full intention to do so, whatever it might cost, and seemed truly glad that God at last, through my advice, had delivered him from this burden; for from time to time the matter had pressed on his conscience that he ought to do it.--I spent this evening in relating to my father and brother some of the Lord's dealings with me in England, particularly how He has graciously provided for my temporal wants in answer to prayer, and they both seemed to feel, for the moment at least the blessedness of such a life.

April 7. I saw brother Knabe this morning, who is still determined to pay the money, though tried by his wife. I exhorted him to steadfastness. I also saw some persons who called on me to hear about England, for every one of whom the Lord gave me a word without any effort. It was especially so last night. A friend of my father, a Roman Catholic, called, and I was enabled to set the truths of the gospel before him, with their blessed effects, without entering upon the Roman Catholic controversy.--A part of this morning I spent in walking about with my father to see one of his gardens, and some of his fields, because I knew it would give him pleasure; and I felt that I ought in every way to show him kindness and attention, as far as I conscientiously could. Tomorrow, God willing, I intend to leave, and to return to England. The Lord, in His rich mercy, in answer to my prayer, has enabled me so to walk before my father, and has also impressed what I have said so far upon his heart,

FIRST PART

as to cause him to say today, "May God help me to follow your example, and to act according to what you have said to me."

April 9. Celle. Yesterday morning I drove with my father to Halberstadt, where, with many tears, he separated from me. I was alone in the mail, which was a great comfort to me. It was a solemn time. I found myself again on the road to Brunswick, which I had traversed twice in the service of the devil, and now I was traveling on it in the name of Jesus. I discerned, in passing, the inn at Wolfenbuttel, from whence I intended to run away, and where I was arrested. How peculiar were my feelings! In the evening we reached Brunswick, from whence we started the same night. During the night I heard a fearfully wicked, most profligate, infidel, and scoffing conversation between the conducteur and a student, and the only testimony I gave was, complete silence all the time. I arrived here this morning at eight, and have been here all the morning, as the mail will not start for Hamburg until four this afternoon. It has been far from well with me in my soul today. That awful conversation last night has been spiritual poison to me. How's very soon do we, even unconsciously, receive evil!

April 10. Hamburg. I arrived here at ten this morning.--April 11. I went on board last night, and at twelve we sailed. This morning at half-past eleven we arrived at Cuxhaven, where we cast anchor, on account of a strong contrary wind.--April 13. Though I desired as much, perhaps, as any of the passengers speedily to get to the end of our voyage, longing to get back again to my work in Bristol, and also to my wife and children, yet I was kept in peace; and whilst some murmured at the contrary wind, the Lord enabled me to lift up my heart in prayer that He would calm it, if it were His holy will, and, accordingly, after a delay of about nineteen hours, we plied again yesterday morning, at seven. At ten I was taken with sea sickness, from which I had been kept during my four previous short voyages in answer to prayer; but this time I on purpose refrained from praying about it, as I did not know whether it was better for my health to be seasick or not. The sickness continued the whole of yesterday. Today I am well. We have fine and calm weather. I consider it a mercy that the Lord has allowed me to be sea-sick.

April 15. Bristol. Yesterday at one we landed in London. In answer to prayer I soon obtained my things from the Custom-house, and reached my friends in Chancery Lane a little before two, where I found a letter from my wife, stating that brother Craik is ill, having an inflammation in the wind-pipe, and therefore, humanly speaking, will be unable to preach for some time. In consequence of this I started immediately for Bristol, where I arrived this morning. I found brother Craik better than I had expected, though completely unable to attend to the ministry of the Word.

April 16. Today brother Craik and I received 11l. 15s. 9d. each, being a legacy left to us some time since. We said once or twice to one another, that perhaps this money might be paid at a time when we much needed it. And so it is just now. May I and all my brethren leave the management of all our affairs entirely to the Lord, who best knows what is good for us; and may it be our concern to seek first the kingdom of God and His righteousness, and all temporal supplies shall be added to us!

May 1. I went to see brother Craik, and found him better, but heard from his medical attendant that he ought not to preach for several months. May 5. My father-in-law has been for several days very ill. May 15. Mr. Groves continues very ill. May 29. This morning brother Craik went into Devonshire for change of air.

June 3. Today we had a public meeting on account of the Scriptural Knowledge Institution for home and abroad. It is now fifteen months, since, in dependence upon the Lord for the supply of means, we have been enabled to provide poor children with schooling, circulate the Holy Scriptures, and aid missionary labours. During this time, though the field of labour has been continually enlarged, and though we have now and then been brought low in funds, the Lord has never allowed us to be obliged to stop the work. We have been enabled during this time to establish three day-schools, and to connect with the Institution two other charity day-schools, which, humanly speaking, otherwise would have been closed for want of means. In addition to this, the expenses connected with a Sunday-school and an adult school have been likewise defrayed, making seven schools altogether. The number of the children that have been thus provided with schooling, in the day-schools only, amounts to 439. The number of copies of the Holy Scriptures, which have been circulated, is 795 Bibles and 753 New Testaments. We have also sent, in aid of missionary labours in Canada, in the East Indies, and on the Continent of Europe, 117l. 11s. The whole amount of the free-will offerings put into our hands for carrying on this work, from March 5, 1834, to May 19, 1835, is 363l. 12s. 0 3/4d.

June 20. Our father is evidently today near his end. June 22. This morning at two our father died. June 23. Both our children are ill. June 24. Our little boy is very ill. June 25. The dear little boy is so ill, that I have no hope of his recovery. The disease is inflammation on the chest. I spoke this evening comfortably at Gideon, on Psalm cxlv. 1-4, thinking it right that neither the death of my father-in-law, nor my dying child should keep me from the Lord's work. The Lord's holy will be done concerning the dear little one. June 26. My prayer last evening was, that God would be pleased to support my dear wife under the trial, should He remove the little one; and to take him soon to Himself, thus sparing him from suffering. I did not pray for the child's recovery. It was but two hours after that the dear little one went home. The eldest and the youngest the Lord has thus removed from our family in the same week. My dear Mary feels her loss much, but yet is greatly supported. As to myself, I am so fully enabled to realize that the dear infant is so much better off with the Lord Jesus than with us, that I scarcely feel the loss at all, and when I weep, I weep for joy.

June 27. My dear wife is graciously supported. May the Lord grant that these afflictions may not be lost upon us! June 28. I preached today both times comfortably. June 29. This morning was the funeral. The remains of our father and infant were put into the same grave.

FIRST PART

July 3. Our taxes are due, and may be called for any day, and for the first time we have no money to pay them, as we were obliged, on account of our late afflictions, to spend the money which we had put by for them. May the Lord in mercy provide! July 6. I was enabled today, by the free-will offerings through the boxes, and by what I had left, to pay the taxes before they were called for. How kind of the Lord to answer my prayer so soon! July 8. This evening I had 5l. sent from Weston-super-Mare. So the Lord has again appeared. May I praise His holy name for this seasonable help, which came when I had scarcely any money left! July 14. Today I had again a suit of new clothes given to me by a brother. My clothes were much worn and old, and our late funeral might have given a second reason for having new ones. But I did not order any, because I had no money to pay for them, and thought it wrong to contract debts.--A fresh paper was brought in today for taxes, which ought to have been asked for many months since. May the Lord give us the means to pay them!

July 15. We had again an especial prayer-meeting for the restoration of brother Craik, who, though well in his general health, is yet unable to preach, or even to converse for any length of time. July 18. I have felt for several days weak in my chest. This weakness has been increasing, and today I have felt it more than ever. I have thought it well to refrain next week from all public speaking. May the Lord grant that I may be brought nearer to Him through this, for I am not at all in the state in which I ought to be, and I think sometimes that our late afflictions have been lost upon me, and that the Lord will need to chastise me severely.

July 22. The last mentioned taxes were called for this morning, just after the Lord had sent us 5l., from a distance of about eighty miles. So the Lord has again of late, repeatedly, in answer to prayer, sent help. May this lead us to trust in Him for the future! July 28. Since the 14th I have felt unwell, and though sometimes a little better, on the whole I have been getting worse and worse. This morning I have seen our medical attendant, who thinks that all the disease arises from a disordered stomach.

July 31. Today brother C-r, formerly a minister in the establishment, who came to us a few days since, began, in connexion with the Scriptural Knowledge Institution, to go from house to house, to spread the truth as a city missionary. [This was a remarkable interposition of God. Brother Craik had before this, for some months, been unable on account of bodily infirmity, to labour in the work of the schools, the circulation of the Scriptures, &c., and my own weakness, shortly after brother C-r's arrival, increased so that I was obliged to give up the work entirely: How gracious, therefore, of the Lord, to send brother C-r, that thus the work might go on! Up to July, 1837, this brother was enabled to continue in his work, and thus this little Institution was in a most important way enlarged as it regards the field of labour.]

August 15. Today dear brother Craik returned from Devonshire, much better in his general health, but not better as it regards his voice.--August 24. I feel very weak, and suffer more than before from the disease. I am in doubt whether to leave Bristol entirely for a time. I have no money to go away for a change of air. I have had an invitation to stay for a week with a sister in the country, and I think of accepting the invitation, and going tomorrow. August 26. Today I had 5l. given to me for the express purpose of using change of air. Aug. 29. Today I received another 5l. for the same purpose.

August 30. Today, for the first Lord's day since our arrival in Bristol, I have been kept from preaching through illness. How mercifully has the Lord dealt in giving me so much strength for these years! I had another 5l. sent, to aid me in procuring change of air. How kind is the Lord in thus providing me with the means of leaving Bristol! September 2. Went with my family to Portishead. September 3 to 5. I read the lives of the English martyrs at the time of the reformation. My spirit has been greatly refreshed. May the Lord help me to follow these holy men as far as they followed Christ! Of all reading, besides that of the Holy Scriptures, which should be always THE book, THE CHIEF book to us, not merely in theory, but also in practice, such like books seem to me the most useful for the growth of the inner man. Yet one has to be cautious in the choice, and to guard against reading too much. At such a time as the present, when my mind and body are too weak for much exertion, as the study of the Word, conversation, writing letters, or walking, &c., I find it most refreshing to read a few pages of this kind, though these last six years I have not read the fifth part, perhaps not the tenth part as much of other books as of the Holy Scriptures.

September 14. We are still at Portishead. I am but little better. I am greatly bowed down today on account of my inward corruptions and carnality of heart. When will God deliver me from this state?! How I long to be more like Him! My present way of living is also a great trial to me. The caring so much about the body; the having for my chief employment eating and drinking, walking, bathing, and taking horse exercise; all this to which I have not been at all accustomed these six years, I find to be very trying. I would much rather be again in the midst of the work in Bristol, if my Lord will condescend to use His most unworthy servant.

September 15. As I clearly understood that the person, who lets me his horse, has no license, I saw, that being bound as a believer to act according to the laws of the country, I could use it no longer: and as horse exercise seems most important, humanly speaking, for my restoration, and as this is the only horse, which is to be had in the place, we came to the conclusion to leave Portishead tomorrow. Immediately after, I received a kind letter from a brother and two sisters in the Lord, who lived in the Isle of Wight, which contained a fourth invitation, more pressing than ever, to come and stay with them for some time. In addition to this, they wrote that they had repeatedly prayed about the matter, and were persuaded that I ought to come. This matter has been today a subject for prayer and consideration to us.

FIRST PART

September 16. We came this morning to the conclusion to leave Portishead today, and that I should go to the Isle of Wight; but we saw not how my wife and child and our servant could accompany me, as we had not sufficient money for traveling expenses; and yet this seemed of importance, as otherwise my wife would be overburdened in my absence, and my mind would not be sufficiently free; and besides this, she also seems to need change of air. The Lord graciously removed the difficulty this evening; for we received most unexpectedly and unasked for 6l. 13s., which was owed to us, and, also, when we had already retired to rest, a letter was brought, containing a present of 2l. How very, very kind, and tender is the Lord!

September 19. This evening we arrived at our friends' in the Isle of Wight, by whom we were most kindly received.--September 21 to 26. Nothing remarkable has occurred. I feel very comfortable in this place, and find my stay here refreshing to my soul. My health is about the same. I am not fit for mental exercise, and am soon fatigued even by conversation. I have read during the last days, with great interest and admiration of the goodness of God, and to the refreshment of my soul, the life of John Newton, and the lives of some of the English martyrs at the time of the reformation.

Sept. 27. Today I am thirty years of age. I feel myself an unprofitable servant. How much more might I have lived for God than I have done! May the Lord grant, that, if I am allowed to stay a few days more in this world, they may be spent entirely for Him! September 29. Last evening, when I retired from the family, I had a desire to go to rest at once, for I had prayed a short while before; and feeling weak in body, the coldness of the night was a temptation for me to pray no further. However, the Lord did help me to fall upon my knees; and no sooner had I commenced praying, than He shone into my soul, and gave me such a spirit of prayer, as I had not enjoyed for many weeks. He graciously once more revived His work in my heart. I enjoyed that nearness to God and fervency in prayer, for more than an hour, for which my soul had been panting for many weeks past. For the first time, during this illness, I had now also a spirit of prayer as it regards my health. I could ask the Lord earnestly to restore me again, which had not been the case before. I now long to go back again to the work in Bristol, yet without impatience, and feel assured that the Lord will strengthen me to return to it. I went to bed especially happy and awoke this morning in great peace, rose sooner than usual, and had again, for more than an hour, real communion with the Lord before breakfast. May He in mercy continue this state of heart to His most unworthy child!

October 8. My strength has been during the last days increasing, but I feel still the symptoms of indigestion. I have been able to speak several times at family prayer, and to expound the Scriptures to the school children, without suffering in consequence of it.

October 9. I have many times had thoughts of giving in print some account of the Lord's goodness to me, for the instruction, comfort, and encouragement of the children of God; and I have been more than ever stirred up to do so since I read Newton's life a few days ago. I have considered, today, all the reasons for and against, and find that there are scarcely any against, and many for it.

October 15. Today we left our dear friends for Bristol. November 15. Brother C-r and I have been praying together, the last five days, that the Lord would be pleased to send us means for the carrying on of the work of the Scriptural Knowledge Institution. This evening a brother gave me 6s. 1d., being money which he formerly used to pay towards the support of a trade club, which he has lately given up for the Lord's sake.--November 18. This evening £30 was given to me; £25. for the Scriptural Knowledge Institution, and £5. for myself. This is a most remarkable answer to prayer. Brother C-r and I have prayed repeatedly together during the last week, concerning the work, and especially that the Lord would be pleased to give us the means to continue, and even to enlarge, the field. In addition to this, I have several times asked for a supply for myself, and He has kindly granted both these requests. Oh that I may have grace to trust Him more and more!--November 20. This evening I took tea at a sister's house, where I found Franke's life. I have frequently, for a long time, thought of labouring in a similar way, though it might be on a much smaller scale; not, to imitate Franke, but in reliance upon the Lord. May God make it plain! November 21. Today I have had it very much impressed on my heart, no longer merely to think about the establishment of an Orphan-House, but actually to set about it, and I have been very much in prayer respecting it, in order to ascertain the Lord's mind.--I received this day, from an unexpected quarter, £5. for the Scriptural Knowledge Institution, in answer to prayer; and I had also £1. 14s. 6d. sent from a distance of one hundred and twenty miles.-November 22. This evening I had sent for the Institution £1. 4s.--November 23. Today I had £10. sent from Ireland for our Institution. Thus the Lord, in answer to prayer, has given me, in a few days, about £50. I had asked only for £40. This has been a great encouragement to me, and has still more stirred me up to think and pray about the establishment of an Orphan-House.--November 25. I have been again much in prayer yesterday and today about the Orphan-House, and am more and more convinced that it is of God. May He in mercy guide me! The three chief reasons for establishing an Orphan-House are:--1. That God may be glorified, should He be pleased to furnish me with the means, in its being seen that it is not a vain thing to trust in Him; and that thus the faith of His children may be strengthened. 2. The spiritual welfare of fatherless and motherless children. 3. Their temporal welfare.

It may be well to enter somewhat more minutely, than my journal does, upon the reasons which led me to establish an Orphan-House. Through my pastoral labours among the saints in Bristol, through my considerable correspondence, and through brethren who visited Bristol; I had constantly cases brought before me, which proved, that one of the especial things which the children of God needed in our day, was, to have their faith strengthened. For instance: I might visit a brother, who worked fourteen or even sixteen hours a day at his trade, the necessary result of which was, that not only his body suffered, but his soul was lean, and he had no enjoyment in the things of God. Under such circumstances I might point out to him that

FIRST PART

he ought to work less, in order that his bodily health might not suffer, and that he might gather strength for his inner man, by reading the word of God, by meditation over it, and by prayer. The reply, however, I generally found to be something like this: "But if I work less, I do not earn enough for the support of my family. Even now, whilst I work so much, I have scarcely enough. The wages are so low, that I must work hard in order to obtain what I need. There was no trust in God. No real belief in the truth of that word: "Seek ye first the kingdom of God, and His righteousness: and all these things shall be added unto you." I might reply something like this: "My dear brother, it is not your work which supports your family, but the Lord; and He who has fed you and your family when you could not work at all, on account of illness, would surely provide for you and yours, if for the sake of obtaining food for your inner man, you were to work only for so many hours a day, as would allow you proper time for retirement. And is it not the case now, that you begin the work of the day after having had only a few hurried moments for prayer; and when you leave off your work in the evening, and mean then to read a little of the word of God, are you not too much worn out in body and mind, to enjoy it, and do you not often fall asleep whilst reading the Scriptures, or whilst on your knees in prayer?" The brother would allow it was so; he would allow that my advice was good; but still I read in his countenance, even if he should not have actually said so, "How should I get on, if I were to carry out your advice?" I longed, therefore, to have something to point the brother to, as a visible proof, that our God and Father is the same faithful God as ever He was; as willing as ever to PROVE Himself to be the LIVING GOD, in our day as formerly, to all who put their trust in Him.--Again, sometimes I found children of God tried in mind by the prospect of old age, when they might be unable to work any longer, and therefore were harassed by the fear of having to go into the poor-house. If in such a case I pointed out to them, how their Heavenly Father has always helped those who put their trust in Him, they might not, perhaps, always say, that times have changed; but yet it was evident enough, that God was not looked upon by them as the LIVING God. My spirit was ofttimes bowed down by this, and I longed to set something before the children of God, whereby they might see, that He does not forsake, even in our day, those who rely upon him.--Another class of persons were brethren in business, who suffered in their souls, and brought guilt on their consciences, by carrying on their business, almost in the same way, as unconverted persons do. The competition in trade, the bad times, the over-peopled country, were given as reasons why, If the business were carried on simply according to the word of God, it could not be expected to do well. Such a brother, perhaps, would express the wish, that he might be differently situated; but very rarely did I see, that there was a stand made for God, that there was the holy determination to trust in the living God, and to depend on Him, in order that a good conscience might be maintained. To this class likewise I desired to show, by a visible proof, that God is unchangeably the same.--Then there was another class of persons, individuals who were in professions in which they could not continue with a good conscience, or persons who were in an unscriptural position with reference to spiritual things; but both classes feared, on account of the consequences, to give up the profession in which they could not abide with God, or to leave their position, lest they should be thrown out of employment. My spirit longed to be instrumental in strengthening their faith, by giving them not only instances from the word of God, of His willingness and ability to help all those who rely upon Him, but to show them by proofs, that He is the same in our day. I well knew that the word of God ought to be enough, and it was, by grace, enough to me; but still, I considered that I aught to lend a helping hand to my brethren, if by any means, by this visible proof to the unchangeable faithfulness of the Lord I might strengthen their hands in God; for I remembered what a great blessing my own soul had received through the Lord's dealings with His servant A. H. Franke, who, in dependence upon the living God alone, established an immense Orphan-House, which I had seen many times with my own eyes. I, therefore, judged myself bound to be the servant of the Church of Christ, in the particular point on which I had obtained mercy: namely, in being able to take God by His word and to rely upon it. All these exercises of my soul, which resulted from the fact that so many believers, with whom I became acquainted, were harassed and distressed in mind, or brought guilt on their consciences, on account of not trusting in the Lord; were used by God to awaken in my heart the desire of setting before the church at large, and before the world, a proof that He has not in the least changed; and this seemed to me best done, by the establishing of an Orphan-House. It needed to be something which could be seen, even by the natural eye. Now, if I, a poor man, simply by prayer and faith, obtained, without asking any individual, the means for establishing and carrying on an Orphan-House: there would be something which with the Lord's blessing, might be instrumental in strengthening the faith of the children of God besides being a testimony to the consciences of the unconverted, of the reality of the things of God. This, then, was the primary reason, for establishing the Orphan-House. I certainly did from my heart desire to be used by God to benefit the bodies of poor children, bereaved of both parents, and seek, in other respects, with the help of God, to do them good for this life;--I also particularly longed to be used by God in getting the dear orphans trained up in the fear of God;--but still, the first and primary object of the work was, (and still is:) that God might be magnified by the fact, that the orphans under my care are provided, with all they need, only by prayer and faith, without any one being asked by me or my fellow-labourers, whereby it may be seen, that God is FAITHFUL STILL, and HEARS PRAYER STILL. That I was not mistaken, has been abundantly proved singe November, 1835, both by the conversion of many sinners who have read the accounts, which have been published in connexion with this work, and also by the abundance of fruit that has followed in the hearts of the saints, for which, from my inmost soul, I desire to be grateful to God, and the honour and glory of which not only is due to Him alone, but which I, by His help, am enabled to ascribe to Him.

November 28. I have been, every day this week, very much in prayer concerning the Orphan-House, chiefly entreating the Lord to take away every thought concerning it out of my mind, if the matter be not of Him; and have also repeatedly examined my heart concerning my motives in the matter. But I have been more and more confirmed that it is of God.

December 2. I have again these last days prayed much about the Orphan-House, and have frequently examined my heart, that if it were at all my desire to

FIRST PART

establish it for the sake of gratifying myself I might find it out. To that end I have also conversed with brother Craik about it, that he might be instrumental in showing me any hidden corruption of my heart concerning the matter, or any other scriptural reason against my engaging in it. The one only reason which ever made me at all doubt as to its being of God, that I should engage in this work, is, the multiplicity of engagements which I have already. But that which has overbalanced this objection in my mind has been:--1. That the matter is of such great importance. 2. That if the matter be of God, He will in due time send suitable individuals, so that comparatively little of my time will be taken up in this service.

This morning I asked the Lord especially, that He would be pleased to teach me through the instrumentality of brother C.; and I went to him, that he might have an opportunity of probing my heart. For as I desire only the Lord's glory, I should be glad to be instructed through the instrumentality of any brother, if the matter be not of Him. But brother C., on the contrary, greatly encouraged me in it. Therefore I have this day taken the first actual step in the matter, in having ordered bills to be printed, announcing a public meeting on December 9th, at which I intend to lay before the brethren my thoughts concerning the Orphan-House, as a means of ascertaining more clearly the Lord's mind concerning the matter. December 4. Brother Craik told me this morning, that his voice is getting a little better. December 5. This evening I was struck, in reading the Scriptures, with these words: "Open thy mouth wide, and I will fill it." Ps. lxxxi. 10. Up to this day I had not prayed at all concerning the means or individuals needed for the Orphan-House. I was now led to apply this scripture to the Orphan-House, and asked the Lord for premises, 1000l., and suitable individuals to take care of the children. December 7. Today I received the first shilling for the Orphan-House. Afterwards I received another shilling from a German brother.

December 9. This afternoon the first piece of furniture was given--a large wardrobe. This afternoon and evening I was low in spirit as it regards the Orphan-House, but as soon as I began to speak at the meeting, I received peculiar assistance from God, felt great peace and joy, and the assurance that the work is of God. After the meeting, 10s. was given to me. There was purposely no collection, nor did any one speak besides myself; for it was not in the least intended to work upon the feelings, for I sought to be quite sure concerning the mind of God. After the meeting a sister offered herself for the work. I went home happy in the Lord, and full of confidence that the matter will come to pass, though but 10s. has been given. December 10. This morning I have sent to the press a statement which contains the substance of what I said at the meeting last evening. [For the sake of those who have not read it before, it is given here.]

Proposal for the Establishment of an Orphan-House in connexion with the Scriptural Knowledge Institution for Home and Abroad.

Since the last Report of the operations of the Scriptural Knowledge Institution for home and abroad was published, the Lord has sent us, in answer to prayer, brother John C-r, formerly a minister of the establishment, as a city missionary, who goes from house to house, among the poor of this city, to converse with them about the things of God, to circulate the Scriptures among them, to get them to come to the adult school, if they cannot read, and to advise them to put their children to our schools, provided they go to no other. It was particularly gracious of the Lord to send this brother, nearly five months ago, as my brother and fellow labourer, Henry Craik, has been for these eight months laid aside from the ministry of the Word on account of bodily infirmity, and has therefore been unable to take an active part in this Institution. Thus I have not only found great help, but I have been greatly encouraged to enlarge the field. That to which my mind has been particularly directed, is, to establish an Orphan-House in which destitute fatherless and motherless children may be provided with food and raiment, and scriptural education. Concerning this intended Orphan-House I would say

1. It is intended to be in connexion with the Scriptural Knowledge Institution for home and abroad, in so far as it respects the Reports, accounts, superintendence, and the principles on which it is conducted, so that, in one sense, it may be considered as a new object of the Institution, yet with this difference, that only those funds shall be applied to the Orphan-House which are expressly given for it. If, therefore, any believer should prefer to support either those objects which have been hitherto assisted by the funds of this Institution, or the intended Orphan-House, it need only be mentioned, in order that the money may be applied accordingly.

2. It will only be established if the Lord should provide both the means for it, and suitable persons to conduct it.

As to the means, I would make the following remarks. The reason for proposing to enlarge the field, is not because we have of late particularly abounded in means; for we have been rather straitened. The many gracious answers, however, which the Lord had given us concerning this Institution, led brother C-r and me to give ourselves to prayer, asking him to supply us with the means to carry on the work, as we consider it unscriptural to contract debts. During five days, we prayed several times, both unitedly and separately. After that time, the Lord began to answer our prayers, so that, within a few days, about 50l. was given to us. I would further say, that the very gracious and tender dealings of God with me, in having supplied, in answer to prayer, for the last five years, my own temporal wants without any certain income, so that money, provisions and clothes have been sent to me at times when I was greatly straitened, and that not only in small but large quantities; and not merely from individuals living in the same place with me, but at a considerable distance; and that not merely from intimate friends, but from individuals whom I have never seen: all this, I say, has often led me to think, even as long as four years ago, that the Lord had not given me this simple reliance on Him merely for myself; but also for others. Often, when I saw poor neglected children running about the streets at Teignmouth, I said to myself: "May it not be the will of God, that I should establish schools for these children, asking Him to give me the means?" However, it remained only a thought in my mind for two or three years. About two years and six months since I was particularly stirred up afresh to do something for destitute children, by seeing so many of them begging in the streets of Bristol, and coming to our door. It was not, then, left undone on account of want of trust in the Lord, but through an abundance of other things calling for all the time and strength of my brother Craik and myself; for the Lord had both given faith, and had also shown by the following instance, in addition to very many others, both what He can and what He will do. One morning, whilst sitting in my room, I thought about the distress of certain brethren, and said thus to myself:--"O that it might please the Lord to give me the means to help these poor brethren!" About an hour afterwards I had 60l. sent as a present for myself, from a brother, whom up to this day I have never seen, and who was then, and is still, residing several thousand miles from this. Should not such an experience, together with promises like that one in John xiv. 13, 14, encourage us to ask with all boldness, for ourselves and others, both temporal and spiritual blessings? The Lord, for I cannot but think it was He, again and again, brought the thought about these poor children to my mind, till at last it ended in the establishment of "The Scriptural Knowledge Institution, for Home and Abroad;" since the establishment of which, I have had it in a similar way brought to my mind, first about fourteen months ago, and repeatedly since, but especially during these last weeks, to establish an Orphan-House. My frequent prayer of late has been, that if it be of God, He would let it come to pass; if not, that He would take from me all thoughts about it. The latter has not been the case, but I have been led more and more to think that the matter may be of Him. Now, if so, He can influence His people in any part of the world, (for I do not look to Bristol, nor even to England, but to the living God, whose is the gold and the silver,) to intrust me and brother C-r, whom the Lord has made willing to help me in this work, with the means. Till we have them, we can do nothing in the way of renting a house, furnishing it, &c. Yet, when once as much as is needed for this has been sent us, as also proper persons to engage in the work, we do not think it needful to wait till we have the Orphan-House endowed, or a number of yearly subscribers for it; but we trust to be enabled by the Lord, who has taught us to ask for our daily bread, to look to Him for the supply of the daily wants of those children whom He may be pleased to put under our care. Any donations will be received at my house. Should any believers have tables, chairs, bedsteads, bedding, earthenware, or any kind of household furniture to spare, for the furnishing of the house; or remnants or pieces of calico, linen, flannel, cloth, or any materials useful for wearing apparel; or clothes already worn; they will be thankfully received.

Respecting the persons who are needed for carrying on the work, a matter of no less importance than the procuring of funds, I would observe, that we look for them to God Himself, as well as for the funds; and that all who may be engaged as masters, matrons, and assistants, according to the smallness or largeness of the Institution, must be known to us as true believers; and moreover, as far as we may be able to judge, must likewise be qualified for the work.

3. At present nothing can be said as to the time when the operations are likely to commence; nor whether the Institution will embrace children of both sexes, or be restricted either to boys or girls exclusively; nor of what age they will be received,

and how long they may continue in it; for though we have thought about these things, yet we would rather be guided in these particulars by the amount of the means which the Lord may put into our hands, and by the number of the individuals whom he may provide for conducting the Institution. Should the Lord condescend to use us as instruments, a short printed statement will be issued as soon as something more definite can be said.

4. It has appeared well to us to receive only such destitute children as have been bereaved of both parents.

5. The children are intended, if girls, to be brought up for service; if boys, for a trade; and therefore they will be employed, according to their ability and bodily strength, in useful occupations, and thus help to maintain themselves; besides this they are intended to receive a plain education; but the chief and especial end of the Institution will be to seek, with God's blessing, to bring them to the knowledge of Jesus Christ, by instructing them in the Scriptures.

GEORGE MULLER.

Bristol, Dec. 10th, 1835.

December 11. I have been enabled to pray all this week with increased confidence concerning the Orphan-House, as it regards means, a house, suitable individuals to take care of the children, furniture, &c. December 16. Brother C-n, whom the Lord has kindly allowed to stay above two months among us, to supply brother Craik's lack of service, left us today. How very gracious has the Lord been to us in this affliction! Many brethren have been sent to us as helpers for a little while-- brother C-t for the greater part of the time, and brother C-n for more than two months. And, in addition to this, when brother Craik and I were both ill, the brethren were kept in peace, and there was a spirit of prayer among them. December 31. This evening we had an especial meeting for prayer and praise. We continued together from seven till after twelve.

There have been received into the church at Gideon during the past year--29

Ditto, Bethesda--30

Altogether--59

Of these 59, 30 have been brought to the knowledge of the Lord through the instrumentality of brother Craik and me. There are now, of those who have been begotten again through us, since we have been in Bristol, at Gideon 63, and at Bethesda 71--altogether 134. Besides this, several have fallen asleep in the faith, who never were in communion with us, and several of our spiritual children have joined other churches, in and out of Bristol, and many are now standing as hopeful characters on the list of candidates for communion. There have been added to the church at

FIRST PART

Gideon, since we came, 125; to Bethesda, 163--altogether 288; so that the number of both churches would have been 356 (68 believers we found at Gideon), had there been no changes; but

Of Gideon are at present

under church discipline 6, of Bethesda, 7, altogether, 13

Do. have fallen asleep 12 do. 5 do. 17

Do. have left Bristol 10 do. 4 do. 14

Do. have left us, but are

still in Bristol 11 do. 4 do. 15

39 20 59

So that there are at present in communion with us 297:--143 at Bethesda, and 154 at Gideon.

As it regards the way in which the Lord, in His faithful love, supplied my temporal wants, during the past year, I mention that I received--

1. In free-will offerings, given through the boxes, as my part £130 3s. 7 1/4d.

2. In free-will offerings given by believers in and out of Bristol, not through the boxes £120 7s. 6d.

3. Towards the house rent I received from brother Craik, in consideration that he has no rent to pay, for nine months £7 10s. 0d.

4. The presents sent to us in clothes and provisions, &c., were worth to us at least £27 0s. 0d.

Altogether £285 1s. 1 1/4d.

January 3, 1836. This morning brother Craik spoke a little in public for the first time after about nine months.

January 6. Today we had three especial prayer meetings, for the full restoration of brother Craik's voice. We had also, on January 7, 8, 9, and 10, especial prayer meetings for brother Craik's full restoration. January 16. Today I put into the press another statement, containing a further account respecting the Orphan-House. [It is here reprinted.]

THE LORD'S DEALINGS WITH GEORGE MÜLLER

Further account respecting the Orphan-House, intended to be established in Bristol, in connection with the Scriptural Knowledge Institution for Home and Abroad.

When, of late, the thoughts of establishing an Orphan-House, in dependence upon the Lord, revived in my mind, during the first two weeks I only prayed, that, if it were of the Lord, He would bring it about; but, if not, that He graciously would be pleased to take all thoughts about it out of my mind. My uncertainty about knowing the Lord's mind did not arise from questioning whether it would be pleasing in His sight, that there should be an abode and scriptural education provided for destitute fatherless and motherless children; but whether it were His will that I should be the instrument of setting such an object on foot, as my hands were already more than filled. My comfort, however, was, that, if it were His will, He would provide not merely the means, but also suitable individuals to take care of the children, so that my part of the work would take only such a portion of my time, as, considering the importance of the matter, I might give, notwithstanding my many other engagements. The whole of those two weeks I never asked the Lord for money, or for persons to engage in the work. On December 5th, however, the subject of my prayer all at once became different. I was reading Psalm lxxxi, and was particularly struck, more than at any time before, with ver. 10: "Open thy mouth wide, and I will fill it." I thought a few moments about these words, and then was led to apply them to the case of the Orphan-house. It struck me that I had never asked the Lord for any thing concerning it, except to know His will respecting its being established or not; and I then fell on my knees, and opened my mouth wide, asking Him for much. I asked in submission to His will, and without fixing a time when He should answer my petition. I prayed that He would give me a house, i.e. either as a loan, or that some one might be led to pay the rent for one, or that one might be given permanently for this object; further, I asked Him for £1000; and likewise for suitable individuals to take care of the children. Besides this, I have been since led to ask the Lord, to put into the hearts of His people to send me articles of furniture for the house, and some clothes for the children. When I was asking the petition, I was fully aware what I was doing, i.e., that I was asking for something which I had no natural prospect of obtaining from the brethren whom I know, but which was not too much for the Lord to grant. As I have stated, that I desire to see clearly the Lord's will concerning the Orphan-House, by His providing both the means and suitable individuals for it, I will now mention how He has been dealing with me in these respects.

December 7, 1835.--Anonymously was given 2s. In the paper in which they were enclosed was written "1s. for the Orphan-House, and 1s. for the Scriptural Knowledge Institution. In the name of the Lord alone lift up your banners, so shall you prosper." 1s. besides was given. December 9. I found 3s. in the box, which I had put up two days before in my room for the Orphan-House, and a large wardrobe given just before the meeting in the evening, when I stated publicly my desire concerning this object before the brethren. After the meeting 10s. was given. Also a sister offered herself at the same time for the work. December 10. This morning I received a letter, in which a brother and sister wrote thus:--"We propose ourselves

FIRST PART

for the service of the intended Orphan-House, if you think us qualified for it; also to give up all the furniture, &c., which the Lord has given us, for its use; and to do this without receiving any salary whatever; believing, that if it be the will of the Lord to employ us, He will supply all our need, &c." In the evening a brother brought from several individuals three dishes, 28 plates, three basins, one jug, four mugs, three salt stands, one grater, four knives, and five forks.

December 12. While I was praying this morning that the Lord would give us a fresh token of His favour concerning the Orphan-House, a brother brought three dishes, 12 plates, one basin, and one blanket. After this had been given, I thanked God, and asked Him to give even this day another encouragement. Shortly after, £50. was given, and that by an individual from whom, for several reasons, I could not have expected this sum. Thus the hand of God appeared so much the more clearly. Even then I was led to pray, that this day the Lord would give still more. In the evening, accordingly, there were sent 29 yards of print. Also a sister offered herself for the work. Dec. 13. A brother was influenced this day to give 4s. per week, or 10l. 8s. yearly, as long as the Lord gives the means; 8s. was given by him as two weeks' subscriptions. Today a brother and sister offered themselves, with all their furniture, and all the provisions which they have in the house, if they can be usefully employed in the concerns of the Orphan-House.

December 14. Today a sister offered her services for the work. In the evening another sister offered herself for the Institution. December 15. A sister brought from several friends, ten basins, eight mugs, one plate, five dessert spoons, six tea spoons, one skimmer, one toasting fork, one flour dredge, three knives and forks, one sheet, one pillow case, one table cloth; also 1l. In the afternoon were sent 55 yards of sheeting, and 12 yards of calico. December 16. I took out of the box in my room 1s. December 17. I was rather cast down last evening and this morning about the matter, questioning whether I ought to be engaged in this way, and was led to ask the Lord to give me some further encouragement. Soon after were sent by a brother two pieces of print, the one seven and the other 23 3/4 yards, 6 3/4 yards of calico, four pieces of lining, about four yards altogether, a sheet, and a yard measure. This evening another brother brought a clothes' horse, three frocks, four pinafores, six handkerchiefs, three counterpanes, one blanket, two pewter salt cellars, six tin cups, and six metal tea spoons; he also brought 3s. 6d. given to him by three different individuals. At the same time he told me that it had been put into the heart of an individual to send tomorrow 100l.

December 18. This afternoon the same brother brought from a sister, a counterpane, a flat iron stand, eight cups, and saucers, a sugar basin, a milk jug, a tea cup, 16 thimbles, five knives and forks, six dessert spoons, 12 tea spoons, four combs, and two little graters; from another friend a flat iron and a cup and saucer. At the same time he brought the 100l. above referred to. [Since the publication of the second edition it has pleased the Lord to take to Himself the donor of this 100l., and I therefore give in this present edition some further account of the donation and the donor, as the particulars respecting both, with God's blessing, may tend to edification. Indeed I confess that I am delighted to be at liberty, in consequence of the death of the donor, to give the following short narrative, which, during her lifetime, I should not have considered it wise to publish. A. L., the donor, was known to me almost from the beginning of my coming to Bristol in 1832. She earned her bread by needlework, by which she gained from 2s. to 5s. per week; the average, I suppose, was not more than about 3s. 6d., as she was weak in body. But this dear, humble sister was content with her small earnings, and I do not remember ever to have heard her utter a word of complaint on account of earning so little. Some time, before I had been led to establish an Orphan-House, her father had died, through which event she had come into the possession of 480l., which sum had been left to her (and the same amount to her brother and two sisters) by her grandmother, but of which her father had had the interest during his lifetime. The father, who had been much given to drinking, died in debt, which debts the children wished to pay; but the rest, besides A. L., did not like to pay the full amount, and offered to the creditors 5s. in the pound, which they gladly accepted, as they had not the least legal claim upon the children. After the debts had been paid according to this agreement, A. L. said to herself; "However sinful my father may have been, yet he was my father, and as I have the means of paying his debts to the full amount, I ought, as a believing child, to do so, seeing that my brothers and sisters will not do it." She then went to all the creditors secretly, and paid the full amount of the debts, which took 40l. more of her money, besides her share which she had given before. Her brother and two sisters now gave 50l. each of their property to their mother; but A. L. said to herself: "I am a child of God, surely I ought to give my mother twice as much as my brother and sisters." She, therefore, gave her mother 100l. Shortly after this she sent me the 100l. towards the Orphan-House. I was not a little surprised when I received this money from her, for I had always known her as a poor girl, and I had never heard any thing about her having come into the possession of this money, and her dress had never given me the least indication of an alteration in her circumstances. Before, however, accepting this money from her, I had a long conversation with her, in which I sought to probe her as to her motives, and in which I sought to ascertain whether, as I had feared, she might have given this money in the feeling of the moment, without having counted the cost. I was the more particular, because, if the money were given, without its being given from Scriptural motives, and there should be regret afterwards, the name of the Lord would be dishonoured. But I had not conversed long with this beloved sister, before I found that she was, in this particular, a quiet, calm, considerate follower of the Lord Jesus, and one who desired, in spite of what human reason might say, to act according to the words of our Lord: "Lay not up for yourselves treasures upon earth." Matthew vi. 19. "Sell that ye have, and give alms." Luke xii. 33. When I remonstrated with her, in order that I might see, whether she had counted the cost, she said to me: "The Lord Jesus has given His last drop of blood for me, and should I not give Him this 100l.?" She likewise said: "Rather than the Orphan-House should not be established, I will give all the money I have." When I saw that she had weighed the matter according to the word of God, and that she had counted the cost, I could not but take the money, and admire the way which the Lord took, to use this poor, sickly sister as an instrument, in so considerable a measure, for helping, at its very commencement, this work, which I had set about solely in dependence upon the living God. At that time she would also have me take 5l. for the poor saints in communion with us. I mention here particularly, that this dear sister kept all these things to herself; and did them as much as possible in secret; and during her life-time, I suppose, not six brethren and sisters among us knew that she had ever possessed 480l., or that she had given 100l. towards the Orphan-House. But this is not all. Some time after this 100l. had been given by her, brother C-r, (who was then labouring as a City Missionary in connexion with the Scriptural Knowledge Institution, and who about that very time happened to visit from house to house in that part of the city where A. L. lived), told me that he had met with many cases, in which A. L. had given to one poor woman a bedstead, to another some bedding, to another some clothes, to another food; and thus instance upon instance of acts of love, on the part of our dear sister A. L., had come before him. I relate one instance more. August 4, 1836, seven months and a half after she had given the 100l., she came one morning to me and said: "Last evening I felt myself particularly stirred up to pray about the funds of the Scriptural Knowledge Institution; but whilst praying I thought, what good is it for me to pray for means, if I do not give, when I have the means, and I have therefore brought you this 5l." As I had reason to believe that by this time by far the greater part of her money was gone, I again had a good deal of conversation with her, to see whether she really did count the cost, and whether this donation also was given unto the Lord, or from momentary excitement, in which case it was better not to give the money. However, she was at this time also steadfast, grounded upon the word of God, and evidently constrained by the love of Christ; and all the effect my conversation had upon her was, that she said: "You must take five shillings in addition to the 5l., as a proof that I give the 5l. cheerfully." And thus she constrained me to take the 5l. 5s. Four things are especially to be noticed about this beloved sister, with reference to all this period of her earthly pilgrimage: 1, She did all these things in secret, avoiding to the utmost all show about them, and thus proved, that she did not desire the praise of man. 2, She remained, as before, of an humble and lowly mind, and she proved thus, that she had done what she did unto the Lord, and not unto man. 3, Her dress remained, during all the time that she had this comparative abundance, the same as before. It was clean, yet as simple and inexpensive as it was at the time when all her income had consisted of 3s. 6d., or at most 5s., per week. There was not the least difference as to her lodging, dress, manner of life, etc. She remained in every way the poor hand-maid of the Lord, as to all outward appearance. 4, But that which is as lovely as the rest, she continued working at her needle all this time. She earned her 2s. 6d., or 3s., or a little more, a week, by her work, as before: whilst she gave away the money in Sovereigns or Five Pound Notes.--At last all her money was gone, and that some years before she fell sleep, and as her bodily health never had been good, as long as I had known her, and was now much worse, she found herself peculiarly dependent upon the Lord, who never forsook her up to the last moment of her earthly course. The very commencement of her life of simple dependence upon the Lord, was such as greatly to encourage her. She related the facts to me as I give them here. When she was completely without money, and when her little stock of tea and butter was also gone, two sisters in the Lord called on her. After they had been a little while with her, they told her that they had come to take tea with her. She said to herself; I should not at all mind to go without my tea, but this is a great trial, that I have nothing to set before these sisters; and she gave them therefore to understand, that their staying to tea would not be convenient at that time. The sisters, however, I suppose, not understanding the hint, remained, and presently brought out of a basket tea, sugar, butter and bread, and thus there was all that was requisite for the tea, and the remainder of the provisions was left with her. She told me, that at that time she was not accustomed to trials of faith, as she afterwards was.

Her body became weaker and weaker, in consequence of which she was able to work very little, for many months before she died; but the Lord supplied her with all she needed, though she never asked for anything. For instance, a sister in communion with us sent her for many months all the bread she used.--Her mouth was full of thanksgiving, even in the midst of the greatest bodily sufferings. She fell asleep in Jesus in January 1844.--I have related these facts, because they tend to the praise of the Lord, and may be instrumental in stirring up other children of God, to follow this dear departed sister in so far as she followed the Lord Jesus; but,in particular, that I may show in what remarkable ways the Lord proved, from the very beginning, that the Orphan-House was His and not mine. I now go on to narrate further how the Lord provided me with means for it.] This evening a sister sent five small forms. December 20. A sister gave me 5l. December 21. A friend sent 1l. Weekly subscription of 4s. December 22. A sister gave me 1l. and a friend sent 2s. 6d. December 23. A brother gave this evening a piece of blind line and a dozen of blind tassels. About ten in the evening, a gentleman brought me from an individual, whose name he was not to mention, 4l., of which I was allowed to take 2l. for the Orphan-House, and to give the other 2l. to poor believers. December 28. During the last four days I had received no offerings, and was rather cast down about it, not knowing why the Lord dealt thus. Yet, in the midst of it, I had a hope, that He was in the mean time working for the Orphan-House, though nothing had been given. I was again stirred up to pray, that the Lord would appear today. A little after, I saw a brother who told me, that ever since he had received the printed proposal for the establishment of an Orphan-House, he had considered the matter, and that he was willing to give for the use of it certain premises, which he built some years since, and which cost him 2,600l., provided there could be raised about 500l., to add to the buildings what may be needed, to fit them for the purpose. There is a piece of ground belonging to the premises, sufficiently large to build thereon what may be required. The buildings are very suitable for an Orphan-House, containing some very large rooms. If, therefore, the Lord should put it into the hearts of His people, who have the means, to give this sum of money, the premises will be given. The reason why they are offered under the above-mentioned condition is, that in the state in which they are now, on account of the peculiar purpose for which they were built, they could accommodate only about 15 children, but, by the proposed addition, would be large enough for 50 or 60. For the present, however, the premises are let, and a notice of six months must be given. If this matter should be brought about by the Lord, my prayer concerning a house, which has been repeatedly brought before Him since December 5th, will have been answered. Yet I leave the matter in the hands of Him, who has the power to give us a place, of which we may take immediate possession,

FIRST PART

or who can put it into the hearts of His children to pay the rent for a house, or to give us the 500l. necessary to complete the building.--Weekly subscription of 4s. December 29. A clergyman gave 10s. December 30. A brother at Sidmouth sent 5l.

January 1, 1836. Through a sister was given 6s., being six different donations; also from herself 1l. as a donation, besides 1s. as a monthly subscription. Also a lady sent through her 1l. 1s. as a yearly subscription. Jan. 2. 4 sister sent 5l. Jan. 3. A gentleman sent 5s, Jan. 4. Weekly subscription of 4s. Through a brother from two friends, 1s. The same brother brought also one dish, three plates, two basins, two cups and saucers, and two knives and forks. Jan. 5. 10s., and 12s. 9d., and 2l. were given. This evening some one rang our house bell. When the door was opened, no one was there, but a kitchen fender and a dish were found at the door, which, no doubt, were given for the Orphan-House.

Jan. 7. 10s. was sent. Jan. 8. 2l. was given, also 10s. A sister offered herself for the work. Jan. 9. From E. G. 1l. 5s., and from a brother 6d. Jan. 10. 2s. 6d. was given. In the paper was written, "Two widows mites for the Orphan-school. In the name of the Lord establish it." Jan. 11. Weekly subscription 4s. Jan. 12. 6d., 6d., 4d., 4d., and 1d. were given. Jan. 14. An old great coat was given; 1l. by a brother. A sister in Dublin offered 2l. 12s. yearly. There was sent a deal box, a small looking-glass, a candlestick, a jug, a basin, two plates, two knives and forks, and a tin dish.

All this money, and all these articles have been given, and all these above-mentioned offers have been made, without my asking any individual for anything; moreover, almost all has been sent from individuals concerning whom I had naturally no reason to expect any thing, and some of whom I never saw. Upon the ground of these facts, therefore, I am clearly persuaded, that it is the will of the Lord that I should proceed in the work, and I shall therefore now state something more definite than I could in the former paper.

1. If the Lord should not provide previous to the middle of February a house in the way of gift, which in a few weeks may be occupied for an Orphan-House, or put it into the heart of some one who loves Him to pay the rent for one, or to lend us one for this purpose, I intend, God willing, to rent certain suitable premises, which are to be had for about 50l. yearly. I purpose to take them for a twelvemonth, for that time would be required, before the building could be finished, should the Lord provide the above-mentioned 500l.

2. It is intended, God willing, to open the institution about April 1.

3. It is purposed to confine the Orphan-house, for the present, to female children. My desire is to help both male and female orphans, and that from their earliest youth; but hitherto the Lord has pointed out only a small commencement. Should it, however, please Him to give me the means, and to increase my faith and light, I shall gladly serve Him more extensively in this way. It has appeared well to me to commence with female children, because they are the more helpless sex, and they need

more particularly to be taken care of, that they may not fall a prey to vice. The house which is to had will accommodate about 30 children, which number I intend to receive at once, should the Lord give me the means to clothe that number, and to furnish the house for so many; but, if not, I purpose, at all events, the Lord willing, to commence the work, though with a smaller number.

4. It is intended to receive the children from the seventh to the twelfth year, and to let them stay in the house, till they are able to go to service.

5. As the children will be brought up for service, they will be employed in useful household work.

GEORGE MÜLLER.

Bristol, Jan. 16, 1836.

Jan. 24. Today brother Craik preached once for the first time. Jan. 30. Today I went to meet two sisters, who were expected from London. I sat down in the coach office, took out my Bible, and began to read; and though in the midst of the noise of the city, the Lord most especially refreshed my soul, so much so, that I remember scarcely ever to have had more real communion with Him, which lasted for more than an hour. It was the love of Christ which led me there. I would gladly have remained at home, to have had time for prayer and reading the Word, especially as I had to leave the house early in the morning. Yet I went for the Lord's sake, and He gave me a blessing: so that, though I had to wait more than two hours, and after all the sisters did not arrive, I was richly repaid. May I but leave myself more and more in His hands! He orders all things well!

February 3. I have been very weak for some days. This evening brother Craik was able to preach instead of me, for the first time at the week meetings. How good is the Lord in restoring him thus far! Feb. 16. Today was a day of thanksgiving on account of brother Craik's restoration. We had three public meetings. Feb. 17. I had been repeatedly praying today far a text, but obtained none. About five minutes before the time of preaching, I was directed to Rev. ii. 19, on which I preached with much assistance and enjoyment to my own soul, without any previous preparation; and the word was felt by many to be a word in season. Feb. 26. This evening both churches met at tea together, with the brethren and sisters who intend to leave us in a few days for missionary work. Feb. 29. This evening we had a meeting on behalf of the missionary brethren and sisters. They were by seven brethren commended to the Lord in prayer.

March 1. This afternoon brother and sister Groves, and the brethren and sisters going with them for missionary purposes, twelve in number, left us for the East Indies. In consequence of the journey to the Continent, at the commencement of last year, four brethren and two sisters have gone out, two brethren in October last, and two brethren and two sisters today. This evening we had again a prayer meeting for

FIRST PART

the dear missionary party. May the Lord soon give us the privilege of seeing some one of our own number go forth. April 21. This day was set apart for prayer and thanksgiving concerning the Orphan-House, as it is now opened. In the morning several brethren prayed, and brother Craik spoke on the last verses of Psalm xx. In the afternoon I addressed our Day and Sunday-School children, the orphans and other children present. In the evening we had another prayer-meeting. There are now 17 children in the Orphan-House.

May 3. I have now been for many days praying for the supply of our own temporal wants, and for the funds of the Scriptural Knowledge Institution; but, as yet, I have had not only no answers to my prayer, but our income has been less than usual, and we have had also but very little coming in for the funds of the Institution. We have not been able to put by our taxes, and expect them daily to be called for. My clothes also are now worse than any I ever wore, and I have also but one suit. May 6. I have now been for some years, and especially these last few months, more or less thinking and praying respecting publishing a short account of the Lord's dealings with me. Today I have at last settled to do so, and have begun to write.

May 16. For these several weeks our income has been little; and though I had prayed many times that the Lord would enable us to put by the taxes, yet the prayer remained unanswered. In the midst of it all, my comfort was that the Lord would send help by the time it would be needed. One thing particularly has been a trial to us of late, far more than our own temporal circumstances, which is, that we have scarcely in any measure been able to relieve the distress among the poor saints. Today, the Lord at last, after I had many times prayed to Him for these weeks past, answered my prayers, there being 7l. 12s. 0 1/4d. given to me as my part of the freewill offerings through the boxes, two 5l. notes having been put in yesterday, one for brother Craik and one for me. Thus the Lord has again delivered us, and answered our prayers, and that not one single hour too late; for the taxes have not as yet been called for. May He fill my heart with gratitude for this fresh deliverance, and may He be pleased to enable me more and more to trust in Him, and to wait patiently for His help! May He also be pleased to teach me more and more the meaning of that word, with reference to my own circumstances:--"Mine hour is not yet came."

A third statement, containing the announcement of the opening of the Orphan-House for destitute female children, and a proposal for the establishment of an Infant Orphan-House, was on May 18th, 1836, sent to the press, and is here reprinted.

Opening of the Orphan-House for Destitute Female Children, established in Bristol, in connexion with the Scriptural Knowledge Institution for Home and Abroad; and Proposal for the Establishment of an Infant-Orphan-House.

In a previous printed account, a statement has been given of the success with which the Lord has been pleased to crown the prayers of His servant, respecting the establishment of an Orphan-House in this city. The subject of my prayer was, that He would graciously provide a house, either as a loan, or as a gift, or that some one might be led to pay the rent for one; further, that He would give me 1000l. for the object, and likewise suitable individuals to take care of the children. A day or two after, I was led to ask, in addition to the above, that he would put it into the hearts of His people to send me articles of furniture, and some clothes for the children. In answer to these petitions, 184l. 2s. 6d. and many articles of furniture and clothing were sent, a conditional offer of a house, as a gift, was made, and individuals proposed themselves to take care of the children, the particulars of which have been given in the statement already referred to, dated Jan. 16, 1836. I shall now proceed to show how, since that time, the Lord has continued to answer my prayers.

January 16, 1836, there was given 6d., six yards of calico, three plates, a cup and saucer, and a jug. January 18, 4s. Jan. 19, a saucepan and steamer, a tin dish, a teapot, some drugget; also 4d., and 1s. Jan. 21. 1l., also 5s. Jan. 22. 2s. 6d. Jan. 23. A brother gave 5s., the first fruits of the increase of his salary. Jan. 24. 5s.; also 1l., and 1l. Jan. 25. A brother promised to give 50l. within a twelvemonth, with the particular object of thus securing the payment of the rent of a house. Thus the Lord has answered the prayer respecting this point. There were also given 1l., 6d. and 4s. Jan. 27. A form was sent. Jan. 28. A deal table was given, also, anonymously, were sent a coal box and 4s., also a bedstead. Jan. 29. Two little waiters, two candlesticks, two chandeliers, two night shades, a tin kettle, a warmer, a bread basket, a fire guard; also one dozen tin cups, six plates, and 1s. 6d.; also 1s., a water jug, six plates, a sugar basin, a teapot, a tea canister, and a knife. Jan. 30. A frying pan, a tea canister, a metal teapot, a tin dish, a pepper box, a flour scoop, a skimmer, a grater, two tin saucepans, a tin warmer, 55 thimbles, five parcels of hooks and eyes; also 1l. Jan. 31. 5l. 5s.; an old white dress and a fur tippet.

February 1. 4s., 2s. 6d., also a sister in the Lord offered today to make the bonnets for the children gratuitously, if any one would buy the straw, and that her husband would make a bedstead, if any one would buy the wood; she also mentioned that they would gladly give both the straw and the wood, if they had the means. Feb. 2. 6d., 2d and out of the box in my room was taken 3s. Feb. 4. 2s. 6d.,6d.; also a desk and a kitchen table; there was also promised a subscription of 8s. annually. Feb. 5. 1s. 6d. Feb. 6. A brother sent 100l., being induced to do so an having had the former paper read to him. Feb. 7. 1l. 2s., 1s., 6d., 2s. 6d., 5s., 2s. 6d., 5s., 2s. 6d., 3l. 10s. Feb. 8. A table and two chairs, 4s., 5l., also 30l. was sent from Ireland; 10s., 10s., 1l. Feb. 9. 1l., 4s. 1d., 10s., 1s. 1d., 1s. 1d., 1s., 1s., 1s., 1s., 1d., 5s., 2s. 6d., 2s. 6d., 2s. 6d., 2s. 6d., 2s. 6d., 6d., 6d., 4d., 4d., 1d., 1s. Feb. 11. Three yards of print, 2s. 6d., 5s.; 5s., 10s. Feb. 12. A clothes' horse, a coffee pot, and 1s.; also a washing tub, a coffee mill, a pepper mill, two dozen pieced of bobbin, three dozen stay laces, two dozen thimbles, two dozen bodkins, 300 needles, a gridiron, six pots of blacking paste, a pound of thread, and a large deal table. Feb. 14. 10s., 1l., put anonymously into Bethesda boxes, for the Orphan-House. Feb. 15. Two glass salt cellars, a mustard pot, a vinegar cruet, and a pepper box, also 4s., 4d., 4d., 4d., 4d., 2s. 6d. Feb. 16. 4d. 1s., 4d., Feb. 17. 5s. Feb. 18. A bedstead, and by two poor persons, 2d. Feb. 19. There were sent from London 34 yards of print, six yards of calico, one dozen pocket handkerchiefs, four pairs of stockings, and two New Testaments. Feb. 20. Two salt

FIRST PART

cellars, two mugs, two plates, also two pocket handkerchiefs. Feb. 21. 1l. Feb. 22. 4s., 1s. Feb. 23. Twelve yards of gingham from two Swiss sisters. Feb. 25. 2s. 6d., 2s. 6d. Feb. 28. 1l. Feb. 29. 1l., 5s., 4s.

March 2. 1l., 1s., 1s. 6d., 1s., 1s., 1s., 1/2d., 2s., 1s., 1s., 2s. 6d.; also out of the box in my room, 1l. 2s. 6d.; two large iron pots were sent anonymously. March 4. 10l., 10s., 3s., 7d., 10s., 2s. 6d., 10s., 10s., 3s.; all these offerings were sent from Clapham; also a desk. March 5. Some fancy worsted and 1s., the produce of the sale of some old map rollers. March 7. 4s., 10s., 5s., 5s., 2s. 6d., 2s. 6d., 2s., 2s. 6d., 5s.; all these offerings were sent from Cleve, also 5s.; also, from a distance of about 100 miles, was sent the valuable and useful present of five pewter dishes, three dozen pewter plates, three dozen metal spoons, two coral necklaces, a pair of coral earrings, and a large gold brooch--the trinkets to be sold for the benefit of the Orphan-House. Also from the same place was sent 10s. "which had been laid up for a time of need, but which were sent because the donor thought that the time of trust in the Lord in Bristol was her time of need to give."

March 10. 8s., 1s. 6d., 2s. 6d., 6d., 6d., 6d., 1d., 4d., 4d., 4d., 5s., 2s. March 11. 1l., 5s. March 13. A little girl sent, from a distance of more than 200 miles, 2s. 6d. March 14. A brother at Plymouth promised to send 20l., also 4s. were given. March 15. 7d., 10s., 6d., 1s., 1s., 1d., 6d. March 16. 1s.; anonymously was sent from London 1l., also 2s. 6d. March 18. 10 s. March 19. 3s., 1s., 4d., 4d., 4d., 4d. March 21. 4s. March 22. 1l. March 23. A large deal box, also anonymously six dishes. March 24. 5s. March 25. A ton of coals. March 27. 1l., 1l., 1l., 10s.; these offerings were sent from Trowbridge, also 10s. From the Isle of Wight, 2l., 2l., 1l., 10s., a large piece of green baize, and two metal spoons. March 28. 1l., 4s., 3d., 3l., 10 s., 6s., 10 s., 2s. 6d., 5s., 5s., also an iron kettle and some drugget. March 29. 1s. 3d., 1s. 3d., 1s., 1s. 6d. March 31. 2s.

April 2. 1s., 2s. 6d., 6d., 6d., also six blankets, two counterpanes, four sheets, eight bonnets, five frocks, six pinafores, with the promise to send also six chemises (sent since). April 4. 4s., 1s., 1s., 8d., 1s., 1d., 1s., 3d., 6s., 2s. 6d., 1l., 1l., 3s., also 14 tippets, three pinafores, one frock, three chemises (two more promised), six flannel petticoats; also six stuff petticoats; also six flannel petticoats (and six chemises promised), also a sheet. April 5. 2l., 7s., 6d., 6d., 4d., 4d., 1d., 4d., 6d. April 6. One dozen of washing basins and one jug. April 7. 2s. 2d., 3s., 1s., 2s. 2d., 1s. 1d. April 8. 10s., 10s., 6d., 1s., 2s., also a bench. April 9. 4d., 4d., 4d., 4d., 2s., also three knives and forks, also some marking ink. April 10. Two patent locks. April 11. 4s. April 12. 1s., 8d., 2s., a jug, also twelve bonnets and six tippets. April 13. A set of fire irons, a tea kettle, a coal box, a tin saucepan, a tripod, a tea pot, three cups and saucers, a wash-hand basin, three small basins, and two plates. April 15. 10s., 10s. April 16. 5l., also 1l. and 22 Hymn Books. Also anonymously were sent two dozen pocket handkerchiefs, also a hymn, "The Orphan's Hope," in a frame. April 17. A cask, also a hundred weight of treacle, and 36 pounds of moist sugar.

April 18, 4s. April 19. 2s. 6d., 1s. April 20. A new bedstead. From Clapham were sent 21l. and 11l., likewise three flannel petticoats, some print, six frocks, four pinafores, seven tippets, 12 caps, 14 chemises, 24 furnished work bags, 12 pocket handkerchiefs, 16 pairs of stockings, one pair of sleeves; besides this, with an orphan child, was sent from Clapham, a complete new outfit.

April 21. 2l., 2s., 1s., 6d., 6d., 6d., 5s., 2s., also two candlesticks, a pepper box, and a handkerchief. April 22. 1s., 10s., 2s. 6d., 2s. 2 3/4d., also a long handled brush and 6d., also an ironing blanket, and 32 yards of flannel. April 23. 2l., 5s., 10s., a cheese, and 18 pounds of beef. April 25. 1s. and eight plates. April 26. 6d., 6d., 5s. April 27. 10d. April 28. 1s., also two tons of coal, also two patch-work quilts, 15 work bags and pin-cushions, 12 needle cases, three little bags, one tippet, two pairs of stockings, one kettle holder, also six pairs of worsted stockings.

May 2. 8s., 1l., 10 s. May 3. 8d., 2s. 6d., and a pair of shoes. May 4. A gentleman and lady, who saw the Institution, left six chemises, seven pocket handkerchiefs, two flannel petticoats, four pairs of stockings, and four pairs of gloves; there were also sent 18 thimbles, a gross of buttons, a gross of hooks and eyes. May 5. 2s. 6d., 1s. May 6. 15 pairs of worsted stockings. May 7. 5s., 2s. 6d. May 8. 5s., 6d., 2s. 6d. May 9. 4s., 10s., 6d., 4d., 4d., 4d. May 10. 6d., 4d., 6d., 6d., 4d., 1d., 4d., 2s. May 11. 1l., 2s. 6d., 1s. May 13. A bonnet, also a dish, sent by a poor person in an almshouse; a well-wisher sent, for little orphan boys, six frock pinafores, six little shirts, six frocks and trousers. May 14. 9 pounds of soap. May 15. S. S. 2s. 6d. May 16. 4s. May 17. Out of the box in the Orphan-House, 3s. 0 1/2d., also 1s.

1. It may be well to state, that the above results have followed in answer to prayer, without any one having been asked by me for one single thing, from which I have refrained, not on account of want of confidence in the brethren, or because I doubted their love to the Lord, but that I might see the hand of God so much the more clearly. For as the work has been begun without any visible support, in dependence only upon the living God, it was of the utmost importance to be sure of His approbation at the very commencement.

2. From this statement, and from that contained in the last printed account, it will be seen how the Lord, in a great measure, has already answered the petition of December 5, 1835; for a house has been given, suitable individuals have offered themselves to take care of the children, and much more furniture, and many more articles of clothing have been sent than I ever had expected. The only part of the prayer, which has not been as yet quite fulfilled, is, that which respects the 1000l., which, however, the Lord, I doubt not, will likewise send in His own time. In the meantime, let my brethren help me to praise Him, that He has sent already more than one half of that sum, and therefore more than for the present has been needed.

3. So far as I remember, I brought even the most minute circumstances concerning the Orphan-House before the Lord in my petitions, being conscious of my

own weakness and ignorance. There was, however, one point I never had prayed about, namely, that the Lord would send children; for I naturally took it for granted that there would be plenty of applications. The nearer, however, the day came, which had been appointed for receiving applications, the more I had a secret consciousness, that the Lord might disappoint my natural expectations, and show me that I could not prosper in one single thing without Him. The appointed time came, and not even one application was made. I had before this been repeatedly tried, whether I might not, after all, against the Lord's mind, have engaged in the work. This circumstance now led me to lie low before my God in prayer the whole of the evening, February 3, and to examine my heart once more as to all the motives concerning it; and being able, as formerly, to say, that His glory was my chief aim, i.e., that it might be seen that it is not a vain thing to trust in the living God,--and that my second aim was the spiritual welfare of the orphan-children,--and the third their bodily welfare; and still continuing in prayer, I was at last brought to this state, that I could say from my heart, that I should rejoice in God being glorified in this matter, though it were by bringing the whole to nothing. But as still, after all, it seemed to me more tending to the glory of God, to establish and prosper the Orphan-House, I could then ask Him heartily, to send applications. I enjoyed now a peaceful state of heart concerning the subject, and was also more assured than ever that God would establish it. The very next day, February 4, the first application was made, and since then 42 more have been made.

4. The house mentioned in the last printed account, which we had intended to rent, having been let before any applications had been made, and nothing more having been done about the premises offered as a gift, on account of the want of money needed to complete the building, I rented, at least for one year, the house No. 6, Wilson Street, as being, on account of its cheapness and largeness, very suitable, and in which, up to March 25th, I had been living myself. Having furnished it for 30 children, we began an April 11th, 1836, to take them in, and on April 21st the Institution was opened by a day being set apart for prayer and thanksgiving. There are now 26 children in the house, and a few more are expected daily. They are under the care of a matron and governess.

5. In the last printed account it was mentioned that we intended to take in the children from the seventh to the twelfth year. But after six applications had been made for children between four and six years of age, it became a subject of solemn and prayerful consideration, whether, as long as there were vacancies, such children should not be received, though so young. For it appeared to me, that if it becomes the saints to care in this way, according to their ability, for those whom God has bereaved of both parents, when they become seven years of age, that it becomes them equally so, to take care of them whilst they are under seven years, and therefore completely unable to help themselves. Further, orphan children are often left to themselves, and thus, at the age of 11 or 12 years, have already made much progress in wickedness. Therefore I came at last to the conclusion to take in the little girls under seven years of age, for whom application had been made. Further, there are exceedingly few institutions in the kingdom, in which infant orphans are received, and provided with scriptural education. Further, it has been repeatedly brought be-

fore me, how desirable it would be to establish also in this city an orphan-house for male children, and there were even the above-mentioned articles sent for little orphan boys. Partly, then, on account of these reasons; and partly, because the Institution already opened will be quite filled in a few days, and applications continue to be made; and partly, because the Lord has done hitherto far above what I could have expected: I have at last, after repeated prayer, come to the conclusion, in the name of the Lord, and in dependence upon Him alone for support, to propose the establishment of an Infant-Orphan-House. It is intended to open this Institution, as soon as suitable premises and individuals, to take care of the children, &c., have been obtained.

a. It is intended to receive into this Infant-Orphan-House destitute male and female infants bereaved of both parents, from their earliest days up to the seventh year, and to provide them with food, clothing, needful attendance, and Scriptural education.

b. It is intended to let the female children stay up to the seventh year in the Infant-Orphan-House, and then to remove them to the Institution already opened, till they are able to go to service.

c. It is also intended, as far as the Lord may help, to provide for the boys, when they are above seven years, though we cannot at present say in what manner.

In proposing the establishment of this second Orphan-House, I do it in the same simple dependence upon God alone, as in the case of the former. And feeling my own weakness, and knowing that it is not in my power to give faith to myself, I ask the brethren to help me with their prayers, that my faith may not fail.

6. To avoid misunderstandings, I would expressly state, that both the last mentioned Institution, and the one already opened, are for orphan children living in any part of the United. Kingdom.

GEORGE MÜLLER.

Bristol, May 18, 1836.

June 3. From May 16 up to this day I have been confined to the house, and a part of the time to my bed, on account of a local inflammation, which keeps me from walking. Almost every day during this time I have been able to continue writing a narrative of the Lord's dealings with me, which had been again laid aside after May 7, on account of a number of pressing engagements. It is very remarkable, that the greatest objection against writing it for the press was want of time. Now, through this affliction, which leaves my mind free, and gives me time, on account of confinement to the house, I have been able to write about 100 quarto pages. May the Lord in mercy teach me about this matter!

FIRST PART

June 8. I am still getting better. The abscess is now open. This affliction has been, by the mercy of the Lord, an exceedingly light one. Not one day have I had severe pain, and not one day have I been kept altogether from working. June 9. I was able to go again today to the Orphan-House, and to read the Scriptures with the children. This day came three more children, who have made up our number, so that there are now thirty in the house.

June 11. I am, by the mercy of God, still getting better, but, as yet, unable to walk about. All this week I have been again enabled to go on writing for the press. June 12. Today the Lord very kindly allowed me to preach again, and that most undeservedly, and much sooner than I could have expected. June 14. This morning, brother C-r and I prayed unitedly, chiefly about the schools and the circulation of the Scriptures. Besides asking for blessings upon the work, we have also asked the Lord for the means which are needed; for on July 1, 17l. 10s. will be due for the rent of school-rooms, and, besides this, we want at least 40l. more to go on with the circulation of the Scriptures, to pay the salaries of the masters, &c. Towards all this we have only about 7l. I also prayed for the remainder of the 1000l. for the Orphan-House.

June 18. We have had, for many weeks past, generally little money for our personal expenses, which has been a trial to us, not on our own account, but because we have thus been able to do but very little for the poor brethren. Today, Saturday, we have 3s. left, just enough to pay for a fly to take me to and bring me back from Bethesda tomorrow, as I am unable to walk. This money we should not have had, but for our baker, a brother, who refused today to take money for the usual quantity of bread, which we daily take.

June 21. This evening brother C-r and I found, that the Lord has not only been pleased to send us, through the offerings which have come in during the last week, in answer to our prayers, the 17l. 10s. which will be due for the rent of two school-rooms on July 1st, but that we have 5l. more than is needed. Thus the Lord once more has answered our prayers.

June 25. Saturday. We have been again helped through this week, as it regards our personal need, and have 3s. left, though we had many shillings to pay for driving about. Now the Lord has put it into the hearts of some of His children, to provide me with a fly every Lord's-day, as long as I may need it.

July 1. Today a suit of new clothes was given to me, which came very seasonably. May this fresh instance of the Lord's loving-kindness lead me to love Him more; and may He also be pleased richly to reward those brethren, who have thus ministered to my need! July 16. Today a brother sent me a new hat, the seventh which in succession has been given to me.

July 28. For some weeks past we have not been able to pay the salary of the masters and governesses a month in advance, but have been obliged to pay it weekly.

Brother C-r and I have lately prayed repeatedly together respecting the funds, but we were now brought so low, that we should not have been able to pay even this weekly salary of the teachers, had not the Lord most remarkably helped us again today. For besides 1l. which was given to us, this evening a brother gave 8l., which sum had been made up by a number of his workmen paying weekly one penny each, of their own accord, towards our funds. The money had been collecting for many months, and, in this our necessity, it had been put into the heart of this brother to bring it. My faith has been greatly strengthened through this circumstance. For before today, though I have never been in the least allowed to doubt the Lord's faithfulness, I did not understand His purpose in His dealings with us of late, in not sending us more than we have needed just to be kept from stopping; and I have sometimes thought, whether it might not be His will, on account of my want of faithfulness in His work, to decrease the field; but now I see, that notwithstanding my unworthiness, His allowing us to pray so frequently, was only that the deliverance might be felt so much the more when it came.

July 29. This evening from six to half-past nine we had again a meeting for inquirers. There came twelve fresh cases before us, and there were six more than we could see. Thus we saw, that the work of the Lord, even as it regards conversion, is still going on among us.

October 1. Today, in dependence upon the Lord alone for means, we engaged a brother as a master for a sixth day school. Last Saturday, for the first time, we were so low in funds, that we needed 1l. more than we had, to pay the salaries a week in advance; but one sister, on account of the death of her father, as we afterwards learned, was kept from calling for her money, and on the next day we received more than was needed to pay her. On account, therefore, of the many deliverances which we have had of late, we have not hesitated to enlarge the field, as another boys' school was greatly needed, there having been many applications for admission standing these several months past.

October 5. This evening 25l. was given to me for the Scriptural Knowledge Institution. Thus the Lord has already given the means of defraying the expenses of the new boys' school for some months to come.

October 19. Today, after having many times prayed respecting this matter, I have at last engaged a sister as matron for the Infant-Orphan-House, never having been able, up to this day, to meet with an individual who seemed suitable: though there has been money enough in hand for some time past for commencing this work, and there have been also applications made for several infant orphans.

October 25. Today we obtained without, any trouble, through the kind hand of God, very suitable premises for the Infant-Orphan-House. If we had laid out many hundred pounds in building a house, we could scarcely have built one more suitable for the purpose. How evident is the hand of God in all these matters! How important to leave our concerns, great and small, with Him; for He arranges all things well! If our work be His work, we shall prosper in it.

November 30. On account, as I suppose, of many pressing engagements, I had not been led for some time past to pray respecting the funds. But being in great need, I was led yesterday morning, earnestly to ask the Lord, and in answer to this petition a brother gave me last evening 10l. He had had it in his heart for several months past, to give this sum, but had been hitherto kept from it, not having the means. Just now, in this our great necessity, the Lord furnished him with the means, and we were helped in this way. In addition to this 10l., I received last evening a letter with 5l., from a sister whom I never saw, and who has been several times used by God as an instrument to supply our wants. She writes thus: "It has been so much on my mind lately to send you some money, that I feel as if there must be some need, which the Lord purposes to honour me by making me the instrument of supplying. I therefore enclose you 5l., all I have in the house at this moment; but if you have occasion for it, and will let me know, I will send you as much more." Besides these two donations, I received today 3l. 3s.

December 15. This day was set apart for prayer and thanksgiving respecting the Infant-Orphan-House, which was opened on November 28. In the morning we had a prayer-meeting. In the afternoon, besides prayer and thanksgiving, I addressed the children of our day-schools and the orphans, about 350, on Ecclesiastes xii. 1. In the evening I gave a further account of the Orphan-Houses, commencing from the time when the last printed account had been issued, dated May 18, 1836. The substance of this account was printed, and is reprinted here for the sake of those who are as yet unacquainted with it.

Further account of the Orphan-House for Female Orphans above Seven Years of Age; and Opening of the Infant-Orphan-House, for destitute Male and Female Orphans under Seven Years of Age.

It is now a twelve-month since the proposal for the establishment of an Orphan-House was first made. Since then the Lord has given me almost all I requested of Him, and in some respects even more. This was in part stated in the last two papers which were printed on this subject dated January 16, and May 18, 1836. Of the 1,000l. which I had asked of God on December 5, 1835, I had actually received on May 18, 1836, 450l. 13s. 6 3/4d.; and besides this, 70l. had been promised by two brethren. As it regards premises, articles of clothing, furniture, &c., I had received even beyond my petition. I have now the pleasure of detailing, still further, how God has continued to answer my prayer since May 18, 1836.

May 19th was given 1l. 23rd 1l. and 4s. There were also sent two buckets and 1s. 24th., 10 s. 6d., 2d., 1s. 6d. 25th, one pound of butter, 2s., 1s., 1s. There was also sent 14s., and in the paper was written: "The history of this money is: A lady was going to purchase a dress. The enclosed sum was the difference between the fashionable one, which took her fancy, and one less fashionable. So she thought, the orphans should profit by this sacrifice of her fancy." May 27th, there was left at my house a sovereign, and in the paper was written: 1 Thess. v. 25." [Pause with me a few moments, dear reader, before going on with the account. In preparing the third edition for the press, I have been struck with the very many cases in which individuals, who are spoken of in this narrative, are no more in the land of the living. So it is with the two donors of the last mentioned sums. The dear sister who would not indulge her fancy in having a more fashionable dress, but who would rather give the fourteen shillings, which thus could be saved, to the orphans, has been with her Lord for more than two years. Will she regret not having indulged her fancy in that instance? Will she now suffer loss on account of it? Surely not!--The dear brother who gave the sovereign, was a gracious devoted clergyman of the City of Bristol. He had written in the paper in which the sovereign was enclosed, "1 Thess. v. 25." ("Brethren, pray for us.") This dear man of God does now no longer need our prayers. He entered into his rest several years ago. Yet a little while, dear believing reader, and, if the coming of the Lord prevent not, we too shall fall asleep in Jesus. Therefore, let us work, "while it is day: the night cometh, when no man can work." And, "Whatsoever thy hand findeth to do, do it with thy might: for there is no work, nor device, nor knowledge, nor wisdom in the grave, whither thou goest."--But how would it be with you, dear reader, if you are unprepared, and should be taken out of the world? Let me beseech you to seek the Lord while He may be found. Jesus died to save sinners. He shed His blood. He fulfilled the law of God, and died the JUST for the UNJUST: and whosoever depends for salvation upon His perfect obedience, and upon His sufferings and death, shall be saved; for God has said it.] May 28th, A fender and two coal scuttles. 29th, 5l. 30th, 4s. Also 2s. 6d., with two gowns and a tippet. The brother who left a sovereign with "1 Thess. v. 25," gave today 10s. more; 2s. 4d. June 1st, from a few sisters in Dublin, nine pocket handkerchiefs, 19 1/2 yards of stuff, and forty-two yards of print. 4th, 5s. 6d., eighteen little books. 5th, 6d., 4d., 4d., 4d. 6th, 4s. 7th, 5s. 1d., 2l. 2s. 6d. 8th, 4d., 1s., 1s., 3s. 9th, six pairs of gentlemen's trousers, two coats, one waistcoat, five pairs of socks, two gowns--all worn. 10th, 1l., also from a friend in Ireland 1l. 12th, S. S. 2s. 6d. 13th, 4s., 5l. 14th, 1s. 1d., 1s., 2s. 6d., 6d., 1s., 2s. 6d., 2s. 6d., 3s. 3d., 1s. 1d., 1s. 1d. 15th, a brother at Plymouth sent 25l., 20l. of which had been previously promised. 18th, 1l., 1d., 6 1/4 pounds of bacon, a form, a chopping knife. 19th, 1l. 1s., 10s.; 12s. by sale of ornaments. 20th, 4s. Also from Teignmouth, 5s., 5s., 2s. 6d., 2s. 6d., 2s. 6d., 2s. 6d., 3l., 10s., 2s. 6d., 1s. 1d., 5s., together with a gown, a boy's pinafore, a pair of socks, coloured cotton for three children's frocks, two babies' bed gowns, and five babies' night caps. 21st, 5l. 10s., 6d., 4d., 2d., 4d., 2d., 6d., 6d., twenty pounds of bacon and ten pounds of cheese. 22d, box in the Orphan-House, 2s. 4d. 24th, 2s. 6d., 3s. 8 1/2d. 27th, 4s. 28th, 2s. 6d., 4s., 4d., 6d., 10s., 6s. 6d. 29th, six straw bonnets. 30th, 5s., 2l. July 4th, 6d., 4d., 4d., 4d., 4s. There was also sent from "two orphans" 48l., 1s. 1d., 10s., 8s. 6d., 2s. 6d., 1s. 1d., 1s. 1d., 1s. 1d., 1s. 4d. 5th, 1s., 1s. 2d., 3d., 4s., 4d., 1s. 6th, six new cane chairs. 7th, 2l., 12s., 10s., 2s. 8th, 1s., 2s. 6d., 3s. 10th, 10s., 10s., 1l., 1l. 11th, 8s., 13s. 12th, 13s. 2d. 13th, 12s. 14th, there were sent six chemises, which had been promised on April 14th. Also fourteen pin cushions. 15th, six night caps and 2 petticoats. 20th, 10s., 5s., 1l., 6d., 2d., 6d., 6d., 4d., 6d., 4d., 2d., 4d. 24th, 1l. 25th, 8s., S. S. 5s. Also 25 3/4 yards of print, 12 little shawls and 16 yards of flannel. 26th, box in the Or-

FIRST PART

phan-House 5s. 9d., 4d. 27th, two pairs of shoes. 28th, 3s. 8 1/2d. 29th, 2s. 6d., 6d., 4d., 4d., 4d. August 1st, 4s., 1l. 10., two chemises, three night caps, and ten pocket handkerchiefs; two chemises, three night caps, and six pocket handkerchiefs. 2nd, 8d., 1s., 1s. 3d., 1s. 3d., 1s., 1s., 6d.., 5s., 2s. 6d., 1s., 1d., 1d., one patch work quilt. 5th, 6s. 8th, 4s. 10th, a box, six canisters, and an inkstand, 13th, 5s. 15th, 1l., S. S. 2s. 6d., 4s. 16th, 6d., 6d., 4d., 4d., 4d., 6d., 1s., 1s. 6d. 19th, 1s. 2 1/2d. 23rd, 1s., 10s., 1l., 2s. 6d. September 1st, 1s. 6d., 2s. 6d., 2s., 1s., 4d., 6d., 4d., 6d., 2s. 6d., 2s. 6d., 1s. 6d., 6d., 6d., 2d., 1l., 1l., twelve chemises, one worn stuff frock, 4d., 4d., a basket of apples, and three pounds of sugar. 3rd, 1l., 5l. 5th, 12s. 7th, 5s., 2s. 6d. 8th, 5s. 13th, 1s., 1s., 1s., 2s. 6d., 2s. 6d., 2s. 6d., 2s. 6d., 2s. 3d., 1s., 1s. 1d., 1s. 1d., 2d., 6d., 6d., 2s. 6d., 6d. 14th, 1l., 10s., 10s., 14 pinafores, a basket of apples. 19th, 8s., 2s. 6d. Box in the Orphan-House 1l. 6s. 1 1/4d., 10s. 20th, 6d., 6d., 4d., 4d., 1d, 4d. 27th, several numbers of the "Record" were sent to be sold for the benefit of the Orphan-House, 4d., 4d., 2s., 2s. 6d. 30th, 1l. was given as "A Thank-offering for spiritual mercies vouchsafed to a child." Also Mr. B-sen., Surgeon, kindly offered, today, to give his attendance and medicine gratuitously to the orphans. October 1st, 6d., 4d., 4d., 4d. A worn cloak. 3rd, 5s., 3s. 3d., 1s. A gallon of dried peas. 4th, 1l. 3s. 6d. 10th, 4s., 1s. 1d., 1s. 1d., 1s. 1d., 1s. 11th, 10s., 2d., 6d., 3s. 3d. 14th, 4 1/2 gallons of beer. 16th, three tippets, 8d., 4d., 5s., 5s., 5s., 2s. 6d., 2s. 6d., 10s., 10s., 2s., 1s., 1s., 2s. 6d., 5s. 17th, 4s. 18th, 10s., 6d., 6d., 4d., 4d., 6d., 1d., 4d., 1s. 19th, 1l. 24th, 4s. 25th, three frocks, two pinafores, two tippets, three pairs of sleeves, 10s., 10s., 4d., 1s. 27th, three tippets. Anonymously was sent by post, 10s., with the request that prayer should be made for the donor, for divine guidance under circumstances of much doubt and anxiety. 29th, 12 cloth tippets. 31st, 4s. November 2nd, 1s. 3d., 1s. 3d., 1s. 4th, two little cloaks, four quarterns of bread. 5th, two turkeys, 6d., 4d., 4d., 4d. There was also given by a brother £100.--£50. of which was previously promised, to ensure the rent for premises. It is a remarkable fact concerning this donation, that I had, in December of last year, repeatedly asked the Lord to incline the heart of this brother to give one hundred pounds, and I made a memorandum of this prayer in my journal of December 12, 1835. On January 25th, 1836, fifty pounds was promised by him, and on November 5, fifty pounds besides that sum was given; but it was not till some days after, that I remembered, that the very sum, for which I had asked the Lord, had been given. Thus we often may receive an answer to prayer, and scarcely remember that it is an answer. When it came to my mind that this prayer had been noted down in my journal, and I showed it to the donor, we rejoiced together; he, to have been the instrument in giving, and I to have had, the request granted. November 6th, S. S. 7s. 6d. 7th, anonymously was sent a ton of coals, 4s., one petticoat, two pairs of gloves, two ruffs. 8th, 5l., 2s. 2d., 3s., 2s. 2d., 2s. 2d., 1s. 6d., 2d., 6d., 1s. 6d., 2s. 6d., 2s. 6d. 14th, there was given 20l. for the Orphan-house, and 20l. for the Infant-Orphan-House. Both papers, in which the money was enclosed, contained these words: "If the Lord prolongs the life of the unworthy giver of the enclosed, the same sum will be given at Christmas."--It has been more than once observed to me that I could not expect to continue to receive large sums; for that persons, when first such an institution is established, might be stirred up to give liberally, but that afterwards one had to look to a number of regular subscribers, and that, if those were lacking, it was not likely that such a work could go on. On such occasions, I have said but little; but I have had the fullest assurance, that it is a small matter for the Lord to incline donors to give liberally, a second or third time, if it were for our real welfare. And accordingly the donor, above referred to, added to the first 50l. another 50l., and the last mentioned benefactor, to the 50l., given on a former occasion, added the just mentioned 40l., with the promise to give another 40l. at Christmas. I would only add on this subject, that there are some subscribers, and even some who give considerably; yet I would state, for the Lord's glory, that if they were twenty times as many, I should desire that my eyes might not be directed to them, but to the Lord alone, and that I might be enabled to take the payment of every subscription as a donation from HIM. On the other hand, if there were no subscribers at all, yet the Lord, who heareth prayer, is rich to give according to our need.--There was given also today, "A widow's mite," 10s.--also 4d. November 14th, 4s., also four ducks. For the Infant-Orphan-House, five frocks, four shirts, four chemises, a bed gown, two petticoats; three quarterns bread. 15th 6d., 6d., 4d., 6d., 4d. 16th, by sale of trinkets, 1l. 5s., 4s. 18th, anonymously were sent a boy's cap, a bonnet, a small piece of print. 19th, four quarterns of bread. 21st, 4s., 2s. 6d. 22nd, 4d., 6d., 6d. 23rd, three frocks, a tippet, six pairs of sheets, three pairs of blankets. 25th, 12 hymn books, a worn cloak, a new tent bedstead. 27th, anonymously put into Bethesda boxes 5s. 28th, 4s. 29th, two turkeys. 30th, 10s., five yards of blanketing, a worn shawl. December 1st, a patch-work quilt and five yards of print, 3d., 10s. 4th, 5l. 5s. 5th, 4s., 1l. 5s. 6th, 6d., 2d., a worn cloak, a petticoat, a piece of linen for window curtains. 8th, box in the Orphan-House 2l. 4s. 1 1/2d. 9th, 1l. Also 1l. with "Mark ix. 36, 37," written on the paper. A most encouraging passage for this work, the force of which I had never felt before.--About a hundred weight of treacle.

I. From this statement it appears, that 770l. 0s. 9 1/2d. has been actually given, and that 40l. is promised. All the money, and all the articles of furniture, clothing, provision, &c., have been given, without one individual having been asked by me for anything, from which I have still refrained, that the Lord's own hand might be clearly seen in the matter, and that the whole might clearly appear as an answer to prayer.

II. After frequent prayer, that, if it were the will of God, He would be pleased to send us a Matron and Governess for the Infant-Orphan-House, this petition also has been answered. In addition to this we obtained a convenient house for the purpose, No. 1, Wilson Street, together with a piece of ground for a play-ground; and we therefore began to furnish it on November 21st, and on November 28th we took in the first children.

III. Of late it has appeared well to us to employ some of the strongest and eldest girls of the Orphan-House in the work of the Infant-Orphan-House, under the direction of the Matron and Governess. From this plan it appeared the following advantages would result. 1st. Thus the wages which we should have to pay to assistants would be saved. 2nd. Without any further expense to the Institution, we should in this way be able to support five or six orphans more. 3rd. If thus the bigger girls of the Orphan-House pass through the Infant-Orphan-House, before they are sent into service, they will be accustomed to nursery work, which is so important for young

FIRST PART

servants. 4th. This plan would allow us to have the bigger girls longer under our care, as we should have full employment for them.

[In the original paper follow eight other paragraphs, containing the audited account and various other points of information respecting the two Orphan-Houses, which, at the time when this Report was issued, were of importance to the donors, but are left out now, as it seems desirable to make this edition of the Narrative as concise as may be. This plan has also been adopted concerning the three previous papers, and will be further adhered to.]

GEORGE MÜLLER.

Bristol, Dec. 20, 1836.

December 31. We had this evening a prayer-meeting to praise the Lord for His goodness during the past year, and to ask Him for a continuance of His favours during the coming year. We continued together till half-past eleven. During the past year there have been received into the church of Gideon, 23 brethren and sisters, and into that of Bethesda, 29--altogether 52. Of these 52, 31 have been brought to the knowledge of the Lord through the instrumentality of brother Craik and me. There have now been admitted into Gideon Church, 79 brethren and sisters who have been converted through our instrumentality, and 86 into the Church of Bethesda: 165 seals to our ministry in Bristol. Besides this, several have fallen asleep in the faith who never were in communion with us; several of our spiritual children are connected with other churches in and out of Bristol; and many are now standing as hopeful characters on the list of candidates for fellowship. There have been added to the church of Gideon, since we came to Bristol, 154; to the church at Bethesda, 193--altogether 347; so that the number of both churches would be 415 (68 believers we found at Gideon), had there been no changes; but:

Of Gideon church are under church discipline 5; of Bethesda 8; altogether 13

Do. have fallen asleep 15 do. 7 do. 22

Do. have left Bristol 12 do. 6 do. 18

Do. have left us, but are still in Bristol . . 9 do. 4 do. 13

41 25 66

There are, therefore, at present, in fellowship with us at Gideon 181, and at Bethesda 168--altogether 349.

The Lord has been pleased to give me during the past year, as it regards my temporal supplies:--

1. In offerings through the boxes £133 8s. 9d.

2. In presents of money, from brethren in and out of Bristol £56 13s. 0d.

3. Through family connexion £5 0s. 0d.

4. Besides this have been sent to us clothes, provisions, &c., which were worth to us at least £30 0s. 0d.

5. We have been living half free of rent during the last nine months, whereby we have saved at least £7 10s. 0d.

Altogether £232 11s. 9d.

January 2, 1837. This evening the two churches had again an especial prayer-meeting, which was continued till half-past ten.

January 5. Today a sister called and told me about the conversion of her father, who, in his eightieth year, after having for many years lived openly in sin, is at last brought to the knowledge of the Lord. May this encourage the children of God to continue to pray for their aged parents and other persons; for this sister had long prayed for the conversion of her father, and at last, though only after twenty years, the Lord gave her the desire of her heart. It was an especial refreshment to my spirit to hear the particulars of this case, as I had known so much of the sinful life of this aged sinner.

January 31, and February 2. These two days we have had especial meetings for prayer and humiliation, on account of the influenza, to acknowledge the hand of God in this chastisement, as the disease is so prevalent in Bristol.

April 8. There are now 60 Children in the two Orphan-Houses, 30 in each.

April 22. The Lord has mercifully stayed the typhus fever in the Orphan-House, in answer to prayer. There were only two cases, and the children are recovering.

April 24. This evening we had a comfortable meeting with 30 brethren and sisters over the Word. (Of late brother Craik and I have frequently set apart an evening, generally once a week, to meet with ten, twenty or thirty brethren and sisters, to take tea with them, and to spend the rest of the evening in prayer and meditation over the Scriptures. We began these meetings chiefly on account of having thus an opportunity of seeing more of the saints, as the greatness of the number of those in communion with us makes it impossible to see them as often in their houses, as it might be profitable, or as often as we desire. We commenced these meetings in our own houses, choosing those in particular, of whom we had seen little. After we had

FIRST PART

had several meetings in our own houses, we were invited by the brethren and sisters, and they have asked others to meet us. Sometimes also we have proposed those for invitation whom we see but seldom. These meetings we have found both for ourselves and others very useful, and they will, no doubt, continue to be a blessing, as long as the Lord shall enable us to precede and follow them with prayer. They are also particularly important as a means of the brethren becoming acquainted with each other, and of uniting their hearts.)

May 13. Today I have had again much reason to mourn over my corrupt nature, particularly on account of want of gratitude for the many temporal mercies by which I am surrounded. I was so sinful as to be dissatisfied on account of the dinner, because I thought it would not agree with me, instead of thanking God for the rich provision, and asking heartily the Lord's blessing upon it, and remembering the many dear children of God who would have been glad of such a meal. I rejoice in the prospect of that day when, in seeing Jesus as He is, I shall be like Him. May 14. Lord's-day. The Lord, instead of chastising me today for the ingratitude and discontent, of yesterday, by leaving me to my own strength in preaching, and bringing temporal want upon me, has given me a good day. I have preached with much assistance and comfort, and the Lord has given me rich temporal supplies: for besides the freewill offerings of 2l. 8s. 10d., a 5l. note was put into my hand for the supply of any want I may have. Thus the Lord melted the heart by love, and made me still more see the baseness of my conduct yesterday. Thanks be to God, the day is coming, when Satan will triumph no more!

May 18. There are now 64 children in the two Orphan-Houses, and two more are expected, which will fill the two houses.

May 28. The narrative of some of the Lord's dealings with me is now near being published, which has led me again most earnestly this day week, and repeatedly since, to ask the Lord that He would be pleased to give me what is wanting of the 100l., for which sum I have asked Him on behalf of the orphans; for though, in my own mind, the thing is as good as done, so much so, that I have repeatedly been able to thank God, that He will surely give me every shilling of that sum, yet to others this would not be enough. As the whole matter, then, about the Orphan-House had been commenced for the glory of God, that in this way before the world and the church there might be another visible proof, that the Lord delights in answering prayer; and as there was yet a part of the 100l. wanting; and, as I earnestly desired, the book might not leave the press, before every shilling of that sum had been given, in answer to prayer, without one single individual having been asked by me for any thing, that thus I might have the sweet privilege of bearing my testimony for God in this book:-- for these reasons, I say, I have given myself earnestly to prayer about this matter since May 21. On May 22 came in 7l. 10s., and on May 23, 3l. On May 24 a lady, whom I never saw before, called on me and gave me 40l. This circumstance has greatly encouraged me; for the Lord showed me thereby afresh His willingness to continue to send us large sums, and that they can even come from individuals whom we have never seen before. On May 26th 3l. 6s. was sent, from two unexpected quarters. On May 27 was sent anonymously, a parcel of worn clothes from London and a sovereign. Today (May 28) I received again 4l. 3s. 6d.; and also a parcel was sent from a considerable distance, containing seven pairs of socks, and the following trinkets, to be sold for the support of the orphans: 1 gold pin with an Irish pearl, 15 Irish pearls, 2 pine, 2 brooches, 2 lockets, 1 seal, 2 studs, 11 rings, 1 chain, and 1 bracelet, all of gold.

June 15. Today I gave myself once more earnestly to prayer respecting the remainder of the 1000l. This evening 5l. was given, so that now the whole sum is made up. To the glory of the Lord, whose I am, and whom I serve, I would state again, that every shilling of this money, and all the articles of clothing and furniture, which have been mentioned in the foregoing pages, have been given to me, without one single individual having been asked by me for any thing. The reason why I have refrained altogether from soliciting any one for help is, that the hand of God evidently might be seen in the matter, that thus my fellow-believers might be encouraged more and more to trust in Him, and that also those who know not the Lord, may have a fresh proof that, indeed, it is not a vain thing to pray to God. As the Lord then has con-descended most fully, and even above my expectations, to answer my prayers, arid to Fill my mouth (Psalm lxxxi. 10,) will you help me, brethren and sisters beloved in the Lord, to praise Him for His condescension. It is a wonderful thing that such a worthless, faithless servant as I am, should have power with God. Take courage from this for yourselves, brethren. Surely, if such a one as I am, so little conformed to the mind of Jesus, has his prayers answered, may not you also, at last, have your requests granted to you. During eighteen months and ten days this petition has been brought before God almost daily. From the moment I asked it, till the Lord granted it fully, I had never been allowed to doubt that He would give every shilling of that sum. Often have I praised Him beforehand in the assurance, that he would grant my request. The thing after which we have especially to seek in prayer is, that we believe that we receive, according to Mark xi. 24. "What things soever ye desire, when ye pray, believe that ye receive them, and ye shall have them." But this I often find lacking in my prayers. Whenever, however, I have been enabled to believe that I receive, the Lord has dealt with me according to my faith. This moment while I am writing (June 28, 1837), I am waiting on the Lord for 17l. 10s., the rent for two school-rooms, which will be due in three days, and I have but 3l. towards that sum. I believe God can give; I believe God is willing to give it, if it be for our real welfare; I also have repeatedly asked God for it; but as yet I cannot in the triumph of faith praise Him beforehand, that He will assuredly give me this small sum. I am waiting at every delivery of letters, at every ring at the bell, for help; I am truly waiting on God, and God alone for it; but as yet I do not feel as sure of being able to pay the rent of those school rooms, as I should, if I had the money already in my pocket.

As the Lord has so greatly condescended to listen to my prayers, and as I consider it one of the particular talents which He has intrusted to me, to exercise faith upon His promises regarding my own temporal wants and those of others; and as an Orphan-House for boys above seven years of age seems greatly needed in this city;

and as also, without it, we know not how to provide for the little boys, in the Infant-Orphan-House when they are above seven years of age; I purpose to establish an Orphan-House for about forty boys above seven years of age. But there are three difficulties in the way, which must first be removed, before I could take any further step in this work. 1. My hands are more than filled already through the work arising from the ministry of the Word, the attending to the ordering of church affairs, and the oversight of 370 brethren and sisters. And yet, in addition to this, I have also the work which comes upon me in connexion with the six day-schools, a Sunday-school, an adult-school, the two Orphan-Houses, and the circulation of the Scriptures. (This latter part of the work is more and more increasing; for merely within the last seven months 836 copies of the Scriptures have been circulated). For these reasons, then, I could not in any degree enlarge the field of labour, except the Lord should be pleased to send us a brother, who, as steward, could take from me the work which arises from keeping the accounts, obtaining and circulating the Scriptures, giving advice in ordinary matters respecting the Orphan-Houses, attending to the applications for admission of children in the Orphan-Houses, &c. But whether there is an Orphan-House for boys established or not, such a brother is greatly needed, even as the extent of the work is now, and I therefore lay it on the hearts of the believers who may read this, to help me with their prayers, that such a brother may be found. 2. In addition to this, it would be needful, before I could take any further step, to obtain a truly pious master for the boys, add other suitable individuals who may be needed to take care of the children. 3. The third thing by which I desire to be assured, that it is the will of God that I should go forward in the Orphan-House is, that He provide the means for such an enlargement of the work. Whilst, on the one hand I would confess to the praise of God, that He has been pleased to give me faith to trust in Him; yet, on the other hand, I desire to be kept from presumption and enthusiasm. I do not intend to wait till thousands are raised, or till the Institution is endowed; but I must have such a sum given to me as is needed to furnish a house for forty boys, and to clothe that number, and to have a little to begin with: without such a sum I should not consider it to be the will of God to enlarge the field. What I ask then from the brethren who may feel interested in seeing an Orphan-House for boys established in Bristol is, that they would help me with their prayers, that if it be the will of God, He Himself would be pleased to remove these three difficulties out of the way.

[Whilst the preceding pages of the first edition of this Narrative were in the press, and before the reception of the last proof sheet for correction, the same friend who gave me on May 24, 1837, Forty Pounds for the orphans, and whom up to that time I had never seen, gave on July 12, 1837, Four Hundred and Sixty Pounds more, being altogether Five Hundred Pounds.]

THE LORD'S DEALINGS WITH GEORGE MÜLLER

REVIEW OF THE LAST FIVE YEARS, THE TIME THAT I HAVE LABOURED IN BRISTOL WITH BROTHER CRAIK.

JULY, 1837.

I. Some of the mercies which the Lord has granted to us during this period.

Concerning all this time I have most especially to say, that goodness and mercy have followed me every day. My blessings have been many and great, my trials few and small. To the praise of God I will mention a few of the many mercies which He has bestowed on me.

1. I consider it one of the especial mercies that, amidst so many engagements I have been kept in the ways of God, and that this day I have as much desire as ever, yea more than ever, to live alone for Him, who has done so much for me. My greatest grief is that I love Him so little. I desire many things concerning myself; but I desire nothing so much, as to have a heart filled with love to the Lord. I long for a warm personal attachment to Him.

2. I consider it likewise a great mercy, for which I can never sufficiently praise God, that, whilst during these last five years so many of His children have fallen into great errors, and even those who once ran well, I, who am so faithless to Him, should have been kept from them. There is scarcely one point of importance, comparatively speaking, respecting which I have had scriptural reason to alter my views, since I have come to Bristol. My views concerning the fundamental truths of the gospel are the same as they were at the end of the year 1829 though I have been more and more established in them during these last five years, and have seen more minutely the mind of God concerning many truths. My relish for the study of the word of God has not decreased.

3. I consider it further an exceeding great mercy, that I have been kept in uninterrupted love and union with my brother, friend, and fellow-labourer, Henry Craik. Very few of the blessings that the Lord has bestowed on him, on me, and on the two churches, whose servants we are, are of greater importance. There is not one point of importance, as it regards the truth, on which we differ. In judgment, as to matters connected with the welfare of the saints among whom we labour, we have been almost invariably at once of one mind. (Lord, to Thee is the praise due for this!!!) We are as much, or more than ever united in spirit; and if the Lord permit, we desire to labour together till He come. Who that knows the proneness in man to seek his own, and to get glory to himself; who that knows that the heart naturally is full of envy; who that is acquainted with the position which we both hold in the church, and the occasions thereby occurring for the flesh to feel offended:--who that considers these things will not ascribe our union, our uninterrupted union and love, entirely to the Lord? Let the brethren among whom we labour praise God much for it! Let the

FIRST PART

brethren everywhere, who may read this, praise God for it! This union has glorified God! This union has sprung from God! But, for this union we depend now as much as ever upon God, and therefore let the brethren pray, that God in mercy would give us grace, to put aside every thing that might hinder it.

4. We have had much joy on account of the scriptural conduct of many of the children of God among whom we labour. The two churches have on the whole shown, in some measure, that even in our day there can be love among the brethren. I do not mean that we have been without trials on account of the behaviour of the saints under our care; nor do I mean to say, that either we or they have followed Christ as we might or ought to have done; but only, that we have been mercifully kept hitherto from great divisions; that the cases in which acts of discipline were needed (as the list at the end of the last two years shows) were so few; that we have had much more joy than sorrow on account of the brethren and sisters:--these are matters, worthy to be noticed among the special blessings which God has bestowed on us during the last five years.

5. Another mercy I mention is, that it has pleased God to keep us from some most awful characters, who either actually had proposed themselves for fellowship, or desired to do so, and who, so far as the testimony by word of mouth went, could fully satisfy us. From several such individuals who lived in open sin, we have been kept, by the Spirit constraining them to confess, and that, perhaps, even against their own will, their wicked deeds, which they were practicing; in other instances we suspected them, and, on making inquiry, found out their sins.

6. Another mercy which the Lord has kindly bestowed on us is, that though neither Brother Craik nor I am strong in body, yet we have been helped through much work; and, at the time when we were laid aside, the Lord made up our lack of service, either by sending help from without, or by putting into exercise the gifts of the brethren among us. At those seasons disunion might so easily have sprung up among the brethren; but the good shepherd of the sheep watched so graciously over the flock, that they were kept together in much love and union, whereby also a testimony was given for God, that their faith stood not in the power of man.

7. Sometimes, when particular trials were laid on us, and things appeared very dark, the Lord most mercifully not only supported us under those trials, but also unexpectedly delivered us much sooner out of them, than we could have at all anticipated. May this especially encourage brethren who labour in word and doctrine, or who rule in the church, to trust in the Lord in Seasons of peculiar trial!

8. My temporal wants have all these five years been most richly supplied, so that not once have I lacked the necessaries of life, and generally I have abounded; and all this without having one shilling of regular income. I am not tired of this way of living, nor have I even for once been allowed to regret having begun to live in this way.

THE LORD'S DEALINGS WITH GEORGE MÜLLER

II. The work of the Lord in our hands.

1. It has pleased the Lord to continue to bless the word preached by us to the conversion of many sinners, and there seems to have been no period during these five years, in which this work has been stopped by Him. There have come again several cases before us lately, in which individuals have been recently brought to apprehend their lost state by nature, and to see

that Jesus of Nazareth alone can save them. The whole number of those who have been converted through our instrumentality in Bristol, and who have been received into fellowship with us is 178; besides this, the Lord has given us many seals to our ministry in this city, but the individuals are now either only standing on the list of candidates for fellowship, or are united to other churches in and out of Bristol, or have fallen asleep before they were united to us.

2. The whole number of the brethren and sisters, now in fellowship with us, is 370: 189 at Gideon, 181 at Bethesda.

3. It is now three years and four months since brother Craik and I began, in dependence upon the Lord for funds, to seek to help the spread of the Gospel through the instrumentality of schools, the circulation of the Holy Scriptures, and by aiding Missionary exertions. Since then there have been circulated through our instrumentality 4030 copies of the Scriptures; four Day-Schools for poor children have been established by us; 1119 children have been instructed in the six Day-Schools, and 353 children are now in those six Day-Schools. Besides this, a Sunday-School, and an Adult-School have been supplied with all they needed, and Missionary exertions in the East Indies, in Upper Canada, and on the Continent of Europe, have been aided. In addition to this the word of God has been preached from house to house among the poor, in connexion with the Scriptural Knowledge Institution, by brother C-r, within the last two years.

4. There have been received into the Orphan-Houses 74 orphans, and there are now 64 in them.

And now, in conclusion, I would say that the reason, why I have spoken so plainly about the sins of my unconverted days, is, that I may magnify the riches of the grace of God, which has been bestowed on me, a guilty wretch. I have weighed much whether I should do so or not, knowing well what contempt it may bring on me; but it appeared to me, after much prayer, that as the object of this little work is to speak well of the Lord, I should say in a few words what I once was, in order that it might be seen so much the more clearly, what He has done for me. I also judged that, in doing so, some, who live at present in sin, might see through my example the misery into which sin leads, even as it regards the present life, and the happiness which is connected with the ways of God; and that they also might be encouraged through what God has done for me, to turn to Him. I have made myself therefore a fool, and degraded myself in the eyes of the inhabitants of Bristol, that you, my dear unconverted fellow sinners, who may read this, may, with God's blessing, be made wise. The love of Christ has constrained me to speak about my former lies, thefts, fraud, &c., that you might be benefited. Do not think that I am a fool, and therefore I have told out my heart in my folly; but I have made myself a fool for the benefit of your souls. May God in mercy, for His dear Son's sake, grant that these pages may be a savour of life unto life to you!

The reason why I have spoken so plainly about some of the sins and errors into which I have fallen since my conversion, and about my answers to prayer, and the supplies of my temporal wants, and some of my family concerns, and the success which God has given to our labours,--is not, because I do not know that it is contrary to worldly custom, and against the interests of my worldly reputation; nor is it, as if I made light of my falls; nor as if I would boast in having had my prayers so often answered, and having been in such a variety of ways used as an instrument in doing the Lord's work; but, I have written what I have written for the benefit of my brethren. I have mentioned some of my sins and errors, that through my loss the brethren who may read this may gain. I have mentioned the answers of prayer, that through them they may be encouraged to make known their requests unto God. I have spoken about my temporal supplies, that through seeing how richly God has supplied my temporal wants, since the commencement of 1830, when I left London, they may be stirred up "to seek first the kingdom of God and His righteousness," resting assured, that, in doing so, He will give them what is needful for the life that now is. I have alluded to some family circumstances, that children of God may be encouraged to cast their family burdens upon the Lord, in order that, in doing so, they may find Him carrying the burdens for them. And lastly, I have written about the success which God has been pleased to grant us in His work, that it may be seen, that, in acting on scriptural principles, we have the Lord on our side, and that our mode of preaching is honoured by Him. If in anything which I have written I have been mistaken (and what human work is there which is free from error), I have been mistaken after much prayer. Whilst writing I have often asked help of God. Whilst revising the work, I have still again and again bowed my knees. I have also frequently entreated the Lord to bless this feeble effort of mine to speak to His praise, and I have not the slightest hesitation in saying, that, from the earnestness and comfort which I have enjoyed in prayer, and from the sincere self-examination of my heart, I know that God will bless this little work. May I ask you then, my brethren and sisters, who have been benefited in reading this book, to help me with your prayers, that it may be blessed to others. May I also ask you, my brethren and sisters, who think I ought not to have published it, to ask God to bless that which you yourselves consider good and scriptural in it.

And, now last of all, brethren beloved in the Lord, remember me in your prayers.

SECOND PART

PREFACE TO THE

FIRST EDITION OF THE SECOND PART.

THROUGH grace I am, in some measure, conscious of my many weaknesses and deficiencies; but, with all this, I know that I am a member of the body of Christ, and that, as such, I have a place of service in the body. The realization of this has laid upon me the responsibility of serving the church in the particular way for which the Lord has fitted me, and this has led me to write this second little volume, if by any means those of my fellow-saints, who have not yet learned the importance and preciousness of dealing with God Himself under all circumstances, may be helped in learning this lesson. Nor did I think that the first part of this Narrative rendered the second part needless, because that contains more especially the Lord's dealings with me as an individual, whilst this gives, more particularly, an account of the remarkable way in which the Lord has helped me in reference to His work in my hands. For this second part carries on the account of the Orphan-Houses, etc., which are under my care, and contains the substance of the Reports previously published, so that any one who wishes to have the account from the beginning up to the end of last year, may be able to obtain it. This latter point alone made it needful for me to think about publishing this second part, as of the Reports for 1838 and 1839, which still almost daily are inquired after, there are only a few copies left, though 2,500 of the one and 3,000 of the other were published and of the Report for 1840 there are also only about 500, out of 4,000, remaining. The being thus able to put the whole account of the work into the hands of an inquiring individual, affords such a one a fairer opportunity of seeing the working of those scriptural principles on which the Institution is established. And, lastly, the Lord's continued blessing upon the first part of the Narrative and the Reports, both to believers and unbelievers, has induced me to publish this second volume, which I now affectionately commend to the prayers of the saints, requesting at the same time their prayers for myself.

GEORGE MULLER.

Bristol, June 14, 1841.

A NARRATIVE OF SOME OF THE LORD'S DEALINGS WITH GEORGE MÜLLER SECOND PART

In publishing the continuation of the Narrative of some of the Lord's dealings with me, I have thought it well to give it in the same form in which the larger portion of the former part is written. I therefore proceed to give extracts from my journal making here and there such remarks as occasion may seem to require. The first, part of the Narrative was carried on to the beginning of July 1837, from which period the Continuation commences.

July 18, 1837. Four trials came upon me this morning, without my having previously had opportunity for secret prayer. I had been prevented from rising early, on account of having to spend part of the night in a sick chamber; but this circumstance shows, how important it is to rise early, when we are able, in order that we may be prepared, by communion with the Lord, to meet the trials of the day.

Aug. 15. Today the first 500 copies of my Narrative arrived, and I had, once more, some conflict of mind whether, after all, I had not been mistaken in this matter. A sort of trembling came over me, and a wish to be able to retrace the step. Judging, however, from the most searching self-examination, through which I had caused my heart to pass again and again, as to my motives, before I began writing, and whilst I was writing; and judging, moreover, from the earnestness in prayer with which I had sought to ascertain the mind of God in the matter, and from the subsequent full assurance which I had had of its being according to His will, that in this way I should serve the Church;--I was almost immediately led to consider this uncomfortable and trying feeling as a temptation, and I therefore went to the box, opened it, brought out some copies, and soon after gave away one, so that the step could not be retraced. [This was the last temptation or struggle I have had of that kind; for, though, very many times since, I have had abundant reason for praising the Lord that He put such an honour upon me, in allowing me to speak well of His name in so public a manner, I have never since, even for one minute, been allowed to regret publishing the Narrative; and almost daily have I been more and more confirmed in the conviction, that the giving such like publications to the church, making known the Lord's dealings with me, is one part of my service towards the saints.]

Aug. 17. Today two more children were received into the Infant Orphan-House, which makes up our full number, 66 in the Girls' and infant-Orphan-Houses.

Aug. 28. When brother Craik and I began to labour in Bristol, and consequently some believers united with us in fellowship, assembling together at Bethesda, we began meeting together on the basis of the written Word only, without having any church rules whatever. From the commencement it was understood, that, as the Lord should help us, we would try everything by the word of God, and introduce and hold fast that only which could be proved by Scripture. When we came to this determination on Aug. 13, 1832, it was indeed in weakness, but it was in uprightness of heart.--On account of this it was, that, as we ourselves were not fully settled as to whether those only who had been baptized after they had believed, or whether all who believed in the Lord Jesus, irrespective of baptism, should be received into fellowship nothing was determined about this point. We felt free to break bread and be in communion with those who were not baptized, and therefore could with a good conscience labour at Gideon, where the greater part of the saints, at least at first, were unbaptized; but, at the same time, we had a secret wish that none but believers who were baptized might be united with us at Bethesda. Our reason for this was, that we had witnessed in Devonshire much painful disunion, resulting, as we thought, from baptized and unbaptized believers being in fellowship. Without, then, making it a rule, that Bethesda Church was to be one of close communion, we nevertheless took care that those who applied for fellowship should be instructed about baptism. For many months there occurred no difficulty, as none applied for communion but such as had either been already baptized, or wished to be, or who became convinced of the Scriptural character of believers' baptism, after we had conversed with them; afterwards, however, three sisters applied for fellowship, none of whom had been baptized; nor were their views altered, after we had conversed with them. As, nevertheless, brother Craik and I considered them true believers, and we ourselves were not fully convinced what was the mind of the Lord in such a case, we thought it right that these sisters should be received; yet so that it might be unanimously, as all our church acts then were done; but we knew by that time, that there were several in fellowship with us, who could not conscientiously receive unbaptized believers. We mentioned, therefore, the names of these three sisters to the church, stating that they did not see believers' baptism to be scriptural, and that, if any brother saw, on that account, a reason why they should not be received, he should let us know. The result was, that several objected, and two or three meetings were held, at which we heard the objections of the brethren, and sought for ourselves to obtain acquaintance with the mind of God on the point. Whilst several days thus passed away before the matter was decided, one of those three sisters came and thanked us, that we had not received her, before being baptized, for she now saw that it was only shame and the fear of man which had kept her back, and that the Lord had now made her willing to be baptized. By this circumstance those brethren, who considered it scriptural that all ought to be baptized before being received into fellowship, were confirmed in their views; and as to brother Craik and me, it made us, at least, still more question, whether, those brethren might not be right; and we felt therefore, that

SECOND PART

in such a state of mind we could not oppose them. The one sister, therefore, who wished to be baptized, was received into fellowship, but the two others not. Our consciences were the less affected by this, because all, though not baptized, might take the Lord's supper with us, at Bethesda, though not be received into full fellowship; and because at Gideon, where there were baptized and unbaptized believers, they might even be received into full fellowship; for we had not then clearly seen that there is no scriptural distinction between being in fellowship with individuals and breaking bread with them. Thus matters stood for many months, i.e. believers were received to the breaking of bread even at Bethesda, though not baptized, but they were not received to all the privileges of fellowship.--In August of 1836 I had a conversation with brother H. C. on the subject of receiving the unbaptized into communion, a subject about which, for years, my mind had been more or less exercised. This brother put the matter thus before me: either unbaptized believers come under the class of persons who walk disorderly, and, in that case, we ought to withdraw from them (2 Thess. iii. 6); or they do not walk disorderly. If a believer be walking disorderly, we are not merely to withdraw from him at the Lord's table, but our behaviour towards him ought to be decidedly different from what it would be were he not walking disorderly, on all occasions when we may have intercourse with him, or come in any way into contact with him, Now this is evidently not the case in the conduct of baptized believers towards their unbaptized fellow-believers. The Spirit does not suffer it to be so, but He witnesses that their not having been baptized does not necessarily imply that they are walking disorderly; and hence there may be the most precious communion between baptized and unbaptized believers. The Spirit does not suffer us to refuse fellowship with them in prayer, in reading and searching the Scriptures, in social and intimate intercourse, and in the Lord's work; and yet this ought to be the case, were they walking disorderly.--This passage, 2 Thess. iii. 6, to which brother R. C. referred, was the means of showing me the mind of the Lord on the subject, which is, that we ought to receive all whom Christ has received (Rom. xv. 7), irrespective of the measure of grace or knowledge which they have attained unto.--Some time after this conversation, in May 1837, an opportunity occurred, when we (for brother Craik had seen the same truth) were called upon to put into practice the light which the Lord had been pleased to give us. A sister, who neither had been baptized, nor considered herself under any obligation to be baptized, applied for fellowship. We conversed with her on this as on other subjects, and proposed her for fellowship, though our conversation had not convinced her that she ought to be baptized. This led the church again to the consideration of the point. We gave our reasons, from Scripture, for considering it right to receive this unbaptized sister to all the privileges of the children of God; but a considerable number, one-third perhaps, expressed conscientious difficulty in receiving her. The example of the Apostles in baptizing the first believers upon a profession of faith, was especially urged, which indeed would be an insurmountable difficulty, had not the truth been mingled with error for so long a time, so that it does not prove willful disobedience, if any one in our day should refuse to be baptized after believing. The Lord, however, gave us much help in pointing out the truth to the brethren, so that the number of those, who considered that only baptized believers should be in communion, decreased almost daily. At last, only fourteen brethren and sisters out of above 180, thought it right, this Aug. 28, 1837, to separate from us, after we had had much intercourse with them. [I am glad to be able to add, that, even of these 14, the greater part afterwards saw their error, and came back again to us, and that the receiving of all who love our Lord Jesus into full communion, irrespective of baptism, has never been the source of disunion among us, though more than forty-four years have passed away since.]

Sept. 2. I have been looking about for a house for the Orphan Boys, these last three days. Every thing else has been provided. The Lord has given suitable individuals to take care of the children, money, &c. In His own time He will give a house also.

Sept. 6. This morning I accompanied a sister, who had been staying a night with us, to the steamer. In answer to prayer I awoke at the right time, the fly came at half-past five, her trunk was got from the vessel in which she came yesterday, and we arrived before the steamer had left. In all these four points I felt my dependence upon the Lord, and He, having put prayer into my heart, answered it in each of these four particulars.

Sept. 15. This evening we had a meeting for inquirers and applicants for fellowship. There were more than we could see within three hours; and when all strength was gone, we had to send away four. Among those whom we saw was E. W., who had been kept for some time from applying for fellowship, on account of not seeing believers' baptism to be scriptural. She wished to be taught, but could not see it. She felt grieved that on that account she could not attend to the breaking of bread, which she did see to be scriptural. As soon as open communion was brought about at Bethesda, she wished to offer herself for fellowship, but was twice prevented by circumstances from doing so. Last Wednesday evening she came to the baptizing, when once more, after the lapse of more than two years, I preached on baptism, which fully convinced her of its being scriptural, and she desires now to be baptized. Her difficulty was, that she thought she had been baptized with the Spirit, and therefore needed no water baptism, which now, from Acts x. 44-47, she sees to be an unscriptural objection.--Though it is only one month this day since my Narrative was published, I have already heard of many instances in which the Lord has been pleased to bless it.

This morning we received a parcel with clothes and some money for the Orphans, from a sister at a distance. Among the donations in money was a little legacy, amounting to 6s. 6 1/2d. from a dear boy, the nephew of the sister who sent the things, who died in the faith. This dear child had had given to him, in his last illness, some new shillings, sixpences, and other smaller silver coins, amounting to the above-mentioned little sum. Shortly before he fell asleep, he requested that this his little treasure might be sent to the Orphans. This precious little legacy is the first we have had.

SECOND PART

Sept. 19. Two things were today particularly impressed upon my heart, and may the Lord deepen the impression. 1. That I ought to seek for more retirement, though the work should apparently suffer ever so much. 2. That arrangements should be made, whereby I may be able to visit the brethren more, as an unvisited church will sooner or later become an unhealthy church. Pastors, as fellow-labourers, are greatly needed among us.

Sept. 28, I have for a long time been too much outwardly engaged. Yesterday morning I spent about three hours in the vestry of Gideon, to be able to have more time for retirement. I meant to do the same in the afternoon, but before I could leave the house I was called on, and thus one person after the other came, till I had to go out. Thus it has been again today.

Oct. 16. For a long time past brother Craik and I have felt the importance of more pastoral visiting, and it has been one of our greatest trials, that we have been unable to give more time to it. This evening we had purposely a meeting of the two Churches, at which brother Craik and I spoke on; I. The importance of pastoral visiting. II. The particular obstacles which hindered us in attending to it. III. The question whether there was any way of removing some of the obstacles.

I. As to the importance of pastoral visiting, the following points were mentioned: 1. Watching over the saints, by means of visiting them, to prevent coldness, or to recover them from backsliding. 2. To counsel and advise them in family affairs, in their business, and in spiritual matters. 3. To keep up that loving familiar intercourse, which is so desirable between the saints and those who have the oversight of them.--These visits should be, if possible, frequent; but in our case there have been several obstacles in the way.

II. The particular obstacles in our case are: 1. The largeness of the number who are in communion with us. One hundred would be quite as many as we have strength to visit regularly, and as often as would be desirable; but there are nearly 400 in fellowship with us. 2. The distance of the houses of the saints from our own dwellings, as many live more than two miles of. 3. The Lord's blessing upon our labours. Not one year has passed away, since we have been in Bristol, without more than fifty having been added to our number, each of whom, in general, needed several times to be conversed with before being admitted into fellowship. 4. That brother Craik and I have each of us the care of two churches. At the first sight it appears as if the work is thus divided, but the double number of meetings, &c., nearly double the work. 5. The mere ruling, and taking care, in general, of a large body of believers, irrespective of the other work, takes much more time, and requires much more strength, than the taking care of a small body of believers, as we, by grace, desire not to allow known sin among us. 6. The position which we have in the church at large brings many brethren to us who travel through Bristol, who call on us, or lodge with us, and to whom, according to the Lord's will, we have to give some time. 7. In my own case an extensive needful correspondence. 8. The weakness of body on the part of both of us. When the preaching is done,--when the strangers who lodge with us are gone,--when the calls at our house are over,--when the needful letters, however briefly, are written,--when the necessary church business is settled;--our minds are often so worn out, that we are glad to be quiet. 9. But suppose we have bodily strength remaining after the above things have been attended to, yet the frame of mind is not always so, as that one could visit. After having been particularly tried by church matters, which in so large a body does not rarely occur, or being cast down in one's own soul, one may be fit for the closet, but not for visiting the saints. 10. Lastly, in my own case, no small part of my time is taken up by attending to the affairs of the Orphan-Houses, Schools, the circulation of the Scriptures, the aiding Missionary efforts, and other work connected with the Scriptural Knowledge Institution.

III. What is to be done under these circumstances? 1. In the days of the Apostles there would have been more brethren to take the oversight of so large a body as we are. The Lord has not laid upon us a burden which is too heavy for us; He is not a hard master. It is evident that He does not mean us even to attempt to visit all the saints as much as is absolutely needful, and much less as frequently as it would be desirable. We mention this, to prevent uncomfortable feelings on the part of the dear saints under our pastoral care, who find themselves not as much visited as they used to be when we came to Bristol, when the number of them was not 70, and now it is about 400, and when in many other respects the work in our hands was not half so much, as it is now, and when we had much more bodily strength. 2. it is therefore evident that there are other pastors needed; not nominal pastors, but such as the Lord has called, to whom He has given a pastor's heart, and pastoral gifts. 3. Such may be raised up by the Lord from our own number, or the Lord may send them from elsewhere. 4. But in the meantime we should at least see whether there are not helpers among us. 5. As to the work itself, in order that time may be saved, it appears desirable that the two churches, Bethesda and Gideon, should be united into one, that the breaking of bread should be alternately, and that the number of weekly meetings should be reduced.

Oct. 21. A few weeks since I had rented a very large and a very cheap house for the Boys' Orphan-House; but as the persons who lived in that neighbourhood threatened the landlord with an action, on account of letting his house for a charitable institution, I, at once, gave up all claim. That which led me to do so, was the word of the Lord; "As much as lieth in you, live peaceably with all men." I was quite sure when I gave up the agreement, that the Lord would provide other premises. On the same morning when this took place, Oct. 5, the Lord, to show His continued approbation of the work, sent 50l. by a sister, who is far from being rich, for the furnishing of the Boys' Orphan-House. Now, today, the Lord has given me another house for the Orphan-Boys, in the same street, in which the other two Orphan-Houses are. Thus, in His own time, He has sent help in this particular also. Indeed in everything, in which I have had to deal with Him alone in this work, I have never been disappointed.

SECOND PART

Oct. 23. Today two young sisters were received into fellowship who have been in our Sunday-School. Thus we begin now to reap fruit in respect of our schools.

Nov. 1. Our Bible-School and Missionary funds having been for some time very low, I had been led repeatedly to ask the Lord for a rich supply, and mentioned several times, though with submission to His will, the sum of 100l. before Him. However, He seemed not to regard the prayer respecting the 100l., but gave to us by little and little what was needed. Yesterday I received a donation of 80l., and today one of 20l., and thus He has kindly given the 100l. By this means we are able to increase our stock of Bibles, which has been much reduced of late.

Nov. 5. Last night I awoke with a great weakness in my head, which kept me a good while awake. I at last got to sleep by tying a handkerchief round my head, and by thus pressing it. Today, however, though weak, I was able to preach, and that with much enjoyment, especially in the evening at Bethesda.

Nov. 6. I feel very weak in my head. This evening it was settled at a meeting of the two churches, assembling at Bethesda and Gideon Chapels, that, for the reasons before given, the two churches should be henceforth united as one.

Nov. 7. My head is so weak, that I see it absolutely needful to give up the work for some time. After I had come this morning to the conclusion to leave Bristol for a while for the purpose of quietness, I received an anonymous letter from Ireland with 5l. for my own personal expenses, and thus the Lord has kindly supplied me with the means for doing so.--I can work no longer, my head being in such a weak stated from continual exertion, so that I feel now comfortable in going, though scarcely any time could have been, humanly speaking, more unsuitable. The Orphan-House for the Boys is on the point of being opened, the labourers therefore are to be introduced into the work;-—most important church matters have been entered upon and are yet unsettled;-—but the Lord knows better, and cares for His work more than I do or can. Therefore I desire to leave the matter with Him, and He graciously helps me to do so, and thus, in the quiet submission to His will, and the willingness to leave the work in His own hands, I have the testimony that I have not been engaged in my own work but in His.

Nov. 8. This morning I left Bristol. When I left my house, I knew not what place to go to. All I knew was, that I must leave Bristol. A Bath coach was the first one I could get, and I took it. My intention was, not to go to brethren, as I needed perfect quietness; but I felt so uncomfortable at the hotel, on account of the worldliness of the place, that I went to see a brother, who with his aunts kindly pressed me to stay with them.--This evening has been a very trying season to me. My head has been very weak; I have greatly feared lest I should become insane; but amidst it all, through grace, my soul is quietly resting upon the Lord.

Nov. 12. Lord's day. I am still staying in Bath. The weakness of my head allowed me to attend but one meeting, and even that distressed my head much.

Nov. 13. I was greatly distressed this evening on account of my head. I prayed earnestly to be kept from insanity.

Nov. 14. I am rather better in my head today.

Nov. 15. I left Bath, and went back to Bristol, as I felt I needed more quietness than I can have in the house of any friends, being continually drawn into conversation, which my head cannot bear.

Nov. 16. Today I went to Weston Super Mare, to take lodgings for myself and family. A sister sent me this morning 5l., by which the Lord has provided me with the means for removing my family.

Nov. 17. Weston Super Mare. This evening my wife and child, and our servant arrived here. Yesterday a sister secretly put two sovereigns in my wife's pocket book. How kind is the Lord in thus providing us with means according to our need! How kind also in having just now sent brother T. to take the work arising from the Schools, Orphan-Houses, &c., just as brother C—r was sent two years ago, shortly before I was completely laid aside!——Today a brother sent me information, that he had ordered one hundred pairs of blankets to be sent to me, for distribution among the poor.

Nov. 23. My general health is pretty good; my head, however, is no better, but rather worse. This evening I was led, through the affliction in my head, to great irritability of temper. Of late I have had afresh painfully to experience in myself two things: 1. that affliction in itself does not lead nearer to God. 2. That we may have a good deal of leisure time and yet fail in profitably improving it. Often had I wished within the last months that I might have more time. Now the Lord has given it to me, but alas! how little of it is improved for prayer. I find it a difficult thing, whilst caring for the body, not to neglect the soul. It seems to me much easier to go on altogether regardless of the body, in the service of the Lord, than to take care of the body, in the time of sickness, and not to neglect the soul, especially in an affliction like my present one, when the head allows but little reading or thinking.——What a blessed prospect to be delivered from this wretched evil nature! I can say nothing respecting this day, and this evening in particular, but that I am a wretched man.

Nov. 24. I am now quite sure that I want more than mere quiet and change of air, even medical advice. My general health seems improved through my stay at Weston, but the disease in my head is increased. I have had many distressing moments since I have been at Weston, on account of fearing that my disease may be the forerunner of insanity; yet God has in mercy sustained me, and enabled me, in some small measure, notwithstanding my great sinfulness, to realize the blessing of being in Christ, and therefore secure for ever.

SECOND PART

Nov. 25. We returned to Bristol. I was at peace, being able to cast myself upon the Lord respecting the calamity which I feared. This evening I saw a kind physician and surgeon, who told me that the disease is either a tendency of blood to the head, or that the nerves of the head are in a disordered state. They also told me that I had not the least reason to fear insanity. How little grateful is my soul for this!

Nov. 29. I am no better. A sister sent me today 5l. also a pickled tongue, fowls, cakes, and beautiful grapes were sent to me. My cup, as to temporal mercies, runs over.——One of the Orphan children died while I was at Weston Super Mare. There is reason to believe that she died in the faith.

Nov. 30. I am not any better. I have written to my father, perhaps, for the last time. All is well, all will be well, all cannot but be well; because I am in Christ. How precious that now, in this my sickness, I have not to seek after the Lord, but have already found Him.

Dec. 1. By the mercy of God my head is somewhat relieved. My liver is in a most inactive state, which, as my kind medical attendants tell me, has created the pressure on the top of the head, and through the inactivity of the liver, the whole system having been weakened, and my mental exertions having been continued, the nerves of the head have greatly suffered in consequence.——This evening was sent to me, anonymously, from a distance, 5l. for my own present necessities. The letter was only signed F. W.——A sister, a stranger, gave to my wife 1l. Thus the Lord remembers our increased expenditure in consequence of my affliction, and sends to us accordingly.

Dec. 4. Yesterday I met with the brethren for the breaking of bread. Today I am not so well. Every time that I meet with them, the nerves of my head are excited, and I am worse afterwards. A sister from Barnstaple sent us 1l. 15s.

Dec. 8. My head is not so well as at the end of last week. I find it difficult to be in Bristol and not to exert my mind. Prayer and the reading of the Word I can bear better than any thing. May the Lord give me grace to pray more! I see as yet scarcely a single reason, so far as I myself am concerned, why the Lord should remove this affliction from me. I do not find myself more conformed to the mind of Jesus by it.

Dec. 9. Two years ago this day, I stated my intention of establishing an Orphan-House, if God should permit. What has God wrought since! 75 orphans are now under our care, and 21 more we can receive. Several more are daily expected. During the last twelvemonth the expenses have been about 740l., and the income about 840l. In addition to this, about 400l. has been expended upon the Schools, the circulation of the Scriptures, and in aiding Missionary purposes. More than 1100l. therefore we have needed during the past year, and our good Lord has supplied all, without one single person having been asked for any thing.

Dec. 12. Today the hundred pairs of blankets arrived. How kind of the Lord to give us the privilege of being instrumental in providing, in this respect, for some of the poor, both among the saints and in the world! This donation came in most seasonably, as, on inquiring into the circumstances of some of the poor, most affecting cases of distress were discovered, on account of the want of blankets. May the Lord give me grace to deny myself, in order to provide for the necessities of the poor! How much may be done even by a little self-denial! Lord, help me!——The blankets were of a very good quality. It is a Christlike spirit in supplying the necessities of the poor, not to ask how little will do for them, but how richly may I possibly supply their need.

Dec. 14. A sister, who a short time since had given me 5l. for my own personal expenses, gave me another 5l. today. How very kind is the Lord in providing so abundantly for us, and giving us far more than we need!

Dec. 16. My head is not at all better, but rather worse. My medical attendants have today changed the medicine. But however kind and skillful they are, however nourishing the food which I take, however much I seek to refrain from over-exertion, and however much I take exercise in the air:——till Thou, my great Physician, Thou, Creator of the Universe, Lord Jesus, dost restore me, I shall be laid aside!——I have been working a little during the last fortnight, but only a little.

Dec. 17.——Lord's day. This morning I saw the 32 orphan girls, who are above seven years old, pass under my window, to go to the chapel. When I saw these dear children in their clean dresses, and their comfortable warm cloaks; and when I saw them walking orderly under the care of a sister to the chapel; I felt grateful to God that I had been made the instrument of providing for them, seeing that they are all better off, both as it regards temporal and spiritual things, than if they were at the places from whence they were taken. I felt, that, to bring about such a sight, was worth the labour not only of many days, but of many months, or years. I felt that it answered all the arguments of some of my friends who say "you do too much."

Dec. 24. This is the seventh Lord's day that I have been laid aside.——This day I determine, by the help of God, no more to send letters in parcels, because I now clearly see that it is against the laws of the country, and it becomes me, as a disciple of Jesus, in every respect to submit myself to the Government, in so far as I am not called upon to do any thing contrary to the word of God.

Dec. 26. Today the same brother who sent me the hundred pairs of blankets, sent me 100l. to purchase as many more blankets as I can satisfactorily distribute.

Dec. 29. Applications for the admission of orphans become more and more numerous. Almost daily fresh cases are brought before us. There are already as many applications for Orphan-Girls above seven years as would fill another house. There are also many more Infant-Orphans applied for than we can take in. Truly this is a large field of labour!

SECOND PART

Dec. 31. This is the eighth Lord's day since I have been kept from ministering in the Word, nor did I think it well, on account of my head, to go to any of the meetings today. Whether I am really getting better I know not, yet I hope I am. My head is yet much affected, though my liver seems somewhat more active.—-This morning I greatly dishonoured the Lord by irritability, manifested towards my dear wife, and that almost immediately after I had been on my knees before God, praising Him for having given me such a wife.

REVIEW OF THE YEAR 1837.

I. There are now 81 children in the three Orphan-Houses, and nine brethren and sisters who have the care of them. Ninety, therefore, daily sit down to table. Lord look on the necessities of Thy servant!

II. The schools require as much help as before; nay, more, particularly the Sunday School, in which there are at present about 320 children, and in the Day Schools about 350.—-Lord, Thy servant is a poor man; but he has trusted in Thee, and made his boast in Thee, before the sons of men; therefore let him not be confounded! Let it not be said, all this is enthusiasm, and therefore it is come to nought.

III. My temporal supplies have been:—-

1. By the Freewill Offerings through the boxes £149 18s. 6 1/2d.

2. By Presents in money, from believers in and out of Bristol £77 4s. 0d.

3. By Presents in clothes, provisions, &c., which were worth to us at least £25 0s. 0d.

4. By Money through family connexion £45 0s. 0d.

5. We have been living half free of rent, whereby we have saved at least £10 0s. 0d.

Altogether £307 2s. 6 1/2d.

I have purposely given here again, as at the close of the former years, a statement of the supplies which the Lord has been pleased to send me during this year, because I delight in showing, both to the world and to the church, how kind a Master I have served even as to temporal blessings, and how so plainly in my ease the Lord has displayed the truth of that word "Whosoever believeth on Him shall not be confounded," not merely by providing the means for His work in my hands, but also by providing for the necessities of myself and family.

January 1, 1838. Through the good hand of our God upon me, I have been brought to the beginning of an other year. May He in mercy grant that it may be spent more in His service than any previous year! May I, through the indwelling of the Holy Spirit, be more conformed to the image of His Son, than has been the case hitherto!—-Last night the brethren had a prayer meeting at Gideon, after the preaching was over, and continued till half-past twelve in prayer; but I was unable to be present.

Jan. 2. During the last night thieves broke into our house, and into the school-room of Gideon Chapel. Being stopped by a second strong door, in my house, or rather being prevented from going any further by our loving Father, who did not allow the hedge which He has set round about us, at this time, to be broken through, nothing was missing, except some cold meat, which they took out of the house.—-They broke open several boxes in Gideon school-room, but took nothing. They left some of the bones, the meat being cut off, in one of the boxes in Gideon school-room, and hung up another in a tree in our garden. So depraved is man naturally when left to himself, that he not only steals his fellowman's property, but also makes sport of the sin! How merciful that God has protected us! My mind was peaceful when I heard the news this morning, thanking God from my heart for preservation, and considering it as an answer to prayer, which had been many times put up to Him, during these last years, respecting thieves.

Jan. 6. I feel very little better in my head, though my general health seems improved; but my kind physician says I am much better, and advises me now change of air. I am most reluctant to go, though on two former occasions when I used change of air, in August 1829 at Exmouth, and in 1835 at Niton in the Isle of Wight, the Lord abundantly blessed me in doing so, both bodily and spiritually. This evening a sister who resides about fifty miles from hence, and who is therefore quite unacquainted with the medical advice given to me this morning, sent me 15l. for the express purpose of change of air, and wrote that she felt assured, from having been similarly afflicted, that nothing would do me so much good, humanly speaking, as quiet and change of air. How wonderfully does God work! I have thus the means of carrying into effect my physician's advice.—-Today I heard of a most remarkable case of conversion through the instrumentality of my Narrative.

SECOND PART

Jan. 7. This is the ninth Lord's day that I have been kept from ministering in the Word. My head is in a distressing state, and, as far as I can judge, as bad as ever. It seems to me more and more clear that the nerves are affected. My affliction is connected with a great tendency to irritability of temper; yea, with some satanic feeling, foreign to me even naturally. O Lord, mercifully keep Thy servant from openly dishonouring Thy name! Rather take me soon home to Thyself!

Jan. 10. Today I went with my family to Trowbridge.

Jan. 12. Trowbridge. This evening I commenced reading Whitfield's life, written by Mr. Philip.

Jan. 13. I have already received blessings through Whitfield's life. His great success in preaching the Gospel is evidently to be ascribed, instrumentally, to his great prayerfulness, and his reading the Bible on his knees. I have known the importance of this for years; I have practiced it a little, but far too little. I have had more communion with God today than I have had, at least generally, for some time past.

Jan. 14. Lord's day. I have, continued reading Whitfield's life. God has again blessed it to my soul. I have spent several hours in prayer today, and read on my knees, and prayed for two hours over Psalm lxiii. God has blessed my soul much today. I have been fighting together with the armies of Jesus, though this is the tenth Lord's day since I have been kept from preaching, and though I have not assembled with the brethren here, on account of my head. My soul is now brought into that state, that I delight myself in the will of God, as it regards my health. Yea, I can now say, from my heart, I would not have this disease removed till God, through it, has bestowed the blessing for which it was sent. He has drawn out my soul much yesterday and today. Lord, continue Thy goodness, and fill me with love! I long, more fully to glorify God; not so much by outward activity, as by inward conformity to the image of Jesus. What hinders God, to make of one, so vile as I am, another Whitfield? Surely, God could bestow as much grace upon me, as He did upon him. O, my Lord, draw me closer and closer to Thyself, that I may run after Thee!—I desire, if God should restore me again for the ministry of the Word (and this I believe He will do soon, judging from the state in which He has now brought my soul, though I have been worse in health the last eight days, than for several weeks previously), that my preaching may be more than ever the result of earnest prayer and much meditation, and that I may so walk with God, that "out of my belly may flow rivers of living water." But alas! if the grace of God prevent not, one day more, and the rich blessings, which He has bestowed upon my soul yesterday and today, will all vanish; but again, if He favours me (and oh! may He do it), I shall go from strength to strength, and I and the saints in Bristol shall have abundant reason to praise God for this my illness.

Jan. 15. I have had since yesterday afternoon less suffering in my head than for the last eight days! though it is even now far from being well. I have still an inward assurance, on account of the spiritual blessings which the Lord has granted to me, that through this affliction He is only purifying me for His blessed service, and that I shall be soon restored to the work.——Today, also, God has continued to me fervency of spirit, which I have now enjoyed for three days following. He has today, also, drawn out my soul into much real communion with Himself, and into holy desires to be more conformed to His dear Son. When God gives a spirit of prayer, how easy then to pray! Nevertheless it was given to me in the use of the means, as I fell on my knees last Saturday, to read His Word with meditation, and to turn it into prayer. Today I spent about three hours in prayer over Ps. lxiv. and lxv. In reference to that precious word! "O thou that hearest prayer," (Ps. lxv. 2.) I asked the Lord the following petitions, and entreated Him to record them in heaven and to answer them.

1. That He would give me grace to glorify Him by a submissive and patient spirit under my affliction.

2. That, as I was enabled now, and only now from my heart, to praise God for this affliction, He would not remove His hand from me, until He had qualified me for His work more than I have been hitherto.

3. That He would be pleased to grant, that the work of conversion, through the instrumentality of brother Craik and myself, might not cease, but go on as much now as when we first came to Bristol, yea, more abundantly than even then.

4. That He would be pleased to give more real spiritual prosperity to the church under our care, than ever we have as yet enjoyed.

5. Having praised Him for the sale of so many copies of my Narrative in so short a time, I entreated Him to cause every copy to be disposed of.

6. I asked Him to continue to let His rich blessing rest upon this little work, and more abundantly, so that many may be converted through it, and many of the children of God truly benefited by it; and that thus I might now be speaking through it, though laid aside from active service.

7. I asked Him for His blessing, in the way of conversion, to rest upon the Orphans, and upon the Sunday and Day-School children under our care.

8. I asked Him for means to carry on these Institutions, and to enlarge them.

These are some of the petitions which I have asked of my God this evening in connexion with this His own word. I believe He has heard me. I believe He will make it manifest, in His own good time, that He has heard me; and I have recorded these my petitions this 14th day of January, 1838, that, when God has answered them, He may get, through this, glory to His name.——[Whilst writing this second part, I add to the praise of the Lord, and for the encouragement of the children of God, that petitions 4, 5, 6, 7, and 8, have been fully answered, and the other petitions, likewise, in part.]

SECOND PART

Jan. 16, Tuesday. A blessed day. How very good is the Lord! Fervency of spirit, through His grace, is continued to me, though this morning, but for the help of God, I should have lost it again. The weather has been very cold for several days; but today I suffered much, either because it was colder than before, or because I felt it more, owing to the weakness of my body, and having taken so much medicine. I arose from my knees, and stirred the fire; but I still remained very cold. I was a little irritated by this. I moved to another part of the room, but felt the cold still more. At last, having prayed for some time, I was obliged to rise up, and take a walk to promote circulation. I now entreated the Lord on my walk, that this circumstance might not be permitted to rob me of the precious communion which I have had with Him the last three days; for this was the object at which Satan aimed. I confessed also my sin of irritability on account of the cold, and sought to have my conscience cleansed through the blood of Jesus. He had mercy upon me, my peace was restored; and when I returned I sought the Lord again in prayer, and had uninterrupted communion with Him. [I have purposely mentioned the above circumstance, in detail, in order to show, how the most trivial causes may operate in suddenly robbing one of the enjoyment of most blessed communion with God.] I have been enabled to pray for several hours this day. The subject of my meditation has been Psalm lxvi.--Verses 10, 11, and 12, are particularly applicable to my present circumstances. God has already, through the instrumentality of this my affliction, brought me into a "wealthy place," and I believe He will bless my soul yet more and more.—-I do not remember any time, when I have had more fervency of spirit in connexion with such a desire to overcome every thing that is hateful in the sight of God, and with such an earnestness to be fully conformed to the image of Jesus. Truly, I have reason to apply to myself verse 16, and "tell what God has done for my soul."--Verse 18 also I can take to myself. I do not regard iniquity in my heart, but it is upright before Him, through His grace, and therefore God does hear my prayers.--What has God done for me, in comparing this 16th of January 1838 with the 16th of January 1820, the day on which my dear mother died.--I have also resolved this day, if the Lord should restore me again, to have an especial meeting at the chapel once a week, or once a fortnight, with the Orphan and Day-School children, for the purpose of reading the Scriptures with them.—-My heart has been drawn out in prayer for many things, especially that the Lord would create in me a holy earnestness to win souls, and a greater compassion for ruined sinners. For this I have been quickened through reading onward in Whitfield's life.

Jan. 17. The Lord is yet merciful to me. I enjoy fervency of spirit. My soul has been again repeatedly led out in prayer this day, and that for a considerable time.--I have read on my knees, with prayer and meditation, Psalm lxviii.—Verse 5 "A Father of the fatherless," one of the titles of Jehovah, has been an especial blessing to me, with reference to the Orphans. The truth, which is contained in this, I never realized so much as today. By the help of God, this shall be my argument before Him, respecting the Orphans, in the hour of need. He is their Father, and therefore has pledged Himself, as it were, to provide for them, and to care for them; and I have only to remind Him of the need of these poor children, in order to have it supplied. My soul is still more enlarged respecting Orphans. This word "a Father of the fatherless," contains enough encouragement to cast thousands of Orphans, with all their need, upon the loving heart of God.--My head has been again in a distressing state today; my soul, however, is in peace. May God in mercy continue to me fervency of spirit!

January 18 to February 2. During this time I continued still at Trowbridge. I was, on the whole, very happy, and habitually at peace, and had repeatedly much communion with God; but still I had not the same earnestness in prayer, nor did I, in other respects, enjoy the same degree of fervency of spirit, with which the Lord had favoured me for several days previous to this period. While the considerable degree of fervency of spirit, which I had had, was altogether the gift of God, still I have to ascribe to myself the loss of it. It is remarkable, that the same book, Whitfield's Life, which was instrumental in stirring me up to seek after such a frame of heart, was also instrumental in depriving me of it, in some measure, afterwards. I once or twice read that book when I ought to have read the Bible on my knees, and thus was robbed of a blessing. Nevertheless, on the whole, even this period was a good season.--My health being not at all improved, it seemed best that I should give up all medicine for a while, and take a tour; on which account I left Trowbridge today and went to Bath, with the object of going from thence to Oxford. I had grace today to confess the Lord Jesus on my way from Trowbridge to Bath, as also twice, lately, in going from Trowbridge to Bristol; but I was also twice silent. Oh that my heart may be filled with the love of Jesus, in order that it maybe filled with love for perishing sinners!

Feb. 3. I left Bath this morning, and arrived in the evening at Oxford, where I was very kindly received by brother and sister ----, and the sisters ----.

Feb. 7. Oxford. I had been praying repeatedly yesterday and the day before, that the Lord would be pleased to guide me, whether I should leave this place or not; but could not see it clearly to be His will that I should do so, and therefore determined to stay. Now, as I am able to have a quiet horse, I shall try horse exercise, if it may please the Lord to bless that to the benefit of my health.

Feb. 10. I have had horse exercise for the last three days, but the horse is now ill. "Mine hour is not yet come," is the Lord's voice to me in this little circumstance.

Feb. 11. This morning I was directed to read Proverbs iii. 5-12, having just a few minutes to fill up before breakfast. I was particularly struck with those words: "Neither be weary of His correction." I have not been allowed to despise the chastening of the Lord, but I begin, now and then, to feel somewhat weary of His correction. O Lord, have mercy upon Thy poor unworthy servant! Thou knowest, that, after the inner man, I desire patiently to bear this affliction, and not to have it removed till it has done its work in me, and yielded the peaceable fruits of righteousness. But Thou knowest also what a trial it is to me to continue the life I am now living. Help, Lord, according to my need!

SECOND PART

On Feb. 8th I sent a letter to the church in Bristol, which, having been preserved, I give here in print, as it shows the way in which the Lord dealt with me during and through the instrumentality of the affliction, and which, with His blessing, may lead one or other of the children of God who are in trial, quietly to wait for the end, and to look out for blessings to be bestowed upon them through the instrumentality of the trial.

To the Saints, united together in Fellowship, and assembling at Bethesda and Gideon Chapels, Bristol.

Trowbridge, Feb. 1, 1838.

Dear Brethren,

Twelve weeks have passed away, since I last ministered among you. I should have written to you repeatedly, during that period, had I not thought it better to put aside every mental occupation which could be deferred, as my head is unfit for mental exertion; but I would now rather write a few lines, than appear unmindful of you. You are dear to me; yea, so dear, that I desire to live and die with you, if our Lord permit; and why should I not tell you so by letter? I will write, then, as a token of brotherly remembrance and of love towards you; and may it be a means of quickening you to prayer on my behalf.

In looking back upon my past life, I know not where to begin, and where to end, in making mention of the Lord's mercies. His long-suffering towards me in the days of my unregeneracy cannot be described. You know a little of my sinful life, before I was brought to the Lord; still you know but very little. If, however, I have much reason to praise God for His mercies towards me in those days, I have more abundant reason to admire His gentleness, long-suffering, and faithfulness towards me since I have known Him. He has step by step led me on, and He has not broken the bruised reed. His gentleness towards me has been great indeed, very great. (Brethren, let us follow God, in dealing gently with each other!) He has borne with my coldness, half-heartedness, and backsliding. In the midst of it all, He has treated me as His child. How can I sufficiently praise Him for this long-suffering? (Brethren, let us imitate our Father, let us bear long, and suffer long with each other!) He has been always the same gracious, kind, loving Father, Friend, Supporter, Teacher, Comforter, and all in all to me, as He was at the beginning. No variableness has been found in Him towards me, though I have again and again provoked Him. I say this to my shame. (Brethren, let us seek to be faithful, in the Lord, towards each other! Let us seek to love each other in the truth, and for the truth's sake, without variableness! It is easy, comparatively, to begin to love; but it requires much watchfulness, not to grow weary in love, when little or no love is returned; yea, when we are unkindly treated, instead of being loved. But as our gracious, faithful God, notwithstanding all our variableness, loves us without change, so should we, His children, love each other. Lord, help us so to do!)

Besides this gentleness, long-suffering, and faithfulness, which the Lord has manifested towards me, and which I have experienced in common with you all, the Lord has bestowed upon me peculiar blessings and privileges. One of the chief is, that He has condescended to call me for the ministry of His word. How can I praise Him sufficiently for this! One who was such a sinner, such a servant of Satan, so fit for hell, so deserving of everlasting destruction, was not merely cleansed from sin and made a child of God through faith in the Lord Jesus, and thus fitted for heaven, and did not merely receive the sure promise that he should have eternal glory; but was also called unto, and, in a measure, qualified for the expounding of the word of God. I magnify Him for this honour!—-But more than this. More than eleven years, with very little interruption, have I been allowed, more or less, to preach the Word. My soul does magnify the Lord for this! More still. The Lord has condescended to use me as an instrument in converting many sinners, and, in a measure at least, in benefiting many of His children. For this honour I do now praise God, and shall praise Him not merely as long as I live, but as long as I have a being. But I do not stop here. I have many other reasons to speak well of the Lord, but I would only mention one. It is my present affliction. Yes, my present affliction is among the many things, for which I have very much reason to praise God; and I do praise Him for it. Before you, before the whole church of Christ, and before the world would I confess that God has dealt in very kindness towards me in this affliction. I own, I have not borne it without impatience and fretfulness; I own, I have been several times overcome by irritability of temper on account of it; but nevertheless, after the inner man, I praise God for the affliction, and I do desire from my heart, that it may truly benefit me, and that it may not be removed till the end has been answered, for which it has been sent. God has blessed me in this trial, and is still blessing me.--As I know you love me, (unworthy as I am of it), and feel interested about me, I mention a few of the many mercies with which God has favoured me during these twelve weeks. 1. At the commencement of my illness, when my head was affected in a manner quite new to me, and when thus it continued day after day, I feared lest I should lose my reason.--This created more real internal suffering than ever I had known before. But our gracious Lord supported me. His precious gospel was full of comfort to me. All, all will be well, was invariably the conclusion, the conclusion grounded upon Scripture, to which I came; yea, all will be well with me eternally, though the heaviest of all earthly trials should coins upon me, even that of dying in a state of insanity.--I was once near death, as I then thought, nearly nine years ago: I was full of comfort at that time; but to be comfortable,--to be able quietly to repose upon God, with the prospect of an affliction before one, such as I have now mentioned,--is more than to be comfortable in the prospect of death, at least for a believer.--Now, is it not well to be afflicted, in order to obtain such an experience? And have I not reason, therefore, to thank God for this affliction?

SECOND PART

Oxford, Feb. 6, 1838.

When I began to write the foregoing lines, beloved brethren, I intended to write but very briefly; but as I love you, and as I have abundant reason to magnify the Lord, my pen ran on, till my head would follow no longer.--I go on now to mention some other mercies which the Lord has bestowed upon me, through my present affliction.

2. Through being deprived for so long a time of the privilege of preaching the Word to sinners and saints, the Lord has been pleased to create in me a longing for this blessed work, and to give me at the same time to feel the importance of it, in a degree in which I never had experienced it before. Thus the Lord has fitted me somewhat more for His work, by laying me aside from it. Good therefore is the Lord, and kind indeed, in disabling me from preaching. Great has been my trial, after the self-willed old nature, not to be able to preach; and long ere this, unfit as I was for it, I should have resumed the work, had I followed my own will; but hitherto have I considered it most for the glory of God, quietly to refrain from outward service, in order to glorify Him by patient submission, till my Lord shall be pleased to condescend to call His servant forth again for active engagements. And then, I know, He will give me grace, cheerfully to go back to the delightful service of pointing sinners to the Lamb of God, and of feeding the church.

3. Through this affliction I have known experimentally in a higher degree than I knew it before, how, if obliged to refrain from active service, one can nevertheless as really and truly help the armies of Jesus, through secret prayer, as if one were actively engaged in the proclamation of the truth.--This point brings to my mind a truth, of which we all need to be reminded frequently, even this, that at all times, and under all circumstances, we may really and truly serve the Lord, and fight for His kingdom, by seeking to manifest His mind, and by giving ourselves to prayer.

4. Through the instrumentality of this affliction the Lord has been pleased to show me, how I may lay out myself more fully for His service in the proclamation of His truth; and, by His grace, if ever restored for active service, I purpose to practice what He has shown me.

5. Through being deprived so much from meeting with the brethren as I have been these thirteen weeks, I have learned somewhat more to value this privilege than I did before. For as my head has been much affected, even through one meeting on the Lord's day, I have seen how highly I ought to have prized the days, when twice or thrice I could meet with the saints, without suffering from it.--Bear with me, brethren, when I beseech you, highly to esteem the opportunities of assembling yourselves together. Precede them with prayer; for only in as much as you do so, have you a right to expect a blessing from them. Seek to treasure up, not merely in your memory, but in your heart, the truths which you hear; for soon you may be deprived

of these privileges, and soon you may be called upon to practice what you hear. Brethren, let us not learn the greatness of our privileges, by being deprived of them.--

I also delight in mentioning some of the particulars in which the Lord's kindness to me has appeared in this affliction, and whereby He has shown, that He does not lay more on us, than is absolutely needful.

1. You know, that since May, 1836, I was able to walk but little. This infirmity the Lord entirely removed, just before I became afflicted in my head. This was exceedingly kind; for air and exercise are the only means, which almost immediately relieve my head. How much greater would have been the affliction, had I not been able to walk about in the air!——Truly, "He stayeth His rough wind, in the day of His east wind." I delight in pointing out the gentleness of the stroke.

Oxford, Feb. 7, 1838.

2. The Lord might have chosen to confine me to my bed, and kept me there in much pain these thirteen weeks, for the sake of teaching me the lessons which He purposes me to learn through this affliction; instead of this, the pain in my head has been so slight, that it would not be worth mentioning, were it not connected with a weakness of the mental faculties, which allows of but little exertion.

3. Further, it might have pleased the Lord to incapacitate me altogether for active service, but instead of this, He has still allowed me, in some small measure, to help by my judgment in some church matters, to write some letters in His service, to speak now and then a word to believers for the furtherance of their faith, and to confess His name repeatedly before unconverted persons, with whom I have met on my journeys. Besides all this, I have had strength for other work connected with the kingdom of Jesus Christ.

4. In one other point the Lord has been especially gracious to me, in that, while I have been unable to preach, unable to write or read much, or even to converse for any length of time with the brethren, He has allowed me always sufficient strength for as much secret prayer as I desired. Even praying with others has been often trying to my head; but prayer in secret has not only never tried my head, but has been habitually (I mean the act of prayer) a relief to my head. Oh! how can I sufficiently praise God for this. How comparatively slight are any trials to a child of God, as long as under them he is enabled to converse freely with his Father! And so sweet has been this communion with my Father, a few times, and so have I been enabled to pour out my heart before Him, that whilst those favoured seasons have lasted, I not only felt the affliction to be no affliction, and could call it, from my heart, sweet affliction; but I was almost unwilling soon to go back to the multiplicity of engagements in Bristol, lest I should not have leisure to continue so much in prayer, meditation, and the study of His word. Shall I not then praise my Father for such dealings with me? Do I not even now see this affliction working for my good? I say, therefore, after the inward man: Father, continue Thy hand upon me, as long as

SECOND PART

it shall seem good in Thy sight, only bless my soul!--—But, brethren, do not mistake me, as if I meant that I prayed habitually with much earnestness. O no! I pray a little habitually, I pray now and then much; but I pray by no means as much as my strength and present time allow me. Therefore ask God on my behalf, that grace may be given me, habitually to pray much; and you will surely be profited by it.--But I could not help alluding to this point, as the Lord's kindness is so particularly seen in this matter.

5. Lastly, I cannot omit mentioning the kindness of the Lord, in opening the houses of some of His children at Bath, Trowbridge, and Oxford for me, during this my affliction. These dear saints have shown me much kindness. But while I would be grateful to them for it, I discern the hand of God in influencing their hearts. Moreover, I have had kind medical attendants. And you, my dear brethren, though I have been unable to minister among you, have continued to supply my temporal wants, for which I thank you, and in all of which I see the gracious, loving hand of my Father, who through all this, as by a voice from heaven, tells me: "My child, even bodily health and strength would I give, were it good for thee." I therefore desire to wait for the good pleasure of my God concerning this point.

Your love will naturally ask, how I now am in body. My disease, as my kind medical friends tell me, is an inactive liver, which causes the pain in the head, and the inability of exerting my mind for any length of time. In addition to this, the nerves of the head seem to have suffered through over-exertion. As medicine had been tried for about ten weeks, and had not given relief, it appeared well, that I should give it up for a time, and simply travel about for the benefit of the air. My own experience teaches me, that this means is beneficial; for it gives almost immediate relief. In consequence of this, I left Trowbridge last Friday, and arrived on Saturday evening at Oxford, where I am staying with dear brother and sister B. I have here all that brotherly love can do for me, and am in every way comfortable. It is now a week since I have given up medicine, and I am at least not worse, if not better; but I think I am a little better. I wait on the Lord to show me His will, as to the place to which I should go next.

As to my inner man, I am in peace, generally in peace, and long for more conformity to the mind of Christ. My chief desire is, that if it shall ever please the Lord to restore me again, to be sent back to active service with increased humility, greater earnestness in the work, greater love for perishing sinners, and a heart habitually influenced by the truths which I preach.--Whether I shall ever be restored for the work, I cannot say with certainty; but, if I may judge from the Lord's dealings with me in former times, I have reason to believe, that I shall yet be allowed to labour again.

In conclusion, dear brethren, pray for my dear brother and fellow-labourer. Esteem him highly in the Lord; for He is worthy of all honour.—-I would write more, for I have much more to speak of; but as I purpose, if God allows me the pleasure, to write again soon, I leave it till then. Farewell.

THE LORD'S DEALINGS WITH GEORGE MÜLLER

Your affectionate brother and servant in the Lord,

GEORGE MULLER.

Feb. 13. These ten days I have been staying in Oxford, though I came only for one or two; but I have stayed to see the Lord's hand leading me away from hence. I have now been led to decide on going to Lutterworth to see brother-—, to converse with him about accompanying him on a journey to the Continent, with reference to Missionary objects. When I had come to this decision, I took another ride, the horse being well again; but now this formerly quiet horse was self-willed and shy, which does not at all suit me in the weak state of my nervous system. As horse exercise had kept me here longer than I had intended to stay, and as I cannot now ride on this horse which before suited me so well, I see, even in this, in itself, trifling circumstance, a confirmation that I had been right in my decision to leave Oxford.

Feb. 16. Lutterworth. I arrived here on the evening of the 14th. I have been decidedly worse since I have been here, and was obliged again to have recourse to medicine. A brother having strongly recommended me, whilst in Oxford, to go to Leamington on account of my health, and having at the same time offered to pay my expenses during my stay there, and being now so very unwell again, and so near Leamington, I decided to-night upon accepting his kindness, provided that my kind physician in Bristol had no objection.

Feb. 17. Leamington. I left Lutterworth this morning, where I have received much kindness. There was no inside place, and I was very unwell; but the fear of being quite laid up at Lutterworth, and becoming burthensome to those dear saints who had received me into their house though a stranger to them; and having still no desirable medical advice; and the remembrance that the Lord had graciously enabled me, even lately, to travel outside in cold weather; induced me to get on the coach, and I rode off in a heavy fall of snow. But God had mercy. After eight miles ride, at Rugby, I obtained an inside place. The rest of the way was crowned with mercies. I had a room to myself at Southam, found a suitable dinner just ready, had an inside place to Leamington, and was preserved by the way, though the coachman was quite intoxicated, and drove furiously.--I had asked the Lord to let me find a suitable and cheap lodging at Leamington, and the first lodging I saw I took, for which I pay only ten shillings weekly. Thus, a few minutes after my arrival, I sat comfortably at my own fireside. How very kind of the Lord!

Feb. 26. Yesterday and today I have suffered again in my head, though I have been on the whole better since I have taken the Leamington waters. But far more trying has been the internal conflict which I have had. Grace fought against evil suggestions of one kind and another, and prevailed; but it was a very trying season. This was much increased by receiving neither yesterday nor today a letter from my dear

SECOND PART

wife. Grace sought out for reasons why she had not written; nevertheless it was a very trying season. Today I earnestly prayed to God to send my wife to me, as I feel that by being alone, and afflicted as I am in my bead, and thus fit for little mental employment, Satan gets an advantage over me.

Feb. 27. God has had mercy upon me. The sore and sharp trial, the very bitter conflict is over.--This morning also I received a letter, which ought to have come yesterday, and which showed me that my dear wife had not been remiss in writing. She announced her purpose of coming today, and God, in mercy to me, brought her safely.

March 3. My head has been on the whole better these two weeks, than it has been for several months; but still I am not well. I have walked every day, for the last thirteen days, between three and four hours a day, and by the mercy of God am able to do so, without much fatigue.

March 11. My health is much the same. I am pretty well, but have no mental energy.--I have read during the last weeks once more, with as much or more interest than ever, I. and II. of Samuel, and I. and II. of Kings.--I have now, after repeated prayer, come to the conclusion, (if brother Craik, to whom I have written, sees no objection, and if my physician thinks it would be beneficial to my health,) to accompany brother--to Germany, that thus; 1, I might aid him by my advice in reference to the object of his journey; 2, that thus, if the Lord will, through the journey and the benefit of my native air, my health might be benefited; and 3, that I might once more have an opportunity of setting the truth before my father and brother.

March 12. I feel quite comfortable in the prospect of going to Germany. I trust it will prove to be as much of God, as it was shown to have been the last time.

March 13. I had a letter today from brother Craik, who thinks it desirable that I should go to Germany, but my physician says that I should not go for a month or two, for that my mind ought not to be burdened. I am in peace, and from this I see that the Lord has made me willing to do His and not my own will. I wrote to brother——the result of today, and have now left it with him, whether he will wait, or go on the 21st, as he purposes.

March 14—20. During these days, as before, I have continued to read the Scriptures with prayer, i. e. turning what I read into prayer, chiefly with a reference to myself. My days generally pass away in peace. It is a trial to me, to have to care so much about my body; but, on the whole, the Lord gives me grace to submit patiently, yet not always. Today I saw again my medical adviser, who wishes me to stay another week.

March 23, Today I received a letter from brother ----. He is not gone, and will wait for me. I have increased assurance that I shall go to Berlin, and have comfort in the thought.

March 24. A few days ago I had particular comfort in meditating on the Lord's prayer in Luke (which came in the course of my meditation), after having been tempted to pass it over, as it had been the subject of my meditation a short time before.--Within the last fortnight I have read with meditation and prayer from the 4th to the 12th chapter of the Gospel by Luke.

April 2. For some time I have been getting weary of my stay here. Yesterday I pleaded especially that word Psalm ciii. 13: "Like as a father pitieth his children, so the Lord pitieth them that fear Him." I begged God to pity me, and to release me from the necessity of staying any longer at Leamington, if it might be. Today I saw my physician, and he has allowed me to leave. Thus the Lord has granted my request.

April 3. My dear Mary left for Bristol, and I for London, on my way to Germany. I was led to read, this morning, Psalm cxxi. with my dear wife before we separated, which we both felt to be very appropriate to our circumstances.

April 6. This evening I went on board the steamer for Hamburg.

April 7. All the day ill from sea sickness.

April 8. Lord's day. I was able to get up this morning, and to take my meals.--Last night I was led to praise God for having made me His child, considering that I was most likely the only one on board that knew Him. This morning, however, I found a sister in the Lord among the passengers, with whom I had much conversation.--At dinner she manifested more grace, in testifying against evil, than I did. At tea time I had grace, in some measure, to speak of Jesus before the company, and to confess Him as my Lord.

April 9. We arrived at Hamburg about one in the morning, having had a most favourable passage of about 48 hours, and at seven I went on shore. It had been repeatedly my prayer, that I might soon find out brother ----, who had gone three days before me to Hamburg; and immediately after my arrival, in answer to prayer, without any difficulty, I found out where he lodged.

April 14. Berlin. We arrived here the evening before last. Having been yesterday and this morning seeking for lodgings, without being able to obtain any that were suitable, I at last became irritated. Surely there was lack of earnest prayer on my part in this matter, and want of patience in waiting the Lord's own time, and want of openness, in not telling brother ---- that I was tired, and that, on account of my weakness, I was unable thus to go about from place to place. At last the Lord directed us to two suitable rooms, and I feel now again comfortable, in my quiet retirement, after having confessed my sin of irritability to the Lord and to brother ----.

SECOND PART

April 15—21. We met several times during this week with certain brethren who desire to give themselves to Missionary service, and prayed and read the Scriptures with them, and made such remarks as seemed to be important in connexion with the work. In addition to this we saw the brethren privately at our lodgings, two, three, or four at a time. But I have still felt the great weakness of my mental powers, and have been only able to attend to this work about three hours a day.--Since my arrival here I have had two letters from my dear Mary. Harriet Culliford, one of the Orphans, and formerly one of the most unpromising children, has been removed. She died as a true believer, several of the brethren who saw her being quite satisfied about her state. Surely this pays for much trouble and for much expense! My wife also mentions some fresh instances of the Lord's blessing resting upon my Narrative.--I am now, after prayer, this day, April 21, quite sure that I should leave Berlin, and go to my father at once, as the work here is too much for my head.

April 22nd. Confirmation-day of the children in Berlin. The son of the person with whom we lodge was confirmed, and in the evening they had the violin and dancing. How awful!—-A few days since I heard that a brother in the Lord, an old friend of mine, and one of the two alluded to in the first part of this Narrative, page 15, was in prison on account of his religious views. This brought afresh before me the privileges which the children of God enjoy in England.--I saw a few days since another brother in prison, who, as an unconverted young man, in the university, was once at a political club, and had his name enrolled, in consequence of this, in the list of the political students. Shortly afterwards he was converted, and gave up all connexion with these political students. He finished his university course and afterwards became a tutor to the sons of a baron. In that family he had been for a considerable time, when one night he was fetched by the police out of his bed and taken to prison, on the ground of this his connexion with the political club three or four years before. [The result was that he was for many months in prison. Now he is a Missionary in the East Indies. I have related this circumstance to remind the reader afresh, that though the Lord freely and fully forgives us all our sins at once when we believe, yet He may allow us to suffer the consequences of them in a greater or less degree.]

April 24. Left Berlin last evening for Magdeburg, Had a long conversation with two deists in the mail. God helped me to make a full confession of His dear Son, in answer to prayer for grace to be enabled to do so. This afternoon I arrived at Heimersleben, the small town where my father lives. Once more then I have met with my dear aged parent, who is evidently fast hastening to the grave, and seems to me not likely to live through the next winter. I arrived just at the time when, the Fair was held in the town. How great, how exceedingly great, the difference in me, as to my feelings respecting such things now, from what they were formerly!

April 25—28. Stay at Heimersleben. The Lord has given me both an opportunity and grace to speak more fully, more simply, and more to the heart of my father about the things of God, and in particular about the plan of salvation, than I had ever done before. I trust that, in judgment at least, he is convinced that there is something lacking in him. All the time of my stay here he has been most affectionate. I spoke also fully again to my poor brother, who is now completely living in open sin. Oh to grace what a debtor am I!—-Brother Knabe, who was the only believer in Heimersleben, as far as I have been able to learn, died about eighteen months since.

April 28. Today I left for Magdeburg. My father accompanied me about eight miles. Both of us, I think, felt, when about to separate, that we were parting from each other, never again to meet on earth. How would it have cheered the separation on both sides, were my dear father a believer! But it made my heart indeed sad to see him, in all human probability, for the last time, without having Scriptural ground for hope respecting his soul.--I arrived in the afternoon at Magdeburg, and went to a brother, a musician in one of the regiments of that fortress, who is on the point of leaving the army to go to the East Indies as a Missionary. In his lodgings I saw another brother, a private soldier, who lives in the barracks, who told me, on my enquiring, that he goes into the sand cellar, which is perfectly dark, in order to obtain opportunity for secret prayer. How great the privileges of those who may freely have both time and place for retirement; but how great, at the same time, our obligation to improve these opportunities!—-This evening at eight I went on board an Elbe-steamer for Hamburg.

April 30. This morning at seven I arrived at Hamburg. Nothing particular happened during the passage, except that we stuck fast, in a shallow part of the river, through the carelessness of one of the sailors; but the Lord heard prayer, and after a little while the steamer could ply again.

May 1. Yesterday and today I spent in an hotel at Hamburg in writing letters. I had also, though staying at an hotel, much real communion with God in reading the Scriptures and in prayer. This evening I embarked for London.

May 4. London. Left Hamburg on the 2nd. Had a fine passage. I have, by the mercy of God, been kept from light and trifling conversation; but I have not confessed the Lord Jesus as plainly as I ought to have done. This afternoon I arrived at the house of my dear friends in London, who received me with their usual kindness. After prayer I see it my duty to leave tomorrow for Leamington, to see my physician there once more, and then to go as soon as I can to Bristol.

May 5. Leamington. Through the mercy of the Lord the journey to Germany, concerning which I had prayed so often, is now over, and I am safely brought back again to this place.--It has been a wet and cold day, but God has in mercy preserved me from injury, though I got wet. I had some conversation with a clergyman on the coach; I confessed the Lord Christ a little, but not plainly enough.--I had asked the Lord to give me a quiet and cheap resting place in my former lodgings, if it might be, and accordingly they were unlet.

May 7. This morning I left Leamington for Bristol. I had grace to confess the Lord Jesus the last part of the way before several merry passengers, and had the honour of being ridiculed for His sake. There are few things in which I feel more entirely

SECOND PART

dependant upon the Lord, than in confessing Him on such occasions. Sometimes I have, by grace, had much real boldness; but often I have manifested the greatest weakness, doing no more than refraining entirely from unholy conversation, without, however, speaking a single word for Him who toiled beyond measure for me. No other remedy do I know for myself and any of my fellow-saints who are weak, like myself, in this particular, than to seek to have the heart so full of Jesus, and to live so in the realization of what He has done for us, that, without any effort, out of the full heart, we may speak for Him.--I found my dear family in peace.

May 8. This evening I went to the prayer meeting at Gideon. I read Psalm ciii, and was able to thank the Lord publicly for my late affliction. This is the first time that I have taken any part in the public meetings of the brethren, since November 6th, 1837.

May 13. Today I was much helped in expounding the Scriptures publicly. When I began I knew not how the Lord would deal with me, whether I should be able to speak or not, as my head is still very weak. But the Lord helped me. I did not feel any loss of mental power. How gracious of the Lord to allow me again to commence serving Him in the ministry of His word.--[For several months after this I preached, on the whole, with much more enjoyment, and with much more earnestness and prayerfulness, than I did before I was taken ill. I also felt more the solemnity of the work.]

June 11. A stranger called on me, and told me, that, many years ago, he had defrauded two gentlemen of a small sum, and that he wished to restore the same with interest. He also stated that he had read my Narrative, and, feeling confidence in me, he requested me to convey this money to those gentlemen, giving me, at the same time, their names and place of abode. He intrusted me with four sovereigns for each of them. At the same time he gave me one sovereign for myself, as a token of Christian love. I never saw the individual before, nor do I up to this moment know his name. I conveyed this money, however, not by post, as he wished but through two bank orders, in order that thus I might be able to show, should it be needful, that I actually did send the money; for in all such matters it becomes one to act with particular caution.--It may be that this fact will be read by some who have, like this stranger, before their conversion, defrauded certain individuals. If so, let them like him, or like Zaccheus of old, restore what they took, and, if they have the means, with interest, or compound interest.

June 13. Last evening my dear wife was taken ill. Often had I prayed respecting her hour, and now was the time to look out for the answer. She continued in most severe sufferings from a little after nine until midnight. Thus hour after hour passed away, until eleven this morning. Another medical attendant was then called in, at the desire of the one who attended her. At three in the afternoon she was delivered of a still-born child.--The whole of the night I was in prayer, as far as my strength allowed me. I cried at last for MERCY, and God heard.

June 14. My dearest wife is alive, but I am depending upon God for her life every moment. She is in much peace. A sister gave me this evening 5l. on account of dear Mary's illness.--[Again we had not thought it well to make pecuniary provision for this time, though at no period of my life had I more abundant means of doing so than during the last few months; but our gracious Father helped us abundantly in this and in other instances, as I shall mention below.]

June 22. Today there was sent to us anonymously, by post, 5l. for our own personal expenses, at this the time of our affliction, when our expenses are so great. The donor accompanied the 5l. note with an affectionate letter to my wife and myself.

July 6. My dear wife, who for more than a fortnight after her delivery was so ill, that the two medical attendants came twice or three times daily, seems now, humanly speaking, likely to recover, and to be given back to me as from the dead. Lord, help me so to receive her!

July 12. From the commencement of the establishment of the Orphan-houses, up to the end of June 1838, the hand of the Lord was seen in the abundance with which He was pleased to supply me with the means for maintaining nearly 100 persons. Now, however, the time is come when "the Father of the fatherless" will show His especial care over them in another way.--The funds, which were this day twelve-month about 780l., are now reduced to about 20l.; but, thanks be to the Lord, my faith is as strong, or stronger, than it was when we had the larger sum in hand; nor has He at any time, from the commencement of the work, allowed me to distrust Him. Nevertheless, as our Lord will be inquired of, and as real faith is manifested as such by leading to prayer, I gave myself to prayer with brother T---- of the Boy's Orphan-House, who had called on me, and who, besides my wife, and brother Craik, is the only individual to whom I speak about the state of the funds. While we were praying, an orphan child from Frome was brought, and some believers at Frome, having collected among them 5l., sent this money with the child. Thus we received the first answer at a time of need. We have given notice for seven children to come in, and purpose to give notice for five more, though our funds are so low, hoping that God will look on our necessities. [Observe how gently the Lord dealt with us, in that, when want approached, He helped at once, in immediate answer to prayer, in order thus to increase our confidence in Him; but, at the same time, to prepare us for sharper trials of our faith.]

June 17 and 18. These two days we have had two especial prayer meetings, from 6 to 9 in the evening, to commend publicly to the Lord the Boys' Orphan-House. The meetings had been deferred until now, on account of my illness. In the morning of the 18th I expounded, with especial reference to children, 1 Samuel iii., before above 550 children, being our Orphan and Day-School children, and, as many as could come, of those belonging to the Sunday-School. What a great work! What an honour to be allowed to provide Scriptural instruction for so many little ones. Lord, help me to make use of my talents for the benefit of the rising generation, and let me serve my generation according to Thy will!——Our funds for the Orphans are now very low. There are about 20l. in hand, and in a few days 30l. at least will be needed; but I purposely avoided saying any thing about our present necessities, and spoke only, to the praise of God, about the abundance with which our gracious Father, "The Father of the fatherless," has hitherto supplied us. This was done in order that the hand of God, in sending help, may be so much the more clearly seen.

July 22. This evening I was walking in our little garden, meditating on Heb. xiii. 8, "Jesus Christ the same yesterday, and today, and for ever." Whilst meditating on His unchangeable love, power, wisdom, &c.--and turning all, as I went on, into prayer respecting myself; and whilst applying likewise His unchangeable love, and power, and wisdom, &c., both to my present spiritual and temporal circumstances:—-all at once the present need of the Orphan-Houses was brought to my mind. Immediately I was led to say to myself, Jesus in His love and power has hitherto supplied me with what I have needed for the Orphans, and in the same unchangeable love and power He will provide me with what I may need for the future. A flow of joy came into my soul whilst realizing thus the unchangeableness of our adorable Lord. About one minute after, a letter was brought me, enclosing a bill for 20l. In it was written: "Will you apply the amount of the enclosed bill to the furtherance of the objects of your Scriptural Knowledge Society, or of your Orphan Establishment, or in the work and cause of our Master in any way that He Himself, on your application to Him, may point out to you. It is not a great sum, but it is a sufficient provision for the exigency of today; and it is for today's exigencies, that, ordinarily, the Lord provides. Tomorrow, as it brings its demands, will find its supply, etc." [Of this 20l. I took 10l. for the Orphan fund, and 10l. for the other objects, and was thus enabled to meet the expenses of about 34l. which, in connection with the Orphan-Houses, came upon me within four days afterwards, and which I knew beforehand would come.]

On July 26 sailed from Liverpool for the East Indies, for Missionary service, twelve German brethren and three sisters, as the result of the journey of brother ---- and myself to the Continent, in April last.

July 27. Yesterday the funds for the Orphans were reduced to 5l. Blessed be God, my confidence in Him was unshaken! I received yesterday 2l. 13s. Today I was going with my family for change of air to Durdham Down, and thought it well, therefore, to take out any money which there might be in the Orphan-Box in my house. When I opened it, I found a ten pound note and three half crowns. I had been waiting on God for means, both yesterday and today, and thus He has again shown how willing He is to help.

Aug. 6. During this week I shall have to pay again at least 35l. for the Orphans, and have but about 19l. towards it. My eyes are up to the "Father of the fatherless." I believe He will help, though I knew not how.

Aug. 7. How graciously has the Lord again appeared, and that in so short a time! How has he sent help, from altogether unexpected quarters! I have been praying yesterday and today earnestly, beseeching the Lord now to appear, and show His power, that the enemies might not say, "Where is now thy God?" I reminded Him especially, that I had commenced the work that it might be seen, that He, even in our day, is willing to answer prayer, and that the provision for our Orphans might be a visible proof to all around us of this truth. And now observe! Last evening brother Craik told me that 10l. had been given him for the work in our hands; 5l. for the Orphans, and 5l. for the School—Bible—and Missionary fund. Today, having to pay 25l., and not having quite enough, when I went to brother T---- for the money which he might have received, as I knew that 25s. had been given to him, I took with me the keys of the boxes in the Orphan-Houses, to see whether the Lord had sent in a little. I opened the box in the Boys'-Orphan-House, and found 1l. 7s. 5 ½d. Immediately after I received from brother T---- 13l. 19s. 10d., the greater part of which, as he told me, had come in within the last few days. Thus our adorable Lord has once more delivered; for I have now even more than enough to meet the current expenses of this week.

Aug. 16. When today the account books of the Boys'-Orphan-House were brought, several days sooner than I had expected them, it was found that there was 1l. 6s. 6d. due to the matron. Besides this, money was to be advanced for housekeeping, and there was only 13s. 5 1/2d. in hand. To this one of those connected with the work added 2l. This 2l. 13s. 5 1/2d. was sent to the matron, whilst we were waiting upon God to send more help. In the evening the boxes at the Girls' and Infant-Orphan-Houses were opened, and in them was found 3l. 7s. 5 1/2d. Thus the Lord has kindly helped us again for two or three days.

Aug. 18. I have not one penny in hand for the Orphans. In a day or two again many pounds will be needed. My eyes are up to the Lord. Evening. Before this day is over, I have received from a sister 5l. She had some time since put away her trinkets, to be sold for the benefit of the Orphans. This morning, whilst in prayer, it came to her mind, I have this 5l., and owe no man any thing, therefore it would be better to give this money at once, as it may be some time, before I can dispose of the trinkets. She therefore brought it, little knowing that there was not a penny in hand, and that I had been able to advance only 4l. 15s. 5d. for housekeeping in the Boys'-Orphan-House, instead of the usual 10l.; little knowing also, that within a few days many pounds more will be needed. May my soul be greatly encouraged by this fresh token of my gracious Lord's faithfulness!

Aug. 20. The 5l. which I had received on the 18th, had been given for housekeeping, so that today I was again penniless. But my eyes were up to the Lord. I gave myself to prayer this morning, knowing that I should want again this week at least 13l., if not above 20l. Today I received 12l. in answer to prayer, from a lady who is staying at Clifton, whom I had never seen before. Adorable Lord, grant that this may be a fresh encouragement to me.

Aug. 23. Today I was again without one single penny, when 3l. was sent from Clapham, with a box of new clothes for the Orphans.

SECOND PART

Aug. 29. Today sixteen believers were baptized. Of all the baptisms which we have had, this was, perhaps, the most remarkable. Among those who were baptized was an aged brother of above 84 years, and one above 70. For the latter his believing wife had prayed 38 years, and at last the Lord answered her prayers in his conversion. Should any believer who may read this, be on the point of growing weary in prayer for his unconverted relatives, because of the answer being delayed, the above fact may be instrumental in stirring up such a one to give himself to prayer with renewed earnestness and strengthened expectation. "In due season we shall reap, if we faint not." There were also amongst those who were baptized a blind brother and sister, and two very young persons.

Aug. 31. I have been waiting on the Lord for means, as the matron's books from the Girls'-Orphan-House have been brought, and there is no money in hand to advance for house-keeping. But as yet the Lord has not been pleased to send help. As the matron called today for money, one of the labourers gave 2l. of his own, for the present necessities.

Sept. 1. The Lord in His wisdom and love has not yet sent help. Whence it is to come, need not be my care. But I believe God will, in due time, send help. His hour is not yet come. As there was money needed in the Boys'-Orphan-House also, the same brother, just alluded to, gave 2l. for that also. Thus we were delivered at this time likewise. But now his means are gone. This is the most trying hour that as yet I have had in the work, as it regards means; but I know that I shall yet praise the Lord for His help. I have mentioned my arguments before Him, and my gracious Lord, "the Father of the fatherless," will send help.

Sept. 3. This morning the Lord again helped by 2l., which another labourer connected with the work gave. This 2l., together with sixpence which had been given anonymously, was sent off to the Girls'-Orphan-House, where all the money must be gone. There came in further 1l. 14s. 8d. in the course of the day, which was given to the matron of the Boys'-Orphan-House.

Sept. 5. Our hour of trial continues still. The Lord mercifully has given enough to supply our daily necessities; but He gives by the day now, and almost by the hour, as we need it. Nothing came in yesterday. I have besought the Lord again and again, both yesterday and today. It is as if the Lord said: "Mine hour is not yet come." But I have faith in God. I believe that He surely will send help, though I know not whence it is to come. Many pounds are needed within a few days, and there is not a penny in hand. This morning 2l. was given for the present necessities, by one of the labourers in the work.--Evening: This very day the Lord sent again some help to encourage me to continue to wait on Him, and to trust in Him. As I was praying this afternoon respecting the matter, I felt fully assured that the Lord would send help, and praised Him beforehand for His help, and asked Him to encourage our hearts through it. I have been also led yesterday and today to ask the Lord especially, that He would not allow my faith to fail. A few minutes after I had prayed, brother T-

--- came and brought 4l. 1s. 5d., which had come in, in several small donations. He told me, at the same time, that tomorrow the books will be brought from the Infant-Orphan-House, when money must be advanced for housekeeping. I thought for a moment, it might be well to keep 3l. of this money for that purpose. But it occurred to me immediately, "Sufficient unto the day is the evil thereof." The Lord can provide, by tomorrow, much more than I need, and I therefore sent 3l. to one of the sisters, whose quarterly salary was due, and the remaining 1l. 1s. 5d. to the Boys'-Orphan-House for housekeeping. Thus I am still penniless. My hope is in God: He will provide.

Sept. 6. This morning the books were brought from the Infant-Orphan-House, and the matron sent to ask when she should fetch them, implying, when they would have been looked over, and when money would be advanced for housekeeping. I said "tomorrow," though I had not a single penny in hand. About an hour after, brother T---- sent me a note, to say that he had received 1l. this morning, and that last evening a brother had sent 29lbs. of salt, 44 dozen of onions, and 26lbs. of groats.

Sept. 7. The time had come that I had to send money to the Infant-Orphan-House, but the Lord had not sent any more. I gave, therefore, the 1l. which had come in yesterday, and 2s. 2d. which had been put into the box in my house, trusting to the good Lord to send in more.

Sept. 8. Saturday evening. I am still in the hour of probation. It has not pleased my gracious Lord to send me help as yet.--The evening before last I heard brother Craik preach on Genesis xii., about Abraham's faith. He showed how all went on well, as long as Abraham acted in faith, and walked according to the will of God; and how all failed when he distrusted God. Two points I felt particularly important in my case. 1. That I may not go any by-ways, or ways of my own, for deliverance. I have about 220l. in the bank, which, for other purposes in the Lord's work, has been entrusted to me by a brother and a sister. I might take of this money, and say but to the sister--and write but to the brother, that I have taken, in these my straits, 20l., 50l., or 100l., for the Orphans, and they would be quite satisfied (for both of them have liberally given for the Orphans, and the brother has more than once told me, only to let him know when I wanted money;) but this would be a deliverance of my own, not God's deliverance. Besides, it would be no small barrier to the exercise of faith, in the next hour of trial. 2. I was particularly reminded afresh, in hearing brother Craik, of the danger of dishonouring the Lord in that very way in which I have, through His grace, in some small measure brought glory to Him, even by trusting in Him.--Yesterday and today I have been pleading with God eleven arguments, why He would be graciously pleased to send help. My mind has been in peace respecting the matter. Yesterday the peace amounted even to joy in the Holy Ghost But this I must say, that the burden of my prayer, during the last days, has been chiefly, that the Lord in mercy would keep my faith from failing. My eyes are up to Him. He can help soon. One thing I am sure of: In His own way, and in His own time He will help. The arguments which I plead with God are:

SECOND PART

1. That I set about the work for the glory of God, i e. that there might be a visible proof, by God supplying, in answer to prayer only, the necessities of the Orphans, that He is the living God, and most willing, even in our day, to answer prayer; and that, therefore, He would be pleased to send supplies.

2. That God is the "Father of the fatherless," and that He, therefore, as their Father, would be pleased to provide. Psalm lxviii. 5.

3. That I have received the children in the name of Jesus, and that, therefore, He, in these children, has been received, and is fed, and is clothed; and that, therefore, He would be pleased to consider this. Mark ix. 36, 37.

4. That the faith of many of the children of God has been strengthened by this work hitherto, and that, if God were to withhold the means for the future, those who are weak in faith would be staggered; whilst by a continuance of means, their faith might still further be strengthened.

5. That many enemies would laugh, were the Lord to withhold supplies, and say, did we not foretell that this enthusiasm would come to nothing?

6. That many of the children of God, who are uninstructed, or in a carnal state, would feel themselves justified to continue their alliance with the world in the work of God, and to go on as heretofore, in their unscriptural proceedings respecting similar institutions, so far as the obtaining of means is concerned, if He were not to help me.

7. That the Lord would remember that I am His child, and that He would graciously pity me, and remember that I cannot provide for these children, and that therefore He would not allow this burden to lie upon me long without sending help.

8. That He would remember likewise my fellow-labourers in the work, who trust in Him, but who would be tried were He to withhold supplies.

9. That He would remember that I should have to dismiss the children from under our Scriptural instruction to their former companions.

10. That He would show, that those were mistaken who said, that, at the first, supplies might be expected, while the thing was new, but not afterwards.

11. That I should not know, were He to withhold means, what construction I should put upon all the many most remarkable answers to prayer, which He had given me heretofore in connexion with this work, and which most fully have shown to me that it is of God.

In some small measure I now understand, experimentally, the meaning of that word "how long," which so frequently occurs in the prayers of the Psalms. But even now, by the grace of God, my eyes are up unto Him only, and I believe that He will send help.

Sept. 10. Monday morning. Neither Saturday nor yesterday had any money come in. It appeared to me now needful to take some steps on account of our need, i.e., to go to the Orphan Houses, call the brethren and sisters together, (who, except brother T----, had never been informed about the state of the funds), state the case to them, see how much money was needed for the present, tell them that amidst all this trial of faith I still believed that God would help, and to pray with them. Especially, also, I meant to go for the sake of telling them that no more articles must be purchased than we have the means to pay for, but to let there be nothing lacking in any way to the children, as it regards nourishing food and needful clothing; for I would rather at once send them away than that they should lack. I meant to go for the sake also of seeing whether there were still articles remaining which had been sent for the purpose of being sold, or whether there were any articles really needless, that we might turn them into money. I felt that the matter was now come to a solemn crisis.-- About half-past nine six-pence came in, which had been put anonymously into the box at Gideon Chapel. This money seemed to me like an earnest, that God would have compassion and send more. About ten, after I had returned from brother Craik, to whom I had unbosomed my heart again, whilst once more in prayer for help, a sister called who gave two sovereigns to my wife for the Orphans, stating that she had felt herself stirred up to come, and that she had delayed coming already too long. A few minutes after, when I went into the room where she was, she gave me two sovereigns more, and all this without knowing the least about our need. Thus the Lord most mercifully has sent us a little help, to the great encouragement of my faith. A few minutes after I was called on for money from the Infant-Orphan-House, to which I sent 2l., and 1l. 0s. 6d. to the Boys'-Orphan-House, and 1l. to the Girls'-Orphan-House.

Brother Craik left Bristol today for a few days in company with another brother. I should have gone with them for the sake of obtaining some quiet for my head; but I must remain, to pass with my dear Orphans through the trial; though these dear little ones know nothing about it, because their tables are as well supplied as when there was 800l. in the bank, and they have lack of nothing.

Today I saw a young brother who, as well as one of his sisters, had been brought to the knowledge of the Lord through my Narrative.

Sept. 11. The good Lord, in His wisdom, still sees it needful to keep us very low. But this afternoon brother T---- called, and told me that one of our fellow-labourers had sold his metal watch, and two gold pins, for 1l. 1s., that 9s. 6d. had come in, and that two of our fellow-labourers had sent two lots of books of their own, 19 and 21 in number, to be sold for the Orphans. What an abundant blessing, that in such a season of trial I have such fellow-labourers! This 1l. 10s. 6d. was given to the Boys'-Orphan-House.

Sept. 12. Still the trial continues. Only 9s. came in today, given by one of the labourers. In the midst of this great trial of faith the Lord still mercifully keeps me in great peace. He also allows me to see, that our labour is not in vain; for yesterday died Leah Culliford, one of the orphans, about 9 years old, truly converted, and brought to the faith some months before her departure.

Sept. 13. No help has come yet. This morning found it was absolutely needful to tell the brethren and sisters about the state of the funds, and to give necessary directions as to not going into debt, etc. We prayed together, and had a very happy meeting. They all seemed comfortable 12s. 6d. was taken out of the boxes in the three houses, 12s. one of the labourers gave, and 1l. 1s. had come in for needlework done by the children.

One of the sisters, who is engaged in the work, sent a message after me, not to trouble myself about her salary, for she should not want any for a twelvemonth. What a blessing to have such fellow-labourers!

Sept. 14. I met again this morning with the brethren and sisters for prayer, as the Lord has not yet sent help. After prayer one of the labourers gave me all the money he had, 16s., saying that it would not be upright to pray, if he were not to give what he had. One of the sisters told me, that in six days she would give 6l., which she had in the Savings' Bank for such a time of need. God be praised for such fellow-labourers!--Up to this day the matrons of the three houses had been in the habit of paying the bakers and the milkman weekly, because they had preferred to receive the payments in this way, and sometimes it had thus been also with the butcher and grocer. But now, as the Lord deals out to us by the day, we considered it would be wrong to go on any longer in this way, as the week's payment might become due, and we have no money to meet it; and thus those with whom we deal might be inconvenienced by us, and we be found acting against the commandment of the Lord, "Owe no man anything." Rom. xiii. 8. From this day, and hence-forward, whilst the Lord gives to us our supplies by the day, we purpose therefore to pay at once for every article as it is purchased, and never to buy anything except we can pay for it at once, however much it may seem to be needed, and however much those with whom we deal may wish to be paid only by the week. The little which was owed was paid off this day.--When I came home I found a large parcel of new clothes, which had been sent from Dublin for the Orphans, a proof that tire Lord remembers us still. We met again in the evening for prayer. We were of good cheer, and still BELIEVE that the Lord will supply our need.

Sept. 15. Saturday. We met again this morning for prayer. God comforts our hearts. We are looking for help. I found that there were provisions enough for today and tomorrow, but there was no money in hand to take in bread as usual, in order that the children might not have newly baked bread. This afternoon one of the labourers, who had been absent for several days from Bristol, returned, and gave 1l. This evening we met again for prayer, when I found that 10s. 6d. more had come in since the morning. With this 1l. 10s. 6d. we were able to buy, even this Saturday evening, the usual quantity of bread, (as it might be difficult to get stale bread on Monday morning,) and have some money left. God be praised, who gave us grace to come to the decision not to take any bread today, as usual, nor to buy any thing for which we cannot pay at once. We were very comfortable, thankfully taking this money out of our Father's hands, as a proof that He still cares for us, and that, in His own time, He will send us larger sums.

Today, a brother kindly paid the bill for medical attendance on my dear wife during her confinement. The same brother also had paid, some weeks since, the second medical attendant, who was called in. Thus the Lord, in various ways, sends help to us, showing continually His fatherly care over us.

Sept. 16. Lord's day afternoon. We met again for prayer respecting supplies for the Orphans. We are in peace, and our hope is in God, that He graciously will appear, though but one shilling has come in since last evening.

Sept. 17. The trial still continues. It is now more and more trying, even to faith, as each day comes. Truly, the Lord has wise purposes in allowing us to call so long upon Him for help. But I am sure God will send help, if we can but wait. One of the labourers had had a little money come in, of which he gave 12s. 6d.; another labourer gave 11s. 8d., being all the money she had left: this, with 17s. 6d., which, partly, had come in, and, partly, was in hand, enabled us to pay what needed to be paid, and to purchase provisions, so that nothing yet, in any way, has been lacking. This evening I was rather tried respecting the long delay of larger sums coming; but being led to go to the Scriptures for comfort, my soul was greatly refreshed, and my faith again strengthened, by the xxxivth Psalm, so that I went very cheerfully to meet with my dear fellow-labourers for prayer. I read to them the Psalm, and sought to cheer their hearts through the precious promises contained in it.

Sept. 18. Brother T. had 25s. in hand, and I had 3s. This 1l. 8s. enabled us to buy the meat and bread, which was needed; a little tea for one of the houses, and milk for all; no more than this is needed. Thus the Lord has provided not only for this day, but there is bread for two days in hand. Now, however, we are come to an extremity. The funds are exhausted. The labourers, who had a little money, have given as long as they had any left.--Now observe how the Lord helped us! A lady from the neighbourhood of London who brought a parcel with money from her daughter, arrived four or five days since in Bristol, and took lodgings next door to the Boys' Orphan-House. This afternoon she herself kindly brought me the money, amounting to 3l. 2s. 6d. We had been reduced so low as to be on the point of selling those things which could be spared; but this morning I had asked the Lord, if it might be, to prevent the necessity of our doing so. That the money had been so near the Orphan-Houses for several days without being given, is a plain proof that it was from the beginning in the heart of God to help us; but, because He delights in the prayers

SECOND PART

of His children, He had allowed us to pray so long; also to try our faith, and to make the answer so much the sweeter. It is indeed a precious deliverance. I burst out into loud praises and thanks the first moment I was alone, after I had received the money. I met with my fellow-labourers again this evening for prayer and praise; their hearts were not a little cheered. This money was this evening divided, and will comfortably provide for all that will be needed tomorrow.

Sept. 20. Morning. The Lord has again kindly sent in a little. Last evening was given to me 1s. 6d., and this morning 1l. 3s. Evening. This evening the Lord sent still further supplies; 8l. 11s. 2 1/2d. came in, as a further proof that the Lord is not unmindful of us. There was in the box of the Girls' Orphan-House 1l. 1s., and in that of the Boys' Orphan-House 1l. 7s. 2 1/2d. One of the labourers, in accordance with her promise this day week, gave 6l. 3s. About eighteen months ago she saw it right no longer to have money for herself in the Savings' Bank, and she therefore, in her heart, gave the money which she had there to the Orphan-Houses, intending to draw it in a time of need. Some time since (she told me this evening) she drew a part of it to buy several useful articles for the Orphan-Houses; now the sum was reduced to 6l. When she found out the present need, she went this day week to the Savings' Bank, and gave notice that she wished to draw her money today. Truly, as long as God shall be pleased to give me such fellow-labourers, His blessing will rest upon the work! This 8l. 11s. 2 1/2d. was divided this evening to supply the three houses, and we thanked God, unitedly, for His help.

Sept. 22. Both yesterday and today we have again assembled for prayer and praise. We are in no immediate want, but on the 29th 19l. 10s. will be due for the rent of the three Orphan-Houses.--Today there was only 4s. 7d. in hand for the other objects of the Institution, though it was the pay-day for some of the teachers. My comfort was the living God. During this week He had helped me so repeatedly and in such a remarkable way, as it regards the Orphan-Houses, that it would have been doubly sinful not to have trusted in Him for help under this fresh difficulty. No money came in this morning. About two, the usual time when the teachers are paid, a sovereign was given, with which I went immediately to brother T. (who attends to this part of the work), to pay at least in part, the weekly salaries. I found that he had received a sovereign in the morning. By means of this sovereign, together with the one which I had received just at the moment when it was needed, we were helped through this day.

Sept. 25. Yesterday and the previous days we have continued to assemble for prayer. In four days the rent for the Orphan-Houses will be due, and we have nothing towards it; also, the housekeeping money in the three houses is now again gone. May the Lord have compassion on us, and continue to send us help! A little came in this morning: there was found 9s. 6d. in the box in my house.

Sept. 27. The 9s. 6d. which came in the day before yesterday, was given to the Infant-Orphan-House. Thus we were helped through that day and yesterday. There was every thing that was needed in the three houses; I had made particular enquiry;

there was meat even for today. We met yesterday again for prayer. Today I was not able to go, on account of indisposition; I sent, therefore, to brother T. to request him to divide the 18s. 6d., (10s. of which had come in last evening, and 8s. 6d. of which we had in hand), between the three matrons. This afternoon I hear of a fresh deliverance which the Lord has wrought. About five weeks ago, a farmer applied for the admission of an orphan-girl, his grand-daughter. As I knew, however, that he had the means of providing for her, and as our Institution is only for destitute orphans, I informed him that the child could only be received, on condition of his paying 10l. a year for her support, (which is about the average expense for the younger girls), and this, quarterly, in advance.4 This morning he came, brought the child, and paid 2l. 10s. in advance, and gave 1l. besides. Thus the Lord has again most seasonably helped us in this our time of need. May He keep the memory of these deliverances alive in our souls, and increase our confidence in Him by every fresh one! In less than two days we have to pay 19l. 10s. for rent! May the Lord keep us looking to Him, and mercifully send help!

Sept. 29. Saturday evening. Prayer has been made for several days past respecting the rent, which is due this day. I have been looking out for it, though I knew not whence a shilling was to come. This morning brother T. called on me, and, as no money had come in, we prayed together, and continued in supplication from ten till a quarter to twelve. Twelve o'clock struck (the time when the rent ought to have been paid), but no money had been sent. For some days past I have repeatedly had a misgiving, whether the Lord might not disappoint us, in order that we might be led to provide by the week, or the day, for the rent. This is the second, and only the second, complete failure as to answers of prayer in the work, during the past four years and six months. The first was about the half-yearly rent of Castle-Green school-room, due July 1, 1837, which had come in only in part by that time. I am now fully convinced that the rent ought to be put by daily or weekly, as God may prosper us, in order that the work, even as to this point, may be a testimony. May the Lord, then, help us to act accordingly; and may He now mercifully send in the means to pay the rent!--Whilst in this matter our prayers have failed, either to humble us, or to show us how weak our faith is still, or to teach us, (which seems to me the most probable,) that we ought to provide the rent beforehand; the Lord has given us again fresh proofs, even this day, that He is mindful of us. There was not money enough in the Girls'-Orphan-House to take in bread, (we give the bread to the children on the third day after it is baked); but before the baker came, a lady called who had had some needlework done by the children, and paid 3s. 11d., and thus the matron was able to take in bread as usual. I found this morning 2s. in the box in my house, our extremity having led me to look into it. One of the labourers gave 13s. This 15s. was divided amongst the three matrons. Thanks to the Lord, there is all which is needed for today and tomorrow.

Sept. 30. We are not only poor as regards the Orphan-fund, but also the funds for the other objects bring us again and again to the Lord for fresh supplies. Today, when we had not a single penny in hand, 5l. was given for the other objects.

SECOND PART

Oct. 2. Tuesday evening. The Lord's holy name be praised! He hath dealt most bountifully with us during the last three days! The day before yesterday 5l. came in for the Orphans. Of this I gave to each house 10s. which supplied them before the provisions were consumed. Oh! how kind is the Lord. Always, before there has been actual want, He has sent help. Yesterday came in 1l. 10s. more. This 1l. 10s., with 4s. 2d. in hand, was divided for present necessities. Thus the expenses of yesterday, for housekeeping, were defrayed. The Lord helped me also to pay yesterday the 19l. 10s. for the rent. The means for it were thus obtained. One of the labourers had received through his family 10l., and 5l. besides from a sister in the Lord; also some other money. Of this he gave 16l., which, with the 3l. 10s. that was left of the above-mentioned 5l., which came in the day before yesterday, made up 19l. 10s., the sum which was needed.

--This day we were again greatly reduced. There was no money in hand to take in bread as usual, for the Boys' and Infant Orphan-Houses, but again the Lord helped. A sister who had arrived this afternoon from Swansea brought 1l. 7s., and one of the labourers sold an article, by means of which he was able to give 1l. 13s. Thus we had 3l.:—1l. for each house, and could buy bread before the day was over. Hitherto we have lacked nothing!

Oct. 4. Thursday. The money of Tuesday helped us through yesterday. Today, when again all was gone, and help was greatly needed, our loving Lord appeared. The books which had been given some time since, by some of my fellow-labourers, were sold for 11s., also an old bedstead for 2s. 6d., and an old sofa for 10s. The boxes were also opened, as I had been told some money had been put in, and 9s. 1d. was found in them. This money was a fresh encouragement to us in our need. By this 1l. 12s. 7d. we were helped through the day.

Oct. 5. This morning, just before I was going to the Orphan-Houses to meet with the brethren and sisters for prayer, 1l. 3s. was brought from Teignmouth. This money seems to have been given some months since to a brother at Teignmouth, but it did not reach me until today. It is a most seasonable help, to defray the expenses of this day, and a fresh proof, that not in anger, but only for the trial of our faith, our gracious Lord delays as yet, to send larger sums.

Oct. 6. Saturday. The Lord has again most kindly helped us. It came to my mind that there were some new blankets in the Orphan-Houses, which had been given some time since, but which are not needed, and might therefore be sold. I was confirmed in this by finding that the moth had got into one pair. I therefore sold ten pairs, having a good opportunity to do so. Thus the Lord not only supplied again our present need for the three houses, but I was also able to put by the rent for this week and the next, acting out the light which He had given us this day week. There came in 9s. 6d., besides 7l. for the blankets. The School fund, also, was again completely exhausted, when today and yesterday came in so much, that not only the weekly salaries could be paid today, but also above 1l. could be put by for rent.

Oct. 9. Through the last-mentioned supplies for the Orphans we were helped up to this day; but today we were brought lower than ever. The provisions would have lasted out only today, and the money for milk in one of the houses could only be made up by one of the labourers selling one of his books. The matron in the Boys'-Orphan-House had this morning two shillings left. When in doubt whether to buy bread with it, or more meat, to make up the dinner with the meat which she had in the house, the baker called, and left three quarters of bread as a present. In this great need, some money having been given to one of the labourers, he gave 2l. of it, by which we were able to buy meat, bread, and other provisions. Nevertheless even this day, low as we had been brought, before this 2l. was given, there had been all in the house that was needed.

Oct. 10. The Lord had sent in so much since yesterday afternoon, that we were able at our meeting this morning to divide 2l. 0s. 2d. between the three matrons, whereby we are helped through this day. But now the coals in the Infant-Orphan-House are out, and nearly so in the other two houses. Also the treacle casks in all the three houses are nearly empty. On this account we have asked the Lord for fresh supplies.

Oct. 11. The "Father of the fatherless" has again shown his care over us. An Orphan from Devonshire arrived last evening. With her was sent 2l. 5s. 6d. The sister who brought her gave also a silver tea-pot, sugar-basin, and cream jug (of the weight of 48 oz.), having found true riches in Christ. There was also in the boxes 9s. One of the labourers paid for a ton of coals. We obtained 16l. 16s. for the silver articles.--Thus we were helped through the heavy expenses of the following days.

Oct. 12. Today seven brethren and sisters were added to us in fellowship, and eight were proposed. May the Lord send helpers for the work!

Oct. 13. For three months past the Orphan fund has been low, yet hitherto we have lacked nothing!

Oct. 15. I knew that there would be money needed this morning, for many things in the Orphan-Houses, and my heart was therefore lifted up to the Lord. Just when I was going to meet my fellow labourers for prayer, I received from Trowbridge 4l. There had come in also at the Orphan-Houses 7s. 3d. To this one of the labourers added 1l. Thus I was enabled abundantly to supply all that was wanted, and to pay for a cask of treacle and a ton of coals. We are now, however, cast again on the love of our Lord for further supplies, as there is neither any thing in hand, nor have the labourers any more of their own to give.

Oct. 16. The day commenced with mercies. I was looking up to the Lord for help, early this morning, when, almost immediately afterwards, brother T. came, and brought two silver table-spoons, and six tea-spoons, which had been left, anonymously, yesterday afternoon, at the Girls'-Orphan-House. This afternoon I received 12l. from Staffordshire. On the seal of the letter, which enclosed the money, was

"Ebenezer." How true in our case! Surely this instance is a fresh "Ebenezer" to us; for hitherto the Lord has helped us.--There was also found a half sovereign in the box at my house. Also a lady left 5s. at the door of the Girls'-Orphan-House, with about 200 pears for the children; and a brother sent 2s., the first fruits of the increase of his wages. Thus I was able to give a larger supply than usual to the matrons.

Oct. 22. Today our funds were again quite low. In the Infant-Orphan-House only 2d. was left, and very little in the other two houses. But the Lord most manifestly again answered prayer. A gentleman from London, who is greatly interested about destitute and neglected children, came over from Bath with two of his sisters to see the Orphan-Houses. He gave 1l. There was 2s. 6d. put into the box at my house, and 6d. anonymously into the box at Gideon Chapel. With this 1l. 3s. I went directly to the Orphan-Houses to relieve the present need. Whilst I was there, the Lord gave still further supplies; for being informed that in the morning some ladies had seen the houses, and put money into the boxes, I opened them and found 3l. 0s. 1d. Thus the Lord, by means of this 4l. 3s. 1d., helped us through the necessities of this day.

Oct. 23. The Lord again sent above 2l., which supplied this day's necessities.

Oct. 24. Today the Lord sent from a most unexpected quarter 5l. The money was given by a relative of two children in the Boys'-Orphan-House. Thus we are helped for two days, and are able to put by the rent for this week.

Oct. 27. Saturday. This day we have been again mercifully helped, though our need has been almost greater than ever. But, thanks to our adorable Lord! this day also we have not been confounded; for there was 6s. in the box at the Infant-Orphan-House, and 6s. came in for things which had been given to be sold. To this one of the labourers added 18s. By means of this 1l. 10s. we have been able to meet all pressing demands, and to procure provisions for today and tomorrow.

Oct. 29. Monday. The Lord has again given us this day our daily bread, though, in the morning, there was not the least natural prospect of obtaining supplies. One of the labourers, who had received some money for his own personal expenses, gave 2l. Some things also, which had been given for sale, had been sold for 18s.; and 6d. had been put into the box at Gideon Chapel This 2l. 18s. 6d. enabled us to meet the expenses of this day. There were also many articles of worn clothes sent.

Oct. 30. This has been again a day of peculiar mercies in reference to the funds. Whilst I was in prayer respecting them, a brother brought 2 1/4 yards of cloth. He had bought it for himself, but, afterwards considering that he had sufficient clothes, he gave it to be sold for the Orphans. This evening a sister gave me 20l., ten of which were for the Orphans, and ten for the other objects. Thus we are helped for this week.

Nov. 4. Lord's day. There was given, by a stranger, last Wednesday evening, at Bethesda Chapel, to one of the sisters, a sovereign for the Orphans, which I received today. Thus the Lord has again begun the week with mercy, and His love surely will help us through it, though again many pounds will be needed.

Nov. 5. Monday. By means of the sovereign which had come in yesterday, and several small donations today and on the past days, together with 2l. 10s. which one of the labourers added of his own, 6l. 2s. 6d. was divided this day between the three matrons, which will supply their need for two days at least.

Nov. 7. The funds are now again completely exhausted. Today I divided 1l. 3s. 8d., which had come in yesterday; thus the necessary wants were supplied. The Lord be praised who has helped us hitherto! One of the Orphans was sent today to service, and the Lord enabled us to give her a suitable outfit.

Nov. 8. Last evening 1l. 4s. came in, which, being divided between the three houses, helped us through this day.

Nov. 10. Saturday. All seemed to be dark, so far as regards natural appearances, at the commencement of this day. But through this day also the Lord has helped us, and enabled us to meet all demands. In the course of the day came in 1l. 8s. 6d. To this two of the labourers added 10s. each, and thus we were brought to the close of one more week, having been able to supply the necessities of 97 persons in the Orphan-Houses, without owing any thing.

Nov. 12. Monday. Sixpence came in this morning, to which one of the labourers added 10s. 6d., to meet the most pressing necessities. This evening I found the 1l. was not enough to take in bread for the Boys'-Orphan-House. The Lord gave us, however, before the day was over, enough to buy the usual quantity of bread; for there was found in the boxes 5s. 9d. and a pair of small gold earrings.

Nov. 13. This morning our want was again great. I have 20l. in hand which has been put by for rent, but, for the Lord's honour, I would not take of it. Nothing had come in, and the labourers had scarcely any thing to give. I went, however, to the Orphan-Houses, to pray with my fellow labourers, and, if it might be, to comfort them, and see what could be done. When I came there, I found that 19s. 6d. had come in this morning. On enquiry I heard that only 2s. 6d. more was needed to carry us through the day. This one of the labourers was able to add of his own. Thus the Lord has again helped us out of our difficulty. One of the labourers gave some things which he could do without, and another gave a workbox to be sold for the Orphans.-- Before this day has come to an end, the Lord has sent in 1l. 2s. 4d. more, so that we have also a little for tomorrow.

Nov. 15. The money which had come in the day before yesterday, supplied the necessities of yesterday also; but today we were brought again very low. I went to the Orphan-Houses, to pray with my fellow-labourers, not without hope that the Lord might have appeared, and sent a little help. When I arrived I found that one of the labourers had sold a few of his books, together with two which had been given by

SECOND PART

another labourer on the 13th, for which he had received 7s. To this one of the labourers added 7s. 9d. This 14s. 9d. supplied the most pressing necessities. When I came home I found 1s. in the box at my house, and soon after received 5s. for a pair of fire screens, which had been given for sale. There were also three baskets of potatoes sent to the three different houses. A sack of potatoes had been ordered, but the brother, who had been desired to bring them, could not conveniently do so today, and thought, as this present had been ordered from him, there would be no immediate need of them; and Oh! how kind of the Lord to order it thus: for had he brought them, the payment would have taken away the money which was intended for the usual quantity of bread. But before the day was over, the Lord helped still further. In the afternoon a gentleman from Bath called at the Boys'-Orphan-House, and gave a cheque for 3l. There was also 1s. given; 2s. 6d. came in for needle-work, and 5s. 6d. for things sold. Thus altogether 4l. 4s. 9d. has been sent by the Lord this day.

Nov. 17. Saturday. Today above 3l. was needed, and as only 15s. 6d. had come in, we found it needful to determine to dispose of a few articles of furniture which we conveniently could do without. One of the labourers gave a good watch to be sold, which she had bought some months since, there being then no time-piece in one of the houses. In consideration of these articles to be sold, I took, for the present necessities of the Orphans, 2l. 10s. of the money which had been put by for the rent, to be replaced when these articles could be sold at a suitable opportunity. Thus we were helped to the close of one more week.

Nov. 19. Today we were again in great need. There had come in only 7s. 6d. for needle-work. The Lord had, however, given to one of the labourers a little money, of which he gave 15s., by means of which we were helped through this day also.

Nov. 20. Today our need was exceedingly great, but the Lord's help was great also. I went to meet with the brethren and sisters as usual. I found that 1l. would be needed to supply the necessities of today, but 3s. only had come in. Just when we were going to pray, one of the labourers came in, who, after prayer, gave 10s. Whilst we were praying, another labourer came in, who had received 1l. Thus we had 1l. 13s.; even more, therefore, than was absolutely needed.

Nov. 21. Never were we so reduced in funds as today. There was not a single halfpenny in hand between the matrons of the three houses. Nevertheless there was a good dinner, and, by managing so as to help one another with bread, etc., there was a prospect of getting over this day also; but for none of the houses had we the prospect of being able to take in bread. When I left the brethren and sisters at one o'clock, after prayer, I told them that we must wait for help, and see how the Lord would deliver us at this time. I was sure of help, but we were indeed straitened. When I came to Kingsdown, I felt that I needed more exercise, being very cold; wherefore I went not the nearest way home, but round by Clarenceplace. About twenty yards from my house, I met a brother who walked back with me, and after a little conversation gave me 10l. to be handed over to the brethren, the deacons, towards providing the poor saints with coals, blankets and warm clothing; also 5l. for the Orphans, and 5l. for the other objects of the Scriptural Knowledge Institution. The brother had called twice while I was gone to the Orphan-Houses, and had I now been one half minute later, I should have missed him. But the Lord knew our need, and therefore allowed me to meet him. I sent off the 5l. immediately to the matrons.

Nov. 23. The above-mentioned 5l., with an addition of 11s. 6d. which had also come in, helped us through the expenses of yesterday and today.

Nov. 24. This again has been a very remarkable day. We had as little in hand this morning as at any time, and yet several pounds were needed. But God, who is rich in mercy, and whose word so positively declares that none who trust in Him shall be confounded, has helped us through this day also. While I was in prayer, about ten in the morning, respecting the funds, I was informed that a gentleman had called to see me. He came to inform me that a lady had ordered three sacks of potatoes to be sent to the Orphan Houses. Never could they have come more seasonably. This was an encouragement to me, to continue to expect help. When I came to the prayer meeting about 12 o'clock, I heard that 2s. had come in, also 1l. for a guitar, which had been given for sale. The payment for this guitar had been expected for many weeks. It had been mentioned among us, repeatedly, that it might come just at a time, when we most needed it: and oh! how true. Also the watch which had been given was sold for 2l. 10s. But with all this we could not have put by the rents for this week, amounting to 30s. One of the labourers, therefore, gave his watch to the Orphan-fund under this condition, that should the Lord not enable us before Dec. 21st to make up this deficiency, it should be sold, but not otherwise, as he needs it in the Lord's service.--[A few days after the Lord gave the means to put by the 30s., and 30s. besides for the next week's rent.] Thus the Lord helped us through this day, and with it brought us to the close of one more week.

Nov. 25. Lord's-day. The Lord kindly remembers us before there is absolute need. A sister who is going to leave Bristol, called on me to bid me farewell, and gave me, in parting, 1l. 10s. for the Orphans. It is remarkable, that almost every donation given within the last four months and thirteen days, since our funds have been low, has come from unexpected quarters, to make the hand of God so much the more manifest.

Nov. 26. Though there had come in yesterday 1l. 10s., yet that was scarcely the half of what was needed this day. But the Lord knew our circumstances, and, as He is wont to do, most unworthy as we are of it, remembered our need. There was given 1l. this morning, and 1s. had been put anonymously into the box at Gideon Chapel; and a lamp, which had been given some time since, had been sold for 10s. Also 1s. 2d. came in for needlework. By means of these several little sums we could meet all the demands of this day.

SECOND PART

Nov. 27. Yesterday afternoon came in 10s., and this morning, by the disposal of some articles, which had been given for sale, 12s. This furnished us with means to procure, for this day also, the necessary supplies.

Nov. 28. This is, perhaps, of all days the most remarkable as yet, so far as it regards the funds. When I was in prayer this morning respecting them, I was enabled firmly to believe that the Lord would send help, though all seemed dark as to natural appearances. At 12 o'clock I met as usual with the brethren and sisters for prayer. There had come in only 1s., which was left last evening anonymously, at the Infant Orphan-House, and which, except 2d., had already been spent, on account of the great need. I heard also that an individual had gratuitously cleaned the time-piece in the Infant Orphan-House, and had offered to keep the timepieces of the three houses in repair. Thus the Lord gave even in this a little encouragement, and a proof that He is still mindful of us. On inquiry I found that there was every thing needful for the dinner in all the three houses; but neither in the Infant nor Boys' Orphan-Houses was there bread enough for tea, nor money to buy milk. Lower we had never been, and, perhaps, never so low. We gave ourselves now unitedly to prayer, laying the case in simplicity before the Lord. Whilst in prayer there was a knock at the door, and one of the sisters went out. After the two brethren, who labour in the Orphan-Houses, and I had prayed aloud, we continued for a while silently in prayer. As to myself, I was lifting up my heart to the Lord to make a way for our escape, and in order to know, if there were any other thing which I could do with a good conscience, besides waiting on Him, so that we might have food for the children. At last we rose from our knees. I said, "God will surely send help." The words had not quite passed over my lips, when I perceived a letter lying on the table, which had been brought whilst we were in prayer. It was from my wife, containing another letter from a brother with 10l. for the Orphans. The evening before last I was asked by a brother whether the balance in hand for the Orphans would be as great this time, when the accounts would be made up, as the last time. My answer was, that it would be as great as the Lord pleased. The next morning this brother was moved to remember the Orphans, and to send today 10l., which arrived after I had left my house, and which on account of our need was forwarded immediately to me. Thus I was enabled to give 6l. 10s. for housekeeping, and to put by 3l. 10s. for rent.

The brother who sent the 10l. for the Orphans, sent likewise 10l. to be divided between brother Craik and me, with the object of purchasing new clothes for ourselves.

Nov. 29. The Lord has greatly blessed our meetings for prayer. They have been instrumental in leading us to much prayer for the children in the Orphan-Houses, in the Day-Schools, and in the Sunday-School. They have led us to prayer for ourselves, for the Day-School Teachers, and for the Sunday-School Teachers, that grace may be given to us so to walk before the children, and so to deal with them, as that the Lord may be glorified by us. We have also often been led to intercede for the believers with whom we are in fellowship, and for the Church at large. We have especially prayed, that our work may lead the church generally to a more simple confidence and trust in the Lord. That these meetings have not been in vain, as regards the procuring of funds, has been already sufficiently seen by the many instances which have been recorded in the foregoing pages. Today, however, we have had another particular proof of this. When we met I found that 10s. had come in yesterday afternoon. When I returned home I found 1l. had come in, and shortly after I received another 1l. In the evening I received 50l., which was sent from Suffolk by a sister who had often expressed how gladly she would contribute more largely to the work which is in our hands, had she the means, and who just now, in this our time of need, has obtained the means to carry out the desire of her heart. I rejoice in the last donation particularly, not because of the largeness of the sum, but because it enables me to pay to my brethren and sisters in the Orphan-Houses the salary which is due to them. For though they are willing to labour without any remuneration, nevertheless "the labourer is worthy of his reward." This donation also proves, that the Lord is willing even now, as formerly, to send large sums. But I expect still larger. The same sister who sent the 50l. for the Orphans, sent, at the same time, 30l. to be divided between brother Craik and me for our personal expenses. How abundantly does the Lord care for us! Truly we serve a kind Master!

Dec. 5. Today there were again a few shillings needed, in the Boys' Orphan-House. That which remained of the £50l. had been divided for housekeeping in the three houses, and was now all spent in the Boys' Orphan-House, and nearly also in the other two houses. The few shillings which were needed in the Boys' Orphan-House, the Lord, however, had previously provided by the little which had come in on December 3 and 4.

Dec. 6. This day our need was again as great as ever, but the deliverance of the Lord was also as manifest as ever. No money had come in, and I knew there would be some needed this morning in all the three houses. That which was required to buy provisions for today, was about 1l.; but there were also coals needed in two houses, and two of the treacle-casks were empty. We gave ourselves, as usual, to prayer. After prayer one of the labourers gave 1l. of the salary which she had received a few days ago; another gave 6s., and 4s. 6d. was taken out of the boxes. Thus we had 1l. 10s. 6d. to divide, and therefore more than was absolutely needed; also one of the labourers had ordered half a ton of coals to be sent to the Boys' Orphan-House, for which he paid himself.

This afternoon I received 100l. from a sister; 50l. for the Orphans, and 50l. for the School—Bible—and Missionary-Fund. This same sister, who earns her bread with her own hands, had given, on October 5, 1837, 50l. towards the Boys' Orphan-House, and gave for the necessities of the poor saints, in August, 1838, 100l. more; for she had been made willing to act out those precious exhortations: "Having food and raiment let us be therewith content." "Sell that ye have, and give alms; provide yourselves bags which wax not old, a treasure in the heavens that faileth not, where no thief approacheth, neither moth corrupteth." "Lay not up for yourselves treasures upon earth, where moth and rust doth corrupt, and where thieves break through and steal: but lay up for yourselves treasures in heaven, where neither moth nor rust doth corrupt, and where thieves do not break through nor steal." Respecting the 50l. which has been given of this sum for the School—Bible—and Missionary-Fund, it is worthy of remark, that we would not order Reference Bibles till we had the means. We had repeatedly prayed respecting this want of Bibles, and particularly again this morning. It had been also much laid on our hearts today, to request that the Lord would enable us to have the Report printed, which we could not do, unless He first sent the means. Lastly, we had also repeatedly asked Him to supply us so largely, if it were His will, as that at the time of the public meetings we might be able to speak again of abundance. For though for some months past the time has been fixed for the public meetings, without any reference to the state of the funds, nevertheless, it might have had the appearance, that we had convened the brethren for the sake of telling them about our poverty, and thus to induce them to give.

Dec. 8, 1838. The Lord closes the third year of this part of the work with blessings. Yesterday was sent 24 yards of flannel, and today were taken out of the box in the Boys' Orphan-House a 5l. note and 3d. Also 2s. was given, and 1l. besides.

Dec. 11, 12, and 13. On the evenings of these three days there were public meetings, at which I gave an account of the Lord's dealing with us in reference to the Orphan-Houses and the other objects of the Scriptural Knowledge Institution. As the work, and particularly that of the Orphan-Houses, was begun for the benefit of the church at large, it appeared well to us, that from time to time it should be publicly stated how the Lord had dealt with us in reference to it; and as on Dec. 9th the third year had been completed, since the commencement of the Orphan work, this seemed to be a suitable time for having these meetings.

Should any one suppose, in reading the plain details of the trials through which we passed during the four months previous to Dec. 9, 1838, respecting the Orphan-Houses, that I have been disappointed as it regards my expectations, as far as the funds are concerned: my answer is, that the reverse is the case. For straits were expected. Long before the trials came, I had more than once stated publicly, that answers to prayer, in the time of need,--the manifestation of the hand of God, stretched out for our help,--was just the very end for which the Institution was established.

I further state, that the Orphans have never lacked any thing. Had I had thousands of pounds in hand, they would have fared no better than they have; for they have always had good nourishing food, the necessary articles of clothing, etc.

It is now (namely on Dec. 10, 1838) four years and nine months since brother Craik and I established the Scriptural Knowledge Institution. The reasons which we had for doing so were, that thus a testimony might be borne that the children of God need not to go to unbelievers to ask them for money; nor require the patronage of the great men of this world in the Lord's work; and that, further, believers generally might be stirred up, to renounce their alliance with the world in the management and promotion of religious objects, and that, lastly, it might be seen, that, without contracting debts, such objects can be carried on.

Painful as it was, and as it still is, to us, to be obliged to differ from so many of our brethren, in these particulars, nevertheless we were called upon to work without them, if we could not conscientiously work with them. May the Lord grant, that the eyes of many of His children may be opened, so that they may seek, in all spiritual things, to be separated from unbelievers, (2 Cor. vi. 14—18), and to do God's work according to God's mind!

I notice briefly the following particulars respecting the first three objects of the Scriptural Knowledge Institution. 1. There is at present (in December, 1838) a Sunday School supported by it, which contains four hundred and sixty-three children. This part of the work calls for particular thanksgiving; for during these last eighteen months the number of the children has been nearly three times as great as it used to be. Five of the scholars have been converted within the last two years, and are now in fellowship with the church, and three of them are teachers in the school. 2. There is in connection with the Institution an Adult-school, in which, since the commencement of the work, above 120 adults have been instructed, and in which at present twelve are taught to read. 3. The Institution has entirely supported, since its commencement, several Day-schools for poor children, and within the last two years six of such: three for boys, and three for girls.--The number of all the children that have had schooling in the Day-schools through the medium of the Institution, since its formation, amounts to 1534; the number of those at present in the six Day. Schools is 342. 4. During the last two years there have been circulated, 1884 copies of the Scriptures in connexion with the Institution, and since the beginning of the work, March 5, 1834, five thousand and seventy-eight copies. 5. For Missionary purposes have been laid out £74. 18s. 4d. 6. The total of the income for the first three objects, during the last two years, was £1129. 13s. 1d. The total of the expenses £1111. 13s. 7 1/2d.

There are, at present, 86 Orphans in the three houses, i. e. 31 in the Girls'-Orphan-House, 31 in the Infant-Orphan-House, and 24 in the Boys'-Orphan-House.

The whole number of Orphans, who have been under our care, from April 11, 1836, to Dec. 9, 1838, amounts to 110.

God's blessing has most manifestly rested upon this part of the work. For, 1. Without any one having been asked for any thing by us, the sum of £2111 5s. 4 1/2d. has been given to us, entirely as the result of prayer to God.

2. Besides this, also, many articles of clothing, furniture, provisions, etc. 3. Without our solicitation three medical gentlemen, (one for each house), have, up to Dec. 9, 1838, kindly given their attendance and medicines gratuitously.

SECOND PART

4. The children have been, on the whole, in good health, and many of them have greatly improved as to their health, since they have been with us. 5. Though most of them had been brought up in a very different manner from what one could desire, yet God has constrained them, on the whole, to behave exceedingly well, so much so that it has attracted the attention of all observers. This can be ascribed only to the good hand of God. 6. There are a few among them, respecting whom we have a comfortable assurance that they care about their souls. 7. There is not one of those who have died, of whom we are without hope, as it regards their eternal welfare; but respecting two of them we have especial reason to rejoice. The elder of the two, Harriet Culliford, about twelve years of age when she died, had been for many months wasting away in consumption. She was, almost during the whole time of her illness, completely careless about the things of God; nothing seemed to make any impression upon her, though a well behaved child in other respects. About a fortnight before her departure, she was brought to know the Lord, gave the fullest evidence, that could be given in her circumstances, of a real change of heart, and departed full of joy at the prospect of being with the Lord, though previously she had been very desirous to be restored again. The younger, Leah Culliford, (both of them of a very consumptive family), fell asleep in Jesus on Sept. 11, 1838. She was but little more than eight years of age; but many weeks before her death she gave evidence to those who were placed over her of a change of heart, and of faith in the Lord Jesus Christ.

The total of the income for the Orphans, from Dec. 9, 1836, to Dec. 9, 1838, has amounted to £1341. 4s. 7d. the total of the expenses to £1664. 4s. 0 3/4d. There was two years ago a balance of £373. 4s. 8 1/4d. in hand, and now the balance is £50. 5s. 3d.

Dec. 16. There was a paper anonymously put into the box at Bethesda Chapel, containing 4l. 10s. In the paper was written "For the Rent of the Orphan-Houses, from Dec. 10 to Dec. 31, 1838. 'O taste and see that the Lord is good: blessed is the man that trusteth in Him!" In order that the reader may be able to enter into the value of this donation, I would request him to read over once more, what I wrote under "Sept. 29 of this year." [The individual who gave this 4l. 10s. for the rent of the Orphan-Houses for the first three weeks after the public meetings, at which the matter about the rent, for the instruction of the brethren, was fully stated, continued for three years, up to Dec. 10, 1841, to give regularly, but anonymously, 1l. 10s. a week for the same purpose, which was exactly the sum required every week for the rent of those three houses. Thus the Lord rewarded our faithfulness, in carrying out the light which He had given us. But the chief blessing, resulting from this circumstance, I consider to be this, that several brethren, who earn their bread by the labour of their hands, have learned through this circumstance, that it is the will of the Lord they should lay by their rent weekly. I beseech those brethren who are not pursuing this course, to do so, and they will soon prove by experience the benefit of acting on Scriptural principles even as it regards this life.]

Dec. 17. Today eleven brethren and sisters were proposed for fellowship. The Lord still uses us as instruments. Truly, our labour in the Lord is not in vain!

Dec. 20. As the expenses for the Orphans have been above 47l. within the last six days, and as but little above 13l. has come in, and as the money for printing the Report had to be kept back, in order that we might not be in debt, we were again to-day very low in funds, though it is but six days since the public meetings. As I knew that tomorrow several pounds would be needed to supply the matrons, I gave myself this morning to prayer. About a quarter of an hour afterwards I received 3l., the payment of a legacy, left by a sister, who fell asleep in Jesus several months since, in Ireland. Besides this I received from the brother, through whom the legacy was paid, 2l. 10s. for the Orphan-Fund. With this 5l. 10s. I hope to be able to meet the expenses of tomorrow.

I observe here that it might have been naturally supposed that every heart would be touched, through what was publicly stated about the remarkable manner in which the Lord had provided for us for nearly 150 days, and that consequently an abundance of means would have come in. To this is to be added, that 50l. 5s. 3d. was in hand on Dec. 10, and that therefore it seemed not likely that we should be in need; and yet, by Dec. 20, we were again so poor, that there was nothing to meet the expenses of the next day, as has just been related. All this came not unawares upon me and my fellow-labourers; for we had been taught to look off from all creature expectations to the living God. It was on this account that, many times in our prayer meetings during November and the beginning of December, we were led to ask the Lord, not to allow us to expect an influx of means because, for the benefit of the Church, our circumstances would be made known at the public meetings. And how kind was it of the Lord to give us prayer about this, and thus to prepare us beforehand; for had we leaned upon natural expectations, we should have been surely disappointed, as only six days after the meetings we were as poor as ever. By the grace of God we are so acquainted with the heart of our Father, that we speak not about these things to excite the compassion of our fellow saints, for we have learned to lean upon God only; but we make known His dealings with us, that others may be led "to taste and see that the Lord is good," and to put their trust in Him.

The sister who left the 3l. for the Orphans, as just alluded to, also left 3l. for the funds of the other objects, 20l. to be divided between brother Craik and me, and 3l. for the poor saints.

Dec. 22. A solemn day. I received today the information from my father that my brother died on October 7th. When I saw him in April this year, he was living in open sin, and in disunion with my father. I cannot learn that his end was different from his life, so that I have no comfort in his death.--Of all the trials that can befall a believer, the death of an unconverted near relative seems to me one of the greatest. "Shall not the judge of all the earth do right?" must be the stay of the believer at such a time, and, by grace, it is my stay now. I know that the Lord is glorified in my brother, whatever his end has been: whether in his last hours, like the thief, on the cross, he was saved, or whether he died in sin and unbelief; yet I do, as to myself, desire from my heart to adore that grace which plucked me as a brand out of the

SECOND PART

burning, many years ago.--May the Lord make this event a lasting blessing to me, especially in leading me to earnestness in prayer for my father!

Dec. 26. From the 21st to this day several small donations had come in for the Orphans, so that we were supplied as we needed. Today there was ten-pence left, after the day's expenses had been met. One hour after the Lord kindly appeared again. 5l. was sent by Q. Q. This money came, just after I had prayed for means.

Dec. 27. Today came in 2l. 12s. 6d., whereby the Lord has again helped us to meet the probable expenses of tomorrow.

Dec. 28. This evening the Lord kindly sent further help, when we were again destitute of the means of providing for tomorrow. I received 20l. (half for the Orphan-Fund, and half for the other funds), with Ecclesiastes ix. 10: "Whatsoever thy hand findeth to do, do it with thy might; for there is no work, nor device, nor knowledge, nor wisdom, in the grave, whither thou goest."

Dec. 29. A sister, having felt herself particularly stirred up about the Orphans, as she writes, sent this evening 7l. five pounds from herself, and 2l. which had been sent from the EAST INDIES. To the Lord this is to be ascribed, who, in answer to our prayers, makes these impressions on the hearts of His children.

REVIEW OF THE YEAR 1838.

1. As to the church.

68 brethren and sisters we found in fellowship, when brother Craik and I came to Bristol.

458 have been admitted into fellowship since, so that the total number would be

526 had there been no changes. But,

31 have fallen asleep.

28 are under church discipline, which is the total number of all the cases of separation from communion within these six years and seven months.

36 have left Bristol

THE LORD'S DEALINGS WITH GEORGE MÜLLER

26 have left us, but are still in Bristol. Only 26 within six years and seven months!

Total 121. There are therefore only 405 at present in fellowship with us. 61 have been added during the last year, of whom 36 have been brought among us to the knowledge of the truth.

II. As to my temporal supplies

The Lord has been pleased to give me during the past year:

1. By the Freewill Offerings through the boxes £151 6s. 8d.

2. By presents in money from believers in and out of Bristol £141 18s. 0d.

3. By money, through family connexion £40 0s. 0d.

4. By presents in clothes, provisions, etc., which were worth to me, at least £12 0s. 0d.

We have been living for six months, half free of rent whereby we have saved at least £5 0s. 0d.

Altogether £350 4s. 8d.

During no period of my life had I such need of means, on account of my own long illness and that of my dear wife, and on account of the many and particular calls for means as during the past year; but also during no period of my life has the Lord so richly supplied me. Truly, it must be manifest to all that I have served a most kind Master, during this year also, and that, even for this life, it is by far the best thing to seek to act according to the mind of the Lord, as to temporal things.

January 1st, 2nd, and 3rd, 1830. We have had three especial church prayer meetings these three days. The year commenced with mercies. In the first hour of the year there came in for the Orphans 2l. 7s., which was given after our usual prayer meeting on December 31, which this time lasted from seven in the evening till after midnight.

Jan. 11. Since December 20, came in several donations for the Orphans, so that we were supplied, before that which we had in hand was quite gone. On the seventh, however, all our money was again expended, when a brother, from the neighbourhood of London, who, is staying here, gave me 10l. Today, when this 10l. was given out, I received from London 3l. 7s., and 4s. besides. Thus the Lord, as our need is, sends help, and all in answer to prayer, without our asking any one.

SECOND PART

Jan. 17. Since the 11th 22 small donations have again come in, by which we have been helped thus far. This afternoon all which was in hand was given for housekeeping, and I was again penniless. The Lord, however, was mindful of this, and in the evening two sovereigns were left anonymously at my house. In the paper was written: "The enclosed are for the use of the Orphan-Houses, from J. H., who thinks he ought to do something for the Institution." J. H. will have in this a proof that the Lord touched his heart to give the money, because there was not a penny in hand for those who are the especial care of Him who is the "Father of the fatherless."

Jan. 20. Ten small donations have come in since the 17th, which have enabled us to provide what was needed for the last three days, and also for today.--For some time past it has appeared to me that the words "Ye have the poor with you always, and whensoever ye will ye may do them good," which the Lord spoke to His disciples, who were themselves very poor, imply that the children of God, as such, have power with God to bring temporal blessings upon poor saints or poor unbelievers, through the instrumentality of prayer. Accordingly I have been led to ask the Lord for means to assist poor saints; and at different times He has stirred up His children to intrust me with sums both large and small, for that especial object; or has, by some means or other, put money at my disposal, which I might so use. In like manner I had been asking again for means a few days since, to be able more extensively to assist the poor saints in communion with us, as just now many of them are not merely tried by the usual temporal difficulties arising from its being winter, but especially from the high price of bread. And now this evening the Lord has given me the answer to my prayer. When I came home from the meeting, I found a brother at my house who offered to give me 10l. a week, for twelve weeks, towards providing the poor saints with coals and needful articles of clothing, but chiefly with bread. [Accordingly this brother sent me two days afterwards 120l.,--whereby very many, especially poor widows, were greatly assisted, chiefly with flour and bread. This money just lasted till the price of bread was reduced from 9 1/2d. to 7 1/2d. Thus, for several weeks, about 150 quarters of bread were distributed weekly, besides what was given in flour, coals, and clothes. I have mentioned this circumstance as an encouragement to those who either have little or nothing at all to give to poor persons, and who yet have a desire to give; and to those who have means, but whose means are not adequate to relieve all the demands made upon them. Had we more grace to plead the words of our Lord, above referred to, we should receive far more from Him to meet the necessities around us.]

Jan. 22. A brother formerly an officer in the navy, Who for Jesus' sake has given up his rank and pay, gave three silver table spoons, three silver forks, and two teaspoons, to be sold for the benefit of the Orphans. The produce of them, with 1l. 5s. which has come in besides, enabled us to meet the expenses of today and tomorrow.

Jan. 26. Saturday. The need of the 24th, 25th, and of today was supplied, partly, by the little that had been left on the 23rd; and partly, by five small donations, by 9s. for the children's needlework, and by 12s. which had come in by the sale of two old silk dresses, which had been given for sale. Now, when we were again penniless, 6s. was given me, just after I had been praying for means.

Jan. 28. Monday morning. We are now quite reduced as to means for the Orphans. The little which is in hand has been put by for rent. How the Lord will help us through this day, I know not; but I have faith in God. He will help us, though I know not how. By God's help I purpose not to take a single penny of what is in hand, because it is due for rent.--This morning and afternoon came in from one individual 4s. 6d., and from a sister, who earns her bread by needlework, 1l. There was also 1l. 0s. 10d. taken out of the boxes in the Orphan-Houses, which our need had led us to open. Thus we were helped through the day, and have 1l. left for tomorrow.

Jan. 29. The 1l. which was left helped us through this day; but in the Boys'-Orphan-House were no means to take in bread. In the evening eight small loaves were sent by a sister who could not possibly know our need, and thus we were supplied.

Jan, 30. A little while after I had been in prayer this morning for means for the Orphans, brother T. brought a silver watch and 5s., which had been given last evening. Also, still further, came in this morning five yards of Indian muslin, a zephyr scarf, a muslin dress, and a gold locket, to be sold. About two hours afterwards was sent 1l.

The individual who last evening gave the silver watch and 5s. for the Orphans, called on me today. She is a servant, who in the house of her master found the first part of this Narrative soon after the publication of the first edition, which the Lord used as the means of her conversion. [She fell asleep in Jesus, after having been 36 years in fellowship with us.]

Jan. 31. There came in this morning 2s. 6d. for the Orphans. This, with 1l. in hand, and 10s. which one of the labourers contributed, was sufficient for this day's necessities.

Feb. 1. There is no money in hand for the Orphans. I am waiting on God. Just when Brother T. had come to tell me that the need for this day would be 19s. 6d., one of the labourers in the work came and gave me 1l.

Feb. 2. There are again no means in hand. One of the labourers gave 1l., but I know not whether 1l. will be sufficient for the necessities of this day. This I do know, however, that the Lord will supply us with more, should more be needed. When I met with the brethren and sisters for prayer, one of the labourers gave his watch, under the condition that 1l., which was needed besides that which we had in hand, should be taken from the rent money which had been put by, till it could be replaced; and, if otherwise, that the watch should be sold at the end of the quarter. Just as we had separated, a sovereign was brought to me, which had been sent to my

SECOND PART

house since I had left it. This was taken instead of the one which had been advanced upon the watch, and thus a speedy answer was granted to our prayers. We have now been brought to the close of one more week.

Feb. 3. Lord's day. A sister sent from her sick bed this evening 2l. for the Orphans, with Ecclesiastes ix. 10. Thus the Lord has supplied our need for tomorrow.

Feb. 4. This afternoon came in two pounds more from the grandmother of two of the Orphans, in answer to prayer, and very seasonably, as the coals in one house are quite out, and nearly so in the other two.

Feb. 5. Today came in 12s., which supplied the necessities of this day.

Feb. 6. Only 10s. 6d. was needed for today, which one of the labourers gave.

Feb. 7. This day has been one of the most remarkable days as it regards the Funds. There was no money in hand, I was waiting upon God. I had asked him repeatedly, but no supplies came. Brother T. called between 11 and 12 o'clock, to tell me that about 1l. 2s. would be needed, to take in bread for the three houses, and to meet the other expenses; but we had only 2s. 9d., which yesterday had been taken out of the boxes in the Orphan-Houses. He went to Clifton to make arrangements for the reception of the three orphans of our sister Loader, who fell asleep on the 4th; for though we have no funds in hand, the work goes on, and our confidence is not diminished. I therefore requested him to call on his way back from Clifton, to see whether the Lord might have sent any money in the mean time. When he came I had received nothing, but one of the labourers, having 5s. of his own, gave it. It was now four o'clock. I knew not how the sisters had got through the day. Just before I went out to preach, 5s. was brought to my house, which I took as a token for good. I had been asking the Lord for a passage of the Word to speak from this evening, and at last was directed to Matt. vi. 19-34, a subject most applicable to our circumstances. After the meeting was over, I went to the Girls'-Orphan-House, to meet with the brethren for prayer, and to give the 5s. which I had received, and to see what could be done. When I arrived there, I found that a box had come for me from Barnstaple. The carriage was paid, else there would have been no money to pay for it. (See how the Lord's hand is in the smallest matters!) The box was opened, and it contained, in a letter from a sister, 10l., of which 8l. was for the Orphans, and 2l. for the Bible Fund; from brethren at Barnstaple, 2l. 11s. 2d.; and from another brother 5s. Besides this, there were in the box 4 yards of merino, 3 pairs of new shoes, 2 pairs of new socks: also six books for sale. Likewise a gold pencil-case, 2 gold rings, 2 gold drops of earrings, a necklace, and a silver pencil-case. On inquiry, how the sisters had been carried through the day, I found it thus: everything was in the houses which was needed for dinner. After dinner a lady from Thornbury came and bought one of my Narratives and one of the Reports, and gave 3s. besides. About five minutes afterwards the baker came to the Boys'-Orphan-House. The matron of the Girls'-Orphan-House seeing him, went immediately with the 6s. 6d. which she had just received, (to prevent his being sent away, as there was no money in hand at the Boys'-Orphan-

House,) and bought bread to the amount of 4s. 6d. The two remaining shillings, with the little which was in hand, served to buy bread for the Girls'-Orphan-House. By the donations sent in the box, I was enabled to give a rich supply to the matrons before the close of the day.

How sweet to see our Father thus caring for us! To a person who has spiritual eyes, what a proof is one such day of the most particular providence of God! And we have had many such days.

Feb. 8. Today the Lord sent still further help, which is remarkable for two reasons in particular. First, we had decided yesterday upon receiving the three little Loaders, though we were so low as to funds. Thus the Lord sent means on their behalf. Secondly, we were brought so low yesterday, and our faith was so much tried, in order that now again the abundance of supplies out of our loving Father's hand, might be so much the sweeter. A sister in the neighbourhood of London sent today in money 1l. 5s., and the following articles for sale; 3 purses, 1 mourning brooch, 1 amber ditto, 1 amethyst stud, 1 cameo ditto, I pair of coral ear rings, 1 coral cross, 1 ring set with a diamond and six rubies, 1 ditto pearl and garnet, 1 ditto garnet, 1 ruby cross, 4 necklaces, and 148 pamphlets and tracts. Also several articles of clothing for the children.

Feb. 13. Since the 8th, five donations, amounting to 9l. 9s., had come in. This afternoon I paid out the last money which we had in hand, and in giving it to brother T. said, we have now again to look to the Lord for further supplies. This evening 5l. was given to me, which had come in under the folio wing circumstances:--

A gentleman and lady visited the Orphan-Houses, and met at the Boys'-Orphan-House two ladies who were likewise visiting. One of the ladies said to the matron of the Boys'-Orphan-House: "Of course, you cannot carry on these institutions without a good stock of funds." The gentleman, turning to the matron, said, "Have you a good stock?" She replied: "Our funds are deposited in a bank which cannot break." The tears came into the eyes of the inquiring lady. The gentleman, on leaving, gave to the master of the boys 5l., which came in when I had not a penny in hand.

Feb. 16. Yesterday came in 17s. 6d. for the Orphans, which, with what was taken out of the boxes today, helped us through; and thus we have been brought to the close of one more week.

March 5. Up to this day, since Feb. 16, the supplies for the Orphans have come in so seasonably, that we were able comfortably to meet all the demands. Today, however, I knew that there would be again several pounds required, as, besides the daily provisions, there were coals needed, the treacle-casks in two houses were empty, and there was but 5s. in hand. I gave myself therefore to prayer this morning. WHILST I WAS IN PRAYER, Q. Q. sent a cheque for 7l. 10s. Thus the Lord has again most seasonably helped us out of our difficulty. There came in still further this day, 1l. 19s. 2d., by the sale of some articles, which had been given for the benefit of the Orphans.

March 6. For some time past the minds of several brethren among us, as well as that of brother Craik and my own, had been much exercised respecting certain questions connected with points of church order and discipline, on account of which brother Craik and I were absent from Bristol during the last two weeks, to give ourselves to prayer and consideration respecting those points. Since our return we have had, these last three evenings, meetings with the saints, before whom we stated the result to which we had been led, after prayer and examination of the Scriptures. The following is an abstract of what was stated at those meetings, which I give here, as this matter forms an important period in my experience about church matters; but the abstract will be of little use, except the reader consider carefully the passages to which reference is made.

I.--QUESTIONS RESPECTING THE ELDERSHIP.

(1) How does it appear to be the mind of God, that, in every Church, there should be recognized Elders?

Ans. From the following passages compared together, Matth. xxiv. 45, Luke xii. 42. From these passages we learn that some are set by the Lord Himself in the office of Rulers and Teachers, and that this office (in spite of the fallen state of the Church) should be in being even down to the close of the present dispensation. Accordingly, we find from Acts xiv. 23, xx. 17, Tit. i. 5, and 1 Pet. v. 1, that soon after the saints had been converted, and had associated together in a Church character, Elders were appointed to take the rule over them and to fulfil the office of under-shepherds.

This must not be understood as implying, that, when believers are associated in Church fellowship, they ought to elect Elders according to their own will, whether the Lord may have qualified persons or not; but rather that such should wait upon God, that He Himself would be pleased to raise up such as may be qualified for teaching and ruling in His church.

(2) How do such come into office?

Ans. By the appointment of the Holy Ghost, Acts xx. 28.

(3) How may this appointment be made known to the individuals called to the office, and to those amongst whom they may be called to labour?

Ans. By the secret call of the Spirit, 1 Tim. iii. 1, confirmed by the possession of the requisite qualifications, 1 Tim. iii. 2-7, Tit. i. 6-9, and by the Lord's blessing resting upon their labours, 1 Cor. ix. 2.

In 1 Cor. ix. 2, Paul condescends to the weakness of some, who were in danger of being led away by those factious persons who questioned his authority. As an Apostle—appointed by the express word of the Lord--he needed not such outward confirmation. But if he used his success as an argument in confirmation of his call, how much more may ordinary servants of the Lord Jesus employ such an argument, seeing that the way, in which they are called for the work, is such as to require some outward confirmation.

(4) Is it incumbent upon the saints to acknowledge such and to submit to them in the Lord?

Ans. Yes. See 1 Cor. xvi. 15, 16, 1 Thess. v. 12, 13, Heb. xiii. 7, 17, and 1 Tim. v. 17. In these passages obedience to pastoral authority is clearly enjoined.

II.--Ought matters of discipline to be finally settled by the Elders in private, or in the presence of the Church, and as the act of the whole body?

Ans. (1) Such matters are to be finally settled in the presence of the Church. This appears from Matth. xviii. 17, 1 Cor. v. 4, 5, 2 Cor. ii. 6-8, 1 Tim. v. 20. (2) Such matters are to be finally settled as the act of the whole body, Matth. xviii. 17, 18. In this passage the act of exclusion is spoken of as the act of the whole body. 1 Cor. v. 4, 5, 7, 12, 13. In this passage Paul gives the direction, respecting the exercise of discipline, in such a way as to render the whole body responsible: verse 7, "Purge out the old leaven, that ye maybe a new lump;" and verse 13, "Therefore put away from among yourselves that wicked person." From 2 Cor. ii. 6-8, we learn that the act of exclusion was not the act of the Elders only, but of the Church. "Sufficient to such a man is this punishment (rather, public censure) which was inflicted of many." From verse 8 we learn that the act of restoration was to be a public act of the brethren: "Wherefore I beseech you that ye would confirm (rather ratify by a public act) your love towards him."

As to the reception of brethren into fellowship, this is an act of simple obedience to the Lord, both on the part of the Elders and the whole Church. We are bound and privileged to receive all those who make a credible profession of faith in Christ, according to that Scripture, "Receive ye one another, as Christ also received us, to the glory of God." Rom. xv. 7.

III.--When should Church acts (such as acts of reception, restoration, exclusion, &c.) be attended to?

Ans. It cannot be expressly proved from Scripture, whether such acts were attended to at the meeting for the breaking of bread, or at any other meeting; therefore

SECOND PART

this is a point on which, if different churches differ, mutual forbearance ought to be exercised. The way in which such matters have hitherto been managed amongst us has been by the Church coming together on a week-evening. Before we came to Bristol we had been accustomed to this mode, and, finding nothing in Scripture against it, we continued the practice. But, after prayer, and more careful consideration of this point, it has appeared well to us that such acts should be attended to on the Lord's days, when the saints meet together for the breaking of bread. We have been induced to make this alteration by the following reasons:--

(1) This latter mode prevents matters from being delayed. There not being a sufficiency of matter for a meeting on purpose every week, it has sometimes happened, that, what would better have been stated to the Church at once, has been kept back from the body for some weeks. Now, it is important that what concerns the whole Church, should be made known as soon as possible to those who are in fellowship, that they may act accordingly. Delay, moreover, seems inconsistent with the pilgrim-character of the people of God.

(2) More believers can be present on the Lord's days than can attend on week evenings. The importance of this reason will appear from considering how everything which concerns the Church should be known to as many as possible. For how can the saints pray for those who may have to be excluded,--how can they sympathize in cases of peculiar trial,--and how can they rejoice and give thanks on account of those who may be received or restored, unless they are made acquainted with the facts connected with such cases?

(3) A testimony is thus given that all who break bread are Church members. By attending to Church acts in the meeting for breaking of bread, we show that we make no difference between receiving into fellowship at the Lord's supper, and into Church membership; but that the individual who is admitted to the Lord's table is therewith also received to all the privileges, trials, and responsibilities of Church membership.

(4) There is a peculiar propriety in acts of reception, restoration and exclusion being attended to when the saints meet together for the breaking of bread, as, in that ordinance especially, we show forth our fellowship with each other.

Objections answered.

(1) This alteration has the appearance of changeableness.

Reply. Such an objection would apply to any case in which increased light led to any improvement, and is, therefore, not to be regarded. It would be an evil thing if there were any change respecting the foundation truths of the Gospel; but the point in question is only a matter of Church order.

(2) More time may thus be required than it would be well to give to such a purpose on the Lord's day.

Reply. As, according to this plan, Church business will be attended to every Lord's day, it is more than probable that the meetings will be thereby prolonged for a few minutes only; but should circumstance required it, a special meeting may still be appointed during the week, for all who break bread with us. This, however, would only be needful, provided the matters to be brought before the brethren were to require more time than could be given to them at the breaking of bread.

N.B. (1) Should any persons be present who do not break bread with us, they may be requested to withdraw, whenever such points require to be stated, as it would not be well to speak of in the presence of unbelievers.

(2) As there are two places in which the saints meet for the breaking of bread, the matters connected with Church acts must be brought out at each place.

IV.--QUESTIONS RELATIVE TO THE LORD'S SUPPER.

(1) How frequently ought the breaking of bread to be attended to?

Ans. Although we have no express command respecting the frequency of its observance, yet the example of the apostles and of the first disciples would lead us to observe this ordinance every Lord's day. Acts xx. 7.

(2) What ought to be the character of the meeting at which the saints are assembled for the breaking of bread?

Ans. As in this ordinance we show forth our common participation in all the benefits of our Lord's death, and our union to Him and to each other (1 Cor. x. 16, 17,) opportunity ought to be given for the exercise of the gifts of teaching or exhortation, and communion in prayer and praise. Rom. xii. 4—8, Eph. iv. 11—16. The manifestation of our common participation in each other's gifts cannot be fully given at such meetings, if the whole meeting is, necessarily, conducted by one individual. This mode of meeting does not however take off from those, who have the gifts of teaching or exhortation, the responsibility of edifying the church, as opportunity may be offered.

(3) Is it desirable that the bread should be broken at the Lord's Supper by one of the Elders, or should each individual of the body break it for himself?

SECOND PART

Ans. Neither way can be so decidedly proved from Scripture, that we are warranted in objecting to the other as positively unscriptural, yet--

(1) The letter of Scripture seems rather in favour of its being done by each brother and sister, 1 Cor. x. 16, 17. "The bread which we break."

(2) Its being done by each of the disciples, is more fitted to express that we all, by our sins, have broken the body of our Lord.

(3) By attending to the ordinance in this way, we manifest our freedom from the common error that the Lord's supper must be administered by some particular individual, possessed of what is called a ministerial character, instead of being an act of social worship and obedience.

[Before brother Craik and I left Bristol for the consideration of the above points, things wore a gloomy appearance. A separation in the church seemed to be unavoidable. But God had mercy, and pitied us. He was pleased to give us not merely increased light, but showed us also how to act, and gave us a measure of wisdom, grace and spiritual courage for acting. The clouds were dispelled, and peace was restored in the church.]

While I was away from Bristol, Samuel Loader, a little orphan boy, died, after a fortnight's residence in the house, and only three weeks after his mother's death. The brethren in the Boys-Orphan-House consider him to have died in the faith.

March 16. Saturday. By the good hand of the Lord we are brought to the close of one more week. I have been able to meet all the current expenses for the Orphans, and to pay, besides this, 10l. for salaries. Thus a part of what has been due for several weeks to my dear fellow-labourers is defrayed. I have especially prayed within the last ten days that the Lord would be pleased to give me the means for this. 2s. 8 1/2d. I have left.

March 18. Monday. Last evening 5l. came in with Eccles. ix. 10. Thus we were again enabled to supply all the necessities of this day.

Pause a few moments, dear reader! Consider how seasonably the Lord sends the supplies! Not once does He forget us! Not once is our need only half supplied! Not once do His supplies come too late! Dear reader, if you have not the like experience of the Lord's watchful care, Oh taste and see that the Lord is good!

March 20. The need of the 18th and 19th was supplied by the 5l. which had come in on the 18th. Today we were again poor and needy, therefore the Lord thought on us, and sent us 3l. 16s. 1 1/2d.

March 22. Some trinkets which had been given, and 12s. which was in hand, supplied the need of today. Yesterday were sent six sacks of potatoes. We were not able to lay in a stock last autumn (as we had done the two previous autumns) on account of want of means, but in no previous year have we had so many sent.

March 23. Today I received a letter from brother T., who is on account of his health in Devonshire, to inform me that a heavy gold chain, a ring set with ten brilliants, a pair of gold bracelets, and 2l. have been given to him. He gave a Report to a brother, who, having read it, was thereby stirred up to prayer, and knowing that his believing sister possessed these trinkets, he asked the Lord to incline her heart to give them up for the benefit of our Orphans, which she soon after did. By means of these donations I am able both to meet the remaining expenses of this week, and also to pay 15l., which still remains due on account of the salaries. My fellow-labourers not only never ask me for any thing, but are willing to part with money, or any thing else in the hour of need; nevertheless, I had asked the Lord about this point frequently, and He has now given me my request, whereof I am glad. I received also this afternoon 5l. 10s., besides a number of things to be disposed of for the Orphans.

March 24. The Lord has again kindly opened His liberal hand today, and given us 6l. 10s. Thus we have wherewith to meet the necessities of tomorrow in the Orphan-Houses.

From March 24 to April 7, came in about sixty small donations. This, with the produce of the sale of the trinkets, supplied all our need for the Orphans.

April 7. Our funds were now again spent, except 15s., though three days ago above 30l. had come in; therefore the Lord has sent in again this day several contributions, altogether 6l. 5s.

April 8. The money which came in yesterday was sent off today for housekeeping in the three different houses, and when I was now again left penniless, there came in 2l. 6s. 10d.

April 9. The 2l. 6s. 10d. was given out today for housekeeping, and I am once more penniless.--A few hours after I had written this, there was given to me by a brother 2l. 10s. When I received this money, I was at the same time informed of the death of one of our sisters, a widow, whose child we can receive.

April 10. Today was sent anonymously from the country 5l. In the evening I received still further 1l. 16s. 6d.

April 11. It is three years today since the first Orphans were received. Good indeed has the Lord been to us during these three years! We have lacked nothing! Again He has sent this day, in a remarkable manner, 5l., with the following letter, addressed to a brother:

"My dear Friend, enclosed are 5l. for the Orphan-Asylum, the history of which is rather interesting. We have a servant who lived some years ago as kitchen-maid in a noble family (i. e. the master a wealthy member of Parliament, the mistress an Earl's daughter.) No perquisites were allowed; but the individual in question acted on the same principle as her fellow-servants, and sold kitchen-stuff for her own benefit, which she thinks might amount to 4l.; and therefore she believes that 5l. would fully repay principal and interest. This money is of course due to her former master and mistress, with whom I have had several interviews on the subject. They were disposed that the money should be given to some charity; and in consequence of reading one of the Reports you kindly sent me, the young woman had a great desire that her own repentance might yield fruit to that work of faith and love. Her wishes have been sanctioned by her former mistress. It is rather remarkable that our truly Christian servant had been converted a year and a half, before this individual sin, calling for pecuniary restitution, had come into her remembrance."

April 13. I conversed with another of the Orphans, who seems to have been truly converted, and who has walked consistently for many months. Tomorrow she will be united with the saints in communion. She will be the third in fellowship with us, and several have died in the faith. How has the Lord owned the work, even in this respect!

April 14. Today 5l. 0s. 8d. came in for the Orphans, 1l. of which is one of the most remarkable gifts that we have ever had. A poor brother, with a large family, and small wages (there are eight in the family, and he had 15s. wages till lately, when they were raised to 18s.) put by this money by little and little of what was given him by his master for beer. This brother, who was converted about five years ago, was before that time a notorious drunkard.

April 30. Today our dear young brother, John Short, only a little more than 14 years old, fell asleep, after having been for several years ill. He had been for several years converted. He was one of our Sunday-School children before his illness. When, many months since, he lost one of his limbs by amputation, he glorified the Lord not merely by the way in which he sustained the severe suffering attending the operation, but also by confessing the Lord, as his strength, in the hour of trial. He was a sweet youth!

July 2. Today was given me, when there was not one shilling in hand, 50l. for the School—Bible—and Missionary-Fund.

July 15. Monday. Today 2l. 7s. 3d. was needed for the Orphans, but we had nothing. How to obtain the means for a dinner, and for what else was needed, I knew not. My heart was perfectly at peace, and unusually sure of help, though I knew not in the least whence it was to come. Before brother T. came, I received a letter from India, written in May, with an order for 50l. for the Orphans. I had said last Saturday to brother T., that it would be desirable to have 50l., as the salaries of all my fellow-labourers are due, the three treacle-casks empty, all the provision stores exhausted, several articles of clothing needed, and worsted for the boys to go on with their knitting. Now the Lord has sent exactly 50l. Moreover this money comes very seasonably, as in three days I shall have to leave Bristol for some days, and can now go comfortably, as it regards leaving means behind.

[In the afternoon of this same day I met at a brother's house with several believers, when a sister said that she had often thought about the care and burden I must have on my mind, as it regards obtaining the necessary supplies for so many persons. As this may not be a solitary instance, I would state, that, by the grace of God, this is no cause of anxiety to me. The children I have years ago cast upon the Lord. The whole work is His, and it becomes me to be without carefulness. In whatever points I am lacking, in this point I am able, by the grace of God, to roll the burden upon my heavenly Father. Though now (July 1845) for about seven years our funds have been so exhausted, that it has been comparatively a rare case that there have been means in hand to meet the necessities of the Orphans for three days together; yet have I been only once tried in spirit, and that was on Sept. 18, 1838, when for the first time the Lord seemed not to regard our prayer. But when He did send help at that time, and I saw that it was only for the trial of our faith, and not because He had forsaken the work that we were brought so low, my soul was so strengthened and encouraged, that I have not only not been allowed to distrust the Lord since that time, but I have not even been cast down when in the deepest poverty. Nevertheless, in this respect also am I now, as much as ever, dependant on the Lord; and I earnestly beseech for myself and my fellow-labourers the prayers of all those, to whom the glory of God is dear. How great would be the dishonour to the name of God, if we, who have so publicly made our boast in Him, should so fall as to act in these very points as the world does! Help us then, brethren, with your prayers, that we may trust in God to the end. We can expect nothing but that our faith will yet be tried, and it may be more than ever; and we shall fall, if the Lord does not uphold us.]

July 16 and 17. These two days we have had two especial prayer meetings, to commend to the Lord five German brethren who for some weeks have been sojourning among us, and who purpose to leave tomorrow for Liverpool, to sail from thence to the East Indies.

July 18. I left this morning with the German brethren, to accompany them to Liverpool.

July 21. Liverpool. This afternoon I preached in the open air on the docks. Truly, it must be a sweet privilege to be permitted frequently to proclaim the glad tidings of the Gospel in the open air, which the Lord does not bestow upon me, as, under ordinary circumstances, I have no strength for this work.--The people were attentive. There was but one who mocked.

July 22. Preached again out of doors.

July 23. I accompanied the five brethren on board this afternoon.

SECOND PART

July 27. Today I had another remarkable proof of the importance of the children of God opening their hearts to each other, especially when they are getting into a cold state, or are under the power of a certain sin, or are in especial difficulty. An individual called on me, who I trust is a brother, with whom I had conversed once before, but felt uncomfortable respecting him. When he called again today, it appeared to me that there was something upon his heart, which, if I could but know, I might be instrumental in benefiting him. I pressed him affectionately to open his heart, assuring him at the same time that the matter which he might speak of should remain in my own bosom. At last I succeeded. [The result of this conversation was, that the advice which I gave him, led him, after three days, to leave for America, where he ought to have been, instead of being in England; and if he has followed my advice, in one other point, the matter which for years had burdened his conscience, and which, no doubt had been the means of keeping him in a low spiritual state, will have no more power over him. Should this fall into the hands of any children of God who have a particular trial or burden, or a guilty conscience, on account of a particular thing, or a besetting sin, etc., on account of which it would be beneficial to open their hearts to another child of God, in whose love, spiritual judgment, etc., they have confidence, I would advise them to do so. I know from my own experience, how often the snare of the devil has been broken, when under the power of sin; how often the heart has been comforted, when nigh to be overwhelmed; how often advice, under great perplexity, has been obtained,--by opening my heart to a brother in whom I had confidence. We are children of the same family, and ought therefore to be helpers one of another.]

Aug. 3. £3. 5s. was required to meet the necessities of the Orphan-Houses this day. The Lord enabled us to meet this demand, partly, by the sale of some Indian muslin, which had been given some months since, but which was only now disposed of; partly, by a few small donations; and partly, by what one of the labourers added of his own. [We have often found that the money for articles, which were put out to be sold, has come in most seasonably. At this time it happened so that a brother, into whose hands the muslin had been put, felt himself stirred up to go and ask the individual who had it for sale whether she had disposed of it. This brother knew nothing about our need at that time.]

Aug. 5. Monday. On Saturday and yesterday morning I had repeatedly asked the Lord to send us help, as there was not a penny in hand for the need of today. Yesterday morning a brother gave me two sovereigns, and in the evening I received two more. Besides this, there was 4l. 10s. anonymously given for three weeks' rent for the Orphan-Houses, also 10s. by a brother, and 9s. came in for needlework of the children; so that altogether 9l. 9s. came in yesterday.

This evening I took tea with a sister who purposes to leave Bristol tomorrow for Van Diemen's Land. [For the comfort of any saints, who may be similarly situated, I mention the following circumstance. The son of this sister was transported many years since. In the course of time he obtained a business of his own in Van Diemen's Land, and wished his mother to come to him. The mother went, and had, in answer to the prayers of the saints, a prosperous voyage. When she arrived, she found her son truly converted. What a joy for the long and deeply afflicted mother! What remarkable means the Lord uses to bestow blessings! Moreover, to mark that the Lord had sent her to her son, she found that a month before her arrival his wife had died, and that she therefore reached him just at the right time, both on account of his children and his business.]

Aug. 7. Today again about 3l. was needed for housekeeping at the Orphan-Houses, which the Lord had sent in since the day before yesterday, so that we were able to meet all the demands.

Aug. 8. Today 1l. 3s. was needed, but only 3s. had come in. The deficiency was supplied by one of the labourers giving a sovereign of his own. Though there is no money in hand, yet are we so little discouraged, that we have received today one orphan boy, and have given notice for the admission of six other children, which will bring the number up to 98 altogether.

Aug. 9. Only 10s. had come in since yesterday, and as 30s. were needed, one of the labourers gave a sovereign.

Aug. 10. Saturday. The need of today is 2l. 10s. but only 10s, has been given since yesterday. One of the labourers, having 2l., gave it, and thus our need was supplied.

Aug. 12. Monday. The Lord has again kindly sent 11l. Of this sum 10l. came in from Q. Q., when again there was not one penny in hand. We have now supplies for about four days.

Aug. 14. Today was very seasonably sent a whole piece of calico and a piece of print.

Aug. 16. All our money is now again gone. Today 1l. 3s. was needed, but only 3s. was in hand. One of the labourers was able to add a sovereign, and thus we were helped.

Aug. 17. Saturday. 5l. was needed today, but only 7s. 6d. had come in. The remaining 2l. 12s. 6d. one of the labourers gave. Thus we were helped to the close of another week.

Aug. 19. Monday. This has been again a day in which our faith has been particularly tried; but even this day we have not been confounded. Not one penny was in hand when the day began. We had therefore now, for more than one hundred persons, again to look to the Lord. But this I must say, to the praise of the Lord, my soul was perfectly at peace. I meant to have gone very early to the Orphan-Houses to meet with my fellow-labourers for prayer; but, as one person after the other called upon me, I was kept from it the whole morning. When brother T. called upon me between 12 and 1 o'clock for money, I had none to give. In the afternoon at four I was able to meet with the brethren and sisters. When I came to the Girls'-Orphan-House, I found that one of those children, for the reception of whom we had given notice, had been brought from Bath, and with him was sent 1l. 5s. After the meeting was over, one of the labourers gave 10s. By means of this 1l. 15s. we were able for this day also to provide every thing needful.

Aug. 20. When we met together this morning for prayer, only one shilling had come in since yesterday, and 2l. at least was needed to meet the expenses of this day. After prayer, one of the labourers gave 10s., and 1s. 1 1/2d. was taken out of one of the boxes. This 12s. 1 1/2d. was divided to meet the momentary need. About an hour afterwards, 1l. 14s. came in, being the payment, in part, of articles which had been sold several months since.

Aug. 21. Nothing had come in since yesterday. 13s. would have been needed to have taken in the usual quantity of bread. After we had prayed, the same labourer who had contributed yesterday and the day before, gave today 5s. more. This helped us to buy milk; but in one of the houses the usual quantity of bread could not be taken in. I have further to notice respecting this time of trial, that I had purposed to have gone yesterday to Bath, to meet today and tomorrow with several brethren, who are met there from various parts of the country, to unite in prayer for the present spiritual necessities of the church at large. However, on account of our present need in the Orphan-Houses, I could not go yesterday, as I did not think it right to let my fellow-labourers bear the trial alone. Today also I have been kept here, as our poverty is greater than ever. Yet (the Lord be praised!) neither have the children in the least lacked this day, nor has my mind been in any degree disturbed. My fellow-labourers also seem quite in peace. We are waiting for deliverance, and we are sure that the Lord, in His own time, will send it.

Aug. 22. In my morning walk, when I was reminding the Lord of our need, I felt assured that He would send help this day. My assurance sprang from our need; for there seemed no way to get through the day, without help being sent. After breakfast I considered whether there was any thing which might be turned into money for the dear children. Among other things, there came under my hands a number of religious pamphlets which had been given for the benefit of the Orphans; but all seemed not nearly enough, to meet the necessities of the day, In this our deep poverty, after I had gathered together the few things for sale, a sister, who earns her bread by the labour of her hands, brought 82l. This sister had seen it to be binding upon believers in our Lord Jesus to act out His commandments: "Sell that ye have (sell your possessions) and give alms," Luke xii. 33; and "Lay not up for yourselves treasures upon earth," Matt. vi. 19. Accordingly she had drawn her money out of the bank and stocks, being 250l., and had brought it to me at three different times for the benefit of the Orphans, the Bible—Missionary—and School-Fund, and the poor saints, About two months ago she brought me 100l. more, being the produce of some other possession which she had sold, the half of which was to be used for the School—Bible-and Missionary Fund; and the other half for the poor saints. This 82l. which she had brought today, is the produce of the sale of her last earthly possession.--[At the time I am preparing the seventh edition for the press, more than twenty-nine years have passed away, and this sister has never expressed the least regret as to the step she took, but goes on, quietly labouring with her hands, to earn her bread.]--But even now, when this money was given, I left it in the hands of the Lord, whether any part of it should be applied for the Orphans. I asked the sister, therefore, whether she wished the money to be spent in any particular way, as she had expressed her wish about the former sums. This time she left it with me, to lay out the money as I thought best. I took, therefore, half of it for the Orphans, and half for the other objects of the Scriptural Knowledge Institution. I have thus been enabled to come to Bath, (after I had sent a more than usual supply to the matrons), to meet, at least for the remaining time, with the brethren who are assembled here for prayer. Before the day is over, I have received 10l. more, while at Bath, from one of the brethren who are assembled here; so that our deep poverty, in the morning, has been turned into a comparative abundance.

Aug. 23. The Lord has sent still further supplies. Another of the brethren gave me this morning 1l., and a third, with whom I drove back to Bristol, 5l.

From Aug. 25 to Sept. 1, there came in above 17l. more.

Sept. 4. I have been led to pray whether it is the Lord's will that I should leave Bristol for a season, as I have for the last fortnight been suffering from indigestion, by which my whole system is weakened, and thus the nerves of my head are more than usually affected. There are, however, two hindrances in the way, want of means for the Orphans, and want of means for my own personal expenses.--Today I have received a cheque from Q. Q. for 7l. 10s. for the Orphans, which came, therefore, very seasonably. Also 4l. besides has came in since the day before yesterday.

Sept. 5. Today a sister sent me 5l. for myself, to be used for the benefit of my health. She had heard that my health is again failing. I do not lay by money for such purposes; but whenever I really need means, whether for myself or others, the Lord sends them, in answer to prayer; for He had in this case again given me prayer respecting means for myself and for the Orphans, that my way might be made plain as to leaving Bristol for a season.

Sept. 6. My body is now so weak, and my head again so affected in consequence of it, and I have found it needful to give up the work at once. I left today for Trowbridge, for three days, intending afterwards to go with my wife into Devonshire, if the Lord permit.

Sept. 7. Trowbridge. This has been a very good day. I have had much communion with the Lord. How kind to take me from the work at Bristol for a season, to give me more communion with Himself. I remembered the Lord's especial goodness to me in this place, at the commencement of last year. How kind has He also been since! I prayed much for myself, for the Church at large, for the saints here and in

SECOND PART

Bristol, for my unconverted relatives, for my dear wife, and that the Lord would supply my own temporal necessities and those of the Orphans:--and I know that He has heard me.--I am surrounded with kind friends in the dear saints, under whose roof I am, and feel quite at home. My room is far better than I need; yet an easy chair, in this my weak state of body, to kneel before in prayer, would have added to my comfort. In the afternoon, without having given a hint about it, I found an easy chair put into my room. I was struck with the kindness, the especial kindness of my heavenly Father, in being mindful of the smallest wants and comforts of His child.--Having had more prayer than usual, I found that my intercourse with the saints at tea was with unction, and more than usually profitable. But this very fact reminds me of my sad deficiencies, and of my great lack of real fervency of spirit. May the Lord carry on His work with power in my soul! Today I had 1l. given to me, half for the Orphans, and half for the other funds. Thus the Lord has begun to answer my prayers; for I expect far more.

Sept. 8. Lord's day. I assembled with a few saints at Trowbridge, and spoke to them in the morning and evening with much assistance. The afternoon I spent at home over the Word and in prayer. God has evidently blessed the Word. He had a purpose in sending me here, both for blessing to myself and to others.

Sept. 9. This morning I conversed with a poor aged sister in the Lord, who for 47 years has been a believer, but who, from want of settling by the written Word only, whether she is a believer or not, has often had doubts about her state before God. However, I brought the Scriptures only before her. [My pressing the Scriptures alone upon her heart, was made such a blessing, that I hear she has not doubted in the same way since.] This aged sister told me she often prays for the Orphans, and for the continuance of means. How many helpers has the Christian in the conflict; yet all are strengthened by ONE who is ALWAYS for us!

This evening I returned to Bristol, to go from hence tomorrow to Exeter, if the Lord permit, on account of my health. I had been earnestly asking the Lord, while I was staying at Trowbridge, that He would be pleased to send in supplies for the Orphans, before I go into Devonshire, and I had the fullest assurance that means would come in before I left Bristol. I therefore asked my wife, on my return, how much had come in, and found that it was only 8l. 9s. 7 3/4d. This was not nearly as much as I had expected, and would not answer the end for which I had particularly asked means, i. e. that I might be able to leave enough for several days. My reply therefore was, according to the faith given to me, and judging from the earnestness and confidence of my prayer, that the Lord would send more before I left. About an hour after, brother Craik brought me 10l., which he had received this evening with Ecclesiastes ix. 10, and also a letter from a brother at Ilfracombe, in which the arrival of a large box, full of articles, to be sold for the benefit of the Orphans, is announced. Thus the Lord has dealt with me according to my faith.

Sept. 10. This morning before I left Bristol came in still further 1l. 16s. 7d., so that I had about 20l. to leave behind for the present need. I found also, on opening the box which has arrived, 65 books, a brace of valuable pistols, and a great many articles of East India linen. How kind of the Lord to send these supplies just now!

After my departure from Bristol I continued to help my fellow-labourers by my prayers. I had the fullest assurance that the Lord would help them, and my hope was not ashamed, as will appear from the following part of the journal.--In the evening of Sept. 10th, we arrived in Exeter, where we were lodged by a brother, who on the following day left for Plymouth. The love of this brother constrained us to remain for five days at his house, though he was absent, leaving us all the house with a sister, as a servant, to ourselves. Though at another time I should have preferred the opportunity of having intercourse with this brother, yet now, in this my weak state of body, the being left alone was the very thing which suited me. I could not but trace the kind hand of God in this circumstance. I was able to speak twice publicly while in Exeter. I rejoiced at what I saw there of the work of God. This city was in the year 1830 especially laid on my heart, when I used frequently to preach there; but then there was a great spiritual deadness.

From Sept. 16th to Sept. 28th we were at Teignmouth my former field of labour. I had not seen the brethren, among whom I used to labour, since May, 1833. The Lord gave me strength, many times to minister in the Word among them, during the time of my stay there. At Teignmouth also, I had, in some respects, reason to be glad, particularly in that I saw some of those truths practised, and that more fully and intelligently, which, though in much weakness and indistinctly, I had sought to set forth whilst labouring there. At Teignmouth also, as well as in Exeter, the saints showed us much love. A brother and sister lodged us during the whole of our stay. May the Lord reward them for their love!--While I was at Teignmouth I received on Sept. 18th, the following letter from brother T., in reference to the work in Bristol:--

Bristol, Sept. 16, 1839.

My dear Brother, I have delayed writing until now, that, as I hoped, I might have additional news to tell you after the Lord's day. And now that my hope has been made good, I rejoice to do so. The Lord has dealt most graciously with us since your departure. The children, brother B. and the sisters are well, and the wants of the Orphans have been abundantly supplied. There has come in altogether 24l. 8s. 6d., &c.

On Sept. 24th, I received another letter from brother T., dated Bristol, Sept. 23rd, in which he writes: "It rejoices me that I have still nothing but the goodness of the Lord to tell you of. That little word 'Ebenezer' is at once our encouragement and our daily song, of which we are not weary. I have received since the last information you had from me 5l. 17s. 4 1/4d., besides 1l. 10s. for the rent of the Orphan-Houses."

On Sept. 28th, while I was at Teignmouth, a brother asked me about the funds for the Orphans, being willing to help, and I had reason to believe considerably, if they were in need. Though I knew not for a certainty that there was one shilling in

SECOND PART

hand in Bristol, yet for the Lord's sake I declined telling him any thing about the funds, in order that the work might evidently be carried on by dealing with the Lord Himself.

On Sept. 28th we left Teignmouth for Plymouth, being taken by the love of a brother from Teignmouth to Newton Bushel in his own little carriage. At Plymouth we found again a kind brother waiting at the coach office, to receive us. He took us to his house and lodged us till our departure, on Oct. 6th. During my stay at Plymouth, I was stirred up afresh to early rising, a blessing, the results of which I have not lost since. That which led me to it was the example of the brother in whose house I was staying, and a remark which he made in speaking on the sacrifices in Leviticus, "That as not the refuse of the animals was to be offered up, so the best part of our time should be especially given to communion with the Lord." I had been, on the whole, rather an early riser during former years. But since the nerves of my head had been so weak, I thought, that, as the day was long enough for my strength, it would be best for me not to rise early, in order that thus the nerves of my head might have the longer quiet. On this account I rose only between six and seven, and sometimes after seven. For the same reason also I brought myself purposely into the habit of sleeping a quarter of an hour, or half an hour, after dinner: as I thought I found benefit from it, in quieting the nerves of my head. In this way, however, my soul had suffered more or less every day, and sometimes considerably, as now and then unavoidable work came upon me before I had had sufficient time for prayer and reading the Word. After I had heard the remark to which I have alluded, I determined, that whatever my body might suffer, I would no longer let the most precious part of the day pass away while I was in bed. By the grace of God I was enabled to begin the very next day to rise earlier, and have continued to rise early since that time. I allow myself now about seven hours' sleep, which, though I am far from being strong, and have much to tire me mentally, I find is quite sufficient to refresh me. In addition to this I gave up the sleeping after dinner. The result has been that I have thus been able to procure long and precious seasons for prayer and meditation before breakfast; and, as to my body, and the state of the nervous system in particular, I have been much better since. Indeed I believe that the very worst thing I could have done for my weak nerves was, to have lain an hour or more longer in bed than I used to do before my illness; for it was the very way to keep them weak.--As this may fall into the hands of some children of God who are not in the habit of rising early, I make a few more remarks on the subject.

I. It might be asked, how much time shall I allow myself for rest? The answer is, that no rule of universal application can be given, as all persons do not require the same measure of sleep, and also the same persons, at different times, according to the strength or weakness of their body, may require more or less. Females also, being generally weaker in body, require more sleep than males. Yet, from what I can learn, it is the opinion of medical persons, that men in health do not require more than between six and seven hours sleep, and females no more than between seven and eight hours; so that it would be rather an exception, for a man to require more than seven and a woman more than eight hours. But my decided advice, at the same time, is, that children of God should be careful not to allow themselves too little sleep, as there are few men who can do with less than six hours sleep, and yet be well in body and mind, and few females who can do with less than seven hours. Certain it is that for a long time, as a young man before I went to the university, I went to bed regularly at ten and rose at four, studied hard, and was in good health; and certain also, that since I have allowed myself only about seven hours, from the time of my visit at Plymouth in Oct. 1839, I have been much better in body, and in my nerves in particular, than when I was eight or eight hours and a half in bed.

II. If it be asked, but why should I rise early? The reply is, to remain too long in bed is 1. waste of time, which is unbecoming a saint, who is bought by the precious blood of Jesus, with his time and all he has, to be used for the Lord. If we sleep more than is needful for the refreshment of the body, it is wasting the time with which the Lord has intrusted us as a talent, to be used for His glory, for our own benefit, and the benefit of the saints and the unbelievers around us. 2. To remain too long in bed injures the body. Just as when we take too much food, we are injured thereby, so as it regards sleep. Medical persons would readily allow, that, the lying longer in bed than is needful for the strengthening of the body, does weaken it. 3. It injures the soul. The lying too long in bed, not merely keeps us from giving the most precious part of the day to prayer and meditation, but this sloth leads also to many other evils.--Any one need but make the experiment of spending one, two, or three hours in prayer and meditation before breakfast, either in his room, or with his Bible in his hand in the fields, and he will soon find out the beneficial effect which early rising has upon the outward and inward man. I beseech all my brethren and sisters into whose hand this may fall, and who are not in the habit of rising early, to make the trial, and they will praise the Lord for having done so.

III. It may lastly be said, but how shall I set about rising early? My advice is, 1. Commence at once, delay it not. Tomorrow begin to rise. 2. But do not depend upon your own strength. This may be the reason why, before this, you may have begun to rise early, but have given it up. As surely as you depend upon your own strength in this matter, it will come to nothing. In every good work we depend upon the Lord, and in this thing we shall feel especially how weak we are. If any one rises that he may give the time which he takes from sleep, to prayer and meditation, let him be sure that Satan will try to put obstacles in the way. 3. Do trust in the Lord for help, You will honour Him, if you expect help from Him in this matter. Give yourself to prayer for help, expect help, and you will have it. 4. Use, however, in addition to this, the following means: a, Go early to bed. If you stay up late, you cannot rise early. Let no society and no pressure of engagements keep you from going habitually early to bed. If you fail in this, you neither can nor ought to get up early, as your body requires rest. Keep also particularly in mind, that neither for the body nor the soul is it the same thing, whether you go to bed late and rise late, or whether you go to bed early and rise early. Even medical persons will tell you how injurious it is to sit up late, and to spend the morning hours in bed; but how much more important still is it to retire early and to rise early, in order to make sure of time for prayer and meditation before the business of the day commences, and to devote to those exercises that part of our time, when the mind and the body are most fresh, in order thus to obtain spiritual strength for the conflict, the trials, and the work of the day. b, Let some one call you, if possible, at the time which you have determined before God that you will rise; or procure, what is still better, an alarum, by which you may regulate almost to a minute the time when you wish to rise. For about 12s. a little German clock, with an alarum, may be bought almost in every town. Though I have very many times been awakened by the Lord, in answer to prayer, almost to the minute when I desired to rise; yet I thought it well to procure an alarum, to assist me in my purpose of rising early: not indeed as if it could give the least help, without the Lord's blessing, for I should remain in bed, notwithstanding the noise of the alarum, were He not to give me grace to rise; but simply looking upon it as a means. c, Rise at once when you are awake. Remain not a minute longer in bed, else you are likely to fall asleep again. d, Be not discouraged by feeling drowsy and tired in consequence of your rising early. This will soon wear off. You will after a few days feel yourself stronger and fresher than when you used to lie an hour or two longer than you needed. e, Allow yourself always the same hours for sleep. Make no change, except sickness oblige you. .

Plymouth, Oct. 1. Today my soul was again especially drawn out in prayer for the dear Orphans. I not merely asked the Lord that He would still continue to supply their need, but I was so fully assured that He had sent the necessary means since I last heard, that I was enabled to praise Him for having done so. Immediately after I had praised Him, but while I was yet on my knees, came another letter from brother T., dated Bristol, Sept. 29, in which he writes thus:

"The Lord's help has been graciously continued to us since I wrote last. Ever since your absence, the supplies have come in so seasonably, that I have not had occasion, until now, of opening the boxes in the Orphan-Houses. There came in, since my last account, from a sister 2s. 6d., with Ecclesiastes ix. 10, 11.. 1s. 6d., through Mr. C. of Bath, 2l. 3s. 4d., from the boxes 14s. 6 1/2d., from A. M. B. 5s. Some apples besides have been given, some old clothes, and a large bath to be sold or used. I gave on Thursday to the sisters 10l., and today for the Boys'-Orphan-House 1l. 10s. After this I have in hand 1l. 3s. 8 3/4d., to be multiplied as the Lord wills. I had written thus far, and was on the point of writing that we expected sister E. home this evening, when the door-bell rang, and sister E. came in, bringing a little packet of money, directed to you, from Hereford, enclosing a letter and ten sovereigns "for your labours of faith and love;" so that the remainder of the barrel of meal has been multiplied somewhat already. It is most seasonable help! It rejoices me that it has come in time, for you to have the intelligence with this letter. I have in hand 19s. for the other funds, therefore it seems well to me, if it should be needed before I hear from you, to take only 5l. for the Orphans; but, if it pleases the Lord to enable us to do without, I shall leave it untouched until you write. In addition to what I have written, I have just received 10s. and 1l. 9s. 3d. How gracious!"

The time from October 6th to the 17th I spent among the brethren at Bideford and Barnstaple, with great refreshment to my own soul, and was also allowed by the

Lord to minister to them. The whole of my stay among the children of God in Devonshire has been very profitable to me. May my soul not lose the blessing of it! How the Lord uses our infirmity of body for the blessing of our souls! In my case also it was instrumental in communicating blessing to others. I was able to speak more frequently in public, while absent from Bristol, than I should have done under ordinary circumstances, had I remained in Bristol.

Barnstaple, Oct. 10. The day before yesterday I had 10s. given to me here for the Orphans; and yesterday 3l., which came in most seasonably, as will appear from the following letter which I received this evening from brother T.

Bristol, Oct. 8th, 1839.

"My dear Brother, we have continued to enjoy the gracious help of the Lord since I last wrote to you. Nearly up to that time the supplies had come in so seasonably, that the previous disbursements had scarcely ever been expended, before I was again able to make a fresh one. Since then, however, we have been twice a little straitened. On Friday evening we were in prospect of Saturday's necessities, and had nothing to meet them, except the money about which I was in doubt from not having received directions from you. I had already used 5l. out of the 10l. which had been sent, and now, after waiting till it was actually needed, we thought it an indication, as none had been sent, that this should all go to the Orphan-Houses. On Monday again more money was needed than I had in hand, but we were in expectation of help. After dinner, as nothing had come in, I thought it well to open the boxes, thinking, that, although I had opened them so recently, I had no right to presume that the Lord had not had time to pour into them. The expectation was not in vain; for in the box at the Boys'-Orphan-House I found 1l. 0s. 1 1/2d., in the box at the Girls'-Orphan-House 7s. 1d. At the latter place I met sister A. who gave me 3s. for things that she had sold. Thus we were most graciously helped through Monday. Then, in the evening, at the meeting I received from sister B. 2s., and through sister C. 11s. I had opened the box at the Infant-Orphan-House on Monday, and found it empty. But today, finding the 13s. insufficient, and being told that something had been put in, I opened it, and found 3s. 6d., which nicely helped us through. And we are now looking to the Lord for more. In the mean time I shall this morning attend to the sale of whatever has been given to be sold. It comforts us to know you are praying for us," &c.

The money which I had received yesterday and the day before yesterday here, at Barnstaple, and two weeks ago at Teignmouth, enabled me now to send off at once 5l.

On Oct. 17th I returned to Bristol, with renewed strength, for active service.

Oct. 17. Bristol. The Lord has been again very gracious as it regards the funds; for during the last three days, while I was at Barnstaple, I received from a sister 5s., two rings, and a brooch. From another sister a gold watch, to be sold for the Orphans. From a brother a seal, two ear-rings, and a brooch. From a third sister sixteen books to be sold; also 4l., the produce of a veil. From a fourth sister 2l. 10s., and from a fifth 1l., and from five others 8s. 9d. In addition to this I found when I came home, that though my fellow-labourers had been greatly tried a few days previous to my return, so much so, that, when the 5l. arrived which I sent from Barnstaple, they were in greater poverty than they ever had been; yet, within the last days, several pounds had come in, and yesterday, over and above all this, arrived 15l. from London for some articles which had been sent there to be sold. What can we render unto the Lord for all His benefits!

Oct. 19. The Lord is still pouring in bountifully! This morning 10l. was sent from Worcester, and a sister brought 7l., being the produce of the sale of ladies' baskets, which she and some other sisters are making for the benefit of the Orphans. This last case shows what various means the Lord uses to provide for our need; yet all comes without one single individual being asked to give help; for to the Lord alone we speak about our need. We are now again comparatively rich, i. e. we have means in hand to meet the current expenses of about eight days, which has been only two or three times the case during the last fifteen months.

Oct. 30. A little boy brought me a letter, given to him by a gentleman and lady in the street, as he said, to take to my house. The letter contained these words with a five pound note: "The enclosed 5l. accept for the benefit of the Orphans, in the name of the Lord Jesus."

Nov. 5. Today an Orphan was brought from Bath, and a lady sent by her servant, the aunt of the child, a sovereign for the Orphans, when there was but 3s. 11d. in hand. It has been thus repeatedly, that when orphans have been brought, and we had no money, or scarcely any, that the Lord sent a little with these poor children. It never is with us any question, whether there is much or little money in hand, so far as it regards the reception of children; but only, whether there is room.

Nov. 8. We are now again quite poor. The Lord gave us to know more than usually from Oct. 17th to Oct. 31st what it is to abound, and now we know again what it is to be poor. It would have been desirable to have had 3l. today, but only 1l. 3s. 11d, was in hand, which I sent off. In our need we were led to open the boxes in the Orphan-Houses, which had not been done for some weeks, and in them was found 16s. 2 1/2d. To this one of the labourers added 9s. By this 2l. 9s. 1 1/2d. we could meet those expenses which needed to be met, and we were thus helped through the day.

Nov. 9. Saturday. 3l. 0s. 6d. was required today, in order comfortably to meet the present demands, but not one penny was in hand. Between ten and eleven I went to the Girls'-Orphan-House, to meet with my fellow-labourers for prayer. Only 2s. had come in. This was all I could leave. There was every thing in the houses which was required for the moment, and I proposed that we should meet again for prayer in the afternoon at four. When we did so, one of the labourers gave 8s. 6d., another 10s., another 5s. 6d., so that I had as much to give to the matrons as would provide comfortably all the necessaries for the children till Monday morning; only the usual quantity of bread could not be taken in. About half an hour, after we had separated, came in 1l. 10s., the produce of the sale of a shawl, which a sister from Devonshire had given for that purpose some days since. Thus we had altogether 2l. 16s., whereas when the day commenced we had no natural prospect of any thing. This is a new sweet encouragement. Besides this, our Father has given us another proof of His continued care, in that twenty sacks of potatoes and a small barrel of herrings have been sent for the Orphans.

Nov. 11. Monday morning. Yesterday, when, as just related, there was not a penny in hand, there was given to me, with Ecclesiastes ix. 10, ten shillings. This morning came in 1l. 10s, more, Soon afterwards a note was sent to me from the Orphan-Houses, to say that the need of today would be 3l. JUST WHILE I WAS READING THE NOTE I received another, including a sovereign, which a sister from Devonshire had given to one of the brethren for the Orphans. Thus I had just the 3l. which was needed. A few minutes after came in 1s. more.

Nov. 12. The need of today was 2l. As only 1s. had been left in hand yesterday, and no more than 6s. had come in, we were again in a strait. But I was not looking at the little in hand, but at the fulness of God. I sent off the little which I had. In the afternoon we met for prayer. I then found that 2s. 6d. had been taken out of the box in the Infant-Orphan-House, and that 4s. more had come in by the sale of some old books. To this one of the labourers added 2s. 3d., all she had of her own. After prayer came in 2s. 6d., which had been given while we were in prayer. In the evening we met again for prayer, when another labourer gave 3s. 4d. Thus, in our deep poverty, we got together this day 1l. 0s. 7d., which supplied our absolute necessities. We were this afternoon so reduced, till the Lord sent a little help, that there were no means to provide breakfast for tomorrow, for the children in the Boys'-Orphan-House.

Nov. 13. Nothing has come in. Our need is even greater today than yesterday, on account of our not having been able yesterday to take in the usual quantity of provisions. In this our need I packed up the books, which had been intended for sale on Aug. 22, when the Lord sent such a rich, supply, before they were actually disposed of. To them one of the labourers added some of his own, and a few other articles. Also some old jackets, which had been sent, were packed up to be disposed of. At twelve I met with my fellow-labourers for prayer.

There was every thing in the houses which was needed for dinner, but there were no means to get milk for tea. (The children have milk and water at tea time.) Three of my helpers went out to dispose of the articles. At four in the afternoon I received the information that 14s. had come in, for some of the things which were disposed of. One of my fellow-labourers had besides disposed of an article of his own for 1l. 5s. This 1l. 19s. enabled us to take in bread as usual, and to defray the other necessary expenses. We had never been lower in means than yesterday and today. Yet my soul, thanks to the Lord! was also yesterday and today in perfect

SECOND PART

peace. My helpers seem also quite in peace. This evening I received 2s. 6d., and 11s. with Ecclesiastes ix. 10. This little money is as precious, as at other times 100l. would have been, because it is a fresh proof that our Father still cares for us. The money was given to me just after I had been speaking on these words: "But I am poor and needy; yet the Lord thinketh upon me." Whilst speaking I was able, in a measure, to realize the preciousness of the truth contained in those words, and after speaking my Father gave me a fresh proof that He is thinking upon me.

Nov. 14. I took the 13s. 6d. which was given last evening, early this morning, to the Orphan-Houses, where I found that 10s. 6d. had come in by the sale of a Hebrew Old and a Greek New Testament, which a brother had given who had more than one copy; and 1s. 6d. for another book. This 1l. 5s. 6d. has been divided, in the hope that our kind Father will remember us before the day is over, and send in more. This afternoon, when we met for prayer, I found that 18s. more had come in for some articles which had been sold. We have had thus 2l. 3s. 6d. this day to divide for housekeeping. By the good hand of the Lord upon us, there has been every thing really needful. May the Lord look upon us, and help us further! Surely, He will do it!

Nov. 15. We are still in deep poverty. Nothing had come in by four o'clock in the afternoon, when I went to meet with my fellow-labourers for prayer. I did not go in the morning, because I knew that there was every thing which was needed till the afternoon. When I came I found that a sister had given 2s. 6d.; a new Bible which one of the labourers had given, who had more than one old copy, had been sold for 10s.; also 2s. had come in, and 1s. 4d. for some other articles which had been sold. This 15s. 10d. supplied that which was absolutely needed for today. We are still of good courage. We are sure that the Lord, in His own time, will deliver us out of the trial; for were our poverty more than a trial of faith, had the Lord in anger shut up His hands, we should not receive any thing at all. But this is not the case. For even this very day two sacks of potatoes were sent by the same brother who sent twenty sacks a few days since, with the promise to send still more. We have no means to lay in a stock for the winter, else we should have bought, perhaps, fifty or sixty sacks; but our kind Father does it for us. There has been also a toy chest of drawers promised for sale.

Nov. 16. Our prayer was last evening, in particular, respecting the necessities of today, as two days' provisions would be needed, it being Saturday. Besides this, about 2l. 10s. was needed to pay the weekly salaries of the brethren and sisters who labour in the Day-Schools. For all these demands there was nothing in hand, nor have we any more needless articles to dispose of; and useful ones we do not consider it right to sell, as our Father knows our need. When we met about twelve o'clock this morning, I found that last evening there had been Bibles unexpectedly sold to the amount of 1l. 11s. 6d., and about 10s. had been given besides. Thus we had nearly enough for the School-Fund. Moreover, 15s. had come in for the Orphan-Fund. A large sea-chest was given by a brother several months since, for the benefit of the Orphans, which had never been disposed of, and which, in this our great need, was sold for 15s. Yet this 15s. was needed to pay what was due for washing; and, therefore, we had still nothing to take in provisions with. It occurred to one of the labourers, that there might be a little advanced on his watch, of the money which had been laid by for rent, as had once or twice before been done; and that the watch might be sold at quarter-day, in case there should not come in enough to make up the deficiency. Yet even this plan we did not any longer think to be quite Scriptural, as he needs the watch in the Lord's service, and as our Lord is so kind, that He would otherwise send us means, were it well for us. In short, it appeared to us quite clear, that while we ought, in such a strait, to dispose of things which we do not need, nothing ought to be disposed of which is needed, in order that the Lord's own deliverance might be so much the more manifest. All we could think of for sale was five pewter dishes, which had been given nearly four years ago, but which were never used, as they were not convenient. These we agreed should be sold. About four o'clock this afternoon I received 2l. 2s., which a brother and sister had brought from Leicestershire. With this I went joyfully to the Orphan-Houses. There I found that 9s. 6d. had come in for the pewter dishes; one of the labourers had given 10s. for the Orphans, and 10s. for the School-Fund. (There had come in 2s. more for the other funds. All demands were met, and there was 1s. 6d. over.) Besides this, one of the labourers had sold a book of his own for 4s., and another labourer gave two pairs of new gloves, and four gentlemen's stocks. One pair of the gloves had been sold. Thus altogether had come in 4l. 2s. 3d., and therefore about 1l. 10s. more than was needed. We are now brought to the close of one more week. This has been, perhaps, of all the weeks the most trying. So much prayer, and so little coming in, I never knew. Yet, by the grace of God, I was sure that help would come, after the trial of faith was over. During the whole of this week, greatly as we have been tried, and though twice no stock of bread could be taken in, yet there has been nourishing food at every meal, and neither the children nor any other person can have perceived our poverty. About 13l. has been spent even this week for housekeeping in the three Orphan-Houses.

Nov. 18. Monday. The Lord has kindly sent in since Saturday evening 3l. 18s. 3 1/4d., and thus our need for today is supplied. On Saturday evening the produce of an orphan-box, 5s. 1 1/4d., was given; and last evening a sister gave two sovereigns to brother Craik, waiting for him a long time in the chapel, till she could see him. She might have delayed giving it till another time, as she had to wait so long; but the Lord knew our need. There were also sent eight sack of potatoes, by the same brother who had sent twenty-two sacks before.

Nov. 19. As there was not enough money in hand for the necessities of today, we were again as poor as on Saturday. Between three and four in the afternoon the milk is generally taken in; but in the Boys'-Orphan-House there was not money enough to meet this small expense. However, the Lord knew our need, and sent us at two o'clock 13s., which helped us comfortably through the day. A sister had purposed in her heart to give 3d. a week for the Orphans, and she felt herself stirred up to bring the yearly amount now, in this our extremity.

SECOND PART

Nov. 20. This has been a day of deep poverty. Nothing but the 13s., above referred to, came in yesterday, which was scarcely enough to meet yesterday's usual need. My mind, by the grace of God, was not at all cast down; but I felt it rather trying, that the abundance of my other engagements had not allowed me to meet with my fellow-labourers, either yesterday or today, for prayer. This evening I had a note from the Boys'-Orphan-House, to state that a lady had sent two dozen of boys' shirts, which she had made herself, with which she sent 5s. to get them washed. This 5s. enabled us to meet that which was absolutely needful. [I mention here, that while our usual current expenses are about 2l. 10s. daily for housekeeping in the three houses; yet we might, in case of need, do for one or two days with as little as yesterday and today, as there are generally potatoes and meat in the house, and a stock of bread for two days, in order that the children may eat stale bread.] Without this 5s. we should have been unable to procure all that was absolutely needed. This our kind Father knew, and therefore He sent it. There were also given two quarterns of bread by one of the bakers, which made up the usual quantity. Moreover five and a half sacks of potatoes were sent by the brother who sent the others, making in all 35 1/2 sacks.

Nov. 21. This morning one of the labourers gave 7s., in order that there might be means to take in milk. Between ten and eleven o'clock we met for prayer, and I found that 10s. had come in for a toy chest of drawers, which in this our great need had been sent for sale. Besides this 6d. had been taken out of the box in the Infant-Orphan-House. This 17s. 6d. enabled us to provide the dinner, and to take in a little bread in two houses, even as much as would be enough for breakfast tomorrow; but there was 4s. 6d. needed to buy bread for the Boys'-Orphan-House, as there was only enough for today. When we met again this afternoon, 3s. had come in, as one of the labourers had sold a few old books. Another labourer gave 1s. 6d., and thus we had also the 4s. 6d., which was needed for bread. After prayer, it was mentioned that a sister, a servant, who is out of a situation, had been this afternoon to see the Orphan-Houses, and had put something into the box at the Girls'-Orphan-House. The box was opened, and half-a-crown was found in it. This money was, in our deep poverty, as acceptable as 50l. at other times might have been. We rejoiced when we saw it, for it was a fresh proof to us, that, not in anger, but only for the trial of our faith, we are so poor. This 2s. 6d. provides us with the means to take in milk tomorrow morning, so that we shall have everything which is needed till after breakfast tomorrow, but then there is neither bread, nor meat, etc. remaining for dinner. Our comfort, however, is: "The morrow shall take thought for the things of itself. Sufficient unto the day is the evil thereof." Matt. vi. 34. We separated very happy in God, though very poor, and our faith much tried.

Nov. 22. Our poverty had now become very great. Greater it had never been. Yet, the Lord be praised! I was as comfortable as ever; for I was sure we were only for the trial of our faith in this state. Had the Lord shut up His hand iii anger, He would not have continued to give us, even during this week, from time to time, tokens of His care over us. I said this morning: "Man's necessity is God's opportunity" is a proverb of the world, and how much more may we, His children, now look to

Him in our great need. I knew we must have help in some way, as now it had come to the greatest extremity, there being in none of the houses anything for dinner, except potatoes, of which we have an abundance. At ten this morning I was informed that a large box, bearing my address, had arrived at one of the Orphan-Houses. I set off immediately, and found it was from the neighbourhood of Wolverhampton. It contained 12l. for the Orphans, 1l. 11s. 10d. for the other Funds, 4 yards of flannel, 9 yards of calico, 12 yards of print, 4 1/2 yards of coloured cotton, 4 yards of stuff, 2 pairs of stockings, and 3 1/4 yards of brown holland. Besides this, there were in it the following articles for sale: 2 decanters and stands, 4 glass salt cellars, 3 scent bottles, a set of cruets and stand, 5 beer glasses, 7 chimney ornaments, 3 tortoise-shell combs, 3 fans, 2 silver vinaigrettes, 2 silver shoe-buckles, 2 waist buckles, 2 silver salt-cellars, 1 pair of knives and forks with silver handles, a small silver toasting fork, 9 silver coins, three gold rings, 4 pairs of ear-rings, 3 brooches, a cornelian heart, a silver seal, 1 pair of silver studs, 1 gold watch key, 1 silver pencil case, 5 pairs of bracelets, 5 necklaces and 1 urn rug. The joy which I and my fellowlabourers had when all these things lay before us, cannot be described; it must be experienced in order that it may be known. It was two hours and a half before the dinner time, when the help was granted. The Lord knew that the Orphans had no dinner, and, therefore, did He now send help.--This morning also a brother sent to the Girls' Orphan-House to ask whether the treacle-cask was empty, and if so, to send it by the messenger, that it might be filled.

Nov. 24. Today 5l. came in again with Ecclesiastes ix. 10, besides 1l. 10s. for the rents.

Nov. 27. Today again some money was needed for housekeeping. But as a little had come in yesterday and today, we had enough.

Nov. 28. Last evening 10s. came in, which was just enough to supply this day's need. We are now again penniless.

Nov. 29. A great part of the articles, which were sent this day week from the neighbourhood of Wolverhampton, have now been disposed of for 5l. 11s.; we are, therefore, supplied for today and tomorrow.

Dec. 2. Since the last money has been given out for housekeeping, only 1l. 12s. has come in but as 1l. 10s. of this had been given for the rents, I had only 2s. in hand, when brother B., the master at the Boys'-Orphan-House, came this morning, and told me that the need of today would be at least 2l. I gave him the 2s. which I had, and proposed that we should pray together for more means. WHILE WE WERE IN PRAYER, a brother called. After prayer brother B. left me, and the brother who had come gave me 5l. As soon as he had left, I went joyfully with the money to the Orphan-Houses, to prevent the bakers being sent away. This evening I received still further 2l. Thus the Lord has richly supplied our need for today and tomorrow.

SECOND PART

Dec. 3. The Lord has remembered again our need for tomorrow. I received today from Liverpool 15s.; and from a brother in the neighbourhood of London, who had been staying here for a season, 5l.; also 1l. by the sale of some articles.

Dec. 4. It has been repeatedly our prayer during the last month and in the beginning of this, that the Lord would be pleased to give us again so much means, before the time of the public meetings, which are fixed for the 10th, 11th, and 12th, of this month, that, when we speak about His dealings with us during this year, we might also respecting the close of it have again to speak, to His praise, of the abundance which we had in hand. At the end of last year we made the same request, and the Lord granted it. Now today, as an answer to this our often repeated request, I received from the East Indies 100l., to be laid out for the Orphans, or the other objects of the Institution. Respecting this money it is to be noticed: 1. The great distance from whence it is sent. 2. That it comes just now, and thus enables us to speak at the meetings of this rich supply after our trials. 3. It furnishes us with means to order Bibles, as one half of the money will be taken for the other funds; there having been a great inquiry for Bibles lately, and we have not been able to meet the demand, for want of means. Respecting this point also we have prayed repeatedly, and now the Lord has answered our petition. How very precious it is to wait on the Lord! What an abundant proof have we in this donation, that all our late straits, as it regards means, were only allowed for the trial of our faith! This evening came in still further 1l. 5s.

Dec. 9. Since Dec. 4 several small donations have come in, so that unto the last day of this fourth year of the Orphan-work the Lord has continued His kindness to us.

On Dec. 10, 11, and 12 we had public meetings, at which the account of the Lord's dealings with us in reference to the Orphan-Houses and the other objects of the Scriptural Knowledge Institution was given. During the whole of the past year, as formerly, the labourers who are engaged in the work had kept their trials and their joys of faith to themselves; but now we considered the time to have come, when, for the benefit of the church at large, and to the glory of our Lord, we should make our boast in Him.--It is now (i. e. on Dec. 10, 1839) five years and nine months since the Scriptural Knowledge Institution has been in operation. In addition to what has been said about the Lord's dealings with us, more especially in regard to the funds, I make a few more remarks, with reference to His kindness to us, in other respects, during the last year. 1. During the last year also we have been enabled to continue to provide all the needful expenses connected with the six Day-Schools, three for boys and three for girls. The number of the children, who are at present in them, amounts to 286. The number of all the children that have had schooling in the Day Schools, through the medium of the Institution, since its formation, amounts to 1795. 2. There are at present 226 children in the Sunday School. 3. There are 14 taught to read in the Adult School, and there have been about 130 adults instructed in that School, since the formation of the Institution. 4. There have been circulated during the last year 514 copies of the Scriptures, and 5592 since March 5, 1834. 5. There has been laid out during the last year 91l. 6s. for Missionary purposes. 6. There have been received into the three Orphan-Houses from Dec. 9, 1838, to Dec. 9, 1839, 16 orphans. There are at present 96 orphans in the three houses. The number of all the orphans, who have been under our care from April 11, 1836, to Dec. 9, 1839, amounts to 126.

I notice further the following points in connexion with the Orphan-Houses.

1. Without any one having been asked for any thing by us, the sum of 3,067l. 8s. 9 1/4d. has been given to us, entirely as the result of prayer to God, from the commencement of the work up to Dec. 9, 1839. 2. Besides this, there have also been sent many articles of clothing, furniture, and provisions, for the use of the Orphans. 3. Without our solicitation, three medical gentlemen (one for each house), have up to this time, kindly given their attendance and medicines gratuitously. 4. The hand of God is most manifest in that we have had so little sickness, considering that so many persons during this autumn have been suffering from fever, etc. Even in this particular I desire publicly to acknowledge the Lord's peculiar kindness to us. 5. Though most of the children have been brought up in a very different manner from what we could desire, yet the Lord has constrained them, on the whole, during this year also, to behave exceedingly well, so much so that it has continued to attract the attention of all observers. 6. That, however, which gives us the chief ground for thankfulness, so far as the children are concerned, is, that in eight of them we perceive decided proofs of a real change of heart and of faith in our Lord Jesus Christ, so that they have been received into church fellowship. We are not surprised that these children, who are from 9 years old and upwards, have been converted; for the conversion of the orphans under our care has been a frequent subject of prayer among us, and that of late more than ever; so that we fully expect, if the Lord shall continue to give prayer for them, that soon many more will be brought to believe in the Lord Jesus.

The total of the expenses, connected with the objects of the Institution, exclusive of the Orphan-Houses, from Nov. 19, 1838, to Nov. 19, 1839, is 542l. 13s. The balance in hand on Nov. 19, 1839, was 18s. 5d. The total of the expenses connected with the three Orphan-Houses, from Dec. 9, 1838, to Dec. 9, 1839, is 960l. 9s. 2 3/4d. The balance in hand on Dec 9, 1839, was 46l. 8s. 1d.

Dec. 24. This morning we wanted again more money for the Orphans than there was in hand. It is only eight days since the last public meeting, when there was a balance of 46l. 8s. 1d. in hand. On this account we disposed of some silver articles and books which had been sent within the last days for the benefit of the Orphans, by which means we have enough for today and tomorrow.

Dec. 31. My health is much better than for years. My mental powers also are as good as they have been at any time during the last three years. I ascribe this to God's blessing, through the instrumentality of early rising, and plunging my head into cold water when I rise.

SECOND PART

REVIEW OF THE YEAR 1839.

I. As to the church--68 brethren and sisters brother Craik and I found in fellowship when we came to Bristol.

573 have been admitted to fellowship since we came to Bristol.

641 would be, therefore, the total number of those in fellowship with us, had there been no changes. But

40 have fallen asleep;

33 are under church discipline

55 saints have left Bristol;

38 have left us, but are still in Bristol;

166 are therefore to be deducted from 641, so that there are only 475 at present in fellowship with us.

During the last year have been added 115, of whom 34 have been brought to the knowledge of the Lord among us.

II. As to my temporal supplies.

The Lord has been pleased to give me during the past year

1. By the Freewill Offerings through the boxes £137 4s. 5d.

2. By Presents in money, from saints residing in and out of Bristol £121 18s. 0d.

3. By Money through family connexion £42 0s. 0d.

4. By Presents in clothes, provisions, &c., which were worth to us at least £12 0s. 0d.

Altogether £313 2s. 5d.

January 1, 1840. Our usual meeting last night was most precious! We continued together from seven till half-past twelve. Of all the similar meetings which we have had, it was, according to my judgment, by far the best. Not more than five prayed; but there was much more real prayer than at former meetings.--This morning, about one hour after midnight, when our prayer meeting was over, I received a paper with some money sealed up in it for the Orphans. A few minutes afterwards I remembered that the individual who gave it was in debt, and I was aware she had been repeatedly asked by her creditors for payment; I resolved therefore, with out opening the paper, to return it, as no one has a right to give whilst in debt. This was done when I knew that there was not enough in hand to meet the expences of the day. About eight this morning a brother brought 5l., which he had received just then from his mother, for the Orphans. Observe, the brother is led to bring it at once! The Lord knew our need, and therefore this brother could not delay bringing the money. A few hours after I received 5l. more, and 8s. 5d., also 2s. 6d., so that we are now again supplied for three or four days.

Jan. 5. Besides the 10l. 10s. 11d, which came in on New-year's day, there came in on the 2nd and 4th 3l. 0s. 7d. But when now we were again without a penny, there came in 5s., and 6d., and 1s. Also 2l. with Ecclesiastes ix. 10, and 1l. 10s. for rent.

Jan. 7. Today, when there were again only a few shillings in hand, as since the 5th had come in only 3s., I gave myself to prayer, when, just after I had risen from my knees, a sister came and brought 1l., as a thank-offering to the Lord for the many mercies of the past year. There came in still further today, by ten different donations and the sale of two Reports, 2l. 17s.

Jan. 8. There were only a few shillings more in hand than was needed for housekeeping today. Nevertheless our kind Father remembered us before the day was over. A sister, a servant, gave me 15s.; also with Ecclesiastes ix. 10, came in 5l. 5s., from two sisters 6s, 1d., and by sale of Reports 3s.

Jan. 22. I have repeatedly asked the Lord for means to be able to order more Bibles, as two sorts were again exhausted. There is moreover scarcely enough money in hand to pay the teachers next Saturday. This afternoon I received from a sister 14l. 2s. 7d., which she had had in the Savings' Bank. She considered that this money would be better used in the Lord's work, than left in the Savings' Bank. Thus I was enabled to order some Bibles.

From Jan. 8th to 22nd came in 34l. 9s. 5d. for the Orphans, and the donations were so seasonable, that always either something was given, or articles which had been given for sale could be disposed of, before the last money had been expended. But as there was today again only very little in hand, I was led to open the orphan-

SECOND PART

box in my house, in which I found two papers, the one containing 10s., the other a 5l. note. In both papers was written Eccles. ix. 10. There came in today still further above 5l. Thus our Lord has sent us what we are likely to need for three or four days to come.

Jan. 25. I have been much in prayer this week about going to Germany: 1, To see certain brethren who purpose to go as Missionaries to the East Indies; and 2, To see my father once more. I am led to go just now, instead of delaying it, because my health is again so failing, that it seems desirable I should leave Bristol at all events, and thus I could continue to serve in the work of the Lord, and yet attend to the benefit of my health at the same time. Lord, keep me from making a mistake in this matter!

Jan, 31, Since Jan. 22 several small donations came in for the Orphans, and several pounds by the sale of silver articles, trinkets, &c. But as I have had to pay out today 11l. 13s., we are now again very poor. For many days past we have been so helped, that money has always come in, before all was spent. Now there is only 1s. 5d. in hand. The Lord will provide! I feel quite comfortable, though in three days I shall have to leave the work for several week.--About three hours after I had written the above, came in 1l. 14s. 1 1/2d. In the afternoon I received still further from Tottenham for the Orphans 10l., and in the evening from Hereford 30l., of which latter sum there was 6l. for the Orphans, and 24l. for the other objects of the Scriptural Knowledge Institution. Thus the Lord will kindly allow me to leave a little money behind on my departure, and I have also a still further answer to my prayer for means to purchase Bibles, for which I have asked the Lord repeatedly, and which he began to answer by the donation which I received on the 22nd. I have received 5l. besides for the other objects.

Feb. 1. I have now felt quite sure for several days past, that I should leave Bristol for a season, and go to Germany. If the Lord permit, I shall leave the day after tomorrow.

Feb. 2. Today and yesterday has come in still further, before my departure, nearly 9l. for the Orphans. How kind of the Lord to send this money just now, on the eve of my leaving home!

Feb. 3. Today I left Bristol for Berlin.

On Feb. 5th I left London in the steamer for Hamburg. Though it had been so very stormy for several weeks past, the Lord gate us a very favourable passage; the first, as the captain said, which they had had for several weeks. We landed at Hamburg on the 7th at five in the afternoon. The porter who carried my things led me, as I afterwards found out, some by-way, either to save a long distance, or to get me into the city with my luggage, though it was after the custom-house hours. I did not understand this at first; but, when we were about to enter the city, he told me that that was not the proper way, but that if I would give to the custom-house officer, whom I should presently see at the entrance into the city, a small fee, he would let me pass. My reply was that I did not wish to do what was unlawful, nor should I give a fee to encourage what was unlawful, and that I would rather go a long way round, than get by such means into the city. Presently we arrived at the place at which the custom-house officer stood, who, on my telling him plainly that I had not the least wish to pass that way, if it were unlawful, saw that I was only a passenger, and that I had no wish to get into the city with goods which are not duty free, and therefore let me pass. This little circumstance proves afresh in how many little things the children of God may act differently from the world, to the glory of their Father, and how in going the Lord's way, we find it to be, even as far as this life is concerned, the easiest path.--About half an hour after, when I arrived at the hotel, a little circumstance served afresh to remind me, that the Christian, like the bee, might suck honey out of every flower. I saw upon a snuffer-stand in bas-relief, "A heart, a cross under it, and roses under both." The meaning was obviously this, that the heart which bears the cross for a time meets with roses afterwards. I applied it to myself, and this little event greatly cheered my heart in this place, where I was without the fellowship of a single believer.

I left Hamburg in the evening of Feb. 8th, travelled all night, all day, and the whole of the second night, and reached Berlin on the morning of the 10th. I confessed not the Lord Jesus on this long journey, which I record here to my shame; nor did I give any other testimony for Jesus in the steamer, than merely refraining from the light and trifling conversation of the party, and all this after I had had on my way from Bristol to London a fresh encouragement in conversing with a gay traveller addicted to drinking, who evidently listened with a measure of attention, and with a desire of having his chains broken.

From Feb. 10th to 20th I was in Berlin. I think it is likely that eight or nine brethren and sisters will go from hence to the East Indies.--After having been greatly helped by the Lord in my work, the first and special object of my journey to the Continent; mercifully kept by Him in the narrow path and in great peace, whilst surrounded with temptations on every side; and after having also seen afresh abundant reason to praise the Lord for all the way in which He had led me since I lived here in 1828 and 1829; I left Berlin on the evening of Feb. 20th for Magdeburg, which I reached on the morning of the 21st, and on the same evening I arrived at my father's house.--In all human probability I now see my dear father the last time. He is evidently much weaker than he was two years ago, and coughs much more. What has the Lord done for me since I lived in the house where I am now! The two rooms where I am now most in prayer, reading the Word, and confessing His name, were those very rooms in which I sinned most, whilst living here many years ago. I have had again opportunity, most fully to bring out the truth about the work of the Lord Jesus before my father, whilst conversing a long time with a woman in his hearing, to whom I showed from the Scriptures, that we are to be saved, not by our own works, but simply by faith in the Lord Jesus, who bore the punishment instead of us, and who fulfilled the law in our room.

SECOND PART

Feb. 24 and 25. I am still at Heimersleben. My dear father is very weak.

Feb. 26. This morning I left Heimersleben. I took leave of my father most probably for the last time. It has been a great pleasure to me, and I consider it a great privilege, to have been permitted by the Lord once more to see my father, once more personally to show him filial love and regard, and once more to set the truth before him. He has been again during the whole of this my stay most affectionate to me, as he was during my two former visits to him since I left the Continent to reside in England. How cheerfully should I have left him this morning, did I know him to be safe in Jesus! But, alas! he as yet is not resting upon Christ, though he is so far religious as to read prayers and the Bible.--After I had left him I went to my faithful and beloved friend, brother Stahlschmidt, at Sandersleben, but found him absent from home.

Brother Kroll, the servant of brother Stahlschmidt, [whom I have mentioned in the first part of my Narrative,] received me with much affection. When this brother first came to Sandersleben in 1829, there was scarcely a single true Christian besides his master in the little town. Soon afterwards he began to hold meetings, which were attended by the two or three who loved the Lord Jesus. These meetings were for a long time suffered to go on quietly; but when the Lord blessed them, and others were stirred up to care about their souls, brother Kroll had to appear before the magistrates, and was forbidden to hold them. When this was of no effect, (as he considered that he ought only to obey earthly rulers in things in which he could do so with a good conscience,) and they continued still to meet together, the police came into one of their meetings, and forced them to discontinue it. When even this availed nothing, the brethren were finally threatened that every one who attended these meetings should pay three thalers, and every one who read or spoke at them should pay five, which is a large sum in Germany for poor people. But notwithstanding all these obstacles, the few poor saints continue their meetings, but in secret, to be unmolested by the police. They have now neither a stated place nor a fixed time for their meetings. On the second and third evenings, whilst I was at Sandersleben, I met with them. On the second evening we were in the room of a poor weaver. The dear brethren would have me sit on the only chair which was in the room. It was a very small room, perhaps twice as large as the loom, which was in it. There were about twenty-five or thirty persons present, many of whom had seated themselves in and under the loom, and the rest sat on two or three little forms. These meetings were very precious. The very fact of going to them with the feeling of having to pay the fine, or to suffer an adequate imprisonment, should one be found there, makes them to be doubly valued; and I believe that the Lord's double blessing rests upon them. I spoke long both times; indeed, as long as I had strength, and the dear people seemed to eat the Word.--I have so circumstantially related these facts, that thereby the children of God in Great Britain may be led more highly to value their religious privileges, and to make good use of them whilst they are continued.

It is worthy of remark, that while the meeting at Sandersleben were permitted to continue, there was no believing clergyman in the little town; but about the time that they were forbidden, the Lord sent a brother who truly preaches the gospel. I had for some hours refeshing and most affectionate brotherly intercourse with Him. May the Lord let His blessing rest upon him, and help him to be a faithful witness for God in that dark neighbourhood!

I had travelled so fast, and stayed so short a time in the places where I had been, that I was obliged to leave Heimersleben without having received the letter which I had expected from my wife there, a matter of no small trial (as those who have been for some time at a great distance from home, know it to be); especially in my case, as, on account of the Orphans and the other work, besides my family, it was of so much importance for me to hear from time to time. I had arranged with my father to have the letter sent to me to Sandersleben, by an express messenger, who could be obtained for a small remuneration. However, hour after hour passed away, on the 27th, and the messenger did not arrive. At last the time was gone by, as it was getting dark, and the person ought to have come at noon. I now lifted up my heart to the Lord, beseeching Him to give me grace to give up my own will in this thing. No sooner had I been brought into such a state, as to be TRULY content and satisfied with the will of the Lord in this matter, than the expected letter was handed over to me. The woman who brought it had lost her way in the morning, on account of a dense fog, which made her so late. I have frequently found, under similar circumstances, that after I had been brought into such a state as to be willing to give up my own will, whereby I was fitted to bear the blessing, the Lord gave me the desire of my heart, according to the truth of that word: "Delight thyself also in the Lord, and He shall give thee the desires of thine heart." Psalm xxxvii. 4.

Feb. 29. This morning I left Sandersleben. Towards the evening I reached Halberstadt, the town where I was from Easter 1816 to June 1821, at the Cathedral Classical School. I went to a certain small inn, known to me from the time that I lived at Halberstadt, both for the sake of quietness and to save expense, as I knew it to be more like a private boarding-house than an inn. After having had my supper, the innkeeper, who seemed to me a quiet and unassuming person, came into the room where I was, and began conversation with me. After a few moments I recognised in him a former schoolfellow of mine. The Lord now enabled me to tell him of my gay life, my conversion, my subsequent going to England, and of some of the Lord's dealings with me there. He listened with great attention, and was evidently affected by what I said. May the Lord bless to him my testimony for Jesus! I was thus afresh reminded of what grace has done for me. How kind of the Lord to direct me to that place!

March 1. This morning I saw an old friend of mine, a missionary to the Jews at Halberstadt. When first he went there he held meetings, which the few Christians of the town attended; but of late he has been obliged by the police to give them up. In that town of about 15,000 inhabitants, with, I think, seven large Protestant churches, there is not one converted clergyman, as this brother told me; and the few Christians that are there are not permitted to assemble themselves together. Brethren, you who live in Great Britain, be thankful for your religious liberty, and make use of it while the days of outward peace last!--About twelve this morning I left by the mail for Brunswick. The Lord enabled me to preach Christ to a young man, a painter, who, for the sake of improvement in his art, had travelled far and wide, and was now returning home from Vienna to his parents. He listened very attentively, in which I had a fresh proof that one never ought to look at natural appearances in proclaiming the truth; for I judged, before I began to speak to him, from his gay appearance, that he would quite laugh at what I might tell him about Jesus.--I saw again this afternoon, at Wolfenbuttel the inn from whence I ran away, when in debt, in the year 1821, and praised the Lord for His goodness to me since that time. Now, this evening, I am at Brunswick, and shall have again, through the Lord's kindness, rest during the night, as the mail does not leave for Hamburg until nine tomorrow morning.

March 8. London. I left Brunswick on the 2nd, and arrived at Hamburg in 24 hours. As there was ice in the Elbe, the London steamer could not get up to Hamburg, and I had therefore to go alone, in a hired carriage to Cuxhaven, about eighty miles, the most expensive journey that ever I made in my life, for it cost above 3l. 10s. Thus I had to travel three days and two nights, with the interruption of only five hours at Hamburg. I reached Cuxhaven at half-past eight in the evening on March 4th.--The fact of having thus to travel from Hamburg to Cuxhaven, that being the only way in which I could have got there in my circumstances, without losing the steamer, showed me afresh how one is step by step cast upon the Lord. A month since the Elbe was cleared of ice, and now, contrary to the expectation of all, the cold had returned to such a degree, that it was a second time innavigable.

March 3. I embarked this morning for London. I had conversation with two Russian Jews, who listened with great interest to all I said to them; but I did not tell them plainly that I believed Jesus of Nazareth to be the Messiah, as I fully purposed to do at the next conversation. After I had left them, they conversed with each other, and I could see from their countenances, that they either took me for a baptized Jew, or for a missionary to the Jews, on account of the peculiar way in which I had conversed with them. Presently one of them came and asked me what I thought of that Jesus. No sooner had I owned Him as the true Messiah and as my Lord and my God, than he began to blaspheme; and from that time, as long as we were on board, they shunned me; and I also felt that all I had to do was to show kindness to them by actions, but no more to converse with them about the Messiah, in order to keep them from blaspheming that holy name which is dear to my heart. My conversation with them had, however, an unexpected effect in another way. At the dinner table I was asked by one of the passengers about those Jews, who they were, etc., as my long conversation with them on the deck had been noticed. This led me, (in order that the conversation might be turned to profitable subjects, and that I might discover whether there was a Christian at the table), to throw out the remark, "how remarkable it is that the Jews, in all parts of the world, can be recognised as such; and are not mixed with other nations," etc. Immediately the captain replied, "this can only be explained by the Scriptures, and shows the Bible to be true," or something to that effect. I now, in agreeing with the captain, followed up the subject, and both after dinner and repeatedly during the passage had long and most interesting conversations with the captain, whom I found to be a true brother in the Lord, and from whom I separated most affectionately on our arrival in London.

On March 7th I landed in London, where I found two letters from my dear wife, from which I saw that up to the last the Lord had been dealing with her, as well as with me, in the greatest kindness, and had given also an abundance for the Orphans during the whole time of my absence.

March 9. I left London this morning, arrived this evening in peace in Bristol, and found my dearest Mary and all in peace. Truly, the Lord has abundantly blessed me and them while I have been from home!

During the whole time of my absence the Lord not only supplied all the need of the Orphans, but on my return I found more in hand than there was when I left. The donations, which came in during my absence, amount to between 80l. and 90l.

March 11. Today I received 19l. 19s., being a legacy left to me by a brother who fell asleep the beginning of last December. How richly does the Lord supply all my own temporal necessities!

March 22. Today, when there was not a penny in hand for the Orphans, I received the following donations: 3l. as the produce of the sale of ladies' baskets, an old crown piece, an old half-crown piece, and a Spanish dollar. Also 1s. With Eccles. ix. 10, was given 2l. 10s.

March 23. Today came in still further 1l. 2s. 6d.

March 25. All money was now again given out, when today came in by the sale of Reports 8s. 9d., and in small donations 1l. 5s. 11d.

March 26. On the 17th of this month I received the following letter, from a brother who several times had been used by the Lord as an instrument in supplying our need, and who also two months since sent 30l.

"I have received a little money from ----. Have you any present need for the Institution under your care? I know you do not ask, except indeed of Him whose work you are doing; but to answer when asked seems another thing, and a right thing. I have a reason for desiring to know the present state of your means towards the objects you are labouring to serve: viz, should you not have need, other departments of the Lord's work or other people of the Lord may have need. Kindly then inform me, and to what amount, i. e. what amount you at this present time need, or can profitably lay out."

At the time when this letter came, we were indeed in need, or at least it was desirable, as far as I had light, to have means, as I was just on the point of establishing an Infant-School, and as again some sorts of Bibles were needed in order to go

SECOND PART

on with the circulation of the Scriptures. Also in the Orphan-Fund there was only 2s. 3 1/2d. Nevertheless I considered that, as I have hitherto acted, (i. e. telling the Lord alone about our need), I ought to continue to do, as otherwise the principal object of the work, to be a help to the saints generally, by seeking to lead them to increased dependence upon God alone, through this Institution, would be frustrated. I answered therefore the letter, in substance, as follows:

"Whilst I thank you for your love, and whilst I agree with you, that, in general, there is a difference between asking for money, and answering when asked, nevertheless in our case I feel not at liberty to speak about the state of our funds, as the primary object of the work in my hands is, to lead those who are weak in faith to see that there is reality in dealing with God alone."

After having sent off the answer, I was again and again led to pray to the Lord in this way: "Lord, thou knowest that for Thy sake I did not tell this brother about our need. Now, Lord, show afresh that there is reality in speaking to Thee only about our need, and speak therefore to this brother, so that he may help us."

Today, in answer to this my request, this brother sent 100l., of which sum I shall take 20l. for the Orphans, and 20l.. for each of the other objects. Thus I have means for establishing the Infant-School, and for ordering more Bibles. Also the Orphans are again supplied for a week; for when the money came in there was not one penny in hand for them.

April 7. This evening I received information from my little half brother that my dear father died on March 30th. He was taken worse a few days after I left him. How kind of the Lord to have allowed me once more to see him! Had I gone to Germany at the time I first intended, he would most likely not have been alive to see me.--As I know not of one believer in the whole town where he lived, I cannot for a certainty ascertain any thing about his state before his death; but that which I do know gives me no proof of his having died in the faith of Christ. As to myself, I am sure of this, that it becomes me to adore that wonderful grace which plucked me as a brand out of the burning, and to say in reference to my dear departed father: "Shall not the judge of all the earth do right?" and in submission to the will of God to be satisfied with His dealings. This, through grace, I am able to do. Every true believer who has unconverted parents, for whose spiritual welfare he is concerned, can understand what joy it would have been to me to have heard a satisfactory account of a true change of heart in my dear father before his end; but as it has been otherwise, I know nevertheless that God will be eternally glorified even in this dispensation. During no period did I pray more frequently or more earnestly for the conversion of my dear aged parent, than during the last year of his life; but, at all events, it did not please the Lord to let me see the answer to my prayers.

April 9. Through the 20l. which came in on March 26, and a number of smaller and larger donations since then, we have had for the last twelve days more than usual. But now today our means were again reduced to 7s. 10d., when the Lord sent in 5l. through a brother in Bristol, who during this year also, as at former times, has been the instrument in the hands of God of repeatedly supplying our need when we were very poor.

We are on the point of sending some money to the East Indies for Missionary objects. Whilst I was on my knees respecting this object, 5l. was brought for it.

April 10. Today came in still further for the Orphans, with Eccles. ix. 10, 5l.; also 2l.

April 19. For several months past it had appeared to brother Craik and me, and to several other brethren who help us in the work of caring for the saints, that a part of the church meeting together at Gideon Chapel was a hinderance to our giving that clear and distinct testimony respecting the principles on which we meet, which we desire to give to the world and to the church at large in this city. As the Lord, however, had so abundantly blessed our labours in that place, in the conversion of sinners, and also in the building up of many saints, we felt that we ought to act in this matter with the greatest prayerfulness and consideration; and we had therefore many meetings for prayer and deliberation with several brethren. On this account it was likewise, that though we came as early as the 17th of January to the conclusion that it would be better to relinquish Gideon as a meeting place, we still deferred the matter for two months and a half longer, before we even mentioned our difficulties publicly. At last, on March 30th, we assembled with all the saints, and brother Craik and I stated to them our difficulties. The following is the substance of what was stated at the meeting.

Brief statement of certain difficulties connected with our continuing to retain the occupancy of Gideon Chapel, Newfoundland Street, Bristol.

In order to enter into the force of the following particulars, it is necessary to keep in mind the position which, as a body of saints, we seem called upon to maintain, in this city, before the church and the world. We meet simply as believers in Christ, without reference to any sectarian distinction, maintaining the Scriptures as our only rule of doctrine and discipline, and affording freedom for the exercise of any spiritual gift which the Lord may be pleased to bestow. We thus hold out a gathering place for all who believe in the Lord Jesus, and desire to confess His name, by obedience to His authority. Whatever impedes us, in this our great work, can only be suffered to continue, if the Lord Himself lays it upon us as a burden or chastisement. Nothing but necessity can justify our putting any obstacles in the way of the saints in this city, who, feeling the obligation of separating from every sectarian bond of union, would desire to meet with us.

SECOND PART

I.

1. There seems no sufficient reason for holding our Lord's day morning meetings, for the breaking of bread, in two different places. See 1 Cor. xi. 20. The number is not too large to assemble in one place, and the extent of locality is not so great as to prevent it, except in the ease of invalids or of very aged persons: and the disadvantages of two meeting places are very serious. In this way of meeting the gifts are needlessly divided, as the gifted brethren are in two places instead of one; discipline is rendered very difficult to be executed, as it can scarcely be ascertained who absent themselves, etc.; and impediments are thrown in the way of mutual intercourse and acquaintance, as the saints sometimes go to the one place, and sometimes to the other.

2. There are only four ways in which we can so arrange as to assemble every Lord's day morning, as a church, together. a, Bethesda may be given up, and the meeting of the saints maybe at Gideon. b, The meetings maybe alternately at each place. c, The meetings may be held at a third place intermediate, in respect of locality, between the two. d, Gideon may be given up, and Bethesda alone become the place of meeting for breaking of bread.

--In regard to the first two of these four arrangements, the size of Gideon puts a complete obstacle in the way, as there would not be sufficient room, were the saints and others, who would still attend, to meet together in that place. The third plan appears to be freest from all objections, could it be accomplished; but there is no one other place to be obtained sufficiently large for our purpose, and therefore, if it be granted that the profit of the saints and the glory of Christ seem to require our having one gathering place, till the number of the saints and the extent of locality on which they reside shall force us to have more than one: the only way in which, for the present, this can be accomplished is by our relinquishing Gideon, and having Bethesda as our only place of meeting.6

II.

But the above are not the only reasons why we should no longer continue to retain Gideon as a meeting place for the church.--We have reason to believe that several of our dear brethren, who have been in the habit of assembling there for worship, do not see with us in reference to the great leading principles on which we professedly meet. Ever since the removal of any restraint upon the exercise of whatever gift the Spirit may bestow, in connexion with the practice of weekly communion at Gideon, there has been dissatisfaction on the part of some. A few have left and gone to other places, some have been in the habit of remaining only as long as there is teaching or exhortation, and then leaving without breaking bread. We have reason to believe that several do not, in heart, acknowledge us as taught of God in regard to the changes, which we have introduced; or, if they feel unwilling to say so, yet they are inclined to retain their old way. Now, spiritual rule can only be continued over those who yield willing subjection: an unwilling submission on the part of those who are in the place "of the ruled," we deem no true subjection at all. Therefore, those who do not believe that matters are conducted amongst us in a Scriptural way, cannot comfortably continue in fellowship with us: and by yielding up to them the use of the Chapel, we take away all just cause of complaint.--On account of these reasons there would be no need of leaving a meeting place under other circumstances; but as, when brother Craik and I came to Gideon Chapel, we found saints there assembled together in fellowship who had contributed towards the purchasing and fitting up of the Chapel, and who had been in the habit of meeting together on different principles, it seems not Christlike either to force our light upon them, or to constrain them to leave us; but to give up the Chapel to them, as they do not, in heart, go along with us. It cannot be expected that, for the sake of pleasing even those whom we love in Christ, we should shrink back from carrying out any truth which the Lord may lead us into; and, therefore, if our brethren cannot heartily go along with us, it is better that nothing should be imposed upon them contrary to their convictions. If it should be said that for the sake of a few we thus separate from many: our reply is, that we separate from none of the saints; we only withdraw from a building, because it appears to us a hinderance to the manifesting of the truth, and, at the same time hold out a gathering place for all who feel that it would be for the edification of their souls, and the glory of God, that they should continue to meet with us. We invite all those who conscientiously can submit to the order which obtains amongst us, to continue in fellowship with us; and we purpose to provide a place of meeting to suit the convenience of the feeble and aged who would feel the distance of Bethesda to be an obstacle to their meeting habitually with the saints there.

III.

But in addition to those already mentioned, there is a third class of difficulties connected with retaining Gideon. The present character of the meeting for the breaking of bread there, is very far from fully exhibiting the principles on which we meet together. Unbelievers sitting among the saints, hinders our appearing to meet for the breaking of bread, and renders it necessary that a disturbing pause should intervene between the act of breaking bread and the other part of the meeting. We cannot have the breaking of bread at the commencement of the meeting, because of the confusion occasioned by the intermixture of those who are not in fellowship with us. To alter

SECOND PART

this, and to request all who are not in fellowship with us (except those belonging to the families of the saints) to sit by themselves, as is the case at Bethesda, would, we fear, produce increased dissatisfaction. Such a request moreover would not be Christlike, as long as from the construction of the building no comfortable sittings were reserved for any besides the saints themselves. Thus, by retaining Gideon, we are under the necessity of either marring our testimony to the church at large, or of deepening the dissatisfaction prevalent among several who are already in fellowship with us.--Again, the very construction of the place renders it unsuitable for a meeting of saints. Part of the sittings being pews, necessarily tends to give the appearance of a distinction between the very poor and the more respectable class. This distinction would need to be done away, and we have every reason to fear that some might feel personally aggrieved by the pews being taken away and replaced with benches. We have only of late understood that some of the pews are looked upon as private property. This is such a violation of the statement that the sittings are all free, that it could no longer be permitted. To require these unscriptural practices to be renounced, we have reason to apprehend, would be considered as an arbitrary act of rule, and might alienate the minds of those of our dear brethren who are still, in heart, attached to that to which they hare been accustomed in former years.

If it can be shown that the above difficulties are capable of being removed, or that any greater evil would attend the yielding up of Gideon than the evils which necessarily accompany our retaining it, then we are bound not to give it up. But, according to our present light, we see no way of reconciling the two objects, viz.: the retaining of Gideon, and the exhibiting a full, unhindered testimony to the truth of God. We repeat it, that we do not separate from any single individual in fellowship with us, we only leave the walls of a building, and invite those who feel called upon to separate from every sectarian system, and to meet where free exercise is afforded for every spiritual gift, to assemble with us at Bethesda.

In the case of those who are in ordinary health, the inconvenience attending the locality of Bethesda is a matter of very little consequence. Half an hour's earlier rising on the morning of the Lord's day, would be sufficient, in most cases, fully to meet the difficulty; and the consciousness, that the glory of Jesus and the true welfare of His church were thereby promoted, would far more than compensate for the amount of self-denial which the inconvenience arising from the distance would impose.--In reference to the weak, the sickly, and the very aged, who reside in the neigbourhood of Gideon, we trust, in the strength of the Lord, to make such ample provision for their comfort on the Lord's day, that they may have no reason to regret that Gideon has been relinquished. Lastly, as it regards the opportunities which will be lost, by giving up Gideon, of proclaiming the truth among believers, as well as preaching the gospel to the world, we intend, according to our ability and the measure of gift amongst us, to open places for those purposes in different parts of the city.

After we had fully stated our minds respecting our difficulties in continuing to meet, as a church, at Gideon Chapel, we were still quite willing to continue to occupy it as a preaching place, provided the brethren whose property the Chapel was (because of their having contributed towards the purchase and fitting up of the building,) were perfectly satisfied with our doing so. If this had been the case, all the difference would have been, that on Lord's day mornings Gideon Chapel would have been shut, and all the church would have met at Bethesda; but we should have been willing not only to preach in Gideon on the Lord's day evenings, and once or twice in the week, but also on the Lord's day afternoons instead of the morning meeting: so that even the unconverted, or the believers of that neighbourhood, who are not in communion with us, should have been no losers.--Whilst nothing was stated by any one, that showed us we had been mistaken in the conclusion to which we had come, a point was mentioned which soon brought the matter to a final decision. It was said that the giving up of one of the principal meetings on the Lord's day would be against the spirit of the trust deeds, as the Chapel was particularly intended to be a preaching place. Now, though we did not see it to be thus, as we meant to preach the Word, as before, at Gideon, if it could be done in perfect harmony with the owners of it; yet it seemed beyond a question that we could not retain the Chapel, whilst we appeared, even in the least to alienate the property from the use for which it was said to have been intended. We, therefore, were confirmed by this in our conclusion to give up the Chapel at once, and that entirely. [In order that the aged and infirm, and invalids who live in the neighbourhood of Gideon, might not be losers by the change, cars were provided, at the expense of the church, to convey them to the meeting for the breaking of bread at Bethesda; and a Chapel was rented in Callow-hill Street, near Gideon, in which, on the Lord's day and Thursday evenings the Word was ministered, It was very kind of the Lord to order it so that this chapel was at once to be had! Two years and a half afterwards, in October, 1842, we rented a still more suitable Chapel, in the heart of the City. On April 19th, 1840, we preached for the last time at Gideon, after having laboured there, with abundant blessing, for about eight years. Only three saints, as far as I know, out of about 250, who used to meet with us at Gideon, remained there. Nor has the Lord ceased to bless our labours since we left.]

April 27. Monday. The Lord knew that we were penniless, and should be in need of fresh supplies today for the Orphans, therefore He moved the hearts of some of His children to remember us, in answer to our prayer. Yesterday I received with Eccles. ix. 10, 5l., and 10s. from a sister who had lent this sum to some one, but never expected it again; and now, having unexpectedly received it, gave it to the Lord for the Orphans. 1l. 10s. was given for the rent of the Orphan-Houses. There was 2s. 6d. put anonymously into the box at Bethesda, and also 1l. This morning I was informed that 5l. had been sent to the Infant-Orphan-House. Thus the Lord has given for our need 13l. 2s. 6d.

Let us pause here a few moments, beloved reader! Let us adore the Lord's kindness! See how seasonably the Lord sends the help. As our need is, so He remembers us. It is not now and then that He is mindful of us, but continually. As

SECOND PART

surely as we stand in need of any thing, He sends it; be it money, provisions, clothes, or any thing else. We may be allowed to be poor, yea, very poor; we may have to pray again and again to our Father before the answer comes; we may be reduced so as to have from mal to meal to wait upon Him; yea, according to all outward appearance, the Lord may seem to have forgotten us:--but, amidst it all, as surely as we really need any thing, in His own time and way does He send help. Perhaps you may say; "But how would you do, in case there were a mealtime to come and you had no provisions for the children, or they really wanted clothes, and you had no money to procure them?" Our answer is, such a thing is impossible as long as the Lord shall give us grace to trust in Him, (for "whosoever believeth on Him shall not be ashamed,") and as long as He shall enable us to carry on the work in uprightness of heart. But should we be ever so left to ourselves as to forsake the Lord and trust in an arm of flesh, or should we regard iniquity in our heart i. e. wilfully and habitually do any thing, either in connexion with the work or otherwise, which is against the will of God, then we may pray and utter many words before Him, but He will not hear us, as it is written: "If I regard iniquity in my heart, the Lord will not hear me." Psalm lxvi. 18. I, therefore, beseech all who love our Lord Jesus and who may read this, to entreat Him on behalf of all of us who are engaged in this work, that He would be pleased to continue to give us faith, and that He would keep us from living in sin.

May 2. Nothing having come in for five days, we were today again penniless. In answer to prayer 5s. 6d. came in, and some trinkets were sent, the names of which the donor does not wish to be known. Thus we were helped through this day.-- Observe here, how the Lord allowed five days to pass away without influencing the hearts of any to send us supplies; but the moment there is real need, the stream runs again.

May 3. Today the Lord sent in again some money for the Orphans. He knew we were penniless, and therefore answered our requests. Besides 1l. 10s. for rent, there came in 1l. 1s. from London, and 2l. from the Isle of Wight.

May 4. By what came in yesterday, we were supplied for today; but the Lord sent today still more, as that which came in yesterday was only enough for today. There was given in money 7l., of which 3l. was the profit of the sale of ladies' baskets, which are made by some sisters in the Lord for the benefit of the Orphans.

Last evening a brother was baptized, who on the first Lord's day of this year came with his intended wife to Bethesda Chapel. Both were in an unconverted state. They both were at the same meeting, through what brother Craik said, made to feel the power of the truth, and, in consequence, were led to Jesus and found peace in Him, and are now both in communion with us.--The Lord still condescends to use us as instruments. Today we conversed with seven persons about fellowship, and had to send away five, being worn out after we had seen the seven, one after the other. Only since April 1st, forty-one persons have come to us to speak about their souls. May the Lord in mercy give us helpers in the work, for truly the harvest is great; and may not our ingratitude for His abundant blessing upon our labours oblige Him to shut up His hands from continuing to use us!

May 6th. This evening I received 10l. for the Orphans, and 10l. for the Infant-School, which we are on the point of opening. Before our little stock is quite exhausted, (for there is yet 2l. left for the Orphans) the Lord has thus kindly sent a fresh supply. Thus also my prayer is answered in being able to give to two of the sisters in the Orphan-Houses some money for their personal expenses.

May 8. There are four believers staying at my house, and today we had only a few shillings of our own money left. I gave myself, therefore, to prayer for means for our own personal expenses. In answer to my request, I received this morning 5l.

May 10. Today five of the Orphans were received into fellowship and baptized. There are now fourteen of them in fellowship.

May 16. The need of today, as we were again penniless, led us to open the boxes in the Orphan-Houses, in which 2l. 0s. 2d. was found. There was given 5s. besides. In the evening came in still further a sovereign from a sister, a servant, with the following lines: The Lord has put it into my heart to send a sovereign to the Orphans. He indeed put it into my heart, which was once at enmity with God and would have said, lay it by, you may want it when you are old; but then I could not look towards heaven and say, I know my Heavenly Father will supply all my need; neither could I say, 'Abba, Father,' for I knew Him not."

May 17. Today the Lord has sent a little more, so that we have enough to meet the demands of tomorrow. There came in altogether 3l. 9s. 6d.

May 22. Several small donations enabled us to supply the necessities of the last four days. When this day commenced, however, there was again not a penny in hand. But my eyes were directed to the Lord, and therefore my heart was at peace; I was fully assured that He would help this day also. About eleven I was informed that there was 19s. 3d. in hand, being the produce of the boys' knitting, and that also some old clothes, given for sale, had been sold for 3s. 6d., and one Report besides for 3d. To this one of the labourers added 4s. of his own, and gave a book besides for sale. Thus we had 1l. 7s., which was enough to meet the demands of this day.

May 26. By the sale of 166 little books which had been given to be disposed of, by a few shillings which came in for the children's needlework, by 4s. which had been taken out of the boxes in the Orphan-Houses, by a little money given by one of the labourers, by 10s. which came anonymously in a letter, and by the sale of some Reports--we were able to meet the demands since the 22nd. Today there was 1l. 2s. 8d. left in hand, but this was not quite enough for the need of the day. In the afternoon came in for needlework 11s. 6d., and there was 5s. left at the Infant-Orphan House. Thus we had enough, and a few shillings left for tomorrow.

SECOND PART

May 26. Nothing had come in. My engagements kept me from going to the Orphan-Houses till seven in the evening, when the labourers met together for prayer. When we met I found that one of them had given 17s., which had been divided between the three houses. This, with the little which had been left yesterday, had procured all necessary articles. We are now very poor.

May 27. We met for prayer, at eleven this morning. No money had come in, but there was enough for dinner in all the houses. This morning the LAST COALS were used in the Infant-Orphan-House, and in the Boys'-Orphan-House there were ONLY ENOUGH FOR TODAY, and there was no money in hand to buy more. In this our need T.P.C. sent a load of coals. How kind of the Lord! A plain proof that not in displeasure, but only for the trial of our faith we are allowed to be so poor. We purpose to meet again at four this afternoon. May the Lord graciously be pleased to send help in the mean time!

Evening. The Lord has had mercy! A person bought some days since several articles, which had been given to be sold for the benefit of the Orphans, and owed 6l. 15s. This morning I asked the Lord to incline his heart to bring the money, or a part of it, as we were in such need. Just as I was going to meet for prayer with my fellow-labourers this afternoon, he came and brought 4l. But our kind Father showed us still further today, that only for the trial of our faith He had for a season withheld supplies; for there was given this evening with Eccles. ix. 10, 5l. There came in also 9s. for articles which had been put into the hand of a sister, who has taken on her the service of disposing of articles which are given for sale. Besides this, there were sent two boxes of new clothes, and some materials for clothes, from sisters in the Lord, residing in Dublin, which articles are worth several pounds. Thus the day, which had begun with prayer, ended in praise. But there is one thing more to be recorded respecting this day, as precious or more so than what has been said: I was today informed that the Lord has begun to stir up several of the boys to care about their souls.

May 28. The Lord has kindly sent in further supplies. A clergyman gave 2l.; and 5s. came in for Reports.

May 29. Today has come in still further 1l. 3s. 2d., and several trinkets which were sent from Barnstaple.

May 30. I took 1l. out of the box in my house.

May 31. When there was again not a penny in hand, the Lord sent in 2l. 2s.

June 6. This is Saturday. Several pounds were needed, as usual, for the Orphans; but there was not a penny in hand. In this our great need F. W., who often has been instrumental in supplying our need, and who lives many miles from Bristol, sent 5l. There came in 5s. besides. Thus we are helped to the close of one more week, in which our faith has been repeatedly tried. In the evening came in further, by sale of articles, 2l., and a donation of 10s.

June 7. Lord's day. Today came in 7l. 1s. 3d., to enable us to meet the necessities of tomorrow.

June 8. This evening eight German Missionary brethren and sisters, whom I have been for some time expecting, arrived in Bristol, on their way to the East Indies.

June 9. Again, when only 2s. 3d. was in hand for the Orphans, there came in from a considerable distance 2l.

June 10 and 11. These two days came in 1l. 0s. 4d., which was enough, with the little which had been left, to procure what was needed.

June 12. When there was nothing in hand, several articles of gentlemen's clothing, all worn, were sent for sale, which, being disposed of for 1l. 17s., we were helped through this day.

June 13. Today's need was met by a box of clothes coming from Worcester, which contained also 3l. 0s. 2d. There was also 11s. taken out of the box in my house.

June 15. 2l. 5s. 3d. came in yesterday and today, by which we were able to meet the necessary demands, and have 5s. left.

June 16. Some articles were sold for 11s., which had been given for sale. This, with the remaining 5s., met the necessities of the day.

June 17. Only 4s. has come in by children's needlework. This is all we have, to meet the need of today, except 2s. 6d., which I found in the box in my house, which our poverty led me to open. Evening. The Lord has had mercy upon us. A sister, to whom some time since some money was left, and whom the Lord has made willing to lay it all out in His service, having received a small part of what is coming to her, brought 5l. 10s. 6d. of it, this afternoon, for the Orphans. There came in still further this evening 2l.

For several days past I had been very poor in reference to my own temporal necessities, as well as in reference to the Orphans. Today we were especially poor, in both respects; but our kind Father remembered not merely the need of the dear Orphans, but gave me also some money for my own personal expenses. The same sister just referred to, who brought 5l. 10s. 6d. for the Orphans, brought me also 7l. for myself.

SECOND PART

June 18. Today a new coat and waistcoat were given to me, for which I had repeatedly asked the Lord, as my clothes are now very old. As surely as I really need any thing, be it in money, or in any other way, my kind Father supplies the need.

June 19. The Lord has poured in still more abundantly today. A brother gave me 10l. for myself. Thus, after a season of more than usual poverty, the Lord sends a more than usual supply. How kind a Master do I serve!

June 21. Again, when there was not one penny in hand, came in today 6l. 10s. for the Orphans.

June 22. Tomorrow, the Lord willing, I purpose, with my wife, to accompany the three German brethren and the five German sisters to Liverpool who purpose to sail from thence. Under these circumstances it is desirable to leave at least a little money behind. This desire of my heart the Lord has granted; for this morning D. C. gave me 5l., and there came in by sale of articles 10s. 5d. In the evening a sister, who has left Bristol today, sent me by her mother 5l., having particularly requested her to let me have the money today, as she knew that I was going away tomorrow.

This evening we had an especial Missionary prayer meeting, at which the brethren and sisters were commended to the Lord.

June 23. This morning we left for Liverpool, where we safely arrived in the evening.

The following extracts give the account of the Lord's goodness in supplying the necessities of the Orphans, while I was away from Bristol.

On June 25, whilst at Liverpool, I received a letter from brother R. B., master at the Boys'-Orphan-House, dated Bristol, June 24th, in which he writes thus:--The money which you left behind, with 1s. 6d. which came in for Reports, supplied the necessities of yesterday and today; but there is nothing in hand to meet the necessities of tomorrow. Our hope is in God, assuredly believing that He will, as in former times, help us in His own time and manner."--

Two days afterwards the following letter came.

"Bristol, June 26, 1840.

"Dear Brother,--Since I wrote to you we have very sweetly proved the mercy and truth of our heavenly Father, When my letter left Bristol, we had not one penny in hand. On the same evening sister gave me a parcel containing 1l. 1s., the produce of the sale of an article. This was sufficient for yesterday. But after this we were again penniless. I went to the meeting in the evening, where brother J. B. gave me a list of names of persons who had given to him for the Orphans, to the amount of 1l. 4s. 1d. I afterwards sold one of your books, one of brother Craik's Renderings, and a

THE LORD'S DEALINGS WITH GEORGE MÜLLER

Report. I also remembered that a few days before 2s. 6d. had been given to me which I had forgotten to use. We therefore had in all 1l. 11s. 7d., which is sufficient to meet this day's necessities. I have just received a sovereign for the Orphans, and besides this a box, containing various articles of clothes which has been sent from Wales, part of which articles are only fit for sale. Thus we have something for tomorrow, if needed.

"Your affectionate brother,

"R. B,"

The arrival of the box of clothes, etc., was announced to me in an affectionate letter from a brother in Wales, who sent them, but whom I do not know personally. What follows will show how seasonably the donation came. On June 30th I received another letter from brother B., dated Bristol, June 29th, 1840, in which he writes "I should have posted my letter by one o'clock, but delayed until it was too late, hoping that I might have to speak of the Lord's goodness as well as of our poverty. Thank God, my hopes have been realized!—Besides the 1l. mentioned in my last letter, in the evening of the 26th 11s. 3d. came in for needlework, and 5s. was given. On Saturday I sold some of the clothes which had been sent from Wales for 1l., and 5s. was given to me for an article which had been sold some time ago. As this was scarcely sufficient, I opened the boxes, and found 3s. 2d. in them. The whole, therefore, which was in hand, amounted to 3l. 4s. 5d., which was enough for Saturday the 27th. This morning, Monday, as nothing had been given to me since Saturday, there were no means to provide for the dinner in the Boys'-Orphan-House; but one of the sisters, having a little money of her own, purchased potatoes and meat with it. At eleven o'clock we met for prayer. The baker came to the Infant-Orphan-House, but no bread was taken. A brother left two quarterns of bread at the Boys'-Orphan-House, as a gift. Soon after I received 1l. through sister L. G., which, as soon as I received, I began to write to you. It was a comfort to me, in our poverty, that you still, united in spirit, prayed with us, although distance separated us in body. I do not know that I ever felt more powerfully the kindness of our Heavenly Father, than when I received this last mentioned 1l. Although we are still poor, and soon shall be again in need, yet, receiving it just at this time, it was very refreshing."

The next day I received the following report about the Orphan-Houses from brother B., dated June 30th.--" According to your request, tomorrow only is the time for me to write, but as the Lord has dealt very bountifully with us, I write today, in order that you may be refreshed by the account thereof. Yesterday afternoon, I received 16s., and this morning I sold some more of the articles sent from Wales, for 8s. 6d., which meets this day's demands."

On July 2nd I accompanied the eight German brethren and sisters to the vessel. Just before they went on board, brother ----, one of the missionary brethren, gave me 6l. 10s. for the Orphans. He had sold his plate while at Bristol, considering that as a servant of Jesus Christ, and as one who desired to preach Jesus to the poor Hindoos, he needed it not, This money was the produce of it, except about 2l., which he had spent in purchasing a few books. In giving it to me said, "The money which we have in the common stock, (being altogether 20l. for the eight) is enough for us. For some months, while we are on board, we need no money at all, whilst you may lay it out; and when we need more, the Lord will again supply our need. The other brethren and sisters have no money of their own, and I desire likewise to have none, The Lord has laid the Orphans particularly on my heart, and therefore you must not refuse to accept it."--This brother little knew how on that very day I had been repeatedly asking the Lord for means. Truly this was one of the most remarkable ways of obtaining money, as it came from a poor German missionary, who, in dependence upon the Lord for his temporal supplies, went to the East Indies. I sent off at once 5l. of this money to Bristol. The next day, July 3, I received at Liverpool the following letter from brother B., dated Bristol, July 2nd.--" Since I last wrote, we have still found that the Lord is faithful to His word. May we never be unfaithful towards Him! On Tuesday evening, June 30th, sister C. brought 11s. 6d. for some articles she sold, and I had received 1s. 6d. for Reports. This, with 8s. that had been put into the boxes, met the absolute necessities of yesterday, Wednesday. As nothing has been given since Tuesday, we are, today, Thursday, very needy. I sold the books I mentioned as being sent, with some others which one of the sisters in the Orphan-Houses gave of her own, for 7s., which bought that which was needful for dinner; but there is no money to take in bread nor milk for one of the houses. We met for prayer. Our hope is in God, trusting that He who has so often helped us in poverty, will still do so. If I write any more I shall be too late to post this letter."

[On my return to Bristol I found, which is not mentioned in the next letter, that the milk was purchased with the money of one of the sisters in the Orphan-Houses.]

On July 4th I received the following letter from Bristol, dated July 3rd.

"My dear Brother,--The last account I sent you left us in the greatest poverty. We had sufficient, it is true, for the time then present; but there was no money to take in bread with. In the afternoon there was an old riding habit sent for the Orphans, which I sold this morning for 7s. I also sold a few books for 5s., two old silver thimbles and a ring for 1s. 6d.; besides this, 1s. 6d. was sent for Reports; making in all 15s. This purchased dinner for the three houses. At twelve o'clock we met for prayer. We were indeed in great need. There was no money either for bread or milk. The coals in all the three houses were used, and in every other respect the stores were in a low state. We had really wanted nothing, but there was scarcely any thing left. Well, while we were in prayer to God, your letter came. One of the sisters opened the door and received it, and after prayer it was given to me. You will be able to conceive the greatness of our joy, on opening it, and finding it to contain 5l. I cannot express how much I felt. During the trial I had been much comforted by the Lord's sending a little token of his love every day. It just proved that He was mindful of us in our poverty, and that when His time was come, He would send us an abundance. I think we all felt your absence a little, although not cast down on that account. Money is very precious to those who, like us, so evidently see the HAND and HEART of our Heavenly Father in bestowing it, The sisters send their love to you.

"Your affectionate brother,

"R. B."

On July 6th I received the following account from Bristol, dated July 5th. "You are, I am sure, often praying for us, and therefore see, in the help we receive, God's gracious answers to your prayers, and therefore you will be refreshed by hearing the account of how matters are with us. On Saturday there was again a little money needed in the Girls'-Orphan-House, for butter and such little articles; but I had none in hand, wherewith to supply this need, until nearly tea time, when 5s. was given to me. In the evening of the same day, at ten o'clock, 10s. was sent through brother J. S. You will see that we are still cast simply on God for the future, without anything to depend on but Himself; and on whom, or on what should children depend, but on their most kind Father."

On July 8th, whilst still detained in the Lord's service at Liverpool, I received from a brother 10l. for the Orphans, which I sent off at once. On the same day, after I had sent off the money, I received the following letter from Bristol, dated July 7.

"The Lord is still pleased to keep us very low. Only 4s. 2d. in money has come in since last I wrote to you. The 10s. I told you of, and this 4s. 2d., I divided among the sisters. But as this was far from being sufficient, and knowing that you had received 6l. 10s. and only sent 5l., I took out of the other funds 1l. 6s. 6d., being all that I could spare, and divided it also. I would not have done so, had it not been needful, and had it not appeared to me that we were not going out of the path of obedience in doing this. There was a sack of flour sent this morning. We are still, we may say, in need, as even the money, which I have divided, was not enough to purchase every thing desirable to have."

On July 11th, whilst at Worcester, I received the following letter, dated Bristol, July 9.

"After writing to you the last time, I got no more money on that day, except 1s. The next day, Wednesday, I received 2s. 6d., and took 2s. out of the box in the Boys'-Orphan-House. Also a sister purchased a Bible, and out of that money I took 3s. 6d. to make up the 30s., to which I alluded in my last letter. This carried us through the day. In the evening of the same day I received 11s. 3d. and 2s., which purchased meat for dinner; and the potatoes in the boys' garden, being now fit for use, we had for dinner. After the dinner was provided we received the 10l. from you, which enabled the sisters again to replenish their stock. Out of the 10l. I kept the 30s., in case I might need it on Saturday for the salaries of the masters and governesses of the Day Schools. We felt the poverty a little more, I think, on account of your absence. I knew the Lord would help, but still I felt tried in some measure. The Lord, by His grace, reproves our waywardness towards Him.

When this letter arrived, there was sent to me, at the same time, from Bristol, 5l. for the Orphans, which I sent off at once. On July 17th I returned to Bristol.

I add a few more words respecting my stay at Liverpool.

--About October 1837 I sent some Bibles and 46 copies of my Narrative to a brother in Upper Canada, who, in dependence upon the Lord for temporal supplies, is labouring as a missionary in that country. About eighteen months afterwards I heard, that this box had not arrived. I then wrote to the shipbroker at Liverpool, (who as agent had to send it to America, and to whom I had paid his commission and the freight), to make inquiry about the box; but I received no answer. About a month afterwards my letter was returned to me, through the Dead-Letter Office, and it was stated on the outside that the individual had left Liverpool, and no one knew where he was gone. Putting all these things together, I had now full reason to think that the broker had, never sent off the box. My comfort, however, was, that though this poor sinner had acted thus, yet the Lord, in His own place and way, would use the Bibles and my Narratives. Now, almost immediately after my arrival in Liverpool, a brother told me, that several persons wished to hear me preach who had read my Narrative; and that he knew a considerable number had been bought by a brother, a bookseller, from pawnbrokers, and sold again; and that some also had been ordered from London when there were no more to be had otherwise. It was thus evident that the shipbroker pawned these Narratives before he absconded; but the Lord used them as I had hoped.--I preached ten times in English and once in German whilst at Liverpool, and I know that several persons were brought to hear me, through having read my Narrative.--The German brethren preached twice in German, there being several German vessels in the port, and a number of German sugar refiners living at Liverpool. Liverpool seems to me especially a place where a brother, who is familiar with French and German, may find an abundance of work among the German and French sailors, in the way of preaching to them, and in the way of distributing French and German Bibles and Tracts.--One of the German missionary brethren found out a brother in the Lord, a native of the same town in Prussia, from whence he himself comes, who repeatedly met with us. This dear sailor was the only believer in the vessel in which he was, and has had to suffer much for the Lord's sake.--When the German brethren and sisters were going on board, I engaged a fly for the purpose of taking all their small luggage. When the man put the luggage into the fly, I was struck by its having a hind boot, which I had never seen before in any fly, which he opened, and into which he put several carpet bags. There were seventeen packages altogether. When we arrived at the vessel it was just on the point of going into the river, with several other vessels, and there were crowds of people standing at the docks. The flyman took out the luggage and was on the point of leaving, when I asked him whether he had taken out all the luggage, which I had not been able to count, because of the pressure of people, and the rapidity with which the packages were taken to the vessel. His reply was, Yes. But all at once, by the good hand of God, I remembered the hind boot, and I asked him to open it. The man, somewhat confused, opened it, and in it were five or six carpet bags. This thing showed me afresh our entire dependence upon the Lord, step by step. I was alone. The crowd was great. The vessel was on the point of sailing: and all without my fault or the fault of any one; but it was so through unforseen circumstances. One minute later, and the bags, in all human probability, would have been lost. For when the brethren had missed their luggage, it would have been too late; for though I had marked the number of the fly when I engaged it, yet that would have profited nothing, when once the brethren were at sea. But the hand of God was for good upon these His children, whose stock of linen was only such as they would need. Such a circumstance should teach one to make the very smallest affairs a subject of prayer; for instance, That all the luggage might be safely taken out of a fly.

On July 10th my wife and I left Liverpool, where we had experienced much kindness, for Worcester, where we stayed a few days, and had again much love shown to us by the saints there.

July 25. Since July 11th the Lord has kindly sent in the supplies for the Orphans, so that we have had always something coming in, before the last which was in hand was spent. Now, today, having paid out this morning 8l. 5s., again nothing was left in hand, when in the afternoon 3l. came in by sale of articles.

July 26. Lord's-day. As I had no opportunity today of preaching in our chapels (there being two brethren ministering among us who are strangers in Bristol), I have preached twice this evening in the open air. Precious as this work is, yet I am sure it is not that to which I am called for a constancy, as I have no strength of body for it. But I have seen afresh this evening how greatly it is needed. The second time I preached, I took my stand in a court, filled with poor people, almost every one of whom was dirty, though it was the Lord's day evening. A woman readily lent me a chair on which I stood, and could thus be heard by the people in the houses behind and before me, and on my right and left hand. Judging from their dirty appearance, I should not suppose any of these poor people had been any where, to hear the Gospel preached throughout the day. How plenteous is the harvest, and how few are the labourers! Lord of the harvest, send Thou, in compassion to poor sinners, more labourers into the harvest! --How well a brother who has some gift, and a measure of strength of lungs, might employ a part of the Lord's days, or of other days, either by reading the Scriptures from house to house to such persons, and making some remarks on them; or by standing up in a court and reading the Scriptures aloud and speaking on them. It is very rarely that one meets with decided opposition on these occasions; at least I have generally in such cases found far more readiness to listen, than decidedly to oppose.

SECOND PART

Aug. 1. A few days since a brother was staying with me, on his way to his father, whom he had not seen for above two years, and who was greatly opposed to him, on account of the decided steps which his son had taken for the Lord. Before this brother left, that precious promise of our Lord was brought to my mind: "If two of you shall agree on earth as touching any thing that they shall ask, it shall be done for them of my Father which is in heaven." Matt. xviii. 19. Accordingly, I went to the brother's room, and having agreed to pray about a kind reception from his father, and the conversion of both parents, we prayed together.--Today this brother returned. The Lord has answered already one part of the prayer. The brother was most kindly received, contrary to all natural expectation. May the Lord now help us both to look for an answer to the other part of our prayer! There is nothing too hard for the Lord!

Since the publication of the third edition, the father of this brother died. He lived above ten years after Aug. 1, 1840, until he was above 86 years of age; and as he continued a life of much sin and opposition to the truth, the prospect with reference to his conversion became darker and darker. But at last the Lord answered prayer. This aged sinner was entirely changed, simply rested on the Lord Jesus for the salvation of his soul, and became as much attached to his believing son, as before he had been opposed to him; and wished to have him about him as much as possible, that he might read the Holy Scriptures to him and pray with him. Let this instance encourage believers, who have unbelieving parents, to continue in prayer for them.

Since the publication of the fourth edition, the mother also died. About sixteen years had elapsed, after her son and I had thus prayed together, before, in her case, the answer was granted; yet she, too, at last, in very advanced years, was brought to trust in the Lord Jesus alone for the salvation of her soul.--I distinctly remember, with what full assurance, that the Lord would answer our united supplication, I went to the room of this brother, to propose prayer, resting upon the promise in Matt. xviii. 19, though the case appeared to be most hopeless.

Aug. 6. Yesterday I was led, by the sense of our necessity, and the knowledge of the Father's heart, like Elijah, to go again and again to Him with my request for help, as there was nothing in hand for the Orphans to supply the necessities of today. Last evening, after the meeting, a brother from Oxford gave me a sovereign for the Orphans; by two other individuals was sent half-a-crown; and by the sale of an article, which had been given many weeks since, but was only disposed of today, came in 5s.: thus, in all, the Lord sent again 1l. 7s. 6d. This morning I heard that 10s. was given yesterday to brother B., so that we were able to meet the demands of today, which are 1l. 15s.

Aug. 7. As there was only 2s. 6d. in hand, I asked the Lord repeatedly yesterday to send us what was needed for today. When I came home last evening from the meeting, 5l. was given to me, which Q. Q. had brought while I was away, to be used as I thought well. This I took for the Orphans, which will supply our need for today and tomorrow.

Aug. 8. Saturday. This evening I was meditating on the 4th Psalm. The words in verse 3: "But know that the Lord hath set apart him that is godly for Himself; the Lord will hear when I call upon Him," I was enabled to apply to myself, and they led me to prayer for spiritual blessings. Whilst in prayer, the need of the Orphans (there being now again not one penny in hand), was also brought to my mind, and I asked the Lord respecting this likewise. ABOUT FIVE MINUTES AFTERWARDS I was informed that a sister wished to see me. She brought 1l. 10s. for the Orphans. Thus the Lord has already kindly sent a little to begin the week with. There was also still further given today, 1s. 11d.; and 5s. 1d. was taken out of the boxes in the Orphan-Houses.

Aug. 10. Monday. The 1l. 17s. which came in on Saturday evening for the Orphans, was not enough for the necessities of today, as 2l. 15s. was required. About noon, the Lord gave through a brother in Bath, who has a relative in one of the Orphan-Houses, 1l. 10s. more, so that we had enough, and a few shillings left. This evening came in 4s. besides, also 15s. 6d. by sale of articles.

Aug. 11. The money which was in hand, with 3s. which was given by one of the labourers, as there was not enough otherwise, helped us through this day.

Aug. 12. One of the labourers gave today 10s. of his own, as nothing had come in. Yet this would not have been sufficient, had there not been sold two pairs of stockings, which had been knitted by the boys, for 4s. 1d., and had not 5s. been found in one of the boxes.

Aug. 13. Yesterday there was given a collection of shells, which was sold today, and supplied the necessities of this day, with an addition of 10s. which a brother gave last evening, and 4s. which was taken out of the box in the Infant-Orphan-House.

Aug. 14. There was nothing at all in hand. I opened the box in my house, and found 1s. 4d. in it, A labourer gave 4s. of his own. There was found 1s, 6d. in the boxes in the Orphan-Houses, and 5s. came in by the sale of a few articles which had been given for that purpose. By this 11s. 10d, we were able to meet the absolute need, but were able to take in only a small quantity of bread.

Aug. 15. There was today the greatest poverty in all the three houses; all the stores were very low, as the income throughout the week had been so small. In addition to this it was Saturday, when the wants are nearly double in comparison with other days. At least 3l. was needed to help us comfortably through the day; but there was nothing towards this in hand. My only hope was in God.

The very necessity led me to expect help for this day; for if none had come, the Lord's name would have been dishonoured. Between twelve and one two sisters in the Lord called on me, and the one gave me 2l. and the other 7s. 6d. for the Orphans. With this I went to the Boys'-Orphan-House about one o'clock, where I found the children at dinner. Brother B. put the following note into my hand, which he was just going to send off:

"Dear Brother,--With potatoes from the children's garden, and with apples from the tree in the play-ground (which apples were used for apple dumplings), and 4s. 6d. the price of some articles given by one of the labourers, we have a dinner. There is much needed. But the Lord has provided and will provide."

There came in still further this day by sale of Reports, 1s., by the box in the Girls'-Orphan-House, 1s., by children's needlework, 6s. 6d., by a donation of one of the sisters in the Orphan-Houses, 6s. Thus we had this day 3l. 6s. 6d. to meet all necessities, and are brought to the close of another week.

Aug. 16. Lord's-day. There came in still further last evening, 3s. by sale of some articles, and today 2s. was given, and 5l.; so that the Lord in His love and faithfulness has given us what we are likely to need tomorrow and the day after.

Aug. 17. There has come in still further 2l.

Aug. 18. This morning a brother who passed through Bristol gave 1l., saying that it had been especially laid on his heart to do so. Thus the Lord has provided a little towards tomorrow. Besides this came in today 1s. 9d.

Aug. 19. By the sale of three pairs of stockings came in 5s. 6d., and from Liverpool was sent 12s. 6d.: this, with what was in hand, was enough for today, and left a little over.

Aug. 20. Today there was not enough money in hand to meet all the demands; but it being known that yesterday several persons had put money into the boxes in the Orphan-Houses, they were opened, and found to contain 1l. 4s. 6d., which was more than sufficient.

I would call upon the believing reader to admire the love and wisdom and power of God in ordering it so that persons should come to the Orphan-Houses just at the time when there is temporal pressure, and should be influenced to put money into the boxes. These little sums have been often the means of helping us in our greatest need. The especial providence of God, as in every other respect, so in this particular point also, is to be seen respecting this Institution, in that so much is anonymously put into the boxes; for there has been no less than 45l. 18s. 9 3/4d. put in during the last two years, from Dec. 10, 1838, to Dec. 10, 1840.

Aug. 22. Saturday. Yesterday there was only 13s. 6d. in hand, which was enough to meet the necessities of the day, but not sufficient to enable us to take in the usual quantity of bread. This morning we were in much need, not only because there were no means for procuring dinner in the Boys' and Girls'-Orphan-Houses, but also because, this being Saturday, we had to procure provisions for two days.

When brother B. went to the Infant-Orphan-House, to make inquiry about the demands for today, he was informed that money had been put into the box there, which was found to be 12s. There came in also in the morning 10s, besides. This 1l. 2s. was more than sufficient to purchase all that was needed for dinner. Between twelve and one o'clock there arrived a parcel from Clapham, which contained several donations for the Orphans, amounting to 2l. 15s., besides a pair of sheets and pillow cases, 4 frocks, 4 handkerchiefs, 4 caps, 1 stuff petticoat, 2 chemises, 6 bags, 1 little shirt, (all new), and several yards of prints and calico. In the evening came a box from Worcester, which contained the following articles for sale: a valuable veil, 2 silver ladles, a silver fork, 2 pairs of new plated candlesticks, a fan, and 2 Italian books. There came also from the neighbourhood of Wolverhampton, 2s. 6d. and seven books. Thus the Lord helped us through this day also, at the commencement of which we were so very poor, and needed several pounds.

Aug. 23. Lord's-day. As we have often found it to be the case, so it is again now. After the Lord has tried our faith, He, in the love of His heart, gives us an abundance, to show that not in anger, but for the glory of His name, and for the trial of our faith He has allowed us to be poor. This morning I received from an aged and afflicted servant, 3l.; and a little afterwards 8l. from Q. Q. From another servant 5s.; also 2s. was put anonymously into the box at Bethesda, besides the 1l. 10s. for rent. Thus the Lord has kindly given today 12l. 17s.

Aug. 29. Saturday. Since last Monday had come in only 2l. by the profits of the sale of ladies' baskets, 1l. 14s. 10d. by sale of articles, 3s. as two donations, and 6d. by Reports. Thus it happened that when this day began, though a Saturday, we had only 7s. in hand. In the course of the morning came in 11s. 9d., and towards the evening 8s. 6d. This day we have been as poor in regard to our stores, as at any time. During the whole of this day, though Saturday, we had only 1l. 7s. 3d, On this account we had to buy a smaller quantity of bread than usual, etc.; nevertheless the children have even this day lacked nothing, and there is a sufficient quantity of wholesome food till breakfast on Monday morning.

For many weeks past very little has come in for the other funds. The chief supply has been by the sale of Bibles. Last Saturday I was not able to pay the whole of the weekly salaries of the teachers in the Day Schools, which, however, does not make me a debtor to them, as it is an understood thing, that they have not to look to me for payment, but to the Lord. Today again only 2s. was in hand, whilst several pounds were needed to pay the salaries. It appeared now plainly to be the will of the Lord that, as all the labourers in the Orphan-Houses know about the state of the funds, so the brethren and sisters who labour in the Day Schools should share the trial of faith and the joy of faith with us. Accordingly we all met, and after I had laid on their hearts, the importance of keeping to themselves, for the Lord's sake, the state of the funds, we prayed together.

Aug. 30. Lord's day. Today the Lord has again bountifully opened His hand for the Orphans. There came in with Ecclesiastes ix. 10, 5l.; from a sister, a servant,

SECOND PART

10s.; and for rent 1l. 10s. Besides this, was anonymously put into the box at Bethesda, 10s. 3d. and 2s. 6d.

Sept. 1. Though there was a good supply given to the matrons yesterday, yet, as the stock of provisions had been so low on Saturday, the money was all spent by last evening; and had the Lord not kindly sent in yesterday 14s., and today 1l. 10s., we should have been again in need.

Sept. 4. The day before yesterday, Sept. 2, came a box from Leeds, from sisters in the Lord whom we have never seen, and of whom until now we have never heard, but on whose hearts the Lord has laid His work in our hands. The box contained a variety of articles, to be sold for the benefit of the Orphans. No money has come in the last two days, except 1s. which was given, and 5s. for things sold. On this account the boxes in the Orphan-Houses were opened, but only 1s. 7 1/2d. was found in them. To supply what was needed today, an article which came in the box from Leeds was sold for 5s. and thus we were helped through the day. The sisters who sent the box from Leeds wrote to us a most affectionate letter, in which they announced this and another box which is to follow, stating how much the Lord had laid the work in our hand on their hearts. They may have little thought, when they sent off the box, that so soon the produce of one of the articles sent by them would supply our need.

Sept. 5. Saturday. Because there had come in so little during the last days, at least 3l. was requisite to supply the need of today. There was, however, not one penny in hand when the day commenced. Last evening the labourers in the Orphan-Houses, together with the teachers of the Day Schools, met for prayer. This morning one of the teachers, who had a little money of his own, brought 1l. 5s. 6d. Thus, as we had hoped, we were enabled to provide for the dinner. In the afternoon all of us met again for prayer. Another teacher of the Day Schools gave 2s, 6d, and 1s. came in besides. But all this was not enough. There was no dinner provided for tomorrow, nor was there any money to take in milk tomorrow, and besides this a number of other little things were to be purchased, that there might be no real want of anything. Now observe how our kind father helped us! Between seven and eight this evening a sister, whose heart the Lord has made willing to take on her the service of disposing of the articles which are sent for sale, brought 2l. 10s. 6d. for some of the things which came a fortnight ago from Worcester, and last Wednesday from Leeds. The sister stated, that though she did not feel at all well, she had come because she had it so laid on her heart, that she could not stay away. Our Father knew our need, and therefore, though so late, He sent this help. Thus we were richly provided with all we needed this Saturday.

Sept. 6. The Lord has kindly sent in today for the Orphans 4l. 5s. 6d. for the need of tomorrow. One pound of this money was given by a servant, who has again and again given of late, and who has thus again and again been the means of supplying our need, when there was either nothing at all, or not sufficient in hand. When she gave me the money to-night, she told me that of late she had had the Orphans particularly laid on her heart. 1l. 3s. was the produce of an orphan-box, which a sister was led so seasonably to send just now.

Sept. 7. This morning a brother from Barnstaple, who came on Saturday evening (that evening when we were so greatly tried, but so graciously delivered), gave me 1l. 0s. 3d., which the love of some saints at Barnstaple had sent for the Orphans, besides 5s. of his own. We have thus enough for today and tomorrow. There came in still further today, 6s. 6d.

Sept. 8. How kindly has the Lord so ordered it that for some time past the income for the school-fund should have been so little, in order that thus we might be constrained to let the labourers in the Day Schools share our joys and our trials of faith, which had been before kept from them! But as above two years ago the Lord ordered it so that it became needful to communicate to the labourers in the Orphan-Houses the state of the funds, and made it a blessing to them, so that I am now able to leave Bristol, and yet the work goes on, so, I doubt not, the brethren and sisters who are teachers in the Day Schools will be greatly blessed by being thus partakers of our precious secret respecting the state of the funds. Our prayer meetings have already been a blessing to us, and united us more than ever in the work. We have them now every morning at seven, and we shall continue them, the Lord helping us, till we see His hand stretched forth, not merely in giving us means for the teachers, but also for other purposes; for we need a stove in one of the school rooms, a fresh supply of several kinds of Bibles and New Testaments, and it is desirable to have means to help Missionary brethren who labour in dependence upon the Lord for the supply of their temporal necessities.

Sept. 9. We are now meeting every morning at seven for prayer. With 5s. which was sent yesterday from the Isle of Wight for the Orphans, we have commenced the day; but I believe that the Lord will help us through this day also.

Evening. About twelve this morning a brother, a stranger, who is staying at Ashton, near Bristol, came with some of his family to the Orphan-Houses. While brother B. was for a few moments out of the room to fetch a key, the visiting brother took the opportunity of secretly putting something into the box at the Boys'-Orphan-House. Brother B., however, perceived it before he could get away from the box, and, the brother being gone, our great need brought it out, when it was found to be 5l. Thus the Lord kindly has provided for the need of today and tomorrow. When this money was given we were exceedingly poor. For not only would there have been no means to take in the usual quantity of bread in one of the houses, but there was no money to take in milk in the afternoon in any of the houses. The Lord knew our need, and therefore just now sent this brother. He gave also 2s, for Reports.

Sept. 10. When now the 5l. of yesterday was again spent, the Lord has kindly sent another 5l. There came in still further 6s. 10d.

SECOND PART

Yesterday came in it. 7s., and today 1l. 15s. 10d. for the other funds. Thus the Lord, in answer to our petitions at the morning prayer meetings, has sent in a little for these funds also.

Sept. 11. The Lord has sent in still further and more richly for the Orphans. This morning 1l. was given to me which had been sent from Trowbridge, and this afternoon a brother who came from Scotland gave me 10l., and brought the following trinkets which were sent by a lady from Scotland:--2 clasps, a ring, 2 pairs of ear-rings, a slide, a pin, a cross, and 2 bracelets, all of gold. In the afternoon came in 3l. by sale of articles.

Sept. 12. The Lord has sent in still more. This morning was sent 10l. through a banker in London, by the order of a sister at Worcester; and 10s. was put into the box at my house. This has been a week of peculiar mercies, as above 40l. has been sent in, besides several articles. We have continued to meet for prayer every morning, from seven to eight.

Sept. 13. Today came in 3l. 8s. 4d.,of which 1l. 10s. 6d. was for some of the articles sent from Leeds.

Sept. 16. Though during the last week above 40l. came in, yet, because the usual expenses for housekeeping were about 15l., and because most of the sisters who labour in the Orphan-Houses had not had for a long time any money for their own personal necessities, we were the day before yesterday again so poor, that only a few shillings were left. The Lord, knowing this, sent in a little money, and, by a sister from the Isle of Wight, 7 rings, 2 brooches, 2 pins, 1 pair of ear-rings, 2 pairs of studs, all of gold, 2 chemises, and 2 babies' shirts. Today arrived from Leeds, from two sisters in the Lord before referred to, a second box, the first having come about a fortnight ago. This second box contained the following articles:--2 silver dessert spoons, a pair of silver sugar tongs, a silver tea caddy spoon, 6 plated forks, 4 knife resters, a cream spoon, 6 Britannia metal tea spoons, a silver watch, a metal watch, a small telescope, 2 cloak fastenings, 11 pencils, a pen case with pieces of sealing wax, 2 pairs of scissors, 6 chimney ornaments, a boa ring, a chess board, 3 purses with 2l. 1s. 4d., 2 silver pocket knives, a silver pencil case, a ditto of brass, a bodkin case, a gold pin, a silver vinaigrette, 125 needles, 1 memorandum case, 5 paper baskets, 18 books, 100 copies of a small English Grammar (unbound), 75 pamphlets, 37 table mats, 120 little tracts, 5 pairs of stockings, 2 pairs of socks, a Thibet shawl, 6 coloured frocks, 4 caps, 9 collars, 8 neckerchiefs, 3 muslin aprons, 5 holland aprons, 4 muslin frocks, 6 babies' ditto, 2 white gowns, 2 remnants of print, 5 habit shirts, a bonnet, a merino apron, a glass trumpet, a taper candlestick, several small pieces of riband and gauze, 4 yards of silk fringe, 7 cases of different kinds of cards, a crape scarf, some lining calico, 13 little boxes, a straw basket, and about 50 other various little articles. It is difficult to describe the peculiar pleasure which I had in unpacking the box, and in finding that all these articles were for the Lord's work.--There came in still further this evening 8s.

Besides other small donations since the 10th, there came into day 5l. for the other funds, as the answer to oft-repeated prayer; also, from Liverpool, 1l. 14s. 8d. Thus the Lord encourages our hearts in this part of the work likewise.

Sept. 17. The need of today for the Orphans was supplied by the little which had come in yesterday, and by the 2l. 1s. 4d. which came in the second box from Leeds. These two boxes from Leeds have been sent most seasonably by the Lord, and thus truly the sisters who sent them have been led by Him to do so, according to what they wrote in a letter, which announced the arrival of the first box; "We feel deeply interested in your concerns, and our anxiety to serve you has increased by every new discovery of the kindness and goodness of God, in providing for your wants. Indeed, we cannot but believe that the Lord has put it into our hearts to help you, and we trust you will honour us, His unworthy servants, by believing that our gift is really His." There came in today 2l. 16s. by the sale of some of the articles sent in the first box from Leeds, and by the sale of some other articles. Thus our need for tomorrow is supplied.

Sept. 18. Today the Lord has sent again 17s. 5d. by sale of some of the articles sent from Leeds, and 2l. 10s. from Leicestershire, and also 4s. for children's needle-work. Thus we had enough for tomorrow, being Saturday.

Sept. 21. Monday. By what was in hand for the Orphans, and by what had come in yesterday, the need of today is more than supplied, as there is enough for tomorrow also.

Today a brother from the neighbourhood of London gave me 10l., to be laid out as it might be most needed. we have been praying many days for the School-Bible—and Missionary Funds, I took it all for them. This brother knew nothing about our work, when he came three days since to Bristol. Thus the Lord, to show His continued care over us, raises up new helpers. They that trust in the Lord shall never be confounded! Some who helped for a while may fall asleep in Jesus; others may grow cold in the service of the Lord; others may be as desirous as ever to help, but have no longer the means; others may have both a willing heart to help, and have also the means, but may see it the Lord's will to lay them out in another way;--and thus, from one cause or another, were we to lean upon man, we should surely be confounded; but, in leaning upon the living God alone, We are BEYOND disappointment, and BEYOND being forsaken because of death, or want of means, or want of love, or because of the claims of other work. How precious to have learned in any measure to stand with God alone in the world, and yet to be happy, and to know that surely no good thing shall be withheld from us whilst we walk uprightly!

Sept. 23. This morning there was again only 10s. in hand for the Orphans. As this was not enough for the day, I opened the box in my house, in which I found 8s. 6d. The boxes in the Orphan-Houses were also opened, which contained 7s. 6 1/2d. There came in also by the sale of a pair of stockings, 1s. 6d. This 1l., 7s. 6 1/2d. was

SECOND PART

enough, and even 3s. more than was absolutely needed. The Lord gave today another proof that He is still mindful of us, for a brother sent half a ton of coals to each of the three houses.

Sept. 24. Yesterday our prayer, in our meeting at twelve o'clock, was especially for the supply of today. I was fully assured that the Lord would send help, as now all our stores were again exhausted. Accordingly, last evening a sister, into whose hands some of the articles, which came in the second box from Leeds, had been put for sale, gave me 1l. 3s. 7d., being the payment for some of them. There came in a donation of 2s. besides. This 1l. 5s. 7d. served for this day. The Lord be praised who has helped us thus!

Sept. 25. It is now half-past eleven. Nothing has come in as yet. How the Lord will help us through the day is not my care; for sure I am He will help. I am just going to meet with my fellow-labourers for prayer. Perhaps the Lord will again, at the time of the meeting, fill our mouths with praise, as He has done so many times. My soul waits on Him for deliverance! How truly precious to have such a Father as we have!

Sept. 26. When I went yesterday to the meeting for prayer, I found that some articles, which had come from Leeds, had been sold for 10s. 9d., and that 2s. 6d. had been taken out of the box in the Girls'-Orphan-Ho use. To this one of the labourers added 10s. of his own. This 1l. 3s. 3d. supplied all we needed yesterday; but there was now again nothing in hand to meet this day's demands, which I knew would be great, on account of its being Saturday. The Lord, however, remembered our Saturday's necessities, and therefore sent in abundantly, so that we had even more than we needed for today, though we required no less than 5l. The way in which He kindly helped us, was this: first, 3l. came in for articles which had been sent from Leeds; afterwards a little boy and girl brought two little Savings' Banks, filled with their little presents, amounting altogether to 15s 1 1/4d. In the evening came in still further 4l. for articles which had been sold, most of which had likewise been sent from Leeds. Thus the Lord sent in altogether 8l. 18s. 1 1/4d. in the course of the day, whilst it commenced without there being a penny in hand.

Sept. 27. Today the Lord has sent in still further 2l. 5s. 8d., of which 15s. 8d. was for articles sent from Leeds, and 1l. with Ecclesiastes ix. 10.

Sept. 29. Yesterday we were again penniless, after the necessities of the three houses had been supplied. Almost immediately afterwards came in 1l. 12s. 2d., sufficient to supply the need of today.

Sept. 30. Today there is nothing in hand. It is now a quarter past eleven, but nothing yet has come in. Nevertheless the Lord will surely help us this day also! About five minutes after I had written the above, I was informed by a note from brother B., that 2l. 10s. 6d. had come in in small donations.

THE LORD'S DEALINGS WITH GEORGE MÜLLER

Oct. 1. It is now again eleven o'clock, and the Lord has not as yet been pleased to send in any thing for the necessities of this day. Let me see now how the Lord will again help us in the love of His heart; for He will surely help, though I know not how.--Evening. When I went to the prayer meeting, I found that only 1s. had come in, but at the same time I was informed that the money, which had been divided yesterday among the matrons, was enough for today also.

Oct. 2. Nothing came in yesterday, nor this morning. In addition to this, I was so engaged, that in the afternoon I had not even time to make inquiry how the Lord had helped. Thus it is often that I can do nothing but quietly go on with my engagements, casting all care upon the Lord. When I came home this evening, the first thing that met my eyes was the following letter from a distance of many miles:

"Beloved Brother,--Five pounds are enclosed as from the Lord, as I believe you stand in need of it for the use of the Orphans. Yours affectionately, F. W.

Truly, the Lord, to whom we had spoken yesterday, had spoken for us, and told this brother that we were in need of money. After having read this letter, my eyes met two others. In the one I was informed by a brother, that he had sold two pairs of fire screens for 8s., and had sent the money. These screens had been for many months in his hands for sale, and now to-day, in this our poverty, a lady came to the shop and bought them. The other letter was from brother B., master of the boys in the Boys'-Orphan-House, which I give here:

"I opened the boxes and found 4s. 1 1/2d. in them. This was far from being sufficient. About four o'clock three persons came to the Orphan-Houses, and put into the box at the Boys'-Orphan-House 7s., into the box at the Infant-Orphan-House 6s., and into the box at the Girls'-Orphan-House 7s. Thus I have had in all to divide 1l. 4s. 1 1/2d., which meets the necessities of the day."

Oct. 3. It was exceedingly kind of the Lord to send in so much yesterday; for the necessities of today, being Saturday, required it all. And now, when there was again nothing in hand, there arrived this evening a large box, sent by a sister at Stafford, whom I never saw, which contained 1l. 5s., and the following articles: 11 gold rings, a silver ring washed, a locket, a gold brooch, 3 single ear-rings, a watch hook, a silver watch-guard, 2 silver-mounted eye glasses, 3 vinaigrettes, 2 purses, a silver buckle, 2 old silver coins, 2 silver pencil cases, 3 pairs of bracelets, 3 necklaces, 2 waist buckles, a bracelet snap, a cloak fastening, a necklace snap, a yard measure, a mourning brooch, 7 pincushions, a snuff box, a small looking glass, 2 china boxes, a china inkstand, 5 china cups and saucers, a china basket, 2 china jugs, a scent bottle, a boa ring, 20 shells, a boy's cap, a pair of snuffers and stand, a little basket, a pair of screen handles, 3 ornamental pens, 5 artificial flowers, 5 glass plates, 5 counter plates, 3 pairs of card racks, a comb, a pair of watch pockets, 12 table mats, 8 paintings, 4 drawings, 2 fans, a pair of garters, 3 pairs of gloves, 3 pairs of silk stockings, 3 veils, a gauze scarf, 6 ladies' bags, 5 silk bands, 2 floss silk scarfs, a gauze handkerchief, 2 silk scarfs, a crape shawl, a silk shawl, 2 muslin capes, 30 yards of worn

SECOND PART

cotton lace, 8 yards of muslin work, 9 yards of print, a pinafore, a frock, a sampler, a pair of socks, a pair of ear-rings, and 17 ladies' dresses.--One thing is particularly to be noticed respecting this donation, that the Lord from time to time raises up fresh individuals to help us in the work, thereby continually reminding us, that He is not limited to any individuals in particular, neither are we, His children.

Oct. 4. Today came in 19s. 4d., by sale of some of the articles sent from Leeds. Thus our need for tomorrow is supplied.

Oct. 5. 7l. 15s. 2d. came in again today, of which 5l. was from a brother whom I have never seen.

Oct. 6. Today came in further by sale of articles which had been sent from Leeds, 3l. 7s. 6d., also 14s. 3d. in small donations.

Oct. 7. 1l. 14s. 2d. came in today in small donations.

It is now five weeks, since we have daily met for prayer. Not indeed merely to ask for means, but for grace and wisdom for ourselves in reference to the work, for the conversion of the children under our care, for grace for those children who stand already on the Lord's side, for a blessing upon the circulation of the Scriptures, for a blessing upon the work, with reference to the church at large, etc. But whilst we thus, as the Spirit led us, prayed for various things, nevertheless the lack of means was that which had brought us day after day together. We asked the Lord to give us the means which are needed for carrying on the Day Schools, for buying Bibles, as several sorts are needed, and to enable us to assist Missionary work in foreign countries. Never at any previous time, since first the work commenced on March 5, 1834, have we had to continue so long a time in prayer for these funds, without obtaining the answer. The Lord, however, gave us grace to "continue in prayer," and keep our hearts in the assurance that He would help. Now, though He delayed long, before He sent us the answer, in His own time He made it manifest, that He had not only not shut His ear against our prayer in anger, but that He had answered them even before we called; for there was sent today, from the East Indies, a bank order for 100l., which had been sent off two months since, therefore several days before we even began to pray. It was left to me to apply this money as it might be needed. As we had so long, and so particularly prayed for these funds, I took the whole of it for them, and not for the Orphan-Fund. --The Lord be praised for this precious answer. It was particularly precious, as leading the dear brethren and sisters who labour in the Day Schools, and who comparatively are little accustomed to this way, to see how good it is to wait upon the Lord.

Oct. 10. All our wants for the Orphans have been richly supplied during this week; and today, on my leaving for Trowbridge in the Lord's service, I was able to send 5l. 5s. 8d. to the sisters, the matrons.

Oct. 11—14. Trowbridge. I have had a good season since I have been here. The Lord has enabled me to rise very early, and I have thus had more than two hours of communion with Him before breakfast, the fruit of which I have felt all the day long. The Lord in mercy continue my enjoyment!--For the last three weeks I had been asked, yea pressed, to come here, to minister among the saints; but I could not clearly see it to be the Lord's will, and therefore did not go. Now I came, assured that it was His will, and have been very happy, and greatly helped in my service here in every way, and I am fully assured that my labour has not been in vain. How good it is, even for this life, according to the Lord's bidding either to go or stay!--I have seen, whilst here, a young woman, the daughter of a brother and sister who were in communion with us, but who have both fallen asleep. While her father was living she hated the truth, but still she came to Bethesda Chapel. One day, whilst there, she was made to feel the power of the truth: and, since the death of her parents, the Lord has granted an answer to their many prayers on her behalf; for she is now standing on the Lord's side. Let believing parents continue in prayer for their children, and let them also continue affectionately and at suitable times to bring the truth before them, and to bring them to the preaching of the Word: and in due season it will be manifested that their labours were not in vain.

Oct. 14. Yesterday, while at Trowbridge, I received from a sister, from the neighbourhood of London, 1l. for the Orphans. In the evening, a sister, a servant, gave me 1s. This morning I gave myself again to prayer respecting the Orphan-Fund, as I had reason to believe that there was nothing in hand in Bristol, except several pounds had come in since I left. Soon after, a sister, a servant, gave me 5s., and, on leaving in the afternoon, a brother gave me 5l. When I came home this evening, I found that only 3l. 10s. 8d. had come in since I left, just sufficient to supply the need up to this evening, so that the help which the Lord gave at Trowbridge, in answer to prayer, came very seasonably to supply the need of tomorrow.

Oct. 20. Tuesday. During these last three days we have again experienced the continued care of our loving Father on behalf of the Orphans. On Saturday evening, when again there was no money at all remaining in my hands, a pair of silver mounted horns was anonymously left at my house. On the Lord's day I received 6l. 1s. Yesterday the Lord sent in still more abundantly; for in the morning came in 12l. from the neighbourhood of Wolverhampton, and in the evening 2l. was given to me by D. C. This morning, a few minutes after I had been thinking that no potatoes had been sent yet for the Orphans, and that we had no money to lay in a stock (for the 14l. which came in yesterday was at once sent off), a brother came and informed me that he had given orders that twenty sacks of good potatoes should be sent to the Orphan-Houses. Thus our kind Father continually cares for us.

Oct. 26. Monday. The Lord has been again very kind to us, during these last days. There came in since Oct. 20, in small donations, 18s. 1d.; for knitting and by sale of stockings, 16s. On Friday last, besides, there were sold stockings to the amount of 17s. 5d. In the evening a brother gave me 5l. This 5l. and the money for the stockings came in very seasonably, as it enabled us to supply the large demands

SECOND PART

of the next day. Yesterday morning, when I took my hat from the rail, I found in one of my gloves a note, containing a 5l. note and the following words: "2l. for the Orphans, the rest for dear brother and sister Muller," There came in still further yesterday 2l. 12s. 6d. Thus we are again supplied for about three days.

In reference to the note which was put into my hat, containing 5l., I just add, that I had repeatedly asked the Lord for means for our own personal expenses, previous to the reception of it, as we had but very little money for ourselves. Indeed the very moment, before I took my hat from the rail, I had risen from my knees, having again asked the Lord for means for ourselves and for the Orphans.

Oct. 30. The evening before last 9s. came in, being the produce of some work which a sister had done for the benefit of the Orphans; and early this morning, while my candle was yet burning, a paper was brought, containing 12s. These two donations, with what little is in hand besides, supply our need for this day.

Oct. 31. Saturday. There was no money in hand, My mind was particularly stirred up to open the box in my house. I did so, and found 1l. 10s. 7d. in it. The boxes in the Orphan-Houses were likewise opened, in which was found 8s. Also a brother from Tetbury gave 2s. 6d. Thus the need of today was supplied.

Nov. 2. Monday. 1l. 11s, is the need of today, and as 1l. 12s. has come in since Saturday evening, we are helped for today.

November 3 and 4. Only 2s. 6d. has come in since Nov. 2nd, but the necessities of these two days were supplied by means of articles which had been given to be disposed of.

Nov. 5. Only 2s. came in yesterday for knitting. We are now, without any thing, cast upon the Lord. The need of today is 1l. 3s., which I am unable to send.-- Afternoon. There came in at three o'clock 4l. for some of the articles which had been sent from Stafford, and which had been sold some time since, so that I was able to send the needful supplies. There came in 6d. besides.

Nov. 7. Saturday. Of the 4l. 2s. 6d. which was in hand the day before yesterday, there was so much left, that, with an addition of 9s. 6d., all the necessities of today could be supplied. This one of the labourers gave.

Nov. 8. Lord's day. Today the Lord has been again very kind, and looked upon us in our poverty. Besides the 1l. 10s. for rent, I received with Ecclesiastes ix. 10, 5l. I was also informed that two large sacks of oatmeal had been sent from Glasgow as a present. In addition to all this, a brother told me that he had it in his heart to give 10l. worth of materials, for winter clothes for the children, leaving the material to my choice, according to the need, so that just what was most desirable might be given. (He, accordingly, sent a few days after, a large pair of good blankets, 32 1/2 yards of mixed beaver, and 10 1/2 yards of blue beaver for cloaks.) There was also

1s. put into the box at Bethesda, with the words, "Jehovah Jireh." These words have often been refreshing to my soul for many years past, and I wrote them with a valuable diamond ring, set with ten brilliants, which was given to the Orphans about twenty months since, upon a pane of glass in my room, which circumstance, in remembrance of the remarkable way in which that valuable ring came, has often cheered my heart, when in deep poverty my eyes have been cast upon "JEHOVAH JIREH"(i.e. the Lord will provide) whilst sitting in my room.

I purposed to have gone to Trowbridge yesterday, and had settled it so on Friday evening with brother ----. But no sooner had I decided to do so, than I felt no peace in the prospect of going. After having prayed about it on Friday evening, and yesterday morning, I determined not to go, and I felt sure the Lord had some reason for not allowing me to feel happy in the prospect of going. I began now to look out for blessings for this day, considering that the Lord had kept me here for good to some souls. This evening I was especially led to press the truth on the consciences of the unconverted, entreating and beseeching them, and telling them also that I felt sure, the Lord had, in mercy to some of them, kept me from going to Trowbridge. I spoke on Genesis vi. 1—5. Immediately after I saw fruit of the Word. An individual fully opened his heart to me. I walked about with him till about ten o'clock, even as long as I had any strength left. [About ten days afterwards a brother told me of a poor drunkard who heard me that evening, and who since then had stayed up till about twelve o'clock every night to read the Scriptures, and who had not been intoxicated since.]

Nov. 11. As only 4s. 6d. had come in for knitting, and 2s. 6d. as a donation for the Orphans since the 8th, we were now again very poor. Today there was 9s. more needed than there was in hand, which one of the labourers gave. There were sent today anonymously, nine sacks of potatoes, a proof that our Father continues to be mindful of us, though we are now again so poor.

Nov. 12. Only 6s. 6d. came in last night, 4s. 6d. of which is the produce of the work of a sister, and 2s. from a poor afflicted sister. This 6s. 6d. was very precious in my esteem, because it showed me afresh our Father's heart towards us, and it was a little to begin the day with. No more has come in this morning, when at twelve I heard from the Orphan-Houses that 1s. 6d. had been received for knitting, and that about eleven this morning a sovereign was left, anonymously, at the Girls'-Orphan House. The paper in which the sovereign was enclosed contained only the letters "A. U. S."--This was a precious deliverance. We have thus enough for today.--Evening. There came in still further today for knitting 3s., and a little girl sent 1s. When I came home this evening, I found that a boy's jacket and a sovereign had been left anonymously at my house. Truly, these deliverances today have been very precious! We have now enough for tomorrow also.

Nov. 14. Trowbridge. Saturday. That which came in the evening before last supplied our need yesterday; but since then nothing has been received, and therefore there were no means to meet this day's demands. I had to go this morning in the

SECOND PART

Lord's service to Trowbridge, feeling assured that His time had now come for my going, and it required indeed looking at the power, wisdom, and love of our Father, comfortably to leave my dear fellow-labourers, there being nothing in hand. My comfort was that the same kind Father who had provided would provide.

Nov. 16. Trowbridge. Monday. This morning I received a letter from Bristol, in which I was informed that on Saturday came in 12s. 6d; also 9s. was given by one of the labourers. Besides this were received 3s. by sale of articles, and three small donations, amounting to 5s. Thus the Lord most mercifully sent in 1l. 9s. 6d., which was enough to supply the absolute need.

Nov. 17. Trowbridge. This morning I had again the report from Bristol about yesterday, in order that, though unable to send means, I might help with my prayers. In a note written in the morning by brother B., and sent to my wife, he writes thus: "I know not whether the Lord has sent in any money for the Orphans or not. I have received none. Sister ---- (one of the labourers) has given half a ton of coals to the Boys'-Orphan-House.

There are coals needed at the Girls'-Orphan-House, and much money for the ordinary expenses. There is sufficient in all the houses for dinner. He has said, 'I will never leave thee nor forsake thee,' so that we may boldly say, the Lord is MY helper." In the afternoon of the same day he writes: "I have delayed writing as long as I could. The Lord has not sent any thing, but the sisters can do without taking in bread, and they had money enough to pay for the milk, except sister ----, who has, however, received a few shillings for some articles of her own, that she sold. Thus we are supplied with the absolute necessities for today." In reference to the last lines I make a few remarks. At first sight it might appear as if it were a failure of the principles on which we act, that now and then individuals who are connected with the work have been obliged to sell articles of their own to procure things which were needed. But let it be remembered, that under no circumstances prayer for temporal supplies can be expected to prevail with the Lord, except we are willing to part with money or any needless articles which we may have of our own. Indeed an Institution like the one under my care should not be carried on by any rich believer, on the principles on which we, by grace, are enabled to act, except it be that he were made willing himself to give of his own property, as long as he has any thing, whenever the Institution is in real need.

Nov. 18. Bristol. This morning at twelve I returned from Trowbridge, where I had been very happy, and where the Lord evidently used me this time. How happy a thing it is to go and to stay with the Lord!--I found that yesterday some money had been put into the orphan-box at my house, which my wife had reason to believe was at least 1l. She therefore sent 1l. which had come in for the rent of the Orphan-Houses, in consideration of this, as she had not the key to the box. This 1l. met the necessities of yesterday, and with 1s. additional, which one of the labourers gave, was also enough for the dinner of today. There came in also yesterday from Clapham, as a token that the Lord allows us only to be poor for the trial of our faith, but not in anger, the following articles of clothing: 6 frocks, 7 pinafores, 4 chemises, 3 pocket handkerchiefs, 2 petticoats, 3 night caps, 4 work bags (all new) a yard of merino, and 12 silk papers. On my arrival at home I opened the box in my house, in which I found 2l. 0s. 6d., so that I had 1l. 0s. 6d. to send off, whereby the usual quantity of bread could be taken in.

Nov. 19. Since Sept. 18, 1838, this has been, perhaps, of all the days the most trying. The poverty has been exceedingly great for the last six days. There had come in no money since yesterday. On this account no bread could be taken in, as far as the natural prospect went. Nor was there any money at three in the afternoon to take in milk for tea, when brother B. came to me. However, we prayed together, and the Lord had mercy. For one of the labourers found that he was able, which he knew not before, to give of his own 10s., so that there were the means to take in the milk, by the time that it is usually brought. This evening about six there came in still further 10s. 3d. by the sale of Reports. Thus, by the good hand of our God upon us, we were able to take in bread as usual. How very kind of the Lord that He sent us an abundance of potatoes and two large sacks of oatmeal, before this season of deep poverty, as to pecuniary means, commenced! May the Lord now in great pity look upon us, for we are in deeper poverty than ever, as with every day it increases, whilst there is no full deliverance. Thanks be to the Lord that my mind has been in peace this day also, though our faith has been so very much tried! Thanks to Him that my mind is in peace now, though there is nothing but want on every side before me, respecting tomorrow! Surely, the Lord will again, in His own time, more fully stretch forth His helping hand!

Nov. 20. Nothing more had come in this morning. It was nearly three o'clock this afternoon, when brother B. called on me, to see whether any thing had come in; but I had received nothing. I was obliged to go out with a brother from Devonshire, and therefore requested him to wait till I returned. About a quarter past three I came back, when, among several persons who were waiting at my house to converse with me, there was a sister whom I much desired to see about some church affair. I did so. When I had ended the conversation with her, about half-past three, she gave me 10l. for the Orphans. More sweet, and more needed, were none of the previous deliverances. Language cannot express the real joy in God which I had. I was free from, excitement. The circumstance did not un-fit me even for a single moment to attend to my other engagements. I was not in the least surprised, because, by grace, my soul had been waiting on God for deliverance. Never had help been so long delayed. In none of the houses was milk for tea, and in one even no bread, and there was no money to purchase either. It was only a few minutes before the milkman came, when brother B. arrived at the Orphan-Houses with the money. Yet even now it was more than an hour before the usual tea time. The Lord be praised for this deliverance! Such a week of deep poverty, as we have had since Nov. 13, we never had before. Yet, thanks to the Lord! we have lacked nothing, and we have been kept from dishonouring Him by unbelief. I further notice respecting this day, that before this 10l. was received there was sent to the Infant-Orphan-House a cart load of clumps of wood, when there were neither coals, nor money to buy any.

SECOND PART

Nov. 21. Saturday evening. The 10l. which came in yesterday afternoon is all expended. Again I have not a penny in hand. We are, however, brought to the close of another week, and have now, a little at least, replenished our provision stock; and should the Lord permit us to enter upon another week, He will surely provide according to our need.

Nov. 22. Lord's day. The Lord has been again mindful of our need, and has sent us in the means to meet the demands of two days. Besides the 1l. 10s. which came in for rent, a brother gave me this morning two sovereigns, a sister from a distance sent it., and a brother, who spent this day with us, put 12s. 6d. into the box at my house, which our need soon brought out.

Nov. 23. This evening were given, after all the money had been again disbursed, 2 gold rings, 5 small silver coins, a silver ring, 5 silver studs, a silver buckle, a pair of ear-rings, a necklace, and a little box.

Nov. 25. As only 3s. 6d. had come in for knitting since the 22nd, we were now again very poor. The boxes in the Orphan-Houses were opened, but only 1s. was found in them. In this our poverty 6l. came in this afternoon for some of the articles which had been sent from Stafford on Oct. 3rd, and which had been sold some time since. This money had been expected for some time, but came in only now, in this our great need. In the evening came in still further 2l. from the East Indies.

Nov. 26. Today were sent from Newport, near Barnstaple, 2 rings, a brooch and 4s.

Nov. 27. This morning I received 4l. from a sister in Dublin, before we were really in need; but this donation came very seasonably to meet the large demands of tomorrow, Saturday, for which there is nothing in hand. There was also taken out of the boxes in the Orphan-Houses, this afternoon, 2l. 12s. 6d.

Nov. 28. Saturday. There has come in again 1l. today. Thus the Lord has bountifully supplied our need during this week, always sending the means without allowing us to be so deeply tried as during the two previous weeks.

Nov. 29. The Lord's loving hand has again today provided richly for the Orphans, for at least two days. There came in altogether 6l. 19s. 6d.

Dec. 1. Today we were so poor as to the Orphan-Fund, that we should not have been able to meet the demands of the day; but the Lord's loving heart remembered us. There came in this morning 5l. 7s. for some of the articles which were sent some time since from Stafford. I have purposely again and again mentioned how the help, which the love of some saints at Leeds and Stafford sent, delivered us, that it might be manifest that those donors were directed by the Lord in this matter.

Dec. 2. When today there was again but little money in hand, because of the disbursements of yesterday, D. C. brought me 2l., which his wife a sister had saved out of housekeeping, for the benefit of the Orphans. About an hour, after I had received this 2l., there was sent, in two post-office-orders, 6l. 4s. 6d. by a sister, being the produce of the sale of some trinkets; of which sum one half is to be used for the benefit of the Orphans, and the other half for my own personal necessities. Thus the Lord has by this donation also provided for myself and family, when we were in much need.

Dec. 5. Saturday morning. Yesterday afternoon a sister left two sovereigns at my house for the Orphans. The Lord in the love of His heart, remembered our Saturday's necessities, and sent in this supply; for there was only 18s. 6d. in hand when this money came, and 2l. 12s. is needed for this day. Evening. As there was now again only 6s. 6d. in hand, I gave myself to prayer, and immediately after I had risen from my knees, 1l. 5s. 6d. was given to me, for things which had been sold, being chiefly articles which had been sent from Stafford. There was also a flute left anonymously at my house, this evening.

Dec. 6. Today there came in still further 2l. 2s. 6d.

Dec. 7. Again 1l. 11s. has come in.

Dec. 9. Morning. This is the last day of the fifth year of the Orphan work. Hitherto the Lord has helped us! This morning there was only 1l. 1s. 9d. in hand, but 1l. 7s. was needed for the supply of today. I therefore opened the box in my house, in which 2s. 6d. was found. This 1l. 4s. 3d. I sent off to the Orphan-Houses. Evening. There came in during this day 1l. 6s. 6d.; out of this I had to pay away 1l. 2s., so that now, at the close of the year, though the balance amounts to 15l. 0s. 6 1/4d., there is only 4s. 6 1/4d. in hand, as the rest has been put by for the rent, which is due up to this time. With this 4s. 6 1/4d. we have now to commence the sixth year, leaning upon the living God, who most assuredly during this year also will help us in every way, as our circumstances may call for it.

At the close of these details (with reference to the year from Dec. 9, 1839, to Dec. 9, 1840) I make a few remarks in connexion with them.

1. Though our trials of faith during this year also have been many, and recurring more frequently than during any previous year, and though we have been often reduced to the greatest extremity, yet the Orphans have lacked nothing; for they have always had good nourishing food, and the necessary articles of clothing, etc.

2. Should it be supposed by any one in reading the plain details of our trials of faith during this year, that on account of them we have been disappointed in our expectations, or are discouraged in the work, my answer is, that the very reverse is the

fact. Such days were expected from the commencement of the work; nay, more than this, the chief end for which the Institution was established is, that the Church of Christ at large might be benefited by seeing manifestly the hand of God stretched out on our behalf in the hour of need, in answer to prayer. Our desire, therefore, is not that we may be without trials of faith, but that the Lord graciously would be pleased to support us in the trial, that we may not dishonour Him by distrust.

3. This way of living brings the Lord remarkably near, He is, as it were, morning by morning inspecting our stores, that accordingly He may send help. Greater and more manifest nearness of the Lord's presence I have never had, than when after breakfast there were no means for dinner, and then the Lord provided the dinner for more than one hundred persons; or when, after dinner, there were no means for the tea, and yet the Lord provided the tea; and all this without one single human being having been informed about our need. This moreover I add, that although we, who have been eye witnesses of these gracious interpositions of our Father, have not been so benefited by them as we might and ought to have been, yet we have in some measure derived blessing from them. One thing is certain, that we are not tired of doing the Lord's work in this way.

4. It has been more that once observed, that such a way of living must lead the mind continually to think whence food, clothes, etc., are to come, and so unfit for spiritual exercises. Now, in the first place, I answer, that our minds are very little tried about the necessaries of life, just because the care respecting them is laid upon our Father, who, because we are His children, not only allows us to do so, but will have us to do so. Secondly, it must be remembered, that, even if our minds were much tried about the supplies for the children, and the means for the other work, yet, because we look to the Lord alone for these things, we should only be brought, by our sense of need, into the presence of our Father, for the supply of it; and that is a blessing, and no injury to the soul. Thirdly, our souls realize that for the glory of God and for the benefit of the church at large, it is that we have these trials of faith, and that leads again to God, to ask Him for fresh supplies of grace, to be enabled to be faithful in this service.

5. My heart's desire and prayer to God is, that all believers, who read this, may by these many answers to prayer be encouraged to pray, particularly as it regards the conversion of their friends and relations, their own state of heart, the state of the Church at large, and the success of the preaching of the gospel. Do not think, dear reader, that these things are peculiar to us, and cannot be enjoyed by all the saints. Although every child of God is not called by the Lord to establish Schools and Orphan-Houses, and to trust in the Lord for means for them; yet there is nothing on the part of the Lord to hinder, why you may not know by experience, far more abundantly than we do now, His willingness to answer the prayers of His children. Do but prove the faithfulness of God. Do but carry your every want to Him. Only maintain an upright heart. But if you live in sin; if you wilfully and habitually do things, respecting which you know that they are contrary to the will of God, then you cannot expect to be heard by Him. "If I regard iniquity in my heart, the Lord will not

hear me: but verily God hath heard me; He hath attended to the voice of my prayer." Psalm lxvi. 18, 19.

6. As it regards the children of God, who by the labour of their hands, or in any business or profession, earn their bread, particularly the poorer classes of them, I give my affectionate yet solemn advice, to carry into practice the principles on which this Institution is conducted, as it regards not going in debt. Are you in debt? then make confession of sin respecting it. Sincerely confess to the Lord that you have sinned against Rom. xiii. 8. And if you are resolved no more to contract debt, whatever may be the result, and you are waiting on the Lord, and truly trust in Him, your present debts will soon be paid. Are you out of debt? then whatever your future want may be, be resolved, in the strength of Jesus, rather to suffer the greatest privation, whilst waiting upon God for help, than to use unscriptural means, such as borrowing, taking goods on credit, etc., to deliver yourselves. This way needs but to be tried, in order that its excellency may be enjoyed.

On Dec. 14, 15, 16, and 25, we had public meetings, at which the account of the Lord's dealings with us during the last year, in respect of the Orphan-Houses, Schools, etc., was given, for the benefit of any who desired to come. The preceding part of the Narrative gives the substance of what was stated at those meetings, in reference to the many answers to prayer which the Lord has granted to us during the past year. There are a few points more, which may be of interest to the believing reader, and which were then mentioned, which I shall now add.

1. There have been, during this year also, six Day Schools for poor children, entirely supported by the funds of the Institution, all of which have been established by us.

Besides this, the rent for the school room of a seventh School, carried on by a sister, who is known to us, has been paid and two other such Schools, out of Bristol, have been assisted with Bibles and Testaments.

The number of all the children that have had schooling in the Day Schools through the medium of the Institution, since its formation, amounts to 2216; the number of those at present in the six Day Schools is 303.

These Day Schools have defrayed, by the payments of the children, about the sixth part of their own expenses.

2. There is one Sunday School entirely supported by the funds of the Institution.

SECOND PART

3. There has been since the formation of the Institution one Adult School connected with it, in which, on the Lord's day afternoons, since that time, about 150 adults have been instructed.

This School has been discontinued at the close of this year, and instead of it it is purposed to have a regular Evening School for adults who cannot read. It is purposed to instruct them for about an hour and a half in reading and writing twice a week, and afterwards to read the Scriptures for a short time to them, and to bring the truth before them. The School will commence at seven o'clock in the evening, and the instruction will be altogether free.

4. The number of Bibles and Testaments which have been circulated through the medium of the Institution, during the last year, amounts to 452 copies.

There have been circulated, since March 5, 1834, six thousand and forty-four copies of the Scriptures.

5. There have been laid out during the last year, of the funds of the Institution, 120l. 10s. 2d. for Missionary purposes.

6. There are at present 91 Orphans in the three houses. The total number of the Orphans who have been under our care from April 11, 1836, to Dec. 9, 1840, amounts to 129.

I notice further the following points in connexion with the Orphan-Houses.

1. Without any one having been asked for any thing by us, the sum of 3,937l. 1s. 1d. has been given to us, as the result of prayer to God, since the commencement of the work. 2. Besides this also, a great variety of provisions, clothes, furniture, etc. 3. Though there has been during this year as much, or more sickness, in the Orphan-Houses, than during any previous year; yet I own to the praise of the Lord publicly, that it has been very little, considering the number of the children.

For the future we purpose, according to the time, means, etc., which the Lord may be pleased to give us, to attend to a fifth object, the circulation of such publications, as may be beneficial, with the blessing of God, to benefit both believers and unbelievers. We purpose either to buy or print tracts for unbelievers, and to sell them, or have them distributed, as opportunity maybe given; and to buy or print such publications, for circulation, as may be instrumental in directing the minds of believers to those truths which in these last days are more especially needed, or have been particularly lost sight of, and which may lead believers to return to the written word of God.

THE LORD'S DEALINGS WITH GEORGE MÜLLER

THE BLESSING OF THE LORD UPON THE WORK IN REFERENCE TO THE SOULS OF THE CHILDREN.

1. During the last fourteen months there have been meetings purposely for children, at which the Scriptures have been expounded to them. At these meetings an almost universal attention is manifested by them, which I thankfully ascribe to the Lord, and upon which I look as a forerunner of greater blessing.

2. During the last year three of the Sunday School children have been received into fellowship.

3. At the end of last year there had been eight Orphans received into communion: during the present year fourteen have been received: in all twenty-two.

4. Of those two who died during this year, one was an infant, and the other a girl about twelve years old. The latter, on the whole, a well behaved child, was for months ill in consumption before she died. The nearer she came to the end of her life, the greater was the solicitude of those under whose care she was, respecting the state of her heart, as she was evidently unprepared for eternity. But now we saw, what never had been witnessed in any other of the children to such a degree. This, on the whole, naturally amiable, meek, and quiet child, manifested not merely complete indifference to the truth, the nearer she came to the close of her life; but also showed much aversion, and, as far as she could, great enmity to the truth. At last she was evidently dying, yet altogether unprepared for death. In this state all the Orphans in the Girls'-Orphan-House were assembled together, and the awful state of this dying child was pointed out to the unbelieving Orphans as a warning, and to the believing Orphans as a subject for gratitude to God on behalf of themselves, that they, by grace, were in a different state; and it was laid on their hearts to give themselves to prayer for their dying companion. The labourers in the work were sustained to hope still, and to pray still, though Charlotte Lee remained opposed to the truth while in this dying state. However, unexpectedly she lived ten days longer, and about two days before her death she was so altogether different, that we have hope in her end.

It was stated in the last year's Report, that we were looking for fruit upon our labours as it regards the conversion of the children, as the Lord had given to us a measure of earnestness in praying for them. The Lord has dealt with us according to our expectations. But I expect far more than what we have seen. While the chief object of our work has been, and is still, the manifestation of the heart of God towards His children, and the reality of power with God in prayer; yet, as we hoped, and as it has been our prayer, the Lord gives to us also the joy of seeing one child after another brought to stand openly on the Lord's side.--As far as my experience goes, it appears to me that believers generally have expected far too little of present fruit upon their labours among children. There has been a hoping that the Lord some day or other would own the instruction which they give to children, and would answer at some time or other, though after many years only, the prayers which they offer up on their behalf. Now, while such passages as Proverbs xxii. 6, Ecclesiastes xi. 1, Galatians vi. 9, 1 Cor. xv. 58, give unto us assurance not merely respecting every thing which we do for the Lord, in general, but also respecting bringing up children in the fear of the Lord, in particular, that our labour is not in vain in the Lord; yet we have to guard against abusing such passages, by thinking it a matter of little moment whether we see present fruit or not; but, on the contrary, we should give the Lord no rest till we see present fruit, and therefore in persevering, yet submissive, prayer, we should make known our requests unto God. I add, as an encouragement to believers who labour among children, that during the last two years, seventeen other young persons or children, from the age of eleven and a half to seventeen, have been received into fellowship among us, and that I am looking out now for many more to be converted, and that not merely of the Orphans, but of the Sunday and Day School children. As in so many respects we live in remarkable times, so in this respect also, that the Lord is working greatly among the children in many places.

I most earnestly solicit all who know the reality of our privilege as the children of God, even that we have power with God, to help us with their prayers, that many more of the children may soon be converted, and that those who have made a profession of faith in the Lord Jesus may be enabled so to walk, as that the name of Jesus may be magnified by them. The believing reader must know how great the aim of Satan will be to lead those children, who, from nine years old, and upward, have been received into fellowship, back again into the world, and thereby seek to lead believers to give up looking for real conversion among children.

The total of the expenses connected with the objects of-the Institution, exclusive of the Orphan-Houses, from Nov. 19, 1839, to Nov. 19, 1840, is 622l. 2s. 6 1/2d. The balance in hand on Nov. 19, 1840, was 13l. 2s. 9 3/4d.

The total of the expenses connected with the three Orphan-Houses, from Dec. 9, 1839, to Dec. 9, 1840, is 900l. 11s. 2 1/2d. The balance in hand on Dec. 9, 1840, was 15l. 0s. 6 1/4d.

Dec. 23. There was sent to us for ourselves, anonymously, a piece of beef, which came very seasonably, as we are just now again very poor.

Dec. 26. This morning a poor brother, who, like ourselves, lives in dependence upon the Lord for his temporal supplies, whilst serving the Lord in the ministry of the Word, and who has been several days staying with us, gave to my wife 3s. 6d., for our own personal necessities, saying, that we might need it. This is indeed a most remarkable donation, both because of the individual from whom it came, and because of its having been given just now; for without it we should not have been able to provide for our temporal necessities this day.

THE LORD'S DEALINGS WITH GEORGE MÜLLER

REVIEW OF THE YEAR 1840.

I. As to the church.

68 brethren and sisters brother Craik and I found in communion, when we came to Bristol.

687 have been admitted into communion since we came to Bristol.

755 would be, therefore, the total number of those in fellowship with us, had there been no changes. But

79 have left Bristol.

55 have left us, but are still in Bristol.

44 are under church discipline.

52 have fallen asleep.

230 are therefore to be deducted from 755, so that there are only 525 at present in communion.

114 have been added during the past year, of whom 47 have been brought to the knowledge of the Lord among us, 24 besides, though they knew the Lord, had never been in fellowship any where; 43 had been at some time or other in fellowship, but most of them with saints not residing in Bristol.

II. As to the supply of my temporal necessities:

1. The Lord has been pleased to send me by the Freewill Offerings of the saints among whom I labour, through the instrumentality of the boxes £128 5s. 10 1/2d.

2. Through saints in and out of Bristol, by presents in money £100 5s. 1d.

3. Through family connection £8 18s. 0d.

4. In provisions, clothes, etc. worth to us at least £5 0s. 0d.

Altogether £242 8s. 11 1/2d.

THIRD PART

PREFACE TO THE FIRST EDITION OF THE THIRD PART.

THE reasons which induced me to publish this third part of the Lord's dealings with me are the same which led me to the publication of the second part, and which are stated in the preface to the first edition of the second part. In addition to those reasons it appeared to me desirable to give some account of my recent labours in Germany, and also to write on a few other points, which I considered of great importance to be made known.

GEORGE MÜLLER.

21, Paul Street, Kingsdown,

Bristol, June 18, 1845.

A NARRATIVE OF SOME OF THE LORD'S DEALINGS WITH GEORGE MÜLLER
THIRD PART

IN the deep consciousness of my entire natural inability for going through the work, which is before me, to the profit of the reader and to the glory of God, I am nevertheless of good cheer in beginning this service; for the Lord has enabled me often to bow my knees before Him, to seek His help respecting it; and I am now expecting His help. He delights in making His strength perfect in our weakness, and therefore will I also, though so weak, look for His strength. And if through this my feeble effort, to show forth the praises of the Lord, good be done (of which I have the fullest assurance, on account of the abundance of supplication which for many months past has been found in my spirit in reference to this service,) I do desire from my inmost soul to ascribe all the honour and glory to the Lord.

I purpose in writing this third part of my Narrative to adopt the same mode which I employed in the two former parts, namely that of giving extracts from my journal, and accompanying them with such remarks as it may be desirable to make for the profit of the reader. The second part carries on the Narrative up to the end of the year 1840, so far as it regards my own personal affairs; but only to Dec. 9, 1840, so far as it regards the Orphan-Houses, and other objects of the Scriptural Knowledge Institution, as on that day the accounts were closed. From this period, then, the Narrative is continued.

Dec. 10, 1840. When the accounts were closed last evening, the balance in hand was 15l. 0s. 6 1/4d., but as nearly 15l. of this sum had been put by for the rent of the Orphan-Houses, the sum really in hand for use was only 4s. 6 1/4d. With this little sum we commenced the sixth year of this part of the work, while there are daily, as usual, more than a hundred persons to be provided for.

--A little boy brought half-a-crown to the Boys'-Orphan-House, this morning, which is the first gift in this sixth year. Thus we had altogether 7s. 0 1/4d. for this day, which was enough to pay for the milk in the three houses, and to buy some bread in one of them. We have never before been so poor at the commencement of the year.

Dec. 11. Only 2s. 6d. more had come in since last evening. There was sufficient for dinner in the Girls' and Infant-Orphan-Houses, but scarcely enough in the Boys'-Orphan-House. This half-crown, therefore, supplied the remainder of the dinner in the Boys'-Orphan-House. But now there was no money to take in milk, in any of the houses, for tea, or to buy any bread. However the Lord helped us through this day also. About one o'clock some trinkets, which had been sent a few days since, were disposed of for 12s., by which the usual quantity of milk, and a little bread could be taken in. [I observe here that there is generally bread for two or three days in the houses, the children eating the bread on the third day after it is baked. When, therefore, we are unable to take in the usual quantity, for want of means, we procure stale bread afterwards.]

Dec. 12. Only 4s. had come in to meet this day's necessities. Thus we should not have had sufficient means to provide for the dinner in the Girls'-Orphan-House, had not 6s. come in this morning, just in time to help us through the difficulty. Still we had no means to buy bread, and a few other little things which were needed. In addition to all this it was Saturday, and therefore provisions for two days needed to be procured. About four o'clock this afternoon, one of the sisters in the Orphan-Houses, to whom I had some days since sent a little money for her own personal necessities, gave 1l. Thus we were able to purchase sufficient provisions to last till breakfast on Monday morning. These last days have been very trying. The poverty has been greater than ever; the Lord, however, has not confounded us, but has, strengthened our faith, and always given us necessaries.

The School-Funds are also now again very low. There was only so much money in hand, as that two of the teachers, really in need, could be paid today. Truly, my dear fellow-labourers in the schools need to trust the Lord for their temporal supplies! [I notice here, that though the brethren and sisters have a certain remuneration, yet it is understood that, if the Lord should not be pleased to send in the means at the time when their salary is due, I am not considered their debtor. Should the Lord be pleased to send in means afterwards, the remainder of the salary is paid up, and also additional assistance is given in time of sickness or more than usual need, as the Lord may be pleased to grant the means. A brother or sister, in connection with this work, not looking for themselves to the Lord, would be truly uncomfortable; for the position of all of us is of such a character, that it brings heavy trials of faith, in addition to the many precious seasons of joy on account of answers to prayer.]

Dec. 13. Lord's day. This morning I received 2l. 10s. Thus, before the last provisions are actually consumed in the Orphan-Houses, I have been able to give fresh supplies.

Dec. 14. Though 2l. 10s. had come in yesterday, there was still not sufficient this morning to buy coals in the Boys' and Girls'-Orphan-Houses. But the Lord kindly supplied us with means for that also; for there were given today six silver tea spoons, and a pair of silver sugar tongs. I received also 1l. 10s. which yesterday had been anonymously given for rent. Thus the Lord, in this particular also, again begins the year with blessings. [As during the two previous years 1l. 10s. a week was anonymously given to pay for the rent of the three Orphan-Houses, so during the whole of this year also, from Dec. 10, 1840, to Dec. 10, 1841, the donor continued the same contribution.] This evening was the first of our public meetings, at which I gave the account of the Lord's dealings with us in regard to this work, during the last year. It was a good season. I felt much assisted by the Lord, and was, through grace, very happy, so that none of those who were present can have read in my countenance that I have nothing at all in hand towards the supply of the necessities of tomorrow. After the meeting this evening 2 1/2d. was left anonymously at my house.

Dec. 15. The day commenced with 2 1/2d. in hand. My eyes were directed to the living God. I was looking out for help. The greatness of our need led me to expect it. About eleven o'clock I received from Barnstaple a 5l. note and half-a-sovereign. Thus the Lord in His faithful love delivered us. Half an hour afterwards I had the report from the Orphan-Houses about the state of things today, which will show how seasonably the money from Barnstaple came. Brother R. B., master at the Boys'-Orphan~ House, wrote that last evening a sister gave 5s. and a cloak, but that there never was less bread in the Orphan-Houses at any time than this morning, and that both in the Boys' and Infant-Orphan-Houses all bread had been, cut up for use.-- We are now waiting on the Lord for means to enable us to have the Report printed. Till He provides, we will, by His help, do nothing in this matter. Though it seems to us important that the account of the Lord's dealings with us in the work should be made known to the saints generally; yea, though this is the primary object of the work; nevertheless it appears to us a small matter for our kind and loving Father, who withholds nothing from His children that is really good for them, to give us the sum which we need for this purpose whenever His time shall have come. We do desire grace even in this thing to acknowledge Him; for His time may not yet have come for us to have the sweet privilege of sending forth far and wide the account of His goodness to us during the past year.

Dec. 16. To-night I received with Ecclesiastes ix. 10, 1l. 10s., and 12s. from another individual; also a Spanish dollar was sent. Thus we have something for the necessities of tomorrow.

Dec. 17. Today came in 3s., and from Bath 4l. 6s. 8d.; also 2l., the produce of the sale of ladies' baskets.

Dec. 19. Only 11s. 2d. has come in since the day before yesterday. As I had to pay out today 6l. 10s., it being Saturday, we have now again only 5s. 9d. left, which is just enough to meet the expense of a parcel, the arrival of which has been announced. Thus we still have no means for printing the Report, The Lord's time seems not yet to have come.

This afternoon came in from Exmouth 1l. 10s. 5d. for the other objects, so that, with what there was in hand, the teachers of the Day-Schools who were in need could be supplied.

Dec. 20. The Lord has again sent in rich supplies. He remembered that there was nothing in hand for the Orphans, and that we, who care for them, desire, through grace, not to be anxiously concerned about the morrow. There came in today altogether 6l. 17s.

Dec. 25. This morning there was 5l. given to me by a brother, to be used as most needed. As there is a little left for the Orphans, but about 5l. needed, tomorrow, for the schools, and there are only a few shillings in hand, I took this money for these funds.

Jan. 1, 1841. Since Dec. 20 has come in not only as much as was needed, but more. Of the donations which were given, I only notice: A sister brought the produce of her silver spoons, which she had sold, having had it laid on her heart to do so through the last public meetings. During this week we have daily met for prayer, for the especial purpose of asking the Lord to give us the means of having the last year's Report printed. It is three weeks since it might have been sent to the press. We felt this now to be a matter of especial importance, as, if the Report were not soon printed, it would be known that it arose from want of means. By the donations which came in during these last days for the Orphans, and by 10l. which was given today for the other funds, we have the means of defraying the expenses of about two-thirds of the printing, and therefore a part of the manuscript was sent off, trusting that the Lord would be pleased to send in more means before two sheets are printed off; but if not, we should then stop till we have more.--Evening. There came in still further 5l.; and also 10s., and 3s.

Jan. 2. Today 18s. came in, and the following articles were sent anonymously to the Girls'-Orphan-House: A smelling bottle, a metal chain and cross, a silver pencil case, a mother-of-pearl ring, a pebble, a necklace clasp, 2 pairs of studs, and 6 chimney ornaments. There were also sent anonymously, this evening, 2 pairs of skates.--There was needed today 1l. 1s. 6d. more than there was in hand, to pay the salaries of the teachers in the Day-Schools. About noon a sister brought three small donations, amounting to 9s.; and a sovereign came by post. Thus our need has been supplied.

Jan. 3. This morning a brooch was given to me, set with a brilliant and 10 small emeralds. The stones are to be sold for the benefit of the Orphans, and the gold is to be returned. I received also the following sums: From a sister in Bristol, 5l.; from the East Indies 2l.; from Devonshire 2l. 10s. and a silver vinaigrette; anonymously put into the boxes at Bethesda 2s., ditto by I. L. 3s. 6d., ditto for rent 1l. 10s.; and by sale of articles 1s. 6d. Thus the Lord has sent in today 11l. 7s., in answer to our united prayer during the last week.

THIRD PART

Jan. 4. Today the following trinkets were given, to be disposed of for the benefit of the Orphans, or on behalf of the other objects. [They were taken for the latter, there being only about 7s. in hand.] Two chains and crosses of soap beads, an amber necklace, a bead necklace, a gold Maltese cross and chain, a Brazilian gold chain, a pearl hair brooch, a pearl cross, a mother-of-pearl buckle, 2 rings, a necklace snap, a moonstone brooch, a brooch of Ceylon stones, a pair of bracelet snaps, a gold brooch, a gilt vinaigrette, a pair of buckles, and a box. [The money which was obtained for the greater part of these trinkets, supplied our need on Saturday, January 9th.]

Jan. 11. Monday. During the last week the Lord not only supplied us richly with all we needed for the Orphans, but enabled us to put by several pounds towards printing the Report. On Saturday evening there was only 3s. 6d. left. On this account I was looking out for answers to my prayers for means, and the Lord did not disappoint me. There came in altogether yesterday 9l. 16s. 4d. We have now enough even for the last part of the Report. Thus the Lord has been pleased to answer our prayers in this respect also. This afternoon when there was again only 2s. 6d. in hand, came in by sale of articles 3l. 9s. 6d., and by a donation 5l.

Jan. 12. Today I have received a letter from a brother, in which he empowers me to draw upon his bankers, during this year to the amount of 1000l., for any brethren who have it in their hearts to give themselves to missionary Service in the East Indies, and whom I shall consider called for this service, as far as I am able to judge. [This power lasted only for that year; but no brethren who seemed to be suitable offered themselves for this service]

Jan. 13. This evening I was called to the house of a brother and sister who are in the deepest distress. The brother had become surety for the debts of his son, not in the least expecting that he ever should be called upon for the payment of them; but as his son has not discharged his debts, the father has been called upon to do so; and except the money is paid within a few days, he will be imprisoned.

How precious it is, even for this life, to act according to the word of God! This perfect revelation of His mind gives us directions for every thing, even the most minute affairs of this life. It commands us, "Be thou not one of them that strike hands, or of them that are sureties for debts." Prov. xxii. 26. The way in which Satan ensnares persons, to bring them into the net, and to bring trouble upon them by becoming sureties, is, that he seeks to represent the matter as if there were no danger connected with that particular case, and that one might be sure one should never be called upon to pay the money; but the Lord, the faithful Friend, tells us in His own word that the only way in such a matter "to be sure" is "to hate suretiship." Prov. xi. 15. The following points seem to me of solemn moment for consideration, if I were called upon to become surety for another: 1. What obliges the person who wishes me to become surety for him, to need a surety? Is it really a good cause in which I am called upon to become surety? I do not remember ever to have met with a case in which in a plain, and godly, and in all respects Scriptural matter such a thing occurred. There was generally some sin or other connected with it. 2. If I become surety, notwithstanding what the Lord has said to me in His word, am I in such a position that no one will be injured by my being called upon to fulfill the engagements of the person for whom I am going to be surety? In most instances this alone ought to keep one from it. 3. If still I become surety, the amount of money, for which I become responsible, must be so in my power, that I am able to produce it whenever it is called for, in order that the name of the Lord may not be dishonoured. 4. But if there be the possibility of having to fulfill the engagements of the person in whose stead I have to stand, is it the will of the Lord, that I should spend my means in that way? Is it not rather His will that my means should be spent in another way? 5. How can I get over the plain word of the Lord, which is to the contrary, even if the first four points could be satisfactorily settled?

This morning (Jan. 13) I had again not one penny in hand for the Orphans, though there was enough for today at the Orphan-Houses, as I had sent yesterday sufficient for two days. The little stock being exhausted, I had been led to the Lord in prayer for fresh supplies, when soon afterwards a brother called on me, who stated, that, in considering the necessities of the poor, on account of the cold season, the Orphans had likewise been brought to his mind, and that he had brought me 15l. for them. This afternoon came in still further 1l. from two sisters, as a thank-offering for many mercies during the past year. Likewise 10l. "From a friend in Christ for the Orphans'-House." Further: by sale of articles 2l. 4s. 6d., by knitting 1l. 4s., by Reports 9d., and by four donations 13s. Thus the Lord has been pleased to send in this day altogether 30l. 2s. 3d., whilst, when the day commenced, I had nothing at all in hand.

Jan. 23. This day commenced without any thing in hand. In addition to this it was Saturday. About nine o'clock Q. Q. called to see me, but, as I was in prayer with my family, she did not stay. About half an hour afterwards she called a second time, gave 5l. for the Orphans, and said, "I bring this because it is Saturday, and it may be needed." This sister was not deterred by not seeing me the first time, because our Father knew we had need of this money. There was likewise 5s. given me this afternoon, and when the sister gave it she said, "I bring this today, because it is Saturday."

Jan. 25. 2l. 19s. 10d. came in yesterday and this morning. When the necessities of the day had been supplied, and there was only 12s. 10d. left, I received a parcel from an unknown donor. It contained 1 lb. and 6 oz. of worsted and 4 sovereigns, with the following note:--"'Your Father knoweth that ye have need of these things.' 'All things whatsoever ye shall ask in prayer, believing, ye shall receive.' An Orphan sends 3l. for the Orphans, and 1l. for Mr. G. Mueller's own necessities, Jan. 23, 1841."

Feb. 1. Today we had not sufficient money for our own personal necessities, when we were helped in the following way. Some months ago several articles were sent to my dear wife from a distance of about 200 miles, which she did not at all need, and which therefore had been placed in the hands of a sister to be disposed of.

THIRD PART

This was only now done, and today, in this our need, the money was brought for them, being 1l.. 10s. 6d.

Feb. 4. Since Jan. 25, there has come in 10l. 14s. 11d. for the Orphans. This morning a brother from Gloucestershire brought me a doubloon, (18 1/2 pennyweights of fine gold,) a Spanish dollar, 2 small Spanish coins, 4 old English crown pieces, 2 old English half-crown pieces, 3 old shillings, 2 old sixpences, and an old twopenny piece. He told me that he had purposed to come a day sooner, but that, though he was quite prepared for his journey, his business did not allow him to leave home, but that immediately, when these coins were given to him for the Orphans, he was able to leave. On his arrival in Bristol, this brother was asked by a gentleman, a fellow passenger, to go with him; but he replied he must go at once to me. On mentioning my name, the Gloucestershire brother was asked whether he did not believe that it was all chance work about the Orphan-Houses. He replied no, and showed him the handful of gold and silver coins, which he had received for the Orphan-Houses, and which he felt himself constrained at once to deliver.--There was also given this day a valuable gold lever watch.--Though these donations of today were not needed to supply the necessities of the children, yet they came very seasonably, and as the answer to many prayers which I had lately offered up to the Lord, to enable me to give 26l. to the labourers in the Orphan-Houses, for their own personal necessities.

Feb. 6. At the close of this week there is nothing at all in hand, either in the Orphan-Fund or in the other funds; but the Lord has enabled me to meet all the expences of the week, which only yesterday and today were above 30l.

Feb. 7. In answer to prayer, when we were without any money for the Orphans, came in today altogether 2l. 18s.

Feb. 10. There came in yesterday and the day before several small donations; also by post, anonymously, a sovereign and a diamond ring from Leamington; but we are now again without means. May the Lord help us!

--Evening. There came in by sale of articles 10s., by sale of Reports 10s., and by a donation 1s. 6d. I also opened the box in my house, in which I found 1l. 0s. 6d. A sovereign had been put in by a brother from Stafford, who had already left my house, but felt himself constrained to return, in order to put in this money.

Feb. 12. Last evening there was left at my house, anonymously, a letter containing two sovereigns, in which was written, "For the Orphan-House 2l." This 2l. is exactly what is needed for today.

Feb. 13. Saturday morning. The Lord sent in yesterday 1l. 15s. which, though not enough for this day, was a little to commence with. Evening. Scarcely had I sent off this morning the 1l. 15s. to the Orphan-Houses, when I received from Clapham 9l. 6s. 6d. and 6 yds. of calico, for the Orphans, so that 1l. more, which was needed to meet this day's demands, could be supplied. There came in also 14s. 6d.

We are very poor in reference to the funds for the other objects, and have now determined to meet daily for prayer, till the Lord may be pleased to send help.

There are now four sisters in the Lord staying at our house. This morning we had only 2s. left of our own money, when there was sent to us for ourselves from Clapham a sovereign and 2 lbs. of tea; and from Manchester 5 shillings' worth of postages. Thus the Lord has kindly helped us for the present.

Feb. 14. The Lord has had pity, and helped us in some measure. A brother gave me 5l. for the first four objects of the Scriptural Knowledge Institution.

Feb. 22. Since the 14th there has come in still further for the first four objects 6s. 1d., 13s. 4d., 2s. 6d., 1l., and 5l., besides what has come in by the sale of Bibles, etc. Thus we have been able to meet all the expenses of this week.

March 4. From February 22 up to this day our necessities in the Day Schools were supplied by thirteen small donations, and by a donation of 8l. from Q. Q. Today I received the following letter

"Dear Brother,

I yesterday happened to meet with one of your Reports of the Orphan Institution for the last year, which I have read with much interest. I was not before at all aware how entirely you subsisted day by day on the good providence of the Lord, and it is very wonderful to see His constant care of such of His children as walk uprightly, and put their trust in Him. It must be very blessed thus to know and feel His care from day to day, in making bread and water sure. I am concerned to find that there was so much need at the time I saw you in ...... and that I did not assist you; but I will delay no longer, for there may be equal need now; and as I find many sums given with the text Ecclesiastes ix. 10, it reminds me, not to put off till tomorrow that which should be done today. Just before I fell in with your Report, I got a little portable money out of the bank, thinking it might be needed in some such way, so without delay I enclose it; the amount is 15l., and I hope that the Lord will direct my mind and incline my heart to help you again at the time of need. I perceive you have a list with the sums received, and the names of the donors open for inspection (though not published, which is well). Please to insert my donation, and any future ones I may give, under the initials A. B."

When this letter arrived, there was not one penny in hand for the Day Schools, whilst two days after about 7l. was needed. As the money was not given for any particular part of the work, it was put to this fund. There was also only 2l. in the Orphan fund. This money came from a considerable distance, and from a brother who never

THIRD PART

had assisted in this work before, whereby the Lord afresh shows how easily He can raise up new helpers.

March 11. From Feb. 13 to this day we have had comparative abundance for the Orphans, as 70 donations of 10l. and under have come in, also many pounds by sale of articles and Reports; but now, when we had again only 13s. 6d. in hand, not half of what is needed to meet the necessities of tomorrow, a sister at Plymouth sent 6l.

March 12. There came in still further today 5l. from "Friends to the Orphan," besides 2s. 6d., 1s. 6d., 10s., and 8s. 6d.

March 18. Today I heard of the conversion of a gentleman, whose believing wife had prayed many years on behalf of her husband. He was a Roman Catholic and a great drunkard. But though he had been a Roman Catholic, he was truly made to rest upon the Lord Jesus alone for salvation; though he had been a great drunkard, the power of the Gospel was seen in his case, for he forsook his evil ways; and though his wife had had to continue to pray for him many years, yet at last the Lord answered the cries of his afflicted handmaid, and gave her the desire of her heart.

As I know it to be a fact, that many children of God are greatly tried by having unconverted relatives, I relate here, for the encouragement of believers who are thus exercised, two precious facts, the truth of which I know, and by which the Lord manifested His power in converting, two of the most unlikely individuals, so far as natural appearance is concerned. Between forty and fifty years ago it pleased the Lord to convert the wife of a farmer at Ashburton in Devonshire, whose husband in consequence became her bitter opposer. This opposition was greatly increased when he had reason to believe that she was going to be baptized. The wife, however, thought that, on account of his great enmity, she would choose a time for being baptized when he was from home. A time was therefore chosen when he was to be absent at a fair in Exeter. The farmer went to the fair; but having learned on Thursday that his wife was to be baptized at eleven o'clock the next morning, in haste to return he rose early on Friday morning, to put a stop to the proceeding. After he had rode several miles, he said to himself, "No, I will not go; let her do what she pleases, I will not care about her at all:" and he therefore rode back again towards Exeter. But after awhile he altered his mind again and said to himself, "Nay, I will go, she shall not have her way;" and he rode again towards Ashburton. He pursued his way, and then changed his mind a third time, and turned towards Exeter; but not long after this, a fourth time he had different thoughts, and determined to ride borne. Now, however, he remembered, that, on account of his having thus gone backwards and forwards, and that for several miles, he had wasted so much time, that he could not possibly be at Ashburton by eleven o'clock, a distance of more than twenty miles from Exeter. Enraged by this thought, he dismounted from his horse on Haldon Common, between Exeter and Teignmouth, cut a large stick out of the hedge and determined to beat his wife with that stick, as long as a part of it remained. At last he reached his home, late in the afternoon, and found his wife had been baptized. In a great rage he now began to beat her, and continued to do so, till the stick in his hand was actually broken to pieces. Having thus most cruelly treated her, her body being full of bruises, he ordered her to bed. She meekly began to undress herself, and intended to go to bed, without saying a word. But when he saw her about to go, he said, "You shall not sleep in my bed any more. Go to the children's bed." She obeyed. When now on the point of lying down on the children's bed, he ran into the kitchen, fetched a piece of wood, threw her down on the bed, and was about to begin again to beat her, when suddenly he let the piece of wood fall, and went away without saying a word. The poor suffering wife saw no more of him that evening or night. On the next morning, Saturday, before she had risen, her husband left the house, and was absent all day till the evening. In the evening the wife gave him to understand when retiring for the night, that, according to his wish, she was again going to sleep in the children's bed, when he meekly said to her, "Will you not sleep in your own bed?" She thought he meant to mock her, and would beat her again, if she did go into her own bed. As, however, he continued in a meek and kind way to desire her to lie down in her usual bed, she did so. All night from Saturday to the Lord's day he lay groaning by her side, turning about in the bed, but having no sleep. On the Lord's day morning he rose early. After awhile he came to her and said, "My dear, it is time to get up: if you will get up and make the breakfast, I will go with you to the meeting." Still the wife thought, he only meant to mock her, and that perhaps he would beat her again, when she was on the point of going to the meeting. Nevertheless she rose, prepared the breakfast, and at last, as he continued meek and kind as before, she made herself ready to go to the meeting. How great was the astonishment and surprise of the people in the small town, where the thing had become known almost to every one, when arm in arm he walked with his wife to the meeting and entered it himself, which he had never done before! After the meeting was over, he related before all persons present, what had passed in his mind between Exeter and Ashburton, how he had most cruelly beaten his wife, how he had ordered her to go to the children's bed, how he had run into the kitchen to fetch a piece of wood to beat his wife a second time, how he had thrown her on the bed for that purpose, and how he had already lifted up his hand with the piece of wood in it, when there was like an audible voice saying to him: "Why persecutest thou me!" The piece of wood had then fallen out of his hand, and he had felt instantly that he was persecuting the Lord Jesus. From that moment his soul had become most distressed. He had been sleepless and miserable during the night from Friday to Saturday. On Saturday morning he had left the house early in the greatest agonies of soul, and had been roving about in the fields and neighbouring villages all the day. He had come home, and spent another sleepless night from Saturday to the Lord's day. And then passed what has been related.

From this time this persecutor became a disciple of the Lord Jesus. He found peace through the blood of the Lord Jesus, by faith in His name, and walked about thirty years in peace and love with his wife, and adorned the gospel of the grace of God.

THIRD PART

His wife outlived him. The husband died more than thirteen years ago. The aged sister told all the particulars of the case to a brother in the Lord, out of whose mouth I heard them; and I have related them faithfully to the best of my knowledge.

Surely the arm of the Lord is not shortened in our days! In a moment He may turn the heart of the greatest persecutor. Think on Paul, think on Manasseh!

The other case of a remarkable conversion, which I am about to relate for the encouragement of the believing reader, occurred in my native country, the kingdom of Prussia, about the year 1820. I relate it as circumstantially as it was brought before me by a brother in the Lord. Baron von K. had been for many years a disciple of the Lord Jesus. Even about the commencement of this century, when there was almost universal darkness or even open infidelity spread over the whole continent of Europe, he knew the Lord Jesus; and when about the year 1806, there was the greatest distress in Silesia among many thousands of weavers, this blessed man of God took the following gracious step for his Lord and Master. As the weavers had no employment, the whole Continent almost being in an unsettled state on account of Napoleon's career, it seemed to him the will of the Lord, that he should use his very considerable property to furnish these poor weavers with work, in order to save them from the greatest state of destitution, though in doing this there was not only no prospect of gain, but the certain prospect of immense loss. He therefore found employment for about six thousand weavers. But he was not content with this. Whilst he gave the bread which perishes, he also sought to minister to the souls of these weavers. To that end he sought to set believers as overseers over this immense weaving concern, and not only saw to it that the weavers were instructed in spiritual things, but he himself also set the truth before them. Thus it went on for a good while, till at last, on account of the loss of the chief part of his property, he was obliged to think about giving it up. But by this time this precious act of mercy had so commended itself to the government, that it was taken up by them, and carried on till the times altered. Baron von K. was, however, appointed director of the whole concern as long as it existed.--This dear man of God was not content with this. He travelled through many countries to visit the prisons, for the sake of improving the temporal and spiritual condition of the prisoners, and among all the other things which he sought to do for the Lord, was this also in particular: He assisted poor students whilst at the University of Berlin, (especially those who studied theology, as it is called,) in order to get access to them, and to win them for the Lord. One day a most talented young man, whose father lived at Breslau, where there is likewise a university, heard of the aged baron's kindness to students, and he therefore wrote to him, requesting him to assist him, as his own father could not well afford to support him any longer, having other children to provide for. A short time afterwards young T. received a most kind reply from the baron, inviting him to come to Berlin; but, before this letter arrived, the young student had heard that Baron von K. was a pietist or mystic (as true believers are contemptuously called in Germany;) and as young was of a highly philosophical turn of mind, reasoning about every thing, questioning the truth of revelation, yea questioning most sceptically the existence of God, he much disliked the prospect of going to the old baron. Still, he thought he could but try, and if he did not like it, he was not bound to remain in connexion with him. He arrived in Berlin on a day when there was a great review of the troops; and being full of this he began to speak about it to the steward of the baron. The steward, however, being a believer, turned the conversation, before the young student was aware of it, to spiritual things; and yet he could not say that it had been forced. He began another subject, and a third, but still it always came presently again to spiritual things. At last the baron came, who received young T. in the most affectionate and familiar manner, as if he had been his equal, and as if young T. bestowed a favour on him, rather than that he was favoured by the baron. The baron offered him a room in his own house, and a place at his own table, while he should be studying in Berlin, which young T. accepted. He now sought in every way to treat the young student in the most kind and affectionate way, and as much as possible to serve him, and to show him the power of the Gospel in his own life, without arguing with him, yea without speaking to him directly about his soul. For, discovering in young T. a most reasoning and sceptical mind, he avoided in every possible way getting into any argument with him, while the young student again and again said to himself: "I wish I could get into an argument with this old fool, I would show him his folly." But the baron avoided it. When the young student used to come home in the evening, and the baron heard him come, he would himself go to meet him on entering the house, would light his candle, would assist and serve him in any way he could, even to the fetching the bootjack for him, and helping him to take off his boots. Thus this lowly aged disciple went on for some time, whilst the young student still sought an opportunity for arguing with him, but wondered nevertheless how the baron could thus serve him. One evening, on the return of young T. to the baron's house, when the baron was making himself his servant as usual, he could refrain himself no longer, but burst out thus: "Baron, how can you do all this! You see I do not care about you, and how are you able to continue to be so kind to me, and thus to serve me!" The baron replied: "My dear young friend, I have learned it from the Lord Jesus. I wish you would read through the Gospel of John. Good night." The student now for the first time in his life sat down and read the word of God in a disposition of mind to be willing to learn, whilst up to that time he had never read the Holy Scriptures but with the view of wishing to find out arguments against them. It pleased God to bless him. From that time he became himself a follower of the Lord Jesus, and has been so ever since.

I continue now the extracts from my journal.

March 19, 1841. It is twelve years this day since I arrived in England. How exceedingly kind and gracious has the Lord been to me day by day ever since! And the Lord has crowned this day also with mercies. I have been for some time again very weak in body, on account of which it appeared to me desirable to change my sphere of labour for awhile, to which I was the more inclined as I purpose to write the second part of my Narrative, for which I need more time than I can well find in Bristol, along with my other engagements. Today I had fully determined to leave, as I am now exceedingly weak; but we had no means for it. This morning, after the exposition of the Scriptures to the Orphan and Day School children, there was given to

THIRD PART

me a check for 15l., of which 5l. is for brother Craik, 5l. for myself, and 5l. for the Orphans, Thus my way, even as to means, is made quite plain.

March 20. Nailsworth. I had purposed to take lodgings in the neighbourhood of Tetbury, passing only a night or so at Nailsworth. When I came here today, and heard about the state of the saints here and in the neighbourhood, I could not but think that the Lord had sent me to this place to labour for a season.

March 21. I ministered twice today among the brethren at Nailsworth, with much assistance from the Lord, and feel already much better from the change of air.

March 22. Truly God has sent me here! Certain matters which have been brought to light through my being here, prove it. May the Lord make it still more abundantly plain that He has sent me here!--There is a small house, which a brother left a few weeks since, but has to pay rent for at least three months longer. He will let me have it rent free, and he and brother--mean to put into it the needful furniture.--Thus the Lord has provided a lodging, not only for me, but also for all my family, who can now join me here.

A sister in the Lord in Ireland, who did not see her acceptance before God, and who was habitually without the assurance that she is a child of God, that she is born again, that her sins are forgiven, and that she shall be saved, in her distress of mind wrote to me about this time. As her case is by no means a solitary one, but as there are so many children of God who do not know that they are children of God; as there are so many whose sins are forgiven who do not know that they are forgiven; and as there are so many who will be saved, who do not know that they will be saved, and who are continually afraid of what would become of them, were they to be taken out of the world:--I have thought it well to say something here on this most important subject.

I. Question. How may I obtain the knowledge that I am a child of God, or that I am born again, or that my sins are forgiven, or that I shall not perish but have everlasting life?

Answer. Not by my feelings, not by a dream, not by my experience being like this or that one's, or unlike this or that one's; but this matter is to be settled, as all other spiritual matters, entirely by the revealed will of God, the written word of God, which is the only rule, the only standard for believers.

II. Question. By what passages, then, for instance, may I make out that I am a child of God, or born again?

Answer. 1. In 1 John v. 1, it is written: "Whosoever believeth that Jesus is the Christ is born of God." The meaning of these words is evidently this, that every one (whether young or old, male or female, one who has lived an outwardly moral or immoral life,) who believes that the poor, despised Jesus of Nazareth, of whom we read in the New Testament, was the promised Christ or Messiah, such a one is no longer in his natural state, but is born again, is born of God, is a child of God. The question therefore is, Do you believe that Jesus, who was born at Bethlehem, and crucified under Pontius Pilate, is the promised Saviour, the Messiah, the one for whom the Jews were to look? If so, you are a child of God, else you would not believe it. It is given unto you to believe it. Millions may SAY that Jesus is the Saviour, the Messiah, but none BELIEVE it except the children of God. It proves me to be a child of God that I believe it; to none besides is it given to believe it, though millions might say so.

Perhaps you say, I do not feel that I am born again, born of God, and I have therefore no enjoyment.

Answer. In order that you may have the enjoyment, which is the result of the knowledge that you are a child of God, that you are born of God, or born again, you must receive God's testimony. He is a faithful witness, He speaks nothing but the truth, and His declaration is, That every one who believes that Jesus is the Christ is born of God. If you receive this testimony of God, you, to whom by grace it is given to believe that Jesus is the Christ, cannot but be happy, from the fact that God Himself says, that you are His child. But if you will wait till you feel that you are a child of God, you may have to wait long; and even if you felt it, yet your feelings would be worth nothing; for either it might be a false feeling, or, though it were real, it might be lost the next hour. Feelings change; but the word of God remains unalterably the same. You have, then, without having had a dream about it, without having had a portion of the word in a more than usual way impressed upon your mind concerning the subject, without having heard something like a voice from heaven about it, to say to yourself: If I believe that Jesus is the promised Messiah, I am a child of God. And then, from a belief of what God declares in this passage concerning you who believe that Jesus is the Christ, even that you are His child, spring peace and joy in the Holy Ghost.

Answer 2. In Galatians iii. 26, it is written: "Ye are all the children of God by faith in Christ Jesus." The question here again is: Do I believe in the Lord Jesus? Do I depend upon Him alone for the salvation of my soul? If so, I am a child of God, whether I feel it or not.

Answer 3. In John i. 11--13, it is written of the Lord Jesus: "He came unto His own, and His own received Him not. But as many as received Him, to them gave He power (or the right or the privilege) to become the sons of God, even to them that believe on His name: which were born, not of blood, nor of the will of the flesh, nor of the will of man, but of God." The question here again is simply this, Have I received the Lord Jesus, i.e., Do I believe in His name? If so, I am born of God, I am a child of God, else I should never have believed in the Lord Jesus; for none but the children of God do believe in Him.

THIRD PART

III. Question. How may I know that my sins are forgiven? Have I to wait till I feel that they are forgiven, before I may take comfort concerning this matter? Or, must I wait till I have in some powerful way a portion of the word of God applied to my mind, to assure me of it?

Answer. This point is again only to be settled by the word of God. We have not to wait till we feel that our sins are forgiven.--I myself have now been a believer for more than nineteen years (i.e. in the year 1845). How long it is, since I have had no doubt whatever about the forgiveness of my sins, I cannot tell with certainty; but this I am quite sure of, that ever since I have been in England, which is now about sixteen years (in 1845), I have never once had a single moment's doubt that my sins are all forgiven; and yet I do not remember that I even once have felt that they were forgiven. To know that they are forgiven, and to feel that they are forgiven, are two different things.--The way to settle, whether our sins are forgiven, is, to refer to the word of God alone with reference to it. In Acts x. 43, it is written concerning the Lord Jesus, "To him give all the prophets witness, that through His name whosoever believeth in Him shall receive remission of sins." All the prophets speaking under the immediate power of the Holy Spirit, bore testimony, that through the obedience and sufferings of the Lord Jesus, whereby He becomes our Saviour or is our Jesus, all who believe in Him for salvation, who depend upon Him and not upon themselves, who receive Him to be the one whom God declares Him to be, should receive the forgiveness of their sins. The questions therefore to be put to ourselves are simply these: Do I walk in utter carelessness? Do I trust in my own exertions for salvation? Do I expect forgiveness for my sins on account of living a better life in future? Or, do I depend only upon this, that Jesus died upon the cross to save sinners--and that Jesus fulfilled the law of God to make sinners righteous? If the latter is the case, my sins are forgiven, whether I feel it or not. I have already forgiveness. I shall not have it merely when I die, or when the Lord Jesus comes again; but I have it now, and that for all my sins. I must not wait to feel that my sins are forgiven, in order to be at peace, and in order to be happy; but I must take God at His word, I must believe that what He says in true, and He says, "That whosoever believeth in the Lord Jesus should receive remission of sins;" and when I believe what God says, peace and joy will be the result.

Again, in Acts xv. 8, 9, it is written with reference to us Gentile sinners: "And God which knoweth the hearts, bare them witness, giving them the Holy Ghost, even as He did unto us; and put no difference between us and them, purifying their hearts by faith." Here we see how the guilt is to be removed from the heart, how we can get a clean heart, obtain the forgiveness of our sins,--even by faith in the Lord Jesus. Depending upon the sufferings of the Lord Jesus in the room of sinners, and depending upon His obedience in fulfilling the law of God, His sufferings are considered as endured by us, His obedience as if found in ourselves: in Him (if we believe on Him) we are considered to have hung on the cross, and therefore were punished in Him, on account of which God, though perfectly holy and just, can forgive us our sins for Jesus' sake, as well as reckon us righteous, through faith in the Lord Jesus, who in the room of those who believe on Him fulfilled the law of God.

I would here by the way especially warn against one error, which is, that persons say, I can believe that Jesus is the Christ, the Saviour, that through Him alone the forgiveness of sins is to be obtained, and I do depend on Him alone for forgiveness, but I desire to know that He is my Christ, my Saviour, and because I am not sure about that, I can have no peace. Now, the Gospel which is preached in the New Testament is not, you must believe that Jesus of Nazareth is your Christ, your Saviour, but that He is the Christ, the Saviour; and if you believe that, you have a right to look upon Him as your Saviour.

IV. Question. How may I know that I shall be saved?

Answer. "If thou shalt confess with thy mouth the Lord Jesus, and shalt believe in thy heart that God hath raised Him from the dead, thou shalt be saved." Rom. x. 9. The point is simply this: Do I confess with my mouth the Lord Jesus? Do I own Him by the confession of my mouth before men, and do I believe in my heart that Jesus of Nazareth who was crucified was not left in the grave, but was raised again by God on the third day? If so, I shall be saved. For while there may be the confession of the Lord Jesus with the month, without the person being finally saved, there does not go along with this the believing in the heart that God has raised Him from the dead, without the person, in whom both are found, being finally saved; for in none but the children of God are these two points found united together. We have here particularly to observe, that it is not written: If thou shalt say that God has raised Him from the dead; but if thou shalt believe in thine heart that God has raised Him from the dead, thou shalt be saved. I have, then, to take God at His word. If I do confess the Lord Jesus with my mouth, and do believe in my heart that God has raised Him from the dead, I shall be saved, though I do not feel it, though I am utterly unworthy of salvation, yea, though I am altogether deserving condemnation. I must not wait till I feel that I shall be saved before I take comfort; but I must believe what God says in this verse, and, out of that, peace and comfort will flow into my soul. Should, however, one or the other of the children of God, believe in his heart the resurrection of the Lord Jesus, if at the same time he has never made confession of the Lord Jesus with his mouth, he cannot be surprised that the assurance about his salvation is wanting to him; yet if both be found in you, my dear reader, God has been gracious to you, you are His child, you shall be saved.

Further, in John iii. 16, it is written: "God so loved the world that He gave His only begotten Son, that whosoever believeth in Him should not perish, but have everlasting life." Notice here in particular: 1. It matters not how great a sinner I am. 2. The promise is positive concerning my salvation, if I believe in the Lord Jesus. 3. I have only to believe in the Lord Jesus. No matter how it may have been with me hitherto; if only now I trust in and depend upon the Lord Jesus for salvation, I shall have everlasting life.

Further, in Acts xvi. 30, 31, it is written: "Sirs, what must I do to be saved? And they said, Believe on the Lord Jesus Christ, and thou shalt be saved."

THIRD PART

Further, in John iii. 36, it is written: "He that believeth on the Son hath everlasting life; and He that believeth not the Son shall not see life; but the wrath of God abideth on him." As assuredly as I depend upon and trust in the Lord Jesus for the salvation of my soul, I shall be saved, I have already everlasting life; for He died, to deliver those who believe on Him from the wrath of God, under which all men are in their natural state; but if I do not believe in the Lord Jesus, the wrath of God, which rests upon all men in their natural state, will finally destroy me, if I remain without faith in the Lord Jesus; for then I reject the one only remedy, in refusing to take Jesus as my substitute, who bore the punishment that He might deliver the sinner from it, and who fulfilled the law of God that He might make the sinner who believes on Him a just one before God.

V. Question. How may I know that I am one of the elect? I often read in the Scriptures about election, and I often hear about election, how may I know that I am a chosen one, that I am predestinated to be conformed to the image of the Son of God?

Answer. It is written: "As many as were ordained, (i.e. appointed) to eternal life believed." Acts xii. 48. The question therefore simply is this: Do I believe in the Lord Jesus? Do I take Him to be the one whom God declares Him to be, i. e. His beloved Son in whom He is well pleased? If so, I am a believer, and I should never have believed, except I had been appointed by God to eternal life--except I had been made by God to be a vessel of mercy. Therefore the matter is a very simple one: if I believe in the Lord Jesus, I am a chosen one,--I have been appointed to eternal life.

Again, in Rom. viii. 29, 30, it is written: "For whom He did foreknow, He also did predestinate to be conformed to the image of His Son, that He might be the firstborn among many brethren. Moreover, whom He did predestinate, them He also called: and whom he called, them He also justified; and whom He justified, them He also glorified." How are we justified, or constituted just ones, before God? By faith in the Lord Jesus. Rom. iii. 20--26. Therefore if I believe in the Lord Jesus, it follows (on account of the inseparable connection of all the precious things spoken of in these two verses), that I have been foreknown by God, that I have been predestinated by Him to be conformed to the image of His Son, that I have been called, that I have been justified, and that, in the sight of God, I am already as good as glorified, though I am not as yet in the actual possession and enjoyment of the glory.

The reason why persons who renounce confidence in their own goodness for salvation, and who only trust in the merits and sufferings of the Lord Jesus, do not know that they are the children of God, that their sins are forgiven, and that they shall be saved, generally arises from one of these things: 1. They do not know the simplicity of the Gospel; or, 2. They seek to settle it by their feeling; or, 3. They wait for some powerful impulse, or a dream, or something like a voice from Heaven to assure them of it, or for some passage being in a powerful way applied to their mind to assure them of it; or, 4. Because they are living in sin. Should the last be the case, then, however correctly we may understand the Gospel; however much we may desire by the Holy Scriptures alone to settle these questions; yea, however much in former times we may have enjoyed the assurance of the forgiveness of our sins, or of our being the children of God, or that we shall be saved: in such a state of heart all peace would be gone, and would not return as long as we live in sin. There may be found much weakness and many infirmities even in the believer who has assurance about these points; but the Holy Ghost does not comfort us, and will not comfort us, if we habitually indulge in those things which we know to be contrary to the mind of God. An upright, honest heart, is of the utmost importance in all divine things; and especially with reference to the assurance about our standing before God.

April 15. From March 12th up to this day we had always a little money in hand for the Orphans, so that there was comparatively no trial of faith. Of the many donations which came in during this period I only mention two, as rather deserving to be noticed, to show what various ways the Lord uses to send us supplies. On March 16th I received from the neighbourhood of London 5l., respecting which the brother who sent it writes, that he was in the habit of giving this sum to his wife, a sister, on her birth days, to lay it out in buying any little thing she liked, and that she this time preferred giving it to the Orphans. On April 3rd a sister gave 5l., which came in most seasonably. She had lost a sum of money, which was afterwards found again, and she felt constrained to give 5l. of it to the Orphans. Now today, April 15, when all was again spent, 3l. came in from Wales.

On Friday, April 30, while I was at Nailsworth, in Gloucestershire, I received the following letter from brother R. B., Master at the Boys'-Orphan-House:

"My dear Brother,

"When I wrote last, on Tuesday evening, there was not one penny in hand. But since then the Lord has most graciously dealt with us. Only 1s. 6d. came in on Wednesday morning; but as there were enough provisions in the house for the day, the sisters experienced no difficulty: it was only necessary to refuse to take in what there was not money to pay for. About six I went out for a walk with the boys, and returned after eight, when I found a letter in which was enclosed 5l., with these words; "From the Lord, for the present necessities of the Orphans." It was indeed for the present necessities. Etc.

"Your Brother,

R. B."

THIRD PART

This letter came after a previous one, in which brother R. B. informed me about the need in the Orphan-Houses, which led me to prayer. When this letter came from brother B., I received at the same time another from Birmingham, in which was enclosed 10l., from a brother, who had sold some of his books. It was from a most unexpected quarter, as that brother is himself, as a servant of the Lord, depending upon Him for temporal supplies. The same post brought me also information of 1l. 4s, 6d., having been sent from Dublin. The sister in Ireland writes that she sends the money now, as we may be in want of even so small a sum. With regard to the above-mentioned 5l., I mention still further that I know from the handwriting who the donor is; and it is remarkable that he had not given or sent the money to me, as he not only knew I was not in Bristol at the time, but that I was in the neighbourhood where he lives. But this was not only of the Lord's ordering, but it was a direct answer to prayer; for knowing the need at the Orphan-Houses, I had been especially led to ask the Lord not to allow the money to be first sent to me in letters or parcels, but to cause it to be directly sent to brother B. How truly precious it is that every one, who rests alone upon the Lord Jesus for salvation, has in the living God a father, to whom he may fully unbosom himself concerning the most minute affairs of his life, and concerning every thing that lies upon his heart! Dear reader, do you know the living God? Is He, in Jesus, your Father? Be assured that Christianity is something more than forms and creeds, and ceremonies: there is life, and power, and reality, in our holy faith. If you never yet have known this, then come and taste for yourself. I beseech you affectionately to meditate and pray over the following verses: John iii. 16, Rom. x. 9, 10, Acts x. 43, I John v. 1.

May 2. A sister who lives near Lutterworth sent me yesterday 5l., which was given for the Orphans by a friend of hers. This 5l. supplies our need today, it being Saturday, for there was only 1l. in hand when this money came.

From March 20th, to May 7th, I spent at Nailsworth, where I prepared the second part of my Narrative for the press, and laboured in the Word. These seven weeks were on the whole, by the help of God, profitably spent in the service of the Lord, and to the benefit of my own soul. There was much love shown to me and my family by the dear saints among whom I was labouring, and I know that my service among them has not been in vain.

Today, May 7, I returned with my family to Bristol.

While I was staying at Nailsworth, it pleased the Lord to teach me a truth, irrespective of human instrumentality, as far as I know, the benefit of which I have not lost, though now, while preparing the eighth edition for the press, more than forty years have since passed away. The point is this; I saw more clearly than ever, that the first great and primary business to which I ought to attend every day was, to have my soul happy in the Lord. The first thing to be concerned about was not, how much I might serve the Lord, how I might glorify the Lord; but how I might get my soul into a happy state, and how my inner man might be nourished. For I might seek to set the truth before the unconverted, I might seek to benefit believers, I might seek to relieve the distressed, I might in other ways seek to behave myself as it becomes a child of God in this world; and yet, not being happy in the Lord, and not being nourished and strengthened in my inner man day by day, all this might not be attended to in a right spirit. Before this time my practice had been, at least for ten years previously, as an habitual thing, to give myself to prayer, after having dressed myself in the morning. Now I saw, that the most important thing I had to do was, to give myself to the reading of the word of God and to meditation on it, that thus my heart might be comforted, encouraged, warned, reproved, instructed; and that thus, by means of the word of God, whilst meditating on it, my heart might be brought into experimental communion with the Lord. I began therefore to meditate on the New Testament from the beginning early in the morning. The first thing I did, after having asked in a few words the Lord's blessing upon His precious word, was, to begin to meditate on the word of God, searching, as it were, into every verse, to get blessing out of it; not for the sake of the public ministry of the Word; not for the sake of preaching on what I had meditated upon; but for the sake of obtaining food for my own soul. The result I have found to be almost invariably this, that after a very few minutes my soul has been led to confession, or to thanksgiving, or to intercession, or to supplication; so that, though I did not, as it were, give myself to prayer, but to meditation, yet it turned almost immediately more or less into prayer. When thus I have been for awhile making confession, or intercession, or supplication, or have given thanks, I go on to the next words or verse, turning all, as I go on, into prayer for myself or others, as the Word may lead to it; but still continually keeping before me, that food for my own soul is the object of my meditation. The result of this is, that there is always a good deal of confession, thanksgiving, supplication, or intercession mingled with my meditation, and that my inner man almost invariably is even sensibly nourished and strengthened, and that by breakfast time, with rare exceptions, I am in a peaceful if not happy state of heart. Thus also the Lord is pleased to communicate unto me that, which either very soon after, or at a later time, I have found to become food for other believers, though it was not for the sake of the public ministry of the Word that I gave myself to meditation, but for the profit of my own inner man. With this mode I have likewise combined the being out in the open air for an hour, an hour and a half, or two hours before breakfast, walking about in the fields, and in the summer sitting for a little on the stiles, if I find it too much to walk all the time.7 I find it very beneficial to my health to walk thus for meditation before breakfast, and am now so in the habit of using the time for that purpose, that when I get into the open air, I generally take out a new Testament of good sized type, which I carry with me for that purpose, besides my Bible: and I find that I can profitably spend my time in the open air; which formerly was not the case, for want of habit I used to consider the time spent in walking a loss, but now I find it very profitable, not only to my body, but also to my soul. The walking out before breakfast is of course not necessarily connected with this matter, and every one has to judge according to his strength and other circumstances.--The difference then between my former practice and my present one is this. Formerly, when I rose, I began to pray as soon as possible, and generally spent all my time till breakfast in prayer, or almost all the time. At all events I almost invariably began with prayer, except when I felt my soul to be more than usually barren, in which case I read the word of God for food, or for refreshment, or for a

THIRD PART

revival and renewal of my inner man, before I gave myself to prayer. But what was the result? I often spent a quarter of an hour, or half an hour, or even an hour on my knees, before being conscious to myself of having derived comfort, encouragement, humbling of soul, &c.; and often, after having suffered much from wandering of mind for the first ten minutes, or a quarter of an hour, or even half an hour, I only then began realty to pray. I scarcely ever suffer now in this way. For my heart being nourished by the truth, being brought into experimental fellowship with God, I speak to my Father, and to my Friend (vile though I am, and unworthy of it!) about the things that He has brought before me in His precious word. It often now astonishes me that I did not sooner see this point. In no book did I ever read about it. No public ministry ever brought the matter before me. No private intercourse with a brother stirred me up to this matter. And yet now, since God has taught me this point, it is as plain to me as any thing, that the first thing the child of God has to do morning by morning is, to obtain food for his inner man. As the outward man is not fit for work for any length of time, except we take food; and as this is one of the first things we do in the morning; so it should be with the inner man. We should take food for that, as every one must allow. Now what is the food for the inner man? Not prayer, but the word of God; and here again not the simple reading of the word of God, so that it only passes through our minds, just as water runs through a pipe, but considering what we read, pondering over it, and applying it to our hearts. When we pray, we speak to God. Now, prayer, in order to be continued for any length of time in any other than a formal manner, requires, generally speaking, a measure of strength or godly desire, and the season, therefore, when this exercise of the soul can be most effectually performed, is, after the inner man has been nourished by meditation on the word of God, where we find our Father speaking to us, to encourage us, to comfort us, to instruct us, to humble us, to reprove us. We may therefore profitably meditate, with God's blessing, though we are ever so weak spiritually; nay, the weaker we are, the more we need meditation for the strengthening of our inner man. There is thus far less to be feared from wandering of mind, than if we give ourselves to prayer without having had previously time for meditation.--I dwell so particularly on this point because of the immense spiritual profit and refreshment I am conscious of having derived from it myself, and I affectionately and solemnly beseech all my fellow-believers to ponder this matter. By the blessing of God I ascribe to this mode the help and strength which I have had from God to pass in peace through deeper trials in various ways, than I had ever had before; and after having now above forty years tried this way, I can most fully, in the fear of God, commend it. In addition to this, I generally read after family prayer larger portions of the word of God, when I still pursue my practice of reading regularly onward in the Holy Scriptures, sometimes in the New Testament and sometimes in the Old, and for more than fifty-two years I have proved the blessedness of it. I take also either then or at other parts of the day, time more especially for prayer.

How different, when the soul is refreshed and made happy early in the morning, from what it is when, without spiritual preparation, the service, the trials, arid the temptations of the day come upon one!

May 29. Today I received from the East Indies 100l.--Notice here, that without any solicitation, simply in answer to prayer, the Lord is pleased to send us from time to time even large sums, and that from such a distance as the East Indies.

June 4. Two or three weeks since, a brother at a distance requested me to let him know the names of my bankers, and the names of their agents in London, in order that he might by means of his bankers send me some money. One day after another passed away, and I heard no more about it. Today I received the following letter

"My dear Brother,

"I have delayed writing to you under the expectation of seeing you at Bristol; but I am not yet suffered to leave ****. I have, by this post, written to ***** of London, desiring them to pay over to Messrs. Robarts, Curtis & Co., in favour of Messrs. Stuckey & Co. of Bristol, to the credit of George Mueller, the sum of fifty pounds. This apply, dear brother, as the Lord gives you wisdom. I am not concerned at my having been prevented for so many days from sending this money: I am confident it has not been needed."

This last sentence is remarkable. It is now nearly three years since our funds were for the first time exhausted, and only at this period, since then, could it have been said in truth, as far as I remember, that a donation of 50l. was not needed. From the beginning of July, 1838, till now, there never had been a period when we so abounded as when this donation of 50l. came; for there was then in the Orphan-Fund and the other funds between two and three hundred pounds. The words of this brother are so much the more remarkable, as, on four former occasions, when he likewise gave considerable donations, we were always in need, yea, great need, which he afterwards knew from the printed accounts.

On the same day came in still further from Hackney 10l., besides several small donations.

July 7, 1841. For some time past brother Craik and I have questioned whether, under our present circumstances, the mode of receiving the free-will offerings of the saints among whom we labour, by means of boxes over which our names were fixed, together with the explanation of the object of the boxes, was any longer the more excellent way. We have at last been quite decided about it, and put today the following short statement into the press.

THIRD PART

To the Saints in Christ Jesus assembling at Bethesda Chapel, Bristol.

"Dear Brethren,

"It has seemed well to us to remove, from the chapel, the boxes appropriated for the reception of the free-will offerings towards our temporal support. In order to prevent misapprehension or misrepresentation, we desire affectionately to lay before you the following statement of our reasons for taking this step.

Upon our first coming to Bristol we declined accepting anything in the shape of regular salary, or by means of seat-rents, from the brethren among whom we were labouring. We did not act thus because we thought it wrong that those who were ministered unto in spiritual things should minister unto us in temporal things; but 1. because we would not have the liberality of the brethren to be a matter of constraint, but willingly; 2. because on the ground of James ii. 1-6, we objected to seat-rents. Boxes were put up for the sake of those into whose hearts God might put it to desire to act according to that word, "Let him that is taught in the Word communicate unto him that teacheth in all good things." Gal. vi. 6.

When the boxes were first put up, we were the only brethren that seemed called to labour in the Word and doctrine. Since then, however, circumstances have considerably altered; and, partly from the change in circumstances, and, partly from increased light in reference to the position of those who minister the Word, we have for some time past felt that it might be well, for certain reasons, that the present mode of receiving the offerings of the saints should be discontinued. At the same time we are very desirous of having it clearly understood, that, in the great principles which led to the adoption of the boxes, in the first instance, we are unchanged: or rather we are more strengthened, by the experience of more than ten years, in the propriety of rejecting seat-rents and fixed salaries.

1. As long as the boxes are there, it ought to be understood for what purpose the money, which is put into them, is applied. This necessity requires that our names should be given, as those who labour in the Word and doctrine. This again has the appearance of elevating ourselves above all the other brethren, and of assuming office to ourselves, instead of just seeking to fill the place which the Holy Ghost may have given us in the body.

2. It may please the Lord increasingly to call and qualify other brethren for the work of ruling and teaching in the church; but still, as long as we are looked upon as we have been hitherto, in consequence of our names being affixed to the boxes, unnecessary difficulties may probably be put in the way of any others being fully recognised by the saints generally as occupying, equally with ourselves, the place in which the Lord may set them.

3. The question may be asked even now, "Are these the only labourers?" and the reply would be that there are others who also labour, but who are not supported

in the same way. This fact is fitted to give the impression to those who do not know us, that we were seeking to keep our place in the church by some outward title, rather than just filling it up in obedience to the Lord, and quietly leaving it with His Spirit to produce subjection unto us on the part of the saints.

4. Lastly, from the manner in which our names appear in public, we have reason to believe that some of the saints look upon us as exclusively the "ministers," and thus that some may have felt themselves neglected because not visited personally by us. The notion that two individuals should be able to exercise pastoral inspection over about five hundred and fifty believers, we consider to be very unsound; but for ourselves we feel that it is a responsibility which we dare not take. According to our gift and strength we desire to rule, teach, and feed the sheep of Christ; but we dare not undertake the personal inspection of all who are already gathered, or may be gathered, simply as believers in the Lord Jesus, in this city.

Thus we have endeavoured very briefly to state our reasons for declining any longer to receive your offerings through boxes publicly put up, and having our names appended to them. We desire grace to serve you more faithfully than ever, and cast ourselves, as we have done hitherto, upon Him who hath said, "If any man serve me him will my Father honour."

HENRY CRAIK, GEORGE MUeLLER

Bristol, July 7, 1841. .

When this alteration was made, I had another proof of the many blessings which are connected with the life of faith. Under other circumstances the question would have naturally arisen in my mind, And what will you do for support, if the boxes are removed? How will the offerings come in? Will any come in? But none of these things troubled me even for a moment. I said to myself, somehow or other the Lord will provide for me. If not through the instrumentality of the saints in Bristol, He will send help by means of those who live elsewhere. All I have to do in this matter is, to serve the Lord and to trust in Him, and He will surely take care of my temporal necessities. And thus it has been since July 1841 also, even as before. The reader may desire to know, how the Lord has since that time provided for my temporal necessities, seeing that the boxes, which were put up in the two chapels for the reception of the free-will offerings, were removed. I therefore state it. 1, I have received, as at former times, some presents in provisions, clothes, etc., from the saints among whom I labour and from other saints. 2, Some of the brethren and sisters among whom I labour have either habitually or from time to time put up some money in paper, and directed it to brother Craik or to me, or to both of us, and have put these little money parcels into one of the boxes for the reception of the offerings of the poor saints, or into the boxes into which the free-will contributions for the rent and expenses of the chapels are put. These little packets have been handed over to us by the deacons, and as they were directed so they have been appropriated, Those which are directed to brother Craik only, are handed over to brother Craik; those which are directed to me only, I appropriate for myself; and those which are directed to both of us, the contents are divided between us. 3, In a few cases, brethren and sisters in communion with us have also given me presents in money. 4, The Lord has also continued to incline the hearts of some of His children, not living in Bristol, to send me presents in money, and again and again even those whom I have never seen, and whose names, sometimes, I do not even know.

The only thing that was a real difficulty in my mind in making this alteration was, not that I should be a loser, and much less that the Lord would not care for my temporal necessities; but lest some of the children of God should find, in the removal of the boxes for the reception of the offerings for brother Craik and me, an excuse for doing nothing at all for our temporal necessities; and lest especially the poor, because they might have only pence or halfpence to give, should be deterred from doing so, and thereby both classes should rob themselves of blessing. It was not, because I feared to lose the gifts of some; for, I can, by the grace of God, say in some measure at least with the apostle Paul, "Not because I desire a gift: but I desire fruit that may abound to your account." Philip iv. 17. My aim also is, by the help of God, to be brought into that state of heart in which the apostle Paul was when he said, "I will very gladly spend and be spent for you; though the more abundantly I love you the less I be loved." 2 Cor. xii. 15. But yet with this desire on my part, I knew that the dear children of God among whom I labour would rob themselves and not me of a blessing, if they did not contribute towards my temporal necessities and I feared, lest this alteration should be used by Satan as an instrument to their injury.

But the mind of God seemed to us, after all, on account of the reasons before stated, that the alteration ought to be made, notwithstanding any possible evils which might result from it.

We are thus in such a position, that there is free room for the Holy Ghost to commend all the various labourers among us, according to the measure of grace and gift given to them, to the consciences of the brethren, not only with reference to their spiritual position in the body, butt also with reference to their temporal need.

Aug. 7. Today we had one sixpence left for our own personal necessities. We needed some money to buy eggs and cocoa for a brother who is come to stay with us, when this brother gave me four shillings, which he had brought for me from the place whence he comes. Thus we are helped for the present.

Aug. 26. After a season of comparative poverty with reference to myself, though always having what was really needful in the way of nourishing food, etc., a brother sent me today 17l. 18s. from a considerable distance, of which half is for the Orphans, and half for my own temporal necessities.

Sept. 2. During the last four months we have had more in hand for the Orphans than we needed. Since July 1838, when for the first time the funds were exhausted, we have had at no period so much money in hand. There was as it were, during these four months, one continual even running of the river of God's bounty, both by presents in money and articles. Of the donations which were received during this period, I mention only the following:--On May 12th I received from Florence, in Italy, the following donations:--3 silver pins and 4 dollars; 3 dollars and a sixpence; 2 Pauls (Italian coins); 5l.; 3 pincushions, 6 penwipers, and a little shawl How abundantly do these donations from Florence prove how easily the Lord is able to provide us with means for His work, even from the most unexpected quarters!--As we had now for several months abounded in a greater degree than at any previous time of the same length during the past three years and three months, so it pleased the Lord after this period to try our faith more severely than during any time since the work first commenced. Indeed, so sharp were the trials of our faith for more than six months after this;--so long the seasons when, day after day, only daily supplies were granted to us, and when even from meal to meal we had to look to the Lord;--so long had we to continue in prayer, and yet help seemed to fail;--that it can be only ascribed to the especial mercy of God, that the faith of those who were engaged in this work did not altogether fail, and that they did not entirely grow weary of this way of carrying on the Lord's work, and go, in despair of help from God, back again to the habits and maxims of this evil world. How my fellow-labourers have felt during all this time, I am, of course, unable to state; but, if I may speak of myself, I joyfully state, to the praise of the Lord, that during all the following months my faith was sustained without wavering, but still so greatly was it tried, that often I had no other petition, but that the Lord would be pleased to continue it, and that He would pity me as a father pitieth his children. In the midst of the trial I was fully assured that the Lord would lighten His hand in His own good time, and that, whilst it lasted, it was only in order that in a small measure, for the benefit of the church of Christ generally, that word might be fulfilled in us--"Whether we be afflicted it is for your consolation." I now give an account of the commencement and progress of our trial of faith during the months which succeeded the time of abundance.

Sept. 3. The money in hand had come to 3l. 5s. I therefore asked the Lord this morning for fresh supplies, and very soon after came a post-office order from Glasgow for 3l.

Sept. 7. 5l. 9s. more had come in since September 3rd, but this morning the last money had been given out. After the great abundance during the last months, now not a farthing was left. I gave myself therefore to prayer, and in the afternoon I received a post-office order from a brother at Plymouth for 3l. In the evening was left at my house a bonnet box from G. T. I., which contained 5s., 4 shirts and 4 handkerchiefs.

Sept. 8. Today came in 4s. from the neighbourhood of Wolverhampton, 2s. 6d. from Bath, and 1l. was given by a brother, who had just arrived from Ceylon.

THIRD PART

Sept. 9. This morning 5l. was sent by a brother, a student in the University of Cambridge, who had read my Narrative; also 13s. 6d. came in besides.

Sept. 18. From the 9th to this day we were comfortably supplied with what we needed. Today, when 3l. was needed, and there was only 1l. 9s. 2d. in hand, 12l. came in from the neighbourhood of Wolverhampton, and 3s. by knitting.

Sept. 25. Saturday. Since the 18th was received, by donations and sale of articles, 5l. 19s. 8d., which enabled us, together with the 12l. 3s. which came in on the 18th, to meet all the expenses. But when I had sent off yesterday what was needed to meet the day's need, nothing at all was left in hand for this day, whilst I knew that above 3l. would be required. The Lord, therefore, in His faithful love sent in yesterday afternoon 11s. 0 1/2d.; this morning 5l. from Plymouth; and 1l. 1s. with several articles of clothing for the Orphans from Clapham. Thus we had about twice as much as was required for this day.

Sept. 26. 2l. 11s. came in today.

Sept. 28. As 2l. was needed for the supplies of this day, and only 1l. 13s. 0 1/2d. was in hand, the boxes in the Orphan-Houses were opened, in which was found 10s. 2d.

Sept. 29, When there was again only 3s. 2 1/2d. in hand towards the need of today, a brother, a commercial traveller, having returned last night to Bristol, brought me two sovereigns, which had been given him for the Orphans by a lady at Marlborough, who had read one of the Reports. There came in still further today 2l. 8s. 6d.

Oct. 1. When I had again not one penny in hand for the necessities of this day, there was brought to me this morning 10s. for the Orphans, which had been sent from Kensington. In the paper, which contained the money, was written: "Your Heavenly Father knoweth that ye have need of these things." "Trust in the Lord." This word of our Lord is to me of more value than many bank notes. About five minutes later I received from an Irish sister 10l., through her banker in London. At the same time I received information from Tetbury that three boxes, containing articles to be disposed of for the benefit of the Orphans, were on the way, and two hours after, 14 small donations were given to me, amounting to 1l. 7s. 4d.--I mention here, as a point particularly to be noticed, that after the season of comparative abundance had come to an end in September, the Lord did not at once allow us to be so sharply tried as we were afterwards. He dealt in the same gentle way with us three years before, when the trials of faith in this part of the work first commenced.

Oct. 6. As only 4l. more had been received for the Orphans since Oct. 1; the last money had now again been given out to supply this day's necessities, when 2l. 15s. came in, being the produce of some of the articles which had been sent from Tetbury. This evening I also received from a brother a sovereign, which his believing wife, on her dying bed, had requested him to give after her decease. There came in likewise this evening by a donation 10s., and by sale of articles 2l. 10s. 5d.

During the last five months we have had comparatively an abundance of means for the other objects of the Scriptural Knowledge Institution also; but now we are again very poor. Just now, in this our great need, a brother, who has learned to esteem the Holy Scriptures above every other book, sent me a box of books, the produce of which supplies our present need for the Day Schools.

Oct. 9. No more than 1l. 2s. 11d, having been received for the Orphans since the 6th, there was only 2l. 3s. 9d. in hand, whilst 4l. was needed, it being Saturday. In the course of the morning 2l. came in for stockings, from a sister who resides five or six miles from Bristol; and in the afternoon another sister sent 1s., and a third brought 5l. The latter had it particularly laid on her heart not to delay till tomorrow the giving of this money, as it might be needed today. Thus the Lord has not only given us enough for today, but also a little to begin the next week with.

Oct. 10. Today we received still further 5l. 9s. 11d. for the Orphans.

Oct. 11. When today again money was needed for the Day Schools, there arrived from Marlborough a box of books, containing 110 volumes and several pamphlets. The produce of the books, together with 1l. 9s. 4d., which came in at the same time, supplied again our present necessities.

Oct. 16. More than 10l. had come in since the 10th for the Orphans; but today there was again only 10s. 11 1/2d. in hand, whilst about 3l. was required. The boxes at the Orphan-Houses were therefore opened, which contained 1l. 1s. In the course of the day also 5s. 5d. was paid for stockings. About seven o'clock this evening sister E. C. brought several small donations, amounting to 1l. 17s. 4d., for the Orphans, and 9s. 8d. for the other funds. Thus we had even for this day 3l. 14s. 4 1/4d.

Oct. 21. As only between 9l. and 10l. had come in since the 16th for the Orphans, we were this day again, as is often the case, without anything in hand, when 12s. 2d. was sent from Exmouth, and 8s. 8d. came in by sale of stockings. There arrived also a box and a basket from Ilfracombe, the contents of which are to be sold for the benefit of the Orphans. Moreover 15s. 6d. was taken out of the boxes in the Orphan-Houses.

Oct. 22. By the money which was yesterday taken out of the boxes, and by 1l. 3s. which came in by disposing of some of the articles sent from Ilfracombe, we were comfortably supplied today.

Oct. 23. We had only 5s. 6d., which I found in the box in my house, 8s. 9d. for stockings, and 9s. which came in morning, besides a few shillings in the hands of the matrons, to help us through the day.

THIRD PART

Oct. 24. Today, when we had not enough to pay the salaries of the teachers in the Day Schools, I received 5l. from a sister at Topsham, which supplied our need.

Oct. 25. Yesterday and today was given 2l. 17s. for the Orphans.

Oct. 26. This afternoon I had only one penny left, when two Orphans arrived from Bath, with whom 5l. 15s. 6d. was brought. At the very moment, while I was receiving this money, I was called on for money from the Girls'-Orphan-House, which I was thus able to send. It has often been so ordered by the Lord, that, whilst we require nothing at all to be paid at the admission of the children, nevertheless that which has been brought with them has been the means of supplying the need, in which we were at the time when they were sent. There came in still further today 1l.

Oct. 29. Today we were again very poor; for not only had I nothing at all in hand, but the provision stores were much reduced. About twelve o'clock a sister gave me 3s. 2d., also from a distance was sent 9d. In the afternoon we were able to dispose of some articles for 3l., which had been sent a long time ago. Three shillings came in for needlework, and 2s. 6d. as a donation. Thus we had 3l. 9s. 5d.--The day before yesterday I had asked the Lord that He would be pleased to send us some potatoes, as we have no means to lay in a stock. This morning I was informed that the same brother who had sent 20 sacks last year, had again ordered 20 sacks to be sent, and 6 sacks have also been given by another individual.

Oct. 30. As this is Saturday, the money which came in yesterday was not quite enough for today. But this morning's post brought, in answer to prayer, from Clapham 10s. and anonymously from Plymouth 10s.

Nov. 1. Yesterday was received altogether 2l. 10s. 3d.

Nov. 2. At a time of the greatest poverty 1l. was sent by a lady from Birmingham. About half an hour afterwards I received 10l. from a brother who had saved up 150l. and put it into a savings' bank, but who now sees that, to devote this money to the promotion of the work of God tends more to the glory of the name of Jesus, than to retain it in a savings' bank upon interest for a time of sickness or old age; for he is assured that should such times come, the same Lord, who has hitherto cared for him whilst in health and strength, and able to work, will also care for him then. The same brother gave me 3l. a fortnight since. This 10l. came in very seasonably; for though we had been able to provide for the absolute necessities of today, yet there was want in many respects, especially as a boy is just going out as an apprentice, who needs tools and an outfit.

Nov. 3. This afternoon two little boys were received, with whom three little girls sent 13s. 6d.

Nov. 4 and 5. 2l. 5s. 1d. more was given.

Nov. 7. When there was now again nothing at all in hand, there came in 2l., being the profit of the sale of ladies' baskets; and also 3l. 1s. 10d.

Nov. 8-11. 4l. 9s. 4d. was received during these four days.

Nov. 12. This morning after the exposition of the Scriptures to the children, 10s. was given to me, at a time when there was not only nothing at all in hand, but when without some help we should not have had every thing that was really needed for today.

Nov. 13. Saturday. This morning I took 1s. out of the box in my house. This one shilling was all there was towards the need of today.--Pause, dear reader, for a few moments! Consider that there are more than a hundred persons to be provided with every thing they require; consider that there is no money in hand; and consider also that this is the case not once nor twice in the course of the year but very frequently. Is it not precious, under such circumstances, to have the living God as a father to go to, who is ever able and ever willing to help as it may be really needed? And to this privilege every one has a title who believes in the Lord Jesus, being as such a child of God. Galatians iii. 26. For though all believers in the Lord Jesus are not called upon to establish Orphan-Houses, Schools for poor children, etc., and trust in God for means; yet all believers, according to the will of God concerning them in Christ Jesus, may cast, and ought to cast, all their care upon Him who careth for them, and need not be anxiously concerned about any thing, as is plainly to be seen from 1 Peter v. 7, Philippians iv. 6, Matthew vi. 25-34. Under these circumstances of need, a silver watch, which only yesterday afternoon had become the property of the Orphan-Fund, was disposed of, whereby we were helped through the expenses of today. The coals are almost gone in each of the houses. Every article of provision, etc., is likewise much reduced. Truly, we are exceedingly poor; nevertheless there are the necessary provisions till Monday morning, and thus we were brought to the close of another week. This afternoon all the labourers met for prayer.

Nov. 14. When we met again this afternoon for prayer, we had reason to praise, for the Lord had sent in means. This morning was given to me 5l., and 6s. had come in by sale of articles. There came also by post a small parcel from Wales, containing a few little articles, which are not to be mentioned, and 2s. 6d.

Nov. 15. Last Friday brother Craik and I had a meeting for inquirers and candidates for fellowship. We saw eight and had to send away ten whom we could not see, our strength being quite gone after we had seen the eight, one after another. This evening we saw seven and had to send away three.

Nov. 16. The last four days we have daily met for prayer, there being no means to pay the teachers in the Day Schools. Besides this, we need a stove in one of the school rooms; also some Bibles and Tracts. Today I received 2l. from a brother at Exmouth.

THIRD PART

As only 2s. had been given yesterday for the Orphans, there was this morning again only 4s. 6d., in hand, which between ten and eleven o'clock I was on the point of sending to the Orphan-Houses, having been called on for money. While I was writing the note to that effect, I received a post-office order for 3l. from a brother at Barnstaple, which was again a most precious deliverance, as our stores had been in every way so much reduced. About two hours later I received 4l. more from a brother at Exmouth, the half of which was for the Orphans, and the other half for the other objects. Through the same brother also was sent with Luke xxii. 32. 1l. for the Orphans. There came in still further today 2l. for stockings, which were bought by two ladies who visited the Orphan-Houses. They also gave 3s. 9d. Also an individual who had removed at four different times the furniture of the Orphan-Houses to and from Westbury, where the children had been, in turn, from Aug. 10 to Nov. 12, while the houses were coloured down and painted inside, charged only 1l. 1s. 10 1/2d., instead of 4l. 2s. 10 1/2d., which would have been the regular charge, and stated that he had long wished to do something for the Orphans, and that he should not have charged even this 1l. 1s. 10 1/2d. had he not had to lay it out in money. Thus the Lord in various ways helps us, and all without our asking any human being, but only in simplicity telling Him day by day our need.

Nov. 18. To day we had again a meeting with inquirers, and saw seven.

Nov. 21. Only 1l. 11s. 4d. came in since the 16th for the Orphans, on account of which there was today again no money at all in hand, and the stores were very much exhausted. How kind, therefore, of the Lord to send in again at this time 2l. 10s.

Nov. 23. Yesterday came in 5s. for stockings, which provided today the means for the breakfast in the Boys'-Orphan-House. A sister sent also a gammon and some peas. Now we are very poor indeed. One of the labourers was able to provide a dinner in the Girls'-Orphan-House out of his own means. In this our great need came in 17s. 6d. by sale of Reports, which money had been expected for some months past, but which the Lord sent just now most seasonably. Besides this, 2s. 6d. was also received for the children's needlework. Thus we were provided for this day also. In the afternoon the Lord gave us a still further proof of the continuance of His loving care over us, now that we are so poor; for a box arrived from Plymouth, containing clothes, trinkets, etc.

Nov. 24. We have been daily meeting for prayer the last twelve days. Today, just before I was going to the meeting, one of the articles, which came in the box from Plymouth yesterday afternoon, was sold for 2l. 2s., which sum supplies us with means for this day. The donors may not have thought, perhaps, that their bounty would so soon be needed.--When I came to the prayer-meeting, I heard of a little circumstance which is worthy of notice. The Infant Orphans took a walk this morning with their teacher. A poor woman came to her, whilst they were walking, and gave her two pence for the benefit of the Orphans, adding "It is but a trifle, but I must give it you." Now, one of these two pence had been needed, by the time I came, to make up the little sum which was required for the bread.--This afternoon was received still further 9d., and also 12s. by the sale of some of the articles which came from Plymouth.

Nov. 25. With 12s. 1d. we began the day, which was not sufficient for all that was required. In the afternoon came in 11s. for knitting. Thus we had enough for this day also.

Nov. 26. One of the labourers gave 5s.; 11s. came in by sale of articles, and 6d. was taken out of the box in my house. Little as this was, yet we were able to procure with it all that was really needful; but now our provision stock is very much reduced.

Nov. 27. This is Saturday, and nothing at all was in hand when the day commenced. My especial prayer had been, that the Lord would, be pleased early in the morning to send us supplies, as otherwise there would not be sufficient for dinner. Accordingly, about 10 o'clock, a parcel came from Clapham, containing 11s. and the following articles: 12 yards of calico, a frock, a chemise, 2 petticoats, a flannel ditto, 2 handkerchiefs, 2 pinafores, a furnished workbag, an old silver thimble, and half a franc. Thus the Lord kindly provided us with means for the dinner, and we took it as a token for good that He would send what else might be needed this day. There came in still further in the course of the afternoon, by sale of an article, given by one of the labourers, 5s.; by sale of some lithographic sketches, given by one of the labourers, 4s. 6d.; by sale of articles given some time since, 16s.; by sale of stockings, 2s. 9d.; and by a donation, 2s. Thus the Lord was pleased to give us in the course of this day 2l. 1s. 3d., while we were in the greatest need in the morning, and without any natural prospect of having the means which were required for the day.

Nov. 29. The Lord has kindly sent in supplies. Yesterday was given altogether 5l. 19s. 7d. These two weeks we have been likewise in the greatest poverty in reference to the Day Schools; but the Lord has almost daily sent in a little to supply the absolute necessities of the brethren and sisters, who are engaged in that part of the work.

Nov. 30. Though 5l. 19s. 7d. had been given, yet, as the stores had been previously so reduced, there was again some more money needed today. 5s. came in by sale of articles, and one of the labourers gave some money of his own. In this time of great need there arrived a parcel, sent anonymously, which contained the following articles: 3 combs, 6 shells, 5 pairs of gilt bracelets, 4 single bracelets, a pair of ditto, a gilt chain, a gilt necklace, a cornelian ditto, a bead ditto, a brooch, a buckle, 2 pairs of earrings, 3 rings, 3 pairs of drops, and a single ear-ring.

Dec. 1. Again there were many shillings needed for this day. At the Boys'-Orphan-House matters stood so in the morning, that, with an addition of eight pence, the dinner could be provided; but there was only seven pence in hand. Brother B. having heard that something had been put last evening into the box at the Girls'-

THIRD PART

Orphan-House, went, and it was found to be one penny, which an aged sister had put in, whereby the present need was supplied. Even the gift of this one penny was thus evidently under the ordering of our kind Father, who not in anger, but for the trial of our faith, keeps us so poor. About ten o'clock this morning was sent by post, half a sovereign. In the letter was written: "From the wife of a clergyman, for the Orphan-Houses, Nov. 30 1841." This donation was truly sweet, as coming from our faithful Lord, though it was not nearly enough. But He had pity on us, and sent in still further today by the sale of stockings 5s., and by the sale of other articles 12s.

Dec. 2. In the course of this morning was sold a part of the trinkets which came on Nov. 30th, for 1l. 4s. 10d. Besides this came in by sale of articles 1s. 6d. Thus was our present need supplied in the afternoon 3l. was sent by a sister from Plymouth, and by a sister in Bristol was given to me 2s.

Dec. 3 and 4. 1l. 10s. 6d. has been received during these two days.

Dec. 6. Yesterday the Lord again, in His faithful love, sent in means for the need of today. A gentleman from Devonshire came to me after the meeting, introduced himself as a brother, and gave me 5l. for the work of the Lord, as it might be needed. I had pleasant brotherly communion with him, but he preferred not to give me his name. Besides this, came in 18s. 11 1/2d. by sale of articles. As this 18s. 11 1/2d. was not enough for the supply of the Orphans for this day, there being nothing at all in hand besides, and 1l. more needed, I took 1l. of the 5l. for the Orphans, and 4l. for the other objects. Through the same stranger I received also 2s. 6d. from a sister. There came in this evening 1l. 3s. besides.

By the 4l. which I took of the 5l. given by the gentleman from Devonshire, the most pressing need with regard to the teachers in the Day Schools is relieved. This stranger gave me also 1l. for Missionary purposes.

Dec. 7. Three weeks and three days we have now been daily meeting for prayer, on account of the state of the funds, and to ask the Lord's blessing upon the work. We have been daily asking Him to supply us with means for the School-Bible-Missionary-and Tract Fund. Now, today, in this our great poverty, was sent by a sister from one of the Northern counties, whom I have never seen, the sum of 50l. of which, according to her wish, 10l. is to be applied to each of these objects, and 10l. for the Orphans. Thus the Lord has been pleased to send us a little help, which is greatly needed for all the objects: for the teachers have had only as much as was absolutely needful, the Bible stock is almost entirely exhausted, the Tract stock is quite exhausted, and to some Missionary brethren we greatly desired to send help, but were unable to do so. Nevertheless, even now we are waiting upon the Lord for further supplies.

When this money came, there was none at all in hand for the Orphans, though for many reasons fresh supplies were much needed. By this 10l., then, the Lord has again helped us for the present. There was likewise sent anonymously by post, 1l.

Dec. 9. Today came in for the Orphans by the sale of stockings 10s. 10d.--We are now brought to the close of the sixth year of this part of the work, having only in hand the money which has been put by for the rent; but during the whole of this year we have been supplied with all that was needed.

During the last three years we had closed the accounts on this day, and had, a few days after, some public meetings at which for the benefit of the hearers, we stated how the Lord had dealt with us during the year, and the substance of what had been stated at these meetings was afterwards printed for the benefit of the church at large. This time, however, it appeared to us better to delay for awhile both the public meetings and the publishing of the Report Through grace we had learned to lean upon the Lord only, being assured, that, if we never were to speak or write one single word more about this work, yet should we be supplied with means, as long as He should enable us to depend on Himself alone. But whilst we neither had had those public meetings for the purpose of exposing our necessity, nor had had the account of the Lord's dealings with us published for the sake of working thereby upon the feelings of the readers, and thus inducing them to give money, but only that we might by our experience benefit other saints; yet it might have appeared to some that in making known our circumstances we were actuated by some such motives. What better proof, therefore, could we give of our depending upon the living God alone, and not upon public meetings or printed Reports, than that, in the midst of our deep poverty, instead of being glad for the time to have come when we could make known our circumstances, we still went on quietly for some time longer, without saying any thing. We therefore determined, as we sought and still seek in this work to act for the profit of the saints generally, to delay both the public meetings and the Report for a few months. Naturally we should have been, of course, as glad as any one to have exposed our poverty at that time; but spiritually we were enabled to delight even then in the prospect of the increased benefit that might be derived by the church at large from our acting as we did.--I now proceed where I left off.

Dec. 11. Since the day before yesterday the following sums came in for the Orphans, whereby the need of yesterday and today has been supplied. A brother gave 2l. A little boy and girl brought the produce of their savings' banks, amounting to 19s. 5d. By the sale of stockings came in 15s. 1d., and by six donations 10s. 6d.

Dec. 13. Yesterday came in 1l. 11s. 6d., and today 10s. By this 2l. 1s. 6d. this day's need has been met. There was also, very seasonably, half a ton of coals sent to each of the three Orphan-Houses.

Dec. 14. Yesterday afternoon a lady sent a sovereign for the Orphans. There came in 15s. 6d. besides. Thus we had enough for this day likewise.

Dec. 15. Having now again nothing in hand for the Orphans, the boxes were opened, in which 4s. 4d. was found. This, with a little which one of the labourers was able to add of his own, helped us through the day.

THIRD PART

From Nov. 12 up to this day, my fellow-labourers in the Church and I have seen thirty inquirers and candidates for fellowship, and some of them we have seen repeatedly. How can we sufficiently praise the Lord for still continuing to use us in His service.

Dec. 16. Nothing at all had come in for the Orphans; but as one of the labourers had last evening, most unexpectedly, received some money from a distance of about two hundred miles, and as the Lord inclined his heart to give of it for the present need, we were supplied for today also.

Dec. 17. In like manner we are helped today.

Dec. 18. Saturday morning. There is now the greatest need, and only 4d. in hand, which I found in the box at my house; yet I fully believe the Lord will supply us this day also with all that is required.--Pause a few moments, dear reader! Observe two things! We acted for God in delaying the public meetings and the publishing of the Report; but God's way leads always into trial, so far as sight and sense are concerned. Nature always will be tried in God's ways. The Lord was saying by this poverty, "I will now see whether you truly lean upon me, and whether you truly look to me." Of all the seasons that I had ever passed through since I had been living in this way, up to that time, I never knew any period in which my faith was tried so sharply, as during the four months from Dec. 12, 1841, to April 12, 1842. But observe further: We might even now have altered our minds with respect to the public meetings and publishing the Report; for no one knew our determination, at this time, concerning the point. Nay, on the contrary, we knew with what delight very many children of God were looking forward to receive further accounts. But the Lord kept us steadfast to the conclusion, at which we had arrived under His guidance.--Now to return to Saturday, Dec. 18th. Evening. The Lord has been very kind to us this day. In the course of the morning 6s. came in. We had thus, with what provisions there were in hand, all that was needed for the dinner, but no means to provide for the next meal in the afternoon. A few minutes after the labourers had met together for prayer this morning, there was given to one of them a sovereign for himself. By means of this, all that was needed for tea could be procured. Another labourer gave 3s. 6d. and two books, which were sold for 4s. There came in still further in the course of the afternoon and evening:--by sale of stockings, 8s. 8d.; by needlework, 8d.; and by sale of articles, 5s. Thus, when we again met in the evening for prayer, we found that the supplies had amounted to 2l. 8s. 2d., enough for all that was required today. But one thing more is to be noticed respecting this day. I was informed that three more of the Orphans have been recently brought to the knowledge of the truth. We have now been meeting daily for prayer during the last five weeks, and thus the Lord has not merely heard our prayers respecting the funds, but has also blessed these children.

Dec. 20. The Lord has again kindly sent fresh supplies. A sister gave 1l.; a servant sent 1l.; another servant, 2s 6d. by sale of articles 13s. 1d. This morning, just before was going to the prayer-meeting, a lady brought 3l.; and 5s. more I received this evening.

Dec. 21. Though 6s. 0s. 7d. had been received yesterday and the day before, there was only 5s. remaining towards the supply of the necessities of today. At one o'clock three little boys gave me the produce of their Orphan-box, which was 4s. 7d. When I came home, I found that 18l. had come in, being a legacy left for the Orphans by a lady who died at the commencement of the year. This money comes in most seasonably, not merely for the supply of the wants of the children, but also as enabling me to give to some of the labourers in the Orphan-Houses supplies for themselves.

Dec. 23. This is now the sixth week that the labourers in the Day-Schools and Orphan-Houses have daily met for prayer. Several precious answers we have already received since we began to meet, as it regards pecuniary supplies, fresh instances of conversion among the children, etc. One of our petitions has been that the Lord would be pleased to furnish us with means for a stove at Callowhill Street School-room. But though we had often mentioned this matter before the Lord, he seemed not to regard our request. Yesterday afternoon, while walking in my little garden, and meditating and praying, I had an unusual assurance that the time was now come when the Lord would answer our request, which arose partly from my being able to believe that He would send the means, and partly from the fact that the answer could no longer be delayed, without prayer having failed in this matter, as we could not assemble the children again, after the Christmas vacation, without there being a stove put up. And now, dear reader, observe:--This morning I received from A. B. 20l., and we have thus much more than is required for a stove.

Dec. 24. On the 22nd and 23rd 2l. 0s. 5d. came in for the Orphans. The need of today was 3l. 10s., but only 3l. was in hand. This afternoon, however, 1l. was sent from Kensington and 1l. from Plymouth. This evening we received still further anonymously 4s., and by knitting 2l. 10s.

Dec. 25. By sale of articles was received 14s. 2d.

Dec. 26. This afternoon I was walking in my little garden, meditating on and turning into prayer Rom. viii. 28-32. When I came to verse 32, the necessity of the Orphans came to my mind, as tomorrow we shall again need more money than there is in hand, and I therefore asked the Lord that He would be pleased to give me a fresh proof that He will "freely give us all things," by supplying our present need. This evening I spoke on the above-mentioned passage, and after the meeting a sister gave to my wife 12l., of which 10l. was for the Orphans, and 2l. for my own necessities. There came in 5s. besides.

Dec. 31. As only 1l. 15s. had been received since the 26th, there was again nothing in hand towards the need of this day. About an hour before the money was

THIRD PART

sent for from the Orphan-Houses, an individual who lives in Redcliff Parish, Bristol, sent 5l. By sale of stockings came in likewise 3s. 6d.

REVIEW OF THE YEAR 1841.

I. In reading over my journal, I find that the Lord has given me during this year many precious answers to prayer, in addition to those which have been recorded in the previous part of the Narrative. I mention the following for the encouragement of the reader: 1, One of the Orphan-Boys needed to be apprenticed. I knew of no suitable believing master, who would take an in-door apprentice. I gave myself to prayer, and brought the matter daily before the Lord. I marked it down among the subjects for which I would daily ask the Lord; and at last, though from May 21 to September I had to pray about the matter, the Lord granted my request; for in September I found a suitable place for him. 2, On May 23rd I began to ask the Lord that He would be pleased to deliver a certain sister in the Lord from the great spiritual depression under which she was suffering, and after three days the Lord granted me my request. 3, On June 15th I began to ask the Lord to deliver a brother at a distance from the great spiritual nervousness in which he found himself shut up, which not only distressed him exceedingly, and in a great measure hindered him in his service towards the world and the church; but which, in consequence, was also a trial to the saints who knew and valued this dear brother. This petition I brought many times before the Lord. The year passed away, and it was not granted. But yet at last this request also has been granted to me and to the many dear saints who, I know, prayed for this dear brother; for though he was for some years in this state, it is now [in 1845] two years and more since he has been quite restored. 4, On June 15th I also began to ask the Lord daily, in His mercy to keep a sister in the Lord from insanity, who was then apparently on the very border of it; and I have now [in 1845] to record to His praise, after nearly four years have passed away, that the Lord has kept her from it. 5, During this year I was informed about the conversion of one of the very greatest sinners, that I ever heard of in all my service for the Lord. Repeatedly I fell on my knees with his wife, and asked the Lord for his conversion, when she came to me in the deepest distress of soul, on account of the most barbarous and cruel treatment that she received from him, in his bitter enmity against her for the Lord's sake, and because he could not provoke her to be in a passion, and she would not strike him again, and the like. At the time when it was at its worst I pleaded especially on his behalf the promise in Matthew xviii. 19: "Again I say unto you, that if two of you shall agree on earth as touching any thing that they shall ask, it shall be done for them of my Father which is in heaven." And now this awful persecutor is converted. 6, On May 25th I began to ask the Lord for greater real spiritual prosperity among the saints, among whom I labour in Bristol, than there ever yet had been among them; and now I have to record to the praise of the Lord that truly He has answered this request; for, considering all things, at no period has there been more manifestation of grace and truth, and spiritual power among us, than there is now while I am writing this for the press (1845). Not that we have attained to what we might; we are far, very far from it; but the Lord has been very, very good to us, and we have most abundant cause for thanksgiving.

II. The state of the church with reference to numbers, etc.

68 brethren and sisters brother Craik and I found in communion, when we came to Bristol.

775 have been admitted into communion since we came to Bristol.

843 would be, therefore, the total number of those in communion with us, had there been no changes. But,

101 have left Bristol.

55 have left us, but are still in Bristol

48 are under church discipline.

67 have fallen asleep.

271 are therefore to be deducted from 843, so that there are only 572 at present in communion.

88 have been added during the past year, of whom 30 have been brought to the knowledge of the Lord among us.

III. The Lord's goodness as to my temporal supplies during this year.

1. The Lord has been pleased to give me by means of the anonymous freewill offerings of the saints, put into the boxes at our meeting places L116 2s. 4 3/4d.

2. By presents in money from the brethren among whom I labour in Bristol L43 9s. 9d.

3. By presents in money from children of God not living in Bristol L53 19s. 0d.

4. By presents in provisions, clothes, furniture, etc., from the saints among whom I labour, worth to us at least L15 0s. 0d.

THIRD PART

5. By presents in clothes, &c., from believers not living in Bristol, worth to us at least L10 0s. 0d.

Altogether L238 11s. 1 3/4d.

Thus during this year also, without asking any one but the Lord for help, with regard to ray temporal necessities, I have been richly supplied with all I needed; yea, I have had much more than I needed.

January 1, 1842. Last night we had our usual prayer-meeting at the close of the year, which this time lasted from seven in the evening till half-past twelve.

Jan. 3. This evening we had a most precious public prayer-meeting. When the usual time for closing the meeting came, it appeared to me that there was a desire to continue to wait upon the Lord. I therefore proposed to the brethren that those who had bodily strength, time, and a desire for waiting still longer upon the Lord, would do so. At least thirty remained, and we continued till after ten in prayer, whilst several brethren prayed. I never knew prayer more really in the Spirit. I experienced for myself unusual nearness to the Lord, and was enabled to ask in faith, nothing doubting.

On the 1st of January came in for the Orphans 1l.7s. 6d.; on the 2nd 10l. 13s. 7d.; and today came in from Plymouth 6l., from Exmouth 5l., from a sister in Bristol 5l., and from the East Indies 2l. I have by this 30l. 1s. 1d. been enabled, as it had been my prayer, to give some money to the other five sisters who labour in the Orphan Houses, for their own personal necessities.

Jan. 4. As we have often found it to be the case, so it is now. After a season of more than usual poverty, comes a time of more than usual abundance. Today the same brother, who has been spoken of under November 2nd, and who has drawn his money out of the Savings'-bank to spend it for the Lord, sent 20l. more of it. There came in also from Guernsey 1l., and 1l. 7s. besides. I am now able to order oatmeal from Scotland, buy materials for the boys' clothes, order shoes, etc. Thus the Lord has been pleased to answer all our requests with respect to the pecuniary necessities of the Orphans, which we have brought before Him in our prayer meetings during the last seven weeks. We have thus had of late an abundance, but the expenses have been great also; for within the last twenty-five days I have paid out above 100l.

Jan. 22. As only little above 32l. had been received since the 4th, there was today again only 1l. 8s. 0 1/2d. in hand, whilst 3l. 8s. was needed, it being Saturday. However, as the Lord has helped us very many Saturdays, when we had still less at the commencement of the day, so it was today also. About an hour before the money was called for, I received from the neighbourhood of Crediton 4l., which came with the especial recommendation of a gentleman and lady to introduce the use of oatmeal in the Orphan-Houses, if we had not done so, and this money was sent towards the first supply. We have, however, used oatmeal now for many months, and have found it decidedly of great benefit to the children As about a fortnight since I had ordered 10l. worth from Glasgow, this money came in most seasonably to supply the other necessities of this day.

Jan. 24. Yesterday the Lord sent in 3l. 5s. 7d., to supply the need of this day.

Jan. 25. There was now again this morning nothing in hand for the Orphans. About ten o'clock there was sent to me, as the produce of an Orphan box, a small necklace, an old sixpence, and 5s. 8d. There came in also by sale of stockings 3s. 9d. As this 9s. 5d. was not enough, the boxes in the Orphan-Houses were opened, which contained 17s. 2d., and thus we were again supplied.

Perhaps, dear reader, you have said in your heart before you have read thus far: "How would it be, suppose the funds for the Orphans were reduced to nothing, and those who are engaged in the work had nothing of their own to give, and a meal time were to come, and you had no food for the children." Thus indeed it may be, for our hearts are desperately wicked. If ever we should be so left to ourselves, as that either we depend no more upon the living God, or that "we regard iniquity in our hearts," then such a state of things, we have reason to believe, would occur. But so long as we shall be enabled to trust in the living God, and so long as, though falling short in every way of what we might be, and ought to be, we are at least kept from living in sin, such a state of things cannot occur. Therefore, dear reader, if yourself walk with God, and if, on that account, His glory is dear to you, I affectionately and earnestly entreat you to beseech Him to uphold us; for how awful would be the disgrace brought upon His holy name, if we, who have so publicly made our boast in Him, and have spoken well of Him, should be left to disgrace Him, either by unbelief in the hour of trial, or by a life of sin in other respects.

Jan. 26. Again there was nothing in hand when the day commenced. In the course of the morning a gentleman from Yorkshire came to the Orphan-Houses. He bought two Reports, and one copy of the "Improved Renderings," put 2s. 6d. into the box at the Boys-Orphan-House, and 3s. into the box at the Infant-Orphan-House. There was also one penny found in the box at the Girls'-Orphan-House. This 6s. 10d. would have provided the absolute necessities for today, but it was desirable to have more means. I therefore opened the box in my house, in which I found a sovereign and a shilling. We were thus comfortably provided.

Jan. 27. Last evening came in 4s. This morning a parcel arrived from E. P., containing 3s., and the following articles: 7 books, a Bible, 6 pairs of socks, 4 pairs of babies' shoes, a purse, a lady's comb, a lady's bag, a pair of knitted over-shoes, and 2 pairs of muffetees. Yesterday afternoon a gentleman came to see the Orphan-

THIRD PART

Houses, and put a sovereign into the box at the Boys'-Orphan-House, which our need has brought out. We have thus 1l. 7s. for this day.--Evening. This afternoon came in still further 2l. from a lady at Kensington, on whose heart the Lord seems to have particularly laid the work.

Jan. 29. The two sovereigns, which came in on the 27th, supplied our need yesterday. When I had again nothing in hand, to meet today's necessities, a sister came last evening, who brought me 1l. 6s., a sovereign from another sister, and 6s. from herself. She said: "I do not know whether the Orphans have a dinner for tomorrow or not, but I had no rest in delaying to bring this money." I had but just then come home from a meeting, and had on the way to my house been lifting up my heart to the Lord, that He would be pleased to remember our need.--This morning was sent from Clapham 1l. 2s. 6d., with 3 frocks, a petticoat, 4 handkerchiefs, and 2 pinafores.

My dear reader, do you indeed recognise the hand of God in all these instances I have given instance upon instance, I have brought before you not this particular case, nor another particular case; but I have purposely shown you how we have fared day after day in our poverty, in order that you may adore the Lord for His goodness to us, and that you yourself may be led to depend upon Him for every thing, should you not have done so before. I affectionately beseech you, not to take these instances as a matter of course. Say not in your heart, This is a charitable Institution; persons know that the maintenance of these many Orphans, and the support of these Day Schools, etc., costs much money; and therefore they will contribute. Nor suffer Satan to rob you of the blessing which the account of the Lord's faithfulness to us, and His readiness to listen to our supplications is calculated with God's blessing, to communicate to you, by allowing him to whisper into your ears, that, because the Report are read by many, donations will of course be coming in, and that not all at once, but gradually, and that this is the way in which we are supplied. Dear reader, it is not thus. Suppose, we have been for some time on the whole bountifully supplied. Suppose, now all is gone. Suppose, the expenses are great, but very little comparatively is coming in. What shall we do now? If we took goods on credit, or if we made known our necessities at such times to the liberal Christians who have means, and who are interested in the work in our hands, then, humanly speaking, there might be little difficulty; but we neither take goods on credit, nor do we speak to any one about our need, but we wait upon God. Now, suppose our expenses are week after week, 30l., 40l., 50l., or 60l.? How are the means to come? Persons might still give; yea, many persons might still give, but it might just happen so, that all the donations that are received at the time when our expenses are most heavy are very small donations; how shall we do then? Sometimes the outgoings have been so great, that if I had sold every thing I possessed, I could not thereby have met the expenses of two weeks. What then is to be done? We wait upon God, and he always helps us, and has done so now [i. e. in 1881] for more than forty-five years with reference to the Orphans, and for more than forty-seven with reference to the other parts of the work.

Feb. 5. Saturday. As only 10l. 10s. 6d. had been received since January 29th, i. e. only so much as day by day was needed to provide necessaries for the Orphans, there is again the greatest need. It is now twelve o'clock, and there are no means as yet to meet the expenses of today. The words in the prayer of Jehoshaphat, "Neither know we what to do, but our eyes are upon Thee," are at this moment the language of my heart. I likewise know not what to do, but my eyes are upon the Lord, and I am sure that He will help this day also. Our kind Father still gives us proofs that He is mindful of our need; for last evening were anonymously sent to my house, 2 waistcoats, a shawl, a net collar, 3 3/4 yards of print, 2 decanters, and Clarendon's History of England. And just now, a small silver book, a pepper box with silver top, and some muslin work have arrived from Birmingham.--Evening. In the course of the morning came in, by sale of articles, 12s. We were able likewise to dispose of one of the articles, which were sent last evening, for 5s. This afternoon one of the labourers gave me 10s., and 3s. came in for needle-work. By means of this 1l. 10s. we were able to supply all that was needed.

Feb. 7. Yesterday was received 1l. 13s. 5d., and today 5s. 6d.

Feb. 8. By what came in yesterday, and the day before, the need of yesterday was supplied, and there is enough in all the houses for the meals of today; but in none of the houses have we been able to take in any bread; and as yesterday also but little could be taken in, there will not remain any for tomorrow; nor is there money enough to take in milk tomorrow morning. There are likewise coals needed in two houses. Indeed, so far as I know, these three years and seven months, since first the funds were exhausted, we were never in greater poverty; and if the Lord were not to send means before nine o'clock tomorrow morning, His name would be dishonoured. But I am fully assured that He will not leave us.--Evening. The Lord has not yet been pleased to send us what is needed for tomorrow, but He has given us a fresh proof that He is mindful of us. Between four and five o'clock this afternoon were sent nine plum cakes, which a sister had ordered to be baked as a treat for the Orphans. These cakes were an encouragement to me to continue to look out for further supplies. There was also found in the boxes at the Orphan-Houses, 2s. 1 1/2d., and 1s. 4d. came in for stockings. These little donations are most precious, but they are not enough to meet the need of tomorrow; yea, before nine o'clock tomorrow morning we need more money to be able to take in the milk. Truly, we are poorer than ever; but, through grace, my eyes look not at the empty stores and the empty purse, but to the riches of the Lord only.

Feb. 9. This morning I went between seven and eight o clock to the Orphan-Houses, to see whether the Lord had sent in any thing. When I arrived there, He had just two or three minutes before sent help.--A brother, in going to his house of business this morning, had gone already about half a mile, when the Lord was pleased to lay the Orphans upon his heart. He said, however, to himself, I cannot well return now, but will take something this evening; and thus he walked on. Nevertheless he could not go any further, but felt himself constrained to go back, and to take to brother R. B., at the Boys'-Orphan-House, three sovereigns. [The donor himself

THIRD PART

stated this to me afterwards.]--Thus the Lord in His faithfulness helped us. Help was never more truly needed, for our poverty was never greater; nor did the help of the Lord ever come more manifestly from Himself; for the brother was gone on a good distance, it was between seven and eight o'clock in the morning, and it was so short a time before money was needed. Consider this, beloved reader, and with us praise the Lord. Praise Him particularly, that He enabled us to trust in Him in this trying hour. There came in besides, today, 7s. 6d.

Feb. 11. The 3l. 11s. 6d. supplied our need the last two days. Today again a few shillings more were needed, which one of the labourers was able to give of his own; but this was only enough to take in the usual quantity of milk, and some bread.

Feb. 12. Saturday. Never since the funds were for the first time exhausted, had there come in less during any week, than during this. We were only able to supply the absolute necessities; but this we were enabled to do. When the meal times came, the Lord always provided what was needful, and, considering the great distress there is now almost everywhere, our dear Orphans are very well provided for. Now this day began not only without there being any thing in hand, but our stores were greatly reduced, and we had to procure provisions for two days. One of the labourers gave 5s. in the morning, to provide the means to take in the milk. I collected together some pamphlets, which had been given for sale, to dispose of them, and they were sold about eleven o'clock for 4s. There came in also by sale of stockings 3s., and 12s. was paid on behalf of one of the Orphans. Thus we were provided with means to procure a dinner, and had a little towards purchasing bread, but by no means enough. All the labourers were together in prayer from half-past eleven till one, and me separated comfortably, with the purpose of meeting again in the evening. When I came home, there was given to me an old broken silver pencil case, which, though worth very little, I took as a fresh proof that our Father was mindful of our need. When we met again this evening, we found that 3s. 6d. had come in by sale of stockings, and 6d. for two Reports. As all this was not enough, a few old and needless articles were disposed of for 4s., also the broken pencil ease for 6d. I say needless articles, for other articles it did not seem right to us to dispose of, in order that the Lord's own deliverance might be manifest. A labourer was also still further able to give 7s. of his own. To one of the labourers 2s. had been owed by a certain individual for more than a twelvemonth, which being paid just now, and given by him for the Orphans, came in most seasonably. Thus we had 1l. 18s. 6d., as much as was needful to procure provisions till after breakfast on Monday morning. However, the Lord helped still further. Between eight and nine this evening, after we had been together for prayer, and had now separated, some money was given to one of the labourers for himself, by which means he was able to give 9s., so that altogether 2l. 7s. 6d. had come in this day. This has been of all the weeks, during the last three years and seven months, one of the most trying, so far as it regards the trial of faith. Thanks to the Lord, who has helped us this day also! Thanks to Him for enabling us already this morning, when we met for prayer, to praise Him for the deliverance, which we were sure He would work!

Feb. 14. Yesterday came in from Wolverhampton 1l. 2s. 6d. and a necklace. There was also given to me 1l. 0s. 6d., which had come in by sale of articles, and 6d. for Reports. In the course of this day came in still further 3l. 2s. 4d.

Feb. 15. By needlework came in 4s. 9d.

Feb. 16. This morning there was now again only sufficient money in hand to take in milk at two of the houses; but as a labourer was able to give 6s. 6d., we had sufficient for the milk, and had also enough, with the provisions that were in the houses, to provide for the dinner. Nothing more came in in the course of the morning, nor was I able to make inquiries how matters stood. In the afternoon between three and four o'clock, having once more besought the Lord to send us help, I sat peacefully down to give myself to meditation over the Word, considering that that was now my service, though I knew not whether there was a morsel of bread for tea in any one of the houses, but being assured that the Lord would provide. For, through grace, my mind is so fully assured of the faithfulness of the Lord, that, in the midst of the greatest need, I am enabled in peace to go about my other work. Indeed, did not the Lord give me this, which is the result of trusting in Him, I should scarcely be able to work at all; for it is now comparatively a rare thing that a day comes, when I am not in need for one or the other part of the work. Scarcely had I sat down to meditate, when a note was sent to me from the Orphan-Houses, in which brother R. B., master of the Orphan Boys, had written thus: "On visiting the sisters in the Infant and Girls'-Orphan-Houses, I found them in the greatest need. There was not bread in one of the houses for tea this evening, and the 6s. 6d. was scarcely enough to supply what was needed for the dinner. I therefore opened the box in the Boys'-Orphan-House, and most unexpectedly found 1l. in it. Thus, through the kindness of the Lord, we were again abundantly supplied as it regards present necessities."--In the evening the Lord, in His love and faithfulness, stretched out His hand still farther. I had expounded at the meeting a part of John xi. The last words of which I spoke were: "Said I not unto thee, that, if thou wouldest believe, thou shouldest see the glory of God?" When the meeting was over, as a fresh proof of the truth of this word, a note was given to me, in which a sick sister sent me 5l. for the Orphans.

Feb. 17 and 18. These two days came in 8s. 2d.

Feb. 19. Saturday. Our means were now again completely spent. Our provision stores, were, perhaps, even more exhausted than on any previous Saturday. There was not the least human likelihood of obtaining menus for sufficient provisions for this one day, and much less for two days. When I went before breakfast to the Orphan-Houses, I found a letter from Nottingham, containing 1s., which had arrived last evening. This was not only a sweet proof that our Father remembered our need, but it was also like an earnest that He would supply us this day also with all we required. In the course of the morning came in by sale of stockings 4s. 11d. In the box at my house I found 1s. One of the labourers gave 4s. 10d. Thus we were provided with those things which were absolutely needed for this day. We met between eleven and twelve o'clock for prayer. When we met again in the evening, a second letter had arrived from Nottingham, with another shilling. This was a further sweet proof of our Father's loving remembrance of our need; but with all this we were still without any means to provide bread for tomorrow, the Lord's day. At eight o'clock I separated from my fellow-labourers, as I expected brother R. C. to arrive a little after eight at my house. I therefore requested one of the brethren to go with me, in order to take back to the Orphan-Houses what the Lord might send in by post or in any other way. It was now half-past eight in the evening, and there was no bread yet in any one of the three houses for tomorrow. A few moments after, brother C. arrived, and he had not been more than about five minutes in my house when he gave me half a sovereign, which he brought for the Orphans. I soon found an opportunity to leave the room for a little, gave the 10s. to the brother whom I had brought with me from the Orphan Houses, and who was waiting in another room; and thus, between nine and ten o'clock, sufficient bread could be bought. Observe! For the trial of our faith the Lord had allowed us to be kept waiting so long. When, however, brother C. had arrived, having money for the Orphans, he could not delay giving it at once, a matter most worthy of notice. This has been a week full of trials of faith, but also full of deliverances.

Feb. 21. Since Saturday evening came in 1l. 8s. 11d. There was also sent from Plymouth, a piece of blond, a piece of quilling net, and eleven pairs of children's stockings, for sale. Thus we were supplied with means for that which was requisite for the beginning of this day; but as our stores had been so reduced at the end of last week, there was not enough for tea this afternoon. Four o'clock had now come, one hour before the usual tea time, when a brother from Somersetshire came to see the Orphan-Houses, and put a sovereign into each of the boxes. Our great need soon brought out the money, and thus we were supplied. [Observe! The brother (as he himself told me a few days after in the course of conversation), had but little time, and therefore rather hastily went over the houses. Had he stayed long and conversed much, as might have been the case, his donations would not have been in time for the tea.] There came in 1s. besides, by needlework done by the children.

Feb. 22. This morning a parcel arrived from the neighbourhood of Manchester, containing 4 old silver thimbles, 1 seal, 2 gold pins, 10 cent (an American coin), a buckle, a watch key, a broken seal, some pamphlets and 549 sheets of Hintwafers.

Feb. 23. We were again in want of means. A few of the articles which had come from Manchester were disposed of, and one of the labourers was able to give enough for what remained to be supplied.--The narrative of time events of these days is most imperfect. The way in which the Lord stretched out His hand day by day, and from meal to meal, cannot be accurately described. To enter fully into it, one need be a witness to His inspecting the stores, so to speak, from meal to meal, and giving us those things which we needed.

Feb. 24. Yesterday the following clothes were sent: 3 pairs of boys' trousers, 2 boys' dresses, 2 frocks, a spencer, 5 pairs of children's stays, a pair of boots, and a few other little articles. The clothes were all much worn, and in other respects not fit for the Orphans; but the Lord used them to supply us with the means for the dinner, as they were disposed of this morning. In the afternoon we again met for prayer. On my way to the Orphan-Houses, between four and five, when I knew that there would not be any bread, at least in one of the houses, for tea, I felt quite peaceful, being fully assured that for this meal also the Lord would provide. On inquiry I found that there was bread enough in the Girls'-Orphan-House, none at all in the Boys'-Orphan-House, but enough in the Infant-Orphan-House both for the Infants and Boys. Therefore we were at this time supplied by the bread which was not needed at the Infant-Orphan-House. We have thus this day also what is absolutely needful. But now there is no bread in any of the houses, nor scarcely any thing else in the way of provisions.

Feb. 25. Greater than now our need had never been. Our trials of faith have never been so sharp as during this week. Indeed, so much so, that most of the labourers felt today considerably tried. Yet neither this day has the Lord suffered us to be confounded. Through a remarkable circumstance one of the labourers obtained some money this morning, so that all the need of today could be amply met. In the afternoon a physician of this city kindly sent 1l. for the Orphans, which was a sweet proof to us, when we met for prayer, that our kind Father had not forgotten us. Also on my way to the prayer-meeting at the Orphan-Houses I received 9s.

Feb. 26. My prayer this morning was in particular, that the Lord would be pleased now to look in pity upon us, and take off His hand. Indeed, for several days my prayer has been that He would enable us to continue to trust in Him, and not lay more upon us than He would enable us to bear. This is now again Saturday. There having been given yesterday a rich supply to the matrons, I knew that not so much as usual would be required this Saturday; still I thought that 1l. 10s. would be needed. Between ten and eleven o'clock this morning a parcel came from Clapham, containing 2l. 2s., with 2 frocks, 2 petticoats, 2 chemises, 2 pinafores, and 6 handkerchiefs (all new.) Thus we were richly supplied for today, for only 1l. 10s. was needed. There was moreover half-a-sovereign put into the box at my house this day by a little boy, and 2s. 6d. came in by sale of articles. Thus we were brought to the close of a week in which more than at any previous time the Lord has been pleased to try our faith. To Him most manifestly we owe it that our faith has not failed completely.

Feb. 28. Yesterday Q. Q. gave me an order for 8l. As it was left to me to lay out the money as I thought well, I put 4l. of it to the School-Fund, and 4l. to the Orphan-Fund. Thus both parts of the work have been again most seasonably helped, as today the teachers in the Day-Schools greatly needed some money for themselves. Today 13s. was received for the Orphans.

March 2. Yesterday I found a sovereign in the Orphan-box at my house; received 9s. 2 3/4d. from three little boys, being the produce of their Orphan-box; 2s. 6d. for Reports; and 1l. 10s., being the profit of the sale of ladies' baskets. Thus we were again supplied for yesterday and today. This evening were also sent, by order of an Irish sister, 33 1/2 lbs. of woollen yarn. Respecting this donation it is to be remarked, that last Saturday we had asked the Lord in our prayer-meeting, that He would be pleased to send us means to purchase worsted, in order that the boys might go on with their knitting.

March 3. Yesterday 5s. came in, and this evening a sovereign, when there was now again great need, there being no money in hand.

March 5. Saturday. It was not a small deliverance, that the Lord sent this morning, between ten and eleven o'clock, 2l. 10s. from Edinburgh, when there were no means in hand to meet this day's necessities, nay, not even the means to procure a dinner, as only 4s. had come in yesterday.--Evening. About eight o'clock a gentleman called on me. He said "I come at a late hour, but I trust not the less acceptable on that account. I bring you a little money for the Orphans." He then gave me two sovereigns. When I requested him to give me his name, he told me, that if the giving of his name would be of any benefit he would do so, but as it would not, I might simply put down in the Report "Sent," for he was sure that the Lord had sent him.--I believe it, for the help came most seasonably and in answer to prayer. There was likewise taken out of the box in my house half-a-sovereign.

March 9. At a time of the greatest need, both with regard to the Day-Schools and the Orphans, so much so that we could not have gone on any longer without help, I received this day 10l. from a brother who lives near Dublin. The money was divided between the Day-Schools and the Orphan-Houses. The following little circumstance is to be noticed respecting this donation:--As our need was so great, and my soul was, through grace, truly waiting upon the Lord, I looked out for supplies in the course of this morning. The post, however, was out, and no supplies had come. This did not in the least discourage me. I said to myself, the Lord can send means without the post, or even now, though the post is out, by this very delivery of letters He may have sent means, though the money is not yet in my hands. It was not long after I had thus spoken to myself, when, according to my hope in God, we were helped; for the brother who sent us the 10l., had this time directed his letter to the Boys'-Orphan-House, whence it was sent to me.

March 11. Yesterday a box arrived from one of the Northern Counties, respecting which the donor had requested that neither the articles which it contained, nor the name of the place whence it came, should be mentioned in the public account. I, therefore, only state here that thus the Lord has again most seasonably helped us, besides giving us a fresh proof, in raising up this new and anonymous donor, that He does not cease to care for us. It is intended to apply the produce of the articles contained in the box partly for the Orphans, and partly for the other objects. Though the box arrived only yesterday, we are even this day helped through means of it; for we disposed today of some of the articles to the amount of 9l. 6s. 6d. Of this sum 7l. 6s. 6d. was divided among the teachers, who much needed it; and 2l. was taken for the Orphan-Fund, without which the need of this day could not have been supplied in the Orphan-Houses.

March 17. From the 12th to the 16th had come in 4l. 5s. 11 1/2d. for the Orphans. This morning our poverty, which now has lasted more or less for several months, had become exceedingly great. I left my house a few minutes after seven to go to the Orphan-Houses, to see whether there was money enough to take in the milk, which is brought about eight o'clock. On my way it was especially my request, that the Lord would be pleased to pity us, even as a father pitieth his children, and that He would not lay more upon us than He would enable us to bear. I especially entreated him that He would now be pleased to refresh our hearts by sending us help. I likewise reminded Him of the consequences that would result, both in reference to believers and unbelievers, if we should have to give up the work because of want of means, and that He therefore would not permit its coming to nought. I moreover again confessed before the Lord that I deserved not that He should continue to use me in this work any longer. While I was thus in prayer, about two minutes' walk from the Orphan-Houses, I met a brother who was going at this early hour to his business. After having exchanged a few words with him, I went on; but he presently ran after me, and gave me 1l. for the Orphans. Thus the Lord speedily answered my prayer. Truly, it is worth being poor and greatly tried in faith, for the sake of having day by day such precious proofs of the loving interest which our kind Father takes in every thing that concerns us. And how should our Father do otherwise? He that has given us the greatest possible proof of His love which He could have done, in giving us His own Son, surely He will with Him also freely give us all things. It is worth also being poor and greatly tried in faith, if but thereby the hearts of the children of God may be comforted and their faith strengthened; and if but those who do not know God, and who may read or hear of His dealings with us, should be led thereby to see, that faith in God is more than a mere notion, and that there is indeed reality in Christianity. In the course of this day there came in still further 13s.

March 19. Saturday. As it has often been the case on Saturdays, so it was this day in particular. We began the day in very great poverty, as only 7s. had come in since the day before yesterday. There was not one ray of light as to natural prospects. The heart would be overwhelmed, at such seasons, were there not an abundance of repose to be found by trusting in God. The trial having continued so long, and our poverty having now come to such a degree, that it was necessary we should have help, in order that the name of the Lord might not be dishonoured, I had proposed to my fellow-labourers that we should set apart this day especially for prayer. We met accordingly at half-past ten in the morning. By that time had come in 4s. 6d., 7s. 6d., and 10s. In the afternoon we met again at three, when 10s. came in. In the evening at seven we met once more, there being yet about three shillings needed, to provide all that was required. This also we received, and even 3s. more than was actually needed came in, just when we were about to separate.

Today we were also very poor with reference to our own personal necessities. In the morning we had only 2 1/2d. left, when a sister in the Lord, who knew nothing about our need, gave us the contents of her purse, being 1l. 7s.

THIRD PART

March 23. This afternoon, when we had no money at all of our own, a brother gave us 3s. for ourselves.

March 25. During the last four days we received 6l. 12s. 2d. for the Orphans. This morning, when we were now again without any thing, a parcel arrived from Clapham, containing 1l. 10s., with a frock, a chemise, 2 petticoats, 2 pinafores, and 2 handkerchiefs (all new). About the same time was sent a post-office order from Bath for 2l. This is no small deliverance. The need has been so great during this week that the matrons, in order that there might be no lack in the way of provisions for the children, have been unable to order even half-a-ton of coals at once, and have been obliged to buy them in very small quantities.

When again we had only 6d. Left for our own personal necessities, I received 9s.

March 26. We are helped to the close of one more week with reference to our own personal necessities. During this week we have had several times not one single penny for ourselves; yet during this week also we have had all that was needed in the way of nourishing food, etc., and we have 3d. left.

March 30. From the 25th up to this day we were poor, with reference to the Orphans but the Lord helped us. This morning a brother from Devonshire came to stay for a few days with me. He gave me two sovereigns for the Orphans, and told me the following facts in connexion with them. Last year he portioned out a piece of ground, for the benefit of the Orphans. Having done so, all the members of the family were gathered together, and he asked with them the Lord's blessing upon the crop that was to be planted. This prayer was often repeated afterwards, while the crop was known to belong to the Orphans; and the ground yielded a good crop. The potatoes were to have been sent, but it was considered better to sell them for the benefit of the Orphans, and now this brother brought the produce. These two sovereigns came in most seasonably, as they were only just in time to supply the dinner and other necessaries of this day; for when I came with the brother from the railway station to my house, I found an Orphan boy waiting for money, and I had nothing in hand. This evening I received still further from a sister 1l. 1s. 5 1/2d.

This morning we had not one single halfpenny left for our own necessities, when two brethren arrived to stay with us for some days, the one from Somersetshire and the other from the North of Devon. The brother from the North of Devon brought 12s. for my own use from Barnstaple, and also gave 1l. to my dear wife this afternoon for our own need. Thus we were again supplied. My mind has been quite in peace on account of our own need, and the only inconvenience that we had in this case was, that our dinner was about half an hour later than usual. Such a thing, as far as I remember, scarcely ever occurred before, and has never occurred since; but suppose it had, it is well, in some little measure, to know from one's own experience the meaning of that word, "I know both how to be abased, and I know how to abound:

everywhere and in all things I am instructed both to be full and to be hungry, both to abound and to suffer need." Philip iv. 12.

March 31. This afternoon 5s. came in from Bath, and from a sister in the Lord in one of the Northern counties 5l. for the Orphans and 15l. for the other objects; and through the same donor 12s. This money arrived when there was again only 5s. in hand for the Orphans, which had come in this afternoon, and when there was particular need of means, as many pairs of shoes needed to be mended, and other extra expenses were to be met. When this money came, there was also great need of fresh supplies for the Day-Schools, on account of which this donation was a precious help from the Lord.

April 2. We received 1l. 19s. 6d. for the Orphans.

April 4. When again our little stock had been exhausted, the Lord was pleased to send in yesterday 5l. through a sister of Bristol; also by sale of articles 10s., and by Reports 5s. Today came in from Kensington 1l.

April 6. As only 3s. more had come in yesterday, the money was now again all gone, when this evening was sent from a distance a post office order for 2l.

April 8. This afternoon, when again much money was needed, we received from Plymouth 1l., and from a donor in Bristol 1l.

April 9. Saturday. Only 1s. 6d. had come in since yesterday afternoon. We needed more money than there was in hand, especially as it was Saturday, but the Lord was pleased particularly to try our faith. In the course of the morning came from some sisters in Dublin, 18 yards of calico, 34 yards of print, 43 balls of cotton, and a pair of worn lady's boots. This donation came most seasonably, as we had been mentioning repeatedly the need of calico and print in our prayers; and the sewing cotton and the pair of boots came at once into use. Moreover, this donation was a sweet encouragement to me to continue waiting upon the Lord. Evening was now approaching, and no money had yet come in for provisions, etc., which would be needed on the Lord's day. About six o'clock, I gave myself once more to prayer with my wife, and requested the Lord in my prayer that if the sister, who in love to Him has taken upon her the service of disposing of the articles which are given for sale, had any money in hand, He would be pleased to incline her heart to bring or send the money this evening. After this I sat down peacefully to read the Scriptures, being assured that this time also the Lord would stretch out His hand on our behalf. About half-past seven o'clock the sister to whom reference has just now been made, came and brought 1l. 10s. 4d., for articles which she had sold, stating that though she was unwell, yet she felt herself constrained not to delay bringing this money. Thus we had all that was needed, and 6s. more. When I arrived with the money at the Infant-Orphan-House, about eight o'clock, I found my fellow labourers in prayer, and while we still continued in prayer a sister sent a large basket of stale bread, being five brown loaves, seven bread cakes, and five French loaves.

THIRD PART

April 11. It is this day six years since the first children were taken in, and, as usual, we are poor this day also; for only 13s. 10 1/2d. has come in since Saturday evening.

April 12. We were never in greater need than today, perhaps never in so much, when I received this morning 100l. from the East Indies. It is impossible to describe the real joy in God it gave me. My prayer had been again this morning particularly, that our Father would pity us, and now at last send larger sums. I was not in the least surprised or excited when this donation came, for I took it as that which came in answer to prayer, and had been long looked for. As it was left to me to use the money as might be most needed, I took one half of it for the Orphan Fund, and the other half for the other funds. We have thus also an answer to our prayer for oatmeal, new shoes, and for means to enable us to have the old shoes mended, means for replenishing somewhat our stores, money for some articles of clothing for the children, and also a little money for the sisters who labour in the Orphan-Houses. How precious to look to the Lord! I was always sure that He would at last send larger sums, therefore had my heart been kept in peace, though my faith had never been more tried than during the last months.

April 14. There was half-a-sovereign taken out of the box at the Boys'-Orphan-House this morning. This afternoon three individuals called on me. One of them gave 6l., 3 collars, and 2 veils, and brought likewise 3 gold rings. Another of them gave me 2s. 6d. After they had left I found in my room on the mantelpiece in a paper 2 sovereigns for my own personal expenses, and in three papers 3 sovereigns for the three Orphan-Houses, and also a fourpenny piece on the floor.

April 30. As since the 14th only little more than 16l. had come in, there was again this day not quite enough in hand to supply all that was needed. However, the Lord sent from Clapham a parcel which contained 10s., 2 frocks, 2 pinafores, 2 handkerchiefs, 2 nightcaps, and 2 pieces of list.

May 1. Today was given by a brother a gold watch with a small gold chain and key. The gift was accompanied by the following note to me:

"Beloved Brother,

"A pilgrim does not want such a watch as this to make him happy; one of an inferior kind will do to show him how swiftly his time flies, and how fast he is hastening on to that Canaan where time will be no more: so that it is for you to do with this what seemeth good to you. It is the last relic of earthly vanity, and, while I am in the body, may I be kept from all idolatry.

"Your affectionate brother,

*****"

May 2. There was now again no money in hand, not even the few shillings which were required to take in the milk tomorrow morning, when a sister gave a sovereign to brother R. B. for the Orphans, whereby we are helped.

May 6. Only 3l. 10s. 2 1/2d. had been received since the 2nd, on which account there would have been only enough means in hand to provide for the breakfast tomorrow morning, when in this our fresh need 80l. was sent by the same brother who has been spoken of under "June 4, 1841," in the details respecting the other funds; and also 6l. from Great Malvern. The half of this 80l. was put to the Orphan Fund, and the other half to the other funds: the donation from Great Malvern was put to the fund for the other objects. There arrived at the same time from the East Indies by post a small parcel, containing 2 pairs of gold ear-rings, a brooch, and 2 rupees. These donations came especially in season, as they enable me to give supplies to the brethren and sisters who labour in the Day Schools and Orphan-Houses for their own personal necessities, besides meeting the wants in other respects.

May 10. 6l. 15s. 10d. more has come in since the 6th. Today, in closing the accounts, we have left at the end of this period of seventeen months, in which we have been so often penniless, the sum of 16l. 18s. 10 1/2d. for the Orphans, and 48l. 12s. 5 1/4d. for the other objects of the Scriptural Knowledge Institution.

The time now seemed to us to have come, when, for the profit of the church at large, the Lord's dealings with us, with reference to the various objects of the Scriptural Knowledge Institution, should be made known by publishing another Report. For, whilst we, on purpose, had delayed it at this time five months longer than during the previous years, and that during a period when we were in deeper poverty than during any previous time; yet, as from the commencement it had appeared to me important, from time to time to make known the Lord's dealings with us, so I judged it profitable still, to seek to comfort, to encourage, to exhort, to instruct, and to warn the dear children of God by the printed accounts of the Lord's goodness to us.

The following are a few additional remarks with reference to the period of the seventeen months previous to May 10, 1842.

1. Though our trials of faith during these seventeen months lasted longer, and were sharper than during any previous period, yet during all this time the Orphans had every thing that was needful in the way of nourishing food, the necessary articles of clothing, etc. Indeed I should rather at once send the children back to their relations than keep them without sufficient maintenance.

2. I desire that all the children of God who may read these details may thereby be led to increased and more simple confidence in God for every thing which they may need under any circumstances, and that these many answers to prayer may encourage them to pray, particularly as it regards the conversion of their friends and

THIRD PART

relations, their own progress in grace and knowledge, the state of the saints whom they may know personally, the state of the church of Christ at large, and the success of the preaching of the Gospel. Especially I affectionately warn them against being led away by the device of Satan, to think that these things are peculiar to me, and cannot be enjoyed by all the children of God; for though, as has been stated before, every believer is not called upon to establish Orphan-Houses, Charity Schools, etc., and trust in the Lord for means, yet all believers are called upon, in the simple confidence of faith, to cast all their burdens upon Him, to trust in him for every thing, and not only to make every thing a subject of prayer, but to expect answers to their petitions which they have asked according to His will, and in the name of the Lord Jesus.--Think not, dear reader, that I have the gift of faith, that is, that gift of which we read in 1 Cor. xii. 9, and which is mentioned along with "the gifts of healing," "the working of miracles," "prophecy," and that on that account I am able to trust in the Lord. It is true that the faith, which I am enabled to exercise, is altogether God's own gift; it is true that He alone supports it, and that He alone can increase it; it is true that, moment by moment, I depend upon Him for it, and that, if I were only one moment left to myself, my faith would utterly fail; but it is not true that my faith is that gift of faith which is spoken of in 1 Cor. xii. 9, for the following reasons.

1, The faith which I am enabled to exercise with reference to the Orphan-Houses and my own temporal necessities, is not that "faith" of which it is said in 1 Cor. xiii. 2 (evidently in allusion to the faith spoken of in 1 Cor. xii. 9), "Though I have all faith, so that I could remove mountains, and have not charity (love), I am nothing"; but it is the self-same faith which is found in every believer, and the growth of which I am most sensible of to myself; for, by little and little, it has been increasing for the last fifty-six years.

2, This faith which is exercised respecting the Orphan-Houses and my own temporal necessities, shows itself in the same measure, for instance, concerning the following points: I have never been permitted to doubt during the last fifty-six years that my sins are forgiven, that I am a child of God, that I am beloved of God, and that I shall be finally saved; because I am enabled, by the grace of God, to exercise faith upon the word of God, and believe what God says in those passages which settle these matters (1 John v. 1-Gal. iii. 26-Acts x. 43-Romans x. 9, 10-John iii. 16, etc.)--Further, at the time when I thought I should be insane (though there was not the least ground for thinking so), as recorded on pages 209, 210, and 223, I was in peace, quite in peace; because my soul believed the truth of that word, "We know that all things work together for good to them that love God." Rom. viii. 28.--Further, When my brother in the flesh, and my dear aged father died, and when concerning both of them I had no evidence whatever that they were saved (though I dare not say that they are lost, for I know it not); yet my soul was at peace, perfectly at peace, under this great trial, this exceedingly great trial, this trial which is one of the greatest perhaps which can befall a believer. And what was it that gave me peace? My soul laid hold on that word, "Shall not the judge of all the earth do right!" This word, together with the whole character of God, as He has revealed Himself in His holy word, settled all questionings. I believed what He has said concerning Himself, and I was at peace, and have been at peace ever since, concerning this matter.--Further, When the Lord took from me a beloved infant, my soul was at peace, perfectly at peace; I could only weep tears of joy when I did weep. And why? Because my soul laid hold in faith on that word: "Of such is the kingdom of Heaven." Matthew xix. 14. Believing, therefore, as I did, upon the ground of this word, my soul rejoiced, instead of mourning, that my beloved infant was far happier with the Lord, than with me.--Further, When sometimes all has been dark, exceedingly dark, with reference to my service among the saints, judging from natural appearances yea, when I should have been overwhelmed indeed in grief and despair, had I looked at things after the outward appearance: at such times I have sought to encourage myself in God, by laying hold in faith on His mighty power, His unchangeable love, and His infinite wisdom, and I have said to myself: God is able and willing to deliver me, if it be good for me; for it is written: "He that spared not His own Son, but delivered Him up for us all, how shall He not with Him also freely give us all things?" Rom. viii. 32. This, this it was which, being believed by me through grace, kept my soul in peace.--Further, When in connection with the Orphan-Houses, Day Schools, etc., trials have come upon me which were far heavier than the want of means, when lying reports were spread that the Orphans had not enough to eat, or that they were cruelly treated in other respects, and the like; or when other trials, still greater, but which I cannot mention, have befallen me in connexion with this work, and that at a time when I was nearly a thousand miles absent from Bristol, and had to remain absent week after week: at such times my soul was stayed upon God; I believed His word of promise which was applicable to such cases; I poured out my soul before God, and arose from my knees in peace, because the trouble that was in the soul was in believing prayer cast upon God, and thus I was kept in peace, though I saw it to be the will of God to remain far away from the work.

--Further, When I needed houses, fellow-labourers, masters and mistresses for the Orphans or for the Day Schools, I have been enabled to look for all to the Lord, and trust in Him for help.--Dear reader, I may seem to boast; but, by the Grace of God, I do not boast in thus speaking. From my inmost soul I do ascribe it to God alone that He has enabled me to trust in Him, and that hitherto He has not suffered my confidence in Him to fail. But I thought it needful to make these remarks, lest any one should think that my depending upon God was a particular gift given to me, which other saints have no right to look for; or lest it should be thought that this my depending upon Him had only to do with the obtaining of MONEY by prayer and faith. By the grace of God I desire that my faith in God should extend towards EVERY thing, the smallest of my own temporal and spiritual concerns, and the smallest of the temporal and spiritual concerns of my family, towards the saints among whom I labour, the church at large, everything that has to do with the temporal and spiritual prosperity of the Scriptural Knowledge Institution, etc. Dear reader, do not think that I have attained in faith (and how much less in other respects!) to that degree to which I might and ought to attain; but thank God for the faith which He has given me, and ask Him to uphold and increase it. And lastly, once more, let not Satan deceive you in making you think that you could not have the same faith, but that it is only for persons who are situated as I am. When I lose such a thing as a

THIRD PART

key, I ask the Lord to direct me to it, and I look for an answer to my prayer; when a person with whom I have made an appointment does not come, according to the fixed time, and I begin to be inconvenienced by it, I ask the Lord to be pleased to hasten him to me, and I look for an answer; when I do not understand a passage of the word of God, I lift up my heart to the Lord, that He would be pleased, by His holy Spirit, to instruct me, and I expect to be taught, though I do not fix the time when, and the manner how it should be; when I am going to minister in the Word, I seek help from the Lord, and while I in the consciousness of natural inability as well as utter unworthiness, begin this His service, I am not cast down, but of good cheer, because I look for His assistance, and believe that He, for His dear Son's sake, will help me. And thus in other of my temporal and spiritual concerns I pray to the Lord, and expect an answer to my requests; and may not you do the same, dear believing reader? Oh! I beseech you, do not think me an extraordinary believer, having privileges above other of God's dear children, which they cannot have; nor look on my way of acting as something that would not do for other believers. Make but trial! Do but stand still in the hour of trial, and you will see the help of God, if you trust in Him. But there is so often a forsaking the ways of the Lord in the hour of trial, and thus the food of faith, the means whereby our faith may be increased, is lost. This leads me to the following important point. You ask, How may I, a true believer, have my faith strengthened? The answer is this

I. "Every good gift and every perfect gift is from above, and cometh down from the Father of lights, with whom is no variableness, neither shadow of turning." James i. 17. As the increase of faith is a good gift, it must come from God, and therefore He ought to be asked for this blessing.

II. The following means, however, ought to be used: 1, The careful reading of the word of God, combined with meditation on it. Through reading of the word of God, and especially through meditation on the word of God, the believer becomes more and more acquainted with the nature and character of God, and thus sees more and more, besides His holiness and justice, what a kind, loving, gracious, merciful, mighty, wise, and faithful Being He is, and, therefore, in poverty, affliction of body, bereavement in his family, difficulty in his service, want of a situation or employment, he will repose upon the ability of God to help him, because he has not only learned from His word that He is of almighty power and infinite wisdom, but he has also seen instance upon instance in the Holy Scriptures in which His almighty power and infinite wisdom have been actually exercised in helping and delivering His people; and he will repose upon the willingness of God to help him, because he has not only learned from the Scriptures what a kind, good, merciful, gracious, and faithful being God is, but because he has also seen in the word of God, how in a great variety of instances He has proved Himself to be so. And the consideration of this, if God has become known to us through prayer and meditation on His own word, will lead us, in general at least, with a measure of confidence to rely upon Him: and thus the reading of the word of God, together with meditation on it, will be one especial means to strengthen our faith. 2, As with reference to the growth of every grace of the Spirit, it is of the utmost importance that we seek to maintain an upright heart and a good conscience, and, therefore, do not knowingly and habitually indulge in those things which are contrary to the mind of God, so it is also particularly the case with reference to the growth in faith. How can I possibly continue to act faith upon God, concerning any thing, if I am habitually grieving Him, and seek to detract from the glory and honour of Him in whom I profess to trust, upon whom I profess to depend? All my confidence towards God, all my leaning upon Him in the hour of trial will be gone, if I have a guilty conscience, and do not seek to put away this guilty conscience, but still continue to do things which are contrary to the mind of God. And if, in any particular instance, I cannot trust in God, because of the guilty conscience, then my faith is weakened by that instance of distrust; for faith with every fresh trial of it either increases by trusting God, and thus getting help, or it decreases by not trusting Him; and then there is less and less power of looking simply and directly to Him, and a habit of self-dependence is begotten or encouraged. One or other of these will always be the case in each particular instance. Either we trust in God, and in that case we neither trust in ourselves, nor in our fellowmen, nor in circumstances, nor in any thing besides; or we no trust in one or more of these, and in that case do NOT trust in God. 3, If we, indeed, desire our faith to be strengthened, we should not shrink from opportunities where our faith may be tried, and, therefore, through the trial, be strengthened. In our natural state we dislike dealing with God alone. Through our natural alienation from God we shrink from Him, and from eternal realities. This cleaves to us more or less, even after our regeneration. Hence it is, that, more or less, even as believers, we have the same shrinking from standing with God alone,--from depending upon Him alone,--from looking to Him alone:--and yet this is the very position in which we ought to be, if we wish our faith to be strengthened. The more I am in a position to be tried in faith with reference to my body, my family, my service for the Lord, my business, etc., the more shall I have opportunity of seeing God's help and deliverance; and every fresh instance, in which He helps and delivers me, will tend towards the increase of my faith. On this account, therefore, the believer should not shrink from situations, positions, circumstances, in which his faith may be tried; but should cheerfully embrace them as opportunities where he may see the hand of God stretched out on his behalf, to help and deliver him, and whereby he may thus have his faith strengthened. 4, The last important point for the strengthening of our faith is, That we let God work for us, when the hour of the trial of oar faith comes, and do not work a deliverance of our own. Wherever God has given faith, it is given, among other reasons, for the very purpose of being tried. Yea, however weak our faith may be, God will try it; only with this restriction, that as, in every way, He leads on gently, gradually, patiently, so also with reference to the trial of our faith. At first our faith will be tried very little in comparison with what it may be afterwards; for God never lays more upon us than He is willing to enable us to bear. Now when the trial of faith comes, we are naturally inclined to distrust God, and to trust rather in ourselves, or in our friends, or in circumstances. We will rather work a deliverance of our own somehow or other, than simply look to God and wait for His help. But if we do not patiently wait for God's help, if we work a deliverance of our own, then at the next trial of our faith it will be thus again, we shall be again inclined to deliver ourselves; and thus with every fresh instance of that kind, our faith will decrease; whilst, on the contrary, were we to stand still in order to see the

THIRD PART

salvation of God, to see His hand stretched out on our behalf, trusting in Him alone, then our faith would be increased, and with every fresh case in which the hand of God is stretched out on our behalf in the hour of the trial of our faith, our faith would be increased yet more. Would the believer, therefore, have his faith strengthened, he must especially, give time to God, who tries his faith in order to prove to His child, in the end, how willing he is to help and deliver him, the moment it is good for him.

I now return, dear reader, to the Narrative, giving you some further information with reference to the 17 months, from December 10, 1840, to May 18, 1842, as it respects the Orphan-Houses, and other objects of the Scriptural Knowledge Institution for Home and Abroad, besides the facts of which mention has been already made.

During this period also--1, Two Sunday Schools were entirely supported by the funds of the Institution. 2, There were two adult schools, one for females, and one for males, entirely supported during these 17 months, in which on two evenings of the week the males, and on two evenings the females were instructed, quite gratuitously, in reading and writing, and were furnished with books and writing materials gratuitously. There were, during these 17 months, 344 adults taught in these two schools, and on May 10, 1842, the number under instruction amounted to 110. The chief object of these adult schools is, to teach grown up persons to read, in order that they may themselves be able to read the Holy Scriptures; but, at the same time, those who teach them take opportunity to point out the way of salvation to them, and, while the word of God is read, they seek to make remarks on the portions which are read.--3, There were, during these 17 months, also six Day Schools entirely supported by the funds of the Institution, three for boys and three for girls. These schools are principally intended to enable persons of the poorer classes of the inhabitants of Bristol, to send their children to school, either entirely free, or on paying only the fifth or sixth part of the expenses connected with the instruction which the children receive; they are also, especially, intended to keep believing parents, who have not much means, from the necessity of sending their children to unbelievers for instruction. On May 10, 1842, the number of the children, who attended these Day Schools, was 363; and the total number, who from the formation of the Institution on. March 5, 1834, up to May 10, 1842, had been instructed in the Day Schools, which are supported by the funds of the Institution, amounts to 2616.--4, During these 17 months, 798 copies of the Holy Scriptures were circulated, and from the commencement of the Institution, up to May 10, 1842, 6,842 copies. 5, During these 17 months was spent for Missionary purposes, the sum of 126l. 15s. 3d. of the funds of the Institution, whereby assistance was rendered to the work of God in Jamaica, in Australia, in Canada, and in the East Indies. 6, At the commencement of these 17 months, i.e. on December 10, 1840, a new object was begun., the circulation of such publications as may be instrumental, with the blessing of God, to benefit both unbelievers and believers. We laid out for this object, during these 17 months, from December 10, 1840, to May 10, 1842, the sum of 62l. 17s. 4d., for which twenty-two thousand one hundred and ninety such little publications were purchased, and of which number nineteen thousand six hundred and nine were actually given away.--7,

There were received into the three Orphan-Houses, from Dec. 10, 1840, to May 10, 1842, 15 Orphans, who, together with those who were in the houses on Dec. 10, 1840, make up 106 in all. Of these, five girls were sent out to service, two boys and one girl were apprenticed, one girl was removed by a lady who had placed her for a time under our care, and one was sent back to his relations, as he was injurious to the other children.

There were on May 10, 1842, 96 Orphans in the three houses, i.e. 30 in the Girls'-Orphan-House, 37 in the Infant-Orphan-House, and 29 in the Boys-Orphan-House. Besides this, three apprentices were supported by the funds of the Institution, so that the total number was 99. The number of Orphans who were under our care from April, 1836, to May 10, 1842, amounts to 144.

I notice further the following points in connexion with the Orphan-Houses.

Without any one having been asked for any thing by me, the sum of 5,276l. 14s. 8d. was given to me from the beginning of the work up to May 16, 1842, as the result of prayer to God. Besides this, also, many articles of clothing, furniture, provisions, &c.--During these 17 months we had very little sickness in the three houses, and not one of the children died. I desire publicly to state this, and in it to acknowledge the hand of God.

The total of the expenditure for the various objects of the Institution, exclusive of the Orphan-Houses, during these 17 months, amounted to 710l. 11s. 5d.; the total of the income amounted to 746l. 1s. 0 1/2d. The total of the expenditure for the three Orphan-Houses, from December 10, 1840, to May 10, 1842, amounted to 1,337l. 15s. 2 3/4d.; the total of the income amounted to 1,339l. 13s. 7d.

May 11, 1842. When the accounts were closed last evening, the balance in hand for the Orphans was 16l. 18s. 10 1/2d., though the actual amount for use at present is only 6l. 8s. 10 1/2d. as 10l. 10s. is put by for the rent.--With this 6l. 8s. 10 1/2d. therefore we had to begin again the work, whilst there were 107 persons to be provided for with all they required.

From May 11 to May 27, we were always so provided for by the Lord, that we received fresh donations before the last money was spent, for there came in 28l. 15s. 8 1/2d.; but now we should not have had sufficient for the need of tomorrow, May 28th, when today there arrived a parcel from Kendal, containing 6 frocks, 5 tippets, 6 pinafores, 6 chemises, 2 shirts, 3 aprons, and the following donations in money: with Ps. xxvii., 10s.; Proverbs iii. 5, 6, 2s. 6d.; from a sister who earns her own, bread by her daily exertions, 10s.; from another individual 10s. There came in also by sale of articles, given for that purpose, 2l. 1s.

May 28. There came in still further today 3l. 4s. 4d., so that we are richly provided, with all we need, and have more than enough.

THIRD PART

June 3. For several days past I had not been particularly led to pray for means for the Orphans. Last evening, however, I did so, as we had now again no money in hand, there having come in only 10l. 2s. 2d. during the last five days; and in answer to my request 2l. 19s. 6d. came in this morning.

June 6. Monday. There was now no money at all in hand. I had therefore asked the Lord for fresh supplies, and since Saturday afternoon the following sums have come in: By sale of articles 1l. 4s., FROM AN AGED SERVANT, ILL IN A MORTAL DISEASE, 4l.; anonymously put into the boxes at Bethesda yesterday, in a small parcel, 11s., a gold ring, 3 small Spanish silver coins, and a small American silver coin; ditto 4d.; by a sister was given 6d., and by another sister 5s.; anonymously put into the box at Callow-hill Street Chapel 2s.

This morning I received from A. B. 50l., to be laid out as it might be most useful. I took the whole of this sum for the other objects, as the disposal of it was left to me, whereby I am enabled to order a fresh supply of tracts, some Bibles and Testaments, and to give something to the brethren and sisters who labour in the Day Schools, who are much in need of some supply. The stock of Bibles, as far as I remember, has never been smaller than it is now, for several years; there is likewise only a small quantity of tracts left, and the demand for them is great on the part of brethren who gratuitously circulate them. How kind therefore of the Lord to give us this supply! If our work be His work, He is sure to provide the means for it!

June 9. On the 7th came in 3s. for the Orphans,--on the 8th 2l. 6s. 2d. Today was sent anonymously from Bath 5l., with the words "Jehovah Jireh." These words are very appropriate; for the money came after I had asked the Lord for some, and is required for our need tomorrow.

June 11. Saturday afternoon. As only 6s. 10d. had come in since the 9th for the Orphans, there remains no money in hand for Monday.--Saturday evening. The Lord has already sent a little towards the need of next week, as an earnest, that during the coming week also He will be mindful of us for this evening came in by sale of articles, 1l. 8s. 7d., and a little boy gave 3s. 7 1/4d.

June 12. There came in further today 7s. 6d.; anonymously 10s.; ditto 2l.; and with Ecclesiastes ix. 10, was given. 10s.

June 15. As since the 12th only 1l. 13s. 6d. had come in, there was now again no money in hand for the need of to-morrow. I gave myself therefore to prayer. Immediately after I had risen from my knees, I was told that some money had been put into the box at my house. I opened the box, and found it to be a sovereign.

June 16. The sovereign which yesterday had been put into the box at my house was not enough. On my morning walk I asked the Lord, therefore, for more means, and when I came home I found that 1l. 16s. had been sent for articles given for sale, There came in still further by sale of articles, 1l. 1s. 6d., and by a donation from Leeds, 2l. 10s. 3d.

June 17. 1l. 18s. 9d. came in today.

June 18. Having had to meet the expenses of the funeral of a dear Orphan boy, who, after having been two years in fellowship with the saints, and walked consistently, had fallen asleep, all means were now again gone, when an Irish lady sent this morning 10l., of which 8l. is to be used for the Orphans, and 2l. for my own personal necessities. Thus we are again supplied for the-present.

June 25. As, besides the 8l. which came in on the 18th, only 9l. 14s. 10 1/2d. had been received since, there was now not sufficient in hand for the expenses of the day; but the Lord, as usual, made it manifest, that He is mindful of our need, and that He hears our prayers. For there was sent today from Clapham a parcel, containing a frock, a pinafore, and 13s. 4d. Also, through the same donors, in the same parcel, were sent from Brighton, 8 frocks, 6 pinafores, 6 handkerchiefs, 3 chemises, 2 petticoats, and 10s. Likewise a Christian lady sent a sovereign; and 1s. 6d. came in by sale of Reports, and 1l. 18s. 0 1/2d. by sale of articles. Thus we were abundantly supplied for the need of today.

July 1. All our money was again spent, as only 8l. 15s. 4d. had come in since the 25th, when last evening an Orphan arrived from Barnstaple, with whom there was sent 2l. 5s. 10d. The Lord has repeatedly ordered it so, that when Orphans have been brought, money has been sent with them, whereby our present necessities have been supplied.--I add here, that we do not require any money to be sent with them, nor is there any interest required to get the children admitted, and much less is the Institution of a sectarian spirit, so that only persons of certain religious views could succeed in making application for the admission of Orphans; but without respect of persons, from all parts of the kingdom, so long as there is room, needy children, bereaved of both parents, may be admitted.--I received today still further 10l. And likewise, by six other donations, came in 1l. 10s. 2d. We are now again for a few days supplied.

July 6, On July 2nd came in 10s.; on the 3rd 2l. 2s. 9d.; on the 4th 1l. 18s.; on the 5th came in four donations from Hackney, amounting to 3l. 6s.; a donation of 2l. from Plymouth; a donation of 4s. from a brother in Bristol; by sale of Reports 5s. 3d.; anonymously was sent from Fairford 3l.; a Christian lady gave 1l., and the following articles were sent from Tottenham: a two-guinea piece, a quarter-guinea piece, a half doubloon, (a Portuguese gold coin), a gold coin of James I., and two gold chains. Likewise this evening came in with Ecclesiastes ix. 10, 3l. 1s. 6d., and 3s. 6d. by sale of stockings. By the donations of yesterday and today I am enabled to meet many needful expenses, such as ordering oatmeal from Scotland, buying peas, rice, Scotch barley, materials for boys' clothes, &c.

THIRD PART

July 9. On July 7, 8, 9, had only come in 3l. 11s., so that now today, Saturday, after I had supplied the matrons with what they needed for today and for tomorrow, all the money was again spent; yet we had been, by the good hand of the Lord, brought through another week, and nothing, that had been needed during the week, had been lacking.

July 11. Monday. Yesterday and today came in 3l. 9s. 6d. This money was quite enough for the need of today; and when now again, after this day's need had been met, scarcely any thing was left, the boxes in the Orphan-Houses were opened, which contained 2l. 3s. 4 1/2d.

July 12. 13s. 9d. came in today.

July 13. When our purse was now again empty, the Lord kindly sent 5l. this morning from Glasgow.

From July 13th to 19th the Lord sent in 22l. 5s. 10d., and on July 19th I left Bristol for a season, being able, through grace, to leave the work in His hands, and feeling assured, that He would provide while I was absent from Bristol; and truly the Lord did not suffer me to be disappointed. For during the time of my absence, from July 19th to Sept. 10th, whilst I was labouring at Barnstaple, and in the neighbourhood of Bideford, the Lord richly furnished us with means, though twice during that period we were quite poor.

From July 19th to Aug. 10th had come in, during my absence, 51l. 3s. 7 1/2d.; but now on Wednesday, Aug. 10th, all the money, except ONE PENNY, was spent in the three Orphan-Houses. Between 9 and 10 o'clock in the evening brother M. brought 7l. to the Boys'-Orphan-House. 5l. of this he had received from Q. Q., 1l. with Ecclesiastes ix. 10, and 1l. from a sister who had received this money from Weymouth. When the latter told brother M. that the money might be applied as most needed, he replied to her, that he would give it to the Orphans, as he believed them to be in need. When brother M. brought the money, he said, that when in prayer in the morning for the Orphans, who had been particularly laid on his heart, he felt assured, that we were in need. Thus this brother not knowing any thing about our circumstances, was led by God to help us with his intercessions.

The whole sum which came in from the 10th to the 26th was 25l. 5s. 3d. On the 26th of August there was now again need of a fresh manifestation of the loving care of our Heavenly Father, as on the coming day, being a Saturday, much was needed, and there were only a few pence in hand. And truly, the Lord did appear on our behalf; for this evening came in 10l. with Eccles. ix. 10.--Behold, you who do not know the Lord, what a precious thing it is, even for this life, to walk with God! Behold also you, dear brethren, who tremble to lean fully and solely upon. Him, that those who trust in Him, according to His word, shall not be confounded!

From Aug. 26th to Sept. 10th came in 22l. 6s. 8 1/2d.

Besides the 98l. 15s. 7d. which had come in, in money, during my absence, many articles of clothes, books, provisions, &c. were given for the benefit of the Orphans; but especially a great quantity of trinkets was sent, to be disposed of for the benefit of the Orphans. When I had all these precious spoils before me, which the power of the love of Jesus had won, I found there were no less in my possession than 31 brooches, 2 gold clasps, a pair of gold bracelets, 33 gold rings, a silver gilt vinaigrette, 16 pairs of gold earrings, 2 gold crosses, a gold chain, a gold thimble, 8 gold seals, a gold watch key, a gold watch, 3 lockets, 2 watch hooks, 2 ornamental ladies' combs, 3 ornamental gold hair pins, 2 silver cups, above 30 necklaces, and many other ornaments; also above 60 old silver coins. I cannot describe how great the joy is, which I have, when I see the Lord Jesus, by means of this Institution, bringing forth one needless article after the other, to be disposed of for the benefit of the Orphans.

From Sept. 10th to 28th the Lord supplied our need richly. There came in altogether during these 18 days 92l. 19s. 4d, Though so large a sum had come in, in so short a time, yet as our expenses also had been great, there was again this day, Sept. 28th, not enough to meet this day's need, when, A FEW MINUTES before I was called on for money, 2l. 10s. was sent from Birmingham.

Sept. 29. There came in by knitting 2s. 6d., and by two donations 7s. 6d. with these words: "J. W. from the Lord" 5s., and "From the Lord" 2s. 6d.

Sept. 30. There was again only 16s. 5 1/2d. left towards the necessities of today, when yesterday afternoon a donor left at my house a good silver watch, which, being disposed of for 6l., supplies us not only for today, but leaves something towards the need of tomorrow.

Oct 1. Yesterday afternoon. 1l. came in from Kensington, and this morning by sale of articles 2s. 6d., and 5s. was put into the box at my house. Thus we had, with what was left, something towards the necessities of this day, but not enough, as this is Saturday. As the Lord, however, had given me both yesterday and this morning prayer and faith with reference to the need, I was looking out for help, when at half past ten this morning a small parcel was anonymously left at my house, which contained a 5l. note, a gold chain, and an old 5s. piece, to be used for the Orphans. The Lord be praised who disposed the heart of the unknown donor at so seasonable an hour to send this donation! Half an hour, after I had received the little parcel, I was called upon for money, and was thus able to supply the need of today, and have something left towards the beginning of the week.--There came in still further today 4l. 1s.; for this afternoon a sister in the Lord sent two half sovereigns, which had been sent to her by two donors in Wales, and which she would not delay sending at once, "as it was Saturday." In the evening about eight o'clock an individual residing in the parish of St. Philip, Bristol, brought a sovereign for the Orphans, and after eight o'clock 2l. 1s. came in by the sale of articles: so that, whilst the day com-

THIRD PART

menced, without there being enough to meet its expenses, we received several pounds more than was needed.

Oct. 8. As since Oct. 2 there had come in by sale of the gold chain, the old 5s. piece, and donations, only the sum of 12l. 16s. 6d., there was (after I had sent yesterday morning the money which was requisite for the day), again only 1s. 6 1/2d. left, towards the need of today, being Saturday. But the Lord, in whom I had particularly again made my boast this morning before four German musicians, was mindful of our need; for, besides half a sovereign coming in from Hereford, the boxes in the Orphan-Houses were opened, in which there was found 2l. 3s. 6d. Thus we have already in the morning the greater part of what is needed for today, waiting upon the Lord for the rest.--Evening. This evening came in still further 1l. 5s. 2d., so that we have all that is needed for today.

Oct. 10. Yesterday were put into the chapel boxes three papers, one with Eccles. ix. 10, containing 1l., and two containing 1s. each. There came in also this morning by the knitting of the Orphan Boys 6s. 6d. Thus we have, with a little that was left on Saturday, all that is required for today, and 3s. 5d. over.

Oct. 11. The Lord has again kindly multiplied the 3s. 5d., which was left after the necessities of yesterday were met. A brother in the Lord from Bath called yesterday at one of the Orphan-Houses and gave 5l. as a donation, besides 8s. 3d. for reports. Also by a clergyman near Cirencester was sent 5s., and this morning came a post office order for 10s. from Crediton, and 6d, was given by a sister in Bristol. My dear Reader, pause and admire the hand of the Lord! Day after day He helps us! His help never fails, nor is it ever too late! We may be poor, very poor; but when the help is really needed, the Lord opens His bountiful hand and supplies our need! The help may come in a variety of ways, but it is certain! It may be that He allows us to wait long on Him, and pray very often, whilst He appears not to be mindful of us; yet in the end, in His own appointed and best time, the help comes. Dear Reader, if you know the Lord, and you have not a similar experience, be it known to you, that you may have the same in your sphere of labour or service, though you may not be called by the Lord to establish Orphan-Houses, or Day Schools, or Adult Schools, or Sunday Schools, or circulate Bibles and Tracts in an extensive way. Make but trial of this way, and you will see how truly precious it is to wait upon the Lord for every thing, even for the bread which perishes. Should you, dear Reader, not be reconciled with God through faith in the Lord Jesus, then you may know, that this precious privilege belongs to him who becomes a child of God by faith in the Lord Jesus, that he may come to his Heavenly Father for everything, and that his Father delights in giving him all he can need, while here in the world.

On. Oct. 12th came in 2l. 7s., and Oct. 13th 6s.

Oct. 15. Saturday. Yesterday arrived from Gloucestershire the following letter:--Oct. 13, 1842.

THE LORD'S DEALINGS WITH GEORGE MÜLLER

"My dear Brother,

As I have no doubt on my own mind, but the Orphans are in present need, the enclosed 5l. is sent by the constraining power of the Lord through me.

Yours affectionately,

*****"

The money came indeed in a time of need; for though we had about enough for yesterday's necessities, there was nothing for today's demands, which are 5l. 5s. There came in besides, yesterday afternoon, from a brother in. Bristol 1l., and from an individual in his employment 10s. Thus we could meet both yesterday's and to-day's need, and are brought to the close of another week. Evening. There came in still further this evening, by sale of articles 2l. 11s. 8d., from Ledbury 1s., and from two sisters in. Bristol 11s. Thus we have something towards the need of another week.

Oct. 19. Wednesday. As only 1l. 2s. had come in since Saturday evening, there was now again not sufficient money in hand for the need of today. I therefore opened an Orphan box in my house, in which I found two sovereigns. The Lord was pleased to send still further, in the course of the day, from the neighbourhood of Droitwich, 8s.; by profit from the sale of ladies' bags, made by a sister for the benefit of the Orphans, 10s.; by a donation 2l. 10s.; by Reports 1s. 3d.; and by another donation, from two ladies, three-pence. These ladies, sisters in the Lord, had it much in their hearts to give considerable sums, and had given in former times gold chains, a brilliant, and many other valuable articles for the benefit of the Orphans, besides money; but now, having no means, through particular family circumstances, they were not ashamed to offer these three-pence. I doubt not that I have their prayers, and I value them more than gold; and I know, that if they had gold for the Orphans, they would give that also. The child of God ought to consider that word for his comfort: "If there be first a willing mind, it is accepted, according to that a man hath, and not according to that he hath not." 2 Cor. viii. 12.

On October 21st came in 1l. 9s. 8 1/2d.

Oct. 24. Monday. The necessities of the 22nd, being Saturday, called for all the money that was left, about 3l. Not one farthing was then remaining in my hands. And now observe, dear Reader, how the Lord helped, and praise Him with me, that He always causes the stream to flow again, when there is need. On the same day on which the last money was given out, the day before yesterday, there was handed over to me 1l. 2s. 9d. for sale of articles. Yesterday I received through a sister, from an Indian gentleman and lady, two sovereigns, and one from herself, being the produce of a piece of work, which she had done for the benefit of the Orphans. A poor brother also gave me 3s. Today I received the following anonymous note:--Oct. 22, 1842.

THIRD PART

"Beloved Brother,

The enclosed 35l. was given to the Lord some time since. It was received for service done according to Eph. vi. 7; and believing that laying up treasures for myself upon earth (having enough for my own necessities without it) would be disobedience to Matthew vi. 19, I put it into your hands. You will kindly dispose of it as the Lord may direct you.

Yours in the Lord Jesus.

You will oblige me by receiving 10l. of the enclosed for your own need, or that of your family."

This money came indeed most seasonably; for though, by the donations of yesterday, today's need had been supplied, nevertheless as about 100 yards of flannel and materials for the boys' clothes are needed, and as many other expenses require to be met, besides the regular daily expenses; we are thus in some measure provided. Half of this money I took for the Orphans and half for the other objects, as they also were in great need. There was likewise yesterday put anonymously into the boxes at Bethesda 1s. and 1l. Still further came in, through the boxes in the Orphan-Houses, 6s. 5 1/2d., from a poor widow 2s. 6d., from another individual 1l., in eight donations through a brother 10s. 3d., and a box of worn clothes.

Oct. 29. The need of today is 5l. 5s. We should not have had enough, humanly speaking, had there not been sent yesterday afternoon 5l. from Hull, as on the 26th and 28th only 3l. 5s. 5d. had come in.; so that there was only 3l. 0s. 6 1/2d. in hand, when this 5l. came. There came in still further today 1l. 12s. 4d. How kindly does the Lord, as it were, day by day inspect our stores! He, in general, does not supply our need for many months at once; in order both that He Himself may often have the joy of our calling upon Him for the supplies we need; and that He may give unto us the joy of obtaining our supplies day by day in answer to prayer; and that thus also other children of God might be encouraged, to wait upon Him for all they may need.

On Oct. 30 was given 11s.

Nov. 1. There would have been again nothing in hand, for the need of this day, had not the Lord kindly sent in yesterday afternoon three donations of 1l., 2l., and 2s. Besides this there came in by sale of stockings 3s. 7d.

Nov. 2. After the demands of yesterday had been met, there remained only 16s. 9 1/2d. in hand, I therefore again besought the Lord, that He would be pleased to send in fresh supplies. Accordingly, about one o'clock, a brother left a note at my house, containing a cheque for 7l., of which 1l. was for the Orphans, 1l. for the other objects, and 5l. for my own necessities. Between two and three o'clock I met another brother in my walk in Redland Fields, who gave me a sovereign for the Orphans; and at four o'clock a sister sent a sovereign for the Orphans. Thus our need for today is supplied and something left.

Nov. 7. Monday. Since the afternoon of the 2nd I received 8l. 9s. 10d. After the necessities of Saturday, the 6th, had been supplied, amounting to between 3l. and 4l., there was once more nothing at all left in my hands, which led me afresh to the Lord in prayer. On the same evening I received, as the answer to my prayers, from a sister 10s., and by sale of articles 1l. 16s. 10d., and this morning there came in still further, by several donations, 2l. 15s. 7 1/2d.

Nov. 9. Again all our money was spent after the expenses of today had been met, when this evening there came in 4l. 1s. by sale of articles, 7s. 9d. by sale of Reports, and 3d. as a donation. A parcel was also given to me this evening, sent by two sisters in the Lord, in Bath, containing the following articles: 5 gold rings, a locket, a gold seal, 15 brooches, a pair of ear-rings, a gold pin, a small telescope, an ornamental comb, 4 pairs of clasps, 2 head brooches, some ornaments of mock pearls, 9 necklaces, 11 bracelets, 4 waist buckles, and a few other articles.

Nov. 15, Yesterday came in from W. D. B. 1l. 1s., from a sister 2s., and through an Orphan box 4s. This 1l. 7s. was all there was in hand, and with out it we should not have been able to provide for the need of today.

Nov. 16. After the need of yesterday had been provided for, and I now again had nothing in hand, I received for Reports 1s., and from a believing clergyman 1l.-- When, this morning, after I had been asking the Lord for means, the post brought none, I fell again on my knees, further beseeching Him to supply me with fresh means, as for several days little had come in. I especially also told Him, that, though the post was now out, yet He could in various ways send help. It was ONLY A FEW MINUTES AFTER, when brother C. B. brought me 1l. 3s. which just then had been given to him for the Orphans. About an hour afterwards two brethren called on me, the one from Wiltshire, the other from Essex, who stayed with me some time, and on leaving gave me 2l. 10s. for the Orphans. In the evening I saw still further that the Lord had not only not disregarded my prayers in the morning, but also that He was not confined to sending means by the post. A sister called on me, and brought me, for several purposes, twelve sovereigns, of which six are to be applied for the benefit of the Orphans. This was not all. A brother brought me 9 silver forks and a silver butter knife, the produce of which I might use as most needed. This also, therefore, might have been applied for the Orphans, but I put it to the funds for the other objects as being more in need. In the evening was still further given to me with Eccles. ix. 10, 4s., and as the profit from the sale of ladies' baskets, 1l.; so that a rich supply has been received this day from the hand of our loving Father.

Nov. 20. When we were now again in very great need on account of means for the other objects, there came in this day from a sister in the Lord, a servant in Dor-

THIRD PART

setshire, 10l., which sum being left at my disposal, to use in any way I thought best, I took it for the School-Bible-Missionary and Tract-Fund.

Nov. 26. Saturday. Only 7l. 16s. 11 1/2d. had come in since the 16th for the Orphans. The day began without any thing in hand. In the course of the morning came in by sale of stockings, 6s. 4d., and through the box at the Boys'-Orphan-House 8d. At two o'clock in the afternoon a believing clergyman sent to two of the labourers in the work 2 sovereigns, of which the one was able to give half the sovereign, and the other the whole sovereign. By this means we were supplied with what was needed today.

Nov. 28. Monday. Yesterday came in from Cheltenham 5s.; with Eccles. ix. 10, 5s.; anonymously was left at the Girls'-Orphan-House a paper, containing the letters E.V. with a crown piece; and anonymously was put into the boxes at Bethesda 1s. There was sent also from Bath, a coral necklace and a gold necklace clasp. By these donations we were supplied today.

Nov. 29. This morning I took a shilling out of an Orphan-box at my house, which was all we had wherewith to commence the day. JUST AT THE MOMENT when the letter bag was sent to me from the Orphan-Houses, with the statement of what would be required for this day, I received a post-office order from Barnstaple for 1l. Thus the Lord, in His faithful love, has sent a little, for which I had been waiting upon Him. Through His grace my heart is looking out for more, for I am sure He will never forsake us.

Nov. 30. Nothing at all has come in since yesterday. But as one of the labourers was able to give 17s., we were supplied with bread and a few other little things, which were needed.

Dec. 1. Nothing had come in, except 5s. for needlework of the Orphans. The labourers had nothing to give of their own, except one of them 1s. 6d.; yet this little supplied the absolute need, which was only milk. We were unable to take in the usual quantity of bread. (The bread is eaten by the children on the third day after it is baked. If we are unable to take in the usual daily quantity of bread, for want of means, we afterwards seek to procure stale bread.) Should it be said that the not taking in the usual quantity of bread would at once prove to the bakers that we are poor; my reply is, that that does not follow, because bread has often been sent as a present, as may be seen in the list of articles, given for the Orphans, at the end of the printed Reports. But perhaps it may be stated: Why do you not take the bread on credit? What does it matter, whether you pay immediately for it, or at the end of the month, or the quarter, or the half-year? Seeing that the Orphan-Houses are the work of the Lord, may you not trust in Him, that He will supply you with means, to pay the bills which you contract with the butcher, baker, grocer, &c., as the things which you purchase are needful? My reply is this: 1, If the work in which we are engaged is indeed the work of God, then He, whose work it is, is surely able and willing to provide the means for it. 2, But not only so, He will also provide the means at the time when they are needed. I do not mean that He will provide them, when we think that they are needed; but yet, that, when there is real need, such as the necessaries of life being required, He will give them; and on the same ground on which we suppose we do trust in God to help us to pay the debt which we now contract, we may and ought to trust in the Lord to supply us with what we require at present, so that there may be no need for going in debt. 3, It is true, I might have goods on credit, and to a very considerable amount; but, then, the result would be, that the next time we were again in straits, the mind would involuntarily be turned to further credit which I might have, instead of being turned to the Lord, and thus faith, which is kept up and strengthened only by being EXERCISED, would become weaker and weaker, till at last, according to all human probability, I should find myself deeply in debt, and have no prospect of getting out of it. 4, Faith has to do with the word of God,--rests upon the written word of God; but there is no promise that He will pay our debts,--the word says rather: "Owe no man any thing;" whilst there is the promise given to His children.: "I will never leave thee, nor forsake thee," and "Whosoever believeth on. Him shall not be confounded." On this account we could not say upon the ground of the Holy Scriptures: Why do you not trust in God that He will supply you with means to pay your debts, which you contract in His service for the necessaries of the Orphans? 5, The last reason why we do not take goods on credit is this: The chief and primary object of the work was not the temporal welfare of the children, nor even their spiritual welfare (blessed and glorious as it is, and much as, through grace, we seek after it and pray for it); but the first and primary object of the work was: To show before the whole world and the whole church of Christ, that even in these last evil days the living God is ready to prove Himself as the living God, by being ever willing to help, succour, comfort, and answer the prayers of those who trust in Him: so that we need not go away from Him to our fellow-men, or to the ways of the world, seeing that He is both able and willing to supply us with all we can need in His service. From the beginning, when God put this service into my heart, I had anticipated trials and straits; but knowing, as I did, the heart of God, through the experience of several years previously, I also knew that He would listen to the prayers of His child who trusts in Him, and that He would not leave him in the hour of need, but listen to his prayers, and deliver him out of the difficulty, and that then, this being made known in print for the benefit of both believers and unbelievers, others would be led to trust in the Lord. Thus it has now been for more than nine years (i.e. in. 1845, when the third part was first published). These accounts have been greatly owned by the Lord. We discern, therefore, more and more clearly, that it is for the church's benefit that we are put into these straits; and if, therefore, in the hour of need, we were to take goods on credit, the first and primary object of the work would be completely frustrated, and no heart would be further strengthened to trust in God, nor would there be any longer that manifestation of the special and particular providence of God, which has hitherto been so abundantly shown through this work, even in the eyes of unbelievers, whereby they have been led to see that there is, after all, reality in the things of God, and many, through these printed accounts, have been truly converted. For these reasons, then, we consider it our precious privilege, as heretofore, to continue to wait upon the Lord only, instead of taking goods on credit, or borrowing money from some kind friends, when we are in need. Nay, we purpose, as God shall give us grace, to look to Him only, though morning after morning we should have nothing in hand for the work--yea, though from meal to meal we should have to look to Him; being fully assured that He, who is now (1845) in the tenth year feeding these many Orphans, and who has never suffered them to want, and that He who is now (1845) in the twelfth year carrying on the other parts of the work, without any branch of it having had to be stopped for want of means, will do so for the future also. And here I do desire, in the deep consciousness of my natural helplessness and dependence upon the Lord, to confess that through the grace of God my soul has been in peace, though day after day we have had to wait for our daily provisions upon the Lord; yea, though even from meal to meal we have been required to do this.--I now go on with extracts from my journal.

Dec. 2, 1842. By the produce of six old silver coins, which I received last evening, and by 9s. 6d. which came in besides, we were able to meet the expenses of today; but now there were before us the heavy expenses of tomorrow, Saturday, which I knew would be particularly great, and there was nothing at all in hand to meet them. In this our need there came in this evening from Lutterworth and its neighbourhood two donations, one of 5l., and the other of 1l. The 1l. was for the Orphans, and the 5l. was left to my disposal, as it might be most needed. I took of it 3l. 12s. 3d. for the Orphans, and 1l. 7s. 9d. for the Day Schools. This afternoon a gentleman passed the Girls'-Orphan-House. The house door being opened, he rolled half a crown into the house. This half crown came in when there was nothing at all in hand. There came in also by knitting of the Infants 6d., by knitting of the Boys 6d., from a poor believing widow 6d., and by sale of a Report 3d. Thus we have 4l. 15s. for the necessities of the Orphans tomorrow (the other little sums have been spent today).

Dec. 5. Monday. On Saturday, Dec. 3, 10s. came in from Brighton., and yesterday 1l. with Eccles. ix. 10, and by a sister from Nailsworth 10s. Also by sale of articles 11s, 6d. Thus we had 2l. 11s. 6d., which was nearly but not quite enough for the necessities of today, as it would be desirable to have a few shillings more. I went, therefore, to see whether there was any money in the two boxes at my house, and I found a sovereign. Thus we had more than sufficient for the need of today, which is 3l. This evening I received 1l. 10s. for articles which had been sold.

Dec. 8. A few little donations which came in on the 6th, together with the little there was in hand, supplied our need on the 7th. On the 6th a shilling was anonymously left on the mantel piece in the Infant-Orphan-House; and one of the Orphans, formerly under our care, but now in service, gave 2s. 6d. These two small donations were most seasonable towards the supply of our need on the 7th. Now this day commenced without our having anything in hand. Just while the Orphan-Boy, who had been sent to my house for money, was waiting, I received from the neighbourhood of Droitwich 10s. This, with 3s. 9d. for Reports, and 6d. for knitting of the Infant-Orphans, and 4s. 6d. which one of the labourers was able to give of his own, helped us through this day.

Dec. 9. There was again nothing at all in hand this morning to meet the expenses of the day. A little after ten o'clock an Orphan arrived from Northam, with whom there was sent for my own personal necessities 10s., and 2l. 2s. 4d. besides. As about this latter sum nothing had been written, I put it to the Orphan-Fund, whereby we are supplied for today, and have a little left towards the need of tomorrow. There was also 6d. in the boxes at my house.

Dec. 10. 1l. was left, after the need of yesterday had been met. This morning, Saturday, when I knew that again several pounds would be needed, and I had therefore been waiting on the Lord, I received about nine o'clock 1l. from a brother, who, on his return from Spain to Devonshire, had been intrusted with it for the Orphans, by a sister in the Lord who lives in London. A few minutes after I had received this sovereign, I had to pay on behalf of one of the apprentices 2l., which took exactly all the money I had, so that there was still nothing to meet the ordinary housekeeping expenses of this day, which I knew would be at least 3l. I gave myself therefore still further to prayer, being fully assured, by grace, that my loving faithful Father would this day also provide me His child with everything I needed. Scarcely was I risen from my knees, when I received a bank post bill from Torquay for 10l.; of which 2l. is intended by the kind donor for my own temporal necessities, and 8l. for the Orphans, so that we have more than enough for this day.--There came in still further this evening, in five small donations, 6s. 10d., by needlework 6s., and by sale of articles 1l. 6s. 6d.

Dec. 11. Anonymously put into the box at Bethesda, 2s. 6d., and from C. M. W. 1l.

Dec. 14. There was now again only ONE PENNY in my hands this morning. About eleven o'clock I received a note, enclosing 2s. and 10s. The brother who kindly brought the note which contained the money, gave at the same time 2s. 6d. for the Orphans. As only 16s. was needed to purchase the necessary provisions for this day, and one of the labourers was able to add 1s. 5d. of his own, we were supplied.

Dec. 15. Only 2s. 3d., the contents of an Orphan-box, 1l. by sale of stockings, and 2s. 1 1/2d. from the boxes in the Orphan-Houses, have come in. This, with 5s. which one of the labourers was able to give, supplied the need of today.

Dec. 16. Nothing has come in. 3s. 5d., which one of the labourers was able to give, was all we had. At six o'clock this evening, our need being now very great, not only with reference to the Orphan-Houses, but also the Day Schools, &c., I gave myself with two of the labourers to prayer. There needed some money to come in before eight o'clock tomorrow morning, as there was none to take in milk for breakfast (the children have oatmeal porridge with milk for breakfast), to say nothing about the many other demands of tomorrow, being Saturday. Our hearts were at peace, while asking the Lord, and assured that our Father would supply our need. WE HAD SCARCELY RISEN FROM OUR KNEES, when I received a letter containing a sovereign for the Orphans, half of which was from a young East India officer, and the other half the produce of the sale of a piece of work, which the sister, who sent the money, had made for the benefit of the Orphans. She wrote: "I love to send these little gifts. They so often come in season." Truly, thus it was at this time.-- About five minutes later I received from a brother the promise of 50l. for the Orphans, to be given during the next week; and a quarter of an hour after that, about seven o'clock, a brother gave me a sovereign, which an Irish sister in the Lord had left this day, on her departure for Dublin, for the benefit of the Orphans. How sweet and precious to see thus so manifestly the willingness of the Lord to answer the prayers of His needy children!

Dec. 17. This morning we three again waited unitedly upon the Lord, as there was not enough for the necessities of the Orphan-Houses for this day. Moreover, the teachers in the Day Schools need supplies. Between ten and eleven o'clock I received by the first delivery a letter, containing half a sovereign with these words: "The young lions do lack and suffer hunger; but they that seek the Lord shall not want any good thing. Dec. 16, 1842." It was not stated whether this money was for my own personal need, or for the Orphans, or any other object. I took it for the Orphans.-- Thus we had enough, except about 2s. 6d., to provide all that was needed for today and tomorrow. Between seven and eight o'clock this evening, a brother sent half a crown to the Boys'-Orphan-House, stating that he had been thinking much about the Orphans in the course of this day, but that he had not had time to send this money sooner. Thus, by the kindness of the Lord, we have the exact sum which is required, and are again brought to the close of another week.--Between nine and ten o'clock this evening came in still further, by the sale of articles, 2l. 7s. Thus the Lord has not only helped us to the close of the week, but given us also a little with which to begin another week.

Dec. 19. Yesterday came in by the profit of the sale of ladies' bags 1l., and in two donations 2l. By this 5l. 7s. which came in since Saturday evening, we should have had enough for the ordinary household expenses of today; but as our stores of oatmeal, rice, peas, and Scotch barley, are either entirely or nearly exhausted, and as some calico for shirts and lining, besides many other little articles are needed, and as especially the teachers in the Day Schools are greatly in need of pecuniary supplies, I had been especially entreating the Lord, that He would be pleased to send us larger supplies. I rose from my knees about half-past ten this morning, and about a quarter to eleven I received a let letter from A. B. with an order for 100l., to be used as most needed in the work. Of this sum I took for the Orphans only 25l., and for the other funds 75l. (in consideration of 50l. having been promised to be paid this week for the Orphans); and thus we are in every way again most seasonably helped. "Bless the Lord, O my soul, and forget not all His benefits!"--There came in still further by three donations 3l. 10s.

On Dec. 20 and 21 there came in 2l. 15s. 3d. for the Orphans.

Dec. 22. Though there had come in above 36l. for the Orphans, during the last four days, yet as our stores needed to be replenished, and there had been several other expenses to be met, we were again today in need of farther supplies, when I received the 50l. for the Orphans, which had been promised during the last week. Thus I was able also to supply the labourers in the Orphan-Houses with some money for their own personal need.

REVIEW OF THE YEAR 1842.

I. As to the church.

68 brethren and sisters brother Craik and I found in communion, when we came to Bristol.

848 have been admitted into communion since we came to Bristol.

916 would be, therefore, the total number of those in fellowship with us, had there been no changes.

But

131 have left Bristol.

59 have left us, but are still in Bristol.

51 are under church discipline.

74 have fallen asleep.

315 are therefore to be deducted from 916, so that there are only 601 at present in communion.

73 have been added during the past year, of whom 27 have been brought to the knowledge of the Lord among us.

II. As to the supply of my temporal necessities:

THIRD PART

1. The Lord has been pleased to send me from the saints among whom I labour in Bristol, in provisions, clothes, etc. worth to us at least L10 0s. 0d.

2. In anonymous offerings in money, put up in paper, and directed to me, and put into the boxes for the poor saints or the rent, at the meeting places L113 1s. 8d.

3. In presents in money, from saints in Bristol, not given anonymously L47 8s. 1s.

4. In provisions and clothes, from saints not residing in Bristol, worth to us at least L10 0s. 0d.

5. In money from saints not residing in Bristol L149 6s. 3d.

Altogether L329 16s. 0d.

Jan. 21, 1843. From Dec. 22 up to this day the Lord was pleased to send in the donations for the Orphans so, that there was always some money received, before all was expended.--The 50l. which was given to me on Dec. 22, and between 50l. and 60l. which had come in since, was now today, Jan. 21, 1843, all spent, after the expenses of today, Saturday, had been met, when there was given to me this evening a silver cup, a gold seal, a broken gold seal, a gold buckle, a watch hook, and a brooch. There came in also by sale of articles 2s. 6d., and by a donation 10s.

Jan. 23. Yesterday came in. 9s. and today 2l. 13s.

Jan. 24. Today came in 5l. 7s. 7d.

Jan. 25. This day I received 3l. 3s. 2 1/2d.

Jan. 28. The last money had been again paid out yesterday morning, when I received 5l. last evening with Eccles. ix. 10. This morning was sent to me from Clapham, 2l. 8s. Thus we were able to meet the expenses of today, which were 4l. 5s.

Feb. 3. Since Jan. 28 there had come in 13l. 5s. 1d., which had fully supplied all our need; but now all was again spent, after this day's expenses had been met, on account of which I gave myself to prayer with my wife this morning. This evening I received in answer to it 7s. by sale of articles.

Feb. 4. This morning a brother gave to me 1l. Thus we have 1l. 7s.; but as this is not nearly enough for today, we have given ourselves still further to prayer, and are now looking for supplies. While I am writing this, the Orphan has brought the letter bag to fetch 2l. 15s., which is the need of today; I am therefore looking out for help to make up this sum --I opened the boxes in my house, in which I found 3s. 6d.

With this 1l. 10s. 6d. I had to send off the boy, waiting for further supplies.--This afternoon, about five, came in by sale of articles 1l. 4s. 7d. Thus we had enough, and one penny more than was needed, and we are brought to the close of another week. O Lord, how can Thy servant sufficiently praise Thee for condescending so to listen to his requests! His soul is amazed at Thy condescension, and yet, not amazed when he considers that Thou doest it for the sake of Thy dear Son, in whom Thou dost continually look upon Thy servant!--There came in still further this evening 2s. 6d.

Feb. 6. Yesterday was intrusted to me altogether for the Orphans 2l. 17s. 6d., in eight different donations. Thus I was able to send the supplies which were needed this day in the Orphan-Houses, which required all that had come in yesterday. When now there was again nothing at all in hand, I received, about one o'clock 10l., with the following lines: "From the widow to the Orphans, a thank-offering to Him who careth for them both." Through the same donor I received at the same time from a lady and gentleman 2l. In the evening came in further 10s., by the profit of the sale of ladies' bags, and 2s. 6d. as a donation.

Feb. 10. As during the last three days only 1l. 6s. had come in., all our money was now again expended, and nothing in hand towards the supplies of tomorrow, Saturday, when I received this afternoon 10s., being the profit of the sale of ladies' bags. This evening came in still further with Eccles. ix. 10, 1l., by sale of articles 2s., and from a brother 2s.

Feb. 11. By what came in yesterday afternoon and evening, we had 1l. 14s. towards the expenses of this day. But, as this was not enough, I asked the Lord still further for help, and, behold, this morning's post brought me a post-office-order for 2l. from Stafford, of which 1l. 7s. 6d. is for the Orphans. Thus we have 3l. 1s. 6d., which is quite enough for this day.

Admire with me, my dear Reader, if you know the Lord, His seasonable help. Why does this post-office-order not come a few days sooner or later? Because the Lord would help us by means of it, and therefore influences the donor just then, and not sooner nor later, to send it. Surely, all who know the Lord, and who have no interest in disowning it, cannot but see His hand in a remarkable manner in this work.-- Nor will the godly and simple minded reader say:--"There is no difference between this way of proceeding, on the one hand, and going from individual to individual, asking them for means, on the other hand; for the writing of the Reports is just the same thing." My dear Reader, there is a great difference. Suppose, that we are in need. Suppose, that our poverty lasts for some weeks or even some months together. Is there not, in that case, a difference between asking the Lord only from day to day, without speaking to any human being not connected directly with the work about our poverty, on the one hand: and writing letters or making personal application to benevolent individuals for assistance, on the other hand? Truly, there is a great difference between these two modes. I do not mean to say that it would be acting against the precepts of the Lord to seek for help in His work by personal and individual application to believers, (though it would be in direct opposition to His will to

THIRD PART

apply to unbelievers, 2 Cor. vi. 14-18); but I act in the way in which I do for the benefit of the Church at large, cheerfully bearing the trials, and sometimes the deep trials connected with this life of faith (which however brings along with it also its precious joys), if by any means a part at least of my fellow believers might be led to see the reality of dealing with God only, and that there is such a thing as the child of God having power with God by prayer and faith. That the Lord should use for so glorious a service one so vile, so unfaithful, so altogether unworthy of the least notice as I am, I can only ascribe to the riches of His condescending grace, in which He takes up the most unlikely instruments, that the honour maybe manifestly His. I add only one word more: Should Satan seek to whisper into your ears: Perhaps the matter is made known after all, when there is need (as it has been once said about me at a public meeting in a large town, that when we were in want I prayed publicly that the Lord would send help for the Orphans, which is entirely false); I say, should it be said, that I took care that our wants were made known, I reply: Whom did I ask for any thing these many years since the work has been going on? To whom did I make known our wants, except to those who are closely connected with the work?--Nay, so far from wishing to make known our need, for the purpose of influencing benevolent persons to contribute to the necessities of the Institution under my care, I have even refused to let our circumstances be known, after having been asked about them, when on simply saying that we were in need, I might have had considerable sums. Some instances of this have been given in the former part of this Narrative. In such cases I refused, in order that the hand of God only might be manifest; for that, and not the money, nor even the ability of continuing to carry on the work, is my especial aim. And such self-possession has the Lord given me, that at the times of the deepest poverty, (whilst there was nothing at all in hand, and whilst we had even from meal to meal to wait upon the Lord for the necessities of more than 100 persons), when a donation of 5l. or 10l. or more has been given to me, the donors could not have read in my countenance whether we had much or nothing at all in hand. But enough of this. I have made these few remarks, beloved Reader, lest by any means you should lose the blessing which might come to your soul through reading the account of the Lord's faithfulness and readiness to hear the prayers of His children.

Feb. 13. Monday. After having paid out on Saturday all there was in hand, though having quite enough for that day, we had now again to look to the Lord for means, as we generally need several pounds on Mondays. At this time also our faithful Lord did not disappoint us. For there came in late on Saturday, by the sale of articles given for sale, 1l. 8s. 11d., and by sale of stockings, knitted by the boys, 5s. I received also since then by the profit of the sale of ladies' bags 10s., by the boxes in my house 1s. 9d., and by two donations 6s. There was also yesterday put into the chapel boxes, half-a-crown with these words: "Trust in the Lord, and wait patiently for Him." Thus we had 2l. 14s. 2d., which was enough for the need of this day.

Feb. 14. I have received nothing since yesterday morning. Nothing therefore was in hand when money was sent for, except 1s. 6d., which was sent up from the Orphan-Houses, by the messenger who came for this day's supplies, and which had been received yesterday at the Infant-Orphan-House. I opened the boxes at my house, in which I found 1s. WHILE THE BOY WAS WAITING FOR THE MONEY, the sister who sells the articles which are given to be sold for the benefit of the Orphans, and who knows nothing about our present need, came and brought 12s. for some things which she had sold. With this 14s. 6d. we are able to supply the need of today, as nothing but some bread and milk require to be purchased.

Feb. 15. 2l. 14s. came in from the neighbourhood of Rotherham, besides 1s. 9d. Thus we had enough for this day.

Feb. 16. Yesterday afternoon I received 9s. from two poor sisters at Portsmouth. This, with 9d., which was left of the money which I received yesterday, after the day's need had been met, was all I had at the commencement of this day. In the course of the morning was sent by a lady of Ashton, 10s. more. Thus we had 19s. 9d., which sufficed for this day.

Feb. 17. Only 2s. 6d. had come in as a donation, and 2s. 4d. by knitting. This 4s. 10d. was all I could send, hoping in the Lord for more. The information I had from the Boys'-Orphan-House was, that the 4s. 10d. supplied the matrons with all that was absolutely needful for today. This evening at nine o'clock I received from sister E. Ch. 8s. 9d. for Reports. This is a most precious help, as without it there would be no means to take in the milk tomorrow morning.

Feb. 18. This morning between seven and eight o'clock I took the money which came in last night, to the Orphan-Houses, so that we were supplied for the breakfast. We had now to look to the Lord for several pounds, to meet the demands of this day, being Saturday. Between 10 and 11 o'clock I again with my wife besought the Lord, entreating Him, that He would be pleased to help us, when a FEW MINUTES AFTER, in this our great need, I received by the first delivery a letter from Barnstaple, containing 5l. for the Orphans. How truly precious, to see thus so manifestly the hand of God day by day stretched out on our behalf!

Feb. 20. Monday. Most seasonable as the help had been, which the Lord so kindly had sent on Saturday morning, and fully as it had supplied our need for that day; yet there was nothing left, after all the expenses had been met, so that we had even on Saturday still further to wait upon the Lord for fresh supplies for this day. Now at this time likewise the Lord has appeared on our behalf. About nine o'clock on Saturday evening arrived by post a small parcel from Yorkshire, which contained 6 pitcher purses, 2 night caps, a watchguard, and 6l. 1s. 4d. Of this money 5l. is to be applied for Missionary purposes, 1s. 4d. for the Orphans, and 1l. as it may be needed. This 1l. I took therefore for the Orphans.

--Yesterday morning I received as a widow's mite 1l. for the Orphans; and into the chapel boxes was put 10s. with Eccles. ix. 10, and also half-a-crown anonymously. Thus the Lord has been pleased to send us altogether 2l. 13s., whereby we are able to meet this day's expenses.

THIRD PART

Feb. 21. We were comfortably helped through yesterday, but having provided for all the demands, there was again nothing left in my hands for today. How kind therefore of the Lord to incline the heart of the same brother, who had given me 50l. a few weeks since, to intrust me with 1l. 2s. 6d. more last night, about nine o'clock! By this donation our need for today is supplied.

Feb. 22. Only 3s. 9d. came in yesterday by sale of Reports. When this morning the letter bag was sent from the Orphan-Houses for supplies, I found a note in it, containing this: "For today there is no need of mentioning any sum, as we can make that do, which the Lord may please to send." The 3s. 9d. was all I had to send, waiting upon the Lord for more--There came in further in the course of the morning by sale of stockings 3s., and by sale of other articles, given for that purpose, 2s. 6d. Our need also led us to open the boxes in the Orphan-Houses, in which we found 11s. 6d. Thus we had a altogether, 1l. 0s. 9d., whereby we were helped through this day.

Feb. 23. Last evening I received from Bath a small parcel, containing a small telescope, a set of mother-o'-pearl counters, 7 silver buckles, and a broken silver brooch. This morning the bag was brought for money, but I had nothing in hand. WHILST THE BOY WHO BROUGHT THE LETTER BAG WAS WAITING, to receive the answer, the sister who disposes of the articles which are given for sale, (and who was no more acquainted with the state of our funds than any other person), brought 11s. 4d. With this we began the day, again trusting in the Lord for further help.

Feb. 24. Nothing more came in, in the course of yesterday morning; but a little after four o'clock I received a letter from Jersey, containing a post-office-order for 1l. for the Orphans. The donor writes thus: "Herewith you will find a post-office-order for 1l., being this year's subscription. I had a desire to defer it to the 1st of June; but owing to my mind having been deeply worked on the present day, that this was the acceptable time, I make no scruple of availing myself of this evening's post, which I hope will be acceptable." Jersey, 20 Feb. 1843--How manifest is the hand of the Lord in this matter! He stirs up this donor, who lives at such a distance, to remember our need, whose money indeed came in a most acceptable time.--Thus we were again helped for yesterday. A few minutes after having received the 1l. from Jersey, a brother near Bruton sent me 15s. The money, given by this donor, being always left entirely to my disposal, I took this 15s. towards the need of the Orphans for today. This morning's post brought me half-a-sovereign from London. The letter contained only these words: "London, Feb. 22, 1843. Psalm xxvii. 14." I put this half-sovereign to the Orphan-Fund. There came in also by knitting 1s. 4d., and through the boxes in my house 6 1/2d. Thus we had for the need of this day again, by the good hand of our Lord upon us, 1l. 6s. 10 1/2d.

Feb. 25. Saturday. Yesterday afternoon and evening 12s. 8d. came in by knitting, and 1s. 9d. besides. This was all we had wherewith to begin the day. There came in still further in the course of today: by the boxes in the Orphan-Houses 5d., by knitting 7s. 8d., by a donation 1s., by sale of Reports 4s., by sale of an article, given for that purpose, 10s., and one of the labourers gave 6s. Thus the Lord gave us again 2l. 5s. 6d. for today's need, and we are helped to the close of another week.--As a fresh proof, that our loving Father is still mindful of us, we received this evening a parcel and a box from Plymouth: the former contained a musical box and a piece of worsted work, the latter 10 china ornaments: all to be sold for the benefit of the Orphans.

Feb. 27. Monday. Nothing at all has come in since Saturday. When therefore this day began, we had no means to provide what was needed. My comfort, however, was, that our Father knew that we were needy, and that kept me at this time also in peace. Between 10 and 11 o'clock this morning I received 1l. 10s. from Guernsey. The brother, who sent the money, writes, that he had delayed in sending it, and hoped that "this was the Lord's time," which indeed it is, for we are thus supplied for this day.

Feb. 28. Yesterday afternoon. 3s. were put into the box in my room, which our need brought out, as again this day began without our having anything in hand. I received still further to day from a brother at Crediton. 2l., being the produce of an Orphan-box in his house.--This evening I was at a Scripture-Reading-Meeting, at a brother's house. On leaving I found half-a-crown in one of my gloves, evidently put there on purpose, which I put to the Orphan-Fund, and it was immediately taken to the Orphan-Houses. Thus we were helped through this day also, but have nothing in hand towards tomorrow. There came in also for knitting 2s. 11d. Thus we had 2l. 8s. 5d. for this day.

March 1. There came in this morning by sale of some articles 1l. 5s. About dinner time a clergyman, who had had one of my Narratives lent to him by one of the labourers in the Orphan-Houses, returned it with 1l. 10s. for the Orphans, from himself and his two sisters. Thus we were again provided with all we needed for today.--This evening the Lord helped still further. I received with Eccles. ix. 10, 3l. From sister M. B. came in 1l., by knitting of the Infant-Orphans 3s. 6d., and by two donations 6s.

March 2. This day the Lord has again looked upon us in His faithful love, and sent us help, whereby I am enabled to replenish our stores with rice, peas, and Scotch barley, and am also able to put by the rent. There was found in the boxes in the Orphan-Houses 2l. 3s. 7d., which had been put in by some visitors, who saw the Orphan-Houses yesterday afternoon. There were also given to me 63 old silver coins, the greater part of them old English coins, the others old Spanish and French coins, also one crown piece current. There came in also by sale of articles and donations, besides the money for the silver coins, 16s. 10d. Thus the Lord has dealt bountifully with us these two days, after many days of poverty.

March 6. Monday. The last money had been given out last Saturday, and only 6d. had come in yesterday, whilst our need for today, I knew, would be about 2l. About a quarter of am hour before I was called on for money, I received from a

THIRD PART

brother at Plymouth a post-office-order for 2l. 11s. 6d., and by the same post, anonymously, a French cambric handkerchief and half-a-crown. Thus our present need was again more than met.

March 7. There came in today 2l. 13s. 10d.

March 8. Today we required 3l. 10s. to supply comfortably all that was needed in the Orphan-Houses, but only 2l. 1s. 10d. was in hand. How kind therefore of the Lord to send me a large donation, whereby we were richly supplied! The particulars of it are these:--On Oct. 25, 1842, I had a long conversation with a sister in the Lord, who opened her heart to me. On leaving me I told her, (because I thought it might prove a comfort to her at some future time,) that my house and my purse were hers, and that I should be glad if she would have one purse with me. This I said, I repeat, because I judged that at some future time it might prove a comfort to her in an hour of trial, having at the same time, (to judge from a circumstance which had occurred two days before,) every reason to believe, that she had not 5l. of her own. This sister, after I had said so, readily took me at my word, and said, I shall be glad of it, adding presently that she had 500l. The moment I heard that, I drew back, and said, that had I known that she had any money, I should not have made her this offer, and then gave her my reason why I had supposed she had no property at all. She then assured me that she possessed 500l., and that she had never seen it right, to give up this money, else she would have done so; but that as God had put this sum into her hands, without her seeking, she thought that it was a provision which the Lord had made for her. I replied scarcely any thing to this; but she asked me to pray for her with reference to this matter. This whole conversation about the money occupied but very few minutes, and it all took place after the sister had risen and was on the point of leaving me.--After she was gone, I asked the Lord, that He would be pleased to make this dear sister so happy in Himself and enable her so to realize her true riches and inheritance in the Lord Jesus, and the reality of her heavenly calling, that she might be constrained by the love of Christ, cheerfully to lay down this 500l. at His feet. From that time I repeated this my request before the Lord daily, and often two, three, or four times a day; but not a single word or line passed between me and this sister on the subject, nor did I even see her; for I judged that it would be far better that she retained this money, than that by persuasion she should give it up, and afterwards perhaps regret the step she had taken, and thereby more dishonour than honour be brought on the name of the Lord. After I had thus for 24 days daily besought the Lord on behalf of this sister, I found her one day, on returning home, at my house, when she told me, that she wished to see me alone. She then said to me, that from the time she had last conversed with me, she had sought to ascertain the Lord's will with reference to the 500l., and had examined the Scriptures, and prayed about it, and that she was now assured that it was the will of the Lord, she should give up this money. After she had told me this, I exhorted her, well to count the cost, and to do nothing rashly, lest she should regret the step she had taken, and to wait at least a fortnight longer before she carried out her intention. Thus we separated. On the 18th day after this conversation. I received the following letter.

THE LORD'S DEALINGS WITH GEORGE MÜLLER

"Dear Brother,

"I believe the Lord has not permitted you to grow weary of remembering me, but that He has still enabled you to bear me upon your heart in His presence. All is well with me, dear brother. Your petitions have been heard and answered; I am happy and at peace. The Lord has indeed manifested His tender care of and His great love towards me in Jesus, in inclining my heart cheerfully to lay all I have hitherto called my own, at His feet. It is a high privilege.

I write in haste to ask you (as we have now one purse) to receive the money at a bank in Bristol; I will direct it to be sent in my name, to be delivered into your hands. Etc."

As this whole circumstance is related only for the profit of the reader, and as I knew that the sister still had my letters on the subject in her possession, I wrote to her, requesting her to send them to me, at the time when I published the last account about the Orphan-House, etc. and extracts of them were given in the last Report, in so far as they might refer to the subject or tend to edification. These extracts are here reprinted. My reply to the above was this:

21, Paul Street, Kingsdown, Bristol,

Dec. 6, 1842.

"My dear Sister,

"Your letter found me in peace, and did not in the least surprise me. Dealing with God is a reality. Saints have power with Him through Jesus. It is now forty-two days since you first mentioned this matter to me. I cannot but admire the wisdom of God and His love to you in allowing me to speak to you as I did [i.e. offering her to have one purse with me; when I thought she had no earthly possessions at all], that thus this great privilege might be bestowed upon you, to give up this little sum for Him. Since that hour I have daily prayed for you, and often thrice or more in the course of the day, that the Lord would make you so happy in Himself, and help you with such faith to lay hold on all which He has given you in Jesus, that you might be constrained by love cheerfully to lay down this little sum at his feet. Thus I prayed again at six o'clock this morning for you. Nor have I had the least doubt from the commencement, that the Lord did hear my prayer; yea, so fully have I been assured that I had the petition, that again and again I have thanked Him that He had answered my prayer, before I saw you eighteen days since, and before your letter came this morning. Moreover, I have been fully assured since you were last here, that He was carrying on His work in your soul with reference to this matter, and that no subtle suggestions of Satan, nor educational prejudices, nor misinterpretations of the Scriptures were able to prevail; for I had asked the Lord, by His Spirit to overcome them in you, and that, if a brother's word should be needed, He would be pleased to incline your heart to write to me: and, as no letter came, I felt fully confident, you were going forward in this matter in peace. When I had seen you this day six weeks, and learned about this little sum, I determined, never to say or write to you another word on the subject, but to leave you in the hands of the Lord. Thus I purposed again during the last eighteen days; for it was not the money given up, that I cared for in you, but the money given up unto the Lord, and from right motives. On this very account I advised you to wait one fortnight longer, though you had come to the conclusion; but now, having done so, and seeing that you are fully purposed in the Lord to be poor in this world indeed, that the more abundantly you may enjoy His riches, His inexhaustible riches, I change my advice. My word now, beloved sister, is this: "Whatsoever thy hand findeth to do, do it with thy might," and "If ye know these things, happy are ye if ye do them."

Delay then no longer, even as also you have no desire to delay: and the Lord will bless you abundantly in doing so, inasmuch as you do it unto Him. As you desire to intrust me with this money, I do not refuse it, knowing many ways to lay it out for Him. Etc." Then only follows the direction how the money is to be paid into my bankers' hands.

On Dec. 18, 1842, I received a reply to my letter, which answer was begun to be written on Dec. 8th, but finished on the 16th. I give a few extracts of the letter: "Since I last saw you, dear brother, I have not had the slightest doubt as to what I ought to do: the word of God has been so clear to me on this head, that I have been kept resting on it; and, in answer to your prayers, no temptation has been allowed to prevail, indeed, I think I may add to arise. But I feel that temptations may come, and that I may in seasons of trial not always have faith to be able to rejoice in this privilege. My heart is so deceitful and my faith so weak, that I shall greatly need your prayers still. Will you then, if the Lord enables you, pray that I may never offend my Father by regretting in the least measure this act of obedience, which He has by His grace inclined me to carry out. I shall pray the Lord still to lay me on your heart. I felt so sure, that you were helped to pray for me, that I had thanked the Lord for His grace. I am glad you did not write, although I much value your advice; but I wished to be led by the Lord alone, after He had used you as the instrument in the first instance, and in such a way too, that I am quite sure He intended to bless you to my soul in this matter. I have asked my heart whether I am really doing this to Him. My heart assures me that I am, and not from any other motive than obedience to the written word. Before I ever saw you I had asked the Lord to make me willing to give this little sum into your hands, if it were His will I should; but His time to make me willing had not then come; even then I had, in a measure given it to you, having written a paper, desiring in case I should fall asleep in Jesus, that you might get possession of it; I had it signed by two witnesses, and I always carried it about with me when I travelled, sealed and directed to you. When I wrote this, I little thought what grace the Lord had in store for me. You will forgive my being thus tedious, but I am sure you will praise the Lord with me for His gracious dealings with me. Etc."--At the end of this letter, which was finished on Dec. 16, the sister tells me, that unexpectedly a hindrance had arisen to her having possession of the money, so that it was not likely it could be paid over to me till about the end of January, 1843.

When this letter came, it would have been naturally a great disappointment to me, as the sister had told me in a previous letter that the money should be paid into my hands, and as just at that time in a variety of ways it was desirable that I should have considerable sums. The Lord, however, enabled me immediately to lay hold on that word, "We know that all things work together for good to them that love God," Rom. viii. 28, and my soul was in peace, though we had only enough money in hand to provide for one or at the most for two days the necessary provisions in the Orphan-Houses. It was but the next day, Dec. 19, 1842, when I received 100l. from A. B., and on Dec. 22, I received 50l. from a brother in Bristol, besides other donations: so that within one week, after I had had grace to delight myself in the will of God, He gave me about 200l., whereby I was able to meet all the heavy expenses of replenishing the stores, &c., on account of which I should naturally have been tried in the payment of the money being delayed.

In reply to the letter, which I received from this sister on Dec. 18, I wrote another on. December 31, 1842, of which I give an extract on this subject. "The hand of the Lord is indeed most manifestly to be seen in this matter, concerning the money: the way in which your own mind was led; my speaking under the circumstances under which I did, when you were already risen to leave the room; the reason why I did so, i.e., mere sympathy with your circumstances, and thinking that some day or other my brotherly offer might be a comfort to you, though you should never need it, and all this when I believed that at that time you did not possess 5l.--I have continued to pray for you, or rather the Lord has enabled me every day once, twice, thrice, or even more, to remember you. The burden of my prayer still has been, that He would be pleased to make you very happy in Himself and enable you to enter into the inheritance which awaits you; further, that you may not be permitted in the least to regret the step which you have taken, but rather consider it a privilege to be permitted to give this little sum back to Him who gave it to you, and who gave Himself for you.-- With reference to the delay, I cannot but rejoice. This gives you abundant opportunity to ponder the matter, and afterwards to state to any (who, judging as those who know not how rich the saints are, might blame you,) that you did not do the thing in haste. I consider this delay to be for the furtherance of the honour of the Lord. You know my advice to you, to wait at least a fortnight. That you have seen much of your unfaithfulness, &c., I consider to be an especial blessing which the Lord has bestowed upon you, lest this step you have taken should become a snare to you. Humblings last our whole life. Jesus came not to save painted but real sinners; but

THIRD PART

He has saved us, and will surely make it manifest. I have a passage laid on my heart for you, read the whole of it carefully: 2 Corinth. viii. 1-9, especially verse 9. Etc."

Day after day now passed away and the money did not come. The month of January was come to an end, and February also, and the money had not come. Thus more than one hundred and twenty days were gone by, whilst day by day I brought my petition before the Lord, that He would bless this sister, keep her steadfast in her purpose and intrust me with this money for His work in my hands. Amidst it all my heart was assured (judging from the earnestness which He had given me in prayer, and that I had only desired this matter to the praise of His name), that in His own time He would bring it about. But I never wrote one single line to the sister on the subject all this time. At last, on the one hundred and thirty-fourth day after I had daily besought the Lord about this matter, on March 8th, 1843, I received a letter from the sister, informing me that the 500l. had been paid into the hands of my bankers.

I now wrote to the sister to inquire, whether she wished the money to be expended upon any particular objects, or whether she would leave me altogether free to expend it, as I might be led.

In reply to this she wrote me: "Dear Brother, I would still leave this little sum in the hands of Him to whom it has been given. May He alone be your guide in disposing of it. If I did express one wish, it would be, that you would make use of a part for your own or your family's present necessity." This latter point I declined entirely, thinking it not wise to take a part of this money for myself, to avoid even the appearance as if in any measure I had sought my own things in this matter, instead of the things of Jesus Christ.

The 500l. were thus portioned out: 100l. for the School-Bible-Tract and Missionary Fund. 50l. for the Employment Fund.8 50l. was taken at once for the Orphan-Fund, and afterwards also the remaining 300l. when, as I shall presently relate, the Lord pointed out to me to go forward in the Orphan work, and to establish a fourth Orphan-house.

I have related the particulars connected with this donation so minutely, in order to show, that though we may have long to wait upon the Lord, yea, though for one hundred and thirty-four days we may have daily the same petition to bring before Him, yet at last He will give us the desire of our hearts, if our petitions are according to His mind. And now I only give a few lines of a letter which I received on. July 3, 1844, from the sister who gave this donation, together with my letters for which I had asked her, in order that I may show her state of mind on the subject, after she had had it more than twenty months before her, and after she had for sixteen months actually given up the money. She writes thus: "I am thankful to say that I have never for one moment had the slightest feeling of regret; but it is wholly of the Lord's abounding grace. I speak it to His praise."

THE LORD'S DEALINGS WITH GEORGE MÜLLER

On March 31, 1843, I called at the Orphan-Houses, to make certain arrangements, and one of the sisters told me by the way, that she had been asked by Miss G, who with her father occupied the house, No. 4, Wilson Street, to let me know that they wished to give up their house, if I would like to take it; but she had replied that it was of no use to tell me about it, for she was sure that I had no thought of opening another Orphan-House. When I came home, this matter greatly occupied my mind. I could not but ask the Lord again and again whether He would have me to open another Orphan-House, and whether the time was now come that I should serve Him still more extensively in this way. The more I pondered the matter, the more it appeared to me that this was the hand of God moving me onwards in this service. The following remarkable combination of circumstances struck me in particular. 1, There are more applications made for the admission of Orphans, especially of late, than we are at all able to meet, though we fill the houses as much as the health of the children and of the labourers will possibly admit. 2, If I did take another house for Orphans, it would be most desirable it should be in the same street where the other three are, as thus the labour is less, and in times of great need we are near together for prayer, the distribution of the money, &c. But since the third Orphan-House was opened in Nov. 1837, there never has been one of the larger houses in the street to be let. 3, There are about fifteen children in the Infant-Orphan-House, whom it would have been well some time ago to have removed to the house for the older girls, had there been room; but when a vacancy happened to occur in that house, there were generally several waiting to fill it up, so that unintentionally the female children in the Infant-Orphan-House remained where they were; but this is not well, nor is it according to my original intention for the Infants were intended only to be left till they are seven years old, and then to be removed to the houses for older boys and girls. This my original plan could be executed better for the future, and at once for the present, were I to open another Orphan-House. 4, I know two sisters who seem suitable labourers for this fourth Orphan-House, and who have a desire thus to be engaged. 5, There are 300l. remaining of the 500l. which I so lately received. This money may be used for the furnishing and fitting up of a new Orphan-House. So much money I have never had in hand at one time during the last five years. This seemed to me a remarkable thing, in connexion with the four other reasons. 6, The establishing of a fourth Orphan-House, which would increase our expenses several hundred pounds a year, would be, after we have gone for five years almost uninterruptedly through trials of faith, a plain proof that I have not regretted this service, and that I am not tired of this precious way of depending upon the Lord from day to day; and thus the faith of other children of God might be strengthened.--But most important, yea decidedly conclusive, as these points were; yet they did not convince me that I ought to go forward in this service, if the Spirit's leading were not in connexion with them. I therefore gave myself to prayer. I prayed day after day, without saying anything to any human being. I prayed two and twenty days, without even mentioning it to my dear wife. On that very day, when I did mention it to her, and on which I had come to the conclusion, after three weeks' prayer and consideration in the fear of God, to establish another Orphan-House, I received from A. B. 50l. and 1l. through him from a sister. What a striking confirmation that the Lord will help, though the necessities should increase more and more. At last, on the 24th day, having been now for several days fully assured, that God would have me go forward in this service, I went to inquire whether Mr. and Miss G. still wished to give up the house. But here I found an apparent hinderance. Having heard no wish expressed on my part to take the house, and the sister in the Orphan-Houses, with whom Miss G. had communicated, not having given her the least reason to think that I should do so, Mr. and Miss G. their altered their plans, and now purposed to remain in the house. However, I was to call again in a week, when I should receive an answer. I was not in the least discomforted by this obstacle. "Lord, if Thou hast no need of another Orphan-House, I have none," was the burden of my prayer. I was willing to do God's will, yea to delight myself in His will. And just on this very ground, because I knew I sought not my own honour but the Lord's; because I knew I was not serving myself, but the Lord in this thing; and because I knew that with so much calm, quiet, prayerful, self-questioning consideration I had gone about this business, and had only after many days, during which I had been thus waiting upon the Lord, come to the conclusion that it was the will of God I should go forward in this service: for, these reasons I felt sure (notwithstanding what Mr. and Miss G. had told me), that I should have the house. I also especially judged, that thus it would be, because I was quite in peace, when I heard of the obstacle: a plain proof that I was not in self-will going on in this matter, but according to the leading of the Holy Ghost; for if according to my natural mind I had sought to enlarge the work, I should have been excited and uncomfortable when I met with this obstacle. After a week I called again on Mr. G. And now see how God had wrought! On the same day on which I had seen Mr. G., he went out and met with a suitable house, so that when I came the second time, he was willing to let me have the one which he then occupied in Wilson Street, and as the owner accepted me as a tenant, all the difficulties were removed, so that after the first of June we began fitting up the house, and in July the first Orphans were received.

Of the donations which came in from March 8 to the end of May, 1843, and which were many, I only notice:

on April 10 a brother gave 5l., which had been saved out of house furnishing, by doing it in a plainer way.

At the end of May, 1843, I entered upon a remarkable part of my life, upon which I must dwell somewhat at length, especially as it will, by God's blessing, still further show the Reader the preciousness of depending upon God for every thing.

It was in September or October 1841, that one day a German lady, a native of Wirtemberg, called on me. She said that she had come to England to perfect herself in English, and purposed afterwards to return to Germany to establish a boarding school for young ladies, and especially for English young ladies. Having heard that I was a German, she came to obtain my advice, and to request me to interest myself for her in getting her pupils to instruct in German, in order thus to support herself while in England. After having conversed with her for some time about these things, and given her the information which she desired, I then spoke to her about the things of God, in which conversation I soon found, that though she might have had some religious feelings from time to time, yet that she did not know the Lord. On leaving me I gave her the first and second part of my Narrative, which I thought she would read because it contained the experience of a German, and thus she would also have exercise in English. I then followed with my prayers the reading of the book, that God would be pleased to bless it to the conversion of her soul. After some time she called on me again, telling me that she had been deeply interested in reading my Narrative, and asked me whether I had any objection to her translating the book into German, with the view of getting it published on her return to Germany. My reply was that I had no right to object to it; for, in so far as translation into another language was concerned, the book was everyone's property. I might have mentioned that I did not think her yet sufficiently acquainted either with the English language or the state of things in England, especially religiously, and that, as she was not converted herself, she could not give the exact translation of the book, though she were qualified with reference to the two former points; but, as I had the spiritual benefit of the individual in view, I thought thus with myself; this person has no employment at present, and by translating this book she will be kept from the many snares connected with idleness; she will by this means also make progress in English, which she is desirous of doing; but, most of all, the fact of translating a book for the press will oblige her more accurately and attentively to consider what is contained in it, than she would be obliged to do, were she simply to read it through several times, and therefore this work may, with God's blessing, be instrumental in doing good to her soul. The last point weighed particularly with me; I therefore did not discourage her, though at the same time I did not encourage her, but left the matter to herself. As, however, she left me with the impression that she was going to translate the book, I asked the Lord to convert her soul in doing so. After a time Mrs. G. called on me again, and brought me a part of the manuscript, that I might read it over. I took it, but could not promise her to read it; for I had little prospect of doing so, for want of time. Nevertheless I read a few pages, which I found rather better translated than I had expected. After this she brought me at two or three other times considerable parts of the translation, which, however, I had never time to read. By this time the winter had passed away, and it was come to March, 1842, when all of a sudden, one Wednesday afternoon, I was seized with sharp pains, something like spasms, which were so acute that, though they passed off after about an hour, they left me so weak, that I was not able to go out to our usual meeting on that evening. About seven o'clock, just when I should have been at the meeting but for this illness, Mrs. G., who for several weeks had been at Trowbridge, to finish the translation, and to instruct a young lady in German, came to take leave of me. She said she now purposed to return to Wirtemberg. Though I was very weak, yet, under these circumstances, I could not decline seeing her, as it would be in all human probability the last time that I should do so. I therefore besought the Lord to strengthen me for this service (which I soon perceived He had done), and, after a short conversation with her about her circumstances, I began to speak to her about her soul, and soon found she was heavy laden, burdened under her sins, and broken in heart. With many tears, she told me that she was a great sinner, an exceedingly great sinner. Every word she spoke gave me the impression, that all she now needed was to have the work of Christ pointed out to her, i.e. the power of His blood in cleansing from all sin, by faith in His name.

THIRD PART

I spent about two hours with her, and she left me with many tears.--I also had said to her at the beginning of the conversation with reference to the translation of my Narrative, that if she still desired to publish it, she should seek to get the assistance of a pious clergyman in Germany, who understood English well--On the next morning about nine Mrs. G. called again upon me, telling me that she could not leave Bristol without seeing me once more. She now spent about three hours more with me, in which she told me that, during the night, which she had chiefly spent in prayer and reading the word of God, she had found peace in the Lord Jesus, and that she was now happy in Him. She further told me, that, after she had translated a part of my Narrative, the Spirit of God began to work upon her heart, by convincing her that she was a great sinner. The further she went on, the more she felt what a sinner she was, till at last, when she was come towards the end of the book, she came to the conclusion to return to Germany. I now gave her some advice in reference to her return, and also what she should do with reference to her spiritual welfare, after her return to Wirtemberg. After this she left me. About two or three weeks after (in April, 1842) I received a long letter from her, written on her way homeward, by which I was still further confirmed that, although Mrs. G. was only a mere babe in Christ, yet that she was a babe, and that a real work of grace had been begun in her heart. I then wrote to her, but from that time till towards the end of May, 1843, I heard no more of her. Towards the end of May, 1843, however, I received a long letter from her, dated Stuttgart (capital of the kingdom of Wirtemberg). In this letter Mrs. G. gave me an outline of her history during the year after she had returned to her country. Suffice it here to say, that she had sought in vain to find Christians with whom she could be united in fellowship according to the truths she thought she saw in my Narrative, and according to what she had seen and heard at our meetings in. Bristol. At last, about New-year, 1843, she became acquainted with a little baptist church, which was separated from the State church, and she was after a time baptized and received into fellowship among them, which took place in Feb. 1843. Soon, however, she found things different, as to church order, etc., from what she had seen amongst us in Bristol, or from what she had learnt from my Narrative, especially with reference to close baptist principles, which in the highest and strongest degree were practised among the brethren at Stuttgart: and she wrote to me, to ask my view about that point, as she felt pained at separating from true believers, because they might not be instructed about believers' baptism. Her letter was accompanied by another letter from one of the brethren of the baptist church, Dr. R--, a solicitor or barrister to the upper tribunal of the kingdom of Wirtemberg. The letter of the latter testified of the gracious spirit of the writer, but also that he likewise held the separating views of close communion, and that he, having read the translation of my Narrative in manuscript, seemed to be drawn and knit to me affectionately, but wished to have, upon Scriptural ground, my views about open communion.

   Before I received these letters, I had been repeatedly asked, during my fourteen years' residence in England, why I did not labour in my native country. The importance also of doing so had been pointed out to me; nor was I myself insensible to this; but my answer had always been: "I must labour where the Lord will have me to be, and as I have never seen it to be the Lord's will, that I should labour in Germany, I ought not to do so." About fourteen months before I received these letters, it had been also more than ever laid on my heart by brother R. C. He had seen something of the religious state of the Continent, and he had heard still more about it, and he had found, almost every where, that when he set truth before brethren, they said, It is Scriptural, you are right; but if we were to practice this, what would be the consequences? what would become of us and our wives and children? or something of that kind. Brother C. therefore came on purpose to see me, on his return from Denmark, to lay it on my heart to visit Germany, on account of my being a native and having been led by the Lord as I had. He told me especially that he considered it of importance that I should publish my Narrative in German, in order that thus the faith of the brethren., with the Lord's blessing, might be strengthened, and that they might be led to act according to the light which they had. All this seemed to me very important: but my answer was as before; I cannot go till the Lord calls me. Scarcely had I read the letters from Mrs. G. and Dr. R--, but I felt: now is the time come when I am to go to Germany; and from that time I gave myself to prayer about it. When I afterwards communicated my feeling on the subject to brother R. C. he said; I am not surprised about it, for from the time that I spoke to you on the subject, I have been constantly asking the Lord to bring it about.

--The reasons that pointed it out to me as the Lord's will, that I ought to go to Germany to labour there for a season, were these. 1, I knew not of one single body of believers, who were gathered on scriptural principles. In all the States of Germany, with scarcely any exception, believers are connected with the State Churches, and the very few believers of whom I had heard that they were separated, I knew to be close Baptists, who, generally, by their most exclusive separate views, only confirmed believers in remaining in the Establishment. Especially of the Baptist Church at Stuttgart I had much reason to believe this. It seemed to me therefore important to go to Germany, and labour there for a season., if it might please the Lord to condescend to use me to put a light on a candlestick, howsoever dimly it might be burning at the first, so that by means thereof the light might be spread in other parts of Germany. 2, As I am a German, and therefore familiar with the language, there seemed to me an especial call that I should take on myself this service, particularly as my experience in connexion with several bodies of believers, during the 13 1/2 years previous to this time, would be of great help in this service. 3, It seemed further to me to be the Lord's will that I should go to Germany, in order that I might publish my Narrative of the Lord's dealings with me (which Mrs. G. had not been able to accomplish), and that not simply in the form of a translation, but so that it should be prepared for the press just as the necessities of the believers in Germany (who, with scarcely any exceptions, are not only connected with the Establishment, but have no idea that there is any where else any thing besides Establishment) might require it. Thus, I judged, something would be given to Germany of the practical working of labouring out of the Establishment; of meeting only as believers in the name of the Lord Jesus, irrespective of any particular religious party or sect, and that in dependence upon the power and presence of the Holy Ghost in the Church of Christ; of dependence upon the Lord alone for every thing; of recognising no other book but the Holy Scriptures for our rule concerning every thing, &c.; and thus my Narrative, if the Lord allowed me to publish it, might be working still, after I had left Germany. 4, Up to that time I had never known an open door for me to labour on the Continent, at least not in Germany; for in the Establishment I neither could labour with a good conscience, according to the light which the Lord had been pleased to give me, nor should I have been permitted to have done so; and I was not acquainted with believers on the Continent out of the Establishment; and as to preaching in the open air, or going somewhere and taking a place for preaching, any thing of this sort was out of the question; for I was too well acquainted with the police of Germany, not to know that that would not be permitted. But now I heard of an open door. At Stuttgart, I judged, I might labour in expounding the truth in this close Baptist Church, and seek to bring these dear brethren out of their sectarian views. 5, But that which in connexion with these four reasons had likewise much influence upon me, was this: During the fourteen years that I had been in England, I had never had my mind drawn to labour on the Continent, and now the very opposite was the case. It was but two or three days before I received those letters from Stuttgart, that I had again expressed my mind as to labouring in Germany, i.e. that I felt no call from the Lord to do it, and had no drawing towards it. Now the case was altogether otherwise. I could not but pray about it; I could not but feel drawn to go to Germany in love to the Lord and in pity towards the poor Church of Christ in that country. Naturally there was nothing inviting; for I saw a hard struggle before me with reference to the brethren who were to be won for the truth, and to be brought out of their errors; in the Continental manners and the long and beautiful journey on the Rhine I saw, through grace, no charm, and certainly I saw nothing in them which would induce me to leave home, but the reverse; the fourth Orphan-House was on the point of being opened, and I, naturally, was very reluctant to be absent from it just then; the labour would be great in Germany, and work would heap up greatly for me in Bristol, during my absence. But with all this:--the leading of my mind to Germany still remained.

The more I prayed about these points, the more I judged it to be from the Lord, that I should go for a season to Germany. It was but a few days, before I had the fullest assurance in my soul, (after much prayer, much self-examination in the fear of God, and after much looking at these five points), that it was the will of God I should go; yet even then I did not speak publicly about it.

After having come to the conclusion, that, as far as I could see, it was the will of God that I should go, I began prayerfully to look at the difficulties there were in the way, which were principally these. 1. the New Orphan-House needed to be opened, and all the work in connexion with it was to be done before I could leave; because I could not judge it to be of God, that this work, which was begun, should remain unfinished, except absolute necessity pointed it out, as otherwise it would be a waste of money, a breach of promise to the relatives whose children were to be received, &c. I therefore asked the Lord to help me through all this work, which was not a little, before I could leave. 2. I judged it for various reasons important, not to leave the work of the Orphan-Houses, Day-Schools, &c., without leaving such a sum of money behind, as would, at least for about two months, defray the probable current expenses for the work, therefore a few hundred pounds I thought it desirable to leave behind, in order that the burden of the work might not be left upon the shoulders of my dear fellow-labourers. I had therefore by prayer to get this sum from the Lord, for the obtaining of which I had no natural prospects whatever. 3. Another obstacle in the way was, want of money for traveling expenses to and from Stuttgart, and means for staying there at least for a time, and that not only for myself, but for my dear wife; for I judged, for various reasons, that it was the will of God she should accompany me in this service, but principally because her health was not equal to being left in Bristol, with the responsibility of the work resting upon her in my absence. This again would require a considerable sum, I mean considerable for me, a poor man. The means I then had of my own as far as I now remember, were not enough, if they had been multiplied by fifty. This obstacle was to be removed by prayer. 4. One of the especial reasons for which I saw it to be the Lord's will that I should go to Germany was, the publishing of my Narrative, at a cheap price (2s. for both parts), or to be given away gratuitously, so that the poor might have it. But this could not be obtained, except I published it on my own account, to avoid the publisher's putting a higher price upon it. Then again, as so much expense of time was connected with printing it, I intended, if once I went to Germany, to print not less than 4000 copies; and what is even that number among the many millions whose language is German. But whence was the money to come for all this; an expense which, though printing and paper are very much cheaper in Germany than in England, yet I knew would cost between one and two hundred pounds. For this, then, also, I, a poor man, betook myself to the living God, being fully assured, that, as He had pointed out to me His will with reference to my going, He would also most assuredly provide the means. Nay, I had a secret satisfaction in the greatness of the difficulties which were in the way. So far from being cast down on account of them, they delighted my soul; for I only desired to do the will of the Lord in this matter. In honesty of heart, I had examined the matter, as standing before God. I wished only to know His will, that I might do it. I judged, it was His will that I should go to Germany, and therefore determined in His fear that I would go. When I therefore saw the difficulties, they cast me not down, but cheered me; for as it was the will of God, according to my judgment, that I should go, I was sure He would remove the obstacles out of the way; and therefore the greater the obstacles, the more abundantly plain the proof, that I had come to a right judgment, if they were removed by prayer; but if after all I had been mistaken, which I could not think I had been, then, the sooner I was undeceived the better. How different such a state of heart, from what it would have been, if somehow or other the love for a Continental tour, or the desire to go up the beautiful Rhine, had beguiled me: then I should not have liked to look at the difficulties, or at least I should have sought to have them removed by my own efforts. But as it was, I did nothing but pray. Prayer and faith, the universal remedies against every want and every difficulty; and the nourishment of prayer and faith, God's holy word, helped me over all the difficulties.--I never remember, in all my Christian course, a period now (in October 1881) of fifty-five years and eleven months, that I ever SINCERELY and PATIENTLY sought to know the will of God by the teaching of the Holy Ghost, through the instrumentality of the word of God, but I have been ALWAYS directed rightly. But if honesty of heart and uprightness before God were lacking, or if I did not patiently wait upon God for instruction, or if

THIRD PART

I preferred the counsel of my fellow men to the declarations of the word of the living God, I made great mistakes.--5. A fifth difficulty in the way was, to find a sister, as matron, for the new Orphan-House, who, as far as I could see, would be suitable; for there were reasons why the sister, of whom I had first thought, could not be engaged for this work. This was no small difficulty in the way, not only as a point important in itself, but also because I could not proceed with the fitting up of the house, &c., till such a sister had been found.

In the beginning of June, I began therefore to give myself to prayer, along with my wife and her sister who lived with us, making it a point, every morning after family prayer, to retire together for the express purpose of asking the Lord to remove these five difficulties, if it were indeed, as I judged, His holy will, that I should labour for a season on the Continent. In addition to this we day by day asked His blessing upon the brethren at Stuttgart among whom I was looking forward to labour, and upon unconverted persons with whom I might come in contact on the Continent in the ministry of the Gospel publicly or privately. We asked Him also especially to prepare the hearts of the brethren in Germany for my service, to help me in writing the book, to bless it, &c. We asked Him further, to be with the Church in Bristol, during my absence, to use my absence as a means of making the gifts, which He had bestowed among us, more abundantly manifest, to help the labourers in the Orphan-Houses and Day-Schools during my absence, &c. Thus we were, morning by morning, waiting upon the Lord, and enlarging our petitions as the Holy Spirit might lead me in prayer. But whilst we were thus day by day waiting upon the Lord, the difficulties, instead of being removed, appeared to increase. For instance: instead of money coming in for the Orphans, the Day-Schools, and the other objects of the Scriptural Knowledge Institution, there was considerably more expended than came in, so that we were getting almost poor. Instead of finding a sister, who seemed suitable as matron for the new Orphan-House, I had the prospect of losing another sister out of the work, who considered it her place to leave Bristol. But notwithstanding all this, my soul was at peace, being fully assured, that I could not be mistaken, as I had come through sincere, patient, and prayerful consideration of the whole matter at last to the conclusion, it was the will of the Lord that I should go to Germany, to labour there in the Word, and publish my Narrative in the German language. Faith therefore saw all the difficulties already removed. Faith could give thanks, while the difficulties yet remained. Faith could triumph, though there seemed the death blow coming, since there not only was no money coming in, but the considerable sums, lately in hand, were rapidly diminishing; and, instead of finding a sister for the new Orphan-House, another sister seemed on the point of leaving. Thus forty days had been passing away, whilst day after day we had been waiting unitedly upon the Lord; but the obstacles were greater than ever, yet my confidence in the Lord, that He would remove the difficulties in His own time, was greater than ever also. It was on July 12 that I said to a sister, being led to it by the certain prospect of one of the dear labourers in the Orphan-Houses going to leave; "Well, my soul is at peace. The Lord's time is not yet come, but, when it is come, He will blow away all these obstacles, as chaff is blown away before the wind." It was only ONE QUARTER OF AN HOUR after, when the following paper was put into my hands, whereby I obtained power over 702l. 3s. 7d.

"1st, The poor brethren and sisters of our dear Lord and Saviour. In connexion with the Employment-Fund or otherwise [i.e. might be given away in connexion with the Employment-Fund or otherwise.]

2nd, Sending help in the Gospel of Christ to the dear brethren in Germany, or publishing the Narrative.

3rd, The dear Orphan-Children.

4th, To complete the payment of the expenses incurred by building a chapel for the meeting of the saints at Barnstaple.

I leave the sums, to be used in these several objects, under the Lord, to the judgment of the Lord's servant, brother Mueller, knowing assuredly that He whose steward he is will direct and guide him in this and every other matter.--His holy name be praised for the REAL JOY I feel today in doing a thing, which a few weeks since was a trying act of obedience. Surely, the statutes of the Lord are right, rejoicing the heart. In keeping of them there is great reward.--July 10, 1843."

Thus three of the hinderances were at once removed; for I was by this sum furnished with travelling expenses, and with what might be required for my stay in Germany, had means to publish 4000 copies of my Narrative, and was able to leave means behind for the work in Bristol, sufficient for at least two months. When I received this note, I was not in the least excited, but took the circumstance as quietly as if it were a matter which could not be otherwise. I had been sure, that, when the Lord's time was come, He would send the means, and according to my faith it was now granted to me; and a proof, that up to the last I did believe, was, that when the money came, it did not surprise me. The 702l. 3s. 7d. was not portioned out (except what was sent to Barnstaple), till my return, as I could not know how much each object might require. It was thus spent. 1, For the chapel at Barnstaple, 80l. 7s. 1d. 2, For poor saints, 112l. 2s., spent in a great measure in providing them or their children with linen and clothes, and for the Employment-Fund, 50l. 3, For publishing 4000 copies of the two parts of my Narrative in German, our travelling expenses to and from Stuttgart, our stay for nearly seven months in Germany, and other expenses connected with my service in Wirtemberg, 267l. 4s. 11d. 4, The remainder of the 702l. 3s. 7d., being 192l. 9s. 7d., I put to the Orphan-Fund, not that so much was in hand on my return from Germany; for I had drawn on the strength of what was in the hands of my bankers.

THIRD PART

Shortly after I had received the 702l. 3s. 7d. on July 12, the Lord was pleased to remove the other difficulties also; for a sister was found for the matron's place in the new Orphan-House, and after this the Lord helped me through the work connected with fitting up the house for the reception of the children. The Lord likewise made it plain to the sister who had purposed to leave her situation, that she should remain in Bristol. Thus all the difficulties were by prayer and faith removed, after we had been, day by day, more than fifty days waiting upon the Lord.

On Aug. 3rd, I received a valuable donation of plate, jewellery, china, linen., books, etc., which was a still further proof of the Lord's readiness to supply all that might be needed during my absence in Germany, and also of His having heard our requests that He would be pleased to send in means before my departure. Most of these articles were readily disposed of, so that, even before I had set out, about 60l. had come in for them.

On Aug. 9, 1843, my dear wife and I left Bristol in company of a German sister, Miss W. The latter, together with a Swiss brother, had been led to see the truth of believers' baptism, and had much wished to be baptized; but as the baptist church at Stuttgart had refused them baptism, except they would promise never to take the Lord's supper any more with unbaptized believers, or with those who belonged to any State Church, to which they could not conscientiously submit, they had undertaken the journey of nearly 800 miles to come to Bristol, to be baptized by me, as they both had read the translation of my Narrative in manuscript, and thus knew that we receive all who believe in the Lord Jesus, though they should not agree with us in all parts of truth. They had arrived in Bristol about a fortnight before my departure for Germany, and were baptized at Bethesda a week after their arrival, when I gave an address in German, and used the words of the German translation of the Holy Scriptures which contain the institution of baptism, as neither the brother nor sister understood English. The brother, who had been a teacher and cashier in a considerable establishment in Wirtemberg for educating young gentlemen, and who had lost his situation when his views with reference to baptism became known, remained in England as teacher of the French and German languages, and the sister travelled back with us to Germany.

During the time of my absence from Bristol, I kept no journal, and therefore I cannot give a minute account of all that transpired, and that might be interesting to the believing reader; but as some letters which I wrote to one of my sisters-in-law are preserved, and also all the letters which I wrote to the brethren in Bristol, among whom I labour, I shall be able by giving these letters, to furnish a pretty full account of my service in Germany up to my return.

The following Letter to my sister-in-law gives some account of a great part of our journey.

THE LORD'S DEALINGS WITH GEORGE MÜLLER

Weinheim, Aug. 19, 1843.

My dear L.,

Thus far we have now been brought through the goodness of the Lord. If you look at the map where Mannheim is, you will, I think, find a small town, called Weinheim, the place where we are now at Mrs. M's. Weinheim forms with Heidelberg and Mannheim a triangle, about 10 miles from Mannheim, and the same from Heidelberg. On the Lord's day evening last I wrote to you from Rotterdam, which letter, I hope, you safely received. On Monday morning at seven, Aug. 14, we left Rotterdam, with sister W. in one of the Rhine steamers, in which we sailed till about half-past eight in the evening, when we arrived at Emmerich, the first Prussian town, where we stopped for the night. The weather was beautiful, as indeed it has been every day of this week. There was nothing remarkable as to natural things, except a large noble river, and on the banks of the river clean pretty cottages of the Dutch people. The Lord enabled me to do a little for Him. I distributed German tracts among those who could read German; but many of them were Dutch persons, who could understand me in speaking to them, but could not read German. I had a long but affecting conversation with four Jews, who, though disagreeing among themselves as to their religious views, were all agreed in their complete rejection of Jesus of Nazareth, as the Messiah, and, as usual, blasphemed. I conversed with many persons, but found only one aged person, who, I think, as far as I could learn, was a christian. After having given him a tract, having heard my testimony for Christ, he came with tears and asked me to sell him another tract. After having told him that I gladly gave him the tract, he then asked me to give him a third and a fourth for the old clergyman and the schoolmaster of his place, and said, Oh! if you could but stop, how glad the old clergyman, a pious man, would be to see you.--There were two other interesting things that day. Very soon after we had started, perhaps two hours after, a gentleman left, to whom I gave a tract in German and English, as he could also read English. He then told me he had seen me reading the Bible, but did not like to interrupt me. I told him my errand to Germany. His reply was: "Brother, the Lord bless thee." On asking him who he was, he told me he was a Baptist minister at Amsterdam, and on his way to the brethren at Utrecht, in Holland. He now much regretted not to have had conversation with me. In the afternoon, a gentleman, an officer on pension, who, with his lady, had heard my confession for Christ, while I was conversing with a person sitting close by, asked me very politely, on his leaving, for a tract.--There were two little cabins in the steamer, each with two berths, one of which I engaged for Mary and myself it being much cheaper than to go on shore, though we should not do so again, as our sleep was greatly interrupted, there being much noise till twelve o'clock, and commencing again soon after three in the mornings, so that for three nights our sleep was greatly interrupted. Yet I do not mention this in the way of complaint, for we have only to sing of mercy. However, as in spiritual things, so in natural things, we learn daily. The noise only arose from the needful occupations, but it could scarcely have been greater than it was, if persons had purposely tried to disturb us.--At half-past five on Tuesday morning the steamer

THIRD PART

began again to ply. While I was sitting on deck, between five and six, reading the Bible, a Dutchman came to me to speak about the things of God. He understood me pretty well, but I understood him only imperfectly. He questioned me about the connexion between faith and works, and how man can believe, being a fallen being in Adam. I fear it was more intellectual than heart-work with him, but I made use of the opportunity, to preach Jesus before all, who through this conversation had been drawn round us. This day also I had opportunities of giving away tracts, and of speaking to several, particularly to a young Prussian soldier, and other young men. But all were dead. Most listened and received the tracts, but there were some who boldly rejected. On the second day we sailed from half-past five in the morning till about half-past ten in the evening, when we arrived at Cologne, where we stopped. Our German sister went on shore, and took leave of us, to go on by another company's vessel, for which she had previously paid; dear Mary and I remained alone on board. The third day we had very few passengers on board. Two Irish gentlemen and an English gentleman came on board, to whom I gave English tracts. One of them soon left, and the other two declared themselves on the Lord's side. Two other Jews, who had come on board, likewise rejected the truth, yet I conversed with them till they blasphemed. This third day we sailed from ten in the morning till about half-past seven in the evening, when we arrived at the Prussian fortress Coblentz. Mary and I now took a little walk. In the town I gave some tracts to a Prussian soldier, for himself and some of his comrades, for having given us some information; and in going back to the steamer we heard an English lady before us speaking English to a little boy who was with her. We joined her, and offered her some English tracts, which she accepted, also some German tracts for the Roman Catholic servant. Today we have seen beautiful scenery. Fourth day, Aug. 17, One of the Irish gentlemen asked me to read to him and his friend a chapter in the Bible. This day also we glided along through most beautiful scenery. Travelling is a very dangerous thing. I would exhort every one, especially to be aware what he is about, before he sets out on a journey. Much as I had prayed about this journey, and sure as I have been and still am, that the Lord sent me on this errand, I was yet made to feel how difficult it is to keep the heart in the right frame whilst looking at such beautiful scenery. It surpassed all I have before seen of the kind. I suppose we have not had less than forty instances of ruined castles, fortresses, &c., brought before us this day; the ancient Roman glory--the glory of the German knights, and of the German emperors, whose works, castles and fortresses we saw in ruins, how loudly does it speak of the changeableness of all earthly things, and yet how pernicious often the effect upon the new nature, while looking at these things. The Rhine is wide, the castles often quite close to the river, and hundreds of millions of vines, you might say, without exaggeration, and tens of thousands of vineyards all along the river for perhaps a hundred miles or more. It is beautiful; but how poor, how very poor this beauty in comparison with Jesus! Through grace I would not pay one shilling to see it again, nor go one mile to see it again, for the sake of seeing it.--On the fourth evening, after having sailed that day from seven in the morning, we arrived about five or six o'clock at Mayence, sister W. having joined us again. We found it very refreshing to have a few hours quiet in an hotel, and then all three together took a walk. In this town, where printing was invented, God's precious word is not valued. Almost all are Romanists. It is a large, magnificent, and busy town, and a strong fortress. The railroad also was just in sight on the opposite side of the river. There was scarcely a trace to be seen of that poverty which you see so often in large towns in England, but all bespoke abundance, though I know there is not the abundance of the English gold. Yesterday morning, Aug. 18, we ought to have left at eight o'clock by the steamer, in which we had taken our places from Rotterdam to Mannheim, but the steamer, by which we ought to have gone, did not arrive. We waited hour after hour, till at last, near four o'clock in the afternoon, we left Mayence for Mannheim by a steamer of another company, having thus to lose the money we had previously paid. We were on board of this steamer about seven hours, till near eleven in the evening, when we arrived at Mannheim. There were at least 14 English passengers on board, besides many Germans and French. I distributed English and German tracts, and had conversation with several. There was a dear young sister, a French lady, with whom I had much conversation. She had been with her little brother to a bathing place near the Rhine. I saw her reading the Epistle to the Romans, and thus took the opportunity to converse with her. She had been at school in Paris till within a few months, and is now, as she has no parents, living with her aunt, a pious woman near Strasbourg. It was very refreshing to be able to help this solitary one, who knew no one on board, and who was very glad to have a little counsel. In parting I gave her a copy of my Narrative, some English tracts, a German tract, and an Orphan Report, as she has begun to learn English, and has a friend, a believer, who understands English well. I had also a pretty long conversation with a German young gentleman, a Roman Catholic, about the way to heaven. This morning, Aug. 19, we called on our sister N. at Mannheim, if it might please the Lord to use us to benefit and restore her soul. We found out her residence after some inquiry, and she seemed very glad to see us. After having our passports signed, and taken up some money from the banker, we left Mannheim at two o'clock in the afternoon, and arrived here at four, where we were very affectionately received by brother T. H. and dear Mrs. M. We are now staying in an old building, formerly a Roman Catholic cloister, where I this evening expounded the Scriptures.

Aug. 20, 1843. This morning I expounded the Scriptures at family prayer in English, then at eleven o'clock we broke bread in the cloister, being five in number, and this afternoon, at four o'clock, I expounded again, when altogether 10 English gentlemen and ladies, who are staying here, were present. Tomorrow morning I purpose to see the pious Lutheran clergyman resident here, and about one o'clock, the Lord willing, we shall leave by the mail and arrive at Stuttgart on Tuesday evening, Aug. 22. The heat has been exceedingly great all the last week, so that we have constantly been obliged to sleep with the window wide open. Farewell, dear helper. Our love to dear sister E. from whom we shall be very glad to hear, and to whom you will please to communicate all in our letters that may be interesting to her. Our tender love also to our own dear child. How gladly should we see and kiss her, but though we cannot do that, yet we pray for her. Love also to S. My especial love to all my

THIRD PART

dear fellow-labourers in the church. My love to all the dear brethren and sisters in the Orphan-Houses and Day-Schools. Our love to all the saints.

Your affectionate brother,

GEORGE MUeLLER.

We are now just 600 miles from Bristol.

I make a few remarks in connexion with this letter.

I found it injurious to my inner man that for three nights I had had very little sleep. My own experience has been almost invariably, that if I have not the needful sleep, my spiritual enjoyment and strength is greatly affected by it. I judge it of great moment that the believer, in travelling, should seek as much as possible to refrain from travelling by night, or from travelling in such a way as that he is deprived of the needful night's rest; for if he does not, he will be unable with renewed bodily and mental strength to give himself to prayer and meditation, and the reading of the Holy Scriptures, and he will surely feel the pernicious effects of this all the day long. There may occur cases when travelling by night cannot be avoided; but, if it can, though we should seem to lose time by it, and though it should cost more money, I would most affectionately and solemnly recommend the refraining from night travelling; for, in addition to our drawing beyond measure upon our bodily strength, we must be losers spiritually. The next thing I would advise with reference to travelling is, with all one's might to seek morning by morning, before setting out, to take time for meditation and prayer, and reading the word of God; for although we are always exposed to temptation, yet we are so especially in travelling. Travelling is one of the devil's especial opportunities for tempting us. Think of that, dear fellow believers. Seek always to ascertain carefully the mind of God, before you begin any thing; but do so in particular before you go a journey, so that you may be quite sure that it is the will of God that you should undertake that journey, lest you should needlessly expose yourself to one of the special opportunities of the devil to ensnare you. So far from envying those who have a carriage and horses at their command, or an abundance of means, so that they are not hindered from travelling for want of means, let us, who are not thus situated, rather thank God that in this particular we are not exposed to the temptation of needing to be less careful in ascertaining the will of God, before we set out on a journey.

Stuttgart, Aug. 30, 1843.

My dear L--,
My last letter I finished on the 20th, and posted it on the 21st at Weinheim. On, Monday morning, Aug. 21, I saw a pious clergyman at Weinheim, a true brother,

and a nice man. But we came, without my seeking it, upon the subject of separation from the state church, for which I could not be sorry, as I had an opportunity of stating truth to him which it may please the Lord to use hereafter. Mrs. ---- gave us a rich silk dress, quite new, and a few silver articles for the Orphans. So even here the Lord makes it manifest that He is mindful of this work. About one o'clock in the afternoon we left Weinheim. At Heidelberg, about ten miles from there, a person came into the mail in which Mary and I were, whom I found out in a few moments to be a brother; and a few minutes afterwards the widow of a much tried pious clergyman, who herself also loves the Lord Jesus, seated herself likewise. We had now, from three o'clock till about half-past nine in the evening, when we arrived at Heilbronn, a most pleasant and profitable time, being all four believers. I told this brother much about England, and also about the Orphans, and on separating from him he gave me a gold coin, about seventeen shillings in value, for the Orphans. It was indeed a most precious gift to me, and a fresh proof in what a variety of ways the Lord is able to send help. We remained the night at Heilbronn, that we might not have to travel the night, left the next morning at eleven o'clock, and reached the apartments of our sister G. about eight in the evening on Aug. 22. We were received in the most affectionate way, and she has done every thing to make us comfortable; but the very great heat and the change of living have hitherto drawn upon both of us. I think, that, with the Lord's blessing, we shall be better after a few days. Indeed I have been rather better yesterday and today. On the same evening of our arrival here I went to the post-office and found your first letter, and last Monday morning I received your second also. The next afternoon, Wednesday, Aug. 23, I went to Brother Dr. B., with whom I spent about two hours; and in the evening from half-past eight till ten o'clock I met the four elders of the Baptist Church at his house. The next evening from half-past eight to ten was a meeting of the little church, which consists of about 50 brethren and sisters, of whom almost all were present. I stated the object of my coming to Germany, in so far as it was wise to do so, and also a little about the church in Bristol. The next evening, Aug. 25th, I expounded the scriptures from half-past eight to ten o'clock. All the meetings are in the evenings from half-past eight to ten, so that we generally come home at half-past ten, and go to bed about half-past eleven. Persons have their supper before they go to the meetings. On Saturday evening we had again a meeting, at which I began to give an account of the Lord's dealings with me, from the beginning, as being the best means of leading me to speak about many important truths. It was desired that I should expound the scriptures at all their usual meetings, i.e. twice on the Lord's days, and twice in the week; and, on all the other evenings, there should be extra meetings, at which I should give an account of the Lord's dealings with me. On the Lord's day therefore I expounded twice with much help, feeling scarcely any difficulty with reference to the German language, though I have not before preached in it for fourteen years and a half. On Monday, Aug. 28th, I went on again with my Narrative, and last night I expounded again with much help. But now, as the truth is beginning to be spoken, the devil will also begin to seek to work. But the Lord Jesus will triumph. There is a great crisis before us. Several have been already attracted by the preciousness of the truth, and others already wish I had never come to Stuttgart. They are not asleep over what I say, and that gives me pleasure. I fear it will come in a very few days to a storm, except the Lord prevent.

THIRD PART

Nor am I quite sure whether the police will allow me quietly to work here, when it gets known what I am doing, as the liberty is not so great as I had thought. But it would have been worth while to have come here, only to have spoken these few times. There is now here on a visit to us an English sister, Mrs. F.

Your affectionate brother,

GEORGE MUeLLER.

Immediately on my arrival at Stuttgart, yea, the very first hour that I was there, so heavy a trial of faith came upon me, that it was one of the sharpest trials which I ever have had. The cause of it I am not at liberty to mention. But so much as this, it was in connexion with my going to Stuttgart, and, humanly speaking, the thing would not have occurred, had I not gone thither. The trial was of a double character; for it was not only the thing itself, great as the trial of my faith was on that account; but it was as though the question were put to me in the strongest way:--Are you willing to make sacrifices in connexion with your service here? And do you really lean upon me, the living God, in your service here? But thanks to the Lord, Satan did not prevail. My heart was enabled to say almost immediately:--"All things work together for good to them that love God." I know this also does work together for my good. I know it is the very best thing for me.--Thus peace was almost immediately restored to me, and I was enabled to leave the matter quietly in the hands of the Lord. Nor was it many days before I could say from my inmost soul, if even then I could have had it in my power to alter the thing, which occasioned the great trial, and the consequences of which were then still remaining, and were remaining all the time while I was in Germany, yet I would not have wished it to be altered. And since my return to England I have again and again had reason to admire the goodness of the Lord in having allowed this thing to be as it was, for it proved in the end in every way good to me. May the believing reader leave himself more and more unreservedly in the hands of the Lord, and he will find it to be just as the writer has found it, i. e. that our greatest trials often turn out to be our greatest blessings.--Had I gone, however, in my own strength to Stuttgart, and had I not been led to treasure up so many petitions in heaven before I went, I should, in all human probability, have been quite overcome by this very first trial.

This was not the only trial which befel me there, but they were so many, so great, and so long continued, that I required every particle of experience, wisdom, and grace, humanly speaking, which the Lord had been pleased to intrust me with. I could not but again and again admire the wisdom of the Lord in having sent me only in the year 1843 to Germany, and not several years before, as I often had been advised to go long before I did. For had I gone without having the experience which I had gathered in my service among the saints during the 13 1/2 years previously, and without having had my soul exercised before God in trials of patience, and hope, and faith, as it has been since November 1830, humanly speaking, I should have been overwhelmed. But, as it was, my soul, through grace, having learned to deal with God about every thing, I was sustained by casting all my care upon Him, and looking to Him for help, and expecting help from Him, though every thing looked dark in every way. And thus it came, that all the difficulties were overcome one after another. But more about this when I come to relate some of the peculiar difficulties in connexion with my service at Stuttgart.

I also mention here, that during the eight years previous to my going to Germany to labour there, it had been laid on my heart, and on the hearts of some other brethren among us, to ask the Lord that He would be pleased to honour us, as a body of believers, by calling forth from our midst brethren, for carrying the truth into foreign lands. But this prayer seemed to remain unanswered. Now, however, the time was come when the Lord was about to answer it, and I, on whose heart particularly this matter had been laid, was to be the first to carry forth the truth from among us. About that very time the Lord called our dear brother and sister Barrington from among us, to go to Demerara, to labour there in connexion with our esteemed brother Strong, and our dear brother and sister Espenett, to go to Switzerland. Both these dear brethren and sisters left very shortly after I had gone to Germany. But this was not all Our much valued brother Mordal, who had commended himself to the saints by his unwearied faithful service among us for twelve years, had from Aug. 31, 1843, (the day on which brothers Strong and Barrington sailed from Bristol for Demerara), his mind likewise exercised about service there, and went out from among us eleven months after. He, together with myself, had had it particularly laid upon his heart, during the eight years previously, to ask the Lord again and again to call labourers from among us for foreign service. Of all persons he, the father of a large family, and about 50 years of age, seemed the least likely to be called to that work; but God did call him. He went, laboured a little while in Demerara, and then, on January 9, 1845, the Lord took him to his rest.--When we ask God for a thing, such as that He would be pleased to raise up labourers for His harvest, or send means for the carrying on of His work, the honest question to be put to our hearts should be this: Am I willing to go, if He should call me I Am I willing to give according to my ability? For we may be the very persons whom the Lord will call for the work, or whose means He may wish to employ.

The Reader will notice, in the preceding letter, that all the meetings in the evening were very late. The time of the meetings was one of the many difficulties with which I had to contend; for if the times had been on purpose ill chosen, they could scarcely have been worse. On the Lord's day mornings the meetings were at nine; thus the mothers of families either could not come at all, or had to hurry through their work, and come without having had any time to themselves. On the Lord's day afternoons they were at two, when the heat of the sun in the summer, which is most oppressive, and the effect of the dinner, both combined together to make the persons sleepy, so that individuals not more than half a yard from me, though interested about what was going on, were sometimes fast asleep. In the evenings the meetings commenced at half-past eight, when persons were not only worn out from working nearly up to that time, but also, in general, had just had a heavy

THIRD PART

supper, which was sure to make them sleepy, thought they might be never so desirous to listen. But, by the grace of God, none of these things moved me. I knew the Lord had sent me to these dear saints, and that, therefore, by His help, I could overcome all these difficulties. And these difficulties were overcome; for after a little while I was able to show to the dear brethren and sisters that the Lord's day morning meeting was too early, and we had it half an hour later. The Lord's day afternoon meeting at two o'clock was entirely given up, on account of its being an unseasonable time, and it being better to have only two meetings instead of three, as almost every one could attend two meetings, which was quite enough for one day, and gave some time for parents to be with their children, or gave some more time than usual for reading the Scriptures, a point at which I aimed from the beginning. For when I came to Stuttgart, I found it just as I have found it in some places in England on my first beginning to labour there, even that the dear brethren and sisters had little relish for the word of God, and as a proof of this never referred to it at the meetings; but, before I left Stuttgart, I had the joy of seeing either all, or almost all, having the word of God open before them whilst I was expounding it.--Instead of the afternoon meeting at two, we met at four o'clock, when the oppression of the heat in the summer is not so great as at two, whereby also the lateness of the evening meeting was avoided on the Lord's days. Also on the week evenings we had the meetings half an hour sooner, that is at 8 o'clock instead of half-past 8, and I affectionately advised the dear saints to take a very light supper on those evenings when we met, that blessing might not be hindered. Earlier than eight on the week evenings, and later than half-past nine on the Lord's day mornings, we could not have the meetings, on account of the habits of the country. It can scarcely be perceived by brethren in England how great the difficulties are, with which brethren have to contend in many foreign countries in seeking to spread the truth, not only on account of the climate, or the police, etc., but also on account of the habits of the people; so that I would affectionately beseech all, who take a hearty interest in the spread of the truth, to help by their prayers all who labour in the word and doctrine in foreign lands, so that through the power of the Holy Ghost they may be enabled to overcome all those hinderances.

I now insert my first letter to the brethren in Bristol, written by me from Stuttgart, soon after my arrival, which will show to the reader my position there more clearly. The letter is, with the exception of a very slight verbal alteration, which I made in revising it for the press, just as it was written.

Stuttgart, Sept. 7, 1843.

To the Brethren meeting at Bethesda and Salem Chapels, Bristol.

My dear Brethren,

It was yesterday four weeks since I left Bristol, and I now write these few lines that you may know how I am situated in the service, on account of which I left

England, in order that thus you may the better be able to remember me in your prayers, according to my need. My journey to this place was full of mercies and blessings in a variety of ways, but I must delay giving you the particulars, till it may please the Lord to allow me again the privilege of labouring among you. I arrived at Stuttgart on Tuesday evening, Aug. 22. On the next evening I met the five brethren who labour here in the little church. On Thursday, Friday, and Saturday also I had meetings with the little church, at which I either expounded the Holy Scriptures or communicated to the brethren things about Bristol, which might be profitable to them. The following Lord's day I spoke twice at their meetings, and in the evening I broke bread in my room with a few saints, as the Baptist church break bread only once a month. On Monday and Tuesday evenings I continued to meet the whole little church. Up to that time all went on quietly; but I knew well that it was only the quietness before a storm, and that shortly a hot battle would commence. And thus it was. On Wednesday last week, i.e. Aug. 30, I was requested to meet the elders of the church. When we came together, the brother who appears to take the lead among them, and who is the only one who speaks at their meetings, told me that the time was drawing nigh when the church would take the Lord's supper, and that they had a rule which they considered to be Scriptural, which was, neither to take the Lord's supper with any one who was not himself baptized by immersion after he had believed, nor with any one who, (though thus baptized himself) would take the Lord's supper with any who had not thus been baptized. Nor did they take the Lord's supper with any brother who would take it with any yet belonging to the state church. After this brother had stated to me his views, I stated my own convictions from the Holy Scriptures on these points, and I was quietly heard for about an hour and a half whilst I was speaking without interruption. The Lord was so with me, that when I came home I did not remember any one thing that I could have wished to have stated which had not been stated. The whole having taken up more than two hours, and it being now past ten o'clock in the evening, we proposed to meet again on the next day, Thursday afternoon, at five o'clock. We did so, and several other brethren besides the elders were present. The subjects were now discussed from the Scriptures. Brother--maintained that no one was born again except he was baptized, no one had a right to say his sins were forgiven, except he were baptized, and also that the apostles were not born again until the day of Pentecost. Whilst seeking to defend these unscriptural statements, he also affirmed that our Lord Himself had been born again at His baptism, and that the last three years of His life He had not been under the law, but had ceased to be under the law when He was baptized. I had been accustomed during the eight days that I had been going in and out among the brethren to hear all sorts of unscriptural statements, into which they had fallen through laying an undue stress upon baptism, and especially through considering baptism as a covenant into which God enters with the believer; but when now the foundation truths of the Gospel were also attacked, when of our Holy Lord it was said that he was born again at his baptism, (which made Him out to be like one of us), and when it was said that He had not been under the law during the last three years of His life;--I saw it needful first of all to see whether we were agreed about the foundation truths of the Gospel. But as we had now been together from five to half-past seven in the evening, and as at half-past eight the public meeting began at which I had to speak, I proposed

THIRD PART

to separate and to meet again on Friday afternoon from five to seven. This was done, I now first of all pressed the first points. Brother--stated in the presence of the elders and six or seven other brethren, that he had made an unscriptural statement, and that our Lord needed not to be born again. I then went to the other point, whether the Lord was under the law up to the time when He died on the cross, or only up to the time when He was baptized. Many passages were brought forward to show that our Lord was under the law up to the last moments of His earthly life, which is clear from Gal. iii. 13, Phil. ii. 8, Heb. x. 1-13, and many other passages. At last he was convinced about this also and acknowledged his error. But many other points, equally unscriptural, he was unwilling to renounce, such as, that baptism is a covenant with God, and that there cannot be forgiveness of sins except individuals have been baptized after believing. He also maintained that I was sinning in breaking bread with unbaptized believers, and with those who belong to the state church, and that if the church here allowed me to break bread with them, they would be defiled, as I made myself a partaker of the sins of others, which sins I brought with me; and other such unscriptural statements were made by this brother. Thus we spent again about two hours and a half in intercourse, whilst this teaching elder and one of the other elders considered me unfit to take the Lord's supper with them on the coming Lord's day, but the two other elders and several other brethren who were present were quite ready to break bread with me, and with any who love our Lord Jesus. Brother--now said, there must be a separation. I then entreated the brethren not to think of a separation. I represented to them what a scandal it would be to the ungodly, and what a stumbling block also to the believers who are yet in the state church. I further told them that I had not come to Stuttgart to make a separation between the brethren, but only to lend them a helping hand according to the ability which the Lord might give me. I lastly said: As we have now spent more than six hours together in intercourse, let us meet together tomorrow evening some hours for prayer. To this the brethren agreed, and we accordingly met on Saturday evening at eight o'clock for prayer. The subject of our prayer was, that the Lord would be pleased to unite us together in the truth, and make it manifest on which side the truth was. After we had thus prayed for about two hours, brother--prayed at the end, and related (in what he called prayer) his experience before his conversion, his conversion, his being convinced about baptism, my coming to Stuttgart, his readiness to receive the unbaptized in consequence of my intercourse with him, and how then a great horror had befallen him, and that now he had come back to his former view, only to receive the baptized, and how now his peace had been restored to him, and that he purposed to live and die in this belief. When we arose I told him that the Lord Himself had decided the matter, and had shown on whose side the truth was; for that he, if in peace, as he had said, could not thus have related his experience, and called it prayer. This prayer tended greatly to show the other brethren that he has not the truth.--I should have stated that I said to the brethren at the commencement of this meeting, that, as I and my wife were the only persons on whose account they could not break bread on the coming day, and as nothing ought to be done in a hurry, to whatever conclusion they might come, we would gladly withdraw ourselves, and break bread in our room. This was not accepted, as there was much disunion among the brethren, as they told me, and had been before I came, and that my coming had now only brought matters to a point. I stated once more, at the end of the meeting on Saturday evening, Sept. 2, that we ought to dread a separation, and that we ought to pray that we might be of one mind, and that I was ready to meet them by day or by night for prayer or searching the Word on the subject. Thus we separated. The next morning, Sept. 3, I spoke again at the meeting, having been by all the elders requested at my arrival here to expound the Scriptures at all their meetings, or to communicate to them any thing that might be profitable. On this morning I spoke principally on the Lord's supper, and on what fits for it; on what is meant by feeding upon Jesus, and what fits for it; on the point that it is not a part of truth, but Jesus round whom believers should unite together; and on the truth, that, if any one is a believer, he is entitled to all the privileges of the saints. These points I had not chosen on purpose for that morning, but they came in course in speaking on Exodus xii., on which chapter I had spoken four times before. After I had finished, I was going to pray at the close, when I was interrupted by brother--, the principal and teaching elder (as to outward authority). He stated that he must contradict me, for I had said: 1, The bread and wine in the Lord's supper meant the body and blood of our Lord, whilst, as he believed, and as the word said, it was the real body and blood of our Lord. 2, He believed that as circumcision made a man an Israelite, and fitted him thus for the partaking of the Paschal Lamb, so without baptism no one is fitted to partake of the Lord's supper, which is set forth by the Paschal Lamb; whilst I had said that every one who believes in Jesus was by this his faith made a spiritual Israelite, and had a right to the Lord's supper and to all the privileges of the children of God. He stated further, that this was against the rules of their church, and that, as I took the Lord's supper with unbaptized believers, and with those who had not quite left the state church, I made myself partaker of their sins, and that therefore, as being defiled with these sins, I could not be admitted to the Lord's supper. From the commencement of his speaking he was very irritated, but now continued in a passionate way: I am ruler in this church, and you (addressing himself to me) are no longer permitted to speak at our meetings. Moreover he said, "Whosoever takes the Lord's supper with Mueller will no longer be considered as a member of the church;" and then in anger he left the meeting. During all this time, the Lord, in the riches of His grace, kept me in perfect peace and calmness. I answered brother--not a single word. When he was gone I fell upon my knees, asked the Lord's blessing upon the word which I had spoken, asked the Lord to forgive brother--, and to teach me what I should do now. After this I dismissed the meeting. When all was over, one of the elders, brother R., one who seeks after truth, and rejoices in the true liberty which the Lord enables me to preach, and one who had been sighing under the iron hand of brother--for a long time; this brother, I say, requested me before all, according to the first arrangement, to continue the meetings and to tell them all that might be profitable to them. He was, however, immediately interrupted by another elder, who sees with brother--, and told that he had no right to do so. I then stated again that I had only come from England in love, and that I would not force myself upon them. I then left.--By the time of the afternoon meeting I had received light from the Lord that I should not go to the meeting. I saw that as I had been cast out, together with all the other brethren who owned me as a brother, and as all my tenderness in seeking to avoid a separation had been useless, I had now on the other hand to go steadfastly

THIRD PART

forward, leaving it with the Lord to decide on which side the truth was. I therefore remained at home. The two elders who were won for the truth, went to the meeting in the afternoon, at which brother--sought to disprove what I had said, and after the meeting they stated that they were purposed to own me and all who believe in the Lord Jesus as brethren in the breaking of bread.--On the same evening seventeen of us met in my room for the breaking of bread, as we were in peace; of these seventeen twelve were belonging to this little Baptist church, two Swiss brethren, one English sister, my wife and I. We had a peaceful meeting. Thus the Lord so soon, so unexpectedly, has brought the matter to a point, though in a painful way. The matter would be, however, more painful, did I not see it of great importance that the disciples who hold the truth should be separate from those who hold such fearful errors as: The forgiveness of sins received through baptism; baptism a covenant between us and God; regeneration through baptism and no regeneration without it; the actual death of the old man through baptism, it being drowned, so that only the body and the new nature are alive; and many other fearful errors, to which these poor deluded brethren have been led by laying such undue stress upon baptism. As to poor brother ----, he had denied some months since the inspiration of Luke, the Acts, and the Epistle of James, which point he only gave up when several brethren stated that they must leave on that account, and he has fallen into many other grievous errors; but there has been no one who has had sufficient spiritual courage steadfastly to resist him. Now there is joy with many that the Lord has set them free.--On Monday last, Sept. 4th, I had again a meeting with the brethren and sisters whose eyes the Lord has opened, and others also came, not belonging to this Baptist church. On. Wednesday I had again a meeting, and today, Sept. 8, and tomorrow evening I purpose to meet the brethren again.--All is only a beginning. But there is a beginning. That which I longed for, the chief object of my journey to the Continent, that there might be also in Germany a little living church, but based on Scriptural principles, which might be a light to other places; the beginning of that has now been made, but it is a small beginning. The minds of the dear brethren have been so darkened through this mixture of error and truth, that about every thing they need instruction. However, the Lord will help further. I am of good cheer, because I know that the Lord is on my side, and that He has sent me here, and that He keeps me here. How gladly would I leave this very day, were it His will; but I know that at present I ought to labour here.--I have so circumstantially and minutely related all to you, that you may the better know how to help me with your prayers. The errors and sins of our brother ---- I have only related, that you the more clearly may see how my coming here is of God, in order that these dear children of God, who have suffered so much for the Lord's sake, and who are sincere, though in much error, might be led on and delivered out of these snares of the devil. But many, unaccustomed to examine Scripture, hold fast the former ways; yet those, who are sincere, the Lord will deliver after awhile. How long I may continue here, I know not; but the moment I see the Lord's leading to England, I shall be delighted to go back. At present my temptation is not to stay longer than I ought to stay; but rather to leave sooner than I ought to leave. Help me, therefore, dear brethren, that I maybe willing to do and suffer all the will of God here. As to further particulars, the Lord willing, you shall have them either verbally or by writing. Should any of you like to write to me, or my dear wife, we shall be glad to hear from you; and if the letters be written on thin paper and left at my house, they will be forwarded to me. We remember you daily in our prayers, as you also, no doubt, remember us. May the Lord bring us in His own time again together in peace. Pray earnestly for all the brethren who labour among you. My dear wife salutes you. The saints here salute you.

I am, dear brethren.,

Affectionately your brother and servant,

GEORGE MUeLLER.

I make the following remarks in connexion with this letter.

1. In the beginning it is mentioned, that on the evening of the day after my arrival I met with the five brethren who laboured in the Baptist church at Stuttgart, that is with the teaching elder or president, the three other elders, and the brother who acted as deacon. At this very meeting, nay at the very commencement even of this meeting, I saw what a difficult position mine would be, and what abundant help I should need from God. That which led me to think so was this. During the day that I had been at Stuttgart, I had perceived, that all the brethren and sisters called one another "Thou," which is in Germany the sign of great familiarity, and which is used between very intimate friends or between parents and children, or husband and wife, or brothers and sisters of the same family, &c. Here now I found that males and females of all ages and different stations in life called one another "Thou." When I therefore met with those five brethren I stated the substance of the following objections, against this practice, not however in the form of objections, but either in the way of affectionate inquiries or brotherly suggestions. My objections against it were these: 1, I did not think it would have, in general, a desirable effect upon believers of different sexes to speak to one another thus in the way of so great familiarity. 2, I did not think it would work well for brethren and sisters in service to speak thus to their master and mistress, especially if it should happen that the mistress was an unbeliever, and therefore not in fellowship with them, and a sister were as a servant to say to her master "Thou." 3, I thought it would not work happily and healthfully for a very young brother and sister to be expected to call aged brethren and sisters "Thou," as if on terms of great familiarity, from the moment they were baptized and thus received among them into fellowship. 4, But that which far more strongly operated upon my mind than any of the previous reasons was this, It seemed to me to substitute an outward form for the inward power and reality. I stated to them, That if the calling one another "Thou" were the result of realizing that all the children of God have one and the self-same Father in heaven, that they are really, and not nominally only, brothers and sisters of the same heavenly family, and heirs of the same precious inheritance, and bought by the same precious blood of the Lord Jesus; if it were the result of these truths being enjoyed and realized within, I should see not the least reason against it, in general; but I feared that it was merely an outward thing,

judging from the fact, that however it might have been with a brother and sister previously, the moment they were baptized they were called "Thou" by every one of their number, and they were expected to call every one "Thou" in return. And I judged it to be a pernicious thing, if thus the "Thou" was forced upon persons; for on the part of those who were comparatively high in life it would be considered sooner or later an unpleasant burden, and on the part of the poorer classes it would lead to carnal gratification in being able to treat those in the way of great familiarity who were considerably above them with reference to this life. The thing itself, then, if done from right motives, from the entering into our position as saints with reference to God and to each other, would be most precious; but the thing done, merely because it was customary among them, and observed in order to keep up uniformity, would work most perniciously.--In reply to my remarks of this kind, it was stated, that the use of the word "Thou" was scriptural, that in the Holy Scriptures we never read, when one single person is spoken to, "You," but always "Thou." To this I answered that it was so, but that we must remember that in the Holy Scriptures we find governors and kings addressed by poor men in the term "Thou;" for this was the only form of speech in use, whilst in Germany, where the "Thou" is not used except to denote near natural relationship or familiarity, it ought not to be used, except there be that inwardly corresponding to what we outwardly seek to convey by the term; else it will lead to formality, if not to hypocrisy, and sooner or later the pernicious tendency of this outward thing, to which there is nothing inwardly corresponding, will most surely be felt. It appeared to me far better not to make any profession of familiarity and intimacy by the use of the "Thou," when the heart does not go along with it, and rather to continue to say to one another "You" till there be the drawing of heart to heart by the love of Jesus, than to force the "Thou" upon the brethren and sisters. I felt the more strongly about this, as I had witnessed more than once among believers in England the injurious effects of doing things because others did them, or because it was the custom, or because they were persuaded into acts of outward self-denial, or giving up things whilst the heart did not go along with it, and whilst the outward act WAS NOT the result of the inward powerful working of the Holy Ghost, and the happy entering into our fellowship with the Father and with the Son. I had seen, when these things had been done from wrong motives, that there had been regret afterwards, and the returning back as much as possible to what had been given up or forsaken. Moreover, though I had been only one day in Stuttgart when we had this meeting, yet I had heard enough of the state of things, to make me think the calling one another "Thou" was in many instances a mere outward form.--My brotherly suggestions were not received, but strongly opposed by two or three out of the five brethren, and it was pretty plainly hinted, that, perhaps, I was too proud to be called "Thou;" and the moment I perceived that, I said that I wished every brother, the very poorest of them, to call me "Thou" (and I encouraged them in doing so, by calling every one "Thou"), but that I could not, with my light, call any of the sisters "Thou," nor did I do so up to the day of my departure.

There was another thing of the same character, that is the kiss. In Germany, as on the Continent generally, the kiss is the sign of affection and familiarity among men as well as among females, and the brethren and sisters at Stuttgart always had been in the habit of kissing one another after having partaken of the Lord's supper, that is all the brethren had kissed each other, and all the sisters had kissed each other. Now this again, if the result of real inward affection, and springing from the entering into our heavenly relationship and oneness in Christ Jesus, would be most beautiful, and would be the "holy kiss" of which the Apostle Paul speaks; but I had no reason to believe that this was generally the case among the brethren and sisters at Stuttgart, but rather that it was merely the result of custom and form, and that it was done because it was expected to be done, for it was the church's order, after the Lord's supper to kiss one another. It was on this ground that it seemed to me to be most pernicious; and I could have known how it would work, even though I had not been actually told, that sometimes sisters had stayed away from the Lord's supper, because they did not feel comfortable in kissing all the female members of the church. When therefore I began to break bread with the brethren, after we had been separated by the close baptists, I did not kiss one brother after the breaking of bread; but I made a point of it to kiss every one of them on that very day at a later meeting, when I left them to go to my lodgings, in order that no one might be able to say it was pride or want of love in me that I had not kissed them. Thus I did on the second Lord's day, and on the third. On the fourth Lord's day a brother said, after the breaking of bread, Brethren shall we give one another the brotherly kiss, and I was then ready at once, like the rest, to kiss all the brethren; but the next time there was no kissing, and thus the mere cold form was banished, and every brother felt free to kiss another brother when his heart bade him to do so, without being bound to it by custom or form.

I have so circumstantially dwelt on these apparently little things, because I think them, in principle, matters of the deepest importance. Every thing that is a mere form, a mere habit and custom in divine things, is to be dreaded exceedingly: life, power, reality, this is what we have to aim after. Things should not result from without, but from within. The sort of clothes I wear, the kind of house I live in, the quality of the furniture I use, all such like things should not result from other persons doing so and so, or because it is customary among those brethren with whom I associate to live in such and such a simple, inexpensive, self-denying way; but whatever be done in these things, in the way of giving up, or self-denial, or deadness to the world, should result from the joy we have in God, from the knowledge of our being the children of God, from the entering into the preciousness of our future inheritance, etc. Far better that for the time being we stand still, and do not take the steps which we see others take, than that it is merely the force of example that leads us to do a thing, and afterwards it be regretted. Not that I mean in the least by this to imply we should continue to live in luxury, self-indulgence, and the like, whilst others are in great need; but we should begin the thing in a right way, i.e. aim after the right state of heart; begin inwardly instead of outwardly. If otherwise, it will not last. We shall look back, or even get into a worse state than we were before. But oh! how different if joy in God leads us to any little act of self denial. How gladly do we do it then! How great an honour then do we esteem it to be! How much does the heart then long to be able to do more for Him who has done so much for us! We are far then from looking down in proud self-complacency upon those who do not go as far as we do, but rather pray to the Lord, that He would be pleased to help our dear brethren and

THIRD PART

sisters forward, who may seem to us weak in any particular point; and we also are conscious to ourselves, that if we have a little more light or strength with reference to one point, other brethren may have more light or grace in other respects.

II. It may be asked, whether I consider brother ----, with all his errors, his fearful errors, to be a brother. My reply is, that so far as my own personal acquaintance is concerned, I am not able to form a judgment about it; but from all I have heard about his godly life formerly for many years, I think there is very much reason to believe that he is a child of God. I have related all this and made it public (which I naturally greatly dislike, on account of brother ---- being my brother, and therefore his sin is my own shame), in order that other children of God may be profited by it. There are two most instructive points connected with the history of the Baptist Church at Stuttgart and of our brother ---- in particular.

1, These children of God had been right in considering believers' baptism to be Scriptural, and in separating from the state church of Wirtemberg. But upon these two points they had laid undue stress. Though believers' baptism is the truth of God; though separation from state churches on the part of children of God who know that a church is "a congregation of believers" is right, because they see in state churches nothing but the world mixed up with some true believers; yet, if these points are made too much of if they are put out of their proper place, as if they were every thing, then there must be spiritual loss suffered by those who do so. Nay, whatever parts of truth are made too much of, though they were even the most precious truths connected with our being risen in Christ, or our heavenly calling, or prophecy, sooner or later those, who lay an undue stress upon these parts of truth, and thus make them too prominent, will be losers in their own souls, and, if they be teachers, they will injure those whom they teach. That was the case at Stuttgart. Baptism and separation from the state church had at last become almost every thing to these dear brethren. "We are the church. Truth is only to be found among us. All others are in error, and in Babylon." These were the phrases used again and again by our brother -----. But God never allows this state of things without chastisement. This spiritual pride had led from one error to another. Oh may it be a warning to me and to all believers who may read this, and may God in mercy give and preserve to them and to me a lowly heart!

2, Another thing, on account of which the church at Stuttgart is a warning, is this: When these dear brethren left the state church of the Kingdom of Wirtemberg, on account of which they had many trials, they did not meet together in dependence upon the Holy Spirit, but they took some Baptist church, whether in H-- or E-- I know not, for a model, and there was to be a teaching elder among them. Instead of being content to own their weakness, and give themselves to prayer that the Lord would be pleased to give them a teacher, brother ---- becomes their teaching elder, and this having been done, he alone speaks at all the meetings (with few exceptions). Now, as his own mind laid such an undue stress upon baptism, and as there was no free working of the Holy Spirit, so that any other brother might have brought out at their meetings what the Lord might have laid upon his heart, what could there have been expected otherwise than that after a time the whole noble little band of disciples, who had taken so trying a stand as to be separated from the state church, should become unsound in the faith. May God grant unto us to be profited by it, dear believing reader, so that in our own church position we do our utmost to give to the Holy Spirit free and unhindered opportunity to work by whom He will!

I have related all these things, painful as they were to me when I was in them, and painful as they are now to me in the remembrance, if it may please God to make them a warning to other dear children of God.

Stuttgart, Oct. 14, 1843.

To the Saints, meeting in the name of Jesus, at Bethesda and Salem Chapels, Bristol.

My dear Brethren,

I have judged that your love to the Lord and to me will make you desirous of knowing further particulars about the work here, and I write therefore a little concerning the state of things here.--Since the date of my last letter I have sought to instruct the dear brethren, who had been led by the Lord to own me as a brother with whom they could and ought to have fellowship, and who, therefore, had been disowned by those with whom they had formerly been associated. The state of things concerning the others, who think they do God service in the way in which they treat us, is very affecting. They not only keep entirely aloof from our meetings, but with those of our number, whom they consider seducers and perverters of the truth, they will not speak, nor greet us again when they are greeted. In this state of things nothing remained for us but to speak to the Lord about them, and I, therefore, proposed last week, that we should have especial prayer meetings for these dear, but awfully deluded, brethren. This was heartily responded to, and we now meet from time to time for especial prayer on their behalf. I mention this that you may help us with your prayers in this particular also. The iron rule, and the want of being able to exercise spiritual judgment is so felt, that only one of the brethren and sisters in the neighbouring little towns and villages, who belonged to the Baptist Church, has ventured to meet with us; but amidst it all I am in peace, knowing that the Lord Himself sent me here, and that the truth at last will assuredly triumph. Indeed I know that except these brethren own the sin of which they have been guilty against me, the Holy Spirit, who has been grieved, will not work among them, and the spiritual death among them will open the eyes of the upright ones. Such an instance came before me last week, when a sister of the Baptist Church came to our meetings, and said that she could not remain any longer where she was, as it was as if God had departed from them. We now meet every Lord's day morning from nine to eleven, for the exposition of the word, and from four to six in the afternoon for the breaking of bread. On Tuesday and Thursday evenings, from eight till nearly ten, I expound the scriptures, and on Wednesday and Friday evenings, from eight to ten, I meet with the brethren to read the scriptures. There is the greatest teachableness among the dear saints with whom I meet; but just because they have been so long fed with error instead of truth, they need to be taught almost every thing. But hitherto the Lord has so helped me, and so made the dear brethren willing to bow before the word of God, that we have gone on most happily, and without any disagreement. The last five meetings of this kind we have spent in considering the truths contained in Romans xii., Ephes. iv., 1 Cor. xii. and xiv., &c. They are now gaining light in apprehending the presence and power of the Holy Spirit in the church, and His indwelling in every individual believer, together with the practical application of these truths; and I cannot but hope, that if the Lord, even now at once, were to remove me from them, they would be able to witness in some measure for God, with regard to their church position. But even these truths will take up several such evenings yet, in order that the dear brethren not only may be grounded in them, but also be profited by my experience in these particulars during the last thirteen years, that they may not fall into the same errors, or be exposed to the same difficulties. When that subject is done with, I have to undertake another work, perhaps as difficult as any I have had since I have been here, and I mention it to you, that you may help me with your prayers, that the Lord would be pleased to give me His especial help in that matter also. I understand that all the dear precious saints with whom I meet, have fallen into the awful error, spread almost universally among even true believers in this country, that at last all men will be saved, and even the devils themselves. This awful error I must attack as soon as the subject which we now consider is finished; but pray earnestly that the Lord would give me such spiritual power, as that these dear brethren may be brought, through God's truth, out of this delusion also. I hope in God concerning this matter. He will help me. He has in so many ways made it so abundantly plain that He Himself sent me here, that He will help me in this matter also.--Last Lord's day we were twenty in number at the breaking of bread, including my dear wife and myself; among them was the first fruit of my labours here, in the way of conversion. She is a young lady of nineteen years, the daughter of the procurator of the upper tribunal, Dr. R, one of the former elders of the Baptist Church, who for my sake was cast out. This young sister was baptized about four miles from here, in a river, about eight o'clock in the evening, by moonlight, as the dear brethren feared the tumult and concourse of the opposers in the day time. I advised her father to baptize her, in order that at once, even in this respect, there might be nothing in the judgment of the dear saints, as if a ministerial person, according to the use of the word in the world, were needed, and also that thus the attention of the police might not needlessly be directed towards me, as they are so particularly opposed to baptism. Hitherto I have been left unmolested and unhindered, although I have been nearly eight weeks here, and although it is becoming known throughout the city, and beginning also to spread throughout the country that I am here.--The work still remains small as to outward appearance, as generally, besides the believers in fellowship, there are not more than about ten or twelve persons present; but I dare not take a large place to meet in, humanly speaking, and judging from what hitherto has been always done, but I must go on quietly instructing the saints, or preaching to the few sinners who come, in the hope that God, through my instructing the brethren, will open the eyes and hearts of others, after I have left. There is one brother among us, who learned the way of God more perfectly in Switzerland, and who often had spoken about it, before I came, but who was neither much listened to, nor received into fellowship, because he was not baptized.--In the mean time I also go on with preparing my Narrative in the German language for the press, having found out that there is sufficient freedom of the press here to allow of my getting it printed; but I make but little progress, as my time is, in a variety of ways, here also taken up, and as I have too little mental strength to continue very long at a time working with my pen. Nevertheless, I have about the fifth part ready for the press. I am more and more assured that Germany needs my service in this respect, and that the Lord has called me for this work. About the time of my return to you I can say nothing, as the Lord has not given me any light concerning it; but this I must say, that my wife and myself shall consider it a happy day indeed, when the Lord allows us to see you again. But, His servants we are, and we desire grace to tarry as cheerfully here, as we shall be glad to go back to Bristol, when the Lord sends us back. Only help us in the mean time with your prayers, (as we also pray for you), that the Lord would enable us in this dark land to glorify His holy name. Farewell, greatly beloved brethren. My heart longs after you to behold you again; yet I am happy here, and will cheerfully wait the Lord's own time here. I repeat, that if any of you have it in your heart to write to us, and will leave the letters at my house, they will be forwarded to me. My dear wife sends her love in Christ to all the dear brethren and sisters.

Your affectionate brother and servant in the Lord,

GEORGE MUeLLER.

I make again a few remarks in connexion with this letter.

I. One of my especial aims in my service among the dear brethren at Stuttgart was, to seek to ground them in the truth. To this end we had, from the beginning of our being separated from the Baptist Church, two meetings in the week, from eight to ten o'clock in the evening, when we considered together, upon the ground of the word of God, those points of truth on which these dear brethren appeared to me most to need instruction. I judged it not enough to expound the Scriptures at their public meetings, but to give an opportunity to any brother or sister, at these private meetings, to state any difficulties that they might have on their minds. At first we considered particularly the great truths of the gospel, so that any remaining errors, connected with fundamental points, might be corrected. After that we began the consideration of Romans xii. 3-8, Ephes. iv. 7-16, 1 Cor. xii. and xiv., and the other passages which stand in connexion with the truths taught in these portions. The brethren had seen almost immediately that, according to the example of the first disciples (Acts xx. 7), it would become us to meet every first day of the week for the breaking of bread. Thus far they had light, and that light, I judged, ought to be carried out at once. We therefore from the beginning met every Lord's day for the breaking of bread, with the exception of two or three who had for a few weeks some

THIRD PART

little doubt remaining on their mind, whether, on account of the frequency of the observance, this ordinance might not lose its beneficial effects; but as we left them free, to act according to the light they had, they soon saw the greatness of the privilege of being allowed so often to show forth the Lord's death, and they therefore met regularly with us.--As, however, on my arrival at Stuttgart, the dear brethren had been entirely uninstructed about the truths relating to the power and presence of the Holy Ghost in the church of Christ, and to our ministering one to another as fellow members in the body of Christ; and as I had known enough of painful consequences when brethren began to meet professedly in dependence upon the Holy Spirit without knowing what was meant by it, and thus meetings had become opportunities for unprofitable talking rather than for godly edifying; and as I felt myself bound to communicate to these dear brethren the experience I had gathered with reference to these very truths since June 1830: for these reasons, I say, I thought it well to spend evening after evening with them over the passages above mentioned. Thus week after week passed away. We broke bread, but it was understood, and I wished it to be understood, that I was the only speaker. This I did that in every possible way I might have opportunity of instructing the brethren, and because they knew not yet what was meant by meeting in dependence upon the Holy Spirit. But, at length, after we had for about eight weeks or more spent two evenings a week together over those passages, and others setting forth the same truths, and full opportunity had been given, carefully to look at all the points connected with them, and when now there seemed a measure of apprehension of the mind of God in those passages, then we met for the purpose of carrying out what the brethren had learned, and therefore, at the next time when we met for the breaking of bread, I took my place among them simply as a brother; yet as a brother who had received a measure of gift for the

benefit of his fellow members, and upon whom therefore responsibility was laid to use that measure of gift, and who, by the grace of God, felt this responsibility laid upon him, and who was willing to act accordingly. I do not mean at all to say that even then this matter was perfectly understood, for a few times still things like these would occur:--A brother read a portion of the Word, and then would say, "Perhaps our brother Mueller will expound to us this portion." Or, a brother might speak a little on a subject, and then would say, "Perhaps our brother Mueller will enter somewhat more fully into this subject." At such times, which occurred twice or thrice, I said nothing, but acted according to the desire of those brethren, and spoke; but afterwards, when we met privately, at our scripture reading meetings, I pointed out to the dear brethren their mistake, and reminded them that all these matters ought to be left to the ordering of the Holy Ghost, and that if it had been truly good for them, the Lord would have not only led me to speak at that time, but also on the very subject on which they desired that I should speak to them.

II. At these scripture reading meetings, of which I had about forty with them, we went on very peacefully and happily, though I had many things to bring before the brethren which were quite new to them, and some points also to which they had been exceedingly opposed. The Lord enabled me to seek His help for this service, and He granted it to me.

III. I never had a moment's hesitation in owning these brethren, and meeting with them at the breaking of bread; for I could not say of any of them that they wilfully held those errors, but that it rather arose from the truth never having been brought before them. I therefore judged, that it was my duty to seek to instruct them in the truth, and then they would be led to renounce their errors.

IV. I had from the beginning great hope that the dear brethren would be brought out of their fearful errors. I never was overwhelmed by the prospect of the difficulties before me, but had confidence in God, that through Him I should conquer. My assurance was built on the following grounds: 1, I considered the remarkable way in which so unexpectedly, and after the overcoming of so many difficulties which had been in the way, I was sent to them. I therefore judged that the Lord had sent me to them for blessing. 2, He had given me grace to pray much for the saints at Stuttgart before I had ever seen them, and He helped me to continue in prayer for them whilst with them. This I judged was, in order that He might answer my request on their behalf. 3, They were not like persons who had had the truth set before them, and wilfully rejected it, but they had never had it set before them. 4, The Lord, in His grace, enabled me to deal patiently with them. They were deeply entangled in error, very deeply. Pressing things hastily upon them, I knew, would only make matters worse; but patiently hearing all their objections; meeting time after time over the Word, and seeking the Lord's blessing in prayer on those meetings both before and after, being willing not to press a point too much at once, but giving time to the Holy Ghost to work upon their hearts; dealing thus with them, even as the Lord had inclined my heart, I judged that He would give me the desire of my heart, and deliver them out of their fearful errors.

V. I cannot help noticing here the strange mistake under which the religious public was with reference to my being at Stuttgart. It was this: Some weeks after my arrival the report was spread, and widely too, (for it was printed in one of the religious periodicals), that I was a Missionary sent by the Baptists in England, to bring back the Baptists in Wirtemberg to the State Church, as it was the view of the Baptists in England that it was not wrong to be united with the State Church. This having been stated in print, (though I knew not of it till I was on the point of returning to England), my stay at Stuttgart, I suppose, was rather liked by religious persons in connexion with the State Church, and it is not at all unlikely that that may have contributed to my being permitted to work quietly week after week, and month after month, without the police in the least interfering with me, though it not only was well known, that I was there, but well known too what I was doing in the way of holding meetings, etc. I recognise the hand of the Lord in allowing this mistake to be made.

VI. For many weeks the number of those who frequented the meetings was very small. Very few, besides those who were in communion with us, attended them. The highly sectarian and exclusive spirit which had been manifested by those brethren, who belonged to the Baptist Church, was a great hindrance in the way; for it was

THIRD PART

naturally supposed that we were of the same mind with them. But after nearly five months had passed away, there began to be a different effect produced. The number of those who attended increased, and increased to more than twice or thrice as many as used to come at first, and, humanly speaking, had I seen it to be the Lord's will to remain one month longer, the result might have been still greater. But as I saw as clearly the time of my departure from Stuttgart as that of my going thither, I was not influenced by any outward appearance; for I felt certain that, for various reasons, I ought to return to my service in Bristol.--In this circumstance also I cannot but see the hand of God. Had the meetings all at once been much attended in the beginning, it might have attracted the attention of the police, and possibly a ticket of permission to reside any longer at Stuttgart might not have been granted to me; but, as it was, there was nothing whatever outwardly to attract the notice of the world, for we were few in number, met in a very poor neighbourhood, and in a poor meeting place, and I had thus opportunity to instruct the saints.

Stuttgart, Nov. 11, 1843.

To the Brethren meeting in the name of Jesus, at Salem and Bethesda Chapels, Bristol

Dear Brethren,

I have judged that it might be profitable to you, with the Lord's blessing, to hear again a few particulars of His work here, and I have also thought that the love you bear me will make you desirous to know how I am, and what the Lord is doing with me, and therefore I again write you a little, which is no burden to me, but a sweet pleasure. Yet I assure you, dear brethren, I need not write to you, in order that I may be reminded of you; for I think of you daily, and pray daily for you, as I am sure you do for us: and it will, indeed, be a sweet pleasure to us and joy in the Lord, to behold your faces again; but, in the meantime, we desire grace, not to feel ourselves as in banishment, but so to realize, that this is our present place of service, and so to walk with Jesus, that we maybe very happy, even now, though so far, and for so long a time absent from you. It is now thirteen weeks and three days since I left Bristol, but I have not, during all this time, even for one single minute, been permitted to question whether the conclusion, that I should serve the Lord for a season in this country, was of Him or not; but during all this time, as also many weeks before I left Bristol, my heart has had the fullest assurance concerning this matter. It has been also very kind of the Lord, that He has not even suffered me to be tempted, through a great variety of trying events, which might have occurred either here or in Bristol, to question my call for this service; but, on the contrary, every day's experience almost, here, confirms my mind, and every letter from Bristol also shows, how that God's finger is in this matter. And thus, my dear brethren, it must be always, when we are taking any step according to the will of the Lord: the result must be peace and blessing. I desire therefore quietly to, tarry here, till the same Lord, who put me at this post, shall call me away from it.

--I now enter upon the narrative of a few facts which I wish to communicate to you, that you may be led yet more highly to prize the spiritual privileges, and especially the religious liberty, which you enjoy in England.--About nineteen months since a brother and sister here, who were connected with the little Baptist Church, (the only body of believers in this country who are separated from the State Church) desired to be united by marriage. As they had conscientious objections to be married according to the usage of the State Church, a statement was sent to the director of this city, the first magistrate, in which this brother and sister expressed their desire and declared that they would submit themselves to everything to which they could with a good conscience, such as having their names three times publicly called at the church, paying the clergyman's fees, &c.; but that they could not conform to the marriage ceremony at the church, and they therefore begged to be exempted from this; and they finally claimed for this the rights of the subjects of the kingdom of Wirtemberg, to whom full liberty of conscience is granted by the constitution of the Government. After a time they received a complete denial to this request from the Ecclesiastical court, called the Consistory. They now gave in a full statement of their views, why they left the State Church, why they could not conform to the marriage ceremony in the State Church, &c., and sent this statement, if I remember right, to the highest court, the ministry of the kingdom. It was again refused. And so also by the king himself. Many months had in the meantime elapsed, and the patience of the brother and sister at last began to fail, and as the sister (at that time) saw scarcely any objection to be married at the church, the brother was at last overcome, and he went and gave in the banns at the church. This was in the middle of June last summer. The nearer, however, the marriage day came, the more tried the brother felt, and all peace left him. At last he came to the conclusion to leave himself quite in the hands of the Lord while in the church, and to do no more than he could do with a good conscience; yet he did not know anything definite, nor did he tell his intended wife anything. He asked the brethren, with whom he was in fellowship, to pray for him, who accordingly met at the time when he was to be married. It was on a Lord's day afternoon after the public service, and several hundreds of people had remained. The clergyman, a believer, who, no doubt, knew of the former expressed conscientious objection of this brother and sister, did not at all use the printed liturgy, but only gave, as I hear, a scriptural address as the occasion called for, which our brother found profitable. After this the brother and sister made the usual solemn declaration that they would take each other as husband and wife, &c. This, our brother considered all that could be required of him as a subject. But now remained the clergyman's blessing and confirmation of the matrimony, which in the literal English translation is as follows: "As you then have solemnly promised to each other conjugal love and fidelity, I therefore confirm in the name of the Father, the Son, and the Holy Ghost, as an appointed minister of the Christian church, this your conjugal union as a union, which according to God's order, is indissoluble. What God has joined together, let no man put asunder." Now, while the clergyman was pronouncing the first of these words, the brother walked a step or two back from the altar, with his wife, and inter-

THIRD PART

rupted the clergyman in words to this effect: "I do not belong to the State Church, and I therefore cannot accept the blessing of the State Church, or the confirmation of the State Church, with reference to our marriage. Our Union was made in heaven, and therefore needs no earthly confirmation. I have gone as far as I could with a good conscience, but further I can do nothing."--The clergyman now stated "I pronounce your marriage as void, and I shall give notice of your behaviour to the magistrates."--The whole matter made a great stir, the people rushed out of the church, and our brother, with his wife, having gone orderly back into their pews, fell on their knees and prayed, and then walked home.--The first thing that now followed was, that the relations on the part of the wife sought to separate the brother and sister by all possible means, removing the furniture out of their intended rooms, sending policemen, and not suffering the brother to live where he had purposed to live after marriage, so that the newly married couple had to take up their abode in the house of a brother in the Lord now in fellowship with us, who is the brother of the young wife. On the next day the newly married brother went to the clergyman, and humbly stated to him, that that, which had occurred on the previous day, was not in the least intended as an insult to him, but that he had been forced to act thus to maintain a good conscience. But he again declared the marriage as void, and said that he should legally proceed against him. Either on the same day, or the day after, our brother and sister had to appear before the director of the city, and after having been for hours examined, the marriage was declared as void, and they were ordered to separate from each other, otherwise the laws against concubinage would be put in force against them. Our brother and sister meekly declared, that they would gladly submit to the Government in every thing, in which they could submit with a good conscience, but that they should not separate from each other, as they considered that they, according to divine and human laws, were married. After some time they had to appear a second time, and, if I remember right, a third, if not a fourth time; but they always gave the same declaration before the city director, and added that they claimed the rights of the subjects of Wirtemberg, according to which there was secured to them perfect liberty of conscience. So the matter remained. Nothing more occurred till Monday, Oct. 23rd, when the said brother was ordered to appear before a court called the "Criminal Court" at half-past two, his wife at three, and the brother who had taken them in and lodged them, at half-past three in the afternoon. I ought to have said before, that all three belong to those saints who for my sake were separated from the Baptist Church here. Brother R. and I therefore met for prayer while they were before the judge, and continued in prayer from half-past two till half-past five. All three experienced the fulfilment of that word: "Take no thought how or what ye shall speak: for it shall be given you in that same hour what ye shall speak." Matt. x. 19. The Lord was very nigh to them. They were able firmly, but meekly, to bear testimony for the truth. Even the sister, though alone before the judge, was greatly helped. She has been, ever since the event at the church, quite of one mind with her husband. The crime alleged against the other brother at this court was, that, after he knew that the magistrates had declared the marriage illegal, he still lodged them in his house; to which he declared that he considered the marriage legal. This led to the reasons, and a long and blessed testimony for the Lord was borne before the judge. The crime alleged against the husband before this court was, that he had intended this as an insult against the church, which he denied, but stated that he had gone as far as he could, and that he would rather suffer any thing than act against his conscience. On Thursday, Oct. 26th, these three dear saints had to stand before the same judge, each again alone, from half-past two till half-past five, whilst brother R. and I were again in prayer for them. The Lord again abundantly helped them. Even the judge, though a Roman Catholic, sought both times to favour them as much as possible, and the investigations of the whole affair were as favourably taken down for them on paper by him, as if a brother in the Lord had written them down. We know how that came. The Lord heard the prayers of His children, and also acted according to the just mentioned promise. To both brethren was permitted to hand in on the next day a written statement, on what scriptural grounds the husband's conscience led him to act as he did; and the other brother, on what scriptural grounds he could not obey the magistrate, in refusing to lodge his sister and brother-in-law, when their marriage had been declared illegal. Brother R. and I now wrote two long statements about the affair with scriptural proofs, which, on the next day, were delivered to the Court. On Friday, Oct. 27, the brother, the husband, had to stand the third time that week before the judge, who, among other things, told him, that until the matter by the proper court was decided, the police would separate him and his wife. Thus the matter stands. Our brother and sister may any day be separated; if so, they will be only separated as long as they are in prison; when they come out, they feel themselves before God bound to come again together; and should the matter be forced, they must leave the country. Moreover, if the matter is pressed, the husband may be from six months to two years imprisoned for the act at the church. But the Lord reigneth, and men can go no further than the Lord gives them permission. Our brother who lodged them is liable to six months' imprisonment; but the Lord reigneth. Nothing is to be done here, except to pray and to be ready to suffer for the Lord's sake, in order that real liberty of conscience may be obtained. Such a case never occured here before. The courts know not themselves what to do. The judge who investigated the case, in order to lay the written investigation before the proper court, said publicly: "I wonder how they will manage this affair." With reference to my own judgment about the matter, it is this: If any brother and sister were now to be married to whom the Lord has given the same light, they should not go at all to the church, but simply give information to the magistrates, have their names called at church, declare themselves ready to pay the fees, and state before the brethren that they mean to consider themselves as united by marriage; and if the government after this oppresses them, to leave the country. I cannot regret that matters have been as they have. The government itself forced our brother, so to say, to do what he did: and good will come out of it for the church.--We are now waiting for what the Lord will do in this matter, and to see whether these dear saints will have to bear imprisonment or not.

Another event has occurred: On Oct. 24th, the elders of the Baptist Church, and therefore two of the brethren with whom I now meet for the breaking of bread, were ordered to appear before the director of the city to hear a communication from the ministers of state with reference to their request about being permitted to marry,

THIRD PART

without going to church. As this order now came to them as being of the Baptist Church, whilst our brethren no longer belong to the Baptist Church, but consider themselves united with all who love our Lord Jesus, they sent a written statement to the director of the city, stating that they had ceased to belong to the Baptist Church. Thus, without our seeking it, the position which we hold, even if it had not been so before, is now made known. Still, hitherto nothing has been done to us, nor any hinderance laid in our way. Indeed a few days since, through a particular circumstance, the city director had my passport put into his hands, with the inquiry whether a ticket of permission to remain in Stuttgart should be granted to me, or not, and there were no objections made. So I still teach and preach Christ freely, and all that the Lord has taught me, although to a very small number; for the people are afraid of us. In the mean time I speak to souls as I may meet them in the fields, or when persons ask for an alms without the city, for in the whole of Stuttgart I never saw one beggar. I also make considerable progress with my Narrative, much more than at the first, and have nearly one-half ready for the press.

When we took our position here of receiving all who love our Lord Jesus, irrespective of their agreeing with us in all points, one brother came among us, who had been always refused by the Baptist Church here, because he was not baptized. After this brother had been about six weeks among us, he himself desired baptism. He was baptized on the evening of Oct. 28. Thus we have been able to give a practical proof of the truth which we hold.

Our number has only been increased by the arrival of our brother T. H., the son of our brother H., whom you know. He resides in the same house with us.--I repeat that it will give us joy to hear from any of you. We remember before the Lord those of you by name, of whom it has been written to us that they are in trial. My dear wife sends her love to all the dear brethren and sisters.

I remain, my dear brethren,

Your brother and servant in the Lord,

GEORGE MUeLLER

P.S.--I only add that the two brothers and the sister, by their meekness and godly walk, much commend the truth, and are precious instruments chosen of the Lord, to carry the truth before the rulers of the land.

Dec. 31, 1843. During this year 75 have been received into communion among us in Bristol, and 13 saints have fallen asleep. Being absent from Bristol, I am not able to give the present exact state of the church there as to numbers.--The Lord has been pleased to give me during this year for my temporal necessities.

1, Through the saints among whom I labour in Bristol, in provisions, clothes, etc. worth to us, at least L10 0s. 0d.

2, Through anonymous offerings in money, put up in paper, and directed to me, and put into the boxes for the poor saints, or the rent, at the meeting places L130 8s. 4 3/4d.

3, Through presents in money, from saints in Bristol, not given anonymously L106 12s. 0d.

4, Through presents in money from saints not residing in Bristol L79 1s. 6d.

Altogether L326 1s. 10 3/4d.

To this is to be added that the expenses connected with our journey to Germany, and with our temporal necessities, and all the various expenses coming on us in connexion with our stay in a foreign land, from Aug. 9, to Dec. 31, were met out of the 702l. 3s. 7d., which had been given to me, as has been stated, for several purposes, but especially also for the expenses connected with my service in Germany.

Is it not again most manifest from this statement, that during the year 1843 also I served a most kind Master even with reference to temporal supplies? And this I delight to show. If I had been striving with all my might to obtain a good income during the year 1843, I could not have had more; for in one way or another the Lord gave me about 400l. without asking any one for any thing, and therefore I had far more than I needed either for myself and family, or for giving me ability to use hospitality. I find it more and more pleasant, even with reference to this life, to walk in the ways of the Lord, and to rely upon Him for all I need; and often, when I recount on my walks for meditation the mercies of the Lord towards me, I am constrained to say to the praise of the Lord, that if I had remained in my unconverted state, and therefore continued a servant of Satan, I could not have been nearly as well off, even with reference to this life, as I am now in the service of the Lord Jesus. I find, that the more the Lord enables me, not to seek my own things, but the things of Jesus Christ, the more He takes care that my temporal necessities shall be richly supplied.

Jan. 1, 1844.--Last evening I met with the whole little church at Stuttgart to tea, and the last hours of the year, till about 12 o'clock at night, we spent together in prayer.

THIRD PART

On Jan. 15th, I wrote another letter to the brethren in Bristol, which is here subjoined.

Stuttgart, Jan. 15, 1844,

To the Saints meeting in the name of Jesus, at Bethesda and Salem Chapels, Bristol.

Beloved Brethren.,

I have it in my heart once more to write to you a little about the work of the Lord here, before my return to you, and I do it the more readily, because I have confidence in your love, being assured that you are as glad to hear from me, as I am to write to you. With reference to all the time since I left you, and in particular with reference to the time since I last wrote to you, I have abundant reason to say, that goodness and mercy have followed us. Never, since I first saw it to be the will of God, that I should labour here for a season, which is now more than seven months, have I been permitted to question, that this conclusion was formed under the guidance of the Holy Ghost; and ever since I left you, which is now five months and six days, every thing has proved, that I left you according to the will of God. It is precious, beloved brethren, to go on an errand when the Lord Himself sends us, and to be at a post where the Lord Himself has placed us for then all goes on well. Far better to wait months, or even years, than to take a step in uncertainty, or being but half assured that it is the will of God, that we should take that step.--But as fully as I was assured that I should leave you for a season, so, as far as I can see at present the mind of the Lord, does it appear to me now, that the time is fast approaching, when our Lord will give us again the great joy and precious privilege of seeing you face to face. Truly, we may say, through grace, and without hypocrisy, "We, brethren, being taken from you for a short time in presence, not in heart;" indeed nothing but grace has kept us here so long. And now the time seems to be fast approaching when we shall leave this, and I am by prayer and labour endeavouring, to see your face soon. If the Lord will, my Narrative, (which, with a particular reference to the spiritual necessities of the Church in Germany, I have been preparing for the press, and is nearly finished), will be printed within five weeks from this day, so that I hope we shall be able to leave this towards the end of February. Yet, in the mean time, there remains much work for me still to do, both with reference to writing and labouring among the brethren here; therefore continue, dear brethren, even as you have done hitherto, to help me with your prayers; and we also, by the help of God, will continue to intercede for you, as we do with joy.

As there have occurred a number of important events among us, since I wrote to you last, I proceed now to give you some account of them.--In the early part of

November last year, brother R., the Doctor of Law, asked me to unite with him and a sister in prayer, as that sister (not one in fellowship with us, but belonging to the State Church) was going to be divorced from her husband, and she had desired that we should spend the time with her in prayer for her husband, while this act would be settled in the judicial court. This sister had had to suffer exceedingly during the space of many years from her husband, who hated her greatly for the Lord's sake. Three times she had been obliged to leave him, because of his awful treatment; but three times, especially through the peace-making efforts of brother R., who was her legal counsellor, she returned to her husband, and lived for a season with him, till at last each time her health sank under the sufferings she had endured from him. At length, about two years since, she left him again, with the intention not to return to him any more. This led to a divorce by law, a thing not uncommon on the Continent; and in that hour in which we met for prayer, the matter was settled. In consequence of this, as she had three children, and brought a comparatively considerable property to her husband, the law proceeded to secure this money for the benefit of herself and children, as the husband had wasted all his own property. This act was settled on December 9th, on which occasion she had to meet her husband at his house with the appointed government officers; and she requested our brother Dr. R., as a friend to accompany her. Brother R. (who had been for fifteen years the peace-maker between this husband and wife, and who had three times succeeded in favour of the husband, though the legal adviser of the wife) was nevertheless greatly hated by the husband, who repeatedly spoke to him in public courts of law thus: "You shall never baptize me." Or, "Now my wife will soon be free to marry her priest," (meaning brother R.,) &c. All this brother R. had been able to bear with the greatest meekness, though thus publicly insulted, when acting as solicitor or barrister at the judicial courts. Now on the 9th of December, brother R., as I said, went with this divorced sister to her husband's house. When all the business was done, the husband came close to brother R., in the presence of several magistrates, put a pistol to his side and fired it at him, then took another pistol, put it to his own breast, fired and sank down dead immediately. But while he himself died immediately, brother R. has been wonderfully preserved. He wore a thick wadded coat, and had four papers in his side pocket, through all of which the ball passed. Then, to show the hand of God, the ball met in the other clothes such obstacles (all being double in that spot,) that it only entered a very little way into the body and lodged upon one of the ribs. After the fire was extinguished, (for our brother's clothes were set on fire, so near had the poor sinner put the pistol to him,) our brother walked home, and shortly after a surgeon extracted the ball, and on the seventh day our brother was so far restored, that the whole little church here could be gathered around his bed, together with his relations, and we united together in praising the Lord for His wonderful help; and on the fifteenth day our brother was already so far restored, that he was able to assemble himself again with us for the breaking of bread. Half an inch higher or lower might have taken his life; but the balls (for the pistol was loaded with two, one of which fell out of his clothes,) though most maliciously so prepared that they might do much mischief on entering the body, found so much resistance that the power, through the soft clothing being every part double in that spot, was spent before touching the body. Surely, the Lord is round about us Even the ungodly in this city have been forced to marvel; but now the

THIRD PART

devil spreads the report that that wicked person shot our brother, because he purposed to marry his wife.

At last also the sentence has come from the judicial court appointed for that business, with reference to the married brother and sister about whom I wrote to you. Both of them are sentenced to fourteen days' imprisonment, and their marriage is declared to be illegal and only concubinage, so that when the imprisonment is over, they will be separated by the police, and sent back to prison, should they still seek to live together as they must do, being married in the sight of God. Further, the brother who lodged them after their marriage, is sentenced to four days' imprisonment, because he helped on, as it is said, concubinage. Finally, the husband is sentenced to pay 4/6 of the legal expenses, his wife 1/6 and the other brother 1/6. If here were only the question about money, or suffering imprisonment, we must bear it, and account it an honour, to suffer for Christ's sake; but as the sentence is, that this marriage is concubinage, which according to God and to man it is not, and as the liberty of the Wirtemberg subjects allows them to appeal to a higher court, and as brother R. can do all this business, I have with brother R. and some other brethren judged, that in this case, like Paul, we ought to appeal to a higher court, if by any means we may keep the government from committing this grievous sin of unjustly punishing those godly persons. Should this, however, be in vain, we must yield to the power, the brethren must bear the imprisonment, and this dear couple must leave the country.

Our position here as saints was unquestionably known from the beginning by the police, who watch us closely; but nothing was officially done in the matter till very recently, which was occasioned in the following way. The Baptist church here have two or three times a year, or as often as the city director (the head of the police) requires it, to give in the list of names of those who belong to the church, who have been added, and who have been separating themselves or have been excluded. At the close of the year that was now done again, when the considerable number who had left it on my account, were noticed by the city director, who then sent for the teaching elder or president of the Baptist church, who told him all about me, and that I had occasioned this business. This now drew forth an order from the city director to brother R., in which he was requested to state--1. Who had separated themselves with him, (names, station in life, and place of abode)?--2. Whether we meant to form a separate church?--3. Who were the elders?--4. And who at present belonged to our number? This was very briefly replied to by giving the names of those who separated themselves, the additional two names of those who have been added since, that we meant to be in communion with all who love our Lord Jesus, and that this was the reason, why we had separated ourselves from the Baptist church. To this no reply has been sent; nor has any one as yet put the least hinderance to my freely teaching and preaching Jesus Christ, though it is now five months and six days since I have been labouring here.

The Lord is also now beginning to work among the brethren belonging to the Baptist church here, in answer to our and your prayers, and those of many other dear saints in England, Switzerland, &c. Several are beginning to feel that their position is not a right one, but none have yet fully and publicly renounced their errors, which, I trust, will soon be the case. May we continue to pray concerning this matter. Moreover, the prejudices against us are wearing off on the part of some other persons, so that the number who attend our meetings is rather increasing. There seem also several who are somewhat concerned about their souls, and a few children of God belonging to the state church come. Another brother was also added to our number about a fortnight ago, so that we are now two-and-twenty altogether, who break bread. This is a small company certainly, but though it be only like a taper on a candlestick, yet there is some light, however little, and I trust that, with God's blessing, this light will be more and more bright in Germany, where it is so much needed. The Lord is also blessing my labours among the dear brethren here, so that they grow in knowledge, and, I trust, in grace also; likewise those errors, of which I wrote to you, are giving way, but they are not overcome fully yet, and I shall have a conflict still about them, before I leave: still the Lord has kept us in peace, by giving me wisdom to deal gently with the brethren, remembering the years in which they were built up in error. Help me also with your prayers, that I may find a bookseller to take my book on commission for sale; for I have offered it to three, and they have refused it. One glimpse was enough for one, in seeing that I did not belong to a State Church. Surely I have conflict here step by step; but God helps, and through Him I shall do valiantly in this thing also; nevertheless I beg your prayers.--And now, finally, I entreat you, beloved pilgrims, help me with your prayers, that I may do and suffer all the will of God here gladly, that I may live to His honour while remaining here, that I may be helped in the remainder of my work, that I may not leave a day before, nor stay a day beyond the Lord's time, and that the Lord would give us a prosperous journey and voyage in His own time. My dear wife unites with me in love to all the dear brethren and sisters. We often pray for you, and remember by name those who are in particular trial through bereavement, or from other causes. Farewell.

Your affectionate brother and servant in the Lord,

GEORGE MUeLLER

I add a few remarks in connexion with this letter:--

I. The wisdom of our brother R., in being present at the judicial settlement of the money affairs of the sister, who was legally divorced from her husband, may be questioned, on account of the expressions used by the husband. As to myself, knowing the particulars more fully than the reader can, I do not for a moment think that the man thought our brother had any intention of marrying his divorced wife, for all these expressions were evidently only used to insult Dr. R.; but my objection would rather spring from this, that I question whether a christian has any business at all

THIRD PART

with such concerns. The Lord in a most remarkable way protected Dr. R.; but this by no means proves that he was in his proper place.

II. I also say a few words more about the brother and sister whose marriage was considered illegal. The appeal to the highest court was of no avail, also the final appeal to the King was useless, and about July, 1844, the brother and sister were imprisoned for fourteen days, and the brother, who had taken them in, four days. The Lord was with them, and blessed them much in the prison, as they wrote me. The brethren had free access to them, and once even the greater part of them met in the prison and broke bread together. This exceeding great leniency was granted to them, I think, through the judge who had to investigate their affairs. When their imprisonment was expired, they were ordered to separate, which however they did not do, considering themselves married in the sight of God. For a long time the government only threatened, without separating them by force; at last, however, in March, 1845, after having taken from him his right of citizenship at Stuttgart, and having thus deprived him of the privilege of carrying on his business as a master cabinet-maker, the husband was taken by force from his wife, and escorted by a policeman to his parish, which is about nine miles distant. This was done after the government had suffered them to live together as husband and wife above twenty months, and after they had had a child more than ten months old, which however the Lord took to Himself about a week before the parents were thus separated. This affair has occasioned the loss of the business of this brother; and if an alteration be not shortly made in the laws of the country, with reference to liberty of conscience concerning marriage, (which they hope for, as they mean to appeal to the representatives of the people,) they purpose to emigrate to England.

Though our brother and sister might have acted more wisely, and not have brought the matter to this public act at the church; yet we must keep in mind that their position had been trying, as for more than a twelve-month they had delayed being married, in hope of obtaining permission from the government not to have to go to the State Church; and as no one of the brethren had ever been thus situated; and as they themselves had not much light, yet wished to maintain a good conscience: on these accounts, I say, we cannot but feel for our brother and sister in their trial, and remember them in love.

Were it again to occur, that a brother and sister of the little church at Stuttgart should desire to be united in marriage, and have conscientious objection to be married in the State Church, I gave it as my judgment to the brethren, that they should humbly and meekly make known their intentions to the city director, have their banns called in the Church, pay the fees of the clergyman, etc., and afterwards make known to the whole little Church that they took each other in marriage, signify the same to the city director, and not go to the State Church. If after this they should not be suffered to live together, then to emigrate.

III. After I had been between two and three months at Stuttgart, and the brethren had been instructed in some measure, both at the public meetings and at the

Scripture Reading Meetings, about many important truths, I at last began decidedly to go forward at our private meetings, after much prayer, to the exposing of the fearful errors, which they almost all held, in thinking that at last all men would be saved, and even the devils themselves. We had not, however, had more than two or three meetings on this subject, when Dr. R. was shot; and as this occasioned his absence for some time, I thought it better not to go on with the subject; and when he was sufficiently restored, it was wished that we should consider all the passages connected with the Lord's supper. As on this point also the brethren needed instruction, I readily yielded the point, judging that I had to show them, by being willing to wait, that I sought not my own gratification, in considering their views about universal salvation. Thus five or six meetings were spent in considering all the portions of the Holy Scriptures which speak about the Lord's Supper. But now, this having been finished, I proposed that we should resume considering the Scriptures, with reference to universal salvation, and I found that they had been led into this error, because 1, They did not see the difference between the earthly calling of the Jews, and the heavenly calling of the believers in the Lord Jesus in the present dispensation, and therefore they said, that, because the words "everlasting," etc., are applied to "the possession of the land of Canaan," and the "priesthood of Aaron," that therefore the punishment of the wicked cannot be without end, seeing that the possession of Canaan and the priesthood of Aaron are not without end. My endeavour, therefore, was, to show the brethren the difference between the earthly calling of Israel and our heavenly one, and to prove from Scripture, that whenever, the word "everlasting" is used with reference to things purely not of the earth, but beyond time, it denotes a period without end. 2, They had laid exceeding great stress upon a few passages where, in Luther's translation of the German Bible, the word hell occurs, and where it ought to have been translated either "hades" in some passages, or "grave" in others, and where they saw a deliverance out of hell, and a being brought up out of hell, instead of "out of the grave." 3, They had taken passages out of their connexion.--The mode which I now pursued was, to refer to all the very many passages which they had written down, and to expound them according to the connexion in which they stood, seeking to show the brethren this connexion. In addition to this, I requested them to allow me to speak on those passages without being interrupted, in order that, being able pretty fully to enter upon this subject, there might be free opportunity given to the Holy Ghost to work conviction in their hearts; and, as they were greatly in favour of universal salvation, they might thus be kept from controversy, to which they would have been inclined, without having heard what I had to say from the Word of God against universal salvation; for I had previously given them full opportunity to bring out their own views. After having thus proceeded for several evenings in our private meetings, I saw that the greater part were fully convinced about the errors they had held, and the others had no desire to contradict, though they had perhaps not grace enough to say plainly that they had been in error. Nor did I in the least enforce that any acknowledgment should be made to me. These meetings took place during the last three weeks of my stay at Stuttgart. Thus, by having received grace from the Lord to deal patiently with the brethren, and to wait upon God even for the right time to attack these errors, I was helped to conquer in this thing also.

THIRD PART

IV. I add also a few words more with reference to my Narrative, which I published at Stuttgart. When I had proceeded a considerable way in preparing it for the press, I found especial help from God, in being directed through a kind brother, whom I had known eight years before at Stuttgart, to a paper manufacturer, from whom I could buy the paper for 4,000 copies on advantageous terms, and also to a very honourable and promise-keeping printer. The printer engaged to print two sheets a week and kept his word to the end, so that as long as six weeks before my departure, I was able to say that, if the Lord would, I should depart on the 26th of February, and on that very day I was able to depart. Important as it was, for many reasons, that I should return to my service in Bristol when I did, I cannot but see the hand of God in directing me to so honourable a person as the printer was, in whom also, I trust, is somewhat of the fear of God.-- It has been often mentioned to me in various places, that brethren in business do not sufficiently attend to the keeping of promises, and I cannot therefore but entreat all who love our Lord Jesus, and who are engaged in a trade or business, to seek for His sake not to make any promises, except they have every reason to believe they shall be able to fulfil them, and therefore carefully to weigh all the circumstances, before making any engagement, lest they should fail in its accomplishment. It is even in these little ordinary affairs of life that we may either bring much honour or dishonour to the Lord; and these are the things which every unbeliever can take notice of. Why should it be so often said, and sometimes with a measure of ground, or even much ground: "Believers are bad servants, bad tradesmen, bad masters?" Surely it ought not to be true that we, who have power with God to obtain by prayer and faith all needful grace, wisdom and shill, should be bad servants, bad tradesmen, bad masters.

When now the Narrative was nearly printed, I had to look out for a bookseller who would undertake the sale of the book on commission. My reason for this was, not the money which might thus be obtained, for truly glad should I have been to have given away all the 4,000 copies at once, had I known of suitable opportunities; but in order that by means of the book-trade the Narrative might be circulated even a thousand miles off or more, where I had no opportunity of reaching. Here now it was again that I met with difficulty, as I had done step by step in the other parts of my service in Germany. Three booksellers refused to undertake the sale of the book. The objection evidently was, that I did not belong to the State Church, and one of them plainly told me so. But by the help of God I was not discouraged. I knew the Lord had sent me to Germany: I knew also that it was His will that I should publish an account of His dealings with me in the German language; for He had so unexpectedly laid this matter upon my heart; He had so remarkably provided the means for it, without my asking any one but Himself for them; He had given me such especial help in preparing the book for the press; He had given me such an abundance of prayer about this part of my service, both many weeks before I left England, and day by day all the months that I had been in Germany. For these reasons it was that I had the fullest assurance that this difficulty also would be overcome. I therefore now began to give myself to prayer with my dear wife concerning this very matter. Day by day we waited upon the Lord for about four weeks, and then I applied to another bookseller, who without any hesitation undertook the sale of the book on commission, so that I retained 2,000 copies for gratuitous distribution, and 2,000 he was to have.

Dear reader, there is no difficulty which may not be overcome. Let us but use the power which we have with God as his children by prayer and faith, and abundant blessings may be drawn down from Him.

V. On my departure from Stuttgart, the number of the brethren who met for the breaking of bread was twenty-five. On the very last Lord's day I had the joy of seeing the third elder of the Baptist Church, who had at first thought me so much in error, come among us, and unite with us in the breaking of bread, having for some time had his mind more and more opened to the truth. The day before I departed, not only the brethren and sisters among whom I had laboured took leave of me with many tears, but also nineteen brethren and sisters of the close Baptist Church came to my lodgings, and affectionately bade me farewell, and many with tears. The Lord indeed, in His rich mercy, had so far answered my prayer concerning this my service, that I left a testimony behind in their consciences.

On Feb. 26, 1844, my dear wife and I departed from Stuttgart, and on March 6th, we reached Bristol. Exceedingly as we had longed to return to Bristol, as soon as we could see it to be the Lord's will; yet so greatly had our hearts been knit to the dear saints whom we left behind, that it was a sad pleasure to depart, and our only comfort was, that we left them in the hands of the good Shepherd.

I resume now the account about the Orphan-Houses, and other objects of the Scriptural Knowledge Institution.

During all the time of my absence from Bristol, the Lord bountifully supplied our need. For though the money, which I was able to leave behind on my departure, would not have supplied the Orphan-Houses with more than about one-half of what was needed, yet the Lord helped so seasonably, and sent in so many donations, that there was not once, during all this time, the least difficulty with reference to means. There came in for the Orphans, between Aug. 9, 1843, and Mach 6, 1844, about 450l., besides very many articles of clothing, pro visions, books, trinkets, old silver, etc.

On Aug. 11th, 1843, A. B. sent 50l., which, being left to my disposal, was put to the School-Bible-Missionary and Tract Fund. I received information about this donation on the evening of Aug. 22nd, during the first hour after my arrival at Stuttgart. It was a precious earnest, that the Lord would also be mindful of the need of the Institution during my absence from England. Indeed, it cannot be described, how sweet to me just then, under the circumstances in which I found myself, in an especial trial of faith to which the Lord called me in that very hour, as before stated, was this fresh proof of the Lord's watchful care over His work in my hands.

THIRD PART

Nov. 21, 1843. At a time when all means were exhausted, and when for many reasons large supplies were needed for the School-Bible-Missionary and Tract Fund, whilst I was daily waiting upon the Lord with my dear wife in Germany, bringing the work in Bristol before Him, and beseeching Him also to give us pecuniary means for it, that His enemies might have no cause for triumphing, was sent to me a letter from Bristol, containing another from the East Indies, in which the writer gave me an order for 100l. for the work of the Lord in my hands, giving me at the same time full liberty to use the money as most needed.

A few days after A. B. sent another 50l. for the work of the Lord in my hands. By these two donations, both of which I put entirely to the funds for these objects, we were not only helped to meet all present demands, but were richly supplied.-- Thus, at so great a distance from the work, we were yet able by our prayers effectually to serve the Institution!--Truly, it is precious in this way to hang upon God! It brings its abundant reward with it! Every donation, thus received, so manifestly comes out of the hands of the Lord Himself.

Dear Reader, just look once more upon this circumstance! Hundreds of miles we were from Bristol, and by our bowing our knees before our Heavenly Father at Stuttgart, we not only could bring down spiritual blessings upon the work in Bristol, but also temporal means. Thus, simply by prayer, we obtained whilst in Germany, for the work of God in Bristol, within about one week, nearly 200l.; for there came in some other donations for the Orphans also.

On Jan. 6, 1844, there came in 50l. from one who is VERY FAR PROM BEING RICH, of which 10l. was given for the School Fund, and 40l. for the Orphans. The donor is satisfied with food and raiment, labouring cheerfully, and wishing rather to spend than to keep, or lay up treasure on earth.

March 25, 1844. After a comparatively great abundance with regard to the Orphans, for a whole year and seventeen days, during which time we were not once in difficulty as to means, which had not been the case for nearly five years previous to the commencement of this period, we are now again quite poor, there being NOTHING AT ALL left in my hands, after I have paid out this day more than 50l. for rent and salaries. But through the grace of God I am able to trust as heretofore in the Lord, and therefore my heart is in peace.--Evening. I received this afternoon 11s. 2 1/2d., 2s. 7d., by sale of articles came in 1l.19s. 9d., by sale of Reports 3s., and by a donation 2s. 2d.

March 26. This morning my wife and I besought the Lord unitedly for means, and received almost immediately afterwards 5l. from Birmingham, in answer to our prayer.

March 27. I received 8s., and there was anonymously put into the box at Bethesda 2s. 6d. This morning at half-past nine a sister came to me, and brought me a sovereign for the Orphans, saying: "Whilst I was lying this morning at six o'clock on my bed, I thought, here I am so comfortable, and perhaps the Orphans may be in need, and I resolved to bring you this." The donation came most seasonably and as the fruit of our prayer.--I received also 1l., the profit of the sale of ladies' bags.

March 30. Saturday. There is 6l. 19s. 9d. in hands This will be at least enough till Monday morning.--There came in this morning 1l. 1s. by a donation, before the money was sent off to the Orphan-Houses, so that I had 8l. 0s. 9d. to send, which will be enough, I suppose, till Tuesday morning.

April 1. There came in since the day before yesterday 1l., which was anonymously put into the box at Salem Chapel, 15s. was given by a young sister as the produce of some work which she had done for the benefit of the Orphans, and 1 6s. came in by sale of articles. Having had this 2l. 11s. coming in I was able to meet extraordinary expenses which came upon me today, not having expected that anything beyond the ordinary housekeeping money would have been needed.

April 2. The need of today was 3l. 0s. 6d. Yesterday I had paid away all the money in hand, but in the afternoon came in by sale of articles 2l. 17s. 5d., by the boxes in the Orphan-Houses 5s. 6d., and by needle-work of the Orphans 4s. 3 1/2d.: so that we were able to meet the demands of today.

April 3. Today 1l. 14s. was required. I opened the boxes in my house, in which I found 3s. 1 1/2d. Thus I had 8s. 10d. with what was left yesterday, and the remainder, being 1l. 5s. 2d., one of the labourers was able to give of his own.

April 4. Last evening was given to me 11s, and 10s.; and this morning 5s. came in. Thus we have 1l. 6s., and the need of today is 1l. 7s. One of the labourers was able to add the 1s.

April 5. Yesterday came in by sale of articles 3l., and this morning I received from Clapham 1l. 10s., and through a believer in Bristol 2l. 6s. This afternoon came in still further from a brother in Bath 5l. We have therefore received altogether this day 11l. 14s. from the bountiful hand of our Heavenly Father.

April 6. One of the labourers in the Orphan-Houses gave me still further today 5l., and from Kensington I received 1l. 6s. We are thus again provided for the probable expenses of two or three days.

April 7. Today a sister gave me 2l. for the express purpose of providing a little treat for the dear Orphans, and 15s. 6d. came in besides.

April 8. It has often occurred in our experience, that after we have had to pass for some time through a season of comparative poverty, in which day by day we have had to wait upon the Lord, our Father alters His way of dealing with us, and opens His bountiful hand, by supplying us for several or many days at once. Thus it is now. During the last three days we received more than was required for each of those days, and it was still more abundantly so today; for this afternoon a person, residing at Keynsham, gave me 1l., and this evening a brother gave me 50l. When I received this 50l., we were not in absolute need, but had enough for two or three days; yet I see the kindness of the Lord in sending this donation, as I had been repeatedly of late praying for means, and as we are thus enabled to do things which are not absolutely needful just now, though desirable, and as we have thus the continued proof of his willingness to send means.

April 14. From the end of Nov. 1843, till about the middle of March, 1844, there was always as much in hand as was needed for the School-Bible-and Tract Fund; for besides the help, which we received through the two donations of 50l. and 100l., a number of smaller donations came in after. But now for some weeks past all means were again gone, and on the last three Saturdays all the usual remuneration could not be given to all the teachers in the Day-Schools. In addition to this, the greater part of the common sort of Bibles and Testaments, for circulation among the poor and for Schools was gone. I had also often prayed for means to assist Missionary brethren. Under these circumstances I received this morning from A. B., who has been already repeatedly referred to, as having been used by the Lord to help us in our need, the sum of 50l.

May 4. Besides the 50l. which was given on April 8th, for the Orphans, and the money we had in hand before the 50l. was given, there has come in since then 36l. 2s. 8d.; but today, Saturday, we have again only 5l. 6s. 6 1/2d. left, which, however, is enough for today, and a few shillings will be left for the beginning of next week.

May 6. On Saturday came in by sale of articles 1l. 11s., and by a donation 10s., and yesterday was put anonymously into the Chapel boxes 2s. 6d. So we have more than enough for the expenses of today.

May 8. By the produce of some little boxes, made by a sister, there came in 5s. 6d., by a donation. 2s. 6d., by the contents of an Orphan-box from Crediton. 6s. 10d., and by sale of articles 10s. By these small donations all that is needed for today is met. The brother, who sent me the 6s. 10d, from Crediton, wrote, that he did not like to wait till this little sum had increased, before he sent it, as it might be just now needed; and thus it was.

May 9. The Lord has again helped for today and tomorrow. Last evening I received through a brother 5s., and this morning the boxes in the Orphan-Houses were opened, in which 5l. 3s. 1 1/2d. was found; some one also bought a Report and gave 1s. for it.

May 13. On the 10th there came in 2l. 1s. 9d., on the 11th 10l. 10s. 4d., on the 12th 5l. was sent from Barnstaple by three sisters, and 3l. 6s. came in besides. By I the income of these three days I was not only able to meet their own demands, but I had enough for today, though I required no less than 13l. 15s.

May 15. Yesterday there was only 1l. 5s. left, not nearly enough for what was required today. When I came home last evening, having spent a part of the afternoon at the Infant-Orphan-House, where I found that several articles were needed, I heard that a gentleman had called and wished to be shown into my room, where he had written a paper, which he had put with some money into the Orphan-box. On opening it I found the paper to contain four sovereigns. Thus we are helped for the present.

May 16. Only 5s. came in, through the boxes at my house.

May 17. Yesterday I paid out all TO THE LAST PENNY I had in hand. When now there was nothing left, 2l. came in by the sale of some books, and 1l. 0s. 6d. by two donations, whereby I was able to meet this day's need.

May 18. This morning 1l. 17s. 10d. came in. We have thus, with the little which was left yesterday, 2l. 15s. 11d. for this day, Saturday but I know not whether that will be enough.--Evening. This evening at six o'clock one of my sisters-in-law returned from Plymouth, where she had been staying for a little while, and brought from a sister in the Lord 2l., from another sister 1l. 15s., and also a parcel from some sisters in the Lord in the neighbourhood of Kingsbridge, containing 14s., and the following articles: a pair of shoes, 3 pairs of socks, 3 pairs of cuffs, a pair of mittens, 3 little mats, a pincushion cover, a comb, 3 books, 4 clasps, 2 brooches, a gold pin, a chain, a vinaigrette, a Turk's head cushion, and 10 yards of calico. Also a parcel from Plymouth, containing 2 veils and a scarf. Also from another sister, 2 netted handkerchiefs.

--The money I took at once to the Orphan Houses, where I found, that, to meet the present expenses, 3l. 10s. more was required than what I had been able to send in the morning, as altogether about 6l. 5s. was needed for this day. How kind, therefore, of the Lord, to send this money so opportunely, though only towards the evening of the day! Thus we had enough, and a little left towards the need of Monday.

May 20. Monday. Yesterday came in 4s. 3d., and today 8s. 5d. As this, together with what had been left in hand, was not quite enough, one of the labourers added 6s. 6d. of his own. Thus we had 1l. 18s. 2d. for the need of today.

May 23. We are still supplied by the day. We had received from the Lord during the last days also what we required, but we were poor, having nothing at all in hand. Under these circumstances with reference to means for the Orphans, and in as great need for the other objects of the Institution, two persons, professed believers, called on me today, who were going from house to house in the street where I live, to ask money for a chapel debt. I remonstrated with them, and sought to show them how the name of the Lord was dishonoured by them, in calling upon the enemies of the Lord for pecuniary assistance towards, what they considered, the work of the Lord. I sought to show them, that if their work were of God, He would, in answer to their prayers, send them help: and if not, ought they not to give up, what was not His work, and not force the matter by calling promiscuously from house to house upon believers and unbelievers. Their reply was: "The gold and silver are the Lord's, and therefore we call upon the unconverted for help for His work." My reply was: "Because the gold and silver are the Lord's, therefore we, His children, need not go to His enemies for the support of His work." Now, at that very moment, while I was thus speaking for the Lord, having then nothing at all in hand for the Orphans or the other objects, the postman brought a small brown paper parcel and a letter. My conversation seemed, for the time at least, fruitless; for those two individuals, having left, went as before from house to house; but when I came back to my room, I found the blessedness of the scriptural way; for that parcel, which the postman had brought, while I was conversing, came from Ireland, and contained two post-office orders for 5l. each, and a worked stool cover; the letter which had been brought, and which was from Seaton, contained 1l. for the Orphans; and 1l. 1s. 5d. had been sent, having been taken out of the boxes in the Orphan Houses: so that altogether, whilst those two persons were with me, 12l. 1s. 5d. had come in. Half of the 10l. I put to the Orphan-Fund, and half to the other funds, there being nothing in hand to supply the teachers in the Day-Schools during this week.

May 24. Today a box with many articles arrived from the neighbourhood of Droitwich, and 1l. 8s. 9d, was received by the sale of articles.

May 25, 6s. 6d. came in.

May 27. Monday. On Saturday, after having supplied the need of that day, which was 5l. 15s., and now again little being left in my hands, a brother from Cork brought me a parcel which contained 6 pairs of children's shoes, a pair of little boots, a pair of list slippers (all new), 2 books, 2 pincushions, a knitted watch pocket, and 102 thimbles. The same brother gave also 10s. 6d. and a book. In the evening a brother gave me 1l.--Yesterday was put into the chapel boxes 10s. with Eccles. ix. 10, and 2s. 6d. besides. By these donations, with what was left on Saturday, I am able to meet the demands of this day, being 2l. 17s.

May 31. By the produce of the sale of stockings, knitted by the Orphan-Boys, by some help which one of the labourers was able to give, by a donation, etc., we were supplied during the last three days. Now this morning, when again in much need, I received a note, which contained 5l. with Eccles. ix. 10. By means of this 5l. I was able to meet the expenses of today, which are 2l. 8s. 3d.

June 1. Yesterday there came in still further 2l.18s. 11d. by sale of articles, and today by needlework, done by the Orphans, 1l. 13s. 9d. Thus I am able (including what remained of the 5l.) to supply the need of this day, which is 5l. 10s.--Still further came in 5s.

June 3. Monday. Yesterday came in 16s. 1 1/2d. This, with what was in hand from Saturday, met the demands of today.

June 4. This morning came in 3l. 2s. 4d. by the sale of a few trinkets and of some pieces of old silver. This was enough for this day's need, and left something over, as only 1l. 16s. was required. This afternoon arrived a parcel from Westmoreland, containing 24 chemises, 2 shirts, 2 petticoats, a pinafore, 5 night caps, 7 pairs of stockings (all new), and 38 1/2 yards of print. Thus we are encouraged day after day, though for many days we have now been again very poor.

June 5. Last evening a brother gave me a dozen of modern silver tea-spoons, which, being this morning readily disposed of at a good price, supplied our need for today.

For several days I have now had day by day especial prayer with some of my fellow-labourers about the work, and particularly for pecuniary supplies; and surely we do not wait in vain upon the Lord. Before this day is over we have had another proof of it. This afternoon a parcel was brought by a brother from London, containing a silver cream jug, a pair of gilt earrings, a gold ring, 2 bracelets, and a muffineer. The same donor sent also a sovereign. The bearer brought also another donation of 2s. 6d. A lady also called this afternoon at the Infant-Orphan-House, to see the Institution, and gave 5s.

June 8. On the 6th came in 16s. 6d. and 3s. 6d.; and yesterday was received, by the sale of the silver cream jug and a few other little articles 4l. 0s. 9d., by the sale of stockings 5s., and by a donation 10s. Thus we had enough for today, though the need was 4l. 19s. 8d., as 4l. 15s. 9d. had come in yesterday, and a few shillings had been left before.

June 10. Monday. Though on Saturday all our necessities were comfortably supplied, yet I had then NOT ONE PENNY left. Our Heavenly Father, however, having given us grace to trust in Him, and not to be anxiously concerned about Monday, gave us, even late on Saturday evening, a proof of his loving tender care over us. The labourers met, as usual, on Saturday evening for prayer, and we continued in prayer from a little after seven till about nine o'clock. After we had separated, a sister, who had been waiting at the Infant-Orphan-House, till our prayer was over, gave 4s., saying that she had intended to give it to me on the Lord's-day morning, but had felt herself stirred up to bring it that evening.--Nothing came in yesterday. I met this morning with some of the labourers again for prayer, as I have now been doing daily for about a fortnight, and we again asked the Lord for help, with regard to the writing of the Report, that He would let His blessing rest upon it, bless the intended public meetings, when the account of the Lord's dealings with us will be given, convert the children, give the needful grace and wisdom to us who are engaged in the work, give us means for the Day-Schools, means for ordering a quantity of oatmeal from Scotland, for colouring down the Orphan-houses, for the supply of the present need, etc. There was only the 4s. in hand for the need of today, which I had reason to believe

THIRD PART

would be about 2l. Now see the Lord's help I just now, at eleven o'clock, when the letter bag is brought for the money for today's need, I receive in it 2l. 7s. 3d., which had been taken by brother R. B. out of the boxes in the Orphan-Houses, and half-a-sovereign, which had been sent by a brother in Suffolk. Thus we have 3l. 1s. 3d., whilst only 1l. 15s. is needed today. In the course of reading the Holy Scriptures in my family this morning, came the word: "Ask, and it shall be given you; seek, and ye shall find; knock, and it shall be opened unto you." (Matth. vii. 7.) I pleaded this word especially with the Lord, while I was again praying, after the family prayer was over, with some of the labourers; and surely He has proved afresh that he acts according to His word.

--Evening. The Lord sent still further help today. This afternoon a person called at the Infant-Orphan-House, and gave 7s., and two ladies met the teacher of the Infant-Orphan-House in the street, and gave her a paper, directed to me, which contained 10s. 2s. was also given by a person at Clifton.

June 12. By what had come in on the 10th we were supplied yesterday and also today, and I had three pence left, after I had sent off to the matrons of the four houses what they needed. I then gave myself to prayer with some of the labourers for the supplies of the present need, mentioning again before the Lord all the many things for which we need His help. About one hour after, I received 10s. for the Orphans from a brother of Guernsey, who has been staying a few days in Bristol.

June 13. Last evening came in still further, by the sale of articles, 2s. 3d.; and 6s. 4d. by the sale of some musk plants, which two sisters in the Lord rear and sell for the benefit of the Orphans; and this morning I received 7s. 11d., being six donations. Likewise two small silver coins were given me, and 1l. 15s. 3d. I received by the sale of articles.

June 14. There came in still further last evening 5s., and this morning by the boxes in the Orphan-houses 18s. 9d. This evening 1l. 10s. was sent with an Orphan, from Carne in Suffolk.

June 18. As only 13s. had come in on the 16th and 17th, we were now extremely poor; but the Lord looked upon our necessity, for 5l. was sent by a Christian lady at Scarborough, and a person from Manchester gave 1l.

June 22. Saturday evening. Only 1s. came in the day before yesterday, and 2s. 6d. was taken this morning out of the boxes in the Orphan-Houses.--This has been one of those weeks, in which I have prayed particularly much for means, and in which the Lord seemed little to regard my requests. But my soul, through grace, has been in perfect peace, being fully assured, that He in His own good time will again send larger supplies. In every way we are now very poor, and it seems desirable that we should have large sums to meet the present circumstances. After much prayer the Lord has closed the week with fresh proofs of His loving tender care over the work, which has been a great refreshment to my spirit. There came in this evening, between eight and nine o'clock, by sale of stockings 9s., by sale of other articles 1l. 8s. 7d., by a donation from an Irish sister 5s., and a physician in Bristol kindly sent me 2l., and his little children 4s.--How can my soul sufficiently praise the Lord for His tender mercies and His readiness to bear the prayers of His servant! All these fresh deliverances in the hour of great need show most clearly, that it is only for the trial of our faith, for our profit, for the profit of others who may hear of it, and for the glory of the Lord, that He sometimes seems not to regard our petitions.

June 24, Monday. Yesterday came in by donations 14s. 8d., anonymously was put into the Chapel boxes 1s., add 3s. was given to ore as the produce of the sale of musk plants. Today two Orphans were brought from Bath; for though we are so poor, the work goes forward, and children are received as long as there is room. The person who brought them put two sovereigns into the boxes at the Orphan-Houses. Thus we have again, with what came in on Saturday evening, more than is needed for today and tomorrow.

June 25. Today I received from Scotland 10l., to be used as most needed, of which I took one-half for the Orphans, and the other half for the other objects. Thus, in our great need, the Lord supplies us from day to day, and hears our prayers, which we daily bring to Him, though there have not yet come in larger sums for oatmeal, salary of the labourers in the Orphan-Houses, colouring down the four houses, etc.; but the Lord in His own time will send means for these expenses also.

June 29. Day after day our great poverty continues; yet day after day the Lord helps us. This evening was received from the neighbourhood of Bideford 7s. 6d., a chess board, and a gold pin. There came in also by the sale of articles 1l. 8s. 3d., and by Reports 1s.

June 30. This evening I received 10l. between nine and ten o'clock, at a time of the greatest poverty. A little boy likewise gave me 6d. this evening, and from a sister I received this morning 10s.

July 3. On the 1st came in 2s., and today, by the boxes in the Orphan-Houses, 2s. 10d., by sale of articles 1s. 9d., and from Suffolk was sent a donation of 2l. 10s.

July 7. It is now about six weeks since I have been daily entreating the Lord, both alone and with some of my fellow labourers, that He would be pleased to send us the supplies which we required, both to meet the ordinary and extraordinary expenses. Of late we have been also especially asking the Lord, that He would be pleased to send a rich supply before the public meetings, (which will commence, if the Lord will, on the 15th) in order that it may be seen that without public meetings, and without publishing fresh Reports, we are yet able, by faith and prayer, to draw down help from the living God. As to ourselves, through grace we should be able to lean upon the Lord, and expect help from Him, though not another Report were written, nor another public meeting held, at which the account about His dealings with us is given. We have given proof of this, in that when the year was up on May 10, 1843,

THIRD PART

no Report was published, and no meetings on the subject were held; and also when the second year had passed away, I still did not publish another account, because a weakness in one of my eyes seemed to point it out that the Lord's time had not yet come, although by forcing the matter I might even then have written the Report. But whilst I do not write the Reports for the sake of obtaining money, nor give the account of the Lord's dealings with us at the public meetings for the sake of influencing persons to help us with their means, nor do so for the sake of exposing our poverty; yet some persons might think so. Our prayer, therefore, had been particularly, that the Lord not only would be pleased to give us what we required day by day, but that He would also send in again largely, in order to show that He was willing to hear our prayers, and influence the minds of His children who have the means, to contribute considerably, though it was now more than two years since the last Report was published. Not that we were anxiously concerned even about this: for in the whole work we desire to stand with God, and not to depend upon the favourable or unfavourable judgment of the multitude; yet our souls longed, in pity to those who might seek an occasion, that even the shadow of ground might be cut off for persons to say:

"They cannot get any more money, and therefore they now publish another Report." My soul, therefore, had assurance that the Lord not only would supply our need up to the time when the accounts were closed and the public meetings would be held; but also that He would send in means more largely than He had done for some time past. And thus it was. When on Saturday evening, July 6th, more money was needed than there was in hand, I received about eight o'clock a post-office order for 2l. from Jersey, of which half is for the Orphans and half for the other objects. There came in also at the same time 4s. 9d. by sale of articles. I received likewise at the same time a small paper box by post, containing four mourning rings (of fine stamped gold), 8 other gold rings, a gold seal, a gold locket, a pearl necklace, 2 brooches, a gold watch key, and a few other little things. This was a valuable donation, but doubly so under our circumstances. And now today A. B. sent 50l., of which I took one half for the Orphans, and the other half for the other funds. Besides the reasons just referred to, why this donation is so seasonable, I would only mention one more: The brother who kindly procures the oatmeal for us in Scotland, had written to say, that he had just now some which was very good, if we liked to have it. We could not say we needed none, for by the time it could be sent our meal would be gone: nothing therefore remained but to continue waiting on the Lord for means. And now, when we needed to send an answer, this 50l. came, so that we were able to order a ton of oatmeal.--1s. besides came in this day.

July 14. This is the last day before the accounts are closed, and this day also the Lord has sent in liberally. Being thus helped day by day up to the last moment of this period, we go on cheerfully to the next, leaning upon the Lord.

It is scarcely needful to state at the close of these details, with reference to the last two years and nine weeks, that, notwithstanding our having been often poor, and very poor, yet the children in the Orphan-Houses have always had the needful articles of clothing and nourishing food; indeed this is sufficiently proved by the healthy countenances of the children. Should any one question, that the children are provided with what they need, he may at any time have the proof of it, by seeing the children at their meals, inspecting their clothes, &c. But those who know what it is to walk in the fear of God, know also, that God would not help us, in answer to our prayers, if we hypocritically stated that the children were well provided with wholesome food, etc., and yet it were not true. Rather than keep the Orphans, whilst we were unable to provide for them, we would send them at once back to their relations.

On July 14, 1844, it was two years and nine weeks since the last public account about the Scriptural Knowledge Institution was given. In that last Report it was stated, that we desired to leave it to the Lord's direction, as to the time when another should be published. When the year was expired, I saw no particular reason to lead me to think that I ought to serve the Church of Christ by publishing a fresh Narrative about the Orphan-Houses and the other objects of the Scriptural Knowledge Institution, neither did I see a leading of the Lord towards this service; and soon after, it pleased the Lord to call me to labour in Germany. Having returned in March 1844, it appeared to me desirable now to publish, at the close of the second year, which would be up on May 10, 1844, a fresh account: partly, because of the 5000 Reports, which had been printed, only a few copies were remaining; partly, because many believers expressed a great desire for some further account of the Lord's dealings with us in the work; partly, because there was now an abundance of profitable matter ready to be communicated; and most of all, because I was longing to show by a public audited account, that the considerable sums, with which I had been entrusted, had been appropriated according to the intention of the donors. But much as I desired, for the above reasons, to have written the Report then, the weakness in one of my eyes already mentioned prevented my doing so, till at last, my eye being better, I was enabled to do so.

I now add a few particulars with reference to the operations of the Scriptural Knowledge Institution, for Home and Abroad, from May 10, 1842, to July 14, 1844. During this period also six Day-Schools for poor children were supported by the funds of this Institution. Besides this, the rent for the school-room of a seventh school, was paid during a great part of this period, and also occasional other assistance was given to this and two other schools.--The number of all the children that had schooling in the Day-Schools, through the medium of the Institution, from March 5, 1834, to July 14, 1844, amounts to 3319. The number of those in the six Day-Schools on July 14, 1844, was 338.

During this period likewise, one Sunday-School was supported by the funds of the Institution.

The number of adults that were instructed from Jan. 1841, to July 14, 1844, in the two adult schools of the Institution, amounts to 734 persons. The average attendance during the winter was from 50 to 70 persons, and in the summer from 20 to 40. The number on the list of adult scholars was on July 14, 1844, eighty persons.

THIRD PART

Books, writing materials, and instruction, are given entirely gratis to the adult scholars.

The number of Bibles and Testaments which were circulated from May 10, 1842, to July 14, 1844, is as follows:--237 Bibles were sold, and 284 Bibles were given away. 146 New Testaments were sold, and 162 New Testaments were given away.--From March 5, 1834, to July, 14, 1844, there were circulated 4,828 Bibles, and 3,357 New Testaments.

From May 10, 1842, to July 14, 1844, was laid out for missionary objects the sum of 234l. 8s. 6d., whereby assistance was rendered to the work of God in Jamaica, in Demerara, in Upper Canada, in the East Indies, in the Mauritius, and in Switzerland.

From May 10, 1842, to July 14, 1844, was laid out for the circulation of tracts the sum of 43l. 9s. 1 1/4d. During this period were circulated 39,473 tracts, and altogether were circulated, from Nov. 19, 1840, to July 14, 1844, 59,082 tracts.

From May 10, 1842, to July 14, 1844, there were received into the four Orphan-Houses, 39 Orphans, who, together with those who were in the houses on May 10, 1842, made up 125 in all. Of these: 1, One girl left the Institution against our will. Her aunt repeatedly applied to me to have her niece, who, having been more than eight years under our care, was now of use to her. I remonstrated with the aunt, and sought to show her the importance of leaving her niece with us for another twelvemonth, when she would be fit to be sent out to service; but all in vain. At last, knowing how exceedingly injurious her house would be for her niece, I told the aunt that I could not conscientiously dismiss the girl to go to her house; but the aunt's influence induced the orphan to leave. May God, in tender mercy, visit the soul of this poor wanderer! Such cases are trying, very trying, but even concerning them faith contains a precious antidote. 2, Two of the children were removed by their friends, who by that time were able to provide for them. 3, One girl, who was received when grown up, we were obliged, after a long season of trial, to send back to her relations, in mercy to the other children. 4, Three girls were sent out to service, all three as believers. 5, Three Orphans died, one as an infant, and two in the faith. One had been more than two years in church fellowship, and had walked consistently. 6, Four boys were apprenticed, two of whom had been several years in church fellowship, before their apprenticeship.

There were on July 14, 1844, one hundred and twenty-one Orphans in the four houses. The number of the Orphans who were under our care from April 1836, to July 14, 1844, amounts to 183.

I notice further the following points in connexion with the Orphan-Houses.

1. Without any one having been personally applied to for any thing by me, the sum of 7748l. 16s. 4 3/4d. was given to me as the result of prayer to God, from Dec.

1835, to July, 14, 1844. 2. Besides this, also, many articles of clothing, furniture, provisions, etc., were given. 3. During these two years and two months we had very little sickness, comparatively in the four houses, though there was so much fever in Bristol. I mention this to the praise of the Lord, who mercifully preserved us.

The total of the income for the Orphan-Houses, from May 10, 1842, to July 14, 1844, was 2489l. 0s. 7 1/4d., leaving a balance of 1l. 11s. 11 3/4d. in hand on July 14, 1844.

--The total of the income for the other objects from May 10, 1842, to July 14, 1844, was 1164l. 18s. 4 1/4d., leaving a balance of 20l. 12s. 7d. in hand on July 14,1844.

I cannot omit mentioning that between. May 10, 1842, and July 14, 1844, there was admitted to communion one of the Sunday-School children, and one of the Day-School children. Likewise 6 more of the Orphans were received into church fellowship, so that up to July 14, 1844, altogether 29 of the Orphans had been admitted. In addition to this, between May 10, 1842, and July 14, 1844, one Orphan, before being received, died in the faith, and another, though but nine years of age, would have been received, had she not been just then removed by her relatives, who took her with them to America. But whilst we desire to receive these instances as precious encouragements from the Lord to continue our service, we cannot but believe, judging from the many prayers the Lord gives us for the dear children and adults under our care and instruction, that that which we see is but an earnest of a far larger harvest in the day of Christ's appearing.--The greatest present visible blessing, which is resting upon the work, consists in what the Lord is pleased to do through the Narratives which are written and published respecting it; for a very considerable number, in various parts of the world, have through them either been converted, or, as believers, led on in the knowledge of God.

To avoid misunderstanding, it may be well to insert the following paragraph, which was written by my beloved brother and fellow labourer Henry Craik, and appended to the last Report.

"Hitherto, my name has been appended to the Report along with that of my beloved brother and fellow labourer George Mueller; but, as the responsibility and management of the work devolve entirely upon him, it has seemed well to both of us, that, for the future, his signature should appear alone.--It is scarcely needful to add, that this alteration does not arise from any kind of disunion or even difference of judgment between us. I would especially recommend to the people of God, into whose hands this brief Narrative may fall, to read, examine and ponder the instructive facts and principles herein stated and illustrated; and I desire that the non-insertion of my name may not be understood as implying anything like a disapproval of the way in which the Scriptural Knowledge Institution has been conducted from the beginning. As the honour of being the instrument in this great and blessed work

THIRD PART

belongs to him, and, in no degree, to me, I feel a satisfaction in the omission of my name, lest, otherwise, I should even appear to glory in 'another man's labour.'

HENRY CRAIK."

Thus far only, for the present at least, do I think it well to continue the accounts of the Lord's dealings with me. But I cannot conclude this third part, without adding some hints on a few passages of the word of God, both because I have so very frequently found them little regarded by Christians, and also because I have proved their preciousness, in some measure, in my own experience; and therefore wish that all my fellow saints may share the blessing with me.

1. In Matthew vi 19-21, it is written: "Lay not up for yourselves treasures upon earth, where moth and rust doth corrupt, and where thieves break through and steal; but lay up for yourselves treasures in heaven, where neither moth nor rust doth corrupt, and where thieves do not break through nor steal: for where your treasure is, there will your heart be also."--Observe, dear Reader, the following points concerning this part of the divine testimony: 1, It is the Lord Jesus, our Lord and Master, who speaks this as the lawgiver of His people. He who has infinite wisdom and unfathomable love to us, who therefore both knows what is for our real welfare and happiness, and who cannot exact from us any requirement inconsistent with that love which led Him to lay down His life for us. Remembering, then, who it is who speaks to us in these verses, let us consider them. 2, His counsel, His affectionate entreaty, and His commandment to us His disciples is: "Lay not up for yourselves treasures upon earth." The meaning obviously is, that the disciples of the Lord Jesus, being strangers and pilgrims on earth, i.e. neither belonging to the earth nor expecting to remain in it, should not seek to increase their earthly possessions, in whatever these possessions may consist. This is a word for poor believers as well as for rich believers; it has as much a reference to putting shillings into the savings' banks as to putting thousands of pounds into the funds, or purchasing one house, or one farm after another.--It may be said, but does not every prudent and provident person seek to increase his means, that he may have a goodly portion to leave to his children, or to have something for old age, or for the time of sickness, etc.? My reply is, it is quite true that this is the custom of the world. It was thus in the days of our Lord, and Paul refers to this custom of the world when he says, "The children ought not to lay up for the parents, but the parents for the children." 2 Cor. xii. 14. But whilst thus it is in the world, and we have every reason to believe ever will be so among those that are of the world, and who therefore have their portion on earth, we disciples of the Lord Jesus, being born again, being the children of God not nominally, but really, being truly partakers of the divine nature, being in fellowship with the Father and the Son, and having in prospect "an inheritance incorruptible, and undefiled, and that fadeth not away" (1 Peter i. 4.), ought in every respect to act differently from the world, and so in this particular also. If we disciples of the Lord Jesus seek, like the people of the world, after an increase of our possessions, may not those who are of

the world justly question whether we believe what we say, when we speak about our inheritance, our heavenly calling, our being the children of God, etc.? Often it must be a sad stumbling block to the unbeliever to see a professed believer in the Lord Jesus acting in this particular just like himself. Consider this, dear brethren in the Lord, should this remark apply to you.--I have more than once had the following passage quoted to me as a proof that parents ought to lay up money for their children, or husbands for their wives: "But if any provide not for his own, and especially for those of his own house (or kindred), he hath denied the faith, and is worse than an infidel." 1 Tim. v. 8. It is, however, concerning this verse, only needful, in childlike simplicity to read the connexion from verse 3 to 5, and it will be obvious that the meaning is this, that whilst the poor widows of the church are to be cared for by the church, yet if any such needy believing widow had children or grandchildren (not nephews), these children or grandchildren should provide for the widow, that the church might not be charged; but that, if a believer's child or grandchild, in such a case did not do so, such a one did not act according to the obligations laid upon him by his holy faith, and was worse than an unbeliever. Not a word, then, is there in this passage to favour the laying up treasures upon earth for our children, or our wives. 3, Our Lord says concerning the earth, that it is a place "where moth and rust doth corrupt, and where thieves break through and steal." All that is of the earth, and in any way connected with it, is subject to corruption, to change, to dissolution. There is no reality, or substance, in any thing else but in heavenly things. Often the careful amassing of earthly possessions ends in losing them in a moment by fire, by robbery, by a change of mercantile concerns, by loss of work, etc.; but suppose all this were not the case, still, yet a little while, and thy soul shall be required of thee; or, yet a little while, and the Lord Jesus will return; and what profit shalt thou then have, dear reader, if thou hast carefully sought to increase thy earthly possessions? My brother, if there were one particle of real benefit to be derived from it, would not He, whose love to us has been proved to the uttermost, have wished that you and I should have it? If, in the least degree, it could tend to the increase of our peace, or joy in the Holy Ghost, or heavenly-mindedness, He, who laid down His life for us, would have commanded us, to "LAY UP treasure upon earth." 4, Our Lord, however, does not merely bid us, not to lay up treasure upon earth; for if He had said no more, this His commandment might be abused, and persons might find in it an encouragement for their extravagant habits, for their love of pleasure, for their habit of spending every thing they have, or can obtain, upon themselves. It does not mean, then, as is the common phrase, that we should "live up to our income;" for, He adds: "But lay up for yourselves treasures in heaven." There is such a thing as laying up as truly in heaven as there is laying up on earth; if it were not so, our Lord would not have said so. Just as persons put one sum after another into the bank, and it is put down to their credit, and they may use the money afterwards: so truly the penny, the shilling, the pound, the hundred pounds, the ten thousand pounds, given for the Lord's sake, and constrained by the love of Jesus, to poor brethren, or in any way spent in the work of God, He marks down in the book of remembrance, He considers as laid up in heaven. The money is not lost, it is laid up in the bank of heaven; yet so, that, whilst an earthly bank may break, or through earthly circumstances we may lose our earthly possessions, the money, which is thus secured in heaven, cannot be lost. But this is

THIRD PART

by no means the only difference. I notice a few more points. Treasures laid up on earth bring along with them many cares; treasures laid up in heaven never give care. Treasures laid up on earth never can afford spiritual joy; treasures laid up in heaven bring along with them peace and joy in the Holy Ghost even now. Treasures laid up on earth, in a dying hour cannot afford peace and comfort, and when life is over, they are taken from us; treasures laid up in heaven draw forth thanksgiving, that we were permitted and counted worthy to serve the Lord with the means with which He was pleased to intrust us as stewards; and when this life is over we are not deprived of what was laid up there, but when we go to heaven we go to the place where our treasures are, and we shall find them there. Often we hear it said when a person has died: he died worth so much. But whatever be the phrases common in the world, it is certain that a person may die worth fifty thousand pounds sterling, as the world reckons, and yet that individual may not possess, in the sight of God, one thousand pounds sterling, because he was not rich towards God, he did not lay up treasure in heaven. And so on the other hand, we can suppose a man of God falling asleep in Jesus, and his surviving widow finding scarcely enough left behind him to suffice for the funeral, who was nevertheless rich towards God; in the sight of God he may possess five thousand pounds sterling, he may have laid up that sum in heaven. Dear Reader, does your soul long to be rich towards God, to lay up treasures in heaven? The world passes away and the lust thereof! Yet a little while, and our stewardship will be taken from us. At present we have the opportunity of serving the Lord, with our time, our talents, our bodily strength, our gifts, and also with our property; but shortly this opportunity may cease. Oh! how shortly may it cease. Before ever this is read by any one, I may have fallen asleep; and the very next day after you have read this, dear Reader, you may fall asleep, and therefore, whilst we have the opportunity, let us serve the Lord.--I believe, and therefore I speak. My own soul is so fully assured of the wisdom and love of the Lord towards us His disciples as expressed in this word, that by His grace I do most heartily set my seal to the preciousness of the command, and I do from my inmost soul not only desire not to lay up treasures upon earth, but, believing as I do what the Lord says, I do desire to have grace to lay up treasures in heaven. And then, suppose after a little while you should fall asleep, some one may say, your wife and, child will be unprovided for, because you did not make a provision for them. My reply is, the Lord will take care of them. The Lord will abundantly provide for them, as He now abundantly provides for us. 5, The Lord lastly adds: "For where your treasure is, there will your heart be also." Where should the heart of the disciple of the Lord Jesus be, but in heaven? Our calling is a heavenly calling, our inheritance is a heavenly inheritance, and reserved for us in heaven; our citizenship is in heaven; but if we believers in the Lord Jesus lay up treasures on earth, the necessary result of it is, that our hearts will be upon earth; nay, the very fact of our doing so proves that they are there! Nor will it be otherwise, till there be a ceasing to lay up treasures upon earth. The believer who lays up treasures upon earth may, at first, not live openly in sin; he in a measure may yet bring some honour to the Lord in certain things; but the injurious tendencies of this habit will show themselves more and more, whilst the habit of laying up treasures in heaven would draw the heart more and more heavenward; would be continually strengthening his new, his divine nature, his spiritual faculties, because it would call his spiritual faculties into use, and thus they would be strengthened; and he would more and more, whilst yet in the body, have his heart in heaven, and set upon heavenly things; and thus the laying up treasures in heaven would bring along with it, even in this life, precious spiritual blessings as a reward of obedience to the commandment of our Lord.

II. The next passage, on which I desire to make a few remarks, is Matthew vi. 33. "But seek ye first the kingdom of God and His righteousness; and all these things shall be added unto you." After our Lord, in the previous verses, had been pointing His disciples "to the fowls of the air," and "the lilies of the field," in order that they should be without carefulness about the necessaries of life; He adds: "Therefore take no thought, (literally, be not anxious) saying, What shall we eat? or, What shall we drink? or, Wherewithal shall we be clothed? (For after all these things do the Gentiles seek;) for your heavenly Father knoweth that ye have need of all these things." Observe here particularly that we, the children of God, should be different from the nations of the earth, from those who have no Father in heaven, and who therefore make it their great business, their first anxious concern, what they shall eat, and what they shall drink, and wherewithal they shall be clothed. We, the children of God, should, as in every other respect, so in this particular also, be different from the world, and prove to the world that we believe that we have a Father in heaven, who knoweth that we have need of all these things. The fact that our Almighty Father, who is full of infinite love to us His children, (and who has proved to us His love in the gift of His only begotten Son, and His almighty power in raising him from the dead), knows that we have need of these things, should remove all anxiety from our minds. There is, however, one thing that we have to attend to, and which we ought to attend to, with reference to our temporal necessities, it is mentioned in our verse: "But seek ye first the kingdom of God and His righteousness." The great business which the disciple of the Lord Jesus has to be concerned about (for this word was spoken to disciples, to professed believers) is, to seek the kingdom of God, i.e. to seek, as I view it, after the external and internal prosperity of the church of Christ. If, according to our ability, and according to the opportunity which the Lord gives us, we seek to win souls for the Lord Jesus, that appears to me to be seeking the eternal prosperity of the kingdom of God; and if we, as members of the body of Christ, seek to benefit our fellow members in the body, helping them on in grace and truth, or caring for them in any way to their edification, that would be seeking the internal prosperity of the kingdom of God. But in connexion with this we have also "to seek His righteousness," which means, (as it was spoken to disciples, to those who have a Father in heaven, and not to those who were without), to seek to be more and more like God, to seek to be inwardly conformed to the mind of God.--If these two things are attended to, (and they imply also that we are not slothful in business), then do we come under that precious promise: "And all these things (that is food, raiment, or anything else that is needful for this present life), shall be added unto you." It is not for attending to these two things that we obtain the blessing, but in attending to them.

I now ask you, my dear Reader, a few questions in all love, because I do seek your welfare, and I do not wish to put these questions to you, without putting them first to my own heart. Do you make it your primary business, your first great concern

THIRD PART

to seek the kingdom of God and His righteousness? Are the things of God, the honour of His name, the welfare of His Church, the conversion of sinners, and the profit of your own soul, your chief aim? Or does your business, or your family, or your own temporal concerns, in some shape or other primarily occupy your attention? If the latter be the case, then, though you may have all the necessaries of life, yet could you be surprised if you had them not? Remember that the world passeth away, but that the things of God endure for ever.

I never knew a child of God who acted according to the above passage, in whose experience the Lord did not fulfil His word of promise "All these things shall be added unto you."

III. The third portion of the divine testimony, on which I desire to throw out a few hints, is in I John i. 3. "And truly our fellowship is with the Father, and with his Son Jesus Christ." Observe!, The words "fellowship," "communion," "coparticipation," and "partnership," mean the same. 2, The believer in the Lord Jesus does not only obtain forgiveness of all his sins (as he does through the shedding of the blood of Jesus, by faith in His name;) does not only become a righteous one before God (through the righteousness of the Lord Jesus, by faith in His name;) is not only begotten again, born of God, and partaker of the divine nature, and therefore a child of God, and an heir of God; but he is also in fellowship or partnership with God. Now, so far as it regards God, and our standing in the Lord Jesus, we have this blessing once for all; nor does it allow of either an increase or a decrease. Just as God's love to us believers, His children, is unalterably the same (whatever may be the manifestations of that love:) and as His peace with us is the same, (however much our peace may be disturbed:) so it is also with regard to our being in fellowship or partnership with Him: it remains unalterably the same, so far as God is concerned. But then 3, there is an experimental fellowship, or partnership, with the Father and with His Son, which consists in this, that all which we possess in God, as being the partners or fellows of God, is brought down into our daily life, is enjoyed, experienced, and used. This experimental fellowship, or partnership, allows of an increase or a decrease, in the measure in which faith is in exercise, and in which we are entering into what we have received in the Lord Jesus. The measure in which we enjoy this experimental fellowship with the Father and with the Son is without limit; for without limit we may make use of our partnership with the Father and with the Son, and draw by prayer and faith out of the inexhaustible fulness which there is in God.--Let us now take a few instances in order to see the practical working of this experimental fellowship (or partnership) with the Father and with the Son. Suppose there are two believing parents who were not brought to the knowledge of the truth until some years after the Lord had given them several children. Their children were brought up in sinful, evil ways, whilst the parents did not know the Lord. Now the parents reap as they sowed. They suffer from having set an evil example before their children; for their children are unruly and behave most improperly. What is now to be done? Need such parents despair? No. The first thing they have to do is, to make confession of their sins to God, with regard to neglecting their children whilst they were themselves living in sin, and then to remember that they are in partnership with God, and therefore to be of good courage, though they are in themselves still utterly insufficient for the task of managing their children. They have in themselves neither the wisdom, nor the patience, nor the long-suffering, nor the gentleness, nor the meekness, nor the love, nor the decision and firmness, nor any thing else that may be needful in dealing with their children aright. But their heavenly Father has all this. The Lord Jesus possesses all this. And they are in partnership with the Father, and with the Son, and therefore they can obtain by prayer and faith all they need out of the fulness of God. I say by prayer and faith; for we have to make known our need to God in prayer, ask His help, and then we have to believe that He will give us what we need. Prayer alone is not enough. We may pray never so much, yet if we do not believe that God will give us what we need, we have no reason to expect that we shall receive what we have asked for. So then these parents would need to ask God to give them the needful wisdom, patience, long-suffering, gentleness, meekness, love, decision, firmness, and whatever else they may judge they need. They may in humble boldness remind their heavenly Father that His word assures them that they are in partnership with Him, and, as they themselves are lacking in these particulars, ask Him to be pleased to supply their need; and then they have to believe that God will do it, and they shall receive according to their need.--Another instance: suppose I am so situated in my business that day by day such difficulties arise, that I continually find that I take wrong steps, by reason of these great difficulties. How may the case be altered for the better? In myself I see no remedy for the difficulties. In looking at myself I can expect nothing but to make still further mistakes, and, therefore, trial upon trial seems to be before me. And yet I need not despair. The living God is my partner. I have not sufficient wisdom to meet these difficulties so as to be able to know what steps to take, but He is able to direct me. What I have, therefore, to do is this: in simplicity to spread my case before my heavenly Father and my Lord Jesus. The Father and the Son are my partners. I have to tell out my heart to God, and to ask Him, that, as He is my partner, and I have no wisdom in myself to meet all the many difficulties which continually occur in my business, He would be pleased to guide and direct me, and to supply me with the needful wisdom; and then I have to believe that God will do so, and go with good courage to my business, and expect help from Him in the next difficulty that may come before me. I have to look out for guidance, I have to expect counsel from the Lord; and, as assuredly as I do so, I shall have it, I shall find that I am not nominally, but really in partnership with the Father and with the Son.--Another instance: There are a father and mother with seven small children. Both parents are believers. The father works in a manufactory, but cannot earn more than ten shillings per week. The mother cannot earn any thing. These ten shillings are too little for the supply of nourishing and wholesome food for seven growing children and their parents, and for providing them with the other necessaries of life. What is to be done in such a case? Surely not to find fault with the manufacturer, who may not be able to afford more wages, and much less to murmur against God; but the parents have in simplicity to tell God, their partner, that the wages of ten shillings a week are not sufficient in England to provide nine persons with all they need, so as that their health be not injured. They have to remind God that He is not hard master, not an unkind being, but a most loving Father, who has abundantly proved the love of His heart in the gift of His only begotten Son. And they have in childlike simplicity to ask Him, that either He would order it so, that the manufacturer may be able to allow more wages; or that He (the Lord) would find them another place, where the father would be able to earn more; or that He would be pleased somehow or other, as it may seem good to Him, to supply them with more means. They have to ask the Lord, in childlike simplicity, again and again for it, if He does not answer their request at once; and they have to believe that God, their Father and partner, will give them the desire of their hearts. They have to expect an answer to their prayers; day by day they have to look out for it, and to repeat their request till God grants it. As assuredly as they believe that God will grant them their request, so assuredly it shall be granted.--Thus, suppose, I desired more power over my besetting sins; suppose, I desired more power against certain temptations; suppose I desired more wisdom, or grace, or any thing else that I may need in my service among the saints, or in my service towards the unconverted: what have I to do, but to make use of my being in fellowship with the Father and with the Son? Just as, for instance, an old faithful clerk, who is this day taken into partnership by an immensely rich firm, though himself altogether without property, would not be discouraged by reason of a large payment having to be made by the firm within three days, though he himself has no money at all of his own, but would comfort himself with the immense riches possessed by those who so generously have just taken him into partnership: so should we, the children of God and servants of Jesus Christ, comfort ourselves by being in fellowship, or partnership, with the Father, and with the Son, though we have no power of our own against our besetting sins; though we cannot withstand temptations, which are before us, in our own strength; and though we have neither sufficient grace nor wisdom for our service among the saints, or towards the unconverted. All we have to do is, to draw upon our partner, the living God. By prayer and faith we may obtain all needful temporal and spiritual help and blessings. In all simplicity have we to tell out our heart before God, and then we have to believe that He will give to us according to our need. But if we do not believe that God will help us, could we be at peace? The clerk, taken into the firm as partner, believes that the firm will meet the payment though so large, and though in three days it is to be made, and it is this that keeps his heart quiet, though altogether poor himself. We have to believe that our infinitely rich partner, the living God, will help us in our need, and we shall not only be in peace, but we shall actually find that the help which we need will be granted to us.--Let not the consciousness of your entire unworthiness keep you, dear reader, from believing what God has said concerning you. If you are indeed a believer in the Lord Jesus, then this precious privilege, of being in partnership with the Father and the Son, is yours, though you and I are entirely unworthy of it. If the consciousness of our unworthiness were to keep us from believing what God has said concerning those who depend upon and trust in the Lord Jesus for salvation, then we should find that there is not one single blessing, with which we have been blessed in the Lord Jesus, from which, on account of our unworthiness, we could derive any settled comfort or peace.

IV. There is one other point which, in connexion with several portions of the word of God, which bear on the subject, I desire to bring before the believing reader, and it refers to the "scriptural way of overcoming the difficulties with which the believer now meets who is engaged in a business, trade, profession, or any earthly calling whatever, which arise from competition in business, too great a number of persons being occupied in the same calling, stagnation of trade, and the like." The children of God, who are strangers and pilgrims on earth, have at all times had difficulty in the world, for they are not at home but from home; nor should they, until the return of the Lord Jesus, expect it to be otherwise with them. But whilst this is true, it is also true that the Lord has provided us in all our difficulties with something in His own word to meet them. All difficulties may be overcome by acting according to the word of God. At this time I more especially desire to point out the means whereby the children of God who are engaged in any earthly calling may be able to overcome the difficulties, which arise from competition in business, too great a number of persons being occupied in the same calling, stagnation of trade and the like.

1, The first thing which the believer, who is in such difficulties, has to ask himself is, Am I in a calling in which I can abide with God? If our occupation be of that kind, that we cannot ask God's blessing upon it, or that we should be ashamed to be found in it at the appearing of the Lord Jesus, or that it of necessity hinders our spiritual progress, then we must give it up, and be engaged in something else; but in few cases only this is needful. Far the greater part of the occupations in which believers are engaged are not of such a nature, as that they need to give them up in order to maintain a good conscience, and in order to be able to walk with God, though, perhaps, certain alterations may need to be made in the manner of conducting their trade, business, or profession. About those parts of our calling, which may need alteration, we shall receive instruction from the Lord, if we indeed desire it, and wait upon Him for it, and expect it from Him.

2, Now suppose the believer is in a calling in which he can abide with God, the next point to be settled is: "Why do I carry on this business, or why am I engaged in this trade or profession?" In most instances, so far as my experience goes, which I have gathered in my service among the saints during the last fifty-one years and a half, I believe the answer would be: "I am engaged in my earthly calling, that I may earn the means of obtaining the necessaries of life for myself and family." Here is the chief error from which almost all the rest of the errors, which are entertained by children of God, relative to their calling, spring. It is no right and Scriptural motive, to be engaged in a trade, or business, or profession, merely in order to earn the means for the obtaining of the necessaries of life for ourselves and family; but us should work, because it is the Lord's will concerning us. This is plain from the following passages; I Thess. iv. 11, 12; II Thess. iii. 10-12; Eph. iv. 28. It is quite true that, in general, the Lord provides the necessaries of life by means of our ordinary calling; but that that is not THE REASON why we should work, is plain enough from the consideration, that if our possessing the necessaries of life depended upon our ability of working, we could never have freedom from anxiety, for we should always have to say to ourselves, and what shall I do when I am too old to work I or when by reason of sickness I am unable to earn my bread? But if on the other hand, we are engaged in our earthly calling, because it is the will of time Lord concerning us that we should work, and that thus labouring we may provide for our families and also be

THIRD PART

able to support the weak, the sick, the aged, and the needy, then we have good and scriptural reason to say to ourselves: should it please the Lord to lay me on a bed of sickness, or keep me otherwise by reason of infirmity or old age, or want of employment, from earning my bread by means of the labour of my hands, or my business, or my profession, He will yet provide for me. Because we who believe are servants of Jesus Christ, who has bought us with His own precious blood, and are not our own, and because this our precious Lord and Master has commanded us to work, therefore we work; and in doing so our Lord will provide for us; but whether in this way or any other way, He is sure to provide for us; for we labour in obedience to Him; and if even a just earthly master give wages to his servants, the Lord will surely see to it that we have our wages, if in obedience to Him we are engaged in our calling, and not for our own sake. How great the difference between acting according to the word of God, and according to our own natural desires, or the customs of the world, will be plain, I trust, by the following case. Suppose I were engaged in some useful trade. Suppose I had the certain human prospect, that within the next three months my labour would bring me in nothing, for certain reasons connected with the state of mercantile affairs. As a man of the world I should say, I shall not work at all, because my labour will not be paid; but as a Christian, who desires to act according to God's Holy word, I ought to say: My trade is useful to society, and I will work notwithstanding all human prospects, because the Lord Jesus has commanded me to labour; from Him and not from my trade I expect my wages. In addition to this the Christian ought also to say, Idleness is a dreadful snare of the devil, he has especial opportunity to get an advantage over the children of God when they are unoccupied; and, therefore, I will work though I have no human prospect of obtaining payment for my labour, but shall get only the cost price of the material, and shall have to give my work for nothing. Moreover the Christian ought to say, Though according to human probability I shall have to labour for nothing during the next three months, yet I will work, because the Lord may speedily alter the state of things, contrary to all human expectation; but whether He be pleased to do so or not, I labour because I am the Lord's, bought by His precious blood, and He commands me to labour.--But there are motives still lower than to be engaged in our earthly calling merely that we may earn the means of obtaining the necessaries of life, why even Christians, true children of God, may be engaged in their calling, such as: to obtain a certain sum of money, and then to retire from business and to live upon the interest; or, to provide something for old age; or, to obtain a certain amount of property, without intending to give up business. If it be unscriptural to be engaged in our calling, merely, even for the sake of earning the means for procuring the necessaries of life for ourselves and family, how much more unbecoming that a child of God should be engaged in his calling for the sake of any of the last mentioned reasons.--This second point, then, Why do I carry on this business? Why am I engaged in this trade or profession? ought first to be settled in the fear of God and according to the revealed will of God; and if we cannot say in honesty of heart, I do carry on my business, I am engaged in my trade, or art, or profession, as a servant of Jesus Christ, whose I am, because He has bought me with His precious blood, and He has commanded me to work, and therefore I work: I say, if we cannot say this in honesty of heart, but must confess that we work on account of lower motives such as, that we may earn our bread, or on account of still lower motives, and such which are altogether unbecoming a child of God, who is not of the world but of God, such as, to obtain a certain sum of money in order to be able to live on the interest without having to work; or, to provide something for old age; or, to obtain a certain amount of property without intending to give up business: if these are our motives for being engaged in our calling, I say, can we be surprised that we meet with great difficulties in our business, and that the Lord in His abounding love to us, His erring children, does not allow us to succeed? But suppose this second point is scripturally settled, and we can honestly say that, because we are servants of Jesus Christ, we are occupied as we are--we have further to consider: 3, Whether we carry on our business, or are engaged in our trade, art, or profession as stewards of the Lord. To the child of God it ought not to be enough that he is in a calling in which he can abide with God, nor that he is engaged in his calling, because it is the will of his Lord and Master that he should work, but he should consider himself in his trade, business, art, or profession, only as the steward of the Lord with reference to his income. The child of God has been bought with the precious blood of the Lord Jesus, and is altogether His property, with all that he possesses, his bodily strength, his mental strength, his ability of every kind, his trade, business, art, or profession, his property, &c.; for it is written: "Ye are not your own; for ye are bought with a price." I Cor. vi. 19, 20. The proceeds of our calling are therefore not our own in the sense of using them as our natural heart wishes us to do, whether to spend them on the gratification of our pride, or our love of pleasure, or sensual indulgences, or to lay by the money for ourselves or our children, or use it in any way as we naturally like; but we have to stand before our Lord and Master, whose stewards we are, to seek to ascertain His will, how He will have us use the proceeds of our calling. But is this indeed the spirit in which the children of God generally are engaged in their calling? It is but too well known that it is not the case! Can we then wonder at it, that even God's own dear children should so often be found greatly in difficulty with regard to their calling, and be found so often complaining about stagnation or competition in trade, and the difficulties of the times, though there have been given to them such precious promises as: "Seek ye first the kingdom of God and His righteousness; and all these things shall be added unto you;" or, "Let your conversation (disposition or turn of mind) be without covetousness; and be content with such things as ye have: for He hath said, I will never leave thee, nor forsake thee." Heb. xiii. 5. Is it not obvious enough, that, when our Heavenly Father sees that we His children do or would use the proceeds of our calling, as our natural mind would desire, that He either cannot at all intrust us with means, or will be obliged to decrease them? No wise and really affectionate mother will permit her infant to play with a razor, or with fire, however much the child may desire to have them; and so the love and wisdom of our Heavenly Father will not, cannot, intrust us with pecuniary means, (except it be in the way of chastisement, or to show us finally their utter vanity,) if He sees that we do not desire to possess them as stewards for Him, in order that we may spend them as He may point out to us by His Holy Spirit, through His word.--In connexion with this subject, I give a few hints to the believing reader on three passages of the word of God. In I Cor. xvi. 2, we find it written to the brethren at Corinth, "Upon the first day of the week let every one of you lay by him in store, as God has prospered him." A contribution for the poor saints in Judea was to be made, and the brethren at Corinth were exhorted to put by every Lord's day, according to the measure of success which the Lord had been pleased to grant them in their calling during the week. Now, ought not the saints in our day also to act according to this word! There is no passage in the word of God, why we should not do so, and it is altogether in accordance with our pilgrim character, not only once or twice, or four times a year to see how much we can afford to give to the poor saints, or to the work of God in any way, but to seek to settle it weekly. If, it be said, I cannot ascertain how much I have gained in the course of the week by my business, and therefore I cannot give accordingly; my reply is this, Seek, dear brethren, as much as possible to bring your business upon such a footing, as that you may be able, as nearly as possible, to settle how much you have earned in your calling in the course of the week; but suppose you should be unable to settle it exactly to the shilling or pound, yet you will know pretty well how it has been with you during the week, and therefore, according to your best knowledge, contribute on the coming Lord's day towards the necessities of the poor saints, and towards the work of God, as He, after your having sought His guidance, may lead you. Perhaps you say, the weeks are so unlike; in one week I may earn three or even ten times as much as in another week, and if I give according to my earnings from my calling during a very good week, then how are such weeks, when I earn scarcely any thing, or how are the bad debts to be met? How shall I do when sickness befalls my family, or when other trials productive of expense come upon me, if I do not make provision for such seasons? My reply is, 1, I do not find in the whole New Testament one single passage in which either directly or indirectly exhortations are given to provide against deadness in business, bad debts and sickness, by laying up money. 2, Often the Lord is obliged to allow deadness in business, or bad debts, or sickness in our family, or other trials, which increase our expenses, to befall us, because we do not, as His stewards, act according to stewardship, but as if we were owners of what we have, forgetting that the time has not yet come when we shall enter upon our possessions and He does so in order that, by these losses and expenses, our property which we have collected may be decreased, lest we should altogether set our hearts again upon earthly things, and forget God entirely. His love is so great, that He will not let His children quietly go their own way when they have forsaken Him; but if His loving admonitions by His Holy Spirit are disregarded, He is obliged in fatherly love to chastise them. A striking illustration of what I have said we have in the case of Israel nationally. The commandment to them was, to leave their land uncultivated in the seventh year, in order that it might rest; and the Lord promised to make up for this deficiency by His abundant blessing resting upon the sixth year. However, Israel acted not according to this commandment, no doubt saying in the unbelief of their hearts, as the Lord had foretold, "What shall we eat in the seventh year? Behold we shall not sow, nor gather in our increase." Leviticus xxv. But what did the Lord do? He was determined the land should have rest, and as the Israelites did not willingly give it, He sent them for seventy years into captivity, in order that thus the land might have rest. See Leviticus xxvi. 33-35. Beloved brethren in the Lord, let us take heed so to walk as that the Lord may not be obliged, by chastisement to take a part of our earthly possessions from us in the way of bad debts, sickness, decrease of business, or the like, because we would not own our position as stewards, but act as owners, and keep for ourselves the means with which the Lord had intrusted us, not for the gratification of our own carnal mind, but for the sake of using them in His service and to His praise. It might also be said by a brother whose earnings are small, should I also give according to my earnings? They are already so small, that my wife can only with the greatest difficulty manage to make them sufficient for the family. My reply is: Have you ever considered, my brother, that the very reason, why the Lord is obliged to let your earnings remain so small, may be the fact of your spending every thing upon yourselves, and that if He were to give you more, you would only use it to increase your own family comfort, instead of looking about to see who among the brethren are sick, or who have no work at all, that you might help them, or how you might assist the work of God at home and abroad? There is a great temptation for a brother whose earnings are small, to put off the responsibility of assisting the needy and sick saints, or helping on the work of God, and to lay it upon the few rich brethren and sisters with whom he is associated in fellowship, and thus rob his own soul!--It might be asked, How much shall I give of my income? The tenth part, or the fifth part, or the third part, or one-half, or more? My reply is, God lays down no rule, concerning this point. What we do we should do cheerfully and not of necessity. But if even Jacob with the first dawning of spiritual light (Genesis xxviii. 22) promised to God the tenth of all He should give to him, how much ought we believers in the Lord Jesus to do for Him; we, whose calling is a heavenly one, and who know distinctly that we are children of God, and joint heirs with the Lord Jesus! Yet do all the children of God give even the tenth part of what the Lord gives them?

That would be two shillings per week for the brother who earns 1l., and 4s. to him who earns 2l., and 2l. per week to him whose income is 20l. per week.

In connexion with I Cor. xvi. 2, I would mention two other portions: 1. "He which soweth sparingly shall reap also sparingly: and he that soweth bountifully, shall reap also bountifully." II Cor. ix. 6. It is certain that we children of God are so abundantly blessed in Jesus, by the grace of God, that we ought to need no stimulus to good works. The forgiveness of our sins, the having been made for ever the children of God, the having before us the Father's house as our home: these blessings ought to be sufficient motives to constrain us in love and gratitude to serve God abundantly all the days of our life, and cheerfully also to give up, as He may call for it, that with which He has intrusted us of the things of this world. But whilst this is the case, the Lord nevertheless holds out to us in His Holy Word motives why we should serve Him, deny ourselves, use our property for Him, etc.; and the last mentioned passage is one of that kind. The verse is true, both with reference to the life that is now and that which is to come. If we have been sparingly using our property for Him, there will have been little treasure laid up in heaven, and therefore a small amount of capital will be found in the world to come, so far as it regards reaping. Again, we shall reap bountifully if we seek to be rich towards God, by abundantly using our means for Him, whether in ministering to the necessities of the poor saints, or using otherwise our pecuniary means for His work. Dear brethren, these things are realities! Shortly, very shortly, will come the reaping time, and then will be the question, whether we shall reap sparingly or bountifully.--But while this passage refers to the life hereafter, it also refers to the life that now is. Just as now the love of Christ constrains us to communicate of that with which the Lord intrusts us, so will be the present reaping, both with regard to spiritual and temporal things. Should there be found therefore in a brother the want of entering into his position as being merely a steward for the Lord in his calling, and should he give no heed to the admonitions of the Holy Ghost to communicate to those who are in need, or to help the work of God; then, can such a brother be surprised that he meets with great difficulties in his calling, and that he cannot get on? This is according to the Lord's word. He is sowing sparingly, and he therefore reaps sparingly. But should the love of Christ constrain a brother, out of the earnings of his calling to sow bountifully, he will even in this life reap bountifully, both with regard to blessings in his soul and with regard to temporal things. Consider in connexion with this the following passage, which, though taken from the Book of Proverbs, is not of a Jewish character, but true concerning believers under the present dispensation also: "There is that scattereth, and yet increaseth; and there is that withholdeth more than is meet, but it tendeth to poverty. The liberal son shall be made fat: and he that watereth shall be watered also himself." Prov. xi. 24, 25.--In connexion with 1 Cor. xvi. 2, I would also direct my brethren in the Lord to the promise made in Luke vi. 38, "Give and it shall be given unto you: good measure, pressed down, and shaken together, and running over, shall men give into your bosom. For with the same measure that ye mete withal it shall be measured to you again." This refers evidently to the present dispensation, and evidently in its primary meaning to temporal things. Now let any one, constrained by the love of Jesus, act according to this passage; let him on the first day of the week communicate as the Lord has prospered him, and he will see that the Lord will act according to what is contained in this verse. If pride constrain us to give, if self-righteousness make us liberal, if natural feeling induce us to communicate, or if we give whilst we are in a state of insolvency, not possessing more perhaps than ten shillings in the pound were our creditors to come upon us; then we cannot expect to have this verse fulfilled in our experience: nor should we give at any time for the sake of receiving again from others, according to this verse; but if indeed the love of Christ constrain us to communicate according to the ability which the Lord gives us, then we shall have this verse fulfilled in our experience, though this was not the motive that induced us to give. Somehow or other the Lord will abundantly repay us through the instrumentality of our fellow men what we are doing for His poor saints, or in any way for His work, and we shall find that in the end we are not losers, even with reference to temporal things, whilst we communicate liberally of the things of this life with which the Lord has intrusted us.--Here it might be remarked: but if it be so, that even in this life, and with regard to temporal things it is true, that "To him that gives shall be given, good measure, pressed down, and shaken together, and running over," and that "He which soweth bountifully shall reap also bountifully," then in the end the most liberal persons would be exceedingly rich. Concerning this remark we have to keep in mind, that the moment persons were to begin to give for the sake of receiving more back again from the Lord, through the instrumentality of their fellow men, than they have given; or the moment persons wished to alter their way, and no more go on sowing bountifully, but sparingly, in order to increase their possessions, whilst God is allowing them to reap bountifully, the river of God's bounty toward them would no longer continue to flow. God had supplied them abundantly with means, because He saw them act as stewards for Him. He had intrusted them with a little which they used for Him, and He therefore intrusted them with more; and if they had continued to use the much also for Him, He would have still more abundantly used them as instruments to scatter abroad His bounties. The child of God must be willing to be a channel through which God's bounties flow, both with regard to temporal and spiritual things. This channel is narrow and shallow at first, it may be; yet there is room for some of the waters of God's bounty to pass through. And if we cheerfully yield ourselves as channels, for this purpose, then the channel becomes wider and deeper, and the waters of the bounty of God can pass through more abundantly. Without a figure it is thus: At first we may be only instrumental in communicating 5l. or 10l. or 20l. or 50l. or 100l. or 200l. per year, but afterwards double as much; and if we are still more faithful in our stewardship, after a year or two four times as much, afterwards perhaps eight times as much, at last perhaps twenty times or fifty times as much. We cannot limit the extent to which God may use us as instruments in communicating blessing, both temporal and spiritual, if we are willing to yield ourselves as instruments to the living God, and are content to be only instruments, and to give Him all the glory. But with regard to temporal things it will be thus, that if indeed we walk according to the mind of God in these things, whilst more and more we become instruments of blessing to others, we shall not seek to enrich ourselves, but be content when the last day of another year finds us still in the body, to possess no more than on the last day of the previous year, or even considerably less, whilst we have been, however, in the course of the year the instruments of communicating largely to others, through the means with which the Lord had intrusted us. As to my own soul, by the grace of God it would be a burden to me to find, that, however much my income in the course of a year might have been, I was increasing in earthly possession; for it would be a plain proof to me, that I had not been acting as steward for God, and had not been yielding myself as a channel for the waters of God's bounty to pass through. I also cannot but bear my testimony here, that in whatever feeble measure God has enabled me to act according to these truths for the last fifty-one years and a half, I have found it to be profitable, most profitable to my own soul; and as to temporal things, I never was a loser in doing so, but I have most abundantly found the truth in II Cor. ix. 6, and Luke vi. 38, and Prov. xi. 24, 25, verified in my own experience. I only have to regret that I have acted so little according to what I have now been stating; but my godly purpose is, by the help of God, to spend the remainder of my days in practising these truths more than ever, and I am sure, that, when I am brought to the close of my earthly pilgrimage, either in death, or by the appearing of our Lord Jesus, I shall not have the least regret in having done so; and I know that should I leave my dear child behind, the Lord will abundantly provide for her, and prove that there has been a better provision made for her than her father could have made, if he had sought to insure his life or lay up money for her.

Before leaving this part of the subject, I mention to the believing reader, that I know instance upon instance, in which what I have been saying has been verified, but I will only mention the following:--I knew many years ago a brother as the manager of a large manufactory. Whilst in this capacity he was liberal, and giving away

THIRD PART

considerably out of his rather considerable salary. The Lord repaid this to him; for the principals of the establishment, well knowing his value to their house of business, gave him now and then whilst he thus was liberally using his means for the Lord, very large presents in money. In process of time, however, this brother thought it right to begin business on his own account, in a very small way. He still continued to be liberal, according to his means, and God prospered him, and prospered him so, that now, whilst I am writing, his manufactory is as large as the one which he formerly managed, or even larger, though that was a very considerable one. And sure I am, that, if this brother shall be kept by God from setting his heart upon earthly things, and from seeking more and more to increase his earthly riches, but shall delight himself in being used as a steward by God, cheerfully communicating to the need of God's poor children, or to His work in other ways, and doing so not sparingly, but bountifully, the Lord will intrust him more and more with means; if otherwise, if he shut up his hands, seek his own, wish to obtain sufficient property that he may be able to live on his interest, then, what he has to expect is, that God will shut up His hands, he will meet with heavy losses, or there will be an alteration in his affairs for the worse, or the like.--I also mention two other cases, to show that the Lord increases our ability of communicating temporal blessings to others, if we distribute according to the means with which He has intrusted us, though we should not be in a trade or business, or profession.--I know a brother who many years ago saw it right not only to spend his interest for the Lord, but also the principal, as the Lord might point out to him opportunities. His desire was not, as indeed it ought never to be, to get rid of his money as fast as possible, yet he considered himself a steward for the Lord, and was therefore willing, as his Lord and Master might point it out to him, to spend his means. When this brother came to this determination, he possessed about twenty thousand pounds sterling. According to the light and grace, which the Lord had been pleased to give he afterwards acted, spending the money for the Lord, in larger or smaller sums, as opportunities were pointed out to him by the Lord. Thus the sum more and more decreased, whilst the brother steadily pursued his course, serving the Lord with his property, and spending his time and ability also for the Lord, in service of one kind or another among His children. At last the twenty thousand pounds were almost entirely spent, when at that very time the father of this brother died, whereby he came into the possession of an income of several thousand pounds a year. It gives joy to my heart to be able to add, that this brother still pursues his godly course, living in the most simple way, and giving away perhaps ten times as much as he spends on himself or family. Here you see, dear reader, that this brother, using faithfully for the Lord what he had been intrusted with at first, was made steward over more; for he has now more than one-third as much in a year coming in, as he at first possessed altogether.--I mention another instance: I know a brother to whom the Lord has given a liberal heart, and who bountifully gave of that over which the Lord had set him as steward. The Lord seeing this, intrusted him with still more, for through family circumstances he came into the possession of many thousand pounds, in addition to the considerable property he possessed before. I have the joy of being able to add also concerning this brother, that the Lord continues to give him grace to use his property as a steward for God, and that he has not been permitted to set his heart upon his riches, through the very considerable increase of his property, but that he continues to live as the steward of the Lord, and not as the owner of all this wealth.--And now, dear reader, when the brethren to whom I have been referring are brought to the close of their earthly pilgrimage, will they have one moment's regret that they have used their property for the Lord? Will it be the least particle of uneasiness to their minds, or will their children be the worse for it? Oh no! The only regret they will have concerning this matter will be, that they did not serve the Lord still more abundantly with their property. Dear reader, let us each in our measure act in the same spirit. Money is really worth no more than as it is used according to the mind of the Lord; and life is worth no more than as it is spent in the service of the Lord.

Whilst the three mentioned points--1, That our calling must be of that nature that we can abide in it with God; 2, That unto the Lord we should labour in our calling, as His servants, because He has bought us with His blood, and because He will have us to labour; 3, That as stewards we should labour in our calling, because the earnings of our calling are the Lord's and not our own, as He has bought us with His blood: I say, whilst these three points are particularly to be attended to in order that the Lord's blessing may rest upon our calling, and we be prospering in it, there are, nevertheless, some other points to be attended to, which I mention in love to my brethren in the Lord, by whom they may be needed. 4, The next point is, that a believer in the Lord Jesus should do nothing in his calling, which is purely for the sake of attracting the world, such as for instance, fitting up his shop or rooms of business in the most costly manner, I do not in the least mean to say that his shop or rooms of business should not be clean, orderly, and of such a character as that there may be no positive hinderance to persons going there. All the needful conveniences that are expected may be there and ought to be there. But if any child of God seek to have the front of his shop, or the interior of his shop, or of his place of business fitted up in a most expensive way, simply for the sake of attracting attention, then let him be aware, that, just in so far as he is trusting in these things, he is not likely to succeed in his calling, because he puts the manner of sitting up the shop in the room of trust in the Lord. Such things the Lord may allow to succeed in the case of an unbeliever, but they will not prosper in the case of a child of God, except it be in the way of chastisement, just as the Lord gave to Israel in the wilderness the desire of their hearts, but sent leanness into their souls. Should any brother have fallen into this error, the first thing he has to do, when the Lord has instructed him concerning this point, is, to make confession of sin, and, as far as it can be done, to retrace his steps in this particular. If this cannot be done, then to cast himself upon the mercy of God in Christ Jesus. 5, Of the same character is: To seek to attract the attention of the world, by "boasting advertisements," such as "no one manufactures so good an article," "no one sells this article so cheap," "we sell the best article in the city," etc. Suppose these statements were quite correct, yet they are unbecoming for a child of God, who has the living God to care for him and to provide for him, and therefore needs not to make use of such boasting, whereby he may seek to ensure custom to himself and keep it from others. The law of love is, "Whatsoever ye would that men should do to you, do ye even so to them." Matt. vii. 12. Now what do I wish in this particular that others should do to me, but that they should not seek to keep away persons from dealing with me; but if I use such like expressions in my advertisements, as have been mentioned, what do they imply but, that I wish all people should come to me, and deal with me. If, however, already under the old covenant it was said, "Thou shalt not covet," how much more sinful and altogether unbecoming is it for us children of God, who are in fellowship with the Father and the Son, to make use of such means, in order to ensure to ourselves pecuniary advantages. But, however much the Lord may allow a man of the world to prosper in using such means, they are only hinderances to the child of God to getting on in his calling, because the Lord sees that they are substituted instead of trust in Himself; and should the Lord for a season allow His child apparently to be benefited by them, it will only be for his chastisement and connected with leanness in his soul. Therefore, my brethren in the Lord, I beseech you to put away all these things out of your calling, lest you should be hindering instead of furthering your real welfare. 6, Likewise of a similar character is the following point, which God may suffer to be a real hinderance to His children in their calling, it is, To seek the very best, (and therefore the most expensive) situations which can be had in a town or city. Now I do by no means intend to say, that in our trade, business, art, or profession, we should seek the most obscure, retired, out of the way place possible, and say, "God will provide, and I need not mind in what part of the town I carry on my calling." There are most assuredly certain things to be considered. The persons who are likely to buy the articles I sell, or employ me, are to be considered, and I have not to say, it matters nothing to me, whether I make them come a mile or two to my house, or to the most dirty and disagreeable part of the town; this would be the extreme in the other way. But whilst there is a certain consideration to be used with reference to those who may employ us in our calling, yet if the trust of the child of God respecting temporal prosperity is in the fact that he lives in the best situation, the Lord will surely disappoint him. He will have to pay a very high rent for the best situation, and yet not succeed, because his trust is in the best situation. He is substituting it for dependence upon the living God for customers. He is robbing his soul not only in not taking the customers as from the hands of the Lord, but he is also obliging his heavenly Father, in the very love of His heart, to cause him to be disappointed, because he is not trusting in Him. If the child of God were saying and acting thus: the best situation would cost me 50l. a year more rent, than one which is not really inconvenient for my customers, nor in an improper neighbourhood, and the like, this 50l. I dedicate unto the Lord, to be paid in instalments for His work, or His poor saints, whenever the rent day comes, such a brother would find himself to be no loser, if this indeed were done in dependence upon the Lord, and constrained by the love of Jesus. But if the 50l. more is paid for rent, and yet the living God, in the very love of His heart, should be obliged to withhold prosperity from His child in His calling, because He sees that he is laying undue stress upon the situation of the house, then not only the 50l. extra rent per year is lost, but also that which the Lord is obliged to withhold from His child besides, in order to teach him the lesson; and thus year after year, by our own fault, we may have scarcely any thing to give for the work of God. 7, The next obstacle to prosperity in our calling which I now would mention is, That children of God often use such expressions as these with reference to their calling: "this is our busy time," or "this is our dead time," which implies that they do not day after day deal with God about their calling, but that they ascribe their having much or little to do to circumstances, or to times and seasons. That the people of the world should do so is not to be wondered at; but that the children of God should act thus, who in the most minute affairs of life should seek the help of God, and deal with God about them, is a matter of sorrow to the spiritual mind, and is altogether unbecoming saints. But what is the result. The Lord, according to the expectations of His children, allows them to be without employment, because they say, "this is our dead season." "He did not many mighty works there because of their unbelief," contains a truth which comes in here. But what is the right way of looking at the matter? It is this: the child of God should say, though generally about this time of the year there is little employment to be expected, looking at it naturally, yet as a want of employment is neither good for the outward nor inward man, and as I only desire employment to serve God in my business, to have to give to those who are in need, or help in other ways the work of God, I will now give myself to prayer for employment, for I can by prayer and faith, as a child of God, obtain blessings from my heavenly Father, though not in the ordinary course of things. If thus the child of God were to say and to act, he would soon have employment in his calling, except the Lord meant to use his time otherwise in His work, which He would point out to him. 8, A further reason, why God may be obliged to resist children of God in their business, may be this, that they with the greatest carefulness seek to obtain persons for their shop who are considered "good salesmen," i.e. persons who have such persuasive ways, as that they gain an advantage over the customers and induce them not only to buy articles for which they ask, whether suitable or not, but that they also induce them to buy articles which they did not at all intend to buy when they came to the shop. Concerning this I notice in the first place, that if the child of God puts his dependence upon the "good salesmen," let him not be surprised if his heavenly Father should be obliged to disappoint him, because He sees His child lean upon the arm of flesh, instead of trusting in the living God; and therefore the business does not succeed. Further, it is altogether wrong for a child of God to induce the customers, by means of such men or women who have a persuasive tongue, to purchase articles whether they suit or not, and whether they are needed or not. This is no less than defrauding persons in a subtle way, or leading them into the sin of purchasing beyond their means, or at least spending their money needlessly. However such sinful tricks may be allowed to prosper in the case of a man of the world, in the case of a child of God they will not prosper, except God allow them to do so in the way of chastisement, whilst leanness and wretchedness is brought into the soul. I knew a case of this kind where it was the whole bent of the mind of a professed believer to obtain such "good salesmen," and where even a Jew was kept outside the shop walking up and down to induce persons to come in and buy; and yet that same professed believer failed twice in his business. 9, Another evil with reference to business, and why children of God do not get on in their calling is, that they enter upon business often without any capital at all, or with too little. If a believer has no capital at all, or only a very small capital, in comparison with what his business requires, then, ought he not to say this to himself: "If it were my heavenly Father's will that I should enter upon business on my own account, then would He not somehow or other have intrusted me with the needful means? And since He has not, is it not a plain indication that, for the present, I should remain a journey-

THIRD PART

man, (or shopman, or clerk, as the case may be)?" In a variety of ways the means might come. For instance, a legacy might be left to him, or money might be given to him by a brother in the Lord for that very purpose, or a brother or sister might propose to the individual to lend him money, yet so that if he were unable to pay it again, they would not consider him their debtor, or in many other ways God might intrust him with means But if in some such way the Lord did not remove the hinderance, and the brother would still go into business, he would, through the bill system and other things connected with the want of capital, not only bring great distress into his mind, and subject himself to the possibility of at last being unable to pay his creditors, whereby dishonour would be brought upon the name of the Lord, but he likewise could not be surprised (as he went into business contrary to the will of God, since He pointed out to him that he was not to do so for want of means,) if he should find that he cannot get on, and that the blessing of God manifestly is wanting. In such a case as this, if it can be done, the retracing our steps is the best thing we can do; but often this cannot be done, as others are involved in the matter, and then we have to make acknowledgment of our sin, and seek God's merciful help to bring us into a right position. 10, But suppose all these nine previous points were attended to, and we neglected to seek God's blessing upon our calling, we need still not be surprised if we met with difficulty upon difficulty, and could not get on at all. It is not enough that we seek God's help for that which manifestly is of a spiritual character; but we should seek His help and blessing by prayer and supplication for all our ordinary concerns in life, and if we neglect doing so, we shall surely suffer for the neglect. "Trust in the Lord with all thine heart; and lean not unto thine own understanding. In all thy ways acknowledge Him, and He shall direct thy paths." Prov. iii. 5, 6.

These few remarks I commend affectionately to the prayerful consideration of all brethren and sisters in the Lord with reference to their calling; for though they are written by one who never was in business himself, yet the truths therein set forth have been learned by him in the school of God, and he has had them abundantly confirmed through his pastoral labours during the last fifty-one years.

And now, farewell, beloved reader.--Very many times have I sought the Lord's blessing before I began preparing this third part for the press, and very many times have I done so while writing it, and now I am most fully assured, that He will abundantly bless this part also, because of the abundance of supplication which He has wrought concerning it by His Spirit in my soul. I ask you also, dear reader, if you know the power of prayer, to unite with me in seeking the Lord's blessing upon this book, and then we shall rejoice together in the answers to our prayers, if not here on earth, at least in the day of Christ's appearing.

END OF THE THIRD PART

THE LORD'S DEALINGS WITH GEORGE MÜLLER

1. My Journal gives the names of the individuals, whom the Lord has used as instruments, in supplying our wants; but it has appeared well to me, for several reasons, not to mention them in print.

2. One bill I had to meet for a brother, the other was for money which in the form of a bill I had sent to the Continent; but in both cases the money was in my hands, before the bills were given.

3. At the beginning the name was, The Scriptural Knowledge Society for Home and Abroad;" but as the Institution was never a Society in the common sense of the word, there being nothing like membership, voting, a committee, &c., it appeared afterwards better to alter the name as above stated, for the sake of avoiding mistakes. I mention, moreover, that in this eighth edition the Institution is spoken of in the way in which it is now existing, without further notice of the alterations which have been made since its establishment on March 5, 1834, as its original character is substantially the same.

4. Only two Orphans were received under such circumstances. Since 1841 we have had no child on such conditions, as we now consider, that, if a relative would be able and willing to pay the average expense for the support of a child, such an Orphan could not be considered destitute. During the summer of 1855, thee Orphans were applied for, and their relatives offered to pay 50l. a year for these children to the funds of the Institution. They were, however, not only not received, but their names were not even entered on the list of those who are waiting for admission, as they could not be considered destitute. Our object is not to obtain funds for the Institution, but to provide by means of it for truly destitute Orphans hence, though 50l. is more than the average expense for three Orphans in a year, we did not receive those three just referred to.

5. The Schoolmasters, as well as the clergymen, in Prussia, are connected with the State.

6. We continued for many months to break bread only at Bethesda, till at last, though it is a large chapel, the body of it was no longer large enough to accommodate all who were in communion with us, so that we were obliged to have the Lord's supper in two places. [Note to the second edition.]

7. Since February, 1849, I hare been obliged to discontinue my walks in the fields entirely, on account of a weakness in my right foot.

8. This little charity business was commenced in connexion with the church assembling at Bethesda and Salem Chapels, Bristol, for the purpose of seeking to provide employment for the poor believers, especially the poor sisters, when they were without work.

THIRD PART

9. The evening before my departure, I had invited a number of believers to tea, to spend some time together in prayer, reading the Holy Scriptures, and in intercourse on spiritual subjects.

10. These were the expenses in 1850 and 1851; but, on account of the high price of almost everything now, in 1856, the average expenses of one day are. 12l. or upwards, for the support of the Orphans.

11. Preaching Tours and Missionary Labours of George Mueller (of Bristol.) By Mrs. Mulller. 1883. London: J. Nisbet and Co., Berners Street. Price 3s. 6d. To be had also at the Bible and Tract Warehouse; at the Scriptural Knowledge Institution for Home and Abroad, No. 34, Park Street; and through all book-sellers.

12. This third volume is still in print. Published by W. Mack, 38, Park Street, Bristol.

13. The Funeral Sermon was afterwards preached and published, and is still in print.

FOURTH PART

PREFACE TO THE

FIRST EDITION OF THE FOURTH PART

Twelve years have elapsed since the period at which the third part of the Narrative of the Lord's dealings with me closes. It has not been for want of matter, that this fourth part has not appeared sooner; but the increased and ever increasing variety of other occupations has kept me hitherto from arranging the materials for the press. Of late, however, I have judged, for the following reasons, that I ought particularly to give myself to this service.

1, It has pleased the Lord so abundantly to bless the former parts of my Narrative to the comfort, encouragement, strengthening, and instruction of those who are young and weak in the faith, and to those unacquainted with the simplicity of the truth, that I consider myself to be the servant of such; and I feel that responsibility is laid upon me, to do what further I can, in this way, to serve them. And this, I confess, I do joyfully; for my spirit has oft times been not a little refreshed during the eighteen years which have elapsed, since I published the first part of my Narrative, by the many hundreds of letters I have received, giving an account of the blessing, which the writers of them have derived from the perusal of it; and I have thus been again and again encouraged to go on with the work.

2, I think it important, that the reader of the first three parts of my Narrative should have a right impression of the work in which I am engaged. He may not be acquainted with the Reports of the Scriptural Knowledge Institution for Home and Abroad, which have been published since 1844, and therefore he may know no more of the work in which I am especially engaged, than the first three parts of my Narrative give him. In that case he would not know how the work has been growing since that period; he would not be aware, that it is now three or four times as large as it was in 1844, and is still more and more increasing. He would not know in that case, that the principles of Holy Scripture on which the work of God in my hands was carried on, when comparatively small, and which then were found to be sufficient, even in these last days, are the same on which it is carried on now, though the work is now so large. This point has especially weighed with me, in desiring the publication of the continuation of the account of the Lord's dealings with me in the form of the first three parts, in order that the Living God may be glorified through this account. I judged, moreover, that, whilst the first three parts may especially furnish, to the believer in the Lord Jesus for his private life subjects for comforting and encouraging reflections; this part, besides doing the same still further, may especially be of help to the servant of Christ labouring for God on a large scale, or to the man of God who seeks to carry on business on a large scale, on Scriptural principles.

3, Though the Reports of the Scriptural Knowledge Institution for Home and Abroad have been issued generally every year or every two years; yet, as they are not bound together, they may be lost in part, and thus the chain be interrupted. Moreover, they contain, sometimes, matters which may be of moment for the time being, but not so important afterwards. The Narrative leaves out such points, and introduces on the other hand things which were scarcely suitable for the Reports. My desire, therefore, has been to give in this fourth part the substance of the Reports, which have been published since July 1844, and to bring thus together in one volume what is contained in these nine different Reports.

4, The Reports give scarcely anything of the dealings of God with me personally, irrespective of the work in which I am engaged; but I have not only to speak well of the name of the Lord with regard to His service, but also with reference to His dealings with me personally and with my family; and I desire to serve the saints in relating to them instance upon instance of His kindness to me, hoping that thus many others may be encouraged more and more fully, unreservedly and habitually to trust in God; yea, to do so in the darkest seasons.

The plan on which I have thought it best to bring the materials before the reader is, to relate in distinct periodical chapters: a, How I have been provided, simply in answer to prayer, with means for the support of the various schools of the Scriptural Knowledge Institution, for the circulation of the Holy Scriptures and Gospel Tracts and for the aiding of Missionary work. b, How I have obtained means for the support of the hundreds of Orphans under my care. c, How the Lord has led me to, and provided me with means for, the building of a large Orphan-House, and how I am now occupied in seeking to build a second still larger. d, To state, periodically, a variety of miscellaneous points in connexion with the operations of the Scriptural Knowledge Institution, in a separate chapter. e, To give separately and periodically a chapter, for relating matters connected with my own personal affairs or the work of the Lord in my hands, not immediately connected with the Scriptural Knowledge Institution for Home and Abroad. As, however, the whole book is intended for the spiritual profit of the believing reader, and to show to those who know not God, by His blessing, the reality of the things of God, there will be found interspersed, throughout the book, such practical remarks, as the subjects may seem to call for.

GEORGE MUeLLER.
21, Paul Street, Kingsdown,
Bristol, June 18, 1856.

A NARRATIVE OF SOME OF THE LORD'S DEALINGS WITH GEORGE MÜLLER
FOURTH PART

Supplies for the School--Bible--Missionary and Tract-Fund, sent in answer to prayer, from July 14, 1844, to May 26, 1846.

Aug. 10, 1844. In the greatest need, when not one penny was in hand, I received 5l. from a brother at Hackney. I took half of this sum for these objects, and half for the Orphans.

Sept. 7. Our poverty has been great ever since the accounts were closed on July 14th. Our Tract and Bible stock is very small, and we have much reduced it on account of sending supplies to Demerara. The rents for the School-Rooms are becoming due, and other expenses are to be met. Under these circumstances I received today with Philip iv. 6, the sum of 50l. The donor writes that he thinks he is directed by the Lord to send the money. How truly is it so! I took of this sum 20l. for the Orphans, and 30l. for these objects.

Oct. 1. This evening I received a bank order for 70l., to be used as the Lord might direct me. This money came in most seasonably, as I am thus able to pay to the six teachers who labour in the six Day-schools, their salaries. I took 30l. of the 70l. for these objects, and 40l. for the Orphans.

Dec. 14. The means for these objects have been very small for some time past. Under these circumstances I received this afternoon from a sister in the Lord, who is near the close of her earthly pilgrimage, a small box, containing five brooches, two rings set with twelve small brilliants, five other rings, one mourning ring, a pair of gilt bracelets, a gold pin, a small silver vinaigrette, some tracts, and a sovereign. The donor stated on a paper, contained in the box, that the produce might be used for the Orphans or otherwise, as I might require. As these funds are in particular need, I took the contents of this little box for them, and the trinkets were soon disposed of.--The sister fell asleep very shortly after. Will she need such ornaments before her Lord? Will she regret having given them for His work? Oh! no.

Dec. 21. Today I have received the following trinkets, the produce of which I was at liberty to use for the Orphans, or my own personal necessities, or the printing of my Narrative, or for the School--, Bible--, Missionary and Tract Fund. I have put the produce to the funds for these objects. A ring set with twelve small brilliants, a ring set with one brilliant, another ring set with one brilliant, a ring set with five brilliants, a paste ring, a large brooch, two large rings, two wedding rings, two other small rings, a ring set with small pearls, three other rings, two gold pins, four gold shirt studs, and a gilt pin.

Dec. 24. I have received still further the following trinkets, the produce of which was likewise taken for these objects, it being left to me to use them as most needed. A small gold chain, a ring set with seven brilliants, five gold seals, an eyeglass silver mounted, a ring set with a head, a gold pin, a gold buckle, a silver pencil case, a gold brooch, a brooch set with small pearls, a set of gold shirt studs, a small gold brooch, nine gold rings, a gold heart, a gilt chain, and a gilt watch-chain.

Jan. 13, 1845. When there was nothing in hand towards our many necessities for these objects, I received today the following valuable donation:--Three forty-franc pieces, two twenty-franc pieces, six five-franc pieces, seven two-franc pieces, eleven one-franc pieces, fourteen half-franc pieces, twenty-one quarter of a franc pieces, and fifty-two other small Italian and French silver coins.

Feb. 3. Today, when I had again nothing at all in hand, I received from W. P. 5l.

Apr. 8. When, once more, I had nothing in hand, I received today from Yorkshire 10l., which, being left at my disposal, I used for these objects.

Apr. 24. Today were sent to me a small old gold watch, a half sovereign, a half guinea piece, two twenty-franc pieces, six small Turkish gold coins, a quarter of a franc, a threepenny piece, a silver toothpick, and a brass pencil-case. The produce of these articles likewise was put to these funds.

May 5. From Scarborough was sent to day 5l. for these funds, at a time when I had again nothing left.

May 6. About six weeks ago intimation was kindly given by a brother that he expected a certain considerable sum of money, and that, if he obtained it, a certain portion of it should be given to the Lord, so that 100l. of it should be used for the work in my hands, and the other part for Brother Craik's and my own personal expenses. However, day after day passed away, and the money did not come. I did not trust in this money, yet, as during all this time, with scarcely any exception, we were more or less needy, I thought again and again about this brother's promise; though I did not, by the grace of God, trust in the brother who had made it, but in the Lord. Thus week after week passed away, and the money did not come. Now this morning it came to my mind, that such promises ought to be valued, in a certain sense, as nothing, i.e. that the mind ought never for a moment to be directed to them, but to the living God, and to the living God only. I saw that such promises ought not to be of the value of one farthing, so far as it regards thinking about them for help. I therefore asked the Lord, when, as usual, I was praying with my beloved wife about the work

FOURTH PART

in my hands, that He would be pleased to take this whole matter, about that promise, completely out of my mind, and to help me, not to value it in the least, yea, to treat it as if not worth one farthing, but to keep my eye directed only to Himself. I was enabled to do so. We had not yet finished praying when I received the following letter:

"Beloved Brother, May 5, 1845.

"Are your bankers still Messrs. Stuckey and Co. of Bristol, and are their bankers still Messrs. Robarts and Co. of London? Please to instruct me on this; and if the case should be so, please to regard this as a letter of advice that 70l. are paid to Messrs. Robarts and Co., for Messrs. Stuckey and Co., for you. This sum apply as the Lord may give you wisdom. I shall not send to Robarts and Co. until I hear from you.

"Ever affectionately yours,

"* * * *"

Thus the Lord rewarded at once this determination to endeavour not to look in the least to that promise from a brother, but only to Himself. But this was not all. About two o'clock this afternoon I received from the brother, who had, more than forty days ago, made that promise, 166l. 18s., as he this day received the money, on the strength of which he had made that promise. Of this sum 100l. are to be used for the work in my hands, and the remainder for brother Craik's and my own personal expenses.--I took of these two sums, i.e. of the 70l. and the 100l., half for the Orphans and half for these objects. When this money came in, there was only very little in hand. The last tracts had been given away, two or three days ago, but I had no money to order more: thus I was able to send off an order for 11,700. Bibles also needed to be ordered, but I had no money: I am now able to order some. It had been much on my heart to send a little help to some Missionary brethren, as a token of affectionate interest, and this I am now able to do. The Lord be praised for His goodness in helping thus so seasonably!

From May 6, 1845, to May 26, 1846, we experienced no difficulty at all as to means, the Lord having always seasonably sent in the supplies, so that, without any one exception, I was always able not only to meet all the demands connected with the Day-Schools, the Sunday-School, and the Adult-Schools, but I was also able to do more, so far as it regards means, in aiding the circulation of Tracts, and helping Missionary efforts, than at any previous period of the same length. Of the donations which came in from May 6, 1845, to May 26, 1846, I only mention the following:-- On June 23, with Philip. iv. 6, for circulation of Tracts and Bibles in foreign lands, or, as needed, 60l. Oct. 12, 150l. On Feb. 26, 1846, I received 200l., of which 100l. was to be used for Missionary work in foreign lands, and 100l. for brethren who labour in England, in the word and doctrine, without any stated salary. In connexion with this donation three points are particularly to be noticed:--I. The day before I received this sum, I had given 5l. to a brother, who was travelling through Bristol, and who was on the point of going out as a missionary, without being connected with any society. When I gave him this 5l. I had but very little in hand, but I said to myself, the Lord can easily give more. And thus it was. 2. Before I received this donation, I had been especially led to ask the Lord, that He would be pleased to condescend to use me more largely in helping missionary brethren. For this I had a still greater desire when I found that the money, which I had sent to British Guiana, at the end of November, 1845, amounted only to a few pounds for each brother who labours there, on account of there being so many. I had, on this account particularly, a desire to be able shortly to send another sum to British Guiana, which was thus granted to me. 3. I had also, from time to time, sought, to help brethren, who labour in dependence on the Lord for temporal supplies in various parts of England, and my desire especially had been, that, even in this particular, the Funds of the Scriptural Knowledge Institution for Home and Abroad might be more extensively useful. And thus, in this particular also, this donation cheered my heart, enabling me to assist, in some measure, several faithful labourers. Concerning this latter point I would especially notice, that whenever God has put it into my heart "to devise liberal things," He has not only blessed me in my own soul in doing so, but has also, more or less given me the means to carry out such a purpose. I mention further here, in connexion with this point, that henceforth, as God shall be pleased to supply me with means, I purpose particularly, in connexion with this work, to endeavour to assist brethren of good report, who labour in the word and doctrine, in the United Kingdom of Great Britain and Ireland, but who have no regular salary. If, therefore, any donations should be given henceforth for that particular object, they shall be, by God's help, applied to that; or, if no donations should be given for that particular object, yet, as God shall be pleased to intrust me with means, I purpose by His help, to have my eye particularly on brethren who preach the Gospel without charge, and who, perhaps, besides, for conscience' sake, have relinquished former stipends or regular emoluments which they had in connexion with doing so. Have we not particularly to strive to be fellow-labourers with those who, seeking not their own things, but the things of Jesus Christ, preach the Word without being chargeable to any one? Many whom I know and love in the truth, are mindful of this; but others may not, perhaps, have sufficiently weighed the matter.

On March 10, 1846, I asked the Lord for still further supplies for missionary purposes, and while I was in prayer a letter came from C. W. with 20l. for missionary purposes. Thus also, about the same time, came in, from the neighbourhood of Ludlow, 2l., and from Keswick 5l. for Missions, besides other smaller donations for the same purpose.

It must not be supposed that these are all the donations which I received for the carrying on these objects from July 14, 1844, to May 26, 1846; but those which are referred to came in under remarkable circumstances, or, more manifestly, as answers to prayer.

I now proceed to give an account of the Lord's goodness in supplying me with means for the Orphans, from July 14, 1844, up to May 26, 1846; though here again

FOURTH PART

only the most remarkable instances, on account of the great number of cases, can be given.

Supplies for the Orphan Fund, sent in answer to Prayer, from July 14, 1844, to May 26, 1846.

July 25, 1844. The need of today for the Orphans is 2l. 5s. As there came in yesterday 2l. as the profit of the sale of ladies' bags, which are made by a sister in the Lord for the benefit of the Orphans; also two donations of 5s. each, through her; 5s. from a poor sister in the Lord; and 1l. from Hackney, in all 3l. 15s.; we have 1l. 10s. left.-- In the course of today the Lord was pleased to send in the following donations:--by the boxes in my house 1l. 10s., in nine small donations 16s. 11d., and the contents of an orphan-box, 3s. 01/2 d. This evening also two Christian servants gave me the following trinkets:--a ring, a gold pin, two brooches, and a silver toothpick. A precious gift, because of its seasonableness, and because it gave me joy in seeing these ornaments given up for the Lord's sake.

Observe, dear reader, only eleven day's after the accounts were closed, we were again in fresh poverty, and had to go on day by day waiting upon the Lord for the necessities of about 140 persons.

July 26. Only 6d. has come in today.

July 27, Saturday. July 1l. 14s. was in hand to begin the day with. With two of my fellow--labourers I besought the Lord between nine and ten o'clock this morning for help, when, at eleven o'clock came in, by sale of articles, given for the purpose, 7s. 3d., by sale of Reports 1s. by sale of ladies' bags 1s. 6d., and by two donations 4s. 6d. There were sent also anonymously, two coats, a pair of trousers, and three waistcoats (worn). When this parcel and money came, I was called on for money from the Orphan-Houses. In the course of the day came in still further, by sale of articles, 10s. Thus we have been helped through this day. Late in the evening was given 2s. 6d. besides.

July 28. This morning, when there was now again only 2s. 6d. in hand, I received from Tavistock 6l.; and this evening from Nailsworth, 2s. 6d.

July 29. Yesterday was anonymously put into the Chapel boxes 2l.; also by A. A. 1l. Thus we are provided for today and tomorrow. There came in still further today 1l., from an orphan-box at Barnstaple 1l., and by the profit of work, done by a sister, 5s. There was likewise given a little box, containing the following articles: a lady's bag, a pair of gloves, a silver fruit knife, a gold seal, a needle book with two farthings, a purse containing two-halfpence, 4 1/2 francs, and a copper coin; a little tortoiseshell box containing two old sixpences, two fourpenny pieces, a shilling, a sixpence, and a pebble; a silver vinaigrette, a seal, two patterns for worsted work, a microscope, and 6 embossed cards. This evening I received two silver pencil cases.

July 30. By the boxes in the Orphan-Houses came in today 2l. 4s. 6d., and by sale of Reports 5s.

July 3l. Immediately after having risen from my knees today, to ask the Lord for further supplies, I received 19s. by sale of stockings, knitted by the Orphan Boys. This evening was given to mc by A. A. 5l., and through ditto 2s.

August 1. This morning I was called on for 5l. for the Infant Orphans, so that again only a few shillings remained, not enough for, the other expenses of today, when I received, in the bag sent for the money from the Orphan Houses, the following donations, 1l., and 1s. 6d., 1s. 1d., 1s. 1d., and 2s. 2d. Likewise came in 1s., and I found 2s. 6d. in an orphan-box in my house. Thus I had enough for today.

Aug. 2. The day began with 2 3/4 d. in hand. A little before ten o'clock in the morning the letter-bag was brought from the Orphan-Houses for money, in which I found a note stating that the need of today was 1l. 17s., but I had only 2 3/4 d. to send. I wrote so to brother R. B. master of the Orphan Boys, intending to request him (to send up again in the afternoon, for what the Lord might have sent in the mean time. When I was going to put the 2 3/4 d into the purse in the bag, I found half-a-crown in the bag, slipped into it before it was opened. This half-crown is a precious earnest that the Lord will help this day also. It was found by me just after I had risen from my knees, having been with some of the labourers in the work in prayer for means. Before I bad yet finished the note to brother B. B., a sovereign was given to me, so that I had 1l. 2s. 8 3/4 d. to send off. About two o'clock this afternoon I received by sale of articles 10s. 6d., by sale of stockings 6s. 8d., and by the sale of ladies' bags 9s. 4d. Thus I could send off the 14s. 6d. which was still needed for today, and had 12s. left.

Aug. 3, Saturday. With the 12s. we began the day. My soul said: "I will now look out for the way in which the Lord will deliver us this day again; for He will surely deliver. Many Saturdays, when we were in need, He helped us, and so He will do this day also."--Between nine and ten o'clock this morning I gave myself to prayer for means, with three of my fellow-labourers, in my house. Whilst we were in prayer, there was a knock at my room door, and I was informed that a gentleman had come to see me. When we had finished prayer, it was found to be a brother from Tetbury, who hail brought from Barnstaple 1l. 2s. 6d. for the Orphans. Thus we have 1l. 14s. 6d., with which I must return the letter-bag to the Orphan-Houses, looking to the Lord for more. Evening. In the afternoon one of the labourers received 6s. for himself, which he gave for the Orphans. This evening I went to the usual prayer meeting, (which is held on Saturday evening at the Orphan-Houses, to ask the Lord's blessing upon the work generally), when I found that 2s. had been put into the boxes in the Orphan Houses in the course of the afternoon; also 7s. had come in by the knitting of the Orphan-Girls, and 3s. 6d. more one of the labourers was able to give. Thus we hail 2l. 13s., which was enough for today. How very kind of the Lord thus to listen to the prayers of His children, and to help us day by day!--We had not yet separated, after our prayer meeting, when a box was brought from Scarborough, containing 5s. and a number of articles. When I came home I found that there had come in still further, by sale of articles given for the purpose, 15s. 10d., and by sale of stockings knitted by the Orphans, 7s. 8d. Thus the Lord has greatly helped us today.

Aug. 5, Monday. There came in from A. A. 1s., and anonymously was yesterday put into the Chapel-boxes 2s. 6d., ditto 2s. 6d.

Aug. 6. Without one single penny in my hands the day began. The post brought nothing, nor had I yet received anything, when ten minutes after ten this morning the letter bag was brought from the Orphan-Houses, for the supplies of today.--Now see the Lord's deliverance! In the bag I found a note from one of the labourers in the Orphan--Houses, enclosing two sovereigns, which she sent for the Orphans, stating that it was part of a present which she had just received unexpectedly, for herself. --Thus we are supplied for today. In the afternoon, when I had now again nothing at all in hand, as I had paid out this 2l., there was brought to me from Oxford 1l. 2s. A sister also gave 2s. 6d.

Aug. 7. There came in, when there was not one penny in my hands, 4s. and 3s. 6d. I only found 3s. in the boxes in my house, 10s. was given as the profit of the sale of ladies' bags, and 2s. 6d. as the produce of "A forfeit-box at a young ladies' school." Likewise were given to me, two gold rings, two gold watch-keys, a pair of earrings, a gold brooch, two waist-buckles, a pair of bracelets, a watch hook, and a broken brooch. Thus we have a little towards the need of tomorrow.

Aug. 8. The money which came in yesterday was not enough for the need of today. The boxes in the Orphan-Houses were therefore opened, as I had understood that some money had been put into them during the last days, and they contained 1l. 4s. Thus we have been supplied this day also.

Aug. 9. It is just now striking eleven o'clock, and I have not yet one single penny towards the need of this day. The bag is brought from the Orphan-Houses for money, but I have nothing to send, and am therefore obliged to return the bag without anything. But my soul is waiting for help. The Lord has so repeatedly helped as again during the last weeks, and so He will surely do this day also. Evening. At half-past twelve this morning I received two notes from two sisters who labour in the Orphan-Houses, the one from the sister who, on the 6th, had sent the 2l., being part of a present which she had received, and who now sent 1l. more. She writes: "The enclosed I thought of applying to another purpose; but His thoughts are not as ours. Please to use it as you think fit." The other sister, likewise one of the labourers, sent 10s. This 1l. 10s. met our need for today.

Aug. 10, Saturday. Only 3d., which had come in yesterday afternoon, by sale of a Report, was in my hands, when the day began. A little after nine o'clock I received a post-office order for 5l. from Hackney, to be used as most needed. Of it I took one half for the Orphans, and the other half for the Day Schools. There came in still further, 2l. 5s., 5s. 10d., 6d., and 3s. 4d.

Aug. 12. Yesterday I received from a sister 5s., with James i. 17., 2s. 6d., 6d. was put into the boxes at my house, and 6d. was given by an aged friend. Thus, with what was left on Saturday, we had 1l. 15s. 5d., which met our need today.

Aug. 13. Nothing has come in, but one of the labourers, to whom 15s. was given last evening to buy herself a new gown, gave that. I am looking for more! The boxes in the Orphan-Houses were opened, in which 5s. was found. Thus we had enough, except 6s., which one of the labourers gave.

Aug. 14. Nothing at all had come in, when the bag was brought from the Orphan-Houses for money, and I had therefore to return it without any. About half an hour after, the labourers had an especial prayer meeting. At this meeting one of the teachers of the Day-Schools gave me 10s., which he had put by to buy himself some little books, but he considered it now not to be the Lord's will to do so, but that he should give this money for the present need in the Orphan-Houses. Another of the labourers in the Orphan-Houses gave 5s. Thus we are provided with the absolute necessaries till tomorrow after breakfast.

Aug. 15. Last evening I received 2s., just after our last public meeting about the Orphan-Houses and other objects of the Scriptural Knowledge Institution, at which I had testified afresh of my reliance upon the living God, though I had not then one single penny in hand for the work, which, of course, was not stated.--Now this morning, between eight and nine o'clock sister L. M. came to me and brought me 30s., which she had received for the Orphans. But this will not be enough for today. Yesterday and this morning, before this money came in, the trial of faith had been very sharp.--Evening. At eleven o'clock I received still further from A. A. 5s., and this afternoon, from one of the labourers, 5s., and from two donors 6d. each.

Aug. 16. Our poverty is extremely great. The trial of faith as sharp as ever, or sharper. It is ten o'clock, and there are no means yet for a dinner. I now thought of some articles which I might be able to do without, to dispose of them for the benefit of the Orphans, when one of the labourers gave me 1l., which she had intended for another object, and which she now considers must be left alone for the present. There was also taken out of the boxes in the Orphan-Houses 1s. 6d., and by knitting came in 2s. 3d., and from A. A. 2s.

Aug. 17, Saturday. The Lord has, in tender mercy, helped us, in sending in 3l. for knitting done by the Orphan Girls, 9s. 10d. for stockings knitted by the boys, 11s. 11d. for things sold, which were given for the purpose, and 10s. 7d. put into the boxes at the Orphan-Houses.

Aug. 18. There was put anonymously into the Chapel-boxes 1s., ditto 2s., ditto 2s. 6d., and A. A. gave 10s.

Aug. 19, Monday. Only 3s. has come in today.

FOURTH PART

Aug. 20. This 3s. was all there was in hand for this day, which was needed at the Boys' Orphan-House towards the dinner. In the other houses nothing was needed, but at the same time Nothing was left towards the next meal. Two o'clock came, and we had nothing yet. After two o'clock I opened the boxes in my house, in which I found a paper containing a sovereign and a half, and 2 half-crowns loose. Of this I took 30s. at once to the Orphan-Houses, whereby we were helped for this day. Our need had not been greater for a long time. Dear reader, join me in admiring and adoring Him, who caused that money to be put into the box, and, I have reason to believe, only a very short time before, and who led my mind to open it, to obtain thus the help which was needed. -- In the afternoon came in still further 3l. 6s. by the sale of some old silver and a few trinkets.

Aug. 21. There came in, by sale of Reports, 5s., and from Tewkesbury 1l. This sovereign came in the greatest need. I took it at once to the Orphan-Houses, and by it we were supplied for the day. When I returned home I found that a little old gold watch had been given in the mean time. There came in also 3s.; and two half-sovereigns were given this evening by two little girls, through a sister in the Lord from Bath.

Aug. 22. The two half-sovereigns, which were given last evening, were all we had at the beginning of today. There was found in the boxes in the Orphan-Houses 5s. 9d., and in a post-office order I received 1l. So we had enough for one more day.--And it is by the day I live. Were I to think of how it will be a year or even a month hence, I should be tried indeed--yea, greatly tried. "Sufficient unto the day is the evil thereof," is my Lord's own precious warrant for this. He will not have me to be anxious about tomorrow, and therefore I cast my cares about tomorrow upon Him. As the weeks pass on, and I go on Saturday evenings to the prayer meetings at the Orphan-Houses, I praise the Lord for having sustained me one more week in this service, by enabling me to look to Him. Yea, as each day closes, I desire to be grateful to the Lord for having sustained my faith and patience, and enabled me to rely upon Him, especially in seasons of such great poverty, lasting for weeks, as we have been in of late. But this I must say to the praise of the Lord, that my soul is kept in peace at such times, and, through the riches of His grace, I am kept from questioning whether He will help me or not. And, indeed, it would be sinful ingratitude, after all the Lord has been doing for me in this work, not to rely upon Him. May He in mercy uphold me to the end in this service, and keep me from dishonouring His holy name, either by unbelief, or in any other way.

Aug. 23. This morning the Lord greatly refreshed my spirit; for after a long-continued trial of faith, and after long and deep poverty, there was sent me from Devonshire a check for 20l. There came in 6s. besides.

Aug. 24. 1l. 19s. 7 1/4 d. came in today.

THE LORD'S DEALINGS WITH GEORGE MÜLLER

Aug. 25. From A. A. I received today 20l. How exceedingly kind of the Lord, in an hour of such great need, on account of all the many and great wants in which I find myself just now, to have sent this sum! There came in 2l. 0s. 6d. besides.

Aug. 26. Received for Reports 1l. 7s., and 3d. besides.

Aug. 28. Altogether 1l. 11s. 2d. came in today.

Aug. 29. Received 2s. 11d. by sale of Reports, and

7s. 6d. from Bath. The brother in Bath, who sent me this money, wrote me that the 7s. 6d. was sent to him with the following letter.

27th August, 1844.

"Sir,

"Part of the enclosed 7s. 6d. did belong to your dear Father, J. L., Esq., value of which I stole from him in my unconverted state.--I, now a believer in Jesus, constrained by love to Him, return it to you with interest, praying that the Lord may richly bless you and yours.

"* * * *."

J. L., Esq. has been dead more than fifteen years, therefore it must be longer than that period since the theft alluded to was committed.-- This 7s. 6d. came in in especially great need; for though 50l. had been given during the last seven days, yet on account of our long-continued poverty, and the heavy expenses which were to be met, this 7s. 6d. was received when there was nothing at all in hand, and was sent off at once to the Orphan-Houses.--This evening, when we were still in great need, and when means were required for tomorrow morning, 10s. was given to me. This money was sent off this evening to the Orphan-Houses, for the need of tomorrow morning. About nine o'clock a sister came to my house, who had been to Shirehampton, and had there received 1l. 10s. 6d. for the Orphans. She gave also the remaining 6d. of the change of two sovereigns. The Lord inclined the heart of this sister to bring the money at once, and we are thus supplied for tomorrow. At half-past nine this evening I received another precious donation of 10s., with the following letter:--

"Aug. 29, 1844.

"The history of this money is this. I did some work in the country some time ago, and thought I should never get the money for it, as I had repeatedly written about it, and could not get it. But some time ago I was asking the Lord to incline the heart of the person who owed me the money, to send it to me, and I told Him, that, if He would do so, I would give 10s. for the Orphans. Three days ago I had such confidence, that I should have the money, that I was enabled to praise the Lord for it; and

FOURTH PART

today I was going up Park Street, and met the person coming with the money. It had been put into the party's heart the day before yesterday to pay me the money. Now, dear brother, I fulfil my promise to the Lord by giving you the money. Help me, dear brother, to praise Him for it, and that I may be enabled to trust Him more than ever I have done yet.

"Yours in Jesus,
"* * *"

This brother is a poor tradesman, himself working with his hands.

Aug. 30. Today 6s. 8d. came in by sale of Reports. This evening I met a sister from Bath, who is staying in Bristol for two or three days. She gave me her purse, and all that was in it, for the Orphans, being 5s., saying, she wanted nothing till she returned to Bath. This goes towards tomorrow's need, which will be at least 4l., and for which we have as yet only 1l. 6s. in hand.

Aug. 81, Saturday. There came in a few shillings besides, last evening and this morning, so that I had 1l. 13s. 8d. to send to the Orphan-Houses; but I find 4l. 5s. is needed.--Evening. There came in still further, in the morning, 5s. 6d., by sale of stockings, 1l. 8s. by sale of Reports, 15s. 1d. by sale of articles given for the purpose,5s. 5d. by sale of ladies' bags. And in the evening was received 2l. 10s. 2d. besides, so that I had 2l. 12s. 10d. more than was actually needed.

Sept. 3, Tuesday. Since Saturday evening there has come in, in donations 18s. 10d., by sale of Reports 2l. 3s. 1d., and by work done by the Orphan-girls 1l. 3s. 8d. Thus, with what was left on Saturday, we have been supplied these two days.

Sept. 4. Only one farthing was in my hands this morning. Pause a moment, dear reader! Only one farthing in hand when the day commenced. Think of this, and think of nearly 140 persons to be provided for. You, poor brethren, who have six or eight children and small wages, think of this; and you, my brethren, who do not belong to the working classes, but have, as it is called, very limited means, think of this! May you not do, what we do, under your trials? Does the Lord love you less than He loves us? Does He not love all His children with no less love than that, with which He loves His only begotten Son, according to John xvii. 20--23? Or are we better than you? Nay, are we not in ourselves poor miserable sinners as you are; and have any of the children of God any claim upon God, on account of their own worthiness? Is not that, which alone can make us worthy to receive anything from our Heavenly Father, the righteousness of the Lord Jesus, which is imputed to those who believe in Him? Therefore, dear reader, as we pray in our every need, of whatever character it may be, in connexion with this work, to our Father in Heaven for help, and as he does help us, so is He willing to help all His children who put their trust in Him. Especially do not think, that because you may not be called by God to establish Orphan-Houses and Schools for poor children, therefore you are not warranted to rely upon God, in all your need; for the blessedness of depending upon the living

God may be enjoyed by all the children of God, though they are not all called by Him to such a work as this Narrative describes. Nor must you suppose, that our only trials in this work arise from want of means, so that, in carrying it on, we have to rely upon God for nothing besides this. I assure you that the want of means is the smallest trial, and that I have had far, far greater exercises of faith on account of other things in connexion with this work than those arising from the want of means. But the trials connected with the want of means I dwell upon so particularly, because that is a matter which can be understood by all, and in which the senses themselves almost force us, so to speak, to acknowledge the hand of God.--Well, let us hear then, how God helped when there was only one farthing left in my hands, on the morning of Sept. 4, 1844.

A little after nine o'clock I received a sovereign from a sister in the Lord, who does not wish the name of the place, where she resides, mentioned. Between ten and eleven o'clock the bag was sent from the Orphan-Houses, in which in a note it was stated that 1l. 2s. was required for today. Scarcely had I read this, when a fly stopped before my house, and a gentleman, Mr. ---- from the neighbourhood of Manchester, was announced. I found that he was a believer, who had come on business to Bristol. He had heard about the Orphan-Houses, and expressed his surprise, that without any regular system of collection, and without personal application to any one, simply by faith and prayer, I obtained 200l. and more yearly for the work of the Lord in my hands. This brother, whom I had never seen before, and whose name I did not even know before he came, gave me 2l., as an exemplification of what I had stated to him.--There came in still further this morning 10s., being profits froth the sale of ladies' bags. From the same donor who had sent the sovereign this morning, I received, two hours later, a box containing the following articles:--Three mourning rings, three other gold rings set with cameos, two gold watch keys, four gold lockets, a gold brooch, a silver snuffbox, six medals, three gold ear-drops, a pair of mourning earrings, a purse, two pairs of babies' shoes, a pair of card-racks, two necklaces, five ornamental hair pins, a wafer-stamp, a paper-knife, two book marks, and a great variety of polished pebbles.--Oh! how good is the Lord, and how seasonably comes His help, in our great, great need, when so much is required for clothes, &c. There came in likewise through a sister in Bath 1l., and 5s. 6d. more. Thus, besides all the articles, which have been mentioned, altogether 4ll. 5s. 6d. has come in this day, at the commencement of which I had only One farthing left.

Sept. 6. Besides the money, spoken of on the 4th, only 6s. 10d. more had come in, so that, after this day's necessities had been met, there was now again nothing at all in hand. Soon after I received 3s. 6d. this also was presently spent, except 9d., when a brother from Essex came, who gave me 2l.

Sept. 7, Saturday. Having had to pay out 10s. more, immediately after the receipt of the 2l., this day began with 1l. 10s. 9d. in hand, whilst the need was 3l. 15s. This 1l. 10s. 9d. I sent off to the Orphan-Houses, trusting in the Lord for more. And this time also my hope in God was not put to shame; for in the course of the morning came in 10s. 6d. by sale of Reports, by a donation 10s., by sale of articles 2l. 8s. 8

FOURTH PART

1/2 d., by sale of stockings 1s. 8d., and by sale of ladies' bags 4s. It was very kind of the Lord to send in this money in the course of the morning, thus providing us not only with the 3l. 15s. which was needed for housekeeping, but enabling us also to meet other unexpected expenses. In the Evening I received still further, after the need of the day had been met, but when all again was expended, a sovereign, four small old silver coins, a pair of coral earrings, and a brooch.

Sept. 8 There was the sovereign in hand which came in last evening, as a little towards the need of Monday, when I received this morning 50l., to be used as most needed. It is impossible to express how seasonably this help came, as, though our daily wants had been met day by day, yet very much is required in the way of clothes, &c. But as the need for the other objects is as great or greater, I took of this sum 30l. for them and 20l. for the Orphans. We are thus greatly encouraged to continue in prayer. Our poverty has scarcely ever lasted longer than now, yet the Lord has helped us as our absolute need has required it. The donor of this 50l. wished me to enter it with the text Philip iv. 6, judging that this text must have been often a refreshment to me in seasons of trial, as indeed it has.

From Sept. 8th to 17th came in 23l. 2s. 6 1/2 d.

Sept. 18. From A. A. 5l., by sale of Reports, 13s. 8d., and by the boxes in the Orphan-Houses 14s. 11d.

Sept. 19. This morning came in 10l. from Scotland. By this 10l., and what came in yesterday, I am able to meet the expenses of today, which were more than 16l.

Sept. 21, Saturday. Yesterday came in from Clapham, at an hour of need, 1l. 12s. 10d., together with several articles, also 1l. from Clifton; and today by sale of Reports, 1l. 15s. 4d., and by sale of articles 14s. 9d. Thus we are brought to the close of another week, though the expenses of it have not been less than 110l. (part of which had been put by beforehand). At the close of the week I have not more than 3s. left but the Lord will provide.

Sept. 22. Lord's-day morning. This morning I received from the neighbourhood of Crediton 10l., and from Sidmouth 10l., of which 8l. is for the Orphans, and 2l. for my own personal expenses. Likewise from A. A. 2s. 2 1/2d., for Reports 4s., and in the Chapel boxes was put anonymously 6d., ditto 2s. 6d. ditto 2s. 6d., ditto 6d. with these words: "Be still and know that I am God." How precious this word, and how have I seen today again the truth of it!--Three days ago a sister in the Lord, who is a servant, came to me, and brought me 9l. 16s. which she had drawn out of the Savings' Bank, considering it the Lord's will that she should not keep it there any longer, but spend it for him. She gave me the money that I might do with it as I thought right. However, I sent her home again with the money, advising her to weigh the matter still further, and to pray still further about it, and to count the cost; and if she was of the same mind, after some days, to come again to me. Now this afternoon this sister came again, with her little all, 9l. 16s. As she had now, for a long time, weighed the matter (according to her own statement), and as there had three days more passed away since I had sent her home again with the money, and as I found her grounded upon Scripture for what she was going to do, I could not refuse the money. See portioned it out thus: 2l. for her father, brother, and sister, 1l. 10s. for the poor believers in fellowship with us, 1l. for the Chapel expenses, and 1l. for missionary purposes. This left 4l. 6s., of which she would give me 2l. which I declined, in order that there might not be even the appearance as if I had persuaded this poor servant to draw her money out of the Savings' Bank. She then wished me to give brother Craik 1l., which I accepted for him, and as I saw she wept, because I would not receive anything for myself, I said I would take a sovereign. This I did, that she might not think I refused her Christian kindness because she was a poor servant. The remaining 2l. 6s. she gave for the Orphans. --By the donations which have come in today I am able to meet almost all the expenses connected with the procuring of many articles of clothing and furniture, for which I have long been praying.

Oct. 1. Since the 22nd many pounds have come in, though not any sums above 5l. Now this evening I have received a bank order for 70l., to be used as the Lord might direct me. The donor wishes me to let him know if anything particular should be connected with this donation. There is indeed much connected with it, as it comes most manifestly in answer to prayer; for thus I am able to supply all that is needed in the way of articles of clothes for the Orphans, for which I have been long waiting upon the Lord, and as the winter is now drawing near, the winter-clothes need to be got ready; further, I am able to have the Boys' Orphan-House painted inside and coloured down, which is much needed; I am able to furnish all the labourers in the Orphan-Houses with some money for themselves, which, on account of our long-continued poverty, I had not been able to do for six months. Yet; though the donation comes in so seasonably, I cannot write to the kind donor thus, lest he should be induced to give more, by my exposing our circumstances, and lest also the hand of God should not be so manifest, in providing me with means for the work, as otherwise it would.

--I took of this money 40l. for the Orphans, and 30l. for the other funds.-- During the last two weeks I have had to pay out for the work about 200l., and this week I shall have to pay out again about 60l. Thus the Lord helps continually.

Nov. 1. Since Oct. 1st there has come in such an abundance, that without any difficulty I have been able to meet all the expenses for the Orphans, though during the week ending Oct. 5th I had to pay out 59l., during the week ending on the 12th above 40l., during the week ending on the 19th nearly 40l., and during the week ending on the 26th about 50l. Of the many donations which came in during this period I will only mention the following: From a small town in the kingdom of Wirtemburg 1s. 8d.; from Nice, in France, 1l.; from a missionary in the East Indies 14l. 12s. 6d. Notice, dear reader, how the Lord sends donations from Wirtemburg, France, and the East Indies! Great, however, as our income had been, we were now again poor, on account of the heavy expenses, when, in answer to prayer, there came in today, from some sisters near Coleford, 2l. 10, by sale of Reports 2s., and from A. A. 10l. 7s. 7 1/2 d. The post was out this morning and nothing had come; but my heart said, the Lord still can send, though the post is out; and these donations were soon after given to me.

Nov. 11. From Nov. 1st up to this day we went on easily. There came in again many donations. Now, however, we were again very poor, having had again very heavy expenses. In this great need a ten pound note was this afternoon put into an Orphan-box in my house. This evening I received also still further, from a brother who labours in Demerara, 1l., and 1l. 10s. besides.

Nov. 13. Yesterday and today came in again more than 10l. Our expenses having again been very great, as during these three days above 30l. had been paid out for the Orphans, we were still poor, notwithstanding the considerable income during the last three days. Under these circumstances a ring was given to me this afternoon, set with one large and six small brilliants. How kind of the Lord, thus to help us continually in the work, and to listen to our supplications, which, day after day, we bring to him! Daring no time, since I have been engaged in this service, have the expenses been heavier than during the last four months; yet the Lord has always given us what we have needed.

Nov. 18. The produce of the ring, together with about 10l, more, which had come in since the 13th, was nearly all gone again, on account of the expenses of the past week having been nearly 50l., when this morning a Christian gentleman from Devonshire called on me, who, on leaving, left a letter on my table, containing two five pound notes, of which five pounds was for the Orphans and five pounds for three other objects. This evening I found a five pound note in one of the Orphan-boxes in my house. Thus we are again helped for the present. The name of the Lord be praised!

Nov. 21. The need of today was 4l. 5s., but there were only a few shillings in hand. I opened the boxes in my house, in which I found a sovereign and a shilling. The sovereign could have been put in only last evening. After family prayer I retired again for prayer, about the work as I do daily, by which means I have been helped not only to meet the very heavy expenses since July 15th, but have been helped through many and great difficulties in other respects, and have been enabled to bring many blessings upon the work. While in prayer, I received a letter from the neighbourhood of Leeds, with 5l. Thus we are helped for today. This afternoon came in still further, by sale of articles 1l. 9s., by the boxes in the Orphan-Houses 1l. 6s. 3 1/2 d.; and this evening I received 5l., being the profits from the sale of a Hymn book, which has been printed for the benefit of the Orphans. Thus we have something for the need of tomorrow also.

Nov. 23. As yesterday's expenses had to be met out of what had come in on the 21st, only 11s. 10d. having come in yesterday, and as the need of today for housekeeping was 4l. 10s., we had not enough in hand. Our precious universal remedy, prayer, was now again resorted to. About ten minutes after, I received a Post-office order from Stafford for 2l. About twelve o'clock this morning came in still further, by the sale of some books and prints, given for the purpose, 3l. 1s., by the sale of other articles 3l. 7s. 9d., by the sale of Reports 1s. 1d., by the sale of ladies' bags 13s. 5d., and by the sale of stockings 2s. 6d. This afternoon came in still further from Glasgow 5l. Thus the day, which commenced when we had not enough in hand for its necessities, has ended in comparative abundance, though there is still little in hand for present use, as we need to provide for the rent of the houses and for the purchase of oatmeal, and therefore put by a part of the money given today. Yet we are brought to the close of another week, having been able to meet all its expenses.

Nov. 24. This morning I received a letter from the neighbourhood of Dublin, with four five pound Post-office orders. Thus the Lord has done according to my expectation; for in our usual weekly prayer meeting last evening at the Orphan-houses with the labourers in the work, I was enabled to praise the Lord, that He would provide for the need of this week also.

Dec. 2, Monday. During the last week the income had been again about 36l. But having had still many extra expenses, and, also to put by money for the rents due on the next quarter-day, there was nothing left at the close of the week. Yesterday came in 5s. 10d., 4d., 5s., 19s. 10d., and 1l. By this money we were able to meet the housekeeping expenses of this day, being only 2l. 5s.; but, having 2l. to pay out, besides the current expenses, and having understood that a brother in the Lord from Birmingham, with two other strangers, had visited the Orphan-Houses, and that money had been put into the boxes, they were opened, and 3l. 3s. 1d. was found in them. Thus I was able to send off the 2l. There came in also this afternoon 10s. for work done by a young lady, and this evening, by sale of Reports, 4s.

Dec. 3. As only 1l. 15s. was required for housekeeping today, we had enough, by what had come in yesterday afternoon and evening, and I had twopence left.

Dec. 4. The Lord has again, in the love and compassion of His fatherly heart, multiplied "the handful of meal in the barrel, and the little oil in the cruse." The twopence have been multiplied more than a thousand fold. Yesterday came in from Clapton 2s. 6d., from the county of Dorset 10l., and from A. A. 10s., being (as the donor writes) "the produce of a needless article of jewelery."

Dec. 7, Saturday. Only 2l. 10s. 10d. having come in during the last two days (among which was a remarkable donation of 10s. from Calv, in the kingdom of Wirtemberg), I had again, after I had paid out yesterday what was required, only 2l. 10s. 3d. left, which I knew would not be half enough for this day. Yesterday afternoon came in from Sherborne 6s. This morning I had an unusually full assurance that the Lord would help us this day again, though I knew that more than 8l. would be needed today, towards which there was only 2l. 16s. 3d. in hand. I praised the Lord repeatedly this morning beforehand for the help which He again would grant this day. By the first delivery arrived 10s. from the neighborhood of Kingsbridge. Thus we had 3l. 6s. 3d.; but for housekeeping we needed 5l. 10s., and for other expenses 3l. 1s. 5d. However, when the Orphan came with the letter-bag, to fetch the money, I received in it a letter from Bath, containing 5l. Thus we had enough, and more than enough, for the momentary need, as to the house-keeping expenses. About twelve o'clock came in the following sums besides: by sale of articles 4l. 5s. 8d., by sale of Reports 8d., by sale of stockings 2s. 2d., by sale of ladies' bags 3s. 9d. This evening came in still further, from Dublin, for Reports 1l. 2s., and 1l. as a donation, together with some prints, some books, etc. for sale. Thus we had all we needed, to help us to the close of the week, and were able to put by some money for the weekly rents and other expenses, to be met on quarter day.

Dec. 9, Monday. Though we had been helped abundantly on Saturday, yet, as some money needed to be put by, we had still nothing for the beginning of this week. Yesterday came in for Reports 7s. 4d., and anonymously was put into the Chapel-boxes 1s. and 2s. 6d. There was also anonymously put into the Chapel-boxes a 50l. note, with these words: "25l. for the Orphan-Houses, and 25l. for clothing and blankets for the poor." Thus we are again most seasonably helped, and are now almost entirely prepared to meet all the expenses coming upon us a few weeks hence.

Jan. 18 1845, Saturday. Since Dec. 9th we had always supplies sent, before the last money was given out; it was a season of rich abundance, for there came in (including the 25l. last mentioned) about 140l. Now, however, this evening, after all the expenses of the day had been met, there was nothing remaining. But admire with me, dear reader, the goodness of the Lord! This very evening He has again kindly supplied us with means for the commencement of another week. The boxes at the Orphan-Houses were opened (our need leading us to do so) in winch was found 10l. 16s., one of them containing a ten pound note. Is it not, dear reader, a precious thing to trust in the Lord? Are not ten pounds, thus received out of the hands of our Heavenly Father, as the result of faith in God, most precious? Will not you also seek to trust in Him, and depend on Him alone in all your everyday's concerns, and in all spiritual matters too? If you have not done so, do make but trial of the preciousness of this way, and you will see how pleasant and sweet it is; and if you have done so in a measure, do so yet more and more, and you will never have cause to regret it. But, perhaps, you are not a believer; if so, you cannot trust in God, and go in all circumstances to Him, as to your Father, except you are first reconciled to him through our Lord Jesus. What you have then to do is, to learn that you are a lost, ruined, guilty sinner, deserving nothing but punishment. But, at the same time, you have to remember that God, in the greatness of His love to sinners, sent His own dear Son, that He, in their room and stead, might bear the punishment due to them, make an atonement for their sins, and fulfil the law of God in their stead, in order that every one, who believes on Him, might obtain the forgiveness of his sins, and be reckoned righteous before God. If you believe in the Lord Jesus, i.e., if you receive Him as the one whom God has declared Him to be, even the Son of God (as to His person), and the Lamb of God that takes away the sin of the world (as to His work), and if you rest upon Him, trust in Him for the salvation of your soul, then all your sins shall be forgiven. Though you have grown old in sin, though your sins have been very many and very grievous, yet the blood of Jesus Christ cleanseth from all sin. Do but believe, and you shall be saved. And when thus you are reconciled to God, through faith in His dear Son, walk before Him as an obedient child, seek in child-like simplicity to go to God for every thing, and do really treat God as your father.

There arrived also this Saturday evening, from the Isle of Wight, a small box, containing 14s. and many articles for sale.

Jan. 20, Monday. 3l. 11s, has come in besides the 11l. 10s., which came in on Saturday evening; but as, in addition to the ordinary house-keeping expenses, I had this afternoon to order material for boys' clothes, all the money which had come in since Saturday evening was now again gone. About an hour afterwards I found that two five-pound notes had been put into one of the boxes at my house, and at the same time I received a bank order for 16l. from a poor missionary brother, who labours about 3,000 miles from Bristol~ in dependence upon the Lord for his temporal supplies. Of this 16l. the sum of 12l. is to be employed in sending him Bibles and New Testaments, and 4l. he gives to the Orphans. What ways has not the Lord to help His children who trust in Him! Who would suppose that a poor missionary would send 4l. for the Orphans, from a distance of 3,000 miles? But rather must the ravens again bring supplies, as in the days of Elijah, than that the children of God, who trust in their Heavenly Father, should not have their need supplied. --Thus the Lord has again given 14l. for the Orphans, when all was gone.

Jan. 25, Saturday evening. We have been helped through the heavy expenses of this week, without lacking any thing; but now we have nothing left.--This evening, about ten o'clock, I received from Barnstaple some articles for sale, and a Spanish dollar, two 1/4 of a franc, and a sixpence; also 1l. and 2l. Also sixpence for Reports.

Jan. 27, Monday. Yesterday I received from F. E. B. 2s. 6d., from "Friends to the Institution" 4l.; and 2s. 6d. was put into the Chapel-boxes anonymously, ditto 10s., ditto 2s. 6d. Thus, by what came in on Saturday evening and yesterday, I am able to meet this day's demands, being 4l. 5s. 6d.--Evening. This afternoon I received from Camerton 5l., of which 3l. is for the circulation of the Holy Scriptures, and 2l. for the Orphans. Thus, as the money goes out, the Lord kindly sends in supplies, and all without speaking to one human being about our necessities, but making them known to Him only; yea, determined, by His help and support, rather to endure many trials, in order that through our difficulties the Church of Christ at large may be comforted, and those who are weak in faith be strengthened, than to go away from the door of our Heavenly Father to that of brethren.

Feb. 1, Saturday. We are brought to the close of another week, and have been supplied with all we needed; but there is now again nothing left.

Feb. 2. When now again there was nothing left last evening in my hands for the beginning of the coming week, there have been today, by two different donors,

FOURTH PART

two five-pound notes put into the Chapel-boxes, ditto 2s. 6d., ditto 2s. 6d., and also 2s. 6d. was given besides. Thus we are again supplied fur the present. O Lord, fill my--heart with lively gratitude for all Thy goodness! Lord help me, not only to trust in Thee more and more, but also to love Thee more and more, seeing that Thou dost condescend to use such a poor sinful servant!

Feb. 8, Saturday evening. Above 30l. has come in during this week; but as there have been bought eight hundred weight of rice and eight bushels of peas, besides meeting the regular housekeeping expenses, again only a few shillings remain.

Feb. 10, Monday. Yesterday 2l. was sent to me, from a physician residing in Bristol; anonymously was put into the boxes at Bethesda Chapel 2s., ditto 1l., and ditto 2s. 6d. Also by A. A. was given to me 7s. 2d. I was thus able, with the few shillings that were left on Saturday evening, to meet the expenses of this day, after which 7s. 10d. remained. This morning I was kept, through pressure of engagements, from having prayer, on account of the work, at the usual time; but at half-past two I united with my beloved wife and her sister in prayer, and I asked the Lord, among other blessings, also for means. As to the latter, we had answer upon answer before the close of the day. For this afternoon 1l. 5s. 9d. arrived from Stirling. This afternoon also five sovereigns were put into the box in my room, which I happened to find out soon after. I received also this evening 5s., which had yesterday been anonymously put into the boxes at Salem Chapel. A poor brother likewise gave me 2s. Still further came in 11s. 5d.

Feb. 11. This morning I received still further a donation of 2l. This afternoon I received, as the profit of the sale of ladies' bags, 1l., and 2l. 17s. 4d. came in by sale of articles.

Feb. 12. After I had sent off this morning the money which was required for the housekeeping of today, I had again only 16s. 2 1/2 d. left, being only about one-fourth as much as is generally needed for one day, merely for housekeeping, so that there was now again a fresh call for trusting in the Lord. In the morning I met again, as usual, with my dear wife and her sister, for prayer, to ask the Lord for many blessings, in connexion with this work, and for means also. About one hour after, I received a letter from Devonshire, containing an order for 22l., of which 10l. was for the Orphans, 2l. for a poor brother in Bristol, and 10l. for myself.--Besides having thus a fresh proof of the willingness of our Heavenly Father to answer our requests on behalf of the Orphans, there is this, moreover, to be noticed. For many months past the necessities of the poor saints among us have been particularly laid upon my heart. The word of our Lord: "Ye have the poor with you always, and whensoever ye will ye may do them good," has again and again stirred me up to prayer on their behalf, and thus it was again in particular this morning. It was the coldest morning we have had the whole winter. In my morning walk for prayer and meditation I thought how well I was supplied with coals, nourishing food, and warm clothing, and how many of the dear children of God might be in need; and I lifted up my heart to God to give me more means for myself, that I might be able, by actions, to show more abundant sympathy with the poor believers in their need; and it was but three hours after when I received this 10l. for myself. --This evening was left at the Infant Orphan-House an anonymous letter, containing a sovereign for the Orphans, with the letters C. T. D.

Feb. 15, Saturday evening. 6l. 1s. 4d. has come in since the 12th. All the wants of this week have been richly supplied, but now there was again scarcely anything left towards the coming week, when this evening, just before I was going to our usual Saturday evening prayer meeting at the Orphan-Houses, a bank post bill for 10l. came to hand, being the gift of an aged clergyman. Thus we have a little for the next week, and we have also been able to order two hundred weight of soap, which it was very desirable to have, in order that there might be no need of using new soap for washing.

Feb. 16. Today the Lord has given still more. Anonymously were put into the Chapel-boxes the following sums: A twenty-pound note, a sovereign, 2s. 6d., and 6s. There was given also by A. A. 3s. 7d., and a lady from Nottingham sent 5s. It was particularly kind of the Lord to send in this rich supply, because soon again a ton and a half of oatmeal will need to be ordered from Scotland, the rents need to be provided for, and I desire soon to be able to give again some money to the labourers in the Orphan-Houses for their own personal necessities.

March 4, Besides the 32l. 7s. 1d. that had come in on the 15th and 16th of Feb., there came in up to this day 38l. 17s. 1d., so that there was not any difficulty to meet all the demands. After I had met the expenses for housekeeping yesterday, all our means were again gone, and there was therefore nothing in hand towards the expenses of today. But the Lord helped us again; for two five-pound notes were found in one of the boxes at my house, whereby I am able to meet the need of this day, which is 3l.

Dear Reader! does your heart admire the hand of God in these instances? Does your heart praise the Lord for His goodness to us? Does it, or does it not? If not, then I beseech you to lay aside this account of His dealings with us, and fall on your knees, and ask God to have mercy upon you, and to soften your heart, that you may be sensible of His goodness to us. Surely if you can read this account of His goodness, and it makes no impression upon you, it is a sign that your heart is not in a right state before God. I do not expect that all the readers will, as much as I do, by the grace of God, see the hand of God in all these matters, though I could wish that they did so, even a thousand times more than I do; but yet all should adore God for His great goodness to us, and should remember that what He does for us, in answering our poor sin-mixed petitions, for the sake of His dear Son, He is willing to do for them also.--Particularly notice, that the help never comes too late. We may be poor, yea, very poor; yet the help comes at the right time. We may have to wait upon the Lord, yea, even a long time; but at last He helps. It may seem as if the Lord had forgotten us, by allowing us to be poor, and very poor, and that week after week; but at last He helps abundantly, and shows that only for the trial of our faith, both for our own benefit and the benefit of those who might hear of His dealings with us, has He allowed us to call so long upon Him. --By the grace of God my heart is not troubled now, whether there be much or little in hand. I am sure, that, in the best time and way, God will send help; and thus it is not only with reference to temporal supplies, but also as it regards other things that we may need, or when we may be in peculiar difficulties in other respects. When boys need to be apprenticed, or situations have to be found for the girls, and there are difficulties in the way, as we never send them out, except to believing masters and mistresses, my soul is yet at peace, because I betake myself to my Heavenly Father. When there have been infectious diseases in the Orphan-Houses, whereby, looking at it naturally, many children might be taken away through death, my soul is at peace, because I cast this burden upon the Lord, and He sustains me. When one or the other of my fellow-labourers have left the work, and I needed their place supplied, and knew of no suitable persons, I have been looking to God for help, and that has kept my heart in peace, though this is no small difficulty, as not only can no hirelings be engaged in this work, but also, in case, the individual is a true child of God, there are yet so many things to be considered as to fitness and call for the work. When all kinds of lying reports have been spread about the work and about myself in connexion with it (though they have been very much less than might have been expected), I have committed my case to the Lord; and such things, instead of casting me down, often have greatly cheered me, because they have been a fresh proof to me, that God is at work, and that, therefore, the devil is angry, and stirs up these lies. When I have had for months to leave the work, as in the year 1838, for about four months, in 1843-4, for seven months, and in 1845, for three months, being called to labour on the Continent, or being ill, as in 1838, my heart has been in perfect peace, committing all the concerns of the whole Institution into the hand of God, considering that it was not my work but His, and that, therefore, I might be without carefulness about it. I seek to believe more and more what God says about Himself in His holy word, and it is this which gives this rest and peace to my heart, not only with reference to all the various objects of the Scriptural Knowledge Institution for Home and Abroad, but also about my own body and soul, my dear wife and child, my other dear relations, the temporal supplies for myself and family, my service in the Church in which I labour, now consisting of more than 700 believers, and the state of the Church of Christ at large.

March 8, Saturday. 11l. 17s. 1 3/4 d. more has come in since March 4th. Thus I have been able fully to meet all the expenses during this week, but now hare again only a few shillings left towards the necessities of the coming week.--Late in the Evening.--After our prayer-meeting this evening four sovereigns were given to me, two for the Orphans, and two for the other objects. This is the beginning of the help which the Lord surely will give during the coming week also.

March 11, Tuesday. Only 17s. 6d. had come in since Saturday evening, and therefore, after the expenses of yesterday had been met, there remained again only a few shillings in hand, on account of which my prayer was, that the Lord would be pleased to send in something for this day. When I came home last evening from the meeting, my dear wife told me, that there was some money in the box in our parlour. I opened it, and found it to contain five sovereigns. Thus we are supplied for today.

March 13. Yesterday I had sent off all the money, which was remaining in my hands, to the Orphan-Houses for housekeeping. Also the boxes were opened in the Orphan-Houses, but only 10 1/2 d. was found in them. We were comfortably supplied yesterday with all that was required, but there was no money at all in hand for today. When the letter-bag was brought this morning for money, I found that the need for housekeeping for today was 2l. 15s.; but there was nothing at all in hand. Therefore, while the boy was waiting at my house, I disposed of some trinkets, which had been sent a few days since, for 2l. 15s. 6d. Thus we had enough, and 6d. over. There came in also 8d. by sale of Reports.-- Evening. This afternoon came in, by sale of articles, 17s. 6d., and by a donation 1l.

March 14. The need of today is 2l. There was 1s. 4d. more needed than I had in hand, when 5s. 6 1/2 d. came in from two Orphan-boxes. Thus we are helped for this day.

March 15. Yesterday afternoon half-a-sovereign was brought to me. In the evening 19s. 4d. came in by sale of articles. But this was not enough for the need of today. While the Orphan boy was waiting for the money, I received the following letter from Bath:--

"Beloved Brother in the Lord,

"My sister E. and myself feel it laid on our hearts to send a little for your need at this time, thinking it must be increased by the severity of the weather. We send the inclosed in much love, and thankfulness to the Lord for permitting us to do it, half for the Orphans, and the rest to be applied as seems good to you. Etc."

The letter contained two sovereigns, of which I took one for the Orphans, and the other for the School fund. (The latter sovereign was needed today towards the payment of the teachers in the Day-schools.) Thus we had all that was needed today for the Orphans. This evening I found a sixpence in the box in my room.

March 17, Monday. The sixpence which I took out of the box in my room on Saturday evening was all there was in hand, when yesterday came in the following donations:

A. A. 1l. 2s. 4 1/2 d., anonymously 6d., ditto 2s. 6d. When this morning I had the bag sent from the Orphan-Houses, I found that the amount needed for housekeeping was 2l. 5s.; but there was only 1l. 5s. 10 1/2 d. in hand. Immediately after, before the bag was fetched, one of my fellow-labourers sent me 1l. for the Orphans, so that we had enough for today, and 10 1/2 d. over. When now only 10 1/2 d. remained, I received from Swansea a letter containing a franc and a half, with the words "Jehovah Jireh."

FOURTH PART

March 18. "Jehovah Jireh" (i.e. the Lord will provide) has been again verified in our experience. 10 1/2 d. remained in hand, and the need of this day was 6l. 3s. But the Lord knew what we should need today, and he helped accordingly. I opened the box in my room, and found a ten-pound note in it. Thus we have more than is needed for the present moment.

March 19. Yesterday afternoon I had to pay out 3l. more, for one of the apprentices. Thus the expenses of yesterday were altogether 9l. 3s. How kind therefore of the Lord to have put it into the heart of the donor of the ten-pound note to give that money just then. And now we had again only 17s. 10 1/2 d. left towards the need of today, which is 3l. 5s. But our most faithful Lord has been again mindful of us at this time also. For there came in yesterday from a lady at Sheffield 1l., by sale of Reports 8d., by the profit from the sale of ladies' bags 15s., and by three donations from Bristol donors 12s. Thus there is again all we need for today, and 6 1/2d. left. Immediately after I had written this in my journal, the Lord began to increase again "the handful of meal in the barrel." I received from Barnstaple 5s.

March 20. Yesterday morning, when I was going to send off the money to the Orphan-Houses, I found 2s. 6d. in the letter bag, slipped in anonymously. I found also 1l. 5s. in the boxes at my house. Thus we have 1l. 13s. 0 1/2 d. for the necessities of today, which I find is sufficient.

March 21. All the money being spent, the boxes in the Orphan-Houses were opened yesterday afternoon, in which were found a sovereign, half-a-crown, and a penny. This is all we have for today.

March 22, Saturday. We were able to get through yesterday with the 1l. 2s. 7d. found in the boxes; but in this way our stores become much reduced. Now, however, was Saturday before us with its heavy expenses, and there was nothing yet to meet them, when I went last evening to our public meeting, to minister in the word. However, my soul has been in peace, by the grace of God, during all this week and the last, though again and again we have had nothing. I have reminded the Lord repeatedly during this week, that it is His commandment to His disciples to be without anxiety, and that I am so, because it is His commandment that I should be so, but that now He also, on His part, graciously would be pleased to continue to help me, as He had done hitherto. And now observe how the Lord again has helped! After the meeting last evening, between 8 and 9 o'clock, when I had nothing at all in hand, towards meeting the necessities of this day, which I had every reason to believe would be several pounds, one of the labourers in the Orphan-Houses gave to my wife 5s., Miss E. N. sent 10s., and a sister in the Lord, who arrived last evening from Hull, put the following letter into the hands of my dear wife, addressed to me:--

THE LORD'S DEALINGS WITH GEORGE MÜLLER

"Hull, March 20, 1845.

"Beloved Brother,

"I send you a small box of articles, which perhaps you can dispose of for the Orphans, and 5l. 5s. 7d. in money. Accept it in the Lord's name as a tribute of love from the brethren here. We shall be always glad to see you if you travel this way.

"In haste,

"Yours affectionately in the Lord,

"* * * *"

The box contained the following articles:--a gold cross, two gold pins, two brooches, three gold rings, a small gold seal, two gold bracelet snaps, a pair of silver studs, a mourning brooch, necklace and ear-rings, a silver pencil case, a stone cross and heart, a gilt waist-buckle, a dozen new cloth caps, two books, two new cotton frocks, three new pinafores, a new white lace veil, two waistcoats, a gown, a pair of lady's boots, three veils, two lace capes, two lace shawls, two muslin aprons, a lady's bag, four waist ribands, three pairs of cuffs, a little scarf, three necklaces; 4l. 5s. 7d. for the Orphans, and 1l. for the circulation of the Holy Scriptures.--Today there came in still further, by sale of articles 8s. 6d., for Reports 8d, and by sale of stockings 6s. 8d. Also from Thornbury 2s. 6d. Thus we have enough for today, and something left.

March 24, Monday. Yesterday and today came in only 7s. 6d. altogether. We have enough for today, and 6s. 6d. left, as the demands were only 2l. 10s.

March 25. When there was again only 6s. 6d. left, 4s. 6d. came in yesterday evening. There was also 5l. put into one of the boxes at my house. This morning I received from a brother from the neighbourhood of Birmingham 2l., and 10s. came in by another donation. Thus I had more than sufficient for the need of today, which is 4l. 15s. There came in still further from Bridgenorth 10s., and from a sister in Bristol 2s. 2d.

March 26. Only 3s. 2 1/2 d. came in today, by the boxes in my house.

March 27. Yesterday morning I sent off for housekeeping all the money I had left. It was enough for yesterday, but only enough. Only 1l came in yesterday, and this morning 4d. This 1l. 0s. 4d. was all I had to send to the Orphan-Houses. There came in 5s, 4d. besides, and thus we were helped through this day also.

March 28. Nothing has come in. While the Orphan Boy was waiting for the bag to be made up, 1l. 5s. 1d. came in for a few trinkets, which I had sent out to be disposed of. This was all I could send.

FOURTH PART

March 29. By the 1l. 5s. 1d. we were helped through yesterday. But there was now again not only nothing at all in hand, but we required the more, as the last two days there had been so little laid out for housekeeping, and also because today was Saturday. However, as the Lord never once has forsaken me in the work during the last eleven years, so it has been at this time also. About five o'clock yesterday afternoon a note was given to me in which was enclosed 5l., which a physician of this city kindly sent. In the evening I received 10s., being the profit from the sale of ladies' bags, and this morning came in still further by the sale of articles 9s. 6d., and by the sale of stockings 13s. There were also last evening, anonymously left at my house, a gold seal, a brass seal, and a pair of gilt ear-rings. There came in still further 10s., and 10s.

March 31. There came in yesterday and today anonymously from Hayes-Town, near Uxbridge, 1l., and 2l. 10s. besides.

April 1. On account of the expenses of Saturday having been great, and of yesterday likewise, there remained again but a few shillings. Our gracious Lord, however, who day after day looks on our need, yea, so to speak, inspects our stores, knew this, and therefore yesterday caused ten pounds to be put into one of the boxes at my house. Last evening came in also still further 1l. 7s. from the Isle of Wight.

April 2. As I had to expend today more than 10l. for the Orphans, I was again reduced to a few shillings, when this morning 15l. was sent to me by two donors from Liverpool. Also at the same time came from the neighbourhood of Worcester 1l.

April 3. After having been comparatively poor, the Lord is now again pouring in means, which come very seasonably for the replenishing of our stores, for the obtaining of certain articles of clothing for the children, etc. Today I received the following donations: 19l. 5s. from the brethren assembling at Bethesda Chapel, Sunderland, from two sisters 6s., from A. A. 18s. 5d., and by sale of Reports 1s. 4d.

April 4. Still further from Sunderland 15s., from Sherborne 8s. 6d., from Sidmouth 1l., and from "S. P., Dublin," 1l. 10s.

April 12, Saturday. 33l. 19s. 7d. more has come in since the 4th. After the expenses of today had been met, there again remained scarcely anything, when, in addition to all the ordinary expenses during the coming week before me, a fresh supply of oatmeal needed to be purchased. The boxes in the Orphan-Houses therefore were opened, but only 1l. 8s. 6d. was found in them. There came in besides from A. A. 7s.

April 13, Lord's-day. This morning I received a letter from Hampstead, containing four post-office orders of 5l. each, of which 10l. is for the poor believers among whom I labour, and 10l. for the Orphans.

April 30. From the 13th to this day came in altogether 57l. 13s. 2d. Thus we were well supplied with all the means which were needed during that time; but yesterday morning I had sent off to the Orphan-Houses the last money I had in hand. In the afternoon a sister in the Lord from Bath called, and gave me a sovereign, when I had not one penny in hand towards the need of today. This morning came in still further 18s. 10 1/2 d, by needlework done by the Orphan-Girls. Also 4d. by sale of a Report. Thus we were supplied for today.

May 1. When this day began I had only half-a-crown in hand, which I had taken last evening out of one of the boxes in my house. When I was this morning, on my usual walk before breakfast, bringing my circumstances before the Lord, I reminded Him of His word, "Take no thought for the morrow ", (i.e. be not anxious about the morrow), and I told Him that yesterday I had not been anxious about today, and prayed that He would now be pleased to help me. I was in perfect peace, though I had not the least natural prospect of having the necessities of today supplied. Of the money put by for the rent I would not take. Our need was my comfort. When I returned to my house at eight o'clock, I found that there bad been sent from the Orphan-Houses 5s., given there, and 2s. 6d. for knitting. Also a person had brought yesterday to the Orphan-Houses the contents of an Orphan-box, which had in his room, having felt himself, as he said, much stirred up to do so. It was 3s. 6d. Also a sister from Worcestershire had sent 10s. Before money was sent for from the Orphan-Houses, I received this morning from Stafford 10s. Thus I had 1l. 13s. 6d, to send to the Orphan-Houses for the need of today.

May 2. A little after I had sent off yesterday all the money to the Orphan-Houses, a brother in the Lord from Cornwall called on me and gave me 1l. In the afternoon a sister, who had received peculiar mercy from the Lord in the way of temporal help, called on me, and gave 10s.; and a christian servant, who had received a fee, gave it, the amount being 2s. Thus I have 1l. 12s. to send for the need of this day.--I had written this in my journal, but the bag was not yet gone, when I received from a distance of about 50 miles for Reports 4s. 1d, and from "a Field Officer" 3l 10s.2d., so that I could send all that was needed today, being 3l.

May 3. Yesterday afternoon I received half-a-crown more, and this morning 3s. by sale of articles, and from Kendal 1l 10s. The money from Kendal came about two minutes before the boy came from the Orphan-Houses to fetch the supply for this day's necessities. It was a most seasonable help, as this is Saturday, and we needed today 3l. 15s., and I had not nearly enough in hand.--There came in further this morning 2l. 1s. 2d. by sale of articles, and in the evening 10s., being the contents of an Orphan-box in the neighbourhood of Coleford. -- We are thus brought to the close of another week, and have a little left towards the heavy expenses of the next, as, besides the usual housekeeping expenses of about 20l., there are ten tons of gravel for the playgrounds to be bought, and a ton of oatmeal.

FOURTH PART

July 10. From May 3rd to this day was a season of comparatively rich abundance. The total amount which was received amounts to 268l. 10s. 6 1/2 d. Immediately after the 3rd, the Lord sent considerable help, so that I was able to meet the extraordinary expenses which are referred to under the last date; for on the 4th came in 6l. 0s. 3d., on the 5th 9s. 6d., on the 6th 70l. and 100l., of which two sums one-half was put to the Orphan-Fund, and the other half to the fund for the other objects. On the 10th of May I had to leave Bristol on account of my health, and was absent three weeks, and had to pay away, for the Orphans, about 100l. within one fortnight after. How seasonably, therefore, came these two donations! When these two sums came in there was only 10s. 3d. in hand, and, as has been stated, ten tons of gravel were needed, and a ton of oatmeal, also money for the apprentices, besides the daily current expenses. Of the other donations, which came in during this period, I only mention: from Negro brethren in Demerara, twelve dollars. All the money, after this long time of comparative abundance, was today, July 10th, reduced to 1l. 6s. 0 1/2 d., and 2l. was needed. The boxes in the Orphan-Houses were opened, in which 16s. 1d. was found. Thus we had enough, and 2s. 1 1/2 d. was left.

July 11. Yesterday afternoon came a box from Newport, in the Isle of Wight, with many articles for the Orphans, and a little money for the other objects. This was a precious encouragement to continue to wait upon the Lord. At the first delivery this morning I received several letters. The first I opened was from a brother in Devonshire, with a post-office order for 8s. for the Orphans. He writes thus; "My box for the Orphans still yields but little, but I have been frequently inquiring of the Lord, when that little should be sent. For the last few days it has appeared to me that the time was come to send it to you, I therefore sent for the amount in an order, which I this day received, and now send, in hope it may be of some help in a time of need." This 8s. was a further precious encouragement.--The next letter which I opened was from a christian gentleman at Edinburgh, containing a bank order for twenty-five guineas, of which twenty guineas are for the work of the Lord in my hands, and five for my own personal necessities. There came in still further today, from brethren at Perth 2l., and from the neighbourhood of Glasgow 5l.

July 12. This morning I received a legacy of 5l. for the Orphans, from the relatives of a dear departed sister in the Lord, who, from the commencement of the work up to her last days, had taken the deepest interest in it. Also from Jersey, together with a gold ring, 4l. Also 3l. 2s. 0 1/2 d. by sale of articles and donations, so that during these two days we have had above 40l. coming in.

From July 13th to 19th, came in 16l. 6s. 8d. more. On July 19th I left for the Continent, to labour for a season in Germany, and returned to Bristol on Oct 11th. For about eight months before this, I had seen it to be the Lord's will that I should go again this year to the Continent for a season, and had made my journey and service a subject of prayer from Nov., 1844. Besides asking the Lord's blessing upon my service, I also sought His help for means, and for this also I had not to wait on Him in vain. For as the Lord had sent me, before I went in 1843, the sum of 702l. 3s. 7d. for various purposes, and for the work in Germany in particular, so He gave me again, on May 3rd, 1845, the sum of 500l, for the work in Germany, yet so, that the surplus which there might be should be employed for the Orphans and other work in my hands. From the conditions under which this donation was given to me, it was obvious then, that whilst on the one hand, when it plainly could be seen that only a certain part of the money would be needed for the present service in Germany, the remainder might be used for the benefit of the Orphans, or the other part of the work; yet, on the other hand, we could not begin at once to apply any part of this money to the objects of the Scriptural Knowledge Institution; for at the commencement I could not know how much might be expended on the service in Germany, particularly as my intention was to do as much as I could for those on the Continent who are in darkness and in the shadow of death, and also as I wished as much as possible to help the Church of Christ in that part of the world. Therefore those who said: "We are quite sure there must be much money in hand for the Orphans, else Mr. Muller would not have gone to Germany," were quite mistaken. Often have I had similar things said to me, or about the work, when we have been in the deepest poverty, simply because in faith a certain step had been taken, or a certain thing had been done, which was connected with great expense. At such times, of course, my fellow-labourers and I have had to be silent. For we could not say it was not so, else it would be exposing our poverty, and would look like asking for help. Therefore we have had to be content with something like this: "Lord, it is said that there is much money in hand, whereby some who would otherwise help us, it may be, are kept from doing so; now, Lord, do Thou nevertheless, as the work is Thine, lay our need, the real state of things, on the hearts of Thy children, that they may help us." Thus it was during my service in Germany in the summer of 1845 also. My fellow-labourers in Bristol and my dear wife and I in Stuttgart, poured out our hearts before the Lord, seeking His help upon the work, and asking Him also for means, and He did not despise our cries. There came in, during the twelve weeks that I was away, for the Orphans alone, 200l. 5s, 5 1/2 d. This, together with what was in hand when I left, and with come money that at the end of my stay in Germany (when I saw that I should scarcely need one half of the 500l.) I could order to be drawn out of my bankers' hands in Bristol, richly supplied all the need, during my absence. But the labourers were repeatedly in straits, and several times the last money was gone; but the Lord refreshed their hearts by seasonable help.--Of the 500l. given for the service in Germany, and for the printing of tracts, there remained 311l. 18s, 1 1/2 d., of which I took for the Orphans 161l. 18s. 1 1/2 d., and for the other objects of the Scriptural Knowledge Institution 150l.

Jan. 17, 1846. From the day of my return to Bristol, on Oct. 11, up to this day, there has been no difficulty at all with regard to means. The many donations which have come in, together with what came to the Orphan-Fund from the surplus of the sum given for the work in Germany, enabled me, without any difficulty, to meet all the expenses, though they were many and great. Of the donations which came in during this period I only refer to the following:

On Nov. 19th heft Bristol to labour for a little while at Sunderland. I had but little money to leave with my dear wife for the work; but my path was plain to go, and therefore my hope was in God, as to the work in Bristol during the meantime, being assured that He would care for it. And thus it was. Rich supplies were granted by Him. On the very next day, after my departure, Nov. 20th, the following anonymous letter was left at my house, containing six five-pound notes and two sovereigns.

"My dear Brother in the Lord,

"About six or eight weeks since, anticipating soon a remittance by a bill, which would become available about a week previous to this date, I was led to ask the Lord what He would desire to do with the money which might remain in my hands when I should receive the money for this bill, and your name was immediately presented to my mind with these words: "the Lord has need of it." I therefore enclose the amount, viz, thirty-two pounds, and remain,

"Dear Brother,

"Yours affectionately in the Lord,

"Nov. 20, 1845. &c. &c."

Look at this, dear reader! Is not the hand of God most manifest in such cases? This unknown donor prays what to do with the money, and my name is brought to his or her mind. See also how seasonable the help!

This 32l. was put to the Orphan-Fund, as there was but little in hand. By this and the other sums which came in during my absence, my dear wife was helped without any difficulty, through all the expenses.

There being now again little in hand, I asked the Lord yesterday (Jan. 16, 1846) that He would be pleased to send in supplies, when almost immediately after a sister in the Lord, who had unexpectedly received a rich remittance from distant relatives, gave me 10l.; and today a lady, who on her way from Cornwall to London was staying for a day or two at Clifton, kindly sent me 20l. Thus we are again supplied at least for a week.

March 2. Goodness and mercy have followed us again in many respects with reference to the work, since the last date, Jan. 17th, up to this day; and with regard to means, there has been again a rich supply granted to us, so that I have been able to meet all the expenses of the work, though they have been for the Orphans alone. 180l. 19s. 1d., and more than 100l. for the other objects, during these six weeks. But there remained now scarcely anything in hand, when I received this morning, from a distance of about 200 miles the following letter with 15l.

THE LORD'S DEALINGS WITH GEORGE MÜLLER

"Beloved Brother,

"Enclosed is the produce of the sale of a pianoforte, which I thankfully send for the Lord's work in your hands, having received blessing to my own soul by means of that work, and not the least in being weaned from some of those things I once found pleasure in. I have been waiting payment of the amount for some time, but, having money now in hand, I send it without further delay, as you may possibly need it now. The 15l. you will kindly allot as you see most desirable. That our God would fulfil in you all the good pleasure of His goodness, and the work of faith with power, that the name of our Lord Jesus Christ may be glorified in you, is the prayer of

"Your affectionate Brother,

"* * * * Feb. 28, 1846. * * * *"

March 18. Up to this day also we have been helped, though but little, comparatively, has come in. When yesterday, March 17, all the means were gone, a brother gave me 1l. as a thankoffering for having received a sum of money unexpectedly, as a dividend from a bankruptcy. In the afternoon I received a half sovereign as the profit of the sale of ladies' bags made by a sister in the Lord for the benefit of the Orphans, and 2s. 6d. was put into an Orphan-box at my house. This morning I received the following letter from Devonshire, together with a Post-office order for 5l.

"Beloved Brother,

"I send you an order for 5l., half of which will you accept for yourself, and the other half appropriate for the Orphans; or, if they happen to be well supplied at present, you may apply it to the building you have in contemplation. Job xxii. 21-30.

"Believe me very affectionately yours,

"* * * *"

The half of this money was taken for the present need of time Orphans. There was also sent 1l. 13s. from Weymouth. Thus we are again supplied for the present need.

March 20. Today I have to send more money for housekeeping to the Orphan-Houses, and the Lord has kindly given me yesterday afternoon and this morning the means for it. Yesterday came in by sale of trinkets, &c., 3l. 8s. 4 1/2 d. and by two donations 2s., and this morning I received 11s, from Marlborough.

FOURTH PART

March 21, Saturday. Since yesterday morning, when I had sent off to the Orphan-Houses the very last penny in hand, the following sums have come in: A sister from Worcester gave 2s. 6d., and in the boxes in my house I found 10l. This morning 10s. came from the neighbourhood of Castle Cary, from a sister in Bristol 2s. 2d., by sale of articles 1l. 15s. 8d., and by sale of stockings 5s. Thus I have been enabled, during this week also, to meet all the expenses, though they have been more than 30l.; and 7s. 6d. is left towards the coming week. My heart is in perfect peace, though there are between 140 and 150 Persons to be provided for (including the teachers and matrons in the Orphan-Houses and the apprentices), and though there is heavy sickness in two of the houses. -- Saturday Evening, The Lord has already increased "the handful of meal in the barrel, and the little oil in the cruse." This afternoon I received 3l. 14s., being the contents of an Orphan-box at Barnstaple. There came in 3s. 6d, besides.

March 26. On the 23rd came in 3l. 2s. 1d. On the 24th and 25th came in 1l. 5s. Yesterday was also taken out of the boxes in the Orphan-Houses 7s. 6d., our need having led to the opening of them, and in the boxes in my house was found 2s. 6d.; but we had not quite enough for the need of today, when about twelve o'clock this morning a box arrived from Chelsea, containing 17s. 0 3/4 d., many ornaments, etc.-- We are thus helped for this day.

March 27. Today came in 4l. 11s. 7d. by sale of articles. Likewise 1s. from a little girl. Thus we are again provided for today.

March 28, Saturday. Yesterday afternoon came in still further from Street, by Sale of Reports 10s. and three donations of 6d., 4d., and 2d. There was likewise given by a sister a small gold watch-chain. This morning I received, by sale of articles 4l.14s. 4d., by sale of Reports 1s., and by sale of stockings 6s. Thus, by the income of this week, and by about 2l. 12s. which I found I had more than was needed for the rent when paying it on the 25th, having to receive drawbacks from the landlords, I have been again able to meet the housekeeping expenses during this week, amounting to 21l. 19s. 10d., besides the rent which is 37l., for which the money had been put by; and I am come to the close of another week, with 17s. 8d. in hand towards the necessities of the next. -- Late on Saturday. There has come in still further this evening from A. A. 11s. 3 1/2 d., and from Mrs. R. 8s.

March 30, Monday. My heart was particularly in peace on Saturday evening after the prayer meeting, though I could leave only a few shillings for each of the four houses towards the housekeeping expenses of this week, where, besides the ordinary expenses, there is also money needed on account of heavy sickness in two of the houses. When I emptied the purse to the last penny, and returned home without anything in hand, I felt fully assured that we should have again abundant reasons for thanksgiving next Saturday, and told my dear fellow-labourers so, And, thus it is. Yesterday was put into the Chapel-boxes for the Orphans 50l., ditto 1s., ditto 10s. This morning I received 5l. from a miner at a distance, an entire stranger.

THE LORD'S DEALINGS WITH GEORGE MÜLLER

Thus our Heavenly Father has helped most seasonably. 1, In giving me means for present necessities as to housekeeping. 2, In providing me with means for the extra need on account of the illness of several children. 3, In giving means for getting a ton and a half of oatmeal from Scotland.

April 4, Saturday evening. On the 2nd I received anonymously from London 1l, besides some money for needlework done by the Orphan-Girls; on the 2nd was sent to me 10l. from Bath, from a lady unknown to me. These two donations I received the very moment I rose from my knees, having asked the Lord for more means, as, on account of the heavy expenses just now, we needed again more money by the end of this week. There was also given on the 2nd 1l. by a lady who had received a present of 10l. from some relations, and gave the tenth part of it to the Orphans. On the 3rd and 4th came in 2l. 10s. 7d. The actual expenses of this week, have been 42l. besides 22l. having been put by for the oatmeal which has been ordered, and we have a little more than 9l. left.

April 18, Saturday. The Lord has been again good to me since the 4th with regard to means, 53l. 14s. 0 1/2 d. having come in during these two weeks. Today, having only 2l. 1s. 5 1/2 d., in hand, towards the supplies of the next week, we made known our requests to God, and while I was in prayer with two of my fellow-labourers, there came a letter, in which F. from London sent 10s. There came in almost immediately after by sale of articles 13s. 8d., and by a sister in the Lord from Brixham, who called this morning, 10s. was given. This afternoon the boxes in the Orphan-Houses were opened, but only 10s. 10d. found in them. 6s, came in besides. This afternoon a brother called at the Boys' Orphan-House, and gave eight sovereigns, saying that he had had a desire to bring this money for some days past, but had been unable on account of his health, but now was pressed in spirit to do so, though scarcely able to walk. The following points are to be noticed concerning the Lord's goodness today. 1, I purpose, on account of my health, and for the sake of procuring time for the writing of the Report, to leave Bristol on Monday, and thus I am able to leave money behind for at least 3 or 4 days. 2, I had been speaking today and yesterday in my prayers to the Lord, "It is buy will that I should not be anxious. I am not, by Thy grace; but, Lord, there are about 140 persons to be provided for in the 4 Orphan-Houses, wilt Thou then help me with means!"--I was able to send altogether 11l. 6s. 11 1/2 d. to the matrons.

April 20, Monday morning. The Lord has helped still further. There came yesterday anonymously from London 5l. with these words: "To Brother Mueller, with the writer's fervent prayer, that the giver of all good may continue to pour down upon him and all his undertakings the abundance of His blessings. Half for his own necessities, and half to be disposed of as he thinks fit." I cannot help noticing here the Lord's double kindness, both towards the Orphans and towards myself. I now need for myself more money than usual, as besides the regular housekeeping expenses at home, I need money for myself and dear wife in going away for the twofold object of our health and my having thus time to write the Report: and the Lord supplies me with means. Thus also I received yesterday 5l. for "change of air," and 5l. was sent to

FOURTH PART

me for myself the day before yesterday from a brother at Winchester, whom I have never seen. I find continually, that, without making provision for extra need, and without reckoning anxiously about the future, the Lord helps me when I need anything. I find it pleasant and precious, even as to this life, to walk in the ways of the Lord.

There came in still further yesterday morning for the Orphans from A. A. 13s. 1d., from a brother 1l., from "A friend at Stirling" 6s., and from an Irish sister 5s.--Thus I could send still further this morning to the matrons, before my departure, 4l. 11s. 1d., so that I am able to leave about 16l. behind, and thus the need is supplied for about five days, humanly speaking; and before that time is gone, I expect to obtain more, by waiting upon God.

This morning, before we departed, I received a letter in which was the following sentence: "With regard to property I do not see my way clearly. I trust it is all indeed at the disposal of the Lord; and if you would let me know of any need of it in His service, any sum under 200l. shall be at your disposal at about a week's notice." This brother meant what he said, I have every reason to believe. I might have written; "The Orphans, my dear brother, are now in need, and it would be a particular comfort to me, as I am going away, if you would send me 190l.," and I doubt not that I should have had it after a week. I preferred, however, to continue, as heretofore, to deal with God alone in this service, that the church of Christ at large still further may be benefited, particularly those who are weak in the faith, or those who are recently brought to the knowledge of our Lord Jesus, in seeing how blessed it is to make known our requests unto God, and that those who trust in Him are not confounded. I therefore wrote to this brother, with regard to his kind offer, that I only speak to the Lord about my need.

May, 9, Saturday. This evening, after an absence of 19 days, we returned to Bristol. During all this time the Lord supplied us with means, but it was almost always by the day. During the last days, in the course of my regular meditation on the New Testament, I came to that precious word: "Casting all your care upon Him: for He careth for you," 1 Peter, v. 7, and, by God's grace, I was able to cast all my care concerning His work on the Lord; and when we returned this evening I found, that for this day also the Lord had not only provided, but there was 1l. 16s. 3 1/2 d. more than was needed.

May 11, Monday. Yesterday a brother from Hackney gave 2l., and 17s. 1 1/4 d. came in besides. Thus, with what was left on Saturday, I was able to send 4l. 13s. 5d. to the Orphan-Houses, to be divided among the four matrons. After having sent this morning to the last penny all the money I had in hand to the Orphan-Houses, I received 200l., which, being left entirely at my disposal, was portioned out thus: 100l. for the present need of the Orphans, 50l. for the other objects, and 50l. for the Building Fund of the Orphan House. How kind of the Lord to help so seasonably; for I have very many and heavy expenses before me, besides the ordinary expenses of about 30l. per week. There are to be bought 4 bags of rice, 4 bushels of peas, 2 cwt.

of soap, material for boys' clothes, the 4 houses are to coloured down, several small sums for apprentices are to be paid, the Report is to be printed, etc. This also is to be noticed: The Lord rewarded me thus, for not exposing our poverty to the brother, who offered on April 20th to give me any sum under 200l., if I would let him know if I needed anything for the Lord's work. Thus we had at least a little more than we should have had, even if I had asked that brother.

May 26. Up to this day, till the last hours before the commencement of our public meetings, at which an account is to be given of the Lord's dealings with us since July 14, 1844, the Lord's goodness has continued in supplying us with means. About 80l. more has come in during the last fifteen days. And this very day, the last of this period, I received 26l. anonymously from Stafford, with an affectionate and encouraging note; 20l. 1s. 6 1/2 d. I took out of the boxes at my house, two ten pound notes having been put in; and several other little donations came in besides.

It is scarcely needful to state, at the close of these details, that, notwithstanding our having been often poor, and very poor, yet the children have always had the needful articles of clothing and nourishing food. Those who know what it is to walk in the fear of God, know also, that God would not help us, in answer to our prayers, if we hypocritically stated that the children were well provided with wholesome food, etc., and yet it were not true.

Account of the New Orphan-House, on Ashley Down, Bristol, from its earliest beginning to June 4, 1846.

I began the service of caring for children who are bereaved of both parents, by death, born in wedlock, and are in destitute circumstances, on Dec. 9, 1835. For nearly ten years I never had any desire to build an Orphan-House. On the contrary, I decidedly preferred spending the means, which might come in, for present necessities, and desired rather to enlarge the work according to the means which the Lord might be pleased to give. Thus it was till the end of October, 1845, when I was led to consider this matter in a way I had never done before. The occasion of my doing so was this: On Oct. 30, 1845, I received from a gentleman, who lived in the street, where the 4 Orphan-Houses were, a polite and friendly letter, in which he courteously stated to me that the inhabitants in the adjoining houses were in various ways inconvenienced by the Orphan-Houses being in Wilson Street. He left to myself the judgment of the case.

This letter I received on Thursday morning, Oct. 30, 1845. Being very much occupied that week, I had scarcely any time to consider time matter. On Monday morning, however, Nov. 3, I set apart some hours for the prayerful consideration of the subject, and after I had besought the Lord to guide me to a right decision, I wrote down the reasons which appeared to me to make it desirable that the Orphans should be removed from Wilson Street, and also the reasons against removing. As far as they are suitable for being stated in print, they were those:

FOURTH PART

I. Reasons for removing from Wilson Street.

1. The neighbours feel themselves inconvenienced by the noise of the children in the play-hours. This complaint is neither without foundation, nor unjust; for many persons are very much inconvenienced by the noise of children, and those living close by the Orphan-Houses must be so during the play-hours, even though the noise be only of that kind, that one could not at all find fault with the dear children on account of it. I should myself feel it trying to my head to live next door to the Orphan-Houses, on that account I therefore ought to do to others, as I should wish to be done by. This point had never before appeared to me in so serious a light.

2 The greatness of the number of the inmates in the houses has several times prevented the drains from acting properly, and thus has a few times affected the water in one or two of the neighbours' houses. With reference to these two reasons, as it regards those living near the Orphan-Houses, these words, "Let not your good be evil spoken of," Rom. xiv. 16, and "Let your moderation (i.e. yieldingness) be known unto all men," Philip iv. 5, seemed to me two important portions of the word of God to be acted out in this matter.

But in addition to the reasons for removing the Orphans from Wilson Street, on account of the unavoidable occasional inconvenience that comes upon the neighbours, there appeared now to me, when once I was led to consider seriously the reasons for removing the Institution from Wilson Street, other reasons for doing so, in connexion with the work itself, which had occurred to me before, but never in so strong a light as now, when the subject was brought more immediately before me by the letter, in which I was politely requested to remove the Orphans from Wilson Street. These reasons are:

1. We have no proper play-grounds in Wilson Street. There is one play-ground, which, however, is only large enough for the children of one house at a time; but as there are children in four houses who ought to have the benefit of it, we can not arrange so that all the children have the full benefit of that play-ground, as the meals, the school-hours, the weather, and other hinderances interfere. The dear Orphans ought, I know, to be trained in habits of industry, but children are children, and need to be treated as such; and they should, on account of their health, have the full benefit of a play-ground. But this they cannot have in Wilson Street: and to take them out into the fields for the benefit of bodily exercise, as we have been in the habit of doing, is often very inconvenient.

2. We have no ground for cultivation, near the Orphan-Houses, and hence there must be more walking for the children, on account of using proper means for keeping them, with the blessing of God in health, than is, in other respects, good for them; because frequent walks easily beget in children habits of idleness, which would be especially felt when boys are apprenticed. But this difficulty cannot be obviated by remaining in Wilson Street, and renting a piece of land somewhere else for cultivation; for to get the children ready and conduct them to the piece of ground,

not only takes a good deal of time, but is connected with other great inconveniences, yea with insurmountable difficulties, so that we found it needful to give up a small piece of ground which we once rented for about two years for the Orphan-Boys, at a distance of about half a mile from Wilson Street. Thus, by removing from Wilson Street, and obtaining premises surrounded by land for cultivation, we should be able to procure a most important moral benefit for the children, by having the opportunity more fully than we now have, of training them in habits of industry, besides giving to the boys occupation which is more suitable for them than knitting, which is now the only employment they have, besides making their beds, cleaning the house, and attending to the cooking of their meals. Moreover, this would be occupation in the open air, which not only would bring their limbs into exercise, but also make walking, for the sake of health, almost entirely needless.

3. If we were to remove from Wilson Street, and obtain premises in the country, we might have all the washing done at home, which now, for want of room, can be only done in part. Thus the girls also would have more laborious work at home, a point of great importance for them, so that they would not feel so much the hardships connected with going out to service.

4. The situation of Wilson Street is perhaps scarcely bracing enough for strengthening the constitution of the Orphans, most of whom, being the offspring of very diseased parents, require a very invigorating place of abode.

5. The present situation is certainly not desirable for the teachers, especially as, when their hours of work are over, they have no garden or fields close to the house, immediately to go into for a little refreshment of body; and for some of them it is too far to go to fields, where they might have bracing air.

6. In times of sickness we are too confined in the houses in Wilson Street. If there were less than 30 children in each house, the average expenses for each child would be too great, it being desirable, as the arrangements are now, that there should not be less than 3 labourers in each house; and yet, if there are 30 children in each house, we are too lull in time of sickness, as we have not a single spare room in any of the houses. Now, though the Lord has during all these years most mercifully helped us through such seasons, yet it has not been without inconvenience, and without also, perhaps, having more of the children in one room, at such times, than on account of health is desirable.

7. Even ordinarily, when there is no sickness, it would be desirable to have more room.

There are no premises to be had in Bristol, or in the immediate neighbourhood, where we could have these advantages; for I have been looking about in all directions for this purpose during the last ten years. But suppose there were a large house to be had in one part of the city, and a second a mile off, and a third and a fourth in other directions, such houses, on account of our peculiar position in the work, would not do. For in seasons of need, the distance of the several houses would render it very inconvenient for the labourers to meet together for prayer, to divide the means that may be in hand, etc. Besides, when in seasons of other peculiar difficulties, connected with the work, I wished to meet all my fellow-labourers, there would arise great difficulty by their being divided in different parts of the city. It would also thus be very inconvenient to persons, who wish to see the work, to go from place to place, in order to have a view of all the Orphan-Houses. But this is not all. The more I have considered the matter, the more am I now persuaded, that no ordinary large houses, built for private families, and therefore only calculated to accommodate 10 or 15 persons, at most, for any length of time in them, will do for charitable institutions of any considerable size, as no ordinary house furnishes the proper advantages of ventilation, a point so needful for the health of the inmates in a charitable institution. There seemed to me, therefore to remain nothing but to build premises for the purpose.

II. Reasons for Remaining in Wilson Street.

1. God hitherto has pointed out the spot most plainly. At the commencement of the work, in 1835, no other house was to be had but No. 6, Wilson Street. Afterwards, when in 1830 the Infant Orphan-House was on the point of being opened, again I was looking about in all directions, and saw many houses, but found none that was suitable, till all at once, most unlooked for, the occupiers of No. 1, Wilson Street were desirous of immediately leaving that house, and I was able thus to rent it. When in 1837 I was on the point of opening the Boys' Orphan-House, I looked about again for a house in all directions; for I knew not at that time, what I have since learned by experience, that it was so important that all the houses should be near together. After seeking long in vain, I at last found a very large house, not far from Wilson Street, which I rented; but when the occupiers of the houses in the neighbourhood heard that that house had been let for a charitable institution, they threatened the owner with an action, which led him to request me to give up the agreement, which, of course, I did immediately. At last, most unexpectedly, after having looked about in vain in all directions, the occupiers of No 3 Wilson Street offered it to me, and I rented it for the Orphan Boys. Lastly, in the year 1843, when I was led to see it to be the will of God to go forward in this work, and to establish time Girls' Orphan-House, No. II, for older girls, one particular feature in the matter was, that the house No. 4, in Wilson Street, bad been offered to me without being sought after, when there had not been for about 6 years one single large house to be let in that street.

[But though hitherto God has pointed out Wilson Street as being the spot where this work should be carried on, may not now the time have come for removing?]

2. Perhaps we might also rent Nos. 2, 5, and 7, in Wilson Street, and use two out of those three houses for Orphan-Houses, and one of them for an infirmary in case of sickness.

[But then, I said to myself, would not the objection, which the neighbours on the opposite side of the street might make, on account of the noise of the children in their play-hours, etc. remain? Also the drains would be still more unsuitable, not being constructed for so many inmates; and to alter them would be a heavy expense. The play-ground would be still less sufficient, if two new houses were added. Lastly, there was no reason to think that we could rent Nos. 2, 5, and 7.]

3. There are these three great objections against building: The considerable sum which is required, and which could be spent for present use upon the Orphans. The pilgrim character of the Christian seems lost in building. The time that it will necessarily take in making arrangements for it.

[Do not all these objections only hold good, I said to myself, if I were needlessly to set about building? If I could rent premises, which are really in every way suitable for the work, and I preferred building, then those objections would apply to the case; but when one is forced to it, it is no more than erecting a large building, because there may be 800 children of God in fellowship who have been hitherto renting a meeting-place, but for certain reasons are obliged to leave it, and cannot rent another. Such could not be accused of needlessly spending money in building instead of renting; nor could it be justly said that they have on that account given up the pilgrim character; nor would it be time wasted if some individuals were to make arrangements about the building of that meeting-place. Therefore these three objections just mentioned, which had been for ten years strongly in my own mind, were removed when once I saw plainly that nothing remained but to build.]

After I had spent a few hours in prayer and consideration over the subject, I began already to see that the Lord would lead me to build, and that His intentions were not only the benefit of the Orphans, and the better ordering of the whole work, but also the bearing still further testimony that He could and would provide large sums for those who need them and trust in Him for them; and besides, that He would enlarge the work so, that, if I once did build a house, it might be large enough to accommodate three hundred Orphans, with their teachers and other overseers and servants needful for the work.--Concerning this latter point, I think it important to remark, that during no period had the number of applications for the admission of Orphans been greater than just before I was led to think about building, so that it was quite painful to me, not to be able to comply with the wishes of all the many persons who applied for the admission of Orphans. There were many waiting for admission, particularly Orphan-Boys.

In the afternoon of November 3rd, 1845, I laid the matter before my fellow-labourers in the Church (eight in number) to get their judgment, whether I ought not to leave Wilson Street, and to build. All judged that I ought to leave Wilson Street, and none saw reasons against building.

FOURTH PART

On Nov. 4th my dear wife and I began to meet for prayer about this matter, and purposed to do so morning by morning. We asked God for clearer light concerning the particular points connected with the subject; and, being assured that it was His will that I should build, I began asking the Lord for means.

On Nov. 7th I judged, having considered the matter more fully, that sufficiently large premises to furnish all needful accommodation for 300 children (from their earliest days up to 15 or 10 years old), together with a sufficiently large piece of ground in the neighbourhood of Bristol, for building the premises upon and the remainder for cultivation by the spade, would cost at least Ten Thousand Pounds. I was not discouraged by this, but trusted in the living God.

We continued meeting for prayer morning by morning for 15 days, but not a single donation came in; yet my heart was not discouraged. The more I prayed the more assured I was, that the Lord would give the means. Yea, as fully assured was I that the Lord would do so, as if I bad already seen the new premises actually before me. This assurance arose not from some vague, enthusiastical feeling, the mere excitement of the moment, but I, from the reasons already related, and especially from the commandment contained in Philip iv. 5. For I saw that I should not act according to the mind of our Lord Jesus, if I did not, as soon as I could, remove the Orphans from Wilson Street, as it had been stated to me in the letter referred to, that their living there was an annoyance to some of the inhabitants in that street. 2. This assurance that I should build an Orphan-House arose further, from the whole way in which the Lord has been pleased to lead me in connexion with the Scriptural Knowledge Institution for Home and Abroad, since its beginning on March 5, 1834, i.e. He has been leading me forward as by an unseen hand, and enlarging the work more and more from its commencement, and, generally, without my seeking after it, and bringing things so clearly before me, that I could not but see that I ought to go forward. 3. Lastly and chiefly, this my assurance, that I should build unto the Lord this House of Mercy, arose also particularly from this, that, having strictly examined my heart as to the motives for doing so, I found that, as before. God, I could say that my only motives were His honour and glory and the welfare of the Church of Christ at large, the real temporal and spiritual welfare of destitute Orphans, and the welfare of all those who might take care of them, in the building to be erected. And finding that, after praying again and again about the matter, I still remained in perfect peace, I judged it assuredly to be the will of God that I should go forward.

On Nov. 15th brother R. C. arrived, to labour for a little while in Bristol, I communicated to him my position with reference to having to remove the Orphans from Wilson Street, and I had his judgment also as to its being of God that I should build. This dear brother's judgment greatly encouraged me. His visit was to me of great help in this particular, especially in stirring me up yet more, to bring everything, in connexion with this matter, before God. He also laid it on my heart to seek direction from God with reference to the plan of the building. He said "You must ask help from God to show you the plan, so that all may be according to the mind of God."

THE LORD'S DEALINGS WITH GEORGE MÜLLER

On Nov. 19th I left with my brother and fellow-labourer, Mr. Craik, for Sunderland, where we arrived on Nov. 20. Here we laboured till Dec. 4, when I left alone for Kendal, to labour there for a few days. All the time that I was at Sunderland, I had very much prayer about the building of the Orphan-House, and I felt all the time fully assured, that God would bring the matter to pass. But thirty days had now passed away, whilst I had been day by day waiting upon God for means for this work, and not a single penny had been given to me. Nevertheless, this did not in the least discourage me, but my assurance, that God in His own time and in His own way would give the means, increased more and more. While I was at Sunderland the portion which came in course of my meditation, on the New Testament, was the beginning of the epistle of James. More than at any period in my life was I struck with these verses: "My brethren, count it all joy when ye fall into divers temptations (i.e. trials) knowing this that the trying of your faith worketh patience. But let patience have her perfect work, that ye may be perfect and entire, wanting nothing." James i. 2--4. It was especially the last verse, "But let patience have her perfect work, etc." which I found of exceeding great importance with reference to the building of the Orphan-House. It led out my soul in prayer day after day, to ask the Lord to increase my faith and to sustain my patience. I had these verses so impressed upon my heart, that I could not but think God meant particularly to bless me by them, with regard to the work before me, and that I should especially need patience as well as faith, I stayed at Kendal from the evening of Dec. 4 to Dec. 8, when I left for Bristol, where I arrived on Dec. 9th. It was now 35 days that I had been day by day bringing this matter before God, as to the various points connected with it, and especially also asking the Lord for means; but nothing whatever had been given to me. On the day after my return I renewed our united prayer meeting with my dear wife. Now observe: on the 36th day, after having begun to pray, on Dec. 10, 1845, I received 1000l. towards the building of the Orphan-House. This is the largest donation that I had received up to that time for the Scriptural Knowledge Institution; but when I received it I was as calm, as quiet, as if I had only received one shilling. For my heart was looking out for answers. Day by day I was expecting to receive answers to my prayers. Therefore, having faith concerning the matter, this donation did not in the least surprise me. Yea, if Five Thousand Pounds, or Ten Thousand Pounds, had been given to me, instead of One Thousand Pounds, it would not have surprised me.

Dec. 13. On the 39th day my sister-in-law, who had been for some weeks absent in London, and who had now returned to Bristol, told me that she had met a gentleman in London, who, having quite recently read with deep interest the Narrative of the Lord's dealings with me, wished to know as many particulars about the work in my hands as he could. Being told by my sister-in-law that I purposed to build an Orphan-House, he, an architect, offered to make the plan, and superintend the building, gratuitously. Unsolicited he pressed this matter upon her with deep and lively interest. I hear also that he is a Christian. The fact, that this offer comes unsolicited and from a Christian architect, shows especially the hand of God. This is the second proof that God will help me in this matter.

FOURTH PART

Dec. 23. This is now the 50th day since I have come to the conclusion to build, and the 49th day since we have been daily waiting upon God for help. Nothing more has come in since Dec. 10th, not even one penny. This morning I have been particularly encouraged by the consideration that the Lord has sent me the 100l. and the promise from that pious architect, whom I have never seen, and of whose name I am as yet in ignorance, not to mock me, but as an earnest that He will give all that is needed.

It seems desirable that we should have a large piece of ground of at least six or seven acres. This piece of ground must be in the vicinity of Bristol. 1. In order that the Orphan-House may be accessible to me, as my place at present is fixed by my other work in Bristol. 2. That the labourers in the Institution and the Orphans may be able to attend our meetings, at least on the Lord's day. 3. That the inhabitants of Bristol may have the benefit of seeing with their own eyes this work of God, which is so manifestly His and not mine. 4. That strangers, who pass through Bristol, may have an easy access to it, for the same reason. But then, such a piece of ground, near Bristol, where there is just now an inordinate desire for building, in the way of speculation, would cost in all human probability between 2000l. and 3000l. Then the building itself, however plain, would not cost less than from 6000l. to 8000l., being for 300 Orphans, besides all their overseers, teachers, and assistants. In addition to this, the fitting up and furnishing the house for between 300 and 400 inmates, would not cost less than 1500l. more. This is indeed a large sum of money which I need; but my hope is in God. I have not sought after this thing. It has not begun with me. God has altogether unexpectedly, by means of the letter before mentioned, led me to it. Only the day before I received the letter, I had no more thought about building premises for the accommodation of the Orphans, than I had had during the ten previous years.--My especial prayer is, that God would continue to me faith and patience. If He shall be pleased to help me, in faith and patience to continue to wait on Him, help will surely come.

Dec. 24. No further donation yet. But my hope in God is unshaken. He most assuredly will help.--I have on purpose not issued any circular in connexion with this matter, in order that the band of God may be the more manifest. To some persons, residing in or out of Bristol, I have spoken about my intention of building, when conversation led to it. Through this, if the Lord please, He can make it known to others, and thus send means for the Building Fund. Or He can send in such an abundance of means for the work which is already in existence, that from that abundance there may be a rich surplus towards the Building Fund. But howsoever God may help, I do desire to see His hand made most manifest. There will be, no doubt, many trials connected with this enlargement of the field of labour (for if with 130 Orphans there has been so much trial of faith, what is to be expected when the number is 300); and therefore I desire to see as clearly as daylight that God Himself is leading me onward.

Dec.29. This is the 56th day since I came to the conclusion to build, and the 55th since I have been day by day waiting upon God concerning it. Only that one donation had come in till this evening, when I received 50l. This donation is exceedingly precious to me, not only because I am sure it is most cheerfully given, nor even because of its largeness, but because it is another precious proof that God will bring about the matter, else He would not give me these earnest. All my business therefore is: to continue in faith and patience to wait upon God. My assurance has been more and more increasing that God will build for Himself a large Orphan-House in this city, to show to the inhabitants, and to all who may read and hear about it, what a blessed thing it is to trust in Him.--Of late I have seen, by God's grace, more and more, how entirely unworthy I am of being used by God for this glorious and honourable service, and I can only say, "Lord here is thy servant, if thou art pleased to use such a one as I am."

Dec. 30, 1845. This morning I came, in course of my reading, to the commencement of the book of Ezra. I was particularly refreshed by the two following points contained in the first chapter, in applying them to the building of the Orphan-House: 1. Cyrus, an idolatrous king, was used by God to provide the means for building the temple at Jerusalem: how easy therefore for God to provide Ten Thousand Pounds for the Orphan-House, or even Twenty or Thirty Thousand Pounds, if needed. 2. The people were stirred up by God to help those who went up to Jerusalem. Thus it is a small matter for Him to put it into the hearts of His children to help me, in desiring to build this house of mercy unto His name.--This meditation I had before breakfast. After family prayer in the morning I had again my usual season for prayer about the building, and at this time it was particularly coupled with thanksgiving for the 50l. received last evening, and with entreating blessings on the donor. I was now looking out for more, as I am doing day by day, when this afternoon I received from a person at Clevedon 2s. 6d., from her grandson 6d., and from the sister in the Lord, who brought the money, the change, which she did not wish back, being another 6d. These donations, though small, are nevertheless very precious to me, as I take them as further proofs out of the hands of God, that He will most assuredly bring this thing to pass. This evening I received One Thousand Pounds towards the Building Fund. When I received this donation, I was as calm, yea as perfectly calm, as if I had received a single penny, because, by God's grace, I have faith in Him, and therefore am looking for answers to my prayers, and am sure that God will give every shilling that is needed.

January 2, 1846. This evening I received from Bideford 11s, towards the Building Fund.

Jan. 3. One of the Orphans gave 6d.

Jan. 6. Received a little bag made of foreign seed, and a shell-flower, to be sold for the Building Fund. The sister who sent these articles wrote to me, that the moment she heard of my intention of building an Orphan-House, this text was before her mind: "Who art thou, O great mountain? Before Zerubbabel thou shalt become a plain."--Zech. iv. 7. Also one of the Orphans sent 4d.

FOURTH PART

Having asked the Lord to go before me, I went out today to look for a piece of ground. The armory which is to be sold had been several times mentioned to me, as a suitable place. I did not think so, yet thought I ought at least to look at it. Having seen it and been confirmed in my judgment about its unsuitableness, I asked the Lord whether I should turn towards the city or towards Stapleton. I felt led to go towards the city, and saw immediately after some fields near the armory. After having made inquiry to whom they belonged, I have been led to write this evening to the owner of them, asking him whether he is disposed to sell them, &c. I am now quietly waiting the Lord's pleasure. If His time is come to answer our requests as to a suitable piece of land, I shall be glad; if it is not yet come, I desire that "patience may have her perfect work, being perfect and entire, wanting nothing."

Jan. 8. This evening I received a reply to my letter. The owner of those fields writes, that, if he did sell them, it would be only for building land, and therefore they will be too dear.

Jan 9. Went this morning once more to see those fields, which seem very suitable. Met there Mr. L., a land agent, who told me that they would be nearly a Thousand Pounds per acre, and therefore too dear. I asked Mr. L. to inform me if he should hear of any suitable land for sale.

Jan. 10. One of the Orphans having received half-a-crown from a cousin, gave 1s. 6d. of it towards building the Orphan-House; a sister in the Lord also gave me 3s., a ring, a pair of gold earrings, and a gold brooch.

Jan. 11. Today I received from a gentleman of Liverpool, who has been staying at Clifton, 5l, and from the sister, through whom this donation was conveyed to me, I received 1l. more towards the Building-Fund.

Jan. 12. Received a case with ladies' working instruments, to be sold for the Building Fund. Two of the Infant Orphans also gave 6d. and 4d.

Jan. 13. Half-a-crown was given today.

Jan. 16. From Bideford 1l. 15s.

Jan. 24. The produce of a knitted handkerchief, sold for 2s, was given today; also 4s. 6d. by sale of two dolls; and some brethren at Barnstaple sent 12l. as a token of their loving interest in this work.

Jan. 26. A sister in the Lord gave 2s. 6d.

Jan. 31. It is now 89 days since I have been daily waiting upon God about the building of an Orphan-House. The time seems to me now near when the Lord will give us a piece of ground, and I told the brethren and sisters so this evening, after our usual Saturday evening prayer meeting at the Orphan-Houses.

Feb. 1. A poor widow sent today 10s.

Feb. 2. Today I heard of suitable and cheap land on Ashley Down.

Feb. 3, Saw the land. It is the most desirable of all I have seen.-- There was anonymously put into an Orphan-box at my house a sovereign, in a piece of paper, on which was written, "The New Orphan-House."

Feb. 4. This evening I called on the owner of the land on Ashley Down, about which I had heard on the 2nd, but he was not at borne. As I, however, had been informed that I should find him at his house of business, I went there, but did not find him there either, as he had just before left. I might have called again at his residence, at a later hour, having been informed by one of the servants that he would be sure to be at home about eight o'clock; but I did not do so, judging that there was the hand of God in my not finding him at either place: and I judged it best therefore not to force the matter, but to "let patience have her perfect work."

Feb. 5. Saw this morning the owner of the land. He told me that he awoke at three o'clock this morning and could not sleep again till five. While he was thus lying awake, his mind was all the time occupied about the piece of land, respecting which inquiry had been made of him for the building of an Orphan-House, at my request; and he determined, that if I should apply for it, he would not only let me have it, but for 120l. per acre, instead of 200l., the price which he had previously asked for it. How good is the Lord! The agreement was made this morning, and I purchased a field of nearly seven acres, at 120l. per acre.

Observe the hand of God in my not finding the owner at home last evening! The Lord meant to speak to His servant first about this matter, during a sleepless night, and to lead him fully to decide, before I had seen him.

Feb. 6. Two dolls were given for sale, and one of them was sold for 3s.

Feb. 7. Received from two of the Orphans 8d. and 4d. Also, one of the labourers in the Orphan-Houses gave 10s, and a poor man 3d.

Feb. 8. I wrote the day before yesterday to the architect, who has offered his help gratuitously.

Feb. 11. Received from a sister in the Lord 5l. Received also from the architect the following reply to my letter:

"My dear Sir,

"It will afford me a gratification, beyond what I can communicate by letter, to lend you a helping hand in the labour of love you are engaged in, and I shall esteem

FOURTH PART

it a very great privilege being allowed to exercise my abilities as an architect and surveyor in the erection of the building you propose to erect for the Orphans. I really do mean what I say, and, if all is well, by the blessing of God, I will gratuitously furnish you with plans, elevations, and sections; with specification of the work, so that the cost may be accurately estimated. I will also make you an estimate and superintend the works for you gratuitously, &c."

Feb. 12. This afternoon a little parcel was brought to my house, containing ten sovereigns and a little slip of paper, on which was written:

"Dear Sir, --I have sent you ten pounds for the New Orphan-House. It is the Lord's doing. Seek not to know my name."

Feb. 14. There came in 8s. 6d. by sale of articles.

Feb. 15. Received the promise that on March 25th should be paid to me 500l. for the building of the Orphan-House.

Feb. 18. Received 1l. from Sunderland.

Feb. 19. The architect kindly came from London. He considers the ground to be most suitable as to situation, drainage, water, &c. --I received also today from a sister 5l.

Feb. 20. Received from a sister 10s., and from a brother 5l. The brother told me that never in his life does he remember to have given any donation with so much real pleasure as this 5l. This is of God. I own God's hand in this. He it is that inclines the hearts of His dear children towards this service. May He only be pleased to continue to give me faith amid patience, and I shall most assuredly see this building erected to the praise of His name!

Feb. 28. Two of the labourers in the Orphan-Houses gave 1s. each--Today the 500l. which had been promised on the 15th, was paid 25 days sooner than promised. I rejoiced in this speed; for I remembered that word:

"Whatsoever thy hand findeth to do, do it with thy might: for there is no work, nor device, nor knowledge, nor wisdom in the grave, whither thou goest."

March 2. Received 2 rings, 6 brooches, 2 mourning brooches, 3 old silver thimbles, a silver guard, a small gold chain, 4 pairs of earrings, 3 polished stones, a bracelet, 3 waist buckles, a silver mounting of a horn, and 2 candlestick ornaments.

March 3. From a brother in the Lord 10l.

March 8. From Clevedon 1s., and from London 6d.

March 13. From a young sister in the Lord 13s. From a little girl at Bath 2s. 6d.--Also 2 babies' pinafores for sale.--4 little frocks, a pair of socks, and 4 pincushions (also for sale).--Likewise a dozen doilies.

March 15. Anonymously 2l. with these lines written in the paper: "Wishing for the privilege of raising a few stones towards erecting the New Orphan-House, the enclosed trifle is sent for that purpose.-- There will doubtless be a conspiracy from beneath, to fight against and to hinder the work; nevertheless let us make our prayer unto our God, and set a watch against them day and night."

March 19. By sale of some articles 1l. 5s 4 1/2 d.

March 22. From a sister in the Lord 10s.

March 25. A pair of knitted cuffs for sale.

March 28. A lady at Clifton gave 2l.

March 31. A brother, having unexpectedly received a sum of money as a dividend from a Bankruptcy, gave 10l. towards the Building-Fund, as "A thank-offering to the Lord."

April 5. Anonymously 1l.

April 7. Four pairs of knitted socks were given for sale; and by a sister in the Lord 10l., as "A thank-offering for mercies received." This 10l. comes at a season of a very great trial of faith, on account of a multiplicity of difficulties in which I am just now, and it is another precious earnest to me from God, that He will give me in every way what I need, after He has sufficiently tried my faith and patience.--There were also given 5 stuffed birds and a pincushion. Also 2 cups, 2 shells, a book-mark, and a watch guard. Also a knitted cloth.

April 27. Anonymously 4s., and by sale of articles 3s. 9d. I received also the following letter from Sunderland:

"Sunderland, April 24, 1846.

"Beloved Brother,

"A year having now elapsed since our chapel was opened, and our God having signally blessed us in all things, the saints here have been stirred up to present a thank-offering to our Father, and to give it for the New Orphan-Houses. I therefore send you in their name, the sum of 17l. Etc."

May 3. From a sister at Bath 10s.

FOURTH PART

May 9. By sale of articles 1s. "A widow's mite" 1l.

May 11. From a brother 50l.

May 21. From Oxford 1l.

May 27. From a sister in Bristol 1l.

June 2. Through a sister 1s. 3d.

June. 4. From Leicestershire 5s., and from a sister in Bristol 2s. 6d.

That which has been stated above concerning the origin of the New Orphan-House on Ashley Down, Bristol, was published in the Ninth Report of the Scriptural Knowledge Institution for Home and Abroad, which was issued in the year 1846. In that Report were added to the above, the following remarks, which I likewise give here again, in order that the reader may have a clear under-standing of the whole, and also the full particulars concerning this Orphan Establishment.

1. The total amount, which has been given for the Building-Fund, up to June 4, 1846, is 2710l. 3s. 5 1/2 d. This is only a small part of what will be needed, but, by the grace of God, I am in perfect peace, being fully assured that God in His own time will send the whole sum which is required. Many and great have already been the exercises of faith and patient since I first began to give myself to prayer about this work, and still greater they may be, before it is accomplished; but God, in the riches of His grace, will help me through them all. It is now (June 4, 1846) 212 days since I first began to pray about this work, and day after day, since then, have I been enabled to continue to wait upon God, and I am more than ever assured that, notwithstanding all my exceeding great unworthiness, God will condescend to use me, to build this House. Had it been the excitement of the moment, the difficulties which have already come upon me in connexion with this work, (which are not stated here, on account of their occupying too much room) would have overwhelmed me; but as God Himself, I trust, led me to this work, so He has helped me, and does help me, and, I doubt not, will help me to the end.

2. The house is intended to be built, so as to accommodate 140 Orphan Girls above seven years of age, 80 Orphan Boys above seven, and 80 male and female Orphans from their earliest days, till they are seven years old, together with all the overseers and teachers, etc. that may be needed. The Infants, after having passed the age of seven, will be removed into the different departments for older boys and girls.

3. The plan of the building is, by the help of God, all but completed. Scarcely anything more remains to be altered.

4. The building, however, will not commence till all the money, which is required, has been received.

5. The land and house will be invested in the hands of about ten brethren, as trustees, who shall be persons well known and of good report.

6. Only such donations, ordinarily, will be put to time Building-Fund as are expressly given for it. I should only depart from this my usual mode, if the Lord by some very great abundance of means corning in, or in other respects were to point out, that money not expressly given for the Building-Fund, was to be appropriated to it. It is therefore requested that donors will kindly state it, if they wish any donation put to the Building-Fund.

Miscellaneous points respecting the Scriptural Knowledge Institution for Home and Abroad, with reference to the period from July 14, 1844, to May 26, 1840.

1. During the whole of this period, 4 Day-Schools, with 278 children in them, were entirely supported by the funds of the Institution. Three Day-Schools besides were assisted. The number of the children that were taught in the Day-Schools, entirely supported by the funds of the Institution, from March 5, 1834, to May 26, 1846, amounts to 3983. During the period from July 14, 1844, to May 26, 1846, 628l. 19s. 4 3/4 d. was spent on all the Schools, which were either entirely or in part supported by the funds of the Scriptural Knowledge Institution. --Further, during this period there were also entirely supported a Sunday-School with 80 children, and an Adult-School with 60 persons attending it. The total number of Adult scholars who received instruction, from the formation of this Institution to May 26, 1846, is 1146.

2. During this period were circulated 269 Bibles, and 171 Testaments; and 5079 Bibles, and 3528 Testaments were circulated from the commencement of the work up to May 26, 1846. 40l. 7s. 10d. was expended of the Funds of the Institution on this object, from July 14, 1844, to May 26, 1840.

3. From July 14, 1844, to May 20, 1846, was laid out for Foreign and Home Missions the sum of 595l. 7s, 9d. Of this sum was spent for Foreign Missions 447l. 17s. 9d, which was divided among 15 brethren and sisters who labour in British Guiana, one brother and sister in Jamaica, 2 brethren in India, one brother in Prussia, and 3 brethren in Switzerland. The remainder, 147l. 10s. was divided among 14 brethren who labour in England without any salary, and in dependence upon the Lord for their temporal supplies. During no period previously was so much of the Funds of this Institution spent on Missionary work, which arose from the fact, that, the more I corresponded with brethren who laboured in the word and doctrine in foreign lands, the more I saw how much they stood in need of assistance, and thus, my heart having been led out in prayer to God on their behalf, that He would be pleased to send me means, whereby I might be able to assist them, He was pleased to do so. This led me to purpose, as God should give me grace, to be still more mindful of them in future, and to seek to be able still more to assist them. The same was the case with regard to those brethren who labour in England, but who have no salary or sti-

FOURTH PART

pend, but trust in the living God for the supply of their daily necessities; I did long to help such brethren, and had no doubt that God would enable me to do so.

When I now, whilst preparing this fourth part of my Narrative for the press, look back to this period, how greatly has God helped me since then even in this particular; for, of late years, he has enabled me to spend on Missionary objects about seven times more than during the period now referred to.

4. There was laid out for the circulation of tracts, from July 14, 1844, to May 26, 1846, the sum of 50l. 9s. 9 1/2 d., for which Fifty-two thousand and three such little publications were bought, which, with 5315 in hand on July 14, 1844, makes 57318, of which number 40565 were circulated The total number circulated from Nov. 19, 1840, to May 26, 1846, amounts to 99647.

5. There were received into the four Orphan-Houses, from July 14, 1844, to May 20, 1840, 30 Orphans, who, together with those who were in the four Houses on July 14, 1844, make up 151 in all. Of these: 1. One child died. 2. One boy left the Institution secretly just when he was ready to be apprenticed, and went to his relatives. [In going over this account, for time sake of preparing it for the press, I cannot help making a few remarks on this case, for the sake of teachers, guardians, and parents, who are greatly afflicted by the bad behaviour of children or young persons. The boy referred to just now gave us for years much sorrow. All means, to bring him into a different state, seemed entirely lost. At last he was going to be apprenticed. His clothes and outfit for leaving the House were already prepared, when he secretly left and at last reached on foot the dwelling-place of an elder sister, in the North of Devon, who is married to a master of a small vessel, a pious man. His sister and brother-in-law were greatly afflicted by his bad behaviour towards his friends in Bristol. There remained, however, now nothing to be done, but that the lad should go with his brother-in-law to sea. After he had been some time at sea, one night there was a terrific storm, so that all hope of the vessel or crew being saved was gone. This poor lad now remembered the instruction which he had received in the Orphan-House in Bristol, and earnestly prayed to God for mercy, and turned to Him. From that time, as the brother-in-law himself told me, this youth was a truly changed character, and proved by his godly deportment for several months afterwards, that he had the grace of God in him; for he continued walking in the fear of God, till about 6 months afterwards, when he was drowned by falling overboard. May this encourage all who labour among the young, patiently to go on in their service. "They that sow in tears shall reap in joy." Ps. 126, 5.] 3. Six children were taken back by their relatives, who by that time were able to provide for them. 4. Six boys were apprenticed at the expense of the Institution, and five other boys, ready to be apprenticed, were sent to their relatives to be apprenticed. 5. Two girls were apprenticed, and eight sent out to service, and one girl was sent to her relatives to serve them.

There were on May 28, 1846, One hundred and twenty-one Orphans in the Four Houses. Besides this, six apprentices were still supported by the Funds of the

Institution, so that the total number was 127. The number of the Orphans who were under our care from April 1836, to May 26, 1846, amounts to 213.

I notice further the following points in connexion with the Orphan-Houses.

1. Without any one having been personally applied to for anything by me, the sum of 13,275l. 6s. 9 3/4 d. was given to me as the result of prayer to God, from the commencement of the work up to May 26, 1846. This sum includes the 2710l. 3s. 5 1/2 d. which up to June 4, 1846, was given towards the Building Fund. (It may be interesting to the reader to know that the total amount which was given as free contributions, for the other objects, from the commencement of the work up to May 26, 1846, amounts to 4833l. 18s. 10 3/4 d.; and that which came in by the sale of Bibles and Tracts, and by the payments of the children in the Day-Schools, amounts to 2097l. 18s. 2 1/2 d.) 2. Besides this, also a great variety and number of articles of clothing, furniture, provisions, etc., were given for the Orphans, as has been stated in the printed Reports. The total expenditure for the Orphans from July 14, 1844, to May 26, 1846, was 2732l. 14s. 1 1/2 d., and for the other objects 1325l. 7s. 7 1/4 d.

In conclusion I cannot but mention, to the praise of the Lord, concerning this period, that four of the Sunday-School children were admitted to communion. Likewise three more of the Orphans were received into church fellowship, so that up to that time, altogether 32 of the Orphans had been admitted. I also mention with peculiar joy, and as a matter for thankfulness, that of those who were apprenticed or sent out to service, from July 14, 1844, to May 20, 1846, ten were believers, most of whom had been for several years in fellowship, before they were sent out to service. But whilst we desire to receive these instances as precious encouragements from the Lord to continue our service, we cannot but believe, judging from the many prayers the Lord gives us for the children and adults under our care and instruction, that that which we see is but an earnest of a far larger harvest in the day of Christ's appearing.

Matters connected with my own personal affairs, or time work of the Lord in my hands, not immediately connected with the Scriptural Knowledge Institution, from January 1, 1844, to May 26, 1846.

Soon after my return from Germany, where I had been labouring for seven months in 1843, and 1844, of which I have written at length in the third part of this Narrative, I had it laid on my heart to go there again for a season; but, before doing so, I felt called upon to prepare for the press a new edition of the first and second parts, and to write the third part of my Narrative. For this, however, a large sum of money was required, as I purposed to print not less than 4000 copies. As I had no money of my own for this object, I gave myself to prayer, and, after having prayed several months respecting it, I received on December 30, 1844, unasked for, the sum which would be needed to accomplish this object.

Dec. 31, 1844. Since Brother Craik and I came to Bristol, 982 believers have been received into communion, making 1050 with the 68 whom we found in fellow-

FOURTH PART

ship. Of these, 97 have fallen asleep, 53 are under church discipline, 56 have left us but are still in Bristol, and 176 have removed from Bristol; so that there are only 668 in communion at present. During this year 73 have been received.

The Lord has been pleased to give me during this year--

1, Through anonymous offerings in money, put up in paper, and directed to me, and placed in the boxes for the poor saints, or the rent, at the two chapels

. L117 11 9

2, Through presents in money, from believers in Bristol, not given anonymously

56 0 6

3, Through presents in money, from believers not residing in Bristol . . .   81 14 6

4, In presents in provisions, clothes, etc., worth to us at least   12 0 0

L267 6 9

To this is to be added, that, for the first two months and six days of this year, my expenses, and those of my dear wife, during our stay in Germany, were met, as also our traveling expenses back, as stated in. the third part of my Narrative. Also during the whole of this year a Christian lady gave to our dear child board and schooling without any remuneration, a present worth to us not less than 50l. On this point I cannot help making a few remarks. I had clearly seen it to be the will of God that my daughter should be brought up at school, and not at home. My reasons for it were these: 1, My dear wife, though well qualified, to instruct our daughter, so far as knowledge goes, was unable, on account of being engaged as my wife in a variety of things connected with the Lord's service, to give herself uninterruptedly to this work; and to do it partially we judged to be injurious to our daughter. 2, I had seen instances in which a home education, for an only child, had turned out very badly. 3, I judged that the mixing with other children would be beneficial to our daughter, provided that intercourse was under proper oversight; as thus a child is in early life introduced into a little world, and things do not all at once come upon a young person, when at last obliged to leave the parental roof. 4, But that which most of all led me to this decision was, that, as in the Church of Christ the Lord has qualified the members of the body for the performance of certain work, and all have not the same gift and service, so, in the same way, certain believers are called and qualified above others, for instructing children, and give themselves to this particular service, and that, therefore, I ought to make use of the qualifications of such, and of their having given their whole time to this particular service.-- These reasons led us to place our dear daughter at school, instead of educating her at home, and we have never had cause to regret the step we took, but on the contrary, have had abundant reason to praise God for it I have purposely made these remarks, as I am fully aware that some believers have different views on this subject, and I desire to serve them with the measure of light and experience I have obtained.

After our daughter had been at school for half a year, I asked for the account, when it was stated to me by the Christian lady in whose establishment she was, that she had a pleasure in educating her gratuitously. However, as I pressed the matter, I obtained the account. It was paid, but the exact sum was returned to me anonymously, which, of course, I found out at once to be from the Christian sister at whose school my daughter was. From that time I could never more obtain the account, though my dear child was about six years longer at school. I refer to this point for this especial reason: God had laid it on my heart to care about poor destitute Orphans. To this service I had been led to give myself; He, in return, as a recompense even for this life, took care that my own beloved child should have a very good education, free of expense to me. I was able, and well able to pay for her education, and most willing to do so; but the Lord gave it gratuitously; thus also showing how ready He is, abundantly to help me and to supply my wants.

January 6, 1845. Today I received the most painful information that a false teacher from Switzerland had found his way among the brethren and sisters at Stuttgart, and that through him several, yea almost all, to a greater or less degree had been drawn aside, and shaken as to the very foundations of their faith.

I cannot describe how bitter the trial was to me to see the Lord thus dishonoured, and my painful service for seven months during the previous year, to all appearance, entirely frustrated. The Lord, however, laid these brethren and sisters on my heart in prayer, so that I was day by day enabled to bring them before God, and also to resolve, that, as soon as my path was made plain, I would go again to Stuttgart for a season.

May 3, 1845. I have seen it more and more clearly of late, that the time is drawing near, when I shall go again to Germany, to labour there for a time; for the brethren who had fallen into grievous errors are now recovering out of them, but need a helping hand to restore them fully, or at least to confirm them in the truth. In addition to this I purpose to publish some tracts in German. But though it is now four months, since I have been daily praying respecting this object, I never had been led to ask the Lord to give me means for it, because I felt assured, that, when His time was come for me to go, He would provide the means; and also because I had never felt myself led to pray about it. Today, however, I asked the Lord that He would provide the means for all that is necessary in connexion with this service; and I had a secret satisfaction in feeling that so much was required, i.e. means for the journey to and fro, means for our stay there, means for the publication of Tracts, means to be left behind for the work in Bristol, to supply the need at least for a time, for I did not wish to go, unless it were the Lord's will, and if so, He would give the means. Now see how the Lord dealt with me! About a quarter of an hour after I had been in prayer with my dear wife respecting this object, and I had now, for the first time, asked Him for means to carry it out, though for four months we had daily prayed

FOURTH PART

together respecting spiritual success in this service, I received a letter containing an order for 500l. In the letter this was written:

"I enclose * * * * 500l., which will be more useful in your hands than in mine. I mean it in the first place for all that is needed preparatory to and attendant upon your journey to Germany, and, whatever the surplus may be, you will apply as you find there is need in the different parts of service under your care." Thus the Lord has fully answered our requests for means, and that so speedily!

On July 19th my dear wife and I left Bristol for Stuttgart. As the letters, which I wrote to the church in Bristol, in which I gave some account of my labours on the Continent, have been preserved, I give them here, as they will furnish the reader with an outline of the Lord's dealings with me during that period.

Stuttgart, Aug. 16, 1845.

To the Saints, meeting in the name of the Lord Jesus at Bethesda and Salem Chapels, Bristol.

Dear Brethren,

It is today four weeks since we left you. As I know that your love to us would like to know how the Lord has been dealing with us since, and as I have abundant reason to speak well of Him on account of His goodness and mercy to us since our departure; I gladly relate to you how it has been with us since we left Bristol It was on Saturday afternoon, July 19th, that we started for London. On the next day, the Lord's day, I ministered twice in London, as also on Monday evening. I was much helped in doing so, especially on the evening of the Lord's day and on Monday evening, and I could not but recognize the hand of the Lord even in this, with reference to my leaving Bristol for a season. On Monday and Tuesday we were much occupied in procuring our passports, and on Wednesday at twelve o'clock we went on board the steamer for Ostend. The Lord mercifully carried us over the sea, although we were both very sea-sick, and about five o'clock the next morning we went on shore at Ostend. Having in a very little time, without any difficulty, obtained our luggage out of the Customhouse, we left by the first train for Cologne, at half-past six, travelled all that day, a distance of about 240 miles, and reached Cologne between nine and ten o'clock in the evening. We then travelled either in the Rhine steamers, on the railroad, or in an omnibus, the four following days also, yet so that we arranged to have time to ourselves, and reached Stuttgart about eight o'clock on Monday evening, July 28th. Of the journey I would mention no more, than that on the last day we travelled with a most lovely and gracious brother, an English clergyman from Sussex, with whom, after two or three hours I was so one in heart, that on getting out of the omnibus, in which we travelled together about 30 miles, in order to walk up a long hill, we walked together arm-in-arm. It was most refreshing to our spirits to find so lovely a brother in this dark land. We spent a few hours together at Stuttgart, and then this dear brother left for the neighbourhood of Munich, the capital of the kingdom of

THE LORD'S DEALINGS WITH GEORGE MÜLLER

Bavaria, where his family is for a season.--I had written from Bristol to one of the brethren at Stuttgart, Brother M--, an Englishman, to look out for furnished lodgings for us, and I therefore called on him the next morning, July 29th, to see how far he had succeeded. I now learned that he had made every inquiry for me, and also advertised in the paper, and applied at an intelligence office, but that he had heard only of three apartments, and even these were unfurnished; for all the lodgings which were to be had were occupied by the deputies of the people, a sort of Parliament in Wirtemberg, who have once every three years their assemblies, and who had been for the last six months assembled in Stuttgart. This was no small difficulty, as to stay at an hotel would have been very expensive, especially just now, as the assembly of the deputies has made a great difference in the hotels also. However, our comfort was, that, as we had come in the name of the Lord, and according to His bidding, and that, after having daily prayed about the matter since the latter part of November last year, He would help in this thing also. We now went to the only lodging out of the three which was at all likely to suit; but we found that this was only to be had on Nov. 10th, and not now, a lady having taken a whole floor of seven rooms, and wishing to let two of them. We saw the two rooms which had been offered, found them furnished, and asked to whom they belonged, when we learned that they were in the use of the owner of the house, who had sold the house, but would have the use of these rooms, as well as those in which he lived, till Nov. 1st. I now affectionately asked him, whether he would not let an have these rooms for a time, offering to pay any price, and give the money before-hand, as I was a stranger to him. He said he would consider it with his wife a few hours. My dear wife and I now gave ourselves to prayer, that, if it were good for us, the Lord would be pleased to incline the hearts of these persons to let us have those two rooms, but I told Him, at the same time, that I should not now press the matter further, having offered what I had; for after all He might have another place for us, where. He wished us to be. After two or three hours I went again, and as we required little as to attendance, and were of quiet habits, and required little alteration to be made in the way of furniture, these persons agreed to let us have those rooms; and that same afternoon we were able to leave the hotel and enter our lodging. And now hear the Lord's goodness in this particular. The dear persons with whom we lodge are both Christians, who are most kind to us, and obliging in every way. Their servant also who waits on us is a most kind person. The house is in a healthy and quiet situation, and not far from our meeting-place, though without the city gates. In a word, we could not have wished better lodgings. And how did we get them? Because all the apartments, usually let out as lodgings, were occupied by these 90 or 100 gentlemen of the Parliament. Moreover, to this house we came, through a mistake having been made; for the rooms we now live in were only intended to be let on Nov. 10th. More, the persons with whom we live are evidently wealthy persons, a surgeon who has retired from his profession, and his wife, and who never had let lodgings. Oh! how kind of the Lord, to let circumstances be as they were, in order that we might, through this very difficulty, obtain such a dwelling-place. Daily we feel the comfort of living with Christians, though these dear persons belong to the State Church. May this little matter lead us all, dear brethren, to leave all our affairs in the hands of our loving Father; He arranges matters as they are best for us.-- During the first three or four days in Stuttgart, I was especially poor

FOURTH PART

and needy, and required every particle of courage not to be overwhelmed by the state of things here. Everything seemed most dark. On Tuesday evening when I went to the meeting, there were but eight present, and all I saw and heard gave me the impression of spiritual desolation, resulting from that false teacher from Switzerland having come among the brethren here. In addition to this, my dear wife was taken very ill during the night from Tuesday to Wednesday, July 29 to 30, so that for two days she kept her bed, and only on the fourth day was pretty well again. It was the result of sea-sickness and the great fatigue of the journey, I think. But the Lord had mercy and brightened the prospect by increasing my faith. In addition to this, circumstances looked better almost immediately after my arrival, and I was constantly comforted by the knowledge, that only according to the Lord's will we were here, and that He would not have sent us, if He had not some purpose to be accomplished by it. The first thing that occurred was, that, in answer to our many prayers in England, on the journey, and here, and also in answer to your prayers, dear brethren, the police gave me permission to stay here, a thing which, looking at it naturally, could not have been expected. Still, this had always been my hope, because to Stuttgart I felt to be my mission. The next thing was, that the moment my arrival became known, the poor scattered sheep were again drawn together, and other persons also, believers and unbelievers, came to the meetings, so that the first evening it was known I should hold a meeting, there were about 20 persons present, and since then there have been repeatedly 40 and upwards. This is a small number for England, but large here, and for our position in particular. The next thing was, our landlady told me that every Monday afternoon a number of pious females met at her house, for two or three hours, to knit stockings for the Moravian missionaries, and requested me to come and speak to them. This I now do every Monday afternoon, expounding the Scriptures to 20 or 25 of these females and our landlord and to an aged brother, who has been in the habit of attending these meetings. This is a new field entirely, and something else to show how the hand of God was in the matter of our lodgings. Still more. On the last two Friday evenings I have attended a meeting, at which about 150 persons, belonging to the State Church, meet together, most of them probably converted, and the others either seeking the Lord, or religiously inclined. To this meeting I have gone for love's sake, to show that I really desire to be united, in spirit, with all who love our Lord Jesus. Now at this meeting also, I have had opportunity to speak both times. In future also, the Lord willing, I purpose to go to this meeting, and to embrace the opportunity which thus I may have of speaking what may be suitable under the circumstances. The character of the meeting is not in every way that which is according to the Holy Scriptures, but these dear brethren must be borne with, in order to help them on. About 8 brethren sit round a table, being more intimately known to each other. They lead the whole meeting as to prayer, giving out a hymn, proposing the portion of the Word of God for consideration, &c. They make remarks on it, and all the other 100 or 200, or more or less, that may be present, listen. As I had called on one of these leading brethren, he asked me to sit at that table, and thus I have the right of speaking, which yet must be used very wisely, as these dear children of God may be able to bear it. But even if I were not to speak at all, my very presence would do good, with God's blessing, as they would see that I am desirous of being united with all who love our Lord Jesus; and I cannot but hope that thus prejudices will wear away, they will come to our meetings, and read my book. The Continent is not like England. Every particle of progress one is able to make here, is highly to be prized. The state of things is most interesting here. Infidelity is most awfully showing itself, regardlessly trampling under foot God's word, and shamelessly and most impudently denouncing the whole as a fabrication; but, on the other side, there is evidently an inquiry after truth, and a seeking to know the truth from the Scriptures themselves, and a beginning to be dissatisfied with cold dead forms. The Lord also begins to work for us in other respects. The parliament of Wirtemberg has also publicly considered the matter of the brother and sister who would not be married at the State Church, and have recommended to the government of the country to consider the matter once more, and also to grant to us the privilege of being able to marry, without going to the State Church, as they had already granted us "the administration of the Lord's Supper and Baptism," as they call it. Thus, with God's blessing, help will come in that way also; and I cannot but hope that this poor little gathering here, in which the devil has recently made such havoc, will yet be to the praise of the Lord, and to the benefit of His church in the German States.--God has blessed my being here in bringing brother R. out of the errors into which he had fallen, having been led away by that false teacher from Switzerland; but this brother reaps now bitterly the fruits of his want of watchfulness: that dear young sister who was converted while I was here before, his youngest daughter, is among those persons in Switzerland, and another of his daughters is engaged to one of these persons--Oh! how important, dear brethren, carefully and prayerfully to compare what we hear with the Word of God. Five days following, three times each day, this false teacher held meetings, and thus overpowered these dear saints completely; for they had no time left to consider and to pray over, and compare with the Holy Scriptures, what they heard, as, in addition to three meetings a day, they lasted till after 11 o'clock at night.--I now attend eight meetings every week. Sunday mornings at nine o'clock, exposition of the Word, and in the afternoon at two we meet for the breaking of bread. The dear brethren have gone back to these unsuitable hours. On Monday afternoon at three the exposition of the Scriptures to those who meet together to knit for the missionaries, and on Monday and Wednesday evenings from 8 to 10 o'clock, Scripture reading meetings, with the saints only who break bread. On Tuesday and Thursday evenings from eight to half-past nine, public exposition of the Word. And on Friday evening from half-past eight to a quarter before ten, I meet with the brethren who belong to the State Church. Besides this, my time has hitherto been much occupied in seeing brethren and sisters privately and the rest of my time, besides prayer and meditation, for my own soul and the work, has been occupied in preparing tracts for the press. Five are already finished. I have translated into German: "The love of God to poor sinners," "The Serpent of brass," and "The two thieves;" and I have written myself two tracts, on "Lydia's conversion," and "The conversion of the jailer at Philippi." In this work I purpose to continue, the Lord willing, while we remain here, either writing or translating tracts, and then seeking myself, as much as I can, whilst here, to circulate them--Oh! help me, beloved brethren, yet more and more with your prayers in all this important service. My position here is more important, and more interesting than ever; for God, "who comforteth those who are cast down," has comforted me, after the first three days of trial, and

FOURTH PART

has given me a larger field for service than I had before.--We remember you daily in prayer, and gladly do so, and shall be truly glad to return to you, as soon as we can see it to be the will of the Lord. Farewell, beloved brethren. My dear wife sends to you her love in Christ. Should any of you wish to write to me, I shall be glad to hear from you; but please to write on very thin paper, on account of the heavy postage. The letters may be left at my house.

Your affectionate brother and servant in the Lord,

George Mueller.

Stuttgart, Sept. 13, 1845.

To the Brethren in Christ, meeting in the name of the Lord Jesus at Bethesda and Salem Chapels, Bristol.

My dear brethren,

It is eight weeks today since we left Bristol, and we have still abundant reason to say, that goodness and mercy have followed us every day. This I have in particular also to say in reference to the last four weeks, even since I wrote to you last. As we desire your thanksgiving to the Lord for His goodness to us, and as we earnestly crave the continuance of your prayers, I write again, especially also as I judge that your love will be desirous of knowing further particulars about us and the work of the Lord in my hands. Since I wrote to you, I have continued to attend eight meetings a week, that is, three for exposition of the Scriptures at our usual in meeting-place on Lord's day mornings and Tuesday and Thursday evenings; the breaking of bread on the Lord's day evenings (as we have altered the hour from 2 in the afternoon to 8 in the evening); two Scripture reading meetings on Monday and Wednesday, at which, as well as at all our other meetings, there is given to every brother as much room for prayer, as there may be a desire for it. Then I attend two other meetings a week, among believers or inquirers who are in connexion with the State Church, one on Monday afternoon at the house where we live, which has increased from about ten to about forty. At this meeting I lead entirely, and am the only speaker. Then there is every Friday evening another meeting, at which about 150 persons assemble, which I have continued to attend, and where I have regularly spoken, together with other brethren. The shyness which there was at first is evidently wearing off, and last evening, when I took leave of them, having been there for the last time before our departure, the brethren were quite cordial. In addition to this, the Lord has opened another new and important field. At the house of an elderly lady of title, of one of the ancient noble families of this kingdom, there is a meeting for ladies who work for charitable purposes. This meeting I have also been requested to attend for the purpose of expounding the Scriptures, whilst the ladies work. I was there last Tuesday afternoon, and shall be there again, the Lord willing, neat Tuesday. To all who attend this meeting I have therefore an opportunity of giving a copy of my Narrative in

German, about forty in all, as well as a copy of the eleven tracts which I have published, and thus the truth, with God's blessing, may be carried into the higher circles of this city, if not of this kingdom. Truly, the Lord gave, at the beginning of my sojourn here, to everything apparently the death-blow, that He might give me a larger field than I had had before. Still it is even now but little in comparison with England, yet it is much for Germany. Indeed I have now as much work day by day as I can do. Persons from the establishment come to see mind converse with me, and I might visit as many as I have time and strength for, and many more, and should be welcome.

Sept. 14. Thus far I had written yesterday morning, when a pious gentleman of rank called on me, who, with his wife, feels the deepest interest about the work of the Lord in Bristol, of which they have gathered information through my Narrative in German. This gentleman has been this morning to our poor meeting place also, and has invited me to his house to meet his friends. Thus a new opening has been given. The remainder of yesterday was spent in seeing visitors, and the evening I spent among brethren belonging to the State Church.--I have now been able to publish eleven different Gospel tracts in German. They are as follows; 1."The love of God to poor sinners," translation from the English, 4 pages. 2. "The Serpent of brass," translation, 4 pages. 3. "The two thieves," translation, 8 pages. 4. "Lydia, the seller of purple," written by me, 4 pages. 5. "The jailer at Philippi," written by me, 12 pages. 6. "The four most important questions answered," written by me, 12 pages. 7. "Grace," translation, 4 pages. 8. "The poor man's best medicine," translation, 6 pages. 9. "Almost and Altogether," translation, 6 pages. 10. "What is a Christian?" translation, 6 pages. 11. "A just God and a Saviour," translation, 6 pages.--Of each of these tracts twenty thousand copies have been printed, there are therefore two hundred and twenty thousand copies ready to be used by the Lord. I tell you all these particulars, dear brethren, that you may now help me with your prayers, that God may be pleased to use and bless them. The especial intention respecting these tracts is, to state the Gospel in a plain and distinct way. Now one of my particular reasons for leaving you for a season, and labouring here was, to publish these tracts, and to circulate myself as many of them as I could. The latter I am now about to do in the following way. I have had a box made which will hold about thirty thousand tracts. This box will be filled and fastened behind the conveyance which I purpose hiring. Our portmanteaus and other packages, as much as room permits, will be filled with copies of my German Narrative. Thus stored we purpose to leave on Wednesday or Thursday, Sept. 17 or 18, giving to each person we meet on the road a tract, and giving away in the towns and villages as many as may be wise, without raising a mob around us. In addition to this, as far as opportunity may allow, I purpose to speak with persons on the road. In this way we purpose to travel on, day after day, giving away tracts, and also my Narrative, so that in every village and town, of a journey of 500 or 600 miles, at least a few copies of my Narrative will be left, besides giving them to passengers on the road, and as many tracts as we can. In order to fill our stores again, I purpose to send to Frankfort a large bale of tracts and books before us, also to Eisleben, where Luther was born, and to Cassel. In this way I hope to be able to give away about 900 copies of my Narrative, and fifty or sixty thousand tracts. In addition to this, I am seeking to place with trustworthy brethren in this country, in

FOURTH PART

Switzerland, and in Prussia, smaller quantities, to be given away as opportunity may occur. Our route, as far as I can see at present, will be this: To Heilbronn, Heidelberg, Darmstadt, Frankfort, Fulda, Erfurt, Eisenach, Eisleben. The last place will be the furthest part of our journey. Then we mean to return towards England by way of Nordhausen, Gottingen, Cassel, Elberfeld, Dusseldorf, and Cologne. The whole tour may take from 20 to 25 days, travelling day after day. All this I write to you, earnestly asking your prayers for us, on account of the following particulars: 1. That the Lord would be pleased so to strengthen us in body, as that we may be able to continue travelling day after day for 20 days or more. 2. That the Lord would be pleased to give us suitable and kind drivers, that we may not have difficulty in our work in that way. 3. That the police may not be permitted to obstruct our service. 4. That our own souls may not suffer through this work, but rather be benefited. 5. That the Lord would be pleased to direct the Tracts and Narratives into the hands of those very persons whom He means to bless by them.

6. That He would also be pleased to allow the weather to be of that kind, if it seem good to Him, that our work may not be hindered.-- Great unforseen hindrances and difficulties we may meet with in this service, yet it has now been with me the subject of prayer for several months, and in the name of the Lord I enter upon it.-- The especial reason why I go towards the North of Germany is, because there this service is mostly needed, and there my Narrative is not at all, or scarcely at all known, as the 200 copies which I sent to a beloved brother in those parts for circulation, he could not conscientiouisly, as he says, circulate; I therefore mean myself to circulate the book there. And further, in those parts public meetings in abundance are held, in which the foundation truths of the Gospel are openly attacked by persons who call themselves "the Friends of Light." There then I mean to distribute among the common people as many thousands of Tracts as I can.--Germany is in great agitation. Light is increasing, there is a shaking in establishments; but there infidelity is also increasing, as well as democracy in politics. I watch with deep interest the state of things in Germany, and were not my position in Bristol what it is, I should remain longer here; but I judge it well to be back again, if the Lord prosper our way, about the 12th of October. Gladly should I have written many more Tracts, they are also greatly needed, especially on subjects which are more particularly of importance for believers; but I cannot now stay longer, and must leave it to a time when the Lord may honour me again to labour for a season in Germany.

Sept. 15. Yesterday I was again interrupted by visitors, so that I could not finish my letter. The gentleman, who called the day before yesterday, called again also yesterday. He was Professor of Medicine in the University of Moscow in Russia, and President of the Evangelical Consistory in that City. He seems deeply interested in the service in my hands. He was twice yesterday at our poor meeting place, and has invited me this evening to his house to meet some friends of his, clergymen and others. Last evening there were present at the meeting for the breaking of bread about 40 persons; besides those who broke bread. Our departure is now fixed for Thursday, Sept. 18th; but after a dry season for 4 or 5 weeks, the Lord has now sent rain, and we are entirely in His hands as to the weather, as a rainy season ill suit our intended service; but our Lord, whose work it is, and not ours, will order this matter also as it shall be for His glory and our welfare. I reckon, beloved brethren, on the continuance of your prayers. We also, by the grace of God, continue to remember you day after day. We shall be glad indeed to behold your faces again, and yet we desire to be happy here, because we are in our Lord's work: and indeed we are happy here also, though so far absent from the hundreds of dear saints whom we have so much reason to love. The little church here consists of 19, of whom 6 do not live in this city, but in two villages at some distance, who can only from time to time come to the breaking of bread. That which they especially now need is, that one or more brethren should labour among them, and I would particularly commend this matter to your prayer, that the Lord would be pleased to appear on their behalf in this particular; for it is not likely that things will go on well among them without pastoral care and without oversight. In some little measure order has now been restored among them, and I hope that the coming of that false teacher among them, nine months since, will finally be used by the Lord for their furtherance. And now, greatly loved brethren, farewell. May the Lord, as we continually pray, give to each of you according to your individual need. My dear wife, who helps me much in the work here in one way or other, sends her love in Christ to you.

Your affectionate brother and servant in our Lord,

George Mueller.

Cassel, Capital of the Electorate of Hesse Cassel, Oct. 1, 1845.

To the saints, assembling in the name of the Lord Jesus at Salem and Bethesda Chapels, Bristol.

My very dear brethren,

I long to tell you of the Lord's goodness to us, since last I wrote you, and though this letter may reach you only three or four days before our arrival among you, still I would wish you to help us in praising the Lord for His goodness to us. I now record His kindness in our service, as far as I remember it, from the day where my last letter heft off. I think it was on Sept. 15th that my last letter was finished. On that afternoon I had the last meeting among the working females in my house. It had then increased to at least sixty, from about 10 at the beginning. The evening of that day I spent among gentlemen and ladies of Stuttgart, at the house of a gentleman who had invited me. There the Lord gave me opportunity of testifying for Him about 2 hours and a half. The next afternoon I had a meeting at which about 25 ladies were working for charitable purposes, at the house of a lady of title. To these and to their absent friends, I gave a copy of my Narrative, 40 in number, as well as a copy of each of the 11 Tracts which I have published. Thus, with the Lord's blessing, the Narrative and the Tracts may work among the higher or highest classes of the kingdom of Wirtemberg. I simply mention this to show, dear brethren, what open doors the Lord has given me, after the apparent death-blow upon everything at the beginning. How important that we should not be discouraged by appearances in the Lord's service! On the same evening the last public meeting among the brethren at Stuttgart was attended by about 80 persons more than any previous time, either at this or my former visit. Thus also the Lord gave still further encouragement. On the following day, Wednesday, Sept. 17th, I took leave of various believers, not in communion with us; among the rest, of two pious clergymen at Stuttgart, who treated me most kindly. This day was occupied with making all the arrangements for our journey, as I had to send many thousands of tracts before us to several places, not being able to carry in our carriage all the books and tracts, which we hoped to circulate on the journey. In the evening that gentleman called once more to see me, in whose house I had spent the Monday evening, and with whom I had become acquainted a few days before, and who, since then, had attended all our meetings. I think I told you before, that he was Professor of Medicine at the Russian University at Moscow, and also President of the Protestant Consistory in that city. This dear brother takes a deep interest in my service, and has offered to circulate 50 copies of my book, and 50 copies of each of the 11 tracts. We parted like old friends.--Our prayer had been for a suitable carriage, and an obliging driver, on which so much of our service depended; but we were so occupied, that I could only order a carriage on the morning of our departure, Thursday, Sept. 18th, and the Lord most signally answered our prayers; for we obtained a driver who was one of a hundred. He drove us three days, and was most obliging, so that we could not have desired a better driver; the carriage also was as if made for our work. At 10 o'clock on Thursday morning we set out, furnished with many thousands of tracts, and about 24,000 sent before us; also carrying with us about 450 copies of my Narrative, and having to take up 350 copies on the way. About 350 copies I was able to circulate at Stuttgart whilst there. I should also say that I found several brethren with whom I could leave smaller quantities of tracts for circulation at Stuttgart and else-where, especially an English brother, Dr. M., who lives at Basle, and who spends his whole time in circulating religious books and tracts, written in German and French. This brother came, three days before our departure, to Stuttgart, so that I could arrange with him. Indeed step by step has the Lord prospered me in my feeble endeavours, mixed with sin as every one of them has been, and made it manifest, that, this time also, He bad sent me to Germany. On Thursday, September 18th, then, we set out, and while yet driving through the city of Stuttgart I began giving away tracts, thus to begin the service at once, lest my hands should be weakened through delay. Whilst going on, we continued offering tracts to the passengers on the road, and giving away now and then a copy of my book, and seeking especially to put some copies of it into every village and town. Thus we went on the first day from Stuttgart to Heilbronn, a distance of about 35 English miles. All went on most quietly. We were able to give away many hundreds of tracts, and about 50 copies of my Narrative, and to a few persons I had the opportunity of speaking a little. The second day's journey was from Heilbronn to Heidelberg. In the large towns we went on most quietly, lest there should be a running together of the people, and the appearance be a political disturbance. On this account I never give away tracts and books in towns, but on the road, or just before I come to towns, or after I have passed through them. Yet now and then I have also given them away in towns in a quiet way; for instance, by going to a baker's shop, and buying a trifle and then giving a book. The second day from Heilbronn to Heidelberg we went on as before in our service, but in the afternoon we were tried in spirit. We observed a carriage at a distance behind us, with a gentleman in it, and his coachman before. He stopped more than once to converse with the people to whom I had given tracts. At last he obtained sight of my book also. Thus he kept on driving behind us. Our nerves were greatly tried by this. By the grace of God we were willing to suffer for His name's sake, even greatly, in this work; yet this matter greatly tried us, not knowing what the result might be. At last the carriage drove before us. Then it stopped, and the gentleman lifted himself up, to have a full look at me, then he ordered his coachman to drive on, and they were soon out of sight. The next thing to be expected was, that in the next town the police would stop us in our service. However, we continued the work, and at last arrived at Heidelberg, without having been stopped, and having given away more books and tracts than even on the previous day. The steady even course of service, under all difficulties, without any one's encouragement, and with the discouragement of many, requires not a little faith! We felt how weak our faith was! The third day's journey was from Heidelberg. We continued again our blessed service. I had opportunity this day to put my Narrative and tracts into the hands of ladies and gentlemen as well as poor persons. Our opportunities for service were very many this day, and things went on quietly in the morning. In the afternoon, however, we were even more tried than the day before. We had travelled through Wirtemberg and also the Grand Duchy of Baden, and were now in the country of Hesse-Darmstadt, when I gave some tracts to some lads of a Grammar School, whom we met before a town. But these lads followed us, accompanied the carriage through the whole town, and some distance out of the town, ridiculing us. We sat quiet, saying nothing at all. Then I was addressed by a mail-guard who had seen me give away tracts and books, and who, having stopped the mail, asked for tracts for himself and the passengers, but evidently in a sneering way. This carried the news of our service before us, as the mail went much faster than we, and therefore our work was known in the next place, and a man ran out on our arrival to ask for books, and in consequence of this the attention of persons was arrested. Nevertheless the Lord helped us to continue the work, though somewhat tried in mind, being aware how much such work is opposed on the Continent. A little while after, a light wagon drove quickly after us, and as I was walking by the side of the carriage, up a hill, a man got out, joined me, and asked for a tract. He then said: "Who has allowed you to distribute these books?" I replied. "Nobody, but I am a servant of Jesus, and I desire to serve my Lord. If, however, you can show me that what I am now doing is against the laws of the country I will give it up. As far as I am aware, it is not." He then asked me, what religion was contained in the tracts. I said not any one in particular, but that there were in them the truths of Christianity, about which alone I cared, as I did not design by these books to increase any particular party. A few words more of this kind passed, and he then left me, drove on before us, and presently turned off from the turnpike road into a little bye road in the wood, where he stopped and read the tract which I had given him, which was, "The conversion of the jailer at Philippi." I went on as before with the work, not tried in spirit, but yet my nerves were much affected by it. We meant only to have gone that day as far as Darmstadt, the

FOURTH PART

capital of Hesse-Darmstadt, but I engaged the driver 15 miles further, to Frankfort-on-the-Main, in order that we might be out of the dominion of Hesse-Darmstadt, if through the mail-guard, or the last-mentioned person, who, to judge from his dress, was a government officer, the matter should be coming before the magistrates. At Frankfort we arrived after ten on Saturday evening, Sept. 20th, having now been able for 3 days to go on with the service. The next day, being the Lord's day, we purposed to rest at Frankfort which we much needed for body and spirit, especially also for the sake of asking the Lord's blessing upon the work up till then, and to ask guidance for our future steps, mud His help and blessing for what remained of our work. We had intended, before we left Stuttgart, to go to Eisleben, such a distance from Frankfort, as would require 4 or 5 days more travelling, and then all the way back to Cologne. But on account of what had occurred the two previous days, we now began again to consider our steps, whether we should go on still further or not. Nature wished to get back to England at once. Nature shrank greatly from the continuance of this service. But after having strengthened ourselves in God, we came to the conclusion, that our first purpose was of God, and that we ought not to alter our plans, except we saw it most clearly to be the will of God; we therefore purposed (as we could only look upon the desire of discontinuing our tour as a temptation), to go on with our service, till by the order of the police we were prohibited. Blessed be God who enabled us to triumph over the temptation! But to Him is all the praise due; for had He not strengthened us in that hour, we should have been as those who, having put their hand to the plough, draw it back. I now set about making arrangements for the journey, as the carriage and horses, which I had engaged for the three previous days, had to return to Stuttgart. Our prayer was for another suitable driver, upon which so very much depended in our service. In this again we experienced most evidently the Lord's willingness to answer prayer; for in the same inn at which our Stuttgart driver had put up, it happened, by the ordering of the Lord, that there was a driver from Cassel, the place where I am now writing, who had taken a family to Frankfort, and who was looking out for a job. With this coachman I agreed, to take us to Eisleben, to stop there a day and a half, while I saw brethren in that neighbourhood, and then to take us to Cassel. This engagement was for eight days. It was the more kind of the Lord to allow me to find this person, as I went from place to place in Frankfort to obtain a conveyance, but could not succeed in that large city; and the only one I could have had, would have been nearly twice as expensive as the one which I hired. On Monday morning, then, Sept. 22nd, we left Frankfort, determined by the help of God to pursue our service, and, if need be, to suffer and to endure hardship in it. Many tracts and books also were given away this day, and in the evening we reached Schluechtern, a small town before Fulda. The next day at Fulda I took up a large bale of tracts and books which I had sent before, and on Tuesday evening we reached Vacha. Up to that time we had had fine weather; but we reached Vacha in a heavy storm, it having rained heavily for 2 hours, and lightened and thundered exceedingly. All night the rain continued, and in rain we left Vacha for Eisenach. Our service now seemed over; but yet I managed now and then to put a copy of my book out of the carriage, when I saw an opportunity that it could be kept pretty dry. By the time we reached Eisenach, which stands on the foot of the hill on which is the old castle called the Wartburg, where Luther translated the Bible, the rain ceased and we had a fine afternoon, and in a few hours were able to give away more than 50 books and many tracts. In the evening we reached Gotha, capital of the small dukedom of Saxe Gotha. On Thursday, Sept. 28th, we came as far as a small town called Arthern, and on Friday, about 1 o'clock in the afternoon, we reached Eisleben. All these five days and a half we went on quietly in our service, none hindering us, giving away many books and tracts. Here now we stopped two days, had some intercourse with brethren, and then left for Cassel, which we reached in two days and a half, arriving here last evening. This morning I have been writing this letter and doing some other things needful for the journey, whilst my dear wife has been all the morning engaged in putting up tracts for the journey. If we can obtain a suitable conveyance, we purpose to leave this afternoon on our way to Elberfeld, and, if the Lord gives us grace, to pursue our service till we come to the Rhine, and then by way of Ostend to cross the sea for England, so that about 3 or 4 days after this reaches you we may have the joy of seeing you again face to face. It will be joy to us indeed to see you all again. Farewell, beloved brethren. My dear wife sends her love in Christ to you all.

Your affectionate brother and servant in our Lord,

George Mueller.

I add a few remarks respecting this my service on the Continent.

1. For about eight months before I left England, I had seen it to be the Lord's will, that I should go again that year to the Continent for a season, and had made my journey and service, during that period, a daily subject of prayer from Nov. 1844. I left Bristol on July 19th and returned on Oct. 11th, 1845.

2. I should have greatly preferred to preach the Gospel in the streets or in the market places in Germany; but for that there was no liberty. I did therefore what I could, in spreading about eleven hundred copies of my Narrative, and tens of thousands of tracts. In this I was particularly encouraged by remembering that that great work, at the time of the Reformation, was chiefly accomplished by means of printed publications.

3. We travelled in a hired carriage for 17 days, each day about 40 or 45 miles. I had a box, containing about thirty thousand tracts, made on purpose, behind the carriage, and in the fore-part several portmanteaus filled with tracts and copies of my Narrative in German. As we went on, my dear wife and I looked out for travellers who were coming, or persons on the road side. It was just the time when the potatoes were taken up, and thousands of people were thus either close to the turnpike road, or only a little way from it. The front of our carriage had glass windows, so that we could see all the persons before us, and on each side. As soon as the carriage was near enough, I held the tracts or a copy of my Narrative out to them, and requested them to accept them or sometimes beckoned the working people to come up to the carriage, which almost without exception they readily did, and then received a book

FOURTH PART

or tract. In case of genteel persons, whom we sometimes met, I repeatedly ordered the driver to stop, and I got out of the carriage, and handed the books or tracts to them. Often also I walked up a hill, and then conversed with the persons whom I joined, or gave tracts more extensively in this way.

4. The reason why we pursued this plan of travelling was, a, that I might myself circulate as many as possible; b, that the tracts and Narratives might be scattered over as extensive a tract of country as possible; c, that I might be able to accomplish it, before the police could prevent it. On the road side, before entering villages and towns, or after we had left them, I gave away freely. Now suppose this came to the ears of the police, as no doubt in many instances it did; before any measures could be taken, we might be at a distance of 5, 10, or 20 miles from the spot; for we travelled, as I said, from 40 to 45 miles daily. This was indeed an expensive way of circulating the tracts, and wearing to body and mind more than can easily be perceived; but it was a most effectual way, and a precious service to be allowed to be engaged in for the Lord. When we had finished our journey, lasting 23 days, we were completely worn out for the time.

5. At first we sometimes threw down the tracts to persons, out of the carriage, when they were not near enough to have them handed to them. This, however, we discontinued on the second or third day; for I judged, that, as we would not throw down Bibles, Testaments, or smaller portions of the Holy Scriptures, so these tracts also, filled with the truth of God, and written for the honour of God, should not be thrown down; and that we would rather not give them at all, than in this way. I purposely notice this, as many Christians are in the habit of throwing tracts out of a carriage, as I did at first. I might put them secretly in drawers, or on the table, or under the table-cover in inns, or elsewhere, where they afterwards might be found; but I could not feel any longer happy in not treating them with all reverence, because they contain the truth of God.

6. Perhaps the reader may ask: What has been the result of this labour in Germany? My reply is: God only knows. The day of Christ will declare it. Judging from the constant labour in prayer during 8 months before we went the second time, and day by day while we were on the Continent, and day by day for a long time after our return, I am warranted to expect fruit, and I do expect it. I expect abundant fruit in the day of Christ's appearing. In the meantime my comfort is, that 220,000 tracts have been circulated, many of which through the providence of God found their way not only into the darkest places of the Continent of Europe, but went also to America and Australia. Further, the 4000 copies of my Narrative in German, are almost all circulated. And again, the publishing of my Narrative in German, led me to do the same in French, which was accomplished about three years later. Further, these tracts were reprinted at Hamburg and at Cologne, and are circulated by other Christians; in addition to which, my having published them in Germany led me to get them stereotyped in England, and they continue to be circulated in many countries.

THE LORD'S DEALINGS WITH GEORGE MÜLLER

7. I only add, we continued our service in a similar way, after we had left Cassel, from whence I wrote the last letter to the church in Bristol; and in many respects it was the most interesting part of the service.

December 31, 1845. There have been received into communion 53 during this year, and 1055 since our coming to Bristol, which, with 68 whom we found in fellowship, makes 1123. Of these, 115 have fallen asleep, 65 have been excluded, 57 left us, and 193 left Bristol; so that there are only 693 brethren and sisters in fellowship at present.

During this year the Lord has been pleased to give to me:--

1. Through anonymous donations in money, put up in paper and directed to me, and placed in the boxes for the poor saints and the rent, at the two chapels
L166 15 10 1/4

2. Through presents in money, from believers in Bristol, not given anonymously
...... 102 18 11 1/2

3. Through presents in money, from believers, not residing in Bristol
138 0 7

4. Through presents in provisions, clothes, etc., worth to us at least . . .
26 3 9

Altogether L433 19 1 3/4

To this is to be added, that my dear child had again during the whole of this year her education free at a boarding school, as stated at the close of the last year, whereby I saved about 50l. Also my traveling expenses to and from Germany, and other expenses, connected with my service in Germany, were paid out of the 50l. to which reference has been made. Adding these two items to 433l., I had at least 500l.

Esteemed reader, what do you think of this? Is it not a pleasant thing, in the end, even for this life, really to trust in God? Verily, thus I have found it to be, and thus do I find it to be, the longer I live. Only there must be real trust in God, and it must be more than merely using words. If we trust in God, we look to Him alone, we deal with Him alone, and we are satisfied with His knowing about our need. Two things I add, as I write my experience and the Lord's dealings with me for the profit of the saints.

1. During the last year I resolved, that, by God's help, I would seek to be more than ever a channel for the Communication of God's bounties, and to communicate to those in need, or to give to the work of God. I acted according to the light which

FOURTH PART

God gave me, and He condescended to make me His steward in one way or another far more abundantly than ever before. Would we wish to have means intrusted to us by the Lord, or to succeed in our trade, business, profession, etc., we must be truly desirous of being His stewards, and only His stewards. Read what I have written at length on this subject within the last twenty pages of the third part of this my Narrative; and, if you have read it before, read it yet again.

2. In looking over my journal, I find that during this year also I was more than once without a shilling, yea without a penny, though my income was about 500l.

April 29, 1846. Today my beloved wife and myself had the inexpressibly great joy of receiving a letter from our beloved daughter, while we are staying in the Lord's service at Chippenham, in which she writes that she has now found peace in the Lord Jesus. Thus our prayers are turned into praises.

About 18 mouths before this I began especially to pray for the conversion of my dear child, and the Lord soon after seems to have begun to work in her heart. I knew little of her state of mind before receiving her letter, for I did not wish to force anything upon her of a spiritual character, but leave her to be attracted by the loveliness of the things of God. After hearing from her in April, 1846, she was not received at once to communion, but, being so young, I judged it desirable to watch the work in her soul. Towards the end of the year, however, my fellow-labourers being fully satisfied, she was baptized and received into communion, when she was 14 years and 3 months old.

Supplies for the School-Bible--Missionary and Tract Fund, sent in answer to prayer, from May 26, 1846, to May 26, 1848.

During no period, from the commencement of the operations of this Institution up to May 26, 1846, was I intrusted by the Lord with such large sums, as during the one to which this chapter refers. I had never had more need of pecuniary supplies than during those two years, on account of the many pressing calls; but, at the same time, I had the exceeding great joy and privilege of being able to respond to them in such a way as I had never before been allowed to do. These remarks apply to all the various objects of the Institution, but especially to the supplies for brethren who labour at Home and Abroad in word and doctrine without being connected with any society, or without having any regular salary for preaching the Word.

On May 26, 1846, after the accounts had been closed, a check for 100l. was given to me, the application of which was left to my disposal. I put half the amount to the fund for these objects, and half to the Orphan-Fund, When the accounts were closed, there was 91l. 4s. 11 3/4 d. in, and for these objects, to which this 50l. was added; therefore I began this period with more means than I had had in hand at any time previously at the beginning of a fresh period; and as was its beginning so was the continuance. It has often struck me, that one especial reason why, on the whole, I was allowed to have so little trial with regard to means for the work during those two years, in comparison with former times, may have been, that thereby the Lord would say that He was willing to give what would be needed when once the New Orphan-House should be built, though the expenses would be about two thousand five hundred pounds a year more than they were before. Another reason also may have been, because in many other ways trials of faith and patience came upon me in connexion with the Institution during those two years, that therefore the Lord may not have exercised me so much by the want of pecuniary means as before. But especially also one reason, why the Lord generally gave me so great an abundance during those two years, seems to me this, that it might be seen, not only how He can help us day by day when we are poor, but also how able and willing He is to cause us to abound, when this is for His honour and for our profit.

June 4, 1846. To day was given to me, just when I rose from my knees, after having asked the Lord for more means, especially for missionary purposes, the sum of 150l., with the request to use of it 50l. for the Orphans, 50l. for labourers in England; and 50l. for labourers abroad.

July 6. Besides several small donations which came in since June 4, I received today 50l., of which one half is intended by the donor for the Orphans, the other half for these objects.

July 16. Today I received One Hundred Pounds from a donor who had lost about one half of his property, and who gives this donation as "A thank-offering to God for having left to him as much as he has." I put one half of this donation to the funds for these objects, and the other half to the Orphan Fund.

Aug. 1. About 24l. more has come in since July 16th. During the last two days I have sent 110l. to Foreign labourers, and 15l. to brethren who labour in England; and having thus begun to reduce our Missionary Fund, the Lord gives fresh supplies. The evening before last was sent to me 5l. from Ludlow. Today I received 5l. from Scarborough, of which 4l. is for Missionary objects, and 1l. for the Orphans. Thus the Lord gives me the desire of my heart, to help more and more the dear brethren who labour in word and doctrine, either in this country or in foreign lands.

From the commencement of this Institution on March 5th, 1834, it had been my desire to employ part of the funds with which I might be intrusted, in aiding missionary brethren in foreign lands, who are not supported by any regular salary; and for several years I have likewise had the desire to assist brethren, labouring in similar circumstances, in Great Britain and Ireland. The Lord also had given me the great privilege to assist such brethren more or less during the time that this Institution had been in operation; but especially He began during the two years, to which this chapter refers, to allow me to do so in a far greater degree than before. I knew it to be a fact, that many brethren, who preach the Word, without having any salary for doing so, or property to live upon, were in need. Now it might be said that such brethren ought to trust in God; that, if they preach Jesus as the only hope for the salvation of sinners, they ought to set them a good example by trusting themselves in God for the supply of their temporal necessities, in order that unconverted persons thereby might be led to trust in the Lord Jesus alone for the salvation of their souls. This is true, quite true. Preachers of the precious good news of salvation to every sinner who puts his trust in the merits of the Lord Jesus, ought indeed themselves to depend upon God, their Lord and Father, for the supply of their temporal necessities; but I also felt that I, as their brother, ought to seek to help them as far as lay in me. To this I set myself more than ever after the beginning of the year 1846, as I knew, that, from particular causes, there was an especial call to help such brethren; and as my own means would go but a little way, I gave myself to more earnest prayer than ever for such brethren. The result was, that, during the two years of this period, the Lord so answered my daily supplications with regard to this particular, that I was honoured to send nearly three times as much to Home and Foreign labourers, as during any previous period of the same length. 1,559l. 11s. 6d. was spent in this way, by which twenty-one brethren were assisted who laboured in Foreign lands, and nineteen who laboured in Great Britain and Ireland. Large as this sum is, in comparison with what I had been able to do in this particular in former years, yet it is small, very small, in comparison with what my heart desired to be able to do for these forty brethren. It has frequently, yea almost always, so happened, that the assistance which God has allowed me to send to such brethren, has come to them at a time of great need. Sometimes they had no money at all left. Sometimes even their last provisions were almost consumed, when I sent them supplies. Some of them are fathers of large families, or have sickly wives and children; some were once well off in this world, but for Christ's sake have become poor; and some have had for Christ's sake their all taken from them. Is it not an honour to help such brethren? I could fill hundreds of pages by giving extracts from the letters of the dear brethren to whom I have sent help, and they would be greatly to the edification of the reader; but I do not feel free to do so.-- As I have not only been labouring for these brethren in prayer that God would intrust me with means and allow me the privilege of helping them, but as I also have asked God to direct me especially to send to those who might be in particular need, in case I could not help them all; and as I have sought by an encouraging word to strengthen their hands in God; there is great reason to believe, that these dear brethren have not only been helped by these pecuniary supplies in a temporal point of view, but also that the fact, of God sending them help in their extremity, has tended to refresh and strengthen their hearts, and to lead them more and more to trust in Him.

Sep. 4. 38l. more has come in since Aug. 1st for these objects, and today there was given to me 305l. 17s. 3d. for Home and Foreign labourers, for present use for the Orphans, and for the other parts of the work. Thus I have again the desire of my heart given to me in being able to assist a number of dear brethren at home and abroad, to whom I desired to send help. Of this sum I took 205l. 17s. 3d. for these objects, and 100l. for the Orphans.

Sept. 9. Since the 4th I have sent out about 60l. already for brethren who labour in England and Foreign lands. This morning I received from C. W. 25l. more for missionary objects.

THE LORD'S DEALINGS WITH GEORGE MÜLLER

Oct. 22. This morning's post had brought no means. Whilst walking in my little garden for meditation and prayer, I said to myself--"Though the post has brought no means, yet the Lord can send even this day rich supplies." It was not two minutes after this, when a letter was handed to me, which had been brought that moment, containing two Fifty Pound Notes and these words: "My little children, let us not love in word, neither in tongue; but in deed and in truth."---40l. for missionaries; Demerara and others, dependant on God for supplies. 10l. for Home missionaries, dependant on God for their support. 10l. for the Orphans. 10l. for the poor of Bethesda and Salem Church. 10l. for Mr. Mueller. 10l. for Mr. Craik. 5l. for Bibles and Testaments. 5l. for rent, &c. of chapels."---Thus I had a fresh answer to my prayers, which had been again brought before the Lord this morning, that He would enable me still more to help the dear brethren who labour at home and abroad in dependence upon Him for supplies.

Dec. 22. During the last two months about 70l. more has come in, chiefly for Missionary purposes. Of these donations, about eighty in number, I only mention that there was given on Nov. 5, the sum of 6l. 14s., being the tenth part of profits arising from shares which a brother has in coal mines. --Now today, Dec. 22, I received 175l. more for these funds, which I took as a further precious answer to my supplications to God, for help for home and foreign labourers, and for means to procure a fresh stock of tracts.

March 7, 1847. Often of late have I besought the Lord that He would be pleased to give me more means for those objects. For more than nine months we have on the whole abounded more than at any time during the thirteen years since this work first began; but now there was only 15l. left for the support of six day schools, two Sunday schools, an adult school, and the circulation of Bibles and Tracts. Often also of late had I entreated the Lord that He would be pleased to condescend to use me still further as a steward, in allowing me to send help to the many dear brethren whom I know labouring at home and abroad without any salary, the need of many of whom I knew. Under these circumstances I received this morning 150l. with the following lines:

"Dear brother,

"I have pleasure in sending you 100l. on account of labourers in the Lord's vineyard at home and abroad, and 50l. for other work in your hands.

"Yours very affectionately,

"* *."

Thus my request was in a measure answered with regard to home and foreign labourers, and by taking half of the 50l. for the schools and the circulation of Bibles

FOURTH PART

and Tracts, I had also something for these objects. The other 25l. I put to the Orphan Fund.

March 12. The 100l. for home and foreign labourers was soon portioned out. The difficulty was not to spend it, but how to make it do, so that all, who seemed to me to need, might get a little. On this account I prayed still further during the last four days for means for home and foreign labourers, and now this morning, when I arose from my knees, after having again asked the Lord about tills matter, I received a letter in which C. W. sent me 30l. for missionaries.

April 5. I have been praying day by day, ever since I was able during the last month to send about 130l. to home and foreign labourers, that the Lord would be pleased soon again to give me means for them, on account of their great need; indeed, all our means were so exhausted, that I had only just enough, for tomorrow evening, to meet the weekly expenses connected with the six day schools, when this morning I received 125l. for these objects. What a precious help! How is my heart refreshed by this seasonable answer to prayer!--Almost immediately after this donation had been given to me, I received a letter from Demerara about the great need among the brethren who labour there, by which intelligence the seasonable help, just received, has become still more precious to me.

Thirteen other small donations came in between April 5th and May 13th, and on May 13th I received 100l. for missionary purposes.

On June 8th was given 100l. for missionary purposes.

June 30. For the whole period, since the accounts were last closed, more than 13 months since, we have not been so poor with regard to these funds as today. Last evening I paid out the last money to the brethren who labour in the day schools, in giving them their weekly salary. Under these circumstances a brother in the Lord, who resides about 200 miles from this, and who had been staying in my house two days, gave me 30l. to dispose of as I thought best, only that missionary brethren should be remembered. I took therefore 15l. for Missions, and the other 15l. for the School--Bible and Tract Fund. What a seasonable help!

July 16. Today was given to me, when now again the money received on June 30th for the schools, &c., had been all but entirely expended (as only little had come in since), the sum of 110l. for these objects.

Aug. 25. Great had been my desire to send fresh supplies to the home and foreign labourers. Day by day had I been again praying for means for them since July 16th. Now also I had nothing in hand for the Bible and Tract Fund; and as to the schools, there was not nearly enough to pay the weekly salaries to the teachers next Tuesday evening, when I received this evening 120l. for these objects.

Aug. 26. This morning I received still further from C. W. 20l. for home and foreign labourers.

Sept. 14. Day by day I am bringing before the Lord the necessities of the home and foreign labourers, whom I seek to help, especially as I found in what great need some brethren were, when a short time since they received the help which the Lord allowed me to send them. Now this afternoon I received from Norwich 5l. 6s. for missionary purposes, and also 2 rings, a cornelian necklace., an amber necklace, and a pair of amber bracelets.

Oct. 4. I have now been again praying much for many days for means for home and foreign labourers as well as for means for the other objects, having very little in hand, and having reason to believe that several of the brethren whom I seek to help are in great need. This evening I received from a brother, as the first fruits of his salary, a sovereign for home and foreign labourers. I take this as an earnest out of the hands of God that He will soon send me more.--Received also 5s.

Oct. S. This morning I received the following letter, at the very moment while I was on my knees, waiting still further upon the Lord for help for the various objects, and especially also for means for home and foreign labourers.

"* * * *, Oct. 3, 1847.

"Beloved Brother,

"The enclosed sum of 30l. is in my hands, and it does not appear that the Lord has need of it here, either for my own wants, or others under my notice. It seems likely that He may have need of it for the help of missionary labourers, who are depending on Himself. Would you kindly dispense it, as you may see good, to any who are labouring in the Word at home and abroad; or if you see other pressing need for it among the saints or for the Orphans, use it rather for them, &c."

I took the whole of this donation for these objects, as evidently coming in answer to prayer for them.

Oct. 12. The very great need of some of the dear brethren who labour in the Word, and whom I seek to assist, had led me again day by day to bring their cases before God. I also needed help for the School--, Bible and Tract Fund. Now this evening the Lord has once more helped me by a donation of 180l., of which I took 40l. for the Orphans, 100l. for home and foreign labourers and 40l. for the School, Bible and Tract Fund. How seasonable and how precious this help! How precious to me as the fruit of many prayers, and how seasonable to many who are in need, and who will be thus assisted! Moreover, I am just now in deep sorrow and great trial, the cause of which I will not mention here; and thus God Himself cheers and refreshes my heart, and tells me by this fresh precious and manifest answer to prayer, that He

FOURTH PART

is mindful of His poor unworthy servant, and of the work in which he is engaged. There came in five small donations besides today.

Dec. 30. When in the greatest need, so that I should not have been able to pay the weekly salaries of the teachers of the day schools next Tuesday, I received today from C. W. 10l., the disposal of which being left to me, I took half of it for the school fund and half for the Orphans.

Dec. 31. The year closes under the smiles of our Heavenly Father upon this work, in giving us another proof that He is indeed mindful of our need and attentive to our supplications. I received today 100l., to be used as most needed. I took of it 50l. for these objects and 50l. for the Orphans. I scarcely ever received a donation more seasonably; for there are only means enough for next week for the teachers, Bibles and tracts are needed, and I have been long waiting upon God for means for home and foreign labourers. But this donation only furnishes me with means for present necessities for the schools, and to order some tracts. As to ordering Bibles and sending help to foreign and home labourers, I must still further wait upon God.

Jan. 1, 1848. Today I received still further, for the benefit of the day schools, the sum of 10l.

Jan. 6. Only 1l. 5s. has come in since the first. This evening 120l. was given to me, of which the donor intends 20l. for home and foreign labourers. The other 100l. was left at my disposal. I took therefore of it 70l. for the Orphans, 10l. for the various schools, 10l. for the circulation of the Holy Scriptures, and 10l. for the circulation of tracts.

Feb. 10. There came in about 65l. more for missionary purposes during the month, of January, and today was given to me a donation of 100l., the disposal of which being left to me, I took half of it for these objects, and half for the Orphans, and thus I am able, after much waiting upon God for it, to send a little more help to brethren who labour in the Word.

April 13. This is only the second time, since May 26, 1846, that the means for these objects have been completely exhausted, though we have been two or three times besides brought very low in funds. The last money there was in hand was spent in paying the weekly salaries of the teachers the day before yesterday. There was therefore nothing for this purpose for next week, nor were there any means for the circulation of Bibles and tracts, and for aiding missionary efforts. Under these circumstances prayer and faith were again resorted to. For my universal remedy in need of any kind is, to make known my requests unto God, and then I seek to believe that God has heard me for His dear Son's sake, and I look out for answers to my petitions, and fully expect them. I had also particularly requested four brethren, masters of the boys' day schools, to help me with their prayers, as I should not be able to pay them their weekly salary, next week, except the Lord were pleased to send in means.-- Thus situated, I received this morning, as the fruit of many supplications, the sum of

90l., which was a great refreshment to my spirit. It being left to me to use this money as needed, I put 50l. of it to the funds for these objects, and 40l. to the Orphan-Fund. Thus we are once more helped, and my heart is encouraged more and more to trust in God.

April 29. One of the labourers gave 10l. for missionary purposes, whereby at least one of the most needy among the brethren who labour in the Word could be helped.--It has pleased God not to allow me, during the last five months, to have the honour of helping the dear brethren, who labour in the Word, to the same extent as the eighteen months before. I confess that I am not worthy to be used any longer by the Lord as a steward, to assist these His servants; still my heart craves after it, and still prays that God would count me worthy for His dear Son's sake to supply me with means for them, as I know they are in great need, and many of them, through particular circumstances, in far greater need than ever.

May 26, 1848. By the Lord's faithful love I have been enabled to meet all the heavy expenses connected with these objects during the last two years, amounting to nearly Two Thousand Six Hundred Pounds, and at the same time owe no one anything, and have a balance of 5l. 19s. 7 1/4 d. left in hand.

Supplies for the support of the Orphans, sent in answer to prayer, from May 26, 1846, to May, 26, 1848.

May 26, 1846. Scarcely ever had we so much in hand, and certainly not for the last eight years, when the accounts were closed, as at this time. This evening I received 100l. It being left to me to apply this sum as I felt led, and as it might be needed, I put half of it to the Orphan Fund, and the other half to the fund for the other objects.

June 4. Today I received 50l. for the Orphans together with 100l. for the other objects. This money came the instant after I had risen from my knees, to ask the Lord for more means, as, on account of needing about 75l. for the printing of the Report, 23l. for oatmeal, 19l. for fittings, 25l. for rent, and 26l. for the sisters who labour in the Orphan-Houses (which sums are shortly to be paid), we shall soon again need more.

Jan. 20, 1847. For the whole of this period since May 26, 1846, therefore nearly eight months, when the accounts were closed, we have had always an abundance of means, and for the greater part of the time about 200l. in hand. The sum of One Thousand Sixty-Five Pounds has come in for the Orphans in less than eight months, to which is to be added the balance of 85l. 4s. 9 3/4 d. in hand when the accounts were closed. Invariably I have thus been able to give to the Matrons of the four Orphan-Houses the money in advance, which was required for the necessities of one week. But now, after having paid away last evening 45l. 5s. for the house-

FOURTH PART

keeping of a week in advance and for other expenses, the money which remains in hand is needed for rent, and oatmeal, which has been ordered from Scotland. This morning therefore I gave myself particularly to prayer with regard to means for present use for the Orphans. How blessed to have the living God to go to! Particularly precious to know Him in these days of widespread distress! Potatoes are too dear for food for the Orphans at this time. The rice, which we have substituted instead of them, is twice as dear as usual; the oatmeal more than twice as dear; and the bread one-half dearer than usual. But the riches of God are as great as ever. He knows that our expenses are great. He knows that a little will not do in these days, when provisions are so dear, as there are about 150 persons to be provided for, including teachers and apprentices. My soul is at peace. -- Evening. About noon I received from a pious physician the following note, with a check for 5l.

"My dear sir, I send you something towards buying bread for the Orphans. The dearness of food must be felt by many; but the Lord in judgment is nevertheless gracious He will sustain. I am your sincere friend and well-wisher.

"* * * *"

From Maidenhead I received still further this evening 5s.

Jan. 21. Having had to pay out this morning 5l. 2s. 6d. for oatmeal for present use, before the arrival of the larger quantity of a ton and a half ordered from Scotland, there was again only 2s. 6d. left of the money which had come in yesterday. About 1 o'clock this afternoon I received 1l. through a Christian lady of Bristol from "a poor gardener." There came in also-still further 1s. by sale of Reports and 1l. 2s. 6d. from London.

Jan. 22. A brother from Devonshire came here on business, to obtain some money which was owed to him. He did not obtain it; but God used him as an instrument to bring me some money, for he gave me 10s. for the Orphans. There came in still further by sale of trinkets and old silver 12l. 8s. 5d.

Jan. 23. By sale of books and some music 2l. 10s.

Jan. 24. Profits from the sale of ladies' bags 1l.--During this period also two sisters kindly made some ladies' bags and baskets, and gave the profits arising from the sale for the benefit of the Orphans.

On the 25th and 26th came in still further 2l. 4s. 1 3/4 d., so that, when in the evening of the 26th at our usual weekly meeting for prayer and conference I met with the brethren and sisters, who labour in the various day schools and Orphan-Houses (then seventeen in number), I was again able, by means of the 26l. 1s. 0 3/4 d., which the Lord had sent in during the week, to give to the four matrons of the Orphan-Houses all the needful supplies for the coming week. That which remained was put by towards the rent of the houses. Our prayer now was, that the Lord would be pleased again to send in fresh supplies, that we might have at the next meeting all that might be needed for the week after.

Feb. 2, Tuesday. When we met this evening for prayer and conference, it was found, that, whilst there had been nothing left in hand after our meeting this day week (except money put by for oatmeal and rent), there had come in altogether during the week 29l. 18s. 18 1/2 d. The way in which the Lord supplied us with those means was as follows: On the 26th and 27th I received 10s., and 10s. as profits from the sale of ladies' bags. On the 27th from London 3l., and also 5s. From C. C. 2l. From Braunton a purse with 6s. From Barnstaple 1l. On the 28th anonymously from London, from J. W. A., 5l. with these words: "From the giver of all, through one of His stewards." On the 29th from Sodbury 2s. 6d. On the 30th from Droitwich 5s. 6d. Also anonymously by post 5s. worth of postages with these words: "A sip of milk and a crust of bread for a poor Orphan." Also from C. C. 10s. On the 31st an old shilling and sixpence, a small silver pencil case, and a pair of small ear-drops.-- Feb. 1. Before breakfast I took a direction in my usual morning's walk, in which I had not been for many weeks, feeling drawn in that direction, just as if God had an intention in leading me in that way. Returning home I met a Christian gentleman whom formerly I used to meet almost every morning, but whom I had not met for many weeks, because I had not been walking in that direction. He stopped me and gave me 2l. for the Orphans. Then I knew why I bad been led thus; for there is not yet enough in hand, to supply the matrons tomorrow evening with the necessary means for housekeeping during another week.--There came in still further today for needlework done by the Orphans 1l. 17s. 7d. Also 4s. 5d., the contents of an Orphan box.--On Feb. 2nd came in 2l. 5s. 11d., by sale of a Report 4d., and by sale of stockings 9s. 3d.--On Jan. 30th a box came from London. It contained 4 brooches, a gold chain, 2 pairs of earrings, 2 gold watch hooks, a locket, a ring, 2 parts of gold chains, a rich silk dress, a silk cloak, a glass bottle, some music, 39 books, 18 knitted doilies, and a pair of knitting pins. Some of these articles were today, Feb. 2, sold for 8l. 2s. 3d.-- There came in further by the sale of articles and Reports, 4s. 1d., by the boxes in the Orphan-Houses and at my house 1l. 2s., and anonymously was sent 5s. worth of postages. Here then, dear reader, you have a specimen how the Lord does week after week supply us--I said 29l. 18s. 10 1/2 d. had come in during the week. As, however, I was informed that the arrival of the oatmeal from Scotland had been announced, and that it was much dearer than I had expected, i.e. nearly three times as dear as formerly, I found that there had not been sufficient money put by, and took therefore in the first place what was yet needed for that. In consequence of this I had only 10l. 14s. left for housekeeping, which I divided among the matrons, being fully assured that the Lord would again send in means, before that was spent. I went home in great peace, though all the money I possessed for present use for the Orphans was only three half-farthings.

Feb. 4. Yesterday nothing had come in. This morning, just before I was going to give myself to prayer about the Orphans, a sister in the Lord sent a sovereign, winch she had received, as she writes, "From a friend who had met the Orphan Boys,

FOURTH PART

and was particularly pleased with their neat and orderly appearance." After having received this 1l., I prayed for means for present use, though not confining my prayers to that. About a quarter of an hour after I had risen from my knees, I received a letter, with an order for 5l. The donor writes, that it is "the proceeds of a strip of land, sold to the railway company." What various means does the Lord employ to send us help, in answer to our prayers!-- About half an hour after having received this 5l., there was sent 10s., being the profits from the sale of ladies' bags. This evening was received still further, by the sale of some trinkets, 1l. 18s. Thus I am able to send all the remainder of the money, which is yet needed for housekeeping up to Tuesday, Feb. 9th.

The Lord's holy name be praised for this fresh precious help!

Feb. 5. 1l. 4s. 10d. has come in today.

Feb. 7. Lord's day. Yesterday nothing had come in. In two days again about 20l. will be needed for housekeeping, and there was only about the tenth part in hand. But I was not in the least disturbed about this. There are also new clothes to be found for the 32 Orphans in the Boys' Orphan-House, which likewise will cost many pounds. That expense also, I believed, God would help me to meet. Now observe the Lord's kindness! On returning this morning from the meeting, I found the following letter containing 50l.

"* * * *, Feb. 6, 1847.

"Beloved Brother,

"Having been led, during the past year, to see the unscripturalness of life insurance, which I had been carrying on for some years previously, I now enclose you the sum which I received from the office, on returning to them my policy, viz. 22l. 8s., and the payment due about this time, eleven guineas, as a thank-offering to the Lord for having, chiefly by means of the work in which you are engaged in Bristol, opened my eyes in some little measure to His will with regard to His pilgrim people here. I ask your prayers on my behalf, dearest brother, amongst the many who must be on your heart, for singleness of eye, to walk with God by faith, that 'the whole body may be full of light,' and that I may not be permitted to darken the little light I have, by serving any other master.

I add also ten pounds, which you will kindly apply to the help of those who are labouring in the Gospel abroad, or if more urgent, at home. Also will you oblige me by accepting six pounds for your own use.

Of several Reports (which you sent me for distribution) I have received payment for three, for which I enclose one shilling. The first items please apply for the use of the Orphan-Houses, as you may see best." &c.

Thus the Lord has given by one donation 34l. for the Orphans.--I have also in this another answer, in receiving 10l. for missionary brethren, for whom I had of late been especially seeking help from the Lord.-- This evening I received still further from C. C. 1l. 10s. 0 1/2 d.

Feb. 9. There was received today by sale of articles 3l. 9s. 8d. When I met again this evening with my fellow-labourers for prayer and conference at one of the Orphan-Houses, it was found that 48l. 12s. 6 1/2 d. had come in for present use for the Orphans during the past week, which commenced with three half-farthings in my hands; so that there was enough for all the expenses connected with the house-keeping of the coming week, and the rest was put by for the rent, the apprentices, and the boys' clothes; and as to the necessities of this day week, when again fresh supplies will need to be given to the matrons, I am looking to the Lord.

Feb. 10. This evening we hare received already a little towards the expenses of the coming week. A brother gave me 10l., of which 5l. are for the poor Irish and 5l. for the Orphans. Also 7s. 1d. from the Orphan-box of a sister.

Feb. 11. Anonymously 2s. 6d. From Nottingham 1l. 15s.

Feb. 12. Anonymously, from a lady, 2l. to buy coals for the four Orphan-houses.

Feb. 13. Anonymously from Islington a half-sovereign. By sale of Reports 8d.

Feb. 14. Through a sister 5s., from C. C. 8s. 3d., and anonymously 2s. 6d.

Feb. 15. From a Scotch sister 1l., by sale of stockings, Reports, and articles 7l. 0s. 4d., from an Orphan- box 3s. O 1/2 d., from Nice 1l., anonymously 10s., from Cork 5s. 2d., and several shillings besides in small donations, &c.--Thus there had come in again by this Tuesday evening, Feb. 16th, 21l. 4s. 2d. during the past week. As, however, I had to put by some money for the boys' clothes and rent, I could only leave 12l. 4s. with the matrons, quite sufficient for a few days; and my hope in God is, that He will send more, before this is gone.

Feb. 17. From the neighbourhood of Bridgewater 10s. 6d., and 1s. 1d. came in besides. On the 18th came in 1l. more.

Feb. 19. This morning I gave myself again to prayer, importuning the Lord that He would be pleased to send more means, as so little had come in during the last two days. Almost immediately, after rising from my knees, I received from Doncaster 3l. 3s. At the same tune I received from Bromyard 5s., and 4s. from Aberystwith. About an hour later came from a sister in the neighbourhood of Wotton-under-Edge 12s. 6d., a lady's bag, and a knitted bread-basket cloth. Thus, with

FOURTH PART

the 12l. 4s. already given to the matrons, we are supplied till next Tuesday evening, the 23rd of February.

Feb. 20. Today came in from the neighbourhood of Castle Cary 10s., by sale of Reports 2l. 6d., and by sale of articles 10s. 6d. Also anonymously a parcel from Tetbury, containing 2 shillings, a gold coin, a silver coin, 2 copper coins, a brass coin, 4 gilt brooches, 2 silver brooches, 3 gold brooches, 5 collars, a waistcoat, a pair of boots, 2 cloaks, and a shawl.

Feb. 21. From C. C. 14s., and 5l. with these words: "Your Heavenly Father knoweth that ye have need of these things," and Philip iv. 19. How true! My Heavenly Father knew that we had need of this, and therefore put it into the heart of this donor to give this 5l. for in two days we shall again require many pounds more than I had this morning. Also how truly is again fulfilled in my experience at this time Philip iv. 19.

Feb. 22. From Westmoreland a half sovereign and 1s. in postages.

Feb. 23. Anonymously a half sovereign. By sale of articles and Reports 3l. 16s. 0 1/2 d., and through an Orphan-box in my house 2s. A lady who met the Orphans today in the fields, gave to one of the girls 2s. Evening. Tuesday. By what the Lord has been pleased to send in during the past week, I have enough to supply the matrons with all which is needed during the coming week and 14s. left.

Feb. 24. From a poor brother 6s.; the produce of an Orphan-box 1s. 7 1/2 d. and a shilling bank token.--Feb. 26. From Bath 2s. 6d., and from Droitwich 9s. 4d.

Feb. 27. Saturday evening. Only these few shillings have come in since Tuesday evening, so that, having had to pay away several small sums besides the housekeeping expenses, since Tuesday, nothing is in hand towards supplying the matrons with housekeeping money next Tuesday.-- Received this evening from C. C. 5l., 6s. 6d. and anonymously from Totness 1s. 6d. worth of postages.

Feb. 28. Today came in still further from the Hot-wells 3s. 6d., and 10l. as the profits of shares which the donor has in a certain concern. How kind of the Lord to help us thus so seasonably in our poverty!

March 1. By work and knitting of the Orphans 1l. 4s. 8d. and from E. N. 10s.

March 2. By sale of articles 8l. 10s. 6d., and by sale of a Report 4d. From H. C. as "A thank-offering to the Lord" 1l. From Manchester 1l. From London 13s. From Staffordshire 1s.--Thus by this evening the Lord has again sent in during the past week 29l. 8s. 11 1/2 d., whereby I had enough to advance the house-keeping expenses to the matrons of the four Orphan-Houses for the coming week, and to meet some other expenses.

March 3. Received 6s. 7d.--March 4. 1l. from the neighbourhood of Stroud, as "a thank-offering to God for partial recovery from sickness."--Also from Bath 5l.--A gentleman gave anonymously to the governess of the Infant Orphans 2l.--I also received the following letter today: "Dear Sir, When my dear brother John died, he had one shilling and fourpence halfpenny owing to him which he intended for the Orphans. As I received it today, I now send it to you. He said 'Jesus will never forsake the Orphans.' M. W." The paper contained 1s. 7 3/4 d. and a quarter of a gilder. This legacy came from a dear boy who I hear died in the faith.--March 5. From Clevedon 2s. 6d.--March 6. The proceeds of an Orphan-box 7s. 1d.

March 7. Only 8l. 17s. 9 3/4 d. had come in since the 2nd, and the day after tomorrow fresh supplies will need to be given to the matrons for house-keeping, Under these circumstances I received this morning 150l., of which the donor intends 100l. for labourers in the Lord's vineyard at home and abroad, and 50l. for other work in my hands. Of this 50l. I took 25l. for the Orphans, and 25l. for the School--Bible--and Tract Fund. Thus we are helped afresh.--There came in besides from C. C. 6s., from a lady 1l., and anonymously 1s. 4d.

March 8. This morning I received still further from Falmouth a bank order for 4l. from a brother "As a thank-offering to the Lord for bringing him safely back to his native land;" 2l. of this amount is for the Orphans, 1l. for Brother Craik, and 1l. for my own personal necessities. Also 10s. from an Orphan-box, and 10s. from a sister.

March 6. By sale of articles and Reports 4l. 13s. 2d., from a poor brother 6d., and through the boxes in my house 1l. 1s. 6d.--This evening, Tuesday, I find that since last Tuesday evening again 44l. 1s. 6 3/4 d. has come in. Thus I have the means to meet all the house-keeping expenses during the coming week, and something will be left to put by towards the rent, the current expenses for the apprentices, &c. How good is the Lord in helping us week after week through the heavy expenses, especially in this season of deep distress and dearness of provisions! To His praise I can say, we have lacked nothing all this winter.

Whilst preparing these extracts from my journal for the press, I remember to have heard the following remarks made with reference to the time about which I am just now writing, namely the season of dearth during the winter of 1846-7: "I wonder how it is now with the Orphans? If Mr. Miller is now able to provide for them as he has, we will say nothing." When I heard such remarks, I said nothing except this: "We lack nothing:" or, "God helps us." Should this fall into the hands of any who have had such thoughts, let them remember that it is the very time for faith to work, when sight ceases. The greater the difficulties, the easier for faith. As long as there remain certain natural prospects, faith does not get on even as easily (if I may say so), as when all natural prospects fail. It is true that during the time of the dearth our expenses were considerably greater than usual it is also true that many persons, who otherwise might have given, were unable to do so, or had their surplus directed into other channels, such as Ireland, &c.; but the gold and silver are the Lord's. To Him

FOURTH PART

we made our prayer. In Him we put our trust. And He did not forsake us.' For we went as easily through that winter as through any winter since the work had been in existence. Nor could it be otherwise; for God had at this very time an especial opportunity of showing the blessedness of trusting in Him. Seek, dear reader, more and more to put your trust in Him for everything, and you will even concerning this life find it most precious so to do.

March 10. I was able, last evening, to meet most comfortably all the expenses for the coming week; yet we had then nothing left, as I put by the rest of the money, that we might not get into debt with regard to the rent, the expenses of the apprentices, &c. When now there was again nothing left for future house-keeping expenses, a Christian lady at a considerable distance informed me by this mornings post, that she has paid into the hands of Messrs. Stuckey and Co. of Bristol, my bankers, the sum of 100l. for my use, for the benefit of the Orphans. By the same post I have received also 10s. from Droitwich. The Lord's holy name be praised for this seasonable help! I have now all the rent for next quarter day, am able to purchase two pieces of calico which were needed, a fresh supply of rice and soap, and to meet other heavy expenses in the way of certain alterations and improvements to be made in the four houses, about which I had repeatedly asked the Lord.

May 1. From March 10th up to this day came in the sum of 132l. 10s. 5 3/4 d. Before the means in hand were expended, the Lord always gave a fresh supply. This evening, Saturday May 1st, I gave myself especially to prayer for means, as we were now again very poor, there being no means to meet the house-keeping expenses on next Tuesday evening, when fresh supplies are to be given to the matrons. About half an hour, after I had risen from my knees, I received from a Friend to the Institution a letter, containing 10l. Of this sum 8s. 5d. is from twenty poor Orphans under his care, who, having read one of my Reports, desired him to send to the Orphans in Bristol their little donations, each having contributed from 2d. to 8d., 5s. 6d. is from an aged Christian, 10s. from a servant of the donor, and 8l. 16s. 1d. from himself, to makeup the 10l.

May 2. There came in still further from C. C. 1l., from a Christian lady 10s., from a Christian servant 5s., and anonymously 10s.

May 4. Today was received for articles and Reports 1l. 16s. 1d., and through the boxes at the Orphan-Houses 16s. 8 1/2 d. Thus I was able this evening, by what had come in since Saturday evening, May 1, to meet the house-keeping expenses of the coming week.

May 11. Another week is gone by. This evening also I have been able to meet all the expenses connected with house-keeping during the coming week, through what has come in since May 4th, but at the same time there is nothing left. Hitherto the children have lacked nothing. Never were provisions nearly so dear since the commencement of the work, as they are now. The bread is almost twice as much as eighteen months ago, the oatmeal nearly three times as much as formerly, the rice more than double the usual price, and no potatoes can be used, on account of their exceeding high price. But though I have now returned from the Orphan-Houses, without any means being left in my hands for further supplies, yet my heart is in peace, in great peace, being sure that the Lord will help.

May 12. The Lord is beginning to help already. This evening I have received 4l. from Scarborough.

May 13. This morning I received 6s. from the neighbourhood of Bideford. This afternoon was given to me 50l., being left to my disposal, as it might be most needed. Being so exceedingly poor as to means for the Orphans, and having heavy expenses to meet, I put this 50l. to the Orphan-Fund for present use. Thus I am able to order oatmeal from Scotland, which is nearly out, put by money for the rent, pay for medical attendance for the children, &c. How good is the Lord, in helping us so seasonably in this time of great dearness of provisions! -- There came in still further today 5s.--On May 14th from O. 1s., "through walking a short distance instead of riding."--On May 16th from C. C. 13s. 1d. From O. 3s. being "the first fruits of increase of wages." From the Isle of Wight 17s. 9d., from Hayle 2l., from Plymouth 15s.--On May 17th from a Christian lady 5s., from E. A. B. 13s. 6d., and from C. B. 13s. 10 1/2 d.--On May 18th by sale of articles and Reports 2l. 6s. 4d. Though thus since last Tuesday evening, May 11th, about 63l. has come in, yet as there have been heavy extra expenses to meet in the course of the week, besides the usual amount required for housekeeping for the coming week, and as I need to put by about 20l. for oatmeal which has been ordered from Scotland, we are again without anything in hand.

May 19. This morning the Lord has again begun to send in a little. I received from Bath 1l., and from a Colonel in the Presidency of Madras 2l.--May 20th. From Worcester 1l., and from a sick little boy 6d.--May 23rd. From C. C. 5l. 2s. 4d. Also a stranger called at the infant Orphan-House, bought books to the amount of 8s. 1d., and gave a sovereign for them.

May 24. By sale of articles came in 3l. 10s. 2d.

May 25. From Shirehampton 2s.

The boxes in the Orphan-Houses contained 1l. 10s 1d. Also an individual from Taunton gave 10s. Lastly there came in by sale of Reports 6d. and from M. W. 6d.--Thus the Lord has again sent in since last Tuesday evening about 161l. This, however, not being nearly enough to meet the house-keeping expenses of the coming week, I could only give a part of what was needed, hoping in God to give me more, before that which is in the hands of the matrons shall have been spent.

May 26. A lady gave 10s.--May 27th. By sale of books, given for the purpose, came in 1l. 11s. 6d., and through an Orphan-box 8s. 6d. This 2l. 10s. received yesterday and today I sent off to the Orphan-Houses.

FOURTH PART

May 28. By sale of Reports 1s., the proceeds of an Orphan-box at Street 2s., from Guernsey 1l.--May 29th. The 1l. 3s., which came in yesterday, was enough for today, Saturday; for only the addition of 1l. was required to help us till Monday morning, and therefore the Lord had sent 3s. more than was needed. Evening. There has come in this day still further 1l. 9s. 7d. by sale of some little trinkets, almost all of which had been given some time since, and which now our poverty led me to pack up and send out for sale. This money likewise was divided among the matrons.

May 30. Lord's day morning. I have just now received, in this our great need, when there was not sufficient in hand to meet the necessities of tomorrow, 6l. 6s. from a Christian gentleman of title at Zurich in Switzerland, a distance of about one thousand miles. What a most seasonable help! Thus I am able to send all the remainder of the supplies, which are needed till Tuesday evening.

In these days of straitness, the question would naturally arise, If, when you have only to care for 130 Orphans, you are so poor, what will you do when there are 300, for whom you are just on the point of building a house? And further, Is it not an indication not to increase the work, seeing you are now so poor with only about one-third of the number of Orphans which you purpose to receive into the New Orphan-House?--I am not tried, however, with such thoughts; for I know that 1, Only for the trial of my faith, as heretofore the Lord allows me now again to be poor. Never at any time have the expenses been so great for the work, as from May 26, 1846, to May 26, 1847; but also never has so much come in in the same space of time during any other period of this work. 2, It is for the profit of the church at large, that we have now again to pass through these days of poverty. 3, I know that it is as easy for the Lord to supply us with all the means that the work will require when once the New Orphan-House is opened, as it is for Him to give us what we need now, though the expenses in all likelihood will then be Two Thousand Five Hundred Pounds a year more than they are at present.

Evening: Received 10s. more anonymously.

June 1. Tuesday, 8l. 9s. 0 1/2 d. more has come in since May 30th, of which, however, only 4l. 9s. 7 1/2 d. remained for house-keeping expenses, during the coming week. This was all I could leave with the matrons, hoping in God to send in more before this is gone.

June 2. This morning I received the following anonymous note from Teignmouth, enclosing two halfsovereigns.

"My dear Brother,

I send you with much pleasure the enclosed trifle, to be disposed of as you judge to be best. Also this precious text, "Only believe," once spoken by the lips of our blessed glorified Head, now above.

Ever yours in Him."

Thus the Lord has already sent me a little help towards what may be needed tomorrow. His name be praised! How true that word: "Only believe."--Evening. This afternoon the Lord has shown afresh in my experience the truth of that word: "Only believe." I received a letter containing 40l., of which 10l. are for Brother Craik and myself, 10l. for Home and Foreign labourers, and 20l. for present use for the Orphans. Thus I am enabled to send the money required for house-keeping for this week, till Tuesday the 8th. Oh, how kind of the Lord to help us again and again!

June 8. There was only about 6l. in hand towards the house-keeping expenses of the coming week, as comparatively little had come in since June 2. In addition to the house-keeping, other expenses needed to be met. Under these circumstances 50l. was given to me this morning to be laid out as most needed, which I took for the support of the Orphans. Thus we are again helped for the present moment.

June 17. Only 12l.16s. 0 1/2 d. has come in during the last 9 days. After having advanced on the 15th the money for one week's house-keeping expenses, and paid also 13l. 10s. for apprentices, all our money was again expended, except that which had been put by for rent and oatmeal, which has been ordered. When we were thus once more quite poor, I received today from a Christian gentleman at Edinburgh, whom God has repeatedly used to help us in times of need, a bank-order for 35l. Of this amount 5l. had been given to him by a lady for the Orphans, 25l. were from himself for the Orphans, and 5l. he kindly intended for my own personal necessities. Oh, how precious thus continually to see the hand of God stretched out on our behalf! Will you not, dear reader, taste and see that the Lord is good, and that it is a blessed thing to put our trust in Him? Whatever your position in life, though you may not be called by the Lord to establish Orphan-Houses and Day-Schools for poor children, or to trust in Him for means for circulating Tracts and Copies of His Holy Word; yet all children of God, whatever their position in the world or in the church, ought to put their trust in God for every thing connected with their body, their soul, their business, their family, their church position, their service for God, &c. And it is impossible to do so, without enjoying the blessedness which results from it, even first that peace which keeps the heart and mind like a garrison, and secondly true liberty with regard to circumstances, times, places and persons.

June 29. Tuesday Evening. Having had nearly 50l. coming in since this day fortnight, I have had the means of meeting all the expenses of these two weeks; but now having paid out what was required for house-keeping for the coming week, all is again gone.

June 30. This morning when, as stated, there was again nothing in hand, I received from Devonshire 20l. for the Orphans.

FOURTH PART

July 1. This morning I received still further from a Bristol donor 10l., and 5l. from M.R. These three donations of yesterday and today came in most seasonably, not only because they came when there was nothing in hand, but also because the Lord willing, I am on the point of leaving Bristol for a few weeks, and am thus able to leave some money behind.

I was absent from Bristol from July 1st to August 2nd. During this time 133l. 11s. 4 1/2 d. was received, and the sums came in so seasonably, that there was not ally difficulty at all experienced with regard to means, because there was always a sufficient amount of money in hand, to furnish the house-keeping expenses each week in advance, besides meeting all other current expenses. At the same time I might say that almost every one of the donations came in most seasonably to help us on, if not from day to day, at least from week to week; and if it were not on account of its taking up too much space, I should mention every one of the donations which form the total amount referred to, but I shall only refer to the following.

July 13. The proceeds of an Orphan-box from Stafford 4l. 7s. 6d. The friend who sent the money wished to know whether it arrived in a time of need. I have had many similar requests, to which I can reply nothing, or say at the most that the answer may be learnt from the next Report. It will be easily perceived, on reflection, that if I said, it came seasonably, that would imply we had little or nothing at all in hand, and what would that again mean but this, "As our expenses are so great, that which you have now sent will be soon gone again, and therefore send us some more, or get some friend to help us." But by this very thing the chief object of this work, "To show how blessed it is to deal with God alone, and how blessed to trust in Him in the darkest moments," would be hindered. It is also for this very reason that I do not publish the accounts very frequently, for instance quarterly, as I have been requested to do; but I am delighted to wait a year, or eighteen months, or two years, or more; and even then I do not publish them for the sake of obtaining money (though unquestionably God has used the Reports as instruments to procure us means), but for the benefit of the Church of God, to refresh, encourage, exhort, and instruct my brethren in Christ; and also because it is needful that from time to time. I should give a public account of the way in which the considerable sums, with which I have been intrusted, have been spent.

Of the donations which came in between Aug. 2nd and 14th (in amount 51l. 16s. 3 1/2 d.), I only refer to the following.--Aug. 9th. A brother, being some time ago, through a particular circumstance, in danger of losing all his property, dedicated to the Lord 50l., if He would be pleased to help him out of the difficulty. Now today I received from that brother, with his explanation of this, 10l. for the Orphans and 5l. for my own personal necessities, being a part of that 50l., as the Lord, in answer to prayer, has delivered him out of the danger.

Aug. 14. Saturday evening. This evening I found that there was only as much money in hand for present use for the Orphans (i.e. 44l.), as there were liabilities upon me for rent, &c. On this account I gave myself particularly to prayer for means for house-keeping expenses, as on Tuesday evening I shall have to give fresh supplies to the matrons. About one hour, after I had risen from my knees, two sovereigns were given to me, which a sister had brought from Ilfracombe.

Aug. 15. Today came in further, from Barnstaple. 5s., anonymously 5l., from C. C. 5s. 4d., from a sister in Bristol 1l., from Clifton 4s., and anonymously 2s. 6d. and 3s. 6d.--Thus the Lord has been pleased to give me already, within twenty-four hours, after I had sought more especially His help for means, the sum of 9l. 0s. 4d. My eyes are now looking to Him for more.

Aug. 16. By sale of articles came in 1l. 10s. 10d.

Aug. 17. Tuesday evening. No more having come in, I have not been able to give to the matrons the housekeeping expenses for the whole week; I hope, however, that the Lord will send more before all is expended which I was able to give, and which will last about three or four days.

Aug. 18. This morning I received from Droitwich a half sovereign, and from Yorkshire 3l. Thus the Lord has already given 3l. 10s.--There was also left at my house this afternoon, anonymously, a pair of silver spectacles; and at the Girls' Orphan-House. No. II were left 3 rings, a brooch, and a pair of ear-rings.--There was also given 2s. 6d.

Aug. 21. Today more money was needed for housekeeping; but having receive nothing yesterday, and having sent off what had come in on the 18th, I gave myself to prayer. And now see the precious answer. By the first delivery this morning a letter came from Birmingham, signed W. R., which contained a half-sovereign, of which the anonymous donor wished 7s. 6d. to be used for the Orphans, and 2s. 6d. for Missions. I also received through two Orphan-boxes 7s. 8d. There came also to hand, three small parcels from Plymouth, one of which contained an old silver watch for the benefit of the Orphans, from a blind Orphan; the other contained two shillings and a franc piece; the third a pair of ear-rings, a brooch, a fourpenny piece, half a franc piece, and an old sixpence.-- About half an hour, after I had received these three little parcels, a gentleman, who did not give his name, left at my house two sovereigns and one shilling. About half an hour after that, a lady called and wished to put some money into the box at my house. I do not know her name. But God knows her, and influenced her in answer to my supplications. May His blessing rest upon her and the unknown gentleman who left the 2l. 1s.! When the box was opened, it contained a paper with half a sovereign. Thus the Lord so kindly in this remarkable manner has helped us in this our time of need, and we have now again all we need for the present.

Evening. Still further help. About two o'clock this afternoon a lady from London, who about a year ago had read the Narrative of the Lord's dealings with me, in passing through Bristol left a sovereign at my house for the Orphans, feeling that she could not go on without doing so.--This evening also I received a letter from Scar-

FOURTH PART

borough with five pounds. Also 1l. came in by sale of articles this evening, and 2s. 6d. as a donation.

Aug. 22. I have received still further today from C. C. 2l. 3s. 3d., from Wolverhampton 10s., and from a brother in Bristol 1l. 1s. Thus altogether 14l. 5s. 3d. has come in during these two days.

All, who have spiritual eyes to see, cannot but observe in reading these facts--1st, the reality of dealing with God Himself directly; 2, the blessedness of trusting in Him; and 3, His most particular providence.

Aug. 23. I prayed still further for means, as I shall need to give a fresh supply to the matrons for house-keeping tomorrow evening, besides meeting other expenses. This afternoon I received from a sister in the Lord a sovereign, half of which she wished me to use for my own temporal necessities, and half for the Orphans. Likewise. 10s. as profits from the sale of ladies' baskets.

Aug. 24. Today came in by sale of articles and Reports 2l. 15s. 10 1/2 d.

Aug. 25. Wednesday. Last evening I was able to advance only a part of the week's house-keeping expenses to the matrons. Today, when I had nothing in hand, a sister in the Lord brought her Orphan-box, which contained 10s. 6 3/4 d. in donations, and likewise 9s. 4d. as the proceeds from the sale of musk plants, reared and sold by her for the benefit of the Orphans. The box contained also a Spanish silver coin. Evening. Precious and encouraging as it was to receive those little sums this afternoon, still, as they came in when no money was in hand, they were only an encouragement to look to the Lord for further supplies, but were not enough to supply our need. However the Lord, in His faithful, loving care over the work, and in His readiness to answer prayer, helped further this evening. There came in 150l., of which I took 30l. for the Orphans, and 120l. for the other objects.

Sept. 6. Since August 25th only 20l. 17s. 0 1/2 d. had come in. On this account there was only 3l. 15s. 5 3/4 d. in hand, and tomorrow evening I have again to supply the matrons with house-keeping expenses. In this need, whilst walking in my little garden, I lifted up my heart to God for means, when, in less than five minutes after, I received a letter from Jersey, containing Five Pounds for the Orphans.--This evening I received still further, from a little girl 3s., from Margate. 10d., anonymously 3s., and 3 dollars from a poor missionary brother in Demerara.

Sept. 7. Further, by sale of articles 3l. 1s. 3d. through the boxes in my house 2s. 6d., and through the boxes in the Orphan-houses, which our need led me to open, 1l. 6s. and a medal. Thus I had for the need of the coming week, at our usual prayer meeting this evening, 14l. 1s. 6 3/4 d., which I divided to the last farthing, with the firm persuasion and hope in God, that, by the time it was expended, He would give more; for it was not enough to meet all the demands of this week.

Sept. 8. the Lord has already sent in a little I received from Weymouth 2l. 10s.

Sept. 10. From a dentist in Bristol 10s.

Sept. 11. From a Christian brother, about 200 miles from Bristol, whom the Lord has repeatedly used to help us in time of need, I received 20l. What a precious help! We have now all we require for this week, and a little towards the expenses of the next.--There came in also from Droitwich 5s.

Sept. 12. Further: From C.C. 10s. 14d., from Clevedon 5s., from Clifton 5s., anonymously 2s., ditto 1s. 5 1/2 d.

Sept. 13. Monday morning. As there will be again money needed for housekeeping tomorrow evening, and as I have not enough in hand to advance for the expenses of a whole week, which I generally now seek to do, I gave myself again to prayer for means, and, while I was on my knees in prayer, there came a letter from Yorkshire, containing 5l. for the Orphans. There was received also, by sale of stockings at the Boys' Orphan-house, 7s. 7d.

Sept. 14. By sale of articles and stockings came in 3l. 10s. 0 1/2 d. From Norwich 1l., and also 2s. 6d. Evening. By these sums we have received altogether since last Tuesday evening 34l. 8s. 5 1/2 d. Thus I have been able to supply the matrons this evening with what they need for the coming week, and that which was left I put by for the rent and current expenses connected with the apprentices, and am now looking out for fresh supplies, as I have again nothing left towards the need of the following week.

My dear reader, if you are tired of going on with this account of the Lord's gracious interpositions for us week after week, or day after day, I beseech you to lay it aside for the present. Take it up at another time. This Narrative is not of an ordinary character. It does not contain anecdotes for amusement; it relates no embellished tales; it gives facts in which the hand of God is seen stretched out on our behalf, as the result of prayer and faith. Seek to admire God, dear reader, in this simple Narrative of Facts, which are related to His praise, and to allure your heart more and more for Him, and which are brought before you in all simplicity to encourage you and to stir you up, if it may please God so to use His servant, to put your whole trust in Him. I judge that it will be the more profitable way to read this account by little and little.

Sept. 15. A brother, who is staying at my house, gave me a silver table spoon and two silver dessert spoons. This is the beginning of fresh supplies from God.

Sept. 16. From the neighbourhood of Glastonbury 5s. Also 5s. worth of postages from Derby.

FOURTH PART

Sept. 17. A. Christian lady at Richmond, having received a copy of my Narrative, read aloud in the hearing of another lady the account about A. L. (page 156 to 160 of part I.) The lady who heard it read was so touched by it, that she sent 10l. for the Orphans. God moved her heart to send me this donation at a time when I had only a few shillings in hand for the use of the Orphans!--There came in still further from Clifton 10s., and from Taunton 5s.

Sept. 19. From C. C. 19s.--Sept. 21. Anonymously from Barnstaple 5s. worth of postages. This anonymous donor has many times sent his donations thus. It may be that twenty or thirty times the same amount has been forwarded in the same way.--Also by sale of articles 1l. 8s. 8d. By the boxes in my house 1l. 0s. 6d. Evening: I was able to supply the matrons only with means for house-keeping for three or four days, being fully assured, that, by the time more is needed, the Lord will send further supplies.

Sept. 24. Friday. After I had paid away on Tuesday evening to the last penny what I had in hand for present use for the Orphans, there came in a pair of ear-rings from Norwich; also 1s. 6d. besides. On Wednesday and Thursday nothing came in; but it was needful that I should send more means to the matrons today. Thus situated I received this morning from Barnstaple. 19s. 4d. and 17s. About three hours after, came in by sale of the 3 silver spoons (given on the 15th), an old silver punch ladle, and a few trinkets lately given, 6l. 14s. 7d. Thus we are once more helped, and I have been able to send all that which was yet needed for house-keeping till Tuesday evening. The Lord be praised for His seasonable help! --Observe, dear reader, we may be poor, very poor; we may have to wait upon God, even again and again we may have to make known our requests to Him; but He helps, always helps.

Sept. 25. From C. C. 1l.--Sept. 27. From a Christian lady 1l.-- Sept. 28. 8s. 4d. came in, also 1l. from Scotland, and 1l. 6s. 4 1/2 d. by sale of articles. Also from Wellington an old half-crown, shilling, and sixpence. 3s. 10d. came in besides. Evening. So little having come in, I was able to give to the matrons only as much as would last for about two days for provisions.

Sept. 29. A young man called this morning at my house and gave 2s. 6d. A brother called and put 2s. 6d. into an Orphan-box in my house. Mrs. W. C: gave 1l. Also Mrs. K. 5s. These donations came in today, after I had twice given myself especially to prayer for means, as we are now in so much need.

Sept. 30. Nothing more having come in, we were in great need today. On this account the boxes in the Orphan-Houses were opened, which contained 1l. 4s. 2d. This evening sister C. gave me 18s. 9 1/2 d., being the contents of her Orphan-box. Also 15s. 11d. came in by knitting of stockings. Thus we were helped for the present.

Oct. 2, Saturday. As today more money was needed, and nothing had come in, one of the labourers supplied the present need till Monday morning, which took 3l.--Evening. This afternoon, when there was nothing at all in my hands for the work, I received from a little boy 1s. This evening a box arrived from Norwich, filled by the contributions of many believers. It contained in money 1l. 10s., and the following articles: 6 brass and copper coins, a gold pin, 5 gold brooches, 3 pairs of ear-rings, 3 pairs of silver clasps, a gold clasp, a gold locket, 2 rings, a pair of silver studs, a broken silver tooth-pick, 4 gilt bracelets, a silver mounted eye-glass, 5 braid watch-guards, a silver washed watch-guard, 4 waist buckles, a pair of gilt ear-rings, 3 mourning necklaces and a pair of ear-rings, a mourning ring set with pearls, 2 brass brooches, a mother-o'-pearl cross and clasps, a silver fruit knife, a pair of coral bracelets, 2 bead necklaces, a snuff-box, 2 little baskets, 12 worked mats, 24 ladies' bags of various kinds, 4 cephalines, 13 book-marks, 8 purses, 5 shells, 45 pin-cushions of various kinds, 17 needle cases, 9 pairs of babies' shoes, 2 babies' hoods, 3 neck ties, 2 knitted cloths, 2 netted mats, 4 pairs of watch pockets, 3 pairs of cogs, 3 little scarfs, 2 collars, a pair of socks, a nightcap, some knitted fringe, some work and lace, 2 silk winders, 3 waistbands, 5 handkerchiefs, 1/4 lb. of tea, 2 pen-wipers, some little playthings, 2 combs, some slate pencils, 3 chimney ornaments, 4 paintings, 3 books, 16 pamphlets, a fan, a little box, 13 chemises, 2 shirts, a frock and cape, a shawl border, 3 bodkin cases, 2 1/2 yards of print, a gown, and a few other little things.--Great indeed was my joy in receiving this box, for it was a fresh proof to me, in this our present great poverty, that the Lord hears our prayers and is mindful of us.

Oct. 3. Lord's day. Today I received from C. C. 10s. 10d., from a sister 3l., being the produce of a piece of work done for the Orphans, and anonymously 2s. 6d. By these donations we are supplied till Tuesday evening.

Oct. 4. From a Christian gentleman I received today 1l.; from a brother, as the first fruits of his salary, 2l., of which 1l. is for the Orphans, and 1l. for home and foreign labourers; from another brother 2s. 6d.; from a sister 5s.

Oct. 5. By sale of articles 1l. 10s. 4 1/2 d. This evening I had only means enough to give to the matrons supplies for one or two days. When I came home from our prayer meeting I found unexpectedly another demand made upon me for 5l., in connexion with the house-keeping expenses, towards which I had nothing, but which it was desirable to meet as soon as possible.

Oct. 6. This morning I received the following letter from Kennington, containing a post-office order for 5l.

* * * *, Kennington, Surrey.

"Beloved and honoured brother in our Lord,

I am permitted to be the unworthy instrument in the Lord's hand of transmitting to you the enclosed post-office order for 5l., to be applied either for the Orphans or your own use, as may be most required at this time, &c.

FOURTH PART

Your affectionate sister in our Lord,

Oct. 5, 1847. * * * *"

I am now able to send off the 5l. about the need of which I was informed late last evening, and am again thus graciously helped at this time also by Him who hears the cries of His children. Do you not discern His hand, dear reader, in this instance?

Oct. 8. Today 10s. more was required towards housekeeping expenses; but nothing had come in since the 6th. One of the labourers was able of his own means to give the amount required.

Oct. 9. Saturday. Yesterday, when there was nothing at all in hand, were given half-a-crown, 2 silk handkerchiefs, 3 pinafores, a baby's shirt, a frock, and 2 children's work-bags.--This morning I found in the boxes at my house 1s. I knew that several pounds would be needed today for provisions, and therefore my eyes were directed to the Lord for help. I received accordingly 13s. 6d. "from a London Postman," and from Cumberland 1l. Thus I had 1l. 17s., but as this was still not enough, one of the labourers added 1l. 3s. of his own, as 3l. was needed. Thus we have enough for house-keeping expenses till Monday morning.

Oct 11. Monday. Yesterday came in from a sister 10s., ditto 4s., anonymously 2s., through an Orphan-box 8s., and from a sister 2s. 6d. Thus we have enough for today's necessities, and 1s. 6d. left.

Oct. 12. There came in yesterday afternoon through the boxes at the Orphan-Houses 5s. 0 1/2 d., and through those at my house 1s. Also by sale of Reports 2s. This morning I received through sister Ch. 1l. 5s. 5d. These donations were very refreshing to my spirit in this time of great need, and though not nearly enough for all we required today, they are nevertheless a precious earnest that the Lord will help us further. -- By the first delivery this morning I received an anonymous letter, containing 5l., with these words:

"It is requested that half of the enclosed sum may be expended on Brother Mueller's own necessities, the other half as he thinks fit, in furtherance of his Christian schemes: and may the blessing of the 'Giver of all good' attend him! Oct. 7, 1847."

I put the half of this 5l. to the Orphan-Fund--There came in still further by sale of articles and Reports 1l. 12s. 6d. Thus we have all that is needed for the present moment.--Afternoon. This afternoon a person from the neighbourhood of Chepstow called and left a half-sovereign. There came in also through needlework, done by the Orphans, 2l. 5s. 4d. Thus we are still further helped for the present moment. But all this is not enough. Larger sums are needed, as oatmeal is to be ordered from Scotland, and several other heavy expenses, besides those for house-keeping, are to be met. Nevertheless the precious proofs, which I have had again today of our Father's loving care over the work, lead me to expect further help.--Evening. This evening at a quarter to ten o'clock I received 180l. Of this sum I put 100l. to the Missionary-Fund, 40l. to the School--Bible and Tract-Fund, and 40l. to the Orphan-Fund for present use. How good is the Lord! How precious this help! How much needed and how seasonable!

From the 13th to the 19th of October came in 8l 6s. 1 1/2 d.

On Oct. 19th I left Bristol with my dear wife, partly, because both of us much needed change of air, and partly, because I had a great desire to labour in the Word for a few weeks in Westmoreland and Cumberland. I was not able to leave more means than enough for about three days for house-keeping expenses. But I could not have stayed in Bristol, though there had been nothing at all in hand; my hope was that God would help during my absence. During all the time of my stay at Bowness in Westmoreland, from Oct. 20th to Nov. 20th, there was day by day, with the exception of the first three days, after my departure, need to wait upon God for daily supplies for the Orphans. In consequence of this, every donation, without exception, which was received daring my absence, came in most seasonably. Partly on account of my health, and partly on account of opportunities for service in Westmoreland and elsewhere, I did not feel it right to return to Bristol sooner than I did, though there was such great poverty; nor could I have done anything in Bristol which I could not do in Westmoreland, as it regards procuring means, since prayer and faith are all the means I make use of to obtain supplies when we are in need. For the encouragement of the reader, and also that those, whom God used at that time to enable us day by day to supply the Orphans with what they needed, may see how they were used by Him to help us, I mention here every one of the donations which came in during my absence, with the exception of the articles.

Oct. 21, 1847. From some poor sisters near Kingsbridge. 4s. 6d., in small donations through Brother F. in Bristol 7s. 5d.--Oct. 22. Anonymously from Walsall 5l., of which 2l. is intended for missions, 1l. for the Building Fund, and 2l. for present use for the Orphans.--From Bath anonymously 10s. with a lace cape.--Oct. 24th. I received while at Bowness 10s., also 1s. and 2s. This 13s. I forwarded at once to Bristol by an order. There was also received in Bristol from Droitwich 10s. and from London 2s. 6d.--Oct. 25th. By sale of articles and Reports 2l. From C. C. 1l. From Wolverhampton 10s.--Oct. 26th. Through the boxes in the Orphan-Houses 1l. 14s. 6d., our need having caused them to be opened.--Oct. 28. By sale of Reports 2s. 4d. Orphan-box in my house 10s. From a Christian gentleman near Crediton 5l. --Oct. 30. By sale of Reports 2s. 6d. By sale of an improved Rendering 9d. From London 10s.--Nov. 1. By sale of articles, stockings, and Reports 1l. 14s. 4d.--Nov. 2. Through a brother at Clevedon 5s. Through the boxes at the Orphan-Houses 3l. 8s. 6d. By sale of a Report and Rendering 10d. From one of the labourers 3s.--Nov. 4. From a sister near Wotton-under-Edge 1l.--Nov. 5. From two donors in the neighborhood of Droitwich 5s. each.--Nov. 6. From sister B. in Bristol 4s. From C. C. 1l. 2s. 5 1/2 d.--Nov. 8. Anonymously by post 5l.--From sister H. C. 3s. --There

FOURTH PART

was also given to me at Kendal, where I had been labouring, by a brother 10s., and by a poor sister 4d. This I sent at once to Bristol by an order.--Nov. 9. From a donor in Bristol 1l. From Switzerland 1l. 4s. 4d. From London 5s. By sale of articles 5l. 14s. 4 1/2 d.--Nov. 11. A lady from Ireland visited the Orphan-Houses and gave 1l. By sale of a Report 4d.--Proceeds of an Orphan-box from the neighbourhood of Launceston 1l. 3s. 9d.--Through an Orphan-box in my house 5s.--Nov. 13. Through the bonds in the Orphan-Houses 10s. 2d. Through Mrs. T.'s Orphan-box 2s, 1 1/2 d.--Nov. 14. From C. C. 5l.--Anonymously 2s. 6d.--Nov. 16. By sale of articles and stockings 2l. 11s. 6d.--Nov. 17. By sale of Reports 1s. Through a box in my house 2s. 6d. By needlework and knitting of the Orphans 1l. 6s. From sister C. 10s. From one of the labourers in the work 5l.--Nov. 19. From P. 2s. 6d.--On Nov. 20th we left Bowness for Keswick in Cumberland. The day before we left, I received at Bowness 5s., 5s., and 1l., also from Kendal 2s. 6d. This 1l. 12s. 6d. I sent off at once to Bristol by an order, knowing that it was needed.--Nov. 21. From C. C. 3l.--Nov. 22. Through the boxes in the Orphan-Houses 7s.--Nov. 23. By sale of articles and stockings 2l. 5s. 9d. From one of the labourers 3l.--Nov. 24. By sale of Reports 3s. 3d. From F. L. in Ireland 1l. From Richmond 1l. 10s.-- From Nov. 20th to 24th we stayed at Keswick. Whilst there I received 10s., 2s., and 1s. 6d. for the Orphans. This 13s. 6d. was at once sent off to Bristol, by an order, as we were still very poor, with regard to means for housekeeping expenses for the Orphan-Houses. But notwithstanding all this great poverty in Bristol, which required that we should day by day wait upon God, for our daily supplies, I did not feel at all led to return home, but had an especial drawing to go to Sunderland to labour there for a little while among the brethren assembling at "Bethesda Free Chapel." We therefore left Keswick on Nov. 24th for Sunderland.--Nov. 26th came in by sale of articles 2s., through the boxes at my house 1L. 2s. 6d., and from Dublin 1l.--Nov. 27. Through a box 8d., by sale of articles 7s., and 2l. from London.-- Nov. 28th. From C. C. 10s. 8d., and by sale of Reports 8d.--Nov. 30. By sale of stockings and articles 1l. 13s. 6 1/2 d. From one of the labourers 1l. 10s. By sale of articles 1s. 11d. --Dec. 1. From one of the labourers in the work 10s.--Dec. 2. From sister F. 5s. By sale of articles 1l. From Newbury 10s. 6d.--Dec. 3. By sale of articles 5s. By profits from the sale of ladies' bags 1l. 19s. 6d. From Kingstown, Ireland, 1l. By sale of a Report 4d.--Dec. 5. From C. C. 1l. Through the boxes in the Orphan-Houses 3s. 10d. By knitting of the Orphans 8s. 6d. From Glasgow 5s.--Dec. 7. By sale of articles and stockings 3l. 7s, 11d. From one of the labourers 2l. From Thornbury 4s.--Dec. 8. From a village near Keswick 10s., and by sale of articles 6d. From one of the labourers 10s. From a donor in Ayrshire 2l.--In the evening of Dec. 8th we returned to Bristol from Sunderland. Day by day while we were at Sunderland also, the Orphan-Fund was very low, but God helped day by day, by sending in the means which have been mentioned; and when we returned there was 1s. 11d, in hand, and 2l. came in that same evening from Plymouth.

Dec. 9. From the neighbourhood of Pershore came in this morning most seasonably 5l., as time need for house-keeping expenses today was 4l., and there was only 2l. 1s. 11d, in hand. This 5l. came in about an hour before the 4l. was needed. There was received further today from Bath, anonymously, 10s., and by sale of articles 2s. 6d.--Will you not, dear reader, unite with me in admiring and praising the

Lord who so seasonably helped all the time that I was away from the work, engaged in His service in another way! Do you not see how precious it is to have God to go to, and to find Him ever willing to help those who trust in Him, wherever they be? Do you not also see again the hand of God so manifestly stretched out on our behalf this day Dec. 9th? 4l. was needed, but only 2l. 1s. 11d, in hand, and, an hour before the 4l. was called for from the Orphan-Houses for house-keeping expenses, the Lord sent that 5l. from Pershore.

Dec. 10. Today I received information, in answer to my inquiry, that 10s., which had been sent to me at Sunderland, were intended for the Orphans. These 10s., together with 3l. 14s. 5d. left in hand yesterday, are sufficient for this day, as the need of today is only 3l. 10s. for house-keeping.

Dec. 11. This morning came in 1l. from the neighbourhood of Cockermouth; thus we had, with the 14s. 5d. left yesterday, 1l. 14s. 5d., which is enough for today.

Dec. 13. Monday. Yesterday I received from C. C. 1l. 10s., from another person 2s., as profit from the sale of ladies' bags 1l., and this morning from Burford 2s. 6d. Thus we have again enough for the house-keeping expenses of today.

Dec. 14. Yesterday we had enough, but nothing over. When there was again nothing at all remaining in my hands, there was yesterday afternoon 1s. put into a box at my house. In the evening came in by sale of stockings and articles 2l. 6s. 6d., and by a donation 10s--In the evening also a sister from Norwich brought 10s., 2s. 6d., 6d., and 3s. She also brought the following articles, to be sold for the benefit of the Orphans: A bottle of extract of spring flowers, a small box of scent bottles, a smelling bottle, 8 common seals, a thimble case, a box of wafers; a china box containing two rings, a mourning brooch, and a bead watch-guard; a pin-cushion, a pair of little cuffs, and a little box. Another parcel containing a pair of worked slippers, 2 little bags, 2 books, 2 aprons, a knitted cloth, 3 pin-cushions, a Shetland shawl, and a pair of card-racks. Further: 2 pairs of cuffs and a necktie. Further: a child's silver rattle, 3 rings, 3 pairs of ear-rings, and 2 necklaces--There was also a parcel sent from Langport, containing two toilette cushions, a pair of worked slippers, 2 fans, 2 children's caps, some gold lace, a pair of silver clasps, 3 brooches, a silver thimble, a brass clasp, and some bits of gold. This morning I received a letter from the neighbourhood of Exeter containing a post-office order for 8s. with these words:

"I had hoped to have accumulated a larger sum in my box for the Orphans, than I have of late been enabled to obtain. I now, however, send it to you, though the amount is small, and should be thankful if it should prove useful for present need, it having been upon my mind for the last day or two that I ought to forward it to you without further delay. I therefore send an order for 8s., &c."

Thus we were supplied for the need of this day. This last 8s. was needed to make up the amount required.

FOURTH PART

Dec. 15. Yesterday afternoon I received 3l. more, of which 2l. was from Madeira, and 1l. from the brother through whom the 2l. was remitted. This 3l. was paid away at once, though not needed for house-keeping, so that I had still nothing for the need of today, when this day began.-- My prayer last evening and this morning had been especially, that the Lord would not only be pleased to send me some money for the house-keeping expenses of today, but also enable me to give at least a little money to eight of the sisters who labour in the four Orphan-Houses, who have not had any money for their own personal necessities for several months. This desire was granted to me, for I received this morning a letter from Wakefield with 20l., in which the donor writes: "I hasten to enclose 20l., which I leave to your disposal; but if the varied funds are so situated as to give no material preponderance of need to any one, I should divide it as under, viz. 10l. to the Orphans, 5l. to yourself and colleague, and 5l. for the Bibles, &c." I took all this 20l. for the Orphans, and have thus the joy of being able to send at least 16l. to those eight sisters, and am also supplied with house-keeping money for today; and as for tomorrow, "my eyes are upon the Lord." The Lord be praised for this precious and seasonable help!

Dec. 16. Yesterday afternoon a brother in the Lord gave 5l. for the Orphans. By this money I was able to defray the expenses of today, and the rest I put away for the rent, so that again we have to look to the Lord for supplies for tomorrow. Yesterday also a person gave half-a-crown to one of the teachers of the Orphans, whilst she was walking out with the children.

Dec. 17. Yesterday afternoon came in 12s. and 5s.--Also a lady and gentleman called at the Girls' Orphan-House No. II. and gave 10s. for a copy of my Narrative. Thus we had a little towards the need of today, but not nearly enough. Before, however, I was called on for money, I received from Worcester 1l. 10s. Thus we were supplied for the need of today.

Dec. 18. Saturday. I had reason to believe that our need for house-keeping today would be about 5l., and I therefore waited upon God for means, and looked out for help. Yesterday afternoon, accordingly, came in by sale of trinkets 1l. 8s. This morning I received from Westmoreland 10l. Also a letter from Edinburgh, containing 15l., with the following lines without name.

"Dear brother in Christ, I enclose 'in the name of Jesus' 15l. 5l. for dear brother Craik, 5l. for dear brother and sister Mueller, for their personal or family expenses, 3l. for the Orphans, and 2l. for the Christian Knowledge Institution. May the peace of God, which passeth all understanding, keep your hearts and minds through Jesus Christ our Lord."

There came in also, at the same time, by sale of Reports 10s. Thus I was able to meet all the house-keeping expenses of today, being 4l. 15s. 0d., and the rest I was obliged to put by for the rent and the expenses connected with the apprentices, so that we have yet again to wait upon the Lord for further supplies for next Monday.

However, we are brought to the close of another week in this service, and He who has helped us thus far will surely help us further.

Monday, Dec. 20. Only 9s. and a small gold pin and ring from Stowmarket having come in since Saturday morning, we had not enough for house-keeping expenses today, which are 2l.; but one of the labourers was able of his own to give 1l. 11s. 0d., to supply the deficiency.

Dec. 21. Yesterday afternoon a brother sent 2l. for the Orphans. In the evening a sister gave 2s, 6d. This morning came in through two Orphan-boxes 14s. 10d.; from Droitwich 10s; and by sale of articles, Reports and stockings 1l. 7s. 9d. Thus we have all that is needed for today, the demand being only 3l. 5s. The rest I put by for rent and the apprentices, and wait upon God for help for tomorrow.

Dec. 22. Yesterday evening came in by sale of Reports 8d., from Plymouth 1s., and from a sister 5s. Our need also led me to open the boxes in the Orphan-Houses, which contained 15s. 2 1/2 d. By sale of articles 2s. 6d. This was all I was able to send this morning to the Orphan-Houses, waiting upon the Lord for more.

Dec. 23. The need of today was 11l., having several expenses to meet besides those of house-keeping, which amounted to 4l. for today. This sum the Lord gave me thus: last evening I received 1l. together with a pair of trousers and gaiters, and a remnant of fustian for the Orphans. But as I knew how much there would be needed today, I waited further upon the Lord this morning for help, and, in ONE MINUTE, after I had risen from my knees, I received a letter from Liverpool with 10l. for the Orphans. The donor writes: "I have had the enclosed Ten Pound Note in my drawer for some time, intending to send it to you for the Orphans; but my time is so occupied, that, at a suitable time, when at my desk, I have overlooked it. I now however enclose it," &c,--How seasonable this help! How exactly to the very shilling what is needed today! How remarkable that just now this donor in Liverpool is led to send the Ten Pounds which had been, according to his own words, for some time in his drawer for the purpose of sending it! All this abundantly proves the most minute and particular providence of God and His readiness to answer the supplications of His children.--I am now looking out again for supplies for tomorrow.

Dec. 24. Last evening came in from Mrs. O. 1l., by knitting 1s. 10d., by sale of stockings 2l. 5s., by four half-sovereigns given to the matrons of the four Orphan-Houses, of which three of them gave their part to the funds, 30s, and by sale of trinkets 1l. 2s. Thus we are supplied till next Monday, i.e. for Christmas day (Saturday) and the Lord's day.

Dec. 27. Monday. Before I was called on for fresh supplies, the Lord, in His great kindness, had given me the means requisite for today. On Christmas Day was brought to me a parcel from Hereford in which I received from A. and Z. 3s., also a little box, a silver vinaigrette., and half-a-crown. Yesterday, Lord's Day. I received

FOURTH PART

from Kendal 5l. 10s. Also from Stoke Bishop 10s.--Thus I have been again able to meet all the expenses of today.

Dec. 28. Yesterday came in by sale of Reports from Bath 2s. 6d., ditto from Street 1s., by the proceeds of an Orphan-box from Street 3s., and anonymously 5s.--Today I received by sale of articles and stockings 1l. 11s. 8d. As this was not quite enough for the necessities of today, the boxes in the Orphan-Houses were opened, and 2l. 1s. 0 1/2 d. found in them. Thus we had again more than four pounds for house-keeping to day, and are supplied with all we need.

Dec. 29. Yesterday evening I met at our usual weekly prayer meeting with all the labourers in the Schools and Orphan-Houses, to seek the Lord's blessing upon the work, and upon the children under our care in particular. Among other points the state of the funds also was a subject for prayer, on account of the great need in every way. For we need money for the schools, as I shall not be able next week to pay to the teachers in the Day Schools their usual weekly salary, except means should come in for them. The stock of tracts and Bibles is also becoming very small. Also for eleven weeks I have scarcely at all been able to send help to home and foreign labourers. This especially we prayed about. And as to the Orphans, I had again only 9d. in hand for house-keeping expenses, which had come in at the meeting. However, my heart, by God's goodness, was at peace, and as I had now with my fellow-labourers been again able to bring all our necessities before the Lord I was looking out for help. After the meeting one of the teachers gave me 1s. 6d. for the Orphans, saying, the Lord will give you more tomorrow morning. This I expected myself; for we were in need for house-keeping expenses for today, and we had been waiting upon God for means. Accordingly this morning, when I had only 2s. 3d. in hand, I received from Devonshire 15l. for the Orphans.--How good is the Lord! How seasonable again this supply! I had been just again in prayer about the work, and about this day's necessities, and at the very moment that I rose from my knees this letter was given to me.--There was also another letter from Essex, containing 1l. 5s. for the Orphans. Thus I was again abundantly supplied for this day, and was able to put by the rest for rent and the expenses connected with the apprentices, trusting in the Lord for fresh supplies for tomorrow.

Dec. 30. When this day began, we were without any thing for the necessities of the day, though I had reason to believe that several pounds would again be required. I was therefore again looking out for fresh supplies. Accordingly, about ten o'clock this morning, a brother in the Lord, who had come last evening to stay for a night in my house, gave me 10l., to be used as it might be most needed. To be noticed in connexion with this donation is: 1, I had, not long since, received a donation from him. 2, This brother had generally stated how he wished his donations to be appropriated, and they had been chiefly for missionary purposes; but this time he left it to me to use this money as most needed, and therefore I could take of it what was needed for the Orphans. 3, We were now extremely poor also with regard to the funds for all the other objects, so that I was obliged to tell the teachers of the Day Schools last Tuesday evening, 28th, that if no fresh supplies came in, I should not be able to give them their weekly salaries, as usual, next Tuesday evening, being now poorer in this particular than I had been for years. How kind therefore of the Lord, not only to give me this money through this brother at this time, but also to dispose his heart to leave the application of it to me as most needed. I took half of it for this day's housekeeping expenses for the Orphans, and half for the School Fund, for the weekly salaries of the teachers next Tuesday.--I also received further this morning a half-sovereign from Droitwich.-- The little that was left, after the house-keeping expenses were met, was put by for rent and the expenses for the apprentices, and I was again, without a penny, looking out for fresh supplies for tomorrow.

Dec. 31, 1847. The last day of another year had now come. Great and many had been the mercies of God to me this year in every way, particularly also in connexion with the Orphans; but now I had again nothing for today, except two shillings which are in one of the boxes in my house. I was, however, by God's grace, able to look out for supplies for this last day of another year also, being fully assured that the Lord would not confound me. And thus it has been, according to my expectation; for, before being called on for money, I received 100l., which was left to me to apply to any part of the Lord's service where there seemed the most need. At the same time I received 5l. for the Orphans from Teignmouth. Of the 100l. I took half for the Orphans and half for the other objects. It was indeed a moat seasonable help! I am thus able to meet all the expenses for house-keeping for today, all the present expenses connected with the apprentices, and am able to give 16l. to eight of the sisters who labour in the Orphan-Houses, for their own personal necessities. How good is the Lord! How can I sufficiently praise Him for this seasonable help! --Evening. Received still further 3s., and from Banbury 17s., and the proceeds of an Orphan-box, being 1l. 2s. 6d. Thus the year closes in blessing and under the manifest help of God.

Jan. 1, 1848. As the old year ended, so the new begins. Early this morning was sent to me 1l. 12s. 0d., being the proceeds of an Orphan-box.--A little later I received from Worcester 1l., and from Scotland 3l.

Jan. 6. On the second and three following days came in many pounds more; but though so much had been received during the last seven days, I sent again today the last money to the Orphan-Houses for house-keeping, as our expenses have been exceedingly heavy during the last few days; and I am therefore again penniless with regard to the necessities of tomorrow. -- Evening. The Lord has been again exceedingly kind, and has again helped in His faithful love. This evening I received a check for 120l., of which 20l. is intended by the donor for missionary purposes, and the other 100l. is left to my disposal, either for the Orphans or the other part of the work. I took therefore 70l. for the Orphans, and 30l. for the Day Schools, and the circulation of Bibles and Tracts. I received likewise from D.D. 5l.

Jan. 25. Besides the seventy-five pounds that had come in on the 6th, the sum of 53l. 18s. 0 1/4 d. more came in up to this day.--Now, after having paid this evening for the house-keeping expenses for one week in advance, all the money in my hands for the Orphans is again gone; yet, by the Lord's goodness, we have our stores

FOURTH PART

pretty well supplied, and besides this the matrons have the current house-keeping expenses for one week in hand. May the Lord in His faithful love send fresh supplies for the coming week!

Jan. 27. This afternoon when there was nothing in hand, I received from Guernsey 2l.

Jan. 28, Received from Plymouth 5l. Also 5s. 6d. from the neighbourhood of Exeter, and 2s. besides. From the neighbourhood of Nottingham 5s.

Jan. 30. By profits from the sale of ladies' baskets 2s.

Jan. 31. One of the labourers in the work gave 10l., and a brother on his way to Ireland 1l.

Feb. 1. By sale of articles and stockings 3l. 19s. 7 1/2 d., anonymously 2d., from sister F. 10s., proceeds of an Orphan-box 12s. 6 3/4 d., by sale of stockings 8s. 5d., and by the boxes at the Orphan-Houses 16s. 9d.--When I went this evening to the Orphan-Houses for our usual prayer meeting on Tuesday evenings, I found that altogether since last Tuesday evening 25l. 2s. 0 1/2 d. had come in; but as there had been many extra expenses to meet during the week, there was only actually in hand 8l. 8s. 4 1/4 d. Of this I gave to each of the matrons 2l. 2s. 1d, being only a part of what would be needed during the week, and had then one farthing left, "like the handful of meal in the barrel."

Feb. 2. This morning on my usual walk before breakfast I felt myself led out of my usual track, into a direction in which I had not gone for some months. In stepping over a stile I said to myself: "Perhaps God has a reason even in this." About five minutes afterwards I met a Christian gentleman who gave me two sovereigns for the Orphans, and then I knew the reason, why I had been led this way. Thus the farthing which remained last evening has been already multiplied.--Evening. This afternoon I received still further from a brother 1l. 1s., also a letter from Portsea containing 1l. 10s. The letter from Portsea contained these words: "Please accept it as another token of the Lord's watchful care for you and yours." How true! How exemplified in this very donation at this time!

Feb. 3. This morning I received by the first delivery three letters, each containing further supplies. The first, from Sherborne, enclosed a post-office order for 1l. 15s., of which 1l. is for missionary purposes, and 15s. for the Orphans. The second, from Yorkshire, contained two half Five Pound Notes, which 10l. is left to my disposal, yet it is requested that a part of it should go to the destitute Irish. I put therefore 5l. to the relief of the Irish, and 5l. to the Orphan Fund. The third letter, from Marlborough, contained 1l. for the Orphans.--Thus I have now all that is needed in the way of house-keeping money for the remainder of this week; but I am now waiting upon God for about 25l. to provide each of the 32 Orphan Boys above seven years old with a new suit of clothes.

THE LORD'S DEALINGS WITH GEORGE MÜLLER

The reader might say, "You are continually in need. No sooner is the one demand met, than another comes. Do you not find it a trying life, and are you not tired of it?" My reply is, It is true I am more or less continually in need in connexion with this work. And if I were to tell out all my heart to the reader concerning it, he would have still more reason to say that I am continually in need. For what I have here written is almost exclusively about the way in which God has been pleased to supply me with money for carrying on the work; but I do deliberately state that this, much as it might appear to one or the other, is by no means the chief thing that I stand in need of from day to day. I will just hint at a few other things. Sickness among the children, very difficult and tedious cases, in which, notwithstanding all the means which are used month after month, yea year after year, the children remain ill. Nothing remains but either to keep them, or to send them to the Parish Union to which they belong, as they have no relatives able to provide for them. The very fact of having cared for them and watched over them for years, only endears them the more to us, and would make it the more trying to send them back to their parish. This is a "need" which brings me to God. Here is prayer required, not only for means which such sick children call for, but for guidance and wisdom from on High.--Sometimes children are to be placed out as servants or apprentices. A suitable place is needed, or else they had better remain under our care. The obtaining of this suitable place is a "need" indeed. It is more difficult to be obtained than money. Sometimes for many weeks have I had to wait upon God, to have this "need" supplied; but He has always at last helped.--Sometimes great has been my "need" of wisdom and guidance in order to know how certain children ought to be treated under particular circumstances; and especially how to behave towards certain apprentices or servants who were formerly in the Orphan-Houses. A "need" in this respect is no small thing; though I have found that in this and in all other matters concerning which I was in "need," I have been helped, provided I was indeed able to wait patiently upon God. That word, "godliness is profitable unto all things, having promise of the life that now is, and of that which is to come" (1 Tim. iv. 8), I have in times almost without number found to be true in my own experience. -- Further, when one or the other of the labourers needed to leave the work on account of health, or for other reasons, I have been at such times in far greater "need" than when I required money for the various objects of the Institution. I could only have such "need" supplied by waiting upon God. I could do nothing but speak to my heavenly Father about this matter, and He has always helped. One of the greatest difficulties connected with this work is, to obtain suitable Godly persons for it. So many things are to be taken into the account. Suitable age, health, gift, experience, love for children, true godliness, a ready mind to serve God in the work and not themselves, a ready mind to bear with the many trials and difficulties connected with it, a manifest purpose to labour not for the sake of the remuneration, but to serve God in their work; surely, to obtain Godly persons, in whom these qualifications, even in some measure, are found combined, is not an easy matter. Not that any one will suppose me to mean that I am looking out for perfect fellow-labourers. Not that any one will suppose that my fellow-labourers are referred to by rue, as if they were without weaknesses, deficiencies, and failings. I am myself far, very far from being without weaknesses, deficiencies, and failings.

FOURTH PART

Moreover, I never expect to find fellow-labourers for this work who have not their weaknesses; but this I do mean to say, that the work of God in my hands is of that character, and, by God's grace, is really carried on with such a true purpose to serve God thereby (however much I and my fellow-labourers may fail), that it is with me a matter of deep moment to find truly suitable individuals for it, in whom, as much as possible, the above qualifications should be found united. And, however much there may be wanting, this is more and more my aim, that I may obtain such helpers; and hence it can be easily perceived bow great my "need" must be again and again on this very account. I do here especially advise, that if any should apply in future for situations in connexion with this work, they would keep these remarks before them; for, by God's grace, it is my purpose never to give to any persons a situation in connexion with the Institution, if they are not suitable for it according to the light which God gives me.--Further, that the labourers work happily together among themselves, and that I go on happily in service with them; that I be their servant, on the one hand, and yet, on the other, maintain the place which God has given me in this work; surely, if any one carefully looks at this, he will at once see, that there is a difficulty and a "need" far greater than any that is connected with money. Oh, how these matters lead one to call upon God! How they continually make one sensible of one's "need!" Truly, I am in need, in continual need. Many more points might be referred to in connexion with this work, in which I am more or less continually in "need;" but I will only mention one it is now many years since I have made my boast in the living God in so public a manner by my publications. On this account Satan unquestionably is waiting for my halting, and, if left to myself, I should fall a prey to him. Pride, unbelief, or other sins would be my ruin, and lead me to bring a most awful disgrace upon the name of Jesus. Here is then a "need," a great "need." I do feel myself in "need," in great "need," even to be upheld by God; for I cannot stand for a moment, if left to myself. Oh, that none of my dear readers might admire me, and be astonished at my faith, and think of me as if I were beyond unbelief! Oh, that none of my dear readers might think, that I could not be puffed up by pride, or in other respects most awfully dishonour God, and thus at last, though God has used me in blessing hitherto to so many, become a beacon to the church of Christ! No, I am as weak as ever, and need as much as ever to be upheld as to faith, and every other grace. I am therefore in "need," in great "need;" and therefore help me, dear Christian reader, with your prayers.

I allow, then, moat fully that I am in continual "need." This is the case with regard to money matters, because the work is now so large. A few hundred pounds go but a little way. There have been often weeks, when my demands have been several hundred pounds a week, and it can therefore easily be supposed that even if large donations come in, they do not last long. But whilst I allow this, I desire that the Christian reader may keep in mind that there are other necessities, and even greater ones than those connected with money.--Should, however, the reader say that he thinks "I must find this a very trying life, and that I must be tired of it," I beg to state, that he is entirely mistaken. I do not find the life in connexion with this work a trying life, but a very happy one. It is impossible to describe the abundance of peace and heavenly joy that often has flowed into my soul by means of the fresh answers which I have obtained from God, after waiting upon Him for help and blessing; and the longer I have had to wait upon Him, or the greater my need was, the greater the enjoyment when at last the answer came, which has often been in a very remarkable way, in order to make the hand of God the more manifest. I therefore solemnly declare that I do not find this life a trying life, but a very happy one, and I am consequently not in the least tired of it. Straits and difficulties I expected from the very beginning. Before I began this service I expected them; nay, the chief object of it was, that the church at large might be strengthened in faith, and be led more simply, habitually, and unreservedly to trust in the living God, by seeing His hand stretched out in nay behalf in the hour of need. I did, therefore, expect trials, great trials and straits; but cheerfully, for the glory of God, and the profit of God's dear children, did I desire to pass through them, if only the saints might be benefited by the dealings of God with me. The longer I go on in this service, the greater the trials of one kind or another become; but, at the same time, the happier I am in this my service, and the more assured, that I am engaged as the Lord would have me to be. How then could I be tired of carrying on the work of God on such principles as I do?

I now return to the extracts from my journal.

Feb. 4, 1848. Yesterday came in still further: from Norwich 1l. and from Devonshire 1l.

Feb. S. From a brother at Hereford 5l.--Feb. 5. From "Friends to Orphans" 2l., and from D.D. 12s 2 1/2 d.--Feb. 5. By sale of articles 2l. 6s. 4d. Evening. Since this day week, when I had only one farthing left, the Lord has been pleased to send in for the Orphans 23l. 16s. 8 1/2 d; but as I have had to pay away more than 10l., besides making up the remainder of what was needed for house-keeping expenses for the past week, there was only 6l. 10s. 10 3/4 d. for the expenses of the coming week, whilst nearly three times as much was required by the four matrons. I divided this little, however, among them, in the full assurance, that, by the time it was consumed, the Lord would send more.

Feb. 9. Today only 2s. 4d. has come in. We are supplied for the present moment, and shall have enough till tomorrow evening for house-keeping expenses; but there is about 25l. needed for boys' clothes, and I greatly desire to give some money to the sisters who labour in the Orphan-Houses.

Feb. 10. This morning was given to me the sum of One Hundred Pounds, which being left entirely to my disposal, I took of it 50l. for the Orphans, and 50l. for the School--, Bible--, Tract--and Missionary Fund.--The Lord be praised for this most seasonable help! I am thus helped for the present for all the various parts of the work, and have especially two precious answers to my prayers concerning the Orphan work, in that I am able to get a new suit of clothes for all the boys, and to give some money to the sisters, who labour in the Orphan-Houses, for their own personal necessities.

FOURTH PART

From Feb. 10th to 22nd came in 21l. 0s. 1 1/2 d. more.

Feb. 25. All money was now again expended. This afternoon I had paid away the last. About an hour after, I received from a brother the contents of his Orphan-box, being 2s. 6d. and a gold watch-key. In the evening was given to me 10l., being the half-yearly profits arising from shares in a certain company. How kind of the Lord thus to help again so soon! As soon as the last money was disbursed, He sent more.

Feb. 29. 4l. 18s. 0d. more has come in since the 25th. This evening I paid away for house-keeping all the money I had, being 12l. 10s. 7d., and returned home with an empty purse, trusting in the Lord to give me again fresh supplies. I shall shortly need again many pounds.

March 1. This morning I received anonymously by post from P. L. A. ten shillings. Evening. This afternoon a check for 25l. was left at my house for the benefit of the Orphans.--Thus we are again supplied for a week for what we need for house-keeping, &c. Oh, how good it is to depend on the faithful love of our heavenly Father, who never forsakes His children who put their trust in Him!

March 17. Since the first of this month there has come in, besides the 25l. given on the 1st, altogether 36l. 0s. 3 1/2 d. Now today all means were again gone, when a brother in the Lord from Gloucestershire called at the Orphan-Houses and bought some tracts and an "Improved Rendering" for 2s. 6d., and gave 17s. 6d. for the Orphans. This afternoon came in further, by sale of articles, 2l. 12s. 9d.

March 18. This morning I received from Chelsea 4l., from Tewkesbury 10d., and this evening from D. D. 5s. 2d., and by sale of articles 5s. There was also 1l. left anonymously at my house.--Thus we are again supplied for 2 or 3 days.

March 21. Tuesday. As during the last three days only 1l. 15s. had come in, I had only 2l. this evening towards the house-keeping expenses of the coming week; but finding that one of the teachers had 5l. in hand for knitting and needlework, done by the children, I added this to the 2l., and we are thus supplied for 2 or 3 days with provisions.

March 23. Evening. When there was now again no money at all in hand, and when I had the prospect of needing fresh supplies tomorrow or the day after, a brother from Switzerland arrived at my house, who brought me 4l., which some brethren at Vevey, in Switzerland, had contributed towards the support of the Orphans. He also was the bearer of 15s. from London. What a variety of ways the Lord uses to supply our need! How remarkable that these Swiss brethren, who are just now in so much trial, should be led to send help towards this work! A few minutes, after I had received this 4l. 15s, there came also to hand a letter from Stafford, containing 4l., of which the donor wished me to take one-half for the Orphans, and the other half for my own personal expenses.

March 24. This morning I received still further from the Swiss brother, who had arrived yesterday afternoon, 18 francs, being a donation from the pupils of a boarding school in Switzerland, and 10 francs from a German brother.--Also from Norwich 13s. 8d. and 2s. 4d.

March 25. This morning I received from O. W. a letter with 20l., which the donor wished me to apply to the help of those labouring in the Gospel, and to the Orphans, if in present need. I took half of this for time Orphans, and half for Home and Foreign labourers. We are thus supplied for the Orphans for about three days.

March 28. On the 26th came in anonymously 3s., ditto 10s., ditto 2s. 6d., ditto 1s. 10d.; and 2l. 7s. besides. This evening I had again to give to the matrons fresh supplies for the coming week, towards which I had only a few pounds, when I received this morning 20l. from a distance of about 200 miles.

Between March 28th and April 12th I received, besides the 20l. referred to, 24l. 0s. 7d.

April 13. Thursday. On Tuesday evening I had given out for house-keeping all the money in hand, being 11l. This was enough for three or four days. This morning I was now looking out for more, having requested the Lord to look upon our necessities; for tomorrow, or at the latest the day after tomorrow, fresh supplies will be needed. Now think, my dear reader, of the Lord's goodness, when I tell you that this very morning I received 90l. for the Lord's work in my hands, the disposal of which sum was entirely left with me. I took of this sum 40l. for the Orphans, and 50l. for the School-, Bible-, Missionary-and Tract Fund.

April 26. Only 18l. 19s. 8 1/2 d. had come in since the 13th. As the income during these thirteen days had been so small, our means were again reduced to 16s., after I had supplied the day before yesterday the means for the house-keeping expenses for this week. Today I received information, that to a sister in Switzerland had been given Fifty Francs for the Orphans. Thus the Lord is in every way showing that He is mindful of us.

April 29. Saturday. The expenses of today, in addition to those for house-keeping, which had been met last Tuesday evening for a whole week in advance, reduced our little stock of means to only a few shillings. In addition to this, Tuesday is approaching, when again about 20l. will be needed. And now see, dear reader, how seasonably the Lord helped us again, and that from most unexpected quarters. This morning I received One Hundred Pounds from a brother, who is himself depending upon God for daily supplies whilst labouring in word and doctrine, but who has lately come into the possession of this sum, and who does not think it right to lay up treasure upon earth. Of this 100l. he wishes me to take 10l. for my own personal necessities, to give to brother Craik 10l., and to take 80l. for the Orphans. Of this 80l. the sum of 50l. has been put to the Building Fund, and 30l. has been taken for pre-

FOURTH PART

sent use for the Orphans. -- But this was not all. There was paid to me today the legacy of 19l. 19s. left to me for the benefit of the Orphans by the late Mrs. B., an individual whom I do not remember ever to have seen in my life, and whom I only know by name. Observe this particular providence! At a time of need, of great need of means, this legacy comes in. The will may have been made years ago, and the testator has been dead several months; but just at this time, when not only the 20l. are needed next Tuesday for house-keeping, but other expenses of about 30l. more are to be met in a few days, this legacy comes in.--Today also I have received besides, 10l. from Wiltshire, 1l. 4s. from Cumberland, 10s. from Birmingham, and 1l. from a donor in Bristol. Thus in one day, in a time of great need, 62l. 13s. has come in, besides 50l. for the Building Fund.

May 11. 10l. 2s. has come in since April 29th. This morning I received from a lady at a considerable distance 16l., and from Wandsworth 5l. These two donations came in especially in answer to prayer, not so much for immediate need as it regards house-keeping, but on account of other heavy expenses which are shortly to be met. I have also repeatedly asked the Lord of late, if it may please Him to send in considerable means, before the accounts are closed on the 26th, so that there might not be even the appearance, as if I wrote another Report, because I could get on no longer without it.

May 26, 1848. On this day the accounts were closed. The total sum which has come in from the 12th to this day, is 40l, 3s. 7d. Thus the Lord closes this period under His manifest help! I have been able to meet all the expenses connected with the support of the four Orphan-Houses during the last two years, amounting to 3,228l. 5s. 11d., owe no one anything, and have on this 26th of May, 1848, 1l. 10s. 3 3/4 d. left in hand.

Further Account of the New Orphan-House, on Ashley Down, Bristol, from May 26, 1846, to May 26, 1848.

Those, who have read the former chapter on this subject, will remember, how I was obliged to think of building an Orphan-House, and how, when once led to this, I felt myself also led to build it large enough for Three Hundred Orphans; and how the Lord, in His great kindness, most manifestly in answer to prayer, gave me a field of about seven acres for the purpose; and how, by various donations, 2,710l. 3s. 5 1/2 d. had been already received on May 26, 1848. I shall now give a further account of the Lord's dealings with me, concerning the New Orphan-House, yet so, that, for the sake of brevity, only a few of the donations will be referred to, and chiefly those which seem more particularly to mark the finger of God.

July 4, 1846. For about three months my faith and patience have been exceedingly tried about the field, which I have purchased for the building of the Orphan-House, as the greatest difficulties arose about my possessing the land after all; but, by God's grace, my heart was kept in peace, being fully assured, that, if the Lord were to take this piece of land from me, it would be only for the purpose of giving me a still better one; for our Heavenly Father never takes any earthly thing from His children except He means to give them something better instead. But in the midst of all this great trial of faith, I could not but think, judging from the way in which God so manifestly had given me this piece of land, that the difficulties were only allowed for the trial of my faith and patience. And thus it was. Last evening I received a letter by which all the difficulties were removed, and now, with the blessing of God, in a few days the conveyance will be made out.

July 6. The reason why, for several months, there had come in so little for the Building Fund, appeared to me this, that we did not need the money at present; and that, when it was needed, and when my faith and patience had been sufficiently tried, the Lord would send more means. And thus it has proved; for today was given to me the sum of Two Thousand and Fifty Pounds, of which Two Thousand Pounds is for the Building Fund, and Fifty Pounds for present necessities, of which latter sum I took one half for present use for the Orphans, and the other half for the School--, Bible--,Tract-- and Missionary Fund. This is the largest donation I have yet had at one time for the work; but I expect still larger ones, in order that more and more it may be manifest to the children of God, that there is no happier, no easier, and no better way for the obtaining of pecuniary means or anything else in connexion with the work of God, than to deal directly with the Lord Himself.

It is impossible to describe my joy in God when I received this donation. I was neither excited nor surprised; for I look out for answers to my prayers. I believe that God hears me. Yet my heart was so full of joy, that I could only sit before God, and admire him, like David in 2 Samuel vii. At last I cast myself flat down upon my face, and burst forth in thanksgiving to God, and in surrendering my heart afresh to Him for His blessed service.

There came in still further today 2s. 6d.

July 10. Received 120l., of which 100l. is intended by the donor for the Building Fund, and 20l. for present use in the work, as most needed. I took of this 20l. one half for the Orphans, and the other half for the other objects of the Institution.

July 11. By sale of articles, given for the Building Fund, came in 5s. 6d.

July 15. From a sister in the Lord 1l., from a Christian gentleman 5l., from a sister 3s., and from another sister an old silver pencil case and 2s.

July 17. From the neighbourhood of Oxford 1l.

July 21. This morning a gentleman from Devonshire, on his way to London, called on me. When he came I was in prayer, having, among other matters, brought also before the Lord the following points: 1, I had been asking Him for some supplies for my own temporal necessities, being in need. 2, I had asked Him for more means for the Building Fund, and besought Him to hasten the matter, on account of the inhabitants in Wilson Street, on account of the welfare of the children and those who have the oversight of them in the Orphan-Houses, and lastly, that I might be able to admit more Orphans, the number of applications being so great. 3, I had also asked the Lord for means for present use for the Orphans, as the outgoings are so great. 4, I had asked for means for the other objects. -- When I saw this gentleman from Devonshire, he gave me 20l., of which 10l. is to be used for the Building Fund, 5l. for present use for the Orphans, 2l. for brother Craik and myself, and the remaining 3l. were left to my disposal, which I applied to the other objects of the Scriptural Knowledge Institution. Thus I received, at the very moment that I had been asking God, FOUR answers to my prayers.

Sept. 7 From a friend, who has many times helped the Orphans almost from the commencement, I received 50l.

Sept. 9. "Let patience have her perfect work, &c.," must be still my motto concerning this service. Our position in Wilson Street, where the Orphan-Houses are now, remains as it was; I also see more and more the desirableness of commencing the building soon, both on account of the Orphans, and their teachers and overseers; particularly also, because so very many applications are made for the admission of very destitute Orphans, and I am unable at present, to receive all who are applied for; and yet the Lord is delaying to send the full amount of means required. I am also asked, when the Building is likely to commence, and can only answer, I do not know. Now this morning I had again, after family prayer, my usual season for prayer about this work, when I brought all these matters in simplicity before the Lord. Immediately, after I had risen from my knees, the following letter was handed to me, containing 60l.

* * * *, Sept. 8, 1846.

"My dear Brother,

I send Sixty Pounds out of the abundance which the Lord has given to me, and of which it seems to me that He has need in the work you are engaged. If you think proper, would you kindly take 25l. for the Building Fund of the Orphan Asylum, 25l. for missionary labourers, 5l. for the present use of the Orphans, and 5l. for your own purse; and may our good Lord bless your labours of love, and give the increase a hundred fold.

Your unworthy brother,

* * * *"

Thus the Lord encourages me, day by day, to continue to wait on Him. His time is not yet come; but, when it is, all that is needed will be given. By God's grace my faith is unshaken. I am as certain that I shall have every shilling needed for the work, as if I had the money already in actual possession; and I am as certain that this house of mercy will be built, as if it were already standing before me.

Oct. 18. Today the Lord has much refreshed my heart by sending from B. B. 5s., from a young sister 2s. 6d., and through an order on a Bristol Bank 120l.

Oct. 19. While I was this morning in the very act of praising the Lord for His goodness, in giving me yesterday the above mentioned donations, and whilst I was again bringing my arguments before Him, why He would be pleased soon to give me the whole sum which is requisite, I received an order for 200l., which was doubly precious, because it was accompanied by an affectionate and encouraging letter.

Oct. 29. This morning I had been again bringing the ease of the Building before the Lord in prayer, entreating Him to hasten the matter, if it might be, when, the very instant I rose from my knees, there was handed to me a letter with an order for 300l.--About an hour after, I received from a sister in the neighbourhood of Wotton-under-Edge 10s. 6d.--"From Saints in the neighbourhood of Kingsbridge" 1l. 5s.--From a sister an old silver thimble.

Nov. 14. By sale of articles 12s.--This evening I received a small morocco case, containing a gold chain, a pair of gold ear-rings, and a gold brooch (being a set), with the following letter enclosed:

"Beloved Brother in Jesus,

The contents of the accompanying casket being in my unconverted days a wedding gift from a very dear husband, has, as you may suppose, been hither-to preserved as beyond price. But since God, in His great mercy revealed to my soul His exceeding riches in Christ, and gave to it more (Oh, how much more!) than He has taken away, they seemed as the Babylonish garment or wedge of gold, which ought not to be in the Israelites' possession. I therefore give up that which the flesh would fain keep, and still prize; but which the spirit rejects, as unworthy a follower of Jesus. Accept then, dear Brother, those toys, once the pride of life, and the food of folly; and use them for the building of the Orphan-House, in which I feel it a privilege to lay one stone; and may the Lord recompense you a hundred fold, yea, a thousand fold, in this your great labour of love, is the prayer of yours affectionately in the best of bonds.

----November 1846. A Sister and a Widow."

The gift was precious to me as a proof of the continued readiness of my Heavenly Father to help me in this work; but doubly so, on account of the circumstances under which it was given, and on account of the state of mind in which the anonymous donor had given these ornaments.

FOURTH PART

Nov. 19. I am now led more and more to importune the Lord to send me the means, which are requisite in order that I may be able to commence the building. Because 1, It has been for some time past publicly stated in print, that I allow it is not without ground that some of the inhabitants of Wilson Street consider themselves inconvenienced by the Orphan-Houses being in that street, and I long therefore to be able to remove the Orphans from thence as soon as possible. 2, I become more and more convinced, that it would be greatly for the benefit of the children, both physically and morally, with God's blessing, to be in such a position as they are intended to occupy, when the New Orphan-House shall have been built. And 3, because the number of very poor and destitute Orphans, that are waiting for admission, is so great, and there are constantly fresh applications made.--Now whilst, by God's grace, I would not wish the building to be begun one single day sooner than is His will; and whilst I firmly believe, that He will give me, in His own time every shilling which I need; yet I also know, that He delights in being earnestly entreated, and that He takes pleasure in. the continuance in prayer, and in the importuning Him, which so clearly is to be seen from the parable of the widow and the unjust judge. Luke xviii. 1-8. For these reasons I gave myself again particularly to prayer last evening, that the Lord would send further means, being also especially led to do so, in addition to the above reasons, because there had come in but little comparatively, since the 29th of last month. This morning, between five and six o'clock I prayed again, among other points, about the Building Fund, and then had a long season for the reading of the word of God. In the course of my reading I came to Mark xi. 24, "What things soever ye desire, when ye pray, believe that ye receive them, and ye shall have them." The importance of the truth contained in this portion I have often felt and spoken about; but this morning I felt it again most particularly, and, applying it to the New Orphan-House, said to the Lord: "Lord I believe that Thou wilt give me all I need for this work. I am sure that I shall have all, because I believe that I receive in answer to my prayer." Thus, with the heart full of peace concerning this work, I went on to the other part of the chapter, and to the next chapter. After family prayer I had again my usual season for prayer with regard to all the many parts of the work, and the various necessities thereof, asking also blessings upon my fellow-labourers, upon the circulation of Bibles and Tracts, and upon the precious souls in the Adult School, the Sunday Schools, the Six Day Schools, and the four Orphan-Houses. Amidst all the many things I again made my requests about means for the Building. And now observe: About five minutes, after I had risen from my knees, there was given to me a registered letter, containing a check for 300l., of which 280l. are for the Building Fund, 10l. for my own personal expenses, and 10l. for Brother Craik. The Lord's holy name be praised for this precious encouragement, by which the Building Fund is now increased to more than six thousand pounds.

Dec. 9. It is now Four Hundred Days, since day after day, I have been waiting upon God for help with regard to the building of the Orphan-House; but as yet He keeps me still in the trial of faith and patience. He is still saying as it were, "Mine hour is not yet come." Yet He does sustain me in continuing to wait upon Him. By His grace my faith is not in the least shaken; but I am quite sure that He, in His own time, will give me everything which I need concerning this work. How I shall be supplied with the means which are yet requisite, and when, I know not; but I am sure that God will help me in His own time and way. In the mean time I have abundant reason to praise God, that I am not waiting on Him in vain; for since this day twelvemonth He has given me in answer to prayer, a most suitable piece of ground, and 6,304l. for the Building Fund, and about 2,700l. for present use for the work, so that altogether I have received, since this day twelvemonth, solely in answer to prayer, the sum of Nine Thousand Pounds. Surely, I am not waiting upon the Lord in vain! By His help, then, I am resolved to continue this course unto the end.

Dec. 22. Today I have again a precious proof that continuing to wait upon the Lord is not in vain. During this month, comparatively little had come in for the Building Fund; yet, by God's grace, I have been enabled, as before; yea, even with more earnestness perhaps than before to make known my requests unto God, being more and more convinced that I ought to seek by earnest prayer soon to be able to begin the building. In addition to this I had also especially besought the Lord to give me means for missionary brethren, and also for brethren who labour in the word in various parts of England and Ireland; as all my means for them were now gone. I had also been waiting upon God for means to order a fresh stock of tracts. I had lastly again and again besought the Lord to give me means for the poor saints in Bristol, of whom there are many, and whose need is now particularly great. Now today the Lord has granted me precious answers to my requests concerning these various objects, for I received this morning one Thousand Pounds with these words: "I send you some money, part of which you can apply to the Orphans and the other objects of your Institution, according to their need, and the rest you can put to the Building Fund. At the present price of provisions your expenses must be large for the Orphans. Please also take 25l. for your own need." As I have about 80l. in hand for the Orphans, I took nothing for present use for them, but took 175l. for the other objects, in order thus to be able to send some help to Home and Foreign labourers, and to order a fresh stock of tracts; and 800l. I took for the Building Fund. I should have taken less for the Building Fund, and more for present use, did it not appear to me the will of God, that with my might I ought to give myself to this part of the work.

Jan. 5, 1847. We have just now much sickness in the four Orphan-Houses, on account of which we are much tried for want of room, and for want of proper ventilation, the houses having been originally built for private families. This has again most practically shown me the desirableness of having the Orphans, as soon as possible, removed to a house built on purpose for them and my heart says, "Lord, how long?" and importunes Him the more, yet, by His grace, without being impatient, but willing to wait His time, which in the end is always found to be the best.

Jan. 9. From a professional Christian gentleman 10l., which I received from him in paying him his account today.

Jan. 10. From a brother in the Lord 80l.--From C. C. 8s. 2 1/2 d.

Jan. 11. From a lady at Bedminster 3l. 10s.

FOURTH PART

Jan. 25. The season of the year is now approaching, when building may be begun. Therefore with increased earnestness I have given myself unto prayer, importuning the Lord that He would be pleased to appear on our behalf, and speedily send the remainder of the amount which is required, and I have increasingly, of late, felt that the time is drawing near, when the Lord will give me all that which is requisite for commencing the Building. All the various arguments which I have often brought before God, I brought also again this morning before Him. It is now 14 months and 3 weeks since day by day I have uttered my petitions to God on behalf of this work. I rose from my knees this morning in full confidence, not only that God could, but also would, send the means, and that soon. Never, during all these 14 months and 3 weeks, have I had the least doubt, that I should have all that which is requisite.--And now, dear believing reader, rejoice and praise with me. About an hour, after I had prayed thus, there was given to me the sum of Two Thousand Pounds for the Building Fund. Thus I have received altogether 9,285l. 3s. 9 1/2 d. towards this work.--I cannot describe the joy I had in God when I received this donation. It must be known from experience, in order to be felt. 447 days I have had day by day to wait upon God, before the sum reached the above amount. How great is the blessing which the soul obtains by trusting in God, and by waiting patiently. Is it not manifest how precious it is to carry on God's work in this way, even with regard to the obtaining of means? From December 10, 1845, to January 25, 1847, being thirteen months and a half, I have received solely in answer to prayer, Nine Thousand Two Hundred and Eighty-five Pounds. Add to this what came in during that time for present use for the various objects of the Institution, and the total is about Twelve Thousand and Five Hundred Pounds, entirely the fruit of prayer to God. Can it be said, therefore, with good ground, that this way of carrying on the work of God may do very well in a limited and small way, but it would not do on a large scale? The fact brought out here contradicts such statements.

June 23. This day the Lord in His great goodness, by a donation of One Thousand Pounds for the Building Fund, has again encouraged my heart abundantly to trust in Him for all that which I shall yet need, to meet the remainder of the expenses connected with the fitting up and furnishing the New Orphan-House, &c.

Jan. 23, 1848. Today I received 350l., concerning which the donor expressed it as his especial wish that I should take 50l. for myself, 50l. should be for brother Craik, 50l., for the Employment Fund, and the remaining 200l. as I pleased. I put this 200l. to the Building Fund, as the donor had not given to this object before, having been prevented through circumstances, and I knew he would like to contribute towards it.

Jan. 30. I received from D. D. 35l., of which 30l. are intended for the Building Fund, and 5l. for the School--, Bible--, Tract and Missionary Fund.

March 19. From Scotland 10l.

THE LORD'S DEALINGS WITH GEORGE MÜLLER

March 21. From the neighbourhood of Dudley 9s. 8d.

March 28. "A thank-offering to the Lord from the Church assembling at Bethesda Free Chapel, Sunderland, for Church mercies during the past year." The amount is 21l. 10s. 10d.

April 29. From Cornwall 50l., from a most unexpected quarter, whereby the hand of God is the more abundantly made manifest.

In the Report, published in 1848, the following account was given respecting the New Orphan-House, which, except a few verbal alterations, is here reprinted.

1, The total amount, which I have received for the Building Fund, amounts to 11,062l. 4s. 11 1/2 d. This sum enables me to meet all the expenses connected with the purchase of the piece of land and with the erection of the house. I stated before that I did not mean to commence the Building until I had all the means requisite for it, and this intention was carried out. It was not until there was a sufficient amount of means to meet all the sums required for the various contractors, that a single thing was done; but when I once had as much as was required for them, I did not consider it right to delay any longer, though I saw then clearly, and have since seen still more clearly, that a considerable sum would yet be needed to complete the work. For whilst in every respect the Building will be most plain and inexpensive, yet it being intended to be the abode of Three Hundred Orphans, with all their teachers and overseers, it necessarily must be a very large Building, and was therefore found to be even somewhat more expensive than I had thought, as the whole (including fittings and furniture) cannot be accomplished for less than Fourteen Thousand Five Hundred Pounds, towards which the Lord has already given me, as stated, Eleven Thousand and Sixty-two Pounds Four Shillings and Eleven Pence Halfpenny. The sum still needed is required for all the ordinary fittings, the heating apparatus, the gas fittings, the furnishing the whole house, making three large playgrounds and a small road, and for some additional work which could not be brought into the contracts. I did not think it needful to delay commencing the Building, though several thousand pounds more would be required, as all these expenses needed not to be met till many months after the beginning of the Building.

2, The work of the Building commenced on July 5, 1847, and has been going on steadily ever since, with the manifest blessing and help of God.--Six hundred and seven days I sought the help of God day by day, before we came so far as to be able to commence the Building; yet at last He gave me the desire of my heart.--The work is now so far advanced, with the blessing of God, that a considerable part of the Buildings has been already roofed in, and the remainder will be ready for being roofed in a few weeks, that is, in July, 1848.

3, The New Orphan-House has been placed in the hands of eleven trustees, brethren in the Lord well known to me, whom I have chosen, that they might watch

FOURTH PART

over the work and care for it, should the Lord Jesus tarry and take me to Himself. The deeds have been enrolled in Chancery.

4, The New Orphan-House is intended to accommodate 140 Orphan Girls above seven years, 80 Orphan Boys above seven years, and 80 male and female Orphans from their earliest days, till they are seven or eight years of age, together with all the overseers, teachers and assistants that may be needed. The Infants, after having passed the age of seven or eight years, will be removed into the different departments for older boys and girls.

Miscellaneous points respecting the Scriptural Knowledge Institution for Home and Abroad, with reference to the period from May 26, 1846 to May 26, 1848.

1, During the whole of this period six Day Schools, with 330 children, were supported by the funds of the Institution; two Sunday Schools were entirely supported by it, and a third was occasionally assisted. Again four from among the Sunday School children were during these two years received into Church Fellowship. The total number of the children who received instruction in the Day Schools of the Institution, from its commencement up to May 26, 1848, amounted to 4519. The number of the Adult Scholars, who were instructed during this period in the Adult School, which was supported by the funds of the Institution, amounted to 292; and the total number of adults who had instruction from March 5, 1834, to May 26, 1848, was 1438. The total of the expenses connected with all these schools, during these two years, amounted to 886l. 1s. 11 1/2 d.

2, During this period were circulated 649 Bibles and 232 New Testaments. There were circulated from March 5, 1834 up to May 26, 1848, 5746 Bibles and 3760 New Testaments. 74l. 9s. 10d. was expended of the Funds of the Institution, during this period, on this object.

3, From May 26, 1846 to May 26, 1848 was expended of the Funds of the Institution on Missionary objects, 1559l. 1l. 6d., whereby 43 labourers in the Gospel, at Rome and Abroad, were assisted.

4, During this period 64,021 Tracts were circulated, and the sum of 63l. 1s. 5d. was expended on this object of the funds of the Institution. The total number of Tracts circulated from Nov. 19, 1840 to May 26, 1848, amounted to 163,668.

5, There were received into the four Orphan-Houses, from May 26, 1846, to May 26, 1848, Fifty-one Orphans, who, together with those who were in the four Houses on May 26, 18413, made up 172 in all. Of these: 1. Five children died, two as decided believers, one not without some hope, and two as infants. This was the greatest number of deaths we had had for many years; and yet how small is even the number five out of 172 within two years, if it be remembered that we received children as young as two years old; and if it be further remembered that the very fact of such young children being bereaved of BOTH parents is, generally, a plain proof that their parents were very sickly and unhealthy persons, as indeed has generally been the case, since the greater part of the parents of these children died in consumption, which I learn from the certificates of their death. 2. One of the Orphans, who had been above ten years in the house, left the Institution without leave, and went to her friends for two or three days; and for an example to the other children was not taken back again, when her friends wished her to return. 3. Three of the elder girls, who had been several years in the house, were taken back to their relatives and not suffered to remain any longer, because of improper behaviour towards their teacher. All three, however, were of an age to go to service, and would have been shortly placed out, had they behaved better. 4. Four of the children were dismissed because of malignant skin or other diseases, remedies having failed: and in these cases, for the sake of the other children, we were obliged to send them back to their relatives till they might be cured. 5. Seven children were taken back by their relatives, who by that time were able to provide for them, after they had been for several years in the Orphan-Houses. Some of them were able to earn their own bread by that time, and were of use to their relatives. I always act on the principle of at once giving up the Orphans, to their relatives, if they say that they are able to provide for them; having continually a considerable number of very destitute Orphans waiting for admission. 6. Nine boys were apprenticed. 7. Twenty-one girls were sent out to service, eight of whom had been for some time believers.

There were on May 26, 1848, One Hundred and Twenty-two Orphans in the Four Houses. The number of the Orphans who were under our care from April 1836, to May 26, 1848, was 264. The total amount of expenditure in connexion with the support of the Orphans from May 26, 1846, to May 26, 1848, was 3228l. 5s. 11d.

I notice further the following points in connexion with the Orphan-Houses.

1. Without any one having been personally applied to for anything by me, the sum of 24,771l. 19s. 8 3/4 d. was given to me as the result of prayer to God from the commencement of the work up to May 26, 1848. This sum includes the 11,062l. 4s. 11 1/2 d, which up to May 26, 1848 had been given towards the Building Fund. (It may be interesting to the reader to know that the total amount which was given as free contributions, for the other objects, from the commencement of the work, up to May 26, 1848, was 7,060l. 14s. 1 3/4 d.; and that which came in by the sale of Bibles and Tracts, and by the payment of the children in the day-schools, amounted to 2,373l. 3s. 7 1/2 d.) 2. Besides this, also a great variety and number of articles of clothing, furniture, provisions, &c. were given for the use of the Orphans.

Matters connected with my own personal affairs, or the work of the Lord in my hands, not immediately connected with the Scriptural Knowledge Institution, from May 26, 1846 to May 26, 1848.

July 21, 1846, In very great need respecting my own personal expenses, and immediately after I had prayed respecting it, I received from a Christian gentleman of Torquay 1l.

FOURTH PART

July 23. Immediately after prayer for my own personal expenses, being in need, I received from the neighbourhood of Leeds 2l.

July 25. While I was on my knees in prayer, asking the Lord for means for myself, 1l. came to me from Bath.

Aug. 5. Being still much in need, and having asked the Lord for means, I received yesterday evening 1l. 0s. 3d., being some money due to me, and today from Teignmouth 1l. as a present.

Dec. 31, 1846. During this year there have been received into Fellowship 66.

The Lord has been pleased to give me during this year

1, Through the boxes. . . . L165 15 1 1/2

2, Through believers in Bristol, not anonymously 81 13 1 1/2

3, Through believers not residing in Bristol 136 14 8

4, Through presents in articles, worth at least 15 0 0

L399 2 11

To this is again to be added, what I have enlarged on in a former chapter, that during the whole of this year also my daughter was, free of all expenses, at a boarding school. This was worth about 50l.

In November, 1847, I had a most remarkable deliverance, which to the praise of the Lord is here recorded, as it is a further illustration of how the Lord watches over His children.

I was labouring for a little while at Bowness and Keswick in the ministry of the Word in October and November When at Keswick, I stayed with my dear wife in a large boarding-house, in which, however, we were then alone, except a single gentleman. Just before we left Keswick, on the morning of Nov. 24th, I heard that the gentleman, lodging in the same house, had shot himself during the night, but was not quite dead. We had not heard the report of the pistol, it being a very stormy night, and the house large. Two days after, I received from a Christian brother at Keswick the following information respecting the transaction.

THE LORD'S DEALINGS WITH GEORGE MÜLLER

Keswick, Nov. 25, 1847.

"Dear Mr. Mueller,

The tender and Almighty care of our loving Father was never more over you, and indeed over all of us, than in your stay at Mrs. . . . .'s. Mr. . . . . . . was quite deranged for two or three days before you left. Without any control, he had been walking about his room for the last two days and nights, with loaded-pistols in his hands. Furthermore he had taken into his head that you were going to kill him. How gracious of God, that he spread His wings over you, and over dear Mrs. Mueller, so that Satan could not break through the fence, to hurt even a hair of your heads. Speaking after the manner of men, there was nothing to have hindered him coming into the room, where we were all at tea, 9 and firing amongst us; but the Lord was our refuge and fortress, and preserved us from danger, which we knew not of. He shot himself in the neck and the breast, but is not dead. He has a strait-waistcoat on. I assisted in cutting his clothes off, and in other little offices, needed at such a time, and told him of Christ's love in dying for poor sinners. 'I know it,' he said. He shot himself the first time about three o'clock in the morning, and again about seven. What a scene his room presented. Pistols lying in gore. Bloody knives, lancets, and razors strewed about the floor." Etc.

I add an extract from a second letter, written by the same Christian brother, because it shows still further, how very merciful the Lord was to us at that time, in protecting us.

"Mr. ---- is still alive, and has been removed by his friends into Yorkshire. It appears, insanity is in his family, his father being at this time in an asylum. It is evident that he had the pistols in his pockets, but of this no one knew until after the occurrence took place. I do not know what time of night you went to bed; but I judge it was about ten. If so, it was at ten o'clock Mr.--came down from his bedroom, after having been there six hours. It was a mercy you did not meet him, as it is plain that he had loaded pistols on his person."

Dec. 31, 1847. There have been received into Fellowship, during this year, 39: and altogether, since Mr. Craik and I began labouring in Bristol, 1157, besides the 68 whom we found in Fellowship. Of these 1225, 143 have fallen asleep, 70 are under church discipline, 78 have left us, and 259 have left Bristol; so that there are only 675 actually in communion.

During this year the Lord has been pleased to give me.

1, Through the boxes. . . .   L140 6 11 1/2

2, Through believers in Bristol, not anonymously 57 3 6

3, Through believers, not residing in Bristol 127 3 6

FOURTH PART

4, By a legacy of L100 Stock . .   73 4 9

5, Through presents in articles, worth to us at least 15 0 0

L412 18 84

To this is again to be added the free education of my dear daughter, at a boarding school, worth to us at least 50l.

In April, 1848, I was enabled, by the help of the Lord, to complete all the arrangements for the publication of the Narrative of the Lord's Dealings with me in the French language; and about September of the same year the book appeared under the following title: Expose de quelques-unes des dispensations de Dieu envers Georges Mueller. Paris, librairie Protestante, Rue Tronchet, 2.

Supplies for the School--Bible---Missionary and Tract Fund, sent in answer to prayer, from May 26, 1848, to May 26, 1850.

When this period of the work commenced, I had for these various objects 5l. 19s. 7 1/4 d. in hand, a sum so small, that, without the help of God, I could not have gone on even for a few days; for during this period our average expenditure for one single day, merely for this part of the work, was as much as the whole balance left in hand. Now see how God carried me through, in meeting the expenditure of the thousands of pounds which were laid out for these objects, irrespective of the Orphan work, from May 26, 1848 to May 26, 1850.

On the very next day, after the accounts were closed, May 27, 1848, I received from Westmoreland 5l., being the first donation during this period towards this part of the work, of which sum one half was intended by the donor for the current expenses of the Orphans, and the other half for these objects. On the following day, May 28, was anonymously put into the Chapel boxes for missions 1s. 6d. and 2d. Now it happened that all the expenses, connected with these objects, during the first two days amounted only to about 3l., which I was able to meet by what had come in and the balance left in hand; and on May 29th I received 100l. As the application of this sum was left to me, I took one half of it for the Orphans, and the other half for these objects.--Thus I was supplied with means to meet the expenses which came on me the following day, May 30th, when I had to pay the weekly salaries of the teachers in the Day Schools.

June 9. Great has been my desire, and many have been my prayers to God, that He would be pleased to condescend to use me still further, in allowing me the privilege of helping brethren who labour in the word and doctrine, at home and abroad, without any salary, as I have been able to do but very little for them comparatively during the last four months. Now at last, in answer to my prayers, I have received this morning 160l. for home and foreign labourers.--The Lord may see it needful, for the trial of our faith, to seem for a season not to regard our supplications; yet, if we patiently and believingly continue to wait upon Him, it will be manifest in His own time and way, that we did not call upon Him in vain.

July 12. My soul has been longing for farther supplies for home and foreign labourers, to whom I have sent of late all I could. Almost all the letters received from the brethren, to whom I have sent money, have shown to me their great need. Some were in the greatest necessity when my remittances were received by them. Under these circumstances a donation of 117l. 2s. 7d. came in this morning, of which I took 50l. for these objects, and 67l. 2s. 7d. for the Orphans.

Aug. 19. Today all the means for home and foreign labourers were again gone. Also for the support of the various schools and the circulation of the Holy Scriptures and Tracts, scarcely anything remained; 48l. were in hand, yet, considering the liabilities for rent, &c., not more than 5l. of this sum at most could be considered available. When I had, therefore, so little, there came in 267l. Thus my heart is made glad, for I am able to send help to many brethren in these days of peculiar distress.

Oct. 26. This evening there was given to me anonymously at Salem Chapel a sealed paper, which contained two sovereigns and these words: "For what most needs." I took this donation for these objects, as I have now scarcely any money left towards paying the weekly salaries of the teachers in the Day Schools next Tuesday. Oct. 31st. We have not been so poor with regard to these objects since the accounts were closed. But I hope in God.

Oct. 28. I received from Calne 2l.

Oct. 30. Received from Bath 1l.

Oct. 31. There having come in this 5l., and 1l. 10s. 9d. besides, by the sale of Tracts, I had enough to pay the weekly salaries of the teachers.

Nov. 4. Saturday. There were now again only a few shillings in hand towards paying next Tuesday the weekly salaries of the teachers in the Day Schools, when I received this morning from the neighbourhood of Leeds 5l.

Nov. 5. There was put into the boxes at Bethesda 2s. 6d.

Nov. 6. Received 1l. 0s. 6d.

No-v. 7. This evening I found, that, by what had come in during the 4th, 5th and 6th in the way of donations, and by the sale of Tracts during this week, there was more than enough to pay the weekly salaries.

FOURTH PART

Nov. 9. Only a few shillings were left in my hands on Tuesday evening, the 7th instant, towards the weekly salaries of the teachers, for the coming week. Also almost all the Tracts are again gone, and it is nearly four weeks, since I paid out the last money in hand for missionary objects. As to this latter point, my heart had been especially longing to be able to send again help to home and foreign labourers, knowing how very great the need of many is. Thus I was situated with regard to means when I received today 1000l., of which sum I took 300l. for these objects, 100l. for the support of the Orphans, and 600l. for the Building-Fund. The Lord be praised for this most precious help, which is doubly precious on account of the seasonable time in which it comes!

Nov. 16. Yesterday and today I have sent out more than one hundred pounds to brethren who labour at home and abroad, and the Lord has sent again further supplies; for I received today from C. W. 40l. for home and foreign labourers.

Jan. 15. 1849. The means for the circulation of Bibles and Tracts, and for all the various Schools, and for helping missionary efforts had now been reduced to 15l. It had been during the last days especially my prayer, that the Lord would be pleased to give me fresh supplies for brethren who labour in the word and doctrine at home and abroad, as I had not been able to do any thing for any of them during the last fortnight, for want of means. I desired also more means for the circulation of Bibles and Tracts, as several thousands of Tracts had been going out during the last few days, and as also quite recently there had been many openings found for the circulation of the Holy Scriptures among very poor persons. Now the Lord has again given me a precious answer of prayer. I received this morning a donation of 200l., to be used as any of the objects of the Scriptural Knowledge Institution might need help. The donor, however, kindly wished me to take 25l. for myself. I took this 175l. for these objects, and thus I am again supplied with means for the various Schools, for the circulation of Bibles and Tracts, and have something for aiding brethren who labour in the word and doctrine, as I purpose to use 100l. for them. The Lord be praised for this precious help!

I have received still farther today for missions 23l. 5s.

Jan. 17. Today I have received still further help from the Lord in a donation of 125l. for these objects. How manifest it is by all these sums, large and small, received from God in answer to prayer, that He does not allow me to call upon Him in vain!

Feb. 19. A brother in the Lord, who had sold his earthly possession, for the purpose of spending the proceeds of it for the Lord, sent me 120l. as a part, of which he wished me to use 100l. for missions, 5l. for the Orphans, 10l. for another object not to be mentioned, to give 2l. 10s. to brother Craik, and to take 2l. 10s. for myself.

Feb. 20. Today I have received still further 200l. of which I took 100l. for these objects, and 100l. for the Orphans, as the disposal of this sum was entirely left to me.--I do especially rejoice in all these considerable donations, partly, because they enable me to assist so many faithful servants of Jesus Christ, who labour for Him in dependence upon Him for their temporal supplies; and, partly, because they prove that the work of God may be carried on in dependence upon Him alone for pecuniary means, not merely on a small but also on a large scale. See! dear Christian reader, without making any effort whatever, simply in answer to prayer, without personal application to any one, all these sums come in. And thus it has now been going on for more than sixteen years, [was written in 1850]. Persons said to me fifteen years ago, that it was impossible to carry on such a work for any length of time, without regular subscriptions; for the interest which was taken in it at first, would wear off. I never believed such statements. I was assured in my inmost soul that, if the work of God was carried on in God's way, that was the best pledge that it would be provided by God with pecuniary means. Thus I have found it ever since March 5, 1834, when this work commenced. For since that time I have received above Forty-four Thousand Pounds altogether, [up to May 26 1850 only]; and the Lord has so enlarged the work and helped me, that during the last three years I have had the privilege of paying away in His service, in connexion with this work, about Twenty-five Thousand Pounds; nor have I had during this period in any one instance to meet a payment, without being previously provided by the Lord with means for it. If it pleased the Lord to condescend to use me further in this way, He could so order it that even a still larger field of labour were intrusted to me, which would require still greater sums. Truly, it must be manifest to all simple hearted children of God, who will carefully read the accounts respecting this Institution, that He is most willing to attend to the supplications of His children, who in their need cry to Him; and to make this manifest is the great object I aim at, through the means of this Institution.

March 13. The same donor who sent me on Feb. 19th the donation of 120l., sent me today 100l. more for missions.

March 15. From C. W. for missions 30l.

April 1. Anonymously through Bethesda boxes 2d. for missions. Anonymously through Salem boxes 30l., with these words: "5l. for dear brother Mueller, 5l. for dear brother Craik, 5l. for the poor, 5l: for the rent, 5l. for missionary work, 5l. for the Scriptural Knowledge Institution." The last mentioned 5l. I took for the circulation of Bibles and Tracts, and for the various Schools.

April 15. Anonymously through Salem boxes 1d. for missions.

April 18. Received 250l., which, being entirely left at my disposal, I took 100l. for the current expenses for the Orphans, and 150l. for these objects. Thus I have especially the joy, in answer to my daily supplications, of being able to continue to assist many home and foreign labourers who labour in the word and doctrine.

FOURTH PART

May 13. Anonymously for foreign missions 1s.

May 23. Received 360l., of which the kind donor wished me to take 10l. for my own personal expenses, and the 350l. were left to my disposal, just as the work of the Lord in my hands might require it. I took therefore one half for the current expenses for the Orphans, and the other half for these objects, and I have thus the means to continue to send help to home and foreign labourers.

May 27. From the same donor, who gave on Feb. 19th 120l., and on March 13th 100l., 20l. more for missions.

Aug. 4. During the last month I had sent to home and foreign labourers about 150l., and many heavy extra expenses had been met for the Schools and the circulation of Tracts, on which account our means for these objects began to be reduced, when I received this morning 200l., which, being left entirely at my disposal as might be most needed, I took for these objects.

Aug. 9. Anonymously 5l. for home and foreign labourers in the Word.

Aug. 30. 50l. from the donor spoken of under May 27th. Half this sum lie intends for the Orphans and half for missions.

Sept. 18. I received 100l., to be used as might be most needed. This sum came after I had repeatedly asked the Lord for more means, as the money in hand for these objects was now less than it had been for several months. I took, therefore, the whole of this sum for these objects.

Nov. 3. The means were now again low, lower than they had been for many months, when I received 200l., which, being left at my disposal as most needed, I took entirely for these objects.

Dec. 7. Before our means were exhausted for these objects, when there. was yet 140l. in hand, I received today a donation of 150l., the disposal of which was left to me, to use it either for the Orphans or any part of the work of God in my hands. I took 100l. for these objects, and 50l. for the Orphans.

Jan. 2, 1850. The new year commences, even as to this part of the work, with new mercies. There was given to me 160l., to be used as might be most needed, of which sum I took 100l. for these objects, and 60l. for the Orphans. Thus, before all means are expended, while there is yet about 100l. in hand, the Lord sends me again a fresh supply, in answer to my daily supplications, whereby I am enabled to go on with the circulation of Bibles and Tracts, the meeting of all the expenses connected with the various Schools, and still further to help preachers of the Gospel at home and abroad.--I take this first donation from the Lord in this new year, as an earnest that He will help me during the whole of this year also in regard to means for these objects.

Jan. 30. During this month I had been especially led to send much assistance to home and foreign labourers. Also in other respects the expenses for these objects had been considerable. On this account the funds for them had been reduced to about 80l., when I received this evening 450l., of which the donor kindly wished me to take 50l. for my own personal expenses, to give to Brother Craik 50l., and to use the other as might be most needed. I took therefore 200l. for the Orphans, 50l. for foreign missions, 25l. for home missionaries, 25l. for the Day Schools for poor children and for the Adult School and the Sunday School, 25l. for the circulation of Gospel Tracts, and 25l. for the circulation of the Holy Scriptures.

Feb. 10. Received 180l., which the donor left to my disposal, as it might be most needed for the work of God in my hands; he only desired in his kindness that I should take 20l. of it for my own purse. As there is a considerable sum in hand at present for the supplies of the Orphans, I took the whole of this donation for tile other objects, whereby I am enabled to go on more and more in aiding missionary work, and in continuing the circulation of Bibles and Tracts.--I have great delight in showing also by this and other instances to which reference has been made, how the Lord is mindful of my own temporal necessities, whilst I endeavour to serve Him, in entire reliance on Him for what I need with regard to this life, without any salary or any regular income whatever, so that He not only gives me as much as I absolutely need, but most bountifully supplies me; for generally I receive from Him far more than 1 need for myself and family.

March 23. During the last six weeks has been paid out for the School--Bible--Tract and Missionary objects alone about 270l., and very little comparatively has been received. On this account came in most seasonably, and very manifestly in answer to prayer, a donation of 152l. 3s. 6d., which I received this morning, and which I took for these objects, to replenish our means for them.

March 30. From C. W. 30l. for foreign missions.

May 3. During the last month but very little was received for these objects, whilst, for missionary purposes alone, 113l. was paid out. Now this morning I received a registered letter, containing 60l. with these words:

"---- May 1, 1850.

"Dear Brother,

"I send you 50l. for the missionaries, and 10l. for the Orphans, having just sold out part of my property in the funds. It pleases me to find that your new Report will soon be out.

FOURTH PART

Believe me to be, dear brother,

Yours truly in Christ,

* * * *"

This donation came after many prayers to the Lord for supplies. The work is now large. The outgoings are great. During the last month were again expended about 500l. for the various objects of the Institution, nor have I any prospect that the expenses will decrease; yea, I have no desire that they should. I have as great satisfaction, as much joy, in writing checks for large amounts upon my bankers, as I have joy in paying over to them checks, or bank orders, or large notes, which I receive from the living God, by means of donors, for this work. For the money is of no more value to me than as I can use it for God; and the more I can pay out for the work of God, the more prospect I have of being again supplied by Him; and the larger the sum is, which I can obtain from Him, in answer to prayer only, the greater the proof of the blessedness and the reality of this mode of dealing directly with the living God, for what I need; therefore, I say, I have as much joy in giving out as in receiving. I have been devoting myself, for instance, with all my might, both of body and mind, but especially by labouring in spirit, to have the Orphan-House filled with children, not only that thus three hundred destitute Orphans, might be lodged, boarded, clothed, instructed, and in every way cared for, bodily, mentally, and spiritually; but also, in order that thus large sums might be needed and expended, and I might have a greater call than ever to draw largely upon the inexhaustible treasures of God. That I do not mean, in thus speaking, to say that money so obtained by prayer may be wasted, will scarcely need to be noticed; for if any one would obtain means from God by prayer only, and then waste them, he would soon find that he is not able to pray in faith for further supplies.

May 7. The donation of 50l. for the missionary brethren, received four days ago, was very refreshing to my spirit, and most manifestly to me another answer to prayer; but it did not hinder me from continuing in prayer for more means, as I have a great desire to spend again, by God's help, considerable sums in connexion with these various objects, in the course of this month. Moreover, I was looking out for answers to prayer, and therefore expected still further means to come in on the 4th, the 5th, and yesterday; and, as I received nothing, I only prayed the more earnestly, instead of being discouraged. And thus it was that I obtained this morning a still further answer to my supplication, in a donation of 150l., of which I took half for the Orphans and half for these objects, as the disposal of the money was left to me.

My dear Christian reader, will you not try this way? Will you not know for yourself, if as yet you have not known it, the preciousness and the happiness of this way of casting all your cares and burdens and necessities upon God? This way is as open to you as to me. Every one of the children of God is not called by Him to be engaged in such a service as that to which He has condescended to call me; but every one is invited and commanded to trust in the Lord, to trust in Him with all his heart, and to cast his burden upon Him, and to call upon Him in the day of trouble. Will you not do this, my dear brethren in Christ? I long that you may do so. I desire that you may taste the sweetness of that state of heart, in which, while surrounded by difficulties and necessities, you can yet be at peace, because you know that the living God, your Father in heaven, cares for you. Should, however, any one read this, who is not reconciled to God, but is still going on in the ways of sin and carelessness, unbelief and self-righteousness, then let me say to such, that it is impossible, that you should have confidence to come boldly to God in such a state, and I therefore ask you to make confession of your sins to Him, and to put your trust for eternity entirely in the merits of the Lord Jesus, that you may obtain the forgiveness of your sins. Again, should any one read this who has believed in the Lord Jesus, but who is now again living in sin, who is again regarding iniquity in his heart, let not such a one be surprised that he has no confidence toward God, and that he does not know the blessedness of having answers to his prayers; for it is written: "If I regard iniquity in my heart, the Lord will not hear me: but verily God bath heard me; He hath attended to the voice of my prayer." Ps. lxvi. 18, 19. The first thing such a one has to do is, to forsake his evil course, to make confession of it, and to know afresh the power of the blood of the Lord Jesus on his conscience, by putting his trust in that precious blood, in order that he may obtain confidence toward God.

Supplies for the support of the Orphans, sent in answer to prayer, from May 26, 1848, to May 26, 1850.

When the accounts were closed on May 26, 1848, I had in hand a balance of 1l. 10s. 3 3/4 d. With this amount then we began, whilst day by day above one hundred and thirty persons were to be provided for in the four Orphan-Houses in Wilson Street. Nor was there any money besides available except what had been advanced to the four matrons in the various Orphan-Houses for the week's house-keeping, which was already more than half expended; and I had on the 30th to advance again many pounds for the following week. Place yourself now, dear reader, in my position, in order that you may the more clearly see the hand of God in what follows.

On the very next day, after the accounts were closed, May 27, 1848, I received from Westmoreland five pounds, half of which sum was intended by the donor for the Orphans, and half for the other objects. This donation I took as an earnest out of the hands of the living God, that during the whole of this period also He would provide for these many Orphans, as He had done in former years.

May 28. Received anonymously 3s. 9 1/2 d., and from A. S. A. 10s. 2 1/2 d.

May 29. Today I have received 100l., which, being left to me as most needed, I took half for the Orphans, and half for the other objects. How kind of the Lord to refresh my heart thus in sending me this seasonable help at the very commencement of this period, as there was so little left in hand when the accounts were closed three

FOURTH PART

days since and how especially kind, as tomorrow evening again nearly 20l. will have to be advanced for house-keeping!

June 20. 8ll. 8s. 4d. had come in since May 26th. Without any difficulty I had been able to meet all the expenses as they occurred; but now all our money was gone, and this evening I had again to advance the means for a week's house-keeping, whilst there was nothing in hand. Now observe, dear reader, how the Lord helped me! Whilst I was in the very act of beseeching the Lord for fresh supplies, two sisters in the Lord called, who desired to see my dear wife for a few minutes. It was for the purpose of giving her fifteen pounds for the Orphans.--About half an hour after, a brother from Devonshire called, who, on leaving, gave me 5l. for the Orphans. This evening I received still further from Norwich 1l. 1s., together with an eye-glass and a parcel of clothes. There was received also 1s. for Reports. Also a Christian brother from Barnstaple gave me half a sovereign. Thus I was able to meet the house-keeping expenses for the coming week, and to order 2 cwt. of soap, which was needed, amounting altogether to 20l. 10s., and have 1l. 2s. left. The day began and I had nothing, and yet the Lord enabled me to meet all its demands, and I have 1l. 2s. over.

June 21. The Lord is already beginning to give fresh supplies towards the need of the coming week. This morning was sent to me from Essex a large silver mug. There has come in further today from Bath 5s., by sale of Reports 1s., by sale of a book 1s., from South Molton 2s. 6d., from a lady near Bristol 5s., and through an Orphan-box 11s. 6d. and a silver thimble.

June. 23. From Merriott 14s. 4d., from Dundry 5s., through A. S. A. 1s. 6d., from a sister 5s., by sale of Reports 3s. 4d, by sale of articles 1l. 4s. 10d., by the children's knitting 4s. 6d., and from the Isle of Wight 14s. 7d.

June 25. Anonymously from Teignmouth 5l., through Bethesda boxes 6d., ditto 2d.

June 26. From L. M. 1s. 1d., brother F.'s Orphan-box 1s. 1d., by profit from the sale of ladies' baskets 10s., anonymously 1s., ditto 6d., ditto 1d.

June 27. By sale of articles 17s. 3d., from Clifton 10s., from a sister 10s., through a box in my room 10s., from Tiverton 5s., and through the boxes in the Orphan-Houses 4l. 5s. 2d.--Thus we have had again this evening, in answer to prayer, all the means required for the housekeeping expenses of the coming week, and have a few shillings left.

July 4. Though this day week I had all the means requisite for advancing the house-keeping expenses for this week, yet, after having done so, there remained only a few shillings. I had therefore again to seek help from God respecting the means requisite for this evening, besides means for other expenses, which in the course of the week might come upon me, as the regular house-keeping expenses are not one half of the whole of the expenses for the Orphans. Now, during this week also, I have been helped by the Lord in the following manner:--

On June 28th I received from Uppingham 10s., and 10s., and 1s. Also by sale of Reports came in 6s.--On June 30th was sent from Tetbury 10s. -- On July 1st a brother in the Lord gave me 10l.--On July 2nd from A. S. A. 1l., and from a sister 5s. Also anonymously 4s., ditto 10s., ditto 1s. 6d.--On July 3rd from a brother 1l.---July 4th. By sale of articles 2l. 3s. 6 1/2 d., and by knitting and needlework 6l. 13s. 10d. -- Thus I was again able to advance this evening the means for the house-keeping expenses of the coming week, and have a few shillings left.

July 6. The more the Lord is pleased to help me, the more, by His grace, I have confidence in Him. Therefore, though there were only a few shillings left the evening before last, I set myself to prayer that God would be pleased to send everything requisite for continuing this work. Accordingly, two ladies left today, anonymously, at the Infant Orphan-House, 2 old foreign gold watches, an old silver watch, a small gold chain, 6 gold mourning rings, a pair of gold earrings, and 2 necklaces. There was also given today 10s., and 2s. 2 1/2 d. came in by sale of Reports.

July 7. From Edmonton 1l. From a Christian lettercarrier 10s., from a sister 2s. 6d., and from M. R. 5l.

July 8. Through sister C. from a friend 2s., from M. 2s., from D. 1s., and from sister F. 1s. 1d.

July 9. From A. S. A. 10s. Also a brother has brought me this evening 5l.

July 10. From Street 2s., through Salem boxes 3d., and by knitting 10s. 9d.

July 11. By sale of trinkets, &c. 14l. 13s. 7d. From Gloucester 1l., from Tenby 1s. 6d., anonymously 5s., and from one of the labourers in the work 3s.--Thus I had again this evening enough to meet the ordinary housekeeping expenses for the coming week, but I am now looking out for fresh supplies to meet the expenses connected with ordering a fresh quantity of oatmeal from Scotland, &c.

July 12. The Lord has quickly given me an answer, and granted the desire of my heart. I received this morning a donation of 117l. 2s. 7d., to be used as the work of God in my hands might require. Of this sum I took 67l. 2s. 7d. for the Orphans, and 50l. for the other objects.

Aug. 1. From July 12th up to this day we were comfortably provided with means; but this evening, at our usual prayer-meeting, I had only 8l. to give to the four matrons towards the house-keeping expenses of the coming week, which I did give in the full assurance that the Lord would provide more by the time that this sum was expended, if not before.-- Now see how God at this time also helped in His faithful love, and thereby proved that we did not call upon Him in vain. On the next

FOURTH PART

day, Aug. 2, I received from London 1l., from Buttevant 1s. 6d., from "a Leamington grocer" 2s. 6d., from Bedminster 5s., and by sale of Reports 10s. 6d.--On Aug. 3rd came in by the sale of Reports 1s., from Langport 7l. 4s., from a very poor widow 2s., and 8s. besides.--On Aug. 5th was received from Mr. G. B. C. 1l. 1s., from Marbury 6d., from Brighton 10s., from Ayrshire 1l., and from Newbury 1l.--On Aug. 6, from the neighbourhood of Wotton-under Edge 7s., and by profit by the sale of ladies' baskets 10s.--On Aug. 7th from a Christian lady 1l., by sale of Reports 1s., from a sister 10s., through the Chapel-boxes 2s. 6d., and 6d., from Tockington 1l. 1s., through the Orphan-boxes in my house 13s. 6d., from Northam 2l., and from Cork 1l. On Aug. 8th by sale of articles 18s. 2 1/2 d. By sale of Reports 8s. Thus I had everything which was requisite for the expenses of the past week, and had this evening, Tuesday, even 7l. left to advance towards the house-keeping expenses of the coming week. My hope and prayer is, that the Lord will be pleased to send in more means before this is gone, as it will only suffice till Friday morning.

Aug. 9. The Lord has been very kind today, and proved afresh that none who trust in Him shall be confounded. There has come in by the sale of Reports 1l. 13s. 10d., by sale of another book given for sale 9d., and from Clevedon 10s., together with a pair of gold ear-drops, a buckle, and a pencil case. This evening, while I was walking in my little garden, lifting up my heart for further supplies for the work of God in my hands, there was given to me a registered letter from Liverpool, containing 20l. for the Orphans. There came also from Lymington 5s. Thus I am able to send the remainder of the money which is needed for house-keeping expenses for this week.

Aug. 10. The Lord has sent in still further supplies in answer to prayer. From a brother I received 1l., from the Isle of Wight 5l., from Bath 5l., from Barking 2 gold seals, 2 pairs of gold ear-rings, 2 gold brooches, a gold snap, a bead necklace, and a small telescope.

Aug. 11. By sale of Reports 1l. 9s. 2d. From Bath 5l.

Aug. 12. From Norfolk 1l. 10s.

Aug. 13. Anonymously 2s. 6d., ditto 6d., ditto 1s.

Aug. 14. By profit from the sale of ladies' baskets 1l.

Aug. 15. Through a box in my house 10s., by sale of articles 15s. 2d., by sale of Reports 2l. 0s. 6d., anonymously 2s., from Keswick 1s., from one of the labourers in the work 10s., and from Chelsea with a great variety of articles 7s. 8d., 7 1/4 d., and 1s. I received also from Bath 2 mourning rings.

Aug. 16, Wednesday. This afternoon I received from a brother, who had sold the greater part of his little property, 20l., of which he wished me to take 10l. for the Building Fund and 10l. for present use for the Orphans. Thus I have received for the

Orphans altogether in money, besides many articles, since yesterday week the 8th, 61l. 15s. 8 1/4 d., whereby I have been enabled to supply the means which were yet needed for house-keeping; and I had likewise sufficient to advance last evening all that is needed for house-keeping for this week, and to meet 38l. 2s. 6d. extra expenses, which have come upon me during the last eight days. How seasonable were, therefore, the various donations which the Lord was pleased to send me since the 8th, and how manifestly did they come in answer to prayer! But now I have again scarcely anything left, which, however, does not cast me down, as I shall go afresh, by God's help, to His inexhaustible treasures.

Aug. 22. Tuesday evening. The Lord has again been pleased to send me since last Wednesday morning 17l. 14s. 9d., so that, together with the little which was left last Tuesday evening, I was able to advance the money needed for house-keeping during the coming week. The Lord was pleased to provide me with means for this in the following manner. On Aug. 17th came in 9s. 10d. from Clifton. On Aug. 18th was received by sale of Reports 2l. 1s., and by a donation from Acklow 1l. Also a brother from Bath left anonymously at the Boys' Orphan-House two sovereigns. On Aug 19th a brother from the neighbourhood of Stroud sent me 5l., of which he kindly wished me to take 1l. for my own personal expenses and to use the 4l. as most needed, which I took for the Orphans. Received also 9s. by sale of Reports. On Aug. 20th I received 6s. 6d. and 6s. 10d., being the contents of two Orphan-boxes, also from the neighbourhood of Keynsham 1l., from the neighbourhood of Royston 1l. and from Batheaston 10s.--Aug. 21. Through a box in my house 1l., from Doncaster 10s., by sale of Reports 18s., and from the Isle of Wight 10s. --Aug. 22. By sale of Reports 17s. 6d, by sale of articles 12s. 3d., anonymously 1s., from Thornbury 2s. 6d., and anonymously 4d. Thus, then, I had all the means requisite, and had 11 3/4 d. left.--Think of this, dear reader! 11 3/4 d. I had left and about 130 persons were daily to be provided for, and yet we did not go into debt at that time for anything, nor do we now, nor have we from the commencement of this work. Nor did I make personal application to any one for anything, nor did I directly or indirectly speak about our need, so that persons might be influenced to give. But why not, you may say, dear reader? Simply because this work has for its first and primary end the benefit of the Church at large and of the unconverted world, to show that there is verily a God in Heaven whose ears are open to those who call upon Him in the name of the Lord Jesus, and who put their trust in Him. Cheerfully have I dedicated myself with all my physical, mental, and spiritual energies to this life of faith upon the living God, for everything that I need in connexion with my own personal and family necessities, and in connexion with the work of God in my hands, if but by any means, through it, multitudes of believers and unbelievers may be benefited. Thousands have been benefited by it already, but tens of thousands my heart longs to benefit. No trial, no difficulty, no hardships, no self-denial, will I, by God's help, count too much, if but this end may be attained.-- I had then, as I said, 11 3/4 d. left. Now observe how the Lord helped me again this time in answer to the supplications which the evening before, Aug. 22nd, my fellow-labourers and myself had offered up to Him.

FOURTH PART

On Aug. 23rd, the very next day, came in early in the morning 4s. 6d. by sale of Reports, and a Christian brother from Barnstaple sent 1l. with Matt. vi. 11 ("Give us this day our daily bread"). Also from Torquay was sent a half-sovereign. From Budleigh Salterton 1l., and from Weymouth 2l. together with a gold brooch. There arrived also a parcel from Stowmarket containing the following little sums; 6d., 7s. 6d., 2s., 2s. 6d., 10s., 6s., and 5s. There came in also from Bath 18s. for Reports. Thus I received altogether that day 7l. 5s. 6d., whereby I was enabled to order 8 cwt. of rice, as I was informed the evening before that our store of rice was exhausted.

Aug. 24. By knitting of the children 2s. 3d.

Aug. 25. By sale of Reports 1s., and from F. B. B. 2s. 6d.

Aug. 26. Saturday. Next Tuesday evening again a considerable sum will be needed for house-keeping, whilst at the beginning of this day I had nothing yet towards meeting this demand. Now observe the kindness of the Lord in helping me again bountifully this day. I received from a sister at Tottenham 2l., from Norton St. Philip's 10s., from a village near Leeds 5l., from Southwell 10s., from Edinburgh 21l., of which the donor kindly wished me to take 6l. for my own personal expenses, and 15l. for the Orphans; and from Thornbury for Reports 10s. 6d., as a donation, 2 old three-penny pieces and 20 copper coins, also 5s. from another donor near Thornbury.

Aug. 27. A half-sovereign was received, but the place of the donor is not to be mentioned; from an aged Christian woman 3l. and a pair of silver shirt buttons; and by sale of Reports 10s.

Aug. 28. From a sister as the profit from the sale of ladies' bags 6s. 6d., anonymously 2s. 6d., by sale of Reports 12s., from Weymouth 2l., also 4s., 1s., and 1s. 6d., and from Ryde 1l.

Aug. 29. Anonymously from Torquay 1l. There came in also by sale of articles 17s. 6d., by sale of Reports 10s. 6d., and from a sister 2s. 6d.--Thus, by the help of God, we have again received by this Tuesday evening 42l. 3s. 9d., while last Tuesday evening there was only 11 3/4 d. left. How kindly has the Lord therefore, in answer to our supplications, increased "the handful of meal in the barrel!" Thus I have been enabled to advance the needful sum requisite for the house-keeping expenses till next Tuesday evening, and to meet several extra expenses. The remainder of the money has been put by for rent, and towards meeting the current expenses connected with the apprentices; and I am now again, without anything on hand, looking to the Lord for fresh supplies.

Now observe, dear reader, how again the Lord helped at this time also, and notice in particular how, from all parts of the country, yea from great distances, and sometimes also from foreign lands, the donations are sent, and most frequently from persons whom I have never seen, whereby the hand of God is the more strikingly made manifest.--I relate now how we were helped in answer to our prayers, this time, when nothing was left.

Aug. 30. Wednesday evening. I had this evening a long season for prayer for the work in which I am engaged, and sought also especially help from God as to means for present use for the Orphans. While I was in prayer, a parcel of clothes was brought from Weymouth for the benefit of the Orphans, and shortly after another parcel. There were also sent 2s. 6d. as a donation, and 1s. 6d. for Reports. A few minutes after I had finished praying, I received an anonymous letter from Teignmouth, containing 1l. and these lines; "The Lord permits me to send you the enclosed. Dear brother, 'Only believe,' 'O how great is thy goodness, which Thou hast laid up for them that fear Thee; which Thou hast wrought for them that trust in Thee before the sons of men.' Yours ever in Him."--How again has been fulfilled in my experience that word "Only believe!" I am now looking out for more, for I shall shortly again need many pounds, for the current expenses for the Orphans.

Aug. 31. Received from Hull 1l. 8s. 10d., of which 16s. 3 3/4 d. is from A. Z., who intends of this, 10s. for the Building-Fund, and the remainder as most needed, which I took for present use for the Orphans. A young man also sent through A. Z. 6s., and the remaining 6s. 6d. is for Reports. This morning also a sister in the Lord from Malvern called on me, who brought from herself and a few other sisters 4l., of which 10s. is intended by a sister for foreign missions, and the rest to be used as most needed, which I therefore took for the Orphans. I also received from Cheltenham 6s., and 10s. for Reports from Teignmouth, 10s. ditto from Street, and 1s. and 6d. as donations from Street.

Sept. 1. Received from several believers at Bowness 3l. 0s. 6d., of which they kindly intend 1l. for myself, 1l. for foreign missions, and 1l. 0s. 6d., for the Orphans.--From A. S. 5l.--By needlework of the children 6s. 1d., from Shirehampton 5s., and from a sister 2s. 6d.

Sept. 2. From Ilfracombe 1l. 10s. From Wakefield 10l. From Windsor 8l. 10s., of which 2l. 7s. is for Narratives and Reports. By sale of Reports 1l. 8s. 8d., and for needlework done by the Orphans 1l. 17s. 2d.

Sept. 4. A very poor Christian widow, having come into the possession of 10l. through the death of her mother, gave 1l. of it for the Orphans.

This sister in the Lord has since fallen asleep. Will she regret the gift now? Our time is short, very short. Let every child of God stand in the place of service in which He has set him, working while it is called today, "for the night cometh when no man can work." Again and again, while looking over my journal, I meet with names of donors, who have fallen asleep. Shortly, dear reader, your turn and mine may also come.

FOURTH PART

Sept. 5. The boxes in my house contained 1l. 6s. There came in also by sale of articles 5l. 1s. 8d., by sale of Reports 14s. 4 1/2 d., through the boxes of the Orphan-Houses 4l. 14s. 9 1/2 d., and from a sister 10s. Thus this evening, Tuesday, it was found that the Lord had sent in again since last Tuesday evening, when there was nothing in hand, nearly 50l., so that I have been able to meet all the extra expenses of the week, and to advance again this evening money for house-keeping for the coming week.

Now see how the Lord helped further for the week after this.

Sept. 6. By sale of Reports 13s. 9d. Sept. 8. From a lady 7s. 6d.

Sept. 9. By sale of a small cask of pickles, given for the purpose, 12s. -- A brother and sister gave 3l., as a thank-offering to the Lord for the conversion of two brothers, in one week, in answer to prayer. From London 5l. By sale of articles 1s. 4d. From Scotland 12s. 6d. for Reports, and 3s. 6d. for the Orphans. From Crediton was sent 10s., 3s. 6d., and 11s.

Sept. 10. By sale of Reports 11s. 8d.--From a sister 2s. 6d., and through ditto 1s. 6d. Anonymously 1s.

Sept. 11. Profit from the sale of bags 10s.--From a brother in London 10s. From Scotland 3l. 18s. 7d. with 1l. for myself.

Sept. 12. Tuesday. By sale of articles 18s. 8d. By sale of Reports 3s. By a donation 1s. Thus again about 20l. has come in during the past week, and, with what remained in hand last Tuesday evening, I have had over and above what is needed for house-keeping expenses for the coming week.--When I came home this evening from our usual weekly prayer meeting for the Lord's blessing upon the various objects of the Scriptural Knowledge Institution, I found that a brother from Tavistock had left at my house 2l. 2s. 6d.

Sept. 13. By sale of Reports 8s. 2d.--From a Christian lady 2 crown pieces and 2 pairs of socks.--From East Coker 1l. 10s., together with many gold articles, &c. Also 1s. 6d. with many articles and some coins. From Belper 10s. for Reports, and 10s. as three donations.

Sept. 15. From Kingstown 5s. as a donation and 10s. for Reports.-- This evening 1l. was left anonymously at my house; and a brother left 2 sovereigns at the Boys' Orphan-Rouse. A little boy gave 8d., and 6s. 6d. came in by sale of Reports.

Sept. 10. From a brother at Clifton 1l. 10s.

Sept. 17. By sale of Reports 13s. A.S.A. 10s. Anonymously 10s. From a sister 2s. 6d. Through a sister 10s.

Sept. 19. Tuesday. A gentleman called on me this morning and gave me half-a-sovereign for the Orphans, but would not give his name.--By sale of articles 3l. 0s. 6d., by Reports 8s. 6d., through the box at my house 1l., by a donation 10s. 6d., and paid on behalf of two Orphans 1l. 15s. Evening. Thus again more than 20l. has come in in money during this week, besides many valuable articles. I was thus able to advance all that was needed for house-keeping, and what was left I put by for rent and material for clothes, which have been ordered, trusting in God for fresh supplies for next Tuesday.

The Lord helped us this time again, as the following shows.

Sept. 20. By sale of a Report 6d.

Sept. 21. From Barnstaple was sent 1l. 5s.--Boxes in my house 10s. 6d.--This morning a Christian from Somersetshire called at my house, and said, he only wished to put something into the Orphan-box, and then put in a sovereign.--From Leicester was sent 1l.--This afternoon a letter was left at my house, containing a five pound note and these words: "From a Believer in the efficacy of the prayer of faith, to be appropriated as Mr. Mueller may think fit." As there was only 3l. 16s. in hand for the Orphans, I took this donation for them.--This evening I had again an especial season for prayer respecting the various objects of the Institution. Almost immediately, after I had risen from my knees, I received from Sunderland 1l.

Sept. 23. From Norwich 10s. From Bath 5l. Through a sister in Bristol 5s.

Sept. 24. Anonymously from Liverpool 10s.--From Stourbridge 1l.-- From A. S. A. 6s. 8 1/2 d. By sale of Reports 2s. 6d. From Cheshire 2l. Anonymously 5s.

Sept. 25. The contents of an Orphan-box 18s. 10d.

Sept. 20. From Brighton 5s. By sale of articles 2l. 6s. 8d. By sale of Reports 1l. 6s. Through Orphan-boxes 5s. 2d. Ditto 2s. 9d. Through the boxes at the Orphan-Houses 2l. 14s. 11d.--Thus the Lord has again sent in about 25l. during the week, whereby I have been enabled to meet all the extra expenses of the week, and to advance for the house-keeping expenses of the coming week.

Sept. 27. When today there was again only a few shillings in hand, I received from Sunderland 2l. 19s. 6d. for Reports. Also from a sister in Bristol 10s. from another 10s. as the profit from the sale of ladies' baskets, and from Plymouth 1l.

Sept. 28. By the sale of trinkets and old silver 9l. 10s.

--From Scarborough 2l. as a donation, and 6s. for Reports.--From Barnstaple 2l. 0s. 9 1/2 d. By sale of Reports 10s.--From a donor in Bristol 1l.

FOURTH PART

Sept. 30. From a Christian gentleman in Bath 1l. From Oswestry 7s. By sale of Reports 12s.

Oct. 1. By Reports 3s. 4d. From A. S. A. 11s. 10d. Anonymously 10s. From Devonshire 6s. 6d.

Oct. 2. From Liverpool 2s. 6d. By Reports 7s. 6d. From a Brother in Bristol 1l.

Oct. 3. By sale of Reports 2s. 6d. and by sale of articles 1l. 9s. 9d. Thus by this evening, Tuesday, again about 28l. has come in, and I have been able to meet all the extra expenses of the work, and advance money for the week's house-keeping; but have now again scarcely anything left.

Oct. 4. By sale of trinkets came in 2l. 17s. 6d.

Oct. 5. From a sister 2s. 6d. From Kingsbridge 1l. 5s.

Oct. 0. By knitting 15s. 3d.

Oct. 7. Received from Sherborne 1l. 9s. 4d. Received also from the neighbourhood of Dartmouth 1l. 0s. 6d. There came in likewise through sister E. Ch. 1l. 5s. 10d.--Also 5l. 14s. 0 1/2 d., being part of the proceeds of a little publication.

Oct. 8. From A. S. A. 5l. Anonymously 1l. Ditto 6s.

Oct. 9. By sale of a Report 6d. From a sister 10s.

Oct. 10. From Cheltenham 10s. By sale of articles 4l. 0s. 1d. By sale of Reports 6s. 2d.--Thus, by this evening, Tuesday, again the sum of 26l. 2s. 8 1/2 d. had come in. I was, therefore, able to meet all the housekeeping expenses of the coming week, besides having paid away 8l. 15s. for apprentices, &c., and have 12s. 8d. left in hand. My heart is assured that the Lord will help further.

Now, dear reader, did the Lord help this time also? Yes, He did. Could it be otherwise? No; for they that trust in the Lord shall never be confounded. Let me then relate to you the way in which God helped us, going on with the extracts from my journal.

Oct. 11. At our meeting yesterday evening we made our supplication to God that He would be pleased to help us further. Immediately after the meeting I received 10s. Also when I came home I found that 6s. had been brought from Gosport for Reports, and 1s. 6d. as the proceeds of an Orphan-box at Gosport. Also 5s. was put by the bearer of the money into an Orphan-box at my house, who also brought a woollen shawl.--Today 1l. was left at one of the Orphan-Houses by "an aged person of a Bristol alms-house," who would not give her name. There came in also by sale of stockings 1l. 4s. 6d. There was likewise left anonymously at my house, an old silver watch, 2 mourning brooches, and 2 gold pins. Thus the Lord has already sent in a little.

Oct. 12. Received in an anonymous letter 1s. 8d. From the Isle of Man 2s. 6d. By sale of Reports 1l. 13s. 6d. Through a brother in Scotland 1l.--From two young gentlemen at Clifton 4s.--From Street 1s. 6d. -- Through an Orphan-box 2s. 1d.

Oct. 13. From some believers near Kingsbridge 1l. By sale of articles 15s. Left at the Boys' Orphan-House 5s.

Oct. 14. From Bideford 2l. By sate of Reports 8s. By children's needlework 19s. 8 1/2 d.

Oct. 15. By sale of Reports 2s. 6d. From A. S. A. 13s. 5d. From Barnstaple 1l. From Yorkshire 5l., with these words: "Please to accept the enclosed 5l., as a thank-offering to God for an answer to prayer, in the conversion of a soul. I should like half of it to go to the Orphans, the other half I leave to your discretion." The other half I put to the Building-Fund.

Oct. 10. From Horsington 10s.--Through the boxes at my house 15s. 0 1/2 d.--From a sister 5s.

Oct. 17. From Reading 1l. By sale of Reports 5s. 6d. By sale of articles 4l. 10s. 6d.--Thus by this evening, Tuesday, the Lord had sent in again 23l. 11s. 3d., whereby I had enough for advancing the house-keeping expenses of the coming week, and the remainder I put by for the rent and the current expenses for the apprentices.

Oct. 18. When now there was again nothing in hand, I received by sale of Reports 12s., by a donation 7s, from Notts 5s. 1d., in small contributions 12s. 3d., and 1s.

Oct. 19. Anonymously from Tottenham a half-sovereign. From Collumpton 8s. 6d. and 11s. 6d.

Oct. 20. By sale of Reports 4s. From Barnstaple 5s. From a sister 2s. 6d., and from Madeley 1s. From Dublin 5s.

Oct. 21. From Clevedon 1l. 10s. From Cirencester 1l. 13s. 4d. and also 3s.--By sale of Reports 1l. 2s. 6d.

Oct. 22. From A. S. A. 11s. 3 1/2 d. Anonymously 10s. Ditto 8d. From a clergyman 10s. From S. 10s. By sale of Reports 1s. 6d. From a sister 5l. Oct. 24. By sale of Reports 5s. 4d. Boxes in the Orphan-Houses 1l. 2s. By sale of articles 3l. 2s. 1d.--Thus by this evening, Tuesday, again 20l. 4s. 11 1/2 d, had been received, and as the

FOURTH PART

expenses of the coming week for house-keeping, together with some extra expenses during the past week, did not amount to more than 18l. 1s. 6d., I had 2l. 3s. 5 1/2 d. left, which I put by for the rent and the current expenses for the apprentices, and am again looking to the Lord for fresh supplies, and again assured that He will help me.

Oct. 31. Since last Tuesday evening it has pleased God again to make it abundantly manifest that we do not wait on Him in vain. Besides many articles, there came in 24l. 4s. 8 3/4 d. As the money which was needed for the house-keeping expenses for the coming week, together with a few other small expenses which I had had to meet during the last week, did not amount to more than 19l. 19s. 3d., there was more than 4l. left, which I put by towards the rent and the expenses for the apprentices, and hope in God for the next week.

Nov. 1. When I came home last evening from our usual weekly prayer meeting, I found 1l. from R. L. H. Thus the Lord has already given a little.--There arrived today a box from Reading, containing the following articles from various donors:

A black feather. Also two pairs of ladies' shoes and a pair of velvet boots. Also two ladies' bags, 2 pairs of bracelets, 2 waistbands, a pair of baby's shoes, 2 neck ribands, and some white lace.--Further, a pair of worked slippers, a thimble case, 2 pin-cushions, a pair of baby's stays, a lady's bag, a pocket-book, a silver brooch, 2 gilt brooches, a gilt seal, and 12 yards of calico.--Further, a box of artificial flowers. Also an urn stand. Further, a bible and prayer book in a case. Further, a little box containing 2 gold rings, a gilt chain, a bead necklace, some mock pearls, and a gilt buckle.--Likewise a paper containing a smelling bottle, a pen knife, a waist buckle, and a card.--Further, a paper containing 2 needle-cases, a purse, 2 little books, 2 medals, a scent bag, a little smelling bottle, 3 pebbles, and 3 mourning necklaces. Another paper, containing 4 gold rings, a gold pin, 2 old silver thimbles, the handle of a silver fruit knife, a snuff-box, 2 silver mounted corks, 7 pin-cushions, a needle-book, a pair of bracelets, a bead purse, a smelling bottle, a silver brooch, a gold brooch, a bead necklace, a pair of compasses, a broken gold watch key, 1 shilling, an old silver thimble, an emery cushion, a gold ring, a cloak fastener, and a little bead bag.-- Another paper, containing a silk scarf, a shawl, and some muslin for night-caps. A paper box, containing a silver-mounted smelling bottle, a toilette cushion, an amethyst brooch, a silver butter-knife, a pair of gloves, and 2 shillings for missions. Another paper, containing 8 1/2 yards of blue print.--Also 50 books and some pamphlets. --Lastly, a gauze dress, a silk dress, a collar, and 3 caps.--I have on purpose given here at full length the contents of this box, to show what a variety of articles, either for sale or for the use of the Orphans, has been sent.--There arrived also today, anonymously, a box from a considerable distance, containing more than one hundred different articles. There was also 5s. in this box, to pay for the carriage. This day also came in by sale of Reports 2s. 6d., and by needlework of the Orphans 19s. 1d.

Nov. 2. From the neighbourhood of Lutterworth a half-sovereign, from a sister in Bristol 10s., through a brother half-a-crown and 4 frocks.

Nov. 3. From S. N. 2s. 6d.

Nov. S. From A. S. A. 8s. Anonymously 2s. 6d. By sale of Reports 1s. 4d.

Nov. 6. By sale of stockings 9s. 2d. From Cumberland 5l. From Ayrshire 1l.

Nov. 7. By sale of articles 2l. 9s. 4 1/2 d., and by sale of a Report 6d. This evening, Tuesday, as only 13l. 3s. 5 1/2 d. had come in during the week, I had only 7l. to advance towards the house-keeping expenses of the coming week, after having met some other expenses. But I hope in God for more, before this is gone, which will only last two or three days.

Nov. 5. By sale of Reports came in 3s., and 2s. 6d. was given by a relative of one of the Orphans.

Nov. 9. Only 5s. 6d. had come in yesterday. Tomorrow more money will be needed for house-keeping. In this our poverty I received this morning One Thousand Pounds. The money being left to me for disposal as it might be most needed, I took of it 600l. for the Building Fund, 300l. for missionary purposes and the circulation of bibles and tracts, and 100l. for present use of the Orphans. I have thus the means which are yet needed for this week's house-keeping expenses, besides being able to meet other heavy expenses which are before me next week.

Feb. 20, 1849. For three months and ten days, since Nov. 9, 1848, the donations have always come in so, that we abounded during the whole period, there having been always fresh donations received, before all the money in hand was disbursed. The total amount that came in during this period was 469l. 14s. 10d. Now today there was no money in hand for advancing the amount needed for the next week's house-keeping. All the money in hand was due for rent, and therefore unavailable, as I never go in debt for anything. In this our need there was given to me this afternoon the sum of 200l., which was left to my disposal for fitting up the New Orphan-House, or for any of the objects in connexion with the Scriptural Knowledge Institution that might be in need. As, however, I have all the means for fitting up and furnishing the New Orphan-House, as far as I know, and as there is no money in hand for present use for the Orphans, I took 100l. for that object, and 100l. for the circulation of Bibles and Tracts, for the Day-Schools, the Sunday-School, and the Adult-School, and for Home and Foreign labourers in the Word.

March 9. The New Orphan-House is now nearly ready. On this account we have to get in large supplies for the children's clothes. Within the last few days I have ordered thousands of yards of material for this purpose, and thousands more will need to be ordered, besides providing a stock of many other things. For this large sums are needed. Under these circumstances I received today a donation of 300l., to be used for the Building Fund, or the current expenses of the various objects, just as it might be most required. As I judge that we have all that is needed for the fitting up and furnishing of the house, and as there is more in hand than usual for the missionary objects, the circulation of Bibles and Tracts, and for the various Schools, and as we have only about 60l. for present use for the Orphans, towards meeting all the heavy expenses before us, I took the whole of this donation for the Orphans, as the donor has kindly left the disposal of the money entirely to me. This donation, coming in just now, has been an exceedingly great refreshment to my spirit; for it is, at the commencement of the great increase of our expenses, in connexion with the 300 Orphans, instead of 120, like an earnest from God, that He will supply us also with means when the demands for the 300 will be more than twice as great as they are now. Through this donation I have means to meet all the expenses which will be incurred in getting in for the new establishment the stores of provisions, soap, material for clothes, haberdashery, and of the many other articles of which it would be desirable to buy our supplies on wholesale terms. The Lord be praised for His kindness!

April 10. Received this afternoon the following letter:--"Dear Brother,

"I have the pleasure today of sowing a little more seed-corn for eternity. Employ the enclosed 50l., if you please, for the support of the Orphans. The remaining 5l. be pleased to divide between yourself and dear brother Craik.

"Yours very truly in Christ,

"* * * *"

From the same donor I had recently had two donations of 120l. and 100l.

April 11. From the brethren at Sunderland, assembling at Bethesda chapel, 10l., as a part of their annual thank-offering to the Lord for Church mercies during the last twelvemonth.

April 18. Today I received a donation of 250l., of which I took 100l. for the Orphans, and the other 150l. for the other objects. Never were the current expenses for the Orphans nearly so great as they are now, but at the same time never was the income nearly so great. Thereby the Lord, as it were, says, that, when the New Orphan-House shall have been filled with Orphans, He will likewise give what is requisite for them. Whilst yet much is in hand, He has been pleased to send this donation.

From April 19th to May 23rd, the Lord was pleased to send in still further many donations.

May 23. Today I received 360l., of which I took half for the current expenses for the Orphans, and half for the other objects. By this donation I am still further provided with means to meet all the expenses connected with the removal of the children into the New Orphan-House, the reception and fitting out of many fresh children, the filling the stores of the New Orphan-House, &c. How does the Lord by all this clearly say, that, when this house shall have been filled with children, He will provide the means for their support!

June 18. Today, as the fruit of the prayers of three years and seven months, the children began to be moved from the four Orphan-Houses in Wilson Street, Bristol, into the New Orphan-House.

June 23. Saturday Evening. This has been indeed a week of great and many and peculiar mercies. All the Orphans with their teachers and overseers have been moved into the New Orphan-House, during Monday, Tuesday, Wednesday, and Thursday; so that there are now about 140 persons under one roof. The Lord has most signally helped.--As I had for more than three years sought the help of God concerning all matters connected with the New Orphan-House, I did expect His help in this particular also; but He has done beyond my expectations. Though only the day before yesterday the last children were moved in, there is already such a measure of order established in the house, by the help of God, as that things can be done by the minute hands of the timepieces. His name is to be praised for this, and my soul does magnify Him for His goodness!--Also with regard to temporal supplies for the dear Orphans, the Lord has been exceedingly kind. On the second day of receiving the children, there was sent 20l. On the third day, an individual, who walked with me through part of the house, said, "These children must consume a great deal of provisions," and, whilst saying it, took out of his pocket a roll of Bank of England notes, to the amount of one hundred pounds, and gave them to me for the Orphans. On the same evening there was also sent for the Orphans a very large cask of treacle, and for their teachers and overseers 6 loaves of sugar. Also a cooper made gratuitously two large new casks for treacle. On the next day I received information that about 10 cwt. of rice had been purchased for the Orphans, which should be sent. Besides this, several small donations have come in. So bountifully has the Lord been pleased to help of late, that I have not only been able to meet all the extraordinary heavy expenses connected with moving the Orphans from Wilson Street into the New Orphan-House, filling the stores of the New Orphan-House, &c.; but I have more than five hundred pounds in hand, to begin house-keeping in the New Orphan-House. How true that word that those that trust in the Lord shall not be confounded! After all the many and long-continued seasons of great trial of faith within these thirteen years and two months, during which the Orphans were in Wilson Street, the Lord dismisses us from thence in comparative abundance. His holy name be praised for it!

In order that this chapter may not be too long, I can only mention of the donations, from June 23, 1849, to May 20, 1850, those which came in under particular circumstances. The total amount received from June 23, 1849, to May 26, 1850, for the current expenses of the Orphans, was 2,102l. 13s. 4 3/4 d.

Aug. 30. Received a Fifty Pound Note with these words: "I send you herewith a Fifty Pound Note, half for the Missions, half for the Orphans, unless you are in any personal need; if so, take 5l. for yourself. This will be the last large sum I shall be

FOURTH PART

able to transmit to you. Almost all the rest is already out at interest." I took half of this 50l. for the Orphans and half for Missionaries. The writer sold some time since his only earthly possession, and sent me at different times sums of 120l., of 100l., of 55l., of 50l, and of 20l. for the work of the Lord in my hands. When he says therefore "the rest is already out at interest," he means that he has given it away for the Lord, which indeed both for time and eternity is the very best way of using the means with which the Lord may be pleased to intrust us, in so far as, considering in the fear of God all our various claims and duties and relationships, we may do so. As this is written for the spiritual profit of the reader, I cannot but add to this extract from my journal under Aug. 30, 1849, that since that time I have received other donations from the same donor, and much larger still. He used for God the means with which He was pleased to intrust him, and, contrary to this brother's expectation, the above 50l. was not the last large donation; for it pleased God soon after, to intrust him with another considerable sum, which he again used for the Lord. This did not at all surprise me; for it is the Lord's order, that, in whatever way He is pleased to make us His stewards, whether as to temporal or spiritual things, if we are indeed acting as stewards and not as owners, He will make us stewards over more. But for more, on this deeply important subject, I must refer the reader to the third part of this Narrative, page 575 to 604.

Sept. 27. From friends at Othery 20l.--This donation is very refreshing to my spirit. Last evening and this morning I had especially besought the Lord, that He would be pleased to continue to send me means, as the expenses are now so great; for there are 107 Orphans in the house, and about 190 persons daily sit down to their meals, and this number is every week increasing. Now, by this donation, which comes not only from an entirely new but also most unexpected quarter, the Lord is, as it were, saying to me, that He will not fail to help me, even when there shall be about 330 persons in the house, for which number it is fitted up.

Oct. S. Yesterday again seven Orphans were received. Every week I am now taking in five, six, seven, or eight; and within the last nine weeks altogether have been received, and about 200 persons sit down daily to their meals. This has greatly increased the expenses already, and they will be still more increased, as I purpose to receive still further 120 Orphans, if God permit, to make up the number 300. Yesterday, after having received the seven children, I again gave myself to prayer for an increase of means. Now today I have received from Devonshire a set of valuable jewels, i.e. a ring set with 5 brilliants, a brooch set with 12 larger and 12 smaller brilliants and 1 large emerald, and a pair of ear-rings, both together set with 10 brilliants and 2 emeralds. The bearer brought also 1l. 10s. 4d. and 10s. 2d., being the proceeds of two Orphan-boxes, likewise 1l. 4s. 6d. At the same time I received from another brother from Devonshire. 4l.; and from a third 16s. 10d.-- Truly the Lord does not allow me to wait upon Him in vain!

Nov. 1. Today I have again received seven Orphans. There are now about 220 persons daily sitting down to their meals in the Orphan-House. Before the seven fresh Orphans were brought, I received a letter from a banker in London, giving me information that a brother in the Lord, living between 200 and 300 miles from hence, had given order to pay me 40l. for the Orphans.--By the same post I received anonymously from London 5/. from the same donor, who has now for several years sent twice every year this amount, of which she kindly wishes me to use half for my own personal expenses, and half for the work of the Lord in my hands. I took the half for the Orphans.--This was not all. In the afternoon, whilst receiving the Orphans, there came in still further 69l. 3s. 8d., also 2s. and a few articles.

Nov. 16. About 260l. has been spent within these 16 days, i.e. since the first of the month, for current expenses for the Orphans alone, and about 120l. for the other objects, making in all about 380l. within half a month. Lord look upon the necessities of Thy servant, seeing that now the outgoings are so large!

Nov. 30. We have been helped through this month most comfortably, though the expenses for the Orphans have been heavier by far, than in any month all the 14 years since this work was commenced, having been 380l. 9s. 2d., and, including the expenses for the other objects, about 540l.

Dec. 4. Today was paid to me a legacy of 50l., left for the benefit of the Orphans.

Dec. 12. Anonymously a Bank Post Bill for 50l. 13s. 6d.

Jan. 9, 1850. Today was sent to me from the Committee of the Cholera Fund in Bristol 20l., which the gentlemen constituting it had voted for the benefit of the twenty children who had lost their parents in the Cholera, and whom I had received into the New Orphan-House.

I had not applied either directly or indirectly for this money; indeed I was reluctant even to give information as to the number of Cholera Orphans received, lest there should be even the appearance as if after all I asked for money, instead of solely trusting in the living God. But some of the gentlemen on the Committee, knowing the fact that I had received many Orphans, made such by means of the Cholera, proposed that there should be paid to the Institution a sovereign on account of each such child received. This sum was especially remarkable to me as a fresh proof of the numberless ways, which God has at His command for providing me with means.

I also cannot help noticing the remarkable coincidence that, at the time God visited this land with the Cholera, in 1849, I had so much room for the reception of Orphans. The Lord was pleased to allow me the joy and sweet privilege of receiving altogether twenty-six children, from ten months old and upward, who lost their parents in the Cholera at that time, and many besides, since then, who were bereaved of their parents through this fearful malady.

FOURTH PART

Jan. 31. Today five more Orphans are to be received. For the last fortnight, comparatively little had come in for the Orphans, i.e. not quite 60l. In the prospect of the Orphans coming today, I said last evening to my dear wife, that the Lord would send us something for them; for I have often found, that either He has sent something with the children, or at the time that they have been received. It was but about ten minutes after I had said so, when I received 450l. (see the account of the income for the other objects), of which I took 200l. for the Orphans. This morning I received further 10l. from a pious countess in Edinburgh, and 10s. from Deptford. Thus the Lord has indeed sent something for the Orphans. It is now seven months and thirteen days since the Orphans began to be received into the New Orphan-House. The expenses for them have been since then Fifteen Hundred and Twenty Pounds; and yet we have this day more in hand, than when the New Orphan-House was opened. Unbelief and natural reason would have said, and did say, If there have often been scarcely any means in hand, while the Orphans were in the rented houses, and only about 120 in number, how will it be when there shall be 300 in the New Orphan-House? But faith's reply was, Our poverty has been only for the trial of our faith, and it will be as easy to the Lord to provide for 300 as for 120 Orphans. And thus we have proved it hitherto, and, no doubt, shall prove it, as long as the Lord shall enable us to trust in Him.

May 25, 1850. The Lord has up to the close of this period helped also for this as well as for the other parts of the work; for during this last week I have received about 62l. for the current expenses for the Orphans. With confidence in the living God I step into the new period, though our expenses are now far heavier than ever they were, being fully assured of His faithfulness. May He be pleased to uphold me during the remainder of my earthly pilgrimage in His fear and truth, and may He graciously be pleased to give me day by day the faith which my circumstances may require.

Closing account as to the way in which the means were obtained for the expenses connected with the erection, fitting up, and furnishing of the New Orphan-House, Ashley Down, Bristol.

At the time where the last chapter, referring to this subject, closes, the New Orphan-House was being built. Part of it was already roofed in, and the remainder was to be roofed not many weeks afterwards. But how much did there yet remain to be done in other respects! A building so considerable as to contain about 300 large windows, would require, even after it was finished, an immense amount of labour, to be fitted up and furnished for 330 persons. Then, after this was done, the settling in of the Orphans and their teachers and other overseers, needed still more abundant help. Further, the obtaining of suitable helpers for this part of the work, was indeed no small matter. Lastly, though the Lord had been pleased to give me already above Eleven Thousand Pounds for the New Orphan-House, yet I needed several thousand pounds more, in order to bring the whole into such a state, as might render the building fit for the reception of the Orphans. And now, in looking back, and finding that I not only was helped in all these matters, but also in every one of them far beyond my largest expectations --does it not become me to say to those who love the Lord Jesus, and into whose hands this account may fall: "0 magnify the Lord with me, and let us exalt His name together!" Each one of the foregoing difficulties which still existed on the 26th of May, 1848, was so great, that if only one of them had remained, and I had not been helped, what would have been the result? But while the prospect before me would have been overwhelming had I looked at it naturally, I was never, even for once, permitted to question what would be the end. For as, from the beginning, I was sure that it was the will of God, that I should go to the work of building for Him this large Orphan-House, so also, from the beginning, I was as certain that the whole would be finished, as if the building had been already before my natural eyes, and as if the house had been already filled with three hundred destitute Orphans. I was therefore of good courage, in the midst of an overwhelming pressure of work yet to be done, and very many difficulties yet to be overcome, and thousands of pounds yet needed; and I gave myself still further to prayer, and sought still further to exercise faith on the promises of God. And now, the work is done, the difficulties are overcome, all the money that was needed has been obtained, and even more than I needed; and, as to helpers in the work, I have obtained even beyond my expectations and prayers. Nearly seven years have passed away already [1856] since the New Orphan-House was opened, and about three hundred and thirty persons sit down in it day by day to their meals.

The Godly reader will feel interested in learning now further particulars, as to how it pleased God to assist me in accomplishing my desires, with reference to the preparation of the House for the reception of the children, and I therefore relate the manner in which I received further pecuniary supplies; and, whilst doing so, will here and there make remarks concerning other points, which may throw light on the subject.

Up to May 26, 1848, I had received altogether towards meeting the expenses connected with the building of the New Orphan-House the sum of 11,062l. 4s. 11 1/2 d. I now state further, some instances, merely as specimens, as to the manner in which it pleased the Lord, to provide me further with means for fitting up and furnishing the New Orphan-House, without applying to a single individual personally for anything, but only giving myself to prayer.

June 8, 1848. I received 5l. 17s. as the "Proceeds from the sale of a Tree for the New Orphan-House."

June 17. Received 5l., of which 4l. 1s. is the proceeds from the sale of "a second tree for the New Orphan-House," and 19s. for present use for the Orphans.--The reader is here called upon to notice that, whilst I had yet to obtain several thousand pounds for finishing the New Orphan-House, all the other current expenses of the various objects of the Institution were going on; and for none of all these pecuniary necessities had I any regular certain income whatever, nor did I seek help from any one but the living God only.

FOURTH PART

June 20. A brother and sister gave four silver table spoons, twelve silver tea spoons, and a pair of silver sugar tongs for sale.

Aug. 7. From a sister in the Lord 200l.--With 2 Cor. viii. 12, 1s. -- Anonymously from J. H. W. 5s., as "a thank-offering to the Lord for His delivering goodness in sickness."--Anonymously 1s.

Aug. 13. From a brother 10s. This brother had worked overtime, and in prayer he told the Lord that, if his employers gave him anything for it, he would give it to the Building Fund, as he had a great desire to contribute something towards this work, from which he had been kept for want of means.

Aug. 16. A brother in the Lord having sold his little earthly property, for the sake of spending the money for the Lord, brought 20l. of the proceeds, of which he wished me to take 10l. for the Building Fund, and 10l. for the orphans.

Aug. 19. It is this day a twelvemonth since the foundation stone of the New Orphan-House was laid, and now the building is up, and almost entirely roofed in. Also part of the inside plastering is already done. How can my soul sufficiently magnify the Lord for all the help which He has been pleased to give, since this day twelvemonth!--As we are now so far advanced, I have been increasingly entreating God, that He would be pleased to give me the means which are yet requisite for fitting up and furnishing the house; for even now I am completely depending upon Him for considerable sums, to accomplish this. But while much is still needed, I have never had, by God's grace, the least misgiving, as to His willingness to give me all I need; on the contrary, I have been assured that, when I actually required the money for the fittings and the furniture, it would come. And now this day the Lord has again proved, to me, how willing Ha is to act according to my faith; for there was given to me this morning 887l. under the kind condition that I should take of it 20l. for my own personal expenses, and the rest for the Building Fund or the present need of the various objects of the Institution, as it appeared best to me. I took therefore 600l. for the Building Fund, and placed 267l. to the School--, Bible--, Tract--and Missionary Fund, with the especial intention of using the greater part of this 267l. for helping home and foreign preachers of the Gospel, who labour without any salary, in dependence upon the Lord for supplies, knowing the need of many to be very great; for cases of especial distress among them had again recently come before me. My soul does magnify the Lord for all His goodness and faithfulness!

Oct. 11. This afternoon I received a letter, containing a check for 50l. with these words: "1 Peter iv. 12-14. The enclosed draft is for Mr. Mueller, to be disposed of according to his own need, and the need of the Orphans under his care. May the 37th Psalm continue to be his solace in the fiery trial through which he is passing." I took the whole of this sum towards fitting up and furnishing the New Orphan-House.

Oct. 16. This evening I received a fifty pound note as a thank-offering to the Lord for numberless mercies during a long course of years. The donor desired that

Brother Craik should have 10l., myself 10l. for my own personal expenses, and 30l. were left to me to dispose of as I thought best, for the work of God in my hands, which sum I put to the Building Fund, with the donor's approval.

Oct. 20. From a lady in Ireland 5s.--By sale of turf and grass 3l. 16s. 2d.

Oct. 24. By sale of articles 4s. 4 1/2 d.--From a Christian gentleman in Devonshire 20l. Day by day I am waiting upon God for means for furnishing the house. The last-mentioned sum I received when returning from the Orphan-Houses from our weekly prayer-meeting, where I had been again seeking from God further help, together with my fellow labourers in the work.

Oct. 25. From sisters in the Lord in Devonshire, 5l., of which they kindly intend one half for the Building Fund, and the other half for present use for the Orphans.

Nov. 8. The Building is now so far advanced by the help of God, that I was able to arrange yesterday with the clerk of the works to purchase today 32 grates for small rooms, two copper furnaces for the wash-house, and two iron furnaces for the scullery. Thus, therefore, the expenses for fitting up the house commence. For all this I had the money in hand, and even some hundreds of pounds more, than the liabilities which are already upon me; yet I want still many hundred pounds to meet all the heavy expenses, connected with fitting up and furnishing so large a building, levelling the ground, making a road through the ground, pitching three large playgrounds, &c. Under these circumstances I received this morning anonymously 50l. for the Orphan-House, with Psalm cxvi. and the request not to notice the post-mark. As I understood the donor to intend this donation for the Building Fund, I took it for that.

Nov. 9. Today the Lord has helped still more abundantly. I have received a donation of One Thousand Pounds, to be used for the Building Fund and the present necessities of the work generally, as the various objects of the Institution might require. Of this donation I took, therefore, 600l. for the Building Fund, 100l. for the present necessities of the Orphans, 200l. for missionary purposes, and 100l. for the circulation of Bibles and Tracts, and for the various Day Schools, the Sunday School, and the Adult School of the Institution. All these manifestations of the Lord's abundant help do not in the least surprise me. I expect help from Him. I know that He listens to my supplications, and that, for the sake of the Lord Jesus, He is willing to help me yet more and more, to the confounding of Satan and to the putting to shame of unbelief.

Nov. 10. Received a bank order for 5l. from the neighbourhood of Tavistock, which, being left to my disposal, I took for the Building Fund.

Nov. 15. From the neighbourhood of Launceston 20l.

FOURTH PART

Dec. 22. Received 100l. This sum being left to my disposal, I took it for the Building Fund.

Jan. 2, 1849. Received from Devonshire 10l., with these words: "A moiety of the first fruits of interest on Bristol Dock Shares from the Town Council of Bristol, towards the New Orphan Building." Thus even the fact, of Bristol being made a free port, was used by the Lord as a means to supply me with this sum.

Jan. 17. The time is now drawing near, when further steps are to be taken to fit up and furnish the house, as more than two-thirds of the rooms are all but ready. Under these circumstances I have prayed the more earnestly, day by day, that the Lord would be pleased to give me the means which are yet needed; and as my heart has been assured from the beginning, and all through these three years and two months, since I first began to pray about this subject, that God would in every way help me in this work, so I have also been particularly satisfied that He would be pleased to provide the means which may be required to meet all the heavy expenses, which yet remain to be met. Now, today I have had again a precious answer to my daily supplications with reference to this work; for I received this evening 600l., concerning which it was desired that brother Craik and myself should each take 50l. for ourselves; the remaining 500l. was left entirely to my disposal; yet an especial reference was made to the heavy expenses connected with fitting up and furnishing the New Orphan-House, towards which I might, either in part, or entirely take this sum.-- After prayer I have decided on portioning out the money thus: 300l. towards fitting up and furnishing the New Orphan-House, 50l. for present use for the Orphans, 50l. for the support of the Day Schools, the Sunday School, and the Adult School, 25l. for the circulation of the Holy Scriptures, 25l. for the circulation of Gospel Tracts, 25l. for Foreign Missions, and 25l. for the Employment Fund.

With reference to the present of 50l. for myself, as mentioned just now, I cannot help calling upon the Christian reader to observe how richly the Lord supplies my own personal necessities. Since 1830 I have had no regular salary nor any stated income whatever I then began to rely upon the living God alone for the supply of all my temporal necessities; and all these many years have never once been allowed to regret this step, nor has the Lord at any time failed me. Often, indeed, I have known what it is to be poor; but for the most part I have abounded. I sought no payment from man for my service for God, whether in the ministry of the Word or as director of the Scriptural Knowledge Institution; but though I did not seek for any payment, the Lord has most abundantly recompensed me, even as to this life. By far the most important point, however, of this my way of living, is, that many of the disciples of the Lord Jesus have had their hearts comforted, and have been encouraged themselves to trust more in God, than they used to do; and it was, moreover, my becoming more experimentally acquainted, through this way of living, with the readiness of God to help, to succour, to relieve, and to answer prayer, which led me in March 1834 to begin the Scriptural Knowledge Institution, and in November 1835 to care about destitute Orphans.

Jan. 26. Anonymously from the neighbourhood of Nottingham "A gold chain."

Jan. 30. From a professional gentleman in Bristol 50l.

Feb. 12. The New Orphan-House is now almost entirely finished. In six weeks, with the help of God, all will be completed. On this account I have been during the last fortnight much occupied in making the necessary arrangements for fitting it up and furnishing it; but the more. I have been occupied about this, the more I have seen how large a sum the whole of the fittings and the furniture will require; and this consideration has led me still more earnestly of late to entreat the Lord, that He would be pleased to give me the means, which may yet be needed for the completion of the whole. Under these circumstances a brother in the Lord came to me this morning, and after a few minutes conversation gave me Two Thousand Pounds, concerning which sum he kindly gave me permission to use it for the fitting up and furnishing of the New Orphan-House, or for any thing else needed in connexion with the Orphans. I have placed the whole of this sum, at least for the present, to the Building Fund. Now, dear reader, place yourself in my position. Eleven hundred and ninety-five days it is since I began asking the Lord for means for the building and fitting up of an Orphan-House. Day by day have I, by His grace, since that time, continued to bring this matter before Him. Without one moment's doubt, or misgiving, or wavering, have I been enabled to trust in God for the means. From the beginning, after I had once ascertained the will of God concerning this work, have I been assured that He would bring it about; yea, as sure have I been from the beginning that He would do so, as if I had already had all the means in hand for it, or as if the house had been actually before me, occupied by the children. But though to faith even three years ago the whole work was accomplished, to sight there remained many and great difficulties to be overcome. Even at the commencement of this day there remained many difficulties, in the way of means, as well as in other respects; therefore. I was on the point of giving myself again especially to prayer, at the very moment when I was informed that the donor of the above mentioned Two Thousand Pounds had called to see me. Now I have the means, as far as I can see, which will enable me to meet all the expenses; and in all probability I shall have even several hundred pounds more than are needed. Thus the Lord shows that He can and will not only give as much as is absolutely needed for His work, but also that He can and will give abundantly. It is impossible to describe the real joy I had in God, when I received this sum. I was calm, not in the least excited, able to go on immediately with other work that came upon me at once after I had received the donation; but inexpressible was the delight which I had in God, who had thus given me the full answer to my thousands of prayers, during these eleven hundred and ninety-five days. I notice further concerning this donation: 1, The donor especially desired me to keep his name entirely concealed; and in order that no one might know who he is, he gave me not an order on a bank, but brought the amount in notes. 2, He had intended to leave me this sum for the benefit of the Orphans after his death, and for years it had been in his last will; but he judged it more according to the will of God to give the money during his life time.

FOURTH PART

March 31. A brother brought me a gold repeater with a gold chain, to which two gold seals and a gold ring were attached, and told me that he desired to give the chain, seals, and ring towards fitting up the New Orphan-House, and wished me to get him for the gold repeater a silver watch, as the love of Christ had weaned his heart from any desire to use a gold repeater. He also stated, that whatever was over and above the sale of the repeater should go for the benefit of the Orphans.

I have thus given a few out of the hundreds of donations, varying from one farthing to 2000l., as specimens, to show how the Lord was pleased to furnish me with the means. The total amount, which came in for the Building Fund, was 15,784l. 18s. 10d. Of this sum 14,914l. 5s. 8d. was received by donations in money, 60l. 19s. 11d. came in by the sale of articles, given for the purpose. 66l. 3s. 10d. by the sale of grass and turf from the field, on which the New Orphan-House was erected. 743l. 9s. 5d. came in for Interest; for I considered that, as a steward of large sums, which were intrusted to me, I ought to invest the money, till it was actually needed; and thus the sum was obtained.

After all the expenses had been met for the purchase of the land, the conveyance of the same, the enrolment of the trust deeds in Chancery, the building, fitting up and furnishing of the New Orphan-House, there remained a balance of 776l. 14s. 3 3/4 d., affording a manifest proof that the Lord can not only supply us with all we need in His service, simply in answer to prayer, but that He can also give us even more than we need. It will be seen how this balance was afterwards used.

Miscellaneous points respecting the Scriptural Knowledge Institution for Home and Abroad, with reference to the period from May 26, 1848 to May 26, 1850.

1, During the whole of this period, five Day Schools, with 329 children in them, were entirely supported by the Funds of this Institution; and some pecuniary assistance was rendered to four other Day Schools. Also a Sunday School, with 168 children, was entirely supported, and another was occasionally assisted. Lastly, an Adult School, with 106 Adult Scholars, was supported during this period. There was expended on these various Schools 851l. 1s. 5 1/2 d. during these two years.--The number of all the children that were taught in the Day Schools through the medium of this Institution, from March 5 1834 to May 26, 1850, amounted to 5114; the number of those in the Sunday Schools amounted to 2200; and the number of the persons in the Adult School to 1737. In all 9051.

2, From May 26, 1848 to May 20, 1850, were circulated 719 Bibles and 239 New Testaments. There was expended on this object, during this period, of the funds of the Institution, 104l. 15s. 11d. There were circulated altogether, from March 5, 1834 to May 26, 1850, Six Thousand Four Hundred and Sixty-Five Bibles and Three Thousand Nine Hundred and Ninety-Nine New Testaments.

3, From May 26, 1848, to May 26, 1850, were spent 2574l. 16s. 6d. of the funds of the Institution for missionary objects, whereby 40 preachers of the Gospel in British Guiana, in the East Indies, in Switzerland, in France, in Germany, in Canada, in Scotland, in Ireland, and in England were assisted.

The reader will notice how greatly this object of the Institution was increased during the last four years previous to May 26, 1850. This arose from the fact, that, in the early part of 1846, the need of certain brethren who laboured in the word and doctrine came before me, and God laid them on my heart to labour for them in prayer, in order that I might obtain means from Him for such brethren to a greater extent than I had done before. Ever since then the Lord has been pleased increasingly to use me in this way. For from May 26, 1846 to May 26, 1848, there was spent for that object nearly three times as much as during any former period of the same length; and during the period from May 26, 1848 to May 26, 1850, I was not only allowed to do as much as before, but to expend even 1016l. 5s. more than during the former period, notwithstanding all the many heavy additional expenses for the various other objects of the Institution.

It is my sweet privilege to state, that the labours of many of these forty servants of the Lord, whom I assisted, were especially owned of God during these two years. There took place very many conversions through their instrumentality. This applies both to those who laboured among idolaters and those among nominal Christians.

4, From May 26, 1848 to May 26, 1850 the sum of 184l. 9s. 4 1/2 d. was expended on the circulation of Tracts. There were circulated during this period 130,464 Tracts. The total number which was circulated from Nov. 19, 1840 up to May 26, 1850 amounted to 294,128.

As the Missionary department was considerably enlarged during these two years, so the Tract Department also increased to nearly three times the extent that it was during the former periods, for which I desire to be grateful to the Lord, and I rejoice in it as a means by which the Lord may be pleased to do much good; indeed already we can say, we are not without fruit.

Besides English Tracts, we circulated many in German and French, also some in Welsh, and a few hundreds in Portuguese and Italian.

On May 26, 1848, there were 122 Orphans in the four Orphan-Houses in Wilson Street, Bristol. There were admitted, before the New Orphan-House was opened, 9 fresh Orphans, making 131 in all. Of these, however, one was taken by her relatives to Australia, to which they emigrated, and wished her to accompany them. Three were sent to their relatives till they might be cured, on account of such diseases as made them unfit to be with other children. Two fell asleep in Jesus as decided believers, of whom the one had been several years in the house and converted some months before her death. The other had been only six months under our

FOURTH PART

care, when she died. Almost immediately after her admission she was found to be in consumption, but the Lord allowed us the joy of winning her soul for Him. Two girls were sent out to service, both as believers. And four boys and one girl were apprenticed. The actual number, therefore, of Orphans who were removed from the four rented Orphan-Houses in Wilson Street, Bristol, on June 18th, 19th, 20th, and 21st, 1849, into the New Orphan-House on Ashley Down, Bristol, was 118. Some of these children had been received when the first and second Orphan-Houses in Wilson Street were opened, and had therefore been with us, at the time of our removal, more than twelve years, and they remained several years afterwards, for we keep them as long as it appears to us good for them, irrespective of expense. Thus we have the joy of seeing very delicate and sickly little children grow up and become healthy young men and women, whilst otherwise, humanly speaking, they might never have been reared, or, at all events have been sickly all their lives for want of a healthy place of abode, of cleanliness, or a sufficient quantity of wholesome and nourishing food. But especially we have in this way the great joy of seeing many of these Orphans brought to the knowledge of the Lord Jesus, through the blessing which God grants to our training them up in His fear from their earliest days. It is never with me a question how much money each child costs, through being retained so long, but only that bodily, mentally, and spiritually they may be benefited through our care. To make them useful for time, and to win their souls for the Lord, are our great aims concerning them.

After the New Orphan-House had been opened, and the 118 Orphans from Wilson Street, with their teachers and other overseers admitted into it, I did not at once receive fresh Orphans; but, in order that all the necessary regulations of the new establishment might be properly made, and especially, in order that I myself might first learn what was the best way of regulating it, we waited five weeks before the reception of fresh Orphans. On July 24th, 1849, this commenced, and from that time up to May 26, 1850, altogether one hundred and seventy Orphans were received, from ten months old and upwards, so that on May 26, 1850, there would have been 288 Orphans in the New Orphan-House, including the 118 removed into it from Wilson Street, had there been no changes. But of this number two young children died, two Orphans were taken back by their relatives, who were by that time able to provide for them. One boy was sent back to his relations, partly on account of epileptic fits, and partly on account of oft-repeated great disobedience, in order that we might thus make an example of him for the benefit of the rest. Three boys were sent to their relatives, as ready to be apprenticed, four boys were apprenticed at the expense of the Institution, and provided with an outfit accordingly; and one girl was fitted out and sent to service.

There were, therefore, on May 26, 1850, only Two Hundred and Seventy-five Orphans in the New Orphan-House; and with the teachers, overseers, nurses, and indoor and out-door servants, &c., the whole number of persons connected with the establishment was Three Hundred and Eight. The total number of Orphans, who were under our care from April 1836, up to May 26, 1850, was Four Hundred and Forty-three

I notice further the following points in connexion with the New Orphan-House.

1. Without any sectarian distinction whatever, and without favour or partiality, Orphans are received. There is no interest whatever required to get a child admitted, nor is it expected that a certain sum be paid with the Orphans. Three things only are requisite: a, that the children have been lawfully begotten; b, that they be bereaved of both parents by death; and c, that they be in destitute circumstances. Respecting these three points strict investigation is made, and it is expected that each of them be proved by proper documents; but that having been done, children may be admitted from any place, provided there is nothing peculiar in the case that would make them unsuitable inmates for the establishment.--I particularly request, that persons will kindly refrain from applying for children, except they are bereaved of both parents, as I can not receive them, if only bereaved of one; for this establishment has been from the beginning, only for destitute children who have neither father nor mother, and there can be no exceptions made.

2. The attention of the reader is called to the name of the Orphan Establishment. It is called the "New Orphan-House." I particularly request that the friends of the Institution will use this name and earnestly beg, in order to avoid mistake, that it may not be called the "Orphan Asylum," as there is about half a mile from the spot, where the "New Orphan-House" has been erected, another charitable establishment, which has been for many years in existence, called the "Female Orphan Asylum." But most of all I earnestly request, that the New Orphan-House be not called "Mr. Muller's Orphan-House." I have now and then been pained by observing that this appellation has been given to it. I trust that none, who recognise the finger of God in this work, will be sinning against Him by giving to me any measure of that honour, which so manifestly and altogether is only due to Him. The Lord led me to this work. He gave me faith for it. He sustained my faith for it to the end. He provided the means. He remarkably helped me through one difficulty after the other. Had He not upheld me in the midst of them all, I should have been surely overwhelmed by them. Therefore, by His help, I will not sin by taking even in the smallest degree that honour to myself, which entirely belongs to Him; and let none be sinning, by giving the least degree of this honour to me, or admiring me, instead of honouring and admiring the Lord.

3. The New Orphan-House was placed in the hands of eleven trustees, chosen by me. The deeds were enrolled in Chancery.

4. The New Orphan-House is fitted up for the accommodation of 140 Orphan Girls above seven years of age, 80 Orphan Boys above seven years, and 80 male and female Orphans from their earliest days, till they are about seven or eight years of age. The infants, after having passed the age of seven or eight years, are removed into the different departments for older boys and girls.

FOURTH PART

5. The New Orphan-House is open to visitors every Wednesday afternoon; but the arrangements of the establishment make it needful, that it should be shown only at that time. No exceptions can be made.--The first party of visitors is shown through the House at half-past two o'clock precisely, God permitting the second at three o'clock; and, should there be need for it, the third and last party at half-past three o'clock.--As it takes at least one hour and a half to see the whole establishment, it is requested that visitors will be pleased to make their arrangements accordingly, before they come, as it would be inconvenient, should one or the other leave, before the whole party has seen the House.--From March 1st to Nov. 1st there may be three parties shown through the House every Wednesday afternoon; but from Nov. 1st to March 1st only two parties can be accommodated, on account of the shortness of the days.

6. Persons who desire to make application for the admission of Orphans are requested to write to me and address the letter to my house, No. 21, Paul Street, Kingsdown, Bristol.

7. Without any one having been personally applied to for anything by me, the sum of 33,868l. 11s. 1 1/4 d. was given to me for the Orphans, as the result of prayer to God, from the commencement of the work up to May 26, 1850.--It may be also interesting to the reader to know that the total amount, which was given as free contributions, for the other objects, from the commencement of the work up to May 26, 1850, amounted to 10,531l. 3s. 3 3/4 d.; and that which came in by the sale of Bibles and Tracts, and by the payments of the children in the schools, up to May 26, 1850, amounted to 2,707l. 9s. 3 1/2 d.--Besides this also a great variety and number of articles of clothing, furniture, provisions, &c., were given for the use of the Orphans.

8. The total of the current expenses for the Orphans from May 26, 1848, to May 26, 1849, was 1,559l. 6s. 9d., and the total of the current expenses for them from May 26, 1849, to May 26, 1850, was only 2,665l. 13s. 2 3/4 d., i.e. only about Eleven Hundred Pounds more than the previous year. To avoid misunderstanding, I would request the reader to keep in mind that, though there were above 300 persons connected with the New Orphan-House, on May 26, 1850, and only about 130 in the rented Orphan Houses in Wilson Street, yet above three weeks of the second year the children were still in Wilson Street, and five weeks afterwards we had only those children who came from Wilson Street into the New Orphan-House; and even when we began to receive fresh Orphans, they came in only four, five, six, seven, or eight a-week, so that only by little and little our expenses increased.--It is also needful, in order to have a correct view of the expenses connected with the Orphans, to take into account the presents in rice, bread, coals, calico, print, shoes, &c., worth about 200l., which were given during these two years.

Matters connected with my own personal affairs, from May 26, 1848, to May 26, 1850.

Dec. 31, 1848. During this year the Lord was pleased to give me--

1. By anonymous offerings in money, put up in paper, directed to me, and put into the boxes for the poor saints or the rent, at the two chapels. L156 7 1

2. By presents in money, from believers in Bristol, not given anonymously . 157 14 6

3. By presents in money, from believers not residing in Bristol . . .   145 0 0

4. By presents in provisions, clothes, etc., from believers in and out of Bristol, worth to us at least 15 16 0

L474 17 7

To this is again to be added, for this year also, as before stated, the free education of my daughter at a boarding school, worth at least 50l.

Dec. 31, 1849. The Lord sent me during this year--

1. By anonymous offerings in money, through the boxes in the two chapels
L149 14 9

2. By presents in money from believers in Bristol, not given anonymously
101 3 0

3. By presents in money, from believers not residing in Bristol   158 19 7

4. By presents in articles, worth at least   3 5 0

L413 2 4

Full account of the reasons which led me to the enlargement of the Orphan work, so that One Thousand Orphans might be provided for.

Having written down at full length the exercises of my mind respecting this deeply important step, I give them here, in the form of a journal, as recorded at the time.

Dec. 5, 1850. It is now sixteen years and nine months this evening, since I began the Scriptural Knowledge Institution for Home and Abroad. This Institution was in its beginning exceedingly small. Now it is so large, that I have not only disbursed, since its commencement, about Fifty Thousand Pounds sterling, but the current ex-

FOURTH PART

penses, after the rate of the last months, amount to above L6,000 a year. I did "open my mouth wide," this very evening fifteen years ago, and the Lord has filled it. The New Orphan-House is now inhabited by 300 Orphans; and there are altogether 335 persons connected with it. My labour is abundant. The separation from my dear wife and child great, on account of my being the greater part of the day at the New Orphan-House; sometimes also by night. But notwithstanding all this, I have again and again thought about labouring more than ever in serving poor Orphans. Within the last ten days this matter has much occupied my mind, and for the last five days I have had much prayer about it. It has passed through my mind to build another Orphan-House, large enough for Seven Hundred Orphans, so that I might be able to care for One Thousand altogether. The points which have led me to this thought are: 1, The many distressing cases of children, bereaved of both parents, who have no helper. I have received 207 Orphans within the last sixteen months, and have now 78 waiting for admission, without having vacancies for any. I had about 60 children waiting for admission about sixteen months since, so about 230 children have been applied for within these sixteen months. But, humanly speaking, for the next sixteen months the number of applications will be far greater, as the work is now so much more widely known; except it be that persons may hear that the New Orphan-House is quite full, and on that account may consider it useless to apply. 2, The constitution of most other charitable Institutions for Orphans makes the admission of a really destitute Orphan, i.e. a child bereaved of both parents, and without an influential friend, very difficult, if not hopeless; for admission by means of the votes of donors precludes really poor persons from having, in most instances, the benefit of these Institutions, as they cannot give the time nor expend the money necessary for obtaining such votes. I have myself seen that certain candidates had several thousand votes. The necessity of this arrangement being continued may be much regretted by many who are connected with such Institutions, but they have no power to alter it. In our case nothing is needed but application to me; and the very poorest person, without influence, without friends, without any expense, no matter where he lives, or of whatever religious denomination, who applies for children born in lawful wedlock, bereaved of both parents, and in destitute circumstances, may procure their admission. Now as the new Poor-law is against giving relief to relatives for Orphan children out of the Poor Houses; and as there is such difficulty for really poor people to get their Orphan relatives admitted into ordinary Orphan Establishments; I feel myself particularly called upon to be the Friend of the Orphan, by making an easy way for admission, provided it is really a destitute case. 3, The confidence which God has caused thousands of His children to repose in me, calls upon me to make use of it to the utmost of my power, and to seek yet more largely to be their almoner. 4, The experience which I have had in this service now for fifteen years, during which time I have gone from the smallest commencement of the work to having at present 300 Orphans under my care, calls upon me to make use of this my experience to the utmost. No member of a committee, no president of a Society, could possibly have the same experience, except he himself had practically been engaged in such a work for a number of years, as I have been. 5, This very experience makes things light to me, under God's help, which were difficult formerly, and which would be very difficult now to many; may I not therefore proceed still further? 6, If 700 more young souls could be brought under regular godly training, (and their number would be renewed from time to time,) what blessed service for the kingdom of Christ, and what profitable expenditure of labour too, with the blessing of God, even for this realm in a civil and moral point of view! 7, But that which outweighs every one of these six reasons, is lastly this: I began this Orphan Work fifteen years ago for the very purpose of illustrating to the world and to the church that there is verily a God in heaven who hears prayer; that God is the living God. (See fully about this in "Narrative of the Lord's dealings with George Muller," under the reasons why I began the Orphan Work in 1835, 1st Part, page 143-146 of the Seventh Edition.) Now this last object is the more fully accomplished the larger the work is, provided I am helped in obtaining the means simply through prayer and faith.

But whilst such thoughts have passed through my mind, there are others of another character. For instance, 1, I have already an abundance of work. 2, My dear wife has already an abundance of work. Her whole time, with little intermission (except for prayer and reading of the Word of God) is occupied directly or indirectly about the Orphans. 3, Am I not undertaking too much for my bodily strength and mental powers, by thinking about another Orphan-House? 4, Am I not going beyond the measure of my faith in thinking about enlarging the work so as to double or treble it? 5, Is not this a delusion of Satan, an attempt to cast me down altogether from my sphere of usefulness, by making me go beyond my measure? 6, Is it not also, perhaps, a snare to puff me up, by attempting to build a very large Orphan-House?

Under these circumstances I can only pray that the Lord in his tender mercy would not allow Satan to gain an advantage over me. By the grace of God my heart says: Lord if I could be sure that it is Thy will, that I should go forward in this matter, I would do so cheerfully; and, on the other hand, if I could be sure, that these are vain, foolish, proud thoughts, that they are not from Thee, I would, by Thy grace, hate them, and entirely put them aside.

My hope is in God; He will help and teach me. Judging, however, from His former dealings with me, it would not be a strange thing to me, nor surprising, if He called me to labour yet still more largely in this way.

The thoughts about enlarging the Orphan Work have not arisen on account of an abundance of money having lately come in; for I have had of late to wait for about seven weeks upon God, whilst little, very little comparatively, came in, i.e., about four times as much was going out as came in; and, had not the Lord previously sent me large sums, we should have been distressed indeed.

Lord! How can Thy servant know Thy will in this matter? Wilt Thou be pleased to teach him!

Dec. 11, 1850. During the last six days, since writing the above, I have been, day after day, waiting upon God concerning this matter. It has generally been more

FOURTH PART

or less all the day on my heart. When I have been awake at night, it has not been far from my thoughts. Yet all this without the least excitement I am perfectly calm and quiet respecting it. My soul would be rejoiced to go forward in this service, could I be sure that the Lord would have me to do so; for then, notwithstanding the numberless difficulties, all would be well, and His name would be magnified.

On the other hand, were. I assured that the Lord would have me to be satisfied with my present sphere of service, and that I should not pray about enlarging the work, by His grace I could, without an effort, cheerfully yield to it; for He has brought me into such a state of heart, that I only desire to please Him in this matter. Moreover, hitherto I have not spoken about this thing even to my beloved wife, the sharer of my joys, sorrows and labours for more than twenty years; nor is it likely that I shall do so for some time to come: for I prefer quietly to wait on the Lord, without conversing on this subject, in order that thus I may be kept the more easily, by His blessing, from being influenced by things from without. The burden of my prayer concerning this matter is, that the Lord would not allow me to make a mistake, and that He would teach me His will. As to outward things, I have had nothing to encourage me during these six days, but the very reverse; for the income, for the various objects of the Scriptural Knowledge Institution for Home and Abroad, has been unusually small, only 6l. 14s. altogether, while the outgoings have been 138l. 11s. 7d. But all this would not weigh the least with me, could I be quite sure that the Lord would have me to go forward.

The especial burden of my prayer therefore is, that God would be pleased to teach me His will. My mind has also been especially pondering, how I could know His will satisfactorily concerning this particular. Sure I am, that I shall be taught. I therefore desire patiently to wait for the Lord's time, when He shall be pleased to shine on my path concerning this point.

Dec. 26. Fifteen days have elapsed since I wrote the preceding paragraph. Every day since then I have continued to pray about this matter, and that with a goodly measure of earnestness, by the help of God. There has passed scarcely an hour during these days, in which, whilst awake, this matter has not been more or less before me. But all without even a shadow of excitement. I converse with no one about it. Hitherto have I not even done so with my dear wife. From this I refrain still, and deal with God alone about the matter, in order that no outward influence, and no outward excitement ay keep me from attaining unto a clear discovery of His will. I have the fullest and most peaceful assurance, that He will clearly show me His will. This evening I have had again an especial solemn season for prayer, to seek to know the will of God. But whilst I continue to entreat and beseech the Lord, that He would not allow me to be deluded in this business, I may say I have scarcely any doubt remaining on my mind as to what will be the issue, even that I should go forward in this matter. As this, however, is one of the most momentous steps that I have ever taken, I judge that I cannot go about this matter with too much caution, prayerfulness, and deliberation. I am in no hurry about it. I could wait for years, by God's grace, were this His will, before even taking one single step towards this thing, or even speaking to any one about it; and, on the other hand, I would set to work tomorrow, were the Lord to bid me do so. This calmness of mind, this having no will of my own in the matter, this only wishing to tease my Heavenly Father in it, this only seeking His and not my honour in it; this state of heart, I say, is the fullest assurance to me that my heart is not under a fleshly excitement, and that, if I am helped thus to go on, I shall know the will of God to the full. But, while. I write thus, I cannot but add at the same time, that I do crave the honour and the glorious privilege to be more and more used by the Lord. I have served Satan much in my younger years, and desire now with all my might to serve God, during the remaining days of my earthly pilgrimage. I am forty-five years and three months old. Every day decreases the number of days that I have to stay on earth. I therefore desire with all my might to work. There are vast multitudes of Orphans to be provided for. About five years ago, a brother in the Lord told me he had seen in an official Report, that there were at that time six thousand young Orphans in the prisons of England. My heart longs to be instrumental in preventing such young Orphans from having to go to prison. I desire to be used by the Lord as an instrument in providing all the necessary temporal supplies, not only for the 300 now under my care, but for 700 more. I desire to alleviate yet further the sufferings of poor dying widows, when looking on their helpless Orphans, about to be left behind. I desire yet further to assist poor persons to whom destitute Orphans are left, and who are unable to provide for them. I desire to be allowed to provide Scriptural Instruction for a thousand Orphans; instead of doing so for 300. I desire to expound the Holy Scriptures regularly to a thousand Orphans, instead of doing so to 300. I desire that thus it may be yet more abundantly manifest that God is still the hearer and answerer of prayer, and that He is the living God now, as He ever was and ever will be, when He shall, simply in answer to prayer, have condescended to provide me with a house for 700 Orphans, and with means to support them. This last consideration is the most important point in my mind. The Lord's honour is the principal point with me in this whole matter; and just because that is the case, if He would be more glorified by my not going forward in this business, I should, by His grace, be perfectly content to give up all thoughts about another Orphan-House. Surely in such a state of mind, obtained by the Holy Spirit, Thou, O my Heavenly Father, wilt not suffer Thy child to be mistaken, much less to be deluded! By the help of God I shall continue further, day by day, to wait upon Him in prayer concerning this thing, till He shall bid me act.

Jan. 2, 1851. A week ago I wrote the preceding paragraph. During this week I have still been helped, day by day, and more than once every day, to seek the guidance of the Lord about another Orphan-House. The burden of my prayer has still been, that He, in His great mercy, would keep me from making a mistake. During the last week the Book of Proverbs has come in the course of my Scripture reading, and my heart has been refreshed, in reference to this subject, by the following passages: "Trust in the Lord with all thine heart; and lean not unto thine own understanding. In all thy ways acknowledge Him, and He shall direct thy paths." Prov. iii. 5, 6. By the grace of God I do acknowledge the Lord in my ways, and in this thing in particular; I have therefore the comfortable assurance that He will direct my paths concerning this part of my service, as to whether I shall be occupied in it or not. Further: "The

FOURTH PART

integrity of the upright shall preserve them; but the perverseness of fools shall destroy them." Prov. xi. 3. By the grace of God I am upright in this business. My honest purpose is to get glory to God. Therefore. I expect to be guided aright. Further, "Commit thy works unto the Lord and thy thoughts shall be established." Prov. xvi. 8. I do commit my works unto the Lord, and therefore expect that my thoughts will be established.--My heart is more and more coming to a calm, quiet, and settled assurance, that the Lord will condescend to use me yet further in the Orphan Work. Here, Lord, is Thy servant!

Jan. 14. Twelve days have passed away since I wrote the last paragraph. I have still, day by day, been enabled to wait upon the Lord with reference to enlarging the Orphan Work, and have been, during the whole of this period also, in perfect peace, which is the result of seeking in this thing only the Lord's honour and the temporal and spiritual benefit of my fellowmen. Without an effort could I, by His grace, put aside all thoughts about this whole affair, if only assured that it is the will of God I should do so; and, on the other hand, would at once go forward, if He would have it to be so. I have still kept this matter entirely to myself. Though it is now about seven weeks, since day by day, more or less, my mind has been exercised about it, and since I have daily prayed concerning it; yet not one human being knows of it. As yet I have not mentioned it even to my dear wife, in order that thus, by quietly waiting upon the Lord, I might not be influenced by what might be said to me on the subject. This evening has been particularly set apart for prayer, beseeching the Lord once more, not to allow me to be mistaken in this thing, and much less to be deluded by the Devil. I have also sought to let all the reasons against building another Orphan-House, and all the reasons for doing so, pass before my mind; and now, for the sake of clearness and definiteness, write them down.

Reasons against establishing another Orphan-House for

Seven Hundred Orphans.

1. Would not this be going beyond my measure spiritually? according to that word: "For I say through the grace given unto me, to every man that is among you, not to think of himself more highly than he ought to think; but to think soberly, according as God has dealt to every man the measure of faith." Rom. xii. 3.

Answer: If the Lord were to leave me to myself, the tenth part of the difficulties and trials, which befall me now in connexion with the various objects of the Scriptural Knowledge Institution for Home and Abroad, would be enough to overwhelm me; but, whilst He is pleased to sustain me, I am able day by day to pass on peacefully, and am carried through one difficulty after the other: and thus, by God's help, even with my present measure of faith, if continued to me, should be enabled to bear up under other difficulties and trials; but I look for an increase of faith with every fresh difficulty, through which the Lord is pleased to help me.

2. Would it not be going beyond my measure naturally with reference to mental and bodily strength? Answer: Of all the objections against establishing another Orphan-House, there is none that weighs more with me than this; I might say, it is the only real difficulty. This, however, too, I am enabled to put aside and to overcome thus: By husbanding my strength, by great order, by regular habits, by lightening the work as much as possible, and by using every help that I can, I have been enabled to get through a vast quantity of work. My immense correspondence of about 3000 letters a-year, I have been enabled to accomplish without a secretary. The entire management and direction, and the whole vast correspondence of the Scriptural Knowledge Institution has devolved upon myself alone these sixteen years and ten months, and I have been thinking that, by seeking for an efficient secretary, an efficient clerk, and an inspector of the schools, I might, with God's help, accomplish yet more, though much of what I have been doing hitherto would need to be done by others. There have been several other arrangements brought before my mind, since I have been exercised about this matter, whereby, with the blessing of God, the work might be lightened. I should certainly need efficient helpers to carry out the plans before me; but with such, I, as director, might be enabled, by God's help, to accomplish yet more.

3. There must be a limit to my work and service. Answer: That is true, and if I were quite sure that the present state of the Scriptural Knowledge Institution were to be the limit, I would at once lay aside this thing; but I am not sure that I am come as yet to God's limit. All these sixteen years and ten months, the work has been constantly progressing, and the Lord has helped me continually; and now my mind is just in the same way exercised, as when fifteen years ago I began the Orphan Work, and as when thirteen years ago it was enlarged, and as when seven years and nine months since it was still further enlarged, and as when five years and two months since I was led to decide on building the New Orphan-House. Under these circumstances, having been helped through all these difficulties, and seeing such a vast field of usefulness before me, and having so many applications for the admission of very destitute Orphans, I long to be used still further, and cannot say that as yet the Lord has brought me to His limit.

4. Is it not like "tempting God," to think of building another Orphan-House for seven hundred more orphans? Answer: "Tempting God" means, according to the Holy Scriptures, to limit Him in any of His attributes by His grace I do not wish to limit His power or His willingness, to give to me, His poor servant, simply in answer to prayer, all the means, and every other help and blessing which I shall need to build another large Orphan-House.

5. You will not get the means for building and fitting up so large an Orphan-House; and, even if you did, how will you, at the same time, get the means for carrying on the work, which already exists? Answer: Looking at the matter naturally, this is indeed a weighty objection.

FOURTH PART

The New Orphan-House, with its 300 Orphans only, cost about fifteen thousand pounds to build and to fit up and furnish, and still the expenses are not all met even now. It will in all probability cost several hundred pounds yet. And this large sum was needed, though the style of the building is most simple, and though the field in which it was built was comparatively cheap. After this rate, a building to accommodate seven hundred Orphans, with the necessary ground attached to it for the cultivation of the vegetables used in the Institution, could not be less than thirty-five thousand pounds. Now, looking at it naturally, where is this great sum to come from? Though I looked at all my friends who have given hitherto, and several have done so very liberally, yet there is no natural prospect whatever of receiving this amount; especially if it be kept in mind that six or seven thousand pounds besides, every year, would be needed for carrying on that which is already in existence. I might, therefore, well tremble, looking at the matter naturally, and say, I shall never have the money for this intended Orphan-House for 700 children; for where is this large sum of thirty-five thousand pounds to come from? And even if I were to get the money, will not persons, in giving means for such a Building-Fund, take it away from what they might have given me for carrying on the work which exists already? But whilst thus, naturally, there is no hope of succeeding, I am not in the least discouraged spiritually; for by faith in the living God I say this: He has the power to give me this thirty-five thousand pounds, and much more, were it needed: and He has the power, in the mean time, to give me also all the large sums required, week after week, for meeting the current expenses for the present state of the work. Moreover, I delight in the greatness of the difficulty, as it respects the large sum needed for building and fitting up such an Establishment; for I desire to be most fully assured, from the very outset, that I go forward in this matter according to the Lord's bidding. If so, He will give me the means; if not, I shall not have them. Nor do I mean to apply to any one personally for pecuniary help, but purpose to give myself to prayer for means, as heretofore.

6. Suppose now, you were even to succeed in getting this large Orphan House built, how will you be able to provide for 700 other Orphans? Answer: There is much weight in this objection, looking at it naturally. I am too much a man of business, and too much a person of calm, quiet, cool calculation, not to feel its force. And indeed, were I only to look at the thing naturally, I should at once be ready to own that I am going too far; for the increase of expenditure for the support of these 700 other Orphans could not be less than eight thousand pounds a-year more, so that the current expenses of the Scriptural Knowledge Institution, reckoning its present state, and including those eight thousand pounds, would be about fifteen thousand pounds a-year. Now, I am free to own, that I have no human prospect of obtaining such a sum year by year. But while matters stand thus, looking at them naturally, I see no difficulty at all in them spiritually. If according to the will of God I am enabled to go about this intended second Orphan House; and if, with His help, I shall be enabled to finish it; He will surely provide for those who are gathered together in it, as long as He shall be pleased to enable me to trust in Him for supplies. And here I look back upon the way in which the Lord has led me and dealt with me. When, about seventeen years ago, I took up, in dependence upon the living God for means, two Charity

Schools, with which the Scriptural Knowledge Institution commenced (and this involved an expense of less than one hundred pounds a-year), I had no certain prospect of being able to meet even that small sum; but God so helped me, that I had shortly six Charity Schools. He helped me then also, and enabled me to meet all their expenses. When, fifteen years ago, I began the Orphan Work, which was connected with far heavier expenses, I had still less prospect, according to natural reason, of being able to meet them; but I trusted in God, and He helped me, and He not only enabled me to meet the current expenses for thirty Orphans in the first house rented for them, but also soon to open another for thirty-six more, and to meet all those expenses; for as I had begun in faith in the living God, and not by putting my trust in my brethren in Christ, so I was not confounded. After I had gone on some time with these Orphans in the two rented houses, about thirteen years ago the Lord was pleased greatly to encourage me and to increase my faith by a donation of 500l. for the Orphans; for up to that period I had never received more than One Hundred Pounds at once. But this kind donor, a stranger to me up to that time, suggested to me the propriety of investing this sum and using only the interest of it, as I could not expect to have the Orphans supported for a continuance in the way they had been till then; for that such Institutions must depend upon regular subscriptions or funded property, otherwise they could not go on. As, however, this was only a friendly hint, and no condition under which the money was given, I took this 500l. towards fitting up a third house for the reception of thirty more Orphans. From that time the work has been increasing more and more, till it came to what it is at present. Now, suppose I had said, seventeen years ago, looking at matters according to natural reason, "the two Charity Schools are enough, I must not go any further;" then the work would have stopped there. Or, if I had had a little more trust in my exertions or my friends, I might have taken at the utmost one or two steps further. Instead of this, however, I looked in no degree whatever at things according to my natural fallen reason, and trusted not in the circle of my Christian friends, but in the living God; and the result has been, that there have been since 1834 ten thousand souls under our instruction in the various Day Schools, Sunday Schools and Adult Schools; several hundred Orphans have been brought up, and many of them from their very tenderest infancy; several hundred thousand tracts and many thousand copies of the Word of God have been circulated; about forty preachers of the Gospel at Home and Abroad have been, for several years, assisted in connection with the Scriptural Knowledge Institution; and a house has been built and fitted up for the accommodation of 300 destitute Orphans, each of whom has neither father nor mother. How blessed therefore it is to trust in God, and in Him alone, and not in circumstances nor friends There is, however, one thing which I must record here, because it has taken place since I last wrote in my journal on this subject on January 2nd. It is this. During these twelve days I have received for the various objects of the Scriptural Knowledge Institution in smaller donations 64l. 15s. 6 1/2 d., also a donation of 150l. and one of 300l. Is not this a plain proof that God is both able and willing to help simply in answer to prayer? Is not human reason confounded by such instances? When I first began to write these exercises of my mind about another Orphan House, I knew not that on January 4th I should receive a donation of 3000l., yet I was fully assured that God was able to support one thousand Orphans as easily as He did the thirty whom I first

FOURTH PART

received in a rented house. Does He not, however, tell me by all this: Go forward, my servant, and I will help thee?

7. But it might be said, suppose you were able by prayer to obtain this large sum for building a house for seven hundred other Orphans; and suppose you were able to provide for them during your lifetime, what would become of this Institution after your death? Answer: I am quite familiar with this objection, having heard it many times as a reason against the way of obtaining the means for the Scriptural Knowledge Institution, simply by trusting in God, without any funded property, and without looking to regular subscribers; but my reply is this. My business is, with all my might to serve my own generation; in doing so I shall best serve the next generation, should the Lord Jesus tarry. Soon He may come again but, if He tarry, and I have to fall asleep before His return, I shall not have been altogether without profit to the generation to come, were the Lord only to enable me to serve my own generation. Suppose this objection were a sound one, I ought never to have commenced the Orphan. Work at all, for fear of what might become of it after my death, and thus all the hundreds of destitute children without father and mother, whom the Lord has allowed me to care for, during the last fifteen years, would not have been taken up by me. The same argument was again and again used to Franke, my esteemed countryman, who at Halle, in Prussia, commenced about A.D. 1696, the largest charitable establishment for poor children that, as far as I know, exists in the world. He trusted in God alone. He went on trusting in God alone. And God helped him throughout abundantly. Simply by trust in the living God the Institutions, resembling a large street rather than a house, were erected, and about two thousand children instructed in them. For about thirty years all was going on under his own eye, until 1727, when it pleased God to take His servant to Himself. At his death these Institutions were directed by his truly pious son-in-law. It is true that, at the latter part of the last century, and during the first part of the present, there was little real vital godliness in these Institutions; still they were a temporal blessing to many tens of thousands of young persons even then. So then for several tens of years they were carried on in a truly Godly way, after Franke's death, and when afterwards there was but little real, vital godliness found in these schools, yet tens of thousands of children were benefited at least for this life. Now these Institutions have existed already 150 years, and are in existence still: and, if the Lord Jesus tarry, are likely, humanly speaking, to exist hereafter, as they have existed hitherto. Suppose then, that dear man of God, A. H. Franke, had listened to the suggestions of unbelief, and said, I must not undertake this work, for what will become of it after my death, then all the blessing which spiritually resulted from it to thousands, and all the temporal benefits which have resulted from it to hundreds of thousands, would have been lost. I add, however, this. The New Orphan House has been placed in the hands of eleven trustees, and has been properly enrolled in Chancery, and so also, should God condescend to honour me further in building for Him this intended house for 700 Orphans, it would likewise be placed in the hands of trustees and enrolled in Chancery. One word in conclusion on this subject: let every one take heed lest, in caring about what will become of the next generation, he forget to serve his own generation. The latter each one should seek to do with his might, and thus it should be with each succeeding

generation; then, though we be dead, yet should we be speaking. A. H. Franke is long since gone to his rest, but he spoke to my soul in 1826, and he is speaking to my soul now; and to his example I am greatly indebted for having been stirred up to care about poor children in general, and about poor Orphans in particular.

8. The last objection which has occurred to my own mind is, that by building another Orphan House, I should be in danger of being lifted up. Answer: I should be in danger of it indeed, and am in great danger, even were I not in the least degree to go forward. Yea, the tenth part of the honour which the Lord has condescended to bestow upon me, and the tenth part of service with which He has been pleased to intrust me, would be enough, if I were left to myself, exceedingly to puff me up. I cannot say that hitherto the Lord has kept me humble; but I can say, that hitherto He has given me a hearty desire to give to Him all the glory, and to consider it a great condescension on His part that He has been pleased to use me as an instrument in His service. I do not see, therefore, that fear of being lifted up ought to keep me from going forward in this work; but that I have rather to beseech the Lord that He would be pleased to give me a lowly mind, and never suffer me to rob Him of the glory which is due to Him alone.

Jan. 25. Great pressure of work has kept me from going on writing my reasons for establishing another Orphan-House till now, but being more and more convinced that it is of God I should do so, I now proceed in writing.

Reasons for establishing another Orphan House for Seven Hundred Orphans.

1. The many applications for the admission of destitute Orphans, which continue to be made, I consider as a call from God upon me, to do all that is in my power to provide a Home and Scriptural Education for a still greater number of Orphans. Nothing but positive inability to go forward ought to keep me standing still, whilst I have almost daily fresh entreaties to receive Orphans. Since I began writings on this subject in my journal, thirty more Orphans have been applied for, from two years old and upwards. I cannot refuse to help, as long as I see a door open, and opened by God, as I consider, to help them.

2. The moral state of the Poorhouses greatly influences me to go forward. I have heard it again and again, from good authority, that children, placed in the Unions, are corrupted, on account of the children of vagrants, and other very bad young people who are in such places; so that many poor relatives of Orphans, though unable to provide for them, cannot bear the idea of their going there, lest they should be corrupted. I therefore judge that, even for the sake of keeping Orphans of poor yet respectable people from being obliged to mix with the children of vagabonds, I ought to do, to my utmost power, all I can to help them. For this reason, then, I purpose, in dependence upon the living God, to go forward and to establish another Orphan House for seven hundred destitute children, who are bereaved of both parents. When writing thus about the Poorhouses, I do not wish it to be understood in the way of

FOURTH PART

reproof; for I know not how these matters could be altered; but simply state the fact that thus it is.

3. In this purpose I am the more confirmed, since it is a fact, that the Orphan Houses already in existence in the kingdom are by no means sufficient to admit even the most deserving and distressing cases, and far less all that it would be well to provide for. Moreover, there is great difficulty connected with the admission of Orphans into most of the ordinary Orphan Establishments, on account of the votes which must be obtained, so that really needy persons have neither time nor money to obtain them. Does not the fact that there were six thousand young Orphans in the prisons of England about five years ago, call aloud for an extension of Orphan Institutions? By God's help, I will do what I can, to keep poor Orphans from prison.

4. In this purpose I am still further encouraged by the great help which the Lord has hitherto given me in this blessed service. When I look at the small beginning, and consider how the Lord has helped me now for more than fifteen years in the Orphan work; and when I consider how He has been pleased to help me through one great difficulty after another; and when I consider, especially, how, as with an unseen hand, almost against my will and former desires and thoughts, He has led me on from one step to another, and has enlarged the work more and more: I say, when I review all this, and compare with it my present exercise of mind, I find the great help, the uninterrupted help, which the Lord has given me for more than fifteen years, a great reason for going forward in this work. And this, trusting in Him, I am resolved to do.

5. A further reason for going forward in this service I see in the experience which I have had in it. From the smallest commencement up to the present state of the establishment, with its 300 Orphans, all has gone through my own hands. In the work itself I obtained the experience. It has grown with the work. I have been the sole director of the work, under God, from its smallest commencement. Now this is not an every day case. No committee member of a society, no president or vice-president of an institution, except they had been situated as myself, could have this experience. Coupled with this is the measure of gift which the Lord has been pleased to give me for such work, and for the exercise of which I am responsible to Him. These things, in connexion with the former reasons, it appears to me, are a call from God to go forward in a greater degree than ever in this work.

6. The spiritual benefit of still more Orphans is another especial reason, why I feel called to go forward. The Orphans, who have been under my care hitherto, were almost all the children of parents who were naturally weak in body, if not consumptive. The very fact of a child being deprived of both parents when four, five, six, or seven years old, shows that, except the parents lost their lives by casualty, they were constitutionally weak. On this account young Orphans, generally speaking, require particular care as to their health. In this respect I desire to care for them; but there is more than that to be attended to. I further heartily desire to keep them from the corrupting and demoralizing effect of the lowest sort of children in the streets, courts

and Unions; but I desire more for them than mere decency and morality. I desire that they should be useful members of society, and that the prisons of the United Kingdom should not be filled with poor, destitute, and homeless Orphans. We bring them up therefore in habits of industry, and seek to instruct them in those things which are useful for the life that now is; but I desire more than this for the Orphans. I cannot be satisfied with anything concerning them short of this, that their souls be won for the Lord. For this reason I long to have them from their earliest days, yea, the younger the better, under my care, that thus, under godly nurses and teachers, they may be brought up in the fear of the Lord. Now as this is the chief and primary aim concerning the dear Orphans, even the salvation of their souls through faith in the Lord Jesus, I long to be more extensively used than hitherto, even that I may have a thousand of them instead of three hundred under my care.

7. But there is one point which weighs more strongly with me than even the last mentioned one. It is this. When I began the Orphan Work more than fifteen years ago, it was for the definite and especial purpose, that, by means of it, the unconverted might see, through the answers of prayer that I received in connection with it, that there is verily reality in the things of God; and that the children of God might have their faith strengthened by means of it, and be encouraged, in all simplicity to deal with God under every circumstance, and trust in Him at all times. But if this would be answered in a measure by the state in which the Orphan Work has been in former times, and more so by what it has been since the erection of the New Orphan House, it would be still more so, by the blessing of God, by my going forward in it to a far greater degree than before. This point, even the glory of God in the manifestation of His readiness to hear prayer, has weighed especially and supremely with me in purposing to enlarge the Orphan Work.

8. Lastly, I am peaceful and happy, spiritually, in the prospect of enlarging the work, as on former occasions when I had to do so. This weighs particularly with me as a reason for going forward. After all the calm, quiet, prayerful consideration of the subject for about eight weeks, I am peaceful and happy, spiritually, in the purpose of enlarging the field. This, after all the heart searching which I have had, and the daily prayer to be kept from delusion and mistake in this thing, and the be-taking myself to the Word of God, would not be the case, I judge, had not the Lord purposed to condescend to use me more than ever in this service.

I, therefore, on the ground of the objections answered, and these eight reasons for enlarging the work, come to the conclusion that it is the will of the blessed God, that His poor and most unworthy servant should yet more extensively serve Him in this work, which he is quite willing to do.

Up to this day, January 25, 1851, I have not spoken to one human being about it. As yet even my dear wife knows not about it. I purpose to keep the matter still for some time entirely to myself, dealing with God alone about it, in order that no outward excitement may be in the least degree a stimulus to me. I still pray to be kept from mistake and delusion in this thing, not that I think I am mistaken or deluded,

FOURTH PART

quite the reverse; but yet I would distrust myself and cling to God, to be kept from mistakes and delusions.

January 31st. For several weeks past I have had no doubt that the Lord would have me to serve Him in the erection and fitting up of another Orphan-House for seven hundred Orphans, and I am quite decided on doing so, with His help, and I am now quiet about it, not because I have the least misgiving in my own mind, but because I know that it is most suitable that I should still for some time continue to deal quietly with God alone about it.

March 5th. Nearly five weeks have passed away since I wrote the last paragraph, and my mind has not been once, during this time, even for a moment, in uncertainty as to what I ought to do. It is now about fifteen weeks since I have been especially praying about this subject, and three months since. I began first to write on the subject in my journal, and about ten weeks since I have had any doubt as to what is the will of the Lord concerning this service. I believe that, altogether unworthy though I am of this great honour, He will condescend to use me further and more extensively than before in caring for destitute children who are bereaved of both parents. And this I purpose to do.

April 5th. Another month has passed away, and my mind is just in the same state as it was when I wrote in my journal on the subject on March 5th.

May 5th. One more month has passed away, and still my mind remains quietly assured that, utterly unworthy though I am to be allowed to go forward in this work, and great though the difficulties are, which must be overcome, yet that it is the will of God I should serve Him in this way. It is now this day five months since I first wrote on this subject in my journal, and longer even than that since it has been before rue, during which time I have day by day prayed concerning this matter.

May 24th. From the time that I began to write down the exercises of my mind on Dec. 5th, 1850, till this day, ninety-two more Orphans have been applied for, and seventy-eight were already waiting for admission before. But this number increases rapidly as the work becomes more and more known.

On the ground of what has been recorded above, I purpose to go forward in this service, and to seek to build, to the praise and honour of the living God, another Orphan-House, large enough to accommodate seven hundred Orphans.

When I published these exercises of my mind, and made known my purpose respecting the intended Orphan-House for 700 Orphans, in the Twelfth Report of the Scriptural Knowledge Institution, the following particulars were added to what has been stated.

1. All this time, though now six months have elapsed since. I first began to be exercised about this matter, I have never once been led to ask the Lord for means for

this work, but have only continued day by day to seek guidance from Him as to whether I should undertake it or not.

2. The means requisite, to accomplish the building and fitting up of a house, which shall be really suitable for my intended purposes, though the building be quite simple, cannot be less than Thirty-Five Thousand Pounds, including fifteen or twenty acres of land round the building for cultivation by the spade, in order to obtain out of our own grounds all the vegetables, which are so important to the health of the children.

3. I do not mean to begin the building until I have the means requisite in hand, just as was the case with regard to the New Orphan-House. If God will condescend to use me in building for Him another Orphan-House (as I judge He will), He will give me the means for it. Now though I have not on my mind any doubt left that it is His will I should do so; yet there is one point still wanting for confirmation, and that is that He will also furnish me, without personal application to any one, with all the means requisite for this new part of my service. I the more need also to my own soul this last of all the proofs that I have not been mistaken, in order to have unquestionable assurance that, whatever trials hereafter may be allowed to befall me in connexion with this work, I did not at my own bidding and according to my own natural desire undertake it, but that it was under the guidance of God. The greatness of the sum required affords me a kind of secret joy; for the greater the difficulty to be overcome, the more will it be seen to the glory of God, how much can be done by prayer and faith; and also, because, when God Himself overcomes our difficulties for us, we have, in this very fact, the assurance that we are engaged in His work and not in our own.

4. It is intended to place this Orphan-House also, as was the New Orphan-House, in the hands of godly Trustees.

5. Orphans from any part of the world, provided they speak English, if bereaved of both parents, lawfully begotten, and in destitute circumstances, are intended to be admitted, as is the ease now, irrespective of any sectarian feeling or preference whatever. Neither entrance money nor any particular interest will be required, in order to obtain a ticket for the admission of destitute Orphans, bereaved of both parents, as long as there is room.

6. Individuals who desire to contribute towards the Building Fund for this intended Orphan-House for seven hundred destitute Orphans, are requested to state that the donation is "for the Building Fund." Indeed concerning all the donations for any part of the Scriptural Knowledge Institution for Home and Abroad, it is requested that the donors will kindly state, for what they wish their donations to be applied; or to say expressly that they leave the application of their donations to me, as the various objects may more particularly need help.

FOURTH PART

Supplies for the School--, Bible--, Missionary and Tract Fund, sent in answer to prayer, from May 26, 1850, to May 26, 1851.

At the commencement of this period it was my purpose to seek help from the Lord that I might be able, in a still greater degree than before, to assist brethren who labour in the Gospel, at Home and Abroad, in dependence upon God for their temporal supplies, and to labour more than ever in the circulation of the Holy Scriptures and of simple Gospel Tracts. The following extracts from my journal will now show how kind the Lord has been in answering my requests, and in furnishing me with the means for carrying out the desire of my heart.

June 7, 1850. Today I have received 50l. for missions from a Brother whose heart the Lord has inclined to spend, as a steward of God, a second property, with which He has intrusted him.

June 10. Received 150l., the disposal of which was left to me. I took half for the Orphans and half for these objects.

June 11. Received from C. W. 50l. for missions.--By these sums which, besides smaller donations, came in within the first fifteen days of this period, I was able to begin to carry out my purpose; and as the Lord enabled me, without anxious reckoning, to go on giving out as He was pleased to intrust me with means, so again He sent further supplies before all was gone. It is a point of great importance in the divine life, not to be anxiously reckoning about the morrow, nor dealing out sparingly, on account of possible future wants, which never may come; but to consider, that only the present moment to serve the Lord is ours, and that the morrow may never come to us.

July 2. 170l. has come in today. The donor kindly gave me permission to use this amount as might be most needed. I took therefore 80l. of it for the Orphans, the other for these objects.

Of the various donations which came in for these objects, between July 2nd and Aug. 13th, I only mention, that I received on Aug. 5th a silver salver, 2 silver table spoons, a silver sugar spoon, and a silver mustard spoon; all to be sold for missionary purposes. On Aug. 13th a Christian Friend gave me 50l., of which I took one half for missionary operations and the other half for the Orphans, as the donation was left at my disposal as most needed.

Aug. 15. Today I have received from the same donor, who sent me on June 7th 50l., another donation of 110l, of which he wishes me to apply 10l. for the use of the Orphans and 100l. for missionary purposes. This day I have also received a donation of 120l., of which I took half for the Orphans, and half for these objects.-- Several other small donations came in on the following day.

Aug. 24. Have received from C. W. 30l., of which the donor kindly intends 10l. for foreign missions, 10l. for the Orphans, and 10l. for my own personal expenses. I have sent out already during this month 170l. to Home and Foreign labourers, and the Lord continues to give me means for this and all the other parts of the work.

Sept. 14. Received again 190l., of which I took half for the Orphans and half for these objects.

Sept. 19. Today I received a registered letter from the donor referred to under June 7th and Aug. 15th containing Four Hundred Pounds and these words:

"Dear Brother,

Herewith I send you 400l., of which three parts are to be expended on missionaries, the rest you may expend on the Orphans, if needed; else the whole to be disposed of to the Lord's ministering servants. I thank you for your prayers that I may not regret this step. Were the Lord to come tomorrow, how glad I should be that the whole was thus sent on before me! . . If yourself or dear brother Craik (to whom give my love in Christ) are at all in need, scruple not to take five pounds each.

Yours in the Lord Jesus,

* * * * *"

I took the whole amount for labourers in the word and doctrine. My soul does magnify the Lord for His condescension in listening to my supplications, and, in answer to them, sending me means, and thus allowing me more and more to help missionary brethren. During the last five weeks I have sent again to them about 300l., but I long to be more than ever their servant. What the donor says about "the money going before him," is in reference to his having now spent two properties for the Lord.

Sept. 27. Still further abundant help. Received from a new donor 200l., which, being left at my disposal as most needed, I took of it 100l. for the Orphans, and 100l. for these objects.

Oct. 9. The Lord condescends to use me more and more as His steward. Today I have again received 200l., which might be used as most needed. I have therefore taken of it 100l. for the Orphans, and the other half for these objects.

Oct. 28. Since Oct. 9th many small donations have come in, chiefly for missions; now today I received again 200l., of which I took one half for the Orphans, and the other half for these objects. By these donations (large and small) the Lord enables me to send more and more help to Home and Foreign labourers. During the

FOURTH PART

last seven weeks, only little, comparatively, has come in for these objects, while several hundred pounds have been expended; yet, through the rich abundance which the Lord had sent me before, I have not only had no lack of means, but had still about 300l. in hand, before this donation was received today. Nevertheless it was very sweet to receive it as the fruit of earnest prayer for several weeks, as so little, comparatively, had come in during the last seven weeks.

Dec. 18. This evening was given to me 90l. As the donor stated in the course of conversation, that he felt especially interested about those brethren who labour in the Gospel in various countries, whom I seek to assist, I took of this sum 60l. for that object, and 30l. for the Orphans.

Jan. 4, 1851. This evening I received Three Thousand Pounds, of which I took half for these objects, and half for the Orphans, as the disposal of it was entirely left to me. I am thus enabled more and more to enlarge the work, and to assist increasingly home and foreign labourers in the Word. When I gave myself more particularly to this part of the work, now about six years since, I had not the least human prospect of being able to do so much; but the Lord has been pleased to condescend to listen to my supplications on behalf of these brethren who trust in Him for their temporal supplies. I am in this way also furnished with means, on a larger scale than ever, to circulate copies of the Holy Scriptures and simple Gospel Tracts, which was always of deep importance, but in these days of increasing darkness more so than ever.

Jan. 11. A further rich supply. I have received 150l., of which I took half for the Orphans and half for these objects, as the disposal of it was left to me.

Feb. 24. The donor, who has spent two properties in the service of the Lord, receiving a present of 100l., sent me today 50l. of it for missions. This instance shows, that if we use the means with which the Lord may intrust us, as stewards for Him, He will make us stewards over more.

Since Feb. 1851, the donor just now referred to has come into the possession of a third property, which likewise, as the two previous ones, he has entirely spent for the Lord.

March 7. Exceedingly little, comparatively, has come in since Jan. 11th; yet, as I had means, I expended them to the full degree in which it appeared to me that the Lord pointed out openings, and, in the meantime, I continued praying for more means. Now the Lord has again given much encouragement for continuing to wait upon Him, by a donation of 200l., received today, of which the donor kindly wishes me to take 20l. for my own personal expenses, and the 180l. to be used as may be most needed, which sum I have divided between the Orphans and the other objects.

April 15. From C. W. 40l. for foreign missions.

April 17. Further supplies for missionary purposes. This evening I found a letter containing a check for 50l., of which the donor intends one half for missionary purposes, and the other for the Orphans.

April 30. Received 200l., of which I took half for the Orphans and half for these objects. Besides the donations above referred to, of a larger kind, I received for these objects more than two hundred other donations in pence, shillings, pounds, five pounds, ten pounds, and upwards, during this period. In order to save room I have refrained from particularizing these smaller sums, and especially because it was my more immediate object to show, by the above, how bountifully the Lord was pleased to furnish me with means for the carrying out my desires concerning these objects. Yea, the Lord so abundantly supplied me with means, that during the whole of this period there came not one single case before me in which it would have been desirable to help, according to the measure of light given to me, or to extend the work, without my having at the same time ample means for doing so. In the midst of the great depression of the times, which was so generally felt, and on account of which, humanly speaking, I also might have been exceedingly tried for want of means, I, on the contrary, at no period of the work for the seventeen years previous had a greater abundance of means. I do on purpose lay stress upon this, because I desire that it may become increasingly known, that there is no easier, no better, and no happier way in the end than God's way, and this in particular also with regard to the obtaining of means, simply in answer to prayer, without personal application to any one. I value all the smaller donations which have not been referred to, as well as the larger ones; and many of them, in the sight of the Lord, may have been greater donations than the hundreds of pounds which have been mentioned; but it appeared to me necessary to give the above facts, as I could not mention every single donation, in order to prove the easy way in which prayer and faith may procure means, if we walk uprightly, and if the work in which we are engaged is really the work of God. Were the obtaining of money my aim, by thus writing, it would be bad policy indeed, to bring out all these instances of rich and most abundant supplies for the work; for persons might be led to think that I need no money, or that, if I did, I should have only to pray and it would soon come in, through some one or other, without their helping me; but since my chief aim in the whole work, and in the writing of these accounts in particular, is, that the blessedness of the life of faith may be seen, and that the hearts of the children of God may be allured more and more to their Heavenly Father, and be led more and more to cast their every care upon Him, and to trust in Him at all times, yea, in the darkest moments, therefore I take pleasure in speaking about this rich abundance which God gave me for His own work.

Some readers may say, And what use was made of the money which was received in this way? Such a one is referred, for a full answer, to the next chapter but one, which speaks of the operations of the Scriptural Knowledge Institution for Home and Abroad; yet I would give to him here a few outlines of the operations of the Institution. By the funds, which were intrusted to me during this period, several hundred poor children and adults were provided with schooling; many hundreds of copies of the Holy Scriptures were circulated; about three hundred thousand Gospel

FOURTH PART

Tracts were distributed; forty-five preachers of the Gospel in the East Indies, British Guiana, Canada, the United States, France, Switzerland, Germany, Ireland, Scotland and England were, to a greater or less degree, assisted with pecuniary help; and, lastly, three hundred Orphans were provided with everything they needed for this life, besides being under continual Scriptural instruction. Thus, at least, fifteen thousand souls were during this period under habitual Scriptural instruction in connection with this Institution, either in the Sunday Schools, Adult Schools, Day Schools, and the Orphan House, or through the preachers of the Gospel referred to.

Supplies for the support of the Orphans, sent in answer to prayer, from May 26, 1850, to May 26, 1851.

When this period commenced, I had more in hand for the Orphans than for many years before, under similar circumstances, the balance for current expenses on May 26, 1850, being 150l. 7s. 10d. Yet, much as this was, in comparison with what the balance had generally been before, how small was the amount in reality! About 300 persons were connected with the New Orphan House, who day by day were to be provided with all they needed, besides several apprentices who also were still to be supported. On this account, the one hundred and fifty pounds in hand would only furnish that which was needed for about fifteen days, as the average expenses of the Orphan Work alone were about Ten pounds daily.10 Place yourself, therefore, dear reader, in my position. Three hundred persons daily at table, and 150l. in hand! Looking at it naturally, it is enough to make one tremble; but, trusting in the living God, as by His grace I was enabled to do, I had not the least trial of mind, and was assured that God would as certainly help me as He had done fourteen years before, when the number of the Orphans was only the tenth part as large. The following record will now show that I was not mistaken; and thus another precious proof is furnished to the believing reader of the truth of that word: "Whosoever believeth on Him shall not be confounded."

On the very first day of this new period I received from a sister in the Lord 6l. Another sister gave me 3l., the price of a piece of work done by her. Thus, as the Lord commenced this period, so He was pleased generally day by day to send me something, either in small or large donations. I can, however, only refer to a few instances, to save space.

Between May 26 and June 30, 1850, God was pleased to send in 193l. 4s. 5d., so that I had more than enough with the balance left in hand, to meet all the expenses.

July 1. Paid an account to a Christian brother, and received 10l. back from him for the Orphans. More than 3l. came in besides.

July 2. Received 170l., of which I took 80l. for the Orphans, the rest for the other objects. 17l. 10s. 1d. came in besides.

THE LORD'S DEALINGS WITH GEORGE MÜLLER

On Aug. 16th I had purposed to leave Bristol for a time, having been for two years and four months uninterruptedly there, in the midst of more work than I had ever had before. I went, not because I was quite unfit for work, but in order that, labouring for a little while in a different air, I might, with the blessing of God, keep off illness. On the 13th, when going to take lodgings in the country, a Christian, residing at a distance, whom I met, by God's ordering, no doubt, gave me at the Railway station, just before starting, 50l., of which I took half for the Orphans and half for missionary purposes. On the 15th I received 110l., of which 100l. was intended for missions, and 10l. for the Orphans; and also on the same day 120l. Both donations were from considerable distances. Besides this I received several small donations, so that within three days, from the 13th to the 16th, came in about 300l. While absent from the work, from Aug. 16th to Sept. 13th, I was able to help by my prayers. This was the heaviest month in the way of current expenses. During no month, all the sixteen years and five months previously, had there been so much expended for current expenses, as in August, 1850; but, by what was in hand on August 1, by what came in, as just related, and by all the many smaller donations, we were most comfortably helped through. While absent I was also enabled to wait upon God for means for the work, besides seeking His blessing in other respects. That this was not in vain, was most evident; for not only did many donations come in while I was away, but, on my return, God so abundantly poured in the means, that, within thirteen days after, I received altogether about One Thousand Pounds; for on the very morning after my return, Sept. 14th, came in 190l., on Sept 19th 400l., on Sept. 17th 31l. 18s. 3d., on Sept. 25th 50l., on Sept. 27th 200l., besides many donations of smaller amounts. Truly I do not wait on the Lord in vain! One thing more I must add here. For several years I had not been so poor, with regard to means for myself, as when going away for change of air. But seeing it to be the will of God that I should go, I was sure that He would help me. Thus it was. On Aug. 13th my dear wife received from a sister in the Lord 5l. for change of air; and from a Christian lady near Bridgewater was sent to me for my own personal expenses 1l., from Cork 2l., and from a brother in Bristol 1l. On Aug. 15th was sent for myself from a considerable distance 18l. 11s. 3d. On Aug. 21st from Glasgow 1l. On Aug. 24th from Sunderland 1s., from Cork 1l., and from Liverpool 10l. Thus the Lord sent me for my own personal expenses such an abundance, that from Aug. 13th to Sept. 13th, 1850, I received altogether 61l. 13s. 6d. Truly I serve a good master, and this I delight to show. Not only with regard to the obtaining of means for the work, in which I am engaged, have I found simple trust in the Lord alone the easiest, the happiest, and the best way; but also in the obtaining of supplies for my own personal necessities.

Nov. 27. For seven weeks the income has been very small, in comparison with what has been expended, both for the Orphans and for the various other objects of the Scriptural Knowledge Institution. There has come in for the Orphans 187l. 16s. 2 3/4 d., and for the other objects 62l. 11s. 1d.; and the expenditure has been for the Orphans during these seven weeks 477l. 2s. 11d., and for the various other objects 394l. 9s. 8d. Therefore altogether 871l. 12s. 7d. has been expended, whilst the income altogether has been only 250l. 7s. 3 3/4 d. Of course, we have not gone into debt, as we never order anything, except we have the means in hand for it. Nor has

FOURTH PART

there been even the least difficulty experienced with regard to means, as the Lord in His kindness had sent in considerable sums just before this season commenced. About 330 persons now sit down to their meals in the New Orphan House, day by day, and the expenses for the Orphans alone are about Ten Pounds daily, and those for the other parts of the work are also about Ten Pounds daily, so that I need to receive after the rate of 20l. a day, in order to go on with the work; but during these forty-nine days there has been only one single day that I have received about 20l., and for the greater part of the time only a few pounds daily, and sometimes even only a few shillings. But what was to be done under these circumstances? I gave myself to prayer. God, whom I have now been enabled to make my refuge, and my only refuge for more than twenty years, I have besought day by day. And when now day by day I still have received only small sums, and sometimes nothing or scarcely anything at all: the only effect that it has had upon me has been, to pray the more earnestly. My confidence in God is not at all shaken. I have never had a thought that He would not help me; nor have I even once been allowed to look upon these seven weeks in any other way than that the Lord, for the trial of my faith, has ordered it thus that only so little should come in. I am sure that, when He has tried me sufficiently, there will come in again larger sums. In the mean time, how good has the Lord been, not only to have given all I have needed, but I have even now money in hand! And as to our stores in the New Orphan-House, they are as full as usual. We have at least 150 sacks of potatoes in the house, 20 sacks of flour, 33 barrels of oatmeal, each containing about 200 lbs., about 300 pairs of new shoes (besides about 900 pairs in use), about ten tons of coal, a large quantity of soap and rice; and so all other parts of the stores in proportion. Indeed while there has been little coming in, I have just ordered articles in the wholesale way as formerly, when our income was perhaps four or five times as much during the same period. My judgment is, that it will now soon please the Lord again to send in larger sums, as He has been pleased to exercise my faith for some time in this way. Let me see the result!

Nov. 28. This morning the Lord has given me a fresh proof, that I had not waited on Him in vain, and that my confidence in Him, as recorded last evening, has not been confounded. I received early this morning a donation of 200l., of which I took one half for the Orphans and the other half for the other objects.

Nov. 30. Evening. I am brought to the close of another month. Great have been the expenses, as I have paid out above 400l. for the Orphans, and above 200l. for the other objects; but I have always had the means to meet every payment.

Jan. 4, 1851. Besides a donation of 1l. from Newton Ferrers, 1l. 8s. from Keswick, 4l. 6s. 9d. from the neighbourhood of Bath, I received also this morning anonymously from Torquay 5s. worth of postages, with these words: "Open thy mouth wide, and I will fill it." I am doing this. I expect much, very much indeed, in every way. I also expect much in the way of means. Evening. This very day the Lord has given me a most precious proof, that He delights in our having large expectations from Him. "My mouth has been filled," according to the portion of Holy Scripture sent to me this morning. I have received this evening the sum of Three Thousand

Pounds, being the largest donation which I have had as yet. I have had very many donations of 100l. and of 200l., several of 300l., one of 400l., several of 500l., some from 600l. to 900l., four of l000l., two of 2000l. and one of 2050l. But I never had more than this given to me at one time; yet I have expected more than 2050l. in one donation, and, accordingly, it has pleased the Lord to give me 3000l. this evening. I now write again that I expect far larger Sums still, in order that it may be yet more and more manifest, that there is no happier, no easier, and no better way of obtaining pecuniary means for the work of the Lord, than the one in which I have been led. How great my joy in God is, on account of this donation, cannot be described; but it is not in the least coupled with excitement. I take this donation out of the hands of the living God; I continually look for His help, and am perfectly assured that I shall have it, and therefore is my soul calm and peaceful, without any excitement, though the donation is so large. This donation is, however, like a voice from heaven, speaking to me concerning a most deeply important matter respecting which I am seeking guidance from the Lord, the building of another Orphan-House. For several years, while the Orphans were living in rented houses in Wilson Street, Bristol, it pleased the Lord to manifest His power by helping us from day to day, and sometimes even from meal to meal; but of late years He has more especially been pleased to show His power by sending us abundant supplies. Should it please Him, however, hereafter to cause us again to be similarly situated, He will surely help; and, by His grace, we will then trust in Him as heretofore. Moreover, though we have not been so low with regard to means, yet my faith has not been without trial even in this particular; but especially in other respects it has pleased God continually to keep my faith in exercise. This sum of 3000l. was entirely left at my disposal, and it was therefore portioned out thus: 1500l. for the Orphans, 500l. for foreign labourers in the Gospel, 500l. for home labourers in the Gospel, 200l. for the circulation of Gospel Tracts, 100l. for the circulation of the Holy Scriptures, and 200l. for the support of Day Schools, Adult Schools, and Sunday Schools.

As an instance to show in what a variety of ways the Lord is pleased to help me with means, I insert here the following kind but anonymous letter, which was left at my house on January 27th, 1851.

"Dear Mr. Mueller,

" I left at Mr. W--'s last week a donation of 1l. 1s. towards the Orphan-Houses, which I hope you received safely. It is indeed encouraging and strengthening to read the account of the many indubitable answers you have had to prayer, and I pray God, dear sir, to strengthen your hands, and prolong your life, if it be His will, that both the servants of Christ and of Satan, the former to their comfort, the latter to their confusion if not to their conversion, may see that God alone reigns, and that the hearts of all are in His hand. I now inclose you some coins (there are 18), which may be disposed of for the Orphan-Houses. Truly we wish you good luck in the name of the Lord.

"Believe me, dear sir,

FOURTH PART

"To remain your unknown but true Friend,

"A Minister of the Church of England."

"N.B. I earnestly solicit an interest in your prayers."

The letter contained a two-guinea piece, a small Portuguese gold coin, 15 silver coins, and a copper coin.

March. 7. Very great have been the expenses for the Orphans of late. During the short month of February alone I spent 386l. for them. For nearly eight weeks, since Jan. 11th, the expenses have been nearly four times as great as the income, which, however, I have been able amply to meet, on account of the previous abundance which the Lord had been pleased to send in. Now, however, after much prayer for means, the Lord has been pleased to refresh my heart by a donation of 200l., referred to under this date in the account of the income for the other objects. I took of this sum 90l. for the Orphans. I received also this day 4l. 10s., being the bequest of a Swiss brother in the Lord, who fell asleep in Devonshire, and who desired that what he left should be sold for the benefit of the Orphans.

April 30. At the morning exposition of the Holy Scriptures at the New Orphan-House, I was led particularly to dwell upon the blessedness of the believer having to do with the living God, and referred, in the way of illustration, to His care in supporting the Orphan Work. Immediately after the exposition was over, I received a donation of 12l. 12s. for the Orphans, another of 200l. (which I took half for the Orphans and half for the other objects), and in the afternoon came in still further through the boxes in the New Orphan-House 2l. 14s. 4 1/2 d. Concerning the donation of 12l. 12s. the hand of the Lord is the more manifest, in that it came from a place whence. I had never received any donation, as far as I know, and towards it a vicar, an archdeacon, and one of the Queen's chaplains contributed, gentlemen entirely unknown to me, and yet they felt thus kindly disposed towards this work.

May 26. I am brought to the close of this period. The work is more and more enlarging. During the last month I have paid out for the Orphans more than 450l., and for the other objects more than 500l., being nearly One Thousand Pounds during one month; and yet I have a greater balance left in hand, through the Lord's kindness, than at the close of any of the previous periods.

Of the several hundreds of donations, large and small, received during this period, I have thus taken a few, to show in what way it pleased the Lord to supply me with means for the Orphan Work.

Miscellaneous Points respecting the Scriptural Knowledge Institution for Home and Abroad, with reference to the period from May 26, 1850 to May 26, 1851.

THE LORD'S DEALINGS WITH GEORGE MÜLLER

1. There were during this period four Day Schools in Bristol, with 286 children in them, entirely supported by the funds of the Institution, and three others in Devonshire, Gloucestershire, and Norfolk, with 180 children in them, were assisted.--Further, one Sunday School in Bristol, with 184 children, was entirely supported, and two others, in Devonshire and Gloucestershire, with 213 children, were assisted.-- Lastly, an Adult School in Bristol, with 90 persons in it, was entirely supported.-- The expenses connected with all these various Schools were, during this period, 379l. 17s.--From the formation of the Institution, on March 5, 1834, up to May 26, 1851, there were 5,343 children in the various Day Schools in Bristol alone, 2,379 in the Sunday School, and 1,896 persons in the Adult Schools, besides the thousands in the Schools out of Bristol, which were assisted.

2. During this period I sought again especially to supply very poor persons, whose character was known by their being visited, with copies of the Holy Scriptures; and also to put copies which are printed with large type in to the hands of aged persons, which seems to me of especial need, as such Bibles are still expensive, considering the means of the poor. There was expended during this period, out of the funds of the Institution, on the circulation of the Holy Scriptures, 150l. 16s. 5d. There were 345 Bibles sold and 899 given away; and 30 New Testaments sold, and 413 given away, during this period. From March 5, 1834, to May 26, 1851, there were circulated 7,709 Bibles and 4,442 New Testaments.

3. During this year was spent of the Funds of the Institution for Missionary objects the sum of 2000l. 11s. 1d. By this sum, forty-five labourers in the word and doctrine, in various parts of the world, were to a greater or less degree assisted. The amount sent to each of these servants of Christ was as follows.

To No. 1. Labouring in British Guiana 91l. 10s.

To No. 2. Ditto 82l.

To No. 3. Ditto 80l. 10s.

To No. 4. Ditto 55l.

To No. 5. Ditto 55l.

To No. 6. Ditto 30l.

To No. 7. Ditto 20l.

To No. 8. Ditto 10l.

To No. 9. Labouring in the East Indies 100l.

To No. 10. Ditto 40l.

FOURTH PART

To No. 11. Ditto 40l.

To No. 12. Ditto 20l.

To No. 13 Ditto 14l.

To No. 14 Labouring in Canada 20l.

To No. 15 Ditto 20l.

To No. 16 Labouring in the United States 30l.

To No. 17 Labouring in France 60l.

To No. 18. Labouring in Switzerland 50l.

To No. 19. Ditto 10l.

To No. 20. Ditto 10l.

To No. 21. Labouring in Germany 10l.

To No. 22. Labouring in Ireland 70l.

To No. 23. Labouring in Scotland 115l.

To No. 24. Labouring in England 130l.

To No. 25. Labouring in England 115l.

To No. 26. Ditto 80l.

To No. 27. Ditto 65l.

To No. 28. Ditto 65l.

To No. 29. Ditto 57l.

To No. 30. Ditto 50l.

To No. 31. Ditto 50l.

To No. 32. Ditto 50l.

To No. 33. Ditto 45l.

To No. 34. Ditto 45l

To No. 35. Ditto 30l.

To No. 36. Ditto 30l.

To No. 37. Ditto 30l.

To No. 38. Ditto 20l.

To No. 39. Ditto 15l.

To No. 40. Ditto 10l.

To No. 41. Ditto 10l.

To No. 42. Ditto 10l.

To No. 43. Ditto 10l.

To No. 44. Ditto 5l.

To No. 45. Ditto 5l.

There was also sent to me anonymously for the support of native preachers of the Gospel in China 11s. 1d., which was forwarded .... 11s. 1d.

The total amount of 2000l. was sent to these forty-five servants of the Lord Jesus in 264 different sums, generally not less than 5l. and not more than 10l. at one time to each, except there were especial reasons pointing to a different course. Almost all these brethren were habitually assisted; a few needed only occasional assistance.

I have great joy, in being able to inform the believing reader, that it pleased the Lord again to let great blessing rest upon the labours of these preachers of the Gospel, whom I sought to assist during this year; which is alike true both with reference to those who labour in our own country and those who preach the Word in foreign lands.

I consider it a great privilege to be permitted to defray in part or altogether, from the funds of this institution, the expenses connected with the voyage and outfit of brethren who desire to go out as Missionaries, or to help them after their arrival in their field of labour; but I do not bind myself to support them habitually, seeing that thus they would be out of the position of simple dependence upon God for their temporal supplies.

FOURTH PART

4. During this period 358l. 7s. 3d. was expended on the circulation of Tracts, and 303,098 Tracts and Little Books were circulated.

The Lord was pleased to give me such an abundance of opportunities for circulating tracts by means of godly men, both in this and foreign countries, that, during this year, I was permitted to send out more tracts than during the whole of the previous ten years taken together. Nor must it be withheld from the reader, as matter for thankfulness, that the Lord was pleased to allow me to hear again and again of instances of conversion, by means of the distribution of these Tracts during this period.

5. On May 26, 1850, there were Two Hundred and Seventy-five Orphans in the New Orphan House on Ashley Down, Bristol. There were admitted into it, during this year, 45 Orphans, making 320 in all. Of these, however, two were removed by their relatives, who were able by that time to provide for them, seven died during the year, five of the elder girls were sent out to service, and six of the elder boys were apprenticed; so that on May 26, 1851, there were 300 Orphans in the New Orphan House. The total number of Orphans who were under our care from April, 1836, to May 26, 1851, is Four Hundred and Eighty-Eight. There came in altogether during this year 4102l. 14s. 9 1/4 d. for the support of the Orphans, and 3,640l. 9s. 1 3/4 d. for the other objects; and, after having met to the full every demand with reference to the Orphans, the balance of 970l. 13s. 11 3/4 d. remained in hand. Also, after having entered into every door, which the Lord was pleased to set before me respecting the other objects, and to do far more than during any one year previously, the balance of 809l. 10s. 6d. remained in hand on May 26, 1851. Verily we do not trust in the Lord in vain!

Without any one having been personally applied to for anything by me, the sum of 38,018l. 4s. 6 1/2 d. was given to me for the Orphans as the result of prayer to God from the commencement of the work to May 26, 1851.--It may be also interesting to the reader to know, that the total amount which was given as free contributions, for the other objects, from the commencement of the work to May 26, 1851, amounted to 13,988l. 11s. 9 1/4 d.; and that which came in by the sale of Bibles and Tracts, and by the payments of the children in the Day-Schools, amounted to 2,890l. 9s. 11 3/4 d.--Besides this, also a great variety and number of articles of clothing, furniture, provisions, &e., were given for the use of the Orphans.

It pleased the Lord greatly to gladden our hearts by the working of His Holy Spirit among the Orphans during this period.

Matters connected with my own personal affairs, or the work of the Lord in my hands, not immediately connected with the Scriptural Knowledge institution, from May 26, 1850, to May 26, 1851.

Dec. 31, 1850. During this year there have been received into Fellowship 57, and altogether, from the time that Brother Craik and I began to labour in Bristol,

1313, which, with the 68 believers whom we found in Fellowship, make 1381. Of these 174 have fallen asleep, 160 have left us during these 18 years and a half, 355 have removed from Bristol, and 80 have been excluded from Fellowship; so that there are at present only 612 in communion.

During this year the Lord has been pleased to give me---

1. By anonymous offerings through the Chapel boxes	L148 11 0
2. By presents in money from believers in Bristol, not given anonymously	86 1 9
8. By presents in money from believers not residing in Bristol	160 0 8
4. By presents in provisions, clothes, &c., worth to us at least	7 11 0
	L402 4 5

Further account of the intended Orphan House for Seven Hundred Poor Children, bereaved of both Parents by

death, from May 26, 1851, to May 26, 1852.

The reader will remember it was stated in the previous chapter on this subject, that I purposed, not in dependence upon my Christian Friends, nor upon former donors, but alone in dependence upon the living God, who, I trust, has called me for it, notwithstanding all my unworthiness, to enlarge the Orphan Work. The Godly reader will now be desirous to learn how far I have been helped, in this my intention, to enlarge the field of labour in caring for the vast numbers of helpless Orphans in our land. I will, therefore, give an extract, in the way of specimens, from the account book, kept for the purpose, together with the remarks and observations which I wrote down at the time of the receipt of the donations, and make also here and there additional remarks, as the occasion may call for.

Before I brought before the public my purpose, I gave the record of the exercises of my mind, on this subject, to a valued Christian friend to read, the only one who, besides my family, knew anything of my intention, before it came before the public. I did this particularly in order that, after waiting for several months in secret upon God for guidance and direction concerning it, I might also have the counsel of a prayerful, judicious, and cautious man of God. When this brother returned the manuscript, he spoke to me words of encouragement concerning this purpose, and gave me a half-sovereign towards the Building Fund for this house for 700 destitute Orphans. This was the first donation, which I received on May 13, 1851, and which, I confess, was a great refreshment and encouragement to me, the more so as it came from so cautious a brother, and after I had been for several months, through secret prayer, assured that I should go forward.

FOURTH PART

On May 28th, 1851, my intention became publicly known, and in the evening of May 29th I received from a Christian lady a sovereign towards the Building Fund.

May 30. One of the Orphans in the New Orphan House gave 6d. for the Building Fund, and one engaged in the work gave an old silver watch for sale and 5s.

June. 1. A brother in the Lord, who gives his donations with the letter "P.," gave me 10s.--I also received a sovereign.--This evening I received still further 4 half-crowns, with very encouraging words and expressions of joy, that I have been led to this purpose of building another Orphan House for 700 more Orphans.--There came to hand also anonymously 3s. Ditto an old shilling, a small American coin, and two shillings. Also from a Christian servant in Clifton 2s. 6d.

June. 3. From one of the Orphans in the New Orphan House 6d., and from another 6d.

June 4. From another Orphan in the New Orphan House, 6d. I received also 8s. 0 1/2 d., which the Orphans in the Girls' School of the New Orphan House gave between them for the Building Fund.

June 5. Through one of the boxes at the New Orphan House twopence and likewise one half-penny. These two small donations are very sweet to me. I take them as a further earnest, out of the hands of my heavenly Father, that He, in His own time, will give me the whole sum requisite. Evening: From a sister from Norwich 2s. 6d. From a sister in the Lord in Bristol 1s.

June. 6. Anonymously 5l. 0s. 1d., with these words: "Towards the Building Fund of the proposed Orphan House 2l., for Brother Mueller 1l. 10s., for Brother Craik 1l. 10s."

June 7. Anonymously 1s. 6d.

June. 8. From a brother 5s.--From one of the Orphans formerly under our care, a believer, a sovereign, of which she intends 5s. for the Building Fund, 5s. for present use for the Orphans, 5s. for Brother Craik, and 5s. for my own personal expenses. How sweet a donation! Anonymously 1s. From "P." 1s. 6d.

June 11. Anonymously, from Sunderland 1l--A lady gave to my daughter at my house 5l., but would not give her name.

June. 12. From Richmond 5l.

I have thus given minutely an account of the income during the first two weeks, after my purpose had become known; but shall now only, for the sake of brevity, refer to some of the donations.

June. 21. Twenty-four days have now passed away since I have been enabled, day by day, to wait with a goodly measure of earnestness and in faith upon the Lord for means; but as yet only a little above 28l. has come in. But I am not discouraged. The less there comes in, the more earnestly I pray, the more I look out for answers, and the more assured I am that the Lord, in His own time, after He has tried my faith, will send me larger sums, and, at last, all I need.

July 27. From a Christian gentleman in Clifton 20l. This donation has much refreshed my spirit. I am, day by day, expecting help from the Lord, in large and small sums as He pleases; but as He is trying my faith, in that only so little as yet has come in, this donation has been very precious.

Aug. 8. From a Christian lady in London 5l.--From Somersetshire 40l.

Aug. 12, Day by day I am waiting upon the Lord for means for this object, and generally more than once a day am bowing my knees before God with reference to it. Moreover, of late I have been enabled, with increasing earnestness, to beseech the Lord, that He would be pleased to send in means for the Building Fund. My soul has been all along at peace, though only so little as yet, comparatively, has come in (in all 127l. 19s. 9d.) and though Satan has, in the most subtle way, sought to shake my confidence, and to lead me to question, whether, after all, I had not been mistaken concerning this whole matter. Yet, though he has aimed after this, to the praise of God I have to confess, that he has not been allowed to triumph. I have especially besought the Lord of late, that He would be pleased to refresh my spirit by sending in some large donation for this part of the work. Under these circumstances, I received this morning the following letter with 500l.:

"* * * * August 8.

"My Dear Brother,

"Trusting that God has indeed called you to this work, viz., caring for poor Orphans, and will not allow you to be deceived as to His will regarding the increasing it, but will greatly use you for His own glory and for blessing to many poor destitute children, it is my desire, and I humbly thank our most gracious God and Father for the ability, to have fellowship with you in this work, as far as He permits. Will you, therefore, use the enclosed check for 500l. for the Orphans, towards the present Establishment or the proposed new one, as you may judge best, or taking any part thereof for one or the other. The Lord Jesus be your counselor, your joy, your strength, your all.

"Affectionately yours,

"* * * *"

FOURTH PART

I took the whole amount for the Building Fund. I was not in the least excited. I look out for means. Even at that very moment, when I received this donation, I was looking out for means, for large donations; and I should not have been surprised if 5,000l. had come in, or more. The Lord be praised for this precious encouragement, which has still further quickened me for prayer!

Aug. 14. From the neighbourhood of Leeds 10l.--From Essex 5l.

Aug. 15. Anonymously from Hull 5s.--From Cornwall a copy of "Greece" for sale.

Aug. 19. From Shirehampton 5l.

Aug. 20. From Mirfield 2l. Also 150l. came in today which, being left at my disposal by the donor, as most needed, I took the whole of this amount for the Building Fund, having sufficient means in hand for the current expenses of the various objects of the Scriptural Knowledge Institution.

Aug. 30. From M. S. 30l., of which the donor desires 20l. to be used for missionary objects, and 10l. for the Building Fund. The donor writes: "My present inducement to remit this is, that God has lately prospered me in business, and I had been putting by for this and a few other similar purposes, intending to make bequests in my will, but am convinced that this is the best course to pursue, if not the only justifiable one, with what I can spare from my business and other necessities."

Sept. 1. From a much afflicted sister seven dolls' bonnets for sale. -- A picture in frame.

Sept. 2. From an individual living in Nicholas Street, Bristol, 1l.-- From a brother in the Lord, in Wandsworth Road, London, 5s., with 1l. for present use for the Orphans, and 15s. for missionary purposes.-- From a poor Christian widow in London 1s., with 1s. for present use for the Orphans.--I am day by day labouring in prayer for this object, and with a goodly measure of fervency of spirit, by the grace of God; and am day by day looking out for answers. These sums last recorded are but small, yet they tell me that my Heavenly Father is not unmindful of my supplications, and of those of His dear children who help me with their prayers, and that, in His own time, He will send me more, and also large sums. I magnify His holy name that He does not in the least allow me to question either His power or His willingness to give me all that I shall need; yea, my soul is as assured that I shall have this my request fully granted, unworthy though I am of it, as if the whole amount were already in my hand.

Sept. 4. From a Christian at Keswick 10s., and a lady through ditto 5s.

Sept. 5. From the neighbourhood of Keswick 1l.--From Hull 1l.-- From Shrewsbury 20l.

Sept. 10. As yet the Lord delays sending in larger sums; but I am looking out for them, and am confidently expecting them. This delay is only for the trial of my faith; after He has tried it, He will help me. Applications for the admission of Orphans continue to be made. Within the last ten days eighteen poor children, bereaved of both parents, have been applied for; and since Aug. 15th, therefore in twenty-six days, thirty-two altogether. My heart longs to be allowed of God to help poor Orphans more extensively than ever. Whence the means are to come for the building of this house for 700 Orphans, I know not; but still, by God's help, my confidence in Him is not shaken. To Him it is a very small matter to give me all I need for this work.

Sept. 11. From Ludgvan 10s. Evening. Only these ten shillings have come in today, but three more Orphans have been applied for, making thirty-five in less than a month. Does not the Lord tell me by this, that He will provide another home for Orphans? I will therefore patiently wait upon Him for the means, and after He has tried my faith and patience, He will show Himself as the bearer and answerer of prayer. Today came in the course of my reading John xiv. 13, 14, "And whatsoever ye shall ask in my name, that will I do, that the Father may be glorified in the Son. If ye shall ask anything in my name I will do it." I pleaded this word of promise, and look for answers, even for the fulfilment of this promise. Nor do I doubt that the Lord Jesus will fulfil this His promise in this my case.

Sept. 12. From Guildford 1l. 8s.--From Bath 1l.

Sept. 13. Patience and faith are still called for, and, by God's grace, my desire is to "let patience have her perfect work," Not one penny has come in today for the Building Fund, but five more Orphans have been applied for, so that now forty in less than one single month have been brought before me, all bereaved of both parents, and all very destitute. Under these circumstances, how can I but fervently labour in prayer that the Lord would be pleased to intrust me with means for building another Orphan-House for 700 Orphans. The more I look at things according to natural appearances and prospects, the less likely is it that I should have the sum which is needed; but I have faith in God, and my expectation is from Him alone. From the beginning I depended upon Him only, concerning this proposed enlargement of the work, and therefore have not been disappointed, though as yet only the fortieth part of what is needed has come in (882l. 18s. 7 1/2 d). But how soon, how very soon can the Lord alter the aspect of things. Even this very evening, while I am writing, He can give me many thousand pounds. I continue therefore, to wait upon God, and seek to encourage my heart by His holy word, and while he delays giving me answers, to be occupied in His blessed service. Of this, however, my soul has not the least doubt, that, when the Lord shall have been pleased to exercise my soul by the trial of faith and patience, He will make bare His arm, and send help. The fact that the applications for the admission of destitute Orphans are so many, does both quicken me to

FOURTH PART

prayer, and is also a great encouragement to me, that the Lord will give me the desire of my heart, to provide another home for these destitute, fatherless and motherless children.

Sept. 19. Received today a donation of 170l., which the donor kindly allowed me to use for the work of the Lord in my hands as I pleased. I therefore took the whole of this donation for the Building Fund, having at present sufficient means in hand for the current expenses of all, the various objects of the Scriptural Knowledge Institution, and feeling called to give myself with my might to prepare for the Building of another Orphan-House.

Sept. 20. About two months since I received a letter, of which I give as much as refers to the subject in hand.

"My Dear Sir,

"I was once a book collector, and turned my attention to our old English Bibles, and, among other editions, perfected, almost sheet by sheet, our first English Coverdale Bible of 1535. It is a sad specimen of time, attention, and money misspent and mis-applied, and as I look upon you as the receiver of cast off idols, whether watch chains, trinkets, or old Bibles, I have purposed for some time sending it to you. * * * * Do with the proceeds as you see fit. I should be glad if a portion were converted into large printed Testaments for the aged, and should be thankful if that, which has been cause of humbling to me, should be converted into the means, through your instrumentality, of raising others.

* * * * *

"Ever yours,

* * * *."

A day or two after the receipt of this letter, a parcel arrived, containing the said Coverdale Bible, of A.D. 1535 and another book; the latter to be sold for the benefit of the Orphans. It was only today that I had an opportunity of disposing of the old Bible, which fetched 60l., together with other books, which had been given for the benefit of the Orphans, which brought 10l. Of the 60l. I took 10l. for New Testaments printed with large type for aged poor persons, and 50l. for the Building Fund.

Oct. 2. Evening. Nothing has come in today for the Building Fund, and very little during the last ten days. I have had just now again a long season for prayer respecting this object. Through the support which I receive from the Lord, I am not cast down, though only so little as yet has come in. The work is His, and not mine;

therefore am I able quietly to leave it in His hands. Were I to look at what has come in hitherto, much though it is, in one sense, it would take, after this rate, about ten years, before I should have the sum needed; but this does not cast me down; for, when the Lord's time is come I expect larger sums. Further, there are peculiar natural obstacles in the way to my receiving donations for this object; for it has now been for several months reported that I have already Thirty Thousand Pounds in hand for the Building Fund, though this day it is actually only 1,139l. 19s. 2 1/2 d. Again and again this has been told me, and therefore, were I to look at things naturally, I should have much reason to be cast down, as the spread of such reports is calculated, humanly speaking, to keep persons from contributing towards this object. Another class of persons, true Christians, and liberal persons too, may be thinking, that the sum required is so large that it is not likely I shall obtain it, and that therefore their contributing towards this object would be useless. But none of these things discourage me. God knows that I have not Thirty Thousand Pounds in hand. God can influence the minds of His dear children towards this intended Orphan-House, whatever their thoughts may have been hitherto on the subject. I therefore seek to "let patience have her perfect work," and go on in prayer, being fully assured, that the Lord will not suffer me to be confounded. I am day by day looking out for help, yea for large sums; and I know I shall have them, after the Lord has exercised my faith and patience. Lord wilt Thou mercifully continue to give unto Thy servant faith and patience!

Oct. 3. From the Forest of Dean 1l.

Oct. 4. From Old Aberdeen 5l.--From Dublin the work for an ottoman and a piece of crochet work.

Oct. 5. Through Bethesda boxes 10s.--From Clifton 7s.--From H. S. 4d.

Oct. 7. From Wellington in Salop 5s. Evening. The trial of my faith and patience continues still. Again very little has come in during the last four days for the Building Fund. But my hope in God, by His help, continues steadfast. I had just now again a long season for prayer, having spent the whole evening alone for the purpose, and am assured that, when God's time shall have come, it will be seen that, even concerning this object, I do not wait upon Him in vain. There are persons again and again asking me, When I am going to commence the building; for, they think that I have all, or nearly all, the means which are required. And there are others who ask me whether I still purpose to build this Orphan-House. To Thee, my Heavenly Father, Thy child turns under these circumstances. Thou knowest how small an amount as yet Thy servant has, in comparison with what is needed; but Thou also knowest that Thy servant did not act rashly and under excitement in this matter, but waited upon Thee for six months in secret, before he spoke about this his intention. Now, Lord, in Thy mercy, sustain Thy servant's faith and patience, and, if it please Thee, speedily refresh his heart by sending in larger sums, for which he is looking, and which he confidently expects!

FOURTH PART

Oct. 8. Through the boxes at the New Orphan-House 2s. 6d., with Psalm xxvii. 14. The words of the passage are these: "Wait on the Lord: be of good courage, and He shall strengthen thine heart: wait, I say, on the Lord." By God's grace I wait on the Lord, and am of good courage, and He does strengthen my heart, in faith and patience to continue to wait on Him, though only so little comes in, being assured that, when the trial of faith and patience is over, He will make bare His arm, and send in larger sums.

Oct. 28. Nothing at all has come in today for the Building Fund, and about 70l. only during the last four weeks. Yet, by the grace of God, I am supported, and have not the least questioning of soul whether I shall have the means or not. I only look upon this delay, on the part of God, in sending me larger sums, as an exercise of my patience and faith, and am sure, that in His own time He will give more largely. Today I have had again three long seasons for prayer respecting the work in my hands; and the greater part of this evening have been in prayer, entreating and beseeching the Lord to help me; and I am now again looking out for means, as I do day by day.

Oct. 29. This morning I received a letter, containing a check for 50l., and these words:

"* * * * Oct. 27, 1851.

"My dear Sir,

I had much pleasure and blessing in perusing the Report you were kind enough to send me some time ago, and am much obliged to you for it. Is it not a privilege to be allowed to obtain future good out of present expending? (Luke xvi. 9)' That when ye fail, etc.' I enclose a check for 50l., of which I should wish 25l. to be used for the New Orphan-House, that which you propose to build.

Yours, dear Sir,

Ever faithfully,

* * * * *"

The other 25l. being left to me, to be disposed of as I thought well, I divided equally between the five objects of the Scriptural Knowledge Institution for Home and Abroad.

By the same post I received also a donation of 10s., with the following letter.

THE LORD'S DEALINGS WITH GEORGE MÜLLER

* * * *, Oct. 27, 1851.

"Dear Mr. Mueller,

I enclose you 10s. worth of postages, as a token of gratitude to the Lord. I had 2l. due to me, and the party told me he would not pay it, except I summoned him. I consulted the Scripture, and found, as a Christian, I must not do that; so I put the case into the hand of the 'wonderful counsellor,' and told the Lord, if He would be pleased to give me the 2l., I would give Him back half of it. Not long after I had a message from the party, to say if I would fetch it, I should have the 2l.; so I went, and he paid me without an unpleasant word. I have sent you one half of the pound (the other half I have designed for another purpose). If you need it, you will please to take it for your own personal use; if it is not needed any other way, I should like the privilege of having a stone in the intended Orphan-House, &c."

I took this 10s. for the Building Fund. The donor is a poor working man. -- This afternoon I received 50l. more from the neighbourhood of London, with these words: "For the missionaries, and where else most needed." I took, therefore, 25l. of it for missions, and the other 25l. for the Building Fund.

Thus the Lord has been pleased this day to refresh my heart greatly in sending these donations, and has given again a manifest proof that yesterday I did not wait upon Him in vain. But I look out for more abundant help, and for larger sums. I cannot help noticing here, that this afternoon the Lord also refreshed my spirit through a donation of 6 pairs of new shoes, which a young man (whom about twelve years ago I received as a very destitute Orphan, and who about five years ago was apprenticed to a shoemaker, and who has lately finished his apprenticeship), brought me for the Orphans, as a small token of his gratitude, as he said. He had himself made the shoes, having bought the leather with the little sums which he had earned in working overtime for his master.

Such instances occur often. I see now, again and again, fruit resulting from my labours in this service. It is not at all a rare thing that I meet with respectable young women, or respectable young men, who, many years ago, were placed, as very destitute Orphans, under my care, and who are now a comfort and help to society, instead of being a pest, which otherwise they might have been. But valuable and pleasant as this is, I frequently meet with far more in them: I find them to be children of the living God, through faith in our Lord Jesus Christ, and see or hear that they walk according to their profession. Thus, in the midst of many difficulties, and with much that, for the present moment, is discouraging, I see abundant fruit. Yet, if even only one soul were won from among these Orphans, how abundantly would all labours, trials, difficulties, and expenditure of money be made up; but, if I know of scores of them already in heaven, and scores of them now on the road to heaven, how can I but go on labouring, esteeming it a privilege to be allowed of God to seek to win more and more of them for Him? Considerations like these are a mighty impulse to me to go forward with regard to the intended Orphan House.

FOURTH PART

Nov. 10. Today I received 200l., of which the donor kindly wished me to keep 20l. for my own personal expenses, and to apply the rest as most needed for the Lord's work in my hands. I took, therefore, 100l. for the Building Fund, and 80l. for missionary objects, the circulation of the Holy Scriptures and Gospel Tracts, and for the support of all the various schools which are supported by the funds of the Scriptural Knowledge. Institution. By this donation my heart has been greatly refreshed for the following reasons:--lst. During the last twelve days very little, comparatively, has come in. 2nd. The first four objects of the Institution, for which I took the 80l., were lower as to funds than they have been during the last ten months, as only 113l. remained in hand. 3rd. I had been praying for supplies for my own personal expenses, in order that I might be able to help in certain cases of need, which were near my heart. This day week, Nov. 3rd, I began particularly to pray about this object. On Nov. 7th there was 5l. put anonymously into the letter box at my house, for my own personal expenses. The note was signed "H." On the same evening I received 2l. more. On Nov. 8th I received 1l. from Keswick. On Nov. 9th 1l. 14s. 6d., and today 20l. Though this is a digression from the immediate subject before me, yet, as I write chiefly for the comfort and encouragement of the children of God, and that their dependence upon God and their trust in Him may more and more be increased, and also that unbelievers may see the reality of the things of God, I take delight in mentioning these cases, to show that He does not merely supply me, in answer to prayer, with means for His work in which I am occupied, but that He also bountifully supplies my own personal necessities, simply in answer to prayer.

Nov. 19. Early this morning came, in the course of my reading through the Holy Scriptures, Heb. v. and vi., and my heart was greatly strengthened by Heb. vi. 15., "And so after he had patiently endured, he obtained the promise." I have not once, even for one moment, been allowed to doubt, either the power or the willingness of the Lord to supply me with all that shall be needed for this other Orphan House, since I came at first to the conclusion that it was His will I should enlarge the work; yet I have often, very often, been led to ask, that He would graciously be pleased to sustain my faith and patience to the end; for great, very great, may yet be the exercises both of my faith and patience, before. I have the desire of my heart granted.

Nov. 28. The following case will especially show in what a variety of ways the Lord is pleased to supply me with means. Today I received from an individual, hitherto an entire stranger to me, the letter which follows:--

* * * *, London, Nov 27, 1851.

"My dear Brother,

I asked the Lord for help with regard to yourself and your work. The other night a stranger called at my house, and left a parcel, declining to give her name, saying, 'Take charge of this for Mr. George Mueller.' The parcel contained 3l. 14s.

9d., two silver spoons, and two silver thimbles; 4s. were added to pay the expenses. May the Lord prosper you, my brother.

Yours affectionately,

* * * * *"

As it was not stated for what object the donation was intended, I took the whole for the Building Fund.

Dec. 8. From A. Z. at Hull 3l. 5s., of which the donor kindly intends 5s. for my own personal expenses. Through this donor also 5s. besides. Both these donations are remarkable. The donor who sent the 3l. 5s., some years ago, when in very poor circumstances, set apart from his earnings 3/4 d. a-day for the Orphans. From that time God was pleased to prosper him; and now he is able to send this 3l. 5s. at once. The donor of the 5s. had about a year ago one of the Reports of the Scriptural Knowledge Institution lent to him, when he was living in much sin, by the brother who sent the 3l. 5s., and this Report was the means of his conversion.

Dec. 28. This morning I received a donation of 200l., which, being left at my disposal, I took one half for the Building Fund, and the other half for the School, Bible, Tract and Missionary Objects.

Jan. 28, 1852. From Torquay 5s.--I received also this morning the following registered letter, enclosing 50l.

"* * * * *Jan. 21, 1852.

"Dear Brother,

"Having this morning received a large present, I hasten to send you 50l., either towards building the New Orphan House, or for the missionary servants of the Lord; as you may deem best.

" Yours very truly in Christ,

"* * * *"

I am especially labouring in prayer, day by day, that the Lord would be pleased to furnish me with the means for building another Orphan House, as the number of applications for destitute children, bereaved of both parents, is increasing more and more: but I have also of late been particularly praying to the Lord for means for missionary brethren, as almost all I have in hand for them is expended. On this account I purpose to take one half of this donation for the Building Fund, and the other half for missionary objects.

FOURTH PART

March 17. Day by day I am waiting upon God for means. With full confidence, both as to the power of the Lord to give me the means, and likewise His willingness, I am enabled to continue to wait. But He is pleased to exercise my faith and patience, and especially has this been the case of late. Not more than 27l. 11s. has come in, during the last four weeks, for the Building Fund. Yet, amidst it all, by the help of God, my heart has been kept looking to the Lord, and expecting help from Him. Now today my heart has been greatly refreshed by a donation of 999l. 13s. 5d., which, being left to my disposal for the work of God, I took of it for the Building Fund 600l., for current expenses for the Orphans 200l., and the remainder for the School, Bible, Tract, and Missionary objects. I cannot describe to any one how refreshing this donation is to my spirit. After having been for weeks, day by day, waiting upon the Lord, and receiving so little, comparatively, either for current expenses or for the Building Fund, this answer to many prayers is exceedingly sweet to my spirit.

March 18. From Mallow in Ireland 5s.--From Torquay 5s.--From Whitby 2l. 3s. 6d., of which 1l. is for the Building Fund, 1l. for present use for the Orphans, and 3s. 6d. for ditto.--From Kingstanley 1l.--From Lichfield 4l. 15s., and 5s.

March 21. From Clifton 5l., with 3s. for present use for the Orphans. -- Through Salem boxes 1s.

March 23. From Driffield 5l.--Received also further 500l., which, being entirely left at my disposal, I took 100l. for the Building Fund, 200l. for current expenses for the Orphans, 50l. for the circulation of the Holy Scriptures, 50l. for the circulation of Gospel Tracts, 50l. for preachers of the Gospel in foreign lands, and 50l. for preachers of the Gospel in England, Ireland, and Scotland.

May 16. From two Christian ladies at Clifton 10s.

May 19. From Bishopwearmouth 5l.

May 20. 149l. 8s. 11 1/2 d., being the proceeds arising from the sale of a book in English, and 40l. 14s. from the sale of a book in French, were given for the Building Fund; and 75l. 18s. 9d., being the balance of a certain account, for present use for the Orphans.

To the donations received during this year, is to be added 64l. 10s. 6d. received for interest; for as a steward of the money, with which I was intrusted for the Building Fund, I felt it right to put out to interest that which came in. Lastly, there remained in hand from the former Building Fund the balance of 776l. 14s. 3 3/4 d., which I added to the present Building Fund, so that on the evening of May 26th, 1852, I had altogether 3530l. 9s. 0 1/4 d.

THE LORD'S DEALINGS WITH GEORGE MÜLLER

I add the following points, which were stated in the Report of 1852, and which are here reprinted for the better information of the readers.

A. Looking at the comparatively small amount yet in hand towards the accomplishment of my purpose, some of my readers may suppose that I am on that account discouraged. My reply is, that I am not at all discouraged, and that for the following reasons.

1. The many donations which the Lord has been pleased to send me during the past year expressly for the Building Fund, have been a proof to me that He condescends to listen to my supplications respecting this part of the work, and to those of His dear children who help me with their prayers; for many, I believe, labour with me in prayer.

2. The delay of the Lord in sending still larger sums, and more speedily, than He has been pleased to do hitherto, I only consider to be for the exercise of my faith and patience. Were the Lord displeased with my intention, He would not have dealt with me as He has, and would not have encouraged me to continue to wait upon Him, by the many donations which were expressly given for this object, and some from most unexpected quarters. This exercise of my faith and patience, however, I believe to be intended not merely for my own individual profit; but through me, also for the benefit of others. By God's gracious help and support I will, therefore, continue to wait patiently, till He shall be pleased more abundantly to send in the means, which I do not in the least doubt life will do.

3. Even when intending to build the New Orphan-House on Ashley Down, Bristol, (which was then an undertaking to me greater far than the second Orphan House now contemplated), I had to wait two years and three months, before I had all the means needed; and great, and many, and varied indeed were the trials of my patience and faith, before that work was accomplished; yet, at last, the Lord so abundantly helped me, and so altogether carried me through all the difficulties, that the house was built, fitted up, furnished, and inhabited, and several hundred pounds remained over and above what was required. And now three years have already elapsed since the house has been inhabited, and the three hundred Orphans in it have no cause to speak of want, but only of abundance. But as the work increases more and more, I am not surprised that my trials of faith and patience should become sharper and sharper, and should last longer and longer; but yet, by His help, will I hope in God, whom I shall have to praise further still, and who will help me further still, on the ground of the worthiness and merits of His holy child Jesus, though I am most unworthy in myself to be helped.

4. One of the things, which especially encourages me to continue to wait upon God, and to labour on in prayer Concerning this object, is the great number of applications which continue to be made for the admission of children who have been lawfully begotten, but who are by death bereaved of both parents, and who are in very destitute circumstances. There were 170 such children waiting for admission a

FOURTH PART

year ago; since then there have been 183 more applied for, making in all 353. Of these, as during the last year but few vacancies have occurred, I have only been able to receive twenty-seven, therefore 326 remain unprovided for. This number would be far greater still, had not many persons been kept from applying to me; for they considered it useless, as the number of Orphans, waiting for admission, was already so great. Now when I consider all the help which the Lord has been pleased to grant me in this His service for so many years, and how He has carried me through one difficulty after another, and when I see one case after another, of the most pitiable Orphans (some less than one year old) brought before me; how can I but labour on in prayer on their behalf, fully believing that God, in His own time, will give me the means for this intended second home for 700 more Orphans, though I know not when the money will be sent, and whom He will honour to be the instruments, whether it will come from many or from few comparatively, and whether more especially from those donors whom God has used in former times, or whether He may be pleased to put it into the heart of those to assist me in this service, whose names I have never heard up to this time.

B. Up to the present I have taken no actual steps towards the erection of the second Orphan-House, nor do I mean to do anything in the way of purchasing the land, &c., until I have a sum in hand which may point out that the Lord's time is come for taking such steps. At present I do not allow my mind to be occupied with such points, but seek to go on step by step, and therefore, in the first place, to wait upon God for a greater amount of means than I have in hand at present; and when the Lord shall have been pleased to grant me this, I doubt not that He will also guide and direct me as to carrying out the desire which, I trust, He has put into my heart, to be still more extensively used as the Friend of the Orphan.

C. I state again that this second Orphan-House is only intended, as the one already built, for children who have been lawfully begotten, who have lost both parents by death, and who are in destitute circumstances; this, however, being the case, children may be received from any place, and the more destitute, the fewer patrons and friends they have to plead their cause, the more likely they are to be received, as neither favour nor partiality is shown in the admission of the children, but their cases are considered in the order in which applications are made. I state again here especially, that no sectarian views prompt me, or even in the least influence me in the reception of children; I do not belong to any sect, and am, therefore, not influenced by sectarianism in the admission of Orphans; but from wheresoever they come, and to whatsoever religions denomination the parents belonged, or with whatever body the persons making application may be connected; and whether those who apply never gave me one penny towards the work, or whether they gave much; it makes no difference in the admission of the children. Now just as it has been thus with regard to the admission of Orphans for more than sixteen years past, so, when God shall be pleased to allow me to accomplish my purpose concerning another Orphan-House, it is still intended to be the same concerning that one also. The New Orphan-House on Ashley Down, Bristol, is not say Orphan-House, not the Orphan-House of any party or sect, but it is God's Orphan-House, and the Orphan-House for any and every poor destitute Orphan who has lost both parents; provided, of course, there be room in the establishment, and that there be nothing so peculiar in the case of the children as to prevent their being received; and exactly thus it is intended to be, God helping, with regard to the Orphan-House for 700 Orphans, now in contemplation.

Supplies for the School--, Bible --, Missionary and Tract Fund, sent in answer to prayer, from May 26, 1851, to May 26, 1852.

At no time during the past eighteen years did I begin a new period with so much money in hand, as was the case at the commencement of this. There was a balance of 809l. 10s. 6d. left for these objects. Long before this balance was expended, however, the Lord was pleased to send in further supplies; so that, during all the year, there did not come before me one single instance in which, according to my judgment, it would have been desirable to help forward Schools or Missionary objects, or the circulation of the Holy Scriptures and Tracts, but I had always the means in hand for doing so.

I will now notice a few of the more remarkable donations

On the third day already, after the accounts had been closed, May 29, 1851, I received a donation of 150l., of which I took one-half for the current expenses for the Orphans, and the other half for these objects. -- This was the first donation in this new period, and was a precious encouragement to me in the work.

July 8. From May 29th to this day have come in twenty-eight donations, varying from 1d. to 15l. Today I received a donation of 150l. of which the donor kindly wished me to take 10l. for my own personal expenses, and to use the rest as the work of God might require it. As I still had an abundance in hand both for the Orphans and for these objects, I took one-half for the current expenses for the Orphans, and the other half for these objects.

Sept. 6. Again fifty-two donations had come in between July 8th and this day, varying from 1d. to 20l., when today a brother who has often manifested his deep interest in the spread of the truth, and who is far from being rich, sent me 80l. for home and foreign labourers in the Word.

Nov. 10. Forty donations have come in for these objects from Sept. 6th to this day, varying from 1 1/2 d. to 25l. Today I received 200l., of which, as stated under the particulars given under this date with reference to the Building Fund, I took 80l. for these objects. This donation came in most seasonably; for now the funds for these objects were lower than they had been for the last ten months, as only 113l. remained in hand.

Dec. 21. The funds for these objects were now reduced to 10l. 14s. 5d., as the twenty-two donations from 4d. to 13l., which had come in since Nov. 10th, did not

FOURTH PART

altogether amount to more than 31l. 9s. 4d., and as much money had been expended. The means in hand were therefore far less than they had been at any time during the last sixteen months, when I received this morning from A. Z., a new donor, by the Clifton post, 10l., which, being left to my disposal, I took for these objects.

Dec. 27. Only 1l. 7s. 6d. had come in since the 21st. After the payments of this day were met, there remained only 10s. 4d. in hand.

Consider this position, dear reader. Only 10s. 4d. in hand, and the expenses for all the various schools were to be met, and the circulation of the Holy Scriptures and of Tracts I desired to go on, and the Fifty preachers of the Gospel, whom I sought to help, my heart desired to help still further. Consider also, that whatever my necessities may be, I never go into debt, nor do I apply to any one personally for any thing, but give myself unto prayer. Now hear how this matter ended.

Dec. 28. When I came home last evening from the New Orphan-House, I found a letter from Gloucestershire, containing a sovereign and a half. The sovereign was half for these objects, and half for the Orphans; and of the half sovereign, 6s. were intended for the Orphans; and 4s. for these objects. Thus I had 14s. more But this morning the Lord has opened His hands still more bountifully. I have received a donation of 200l. -- The disposal of the money was left to me. I took therefore one half for the School --, Bible --, Missionary and Tract Objects, and the other half for the Building Fund.--This donation has been a very great refreshment to my spirit. During the last six weeks very little has come in, and though we had lacked nothing (for only a few days since I paid for sixty thousand Tracts at once), yet we were now poorer than we had been for two or three years, with regard to means for these objects. This, however, did not in the least cast me down; for I knew it was only for the trial of my faith and patience, and that, when the trial was over, the Lord would again send in bountiful supplies. This He has now commenced to do, but I expect much more than this. Indeed I am looking out daily for the Lord's help.

Jan. 1, 1852. The old year closed with manifestations of God's loving help, in the way of means, and the new begins in the same way. Last evening I received 4s. 5d. for these objects, and this morning, when I paid an account, I had 10l. returned for the Schools.--In the course of the day I received still further from Sherborne 3l., of which the donor wished 1l. to be taken for the Orphans, 1l. for missions, and 1l. for my own personal expenses. I received also anonymously from Aberdeen 4s. for the Orphans, with 2s. for missions.

Jan. 2. Further: 5l. for the Schools in Bristol.

Jan. 19. All our money for missionary objects, for the circulation of Bibles and Tracts, and for the support of the various Schools was now again spent, as only very little, comparatively had come in since Dec. 28th. The last money which I had, I sent off by the mail steamer to Demerara, which left two days since. Under these circumstances, I received this evening 20l., which I might either use for the Orphans, or for missionary objects, according to the donor's wish. I took it for missionary objects. But I am looking out for larger supplies, as I have many openings, profitably to lay out considerable sums for missionary objects, and for the circulation of Bibles and Tracts. It is remarkable, that, while I have received from the donor of this sum from time to time donations for the Orphans, I had not received anything for missionary objects for a very long time. But I have again and again prayed for help for this part of the work, and this point makes the answer to prayer only the more manifest.

Jan. 21. After still further repeated waiting upon the Lord for means, especially for missionary objects and for the circulation of the Holy Scriptures and Tracts, I received today from Somersetshire 20l., of which the donor intends 10l. for foreign missions and 10l. towards the support of the Orphans.

Jan. 22. From London 4l. for missions.

Jan. 23. 50l., of which half is for missions, and half for the Building Fund.

Jan. 26. 500l. was left at my disposal. I took the whole for these objects.

This donation came in most seasonably, enabling me to go on helping preachers of the Gospel, and also to go on with the circulation of Bibles and Tracts.

March 17. Before all means were gone, when there was yet about 160l. in hand, there came in again today for these objects 199l. 13s. 5d.

March 23. 200l. more came in today.

March 26. From three brethren 20l. for missions.--On the same day from a missionary box at Old Aberdeen 2l.

May 12. The 26 donations which have come in for these objects, since March 26th, were small. Today I received from Cornwall 50l., of which the donor wished me to take 10l. for my own personal expenses; the rest being left at my disposal I took the whole for these objects.

May 15. Received 20l. for missions.

May 19. When nearly all the means for these objects were exhausted, I received 250l., of which I took for these objects 200l., and 50l. for the current expenses for the Orphans.

Thus I have given some instances to show how the Lord was pleased to supply me during another year.

FOURTH PART

Supplies for the support of the Orphans, sent in answer to prayer, from May 26, 1851, to May 26, 1852.

When this period commenced, I had in hand for the current expenses for the Orphans 970l. 13s. 11 3/4 d. We had never had so large a balance for the other objects at the commencement of any new period, as was the case at the commencement of this, and so it was also with regard to the Orphan work. This arose from the fact, that, only a little more than four months before the accounts were closed, a donation of 3000l. had been given, which, being equally divided between the Orphan Fund and the Fund for the other objects, had left so large a balance in hand. But though there was this large balance to begin with, dependence upon God was still required day by day, as the pecuniary help is only a very small part of that which is needed; and even as to means, this sum would not have lasted long, had the Lord not sent in further supplies. This, however, He did; and thus it was, that, while there were other trials, varied and many, yet, as to means, we experienced for a long time scarcely any difficulty at all. I will now very briefly notice some cases in which God helped us with means for the support of the Orphans, in answer to prayer.

May 27, 1851. The first donation of this new period came from an aged Godly clergyman, whom, up to that time, I had never seen, but to whom my heart had been much knit through correspondence. The donation consisted of 5l. from himself, and 1s. 6d. from three poor persons through him.

July 3. A brother and sister, having had a legacy left to them, though very far from being rich, sent 50l. out of it for the Orphans, as they desire to use the money with which the Lord may intrust them for Him.

Oct. 2. From the ladies who constitute the Bristol Dorcas Society, the value of 215l. in flannel and unbleached calico.

Feb. 10, 1852. When the accounts were closed, there was in hand 970l. 13s. 11 3/4 d., and there has come in since then 1242l. 19s. 8d. Up to this time, I had had an abundance of means, to meet all the current expenses of the New Orphan-House, and there was still 126l. 3s. 8 1/2 d. in hand. But though I had this, the certain expenses of this week alone were. 102l. 0s. 4d., besides what might be otherwise needed. Under these circumstances, a Godly merchant at Clifton gave me this evening, through his son, a Fifty Pound Note for the benefit of the Orphans. This donation has greatly refreshed my spirit; for though we were not in actual need, there being 126l. 3s. 8 1/2 d. in hand, to meet the expenses of 102l. 0s. 4d., which I expected to come upon me this week, yet there would then only have been left 24l. 3s. 4 1/2 d. towards meeting the current expenses of an establishment with more than 300 inmates. There had not been so little in hand since the New Orphan-House was first opened. How kind, therefore, of the Lord, to put it into the heart of this donor, who is not personally known to me, to contribute this sum!

March 16. From Feb. 10th up to March 8th the income had been comparatively small, only about 130l. altogether having been received for the current expenses for the Orphans. This, with what was in hand on Feb. 10th, was, therefore, so reduced, that on March 8th I had only been able to advance 15l. for house-keeping expenses, instead of 30l., which I had for a long time been in the habit of doing. After having paid away this 15l., I had only about 5l. left. Before this 15l., however, was quite spent, I had received so much, that on the 12th I could advance. 10l. more for house-keeping. Now this money was all gone, and today, March 16th, more money was needed, but there was none in hand, except the balance which was last year left from the Building Fund, which I was most reluctant to use, and concerning which I asked the Lord that there might be no need for using it, as I wished to take it for the intended Orphan-House, the number of destitute Orphans who are waiting for admission being so great. Now observe how God helped me! Just before I was called on for more money, I received this morning from a noble Lady as her own gift and that of two of her friends 15l., and also 4s. 1 1/2 d. was given to me as the contents of an Orphan-box. Thus I was able to advance again 15l. for house-keeping.

March 17. For about six weeks past the Lord has been pleased to exercise my faith and patience much. Very little, comparatively, has come in for the Building Fund and the current expenses for the various objects; but now He has this day greatly refreshed my spirit by the donation of 999l. 13s. 5d., referred to under the Building Fund, which, being left to me for the Lord's work, to be used as I think best, I took of it for the current expenses for the Orphans 200l.; so that again, before the money, which came in yesterday, is expended, fresh supplies are received. I have been particularly also refreshed by this donation, in that I am not obliged to use the balance of the former Building Fund, but can let that remain for the present Building Fund.

May 26, 1852. Since March 17th no further difficulties have been experienced with regard to means; for though the expenses have amounted since then to about 700l., the Lord has bountifully supplied me with all I needed; for I received another donation of 200l., one of 75l. 18s. 9d., one of 50l., two of 10l., eighteen of between 5l. and 10l., besides many between 6d. and 5l.--Thus I am helped to the close of another year, during which the Lord has enabled me, through waiting upon Him, and looking to Him for help, to supply all the current expenses of the New Orphan-House with its 300 Orphans and all their overseers, teachers, nurses, etc.; the circulation of the Holy Scriptures and Tracts has been going on as before; the various schools have been supported; the same amount as during the past year, or rather more, has been expended for missionary objects; and yet, over and above all this, I have been enabled to gather a goodly sum for the Building Fund of the intended Orphan-House.

Have I not therefore abundant reason to praise the Lord for His goodness, to trust in Him for the future, to speak well of His name to my fellow-believers, and to encourage them, more and more to rely upon the Lord for everything?

FOURTH PART

Miscellaneous points respecting the Scriptural Knowledge Institution for Home and Abroad, with reference to the period from May 26, 1851, to May 26, 1852.

1. During this period there were entirely supported by the funds of the Institution four Day Schools in Bristol, with 248 poor children in them, and three others in Devonshire, Monmouthshire, and Norfolk, were assisted.--Further, one Sunday School in Bristol, with 243 children, was entirely supported, and two others in Devonshire and Gloucestershire, with 230 children, were assisted.--Lastly, one Adult School in Bristol, with 120 Adult Scholars, was entirely supported during this period.--From March 5, 1834, up to May 26, 1852, there were 5,525 children in the Day Schools in Bristol, 2,600 in the Sunday School, and 2,033 grown up persons in the Adult School.--There was expended of the Funds of the Institution, for these various Schools, during this period, 360l. 1s. 9d.

2. During this period there was expended of the Funds of the Institution 207l. 3s. 1d. for the purpose of circulating the Holy Scriptures, especially among the very poorest of the poor. There were issued during this period 1,101 Bibles and 409 New Testaments.--There were altogether circulated from March 5, 1834, up to May 26, 1852, Eight Thousand Eight Hundred and Ten Bibles, and Four Thousand Eight Hundred and Fifty-one New Testaments.

For two years previous to May 26, 1852, it was on my heart, to seek to make some especial effort for the spread of the Holy Scriptures and for the spread of simple Gospel Tracts, in a way and for a purpose which would not be accomplished by the giving of copies of the Holy Scriptures, or the giving of Tracts to poor persons. My wish was, to put believers of the higher classes in the way of obtaining cheap pocket Bibles for the purpose of giving them away as presents to more respectable persons, as well as furnishing them with the opportunity of purchasing Bibles and New Testaments, at a cheap rate, for giving them away among the poor; and of furnishing believers in the higher classes, who are Tract distributors, with an opportunity of purchasing simple Gospel Tracts for circulation. Connected with this I desired, especially, to present the truths of the Gospel, in print, before genteel persons, whom I had not the same opportunity of reaching as poorer persons to whom Tracts and Bibles might be given. To this my attention was turned on account of the mighty efforts which were made to take away the Holy Scriptures, and to spread Tracts which contain most pernicious errors. Up to this time we had never had, to any considerable extent, a depository for Bibles and Tracts. The circulation of Tracts had been almost exclusively by gratuitous distribution; and thus it had been also, for some years previously, with reference to the circulation of the Holy Scriptures.--For a very long time, however, we could not meet with a suitable house, till at last, after much prayer, and waiting for more than a year, convenient premises were obtained by renting No. 34, Park Street, Bristol. On April 29, 1852, this Bible and Tract Warehouse was opened with prayer.

3. During this year there was spent of the funds of the Institution, for missionary objects, the sum of 2005l. 7s. 5d. By this sum fifty-one labourers in the word and doctrine, in various parts of the world, were to a greater or less degree assisted.

It is a subject of joy and thankfulness to me, to be able to inform the believing reader, that the Lord was pleased to grant again much blessing upon the labours of these brethren during this year. Many sinners were converted through their instrumentality, some of whom had been in a most awful state. This remark applies both to foreign and home labourers.

4. There was laid out for the circulation of Tracts, from May 26, 1851, to May 26, 1852, the sum of 356l. 11s. 3 1/2 d. There were circulated during the year 489,136 Tracts.

The total number of Tracts, which were circulated from the beginning up to May 26, 18152, was 1,086,366.

The Lord is pleased to increase this part of the work more and more.

It is not merely, however, of the increase in the number of Tracts that I have to speak. I heard during this year of one case after another, in which the tracts, with which the Lord enabled me to furnish the many brethren who circulate them, were used by Him in the way of communicating great blessing to believers, or as instruments of conversion to unbelievers. I would indeed with all my might seek to spread the truth of God by means of these little publications in greater and greater numbers; but I would follow them also, day by day, with my prayers, and never trust in the numbers which have been issued, but in God, to Grant His blessing, without which all these efforts are in vain.

A great number of believers, in various parts of the world, aid me in the circulation of tracts. Up to April 1852, however, almost all the tracts which were circulated were given away gratuitously, but, as has been stated already, there was then more particularly commenced the sale of Tracts also, in connexion with the sale of Bibles, at the Bible and Tract Warehouse, No. 34, Park Street, Bristol.

5. On May 26, 1851, there were. Three Hundred Orphans in the New Orphan House on Ashley Down, Bristol. From that day up to May 26, 1852, there wore admitted into it twenty-seven Orphans, making 327 in all. Of these 327, nine died during the year; one Orphan was sent to Christian relatives, who by that time were able to provide for him, and who felt it their duty to do so; one was sent to relatives on account of being in such a state of health that the Establishment was an unsuitable place for her; three of the elder girls, who were able to earn their bread by entering service, but who could not be recommended to any situation, after they had been long borne with, were at last sent in disgrace from the Establishment to their relatives. This course was adopted as a last remedy with regard to themselves, and as a solemn warning for all the children in the Establishment. Four girls were with com-

FOURTH PART

fort sent out to service, and nine boys were apprenticed at the expense of the establishment. This makes the removals as many as the reception of new Orphans, so that the number was still 300 in the New Orphan House, on May 26, 1852. The total of the expenses, connected with the support of the Orphans, from May 26, 1851, to May 26, 1852, was 3035l. 3s. 4d. The total number of Orphans under our care from April 1836, to May 26, 18152, was Five Hundred and Fifteen.

I notice further the following points in connection with the New Orphan House.

1. Without any one having been personally applied to for anything, by me, the sum of 42,970l. 17s. 6d. was given to me for the Orphans as the result of prayer to God from the commencement of the work, up to May 26, 1852. It may be also interesting to the reader to know, that the total amount, which was given as free contributions, for the other objects, from the commencement of the work up to May 26, 1852, amounted to 15,976l. 10s. 6 1/4 d.; and that, which came in by the sale of Bibles and Tracts, and by the payments of the children in the Day-Schools, amounted to 3,073/. 1s. 9 3/4 d. Besides this, also a great variety and number of articles of clothing, furniture, provisions, &c., were given for the use of the Orphans.

2. During no period of the work had we such great affliction in the way of sickness in the Orphan Establishment as during this. For nearly four months the scarlet fever and other diseases prevailed, so that more than one hundred children were seriously ill during this period, and at one time there were 55 Orphans confined to their beds. But the Lord dealt very mercifully with us. Only 5 died in consequence of the scarlet fever, though we had 64 decided cases.

3. Several of the Orphans who left the Establishment during this year went away as believers, having been converted some time before they left; one also who died gave very decided evidence of a true change of heart by faith in our Lord Jesus; several who in former years were under our care, as we heard during this year, took their stand openly on the Lord's side, and dated their first impressions to the instructions received whilst with us; and lastly, of those under our care, there were not a few whose spiritual state gave us joy and comfort. Thus, amidst many difficulties and trials and some discouragements, we had abundant cause to praise God for His goodness, and to go forward in the strength of the Lord.

Matters connected with my own personal affairs.

Dec. 31, 1851. During this year the Lord was pleased to give me--

1. By anonymous offerings through the Chapel boxes   L157 4 0 3/4

2. By presents in money from believers in Bristol, not given anonymously   135 5 4

3. By presents in money, from believers not residing in Bristol   156 6 9

THE LORD'S DEALINGS WITH GEORGE MÜLLER

4. By presents in provisions, clothes, &c., worth to us at least   16 17 0

                                                                       L465 13 1 3/4

Admire, dear reader, the Lord's kindness towards me, in that again, during this year also, Ha has so abundantly supplied me with means for my own personal and family necessities, without any regular salary or other stated income whatever, simply in answer to prayer.

Further account of the intended Orphan House for Seven Hundred Poor Children, bereaved of both parents by death, from May 26, 1852, to May 26, 1853.

In the last chapter on this subject, it was stated, that on May 26, 1852, 1 had actually in hand towards this object 3,530l. 9s. 0 1/4 d.; and now I go on to relate how the Lord has been pleased to help me further since then; but, for the sake of brevity, I can only refer to the more remarkable donations.

June 18. Received 5s. 7d. from the Orphans in the Girl's Department of the New Orphan House, in commemoration of the anniversary of the opening of the New Orphan House, which took place this day three years. Received also 3s. 9d. from the Orphan Boys. These little sums from these children have given me much joy. I likewise received this day a donation of 200l., of which the donor kindly wished me to keep 20l. for my own personal expenses, and to use the 180l. as might be most needed. I took of this sum 60l. for the Building Fund, 60l. towards the support of the 300 Orphans, and 60l. for the various other objects of the Scriptural Knowledge Institution.

June 22. Today I was informed that there had been paid into the hands of my bankers 500l. This sum is from a donor whom I have never seen, but whom God evidently has led, in answer to my daily supplications, and to those of my fellow-labourers, to help me in His service. This donation has exceedingly refreshed my spirit, and has led me to expect more and more help from God. As this 500l. is left at my disposal, I took of it one-third for the Building Fund, another third for the current expenses for the 300 Orphans, and the last third for the School--, Bible--, Tract--, and Missionary Fund of the Scriptural Knowledge Institution.

July 1. 50l. The money being left to my disposal, I took half for the Building Fund--and half for the School--, Bible--, Tract-- and Missionary Objects.

July 29. Received from one of the Orphans, formerly under our care, the following lines: "Dear Sir, will you please to accept the enclosed silver chain for the Building Fund, and the 3s. 6d. for your personal use, from your grateful Orphan, * * * *." This donation gave me much joy.

FOURTH PART

Aug. 6. From an Irish friend 53l., "As a small acknowledgment of the donor's gratitude to his Heavenly Father for enriching him with the unsearchable riches of Christ, and to his dear Redeemer for loving him, and giving Himself for him."

Aug. 13. From the neighbourhood of London 50l.

Aug. 21. From Southport a gold ring--I received also today the following letter from Madras, East Indies, enclosing a donation of 50l. for the Building Fund.

"* * * * * Madras, 9th July, 1852.

"Dear Brother,

"Some time in the year 1842 or 1843 I met with 'The Lord's dealings with George Mueller,' and, after rending it, was moved to send you something; but at that time I had not the means. In fact, I had lent, what little money I had, to a person who was unable to repay me, and I was nearly destitute. The good hand of God has been on me since that time, and I have often wondered whether George Mueller was still in the flesh but never had the resolution to inquire. Last December I met in a friend's house the Twelfth Report, and, after reading it, resolved to cast a mite into the Lord's treasury towards building the Orphan-House for Seven Hundred children; and may the God of Jacob, that has fed me all my life long, unto this day, accept of it, as an acknowledgment of the thousandth part of the mercies I have received at His hands. I therefore enclose a bill of exchange * * * *. Value of bill Seventy Pounds sterling. * * * * I have often mentioned you by name in my appeals to the throne of grace; and if I meet you not on earth, I hope I shall in those regions where we shall see the Lamb on His throne and in His Father's kingdom, and where there is no more sin or sorrow.

My dear Brother,

"Ever yours,

"* * * * *"

This donation and letter have exceedingly refreshed my spirit, and quickened me yet further to prayer.

Pause a few moments dear Reader. See how faith and prayer bring means from individuals whom we have never seen, whose very names we have never heard of, and who live at a distance of more than Ten Thousand miles from us. Do you not see that it is not in vain, to make known our requests to the Lord, and to come to Him for everything? When it was first laid on my heart, to build a second Orphan-House for 700 destitute children, bereaved of both parents by death, simply in dependence upon God alone for means, could I have looked for this 70l. from this Christian brother at Madras? Verily not, for I did not even know of his existence. Had I other friends, from whom to expect the large sum which will be needed to accomplish this? No, on the contrary, all human probability was against my ever receiving this large sum. But I had faith in God. I believed that He was able and willing to give me what was needed for this work; and solely in dependence upon Him I purposed to build another Orphan-House. But now see bow God has helped me further; for after I had received this donation of 70l., I had still only 4,127l. 12s. 6 3/4 d. in hand, in other words, only a little more than the ninth part of the sum which, as far as I am able to calculate, will be needed to accomplish my object.

Aug. 30. During this month again fourteen destitute Orphans have been applied for, none of whom we can receive, because the New Orphan-House is full. There are now 356 Orphans already waiting for admission, from six months old and upwards, each bereaved of both parents by death.

Sept. 8. During the last five days, only 2l. 14s. had come in for the Building Fund, and only 9l. 1s. altogether for the current expenses for the various objects of the Scriptural Knowledge Institution. Such seasons try my faith and patience; but, by the grace of God, they do not discourage me. He helps me to continue in prayer, and to look for answers, and for a time when He will help again bountifully. During the past eighteen years and six months, which I have been occupied in this service, I have again and again found, that, after a season, during which very little has come in, and my faith has thus been tried, the Lord has generally the more bountifully helped afterwards. Thus it has been again this day. I have received a donation of 280l. 10s. 6d., of which the donor kindly wished me to take 20l. 10s. 6d. for my own personal expenses, and to use the 260l. as the work of the Lord in my hands might require. I took of this sum one-third for the Building Fund, one-third for the current expenses for the Orphans, and one-third for the other Objects. Thus I had at once a four-fold answer to prayer; 1, Means for my own personal expenses, about which I had been asking the Lord; 2, Means for the Building Fund, for which I am day by day labouring in prayer; 3, Means for the current expenses for the Orphans, which were greatly needed; and 4, Means for the other Objects, which were entirely exhausted.

Sept. 28. From Melbourne, in Australia, 50l., from a believer in the Lord Jesus, whose name even I did not know up to the time that I received this donation.-- See, dear Reader, how the Lord helps me, in answer to prayer. Do you not perceive that my fellow-labourers and myself do not wait upon the Lord in vain? Be encouraged by this! Go for yourself, with all your temporal and spiritual wants, to the Lord. Bring also the necessities of your friends and relatives to the Lord. Only make the trial, and you will perceive how able and willing He is to help you. Should you, however, not at once, obtain answers to your prayers, be not discouraged; but continue patiently, believingly, perseveringly to wait upon God: and as assuredly as that, which you ask, would be for your real good, and therefore for the honour of the Lord; and as assuredly as you ask it solely on the ground of the worthiness of our Lord Jesus, so assuredly you will at last obtain the blessing. I myself have had to

FOURTH PART

wait upon God concerning certain matters for years, before I obtained answers to my prayers; but at last they came. At this very time, I have still to renew my requests daily before God, respecting a certain blessing for which I have besought Him for eleven years and a half, and which I have as yet obtained only in part, but concerning which I have no doubt that the full blessing will be granted in the end. So also, when I was led to build the New Orphan-House, and waited upon the Lord for means for it, it took two years and three months, whilst day by day I brought this matter before Him, before I received the full answer.--But to return to my journal. This donation of 50l. from Melbourne, refreshed my spirit greatly, and quickened me yet further to prayer.--On the same day I received from Sheffield 5l., and from Tottenham 10l.

Oct. 31. Thirteen more Orphans have been applied for during this month.

Nov. 3. This evening I received a check for 300l. for the Building Fund. -- I am continually looking out for help, and am sustained in waiting upon God, and in being enabled daily, and generally several times every day, to bring the matter about the Building Fund before Him. I know that God hears me, on the ground of the worthiness of the Lord Jesus, and that at last He will give me the full amount needed for accomplishing this work. How the means are to come, I know not; but I know that God is almighty, that the hearts of all are in His hands, and that, if He pleaseth to influence persons, they will send help. In this donation of 300l., received this evening, I have seen afresh, how easily God can send means. The donor, who sent it, was not even known to me by name this day month; but, on Oct. 12th, he sent me 200l. for the Orphans, and now 300l. for the Building Fund. Nothing had come in during the former part of the day; still, I was looking out, and, when I returned from the Orphan-House, found that this 300l. had arrived at my house. But I expect far larger sums.

Nov. 11. From London three boxes and two parcels of books, containing 275 volumes in all, to be sold for the Building Fund.

Nov. 16. 50l.--From the neighbourhood of Stroud 10s.--From one of the former Orphans 10s., being part of her first quarter's wages. Sent as a token of gratitude.

Nov. 19. 200l., which, being left to my disposal, I took of it 100l. for the Building Fund, 60l. for preachers of the Gospel at Home and Abroad, 20l. for the circulation of the Holy Scriptures, and 20l. for the circulation of Tracts.

Nov. 21. From Malta 5l.

Nov. 27. "From the neighbourhood of Leominster, as a thank-offering," 2l. Day by day I am waiting upon God, concerning this object. I firmly believe that the Lord will give me all I require for the accomplishment of it though I am utterly unworthy. I believe that I shall also have large sums, very large sums, when the Lord has been pleased sufficiently to exercise my faith and patience. Today I received 250l., the disposal of which was left to me. I took, therefore, 125l. for the Building

Fund, 25l. for current expenses for the Orphans, 40/. for the home and foreign labourers in the Word, whom I seek to assist, 20l. for gratuitous circulation of the Holy Scriptures among very poor persons, 20l. for gratuitous circulation of Gospel Tracts, and 20l. for all the various Day schools, Sunday schools, and the Adult school, which the Scriptural Knowledge Institution either assists or entirely supports.

Nov. 30. During this month, again 25 children, bereaved of both parents by death, lawfully begotten, and in destitute circumstances, have been applied for, not one of whom I have any prospect of being able to admit until the Lord shall have been pleased to enable me to build another Orphan-House. The many Orphans waiting for admission, whose number is increasing every month, lead me to continue in earnest supplication, that the Lord would be pleased to furnish me with means for the erection of another Orphan-House. Nor do I doubt that He will help me.

Jan. 3. From the neighbourhood of Stroud 1l. 15s. 3d.--Anonymously in a letter 8d.--From Newtown Limavady 1l.--Also 252l. 17s. 1d., which, being left to my disposal, I portioned out thus: 75l. for the Orphans, 75l. for the School, Bible, Missionary and Tract Fund, and 102l. 17s. 1d. for the Building Fund.

Jan. 4. From London 2s. 6d.--Day by day I have now been waiting upon God for means for the Building Fund for more than nineteen months, and almost daily I have received something in answer to prayer. These donations have been, for the most part, small, in comparison with the amount which will be required for the completion of this object; nevertheless they have shown that the Lord, for the sake of His dear Son, listens to my supplications and to those of my fellow labourers and helpers in the work; and they have been precious encouragements to me to continue to wait upon God. I have been for many months assured that the Lord, in His own time, would give larger sums for this work; and for this I have been more and more earnestly entreating Him, during the last months. Now at last He has abundantly refreshed my spirit, and answered my request. I received today the promise, that, as the joint donation of several Christians, there should be paid to me a donation of Eight Thousand and One Hundred Pounds for the work of the Lord in my hands. Of this sum I purpose to take 6,000l. for the Building Fund, 600l. for the current expenses for the Orphans, and 1,500l. for the other objects of the Scriptural Knowledge Institution for Home and Abroad. [This joint donation of several Christians was paid in four installments during January, February, March, and April.]

It is impossible to describe the spiritual refreshment which my heart received through this donation. Day by day, for nineteen months, I had been looking out for more abundant help than I had had. I was fully assured that God would help me with larger sums; yet the delay was long. See how precious it is to wait upon God! See how those who do so, are not confounded! Their faith and patience may long and sharply he tried; but in the end it will most assuredly be seen, that those who honour God He will honour, and will not suffer them to be put to shame. The largeness of the donation, whilst it exceedingly refreshed my spirit, did not in the least surprise me; for I expect great things from God. I quote a paragraph from the Twelfth Report,

FOURTH PART

page 27, where under Jan. 4, 1851, this will be found written: "I received this evening the sum of Three Thousand Pounds, being the largest donation which I have had as yet. I have had very many donations of 100l. and of 200l., several of 300l., one of 400l., several of 500l., some of from 600l. to 900l., four of 1,000l., two of 2,000l., and one of 2,050l., but never had more than this given to me at one time; yet I have expected more than 2,050l. in one donation, and, accordingly, it has pleased the Lord to give me 3,000l. this evening. I now write again that I expect far larger sums still, in order that it may be yet more and more manifest, that there is no happier, no easier, and no better way for obtaining pecuniary means for the work of the Lord, than the one in which I have been led." This, you perceive, dear Reader, was written more than two years ago. Since then I have again received many considerable donations, besides thousands of pounds in smaller sums. And now the largest donation of 3,000l., was surpassed by the one of 8,100l. Have I then been boasting in God in vain? Is it not manifest that it is most precious, in every way, to depend upon God? Do I serve God for nought? Is it not obvious that the principles on which I labour, are not only applicable to the work of God on a small scale, but also, as I have so many times affirmed during the past nineteen years, for the most extensive operations for God? I delight to dwell upon this, if, by any means, some of my beloved fellow believers might be allured to put their whole trust in God for every thing; and if, by any means, some unbelievers thereby might be made to see that God is verily the living God now as ever, and might be stirred up to seek to be reconciled to Him by putting their trust in the atonement of the Lord Jesus Christ, and thus find in God a friend for time and eternity.

Feb. 19. Saturday Evening. The Lord has been pleased to send in the means as sparingly this month, as He was pleased to send them in abundantly during the last. But this is for the trial of my faith and patience. While, however, these graces are exercised by the Lord, He kindly sustains both. With unshaken confidence and joyful anticipation am I, by the help of God, enabled to go forward day by day, looking on to the day when I shall have the whole amount requisite for this object, just as it was with reference to the building of the New Orphan House on Ashley Down. I know that I shall not be confounded; for I trust in God, and for the honour of His name proposed the building of this second Orphan House. Yet my soul longs, to be able to declare to the Church of Christ at large, that I have obtained an answer to this my oft repeated request, which again and again, every day, is brought before Him, and in which request my fellow labourers in the work join. Moreover, I long to be able to show to an unbelieving world afresh, by this my petition being granted, that verily there is reality in the things of God. And lastly, I long to be able to commence the building of this second Orphan House, because there are now 438 Orphans waiting for admission. I have not yet received anything today for this object; but the Lord can even now give me something this evening; but be that as it may, I know that, when His time is come, and when my patience has been sufficiently exercised, He will help me abundantly. That word respecting Abraham: "And so, after he had patiently endured, he obtained the promise," (Hebrew vi, 15), has been repeatedly a precious word to me during the last days, it having come of late in the course of my reading through the New Testament.

Feb. 23. This evening, after another long season of prayer respecting the work of God in my hands, and especially also, that it might please the Lord to give me soon what I need for the Building Fund, so that I may be enabled to take active steps in the erection of another Orphan House, came in the course of my reading and meditation James I. This forcibly reminded me of the close of November and the beginning of December in 1845, when, whilst labouring for a season in the Word at Sunderland, this portion also came in the course of my meditation on the whole New Testament. James i, 4: "But let patience have her perfect work, that ye may be perfect and entire, wanting nothing," was then particularly impressed on my mind as a portion which I should need to keep before me. I was at that time, day by day, waiting upon the Lord for means and every other help which might be needed in connexion with the Orphan House, which I had purposed to build in dependence upon the Lord for help. I had not the least doubt that God would help me through all the difficulties connected with this work. I felt as sure that He would enable me to accomplish this work, as if I had actually seen the house before me, inhabited by Orphans; but I had reason to believe, at the same time, that great and many and varied would be my trials of faith and patience, before all would be accomplished. I had not at that time one single shilling in hand towards this work, but often, even then, whilst staying at Sunderland, and meditating on this first chapter of the Epistle of James, did I praise God before hand, that He would give me everything I should need in connexion with this intended Orphan House. Now this evening, February 23, 1853, I am writing in that very house, the New Orphan House, with its 300 Orphans, about which I was then praying. Nearly four years it has been already inhabited by Orphans. And I now say again, "Let patience have her perfect work," with reference to the intended Orphan House for 700 more Orphans; but also, at the same time, am I assured that the Lord will enable me to accomplish this also.

March 14.--From Scotland 200l., of which the donor kindly wished me to give 10l. to Mr. Craik, to take 10l. for my own personal expenses, and to use the 180l. as most needed. I took, therefore, 100l. for the Building Fund, and 80l. for the current expenses for the Orphans. This donation has been a great refreshment to my spirit; for since Jan. 4th only little, comparatively, has come in either for the Building Fund or for the current expenses.

March 29. For nearly three months the Lord has been pleased to exercise my patience by the comparatively small amount of means which has come in. It was more an exercise of patience than of faith; for, during all this time, we not only abounded, with regard to means for the current expenses, through the large sums, which had come in at the beginning of the year, but I had also even now considerable sums in hand, for the current expenses of the various objects. Still, though not actually in need of means, yet my spirit had been enabled to labour on in prayer for means for the Building Fund in particular, and also for means for current expenses, in order that it may become more and more manifest, what a happy, easy, and successful way this is. Now, this evening, when I came home, I found that 300l. had come in. This is a great refreshment to my spirit.--As the amount is left to my dis-

FOURTH PART

posal as may be most needed, I have taken one half of it for the Building Fund, and the other half for the current expenses for the Orphans. The other objects abound at present with means, and even for the Orphans I have yet above 200l. in hand.

April 20. Received from a most unexpected quarter 100l., which I took half for the Building Fund, and half for the Orphans, as the other objects were not in immediate need of means. This donation has much refreshed my spirit.

May 14. Received 260l., of which I took 100l. for the Building Fund, and 160l. for the current expenses for the Orphans.

May 26. From Gloucester 5s.--Through the box at the Bible and Tract Warehouse in Park Street, Bristol, 2l. 11s. 10d.--By sale of an old gold watch, a few trinkets, some old silver coins, and some small pieces of broken silver articles, 10l. 7s. 8d.--Also 80l. 15s. 11d., being the proceeds arising from the sale of a work published in English and 2l. 10s., being the proceeds arising from the sale of a work published in French; were given to the Building Fund.--To these sums is to be added 334l. 16s. 9d., received during this period for interest; for I felt it my duty, as has been stated before, to invest the money given to me for the Building Fund until actually required.

Thus closes this period, from May 26, 1852, to May 26, 1853. All the donations received during this period for the Building Fund, together with the 3530l. 9s. 0 1/4 d. in hand, on May 26, 1852, made the total of 12,531l. 12s. 0 1/4 d. in hand on May 26, 1853.

The following paragraphs were printed in the Report of 1853, respecting the intended Orphan House, which are here reprinted for the better understanding of the subject.

A. Besides having the means to meet all the demands which came upon me in connexion with the various objects of the Scriptural Knowledge Institution for Home and Abroad; and besides enlarging almost all of them considerably, so that the sum of 7035l. 12s. 0 1/2 d. altogether was expended; I have been enabled to add, during the past twelvemonth, 9,001l. 3s. to the Building Fund. The total sum, which God has been pleased to give to me, during the year, both for current expenses and the Building Fund, amounts to 16,042l. 8s. 11d.

B. It is true that very much yet is needed for the Building Fund, before I shall be enabled to accomplish the desire of my heart, in building another House for 700 more Orphans. I may have also yet many trials of faith and patience to pass through; but what the Lord has done for me during the past 24 years in particular, and all His dealings with me in connexion with the Scriptural Knowledge Institution; and all His help afforded for building the New Orphan House on Ashley Down, Bristol, which has been now already inhabited for four years encourage me to continue to wait upon God. By His grace I am not tired of waiting upon Him for means. Yea, I confess to

His praise, that, the longer I live, the more I am practically assured of the blessedness of waiting upon God for every thing.

C. There is no decrease as to the application for the admission of Orphans. This, in addition to all the help and support which the Lord has granted to me for these many years in the work, and in addition to the means received for the Building Fund during the past year, encourages me greatly, to continue to wait upon God for help, to be enabled to build another Orphan House for 700 Orphans. On May 26, 1852, there were 326 Orphans waiting for admission. Since then there have been 184 Orphans applied for, making in all 510. Of these, as only few vacancies have occurred during the past year, not more than 13 could be received into the New Orphan House, and 17 besides, as I have been informed by applicants, were otherwise provided for, so that 30 are to be deducted from 510, which leaves 480 Orphans waiting for admission. Many of these are very young, some even under one year old. But I have the fullest reason to believe, that many persons are kept from applying for the admission of Orphans, because there are already so many waiting, else the number would be greater still. With such a number of poor destitute Orphans before me, bereaved of both parents by death, how can I but labour on in prayer for means, for the accomplishment of this object; and I have not the least doubt that, after the Lord may have been pleased to exercise my faith and patience yet somewhat more, unworthy though I am of it, He will condescend to grant the request for the whole amount of the means which are needed for the building of this second Orphan House, in answer to the supplications which my fellow-labourers and myself continually bring before Him.

D. It must not be supposed that I am discouraged, because two years have elapsed since I first began to receive donations towards this object, and as yet only 12,531l. 12s. 0 1/4 d. is in hand. I expected trials of faith and patience, both for my own profit, and for the benefit of others, who might hear of the Lord's dealings with me. I was not without trials, yea, not without many trials of faith and patience, in building the New Orphan House for 300 Orphans; nor did I obtain the means then till after the lapse of two years and three months; therefore, in seeking to build this house for 700 Orphans, I am not surprised that I should have to wait patiently. But of this I have never had a doubt that, after the Lord had sufficiently tried my faith and patience, He would supply me with all I need. I therefore wait His time. Moreover, the Lord, in a very short time, can give me all I need, it is not necessary that twice or thrice as much time as has already elapsed should have to pass away, before I am in a position to be warranted to

take active measures; yet, be this as it may, by the grace of God I am content to wait His time.

E. Should it be asked, whether I intend to wait till I have the whole sum of Thirty-Five Thousand Pounds, which will be needed; or whether I purpose to begin the building before; my reply is this I do not purpose to delay the beginning of the building till I have what is required for fitting up and furnishing the house, which is

FOURTH PART

included in that sum; for I may well trust in the Lord for that amount whilst the House is being built; but as I, on Scriptural grounds, neither for my own personal expenses, nor for the work of God, go into debt, I should not begin building, till I have sufficient to meet the amount of the contracts of the builders, for which, together with the land, I consider not less than 25,000l. would be needed, so that I have just half the amount requisite for that.

Supplies for the School--, Bible--, Missionary and Tract Fund, sent in answer to prayer, from May 26, 1852, to May 26, 1853.

On May 26, 1852, when the accounts were closed, there was left in hand for these objects the balance of 45l. 5s. 7 1/2 d. Before this balance was expended, I received, on May 27, 1852, from the neighbourhood of Whitehaven, 2l. 10s. for missions. On May 29, from Belper 5s. 7d. for missions. On May 30, through Bethesda boxes 2s. 6d. and 4d. for missions. On June 7th, I received from Somersetshire. 10l.; and on the same day I found that a Christian bookseller in London had, paid into the hands of my bankers 34l. 14s. 4d., which he had been ordered to pay to me, on behalf of a Christian gentleman, to whom this amount was due. This sum I took for these objects. But the Lord helped still further. June 8. 10l. from Y. Z.--June 13. From Y. Z. 33l. 3s. Through Bethesda boxes for missions 1s. Ditto 1s. Through Salem boxes 1s. 8d. From "P." 1s. Ditto 4d. --June. 15. From one engaged in the work 1l. -- June 16. From Clifton 4d.--June 18. From W, W. 10l. "for missionary brethren, labouring in dependence upon God for their temporal supplies." Also 200l. came in, of which I took 60l. for these objects, as stated with reference to this donation, in giving an account of the donations for the Building Fund.--June 22. 500l. came in, as stated under Building Fund, of which one-third or 166l. 13s. 4d. was taken for these objects.

This is just a specimen of how the Lord helped me, week after week, to meet the expenses during this period. About Six Hundred Pounds a month, or above Seven Thousand Pounds during the year, I had to expend for the various objects of the Institution; but I had sufficient to meet every demand; and over and above I was helped by the Lord to increase the Building Fund Nine Thousand Pounds above what it was the year before. The current expenses of the Institution were never so great during the previous nineteen years; but the extent of its operations, and the means which the Lord was pleased to send in, were also never so great.

I stated, however, before, that I could not give here in detail an account of every donation. I, therefore, single out a few more instances, to show the manner in which the Lord helped me.

Aug. 4. The funds for these objects were now reduced to about 4l.; but there was much required in order to be able to go on with the circulation of the Holy Scriptures and Tracts, and to assist missionary brethren; when I received this evening 200l., which was left to me to be applied as seemed best to me. I took therefore one half for the current expenses for the Orphans, and the other half for these objects, and was thus again supplied for the present.

Aug. 14. 20l. for missions from W. W.

Sept. 8. Little, comparatively, has come in since August 4th. Only twenty-seven donations altogether, of which only a few were rather large sums. Therefore all our means were now gone. On the 3rd of this month I sent out 40l. to six brethren who labour in the Word, and would on that day have sent out 35l, more to other six brethren, but had not the means; and, therefore, could only wait upon God. I also desired to order more Bibles and Tracts; but had to delay this likewise, as I would not go into debt for them. Now this morning I received 280l. 10s. 6d. [referred to under the Building Fund], of which 86l. 13s. 4d. was taken for these objects. Thus I am helped again for the present, and look for further supplies.

Oct. 9. Only nineteen donations, almost all small, have come in for these objects since September 8th. For the last three days I have especially desired means for these objects. Gladly would I have helped brethren who labour in the Word at home and abroad; but was unable to do so, and could only pray for means. Now this morning the Lord gave me the desire of my-heart in this respect. I received a donation of 230l. 15s., which, being left at my disposal, I took one half for these objects, and the other half for the current expenses for the Orphans.

Nov. 3. "From an Irish friend" 10l. for missions.--I have particularly prayed within the last few days for means for missionary objects, as all means are gone; therefore this donation is very refreshing as an answer to prayer. But I expect more, as I desire to send out shortly 200l. at least to brethren who labour in the Word.

This I wrote, as the date shows, on November 3rd, and that which follows will now show to the Reader, that I did not wait upon God in vain. During no period, within the nineteen years previously, was I enabled to do so much in the way of aiding missionary operations, as during this period; and during no previous period so much in the circulation of the Holy Scriptures and Tracts, as during this; yet once or twice all the means for these objects were expended, and I had to stand still and to wait upon God for further supplies. The servant of Christ, who knows that he is not occupied about his own work, but about that of his master, can, however, be quiet, and ought to be quiet, under such circumstances, in order to prove that he is only the servant and not the master. If he cannot be quiet, and if, in the restlessness of nature, he will work and take steps when he ought to stand still, and wait upon God; then let him suspect himself, and let him see well to it, whether the work in which he is engaged is God's work or not; and whether, if it be God's work, it is done for the honour of the Master or for the honour of the servant. In this case God abundantly recompensed me for standing still for a little, and for calling upon Him. I had not to wait long, before He was pleased to help me. I now go on with my journal, to show to the Reader how the Lord answered prayer in this instance.

FOURTH PART

Nov. 5. Received from Okehampton six silver tea spoons, to be sold for foreign missions.

Nov. 6. Received 5l. with the following words: "Enclosed is a Post Office Order, drawn out in your favour by * * * * *, Three Pounds of which my dear husband is constrained to send to you for foreign missions. The other two I send; one for your own personal expenses, and the other to be used for the Orphans, as their need may require, &c."

I have especially prayed, for several days past, for help for brethren who labour in the Word at home and abroad, as I have no means left for them, and could lay out at once 200l. or 300l. on their behalf. Therefore this donation is particularly precious. But I expect more.

Nov. 7. From Braunton 2l. for missions.--Anonymously 2s. 6d. for missions.

Nov. 10. From some believers at Ludlow 8l. 14s. for foreign missions.

Nov. 11. During the last ten days I have especially asked the Lord for means for home and foreign labourers. This also was particularly dwelt upon at our usual weekly prayer meeting of the labourers in the work on Saturday the 6th of November. Now today I received 237l. 10s. for the work of the Lord in my hands. As the application of the money was left to me, I took the whole of this amount for home and foreign labourers in the Word, as they, greatly need help; and I expect by tomorrow evening to have sent out the whole amount.--In the course of my reading through the Holy Scriptures there came today John xvi. 23, "Verily, verily I say unto you, whatsoever ye shall ask the Father in my name, He will give it you." I turned to my Father in heaven and said: "Be pleased, Holy Father, to hear me for the sake of Thy Holy Child Jesus, and give me means for these dear brethren who labour in the word and doctrine, whom I seek to help." In about half an hour afterwards I received this 237l. 10.

Nov. 18. Today were paid to me two legacies, left by a lady at a distance whom I have never seen, and whose name even I had never heard, till I was informed about the payment of the legacies. I received the legacy of 100l. for the Orphans (being 101l. 4s. with the interest due), and 50l. for the various Schools for poor children under my direction (being 50l. 12s. with the interest due.)--In portioning out yesterday the means for the brethren who labour in the Word at home and abroad, to whom I desire to send help, I found that the 237l. 10s. was not enough, and also that I needed more means for the various Schools and the circulation of Bibles and Tracts. On this account the payment of this legacy of 50l. 12s. for the Schools came in very seasonably. But the Lord helped still further this evening by a donation of 60l., the application of which is entirely left to me. I have therefore taken of it 20l. for missionary brethren, 20l. for the circulation of the Holy Scriptures, and 20l. for the circulation of Gospel Tracts.

THE LORD'S DEALINGS WITH GEORGE MÜLLER

Nov. 19. From Yorkshire 3l. for foreign missions.--From Cumberland 13s. 10d. for missionaries in Demerara--Also 200l., left to my disposal, as I might be directed by the Lord. I took of it 100l. for the Building Fund, 60l. for foreign and home labourers in the Word, 20l. for the circulation of the Holy Scriptures, and 20l. for the circulation of Gospel Tracts.--During the last eight days I had sent out 252l. to home and foreign labourers in the Word, and 65l. I had paid out for the circulation of Tracts and the Holy Scriptures. I desired, however, still further means for brethren who labour in the Word, for I wished to send out at once 70l. more, and also to lay out more on the circulation of the Holy Scriptures and Gospel Tracts; but I had only about 90l. altogether left for these various objects, when I received today the 3l., the 13s. 10d., and this 200l. The Lord be praised for this help, and may He recompense the donors.

You see, dear Reader, by these instances, that we are richly recompensed for our waiting upon God. You perceive the readiness of His heart to listen to the supplications of His children who put their trust in Him. If you have never made trial of it, do so now. But in order to have your prayers answered, you need to make your requests unto God on the ground of the merits and worthiness of the Lord Jesus. You must not depend upon your own worthiness and merits, but solely on the Lord Jesus, as the ground of acceptance before God, for your person, for your prayers, for your labours, and for every thing else. Do you really believe in Jesus? Do you verily depend upon Him alone for the salvation of your soul? See to it well, that not the least degree of your own righteousness is presented unto God as a ground of acceptance. But then, if you believe in the Lord Jesus, it is further necessary, in order that your prayers may be answered, that the things which you ask of God should be of such a kind, that God can give them to you, because they are for His honour and your real good. If the obtaining of your requests were not for your real good, or were not tending to the honour of God, you might pray for a long time, without obtaining what you desire. The glory of God should be always before the children of God, in what they desire at His hands; and their own spiritual profit, being so intimately connected with the honour of God, should never be lost sight of, in their petitions. But now, suppose we are believers in the Lord Jesus, and make our requests unto God, depending alone on the Lord Jesus as the ground of having them granted; suppose also, that, so far as we are able honestly and uprightly to judge, the obtaining of our requests would be for our real spiritual good and for the honour of God; we yet need, lastly, to continue in prayer, until the blessing is granted unto us. It is not enough to begin to pray, nor to pray aright; nor is it enough to continue for a time to pray; but we must patiently, believingly continue in prayer, until we obtain an answer; and further, we have not only to continue in prayer unto the end, but we have also to believe that God does hear us, and will answer our prayers. Most frequently we fail in not continuing in prayer until the blessing is obtained and in not expecting the blessing. As assuredly as in any individual these various points are found united, so assuredly answers will be granted to his requests.

From what I have stated, the Reader will have seen that my prayer had been especially, that the Lord would be pleased to furnish me with means for the circula-

FOURTH PART

tion of Bibles and Tracts, and for missionary operations; and it has been shown how He granted this my request through the large sums which He sent me (entirely unasked for, so far as man is concerned), on November 11, 13 and 19; but even this was but little in comparison with what He did for me afterwards, when He was pleased to place far greater sums at my disposal for these objects, to which reference has been already made, when speaking about the donations which came in for the Building Fund on November 27, 1852, and on January 3 and 4, 1853.

Thus I was carried through all the expenses for these various objects, and was enabled to enter into every open door which the Lord set before me for circulating the Holy Scriptures and Tracts, and for aiding missionary operations; and not only so, but was enabled to do for these various objects more then during any one period within the nineteen previous years.

Means for the support of the 300 Orphans already under our care, sent in answer to Prayer, from May 26, 1852, to May 26, 1853.

When we began this period, we were not only not in debt, but had in hand the balance of 134l. 8s. 10 3/4 d. To those who are in very poor circumstances, this amount would appear a considerable sum, and they might think, this sum would last a long tine. Such need, however, to know, that it would only furnish the current expenses of two weeks, and that often in one week much more than that sum has been disbursed for the Orphans. To those, on the other hand, who would say, "This is very little, and what will you do, with so small a sum in hand, when day by day 330 persons need to be provided for?" our reply is, God is able to send us more, before this sum is gone. We seek for grace, to live by the day. We seek to be enabled to attend to the commandment and affectionate counsel of the Lord, to be anxious about nothing. It was in this way that no care came over our mind with regard to the future, when we looked at this large Orphan Establishment, with all its large daily wants; for we were assured, that the Lord would surely give us something before all was expended. And thus it was.

I will now furnish the Reader with a few instances from my journal of the particular providence of God, manifested in caring for us, and granting us help in answer to our prayers; for I do especially desire it to be understood, that, though the work is now so very much larger than it was in former years, and therefore far larger sums are needed than before; yet the principles of trusting in God, and depending upon Him alone, are now acted upon as formerly, only with this difference, that year by year, by the grace of God, my soul becomes more and more rooted and established in them. It would therefore be entirely a mistake, to suppose that it is no longer a work of faith. If it was formerly a work of faith on a small scale, it is now a work of faith on a large scale. If we had trials of faith formerly, about comparatively little things; we have now trials of faith about comparatively great things. If we formerly hind no certain income, so now have we none. We have to look to God for every thing in connexion with the world, of which often, however, the pecuniary necessities are the smallest matter; but to Him we are enabled to look, and therefore it is, that we are not disappointed.

During the very first month, from May 27th to June 27th, 1852, there came in, by ninety-two different donations or sums, 354l. 1s. 5d.: so that we had, after a month, more in hand than before. Unbelief, which said, what will you do with so little as 134l.? was therefore confounded. The Lord increased thus little, before it was expended.

June 29, 1852. Today I received one of the most remarkable donations which I ever had. I give the whole account, without the name of the donor.

"Lyons, June 24, 1852.

"Dear Brother in Christ,

"It is now several years, that I read with great interest, and I hope with some benefit to my soul, the account of your labours and experiences. Ever since then your work was the object of many thoughts and prayers, and I gave many copies of your book to Christian friends. One of them has read it in Syria, on Mount Lebanon, where he is for commercial business; and, whilst praying for you and your clear Orphans, the Lord put it in his heart to send you 2l., to which my husband added two others: and we beg you to accept that small offering in the name of the Lord. If you have published anything of the Lord's dealings with you since the year 1844, we shall be very happy to receive it. You could forward it to Messrs. * * * *, London, for * * * * of Lyons. And now, dear Brother, may the grace and peace of the Lord rest on you and your dear home's inhabitants.

" Affectionately yours in the Lord,

* * * *"

I have had donations from Australia, the East Indies, the West Indies, the United States, Canada, from the Cape of Good Hope, from France, Switzerland, Germany, Italy, &c.; and now comes also this donation from Mount Lebanon, with the prayer of a Christian brother, whose name I never heard, nor know even now. See, dear Reader, this is the way in which the Lord has helped me in this precious service for twenty-two year's [1856]. With my fellow-labourers, or without them, and they without me, our prayers are offered up unto the Lord for help, and He is pleased, for Jesus' sake, to listen to our supplications, and to influence the hearts of some of His children known to us or not, to send us help. The donors may be rich or poor; they may live near or at a distance of more than ten thousand miles; they may give much or little; they may have often given before or never; they may be well known to us or not at all; in these and many other things there may be constant variations; but God continually helps us; we are never confounded. And why not? Simply

FOURTH PART

because we are enabled, by time grace of God, to put our trust in Him for what we need.

On the very next day, June 30th, I received another donation from a believing farmer in Jersey of 3l. 1s., which, with 15s. sent by him on June. 8th, were the proceeds of a small field of potatoes, which he had cultivated for the benefit of the Orphans. See in what various ways the Lord helps me! This dear man sent me once more in April 1853, with an affectionate letter in French, 2l. for the Orphans, and shortly afterwards fell asleep in Jesus. While writing this account, I met with many names of worthy disciples of the Lord Jesus, who have entered upon their rest, since I received their donations; may this speak to my heart, and to the heart of the reader, and may we learn the lesson which God intends to teach us thereby!

July 10. 50l. from Liverpool.

Aug. 4. Today I received 200l., of which I took one half for the Orphans, and the other half for the other objects, the disposal of this sum being left with me. This is a precious answer to prayer. There will be about 400l. required during this month for the current expenses for the Orphans, but there was only about 170l. in hand, when this donation came in.

As the 127 donations, which had come in since Aug. 4th, were of a smaller kind, we had on Sept. 8th scarcely anything left, when I received the 280l. 10s. 6d., spoken of (Sept. 8th, 1852) under the Building Fund, of which 86l. 13s. 4d. was taken for the current expenses for the Orphans.

Oct. 7. This evening there was only 8l. left in hand for the current expenses for the Orphans. Hitherto we had generally abounded. But though much had come in, since the commencement of this new period, yet our expenses had been greater than our income, as every donation almost of which the disposal was left with me, had been put to the Building Fund. Thus the balance in hand on May 26, 1852, notwithstanding the large income since then, was reduced to about 8l. I therefore gave myself particularly to prayer for means, that this small sum might be increased. When I came home this evening from the New Orphan House, I found a letter from London, containing 2l., being two donations from Kelso, of 1l. each, and another letter from Peterborough, containing 1l.

Oct 8. This morning I received 5l. 5s. more from Willenhall. Thus the Lord has already been pleased to add 8l. in to the little stock in hand, which is now increased to 16l. 5s.--Another 6d. was added, by sale of a Report.--This evening the matron told me that tomorrow she would need to have more money. I generally advance 30l. at a time for housekeeping expenses, but I had now only 8l. 14s. left, as I had to pay out this afternoon 7l. 11s. 6d. This I purposed to give to her, should it not please the Lord to give more in the meantime, being assured that, before this amount was gone, He would give more. My prayer to the Lord, however, was that He would be pleased to send help, and I looked out for means. When I came home this evening

I found a letter from Gosport, containing 1s., which a little boy has sent for the Orphans, having received it as a reward for picking up a ring, and giving it to the owner. Also a letter from Kingstown, Ireland, containing a Post-office Order for 1l. 7s., of which 1l. 2s. 6d. are for the Building Fund, and 4s. 6d. for Reports. I likewise received 6d. for missions and 6d. for the Orphans, from two boys in the neighbourhood of Stroud. Thus I have 9l, to advance tomorrow for house-keeping.

Oct. 9. This morning Luke vii. came in the course of my reading before breakfast. While reading the account about the Centurion and the raising from death of the widow's son at Nain, I lifted up my heart to the Lord Jesus thus: "Lord Jesus, Thou hast the same power now. Thou canst provide me with means for Thy work in my hands. Be pleased to do so." -- About half an hour afterwards I received 230l. 15s. Also 1s. This 230l. 15s. was left at my disposal. I took one half for the current expenses for the Orphans, and the other half for the other objects, and am now amply provided for meeting the demands of this day.

The joy which such answers to prayer afford, cannot be described. I was determined to wait upon God only, and not to work an unscriptural deliverance for myself. I have thousands of pounds for the Building Fund; but I would not take of this sum because it was once set apart for that object. There is also a legacy of 100l. for the Orphans two months overdue, in the prospect of the payment of which the heart might be naturally inclined to use some money of the Building Fund, to be replaced by the legacy money, when it comes in; but I would not thus step out of God's way of obtaining help. At the very time when this donation arrived, I had packed up 100l. which I happened to have in hand, received for the Building Fund, in order to take it to the Bank, as I was determined not to touch it, but to wait upon God. My soul does magnify the Lord for His goodness.

This last paragraph is copied out of my journal, written down at the time, I add a few words more to the last sentences.

The natural mind is ever prone to reason, when we ought to believe; to be at work, when we ought to be quiet; to go our own way, when we ought steadily to walk on in God's ways, however trying to nature. When first converted, I should have said, What harm can there be to take some of the money, which has been put by for the Building Fund? God will help me again after some time with means for the Orphans, and then I can replace it. Or, there is this money due for the legacy of 100l. This money is quite sure; may I not, therefore, on the strength of it, take some from the Building Fund, and when the legacy is paid, replace the money which I have taken? I know that many would act thus. But how does it work, when we thus anticipate God, by going our own way? We bring, in many instances, guilt on our conscience; but if not, we certainly weaken faith, instead of increasing it; and each time we work thus a deliverance of our own, we find it more and more difficult to trust in God, till at last we give way entirely to our natural fallen reason, and unbelief prevails. How different, if one is enabled to wait God's own time, and to look alone to Him for help and deliverance! When at last help comes, after many seasons of

FOURTH PART

prayer it may be, and after much exercise of faith and patience it may be, how sweet it is, and what a present recompense does the soul at once receive for trusting in God, and waiting patiently for His deliverance! Dear Christian reader, if you have never walked in this path of obedience before, do so now, and you will then know experimentally the sweetness of the joy which results from it. I now return to Oct. 9, 1852.

Received still further today, from Cirencester, 2l., and also 10l.

Oct. 10. From two little girls at Clifton, 5s.--By sale of a silver watch given for the purpose, 1l. 10s,--From a donor in Maryport Street, 3s. 4d.--Through Bethesda boxes 1s. Ditto 2s. 6d. Ditto a sovereign.--From a believer in Bristol 5s.--By sale of empty oatmeal barrels, 15s.

Oct. 11. From Sutton Points, 13s. 7d. --Through the boxes in the New Orphan House, 3s.--From an Orphans formerly under our care, and now in service, 10s., with 10s. for the Building Fund.--From a Christian lady, recently come from Edinburgh, 1l.--Through a Christian lady, staying at Clifton, 5s.

Oct. 12. By sale of rags and bones 12s. 6d. [I copy literally from the receipt book. We seek to make the best of every thing. As a steward of public money, I feel it right that even these articles should be turned into money; nor could we expect answers to our prayers if knowingly there were any waste allowed in connexion with this work. For just because the money is received from God, simply in answer to prayer only, therefore it becomes us the more, to be careful in the use of it].-- By sale of Reports 5s.--From an Orphan box at Plymouth 3s., together with 8s. as a donation added, and 9s. for Reports. Still further help: This afternoon a lady of Clifton called at my house, and brought a check for 200l., which a gentlemen, whose name even I had never heard of, had sent her for the benefit of tine Orphans. We are not now in actual need, yet as 62l. lies already been paid out of what I have received since the 9th, and as other heavy payments are before me, in a few days, it is particularly kind of the Lord, to send this donation from a perfect stranger.

Nov. 13. Today was paid to me the legacy for the Orphans, to which reference has been made. I had no doubt it would come in in good time. Thus it is. The expenses are heavy, week after week. The day after tomorrow, I shall have again to pay out above 100l. for the Orphans.

On Dec. 20th, in the evening, I had only 16l. 9s. left. Think of this, dear Reader. So little, for so large an Establishment! From Dec. 20th to the evening of Dec. 26th, there came in only about 18l.; and as I had paid out above 13l., I could only advance 15l. for house-keeping on Dec. 27th, instead of the usual 30l., and had then about 5l. left for petty expenses. I knew that on the 31st I should have to advance again at least 20l. for house-keeping. Now see how the Lord was pleased to send in the means from the morning of Dec. 27th to Dec. 31st. Dec. 27. From Alcombe, near Minehead, 10s.--From a poor widow in Bristol, 5s.-- Anonymously 1l. Ditto a sovereign, with these words: "An Orphan's mite for the Orphan House."--

THE LORD'S DEALINGS WITH GEORGE MÜLLER

From Clifton, 1s., and 1s. besides.--Dec. 28. From Newport, in Monmouthshire, 10s. and 10s.--From Birmingham, 2l. 10s. with the same for my own personal expenses.--From Boscrea 7d. from three children.--From Lenwade, 10s.--Dec. 29. From B. B. at Leamington 5l.--Anonymously, from London, 2s. 5d.--From three sisters 10s., 5s., 1l., also 10s. 8 1/2 d.--By sale of Reports, 3s. --Through the boxes in the New Orphan House 1l. 6s. 9 1/2 d.--Dec. 30. By sale of Reports 2s. 6d.--From Clifton 5l.--From two Christian ladies in Buckinghamshire 20l.-- From some pupils on Kingsdown 5s. Thus I had on Dec. 31st money enough to advance 25l. for housekeeping expenses, besides having had the means to pay away 20l. 5s. 9d. After I had given out the money in advance for house-keeping expenses, I had, at the close of the year, not 2l. left. But my mind was in full peace. Now see how, before the 25l. which had been advanced was expended, and before other expenses came upon me, the Lord was pleased to send in the means from the 1st to the 4th of January, 1853.--Jan. 1. Anonymously 1s.--From Sherborne, 1l.--From Colchester 10s.-- From Manchester 10s.--From a distance 1l. 2s. 6d.--From Glouchstershire 14s. 6d.--From a brother in the Lord in Bristol 3l. 12s., together with 5s. 7d. from his Orphan box. This brother had it on his heart, more than a twelvemonth ago, to dispose of an article for the benefit of the Orphans, but could not meet with an opportunity till today. Thus, in this time of need, the Lord sends in this money.-- Jan. 2. By sale of Reports 12s.--From two Christian sisters 5s., as a thank offering to the Lord for the mercies of the past year.--From a lady at Clifton 10s.--From a Brother in Bristol 1l.---From Torquay 3s., with 3s. for Reports.--From Worcester 2s. 2d.--From a brother in Bristol 3l.--Jan. 3. From Waterford 1l.--From Liverpool 5l.-- Also the 75l. being part of the 252l. 17s. 1d. spoken of under the Building Fund.--From Clifton 10s.--Through Salem boxes 2s. 6d.-- From "P." 1s. Jan. 4. From Ryde 2l.--From Tottenham 10s. Thus God helped me in a time of great, great need. But before this 4th of January was over, He did far more than ever in the way of supplying me with means, for the largest of all the donations I had ever had, and of which mention has been made before, was given to me, of which 600l. was portioned out for the current expenses for the Orphans.

    I have been thus particular in this last paragraph, on purpose, to give a practical illustration that those are entirely mistaken who suppose that the work is now no longer a work of faith, as it used to be in former years. It is true, we have now a larger income, then we used to have in the years 1838, 1839, and 1840; but it is also true that our expenses are three times as great. We have no regular income now; even as we had not then. We ask no human being now for help; even as we did not then. We depend alone upon God, by His grace even as we did then. Who is there in the whole world who will state that I ever asked him for help in this Orphan work, from its commencement, on Dec. 9, 1835, up till now? Now, as we have no funds to live upon; as we have no regular subscribers or donors upon whom we could depend; as we never ask help from man but God alone; and as, finally, we never did go into debt for this work, nor do we now: why is it not now a work of faith as formerly? Will those, who say it is not, place themselves in my position, when, at the close of the year 1852, I had not two pounds left, and about 330 persons were day by day to be provided for, with all they need, and prove whether it is now anything else than a work of faith? Every one, except those who are determined not to see, will have no

FOURTH PART

difficulty in perceiving that now, as formerly, one could only be kept from being overwhelmed in such a position by looking day by day to the Lord, and that not merely for pecuniary supplies, but for help under the numberless difficulties, which continually are met with in such a work.

On account of the abundance which came in at the beginning of the year, together with what was received afterwards, there was not the least difficulty felt, in the way of means, for many weeks afterwards. Of the donations that came in from Jan. 5 to April 20, and which amounted altogether to 648l. 8s. 8 1/4 d., in 314 different sums, large and small, I will only mention the following: Jan. 25. From an aged Christian merchant at Clifton 50l.--From a Christian merchant in London 20l., on Feb. 11.

April 20. In the prospect of having to pay away yet about 500l, before the accounts are closed on May 26th, and having only 236l. in hand, I asked the Lord especially this evening, that He would be pleased to help me with means for the current expenses for the Orphans, for which I might have far more in hand had I not with all my might given myself to the Building Fund, in order to be soon able to commence the building of this second Orphan House. Now, this evening, I found that a donation of 100l. had come in at my house during my absence, the disposal of which was entirely left to me. I took not the whole of this donation for the current expenses for the Orphans, but only one half, and the other half for the Building Fund. The funds for the various Schools, for the circulation of the Holy Scriptures and Tracts, and for missionary objects, need nothing for at least six weeks to come. This donation has greatly refreshed my spirit, especially as it came from a most unexpected quarter.

Before the accounts were closed, I received, between April 20th and May 26th, 1853, in just One Hundred different sums, 422l. 3s. 11 1/2 d. more, so that I was able amply to supply all demands, and had the balance of 117l. 10s. 9d. left in hand. It was chiefly through a donation of 260l., given to be employed as most needed, spoken of under the Building Fund Income on May 14th, 1853, of which I took 160l. for the Orphans, that we

had so large an amount in hand. This donation was indescribably precious, as it not only, in conjunction with the other money which came in, carried me easily through all the expenses which absolutely needed to be met, and which were heavier than they ever had been during any month since the Orphan work had been in existence; but also enabled me to do things which were most desirable, though not absolutely needful.

How can I sufficiently praise, and adore, and magnify the Lord, for His love and faithfulness, in carrying me thus from year to year through this His service, supplying me with all I need in the way of means, fellow labourers, mental strength, and, above all, spiritual support! But for His help and support, I should be completely overpowered in a very short time; yet, by His help, I go on, and am very happy spiritually, in my service; nor am I now generally worse in health than I was twenty years ago, but rather better.

Miscellaneous Points respecting the Scriptural Knowledge Institution for Home and Abroad, with reference to the period from May 26, 1852, to May 26, 1853.

1. During this period there were four Day Schools, with 235 children in them, entirely supported by the funds of the Institution. Further, one Sunday School in Bristol, with 150 children, was entirely supported, and three others in Devonshire, Somersetshire, and Gloucestershire, with 280 children, were assisted. Lastly, one Adult School, with 103 Adult Scholars, was entirely supported by the funds of the Institution. There were under our care, from March 5, 1884, to May 26, 1853, in the various Day Schools, 5686 children, in the Sunday School 2673 children, and in the Adult School 2132 persons. There was expended of the funds of the Institution, during this year, for the various Schools, 349l. 12s. 11d.

2. During thus year there was laid out of the funds of the Institution, on the circulation of the Holy Scriptures, 431l. 5s. 1 1/2 d., and there were circulated 1,666 Bibles and 1,210 New Testaments.--There were circulated from March 5, 1834, up to May 26, 1853, 10,476 Bibles, and 6.061 New Testaments.

For several years past this part of the work has appeared more and more important to me, on account of the fearful attempts which have been made by the powers of darkness to rob the church of Christ of the Holy Scriptures. I have on this account sought to embrace every opportunity to circulate the Holy Scriptures in England, Ireland, Canada, British Guiana, the East Indies, China, Australia, &c. Every open door which the Lord was pleased to set before me in these or other parts of the world, I have joyfully entered; yea, I have counted it a privilege, indeed, to be permitted of God to send forth His Holy Word. Many servants of Christ, in various parts of the world, have assisted me in this service, through whose instrumentality copies of the Holy Scriptures have been circulated. Our endeavour has been, to place the word of God in the hands of the very poorest persons, and also, in particular, to supply very aged persons with copies of the Scriptures, printed in large type, as such copies still remain expensive, considering the means of the poor. Nor have our efforts been in vain. For we had several cases of direct conversion, simply through circulating the Holy Scriptures, brought before us during this year. But we are fully assured, that the fruit which we have seen, as resulting from this part of the world, is but little in comparison with what we shall see in the day of Christ's appearing. The disciples of the Lord Jesus should labour with all their might in the work of God, as if everything depended upon their own exertions; and yet, having done so, they should not in the least trust in their labour and efforts, and in the means which they use for the spread of the truth, but in God; and they should with all earnestness seek the blessing of God, in persevering, patient, and believing prayer. Here is the great secret of success, my Christian Reader. Work with all your might; but trust not in the least in your work. Pray with all your might for the blessing of God; but work, at the

FOURTH PART

same time, with all diligence, with all patience, with all perseverance. Pray then, and work. Work and pray. And still again pray, and then work. And so on all the days of your life. The result will surely be, abundant blessing. Whether you see much fruit or little fruit; such kind of service will be blessed. We should labour then, for instance, with all earnestness in seeking to circulate Thousands of copies of the Holy Scriptures, and Hundreds of Thousands of Tracts, as if everything depended upon the amount of copies of the Holy Scriptures and Tracts which we circulate; and yet, in reality, we should not in the least degree put our dependence upon the number of copies of the Holy Scriptures, and upon the number of Tracts, but entirely upon God for His blessing, without which all these efforts are entirely useless. This blessing, however, should be sought by us habitually and perseveringly in prayer. It should also be fully expected.

3. During this year there was spent of the funds of the Institution for missionary objects 2,234l. 2s. 6d. By this sum fifty-four labourers in the word and doctrine, in various pants of time world, were to a greater or less degree assisted.

During no period within the nineteen years previous to May 26, 1853, was so large a portion of the funds of the Institution expended, in one year, upon Missionary Objects, as during this year; and in every single case I was enabled to help to the full amount of what appeared desirable. Refreshing as this is, and thankful as we desire to be to the Lord for it; yet it were but a very little thing, had there not been corresponding results. But I have to record to the praise of the Lord, and to the enjoyment of the Christian Reader, that not five, nor ten, nor fifty souls only were won for Him through the instrumentality of these fifty-four dear brethren, but hundreds. I received a great number of letters from these labourers in the Word, both at home and abroad, which brought me heart-cheering intelligence. Thank the Lord for this together with me, dear Christian Reader, and continue to help these esteemed brethren with your prayers, some of whom labour for the Lord under peculiar difficulties.

I would repeat that I consider it a great privilege to be permitted to defray in part or altogether, from time funds of this Institution, the expenses connected with the voyage and outfit of brethren who desire to go out as Missionaries, or to help them after their arrival in their field of labour; but I do not bind myself to support them habitually, seeing that thus they would be out of the position of simple dependence upon God for their temporal supplies.

4. There was laid out for the circulation of Tracts, from May 26, 1852, to May 26, 1853, the sum of 555l. 16s. 7 1/2 d.; and there were circulated within this year 733,674 Tracts.

The total number of Tracts circulated up to May 26, 1853, was One Million Eight Hundred Twenty Thousand and Forty.

The Lord is pleased to increase this part of the work more and more, as will be seen by a comparison of the years in which this part of the Institution has been in operation. From Nov. 19, 1840, to May 10, 1842, the first period that the circulation of Tracts was in operation in connexion with the Scriptural Knowledge Institution for Home and Abroad, there were circulated 19,609 from May 10, 1842, to July 14, 1844, 39,473; from July 14, 1844, to May 26, 1846, 40,565; from May 26, 1846, to May 26, 1848, 64,021; from May 26, 1848, to May 26, 1850, 130,464; from May 26, 1850, to May 26, 1851, 303,098; from May 26, 1851, to May 26, 1852, 489,136; and during this period 733,674.

In these increased opportunities to spread the truth, we rejoice. Moreover, we would, by the help of God, seek to labour still far more abundantly in this particular also, and would seek to press into every open door, which the Lord may set before us. Yea, we would labour, as has been stated before, as if everything depended upon our diligence and carefulness in the use of the means; whilst, in reality, we would not depend upon them in the least degree, but only upon God for His blessing. This blessing of God we have been enabled to seek upon the labours of missionary brethren, the circulation of time Holy Scriptures, and upon the distribution of Tracts. As the days come, so our heart is drawn out in prayer for blessing upon these objects, in connexion with the various Schools and the Orphan Work. How, then, could it be otherwise, but that sooner or later there should come showers of blessing? Thus it was during this year. This year stands alone, in that more money came in, than during any year previously. It stands alone, in that the operations of the Scriptural Knowledge Institution were extended beyond whatever they mad been before. But it stands alone, also, in the abundant blessing, which God granted to our efforts, and which was greater than during any previous period. And, as in other respects, so in particular likewise, the gratuitous distribution of Tracts was abundantly owned of God. Instance upon instance, not 2, nor 5, nor 10, but many, in the way of conversion, and also of blessing to believers, was I informed of by those Godly brethren, who in various parts of the world, aid me in this service. How can I sufficiently magnify the Lord for this! By His grace I would desire to labour on, though I were not to see one single instance of blessing, being assured that "in due season we shall reap," and that our "labour is not in vain in the Lord;" yet how kind of the Lord, to grant such abundant blessing to rest upon our labours!

Often, I fear, Tract distributors have expected little result from their labour; and therefore they have seen little fruit. According to their expectation, they have received. Often, also, I fear, the mere distribution of Tracts has been rested in, and the work done has been estimated by the number of Tracts which were circulated, without earnestly preceding their circulation with prayer, and without earnestly following them with prayer, may I, therefore, be allowed to caution my fellow-believers on these two points? Look out for blessing, but seek also the blessing earnestly in prayer; and you will not fail to receive abundantly.

Should any believer be discouraged, because he has not had much fruit resulting from the circulation of Tracts, let such a one, with renewed earnestness and prayerfulness, go on in his work; let him also expect fruit, and he will surely reap abundantly; if not now, at least in the day of Christ's appearing.

FOURTH PART

5. At the beginning of this period, there were Three Hundred Orphans in the New Orphan-House on Ashley Down, Bristol. During the year there were admitted into it 13 Orphans, making 313 in all. Of these 313, (we own it with thankfulness to God,) not one died during the year; for not a single death occurred for about 15 months. One of the Orphans, who had been received after he had long had his own way, and who having long been borne with, and repeatedly been received back again on a confession of sorrow, at last ran away again, and had then to be placed by his relatives in the Union. One Orphan was sent to relatives, who were by that time able to care for her. Five girls were, at the expense of the Establishment, fitted out for service or learning a business, and were sent out;--also six boys were, at the expense of the Establishment, fitted out and apprenticed. Thus makes the number removed as great as the number received, so that there were still 300 Orphans in tire New Orphan-House on May 26, 1853. The total number of Orphans, who were under our care from April, 1836, to May 26, 1853, was Five Hundred and Twenty-eight.

I notice further the following points in connexion with the Orphan Work.

a. Without any one having been personally applied to for anything by me, the sum of 55,408l. 17s. 5 3/4 d. was given to me for the Orphans, as the result of prayer to God, from the commencement of the work up to May 26, 1853.--It may be also interesting to the reader to know, that the total amount given for the other objects, from the commencement of the work up to May 26, 1853, amounted to 19,163l. 14s. 1 1/2 d.; and that which came in by the sale of Bibles and Tracts, and by the payments of the children in the Day Schools, amounted to 3,490l. 7s. 1 3/4 d.-- Besides this, also a great variety and number of articles of clothing, furniture, provisions, &c., were given for the use of the Orphans.

b. Our labours continued to be blessed among the Orphans.

c. The expenses in connexion with the support of the 300 Orphans and the apprentices during this year, were 3,453l. 15s. 1 1/2 d.

Matters connected with my own personal affairs, or the work of the Lord in my hands, not immediately connected with the Scriptural Knowledge Institution, from May 26, 1852, to May 26, 1853.

Dec. 31, 1852. During this year 35 believers have been received into fellowship. When Brother Craik and I began to labour in the Word in Bristol, we found 68 in fellowship. Since then there have been received into communion altogether 1,403, so that the total number would be 1,471, had there been no changes. But 64 are under church discipline, and separated, for the present, from fellowship; 154 have left us (some of them, however, in love, and merely through circumstances); 421 have left Bristol to reside elsewhere; and 197 have fallen asleep. So that there are at present only 635 actually remaining in communion.

THE LORD'S DEALINGS WITH GEORGE MÜLLER

The Lord has been pleased to give unto me during this year--

1. Through believers in and out of Bristol, in provisions, clothes, etc., worth to us at least   9 0 0

2. Through anonymous offerings in money, put up in paper and directed to me, and put into the boxes for the poor saints or the rent, at the chapels
                                                                                                     157 11 4 1/2

Carried forward   L166 11 4 1/2

Brought forward   L166 11 4 1/2

3. Through presents in money, from believers in Bristol, not given anonymously
                                                                                              ..   121 5 2

4. Through presents in money, from believers not residing in Bristol   157 12 2

                                                                                                     L445 8 8 1/2

My brother-in-law, Mr. A. N. Groves, of whom mention has been made in the first part of this Narrative, as having been helpful to me by his example when I began my labours in England in 1829, in that he, without any visible support, and without being connected with any missionary society, went with his wife and children to Bagdad, as a missionary, after having given up a lucrative practice of about 1500l. per year, returned in Autumn 1852, from the East Indies, a third time, being exceedingly ill. He lived, however, till May 20th, 1853, when, after a most blessed testimony for the Lord, he fell asleep in Jesus in my house. I should more fully dwell on this to myself amid my family's deeply important event, had not a very full biography been published by the widow of my dear brother-in-law, in which also full particulars are given of the last days of this servant of Christ. I therefore refer the reader to the deeply interesting memoir, which has been published at Nisbet's, London, and may be had at the Bible and Tract Warehouse of the Scriptural Knowledge Institution for Home and Abroad, 84, Park Street, Bristol, and through all booksellers, under the title: Memoir of the late Anthony Norris Groves, second edition, with a portrait, cloth, 4s. 6d.; fine paper, cloth, 6s. 6d.

Further account respecting the intended Orphan-House for Seven Hundred Children, bereaved of both parents by death, from May 26, 1853, to May 26, 1854.

In the last chapter on this subject I stated, that, on May 26, 1853, I had actually in hand, towards the accomplishment of my object, the sum of 12,531l. 12s. 0 1/4 d. I will now give some further particulars as to the manner in which it pleased

FOURTH PART

the Lord to supply me with means, but must confine myself to those donations which more specially may call for notice.

June 28, 1853. From Wakefield 40l., with 5l. for Mr. Craik, and 5l. for my own personal expenses.--Also 220l. from the West of England, of which the donor kindly wishes me to take 20l. for my own private expenses, and to use the 200l. as might be most needed. I have taken, therefore, 100l. for the Building Fund; 60l. for missionary operations, the circulation of Bibles and Tracts; and 40l. for the Orphans.

July 14. Received 541l. 10s., which being left to me as most needed, I took 100l. for the current expenses for the Orphans, 100l. for the other objects, and 341l. 10s. for the Building Fund. Being just now in great family affliction, this kindness of the Lord has been a great refreshment to my spirit.

July 15. From Clifton 1s.--Received also 110l. from one who counts it an honour to have this sum to lay down at the feet of the Lord Jesus. I took of this amount 60l. for the Building Fund, and 50l. for the circulation of the Holy Scriptures and Tracts, and for missionary objects.

I cannot help remarking here, that the Lord has used some of the most unlikely persons during the past twenty-two years, in providing me with means for His service. So it was particularly in the case of this brother in the Lord, from whom I received the last-mentioned donation of 110l. I had not the least natural expectation of receiving this sum, when this brother, sitting before me at the New Orphan-House, took out of his pocket a packet of Bank Notes, and gave to me this amount, reserving to himself, as his whole property in this world, a smaller sum than he gave to me, because of his joy in the Lord, and because of his being able to enter into the reality of his possessions in the world to come. I delight in dwelling upon such an instance, because 1, it shows that there is grace, much grace, to be found among the saints even now; 2, it shows the variety of instrumentality which the Lord is pleased to employ, in supplying me with means for His service; and 3, because it so manifestly proves that we do not wait upon Him in vain, when we make known our requests to Him for means.

July 20. From Philadelphia, in the United States, 5l.

Aug. 20. From the neighbourhood of Mallow in Ireland 17s. 6d, and 2s. 6d.--Anonymously from a "Brother Christian and Well-wisher," through his bankers in London, 100l.

Aug. 27. From Caistor 5s.--From Gumeracka, near Adelaide, Australia, 2l. 10s. From the same place 10s.--From Cheltenham 2s. 6d.--From Frampton-on-Severn seven silver coins.

You see, esteemed reader, how much variety there is in the kind of donations as well as in the amount, the places whence they are sent, and the friends who send them. But all these donations come from the living God. All come to us in answer to prayer, and are received by us as answers to prayer; and with every donation, however small, we receive thins a fresh encouragement, to continue in prayer, and have, as it were, another earnest from our Heavenly Father, that at last He not only will give larger sums, but the whole amount which is needed for the Building Fund. Every one of these donations comes unsolicited. Ever since the Orphan Work has been in operation, we have never asked any one for anything. Be therefore, dear reader, encouraged by this, to make trial for yourself, to prove the power of prayer, if you have never done so before.

Dec. 31. This is the last day of another year. Two years and a half I have new been day by day seeking the Lord's help in player for this object. He has also been pleased to give us many proofs, that He is remembering our requests, still as yet I have only 13,670l. 11s. 7 3/4 d. in hand. Considerably more than double this sum will be needed. But, by the grace of God, I am not discouraged. The Lord is able and willing to help us. This is my comfort. In His own time the Almighty God will manifest His power. In the meantime I desire to continue to wait upon Him, and to receive every fresh donation, however small, as an earnest, that in His own time He not only will give larger sums, but the whole amount needed for this object.

Jan. 17, 1854. This day I received the promise, that there should be paid to me, for the work of the Lord in my hands, 5,207l., to be disposed of as I might consider best.

This large donation was shortly after paid to me, and was portioned out thus: For the Building Fund 3000l.; for the support of the 300 Orphans 707l.; for foreign missions 500l.; for labourers in the Word in England, Ireland and Scotland 500l.; for the gratuitous circulation of the Holy Scriptures among the poor 200l.; for the gratuitous circulation of Gospel Tracts 200l.; and for the various schools, supported or assisted by the Funds of the Scriptural Knowledge Institution, 100l.

Behold, esteemed reader, the goodness of God! Behold also the recompense, which sooner or hater, the Lord gives to His children, who wait upon Him and trust in Him Often it may appear that we wait upon the Lord in vain; but, in His own time God will abundantly prove, that it was not in vain. Go on therefore, Christian reader, to wait upon the Lord. Continue to make known your requests to Him; but do also expect help from Him. You honour God, by believing that He does hear your prayers, and that He will answer them.

The joy which such answers to prayer give, cannot be described; and the impetus which they thus afford to the spiritual life is exceedingly great. The experience of this happiness I desire for all my Christian readers. Nor is there anything to hinder any believer from having these joys. If you believe indeed in the Lord Jesus for the salvation of your soul, if you walk uprightly and do not regard iniquity in your heart, if you continue to wait patiently, and believingly upon God; then answers will surely be given to your prayers. You may not be called upon to serve the Lord in the way

FOURTH PART

the writer does, and therefore may never have answers to prayer respecting such things as are recorded here; but in your various circumstances, as to your family, your business, your profession, your church position, your labour for the Lord inn army way, you may have answers as distinct as any here recorded.

Should this, however, be read by any who are not believers in the Lord Jesus, but any who are going on in the carelessness or self-righteousness of their unrenewed hearts, then I would affectionately and solemnly beseech such, first of all to be reconciled to God by faith in the Lord Jesus. You are sinners. You deserve punishment. If you do not see this, ask God to show it unto you. Let this now be your first and especial prayer. Ask Him also to enlighten you not merely concerning your state by nature, but especially to reveal the Lord Jesus to your hearts. God sent Him, that He might bear the punishment, due to us guilty sinners. God accepts the obedience and sufferings of the Lord Jesus, in the room of those who depend upon Him for the salvation of their souls; and the moment a sinner believes in the Lord Jesus, he obtains the forgiveness of all his sins. When thus he is reconciled to God, by faith in the Lord Jesus, and has obtained the forgiveness of his sins, he has boldness to enter into the presence of God, to make known his requests unto God; and the more he is enabled to realize, that his sins are forgiven, and that God, for Christ's sake, is well pleased with those who believe on Him, the more ready he will be to come with all his wants, both temporal and spiritual, to his Heavenly Father, that He may supply them. But as long as the consciousness of unpardoned guilt remains, so long shall we be kept at a distance from God, and especially also as it regards prayer. Therefore, dear reader, if you are an unforgiven sinner, let your first and especial subject of your prayer be, that God would be pleased to reveal to your heart the Lord Jesus, His beloved Son.

March 5. To day it is twenty years since the Scriptural Knowledge Institution for Home and Abroad made its beginning. When I look back upon that day, with reference to this work, I desire with gratitude to exclaim, What has God wrought! His name be magnified for it! I desire to take courage from all His former goodness, and to go on in His service.

March 6. Received 131l. 1s. 3d., which being left at my disposal, I took 31l. 1s. 3d. for the Building Fund, and 100l. for the support of the Orphans.--Through Bethesda boxes, as a thank-offering for the mercies of the past month, 2s. 6d.

April 22. From London, six knives, nine silver forks, three silver table spoons, three silver dessert spoons, three silver tea spoons, one silver salt spoon, a silver pencil case, three penholders, one mounted in silver and two in gold, and a penknife.

May. 3. Anonymously, through banker's in London, 100l.--May 8. Through Bethesda homes, 2s. 6d., as "A thank-offering to the Lord for the mercies of the past month."

THE LORD'S DEALINGS WITH GEORGE MÜLLER

Month after month, for some time past, 2s. 6d. has been given as "A thank-offering for the mercies of the past month," I am delighted with this. Not yearly only may the saints bring their offerings to the Lord, as He may have prospered them, but monthly. Yea the Holy Ghost, by the Apostle Paul, gives this exhortation to the believers of the Church at Corinth, concerning offerings for the poor saints; "Upon the first day of the week let every one of you lay by him in store, as God hath prospered him." I Cor. xvi. 2. As the Lord had prospered them, so were they not merely yearly, or monthly, but even weekly to contribute to the support of the poor. We are strangers and pilgrims on the earth. The time of our pilgrimage here is very uncertain. The opportunities which the Lord gives us for His service are therefore readily to be embraced. All here below is most uncertain. How long we may have the opportunity to work for the Lord, who can tell? Therefore the present hour is to be used with all our might. As an encouragement for all this, we have to look to the return of our Lord Jesus.

May 26. 82l. 18s. 4d., being the proceeds arising from the sale of a work published in English, and 14s. 3d., from the sale of a work published in French, were given for the Building Fund.

Thus closes the period from May 26, 1853, to May 26, 1854. The whole income for this object during the year was 5,285l. 7s. 5d., which, together with the 12,531l. 12s. 0 1/4 d. in hand on May 26, 1853, made the total of 17,816l. 12s. 5 1/4 d. in hand on May 26, 1854.

I add the following remarks, with reference to the intended Orphan House for 700 Orphans, which appeared in the Report for 1854, and which are here reprinted.

A. During this year the current expenses, for the various Objects of the Scriptural Knowledge Institution for Home and Abroad, amounted to 7,507l. 0s. 11 1/2 d., being 471l. 8s, 11d. more than during any previous year; yet the Lord not only enabled me to meet them all, but to add the sum of 5,285l. 7s, 5d. to the Building Fund.

B. There is yet a large sum required, before I shall be enabled to build another house for 700 Orphans; nor have I now, any more than at the first, any natural prospect of obtaining what is yet needed; but my hope is in the living God. When I came to the conclusion that it was the will of God I should build another Orphan House, I had not only no natural prospect of obtaining the 35,000l. which would be needed for thus object, but also no natural prospect of being able to provide for the necessities of the 300 Orphans already under my care. Three years have elapsed since then, and I have had all I needed for them, amounting to about 10,500l., and 17,816l. 19s. 5 1/4 d. I have received for the Building Fund. May I not well trust in the Lord, for what is yet needed for the Building Fund? By His grace I will do so, and delight in doing so; for I know that at last all my prayers will be turned into praises concerning this part of the service.

FOURTH PART

C. There is one point which is particularly an encouragement to me, to go on waiting upon the Lord for the remainder of the means, which are required, viz.: applications for the admission of Orphans continue to be made. On May 26, 1858, there were 480 Orphans waiting for admission. Since then 181 more have been applied for, making in all 661. Of these, however, thirty have been admitted during the past year into the New Orphan-House, and twenty-nine have been otherwise provided for, so that there are actually 602 waiting for admission. These children are from three months old and upwards, and all bereaved of both parents by death.

Supplies for the School --, Bible--, Missionary and Tract fund, sent in answer to prayer, from May 26, 1853, to May 26, 1854.

On May 26, 1853, there was left in hand for these objects a balance of 67l. 17s. 7 3/4 d.

June 13. When I had very little in hand, comparatively, there being about 30l. left, as little only had come in since May 26th, I received a donation of 301l., of which I took 201l. for the support of the Orphans, and 100l. for these objects. How much is there needed, to go on with all these various objects, and to press into every open door, which the Lord may set before me! How kind, therefore, of Him, to have sent me this sum!

July 14. Only about 150l. had come in for these objects since June 18. But though I had not much in hand, I sent out 65l. on the 11th, three days since, for missionary objects, being assured that the sowing would bring the reaping. On the very next day, July 12th, I received from Chelsea 5l. and also 10s. From the north of Devon 10l. Anonymously 5l. From Norwich, for foreign missions, 5l. The day after that, July 13th, I received from the neighbourhood of Leeds 10l., and from Oakhill 1s. Now today I received the 541l. 10s., spoken of under the Building Fund, of which I took for these objects 100l.

July 15. Today the Lord has been pleased to give still more. I have received 20l. for the Schools and 50l. for these various objects.

Sept. 15. During the last two days I sent out 85l. to brethren who labour in the Word at home and abroad; and during the first half of this month have already sent to them 174l. During the last two days, whilst sending out almost the last pound in hand for missionary objects, I felt quite comfortable in doing so, and said to myself: "The Lord can give me more." So it has been. This morning I have received from Weston Super Mare, in a registered letter, 100l. with these words: "The enclosed 100l. for missionaries to the heathen, from H. E. H., Western Super Mare, Sept, 14th." This is particularly refreshing to me, as I desired still to send out during this month about 200l. to other brethren.

Oct. 15. During the last six weeks little only, comparatively, has been received for these objects; but I have sent out much for missionary objects, and for the circulation of the Holy Scriptures and Tracts. Thus the funds for these various objects were this morning reduced to 29l. 15s. 6 1/4 d. Yet my heart desired to send out, before the close of this month, a considerable amount to preachers of the Gospel, and to spend further sums on the circulation of the Holy Scriptures and Gospel Tracts. This my desire has been in a measure already granted, for I received this morning 192l. 1s. Of this sum I took 100l. for these objects, and the remainder for the current expenses for the Orphans. The Lord be magnified for this kindness! There was also much need for fresh supplies for the Orphans, when this donation was received. With more than usual exercise of faith and patience have I had to wait upon God for the last four weeks, during which time the income has been very little and the outgoing very great.

Dec. 8. Today I received three autographs of King William IV., one of Sir Robert Peel, and two of Lord Melbourne (with six postage stamps), to be sold for the funds of the Scriptural Knowledge Institution.--See what a variety of donations the Lord sends us for the support of the work!

Dec. 11. For several years I have not been so poor for these objects, as during the last six weeks. Day by day have I besought the Lord for more means, and almost daily has He also sent in something; yet the income has not been adequate to help the 56 brethren, whom I seek to assist as preachers of the Word at home and abroad, in the measure I have desired. I had reason to believe, that several were in need, but I had nothing to send to them, and could only labour on in prayer, finding relief in the knowledge that God could help them irrespective of my instrumentality, and make this their trial of faith and patience a blessing to their souls, even as I have found this season profitable to myself. But now at the last the Lord has refreshed my spirit exceedingly, by a donation of 300l., left at my disposal; of which I have taken 150l. for these objects, and 150l. for the Orphans, for whom also fresh supplies were greatly needed, so much so, that we had not once been so poor since the New Orphan-House was first opened.

Jan. 17, 1854. Received from an anonymous donor, through London bankers, a Bank Post Bill for 50l. "for general purposes." I took of this amount one half for these various objects, and the other half for the benefit of the Orphans. This donation came at a time of great need.

But the Lord helped me still mere bountifully; for I received also, on that day, the promise of the donation of 5,207l., spoken of already under the Building Fund, and of which donation I took for these objects altogether 1,500l. whereby I was so abundantly helped, that, with what the Lord was pleased to send in besides for these objects, up to May 26, 1854, I was enabled to meet all their many and heavy expenses.

The following circumstance is so remarkable, that I give it at full length as an illustration of the various ways, and the remarkable manner, in which the Lord is pleased, in answer to prayer, to supply me with means.

FOURTH PART

On Aug. 9th, 1853, I received a letter, from a Christian brother, accompanied by an order for 88l. 2s. 6d. on his bankers, of which 3l. 2s, 6d. were the proceeds of an Orphan-Box in a meeting place of believers, and 85l. from a poor widow, who had sold her little house, being all her property, and who had put 90l., the total amount she had received, into that Orphan-Box two months before, on June 9, 1853. In this box the money remained till it was opened, and then the 90l., with a few lines, without name, were found in it. As, however, the fact of her intending to sell the house, and sending me the money, for the Lord's work, had been known to the brother, who sent me the money, he did not feel free to send it to me, without remonstrating with her through two brethren, whom he sent with the money, offering it again to her; for he knew her to be very poor, and feared that this might be an act of excitement, and therefore be regretted afterwards. These brethren could not prevail on her to receive back the money, but they did persuade her to receive back 5l. of the amount, and then the brother, referred to, felt no longer free to keep the money from me, but sent me the 85l.

On the receipt of this I wrote at once to the poor Godly widow, offering her the traveling expenses for coming to Bristol, that I might have personal intercourse with her; for I feared lest this should be an act of excitement, and the more so, as she had received back 5l. of the sum. This sister in the Lord, a widow of about 60 years of age, came to Bristol, and told me in all simplicity how ten years before, in the year 1843, she had purposed that, if ever she should come into the possession of the little house in which she lived with her husband, she would sell it, and give the proceeds to the Lord. About five years afterwards her husband died, and she, having no children, nor any particular claim upon her, then sought to dispose of her little property. However one difficulty after the other prevented her being able to effect a sale. At last she felt in particular difficulty on account of her inability to pay the yearly ground rent of the house and garden, and she asked the Lord to enable her to sell the property, in order that she might be able to carry out her desire, which she had had for ten years. He now helped her; the house was sold, the money paid, and she put the whole 90l. into the Orphan Box for me, being assured that the Lord would direct me how best the money might be used for Him.--I still questioned her again and again to find out, whether it was not excitement which had led her to act as she had done; but I not only saw that her mind had been fully decided about this act for ten years before, but that she was also able to answer from the word of God all the objections which I purposely made, in order to probe her, whether she had intelligently and from right motives acted in what she had done. At last, being fully satisfied that it was not from impulse nor under excitement that she had given the money, I stated to her something like this: "You are poor, about sixty years old, and therefore decreasing in strength, may you not therefore keep this money for yourself?" Her reply was: "God has always provided for me, and I have no doubt He will do so in future also. I am able to work and to earn my bread as well as others, and am willing to work as a nurse, or in any other way." What could I say against this? This was just what a child of God would say, and should say.--But the greatest of all the difficulties about accepting the 85l. remained in my mind. It was this. The house had been sold for 90l. The whole amount had been put into the box, but, on the persuasion of the two brethren who were requested to remonstrate with this widow, she had been induced to take back 5l. out of the 90l. I therefore said to myself, might she not be willing, after a time, to take back the whole 90l., how therefore can I feel happy in accepting this money. On this account I particularly laid stress upon this point, and now learned the circumstances under which she had been induced to take back this 5l.

The two brethren who had called for the purpose of pointing out the propriety of receiving back again the 90l., or part of it, told her that Barnabas sold his land, but afterwards lived with others on that which he and others had thrown into the common stock, and that therefore she might receive at least part of the 90l. back again, if she would not take the whole. She then said to herself that, "as a child of God she might take the children's portion," and, as she had given to God this 90l., she might receive 5l. back again. She told me, that she considered the brethren had shown her from the Holy Scriptures what she might do, and therefore she had taken this 5l. I did not myself agree with the judgment of those brethren who had said this (as there is no evidence that Barnabas ever was supported out of the common stock, the proceeds of the sale of houses and lands, out of which the poor were supported); but I purposely said nothing to the widow, lest she should at once be induced to give me this 5l. also. She had, however, this 5l. untouched, and showed it to me; and before leaving she would make me take 1l. of it for the benefit of the Orphans, which I did not refuse, as I had no intention to keep the 85l. She also gave me a sixpence for the Orphans, which some one had given her for herself, a few days before.

I now asked her, as this matter concerning the remaining of the 5l. was satisfactorily explained, as far as it respected her own state of heart, what she wished me to do with the money, in case I saw it right to keep it. Her reply was, that she would leave that with me, and God would direct me concerning it; but that, if she said any thing at all, she should most like it to be used for the support of brethren who labour in the Word without salary, and who hazard their lives for the name of Christ. She wished me to have a part of the money; but this I flatly refused, lest I should be evil spoken of in this matter. I then offered to pay her traveling expenses, as she had come to me, which she would not accept, as she did not stand in need of it. In conclusion I told her, that I would now further pray respecting this matter, and consider what to do concerning it. I then prayed with this dear Godly woman, commended her to God, separated from her, and have not seen her since.

I waited from Aug. 9, 1853, to March 7, 1854, when I wrote to her, offering her back again the whole 85l., or a part of it. On March 9, 1854, just seven months after I had received the money, amid just nine months after she had actually given it, and ten years and nine months after she had made the resolution to give her house and garden to God, I heard from her, stating that she was of the same mind as she had been for years. I, therefore, disposed of the money, to aid such foreign missionary brethren as, according to the best my knowledge resembled most the class of men whom she wished to assist.

FOURTH PART

The reasons, why I have so minutely dwelt upon this circumstance, are: 1, If, as a steward of the bounties of the children of God, I should be blamed for receiving from a poor widow almost literally her all, it may be seen in what manner I did so. To have refused, on March 9, 1854, also would be going beyond what I should be warranted to do. 2, I desired also to give a practical illustration, that I only desire donations in God's way. It is not the money only, I desire; but money received, in answer to prayer, in God's order. 3, This circumstance illustrates how God helps me often in the most unexpected manner. 4, I have also related this instance, as a fresh proof, that even in these last days the love of Christ is of constraining power, and may work mightily, as in the days of the Apostles. I have witnessed many such instances as this, during the twenty years I have been occupied in this my service. Let us give thanks to God for such cases, and seek for grace rather to imitate such Godly men and women than think that they are going too far.

I cannot, however, dismiss this subject, without commending this poor widow to the prayers of all who love our Lord Jesus, that she may be kept humble, lest, thinking highly of herself, on account of what she has been enabled to do, by the grace of God, she should not only lose blessing in her own soul, but this circumstance should become a snare to her. Pray also, believing Reader, that she may never be allowed to regret what she has done for the Lord.

May 23. Yesterday I looked over the list of the 56 labourers in the Word, whom I seek to assist, in order to see to whom it would be desirable to send help; and, having drawn out a list, with the respective amounts for each, I found that it would be desirable to send out this week 327l., but I wanted at least 50l. more, to be able to accomplish this. Accordingly I gave myself to prayer, if it might please the Lord to send me the means. And now, this morning, in answer to prayer, I received anonymously from bankers in London 100l., which the donor desired to be applied for the current expenses for the Orphans, and for labourers in the Gospel at Home and Abroad. I took therefore 50l. for the Orphans, and 50l. for home and foreign labourers.

By the same post I received also from the neighbourhood of Shrewsbury 10l., the disposal of which being left to me, I took for missionary objects.--I have now the desire of my heart granted, being able to send out the full amount of what it yesterday appeared to me desirable that I should send to the brethren whom I seek to help.

Means for the support of the 300 Orphans, already under our care, sent in answer to prayer, from May 26, 1853, to May 26, 1854.

At the commencement of this period, there was in hand the balance of 117l. 10s. 9d. This was the visible support, in the way of pecuniary means, which we had to look to for 320 inmates in the New Orphan House, whilst often two or three days might call for such an amount as this. But we hoped in God, as in former years, and, by His grace, were upheld, and our faith was not allowed to fail, though it was not a little tried, as the following pages will show.

Of the donations which came in between May 26, and June. 13, 1853, I will only mention the following. On June 1st I received from Cape Town 2l. for the Orphans, and 3l. for tracts. On June 8th I received from Rhode Island, United States, 20 dollars and 5 dollars (4l. 15s. 9d. English), when I had scarcely anything left for the Orphans. Observe, dear Reader, from Africa and from America the Lord sends help to us, yea from almost all parts of the world. Thus is He saying to us more and more; "Only believe." On June 10th I received 5l. from a brother in the Lord at a distance, as a thank-offering to God, that, having been thrown from his horse, he had not been killed, but only greatly hurt.

June. 13. We were now very poor. Not indeed in debt, nor was even all the money gone; for there was still about 12l. in hand; but then there needed to be bought flour, of which we buy generally 10 sacks at a tine, 300 stones of oatmeal, 4 cwt. of soap, and there were many little repairs going on in the house, with a number of workmen, besides the regular current expenses of about 70l. per week. Over and above all this, on Saturday, the day before yesterday, I found that the heating apparatus needed to be repaired, which would cost in all probability 25l. It was therefore desirable, humanly speaking, to have 100l. for these heavy extra expenses, besides means for the current expenses. But I had no human prospect whatever of getting even 100 Pence, much less 100l. In addition to this, today was Monday, when generally the income is little. But, in walking to the Orphan House this morning, and praying as I went, I particularly told the Lord in prayer, that on this day, though Monday, He could send me much. And thus it was. I received this morning 301l. for the Lord's service, as might be most needed.--The joy which I had cannot be described. I walked up and down in my room for a long time, tears of joy and gratitude to the Lord running plentifully over my cheeks, praising and magnifying the Lord for His goodness, and surrendering myself afresh, with all my heart, to Him for His blessed service. I scarcely ever felt more the kindness of the Lord in helping me.--I took of this money 201l., for the current expenses for the Orphans, and 100l. for missionary objects, the circulation of the Holy Scriptures and Gospel Tracts, and for the various Schools.

Of the donations which came in between June 13th and Aug. 31st, amounting to more than 600l., I will only mention: 50l., through a most unexpected circumstance, from Glasgow, on June 29th. 2l. from Sunderland on July 23rd, of which 1l was made up, by an individual putting by one half-penny daily for the Orphans, and a poor widow one penny per week. -- On Aug. 19th I received from a Christian Negro in Demerara an old silver watch, a gold pin and brooch, and Five Dollars.

Aug. 31. When there was less than 20l. in, hand, I received today a donation of 220l., of which the donor kindly wished me to take 20l. for my own personal expenses, and to use the other for the work of the Lord as most needed. I therefore took 150l. for the Orphans, and 50l. for the other objects, and was thus enabled to advance today 30l., as usual, for the house-keeping expenses; money being called for, which, otherwise, I should not have been able to supply.

Of the donations received between Aug. 31st and Oct. 24th, amounting to about 550l., I only notice 2l. 7s. 6d. "From South Africa," 1l. from Malta, and 6s. 4d. from Demerara.

I will now minutely relate the Lord's dealings with us, with reference to meeting the expenses for the 300 Orphans, for about three weeks, as a specimen of how the Lord was pleased to help us during a period when the flour was twice as dear as for several years before, and when other expenses were much greater than usual.

Oct. 24. This afternoon I was called on to advance more house-keeping money; but as I had only about 26l. altogether in hand, I could only give 20l. this time, instead of the usual 30l. I had then about 6l. left for all the many other expenses, large and small, connected with the Establishment, and which are not included in the ordinary house-keeping expenses. Before the day is over, I have received this evening the following amounts Through Salem boxes 1s. By sale of Reports 5s. 1d. with 10s. as a donation. Both sums from Waterford.--From a donor in Bristol 1l.--From Bayswater 5l.

Oct. 25. From an Orphan-box in Bristol 4s.--From Warminster 1l. 1s. -- From Seven Oaks 1l.1s. 6d. This was an old debt, owed for a long time to the donor. He expressed in prayer that, if the Lord would cause the money to be paid, it should be sent to me; and almost immediately afterwards it was paid.--From Durham 12l., being a dividend on shares in gas-works.--From Braunton 5s.--From Balham Hill, London, 1l. 10s., with a variety of articles to be sold for the benefit of the Orphans.--By sale of Reports 2s.

Oct. 26. From Keswick 7s. 6d., 2s. 6d., 1s. 6d., and 3s.--By sale of Reports 1l. 2s. 11 1/2 d.--By sale of some silver coins, a few tea spoons, and a few trinkets 5l.--By sale of Reports 9s.--There was found in the visitor's room at the New Orphan House a four-penny piece.--Through the boxes in the New Orphan House 4l. 14s. This afternoon was the time in the week when visitors see the establishment. It was a wet afternoon, but still above 60 persons went over the house. Being in great need of means, of which the visitors, however, could perceive nothing, as all our stores were full as usual, I asked the Lord, that He would be pleased to put it into their hearts to put money into the boxes: and this sum I found in them this evening.--Yesterday it was necessary to purchase ten sacks of flout, which, being just now twice as dear as darning the last years, cost 27l. 10s.; and this day it was needful to spend 8l. 1s. 2d. for smith's work. How kind, therefore, of the Lord to have sent me today, yesterday, and the afternoon of the day before yesterday, 34l. 11s, 4 1/2 d. Thus, with the 6l. left before, I am able to meet these two items of above 35l., and have about 5l. left.

Now observe how the Lord further helped, when I had only Five Pounds left.

THE LORD'S DEALINGS WITH GEORGE MÜLLER

Oct. 27. By sale of Reports 3s.--From West Brixton 5s., and 5s. from Scotland.--Through a box in the New Orphan House 6d.--By sale of a Report 6d.

Oct. 28. "From Friends of Petersham" 1l. 2s. 6d., and from Richmond 7s. 6d.--From the neighbourhood of Stourbridge. 1l.--From Wells 3s. -- From a clergyman at Weston-super-Mare 5l.--Anonymously from Scotland 6d.--From a brother in the Lord 1l., with two pewter plates. -- From Clifton 10s.--From Hackney 1s.

Oct. 29. From Chilton Polden 5s., as "A thank-offering that the donor's children have not been left Orphans."--From Kingsbridge 5s. 6d.--From Glasgow 7s. 6d.--By sale of articles and Reports 2l. 10s.--From Royston 1l.

Oct. 30. From Lichfield 2s. 6d. and 3s. 8d.--From a medical gentleman in Bristol 1l.--From Clifton 3s.

Oct. 31. This afternoon more money was required for house-keeping. By the donations which had come in since the 27th, I was able to pay away 7l. 13s., and 1l. 2s., and had 12l. 17s, 2d. besides. This I gave to the last penny for house-keeping, and had now literally not one penny left in hand for the current expenses for the Orphans.

This evening I received, when I had nothing in hand: from Clifton 1l. -- From a sister in the Lord in Bristol 2s. 6d.--Through Bethesda boxes 5s., "from servants in Scotland,"--From Wiveliscombe 1l.-- From Clifton 10s.--Through the Chapel boxes 2s.--A pair of silver-mounted spectacles and 2s. 6d. from Clifton.

Nov. 1. By means of those little sums, which came in last evening, I was able to let the matron have further 2l. 17s. early this morning. Thus we were able to meet this day's demands. There came in further today: By sale of old clothes 6s. 4d., and from Launceston, by sale of Reports, 7s. 6d.--There was put into the letter box at my house anonymously, 1s. 6d., with these words: "I had worked hard for this money, and could not get paid. A thought passed lately through my mind, if I ever get it, I will devote it to some charitable purpose. To my surprise, without asking for it, it is paid. I now send it for the Orphans."--Evening. By sale of Reports 3s.--From Spaldwick 2s. 6d. and 1s.--From the neighbourhood of Arundel 11s. 6d.

Nov. 2. From Hull 5s.--From Knapp 1s.--From Gosport 2l.--From six servants at Hampton Court Palace, a parcel, containing a variety of articles, for the use of the Orphans, or to be sold for their benefit, with 4s. --Through the boxes in the New Orphan House 1l. 16s. 5 1/2 d. Given also by a visitor from Cornwall 10s., Ditto by another 10s., Ditto by another 2s. 6d., Ditto by another 1s.--By sale of Reports 6s.-- I was thus further able to advance last evening for house-keeping expenses 1l. 0s. 4d., this morning 3l. 1s., and this evening 3l. 12s. 11 1/2 d. Thus, though we are living by the day, as it respects supplies out of the hands of our Heavenly Father, yet we have lacked nothing!

FOURTH PART

Received further 12s. by sale of Reports.

Nov. 3. From Helensburgh 2s. and 6d.--From Bideford 12s.--From Islington 2l.--From Clifton Park 5l.--By sale of some books 3l. -- From a donor in Bristol 5l. From Norwich 5s.--Thus we have wherewith to meet the expenses for today and tomorrow, and, it may be, of the day after tomorrow. At all events, before this is gone, the faithful Lord will send in more.

Nov. 4. By sale of old clothes 11s. 2 1/2 d.--From Whitby 1l. Ditto 5s.--From Bodmin 1s.--By sale of rags 7s. 3d. [I transcribe from the Income book. We think it right to turn every thing to account, so that nothing be wasted, and that the expenses of the Institution be not needlessly increased.]

Nov. 5. From Swansea 5s.--From Willenhall 5s.--From Bridgewater 5s.--From Worcester 5s. and 1s.--Evening, Saturday. Thus we have had during another week everything needed.

Nov. 7. There came in yesterday 1s. from Stafford, and 3s. from Worksop. -- To day from Kilkenny 1l.--When I had nothing at all in hand, having paid out the last money today, and when more would be needed this evening or tomorrow morning, I received this afternoon, from a most unexpected quarter, 6l. This morning the matron had between 11l, and 12l. in hand for house-keeping expenses, but, by the time I arrived at the New Orphan House, it had all been expended through unexpected demands, so that she had had to add half a crown of her own. I had received, however, this morning, at the very time while I was in prayer for means, 1l. from Kilkenny, which, with, 9s. 3 1/2 d. besides, in hand, I gave to her. Now this afternoon came in the 6l., and we have thus a manifest answer to prayer. The Lord be magnified.-- Evening. Through Salem boxes 1s. Through Bethesda boxes 2s. 6d. Do. 6d. From P. 2s. 6d.

Nov. 8. From Guildford 1l. 1s.

Nov. 9. By sale of Reports 3s. 6d.--From Clonmell 9s. 5d.--Our need of means is great, very great. The Lord tries our faith and patience. This afternoon, a brother and sister in the Lord, from Gloucestershire, called to see me at the New Orphan House, before going through the house. After a few minutes I received from the sister a sovereign, which she had been requested to bring to me for the Building Fund, and she gave me from herself 1l. for my own personal expenses, and 1l. for tine Building Fund, and her husband gave me 5l. for the Orphans, and 5l. for Foreign Missions. Thus the Lord has refreshed my spirit greatly; but I look for more, and need much more.--Evening. By sale of Reports 13s. 2d. By the boxes in the New Orphan House 3l. 1s. 10 1/2 d. I received also this evening from Walmer 10l., of which the donor kindly wished 2l. to be used for the personal expenses of my family, and the rest for missionary work and the support of the Orphans. I took therefore one half for missions, and the other half for the Orphans.

Nov. 10. From Oakhill 5s.--By sale of Reports 15s. 10d.--From Swansea 10s., 4s., and 6s.--From Anglesey 5s. and 2s. 6d.--From Bath 2l.

Nov. 11. Anonymously from Banbury 1l.

Nov. 12. From Bideford 1l.--From Perth 1l. This evening, while praying for means, came a little parcel, containing Ten Sovereigns, from a Christian lady, living not far frown the New Orphan House. This was a very great refreshment to my spirit. Also from Clydach 10s. and 1s.

Nov. 13. Further precious help. Received this morning through Bankers in London, an anonymous donation of 50l. in a Bank Post Bill, with the words: "To be applied to general purposes; to be used as you may judge best." I took therefore the whole of this donation for the current expenses of the Orphans. A most welcome and refreshing donation, the fruit of many prayers, as just now the expenses are very great, and there were no means in hand to meet them! From Clifton 16s. 5d. From Easton 5l.

Nov. 14. From Melton Mowbray 2s. By sale of Reports 1s.--From Norwich 2s. 6d. Ditto 2s. 6d.--From Kingsbridge two brooches--Through the boxes at Bethesda 1s.--From Clevedon 1l.--From F. E. B. 2s. 6d.

Nov. 15. Anonymously from Nottingham 10s.--From Cheltenham 5l.-- From the Isle of Wight 10s.--This evening I received from a Christian lady a brooch set with amethysts, another brooch set with eight brilliants and six other small diamonds, and a small gold necklace. My heart was exceedingly refreshed by this donation, not only because we arc still in need of supplies on account of our heavy daily expenses just now; but also because this valuable donation consists of articles which the Christian donor can spare, without the slightest inconvenience.

Nov. 16. Anonymously in postages 3s. 6d.--From London 10l., with 5l. for my own expenses.--By sale of Reports 7s.--Left by a visitor from Aberdeen, at the New Orphan House 10s. Through the boxes at the New Orphan House 2l. 11s. 6 1/2 d.--From South Brent 1s. 6d.

I have thus given, minutely, the manner in which the Lord was pleased, for 24 days in succession to supply us with means for the Orphans, from which the spiritual reader may easily perceive our position. Thus it was with us not merely during the 24 days of which I have now given the history, but also to a greater or less degree at other times during this year. But I refrain from giving minutely the account of every day, for the sake of brevity.

The particular end, why I have been so minute, is to show that the work is now, as much as ever, a work carried on entirely in dependence upon the Living God, who alone is our hope, and to whom alone we look for help, and who never has forsaken us in the hour of need. There is, however, one thing different with reference

FOURTH PART

to this year, when compared with former years, and that is, that, while our trials of faith during this year were just as great as in previous years, the amount needed in former times was never so great as during this year, especially as the bread during the greater part of this year was about twice as dear as for several years before.

But then, it may be said, if you have had this trial of faith, with these 300 Orphans, why do you seek to build another Orphan House for 700 more, and thus have a thousand to care for? Will you not have still greater trials of faith?

My reply is: 1, God has never failed me all the 20 years of this my service. 2, I am going on as easily now, with 300 Orphans, as with 30, the number with which I commenced. Their number is ten times as large, as it was at the first; but God has always helped me. 3, Trials of faith were anticipated, yea were one chief end of the work, for the profit of the Church of Christ at large. 4, I had courage given me to go forward, solely in dependence upon God, being assured that He would help me; yet I waited in secret upon Him for six months, before I made this my intention known, in order that I might not take a hasty step; and have never regretted having gone forward. 5, But it needs to be added, that the very abundance which the Lord gave me at the time, when my mind was exercised about this matter, was a great confirmation to me, that I had not mistaken His mind. And even during this year, how great has been His help; for the income for the work altogether has been 12,785l. 15s. 7 1/4 d. I am therefore assured that the Lord will, in His own time, not only allow me to build another Orphan House, but that He will also, when He shall have been pleased to fill it, find the means to provide for these children.

I give now a brief reference to some of the more remarkable donations which came in between Nov. 16, 1853, and May 26, 1854.

Jan. 1, 1854. Received three old guinea pieces, with the following words: "The enclosed has been too long held in reserve, as an esteemed memento from a dear departed parent (for which may the Lord grant a pardon). A conviction of its wrong overpowers the natural desire, of its being retained, and not expended to the glory of God: for which purpose it is now sent to dear Mr. Mueller, as a new year offering, to be used in the way he thinks most conducive to the same,"--In this instance I had a double answer to prayer; for we were not only much in need of means, when the donation came in, but I had also again and again asked the Lord to incline the hearts of His dear children to send me their jewellery, their old gold and silver coins, and other valuable, but needless, articles, to be turned into money for the work of the Lord.

Jan. 17. Memorable day. Today, in much need, was received from Glasgow 10l., with 10l. for Mr. Craik, and 10l. for my own personal expenses. -- There came in also, a Bank Post Bill for 50l., anonymously, through London Bankers, which amount was taken half for the Orphans and half for the other objects.--Likewise from Stroud 10s.--From Reading 6s. 3d.--From Gloucester 2s. 6d.--But the Lord over and above all this, allowed me to have this day the promise of that large donation which has been spoken of under the Building Fund, of which 707l. was taken towards the support of the Orphans, by which, together with 1,119l. 8s. 2 1/2 d. which came in for the support of the Orphans from Jan. 17 up to May 26, 1854, we were helped to the close of this period.

March 1. There was left to me, for the benefit of the Orphans, a year ago, by an individual in Bristol, whom I had never seen, a legacy of 100l., which was paid this day, less 10l. legacy duty.

April 9. This morning I received from an anonymous donor, through Bankers in London, a Bank Post Bill for 50l., the application of which was left to me. I took the whole of it for the support of the Orphans. This donation has been a great spiritual refreshment to me, as the expenses for the Orphans are now so very great, and as for five weeks no large sums have come in.

April 17. Received 150l., of which the donor kindly wished me to take 20l. for my own personal expenses, and to use the rest as might be most needed for the Lord's work in my hands. I took, therefore, 100l. for the current expenses for the Orphans, and 30l. for the other Objects. -- This donation has greatly refreshed my spirit, as the expenses for the Orphans were never so great at any period, since the work commenced, as during the last six mouths, on account of the high price of provisions; and as the income, compared with the expenses, has been small of late, though considerable, were not the expenses so very great.

May 14. This morning I have received 150l., of which I have taken for the current expenses for the Orphans 100l., and for the other objects 50l.--Tomorrow I shall have to pay out for the Orphans 107l. 4s. The total amount I had in hand for them, before this donation was received, was only 120l. How kind, therefore, of the Lord to replenish our means again, before they were almost entirely exhausted!--I received, also, this morning from Clifton 5l.

During the following 12 days there came in further 107l. altogether for the support of the Orphans.

Miscellaneous points respecting the Scriptural Knowledge Institution for Home and Abroad, with reference to the period from May 26, 1853, to May 26, 1854.

1. During this year 4 Day Schools, with 202 children, were entirely supported by the funds of the Institution. Further, one Sunday School in Bristol, with 137 children, was entirely supported, and three others in Devonshire, Somersetshire, and Gloucestershire, with 300 children, were assisted. Lastly, one Adult School, with 154 Adult scholars, was entirely supported. The total amount which was spent during this year, in connexion with these schools, was 359l. 15s. 10 1/2 d.--The number of all the children, who were under our care, merely in the schools which were entirely supported by this Institution, from March 5,1834, to May 26, 1854, was 5,817 in the

FOURTH PART

Day Schools, and 2,748 in the Sunday Schools, and 2,315 persons in the Adult School.

2. During this year was expended on the circulation of the Holy Scriptures, of the funds of the Institution, 433l. 2s. 9d. There were circulated during this year 1890 Bibles and 1288 New Testaments; and from the commencement of the work up to May 26, 1854, Twelve Thousand Three Hundred and Sixty-six Bibles, and Seven Thousand Three Hundred and Forty-nine New Testaments.

3. During this year there was spent of the Funds of the Institution for Missionary objects the sum of 2,249l. 10s. 8 1/2 d. By this sum, fifty-six labourers in the word and doctrine, in various parts of the world, were to a greater or less degree assisted.

During this year, the Lord was pleased to bless again abundantly the labours of many of those servants of Christ, who were assisted through the funds of this Institution, and this has been the case in foreign countries as well as at home.

4. There was laid out for the circulation of Tracts, from May 26, 1853, to May 26, 1854, the sum of 563l. 5s. 0 1/2 d.; and there were circulated 869,636 Tracts.

The total number of all time Tracts circulated from the beginning up to May 26, 1854, was Two Millions Six Hundred and Eighty-nine Thousand Six Hundred and Seventy-six.

We desire to be grateful to the Lord, that, during no period previously we were enabled to circulate more Tracts, and more copies of the Holy Scriptures, and aid to a greater degree missionary labours, than during this period; yet we would not rest in that. It is the blessing of the Lord upon our labours which we need, which we desire, and which, by His grace, we also seek. If never so many millions of Tracts, yea even copies of the Holy Scriptures, were circulated, and the Lord did not give His blessing, all these efforts would produce no results to the glory of His name. Yea, if even tens of thousands of preachers of the gospel could be supported with means, in the darkest places of the earth, and they enjoyed not the blessing of the Lord upon their labours, they would labour in vain. For this blessing God will be asked, in order that He may bestow it; but, when it is sought at His hands, He delights in giving it. By God's help we were enabled to seek this blessing, and we obtained again precious answers to our prayers, during this year. It is not merely that the Lord was pleased to give us answers to our prayers with regard to means for carrying on the work; but also in that the various objects of the Scriptural Knowledge Institution were abundantly blessed to the conversion of very many souls; and this was particularly also the case again with reference to the circulation of Tracts.

If any of the Christian Readers are in the habit of circulating Tracts, and yet have never seen fruit, may I suggest to them the following hints for their prayerful consideration. 1, Seek for such a state of heart, through Prayer and meditation on the

Holy Scriptures, as that you are willing to let God have all the honour, if any good is accomplished by your service. If you desire for yourself the honour, yea, though it were in part only, you oblige the Lord, so to speak, to put you as yet aside as a vessel not meet for the Master's use. One of the greatest qualifications for usefulness in the service of the Lord is a heart, truly desirous of getting honour for Him. 2, Precede all your labours with earnest, diligent prayer; go to them in a prayerful spirit; and follow them by prayer. Do not rest on the number of Tracts you have given. A million of Tracts may not be the means of converting one single soul; and yet how great, beyond calculation, may be the blessing which results from one single Tract. Thus it is also with regard to the circulation of the Holy Scriptures, and the ministry of the Word itself. Expect, then, everything from the blessing of the Lord, and nothing at all from your own exertions. 3, And yet, at the same time, labour, press into every open door, be instant in season and out of season, as if everything depended upon your labours. This, as has been stated before, is one of the great secrets in connexion with successful service for the Lord; to work, as if everything depended upon our diligence, and yet not to rest in the least upon our exertions, but upon the blessing of the Lord. 4, This blessing of the Lord, however, should not merely be sought in prayer, but should also be expected, looked for, continually looked for; and the result will be, that we shall surely have it. 5, But suppose, that, for the trial of our faith, this blessing were for a long time withheld from our sight; or suppose even that we should have to fall asleep, before we see much good resulting from our labours; yet will they, if carried on in such a way and spirit as has been stated, be at last abundantly owned, and we shall have a much harvest in the day of Christ.

Now, dear Christian Reader, if you have not seen much blessing resulting from your labours, or perhaps none at all, consider prayerfully these hints, which are affectionately given by one who has now for about thirty years [in 1856] in some measure sought to serve the Lord, and who has found the blessedness, of what he has suggested, in some measure in his own experience.

5. At the beginning of this period, there were Three Hundred Orphans in the New Orphan House on Ashley Down, Bristol. During the year there were admitted into it 30 Orphans; making 330 in all. Of these 330, four died, three were received back again by their relatives, who by that time were able to provide for them, 17 boys were, at the expense of the establishment, fitted out and apprenticed, and eight girls were fitted out and sent to situations, at the expense of the Establishment; so that there were only 298 Orphans in the house at the close of the period. The total number of Orphans, who were under our care from April, 1836, to May 26, 1854, was Five Hundred and Fifty Eight.

I notice further the following points in connexion with the New Orphan House.

A. The expenses during this year, for the support of the Orphans, were 3,897l. 2s. 0 1/2 d.

FOURTH PART

B. Without any one having been personally applied to for anything by me, the sum of 64,591l. 6s. 11 1/4 d. was given to me for the Orphans as the result of prayer to God from the commencement of the work up to May 26, 1854.--It may be also interesting to the reader to know that the total amount given for the other objects, from the commencement of the work up to May 26, 1854, was 22,268l. 2s 11 1/4 d.; and that which came in by the sale of Bibles and Tracts, and by the payments of the children in the Day Schools, from the commencement up to May 26, 1854, amounted to 3,989l. 4s. 5 3/4 d.--Besides this, also, a great variety and number of articles of clothing, furniture, provisions, &c., were given for the use of the Orphans.

C. Our labours continued to be blessed among the Orphans. We saw also again fruit of our labours, during this year, with regard to Orphans who formerly were under our care.

Matters connected with my own personal affairs, from May 26, 1853, to May 26, 1854.

In July 1853 it pleased the Lord to try my faith in a way in which before it had not been tried. My beloved daughter, an only child, and a believer since the commencement of the year 1846, was taken ill on June 20th. This illness, at first a low fever, turned to typhus. On July 3rd there seemed no hope of her recovery. Now was the trial of faith. But faith triumphed. My beloved wife and I were enabled to give her up into the hands of the Lord. He sustained us both exceedingly. But I will only speak about myself. Though my only and beloved child was brought near the grave, yet was my soul inn perfect peace, satisfied with the will of my Heavenly Father, being assured that He would only do that for her and her parents, which in the end would be the best. She continued very ill till about July 20th, when restoration began. On Aug. 18th she was so far restored, that she could be removed to Clevedon for change of air, though exceedingly weak. It was then 59 days mince she was first taken ill.

While I was in this affliction, this great affliction, besides being at peace, so far as the Lord's dispensation was concerned, I also felt perfectly at peace with regard to the cause of the affliction. When in August 1831 the hand of the Lord was heavily laid on me in my family, as related in the first part of this Narrative, I had not the least hesitation in knowing, that it was the Father's rod, applied in infinite wisdom and love, for the restoration of my soul from a state of lukewarmness. At this time, however, I had no such feeling. Conscious as I was of manifold weaknesses, failings, and shortcomings, so that I too would be ready to say with the Apostle Paul, "O wretched man that I am;" yet I was assured that this affliction was not upon me in the way of the fatherly rod, but for the trial of my faith. Persons often have, no doubt, the idea respecting me, that all my trials of faith regard matters connected with money, though the reverse has been stated by me very frequently; now, however, the Lord would try my faith concerning one of my dearest earthly treasures, yea, next to my beloved wife, the dearest of all my earthly possessions. Parents know what an only child, a beloved child is, and what to believing parents an only child, a believing child must be. Well, the Father in heaven said, as it were, by this His dispensation, Art thou willing to give up this child to me? My heart responded, As it seems good to Thee my Heavenly Father. Thy will be done. But as our hearts were made willing to give back our beloved child to Him who had given her to us, so He was ready to leave her to us, and she lived. "Delight thyself also in the Lord; and He shall give thee the desires of thine heart." Psalm xxxvii. 4. The desires of my heart were, to retain the beloved daughter, if it were the will of God; the means to retain her were, to be satisfied with the will of the Lord.

Of all the trials of faith that as yet I have had to pass through, this was the greatest; amid by God's abundant mercy, I own it to His praise, I was enabled to delight myself in the will of God; for I felt perfectly sure, that, if the Lord took this beloved daughter, it would be best for her parents, best for herself, and more for the glory of God than if she lived: this better part I was satisfied with; and thus my heart had peace, perfect peace, and I had not a moment's anxiety. Thus would it be under all circumstances, however painful, were the believer exercising faith.

Dec. 31, 1853. During this year the Lord was pleased to give me

1. By anonymous donations through the boxes	. L177 9 7 1/2
2. Through donations from believers in Bristol, not anonymously	143 3 0
3. Through donations from believers not residing in Bristol	299 16 1
4. Through presents in clothes, provisions, &c., worth at least	18 3 0
	L638 11 8 1/2

Further account respecting the intended Orphan I-louse for Seven Hundred Poor Orphans, bereaved of both Parents by death, from May 26, 1854, to May 26, 1855.

On May 26, 1854, I had actually in hand for this intended Orphan House, as has been stated in the last chapter on this subject, 17,816l. 19s. 5 1/4 d. I will now relate further, how the Lord was pleased to supply me with means, but can only refer, for the sake of brevity, to a few instances out of many. The receipts of the first month of this year, however, shall be given entirely, as a specimen.

May 29, 1854. Through Salem Chapel boxes 6d.

May 31. From Finchdean 5l.

June 1. Through the boxes at Bethesda Chapel 1l.--Ditto from P. and M. E. 10s.--From London 1s. 6d.

FOURTH PART

June 4. A gold dollar piece and nearly two pennyweights of Californian gold dust.

June 5. Through Bethesda Chapel boxes 2s. 6d. as a thank-offering to the Lord for the mercies of the past month.--Through Salem Chapel boxes 1s.--Ditto 6d.--From P. 2s.

June 7. Anonymously through London Bankers 100l.--Through the boxes at the New Orphan House 1s.

June. 8. From E. 2s. 6d.--Anonymously 2s.

June. 12. Through Bethesda boxes 3s.--Ditto 1s.--Ditto 1l.-- Through Salem boxes 6d.

June 14. Through the boxes at the New Orphan House 5s.--Ditto 1/4 d.

June 17. By sale of articles 17s. 7d.

June 18. 3s.--5s.

June-19. 15s.

June 22. A muslin cap, a cape, some worked trimming, and two bags, to be sold for the Building Fund.

June 25. From Glasgow 2s. 6d.--From K. C. 10s.

June 26. Anonymously 2s. 2d.--Through Salem boxes 6d.--From P. 1s.

These were but little sums, esteemed reader, in comparison with the total amount required for the accommodation of 700 more Orphans; yea, they were even small in comparison with what was still required, though I had then nearly 18,000l. in hand. But as it had been given to me, by God's grace, to expect help from Him, yea, the full help needed for this object, so the additional income of a few pounds, of a few shillings, yea of a penny or two, was an encouragement to me for further waiting upon Him, as every donation, the smallest even, brings me nearer the time when all my prayers concerning this object also shall be turned into praises.

July 1. A large gold brooch, set with two carbuncles, to be sold for the Building Fund.

July 2. Anonymously through London Bankers 100l.--From Bury 10s.

July 19. A silver tea pot.

Sept. 27. From one of the former Orphans, now in service, 5s.--From the Orphan Girls, now under our care, 15s. for the Building Fund.-- From the House Girls, i.e. the elder female Orphans, who are more particularly engaged in doing household work, for the purpose of being thus trained for situations, I received likewise 11s.--From the Infant Orphans was also received for the Building Fund today, 6s. 8d.; and from the Orphan Boys 15s, 0 1/2 d.--Oct. 4. From two little factory girls 1s. 7d.

Oct. 28. From Halifax in Nova Scotia 7l.

Nov. 25. From the neighbourhood of Wheatley 10l.

Dec. 8. From various believers at Hull 12l. 12s.

Dee. 30. From Orleans, in France, five francs.

Thus ended the year 1854. Only 426l. 16s. 4d. altogether had come in for the Building Fund from May 26 up to the end of the year. My faith and patience were therefore tried; but, while they were tried, they were, by God's grace, sustained. Day by day I had been enabled from May 26 to Dec. 31, 1854, as well as during the three years previously, to bring this object before the Lord in player; and day by day, by God's grace, my heart had been fully assured, without wavering, that He, in His own time, would not only give larger sums, but the whole amount required. I desired only His honour in the building of premises for 700 more destitute Orphans, bereaved of both parents; and as God, who cares infinitely more for poor Orphans than I do, did not consider the time to have come for the building of another house, I might well be quiet. My heart longed indeed to begin to build; for there were not only 602 Orphans waiting for admission, when the last report was published but there had been application made for 125 more since then, so that on Dec. 31, 1854, 714 were waiting for admission, as only 13 could be received of the total number of 727, no more vacancies having occurred. But though it was so, I judged it was the will of God, that, by patiently waiting His own time, I should glorify Him.--I now proceed to relate how the Lord further dealt with me.

Jan. 1, 1855. 6s. 3d.--From an Orphan 1s., Ditto 1s.--From Manchester 10s.--From three children in Ireland 5s.--Anonymously from Culworth 1l.--From P. 2s. 6d.

Jan. 8. On this day I received from several Christian friends the promise, that 5,700l. should be paid to me for the work of the Lord in which I am engaged.--This donation was paid to me, in different installments, by the middle of April. I took of this sum, for the Building fund 3,400l., for the support of the Orphans 900l., for missionary objects 1,000l., for the circulation of the Holy Scriptures 150l., for the circulation of Tracts 150l., and for the various day schools, Sunday schools, and the adult school 100l. Thus the Lord is hastening on the time when the building may be commenced. His name be magnified! How refreshing this help was, and how seasonable with regard to all the various objects, can scarcely be described. The Lord

FOURTH PART

may allow us, to have our faith and patience tried; but if we are enabled to continue to look to Him, and to trust in Him alone, a rich recompense will result from doing so.

Jan. 11. From a distance of several hundred miles 13l. 15s, with a letter containing the following paragraph: For the last six months, we (i.e. the donor and his wife) have laboured in prayer for the different departments of the Scriptural Knowledge Institution, and especially that our Heavenly Father would be pleased this year largely to increase the Building Fund, and let the work proceed. Two months ago, while continuing in prayer, it was laid upon our minds, that we should set apart, whatever monies the Lord might send us between that time and the new year. The sum contained in the order is what the Lord has given us and we rejoice in being able to send it." What various ways has the Lord to help us! The donor of the 13l. 15s. is a brother who serves the Lord in the ministry of the Gospel among very poor and wretched persons, whilst he labours in dependence upon Him for his temporal supplies. He has been greatly encouraged by the accounts of the Lord's dealings with the Scriptural Knowledge Institution; and now he is a fellow-helper in prayer, and, as this instance shows, also in contributing out of that which the Lord gives to him as the fruit of prayer. This donation greatly refreshed my spirit; for it is so manifest a proof that the Lord is mindful of this work, that He surely, in His own time, will provide for the accommodation of 700 more Orphans, and that thus this dear donor's prayers, and our prayers, will be turned into praises.

Feb. 7. From London 400l., of which the donor kindly wished me to keep 20l. for my family expenses, and to lay out the 380l. for the Lord's work, as I might think best. I took therefore 100l for the Building Fund, 140l. for the support of the Orphans, and 140l. for the other objects.

Feb. 10. Received 197l. 17s. 3d., of which the donor kindly wished me to take 20l. for my own expenses, and the rest to be used as might be most needed for the Lord's work. I took therefore 57l. 17s. 3d. for the Building Fund, 60l. for the support of the Orphans and 60l. for the other objects.

March 28. From one of the Orphans, formerly for many years under our care, but now in service, 10s., with the following letter:

"Dear Sir,--Will you graciously accept this mite from one who thinks of you and yours with gratitude. It is indeed a very small sum. I regret that I have no more to bestow upon such a noble work. It will perhaps put a corner stone in the wall of the intended Orphan House. I think I should like to labour for the Lord in that blessed house, if it is His own will, and be the means in the Lord's hand of bringing many of the dear Orphans to know the truth as it is in Jesus. It was in the Orphan House in Wilson Street, 1846, that first the light of life dawned upon my benighted soul. It was there, that I first learned to call God my Father. I have need therefore to love the Orphan House, not only as concerning temporal things, but especially as its being my spiritual birth-place. May the Lord reward you, dear Sir, for all you have done for me. I am sure He will.

"I am, dear Sir, yours most respectfully,

"* * * * * * * *"

I have at full length inserted this letter out of very many of that kind, received during the past twenty years, that I have been engaged in the Orphan work, for many of the Orphans who have been with us since. April 11, 1836, have not only been fitted for this life, through being under our care, but have been manifestly brought to the knowledge of the Lord.

April 22. 50l., with 50l. for the labourers in the Gospel.

May 6. From Clifton 20l., with 10l. for missions.--May 26. By the sale of a publication 69l. 18s. 1 1/2 d.--To the sums received during this year is to be added 767l. 7s. 0d., received for interest. Thus ends the period from May 26, 1854, to May 26, 1855. The amount which came in during this year for the Building Fund, together with the 17,816l. 19s. 5 1/4 d. in hand on May 26, 1854, make the total of 23,059l. 17s. 8 1/4 d. in hand on May 26, 1855.

In. addition to what has been stated relative to the income for the Building Fund during this year, I furnish the Reader with the following particulars respecting the building for 700 Orphans, reprinted from the Report for 1855.

When I had received the kind information, in January 1855, respecting the donation of 5700l., which should be paid to me by several Christian friends, of which I was at liberty to take such portion for the Building Fund as I might deem desirable, I judged that, though I had not such an amount of means in hand as I considered necessary before being warranted to begin to build, yet that I might make inquiries respecting land. Accordingly, I applied in the beginning of February for the purchase of two fields which join the land on which the New Orphan-House is built. On these two fields I had had my eye for years, and had purposed to endeavour to purchase them, whenever I might be in such a position as to means for the Building Fund, that it would be suitable to do so. I found, however, that, according to the will of the late owner of these fields, they could not be sold now. Thus my prospects were blighted. When I obtained this information, though naturally tried by it and disappointed, I said, by God's grace, to myself: "The Lord has something better to give me, instead of these two fields;" and thus my heart was kept in peace. But when now the matter was fully decided that I could not obtain those fields, which had appeared to me so desirable for the object, the question arose, what I was to do for the obtaining of land. Under these circumstances some of my Christian friends again asked, as they had done before, why I did not build on the ground which we have around the New Orphan-House? My reply was, as before, that it could not be done:--1. Because it

FOURTH PART

would throw the New Orphan-House for nearly two years into disorder on account of the building going on round about it. 2. There would not be sufficient room without shutting in the present house to a great extent. 3. That, as the New Orphan-House stands in the centre of our ground, there would not be sufficient room on any of the sides for the erection of a building so large as would be required.--I was, however, led to consider whether there was any way whereby we could accomplish the building on the ground belonging to the New Orphan-House. In doing so, I found that--1. By having a high temporary boundary made of old boards, the building ground could be entirely distinct from the present establishment. 2. By building on an entirely different plan from that of the present house, we should not only have room enough; but that also, 3. The present house would not be so enclosed that the health of the inmates of the establishment would thereby be injured.

But there was in connexion with this another point, which now came under consideration in addition to the particulars already mentioned: it was this. Though for four years past I had never had a doubt as to its being the will of God that I should build accommodation for 700 more Orphans; yet, at the same time, I had for a long time seen the desirableness of having two houses, instead of one, for the 700 Orphans. This previously formed judgment of having two houses for 350 Orphans in each, or 400 in the one, and 300 in the other, led me now to see whether there could be another house built on each side of the present New Orphan-House, and I judged, from measuring the ground, that there was no objection to this plan. I then called in the aid of architects, to survey the ground, and to make a rough plan of two houses, one on each side, and it was found that it could be accomplished. Having arrived thus far, I soon saw, that we should not only save expense by this plan in various ways, but especially that thus the direction, and inspection of the whole establishment would be much more easy and simple, as the buildings would be so near together. This, indeed, on being further considered, soon appeared to be a matter of such importance, that, even if land could be had but a quarter of a mile off, the difficulties would be greatly increased thereby. At the same time I found, that we still should retain so much land for cultivation by the spade, as would furnish some out-door employment for many boys, and would produce such vegetables as are the most important for young children, to have fresh out of the ground; or that we could easily rent a piece of ground near for that purpose, though it could not be bought.

The result, then, at which I have arrived at present is this, that, having seen what could be accomplished on the ground which we have already, I decided to build, without any further delay than was necessary for preparing the plans, at the South side of the New Orphan-House, another house for 400 children. The plans are now ready, and in a very short time, God willing, i.e. as soon as all tine necessary preliminary arrangements can be made, the building will commence, which I think will be in the early part of July of the present year, (i.e. 1855). Indeed, the first actual steps are already taken, since, on May 29th, the sinking of four wells for the new house was commenced.

THE LORD'S DEALINGS WITH GEORGE MÜLLER

This house is intended for 400 female Orphans, bereaved of both parents, from their earliest days, until they can be placed out in service. With regard to the other house for 300 Orphans, to be built at the North side of the New Orphan-House, nothing definitively can be stated at present. There is enough money in hand to build, fit up, and furnish the house for 400 Orphans, and it is expected that something will be left; but there is not sufficient money in hand, at present, to warrant commencing the building of both. As soon, however, as there is, I shall be delighted to take active measures with regard to that for 300 Orphans also. I do not ask persons to help me with their means. I speak to the Lord about my need in prayer, and I do not wait upon Him in vain. At the same time I feel it right to state, that there is a loud and an abundant call for caring for destitute Orphans. On May 26, 1854, there were 602 waiting for admission, each bereaved of both parents by death. Since then 197 more have been applied for, making in all 799. Of these I have been able to receive only 39 during the past year, and 45 who were waiting for admission have been otherwise provided for, or have died since application was made for them; so that still 715 Orphans are waiting for admission, from three months old and upward. But this number, I state unhesitatingly, would be much larger, had not very many persons refrained from making application, because they judged it would be of no use, as there are already so many waiting for admission. Indeed there is every reason to believe, that there are many tens of thousands of destitute Orphans in this country. And what provision is there in the way of Orphan establishments, it may be asked? At the last census in 1851, there were in England and Wales 39 Orphan Establishments, and the total number of Orphans provided for through them, amounted only to 3764; but at the time the New Orphan-House was being built, there were about 6000 young Orphans in the prisons of England. To prevent their going to prison, to prevent their being brought up in sin and vice, yea, to be the honoured instrument to win their souls for God, I desire, by His help, to enlarge the present establishment, so as to be able to receive 1000 Orphans; and individuals who purpose not to live for time but for eternity, and look on their means as in the light of eternity, will thus have an opportunity of helping me to care for these children. It is a great honour to be allowed to do anything for the Lord. We can only give to Him of His own; for all we have is His. When the day of recompense comes, the regret will only be, that we have done so little for Him, not that we have done too much.

Supplies for the School --, Bible ----, Missionary --, and Tract Fund, sent in answer to prayer, from May 26, 1854, to May 26, 1855.

On May 26, 1854, when the accounts were closed, there was in hand 55l. 15s. for these objects. I now mention a few of the instances in which the Lord, in answer to prayer, supplied us with means.

July 6, 1854. As only about 100l. had come in for these objects during the past five weeks, all our means were now expended. I desired to help brethren who labour in the Word, but was unable to do so, when I received today 50l. from London, which, being left to my disposal, I took half of it for these objects, and half for the support of the Orphans.

FOURTH PART

July 8. Further, from the North of Devon 14l.

July 12. Day by day I have been waiting upon the Lord for means for home and foreign labourers in the Gospel, for whom I had no means, though greatly desiring to send them help. Today I received, as the fruit of many prayers, from London the sum of 100l., of which I took 50l. for the Orphans, and 50l. for these objects. It was the more remarkable that this donor should have sent me help at this time, as I had received 25l. from him on the first day of this month.

About this time I received several other donations for missions.

On July 24th I received a small plate-chest, containing 14 table spoons, 6 dessert spoons, 11 tea spoons, 2 gravy spoons, 2 sauce ladles, 12 forks, 4 salt cellars, 4 salt spoons, a pepper box, a pair of sugar tongs, a wine funnel, a cream jug, a small salver, a small goblet, a larger ditto, fish knife, and a coffee pot, all of silver, 3 pairs of plated nut crackers, a plated salver and a pewter can. The donor, who desires to be his own executor, wished me to sell these articles, keep 10l. for myself, and to use the rest for missionary objects. The contents of the box realized 44l. 5s. 10d., and I was thus enabled on August 1, 1854, to send 40l. to seven brethren labouring in British Guiana; and about ten weeks afterwards I heard that the Lord had sent them this help at a time of great need.--On July 25th from Kendal 1l. for missions.--On July 26th from a visitor at Clifton 30l. for missions.--From Bath 10s.--From Hackney 10s.--From Brosely 2s. 6d.--July 29. From Whitehaven 2l. 5s. 6d. for missions.--July 30. From Uppingham 2s. 6d.--August 8. 40l from a distance, of which 30l. was for missions.--August 18. From C. W. 20l. for missions.

I had thus the joy of being able to send assistance to some of the brethren whom I desire to help as labourers in the Gospel at Home or Abroad; yet all this was little in comparison with what I desired to do. For several months, during this period, that is in June, July, August and September, up to October 17th, I was day by day waiting upon the Lord for means for labourers in the Word, as I had reason to believe that many of them were in need; but little only, comparatively, came in. I was able to send up to October 17th not more than about one half of what I had been able to send them for several years previously. My desire to help these dear brethren was as great as ever. My earnestness in prayer for them, by God's grace, had not decreased. Their need, I had full reason to believe (and in some instances I knew) was great. I could, therefore, only conclude that the Lord allowed these dear brethren thus to have their faith tried, in order that they might the better become acquainted with himself. At last, however, the Lord refreshed my spirit greatly, first on October 17th, and then especially by that large donation at the commencement of the year 1855, of which I took a considerable portion for missionary objects, so that, especially during the last five months of this period, I was able to send help to brethren who labour in the Gospel to such an extent, as that about the same amount was disbursed for that object as for several years previously, but a greater amount for the circulation of the Holy Scriptures and Tracts than formerly. Of the donations for these objects between Aug.

THE LORD'S DEALINGS WITH GEORGE MÜLLER

18 and Oct. 17, 1854, I only mention the following--On Sept. 21st, anonymously from Exmonth, a bank post bill for 20l., of which the donor designed 10l. to be applied to the Missionary Fund, 5l. for the Orphans, and 5l. where most needed, or for my own necessities, as a thank-offering for unmerited mercies. This latter 5l., left for my disposal, I took for the circulation of the Holy Scriptures and Gospel Tracts. I wrote in my journal concerning this donation: "A precious answer to prayer! Great, great is the need."--On Sept. 23rd a deeply-afflicted mother left at my disposal 20l. I took it for missionary objects, the circulation of the Holy Scriptures and Gospel Tracts; for which objects much then was needed. Almost all the Tracts for gratuitous circulation were gone, and many brethren who labour in the Word I desired to help, but had not the means.--Sept. 26. From Kensington 11l., which was taken for the circulation of Tracts and missions, as the disposal of it was left with me.--From Worcestershire 8l. 6s. 7d., being the balance of an account. It was taken for missions and the circulation of Gospel Tracts. A most seasonable help!--Sept. 28. "From two of God's children who can say, 'Our hearts trusted in Him, and we are helped,'" Psalm xxviii. 7, 1l. for missions, 1l. for the Orphans, with 1l. for myself.--Sept. 30. This morning, at our usual prayer meeting with my fellow-labourers, the need of brethren, who labour in the Word, was again especially brought before the Lord, as I had reason to believe many were in need, and I had nothing to send them. This evening I received from Shropshire 2 gold chains, a diamond brooch, and a topaz brooch, with the request of the donor to sell them for the benefit of brethren who labour in the Word. This donation has greatly refreshed my spirit, but I look out for more, far more.--Oct. 4. From E. B. 5l. for missions.--From a Missionary box at Stroud 3l. 0s. 7d.--Oct. 8. From a distance 20l. for brethren who labour in the Gospel at Home and Abroad, 40l. for the Orphans, and 20l. for my own expenses. Precious answer to prayer. Great, great is the need for labourers in the Word. I had, therefore, particularly again waited upon the Lord yesterday, together with my fellow-labourers, for this object.--From B. S. 1l. for missions.-- Oct. 11. From Austin Friars, London, 20l.--Oct. 12. From Philadelphia 1l. From Cotham Lane 1l.--Oct. 14. 2s. 6d.--From Weymouth was received 2l., the disposal of which was left to me. Having just sent out, to the last pound, 40l. to Demerara, I took it for Missionary objects.

Oct. 17. This morning at family prayer, came, in the course of reading, Exodus v, which shows, that, just before the deliverance of the Israelites out of Egypt, their trials were greater than ever. They had not only to make the same number of bricks as before, but also to gather stubble, as no straw was given them any longer. This led me, in expounding the portion, to observe, that even now the children of God are often in greater trial than ever, just before help and deliverance comes. Immediately after family prayer it was found, that by the morning's post not one penny had come in for the work of the Lord in which I am engaged, though we needed much, and though but very little had come in during the three previous days. Thus I had now to remember Exodus v, and to practise the truths contained therein. In the course of the day nothing was received. In the evening I had, as usual, a season for prayer with my dear wife, respecting the various objects of the Scriptural Knowledge Institution, and then we left the New Orphan House for our home. When we arrived at our house, about nine o'clock, we found that 5l. and also 5s. had been sent from

FOURTH PART

Norwich in two Post Office Orders for the Building Fund, and that 8l. 3s. 11d. had been sent in for Bibles, Tracts and Reports, which had been sold. This called for thanksgiving. But a little later, between nine and ten o'clock, a Christian gentleman called and gave me 1l. for the Orphans and 200l. for foreign missions. He had received these sums from an aged Christian woman, whose savings as a servant, during her whole life, made up the 200l., and who, having recently had left to her a little annual income of about 30l., felt herself constrained, by the love of Christ, to send the savings of her whole life for foreign missions. This gentleman stated to me at the same time, that she had never had more than 5l. or 6l. wages a year, during her whole life. Moreover, out of this she has sent me, year by year, 1l. or more for the benefit of the Orphans, for many years; though I never knew her circumstances till now, as she resides at a distance, and I have never seen her. What various ways has the Lord to supply us with means! I add the following remarks: 1, For several months past no donation as large as 200l. has been received, a circumstance which has not occurred for about ten years past. 2, Now an aged servant is used by the Lord to send this donation as the fruit of her earnings, from about fifty years' service. 3, Our especial prayer had been again and again, that the Lord would be pleased to send in means for missionary brethren, as I had reason to believe they were in much need of help; and only at eight o'clock this evening I had particularly besought the Lord to send help for this object. By the last mail I had sent off 40l. to British Guiana, to help seven brethren there in some measure. This amount took the last pound in hand for this object. How gladly would I have sent assistance to other brethren also, but I had no more. Now I am in some degree supplied for this object. 4, Very recently our tracts for gratuitous circulation were almost entirely gone; but, before they were quite exhausted, the Lord sent more means, so that about 200,000 could be ordered.

Oct. 23 Received 149l. 8s., the disposal of which was left with me. I took of it 100l. for the support of the Orphans, for whom I had not 5l. in hand, when it came, and the remainder for these objects, for which still much is needed, in order to help labourers in the Gospel at home, as well as foreign labourers, and in order to go on with the circulation of the Holy Scriptures and Tracts, and to meet the expenses for the various schools. This morning I had also the promise, that in about a month 400l. should be paid to me for the work of the Lord. Thus, after a season of several months, during which scarcely any large sums have been received, the Lord is pleased, in answer to many prayers, to cause the streams of His bounty to flow again more abundantly.

Oct. 26. From a visitor at Clifton 50l., which I took for the School, Bible, Missionary, and Tract Objects.

Nov. 27. In great need there came in 100l., which was left to my appropriation as it might be most required. I took, therefore, 50l. for the Orphans, for whom there was scarcely anything in hand, and 50l. for these objects, for which we needed much in every way.

THE LORD'S DEALINGS WITH GEORGE MÜLLER

Dec. 30. Received 100l., when in the greatest need for these objects, and for the support of the Orphans. I took one-half for these objects, and the other for the Orphans, and am thus again helped, in answer to many prayers.

Jan. 1, 1855. As the year closed with mercies, so another has commenced with mercies. I received from one engaged in the work 2l. for missions. -- From M. E. for missions 5s.--From E. 0. 5s.--From M. A. E. 4s. 4d.--From B. S. 1l. for missions.-- Also 10l. for the support of the Day Schools.

Jan. 2. From a few believers in Huntingdonshire 15s. 2d. for missions.

Jan. 3. From two Christian ladies in London 10l. for missions, with 10l. for the Orphans.

Thus we were helped till I received on Jan. 8th the promise of the donation of 5,700l., of which, as has been stated, 1,400l. was taken for these objects. This, with what came in besides, from Jan. 8, to May 26, 1855, enabled me so amply to meet every demand afterwards, that no further difficulty was experienced during this period, in the way of means.

Means for the support of the 300 Orphans, a/ready under our care, sent in answer to prayer, from May 26, 1854, to May 26, 1855.

At the beginning of this period there was in hand a balance of 123l. 0s. 7 1/2 d. To the poorer class of readers this might appear a considerable sum; but to such we would say, that often the expenses of three or four days are more than this for the Orphan Establishment, with which 335 persons are connected; and, certainly, the average expenses, even if no extraordinary demands were to be met, amount to about Twelve Pounds per day in these dear times; and therefore 123l. would only be enough for about ten days. We had then, so far as regarded visible/e support, only enough for about ten days; but whilst we had so little as to visible support, we looked by faith to Him who is invisible, the Living God, who has upheld this work for so many years. We believed that He would help us still; and we were not confounded, though our faith was again and again tried. I can, however, give only a few out of the many instances which might be recorded.

June 15, 1854. Though this is only the third week since the new period commenced, yet as only about 60l. had come in for the support of the Orphans, in addition to the balance of 123l. 0s. 7 1/2 d., we were today reduced to less than Five Pounds. This had led to much waiting upon the Lord: and again He gave a gracious answer to prayer. I received 151l. 5s. 8d., which, being left to my disposal, I took the whole for the support of the Orphans. Also from two little girls was sent to me 8s., with the information that one of their sisters had set apart a swarm of bees, the honey of which should be sold for the benefit of the Orphans. Thus the Lord has again helped in the hour of need.

FOURTH PART

July 12. Our means were now again reduced to about 30l., as only about 150l. had come in since June 15. In addition to this, we had very heavy expenses before us. This morning, in reading through the book of Proverbs, when I came to chapter xxii. 19-- "That thy trust maybe in the Lord," &c., I said in prayer to Him: "Lord, I do trust in Thee; but wilt Thou now be pleased to help me; for I am in need of means for the current expenses of all the various objects of the Institution." By the first delivery of letters I received an order on a London bank for 100l., to be used for all the various objects, "as the present need might require." I took, therefore, 50l. for the support of the Orphans, and 50l. for the other objects, which are also in great need. Received also from Wandsworth Road 1l. 10s. 8d.; and in the course of the day 2l. 3s. 3d., through the boxes at the New Orphan House. Thus we are again helped for the present.

July 19. For some time past I have been under an engagement to leave Bristol at the end of this month, or in the beginning of August, for about four weeks, to labour at Sunderland. On this account I have besought the Lord during the last days that He would be pleased to send me some means for my own expenses, but especially that I might be able to leave some money behind, to last at least for some time. Yesterday the Lord was pleased to begin answering my request, in sending means for the support of the Orphans. I received from Lymington 5l.--From Tregenda 10s.--From Thetford 10s.--From Perth 1l.--From Kilmarnock 5l.--By sale of Reports 18s. 10d.--Proceeds of an Orphan Box 1l. 5s. 9 1/2 d. Today I have received from South Brent 1s. -- From Middlesex 50l.--Ditto 18s.--From Clifton 5l.--From Dudbridge 8s.--Through the boxes in the New Orphan House 7l. 1s. 3d. -- By sale of Reports 1l. 8s.--Returned on paying an account 2s. 4d. -- From a visitor at Clifton 50l. and a gold chain. The donor kindly wished me to retain 10l. for my own expenses.--From Kingsbridge 2s.

Thus the Lord began to answer prayer; but I expected more, and He sent me more on the following days. I record the income for the Orphans:--

July 20. From Homerton 3l. 3s.--Anonymously from Birmingham 1s.--Anonymously left at my house 5l.

July 21. From Bideford 10s.--By sale of Reports 1s.--From Tavistock 4s. 9d.--In a box from Tavistock, containing specimens of ores, &c. 3s.

July 22. From Wotton-under-edge 10s.--By sale of Reports 7s.--From West Brixton 2l.--From the Isle of Wight 1s. 6d. and 3s. 6d.--By sale of Reports 2s.--From Chippenham 2l. 10s.--From College Green, Bristol, 10s.

July 23. From Bodmin 5s. and 1s.--From Clifton 5s. Ditto 5s. Ditto 1l. Ditto 1l.

July 24. From Dudley 1l. 0. 6d. Ditto 1s. 8d.--From Clifton 10s.-- With James i. 17l. 2s. 6d.--From P. 2s. 6d.--Through Salem boxes 1s. Ditto 6d.--From Stourbridge 1s. 6d.--From Hastings 1l. 10s. -- From H. B. Esq. 2l.

July 25. From Wells 3s.--12s.--2s. 6d.--From Kendal 2l.-- From London 10l.

July 26. Through the boxes at the New Orphan House 5l. 18s. 11d.--By sale of Reports 14s. Ditto 6s.--From Torquay 3s. 4d.--From the neighbourhood of Newton Abbot 11s., with three silver pencil cases, and two pieces of old silver.--From a visitor at Clifton 100l., of which the donor wished me to take 20l. for myself, and to use the other as most needed. I took, therefore, 50l. for the Orphans, and 30l. for missions and the circulation of the Holy Scriptures and Tracts.--From Hackney 1l. 5s.--From Taunton 2s. and 1/4 lb. of tea.--There were anonymously left at the New Orphan House two vases, a Chinese tea caddy, a mosaic box, a ring set with a ruby and two brilliants, a double gold serpent bracelet, a large cameo brooch, a silver snuffbox, a double gold pin set with two brilliants, a pair of gold ear-rings, a pair of gold ear-rings set with pearls and emeralds, a gold brooch set with pearls and emeralds, a gold pin set with pearls and garnets, three gold shirt studs, a large gold cameo ring, a gold masonic medal, a pair of small gold ear-rings, a gold ring set with topazes, a gold watch ring, and a rupee. (These valuable articles did not merely refresh my spirit on account of their value; but they came as an answer to prayer for means, and also that the Lord would incline the hearts of His children to send such valuable, but needless, articles.) There were also given by the same donors, six Indian table mats, a white lace scarf, a black lace cap, and two pamphlets.

July 27. "20l. tendered as a thank-offering for singular deliverance at Llanberis." Ditto 1s. for a Report. --From Reading 1l.--From a Christian gentleman of Edinburgh, then near Glasgow, 3l. Through ditto 1l. Ditto 1l.--From Grundisburgh 5s. Ditto 1s. Ditto 6d.-- Anonymously in postages 2s. 6d.--From Bath 5s.--From Chillington 10s. 6d.--From Nottingham 10s.

July 28. From Pentonville 1l., with a little box of articles.--From Yeovil 1s. and 3s. 6d.--From Cannock 5l.--From Blackrock 12s.

July 29. From Higham Ferrers 10s.--From G. D. 1s.--From Colsterworth 10s.--From Wellesborne 10s.--Anonymously 2s.--By sale of Reports 3s. 6d.--From Whitehaven 2l. 14s. 6d.--By sale of a Report 6d.--From Largs 4l.--"From an Orphan Sailor" 2l.

July 30. From Uppingham 2s. 6d.--From Newton Ferrers 2s. 6d.

July 31. From Lenten 6s. 6d.--From Edinburgh 3l. 10s.

Aug. 1. From London 1l. Ditto 1s. 6d. Ditto 5l.--From Chillington 2s. -- From Broseley 5s.--From Warmley 5s. and an old silver watch.-- A little gold dust from a dying believer.--From F. E. B. 2s. 6d.-- From Barnstaple 1l. 3s.--From Northam 5s.--

FOURTH PART

From Hereford 10s. --By sale of Reports 1s. 6d.--From Newport, near Barnstaple, 1l. 10s.--From Barnstaple 1l. 10s.--From P. 2s. 6d.--Through Bethesda boxes 3s. 6d.--By sale of articles 4l. 13s. 3d. --By sale of Reports 10s.

Aug. 2. By sale of Reports 1l. 0s. 6d.--Anonymously 3s.--From Bath 1l. 10s.--From Ilfracombe 10l.--From Mundesley 2l.--Anonymously given at the New Orphan House 1l. Ditto 1s.--From Kilmersdon 6s.

Aug. 3. By sale of Reports 3s. 6d.--From Birmingham 6s. 6d.-- Through the boxes at the New Orphan House 3l. 18s. 3d.--From Chapletown 10s.--From London 5l.--From Tavistock 2s. 6d.-- Returned on paying an account 2s. 4d.--By sale of Reports 2s. 6d.-- By sale of trinkets 38l. 11s. 6d.--By sale of Reports 12s. 10d.--Received also a letter from the neighbourhood of Gumeracha, in Australia, enclosing a bank order for 10l., of which 2l. was intended for aged or blind saints in Bristol, 1l. for Bibles and Testaments, and 7l. for the Orphans or the other objects of the Scriptural Knowledge Institution. I took this 7l. for the Orphans.

Aug. 4. From Plymouth 2l.--From Ilfracombe 10s.--From London 1l. 13s. 4d.

Aug. 5. From Manchester 10s.--By sale of Reports 3s. 4d.

Aug. 6. From Greenock 5l.--From Cockermouth 1l.--From Islington 1l. 1s.--From Child Okeford 2s. 6d.--From Clifton 2s. 6d. and 3s. -- From Horfield Road 10s. --From Henbury 2l.

Aug. 7. From Melton Abbot 3s.--From Cheltenham Road, Bristol, 1l. 1s. --From Islington 1l. 4s.--By sale of articles 17s. 3 1/2 d.--From Fowey 5l.--Through Bethesda boxes 6s. 8d.--From St. Philip's, Bristol, 5s.--From three children 8s. 6d.--From Clifton 1l. 10s.--Through Salem boxes 1s.

Aug. 8. From Lichfield 1l. Ditto 5s.--By sale of books 4l.--From Calstock 2s. 6d.--From Freshwater 1l.

Aug. 9. Anonymously 10s.--By sale of Reports 2s.--From Yaxham 1l. -- From Gravesend 1l. Through the boxes in the New Orphan-House 4l. 5s. 10d.--From Norwich 16s.--From a brother in the Lord 5l. 17s. 4d. -- From Plymouth 10s.--By sale of Reports 14s. 6d.

Thus the Lord, in answer to prayer, had supplied me so bountifully, that, when I left home on August 10th, I could leave sufficient in the bank to last for a little time, and I hoped in God that, by the time that was gone, He would kindly give more. And thus He did. I have also given the income for the Orphans day by day, for the above 23 days, in order that thus the Reader may see how, in large and small sums, and from various parts of the world, the Lord is pleased to send in the supplies.

THE LORD'S DEALINGS WITH GEORGE MÜLLER

I shall now give a few more instances in which the Lord manifestly, in answer to prayer, helped us in the time of need.

Aug. 26. A Christian widow, having had left to her by a friend a few articles, among which was a diamond brooch, sent it to me for the benefit of the Orphans, and thus had the desire of her heart granted, which she had often had, to be able to send something for them. On the other hand, we receive it in answer to prayer, as there is very little in hand for the Orphans, and as I have again and again asked the Lord to lead His children to send me such articles for His own work.--There came in also from Kirriemuir 1l.--From Kingsbridge a guinea piece, also 1l. From the neighbourhood of Hyde 10s.

Aug. 27. From Douglas 1l.--From the neighbourhood of Sunderland 5s. --From Sunderland 5s.--Through Salem boxes 1s.--With James, 1, 17, 2s. 6d.--From H. T. and E. E. 2s.

Aug. 28. From Captain J. K., Royal Navy, 2l.--From Mr. C. K. 2l.-- From Mr. P. 1l.--From Bury 10s.

Aug. 29. From Sunderland 1l. Ditto 1s.--From Gloucester 6s.--By sale of articles 1l. 4s.--From one engaged in the work 2l.--From the neighbourhood of Crencester 1l.

Aug. 30. From the neighbourhood of Southampton 5l.

Aug. 31. Anonymously, through the boxes at Bethesda chapel, Sunderland, 5l.--From Ilfracombe 2s. 6d.--Through the boxes at the New Orphan-House 5l. 1 1/2 d.--By sale of Reports 16s.--From one engaged in the work, as a thank-offering for journeying mercies, 10s. -- From the neighbourhood of Sudbury in Derbyshire 10l. --From Grosmont 5s.--From Hayle 1l.--By sale of the above-mentioned brooch 6l. 11s.

Sept. 1. From the Isle of Wight 2s. 6d.--From Birmingham 5l.--From Bath 5l.--From a Christian lady in Bath 10l.

See, dear reader, how good the Lord is, and how ready to help in answer to prayer! I was then 300 miles from the work in which I am more especially engaged; but the Lord's assistance was to be obtained in this distant place. Day by day I sought His help while absent, and day by day I received intelligence from Bristol. And thus, my fellow-labourers in Bristol, and I at Sunderland, were seeking the help of the Lord, and He did condescend to listen to our supplications on account of His dear Son, the Lord Jesus, and to grant us our requests.

On this day, Sept. 1st, I also received a precious letter, enclosing a Post-Office Order for 2l. 14s., from a donor, who, for many years, took a lively interest in the work in which I am engaged. This letter was doubly precious, not only because of its containing 2l. 14s., which came just then so particularly in answer to prayer, as since

FOURTH PART

August 2 6th, I had been especially looking to the Lord for means, there being then scarcely any thing left; but also because it so strikingly proved the power of the divine life.

* * * * Aug. 30, 1854.

"Dear Mr. Mueller,

"Having been a constant sufferer now for a year, the money I send you is (humanly speaking) consequently less; and as there is likely to be a crisis soon, in the shape of a large abscess, and I know not what the Lord is about to do with me, I send you all the money I have in hand; and if it should be the last may the Lord add a double blessing to it. The Lord does not want my poor help to do His own work; but I feel priviledged to be allowed to contribute, if it is but a nail, or a cup of milk, to His service. My peace is great--that is, His peace is with me, though tribulation, to some extent, is mine also. I desire your prayers, and remain,

"Yours in our precious Lord,

"* * * * *."

"P.S.--I expect to be able to send a box of, it may be, almost useless articles soon. Whither shall I send it?"

This Christian lady, whom I have never seen in the body, though I corresponded with her for many years, has entered into her rest. She fell asleep at the beginning of the year 1855. In looking over my account books, I meet again and again with the name of one and another who has finished his course. Soon dear Reader, your turn and mine may come. Are you prepared for eternity? Affectionately I press this question upon you. Do not put it away. Nothing is of greater moment than this point; yea, all other things, however important in their place, are of exceedingly small importance, in comparison with this matter. Do you ask, how you may be prepared for eternity, how to be saved, how to obtain the forgiveness of your sins; the answer is, believe in the Lord Jesus, trust in Him, depend upon Him alone as it regards the salvation of your soul. He was punished by God, in order that we guilty sinners, if we believe in Him, might not be punished. He fulfilled the law of God, and was obedient even unto death, in order that we disobedient, guilty sinners, if we believe in Him, might, on His account, be reckoned righteous by God. Ponder these things, dear Reader, should you have never done so before. Through faith in the Lord Jesus alone can we obtain forgiveness of our sins, and be at peace with God; but, believing in Jesus, we become, through this very faith, the children of God; have God as our Father, and may come to Him for all the temporal and spiritual blessings which we need. Thus every one of my readers may obtain answers to prayers, not only to the same extent that we obtain them, but far more abundantly. It may be that few, comparatively, of the children of God are called to serve the Lord in the way of establishing Orphan-Houses, &c.; but all of them may, yea, are called upon to trust in God, to rely upon Him, in their various positions and circumstances, and apply the word of God, faith, and prayer to their family circumstances, their earthly occupation, their afflictions and necessities of every kind, both temporally and spiritually; just as we, by God's help, in some little measure seek to apply the word of God, faith, and prayer to the various objects of the Scriptural Knowledge Institution for Home and Abroad. Make but trial of it, if you have never done so before, and you will see how happy a life it is. You may, perhaps, pity the writer, and think how he must be burdened day by day, and full of care and anxiety; and you may think that he cannot have any quietness and peace, but is worn down by the constant questionings, how the expenses for the various schools are to be met; how further money is to be obtained for the circulation of the Holy Scriptures and Tracts; how the many preachers of the Gospel at Home and Abroad, who are assisted by the Institution, may once more be helped; how the 300 Orphans are to be provided with all they need; how situations for the elder female Orphans are to be found; how suitable places may be obtained for the elder male Orphans when they are ready to be apprenticed, and so on. Now here is just the true state of the case:-- We are not insensible to any of these points; we do feel them. We do not put them away lightly and treat them with indifference; but we look them in the face and feel their deep importance. At the same time, while we neither treat them with indifference, nor attempt to carry them in our own strength, we do, by God's grace, cast our burdens upon Him, trust in Him; and thus are kept in peace in the midst of numberless difficulties, and almost constant trials of one kind and another. Truly I prefer by far this life of almost constant trial, if I am only able to roll all my cares upon my Heavenly Father, and thus become increasingly acquainted with Him, to a life of outward peace and quietness, without these constant proofs of His faithfulness, His wisdom, His love, His power, His overruling providence, &c.

Of the donations which came in between Sept. 2nd and Nov. 5th, amounting to about 600l., in 346 different sums, I mention only, for the sake of brevity, the following.

Sept. 2. From an anonymous donor through Mr. B. at Geneva, by the hands of Count G., 1l. 15s.--Sept. 6. Received from Clerkenwell 50l., to be used one half for missions, and the other half as I thought best. I took the one half for the support of the Orphans, and find the following remark in my journal respecting this donation: "What a precious answer to prayer! Since Aug. 26th we have been day by day coming to the Lord for our daily supplies. Precious, also, on account of missionary brethren, whom I seek to help, for whom there was nothing in hand when this donation was received!"--Sept. 22. From Crediton 3l. 4s. 8d., as "a thank-offering to God for the very fine harvest which in mercy He has been pleased to grant."

Nov. 5. There was now again only about 5l. in hand for the support of the Orphans, when I received 2l. 10s. for them, and 2l. 10s. for myself, from a donor in London, whom the Lord has been pleased to raise up during the last two years, and who since then has been often used as an instrument in helping the work at times of

FOURTH PART

need. A brother in the Lord also gave me 5l. this morning, saying, "I have of late had the Orphans much laid on my heart."--From Clifton 1l. 10s.--From H. C. 3s. --From F. M. 5s.

Nov. 6. Further help. From the Isle of Wight 5s.--Through Bethesda boxes 2s. 6d.--Ditto 6d.--From P. 1s.--Through Salem boxes 1s. -- From a Gloucestershire Farmer 20l., of which he intended 10l. for missions, and the other 10l. to be used as most needed. I took it for the support of the Orphans.

Nov. 7. By sale of Reports 4s. 10d.--Anonymously from York 5s.-- Received back on paying an account 3s. 7 1/2 d.--From a relative of one of the Orphans 1s.--Having had to pay out 18l. for house-keeping expenses, and having had to meet a few little expenses besides, we had again only about 5l. left, as was the case three days ago, when I received this afternoon 5l. from a Bristol donor.--Also 1l. from London.

Nov. 15. Our means were now again gone. We had scarcely anything in hand, with very heavy expenses before us, when this morning a Christian gentleman from Yorkshire called on me, and gave me 50l. for the current expenses for the Orphans. This was a most precious encouragement to prayer! There came in further today from Manchester 9s. 6d.--By sale of Reports 11s. 6d.--Through the boxes in the New Orphan-House 2l.7s. 11d.--Returned on paying an account 3s. 1 1/4 d.--From Exeter 1l. 10s.

Nov. 22. A Brother in the Lord from Manchester came to see the New Orphan-House, and gave 10l., which came in a time of great need.

Nov. 27. 100l. was sent in the greatest need, from a considerable distance, of which I took 50l. for the Orphans, and 50l. for the other objects.

Dec. 20. As since Nov. 27 only about 200l. has come in, I found this evening that our means for the support of the Orphans were reduced to 10l. 9s. 8d, whilst our current expenses of late have been about 12l. daily, on account of the high price of provisions. This led to earnest prayer, that the Lord would be pleased to help us.

Dec. 21. The Lord has already sent a precious answer to the prayer of last evening. I received today from a noble Lady 10l.--From Devonshire 15l.--By sale of Reports 6s. 6d.--From Birmingham 2s. -- By sale of a few coins, etc. 19s. 1d.--From Monmouthshire 8s.-- By sale of Reports 2s. 6d.--From Worksop 10s. 6d.--Returned on paying an account 3s. 3 3/4 d.

Dec. 23. From Cheltenham 2s. 6d.--From London 10s.--From Clondegad 10s.--By sale of articles 3l. 16s. 5d. By sale of a Report 6d.-- From Edinburgh 5l.

Dec. 24. Anonymously 1l.--From Barking 6s.--From Blackheath Hill 6s.

Dec. 25. From B. S. 2s.--Through Bethesda and Salem boxes 7s.-- From P. 2s.

Dec. 26. From a brother in the Lord 6l.--From O. O. at Plymouth 10s.

Dec. 27. From two believers at Plymouth 10s.--From Kingsbridge 10s. -- From Falmouth 1s.--From a little girl 3d.--By sale of Reports 6s.--Through the boxes in the New Orphan-House 1l. 14s. 4d.

Dec. 28. From Adelaide, Australia, 5l.

Dec. 29. From Torquay 5s.--From Exmouth 10s.--From Fulbeck 5s.-- From Sherborne 2s.

Dec. 30. At the beginning of this day our money was again reduced to 19l. 2s. 1 1/2 d. for the current expenses for the Orphans, whilst I had before me the prospect of having to advance this day 30l. for house-keeping expenses, in order that we might go with ease through the work, and in order that all expenses might be met. Now see how the Lord helped us during this day. There came very early this morning, from the neighbourhood of Norwich, a box, containing the following articles. A prize medal, 2 salt cellars, 6 pencil cases, 5 thimbles, 2 fruit knives, a watch chain, 2 vinaigrettes (all of silver), a black necklace, a silver chain, 2 silver toothpicks, some pieces of silver, 2 pairs of gilt bracelets, a pincushion, 4 snaps, a pair of gold earrings, a tortoiseshell comb, a pocket comb, a reading glass, a box of paints, a bag of coral and other beads, 2 smelling bottles and 2 gilt chains. Likewise, from another donor, a silver stock buckle, 2 pairs of shoe buckles, 2 pencil cases, a piece of silver chain, 2 seals, a brooch pin, 2 small gold pins, 6 small silver coins, a metal coin, a small silver medal, a thimble, a pair of silver studs, 9 pairs ditto set with Bristol stone, and a gold earring. There was sent with these articles likewise. 1l., and from a poor woman 6d.--In the course of the day came in further: From Islington 6s.--From A. W. 2s.--From Islington 5s., with 8 chemises and 4 shirts.--Also from a great distance 100l., which being left at my disposal, I took one half for the Orphans, and the other half for the other Objects.--By sale of articles 2l.-- Also 2s. 6d., and 2s. 8 1/2 d. from an Orphan-box.--Thus I was enabled to advance this evening 30l. for house-keeping as needed.

This was the last time, during this period of the Institution, that we were brought so low as to means; for the Lord sent in on Dec. 31 6l. 10s.; on Jan. 1, 1855, in twenty-eight different donations, 14l. 4s. 6d.; on Jan. 2nd 17l. 8s. 3d.; on Jan. 3rd 15l. 1s. 3d.; on Jan. 4th 34l. 11s. 8d., and so on, till the large donation was given of which, as has been stated, 900l. was taken for the current expenses for the Orphans. This, with what came in from Dec. 30th 1854, up to May 26th, 1855, for the support of the Orphans, enabled me to meet all the demands without any difficulty, during the remaining five months. Of all these donations, making, up the total of 2226l. 10s. 7 1/4 d., I refer only to the following.

Jan. 1, 1855. From a clergyman in South Africa 1l.

FOURTH PART

Jan. 4. From a Christian merchant at Clifton 30l. for the Orphans, with 10l. for myself, and 10l. for poor believers.

There have been many instances, in which, along with the donations for missions, or for the support of the Orphans, or the Building Fund, there were also presents in money sent for my own personal expenses, or those of my family. These instances I have gladly recorded, as they came in connexion with the donations referred to, because they afforded me an opportunity of speaking well of the kindness and faithfulness of the Lord in supplying my own personal or family need. It is now [i.e. in 1856] above Twenty Five years, since I have not had any regular income whatever. In the year 1830, I saw it to be the Lord's will to give up my regular income in connexion with the ministry of the Word, and to trust in Him, alone for the supply of all my temporal necessities. I have been enabled to continue in this path, and have not been allowed to regret the step which I then took. Thus it is also in my position as director of the various objects of the Scriptural Knowledge Institution. I have no salary in this position; but the Lord abundantly supplies my need; yea, though there are many expenses connected with this very position, He abundantly meets all my wants, and gives me far more than I need. If with all my might I had sought to obtain a lucrative place, either as a preacher of the Gospel, or in some other way, I should not have had more, I have reason to believe, if as much, as, unsought, unasked for, so far as it regards man, I receive day by day out of the loving hand of my Heavenly Father. When I look at His kindness to me in saving my guilty soul, I am overwhelmed with the boundlessness of His love and grace towards me in Christ Jesus; and when I look at His kindness to me, even as it regards temporal things, I know not where to begin, nor where to end, in speaking well of His name. I do desire to magnify Him, and therefore declare in this public way His great goodness to me in thus so abundantly supplying my temporal necessities; and I do so also, if it may please God, by this means, to encourage the hearts of His children more and more unreservedly to trust in Him. It is now above twenty-five years since I have asked help for myself from any human being; but God has been indeed my helper. And now the very work even with which I am connected, respecting which I had every reason to believe, when I commenced it, that it would be connected with great expenses to myself, as well as be the means, looked at naturally, of decreasing my own income, God has, though unsought for on my part, used as the instrument to bring along with it many supplies for myself also, thus not only abundantly meeting my increased expenses, but giving me far more than I need for myself. How great is His goodness! Dear Christian Reader, be encouraged by this! Do but trust in God with all your heart, and you will find that you will not be confounded. Only let it be trust in God, not in man, not in circumstances, not in any of your own exertions, but real trust in God, and you will be helped, in your various necessities.--I refer to a few more of the donations.

Jan. 25. From various believers at Melbourne, Australia, 20l. for the Orphans, and 20l. for the other objects.

THE LORD'S DEALINGS WITH GEORGE MÜLLER

Feb. 23. Received a very valuable gold watch, a gold watch chain, 2 gold watch keys, a gold seal, a silver mustard pot and spoon, a silver salt stand, a scent bottle, a china basket, 3 china jugs, a china cup and saucer and mug 2 taper candlesticks, a ring stand, 2 spill cups, a card stand, a lamp, a claret jug, a pair of decanters, 6 hock glasses, 14 claret glasses, 6 finger glasses, and a set of china tea things. The donor has found true riches and peace to his soul in the Lord Jesus; and he is thus led to send these articles for the benefit of the Orphans.

April 18. 100l. from a distance, of which the donor kindly intends 20l. for myself, and 80l. for the benefit of the Orphans.

May 5. 219l. 9s. 4d. from a distance, of which the donor kindly wished me to keep 19l. 9s 4d. for myself, and to use the other as it might be required for the Lord's work. I took 100l. for the support of the Orphans, and 100l. for the other objects. This donation was especially refreshing to my spirit, because of its coming at this period, when the outgoings are very great.

May 26. Towards the close of this day it was found that the balance left in hand, for the support of the Orphans, was 110l. 17s. 8 1/2 d., as the amount with which we should have to begin the new period in providing for the necessities of the Orphans. Before leaving the Orphan-House, I had my usual daily season for prayer with my dear wife. Having praised the Lord for His goodness to us and the work, in helping us during another year, and having sought His blessing upon the various objects of the Institution, we commended ourselves again to Him, especially, with reference to means for the coming year, and entreated Him also to sustain our faith to the end of our course; for the longer I go on in this path, the more I feel my entire dependence upon the Lord and my need of being sustained by Him. When we arrived home, we found two more donations, the last of the present period, sent for the benefit of the Orphans; one being two little dresses, a piece of print, a piece of calico, and 20 pocket handkerchiefs; the other a small gold Geneva watch, quite new. We took these two last donations as the Lord's earnest that He would be with us during the coming period also, and with good courage looked forward to it, by His grace.

I add a few remarks to this part of the Narrative:--1. Should any one suppose, on account of its having been stated in the previous pages that we were repeatedly brought low as to means, that the Orphans have not had all that was needful for them; we reply, that never, since the work has been in existence, has there a meal-time come, but the Orphans have had good nourishing food in sufficient quantity: and never have they needed clothes, but I have had the means to provide them with all they required. Persons living in Bristol can easily satisfy themselves as to this, not only by seeing week after week our stores for food and clothes; but also the dress and the healthy countenances of these hundreds of children (though very many of them were received in a very weak and diseased state) will amply prove what I state. 2. Never since the Orphan work has been in existence, have I asked one single human being for any help for this work; and yet, unasked for, simply in answer to prayer, from so many parts of the world, as has been stated, the donations have come

FOURTH PART

in, and that very frequently at a time of the greatest need. Were I to state what is not true, persons could easily convict me; to say nothing of the fact that God, whose name I have continually connected with this work, would disown me as an awful deceiver, and bring this work to nought; but if these things are true, as indeed they are, will not my readers own the hand of God, will they not recognize the minute particular providence of God, and the readiness of His heart to listen to the supplications of those who come to Him with their requests in the name of the Lord Jesus? I do not seek a name for myself in connexion with this work; I do not wish to draw attention to myself, and am indeed sorry when persons have had their attention directed only to me; but I do seek honour for my Heavenly Father, and I do desire that His hand may be owned in this work.

Miscellaneous points respecting the Scriptural Knowledge Institution, for Home and Abroad, with reference to the period from May 20, 1854, to May 26, 1855.

1. During this year four Day Schools in Bristol, with 184 children in them, were entirely supported by the funds of the Institution; and several other Day Schools in Devonshire, Cornwall, Suffolk, Ireland, and Scotland were assisted with copies of the Holy Scriptures. Further, one Sunday School in Bristol, with 158 children, was entirely supported, and seven others, in Cornwall, Devonshire, Somersetshire, and Gloucestershire, with about 400 children in them, were assisted. Lastly, one Adult School, with 183 Adults, was entirely supported during this year.-- The amount expended, during this year, on these various Schools, was 338l. 2s. 5d.

In connexion with all these Schools, I would suggest the following important matter for prayer. From March, 1884, to May, 26, 1855, there were 5,956 children in the Day Schools. In the Adult School there were 2,459 persons. The number of the Sunday School children amounted to 2,817. Thus, without reckoning the Orphans, 11,232 souls were brought under habitual instruction in the things of God in these Schools; besides the many thousands in the Schools in various parts of England, Ireland, Scotland, British Guiana, the West Indies, the East Indies, &c., which were to a greater or less degree assisted. Now, what I would especially request is, that all the disciples of the Lord Jesus, who take an interest in this work, would help me and my fellow-labourers with their prayers, that not only those who are at present under our instruction may be spiritually benefited, but particularly also, that God would be pleased to work mightily in the hearts of those who were once under our care, in bringing to their remembrance the truth which was then set before them. I am the more induced to make this request, as we frequently meet with young men or young women, who many years ago were under our care and instruction, who thankfully own the benefit they received when with us, and who are now believers in the Lord Jesus, though at the time they had given us little or no hope. Thus has the Lord afterwards been pleased to cause the seed to spring up and to bear fruit to His praise. During this year also we had again and again most encouraging instances of this kind brought before us.

THE LORD'S DEALINGS WITH GEORGE MÜLLER

The total sum expended during the 21 years, from March 5, 1834, to May 26, 1855, in connexion with the Schools, which were either entirely, or in part supported by the funds of this Institution, amounted to 7,204l. 12s. 8 1/4 d.

2. Great have been the efforts, made of late years, to spread error; therefore the disciples of the Lord Jesus should be especially active in seeking to spread the truth. Fearfully great, in particular, have been the efforts to rob the Church of Christ of the Word of God; on this account, all who love our Lord Jesus in sincerity, should seek, according to their ability, to spread the Holy Scriptures. On account, therefore, of the especial attempts made, of late years, once more to deprive the Church of Christ of God's unerring Holy Word, I have had it particularly laid upon my mind, in every way to embrace opportunities for circulating it, and especially to place it in the hands of the very poorest of the poor. In this way, not only in England, Wales and Scotland, but particularly in Ireland, we have sought to circulate the Holy Scriptures. And not only there, but also in Canada, British Guiana, the East Indies, Australia and China. Every open door, which the Lord was pleased to set before us, I have endeavoured to press into; and, in this service have been helped by many servants of Christ, who have sought out the most destitute persons, desirous of possessing a copy of the Holy Scriptures. With this we have also particularly sought to combine the supplying of aged persons, who are poor, with copies printed in large type. Our efforts have not been in vain. We have had instances brought before us of direct conversion, simply through reading the Holy Scriptures. Again, during this year also, our labours were owned in this part of the work. But though we have seen some fruit, we believe that the greater part by far will be manifested in the Day of the Lord. It has been given to us, by the help of the Lord, day by day to seek His blessing upon the circulation of the Holy Scriptures, and therefore we believe that our labour will not be in vain. We expect results.

The number of Bibles, New Testaments, and Portions of the Holy Scriptures, circulated from May 20, 1854, to May 26, 1855, is as follows:

693 Bibles were sold.

890 Bibles were given away.

950 New Testaments were sold.

748 New Testaments were given away.

82 copies of the Psalms were sold.

186 other small portions of the Holy Scriptures were sold.

There were circulated from March 5, 1834, to May 26, 1855, through the medium of this Institutions 13,949 Bibles, 9047 New Testaments, 188 copies of the Psalms, and 789 other small portions of the Holy Scriptures.

FOURTH PART

The total amount of the funds of this Institution, spent on the circulation of the Holy Scriptures, from March 5, 1834, to May 20, 1855, is 3389l. 10s. 1d. The amount spent during this year, 476l. 12s. 3d.

3. During this year there was spent of the funds of the Institution for missionary objects, the sum of 2081l. 3s. 2d. By this sum Fifty Seven Labourers in the word and doctrine, in various parts of the world, were to a greater or less degree assisted.

With reference to this part of the operations of the Institution, I have especially the joy of being able to communicate to the Christian reader, that the Lord was pleased, during this year, abundantly to bless the labours of many of the brethren whom I assisted. Again and again I had refreshing intelligence as to the fruit which resulted from their efforts. Many souls were brought to the knowledge of the Lord, through their labours during this year. And such heart-refreshing intelligence came to me not only from those labouring in various parts of the United Kingdom, but also from those who are serving the Lord in foreign countries. This calls for especial praise; but at the same time I would commend these dear brethren to the prayers of the saints, that they may be upheld by the Lord with reference to their bodily and mental strength, and especially that they may be sustained with patience, faith, love, perseverance, and endurance; for great and many are their difficulties. I would especially also request all, who love the Lord Jesus, to pray for more labourers in the Gospel; for I hear continually of fields which are unoccupied, and of open doors not entered into for lack of labourers.

The total amount of the funds of the Institution, spent on Missionary operations, from March 5, 1834, to May 20, 1855, was 16,115l. 0s. 5 1/2 d.

4. The fourth object of the Institution is, the circulation of such publications as may be beneficial, with the blessing of God, to benefit both believers and unbelievers. As it respects tracts for unbelievers, I seek especially to aim after the diffusion of such as contain the truths of the Gospel clearly and simply expressed; and as it respects publications for believers, I aim after the circulation of such as may be instrumental in directing their minds to those truths which in these last days are more especially needed, or which have been particularly lost sight of, and may lead believers to return to the written Word of God.

There was laid out for this object, from May 26, 1854, to May 26, 1855, the sum of 624l. 8s. 4d.; and there were circulated within this year 895,034 Tracts and Books.

The total number of all the Tracts and Books circulated from the beginning up to May 26, 1855, was 3,584,710.

The total amount of means, expended on this object, from Nov. 19, 1840, to May 26, 1855, is 2868l. 15s. 6 3/4 d.

THE LORD'S DEALINGS WITH GEORGE MÜLLER

We desire to be truly thankful to the Lord, for having intrusted us with means, and given us open doors, for the circulation of so many copies of the Holy Scriptures, and so many thousands of Tracts; and for having enabled us to assist again to such an extent preachers of the unsearchable riches of Christ; but we do not rest in this. Our trust was in the Lord for His blessing upon our efforts. Nor has He allowed us to wait upon Him in vain, during this year. We had not only very many answers to our prayers with regard to the obtaining of means, but also many answers to prayer as it respects fruit resulting from our labours. Thus also with reference to the circulation of Tracts. Again and again instances came before us in which souls were converted through the Tracts, which the Lord had allowed us to send out during the year. Among others, I would only mention, that an actor on the stage, to whom one of them was given, was brought to the knowledge of the Lord.

Tract distributors, who can afford to pay for Tracts, and who desire to procure Tracts from us, may obtain them for this purpose with a discount of one-half, or 50 per cent., from the retail price. I state this, as many believers may not like to give away that which cost them nothing, and yet may, at the same time, wish to obtain as much as possible for their money. Applications for this should be made verbally or in writing to Mr. Stanley, at the Bible and Tract Warehouse, No. 34, Park-street, Bristol. To him, also, application may be made for specimen packets containing an assortment of the Tracts and small books which are kept. By sending 3s., 5s., 7s., or 10s. in postages to Mr. Stanley, No. 34, Park Street, Bristol, packets will be sent to any part of England, Wales, Ireland, Scotland, Jersey, Guernsey, &c., post paid, containing specimens to the amount of the postages sent.

A catalogue of the various books and tracts, sold at the above Warehouse, with their prices, may be had there, by applying either personally or by letter to Mr. Stanley.

5. The fifth object of the Institution is, to board, clothe, and Scripturally to educate destitute children who have lost both parents by death.

At the commencement of this period there were 298 Orphans in the New Orphan House on Ashley Down, Bristol. During the year there were admitted into it 39 Orphans, making 337 in all. Of these 337, two died during the year. Only two! We record this with particular gratitude. And even these two died through water on the brain. God helping us, we desire to trace His hand in everything; at the same time, the longer I am engaged in the Orphan work, and see the effects which are produced by regular habits, cleanliness, nourishing food, proper clothing, good ventilation, a healthy locality, &c., the more I am convinced, that at least one-half of the children among the poorer classes die for want of proper attention. I do not state this to find fault with them, but rather mention it in the way of pity and commiseration, to draw the attention of the public to the fact. If anywhere the mortality among children should be great, humanly speaking, it should be so among us, because we generally receive the children very young, and also, because the very fact of these children, while so young, having been bereaved of both parents by death, shows that their parents, generally speaking, were of a very sickly constitution. Indeed the greater part of the Orphans whom we have received, lost one or both parents through consumption. And yet, though such is the case, we have seen again and again, how children who came to us in a most diseased state, have, through proper attention, by the blessing of God, been brought out of that state, and are now very healthy. But we often receive children whose countenances at once show that they have not had sufficient food, or were in other respects greatly neglected. It was only as late as April 26, 1855, that the turn of 4 children came, to be received, all of the same family, from 5 to 9 years old. When these children were brought, it was evident that they were in a most deplorable state of health from the want of proper food. This was now the painful difficulty in which we found ourselves; if we received them, it was not at all unlikely, humanly speaking, that we should have great trial with them on account of their health, as they had been so long neglected; and yet, if we did not take them, they would, we had great reason to fear, very shortly sink under their position. Trust in God decided the matter. We received all four, hoping that, by God's blessing, they would be thus rescued from sinking under their circumstances. The eldest of the four, a boy of above nine years old, was for the first evening or two so weak, that he could not walk up stairs to the dormitory without stopping. This disappeared, after he had had the food of the New Orphan House for a few days; and now all the four are so greatly improved, that they do not look at all like what they were on April 26th, 1855. I have so minutely entered into this one case out of very many of the kind, which have come before me in connexion with the Orphan work during the last 20 years, in order to show how deeply important it is to care for such destitute Orphans, to rescue them, humanly speaking, from misery or premature death, to say nothing now with reference to their spiritual welfare, which is paramount with us.

Besides the two who died out of the 387, we were obliged to expel one from the establishment. This boy was admitted on Oct. 4, 1849. He was then not quite eight years old; but though so young, it was soon found out that he was old in sin, for he was a confirmed liar, thief, &c. He gloried in it among the other boys, and told them that he had belonged to a juvenile gang of thieves, before he had been admitted into the Orphan House, that he had often stolen from the ships iron, brass, &c., and sold it. We thought at first that he spoke thus merely in the way of boasting, but it proved but too true, that he was experienced in such matters; for twice he ran away from the Orphan House, carrying off things belonging to the other children. Moreover, he could pick locks, &c. We received him back twice, after having run away, hoping that, by bearing with him, admonishing him, speaking to him privately, praying with him, and using a variety of other means, he might be reclaimed; but all in vain. At last, having borne with him, and tried him for five years and four months, he was solemnly, with prayer, before the whole establishment, expelled, if by any means this last painful remedy might be blessed to him. Yet we follow even this poor young sinner with our prayers, and hope that yet the Lord may show him his evil ways, and give us even now joy concerning him, as we have had before in a similar instance. This case afresh deeply impressed upon me the importance of caring for

Orphans from their earliest days; for this poor boy, when but eight years old, was already greatly practiced in stealing.

One of the children, after having been five years and one month under our care, was taken back by the relatives who had placed him with us, as they were by that time able to provide for him. One of the girls was sent out to learn a business, one as a junior teacher in a school, and 13 to take situations; and 21 boys were apprenticed. These 40 vacancies thus occasioned, left at the end of the year only 297 children in the New Orphan House. The total number of Orphans, under our care from April 1836, to May 26, 1855, was 597.

I notice further the following points respecting the New Orphan House.

1. Persons who desire to make application for the admission of Orphans, are requested to write to me, and address the letter to my house, No. 23, Paul Street, Kingsdown, Bristol.

2. I again state, as it regards the funds, that the income for the Orphans is kept distinct from that for the other objects. Donors may therefore contribute for one or the other of the objects exclusively, or have their donations equally divided among them all, just as it may appear best to themselves. If any of the donors would wish to leave the application of their donations to my discretion, as the work of God in my hands more especially may call for it at the time, they are requested, kindly to say so, when sending their donations.

3. The expenses for the Orphans, during this year, were 4304l. 4s. 7 1/2 d.

4. Without any one having been personally applied to for anything by me, the sum of 74132l. 6s. 10 3/4 d. was given to me for the Orphans, as the result of prayer to God, from the commencement of the work up to May 26, 1855, which sum includes the 15,055l 3s. 2 1/4 d. paid for the building, fitting up, and furnishing of the present New Orphan House, the 23,059l. 17s. 8 1/4 d., in hand on the 20th May, 1855, for the Building Fund, and the 116l. 17s. 8 1/2 d., the balance for the current expenses.--It may also be interesting to the reader to know that the total sum, given for the other objects, from the commencement of the work up to May 26, 1855, amounted to 25,239l. 8s. 10 3/4 d.; and that which came in by the sale of Bibles and Tracts, and by the payment of the children in the Day Schools, from the commencement, amounted to 4531l. 12s. 10 3/4 d.-- Besides this, also a great variety and number of articles of clothing, furniture, provisions, &c., were given for the use of the Orphans.

5. I have the joy of being able to state that we have great cause for thankfulness, that, in the midst of many difficulties, our labours among the Orphans continue to be blessed, and that, especially, again and again instances now come before us in which those, who were formerly under our care, declare themselves on the Lord's side.

FOURTH PART

6. Besides being able to meet the expenses for the Orphans and the other Objects, amounting altogether to 7832l. 7s. 0 1/2 d. during this year, I was able to add to the Building Fund 5242l. 18s. 3d. The total income during the year was 13,054l. 14s. 4d.

7. The articles given for the benefit of the Orphans, are sold by Miss Stevens, on the first floor of the Bible and Tract Warehouse of the Scriptural Knowledge Institution, No. 34, Park Street, Bristol.

Matters connected with my own personal affairs, or the work of the Lord in my hands, not immediately connected with the Scriptural Knowledge Institution, from May 26, 1854, to May 26, 1855.

Dec. 31, 1854. During this year there have been received into fellowship 61.

The Lord has been pleased to give me during this year--

1. In provisions, clothes, etc., worth at least   8 14 0

2. In anonymous offerings in money, put up in paper and directed to me, and put into the boxes for the poor saints or the rent, at the chapels . .   191 1 11 1/2

3. In presents in money, from believers in Bristol, not given anonymously. 143 12 10

4. In money, from believers not residing in Bristol 854 2 7 1/2

                                                                   L697 11 5

Some of my readers may be ready to exclaim, 697l. 11s. 5d.! What a large sum! Not one out of a hundred ministers has such a large salary, nor one out of twenty clergymen such a good living! Should you, esteemed reader, say so, my reply is: Indeed mine is a happy way for the obtaining of my temporal supplies; but if any one desires to go this way, he must--

1. Not merely say that he trusts in God, but must really do so. Often individuals profess to trust in God, but they embrace every opportunity, directly or indirectly, to expose their need, and thus seek to induce persons to help them. I do not say it is wrong to make known our wants; but I do say it ill agrees with trust in God, to expose our wants for the sake of inducing persons to help us. God will take us at our word. If we say we trust in Him, He will try whether we really do so, or only profess to do so; and if indeed we trust in Him, we are satisfied to stand with Him alone.

2. The individual who desires to go this way must be willing to be rich or poor, as the Lord pleases. He must be willing to know what it is to have an abun-

dance or scarcely anything. He must be willing to leave this world without any possessions.

3. He must be willing to take the money in God's way, not merely in large sums but in small.--Again and again have I had a single shilling given or sent to me. To have refused such tokens of Christian love, would have been ungracious.

4. He must be willing to live as the Lord's steward.--If any one were to begin this way of living, and did not communicate out of that which the Lord gives to him, but hoard it up; or, if he would live up to his income, as it is called, then the Lord, who influences the hearts of His children, to help him with means, would soon cause those channels to be dried up. How it came that my already good income still more increased, so as to come to what it is, has been stated in the early part of this volume; it was when I determined that, by God's help, His poor and His work should more than ever partake of my means. From that time the Lord was pleased more and more to intrust me with means for my own purse. I request the reader carefully to read over once more all I have said in the first volume of this Narrative, third part, from page 575 to 604, on Matthew 6, 19-21, on Matthew 6, 33, and on "Stewardship."

Various reasons might have kept me from publishing these accounts; but I have for my object in writing, the glory of God, and therefore delight in thus showing what a loving master I serve, and how bountifully He supplies my necessities; and I write for the comfort and encouragement of my fellow believers, that they may be led to trust in God more and more, and therefore I feel it due to them to state, how, even with regard to this life, I am amply provided for, though that is not what I seek after.

Further account respecting the intended Orphan Houses for Seven Hundred Poor Children, bereaved of both parents by death, from May 26, 1855, to May 26, 1856.

On May 20, 1855, I had in hand for this object 23,059l. 17s. 8 1/4 d., as stated in the last chapter on this subject. I now relate how the Lord was pleased to supply me further with means, but must confine myself, for the sake of brevity, to some of the more remarkable donations.

June. 20. A silver medal "given to the donor for being engaged in the taking of Java; but he desires to lay down his honour at the feet of the Lord Jesus, and to have this medal used to lay a stone in the new building."

Aug. 4. From S. S. 5l., with 5l. for the circulation of the Holy Scriptures, 5l. for Missions, and 5l. and the following articles for the support of the Orphans: A pair of gold mounted bracelets, a pair of jet bracelets, an iron watch guard, a pair of iron bracelets and waist buckle, a small gold seal, a ring, 2 pencil cases, a gold brooch, a purse and some mock pearls and beads.

FOURTH PART

Aug. 22. From Devonshire 100l.

Nov. 21. From Ipswich 2l., "The property of a dear child now in heaven."

Nov. 23. From London 50l., with 5l. for the circulation of Bibles and Tracts, 5l. for the Schools, 10l. for Missions, 10l. for the Orphans, 10l. for Mr. Craik, and 10l. for my own expenses.

Dec. 5. This evening I had the kind offer, unsolicited, that all the glass required, for about 300 large windows in the new house, which is now being built, should be gratuitously supplied. It is worthy of notice that the glass was not contracted for, this time, as in the case of the house already built. This, no doubt, was under the ordering of our Heavenly Father, who knew beforehand that this offer would be made.

Jan. 10, 1850. From Liverpool: A ring set with a brilliant, a gold bracelet, a Maltese bracelet, a brooch, a Maltese silver clasp and belt, a garnet ring, a pair of gold ear-rings, a box of whist markers, and German cross and chain.

Feb. 19. Now at last the Lord has been pleased, in answer to many prayers, to give me today 3000l., which being left to my disposal for the work of the Lord, I took for the Building Fund 1700l., for the support of the Orphans 300l., and for Missionary objects, the circulation of the Holy Scriptures and Tracts, and the support of the various Schools in connection with the Scriptural Knowledge Institution 1000l. How I feel at such times cannot be described, when in answer to many prayers, the Lord is pleased to open His bountiful hands, and to prove so abundantly how willing He is to listen to the supplications of His children who put their trust in Him, though it may be needful, for their own good and that of others, that for a season He seem but little or not at all to regard their supplications.

March 18. Received 4000l., which was left at my disposal as the work of the Lord might require it. I took of this sum 3000l. for the Building Fund, and 1000l. for Missions, the circulation of Bibles and Tracts, and the various schools, supported by the Institution.--This donation is the fruit of many prayers, and of much looking to the Lord for answers. His holy name be magnified for it. I am thus drawing nearer and nearer the time when I shall have obtained from the Lord everything needed for this object. I have not had, from the beginning, by God's grace, one moment's doubt, that in His own time, He would give me all that is required.

May 26. By sale of a publication in French 3l.--By sale of a publication in English 69l. 1s. 10d.--To these donations is to be added 911l. 8s. 1d., received during this year for interest.

I add a few remarks.

A. Up to May 20, 1856, the total income for the Building Fund was 29,297l. 18s. 11 1/2 d., so that only about 5700l. more will be required, as far as I am able to see, in order to accomplish to the full my purpose respecting the accommodation for 700 more Orphans.

B. The house for 400 female Orphans, commenced in August, 1855, is expected, with God's blessing to be ready by about Midsummer 1857 for the reception of 400 Orphans.

C. As soon as my path is made plain, God willing, the other house for 300 Orphans will also be commenced; but I cannot state, at present, any further particulars respecting this.

Supplies for the School--, Bible--, Missionary and Tract Fund, sent in answer to prayer, from May 26, 1855, to May 26, 1856.

On May 26, 1855, when the accounts were closed, there was in hand 41l. 6s. 11 1/2 d. for these objects. On June 5, 1855, therefore only a few days after the commencement of the new period, when only 1l. 0s. 6d. altogether had come in for these objects, in 8 different donations, I received 211l. 9s. 5d., of which the donor kindly wished me to retain 11l. 9s. 5d. for my own expenses, and to use the 200l. for the work of the Lord, as might be needed. I took, therefore, 100l. for the support of the Orphans, and 100l. for these objects, and had thus some means, to go on with the work. This donation was a great refreshment and encouragement to me, at the commencement of this new period.

July 12. Since June 5th little only, comparatively, has come in. All the donations for these objects were under 5l. Today, however, the Lord, in answer to many prayers, has sent me 200l., to be used as needed. I took of this donation 100l. for the Orphans, and 100l. for these objects, and have thus the means of being able to send some help to brethren who labour in the Gospel.

Aug. 9. Having had heavy expenses the last ten days, in order to help foreign labourers in the Gospel, and to procure supplies of Bibles, Testaments, and Tracts, our means for these objects were now reduced to 7l. 7s. 10 1/2 d. Yet I desired far more to help brethren who labour in the Word, as the greater party of them had not yet been supplied. I therefore besought the Lord, that He would be pleased to send in means. When I came home this evening from the New Orphan House, I found the following letter, from the same believing farmer, whom the Lord has several times used in previous years, to help me when in need.

"* * * * Aug. 8, 1855.

"Dear Brother in Christ,

FOURTH PART

"I feel stirred up to help you in the work in which you are engaged, and therefore beg your acceptance of the enclosed Twenty Pounds, to be used in any way you please, trusting God will direct you.

Yours affectionately in Christ,

"* * * *"

I took the whole amount for Missionary objects and the circulation of Bibles and Tracts.

Aug. 25. The outgoings from these objects have been great, during this month, and the income comparatively small. On this account the means for these objects were reduced today to a few shillings. As the opportunities for the gratuitous circulation of the Holy Scriptures and Gospel Tracts, however, continued to be great, and as I had been only able to send out about the third part as much to labourers in the Gospel, as I could have desired, my prayer during this week had been especially for means for this object. Now the Lord has somewhat helped us. I have received today a donation of 203l. 14s., the whole of which I took for these objects, as the application of it was left with me. The Lord be magnified for this precious help! I shall be able to send at least 150l. of this sum to labourers in the Gospel.-- About 3 hours, before this donation was received, I had been asking the Lord, if He would not condescend to use me as an instrument, at this time, in helping these brethren, He would kindly in some other way supply them with means.

Sept. 1. From Dublin 5l. for missions.

Sept. 11. From C. W. 20l. for foreign labourers in the Gospel. A precious help in answer to many prayers.

Sept. 20. Received 190l., of which I took 100l. for these objects, in order to be able to send some help to brethren who labour in the Word, and to have means for going on with the circulation of Bibles and Tracts; and the remaining 90l. I took for the support of the Orphans. Precious help, the fruit of many prayers!

Sept. 30. From Clerkenwell for missions 10l.

Oct. 13. 20l. from Austin Friars, London. I had been praying again and again for more means for these objects, and had sent out 100l. within the last few days to brethren who labour in the Word, but desired to send out more.

Oct. 23. From London 20l.

Nov. 6th. Since Oct. 16th I had not been able to send any further help to brethren who labour in the Word, much as I desired to do so, having only means enough to meet the necessary demands for the Schools, and the circulation of Bibles and

Tracts, which amounted, from that time, to about 120l. But I prayed daily for means for missionary objects and the circulation of Bibles and Tracts. Today I received 180l., the whole of which I have taken for these objects, as the disposal of it was left to me, having great reason to believe that many labourers in the Gospel are in need of help, and having still so many openings for the circulation of the Holy Scriptures and Tracts. The Lord be magnified for this precious answer to prayer!

Dec. 13. During November I was enabled to send 200l. to brethren who labour in the Gospel at Home and Abroad, and also 197l. in October; but during this month I have as yet been only able to send out 12l. My often repeated prayer has been, that the Lord would give me the joy and privilege of sending out a considerable sum during this month also. This prayer was again repeated, when I rose this morning, and saw the windows covered with ice; for I thought then of the needy brethren in this cold weather, connected with the high price of provisions. It was not long after, when I received 153l., to be used in the Lord's service, as most needed. I took of this, 100l. for brethren labouring in the Gospel at Home and Abroad, and 53l. for the support of the Orphans, and thus have the joy of being able to send at least 100l. at once, waiting upon the Lord for more.

Jan. 31, 1850. As the fruit of very many prayers, I have received today 100l., the whole of which I have put to these funds, the application of the money being left with me; as there was nothing at all left now for the circulation of Bibles and Tracts, and the various Schools, and as I had often asked the Lord to allow me further the joy of sending help to brethren who labour in the Word, to whom since Dec. 14th I had been able to send scarcely anything.

From this time there were no further difficulty experienced with regard to means, for these objects, as on Feb. 19th there was received the donation of 3000l., and on March 18th the donation of 4000l., of each of which, as stated before, I took 100l. for the School--, Bible--, Missionary--and Tract objects, whereby, together with what came in besides, I was not only carried to the close of this period, but was enabled to expend more on Missionary objects, and the circulation of the Holy Scriptures and Tracts, than during any previous year, since the Institution commenced in March, 1834. Let it be especially observed by the Godly reader, that not only does this work continue to exist, after more than 22 years, carried on solely through the power of prayer and faith in the Living God; but also year by year its operations have been extended. Unbelief is thus put to shame. It is plainly proved that the work of God can be carried on simply by trust in God. If our work is indeed the work of God, faith and prayer will be found efficient agents; and if they are not efficient, we may well question, whether we do indeed make use of them; or, if we do, whether the work, in which we are occupied, is truly the work of God.

Notice here also, that not only was I enabled, simply through prayer and faith, to procure means for a greater amount of operations than during any year since March 1834; but, over and above all this, I was able to add to the Building Fund during this year 6238l. 1s. 3 1/4 d., whilst the income for the support of the Orphans was

FOURTH PART

4070l. 18s. 1 1/4 d., and the income for the other objects 4279l. 6s. 6 1/4 d. The total amount, therefore, which the Lord was pleased to send in during the past year, was 14,588l. 5s. 10 3/4 d. Behold, dear Reader, how effectual this way is for the obtaining of means; for the amount is large. Behold too, how pleasant a way it is; for I have not to encounter unpleasant refusals, in applying for money. Behold how cheap a way; for it involves none of the heavy expenses, usually attendant on the collection of contributions; for all I do is, to make known the work in which we are engaged, by means of the Reports, which are for the most part sold for the benefit of the Orphans, and they actually brought in during this year, as the audited accounts show, a little more than they cost.

But, perhaps, you say, Yes, it is just these Reports, why there is nothing at all remarkable in the matter. Our reply is: We do not pretend to miracles. We have no desire even, that the work, in which we are engaged, should be considered an extraordinary one, or even a remarkable one. We are truly sorry that many persons, inconsiderately, look upon it almost as a miraculous one. The principles on which we are acting are as old as the Holy Scriptures. But they are forgotten by many; and they are not held in living faith by others; and by some they are not known at all; nay, they are denied even to be Scriptural by not a few, and are considered as wild and fanatical. It is ascribed to my being a foreigner that I succeed so well, or to the novelty of the thing, or to some secret treasure to which I have access; but when all will not account for the progress of the work, it is said, the Reports produce it all. My reply to these different objections is: My being a foreigner, looked at naturally, would be much more likely to hinder my being intrusted with such large sums, than to induce donors to give. As to the novelty procuring the money, the time is long gone by for novelty, for this is June 1856, and the work commenced in March 1834. As to the secret treasure to which I have access, there is more in this supposition than the objectors are aware of; for surely God's treasury is inexhaustible, and I have that (though that alone) to go to, and have indeed drawn out of it, simply by prayer and faith, more than 113,000l. since the beginning of the work. But now as to the last objection, that the Reports are the means by which all the money is obtained: let us consider this a little, for I do heartily desire that the Reader may not lose the blessing, which this Institution is intended to convey to his soul. My reply is: There is nothing unusual in writing Reports. This is done by public Institutions generally, but the constant complaint is, that Reports are not read. Our Reports are not extraordinary as to the power of language, or as to striking appeals to feelings. They are simple statements of facts. These Reports are not accompanied by personal application for means; but they are simply sent to the donors, or to any other individuals who wish to have or purchase them. If they produce results, which Reports generally do not, I can only ascribe it to the Lord.

I do not mean to say that God does not use the Reports as instruments in procuring us means. They are written in order that I may thus give an account of my stewardship, but particularly, in order that, by these printed accounts of the work, the chief end of this Institution may be answered, which is to raise another public testimony to an unbelieving world, that in these last days the Living God is still the

Living God, listening to the prayers of His children, and helping those who put their trust in Him; and in order that believers generally may be benefited and especially be encouraged to trust in God for everything they may need, and be stirred up to deal in greater simplicity with God respecting everything connected with their own particular position and circumstances; in short, that the children of God maybe brought to the practical use of the Holy Scriptures, as the word of the Living God.-- But while these are the primary reasons for publishing these Reports, we doubt not that the Lord has again and again used them as instruments in leading persons to help us with their means. For as we continually stand in need of considerable sums, and as even hundreds of pounds go but a very little way, I entreat the Lord day by day, and generally several times every day, to supply me with means, to speak to the hearts of His dear children, and to constrain them by the love of Christ to help me out of the means, with which He has intrusted them; and so it comes to pass, I doubt not, that the Lord again and again works by His Spirit in the hearts of those who have read or heard the Reports. But whether we are supplied with means through the Reports or irrespective of them; in either case it is God, who is working for us, and it is to this I wish to direct the mind of the Reader.

Means for the support of the 300 Orphans already under my care, sent in answer to Prayer, from May 26, 1855, to May 26, 1856.

When this period commenced, I had 116l. 17s. 8 1/2 d. in hand for the support of the Orphans, an amount so small, looking at it naturally, that one would be ready to say, there would be soon nothing in hand. Thus indeed it would have been, had the Lord not been pleased further to send in means; but He, in His fatherly care, never ceased to remember our need and to provide for its supply. The expenses were very heavy, month after month, not only because of the greatness of the Establishment, but in particular also on account of the high price of provisions, which prevailed during the whole of last year; yet, notwithstanding this, there was not a single year, since the Orphan work commenced, in which I went on with greater ease regarding means, than during the last period. At the close of the first month, June 26th, though the expenses had been great, there remained 192l. 9s. 11 1/2 d. in hand. At the close of the second month, July 26th, there was a balance left of 259l. 4s. At the close of the third month, Aug. 26th, there was left a balance of 291l. 19s. 2d. And in like manner the Lord was pleased to supply me with means, month after month, so that when He was pleased to give me on Feb. 19th the donation of 3000l., above referred to, I had still 160l. in hand for the support of the Orphans. It is particularly worthy of notice, that the income for the support of the Orphans was not supplied by some very large donations, previous to the one of 3000l.; for there was no period for about ten years, when I received fewer large donations for the support of the Orphans, than during the last. It was supplied by many donations of 1l., 2l., 5l., 10l., 20l. and upwards, but not exceeding 100l., except one of 117l. 10s. 0d. received on May 3rd, and the 300l. which I took for the Orphans out of the 3000l. And again it is remarkable, that while up to Feb. 19th we had always abounded, and were never brought low, but generally had had about 200l in hand; almost immediately after the reception of the 3000l., out of which I took 300l. for the support of the Orphans, the

FOURTH PART

balance, before in hand, was all expended, and more money required; so that I had soon to use a part of the 300l., whereby the hand of God in that large donation was so much the more made manifest; and yet, again, this 300l., with what the Lord was pleased to send in besides between Feb. 19th and May 26th, not only met all the remaining heavy expenses, but left in hand a balance of 167l. 18s. 11 3/4 d.

Observe, dear Reader, while we were in rented houses in Wilson Street, we had our faith greatly tried, year after year, though the expenses were only about one-third as much, as during the past year. And thus also it has been again and again, since the New Orphan House was opened in 1849; but during the past year we were entirely free from trial of faith regarding means for the support of the Orphans, though not without many trials of faith and patience on other accounts. The Lord takes His own way, and therefore He allows this year to stand by itself, in this particular. On this I delight to dwell; for I desire that the hand of God may be recognised in this work, whether it be by His power being manifested in sustaining us in our poverty from day to day, or by His causing us to go on easily with regard to means for a day, or a month, or a year. You see, then, that while there was but like "a handful of flour in the barrel," at the commencement of the period, the Lord was pleased to make it last for a whole year, and yet, at the end of the year, there was more than at the beginning; and during the whole year all these hundreds had been fed, clothed, and provided with everything needful; apprentices had been placed out and premiums paid for them, and their outfit and that of the young women going out to service had been provided at the expense of the Orphan Establishment. What an answer does all this furnish to unbelief which said, when I was going to build the New Orphan House, How will you find the means for the support of these 300 Orphans? Or, when unbelief said, How will you be able to support a thousand Orphans?

I will now out of the very many donations, received during this year, single out a few, and make here and there remarks, as the subjects may call for it.

June 1, 1855. The balance left when the accounts were closed, was only enough to supply the average expenses of ten days for the support of the Orphans, and there had only been received during the last 5 days 14l. 13s. 7d. How kind therefore of the Lord, to send me today 50l. from Liverpool, 1l. from Preston, and 10s. from Milton Abbot!

June 5. 5l. from Lincolnshire "As a thank-offering to the Lord for preserving the only child of a widow from the path of the destroyer."

June 8. A gold chain, some books for sale, and 15l.

June 19. 5l. as "A thank-offering to the Lord for preservation when thrown out of a gig."

July 10. From Worcestershire 25l.

July 12. Received from a great distance 200l., of which I took 100l. for the support of the Orphans, and 100l. for the other objects. There has also come in today 20l. from Norwich, 1l. from Bath, 4s. from Chepstow, 7s. 6d. from Mallow, 1l. from Dublin, a gold seal and sixpence, and 13s. and 6s. 9d. besides. The Lord's kindness is great in this, as a fresh supply of oatmeal, flour, &c., will need to be paid for, other heavy expenses have to be met, and there is not much in hand.

July 14. An Israelitish gentleman, an entire stranger, brought to my house this morning 5l. for the support of the Orphans. See in what a variety of ways the Lord is pleased to supply us with means, and all unsolicited, simply in answer to prayer!

Aug. 17. From Messrs. * * * 7l. 10s. 0d., being a portion of the money received for showing the "British Empire" before she left Bristol. Observe again, esteemed Reader, what a variety of ways the Lord uses to supply me with means; for I had not before even heard of the name of this vessel, nor did I know her owners, even by name; yet God inclines the heart of these gentlemen to send me this 7l. 10s. 0d. towards the support of the 300 Orphans.--Anonymously from Wilton 4s., as "A thank-offering to God for His mercies on a journey."

Aug. 21. From Worcestershire 30l.

Sept. 6. From the Bombay Presidency 25l.

On Sept. 12, were sent by the donor who gave so valuable a donation of jewellery on July 26, 1854, the following articles of jewellery, etc., being the last she possessed, and which the love of Christ led her to give up: A valuable dressing case, 2 little boxes, 2 pomatum pots, a gold thimble, a large gold brooch set with a ruby and 2 brilliants, a gold star necklace set with a brilliant, a gold bracelet, a gold watchguard, a gold cross, 2 rings set with pearls, a ring set with pearls and small rubies, a ring set with 2 brilliants, a ring set with 3 rubies and 2 brilliants, a pair of gold earrings and brooch set with pearls, a large ivory brooch, a silver brooch set with pearls, a silver pencil case, a paste brooch, 5 loose crystals, and some small carved ornaments.

Sept. 26. Received a large cask containing the wearing apparel of the late Mrs. H. at J. in the county of Leicester, which this lady, by her will, had bequeathed to me for the benefit of the Orphans.

Oct. 3. Received the following letter.

"* * *, Oct. 8, 1855.

Dear Mr. Mueller,

The enclosed check for 8l. 1s. 4d. is chiefly the product of a sale for the Orphans, which we held on our sister's wedding-day, and hoping it will be acceptable,

FOURTH PART

We remain,

Your's affectionately,

* * * * *."

The Orphans on Ashley Down were to be benefited by the day of gladness in this Godly family.--The Godly principle, which brought this donation, refreshed my spirit above the money, and, I doubt not, will refresh other Godly readers.--Let me here say, by the way, to believing parents, Seek to cherish in your children early the habit of being interested about the work of God and about cases of need and distress, and use them too at suitable times, and under suitable circumstances, as your almoners, and you will reap fruit from doing so.

Oct. 10. From Surrey 5s. and a gold chain.--From a shepherd in Australia, who had read my Narrative while tending his flock, 12s.-- See how the lady near London sends her gold chain, and the shepherd in Australia his 12s.--Thus the Lord, in the greatest variety of ways supplies me with means, for the greater part through entire strangers. Thus I received one hundred pounds after another, anonymously, through London bankers, until a particular circumstance made known to me the name of the kind Christian donor, whom I have seen but once years ago, and who had, at the same time, sent me considerable donations with his name, whilst his bankers, anonymously, sent his still larger donations of many hundred pounds. I dwell upon this fact, that the reader may be led to own increasingly the hand of God in this work; for I desire that He may be honoured, that His hand may be recognised, and that attention may be drawn to Him, and not to me. It gives me no joy but sorrow, if persons admire me, in connexion with this work, as if I did anything great; as if I acted in a remarkable way. What is it that I do? I simply desire, through this work, to direct the attention of those who need it to the precious truth, that God is unchangeably the same, and that those who take Him at His word, as given to us in the Holy Scriptures, will find how unspeakably blessed it is, even for this life, to do so. To bring back to the written word of God those of His children, who practically have departed from it, and to sound again and again in the ears and consciences of the unbeliever that there is verily a living God who listens to the prayers of those who put their trust in Him, is, as I have often before stated, the great end of this work.

Oct. 11. To day I received, unsolicited, a kind and useful present of flannel and calico, to the amount of 10l., from the ladies constituting the Bristol Dorcas Society.

Oct. 18. "Articles forwarded by friends at a distance," an anonymous but most valuable donation, the particulars of which I am not at liberty to state.--The kind unknown donor or donors should, however, know, that very many pounds have been realized through the sale of these articles, and that they were almost all readily sold.

I cannot help noticing here, how much help the Lord has given us, in disposing of the articles, given for the benefit of the Orphans, and what a considerable sum has come to the funds of the Institution through the fact that believers have been led to send their needless articles. There came in by the sale of articles during the past year, for the Building Fund 21l. 16s. 7d., for missionary objects 15l. 6s. 4d., and for the support of the Orphans 426l. 14s. 9d.

Oct. 27. From Devonshire 4l. "The proceeds of the sale of the Orphans pig." A young pig bought, fattened and sold for the benefit of the Orphans, and this 4l. was sent as the proceeds.

Nov. 3. From St. Leonard's-on-Sea 50l.

Nov. 4. A ring set with 5 brilliants.

Nov. 16. From Yate 10l. and also 5s.

Nov. 19. From New York 25l. From Bath 10l.

Flour is now 65s. per sack. When we began to bake in the New Orphan House, it was from 27s. to 32s. We bought at one time 20 sacks at 27s. Now it is 65s. But the Lord provides us with all we need, though other provisions are also expensive, as well as flour.

Dec. 11. From the north of Devon a brooch, set with an emerald and 10 brilliants.--I took this as a further answer to my prayers, for gifts of diamonds, etc.

Jan. 4, 1856. 42l. 4s. 6d. with these words; "This is the answer of prayers, we have of late without ceasing offered up on behalf the Orphans."--This is one of the most remarkable donations received during the whole year. A brother and sister in the Lord, who labour for Him in seeking to win souls, whilst depending upon Him for all they need, gave themselves to prayer on behalf of the Orphans, and that which the Lord gave them towards the close of the yean 1855, in answer to prayer, enabled them to send this 42l. 4s. 6d. See, dear Reader, that the saints have power with God. This brother and sister have been greatly encouraged by this work, and now, even in the way of means, though they are poor themselves, this work reaps the fruit of their prayers. Be encouraged, then, for yourself to trust in God for all you may need.

Jan.30, 1l. 5s. from Stroud, as "a thank-offering for 25 years of family mercies."

Feb. 3. From Worcestershire 30l.

FOURTH PART

Feb. 0. From George Town, Demerara, 10 dollars.--From South Town 5l and also 5s.--From Liverpool 50l.

Feb. 9. From Adelaide, Australia, 2l. and also 10s.

Feb. 15. From Hornley, Staffordshire, 20l.

April 5. Received 74l. 9s. 1d., which being left to my disposal for the Lord's work, I took the whole for the support of the Orphans.

April 9. From Worcestershire 50l.

April 19. 1l. from the Grand Duchy of Baden.

I have thus, out of more than 2000 donations, taken a few, to show in what way the Lord is pleased to supply me with means.

Miscellaneous points respecting the Scriptural Knowledge Institution for Home and Abroad, with reference to the period from May 26, 1855, to May 26, 1856.

1, During this year 4 Day Schools in Bristol, with 203 children, were entirely supported by the funds of the Institution; and nine Day Schools, in Devonshire, Cornwall, Gloucestershire, Norfolk, Scotland, British Guiana and Africa, were assisted.--Further, one Sunday School in Bristol, with 158 children, was entirely supported, and eight others, in Gloucestershire, Devonshire, Middlesex, Canada and British Guiana, were assisted.--Lastly, one Adult School in Bristol, with 158 Adult scholars, was entirely supported, and two other Adult Schools, in Kent and Norfolk, were assisted. The amount spent during this year, in connexion with these schools, was 348l. 5s. 11 1/4 d.; and the sum total expended during the last 22 years in connexion with the schools, either entirely, or in part, supported by the funds of this Institution, amounts to 7552l. 18s. 7 1/2 d.--The number of children, who were under our care, merely in the Schools, entirely supported by this Institution, from March 5, 1834, to May 20, 1856, was 6104 in the Day Schools, 2911 in the Sunday Schools, and 2611 persons in the Adult School. Thus, without reckoning the Orphans, 11,626 persons have been brought under habitual instruction in the things of God in these various Schools; besides the many thousands in the Schools in various parts of England, Ireland, Scotland, British Guiana, the East Indies, etc., which have been to a greater or lesser degree assisted.

2, During this year was expended on the circulation of the Holy Scriptures, of the funds of this Institution, 496l. 10s. 0d. There were circulated during this year 2175 Bibles, 1233 New Testaments, 119 copies of the Psalms, and 155 other small portions of the Holy Scriptures.-- There have been circulated since March 5, 1834, through the medium of this Institution, 16,124 Bibles, 10,280 New Testaments, 307 copies of the Psalms, and 944 other small portions of the Holy Scriptures.--The sum

THE LORD'S DEALINGS WITH GEORGE MÜLLER

total spent on the circulation of the Holy Scriptures, since March 5, 1834, is 3880l. 0s.1d.

3. During this year there were spent of the Funds of the Institution for Missionary objects 2501l. 9s. 1d. By this sum, sixty one labourers in the word and doctrine, in various parts of the world, were to a greater or less degree assisted. The amount sent to each of these servants of the Lord is as follows.

To No. 1. Labouring in British Guiana (a European) 171l.

To No. 2. Ditto (Ditto) 110l.

To No. 3. Ditto (Ditto) 62l.

To No. 4. Ditto (Ditto) 58l.

To No. 5. Ditto (Ditto) 48l.

To No. 6. Ditto (Ditto) 33l.

To No. 7. Ditto (Ditto) 8l.

To No. 8 Ditto (A Native) 17l.

To No. 9 Ditto (Ditto) 14l.

To No. 10. Labouring in China (a European) 14l.

To No. 11. Labouring in the East Indies (a European) 60l.

To No. 12. Ditto (Ditto) 40l.

To No. 13. Ditto (Ditto) 25l.

To No 14. Ditto (a Native) 15l.

To No. 15 Labouring in Canada 90l.

To No. 16. Ditto 70l.

To No. 17. Labouring in Belgium 45l.

To No. 18. Labouring in Switzerland 30l.

To No. 19. Labouring in France 30l.

FOURTH PART

To No. 20. Labouring in Ireland 60l.

To No. 21. Ditto 45l.

To No. 22. Labouring in Scotland 60l.

To No. 23 Labouring in England 90l.

To No. 24. Ditto 80l.

To No. 25. Ditto 60l.

To No. 26. Ditto 60l.

To No. 27. Ditto 58l.

To No. 28. Ditto 50l.

To No. 29. Ditto 50l.

To No. 30. Ditto 50l.

To No. 31. Ditto 50l.

To No. 32. Ditto 45l.

To No. 33. Ditto 45l.

To No. 34. Ditto 45l.

To No. 35. Ditto 40l.

To No. 36. Ditto 40l.

To No. 37. Ditto 40l.

To No. 38. Ditto 35l.

To No. 39. Ditto 35l.

To No. 40. Ditto 35l.

To No. 41. Ditto 35l.

To No. 42. Ditto 30l.

To No. 43. Ditto 30l.

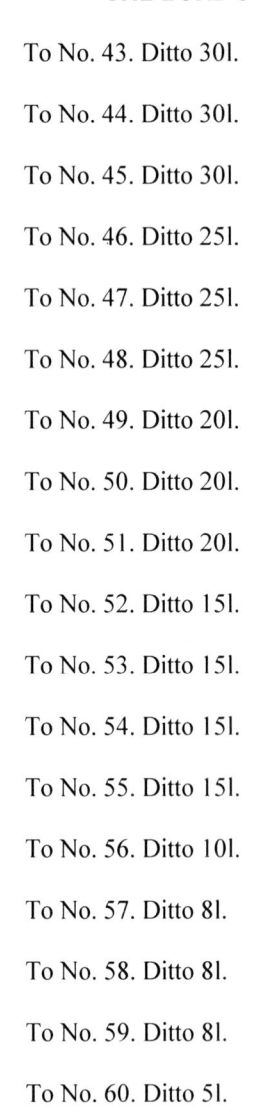

To No. 44. Ditto 30l.

To No. 45. Ditto 30l.

To No. 46. Ditto 25l.

To No. 47. Ditto 25l.

To No. 48. Ditto 25l.

To No. 49. Ditto 20l.

To No. 50. Ditto 20l.

To No. 51. Ditto 20l.

To No. 52. Ditto 15l.

To No. 53. Ditto 15l.

To No. 54. Ditto 15l.

To No. 55. Ditto 15l.

To No. 56. Ditto 10l.

To No. 57. Ditto 8l.

To No. 58. Ditto 8l.

To No. 59. Ditto 8l.

To No. 60. Ditto 5l.

To No. 61. Ditto 5l.

There was also expended for fitting up, or renting, lighting, cleaning, &c., some preaching rooms in spiritually dark villages in Devonshire, Gloucestershire, and Somersetshire, 38l. 9 1

Respecting this part of the work there is great cause for thanksgiving. It has pleased the Lord abundantly to bless the labours of many of these servants of Christ whom I have assisted. Very many souls have been won through them during the past year. On the labours of some in particular, both at home and abroad, an unusual

FOURTH PART

blessing has rested. But whilst I say this to the praise of the Lord, I add the earnest entreaty also, to the believing reader, to supplicate for these dear brethren, that it may please God to give unto them strength of voice, mind and body for their service; but, above all, to renew them in their inward man day by day, and to make them happy in Himself, so that they may out of a happy heart, which is under the power of the truth, set forth the unsearchable riches of Christ. I also request the prayers of the believing reader for an increase of labourers, especially for foreign countries, as almost everywhere there is a great lack of them, and from time to time through death or ill health they are removed from their post of service.

Though more has been expended this year of the funds of the Institution, than during the previous year, for Missionary objects; yet I long to be permitted to do far more than this.

The sum total expended on Missionary operations, of the funds of the Institution, since March 5, 1834, is 18,616l. 9s. 6 1/2 d.

4, There was laid out for the circulation of Tracts, from May 26, 1855, to May 26, 1856, the sum of 791l. 1s. 0 1/2 d., and there were circulated 812,970 Tracts and Books.--The sum total expended on this object, since. Nov. 19, 1840, amounts to 3659l. 16s. 7 1/4 d.--The total number of all the Tracts and Books circulated since Nov. 19, 1840, is 4,397,680.

During this year, as for many years past, there has not been a single open door set before us, where we could profitably have circulated the Holy Scriptures, or given away Tracts, but the Lord has also been pleased to enable us to enter those doors. These opportunities have of late years increased more and more, but the Lord has also been pleased, along with them, to give increased means; and, we doubt not, He will yet further open His bountiful hand, and supply us with means for the circulation of the Holy Scriptures and Gospel Tracts.

I have heard again and again of instances, during the past year in which it had pleased the Lord to bless the circulation of those Tracts and little books, which He had allowed us to issue.

5, At the beginning of this period, there were 297 Orphans in the New Orphan House. During the past year, there were admitted into it 25 Orphans, making 322 in all. Of these 322, one died. Only one! She had been nine years under our care, and we had the great joy of seeing her depart this life as a decided believer in the Lord Jesus. One boy we were obliged to expel from the Institution, after we had long borne with him, but we follow him still with our prayers. 13 boys were fitted out and apprenticed at the expense of the Establishment. Seven girls were sent to service and one was apprenticed, each having been provided with an outfit, at the expense of the Establishment. Several of those who left the Orphan House, we had the joy of sending out as believers. These 23 vacancies, thus occasioned, left on May 26, 1856, only 299 Orphans under our care. This one vacancy, however, was the very next Friday filled up. The total number of Orphans, who have been under our care since April 1836, is 622.

I notice further the following points respecting the Orphan work:

1, At the beginning of this period, there were 715 Orphans waiting for admission. Since then 201 more destitute Orphans, bereaved of both parents by death, and some only a few months old, have been applied for to be admitted, making 916 in all. Of these 916, we were only able to receive 25, as has been stated, and 44 either died or were otherwise provided for, as their relatives or friends informed us; so that there are still 847 waiting for admission. Dear Reader, think of these 847 destitute Orphans, bereaved of both parents! As for myself, I have now before me the most pleasant and heart-refreshing prospect, if the Lord permit, of being able to receive 400 of them about June or July 1857, and also of being permitted to build the third house for 300 more.

2, The average expense for each of the Orphans under our care, during the past year; amounted to 12l. 6s. 8d.

3, Without any one having been personally applied to for anything by me, the sum of 84,441l. 6s. 3 1/4 d. has been given to me for the Orphans, as the result of prayer to God, since the commencement of the work. The total sum given for the other objects, since the commencement of the work, amounts to 28,904l. 11s. 3 3/4 d.; and that which has come in by the sale of Bibles and Tracts, and by the payments of the children in the Day Schools, from the commencement up to May 26, 1856, amounts to 5,145l. 17s. 0d. Besides this, also a great variety and number of articles of clothing, furniture, provisions, etc., have been given for the use of the Orphans.

4, The Lord is pleased to continue to allow us to see fruit in connexion with the Orphan work, and we hear still again and again of cases, in which those, who were formerly under our care, have been led to declare themselves openly for the Lord, besides those, in whom we saw the work of grace manifestly begun, before they left the Orphan House.

5, The total of the current expenses for the Orphans and the various other objects of the Institution, was 8166l. 8s. 5 1/4 d. during the past year.

Matters connected with my own personal affairs, from May 26, 1855, to May 26, 1856.

Dec. 31, 1855. During this year the Lord has been pleased to give me

1. By anonymous donations through the boxes L202 10 9 1/4

2. Through donations from believers in Bristol, not anonymously . . 149 13 9

FOURTH PART

3. Through donations from believers not residing in Bristol . . . 301 15 8

4. Through presents in clothes, provisions, etc., worth at least . . . 12 16 0

L726 10 2 1/4

This, dear Reader, is the writer's statement after having acted on these principles for more than 25 years. You see, not for a week, a month, or even a year, how the writer has been dealt with by the Lord, after he had set out in this way; but, in all simplicity he has related to you, how it has been with him year after year. And now, after more than 25 years, he is still acting on these principles, and is more than ever convinced of their truthfulness and their blessedness; and he is delighted in being able to prove to you, to God's honour, that even for this life he has been no loser by acting out the light which the Lord has been pleased to give to him.

May 26, 1856. Yesterday evening it was 24 years, since I came to labour in Bristol. In looking back upon this period, as it regards the Lord's goodness to my family and myself, the Scriptural Knowledge Institution, and the saints among whom I seek to serve Him, I exclaim, What has God wrought! I marvel at His kindness, and yet I do not; for such is His manner; and, if it please Him that I remain longer on earth, I expect, not fewer manifestations of His love, but more and more.

Since my beloved friend and fellow labourer and I first came to Bristol, 1586 believers have been received into fellowship, which number, with the 68 we found in communion, makes 1654. But out of that number 252 have fallen asleep, 53 have been separated from fellowship, 145 have left us, some however merely through circumstances, and in love, and 510 have left Bristol; so that there are only 694 remaining in communion.

Farewell, Christian Reader. I reckon it one of the greatest privileges which the Lord has been pleased to bestow upon me to be able to finish this volume. Remember the writer in your prayers. He greatly needs them. Numberless are his difficulties and trials, as well as his joys and blessings! Pray that he may be helped of God to finish his course with joy, and to continue his service without growing weary.

The End.

Also from Benediction Books ...

Wandering Between Two Worlds: Essays on Faith and Art
Anita Mathias
Benediction Books, 2007
152 pages
ISBN: 0955373700

Available from www.amazon.com, www.amazon.co.uk
www.wanderingbetweentwoworlds.com

In these wide-ranging lyrical essays, Anita Mathias writes, in lush, lovely prose, of her naughty Catholic childhood in Jamshedpur, India; her large, eccentric family in Mangalore, a sea-coast town converted by the Portuguese in the sixteenth century; her rebellion and atheism as a teenager in her Himalayan boarding school, run by German missionary nuns, St. Mary's Convent, Nainital; and her abrupt religious conversion after which she entered Mother Teresa's convent in Calcutta as a novice. Later rich, elegant essays explore the dualities of her life as a writer, mother, and Christian in the United States-- Domesticity and Art, Writing and Prayer, and the experience of being "an alien and stranger" as an immigrant in America, sensing the need for roots.

About the Author

Anita Mathias was born in India, has a B.A. and M.A. in English from Somerville College, Oxford University and an M.A. in Creative Writing from the Ohio State University. Her essays have been published in The Washington Post, The London Magazine, The Virginia Quarterly Review, Commonweal, Notre Dame Magazine, America, The Christian Century, Religion Online, The Southwest Review, Contemporary Literary Criticism, New Letters, The Journal, and two of HarperSanFrancisco's The Best Spiritual Writing anthologies. Her non-fiction has won fellowships from The National Endowment for the Arts; The Minnesota State Arts Board; The Jerome Foundation, The Vermont Studio Center; The Virginia Centre for the Creative Arts, and the First Prize for the Best General Interest Article from the Catholic Press Association of the United States and Canada. Anita has taught Creative Writing at the College of William and Mary, and now lives and writes in Oxford, England.

"Yesterday's Treasures for Today's Readers"
Titles by Benediction Classics available from Amazon.co.uk

Religio Medici, Hydriotaphia, Letter to a Friend, Thomas Browne

Pseudodoxia Epidemica: Or, Enquiries into Commonly Presumed Truths, Thomas Browne

Urne Buriall and The Garden of Cyrus, Thomas Browne

The Maid's Tragedy, Beaumont and Fletcher

The Custom of the Country, Beaumont and Fletcher

Philaster Or Love Lies a Bleeding, Beaumont and Fletcher

A Treatise of Fishing with an Angle, Dame Juliana Berners.

Pamphilia to Amphilanthus, Lady Mary Wroth

The Compleat Angler, Izaak Walton

The Magnetic Lady, Ben Jonson

Every Man Out of His Humour, Ben Jonson

The Masque of Blacknesse. The Masque of Beauty,. Ben Jonson

The Life of St. Thomas More, William Roper

Pendennis, William Makepeace Thackeray

Salmacis and Hermaphroditus attributed to Francis Beaumont

Friar Bacon and Friar Bungay Robert Greene

Holy Wisdom, Augustine Baker

The Jew of Malta and the Massacre at Paris, Christopher Marlowe

Tamburlaine the Great, Parts 1 & 2 AND Massacre at Paris, Christopher Marlowe

All Ovids Elegies, Lucans First Booke, Dido Queene of Carthage, Hero and Leander, Christopher Marlowe

The Titan, Theodore Dreiser

Scapegoats of the Empire: The true story of the Bushveldt Carbineers, George Witton

All Hallows' Eve, Charles Williams

The Place of The Lion, Charles Williams

The Greater Trumps, Charles Williams

My Apprenticeship: Volumes I and II, Beatrice Webb

Last and First Men / Star Maker, Olaf Stapledon

Last and First Men, Olaf Stapledon

Darkness and the Light, Olaf Stapledon

The Worst Journey in the World, Apsley Cherry-Garrard

The Schoole of Abuse, Containing a Pleasaunt Invective Against Poets, Pipers, Plaiers, Iesters and Such Like Catepillers of the Commonwelth, Stephen Gosson

Russia in the Shadows, H. G. Wells

Wild Swans at Coole, W. B. Yeats

A hundreth good pointes of husbandrie, Thomas Tusser

The Collected Works of Nathanael West: "The Day of the Locust", "The Dream Life of Balso Snell", "Miss Lonelyhearts", "A Cool Million", Nathanael West

Miss Lonelyhearts & The Day of the Locust, Nathaniel West

The Worst Journey in the World, Apsley Cherry-Garrard

Scott's Last Expedition, V1, R. F. Scott

The Dream of Gerontius, John Henry Newman

The Brother of Daphne, Dornford Yates

The Downfall of Robert Earl of Huntington, Anthony Munday

Clayhanger, Arnold Bennett

The Regent, A Five Towns Story Of Adventure In London , Arnold Bennett

The Card, A Story Of Adventure In The Five Towns , Arnold Bennett

South: The Story of Shackleton's Last Expedition 1914-1917, Sir Ernest Shackketon

Greene's Groatsworth of Wit: Bought With a Million of Repentance, Robert Greene

Beau Sabreur, Percival Christopher Wren

The Hekatompathia, or Passionate Centurie of Love, Thomas Watson

The Art of Rhetoric, Thomas Wilson

Stepping Heavenward, Elizabeth Prentiss

Barker's Delight, or The Art of Angling, Thomas Barker

The Napoleon of Notting Hill, G.K. Chesterton

The Douay-Rheims Bible (The Challoner Revision)

Endimion - The Man in the Moone, John Lyly

Gallathea and Midas, John Lyly,

Mother Bombie, John Lyly

Manners, Custom and Dress During the Middle Ages and During the Renaissance Period, Paul Lacroix

Obedience of a Christian Man, William Tyndale

St. Patrick for Ireland, James Shirley

The Wrongs of Woman; Or Maria/Memoirs of the Author of a Vindication of the Rights of Woman, Mary Wollstonecraft and William Godwin

De Adhaerendo Deo. Of Cleaving to God, Albertus Magnus

Obedience of a Christian Man, William Tyndale

A Trick to Catch the Old One, Thomas Middleton

The Phoenix, Thomas Middleton

A Yorkshire Tragedy, Thomas Middleton (attrib.)

The Princely Pleasures at Kenelworth Castle, George Gascoigne

The Fair Maid of the West. Part I and Part II. Thomas Heywood

Proserpina, Volume I and Volume II. Studies of Wayside Flowers, John Ruskin

Our Fathers Have Told Us. Part I. The Bible of Amiens. John Ruskin

The Poetry of Architecture: Or the Architecture of the Nations of Europe Considered in Its Association with Natural Scenery and National Character, John Ruskin

The Endeavour Journal of Sir Joseph Banks. Sir Joseph Banks

Christ Legends: And Other Stories, Selma Lagerlof; (trans. Velma Swanston Howard)

Chamber Music, James Joyce

Blurt, Master Constable, Thomas Middleton, Thomas Dekker

Since Yesterday, Frederick Lewis Allen

The Scholemaster: Or, Plaine and Perfite Way of Teachyng Children the Latin Tong , Roger Ascham

The Wonderful Year, 1603, Thomas Dekker

Waverley, Sir Walter Scott

Guy Mannering, Sir Walter Scott

Old Mortality, Sir Walter Scott

The Knight of Malta, John Fletcher

The Double Marriage, John Fletcher and Philip Massinger

Space Prison, Tom Godwin

The Home of the Blizzard Being the Story of the Australasian Antarctic Expedition, 1911-1914, Douglas Mawson

Wild-goose Chase , John Fletcher

If You Know Not Me, You Know Nobody. Part I and Part II, Thomas Heywood

The Ragged Trousered Philanthropists, Robert Tressell

The Island of Sheep, John Buchan

Eyes of the Woods, Joseph Altsheler

The Club of Queer Trades, G. K. Chesterton

The Financier, Theodore Dreiser

Something of Myself, Rudyard Kipling

Law of Freedom in a Platform, or True Magistracy Restored, Gerrard Winstanley

Damon and Pithias, Richard Edwards

Dido Queen of Carthage: And, The Massacre at Paris, Christopher Marlowe

Cocoa and Chocolate: Their History from Plantation to Consumer, Arthur Knapp

Lady of Pleasure, James Shirley

The South Pole: An account of the Norwegian Antarctic expedition in the "Fram," 1910-12. Volume 1 and Volume 2, Roald Amundsen

A Yorkshire Tragedy, Thomas Middleton (attrib.)

The Tragedy of Soliman and Perseda, Thomas Kyd

The Rape of Lucrece. Thomas Heywood

Myths and Legends of Ancient Greece and Rome, E. M. Berens

In the Forbidden Land, Henry Savage Arnold Landor

Across Unknown South America, by Arnold Henry Savage Landor

Illustrated History of Furniture: From the Earliest to the Present Time, Frederick Litchfield

A Narrative of Some of the Lord's Dealings with George Müller Written by Himself (Parts I-IV, 1805-1856), George Müller

The Towneley Cycle Of The Mystery Plays (Or The Wakefield Cycle): Thirty-Two Pageants, Anonymous

The Insatiate Countesse, John Marston.

Spontaneous Activity in Education, Maria Montessori.

On the Art of Writing, Sir Arthur Quiller-Couch

The Well of the Saints, J. M. Synge

Bacon's Advancement Of Learning And The New Atlantis, Francis Bacon.

Catholic Tales And Christian Songs, Dorothy Sayers.

Two Little Savages: Being the Adventures of Two Boys who Lived as Indians and What they Learned, Ernest Thompson Seton

The Sadness of Christ, Thomas More

The Family of Love, Thomas Middleton

The Passing of the Aborigines: A Lifetime Spent Among the Natives of Australia, Daisy Bates

The Children, Edith Wharton

A Record of European Armour and Arms through Seven Centuries., Francis Laking

The Book of the Farm: - Detailing The Labours Of The Farmer, Steward, Plowman, Hedger, Cattle-Man, Shepherd, Field-Worker, and Dairymaid. (Volume I). by Henry Stephens

The Book of the Farm: - Detailing The Labours Of The Farmer, Steward, Plowman, Hedger, Cattle-Man, Shepherd, Field-Worker, and Dairymaid. (Volume II). by Henry Stephens

The Book of the Farm: - Detailing The Labours Of The Farmer, Steward, Plowman, Hedger, Cattle-Man, Shepherd, Field-Worker, and Dairymaid. (Volume III). by Henry Stephens

The Naturalist On The River Amazons, by Henry Walter Bates

and many others…

Tell us what you would love to see in print again, at affordable prices!
Email: **benedictionbooks@btinternet.com**

Lightning Source UK Ltd.
Milton Keynes UK
UKOW031503061211

183298UK00001B/69/P